A History of the Roman Equestrian Order

In the Roman social hierarchy, the equestrian order stood second only to the senatorial aristocracy in status and prestige. Throughout more than a thousand years of Roman history, equestrians played prominent roles in the Roman government, army and society as cavalrymen, officers, businessmen, tax-collectors, jurors, administrators and writers. This book offers the first comprehensive history of the equestrian order, covering the period from the eighth century BC to the fifth century AD. It examines how Rome's cavalry became the equestrian order during the Republican period, before analysing how imperial rule transformed the role of equestrians in government. Using literary and documentary evidence, the book demonstrates the vital social function which the equestrian order filled in the Roman world, and how this was shaped by the transformation of the Roman state itself.

CAILLAN DAVENPORT is Senior Lecturer in Roman History at Macquarie University. He was educated at the University of Queensland and at the University of Oxford. He has been a Junior Fellow of the Australian Centre for Ancient Numismatic Studies, a Rome Awardee at the British School at Rome, and an Australian Research Council DECRA Fellow.

T0381534

A History of the Roman Equestrian Order

CAILLAN DAVENPORT

Macquarie University, Sydney

CAMBRIDGE
UNIVERSITY PRESS

CAMBRIDGE
UNIVERSITY PRESS

Shaftesbury Road, Cambridge CB2 8EA, United Kingdom

One Liberty Plaza, 20th Floor, New York, NY 10006, USA

477 Williamstown Road, Port Melbourne, VIC 3207, Australia

314–321, 3rd Floor, Plot 3, Splendor Forum, Jasola District Centre, New Delhi – 110025, India

103 Penang Road, #05–06/07, Visioncrest Commercial, Singapore 238467

Cambridge University Press is part of Cambridge University Press & Assessment, a department of the University of Cambridge.

We share the University's mission to contribute to society through the pursuit of education, learning and research at the highest international levels of excellence.

www.cambridge.org
Information on this title: www.cambridge.org/9781009376228

DOI: 10.1017/9781139506403

First published 2019
Reprinted 2020
First paperback edition 2023

A catalogue record for this publication is available from the British Library

Library of Congress Cataloging-in-Publication data
Names: Davenport, Caillan, 1981– author.
Title: A history of the Roman equestrian order / Caillan Davenport.
Description: Cambridge, United Kingdom ; New York, NY : Cambridge University Press, 2019. | Includes bibliographical references and index.
Identifiers: LCCN 2018042047 | ISBN 9781107032538 (alk. paper)
Subjects: LCSH: Equestrian order (Rome) | Social classes – Rome. | Elite
Classification: LCC DG83.3 .D37 2019 | DDC 357/.10937–dc23
LC record available at https://lccn.loc.gov/2018042047

ISBN   978-1-107-03253-8   Hardback
ISBN   978-1-009-37622-8   Paperback

For my parents

Contents

Figures

Tables

Acknowledgements

This book has its origins in my University of Oxford D.Phil. thesis, 'The Senatorial and Equestrian Orders in the Roman Army and Administration, AD 235–337', which was examined and passed in December 2009. Material from the original thesis constitutes the core of Chapters 11 and 12 of the present work, as well as parts of Chapters 6 and 7, though it has been substantially rewritten and revised in subsequent years. I am enormously grateful to the Trustees of the John Crampton Travelling Scholarship for their financial support, without which it would have been impossible for me to spend three years at Oxford pursuing my academic dreams. I owe a great debt to my D.Phil. supervisor, Alan Bowman, for his helpful advice and feedback during the process of writing the thesis, and for his steadfast support of my research and career in the years since. My thesis examiners, Roger Tomlin and John Wilkes, offered sage and benevolent criticism of the thesis' arguments and advice on publication possibilities. Peter Thonemann and Neil McLynn provided helpful 'big picture' thoughts during Oxford's transfer of status and confirmation processes. I have also benefited enormously from discussions with Richard Duncan-Jones, who has shown great kindness towards a young scholar. The Faculty of Archaeology, History, and Letters of the British School at Rome generously granted me a Rome Award for three months between October and December 2008. My stay at the BSR proved to be a transformative period for my research, giving me greater appreciation of the significance of the epigraphic and monumental evidence for the equestrian order; the impact of my time in Italy can be seen throughout this book. Thanks go to Sue Russell for making the BSR a true home away from home in this period. I am very grateful to Maria Pia Malvezzi and Stefania Peterlini from the BSR for their tireless efforts to gain permission for me to view and photograph monuments over many years.

The University of Queensland supported this book through a New Staff Start-Up Grant and a Faculty of Arts Research Excellence Award. These funds enabled me to employ research assistants, visit sites and museums in Europe, make several return visits to the British School at Rome, and attend overseas conferences. I am grateful to the successive Heads of the

School of Historical and Philosophical Inquiry (formerly the School of History, Philosophy, Religion and Classics), Clive Moore and Martin Crotty, for their support in ensuring that I had a reduced teaching load in the early years of my appointment. The School's Research Incentive Scheme provided funds to assist with the cost of photographic permissions. My undergraduate teachers at the University of Queensland inspired me to follow an academic career. I would particularly like to thank Tom Stevenson and Tim Parkin for their support and encouragement, and Brian Jones, whose research and teaching on Roman history and Latin inspired me to become a Roman historian (and led me to indulge in the delights of prosopography). Steven Cosnett and Nicola Linton have been exemplary research assistants, providing valuable support by cataloguing literary and epigraphic sources. Nicola's work was partially funded by a University of Queensland Summer Research Scholarship. I would like to thank the Document Delivery team at the University of Queensland Social Sciences and Humanities Library for their efforts in acquiring books and articles for me over many years. They are worth their weight in gold. It is particularly important to acknowledge these debts to the University of Queensland since this book will appear after I have moved to my new home at Macquarie University in Sydney.

Michael Sharp at Cambridge University Press has been consistently helpful; I would particularly like to thank him and the Delegates of the Press for showing such faith in this project. The three readers for the Press who reviewed both the original proposal and the final manuscript provided a wealth of useful advice and feedback, for which I am extremely grateful. Their detailed criticisms have improved the book immeasurably and transformed it in many ways. Hannah Cornwell offered helpful feedback on the late Republican and Augustan chapters, and Tom Stevenson has always been a generous sounding-board for my ideas on this period. I am grateful to Annika Kuhn for allowing me to cite her excellent D.Phil. thesis on senatorial and equestrian rank in Asia Minor. Chris Mallan, a true gentleman and a scholar, has read every chapter of this work, multiple times, and often at very short notice. I have benefited enormously from his critical eye, and from his steadfast friendship over many years. Meaghan McEvoy read the manuscript, offering numerous insightful suggestions, especially on the later Roman empire. I am very grateful to my copy-editor, Mary Starkey, for her meticulous attention to detail. None of the people named above bear responsibility for the arguments advanced in this book, and its many imperfections.

For their assistance with images and permissions, I am grateful to Julia Lenaghan and R. R. R. Smith (Aphrodisias Excavations), Amy Taylor (Ashmolean Museum, Oxford), Iain Calderwood (British Museum, London), Alessandra Giovenco (British School at Rome), Manfred Schmidt and Marcus Dohnicht (CIL, BBAW), Ramona Rütt (DAI, Arachne Database), Ulrich Mania (DAI, Istanbul), Daria Lanzuolo (DAI, Rome), Federico Fischetti (Gallerie Estensi, Modena), Zeynep Kızıltan (Istanbul Archaeological Museum), Ramona Messerig (Landesmuseum, Mainz), Dominique Darde (Musée archéologique, Nîmes), Parisi Presicce and Angela Carbonaro (Musei Capitolini, Rome), Rosanna Di Pinto (Musei Vaticani, Vatican City), Isabella Nobile and Valentina Catelli (Museo Civici, Como), Ruth Bowler (Walters Art Museum, Baltimore), and Rea Alexandratos (Warburg Institute, London).

Throughout the eleven years of research and writing the thesis and this book, many friends and colleagues in Oxford, Rome, and Brisbane have done their best to distract me from spending too much time with the *equites*, including Ross and Ali Williams, Ceri Hunter, Jennifer Sigafoos, Alexandra Sofroniew, and all members of the Tuesday night pub quiz team (Oxford), Beth Munro and Christina Triantafillou (Rome), Chris Mallan, Helen Tanner, Jennifer Manley, Liz Townsley, Rashna Taraporewalla, Shushma Malik, Amelia Brown, and Alastair Blanshard (Brisbane), while Liz Pullar, Lynn Petrie, David West, and Leilani and Malcolm House have been wonderful travel companions in Greece, Turkey, and Italy. To my darling wife, Meaghan McEvoy, I owe more than I can say. Meaghan has enriched my life in countless ways; her unceasing and unconditional love and support mean the world to me. Finally, this book is dedicated to my parents as a small token of thanks, for everything.

A Note on Translations

Most translations of ancient literary works and documents in this book are my own, except where otherwise specified in the footnotes.

Abbreviations

AE	*L'Année épigraphique*, Paris (1888–present).
ANRW	Temporini, H. (ed.) (1972–88), *Aufstieg und Niedergang der römischen Welt*, Berlin.
BGU	*Aegyptische Urkunden aus den staatlichen Museen zu Berlin, Griechische Urkunden*, Berlin (1895–2005).
CAH IX²	Crook, J. A., Lintott, A. and Rawson, E. (eds.) (1994), *The Cambridge Ancient History*, vol. IX: *The Last Age of the Roman Republic, 146–43 BC*, 2nd edition, Cambridge
CAH X²	Bowman, A. K., Champlin, E. and Lintott, A. (eds.) (1996), *The Cambridge Ancient History*, vol. X: *The Augustan Empire, 43 BC–AD 69*, 2nd edition, Cambridge.
CAH XI²	Bowman, A. K., Garnsey, P. and Rathbone, D. (eds.) (2000), *The Cambridge Ancient History*, vol. XI: *The High Empire, AD 70–192*, 2nd edition, Cambridge.
CAH XII¹	Cook, S. A., Adcock, F. E. and Charlesworth, M. P. (eds.) (1939), *The Cambridge Ancient History*, vol. XII: *The Imperial Crisis and Recovery, AD 193–324*, Cambridge.
CAH XII²	Bowman, A. K., Cameron, A. and Garnsey, P. (eds.) (2005), *The Cambridge Ancient History*, vol. XII: *The Crisis of Empire, AD 193–337*, 2nd edition, Cambridge.
CAH XIII	Cameron, A. and Garnsey, P. (eds.) (1998), *The Cambridge Ancient History*, vol. XIII: *The Late Empire, AD 337–425*, 2nd edition, Cambridge.
ChLA	Bruckner, A. and Marichal, R. et al. (eds.) (1954–present), *Chartae Latinae Antiquiores*, Lausanne.
CIL	Mommsen, T. et al. (eds.) (1862–present), *Corpus Inscriptionum Latinarum*, Berlin.
CJ	Krüger, P. (ed.) (1892), *Corpus Iuris Civilis Volumen Secundum: Codex Iustinianus*, 5th edition, Berlin.

CLE	Bücheler, F. and Lommatzsch, E. (eds.) (1930), *Carmina Latina Epigraphica*, 2nd edition, Leipzig.
Corinth VIII.2	West, A. B. (ed.) (1931), *Corinth: Results of Excavations Conducted by the American School of Classical Studies at Athens*, vol. VIII, Part II: *Latin Inscriptions 1896–1926*, Cambridge, MA.
Corinth VIII.3	Kent, J. H. (ed.) (1966), *Corinth: Results of Excavations Conducted by the American School of Classical Studies at Athens*, vol. VIII, Part III: *The Inscriptions, 1926–1950*, Princeton.
CTh.	Mommsen, T. and Meyer, P. M. (eds.) (1905), *Theodosiani Libri XVI cum Constitutionibus Sirmondianis et leges novellae ad Theodosianum pertinentes*, Berlin.
Eph. Ep.	Mommsen, T. et al. (eds.) (1872–1903), *Ephemeris Epigraphica: Corporis Inscriptionum Latinarum Supplementum*, Berlin.
FGrH	Jacoby, F. et al. (eds.) (1923–present), *Die Fragmente der griechischen Historiker*, Berlin and Leiden.
FHG	Müller, C. (ed.) (1878–85), *Fragmenta Historicorum Graecorum*, 4 vols., Paris.
I. Ankara	Mitchell, S. and French, D. (eds.) (2012), *The Greek and Latin Inscriptions of Ankara (Ancyra)*, vol. I: *From Augustus to the End of the Third Century AD*, Munich.
I. Aph.	Reynolds, J., Roueché, C. and Bodard, G. (eds.) (2007), *Inscriptions of Aphrodisias* URL: http://insaph.kcl.ac.uk/iaph2007
I. Didyma	Wiegand, T. (ed.) (1958), *Didyma 2: Die Inschriften*, Berlin.
I. Eph.	Wankel, H. et al. (eds.) (1979–81), *Die Inschriften von Ephesos*, 8 vols., Bonn.
I. Ilion	Frisch, P. (ed.) (1981), *Die Inschriften von Ilion*, Bonn.
I. Keramos	Varinlioğlu, E. (ed.) (1986), *Die Inschriften von Keramos*, Bonn.
I. Magn.	Kern, O. (ed.) (1900), *Die Inschriften von Magnesia am Maeander*, Berlin.
I. Perge	Şahin, S. (ed.) (1999–2004), *Die Inschriften von Perge*, 2 vols., Bonn.
I. Prusias	Ameling, W. (ed.) (1985), *Die Inschriften von Prusias ad Hypium*, Bonn.

I. Selge	Nollé, J. and Schindler, F. (eds.) (1991), *Die Inschriften von Selge*, Bonn.
IDR III.2	Russu, I. I. and Pippidi, D. M. (eds.) (1980), *Inscriptiones Daciae Romanae III. Dacia Superior 2. Ulpia Traiana Dacica (Sarmizegetusa)*, Bucharest.
IG	*Inscriptiones Graecae*, Berlin (1890–present).
IGBulg.	Mihailov, G. (ed.) (1956–97), *Inscriptiones Graecae in Bulgaria repertae*, 5 vols., Sofia.
IGR	Cagnat, R. et al. (eds.) (1906–27), *Inscriptiones Graecae ad Res Romanas pertinentes*, 4 vols., Paris.
ILAfr.	Cagnat, R. and Merlin, A. (eds.) (1923), *Inscriptions latines d'Afrique*, Paris.
ILAlg.	Gsell, S. and Pflaum, H.-G. (eds.) (1922–23), *Inscriptions latines d'Algérie*, 2 vols., Paris.
ILLRP	Degrassi, A. (ed.) (1963–5), *Inscriptiones Latinae Liberae Rei Publicae*, 2 vols., Florence.
ILS	Dessau, H. (ed.) (1892–1916), *Inscriptiones Latinae Selectae*, 3 vols., Berlin.
Inscr. It. XIII	Degrassi, A. (ed.) (1937–63), *Inscriptiones Italiae XIII: Fasti et Elogia*, 3 vols., Rome.
IRT	Reynolds, J. M. and Ward-Perkins, J. B. (eds.) (1952), *The Inscriptions of Roman Tripolitania*, Rome.
LIA	Ehmig, U. and Haensch, R. (eds.) (2012), *Die lateinischen Inschriften aus Albanien*, Bonn.
LSA	Smith, R. R. R. and Ward-Perkins, B. (eds.) (2012), *The Last Statues of Antiquity Database.* http://laststatues.classics.ox.ac.uk
LTUR	Steinby, E. M. (ed.) (1993–9), *Lexicon Topographicum Urbis Romae*, 6 vols., Rome.
M. Chr.	Mitteis, L. and Wilcken, U. (eds.) (1912), *Grundzüge und Chrestomathie der Papyruskunde*, vol. II: *Juristischer Teil*, Part II: *Chrestomathie*, Berlin and Leipzig.
ME	*Monumentum Ephesenum* in Cottier, M. et al. (eds.) (2008), *The Customs of Law of Asia*, Oxford.
OGIS	Dittenberger, W. (ed.) (1903–5), *Orientis Graecae Inscriptiones Selectae*, 2 vols., Leipzig.
OLD	Glare, P. G. W. (ed.) (2012), *Oxford Latin Dictionary*, 2nd edition, 2 vols., Oxford.

ORF⁴	H. Malcovati (ed.) (1976), *Oratorum Romanorum Fragmenta*, 4th edition, 2 vols, Turin.
P. Berl. Leihg.	Kalén, T. and Tomsin, A. (eds.) (1932–77), *Berliner Leihgabe griechischer Papyri*, Uppsala.
P. Berol.	*Papyrus Berolinensis* (Berlin papyri). Inv. 8334 published in Körtenbeutel, H. (ed.) (1940), *Ein Kodizill eines römischen Kaisers*, Berlin.
P. Dura	Welles, C. B., Fink, R. O. and Gilliam, J. F. (eds.) (1959), *The Excavations at Dura-Europos: Final Report V, Part 1: The Parchments and Papyri*, New Haven.
P. Euphr.	Feissel, D. and Gascou, J. (1995), 'Documents d'Archives romains inédits du moyen Euphrate', *Journal des Savants*, 65–119.
P. Flor.	Vitelli, G. and Comparetti, D. (eds.) (1906–15), *Papiri greco-egizii, Papiri Fiorentini*, Milan.
P. Giss.	Eger, O., Kornemann, E. and Meyer, P. M. (eds.) (1910–12), *Griechische Papyri im Museum des oberhessischen Geschichtsvereins zu Giessen*, Leipzig and Berlin.
P. Harr.	Powell, J. E. et al. (eds.) (1936–85), *The Rendel Harris Papyri of Woodbrooke College, Birmingham*, Cambridge.
P. Hib.	Grenfell, B. P. and Hunt, A. S. (eds.) (1906), *The Hibeh Papyri I*, London. Turner, E. G. and Lenger, M.-T. (eds.) (1955), *The Hibeh Papyri II*, London.
P. Lond.	Kenyon, F. G. et al. (eds.) (1893–1974), *Greek Papyri in the British Museum*, London.
P. Mert.	Bell, H. I. et al. (eds.) (1948–82), *A Descriptive Catalogue of the Greek Papyri in the Collection of Wilfred Merton*, London.
P. Oxy.	*The Oxyrhynchus Papyri*, London (1898–present).
P. Stras.	*Griechische Papyrus der kaiserlichen Universitäts- und Landes-bibliothek zu Strassburg*, Leipzig, Paris and Strasbourg (1912–89).
PLRE	I Jones, A. H. M., Martindale, J. R. and Morris, J. (eds.) (1971), *The Prosopography of the Later Roman Empire*, vol. I: *AD 260–395*, Cambridge.

PME	Devijver, H. (ed.) (1976–2001), *Prosopographia militiarum equestrium quae fuerunt ab Augusto ad Gallienum*, 6 vols., Leuven.
PSI	*Papiri greci e latini*, Florence (1912–present).
RE	Pauly, A. F., Wissowa, G. and Kroll, W. et al. (eds.) (1893–1980), *Real-Encyclopädie der classischen Altertumswissenschaft*, Stuttgart.
RECAM IV	McLean, B. H. (ed.) (2002), *Greek and Latin Inscriptions in the Konya Archaeological Museum (Regional Epigraphic Catalogues of Asia Minor IV)*, London.
RG	Cooley, A. E. (ed. and trans.) (2009), *Res Gestae Divi Augusti: Text, Translation, and Commentary*, Cambridge.
RIB	Collingwood, R. G. and Wright, R. P. (eds.) (1965), *The Roman Inscriptions of Britain*, vol. I: *Inscriptions on Stone*, Oxford.
RIC	Mattingly, H., Sydenham, E. A. et al. (eds.) (1923–present), *Roman Imperial Coinage*, London.
RPC IV Online	Howgego, C., Heuchert, V. and Yarrow, L. M. (eds.) (2006), *Roman Provincial Coinage*, vol. IV: *The Antonine Period*. http://rpc.ashmus.ox.ac.uk/
RS	Crawford, M. H. (ed.) (1996), *Roman Statutes*, 2 vols., London.
SB	Shackleton Bailey, D. R. (ed.) (1965–80), *Cicero's Letters*, 6 vols., Cambridge. (Shackleton Bailey's numbering is cited in square brackets following the traditional reference.)
SCPP	Eck, W., Caballos, A. and Fernández, F. (1996), *Das senatus consultum de Cn. Pisone patre*, Munich.
SEG	*Supplementum Epigraphicum Graecum*, Leiden and Amsterdam (1923–present).
*SIG*³	Dittinberger, W. et al. (eds.) (1915–24), *Sylloge Inscriptionum Graecarum*, 3rd edition, Leipzig.
Tab. Vind. II–III	Bowman, A. K. and Thomas, J. D. (eds.) (1994–2003), *The Vindolanda Writing Tablets*, vols. II–III, London.

TAM	*Tituli Asiae Minoris*, Vienna (1901–present).
vdH^2	van den Hout, M. P. J. (1988), *M. Cornelii Frontonis Epistulae,* 2nd edition, Leipzig.
W. Chr.	Mitteis, L. and Wilcken, U. (eds.) (1912), *Grundzüge und Chrestomathie der Papyruskunde*, 2 vols., Lepizig and Berlin.

Introduction: Charting the History of the Equestrian Order

Aims and Rationale

This book is an institutional and social history of the equestrian order (*ordo equester*) in the Roman world. It charts the history of the equestrians (*equites*) in their various guises from the eighth century BC to the fifth century AD. We begin with the mounted aristocracy of the Regal period and the cavalry of the early Republic, as the Romans regarded these warriors as the ancestors of the later equestrian order. The order itself only emerged as a constituent status group within the Roman state (*res publica*), distinct from both the senate and the plebs, in the late second century BC. Membership of the equestrian order in the Republican period included tax-collectors, businessmen, jurors, and military officers. The *equites Romani* were distinguished by their own status symbols, such as gold rings and the tunic with a narrow stripe, ceremonies with religious and political meaning, and privileges such as front-row seats of the theatre. In the age of the emperors, the ranks of the *equites* included governors, financial administrators and other officials, as Augustus and his successors gave them an important role in the management of the *res publica* alongside senators.[1] Over the course of the imperial period equestrian rank was subdivided into further status grades, of which the higher could only be obtained by service in the army or administration. The proliferation of titles and honours bestowed by the Roman state meant that by the mid-fourth century AD the status of *eques Romanus* had become the least prestigious of these imperial perquisites, though it still retained inherent

---

[1] 'Republic', 'empire', 'imperial period', 'principate' and similar expressions are terms of modern convenience given to specific periods to give shape to our narrative of Roman history. However, in both the 'Republic' and 'empire', the Romans themselves referred to their state as the *res publica*, and recognised the emperor as operating within this system. The 'imperial period', therefore, right through to the fall of Constantinople in 1453, was what we might call a 'monarchical *res publica*'. For this argument, see Kaldellis 2015: 1–31.

value by offering immunities above the level of ordinary citizens. In one form or another, the privileged citizens called *equites* constituted a fundamental part of the socio-political hierarchy of the Roman state for more than a thousand years of history.

The equestrian order has not lacked modern commentators. Fundamental aspects of its social and political history were established by Mommsen in his monumental three-volume *Römisches Staatsrecht* (1871–8). The first independent history of the equestrian order came with Stein's monograph *Der römische Ritterstand*, published in 1927. Stein's work began with the origins of the order proper in the late Roman Republic, but the book primarily focused on equestrians in the imperial period. His research was based on a pioneering prosopographical analysis of *equites* derived from the epigraphic evidence. This demonstrated the analytical potential inherent in Mommsen's *Corpus Inscriptionum Latinarum* and other corpora of inscriptions for prosopographical research and social history. The Regal period and the Republic gained greater attention in Hill's *The Roman Middle Class in the Republican Period* (1952), which, despite its misleading title, was an important and fundamental scholarly work. Hill's book was, however, soon surpassed by Nicolet's seminal *L'ordre équestre à l'époque républicaine (312–43 av. J.-C.)*. The first, analytical volume was published in 1966, followed by a detailed and expansive prosopography of Republican *equites* in 1974. In the course of more than one thousand pages, Nicolet put the study of equestrians in the Republican period on a new footing, especially the ideological function of the order and its relationship with the senatorial order. Nicolet's work was complemented by Badian's short but incisive book of 1972, *Publicans and Sinners*, which brought to life the role played by businessmen and tax-collectors in the administration of the expanding Republic.

In the second half of the twentieth century the imperial period received two new prosopographical corpora which updated and extended the work of Stein. Pflaum harnessed the large number of inscriptions recording equestrian careers to produce his fundamental study of the procuratorial service. *Les procurateurs équestres sous le Haut-Empire Romain* was published in 1950, followed by three volumes of detailed prosopography, *Les carrières procuratoriennes équestres sous le Haut-Empire Romain* in 1960–1, with a further supplement in 1982. The career patterns of *equites* identified by Pflaum have been the subject of some criticism, and not all his conclusions should be accepted, but his study of the material remains unparalleled. The equestrian military officers of the empire were painstakingly assembled by Devijver in his six-volume work *Prosopographia militiarum equestrium quae fuerunt ab Augusto ad Gallienum* (1976–2001). Devijver accompanied this with a series of important articles on the officers and their career, known as the *militiae equestres*.

The work of both Pflaum and Devijver provided an essential foundation for a new socio-political study of imperial *equites*, along the lines of that which Nicolet produced for the Republic. This was Demougin's two-part study, *L'ordre équestre sous les Julio-Claudiens* (1988) and *Prosopographie des chevaliers romains julio-claudiens (43 av. J.-C.–70 ap. J.-C.)* (1992a). Starting with the triumviral period, where Nicolet had concluded his research, Demougin examined the pivotal transformation of the order from Republic to empire and the foundation of the imperial system of equestrian administrative posts. The economic and social world of the equestrian order in the empire has been the subject of a number of important studies by Duncan-Jones, culminating in his 2016 monograph, *Power and Privilege in Roman Society*. Finally, the political and ceremonial function of *equites* in the early empire received renewed attention in Rowe's incisive 2002 book, *Princes and Political Cultures: The New Tiberian Senatorial Decrees*. Rowe demonstrated the vital and important role played by the *ordo* in shaping the political culture of the imperial state, which was not solely determined 'top-down' by the emperors themselves, but also by the willing participation of *equites* individually and collectively. My research stands on the shoulders of these works and those of many other scholars, not only in terms of the prosopographical catalogues of *equites* which they compiled, but also their interpretations of the literary and documentary evidence for the equestrian order.

This book aims to make a contribution by offering a new history of the *equites* and equestrian order from the Regal period to Late Antiquity, the first time (to my knowledge) that this has been attempted since Stein. There are three main aims of this book. The first is to study the many different capacities in which equestrians served the Roman state – as cavalrymen, army officers, jurors in the criminal courts, and financial administrators (to name just a few). We will assess why the official positions available to members of the equestrian order increased significantly over time, especially during the late Republic and the imperial period. The second aim is to examine how membership of the equestrian order functioned on an individual and collective level, in order to discover what it meant to be an *eques Romanus* in the Roman world. In pursuing these first two aims, the book not only moves chronologically from Republic to empire, but also geographically, comparing the significance and function of equestrian status and the positions held by *equites* in the city of Rome, Italy, and in the provinces. We will examine the commonalities that united the *equites*, as well as areas of fragmentation among its members and resistance to adopting equestrian status.

The third and final aim is to examine the wider sociological function of the equestrian order. We will ask why the order and its members constituted such an important part of Roman society, and why the title of *eques* remained an enduring mark of distinction for many centuries, even after equestrians ceased to be the state cavalry. The Romans were well known for retaining official titles, such as *quaestor* or *praefectus praetorio*, long after the original function of the position had changed. But the survival of the equestrian order and the distinction conveyed by membership represented more than mere administrative inertia; it speaks to a much deeper attachment to what the order represented. Indeed, the chronological framework of the book is designed to allow readers to trace the evolution of the equestrian order over the *longue durée*. Although this type of narrative history has largely fallen out of fashion, it remains a powerful way of assessing and explaining continuities and changes over time.[2] The wide chronological scope of the book, covering over one thousand years of Roman history, enables us to place the evolution of the equestrian order in the context of the transformation of the Roman state itself, which changed from monarchy under the kings into a *res publica*, and then into a curious hybrid, the 'monarchical *res publica*' (better known as the empire). The equestrian order shares many similarities with other elite status groups in pre-modern societies, but it has a unique character and developmental trajectory that can only be explained in the framework of the evolution of the Roman state itself. This is where we will begin our analysis.

The Equestrian Order in Historical Context

Comparative approaches to the civilisations of the ancient world have been especially popular in recent years.[3] This is not merely a fashionable trend, but represents an important step forward in historical analysis for ancient historians. Comparative history has all too often been the domain of

---

[2] Heather 2005 is a recent successful example (though the intended readership is much broader than this book).

[3] See, for example, Raaflaub and Rosenstein 1999; Mutschler and Mittag 2008; Scheidel 2009d and 2015; Arnason and Raafluab 2010; Bang and Scheidel 2013.

sociologists, political scientists and modern historians rather than classicists, but it has significant potential for understanding the societies and cultures of Greece and Rome.[4] As Scheidel has aptly put it, 'only comparisons with other civilisations make it possible to distinguish common features from culturally specific or unique characteristics and developments'.[5] Put another way, comparative history allow us to ask the question: what was 'Roman' about the Roman empire? The aim of this introductory chapter is to examine the history of the equestrian order in comparative perspective, in order to ascertain similarities and differences with comparable status groups in other pre-industrial societies. Throughout the introduction and the book as a whole, I will use the terms 'status group' or 'order' to describe the *equites* in preference to 'class', just as the Romans themselves did when they used the word *ordo*. Class is a term of economic stratification, whereas the equestrian order was an elite group that was defined by a range of criteria, of which financial wealth was but one.[6] The discussion herein will necessarily involve some simplification of complex historical phenomena in order to highlight essential points of comparison, but it is hoped that the rewards will outweigh any potential negatives that come with generalisation.[7] It also functions as a microcosm of many of the key sociological arguments presented in the book. In order to avoid repetition, the reader will be referred to specific chapters where the evidence is laid out in detail.

Monarchy and Aristocracy

We begin with Rome as a monarchy. The period from the eighth to the sixth centuries BC, traditionally described as the Regal period, is fiercely debated and is in large part unrecoverable. The Romans themselves believed that they were ruled by seven kings from the foundation of Rome by Romulus (commonly placed in 753 BC, though there were other contenders) to the expulsion of Tarquinius Superbus in 509 BC. Romulus himself is said to

[4] I have benefited from many such studies which take in the broad sweep of human history, especially Mosca 1939; Powis 1984; Mann 1986; Kautsky 1997; and Crone 2003.

[5] Scheidel 2009a: 5.

[6] See Weber 1968: 930–2 and Crone 2003: 101–4 for the basic definitions, and Cohen 1975: 261–7, Demougin 1988: 1–3, and Finley 1999: 49 for their relevance to ancient Rome and the equestrians. However, it is appropriate to use the term 'ruling class' in terms of 'ruling elite', as is common in scholarship by sociologists and political scientists (Mosca 1939: 50; Mann 1986: 25, 270).

[7] Note especially the sage remarks of Matthews 2000b about the complexities that lie beneath broad terms such as 'elite'.

have founded the *Celeres* or 'swift ones', composed of three hundred mounted warriors, whom Pliny the Elder identified as the ancestors of the equestrian order.[8] That the historical kings of Rome were supported by a mounted aristocracy is beyond doubt, though they were probably not a national army, but the personal followers of the king (*rex*). During this period central Italy was home to clans of warrior aristocrats who ranged widely across the region, competing with each other for influence and for kingship in cities such as Rome. It was not until the fifth century BC, a period traditionally identified as the beginning of the *res publica*, that these warrior clans were transformed into landed aristocracy. They preserved their military supremacy by acting as the cavalry of the new state, rather than the king's personal army. Early Rome was not unique in being dominated by a militaristic aristocratic elite; this was a fundamental characteristic of most pre-industrial monarchical societies.[9] Wealth and the ability to equip oneself and one's followers for campaigns has traditionally provided the basis for distinctive elite identity founded on martial valour. In many historical societies, aristocrats socialised their sons to follow in their footsteps by training them in military arts.[10] This helped to create a shared elite system of values, or ideology, which has traditionally provided a more enduring foundation for uniting aristocrats into a coherent social group than landed wealth alone.[11] We can obverse this ideology in the case of the knights of medieval Europe and their chivalric code or the Japanese mounted archers whom we call Samurai, who pursued a ritualised combat unique to their sense of valour and masculinity (to name just two examples).[12] In the Roman world, the culture of military excellence was displayed in the tombs and prestige goods of the warrior aristocracy of the Archaic period. Such military aristocracies exerted their power through what Max Weber called 'traditional authority', a supremacy that derived from accepted customs and norms rather than the rule of law.[13]

[8] The process of evolution described here is discussed in detail in Chapter 1.

[9] Mosca 1939: 53–6, 222–3; Bendix 1978: 231; Kautsky 1997: 144–50; Crone 2003: 26, 42–3; Wickham 2005: 158, 175.

[10] Mosca 1939: 61; Ferguson 1999: 406. For specific examples, see Briant 1999: 113–16 on Achaemenid Persia, and Spence 1993: 198–202 on the *hippeis* of Classical Athens.

[11] On group solidarity defined by ideology, see Mann 1986: 519.

[12] Knights: Barber 1995: 26–7; Kaeuper 2009: 94–115. Samurai: Farris 1999: 60–6; Friday 2003: 103–7, 137–40. Momigliano 1966: 16–17 rejected comparisons between early Roman cavalry and the knights of medieval Europe, but this cannot be sustained in the light of the clear connection between aristocracies and cavalry in world history (thus Cornell 1995: 446 n. 31).

[13] Weber 1968: 226–7.

The specific association between cavalry and the aristocracy was not unique to Rome. In the pre-industrial societies of Europe, the Near East and Asia (commonly referred to as the 'Old World'), the ability to tame and breed horses and then deploy them in battle was one of the primary distinguishing features of wealthy military elites.[14] Chariot warfare was the pre-eminent form of aristocratic display and combat in Greece and the Near East from the eighteenth century BC until the seventh century BC.[15] This is demonstrated, for example, by the predominance of chariots in Homer's *Iliad*.[16] By the seventh century BC the civilisations of Greece and the Near East had largely made the transition from fighting from chariots to cavalry warfare. This was the result of horseback riding spreading south from the Eurasian steppe, where it had first developed in the ninth century BC.[17] The employment of chariots did not die out entirely in the Near East, with scythed chariots being used by the Achaemenids and the Seleucids, for example, but it was still very limited in comparison with horseback riding.[18] The shift from chariot to cavalry did not happen simultaneously throughout the Old World. In Asia, chariot warfare remained widespread for longer, with the Chinese aristocrats of the 'Springs and Autumns' period (722–481 BC) riding in their chariots with bows and arrows.[19] In Italy itself, the transition from chariot to horseback during the Archaic period was heavily influenced by contacts with Greek colonies. Although Athens, Sparta and Corinth only adopted cavalry units in the fifth century BC, there had long been a tradition of an aristocratic cavalry elite in good horse-rearing regions such as Thessaly, Boeotia and Macedonia from an early date.[20] The oldest Greek colony in Italy was Cumae, founded in the eighth century BC by settlers from Euboea, and the presence of an aristocratic cavalry cohort in this colony clearly influenced the appearance of a similar elite, famed for their prowess on horseback, in nearby Capua by the sixth century BC.[21] There were several regions in

---

[14] Ferguson 1999: 424; Bachrach 1999: 292–4; Raber and Tucker 2005.   [15] Drews 2004: 51–4.

[16] Drews 2004: 72. Cf. Kelder 2012, marshalling the limited evidence for cavalry in Mycenaean Greece.

[17] Drews 2004: 99. Pre-conquest 'New World' civilisations did not have horses, but there were other ways of differentiating aristocratic combatants in Aztec society (Hassig 1999). Among the ancient Maya, however, elites and non-elites did not even use different weapons (Webster 1999: 343–6).

[18] Sabin and De Souza 2007: 417–18.

[19] Yates 1999: 18–20. Cavalry became important in the subsequent 'Warring states' period (Graff 2002: 21–2).

[20] Spence 1993: 176–8; Sekunda 2013: 201. On Thessalian horses, see Hyland 1990: 16–17. For the emergence of Athenian cavalry in the fifth century BC, see now Spence 2010.

[21] Nicolet 1962; Frederiksen 1968.

Italy, such as Tuscany and Apulia, that were good for horse-rearing and made the emergence of mounted warfare on the peninsula possible, with the proviso that cavalry service was restricted to those wealthy enough to breed and equip horses.[22] It is in this context that we can place the rise of the mobile and mounted warrior aristocracy of Latium, and Rome itself, during the Regal period.

The *Res Publica*

The Roman *res publica* took shape in the fifth and fourth centuries BC after the expulsion of the kings, but it was a system of government and social organisation that was constantly evolving.[23] The name *res publica* meant that the state was essentially 'public property'.[24] At the beginning of the *res publica*, cavalry of the state was supplied by the wealthiest citizens, who were classified as *equites* during the quinquennial census. This meant that the *equites* no longer constituted a group that derived its power from 'traditional authority', as the warrior elites did, but now formed an 'occupational status group', defined by their official function, according to Weber's categories of status.[25] The appropriate Latin word for this new status group was *ordo* (plural: *ordines*) for which the English 'order' is a suitable translation, even if the basic concept does not translate well to our modern social hierarchy. An *ordo* was 'a body of people [with] the same political or social status' as defined in relation to their place within the Roman state.[26] The Romans thus conceived of their *res publica* as being composed of several *ordines* rather than economic classes.[27] Since the early Roman state organised its citizenry along military lines (as shown by the structure of the *comitia centuriata*), the earliest *ordines* were the *equites* (the wealthiest who fought on horses), the *pedites* (the citizen infantry), and the *proletarii* (the non-fighting poor).[28]

How did military elite of the *equites*, which represented one of Weber's true occupational status groups, diversify and transform into an aristocracy which was not solely defined by martial valour? Originally there were only

---

[22] Frederiksen 1968: 10; Hyland 1990: 17, 188.

[23] On the evolution of the *res publica*, see Hillard 2005 and Flower 2010.

[24] Judge 1974: 280–1; Hammer 2014: 30–1.

[25] Weber 1968: 306. Note especially Stein 1927: 1, who describes the equestrian order as an economic, social and juridical 'status group' (*Stand* in German).

[26] OLD s.v. *ordo* 4; Nicolet 1974: 175.   [27] Nicolet 1974: 175–6; Cohen 1975; Finley 1999: 45.

[28] Cohen 1975: 281. On military organisation as a basis for social hierarchy, see Ferguson 1999: 400.

1,800 cavalrymen, known as the *equites equo publico*, whose horses were supplied at state expense. In 403 BC the state permitted any male citizen who met the highest census qualification to serve as an *eques*, so long as he provided his own horse.[29] However, over the course of subsequent centuries, the Roman state came to rely on auxiliary troops as cavalrymen, meaning that the *equites* themselves now only served as officers. Although military prowess remained important to the collective identity of the *equites*, it began to be rivalled by other sources of prestige, such as the pursuit and display of wealth through land ownership, business ventures and tax collection, as well as excellence in literature, rhetoric and oratory. This meant that the original cavalry aristocracy transformed into a wealthy ruling elite. Such a development was not unique to Rome; indeed, it can be described as a characteristic feature of the evolution of societies as they become more politically and economically complex.[30] By the mid-second century BC the Roman aristocracy was composed of elites who rejoiced in the title of *equites* even if they no longer constituted the main body of the cavalry. What had begun as an occupational status had become a mark of distinction.

The *equites* were composed of senators (of whom there were only 300), and all non-senators who also met the property qualification for cavalry service. The situation changed in the last decades of the second century BC, when members of the eighteen equestrian centuries were forced to relinquish their horse upon admission to the senate, and thus ceased to be *equites*. This measure was soon followed by a series of laws which gave the remaining (non-senatorial) *equites* a prominent and separate role in politics as jurors in the criminal courts. These two developments were the catalyst that forced a separation between senatorial and non-senatorial elites in terms of status distinctions, which had been simmering for centuries.[31] In the new hierarchy of the *res publica*, there was a clear distinction between the senatorial order (*ordo senatorius*) and the equestrian order (*ordo equester*). These *ordines* were superior in status and prestige to the third order, the people or ordinary citizens (*plebs*). Although the Romans continued to be organised in the military organisation of the *comitia centuriata* for voting purposes, the new social hierarchy replaced the old *ordines* of *equites*, *pedites* and *proletarii* of the early

---

[29] This discussion summarises the conclusions of Chapter 1.
[30] Mosca 1939: 57; Bottomore 1993: 29.
[31] Weber 1968: 306 notes how the acquisition of political influence often results in the formation of new status groups.

Republic.[32] The change does not mean that the equestrian order constituted in any sense an economic 'middle class'; rather, they were the second
tier of the Roman aristocracy.[33] The distribution of the wealth acquired by
the expanding Roman state in the Republican period shaped this two-tier
aristocracy. The profits of empire were disproportionally allocated to
affluent elites (senators and equestrians), rather than to ordinary
citizens.[34] Indeed, in Polybius' description of the Roman state and the
relationship between the senate, the consuls and the people as organs of
government, 'the people' are largely wealthy non-senators, rather than the
plebs.[35] The emergence of the equestrian order therefore gave these rich
non-senators an official status within the framework of the *res publica*,
elevating them above the other citizens.[36]

This was not a premeditated decision by any individual or group, of
course, but the result of long-term evolution. Indeed, sociological studies
of aristocracies have shown the vital function they perform in providing
states with their essential structure and cohesion.[37] When viewed in historical perspective, we can see that the two-tier aristocratic structure of the
Roman state was not a novel form of social organisation. As Mosca has
observed, 'below the highest stratum in the ruling class there is always . . .
another that is much more numerous and comprises all the capacities for
leadership in the country'.[38] In both the Republican and imperial periods
the equestrian order constituted the main source for new senators, who
numbered between 300 and 600, depending on the time period. There were
probably 15,000 *equites* in each generation in the first century BC, rising to
20,000–30,000 in the principate.[39] Moreover, the senate itself was not
a closed and exclusively hereditary aristocracy.[40] Entrance into the senate
and equestrian order was based upon financial and moral evaluation by the

---

[32] Cohen 1975: 281.
[33] Cohen 1975: 265; De Ste. Croix 1981: 42, 339–40; Finley 1999: 49–50. It is unfortunate that Hill
     1952, which was otherwise a very important book for its time, refers to the equestrians as the
     'middle class'. The true 'middle class' of ancient Rome, if we can apply such a concept to the pre-
     modern world, formed part of the *plebs*. See Harris 2011: 15–26 and E. Mayer 2012: 8–14 for
     methodological and theoretical reflections on the issue. They suggest that it is possible to think
     in terms of economic classes in Rome, even if the Romans themselves did not conceptualise
     their society in this way.
[34] Mann 1986: 256.   [35] This is discussed further in Chapter 1.
[36] On the role of states in organising social hierarchies, see Poulantzas 1978: 127.
[37] See, for example, Weber 1968: 305–7; Zmora 2001: 1–2; Scheidel 2013: 19–20.
[38] Mosca 1939: 404.   [39] See Chapters 1 and 5.
[40] Hopkins and Burton 1983. For the basic principle of aristocratic replenishment, see also Mosca
     1939: 413.

censors, and later by the emperors.[41] Therefore, the evolution of the separate senatorial and equestrian orders in Rome is consistent with historical trends more broadly.[42] The *ordo equester* performed the sociological function of ensuring that a wide range of wealthy elites were invested in the *res publica*.[43]

We have already discussed above in the context of warrior aristocracies the need for status groups to be given meaning and unity through shared values and ideology. This sense of purpose has been styled 'immanence' by Mann.[44] In the case of the new *ordo equester*, it inherited the martial virtues, ceremonies and status symbols that had previously belonged to the aristocratic cavalry.[45] Even though the equestrians of the late Republic were not all cavalrymen (though some did serve as officers), these militaristic attributes, such as the annual parade on horseback through the city of Rome, helped to provide them with a distinctive ideological purpose which they otherwise might have lacked. For the equestrian order, 'there was genuine social-psychological meaning' in the title of *eques*, as Finley put it. This meant that as a collective unit *equites* became something more than publicans, businessmen, orators, grammarians, army officers, or small-town Italian elites, but the inheritors of a long and proud tradition of service to the state.[46] Their outward *raison d'être* was not the acquisition of wealth, but displaying their *virtus* in order to defend Rome and its interests.[47] This enabled the *equites* to assume a place in the *res publica* alongside members of the senate, whose own ideological purpose was to serve the state *domi militiaeque*. This literally means 'at home and abroad', and refers to both civilian magistracies and positions of military command.

The dissonance between the ideological expression that underpinned the collective identity of the *ordo equester* and the day-to-day lives of most *equites* was not a problem, but rather a source of strength. As Hillard has

[41] Of course, this did not stop the impulse towards a hereditary aristocracy in Rome, in the sense that senators' sons were usually *equites*, and thus part of the upper strata of society. In the imperial period Augustus formally extended senatorial dignity to the family members of senators, though descendants still had to be formally adlected into the senate itself. These developments are discussed in Chapters 4 and 5.

[42] There appears to be no consistency in the methods of stratification of society: sometimes there is strict legal definition of different status groups, as with the senatorial and equestrian orders, while at other times no such juridical criteria are imposed (Eisenstadt 1993: 84–6).

[43] Note in this regard the comments of Hillard 2005: 6 and Flower 2010: 11–12 on the *res publica* as an ideological concept that promoted Roman unity by including all citizens, even though in reality they were sharply divided by status.

[44] Mann 1986: 519. See also Weber 1968: 935.   [45] For discussion, see Chapter 3.

[46] Finley 1999: 46.

[47] M. I. Henderson 1963: 61. For ideology and group solidarity, see Mann 1986: 519, and as far as state service is concerned, Kautsky 1997: 169–71.

noted, Roman public ideology in all its forms was effectively 'theatre' – not in the sense of a performance devoid of meaning, but as 'a reflection of communal values'.[48] These ceremonies and symbols thus served a very real purpose, giving the *ordo equester* its social and political immanence. In pre-modern societies, regimes or social groups that lacked a coherent ideology tended to crumble or wither away.[49] It was very common, therefore, for military accomplishment to be retained as a basis for group cohesion, even though the elites concerned subsequently acquired sources of prestige beyond martial valour.[50] For example, the evolution of a mounted aristocracy into a status group defined by the state, as was the case with Rome's *ordo equester*, finds a parallel in the transformation of knights in medieval Europe.[51] However, medieval knighthood subsequently took a very different trajectory in that it became a hereditary nobility, in a way that the equestrian order never did.[52]

We have thus far identified here many aspects of the Roman aristocracy of the Republic that are common to pre-modern societies. Firstly, elite groups shared common values, which gave them an ideological purpose. Secondly, we have observed that complex societies usually had a larger secondary group of aristocrats beneath the top rank of the elite. However, it is important to emphasise that it was not inevitable that the equestrian order would emerge in precisely the way that it did. Instead, its evolution can only be explained by situations specific to Rome itself. In this context, it is instructive to compare the Roman Republic with Classical Athens and its democratic system of government. These two states not only existed contemporaneously within the Mediterranean, but they were also largely exceptional in the global context of the pre-industrial world, since the natural evolution of societies usually resulted in monarchical rather than republican or democratic constitutions.[53] Yet the cavalry aristocracy in each state evolved in fundamentally different ways. Like the Roman Republic, Athenian society was divided into distinct status groups organised on a timocratic basis from the time of Solon onwards.[54] Even after the Solonic hierarchy ceased to be relevant, cavalry service remained the

---

[48] Hillard 2005: 4.

[49] See the comments of Crone 1980: 62–71 on the early 'Abbāsids' failure to create a 'political rationale' for their state.

[50] Kautsky 1997: 169–77.   [51] Duby 1976: 356; Barber 1995: 43; Zmora 2001.

[52] Duby 1980: 295.

[53] Crone 2003: 42. One cannot avoid thinking of Polybius' anacyclosis in this context (Polyb. 6.4.1–9.14). For Republics in world history, see Everdell 2000.

[54] Raaflaub 1999: 135.

preserve of the wealthiest citizens who could afford horses.[55] The cavalry
was therefore the domain of rich, young aristocrats who trained together
and performed in public displays and festivals, in a comparable manner to
the Roman *equites* who marched in an annual parade through the city of
Rome.[56] However, Athenian democratic ideology meant that the cavalrymen were not celebrated in the same way as the *equites*. Horse riding
possessed strong monarchical overtones for the Athenians, as it was associated with autocratic states such as Macedon and Persia.[57] The rise of the
hoplite infantry in the seventh century BC was idealised as the triumph of
popular political participation over autocracy, even if the so-called hoplite
revolution was really a much more gradual process than our sources would
have us believe.[58] Henceforth, it was the citizen infantryman who demonstrated true *andreia*, the Greek equivalent of *virtus*, not the cavalryman.[59]
Athens' democratic ideology did not always live up to its lofty claims of
equality, and there was certainly debate and discussion as to whether
democracy was always the best form of government, especially among
elites, though this never produced any long-term social change.[60]
The nature of the Athenian political system therefore meant that the
citizens who served in the cavalry did not cohere into a distinct status
group.

 Why did the evolution of the cavalry elite in Rome take a different path?
Rome was not a democracy in the same manner as Athens, but it was still
formally a *res publica* in which the people exercised authority in matters
such as declaring peace and war, authorising legislation, and deciding
capital crimes.[61] The answer must be that the Roman Republic was
a 'mixed constitution', as Polybius divined, which depended on a balance

---

[55] Kamen 2013: 3 rejects the use of the term 'order' for Athenian social groups because of the
Roman associations.

[56] For this, and much of what follows, see Spence 1993: 181–230.

[57] Spence 1993: 193–5; Finley 1999: 47. For an example of 'democratic anxiety' about the cavalry
in practice, see Blanshard 2010: 214–18.

[58] Lintott 2001: 158–60; Raaflaub 1999: 132.

[59] This is widely acknowledged by scholars, e.g. Spence 1993: 165–76; Raaflaub 1999: 137; Low
2002: 104–6; P. Hunt 2007: 126–7. We must be careful not to oversimplify, however, given the
prominence of cavalry on monuments such as the Parthenon frieze: they were not excluded
from Athenian civic pride altogether. See Spence 1993: 202; Balot 2006: 820.

[60] Balot 2006: 82–3, 89–90, 177; Spence 2010: 116. Low 2002 offers a sensitive appreciation of the
ways in which cavalry service could both cohere and conflict with Athenian political ideology in
the early fourth century BC. On the difference between ideology and practice in articulating
status in Classical Athens, see Kamen 2013.

[61] Polyb. 6.14.4–12; Lintott 1999: 199–208; Millar 2002: 32–3. Indeed, in a series of important
articles and books, Millar has emphasised the democratic elements of the Roman system which
were previously neglected (Millar 1984, 1986, 1998, 2002).

between democratic, oligarchic and monarchical elements.[62] Indeed, after the Regal period the heads of the warrior aristocratic clans continued to exert influence and dominate political affairs and senior magistracies into the Republican period.[63] This meant that aristocratic ideology was not regarded with suspicion in Rome, as it was in Greece, but formed an essential part of defining social identity and hierarchy within the *res publica*.[64] Equestrian status gave wealthy, landed aristocrats who could not be (or did not want to be) enrolled in the senate an official status and public identity. This returns us to the sociological reason for the consolidation of the equestrian order as a status group, namely that it offered a way for elite non-senatorial citizens to be recognised and honoured within the *res publica*. The only way for Athens to give prominence to its aristocratic elites in the same manner was to change its whole system of government from democracy to oligarchy; attempts to do so did not meet with long-term success.[65]

We have thus far examined the cultural and sociological reasons for the evolution of the *ordo equester*, but it is equally important to recognise the importance of individual politicians in its development.[66] The *ordo*'s emergence as a status group distinct from the senate in the late second century BC was also the result of Gaius Gracchus' law regarding the composition of juries in the extortion court. This law empanelled equestrian citizens with no senatorial relations to sit in judgement on the conduct of senatorial governors. Although equestrians had been previously involved in political conflicts with senators about the issue of tax contracts, this is the first time that equestrians were given official posts in the civilian political sphere of Rome itself (as opposed to officer commands in the army).[67] The change can be attributed to the vision of Gaius Gracchus as a reformer who, among other things, wanted to hold senators to account for their conduct. The empanelment of equestrian jurors initiated much more significant tension between senators and equestrians, as it meant that the senators had to answer to *equites* for the first time. The conflicts between senators and equestrians in the late Republic were thus largely

---

[62] Polyb. 6.11.1–18.8. The constitution was not designed with this balance in mind, like that of Lycurgus of Sparta, but evolved over time (Polyb. 6.10.1–13). North 1990: 20–1 argues that for all Rome's 'democratic' features, Sparta actually bears a greater resemblance to the Roman Republic than does Athens.

[63] See Chapter 1.

[64] Moreover, as Hillard 2005: 3–4 notes, competition between elites was an inherent part of the political culture of the Roman Republic.

[65] Brock and Hodkinson 2001: 16–17.   [66] Mann 1986: 531–2.

[67] These two laws are discussed at the end of Chapter 1.

the result of the new political role which Gaius Gracchus had bestowed upon the *equites*, rather than any class conflict.[68] Indeed, the story of the equestrian order in the first century BC, as illuminated through the works of Cicero, focuses on the question of how the order's new political authority should be integrated into the framework of a *res publica* in which they had previously been merely an order defined by wealth and status.[69] In Weberian terms, the *ordo equester* was transformed from an occupational status group to one with political power and influence.[70] However, it is important to sound a note of caution here, as the *equites* do not entirely map on to Weber's characterisation of a political status group. This is because the political influence of the *equites* was primarily reactive, in the sense that they did not, and could not, pursue their own policies, and only intervened as a collective in matters that directly affected their interests.[71]

The Monarchical *Res Publica*

In the late first century BC the monarchical element within the *res publica* became more pronounced with the rise of powerful aristocrats or 'dynasts' such as C. Iulius Caesar, Marcus Antonius, and Octavian, who became Augustus in 27 BC. Although Augustus is traditionally referred to as the 'first emperor' of Rome in modern historical discourse, this appellation is one of hindsight. For the Romans of the 'Augustan age', their state was still a *res publica*, albeit one in which the monarchical power of the consuls was gradually being invested in one man.[72] Therefore, as Kaldellis has argued, the Roman state was a 'monarchical *res publica*'.[73] The evolution of the Roman state had important ramifications for the equestrian order. For, like many monarchs, Augustus tried to ensure that the elites were dependent on him for their sources of prestige, as a way of consolidating his rule.[74] Firstly, Augustus ensured that equestrians had

---

[68] Note in this regard the important comment of Kautsky 1997: 49 that aristocratic empires did not have 'class conflict', but rather political disputes between aristocrats.

[69] See Chapter 2.

[70] Weber 1968: 306, defining a political status group as one that emerges 'through monopolistic appropriation of political . . . powers'. The *equites* cannot be described in these terms, although they did have political influence.

[71] Badian 1962: 224.   [72] Flower 2010: 12–15.

[73] Kaldellis 2015: 22–31. See also Bang 2011, who, in a stimulating essay points out that the early Roman empire was not alone in being a state in transition, and that compromise between different aspects of government was often a feature of monarchical states.

[74] Bendix 1978: 219–20; Eisenstadt 1993: 132–4; Crone 2003: 64–6. An excellent example is the medieval ceremony of dubbing performed by emperors, kings and princes (see Duby 1980:

a clearly defined place within his *res publica*. He personally supervised the enrolment of new members, laid down strict moral and social standards, opened up new priesthoods to *equites*, and created links between the order and his own family.[75] Over the course of the first century AD, as the new monarchical *res publica* took shape, equestrian rank essentially became the gift of the emperors. The number of *equites* increased significantly, encompassing the most prestigious elites from the provinces. The imperial *ordo equester* probably numbered about 20,000–30,000 members in each generation.[76] The measures of Augustus and his successors represented a process of 'domestication', which made the *equites* – thousands of wealthy non-senatorial elites from Italy and the provinces – dependent on the emperor for honours and privileges.[77]

Secondly, Augustus and his successors not only employed equestrians as military officers, but also deployed them in a range of civilian procuratorial positions, such as financial administrators and provincial governors. This gave equestrians access to a large range of government offices that were no different to those performed by senators.[78] This meant that *equites* could now claim to serve the state *domi militiaeque* like senators. This ideology of service was enshrined in monuments and inscriptions which listed their army commands, administrative positions, priesthoods and other honours.[79] However, the number of available procuratorships was very limited. In the Augustan period there are fewer than 30 positions attested, and although the number increased to more than 180 in the mid-third century AD, this was still a very small amount compared to the size of the equestrian order.[80] Therefore, it is probable that only 600 out of 20,000–30,000 equestrians in each generation were able to hold procuratorships.[81] Competition was very fierce, and became more so the further one was rose through the hierarchy, since there were fewer senior posts available. Even one position in the imperial service was therefore a major honour, and a sign of imperial favour.[82] The *equites* who did hold procuratorships constituted an elite group within the *ordo*, which Tacitus

---

300–1; Barber 1995: 36). Note also the way in which the Aztec king Moteuczoma Ilhuicamina gave titles of nobility to military men, thus binding them to him (Hassig 1999: 372). This was a general historical trend across Old and New World societies.

[75] See Chapters 8, 9 and 10.   [76] See Chapter 5.

[77] For the principle of 'domestication', see Elias 1982 and 1983. For its application to the Roman world, see Bang 2011: 107–8, 2013: 430; Weisweiler 2015. As Rosenstein 2009: 39–40 points out, senatorial aristocrats had to 'collaborate' with the emperors in order to receive honours from them.

[78] See Chapters 4, 6 and 7.   [79] This is discussed in Chapters 6–7.   [80] Pflaum 1950: 105.

[81] Bang 2011: 124.   [82] See Chapters 5 and 7.

called the *equestris nobilitas* ('equestrian nobility').[83] In sociological terms they comprised a 'service aristocracy', an elite whose members receive titles and status not because of their birth, but as a result of the positions they hold within the state.[84] From the second century AD members of the equestrian order in official positions gained a range of new titles (such as *vir egregius*, 'excellent man'), which indicated that they were superior to other *equites*.[85] This process was a fundamental part of the monarchicalisation of the Roman state.[86]

The gradual evolution of the equestrian order – or more accurately, part of the order – into a 'service aristocracy' finds parallels in other pre-modern societies. As Mosca stated, 'aristocratic autocracies almost always develop into more or less bureaucratic autocracies'.[87] As these states evolved and became more bureaucratically complex, they needed a broader range of leaders and officials, which could only be drawn from the ruling class.[88] For example, the knights of medieval Europe acquired judicial and administrative roles by virtue of their social standing and prestige, which broadened their influence beyond the military sphere.[89] However, as we pointed out earlier, it is important to emphasise that the precise reasons for the evolution of service aristocracies are specific to the individual civilisations. In Rome the integration of the equestrian order into civilian government was prompted by Gaius Gracchus' laws assigning them roles as jurors in the criminal courts. This process was dramatically accelerated by Augustus' desire to appoint *equites* to administrative positions alongside senators. Indeed, Augustus' employment of *equites* in some posts, such as the newly created prefecture of Egypt, was motivated by the fact that they were not members of the senatorial aristocracy. The selection of *equites* was prompted by the belief that they would be loyal to Augustus, and would not be regarded as viable rivals for the purple.[90] In the

---

[83] Tac. *Agr.* 4.1.

[84] For discussion of aristocracies of service, see Mosca 1939: 60; Kautsky 1997: 127–32; Crone 2003: 67–8. Not all states were successful in forming aristocracies of service: note the failure of the 'Abbāsids to achieve this (Crone 1980: 70–1).

[85] See Chapter 7. For the practice of aristocrats demanding ever more precise status distinctions to mark themselves out from their peers, see Kautsky 1997: 213–17.

[86] On ruling ideology providing the basis for the cohesion of state functionaries, see Poulantzas 1978: 154–6; Mann 1986: 269–70.

[87] Mosca 1939: 405.

[88] See Kautsky 1997: 92–5 on the 'meritocracy' of the Chinese bureaucratic exams: most successful candidates were already elites or had elite connections. Scheidel 2009b: 19 also notes the role played by recommendations and patronage in the Chinese system in a manner similar to Rome.

[89] Barber 1995: 41–3. See also Bang and Turner 2015: 17–18 on Han China.

[90] This is explored in Chapter 4. Men of equestrian rank from the administration or officer corps would become viable candidates for the purple in the third century AD, on which see Chapters 11–12.

Republican period the expansion of the equestrian order gave wealthy non-senatorial elites a reason to be invested in the state. This principle still applied in imperial Rome, but it was intensified by a new actor, the emperor, who not only wanted these elites to be tied to the *res publica*, but also to him personally.

The combined senatorial and equestrian aristocracy of the Roman empire has sometimes been characterised as a fundamentally 'civilian' rather than 'military' elite, which represented something of a historical anomaly, paralleled in the pre-industrial world only by China.[91] The unified Chinese empire of the Qin and Han period (221 BC–AD 220) certainly saw a civilian aristocracy and its ideology take hold, in comparison to the previous periods of 'Warring States'.[92] The new social hierarchy was based on the old military model, but the ideology promoted by court intellectuals emphasised the personal virtue of the Chinese emperors and the maintenance of peace and prosperity through their rule.[93] There are some evident points of connection here with Rome, most notably the inheritance of a military social structure (the *comitia centuriata* of Rome), the virtues of the ruler (the *civilis princeps* in Roman thought), and the message of peace (*pax Romana*).[94] But it is problematic to think of the ruling elite of both empires as exclusively 'civilian'.[95] Rome's senatorial and equestrian orders were certainly not a warrior aristocracy, but the army remained an important part of their careers and representation. First and foremost, they aspired to serve the state *domi militiaeque*, in both civilian and military capacities. Army commands still carried significant cachet and prestige for the equestrians, who were drawn from the municipal elites of Italy and the empire.[96] All members of the equestrian order in the imperial period were still eligible to march in the annual

---

[91] Mann 1986: 270; Wickham 2005: 158. For example, see Leyser 1994: 67 on knighthood in the ninth century AD: 'There were no civilians in this lay nobility. A non-belligerent lay noble was a monster just like an armed priest.' These dynamics crossed east–west lines. For example, the Chinese aristocracy differed significantly in its ideological outlook and cultural values from the Japanese warrior caste of the Samurai, which had more in common with the knights of medieval Europe in some ways (Holcombe 1994: 56–8, 72; cf. Friday 2003: 10, emphasising the contrast between the Samurai and the Japanese civilian government more generally).

[92] For the 'great convergence', which refers to the establishment of a stable, unified monarchy in both China and Rome, see Scheidel 2009b: 17–18.

[93] Yates 1999: 33–4; Rosenstein 2009: 41–2.

[94] Mittag and Mutschler 2008: 442, in their comparison of imperial Rome and Han China, note that the development of an ideology of peace was common in societies that have reached their geographical extent.

[95] Bang and Turner 2015: 20–2 make important remarks on elites in Han China, drawing attention to military careers or aspects of martial ideology that have been undervalued by scholars.

[96] See Chapter 6.

parade in Rome, the *transvectio equitum*, a legacy of the days when the *equites* were the cavalry. This parade, as well as a range of other ceremonies, continued to emphasise the military origins of the *ordo* and the *virtus* of its members. This ideology gave the *equites* their sense of purpose, or 'immanence'.[97] The same point can be made about the senate, whose members continued to serve in military commands until the mid-third century AD. The senatorial and equestrian aristocracy of the empire cannot therefore be characterised entirely as 'civilian', as its members aspired to serve the state in whatever capacity they were required, whether that was as officers or officials.[98]

Military and Civilian Identities

The third century AD witnessed a challenge to this paradigm with the emergence of a new military elite from the ranks of the army itself. Its members were soldiers promoted directly to officer commands who became equestrians as a result of their appointments (rather than equestrian rank being a precondition for their selection in the first place).[99] These officers served alongside *equites* from the municipal elites, but came to constitute a significant force their own right in the middle decades of the third century. A series of military crises led the emperor Gallienus to appoint these officers to senior army posts in preference to senators, who effectively lost the right to command troops in battle. From the late third century AD most emperors emerged from within this military cadre, rather than the senatorial aristocracy, as martial accomplishment became a prime criterion for appointment to the imperial office. Matthews has argued that the soldiers who became generals and emperors possessed an 'alternative value system' to the existing senatorial and equestrian elites and their *domi militiaeque* ideology.[100] There were certainly social and cultural divisions between men reared in the army, on the one hand, and blue-blooded aristocrats and civilian bureaucrat elites, on the other. Comments about the boorish and uncivilised nature of Danubian emperors, such as the Tetrarchs and the Valentinians, are common in our literary sources.[101]

---

[97] See Chapter 8.
[98] Powis 1984: 43–62 shows how martial capabilities continued to coexist alongside other civilian markers of aristocratic ideology as pre-modern states evolved.
[99] This process is discussed in detail in Chapter 11.
[100] Matthews 2000b: 436–8; P. Brown 2000: 332–3.
[101] Tetrarchs: Victor, *Caes.* 40.12, with Lact. *DMP* 19.6 on Maximinus Daza. Valentinian I and Valens: Amm. 29.3.6, 31.14.5, with commentary of Lenski 2002: 86–8.

But there were also attempts at integration. The soldier emperors of the third and fourth centuries claimed to espouse the senatorial and equestrian *domi militiaeque* ethos.[102] These Danubian emperors ensured that their sons were sufficiently educated to be able to interact on an equal footing with the senatorial aristocracy, as shown by Valentinian I's employment of Ausonius as tutor to Gratian.[103]

Similar points can be made about the generals themselves. In the mid-fourth century AD senior military commanders were granted senatorial status, which made them part of the wider aristocratic stratum of the *viri clarissimi*.[104] Despite their origins in the camps, the generals of the later Roman empire still sought validation through civilian honours in the gift of the emperor, such as equestrian or senatorial status, the ordinary consulship, marriages and connections with established aristocrats, and the acquisition of land, wealth and power at court.[105] Nor was the process entirely one way, as the elites of the cities and senate adopted or appropriated martial virtues. Members of the curial classes continued to seek officer commands in the Roman army alongside soldiers who rose from the ranks, and senatorial aristocrats appropriated martial dress and symbols as part of their panoply of prestige.[106] Therefore, the new army elites and the existing equestrian and senatorial aristocracies adopted aspects of each other's life and *habitus*. The result was that both groups espoused civilian and military values to some degree, encouraging a sense of cohesion and preventing the rise of an absolutely separate warrior aristocracy.[107] This was a very different situation from that which prevailed in Latium during the Regal period, when Rome and its environs were dominated by warlords and their retinues.

Throughout all these changes, the *ordo equester* formally remained a constituent part of the *res publica*. But equestrian rank was now divided into a series of status grades, of which that of *eques Romanus* was the

---

[102] Davenport 2015a; 2016.   [103] McEvoy 2013: 106–7.   [104] See Chapter 12.
[105] Wickham 2005: 158; Halsall 2007: 92–3, with P. Brown 1992 and Näf 1995 on senatorial values. For a case study of a barbarian family and expressions of their identity in Roman politics, see McEvoy 2016 on the Ardaburii of the fifth century AD. See also Demandt 1980 on the connections and networks of the military elites more generally.
[106] Halsall 2007: 109–10, 350–1, 474–5, 484.
[107] The army officers of the later Roman empire were therefore quite different from the Huns (see Maenchen-Helfen 1973: 190–9). One might also compare the situation in Rome with medieval China. The ascension of military elites and their emperors under the Song, Qi, Liang and Chen dynasties did not result in the change of overall imperial ideology or aristocratic values. The new martial corps instead adopted the aristocratic lifestyles that had already been established in the Han period. See Holcombe 1994: 21, 36, 56–8, 72; Graff 2002: 90–3, 115–16, 256; Scheidel 2009b: 21–2.

lowest. Officers, administrators and curial elites sought the higher ranks of *egregius* and *perfectissimus* which offered greater privileges and immunities. This meant that although equestrian status continued to be valuable, it is doubtful that all its holders identified themselves as part of an 'equestrian order'.[108] Moreover, over the course of the fourth century AD, senatorial status was gradually extended to administrative posts, provincial governorships and military commands. After the early decades of the fifth century AD the only equestrians in the Roman world were junior bureaucrats within the imperial administration, members of honoured corporations (such as the shipmasters) and municipal elites who had not been fortunate enough to acquire the senatorial rank of *clarissimus* they craved. Equestrian status remained an important distinction for these individuals, as they were *honestiores*, who were immune from base punishments. But it did not offer the same social value as it had for the *publicani* of the late Republic or Augustus' procurators. The ceremonies that had bound and united the *ordo equester* as an order gradually ceased to take place over the late empire. In particular, the connection between equestrian rank, *virtus* and martial valour in Roman public life disappeared. This can at least in part be attributed to the militarisation of the Roman administration in general, as all functionaries were said to be pursuing their *militia*, or 'military service'. But it was also the case that the ethos of serving the *res publica* in civilian and military capacities now belonged to the united senatorial order into which the senior administrators, governors and generals had been promoted.

Monarchy and Aristocracy (Reprise)

It was only with the gradual breakdown of the western Roman empire as a distinct political organisation that the aristocracies of western Europe became more ostentatiously military, as civilian administrative opportunities declined. In fifth-century AD Gaul some aristocrats took up arms in order to defend the Roman state, attempt to usurp authority for themselves, or support the cause of the incoming barbarians.[109] The successor states that emerged from the shell of the western empire, such as the Visigothic, Burgundian and Merovingian realms, were monarchies. They were constantly on a war footing, so the ideology of kingship was firmly

---

[108] See Chapter 12.
[109] Halsall 2007: 494–6, 2010: 375–6. For aristocrats turning towards the German invaders, see Wickham 1984: 18–19.

based on success in war rather than personal character or civilian virtues.[110] The most important men in the social hierarchy were those who could support the kings in battle.[111] The combined civilian–military senatorial career ceased to be an option for Gallic aristocrats, since there was no longer any Roman *cursus* which took them to consulships or prefectures in the sixth century.[112] The only civilian careers were ecclesiastical ones.[113] These changes in central and southern Gaul between the late fifth and sixth centuries AD resulted in aristocratic *habitus* becoming increasingly martial in nature.[114] In the region to the north of the Loire river there also emerged a new aristocracy of service, with a distinctive militaristic ethos, dependent on the Merovingian kings. By the seventh century AD, a hereditary military nobility can be found throughout Gaul, or Francia, as it was then known.[115]

Similar reasons lay behind the militarisation of the aristocracy in Italy in the late sixth and seventh centuries AD.[116] The Italian senatorial elite had originally prospered after there had ceased to be a western Roman emperor, since their new Ostrogothic overlords maintained existing structures, and furnished the army and military elite from their own ranks.[117] However, the collapse of Ostrogothic rule and the Byzantine invasion of Italy resulted in 'the eclipse of the senatorial aristocracy and the institutions associated with it' by the seventh century AD, as Brown has shown.[118] As with post-Roman Gaul, military fiefdoms arose throughout Italy.[119] The collapse of the Roman state and its institutions resulted in the demise of its aristocratic civilian values as well. The states that replaced the empire in the west were not *res publicae*, but were unashamedly autocratic regimes ruled by warrior kings. In the Roman eastern (or 'Byzantine') empire, the continuance of the civilian institutions and ideals of the *res publica* delayed

---

[110] For military theology, see McCormick 1986. See also I. Wood 1994: 66–70; Halsall 2007: 489–90.

[111] The late Roman empire in the west was also on a war footing, but generals were appointed to deal with these crises. They were given senatorial rank, and thus no distinct military caste emerged.

[112] Wickham 1984: 21.

[113] Mathisen 1993: 32, 53, 89–104, 125–31, 136–9. For the local nature of administration and careers, see also I. Wood 1994: 60–1; Halsall 2007: 480–2.

[114] Wickham 2005: 174–7. For military grave goods and masculinity, see Halsall 2010: 357–81.

[115] Wickham 2005: 179–85, 194–5, 200–1. See also Fouracre 2000 on the debate about the nature of the aristocracy in post-Roman Gaul.

[116] T. S. Brown 1984; Wickham 2005: 207, 239.

[117] This picture is broadly true, though exceptions can always be found: B. Swain 2016: 215–18.

[118] T. S. Brown 1984: 46–61 (quotation at 61); Barnish 1988.

[119] T. S. Brown 1984: 83, 125. Ecclesiastical careers appear to have been less attractive to the senatorial aristocracies of Italy as opposed to those of Gaul (Barnish 1988: 138–40).

the development of a true military aristocracy.[120] The process of change in Byzantium only began in the seventh century AD, as a result of the demise of the old senatorial order, the pressures of near-constant warfare, the creation of the military themes as the basis of imperial administration, and the increasing influx of outsiders such as Armenians into the imperial service as commanders.[121] The emergence of a hereditary Byzantine military aristocracy, however, was a product of the Komnenian age, a development which went hand in hand with a renewed emphasis on the martial virtues of the emperor.[122] The reconfiguration of networks of power and patronage in this period saw the disappearance of the old senatorial elite.[123] Therefore military aristocracies, such as those that existed in the Regal period, only returned to the Mediterranean world when the successor kingdoms established themselves in western Europe and the eastern, Byzantine empire shed the structures and institutions of earlier history, becoming more of a medieval monarchy.

A New Equestrian Order

The memory of Roman institutions continued to exercise a powerful hold on the European imagination. For example, in the twelfth century AD Arnold of Brescia was part of a movement called the Roman Commune, which wished to revive the Roman *res publica* together with its senate and equestrian order as part of an attempt to break the power of the Papacy.[124] But the Roman concept of the equestrian order also played an influential role in shaping the identity of medieval knights, who were envisioned as a discrete *ordo* within the social hierarchy. Knights were distinguished by the their own ceremonies, such as the ritual of dubbing, and status symbols, like the belt (*cingulum*).[125] The association between knights and the *ordo equester* actually stemmed from religious discourse. The medieval Christian Church conceived of society in terms of *ordines*, which it

---

[120] For the Byzantine state as a *res publica*, see Kaldellis 2015.

[121] Haldon 1990: 388–97, 2004: 213–15; Wickham 2005: 236–9.

[122] Kazhdan and Wharton Epstein 1985: 62–70, 110–16. See also Cheynet 2006: 5; Haldon 2009: 192.

[123] Haldon 2004: 225–6 notes that all senators were directly appointed by the emperor by the ninth century AD, which put an end to the 'hereditary clarissimate'.

[124] Bumke 1977: 110–11. Luscombe and Evans 1988: 314–15 draw attention to the larger intellectual and cultural significance of this movement.

[125] Barber 1995: 26–37. On the ceremonies, see also Leyser 1994: 57; Kaeuper 2009: 146.

inherited from the Roman world.[126] Christian intellectuals encouraged the notion that knights were an *ordo* serving Christ, which gave a theological justification to their professional pursuit of warfare.[127] The ritual of dubbing, through which men became knights, was transformed into a sacred ceremony, which was referred to as an 'ordination', akin to that of priests.[128] The new equestrian order (*ordo equestris* in Medieval Latin) of knights therefore had God's blessing to participate in military campaigns to preserve Christendom, most notably the Crusades.[129] The association with the Roman equestrian order was encouraged by medieval monarchs, who themselves wished to appropriate the legacy of the Roman emperors.[130] The emergence of a mounted warrior aristocracy in medieval Europe should of course be attributed to basic historical and sociological trends which we have already described, such as the association between elites and horseback riding, and the cohesion of such cavalry elites around monarchs. But their ideological sense of purpose, or immanence, was directly indebted to Rome and the memory of the *ordo equester*.

Structure of the Book

This book is divided into four parts. In Part I, after a brief foray through the age of the kings, we focus on the Roman Republic. Chapter 1, 'Riding for Rome', analyses the beginnings of equestrians as the cavalry of Rome, and the importance of courage and valour on horseback to the formation of aristocratic identity. We then move on to explore how equestrians came to form their own order as a constituent part of the *res publica*, separate from both the senate and the people. In Chapter 2, 'Cicero's Equestrian Order', we view the events of the first century BC through the eyes of Marcus Tullius Cicero, whose letters, speeches and treatises form the bulk of our evidence for equestrians in the late Republic. This chapter examines how Cicero's own portrait of the equestrian order, and the jurors, *publicani* and businessmen in its ranks, reflects contemporary uncertainty about the place of the new order within the Roman state. Chapter 3, 'Questions of Status', largely covers the same time period as Chapter 2, but from a slightly different perspective. In this chapter we analyse the new status symbols that came to define membership of the equestrian order, such as the census qualification, gold ring, reserved seats in the theatre, and the narrow-

---

[126] Duby 1980: 295.   [127] Morris 1978; Kaeuper 2009: 55, 137–45.
[128] Chenu 1968: 225–6; Duby 1980: 295–7.   [129] Luscombe and Evans 1988: 308–9.
[130] Jackson 1990: 104 on knighthood and the imperial ambitions of Frederick Barbarossa.

striped tunic. The significance of equestrian status is discussed not only from the perspective of Romans of established backgrounds, but also from the viewpoint of new entrants into the order.

Part II focuses on the institutional changes to the equestrian order in the monarchical *res publica*. Chapter 4, 'Pathways to the Principate', shows how the coming of monarchy under Augustus gave equestrians new opportunities to serve the state that had not existed under the Republic. In Chapter 5, 'An Imperial Order', the focus turns to equestrian status itself, and the way in which it came to be regarded as an imperial benefaction over the course of the first century AD. We study how equestrian rank was expressed throughout the provinces, as well as its inherent value to Roman citizens in regions as diverse as North Africa and Asia Minor. Chapters 6 and 7 form a linked pair: '*Cursus* and *Vita* (I): Officers' and '*Cursus* and *Vita* (II): Administrators'. These chapters analyse how the imperial system established by Augustus and augmented by his successors enabled equestrians to spend their lives serving the state in officer commands and administrative posts, rising through the ranks to the great prefectures at the imperial court itself. The evolution of an equestrian career structure was articulated in the public sphere by the large numbers of honorific and funerary monuments which featured inscriptions recording posts and honours bequeathed by the emperor. The new government hierarchy enabled equestrians to have careers in the army and administration similar to those pursued by senators, which resulted in the emergence of a service elite among the *ordo equester* at large. But not all equestrians desired long careers, and instead were content with one or two posts, or even an honorific title, which functioned as a mark of imperial favour.

Part III, 'Equestrians on Display', is devoted to three studies of the performative, cultural and religious aspects of the equestrian order, focusing mainly on the imperial period, but integrating material from the Republic as well. Chapter 8, 'Ceremonies and Consensus', looks at how equestrian status was articulated at a collective level, through parades and public displays, as well as its associations with the emperor and his family. In Chapter 9 we move to the theatre, arena and circus in 'Spectators and Performers'. Here we examine exactly why so many members of the equestrian order wished to perform on stage or fight as gladiators, and how the state tried to regulate this behaviour. This is paired with an analysis of the equestrian privilege of sitting in the first fourteen rows of the theatre, and how this functioned as a mark of social status in Rome and the provinces. Then, in Chapter 10, 'Religion and the *Res Publica*', the focus turns to the official priesthoods reserved for equestrians in Rome and its sacred periphery, in particular at cult sites in Latium. We show how these religious offices offered equestrians different, but complementary, honours and dignity to the military and administrative commands.

Part IV takes us into the late empire, and the equestrian order's final transition. Chapter 11, 'Governors and Generals', focuses on the transformation of the Roman army and administration in the third century AD, and particularly the ways in which equestrians came to replace senators as military commanders and provincial administrators. The chapter also examines the rise of new men into the equestrian order from the ranks of the army. Chapter 12, 'The Last *Equites Romani*', analyses the fragmentation of equestrian status, as traditional qualifications for the order were discarded, and the order itself transformed into a series of official status grades. Equestrians who served in the army and the administration emerged anew as senators, while equestrian status itself assumed a quite different place in the social hierarchy. The longevity of the equestrian order across more than a thousand years of Roman history can be attributed to the fact that it gave honour and dignity to wealthy elites who were not senators, but still desired a place within the *res publica* at large. This connection gained greater impetus in the monarchical state, as the emperors assumed the prerogative of bestowing equestrian status, creating a way of rewarding the cream of the provincial aristocracy and integrating them into the imperial system.

PART I

The Republic

1 | Riding for Rome

Introduction: Uncle Pliny's History

C. Plinius Secundus (or Pliny the Elder, as he is better known) is widely remembered today as the most prominent victim of the eruption of Mount Vesuvius, which destroyed Pompeii, Herculaneum and surrounding areas in AD 79. As prefect of the imperial fleet stationed at Misenum, Pliny mounted a heroic rescue effort, only to die of asphyxiation on the beach at Stabiae. The tale of the eruption and Pliny's unfortunate demise are memorably described in two letters written some years later by his rather bookish nephew, Pliny the Younger. These letters continue to be read in classrooms at schools and universities today.[1] Yet there is much more to Pliny the Elder's eventful life than his famous death. He was a prodigious author, penning works on cavalry combat; Rome's German Wars; a history continuing the account of Aufidius Bassus; and his surviving magnum opus, the thirty-seven-book *Natural History*, a compendium of essential facts and figures about the world in which he lived.[2] This vast output emerged during the course of his career in the Roman imperial army and administration, as a military officer, cavalry commander and imperial procurator.[3] Such positions were only open to Pliny because he was a member of the equestrian order.

No Roman ever wrote a history of the equestrian order (that we know of), but Pliny the Elder came closest. In Book 33 of his *Natural History*, Pliny turned to the subject of metals. As part of his discussion of gold, he embarked on a history of the *anulus aureus*, which was worn by equestrians in the early imperial period as a symbol of their privileged status within the Roman social hierarchy.[4] This led Pliny in turn to write a potted history of the equestrian order, covering essential topics such as the beginnings of Rome's cavalry, the judicial roles of equestrians, the right to wear the gold

---

[1] Pliny the Younger, *Ep.* 6.16, 6.20.   [2] For Pliny the Elder's *History*, see now Levick 2013.
[3] Pliny the Younger, *Ep.* 3.5 provides a memorable portrait of his uncle.
[4] Pliny the Elder, *NH* 33.18.

ring, and the changing names of the *equites*.[5] But this was no straightforward chronological account, for Pliny's focus remained very much on gold, luxury and their corruptive and corrosive effects. The formation of the *ordo equester* and the use of the gold ring as a status symbol was just one aspect of this larger point.[6] Pliny omitted key developments and pieces of legislation which were necessary to provide a coherent history. This has caused significant frustration to modern historians trying to chart the evolution of the *ordo equester*.[7] But although Pliny's account lacks the precise chronological pointers and specific details we might wish for, it does provide an authentic sense of the way in which equestrian status was continuously being redefined, shaped and challenged at both an individual and collective level in the Roman world.

Unlike the senate and the people, the equestrian order was not a constituent element of the Roman state at the very beginning of its history, but only emerged as a 'third part' (*tertium corpus*) of the *res publica* in the late second century BC.[8] The order's origins in the Regal period and the early Republic, as recounted by Pliny and other Roman authors, were largely invented in the second century BC as a way of providing the equestrian order and its members with antiquity and tradition to match their new corporate identity. The aim of this chapter is to analyse how the mounted warrior elites of the Regal period transformed into a cavalry aristocracy of *equites* in the early Republic, and how the *equites* then fragmented into distinct senatorial and equestrian orders. This process will involve continuous sifting of the literary sources in order to try and distinguish invented traditions from historical reality.

Aristocrats on Horseback

The Romans believed that their city had been ruled by seven kings between the mid-eighth century and the late sixth century BC. The first of these was Romulus (r. 753–716 BC), who had a squadron of 300 skilled horsemen, called the *Celeres* ('swift ones').[9] According to Pliny the Elder, these cavalrymen were the forerunners of the equestrian order.[10] There were

---

[5] Pliny the Elder, *NH* 33.18–36.   [6] Wallace-Hadrill 1990a: 91.   [7] Brunt 1988: 515–16.
[8] Pliny the Elder, *NH* 33.33. For the formation of the equestrians into an *ordo*, see the last section of this chapter and Chapter 3.
[9] All regnal dates for the kings are traditional, and it would be unwise to place too much faith in them.
[10] Pliny the Elder, *NH* 33.35.

various stories in circulation regarding the origins of this name. It was said either to derive from their rapid speed (the Latin adjective *celer* means 'swift'); the Greek word κέλης ('riding steed'); or the cavalry's commanding officer, a man named Celer, who had been responsible for murdering Remus on the orders of Romulus.[11] Pliny was not alone in arguing that the *Celeres* were the distant ancestors of *equites Romani*, indicating a general willingness of later Romans to believe that the *ordo* could be traced back to the foundation of the city of Rome itself.[12] In Livy's history, *From the Foundation of the City*, the cavalry is said to have been composed of three centuries, each with 100 riders. These were named the *Ramnenses*, the *Titienses* and the *Luceres* after the three original tribes.[13] The number of cavalry centuries was said to have been doubled to six by one of Romulus' successors, Tarquinius Priscus (r. 616–578 BC), in order to combat the threat from the Sabines.[14] The most radical expansion and organisation of the army was attributed to the king Servius Tullius (r. 578–534 BC). He was the traditional creator of the 'Servian Constitution', which divided all Roman citizens into 193 centuries for military service based on their property.[15] This also formed the basis for the *comitia centuriata*, in which all Roman citizens met to pass legislation, judge capital cases, and declare peace and war. In this assembly there were eighteen centuries of *equites*, a title that Pliny tells us came from their ownership of *militares equi* ('military horses').[16] These stories, which attributed specific developments to individual kings, served a purpose in explaining the origins of political and military institutions to Romans of the late Republic and early empire. But their historicity is highly suspect.

What then can we say about Rome's early history, and the place of the cavalry within the state? Archaic Rome was certainly ruled by kings, even if we do not accept that all the traditional seven kings were genuine historical figures (there may indeed have been many more than seven).[17] The aristocratic elites of Latium and Etruria were a warrior group, which

---

[11] Servius s.v. *Aen.* 11.603. For the different traditions about Celer himself, see Wiseman 1995b: 9–10.

[12] *Celeres* and *equites*: Pomp. *Dig.* 1.2.2.15, 2.15.9; Festus 48 L, as well as Servius in the preceding note. Some authorities described the *Celeres* as a bodyguard: Livy 1.15.8; Plut. *Rom.* 26.2; Dion. Hal. 2.13, 2.29, 4.71, 4.75.

[13] Livy 1.15.3. The names are Etruscan in origin (Ogilvie 1970: 80).

[14] Festus 452 L; Livy 1.36.2, 7–8; Cic. *Rep.* 2.36.

[15] See Cornell 1995: 179–81; Lintott 1999: 55–63.

[16] Pliny the Elder, *NH* 33.29. Within this group of eighteen, the older centuries were known as *sex suffragia* ('six voting groups') – allegedly from the time of Tarquinius Priscus onwards – because they played a privileged role in the voting process (Cic. *Rep.* 2.39).

[17] Cornell 1995: 119–20, 140.

derived status and prestige from their martial achievements.[18] Archaeological and artistic evidence from burials dated to the seventh century BC reveal both the existence of cavalrymen and the use of chariots, though the latter seem to have been used in displays of prestige rather than ridden in battle.[19] These mounted warrior elites were organised in clan groups. Although the clans originated in specific city-states, they were also highly mobile, competing with other groups for influence throughout the region at large, as Cornell and Armstrong have shown.[20] The aristocratic clans indigenous to Rome itself have been styled 'proto-patricians', the forerunners of the noble families of the Republican age, by modern historians.[21] But Roman kingship was not hereditary, and it was usually held by men who were not native to the city.[22] Therefore the *rex* was selected from among the wider regional aristocracy, rather than the 'proto-patricians'. The primary responsibilities of the *rex* fell into the spheres of justice, religion and warfare. He therefore controlled Rome's 'foreign policy', supported by his own clan group, which constituted the army.[23] These mobile aristocratic clans are attested throughout the sixth and into the fifth century BC, and thus straddle the traditional division between the Regal and Republican periods marked by the 'expulsion of the kings' in 509 BC.[24] The real break seems to have been the demise of the *rex*, after which he was replaced by magistrates known as praetors. This was a post for which leaders of aristocratic clans could compete via election.[25] Over the course of the fifth century BC the warrior elites became increasingly Rome-focused rather than trans-regional, a change that marked their transition into the patriciate of the Roman social order.[26]

Where does this leave the cavalry? Alföldi argued that Romulus' *Celeres* were identical with the patrician aristocracy of Regal Rome.[27] We need to nuance this argument in the light of the evidence for a mobile, regional mounted aristocracy in Latium and the fact that the warlords competed for the kingship of Rome. The consolidation of the Roman patriciate only

---

[18]   Frederiksen 1968: 15–16; D'Agostino 1990: 71–5, 81.

[19]   For discussion of the evidence and its limitations, see Frederiksen 1968: 15–16; D'Agostino 1990: 69–71; Cornell 1995: 81–2; Barker and Rasmussen 1998: 260–1; J. Armstrong 2016: 69–70.

[20]   Cornell 1995: 143–50; J. Armstrong 2016: 53–4, 57–8, 70–1.

[21]   J. Armstrong 2016: 54, 96–7. On the early patriciate, see Cornell 1995: 142–3; Richard 1995: 110–11.

[22]   Cornell 1995: 141–3; Rawlings 1998: 104–7; J. Armstrong 2016: 60–1, 86–93.

[23]   J. Armstrong 2016: 59, 73.

[24]   Cornell 1995: 144–5; Rawlings 1998: 110–12; J. Armstrong 2016: 71, 130–1, 134–46.

[25]   J. Armstrong 2016: 129–36, 172–6.   [26]   J. Armstrong 2016: 54, 73, 84, 134–5, 148.

[27]   Alföldi 1952: 87–92, 1968: 450–2. The view is followed by Alföldy 1984: 7 in his standard work on Roman social organisation.

happened over several centuries. The *Celeres* themselves are clearly fictional, much like Romulus and the other myths of early Rome.[28] However, the motivations that lie behind the myths are just as interesting as the reality. The tradition that made the *Celeres* the ancestors of the *equites Romani* probably took root in the late second century BC, when the equestrian order became its own *ordo* distinct from the senate. As part of this process, stories were created to give the equestrians their own part to play in early Roman history.[29] If the *equites Romani* were truly to be regarded as the 'third part' in the *res publica*, as Pliny the Elder stated, then they had to be there at the very beginning, alongside the senate and the people, riding for Romulus.

The same point can be made about the *comitia centuriata*, which was attributed to the king Servius Tullius. Most scholars now agree that such a schematic organisation of Roman society is likely to have been the result of slow change over time, rather than the initiative of one *rex*.[30] We have already remarked that the fifth century BC saw warrior elites becoming more settled in Rome itself. As part of this process, landowning became a more important source of wealth and prestige, transforming the mobile clan groups into a landed aristocracy.[31] This transformation was paralleled by what Armstrong has called the formation of a 'community-based' army at Rome (as opposed to the *rex*'s personal army).[32] The notion of a timocratic military hierarchy therefore probably dates from the end of the fifth century BC, when Rome began to pay its soldiers for the first time.[33] In this army, the new wealthy landed aristocracy constituted the cavalry.[34] The status symbols that later came to be associated with the equestrian order, such as the *trabea* and the *anulus aureus*, were originally patrician or senatorial attributes – that is, they were the emblems of the new landed aristocracy.[35] This interpretation preserves Alföldi's association between the patricians and the cavalry, but moves it from the Regal period to the early Republic, the point at which a stable aristocratic group actually emerged in Rome. The precise composition of the various centuries in the *comitia centuriata*, as described by Livy and Dionysius of Halicarnassus, must relate to the assembly of the middle Republic in the

---

[28] Cf. Hill 1938.　[29] Ogilvie 1970: 83.　[30] Cornell 1995: 181; J. Armstrong 2016: 80–1.

[31] J. Armstrong 2016: 153–63.　[32] J. Armstrong 2016: 163–4.

[33] Cornell 1995: 187–90. It should be noted, however, that there was as yet no Roman coinage, which meant that the troops were paid in 'uncoined metal' (Burnett 2012: 298).

[34] Hill 1952: 5; Grieve 1987: 308–11. Cf. the more sceptical Cornell 1995: 250–1, who does not believe that the patricians were the cavalry.

[35] Alföldi 1952: 13–72 is fundamental. See also Hill 1952: 215; Nicolet 1974: 139–43; Kolb 1977b: 246–7; Oakley 2005a: 636–7.

fourth and third centuries BC.[36] The creation of the assembly was later ascribed to Servius Tullius because of the Roman habit of associating their significant political and religious institutions with specific kings and their characters.[37]

In reality, the transition from the Regal period to the Republic was much less sudden than the 'expulsion of the kings' in 509 BC might suggest. The concept of a definitive break in this year emerged from the ideology of the new *res publica*, in which the state belonged to all Roman citizens and individual and collective *libertas* was championed.[38] Instead the change was much more gradual. The sixth and fifth centuries BC witnessed the transformation of a mobile, mounted warrior elite ruled by one of their peers as a *rex*, to a landed aristocracy whose members competed with each other for election to the highest magistracies. In the new *res publica* the citizen body was its army, with the inevitable corollary that the wealthiest citizens served on horseback. This division was enshrined in the timocratic *comitia centuriata*, which gradually evolved over time before reaching the developed stage described by Livy and Dionysius some time in the fourth or third century BC. In this assembly, which represented both army and state, the most privileged members were the wealthy aristocrats called *equites*.

The Equestrian Census

The enrolment of Roman citizens in the *comitia centuriata* was the responsibility of two senior magistrates, known as the censors.[39] During the census, conducted every five years, the censors distributed all male citizens aged seventeen and over into classes according to their property qualification.[40] There were eighteen centuries of the *equites*, who were chosen from the wealthiest members of the state. They were expected to enlist as cavalrymen for ten years, which was also the minimum service requirement for all citizens who intended to embark on a public career.[41] The precise amount of the property qualification that enabled citizens to serve as *equites* in the Republican period remains uncertain. We are largely dependent on later accounts. Dionysius of Halicarnassus wrote that

---

[36] Nicolet 1974: 18–19; Cornell 1995: 179–81; Lintott 1999: 55–60; Forsythe 2005: 111.

[37] Beard, North and Price 1998: 3–4, 60–1.   [38] Mouritsen 2001: 11–12; Hammer 2014: 53.

[39] The office of censor was instituted in 443 BC, according to Livy 4.8.3; Dion. Hal. 2.62. At some unspecified point the census began to be taken every five years (Lintott 1999: 115–17).

[40] Nicolet 1974: 73–5; McCall 2002: 8.   [41] Polyb. 6.19.1–4.

Romans in the equestrian centuries were selected 'from those who possessed the greatest census rating and were of noble birth' (ἐκ τῶν ἐχόντων
τὸ μέγιστον τίμημα καὶ κατὰ γένος ἐπιφανῶν), while Cicero likewise stated
that they possessed 'greatest census rating' (*censu maximo*).[42] The highest
census rating on record is the 100,000 *asses* of the first infantry class, the
prima classis. The classification of citizens according to *asses* cannot pre-
date the introduction of coinage at Rome in the third century BC, though
this certainly does not preclude earlier timocratic divisions on the basis of
wealth, since Rome used uncoined metal prior to this point.[43]
The statements of Cicero and Dionysius would seem to suggest that the
equites in the early third century BC required the same property qualification as the *prima classis*.[44] The privilege of being selected as a member of
the equestrian centuries was therefore dependent on other factors in
addition to wealth alone. In choosing Roman citizens for this honour,
the censors took into account their physical fitness for military service,
their character and moral suitability.[45] The censors are known to have
exercised significant care in enrolling or expelling citizens from the centuries, and did not use these powers indiscriminately or without reason.[46]

Over time, however, the census qualification for *equites* increased so that
it was set above the level of the *prima classis*.[47] This higher level was
probably introduced by the time of the Second Punic War at the end of
the third century BC.[48] The change might be connected to the reorganisation of the Roman coinage system that accompanied the introduction of
the *denarius* in 211 BC.[49] The evidence for the raising of the qualification
comes from Polybius, who penned his account of the composition of the
Roman army in the second century BC. He stated that the cavalry for each
legion was selected by the censor 'according to wealth' (πλουτίνδην),
implying that by this time there was a higher standard for *equites* above
that required by the infantry in the *classes*.[50] Livy's account of the events of
214 BC, when citizens had to provide slaves to serve as rowers in the

---

[42] Dion. Hal. 4.18.1; Cic. *Rep.* 2.39. Livy 1.43.8 has the vague statement that they were selected 'from among the leading men of the state' (*ex primoribus civitatis*).
[43] For this process, and the reasons behind it, see Burnett 2012.
[44] Hill 1939, 1952: 8; Walbank 1956: 700; Rathbone 1993: 149 n. 25.
[45] Livy 4.8.2–3; Polyb. 6.20.9. See also Hill 1952: 34; Lintott 1999: 119. The first description of the censors enrolling *equites* dates to 312 BC (Diod. Sic. 20.36.5), though this could hardly be the first time it had taken place (Hill 1952: 37). For the censors' moral powers, see Astin 1988.
[46] Astin 1988: 26–8.   [47] Rosenstein 2008: 7 n. 33.   [48] Nicolet 1974: 47–68.
[49] For the *denarius*, see Woytek 2012: 315–16.
[50] Polyb. 6.20.9; Gabba 1976: 126–8, though strangely he does not believe that this applied to the *equites equo publico*, only the *equites equo suo*. They surely must have had the same rating, as noted by Nicolet 1974: 54–5.

Roman fleet, provides an indication of the potential amount of the higher equestrian census. At this moment of national crisis, citizens rated by the censors as possessing 100,000 *asses* were required to furnish three slaves for the fleet, those with more than 300,000 *asses* had to provide five, men with more than 1 million *asses*, seven, and senators, eight.[51] We need not necessarily assume that these figures matched specific property qualifications, since the senate may simply have imposed these levels on an ad hoc basis.[52] But they do show that citizens could be easily divided at higher levels above the 100,000 *asses* required for membership of the *prima classis*.

Can we get any closer to determining the precise level of the equestrian census? The most familiar figure is the near-canonical 400,000 sesterces qualification, which first appears in one of Horace's *Epistles*, dated to 20/19 BC.[53] Rathbone has noted that this census rating is only ever described in sesterces, which indicates that this specific level probably post-dated 141 BC.[54] That year saw the Romans re-tariff their coinage, which devalued the *as* as a unit of currency, and the administration henceforth switched to calculating 'state payments and official assessments of value' from *asses* to sesterces.[55] Crawford has therefore proposed that this change saw the equestrian census qualification switch from 400,000 *asses* (pre-reform) to 400,000 sesterces (post-reform).[56] Horace's reference to the 400,000 sesterces certainly implies that it was a commonly accepted figure for some time, and dates at least as far back as the *lex Roscia* of 67 BC.[57] We cannot be sure, however, whether it was instituted at an earlier period, either at the time of the reform of 141 BC or some other date before 67 BC.[58] Nor can we conclusively state that the census level did not change multiple times. What we can say is that the *equites* initially possessed the same census rating as the infantry in the *prima classis*, but it was subsequently raised above the level of the *pedites*, probably by the time of the Second Punic War. The census figure

---

[51] Livy 24.11.7–8.

[52] It has been suggested that 1 million *asses* was the qualification for *equites* based on the Livy passage (Nicolet 1974: 63–6; Wiseman 1971: 66; Gabba 1976: 125–8; McCall 2002: 3–5), but this cannot be the case (Brunt 1971: 700; Crawford 1985: 149). See Rathbone 1993: 149 n. 25 for other situations in which taxes were imposed at levels that do not match up with census ratings.

[53] The figure of 400,000 sesterces appears in Hor. *Epist.* 1.57–9 (R. Mayer 1994: 10–11). This is discussed further in Chapter 3.

[54] Rathbone 1993: 149 n. 25.

[55] Woytek 2012: 320. For the reasons behind this re-tariffing, see Kay 2014: 103–4.

[56] Crawford 1985: 147–51. See also Briscoe 2008: 287.

[57] This is discussed in detail in Chapter 3. Cf. Brunt 1988: 146; Kay 2014: 12, 287, who assume that the *lex Roscia* of 67 BC set the census level at 400,000 sesterces.

[58] Rathbone 1993: 149 n. 25 suggests 129 BC, the year in which the *equites* were separated from the senators, as a date for its introduction.

was converted from *asses* to sesterces after the coinage re-tariffing of 141/
140 BC. By the time of the late first century BC, the level was set at 400,000
sesterces.

Although wealthy and privileged, the *equites* in the eighteen centuries
were not expected to pay for their own horses. Instead, each man was
provided with a horse at state expense, described as an *equus publicus*.[59]
According to tradition, these *equites equo publico*, as they were known,
were each allocated 10,000 *asses* from the treasury to purchase a horse (an
amount called the *aes equestre*), as well as a further 2,000 for its upkeep (the
aes hordiarium).[60] The funds for this support came from a tax on widows
and orphans.[61] As befitted their high standing, the eighteen centuries of
equites equo publico initially had the privilege of voting first in the centuriate assembly, before even the *prima classis*, though this had changed by
the third century BC.[62] Something that was not altered, even as Rome's
territory expanded throughout Italy, was the number of *equites equo
publico* selected by the censors. This remained fixed at 1,800 throughout
the Republican period (one hundred *equites* for each of the eighteen
centuries).[63] Three hundred of these *equites equo publico* were initially
assigned to each of the first four legions.[64] This soon proved to be insufficient, and so from 403 BC all Roman citizens who possessed the necessary
property qualification were permitted to serve in the cavalry, though they
had to provide and maintain their steeds themselves (and thus were known
as *equites equo suo*, 'cavalry on their own horse') and were not enrolled in
the equestrian centuries in the *comitia centuriata*.[65] The *equites equo suo*
eventually came to outnumber the *equites equo publico* quite considerably.
By 225 BC, during the Second Punic War, Rome and Campania had a total
23,000 men qualified to serve in the cavalry as *equites*, but only 1,800 of
these would have been officially enrolled in the equestrian centuries as

[59] The original 300 *equites* received two horses each, but this changed at some unknown point
(Momigliano 1966: 17).
[60] Livy 1.43.9, discussed by Hill 1952: 11–12; Nicolet 1974: 36–7; Ogilvie 1970: 171–2. The *aes
equestre* was still granted in the time of Cato the Elder (Hill 1943).
[61] Livy 1.43.9 (widows only); Cic. *Rep.* 2.36.1 (widows and orphans).
[62] Livy 1.43.9; Ogilvie 1970: 173. In the late third century BC this role was given to one of the
centuries of the first class selected by lot, known as the *centuria praerogativa* (Momigliano 1966:
18; Grieve 1987: 313–17). The *sex suffragia* then voted after the first class, but before the second
class (Cic. *Phil.* 2.82–3; Livy 43.16.14).
[63] Livy 1.43.8; Dion. Hal. 4.18.1; L. R. Taylor 1966: 85–6. Cf. Nicolet 1974: 113–19, proposing that
there were 2,400 *equites* in the centuries.
[64] Polyb. 6.20.9.
[65] McCall 2002: 2–3. Livy 5.7.4–13 dates the introduction of the *equites equo suo* to 403 BC, during
the war with Veii (supported by Ogilvie 1970: 642; cf. Nicolet 1974: 54–5). Rosenstein 2008: 7
suggests there was a lesser qualification for cavalry service *equo suo*.

equites equo publico.[66] The increase in the number of Romans who could
serve as cavalry enabled a greater proportion of wealthy citizens to participate in the state at an elite level, and receive recognition for their efforts.
The disparity in numbers between the *equites equo publico* and the *equites
equo suo* demonstrates the prestige that the public horse bestowed on its
holders. However, both groups were considered to be, and were commonly
referred to, as *equites.*[67] They constituted an aristocracy united by military
service to the *res publica*.

The Composition and Cohesion of the *Equites*

The *equites* encompassed both senators and non-senatorial citizens within
their numbers until 129 BC. All senators were *equites equo publico*, retaining both their public horse and place in the eighteen centuries.[68] This was
because the *comitia centuriata* and the senate were fundamentally two
separate political institutions, the *comitia* being an assembly made up of
all citizens, while the senate was an advisory council.[69] This meant that 300
of the available 1,800 available positions in the equestrian centuries were
always occupied by senators.[70] The remaining *equites equo publico* were
either senators' sons or other male relations, such as cousins or nephews, or
wealthy citizens with no senatorial relatives.[71] The wider group of *equites
equo suo* would have been more heterogeneous in origin, though they were
still wealthy, since they had to meet the equestrian property qualification.
This means that there was no firm dichotomy between senators and

---

[66] Polyb. 2.24. On the accuracy of the historian Polybius' figures for the composition of the Roman
army during the Second Punic War, see the comments of Walbank 1956: 196–9.

[67] Stein 1927: 5–6.

[68] A point explicitly made in Cic. *Rep.* 4.2. See the discussion of Nicolet 1974: 75–83. The censors
selected senators in accordance with *lex Ovinia*, passed in the late fourth century BC, the terms
of which are unfortunately obscure (Cornell 1995: 369–70; Lintott 1999: 68–72). The
quaestorship did not confer membership of the senate until the Sullan reform (Lintott
1999: 136).

[69] For the senate's powers, see Lintott 1999: 65–8.

[70] Stone 2005: 75–6 argues that the 300 senators constituted three centuries of the *sex suffragia*.

[71] The precise numerical breakdown of these groups is uncertain, though of course senators could
account for no more than 300 of the 1,800 *equites equo publico*. It is the number of senatorial
relations and those with no senatorial connections whatsoever that remains elusive. Hill 1952:
46 estimated that about half the *equites equo publico* were not related to senators, which seems
a fair approximation. These three groups are naturally a simplification of complex social
networks, as Nicolet 1974: 253–69 observed in his discussion of senatorial and equestrian
relationships. But they are nevertheless important for conceptualising the changes that
occurred later.

equites: senators were *equites*. They were united by the ethos of serving the *res publica* in whatever capacity they were asked to do so, *domi militiaeque*. This literally means 'at home and on campaign', and encapsulates the variety of civilian and military roles that senators were expected to fill either as magistrates, pro-magistrates or in their capacity as citizens.[72]

It is important to emphasise this point because Livy's history is quite misleading on the matter, describing the *ordo equester* as if it constituted a separate and defined group between the *ordo senatorius* and the *populus Romanus* even in the early and middle Republic. Livy's first use of the term appears in his account of the year 440 BC, in which he labelled Spurius Maelius a wealthy man from 'from the equestrian order' (*ex equestri ordine*).[73] Such an expression is anachronistic for the mid-fifth century BC, and Livy's account is shaped by his own conception of the separate equestrian order as it was in the Augustan age, when the *princeps* gave new emphasis to the position of equestrians within the *res publica*.[74] In Livy's version of the events of 403 BC, during which citizens volunteered to serve in the cavalry on their own horses for the first time, he writes how the senators paternalistically lavished praise on the *equites* and the people.[75] Even more striking is Livy's account of the year 210 BC, when a plan to provide money for the fleet is hailed by each constituent part of the state: 'the equestrian order followed the consensus of the senate, the plebs that of the equestrian order' (*hunc consensum senatus equester ordo est secutus, equestris ordinis plebs*).[76] Anyone familiar with the language of Augustan and Tiberian honorific decrees can see the influence of later, imperial political discourse at work here.[77] No Roman of the third century BC would have conceived of an equestrian order, let alone one that was distinct from the senate.

What we instead find in the early Republic is a united cavalry aristocracy of *equites*, who constituted a Weberian occupational status group, defined by their official function.[78] Such groups typically give meaning to their position through honours, status symbols and ideology, as discussed in the Introduction to this book. The Roman aristocracy was defined by

---

[72] Sall. *Cat.* 9.1–3 traces a connection between this ideology of service and the functioning of the *res publica*. For the senatorial career, see Rosenstein 2007, 2009: 35–9. On the expression *domi militiaeque* and its meaning, see further Drogula 2015: 47–56, and Humm 2015: 346 on its frequent use in Livy.

[73] Livy 4.13.1.

[74] Hill 1952: 45–6; Nicolet 1974: 163–7; Oakley 2005a: 636–8; Briscoe 2012: 439. Cf. the more optimistic conclusions of Hill 1930, defending, *inter alia*, the characterisation of Maelius.

[75] Livy 5.7.5–13. On the use of political language in this section, see Ogilvie 1970: 643.

[76] Livy 26.36.12.   [77] This will be discussed in Chapter 8.   [78] Weber 1968: 306.

equestrian *virtus* – an essentially untranslatable word that meant 'courage' or 'valour', but also represented the sum total of what it meant to be a Roman man (a *vir*).[79] Rome placed great emphasis on celebrating the achievements and victories of its cavalry in the fifth and fourth centuries BC. Traditionally, the first of these was the Battle of Lake Regillus, fought either in 499 or 496 BC, in which Rome secured victory over the Latin League thanks to the miraculous appearance of the Dioscuri, Castor and Pollux, at a crucial moment.[80] To honour their contribution to the battle, the Temple of Castor and Pollux (sometimes known as the Temple of the Castores) was erected on the south side of the Roman forum, where it was formally consecrated in 484 BC.[81] The Dioscuri became the patron deities of Rome's cavalry, and featured prominently on coinage, the only mounted warriors to be so honoured.[82] According to Dionysius of Halicarnassus, an annual parade of the Roman cavalry (called the *transvectio equitum*) was instituted shortly after the Battle of Lake Regillus. The *equites equo publico* paraded through Rome wearing the *trabea* (a short red or purple toga) and riding on white horses distinguished by ceremonial bosses, called *phalerae*.[83] The *transvectio* represented a celebration of the wealthiest and most distinguished citizens in the *res publica* as a coherent social group.[84] The date for this celebration was 15 July, which was the day of the victory at Lake Regillus and the festival of Castor and Pollux.[85] However, there was also a second tradition, which features in Livy, Valerius Maximus and Pseudo-Aurelius Victor, which ascribed the institution of the *transvectio* to the censor Q. Fabius Maximus Rullianus in 304 BC.[86] As a way of reconciling these different stories, it has been plausibly argued that Rullianus did not invent the ceremony, but transformed the parade from a celebration for the Roman cavalry to one exclusively for the *equites equo publico*.[87] This may have been a reaction to the growing numbers of citizens

---

[79] See the important discussions of Massa-Pairault 1995; McCall 2002: 6–9; McDonnell 2006: 154–8, 185–95, 248–58.

[80] Dion. Hal. 6.13.1–4; Plut. *Cor.* 3.2–4; Cic. *De Nat. Deorum* 2.6; Livy 2.19–20 (omitting the appearance of the Dioscuri); Nicolet 1974: 19–20. The parade is discussed in further detail in Chapters 5 and 8.

[81] Livy 2.24.5 gives the date of the dedication as 15 July, though other authorities (such as Ovid, *Fasti* 1.705–6) give 27 January.

[82] Forsythe 2005: 186; McDonnell 2006: 249–50. Archaeological evidence attests wider veneration of the Dioscuri throughout Latium (Massa-Pairault 1995: 46–7).

[83] Mommsen 1887–8: III, 513; Kolb 1977b: 246–7.

[84] Nicolet 1974: 44–5; Massa-Pairault 1995: 58; McDonnell 2006: 187–8.

[85] Dion. Hal. 6.13.4; Weinstock 1937a: 15.

[86] Livy 9.46.15; Val. Max. 2.2.9; Ps.-Aur. Vict. *Vir. ill.* 32.3.

[87] Weinstock 1937a: 7–18, 1937b: 2182; McDonnell 2006: 187–8; Sumi 2009: 130. This may have been given added impetus by the reorganisation of Rome's cavalry during the Samnite Wars of the mid-fourth century BC (Oakley 2005a: 644–5).

serving as *equites equo suo*, thus forming an attempt to delineate more precisely the prestige of the eighteen centuries and their members.

In addition to these collective ceremonies, equestrian *virtus* was also celebrated on an individual level in the fourth century BC. There are a number of stories of aristocratic Romans excelling in single combat on horseback from this period. In particular, from the 340s BC onwards all such accounts of monomachy included mounted combatants.[88] One of the most memorable tales featured T. Manlius Torquatus, the son of the consul of the same name, who disobeyed his father's command to hold the ranks against the Latin enemy, and engaged in single combat.[89] His act of insubordination was prompted by a challenge from the Tusculan warrior Geminus Maecius, who offered to show him 'how superior a Latin cavalryman was to a Roman' (*quantum eques Latinus Romano praestet*).[90] In a display of equestrian skill, Torquatus managed to spear Maecius' steed between the ears, unseating his opponent and flinging him to the ground. The elder Manlius Torquatus subsequently had his son executed for disobeying orders, sending a message to all Romans who would seek to break ranks. This story shows that Manlius and other young men derived great pride from their horsemanship, which formed part of their socialisation into the aristocracy.

Young men must have spent considerable time practising the combat skills that would allow them to excel in feats of equestrian *virtus*. McDonnell has argued that the increasing wealth, resources and slaves acquired by Rome in this period allowed the aristocratic youth the time and space to devote to such tasks.[91] It is surely no coincidence that honorific statues of Roman generals on horseback, commemorating equestrian *virtus* in monumental form, were first dedicated in the fourth century BC.[92] In 338 BC, equestrian representations of the consuls C. Maenius and L. Furius Camillus were erected in the Roman forum as a way to paying tribute to their successful victories against the Latin League.[93] As Livy pointed out, such monuments were not common in Rome before this time.[94] But they were soon joined by an equestrian statue in front of the

---

[88] McCall 2002: 84–5; McDonnell 2006: 189–93. Oakley 1985: 397 argues that such duels occurred on a yearly basis.

[89] Livy 8.7.1–22; Oakley 1985: 394 discusses this and other versions of the story.

[90] Livy 8.7.7.   [91] McDonnell 2006: 193–5.

[92] The statue of Cloelia, purportedly erected in 506 BC, is probably not historical (Livy 2.13.11, with the comments of Ogilvie 1970: 268).

[93] As Oakley 1998: 535 notes, the final defeat of the Latin League merited this new type of honour.

[94] Livy 8.13.9. There has been some debate about the historicity of these statues: Wallace-Hadrill 1990b: 172 regards them as 'annalistic fantasy', but they are accepted by other scholars, notably Tanner 2000: 29; Oakley 1998: 533–5; Oakley 2005b: 575; McDonnell 2006: 155–6.

Temple of Castor and Pollux, honouring Q. Marcius Tremulus (consul of 306 BC) for his defeat of the Hernici.[95] Pliny the Elder wrote that the custom of dedicating equestrian statues was borrowed from the Greeks, who erected them to honour sporting heroes in horseback and chariot racing.[96] The decision to use this style of monument to commemorate military victories was a Roman innovation, which demonstrates the importance of the cavalry to the continuance of the *res publica*.[97] Equestrian *virtus* represented one of the fundamental qualities of the Roman aristocracy, providing these wealthy elites with a cohesive *raison d'être*.

Political Conflict and Status Differentiation

The unity of the *equites* started to fragment in the middle Republic. Senators had always been distinguished from other *equites* by virtue of their membership of the *curia*, and senatorial magistrates even more so through holding high office, but this does not seem to have resulted in any serious problems or divisions in the fifth or fourth centuries BC. However, the differences in status between senatorial and non-senatorial *equites*, both within the equestrian centuries and among the *equites* at large, became more pronounced in the middle Republic. The greater differences between these groups stemmed from a series of interrelated developments in the third and second centuries BC. Firstly, there were disputes between senators and non-senators over commercial and trading interests and the letting of public tax contracts. This was not because the non-senatorial *equites* had any revolutionary or innovative political agenda which promoted conflict: they did not, and could not, institute any form of policy. But they did oppose any measures that would affect their interests in the commercial sphere.[98] Secondly, the senators wished to delineate their superior status within the *equites* at large, a status which not only derived from membership of the *curia*, but also their eligibility for magistracies and the associated commands that came with them. They could truly claim to serve the *res publica* in all fields of excellence *domi militiaeque*. Roman citizens with the equestrian census qualification remained fundamentally the same types of people that they

---

[95] Livy 9.43.22; Cic. *Phil.* 6.13; Pliny the Elder, *NH* 34.23.   [96] Pliny the Elder, *NH* 34.19–20.

[97] Massa-Pairault 1995: 50; McDonnell 2006: 154–6; Spencer 2007: 93. For other Roman adaptations of Greek commemorative forms, see Wallace-Hadrill 1990b.

[98] See Badian 1962: 224; Meier 1966: 65–9.

had been in the early Republic, but the differences within the *equites* soon became more apparent.[99]

(i) Trade and Taxes

The first issue that merits consideration is the disparity between senatorial and non-senatorial *equites* in the financial and trading arena. The expansion of Rome's territorial empire in the third century BC, not to mention its increasing political influence throughout the Mediterranean, brought with it new commercial opportunities.[100] But legislation passed in 218 BC, shortly before the outbreak of the Hannibalic War, dramatically limited the capacity of senators to take advantage of these prospects. In this year, Q. Claudius, tribune of the plebs, secured the passage of the *lex Claudia*, which forbade senators or their sons from owning a ship capable of carrying more than 300 amphorae.[101] It is difficult to discover the motivations behind such a specific law. Livy presented it as a moral measure, designed to uphold the traditional view that the only respectable way for senators to earn money was through land owning and agriculture.[102] Involvement in trade was frowned on, unless one was dealing with the profits of one's own estate.[103] A ship of 300 amphorae could transport surplus wine, olive oil and other products for local markets, but would not provide a solid basis for significant commercial operations.[104] The fact that larger ships were specifically forbidden by the *lex Claudia* suggests that senators were already making profits from such ventures by the time the law was passed in the late third century BC.[105]

The senators would have had competition from non-senatorial *equites* and other wealthy citizens who also possessed extensive land holdings in

---

[99] This argument is indebted to the classic account of Brunt 1988: 144–50 on the late Republic, as the fundamental principles remain relevant to the earlier period.

[100] Badian 1972: 11–47; D'Arms 1981: 33–4; Kay 2014: 8–18. Gruen 1984: 302–3 discusses Romans and Italians involved in the Greek east from the early third century BC.

[101] Livy 21.63.2–4. Three hundred amphorae represents c. 7,700 litres of wine or 5,985 kg of grain per ship (Rosenstein 2008: 16 n. 75).

[102] This is plausible since moral reasons lay behind many Roman laws that were ineffective in practice. See D'Arms 1981: 31; Gruen 1984: 300–1.

[103] The *locus classicus* is Cato, *De Agr.* pref. 1–4. For the ideological issues, see Badian 1972: 50–3; D'Arms 1981: 20–31; Rosenstein 2008: 18–19. Money lending was also technically frowned upon, but it did not stop senators and *equites* in both the Republican and imperial periods (Andreau 1999a: 12–14).

[104] Wiseman 1971: 79.   [105] D'Arms 1981: 33; Gruen 1984: 307.

Italy and wished to sell their goods on the market.[106] There must have been intense rivalry between these sellers, since, as Rosenstein has recently shown, land owning in and of itself was not a lucrative business.[107] It is plausible, therefore, that this competition for a share of the market (not mentioned by Livy) meant that non-senators, both those who were *equites* and other wealthy individuals, lobbied Q. Claudius to introduce a law that would curtail the business efforts of their senatorial rivals.[108] The measure was understandably unpopular among the senate. According to Livy, only the consul C. Flaminius supported Claudius' proposal.[109] Of course, the *lex Claudia* did not actually prevent senators from engaging in trade and other commercial activities, since they continued to pursue such interests through relatives, agents and middlemen (including *equites*).[110] Cicero spoke of the law falling into abeyance by the first century BC, though the ideological thinking that underpinned it did not, and the law was reinstituted by Iulius Caesar in 59 BC.[111] These considerations do not undermine the fact that the *lex Claudia* was a piece of legislation that exposed a key point of difference between senators and their sons and other non-senatorial *equites*.[112] This enables us to understand how the interests of these groups might coalesce on some occasions, but diverge on others.

At the end of the third century BC, about the same time as the passing of the *lex Claudia*, a group of individuals known as *publicani* makes its first appearance in the annals of Livy, though they must have existed well before this.[113] The *publicani* were contractors employed to carry out services concerned with the *publica* ('public property') of the Roman state.[114] The censors were responsible for letting out the contracts, which could include supplying the army or navy, constructing or maintaining public buildings, and collecting taxes and customs duties.[115] The more obscure contracts included the feeding of the sacred geese on the Capitoline, the

[106] For land holding as the basis of equestrian wealth, see Nicolet 1974: 285–311; Brunt 1988: 163. For non-senatorial *equites* and other businessmen as competition for senators, see Rosenstein 2008: 5, 20.

[107] Rosenstein 2008: 18–24.

[108] Hill 1952: 88; Yavetz 1962: 339–42; Nicolet 1980: 80–1; D'Arms 1981: 31–3.

[109] Livy 21.63.4. Yavetz 1962: 341 regarded Flaminius as the real mastermind behind the *lex Claudia*.

[110] Wiseman 1971: 77–82; Shatzman 1975: 99–103; D'Arms 1981: 34–47.

[111] Cic. II *Verr.* 5.45; *Dig.* 50.5.3 (Scaevola).

[112] The interpretation of Hill 1952: 51 that these non-senatorial *equites* constituted a 'middle class' is anachronistic, though there is much else of value in his analysis.

[113] Badian 1972: 16; Gruen 1984: 299–300. Livy's first references to *publicani* are dated to the period of the Second Punic War (e.g. Livy 23.48.9–11, 25.1.2–4, 25.3.8–5.1).

[114] Badian 1972: 15–16; Nicolet 1974: 320–1.   [115] Polyb. 6.17.2; Brunt 1988: 149–50.

paving of fountain bases, and the cleaning of Rome's sewers.[116] *Publicani* could be organised into corporations, called *societates* in Latin, but contracts were also let on an individual basis.[117] Many *publicani* were either *equites equo publico* or *equites equo suo*, and they thus constituted a prominent and vocal group within the wealthy members of the centuriate assembly.[118] When we first meet the *publicani* in 215 BC, they are being enlisted by the senate to help supply the army in Spain with clothes, food and other necessary items in a period of crisis.[119] Three *societates*, comprising nineteen individuals, bid for the right to supply the army, but insisted that they should be excused their military service during the period of their contracts, and prescribed that the *res publica* would be responsible for any losses they suffered.[120] This episode illustrates the dependency of the Roman state on the *publicani*. But the relationship extended both ways. All contracts were let by the censors and administered by the senate, so the *publicani* relied on senatorial support for their continued employment.[121] This point is explicitly made by Polybius in his discussion of the division of power in the Roman constitution, which worked precisely because of the interdependency of the consuls, senate and people.[122] When he wrote about how 'the people' (ὁ δῆμος) relied on the senate, his discussion exclusively focused on the letting of public contracts.[123] This means that in this context Polybius did not have the entire *populus Romanus* in mind when he referred to 'the people', but rather the wealthiest non-senatorial citizens.[124]

When the interests of senatorial and non-senatorial *equites* did not align over the letting of public contracts, political conflict could occur, because the *publicani* and other equestrian businessmen resisted any attempt to curtail their financial activities in the provinces.[125] The events of the censorship of Ti. Sempronius Gracchus and C. Claudius Pulcher in 169 BC provide evidence for such fault-lines. Gracchus and Pulcher were

---

[116] Livy 5.23.7, with Badian 1972: 16 (Juno's temple and its geese); Livy 39.44.4–5 (paving and sewers).

[117] For the importance of individual *publicani*, see J. S. Richardson 1976 and Erdkamp 1995.

[118] Nicolet 1974: 318–20.   [119] Livy 23.48.4–12.   [120] Livy 23.49.1–3.

[121] The censors let the public contracts, but the senate was also involved in their administration (Walbank 1956: 694–5; Lintott 1999: 119–20).

[122] Polyb. 6.11.1–18.8, with discussion in Walbank 1956: 673–97.   [123] Polyb. 6.17.1–6.

[124] For Walbank 1956: 692, 'the people' are the *publicani*, for Brunt 1988: 148, they are the *equites*. Nicolet's 1980: 213 description of them as 'the rich' may be the most appropriate, because of the difficulty in ascertaining how many *publicani* were *equites*, and vice versa.

[125] Brunt 1988: 148–9. Senators were forbidden to act as *publicani* (Nicolet 1974: 327–31), though former publicans could become senators (see the list in Wiseman 1971: 197–8).

very stringent in their review of the equestrian centuries, depriving many *equites* of their public horses. Livy says that the censors 'offended the equestrian order' (*equestrem ordinem offendissent*) by this measure, but then compounded their injury by decreeing that the *publicani* who had been granted contracts by their predecessors were ineligible to bid again.[126] Livy's account is misleading in its use of the term *ordo equester,* and in equating the *publicani* with the *ordo.*[127] However, if we regard the offended parties as non-senatorial *equites,* the situation becomes more understandable, since this group included both *publicani* and associates of *publicani.*[128] In response to the censors' actions, the *publicani* recruited a tribune, P. Rutilius, to propose a law that the contracts let by Gracchus and Pulcher should be declared null and void; Rutilius also moved that the two men should be put on trial. When voting began, eight out of the first twelve centuries of *equites equo publico,* along with a number of those in the *prima classis,* voted to condemn Pulcher.[129] This is surely an indication of the number of *publicani,* their associates and sympathisers within the equestrian centuries and in the first class of the *comitia centuriata* (which would have included the *equites equo suo*). In response to this outrage, in 167 BC the senate decided not to annexe the kingdom of Macedonia as Roman territory in order to explicitly deny the *publicani* any contracts for the mines or the timber in the forests.[130] This demonstrates that the senate acknowledged that they depended on the *publicani* for administrative and economic purposes, but were not about to be held hostage by them. The affair exposed the divisions within the upper echelons of Roman society, and especially between senatorial and non-senatorial *equites.*[131] This was not in any sense class struggle between aristocrats and a 'middle class', but a political clash between different

---

[126] Livy 43.16.1–2. Their predecessors were Q. Fulvius Flaccus and A. Postumius Albinus, censors in 174 BC, but we do not know the circumstances surrounding their letting of the contracts (Badian 1972: 39–40).

[127] Nicolet 1974: 318–19; Briscoe 2012: 439.

[128] See Nicolet 1974: 344–6 for a list of equestrian *publicani,* but most of the evidence comes from the first century BC.

[129] Livy 43.16.3–14. See also Cic. *Rep.* 6.2; Val. Max. 6.5.3. Only twelve of the eighteen centuries are mentioned at this stage in the voting, because the *sex suffragia* now voted after the first class (Briscoe 2012: 445).

[130] Livy 45.18.3–5; Badian 1972: 40–1; Gruen 1984: 306; Brunt 1988: 150. It has been suggested that the senate's reaction may be anachronistic and more appropriate for the first century BC (J. S. Richardson 1976: 143–4; Briscoe 2012: 659–60), but I do not see why this should be the case.

[131] Of course, the fact that four centuries of *equites equo publico* did not vote to indict Pulcher shows that there was no direct equation between equestrians and the *publicani.*

elite groups over how best to distribute the rewards and profits of Rome's expanding empire.[132]

What is striking about the disputes over the letting of public contracts is that such conflicts were not sustained year in year out. Clashes only occurred when the *publicani* had grievances. At other times, the system worked as Polybius laid out, and *publicani* certainly had supporters within the senatorial ranks, as the events of 184 BC demonstrate. In that year the censors M. Porcius Cato and L. Valerius Flaccus had decided to let out contracts at rates that would not provide sufficiently large profit margins for the *publicani*.[133] In response, the *publicani* entreated the senate to ask the censors to reconsider, and found a senatorial advocate, T. Flamininus, who spoke on their behalf in the *curia*.[134] The *publicani* and *equites* therefore did not function as a pressure group that proposed policies of their own. Instead, as Badian and Meier have shown, they were primarily reactive, intervening only when their position was threatened.[135] Their chief political concern in the middle Republic was to ensure that their opportunities for profit were not curtailed, so they could benefit from Rome's new empire.

(ii) Status Symbols

The senatorial *equites* were distinguished from other *equites* by their membership of the *curia*, their election to civilian magistracies, and their employment in the military commands attached to these magistracies.[136] Their service to Rome as administrators of justice and generals in the field meant that senators possessed a coherent group identity and *raison d'être*. This distinguished them from other *equites* who held officer posts in the army but did not stand for magistracies. The middle Republic saw the introduction of new privileges that highlighted the status and prestige of these senators, explicitly distinguishing them from other non-senatorial *equites* in the public sphere, as Rawson and Wiseman have shown.[137] The first of these privileges was ceremonial. For example, only senators dined at state expense during the *ludi Romani* and *ludi Plebeii*, the games staged in honour of the Capitoline triad. A new senatorial priestly college,

---

[132] This is discussed in the Introduction.
[133] Livy 39.44.7–8, as interpreted by Briscoe 2012: 367.
[134] Plut. *Cato Maior* 19.2, *Flam.* 19.3. As Gruen 1984: 305 points out, Cato had strong senatorial support, and Flamininus may have been motivated by personal animosities (Astin 1978: 85).
[135] Badian 1962: 224; Meier 1966: 65–9, 94.
[136] See Rosenstein 2007 on this configuration of the senatorial career.
[137] E. Rawson 1971: 16–17; Wiseman 1971: 68.

the *tresviri epulones*, was instituted to oversee these dinners in 196 BC.[138] Even more importantly, in 194 BC senators were given the right to sit in separate seating in the theatre during the *ludi Romani*. Previously they had had to compete with the masses for seats, and this move won the censors of the day great popularity with their senatorial peers.[139] The *equites*, on the other hand, would not acquire their own reserved seats until the *lex Roscia* was passed in 67 BC.[140]

Official dress and associated status symbols also played a crucial part in distinguishing senators from other *equites*. It is true that as *equites equo publico*, senators continued to participate in the annual *transvectio equitum* wearing the purple *trabea*, a sign of regimental unity.[141] There were distinctions, however. For example, the ceremonial *phalerae* awarded for military valour were usually silver, but those on the horses of senatorial magistrates were gold.[142] Outside the ceremony of the *transvectio equitum*, members of the *curia* could be identified by their tunic with the broad stripe, or *latus clavus*.[143] Tradition ascribed its introduction as senatorial dress to King Tullus Hostilius, but the *latus clavus* was originally worn by men of differing social status.[144] Livy, in his account of 203 BC, writes of the senate sending gifts to the Numidian king Masinissa including two purple cloaks, tunics with the *latus clavus*, two horses with their *phalerae*, and two sets of equestrian armour.[145] This description suggests that the senate gave Masinissa two sets of an *eques'* parade uniform, but it does not make clear whether this was the dress intended for a specifically senatorial *eques*.[146] There are solid grounds, however, for supposing that the *latus clavus* came to be an exclusively senatorial dress by the end of the second century BC. Diodorus Siculus referred to the slave Tryphon putting on the *latus clavus*, thus claiming senatorial status, when he was the leader of the servile revolt in Sicily (104–101 BC).[147] The *latus clavus* is abundantly attested as a senatorial attribute in the first century BC, when it

---

[138] See Livy 33.42.1, for the *tresviri epulones*. The banquets are described by Gell. *NA* 12.8.2; Livy 38.57.5; Briscoe 2008: 202.

[139] Livy 34.44.5. Livy's earlier comment (1.35.8) that Servius Tullius assigned senators and *equites* seats at the circus is plainly anachronistic (Ogilvie 1970: 149–50).

[140] See Chapters 3 and 9 for discussion of this matter.   [141] Kolb 1977b: 246–7; Stone 2005: 69.

[142] For the *phalerae*, see Polyb. 6.39.3; Livy 39.31.17; McCall 2002: 83–4. For the argument about gold and silver decorations, see Oakley 2005a: 639. By the Augustan period, *phalerae* were awarded to infantrymen, who wore them on the chest (Maxfield 1981: 92–5).

[143] Rothfus 2010: 436. Livy 9.7.8, a reference to the *latus clavus* being worn in the fourth century BC, is anachronistic (Hula 1900: 7).

[144] Pliny the Elder, *NH* 9.127, 9.136, 33.29.   [145] Livy 30.17.3.   [146] Hula 1900: 7.

[147] Diod. Sic. 36.7.4.

differentiated the members of the *curia* from the equestrians with the narrow stripe, or *angustus clavus*.[148]

The other significant status symbol that was transformed during the middle and late Republic was the *anulus aureus*. This had originally been worn by the *nobiles*, who constituted an elite within the senatorial order.[149] In 304 BC, in protest at the election of the freedman's son Cn. Flavius to the tribunate of the plebs, the *nobiles* removed their gold rings and their equestrian decorations, the *phalerae*.[150] This does not indicate that all senators, or even all *equites equo publico*, joined in this protest – as Pliny the Elder pointed out, we are strictly dealing with the *nobiles*, men of consular ancestry within the senate.[151] Nevertheless, the *anulus aureus* had gained wider currency as a senatorial symbol by the Second Punic War, since Hannibal's brother Mago, so the story goes, was able to display gold rings claimed from dead bodies at the Battle of Cannae in the Carthaginian senate.[152] Mago told the Carthaginian senate that 'no one except the *equites*, and only the first among those, wore this symbol' (*neminem nisi equitem atque eorum ipsorum primores id gerere insigne*).[153] This indicates that the gold ring was no longer confined to the *nobiles*, but was worn by senators as well, since they could justifiably claim to be the leaders of the *equites*.[154]

Livy's account of the events of 169 BC certainly suggests that the gold ring had become a senatorial symbol by the mid-second century BC. In that year the 'chief men of the state' (*principes civitatis*) removed their rings when they put on mourning dress to protest the votes of the eight equestrian centuries against Claudius Pulcher the censor.[155] If Appian is correct, military tribunes wore gold rings in the mid-second century BC, in contrast with the iron ones worn by ordinary soldiers.[156] Senators still made up the majority of military tribunes at this point in time.[157] Therefore, it is apparent that the gold ring, which was previously

---

[148] Varro, *LL* 9.79. The *angustus clavus* is discussed in Chapter 3.

[149] Alföldi 1952: 34; Kolb 1977b: 247.

[150] Livy 9.46.12; Pliny the Elder, *NH* 33.17–18; Stein 1927: 31–2. The fact that the wearing of rings is ascribed specifically to *nobiles* suggests that Livy's earlier reference (9.7.8) to senators removing their tunics with the *latus clavus* and the gold ring is anachronistic (Oakley 2005a: 111–12).

[151] Pliny the Elder, *NH* 33.18. Though the story is common to both, Pliny does not seem to have used Livy (Oakley 2005a: 636).

[152] Livy 23.12.1–2.   [153] Livy 23.12.2.

[154] Pliny the Elder, *NH* 33.20–21; Oakley 2005a: 638–9.

[155] Livy 43.16.14; Scholz 2005: 419. See also Livy 26.36.5 for the association between senators and gold rings.

[156] App. *Pun.* 104.

[157] This is based on the research of Suolahti 1955: 243. In the period 218–134 BC, fifty-five noble tribunes are attested, ten others of senatorial background, and eighteen non-senatorial *equites*.

a privilege restricted to the patrician aristocracy, had spread to the senatorial elite.[158] Pliny the Elder was surely correct to emphasise the slow rate of adoption of the gold ring by senators, noting that not all senators wore them even at the time of the Social War, with even ex-praetors preferring iron rings.[159] This statement may of course have a moral point, since Pliny connected the spread of gold and other, more ornate, rings to the Roman fondness for luxury.[160] What is clear, however, is that the middle Republic was a transitional period in which senatorial and non-senatorial *equites* were being more closely distinguished by their privileges and status symbols, such as seating arrangements in the theatre, their dress and personal adornment. This was an outward reflection of the fact that senators wanted to be acknowledged as a superior status group. They could lay claim to a distinct ideology of service to the state *domi militiaeque* by virtue of their magistracies and associated civilian and military responsibilities. Such a development was in many ways inevitable, for it is a truism that as aristocracies increase in numbers, there is correspondingly a greater need for status differentiations among their members.[161] In the Roman world this trend was to play a crucial part in giving birth to a distinct equestrian order as a constituent element of the *res publica*.

The Decline of Cavalry Service

Perhaps the most significant development resulting in status differentiation between senators and non-senatorial *equites*, and greater heterogeneity among the non-senatorial *equites* themselves, is the decline in actual cavalry service. This was partially the result of changes within the Roman army itself, most notably a growing reliance on auxiliary cavalry composed of Rome's allies, rather than its citizens. Like the legions, the auxiliaries were not permanent standing units, but had to be levied for specific campaigns.[162] The number of auxiliary horsemen in the Roman army grew dramatically over the course of the third and second centuries BC, so that they came to outnumber the citizen *equites*, both those who possessed the public horse and those serving at their own expense.[163] Writing in the second century BC, Polybius declared that the army consisted of three times as many auxiliary horsemen as Roman citizens.[164]

---

[158] Kolb 1977b: 248.   [159] Pliny the Elder, *NH* 33.21.
[160] Pliny the Elder, *NH* 33.22. For the moralistic agenda, see Hawley 2007: 106–7; Wallace-Hadrill 2008: 349–51.
[161] Mosca 1939: 402.   [162] Prag 2011: 16–22.   [163] McCall 2002: 108–10.
[164] Polyb. 6.26.7; Walbank 1956: 709.

At the same time, wealthy *equites* began to seek alternate sources of status and prestige outside military service, as McCall and McDonnell have both cogently argued.[165] The influx of wealth and resources from Rome's expanding empire meant that all citizens in Italy were exempt from paying *tributum* (direct tax) from 167 BC onwards. The wealthiest Romans embraced the development of substantial estates, and richly adorned houses and villas became a new arena of social competition. This was particularly a result of cultural influences from Greece, which began to permeate Roman society in this period. Contact with the Greeks also brought renewed interest in studying law and oratory, which emerged as valid new ways for *equites* to make their mark in public life. These social and cultural changes did not necessarily supplant equestrian cavalry service – military *virtus* remained a key part of the outward expression of the *equites*' individual and collective identity – but it did mean that the army was not the single unifying factor it had been in the past. This transformation from a group based on martial prowess to one founded on the acquisition of wealth is typical of the evolution of aristocracies in pre-modern states.[166] This change in turn typically led to the diversification in sources of personal prestige beyond military status.[167] We can see such a development in the middle Republic, as *equites* became a heterogeneous collection of wealthy citizens among whom military service was merely one aspect of their lives.

In the third and early second centuries BC *equites* were expected to complete their ten years of military service, and had to face the consequences if they failed to fulfil their obligations.[168] In 252 BC, during the First Punic War, 400 *equites equo publico*, a substantial proportion of the equestrian centuries, were deprived of their public horses for failing to finish building fortifications as they had been ordered.[169] This strong connection between the *equites* and their obligation to serve the *res publica* continued in the Second Punic War. It is certain that members of the equestrian centuries fought at the Battle of Cannae. Many of them were senators serving as tribunes.[170] There were probably 1,200–2,400 citizen cavalry, composed of both *equites equo publico* and *equites equo suo*,

---

[165] McCall 2002: 114–36; McDonnell 2006: 259–65, 2011, whose arguments I follow closely in the following section.

[166] Mosca 1939: 56–7; Bottomore 1993: 29.   [167] Kautsky 1997: 169–77.

[168] The ancient sources show that it continued to be a requirement until the first century BC (Polyb. 6.19.1–5; Plut. *C.G.* 2.5.)

[169] Val. Max. 2.9.7; Front. *Strat.* 4.1.22.

[170] Nicolet 1974: 76. Livy 22.49.16–17 does not specifically mention *equites equo publico*, though they are to be understood.

involved in this battle.[171] Attempts to desert the state in the aftermath of
the disaster were severely punished. In 214 BC the quaestor M. Metellus
was one of many *equites* who had his *equus publicus* confiscated by the
censors because they planned to abandon Italy after Cannae.[172] These
punishments continued in 209 BC, during the censorship
of M. Cornelius Cethegus and P. Sempronius Tuditanus. The censors not
only deprived the *equites* who fled from Cannae to Sicily of their public
horses, but also commanded that they should continue to serve for
a further ten years by funding their own steeds, regardless of the years
they had already served.[173] *Equites* were rarely allowed to forgo their
military obligations, except in exceptional cases, such as that of the *publicani* mentioned above.[174] In 186 BC the censors decided to reward
P. Aebutius for his role in exposing the Bacchanalia by excusing him
military service and not giving him an *equus publicus*.[175] But this appears
to have been a unique decision. The valour of the Roman cavalry as a whole
continued to be celebrated in the early second century BC. In 180 BC,
during a hard-fought battle between the Romans and the Celtiberi in which
the barbarians were getting the upper hand, the consul Q. Fulvius Flaccus
exhorted the *equites* to turn the tide. The citizens' charge against the
Celtiberi was such an exhibition of *virtus* that they inspired the auxiliary
cavalry to rise to the occasion, and together they defeated the tribesmen.[176]
Flaccus made a vow to build a Temple of Fortuna Equestris ('Equestrian
Fortune') when he returned to Rome, and it was formally dedicated in
173 BC.[177] The temple was a triumphant symbol of equestrian *virtus*, but it
was erected at a time when the nature of military service for *equites* had
already begun to change.

The growing reliance on auxiliary cavalry meant that *equites* tended to
be promoted rapidly to serve as officers, rather than as regular cavalrymen
as in the past. The main command posts were *tribunus militum* (military
tribune in a legion) and *praefectus* (prefect of citizen cavalry or of allied
units). The tribunes of the first four legions (twenty-four in total after
207 BC) were all elected officials. Of these, only ten tribunes needed to have
served the full ten years before election; only five years' service was

[171] For the figures, see McCall 2002: 36.   [172] Livy 24.18.6–7, 24.43.2–3; Val. Max. 2.9.8.
[173] Livy 27.11.13–15.   [174] Cf. Nicolet 1974: 74; Livy 23.49.1–3, discussed above.
[175] Livy 39.19.3–4. Aebutius' father had previously completed his military service with a public
horse (*publico equo stipendia*) (Livy 39.9.2–3). A. Watson 2005 and O. F. Robinson 2007: 24
suggest that this was a double-edged reward, since Aebutius would not be eligible for senatorial
magistracies if he did not serve in the army, but this does not seem to be the sense of Livy's text
(Briscoe 2008: 237, 287).
[176] Livy 40.40.1–9.   [177] Livy 40.40.10, 40.44.8–12, 42.10.5.

sufficient for the remainder.[178] For all other tribunates, the qualifications were less stringent – commanding officers could appoint whomever they wished to these posts.[179] These officer positions remained attractive to leading senatorial families, both patrician and plebeian, until the first century BC, because of the prestige they offered their holders.[180] *Equites* were also appointed as prefects in command of the citizen cavalry and the auxiliary units provided by the allies.[181] There does not seem to have been any consistency as far as the auxiliaries were concerned, however, since sometimes they were commanded by equestrian *praefecti*, and at other times by senatorial legates, depending on the needs of the particular campaign.[182] The office of *tribunus militum*, especially of the first four legions, appears to have been slightly more prestigious than that of *praefectus*, which consequently attracted fewer men from the noble senatorial families.[183] The emphasis on physical fitness for *equites equo publico* was maintained, since they were still serving officers.[184] M. Porcius Cato (the Elder), censor in 184 BC, believed that Romans were becoming too soft and not living up to the standards of their ancestors, and delivered harsh speeches against men whom he deprived of their *equus publicus*.[185] Cato thought that a man should lose his *equus publicus* if the horse was skinny and ill-groomed or if the man himself was too fat, and it was for this reason that he confiscated the public horse from the portly L. Veturius.[186] Cato also advocated an increase in the numbers of *equites equo publico* from 1,800 to 2,200. The precise reasons behind this proposal are unknown, but they were surely connected to his belief that the *equites equo publico* were a vital constituent part of Rome's army, even if they were now officers rather than regular cavalrymen.[187]

The equestrian ideology of *virtus* displayed through military service remained important, but it was not always borne out in reality, since wealthy Roman citizens retained their *equus publicus* as a symbol of their status even after they had ceased to be a part of the army. The senatorial

[178] Polyb. 6.19.2; Suolahti 1955: 51–3, connecting these regulations with the *lex Villia Annalis* of 180 BC regulating senatorial magistracies.
[179] Suolahti 1955: 56–7.
[180] See the prosopographical research and conclusions of Suolahti 1955: 57–141.
[181] Suolahti 1955: 202–4; Polyb. 6.26.5. For the auxiliary units, three *praefecti* would be assigned to each of the four consular legions, and they would be appointed in addition to the allies' own officers (Suolahti 1955: 200–1; Walbank 1956: 709).
[182] Prag 2007: 84–5, 2010: 102–5.   [183] Suolahti 1955: 275–9.   [184] Giovannini 2010: 356–7.
[185] Astin 1978: 88–9, 96–7; McDonnell 2006: 260–1; Livy 39.42.6.
[186] Astin 1978: 81–2; Aulus Gell. *NA* 4.12.1–3, 6.22.3–4. Veturius: Cato, *ORF*⁴ 8, 72–82; Plut. *Cato Maior* 9.5.
[187] Cato, *ORF*⁴ 8, 85–6; E. Rawson 1971: 16.

members of the equestrian centuries did not serve as regular cavalrymen, and former magistrates were not even appointed as officers, except in exceptional circumstances, such as at the Battle of Cannae.[188] Still, senators retained their *equus publicus* beyond the age of regular military service, and Livy treats the removal of the public horse as a rare and sensational event.[189] In 204 BC both the censors, M. Livius Salinator and C. Claudius Nero, still held their *equus publicus*.[190] Valerius Maximus tells us that this was 'on account of the vigour of their age' (*propter robur aetatis*), though both had already been consul, and Salinator at least was around fifty years old.[191] In a situation remembered chiefly for its farcical nature, Salinator and Nero attempted to settle old grudges by depriving each other of their *equus publicus*, though age or infirmity was never given as grounds for doing so.[192] In 184 BC Cato turned his attention towards the senator L. Cornelius Scipio Asiagenes, whom he divested of his *equus publicus*.[193] Plutarch states that this was the result of Cato's hostility towards the Scipios, but the censor publicly claimed that Asiagenes was no longer suitable for cavalry service.[194] Asiagenes would not have been very old at this time, and was probably in his mid-forties, but, since he had been consul, he would no longer have served as a regular cavalryman anyway.[195] He, like other senatorial magistrates, had retained the *equus publicus* merely as an honour, a symbol of his superior status. There was consequently a growing gulf between senior members of the equestrian centuries – senators such as Salinator, Nero and Asiagenes, who had long since ceased to serve in the cavalry – and more junior members, who did continue to do so, if only as officers. One thing that senatorial and non-senatorial *equites* did have in common was that they were quite distinct from the auxiliary units that came to make up the majority of Rome's cavalry forces over the course of the second century BC. The *equites* could no longer claim to be the coherent fighting force that they had been in the early days of the Republic, but were now a privileged cadre of officers and former officers.

At the same time as the nature of military service changed, senatorial and non-senatorial *equites* embraced the financial opportunities offered by Rome's growing empire. Kay has argued that the flow of new income into

---

[188] Hill 1952: 42; Briscoe 2008: 363.   [189] Crawford 1992: 200.   [190] Livy 29.37.8.

[191] Val. Max. 2.9.6; Nicolet 1974: 75.   [192] Livy 29.37.8–17.

[193] Livy 39.44.1; Plut. *Cato Maior* 18.1; Ps.-Aur. Vict. *Vir. Ill.* 53.2.

[194] Plut. *Cato Maior* 18.1; Hill 1952: 43–4; Briscoe 2008: 363. As Astin 1978: 81 points out, Asiagenes was not expelled from the senate, so physical unfitness is the only possible reason Cato could have given without casting doubt on his *mores*.

[195] For his age, see Nicolet 1974: 75.

Rome in the course of the second century BC concentrated wealth in the hands of a much smaller elite than had previously been the case.[196] This led to greater competition among prosperous Romans for access to the rewards of empire, as we have already seen in the case of the *publicani*. The *crème de la crème* who sat at the top of the financial pyramid wanted to articulate their status by displaying their riches.[197] However, there was tension between the old aristocratic value system, defined by *virtus*, and the drive to acquire wealth and luxury objects. We can see this conflict in action during the censorship of P. Cornelius Scipio Aemilianus in 142 BC. Aemilianus deprived several *equites* of their public horses, including Ti. Claudius Asellus, whose ancestor had had a valiant military career in the Second Punic War.[198] Asellus also defended his own record as a Roman *eques*, boasting 'that he had travelled throughout the provinces in the course of his military service' (*omnis se provincias stipendia merentem peragrasse*).[199] Although Aemilianus' colleague, L. Mummius, later restored Asellus' *equus publicus*, the wronged man brought the censor to trial in 140 BC.[200] The fragments of Aemilianus' speeches delivered during the trial reveal that the censor's reasons for removing Asellus' public horse were based on his lifestyle, particularly his 'malice' (*malitia*) and 'profligacy' (*nequitia*). He accused Asellus of squandering his inheritance and spending more money on a single whore than the entire value of the equipment of his Sabine estate.[201] Although *equites* had certainly been deprived of their public horse for such reasons before, there was greater tension in the second century BC because more *equites* became engaged in the pursuit of wealth, which was seen in some quarters as incompatible with their status.

Many of our specific examples of extravagant *equites* come from the first century BC, a period which is rich in literary testimony. They include Carvilius Pollio, the first Roman to decorate banqueting couches in silver and gold in the Punic fashion. This was an innovation, since previously such furniture had only been made from bronze. Pliny the Elder cited Cornelius Nepos' claim that there were only two silver banqueting couches in Rome before the time of Sulla.[202] Romans of the second century BC evinced moral anxiety about extravagant private houses, yet this did not

---

[196] Kay 2014: 288–91.   [197] McCall 2002: 123–7.

[198] Gell. *NA* 3.4.1. For the ancestor, see Livy 23.46–7, 27.41.7, 28.11, 29.11–12.

[199] Cic. *Orat.* 2.258. Astin 1967: 256 dates this to Aemilianus' censorship.

[200] Astin 1967: 175–7. For the restoration of the *equus publicus*, see Cic. *Orat.* 2.268.

[201] Gell. *NA* 6.11.9; see also *NA* 2.20.6; Nicolet 1974: 836–8; Astin 1967: 120.

[202] Pliny the Elder, *NH* 33.144, 146. The change is borne out by the archaeological record: Wallace-Hadrill 2008: 422–35.

prevent their construction.[203] L. Licinius Crassus, the orator and consul of 95 BC, was the first to have columns of foreign marble in his house; but the magnificence of Crassus' residence was surpassed by that of the *eques* C. Aquilius on the Viminal hill, which was said by everyone to be the most beautiful house of its time.[204] The cultivation of wealth and property offered *equites* new ways to articulate their status in the second century BC. This was not necessarily incompatible with military service for the *res publica*, as the case of Ti. Claudius Asellus demonstrates, but it was perceived by conservative Romans as a threat to aristocratic traditions of equestrian *virtus*.

The final aspect that needs to be considered is the growth in oratory and rhetoric as a source of personal prestige.[205] One of Cn. Naevius' plays, written in the third century BC, featured a derogatory comment about novice orators as 'stupid young men' (*stulti adulescentuli*).[206] But things soon began to change, and public speaking became one of the defining qualities of a Roman citizen, alongside military and political prowess.[207] According to Cicero, the first Roman to really make a name for himself as an orator was M. Cornelius Cethegus (*cos.* 204 BC), who was praised for his eloquence by Ennius.[208] Cicero placed the growth of oratory in the period after Rome had established its empire, and especially after its citizens had been exposed to Greek oratorical techniques.[209] The growing interest in oratory and rhetoric could be deployed in the legal arena, which emerged as a new and important field of social and political competition. In 204 BC the *lex Cincia* set limits on the payments that could be made to a legal advocate. The fact that advocacy needed to be legislated suggests that it was becoming a more common profession in this period.[210] It may be no coincidence that Cato the Elder, himself an *eques equo publico*, earned a reputation early in his career as an advocate, and was famed for this as well as his military service.[211] By the end of the second century BC the *eques* M. Iunius Brutus performed military service, but then chose to pursue a legal career rather than seeking senatorial magistracies.[212]

[203] M. Nicols 2010.   [204] Pliny the Elder, *NH* 36.7 (on Crassus), *NH* 17.2 (on Aquilius).
[205] McCall 2002: 118–23.   [206] Cic. *Sen.* 20.   [207] G. Kennedy 1972: 37–8.
[208] Cic. *Brut.* 57–61. Cicero *Brut.* 61 cited only a few early works he considered worth reading, notably the speech of App. Claudius Caecus concerning the peace with Pyrrhus from 280 BC, and a collection of funeral orations he owned – hardly a ringing endorsement of early Latin rhetoric. G. Kennedy 1972: 27 points out that Cicero is likely to have only read Caecus' oration as transmitted in Ennius' *Annales*.
[209] Cic. *Orat.* 1.14.   [210] For discussion of the law, see Shatzman 1975: 70–3.
[211] Plut. *Cato Maior* 1.4, 6. For later speeches, see Gell. *NA* 10.3.14–17.
[212] Cic. *Orat.* 2.226, *Brut.* 130, *Off.* 2.50; Nicolet 1974: 918.

The study of Latin language for its own sake was also attractive to *equites*. Cato, so Cicero thought, was the earliest orator 'whose writings ought to be made known' (*cuius quidem scripta proferenda*), and Quintilian describes him as the first Roman to write on rhetoric.[213] Romans initially regarded formal training in rhetoric with suspicion, as illustrated by the fact that a senatorial decree was passed in 161 BC expelling philosophers and rhetoricians from Rome.[214] Presumably the senators were anxious about the threat these men posed to traditional values.[215] But by the end of the second century BC, L. Aelius Stilo Praeconinus, an *eques*, helped to lay the foundations for the study of Latin grammar.[216] Other *equites* can be cited in this context, such as C. Lucilius, the inventor of satire, and the tragic poet and orator C. Titius, who flourished around 161 BC.[217]

It is important to note that none of these fields of endeavour was incompatible with military service, and many *equites* actually combined them. The satirist Lucilius, mentioned above, served with Scipio Aemilianus at Numantia.[218] Cicero's uncle, L. Tullius Cicero, who died in 102 BC, was a companion of M. Antonius in Cicilia, and well known for his erudition.[219] Moving forward into the first century BC, L. Orbilius Pupillus was *eques* in the cavalry, and then returned to his studies, eventually making his mark in Rome when Cicero was fifty years old.[220] Finally, even the *publicani* saw military service. Cn. Plancius, the president of a society of publicans, served as a military tribune in Spain in the 90s BC.[221] The point is not that cavalry service for *equites* disappeared in the second century BC – it obviously did not – but that a wide range of other ways to gain and display prestige emerged. This meant that active military careers ceased to be the one defining factor for all *equites* in reality, even if *virtus* retained its ideological importance.

The various pathways and avenues for success available to elite Romans emphasised the differences among both the senatorial and non-senatorial *equites*, rather than the similarities that unified them as a wealthy aristocratic social stratum. Senators were distinguished by their superior status as members of the *curia*, their service in civilian and military positions

---

[213] Cic. *Brut.* 61; Quint. *Orat.* 3.1.19. Cf. Cic. *Brut.* 293–4, in which 'Brutus' is less enthusiastic about Cato, especially when compared to his Greek predecessors in the field of oratory.
[214] Gell. *NA* 15.11; Suet. *De Rhet.* 1. A similar edict, cited by both these authors, was issued by the censors in 92 BC.
[215] For discussion, see G. Kennedy 1972: 53–5.
[216] Cic. *Brut.* 205; Suet. *Gram.* 3.1; Pliny the Elder, *NH* 33.29.
[217] Lucilius: Nicolet 1974: 926–9. Titius: Nicolet 1974: 1040–1; Cic. *Brut.* 167.
[218] Vell. Pat. 2.9.4.   [219] Cic. *Orat.* 2.2–3.   [220] Suet. *Gram.* 9; Hor. *Sat.* 1.10.8.
[221] Cic. *Planc.* 32.

domi militiaeque, as well as their new symbols of rank, such as the *latus clavus* and *anulus aureus*, and the privilege of having reserved seats at the theatre. Non-senatorial *equites* were able to participate in commerce and trade without fear of punishment, and accumulated vast wealth by doing so. Senators, on the other hand, had to work through middlemen in commercial affairs. The power and influence of the *publicani* emphasised the political capital invested in the *equites*, who often came into conflict with their senatorial coevals over the management and distribution of the profits of empire. Finally, over the course of the middle Republic, Rome progressively relied more and more on auxiliary cavalry units, rather than citizen *equites*, who now tended to serve only as officers. Rome's expansion throughout the Mediterranean and the influx of wealth into Italy, together with other cultural changes, created new avenues for aristocratic prestige alongside military service. *Equites* now vied with each other over wealth, land and houses, or through their accomplishments in law and oratory. Taken together, these developments not only sharpened the distinctions between senatorial and non-senatorial *equites*, they also resulted in the *equites* becoming more diverse as a social group. The *equites* would remain a heterogeneous group of wealthy elites for the rest of their history. From this point on, the question became how to give them a sense of collective purpose and importance in the *res publica*.

Two Tribunes, Two Laws

The end of the second century BC witnessed the creation of a separate equestrian order, distinct from the senate, which represented the culmination of these developments. Two pieces of legislation provided the catalyst. The first, passed in 129 BC, compelled senators to surrender their public horses and membership of the equestrian centuries.[222] The only evidence for this measure comes in a passage from Cicero's *De Re Publica*, written in the 50s BC.[223] It is conventionally called the *plebiscitum reddendorum equorum* ('the plebiscite for the returning of horses') based on Cicero's

---

[222] This interpretation is widely accepted, e.g. Stein 1927: 1–4; Hill 1952: 15; M. I. Henderson 1963: 70–1; Badian 1972: 56–7; Gabba 1976: 128; Brunt 1988: 146. Cf. Nicolet 1974: 107–11, 513–15, who dates the measure to some time after 123 BC.

[223] Cf. Lintott 1994: 75, who argues that the measure was actually intended to abolish the *equus publicus* altogether. The traditional interpretation has likewise been contested by Giovannini 2010: 360–4, who argues that senators continued to vote in the equestrian centuries until the end of the Republic. But this proposal is not convincing in the light of literary sources that give no hint of this (e.g. Cic. *Phil.* 6.13, 7.16).

description of it. The *De Re Publica*, which now only survives in fragments, was conceived as a political and philosophical discussion between P. Cornelius Scipio Aemilianus and eight other leading Romans in the early months of 129 BC, prior to Aemilianus' untimely death in somewhat suspicious circumstances.[224] In a fragment of book four of the *De Re Publica*, Scipio makes the following comment:

How fitting is the orderly distribution into ages and classes and cavalry. This last includes the votes of the senate, although too many people now foolishly want this useful custom to be eliminated in seeking a new form of bribe through a bill on returning their horses.[225]

Cicero's historical dialogues were thoroughly researched to ensure their accuracy, so it is unlikely that he would have included this statement in the *De Re Publica* if such a piece of legislation was not under discussion in 129 BC.[226] Moreover, evidence from the late second and first century BC shows that senators did indeed cease to be members of the equestrian centuries.[227] But why was this measure proposed in the first place, since, as we have seen, the *equus publicus* remained a status symbol jealously guarded by senators? Badian's argument that it was intended to give the *equites* 'a conspicuous corporate identity, as a counterweight to the senate' in the aftermath of the tribunate of Ti. Sempronius Gracchus, seems to go too far and to anticipate the legislation of his brother Gaius.[228]

However, this does not mean that we should dismiss the impact of the events of 133 BC on Roman politics altogether, since the aftershocks continued to reverberate in 129 BC.[229] There was, as we discussed above, growing tension between the senatorial and non-senatorial *equites* over the course of the second century BC, especially in commercial affairs and the letting of contracts to the *publicani*. The best explanation for the law of 129 BC is that it served as a 'bribe' for wealthy citizens who possessed the

---

[224] Zetzel 1995: 3–13.
[225] Cic. *Rep.* 4.4.2: *quam commode ordines discripti aetates classes equitatus, in quo suffragia sunt etiam senatus, nimis multis iam stulte hanc utilitatem tolli cupientibus, qui novam largitionem quaerunt aliquo plebiscito reddendorum equorum*. The translation is that of Zetzel 1999: 79–80, though I have rendered *largitionem* as 'bribe' rather than 'dole'.
[226] Badian 1972: 56; Stone 2005: 77.
[227] Nicolet 1974: 104–6. The most explicit example of this is from 70 BC when Cn. Pompeius Magnus resigned his public horse and entered the senate (Plut. *Pomp.* 22). Cf. Giovannini 2010: 359, who argues that this was customary, but not necessary.
[228] Badian 1972: 58–60. M. I. Henderson 1963: 70–1 and Stone 2005: 78–9 argue that the law was the work of Gaius Gracchus or one of his associates, which seems to anticipate the events of 123 BC.
[229] For the political climate of 129 BC, see Beness 2005.

equestrian *census*, but not the *equus publicus*, and who would now be able to gain access to the 300 places in the equestrian centuries vacated by the senators.[230] Whoever proposed the law – and the consensus is that it was probably an ambitious tribune of the plebs – would win support among the newest members of the equestrian centuries, thus enhancing their career prospects and future political programme.[231] The new law would allow more Romans to share in the elite status that came with being an *eques equo publico*.[232] After this point we cannot speak of senatorial and non-senatorial *equites*, since senators were no longer eligible to be *equites*.

Although the law of 129 BC removed senators from the centuries of *equites equo publico*, it did not give the *equites* any specific political role in the Roman state, beyond the usual right to vote in the *comitia centuriata*. That came in 123 BC, during the tribunate of C. Sempronius Gracchus (henceforth, for simplicity, referred to as Gaius Gracchus). It was prompted by the maltreatment of provincials by Roman senatorial officials. This problem had first reared its head in Roman politics in 171 BC, when residents of Spain complained about the conduct of senatorial governors.[233] In 149 BC the tribune L. Calpurnius Piso Frugi established the first permanent court, or *quaestio perpetua*, to try cases of *repetundae* (which literally means 'things that must be recovered', but is usually translated as provincial maladministration or extortion). The senatorial governors would be tried by juries of their peers (i.e. other senators). If convicted, the senators had to repay the amount they had taken from the provincials, with no other penalty imposed.[234] But this court did nothing to stem incidences of corruption by senatorial governors.

In 123 BC the tribune Gaius Gracchus passed the *lex Sempronia de repetundis* ('the Sempronian law on provincial maladministration') to establish a stricter court to hear these cases.[235] A fragmentary copy of Gracchus' law has been found preserved on a bronze tablet (the *Tabula Bembina*), which specifies the terms of the legislation in precise detail.[236] The opening sections show that the *quaestio* was set up to indict senators,

---

[230] This argument has gained acceptance: Hill 1952: 106; Wiseman 1970b: 79, 1973: 191–2; Stockton 1979: 94; Crawford 1992: 201. The new *equites equo publico* would presumably have to have waited until the next censorship in 125 BC to be formally enrolled.

[231] Wiseman 1973: 192. Cf. Nicolet 1974: 109–11, who acknowledges the benefit to *equites* and the electoral ramifications.

[232] McDonnell 2006: 254.   [233] Livy 43.2.1–3.4; J. S. Richardson 1987: 1.

[234] Cic. *Brut.* 106; Stockton 1979: 139–40; J. S. Richardson 1987. Senators served as judges in the vast majority of civil and criminal courts as a matter of course (Brunt 1988: 197–8).

[235] For the date, see Stockton 1979: 230–6; Brunt 1988: 214–15.

[236] *RS* 1, edited by Crawford 1996, superseding all previous versions of the text.

their immediate relatives, or senatorial magistrates.[237] The crucial aspect of Gaius' legislation is that it specified that the jurors would no longer be drawn from the senatorial order. Most of the ancient sources state that the *album* (panel) of *iudices* (jurors) in this court was composed solely of *equites*.[238] The *Tabula Bembina* preserves the precise terms of the law, which explicitly delineated those who were ineligible to serve on the juries:

Concerning [the selection of] 450 men every year. [The praetor ---, within the ten days next after each] of them shall have begun that magistracy, [he] is to see that he chooses 450 men in that way, who in this [state ---,] provided that he do not choose any of those, who may be or may have been tribune of the plebs, quaestor, *IIIvir capitalis*, tribune of the soldiers for any of the first four legions, *IIIvir* for the granting and assigning of lands, or who may be or may have been in the senate or who [may have received] a payment [or may have been condemned in a *quaestio* and *iudicium publicum*, in relation to (either of) which it may not be lawful for him to be enrolled in the senate, or who] may be [younger than 30 or older than] 60 years, or who [may not have his domicile] in the city, at Rome, or nearer the city of Rome [than one mile,] or who may be the father, brother or son [of any of those magistrates,] or of a man who may be or may have been in the senate, or who shall be overseas.[239]

Gaius Gracchus' law therefore prescribed that the praetor should not select senators, or men who have held magistracies associated with the senate, to serve on the *album* of jurors. At this point in history, the posts of tribune of the plebs and quaestor did not confer membership of the senate, but they were obviously perceived to be 'senatorial' in nature, to the extent that their occupants could not be relied upon to be sufficiently impartial when

---

[237] *RS* 1, ll 1–3, though they could not be tried while still holding *imperium*: ll. 8–9. As Brunt 1988: 198, 202 points out, the list of magistrates eligible for prosecution would mean that some *equites equo publico* could indeed be tried under the terms of the law.

[238] Cic. I *Verr.* 38; Diod. Sic. 34/5.25.1; Vell. Pat. 2.13.2, 2.32.3; Tac. *Ann.* 12.60; App. *BC* 1.22. Cf. Plut. *C.G.* 5.2, *Comp.* 2.1, who states that jurors were selected from senators and *equites*, and Livy, *Per.* 60, who refers to *equites* being admitted to the senate. On the basis of this, Brunt 1988: 236–8 argued that a mixed jury applied to all courts except the extortion court.

[239] *RS* 1, ll. 15–17 (trans. Crawford 1996: 86): *de CDL vireis quot annis [legundis. praetor, --- is in diebus X proxum(eis), quibus | quis]que eorum eum mag(istratum) coiperit, facito utei CDL viros ita legat, quei ha[c ceivitate ---, d]um ne quem eorum legat, quei tr(ibunus) pl(ebis), q(uaestor), IIIvir cap(italis), tr(ibunus) mil(itum) l(egionibus) IIII primis aliqua earum, trium vir(um) a(gris) d(andis) a(dsignandis) siet fueritve, queive in senatu siet fueritve, queive merc [edem ceperit quaestioneve ioudicioque puplico condemnatus siet quod circa eum in senatum legei non liceat queive minor anneis XXX | maior a]nnos LX gnatus siet queive in urbe Romae propiusve urbem Roma[m p(assus) m(ille) domicilium non habeat, queive eorum quoius mag(istratuum),] queive eius, quei in senatu siet fueritve pater frater filiusve siet queive trans mare erit.* The restorations in square brackets are supported by the near identical lines 12–15, which refer to the selection of jurors in the year the law was passed.

judging senators.[240] The same principle evidently applied to the *IIIviri capitales* and the three men serving on the Gracchan land commission, as well as the elected tribunes of the first four legions. Finally, the legislation proposed that jurors could not be fathers, brothers or sons of senators or magistrates.[241] The overall aim of Gracchus' law was to ensure that senators, or men with senatorial connections, would not be able to sit in judgement on their peers.

This section of the law, which specifies in great detail precisely who could not be jurors, survives relatively intact. But the positive qualification, prescribing who could serve as jurors, is no longer extant (it originally came after 'who in this state').[242] Given that we know from later literary sources that the Gracchan jurors were *equites*, there are two different ways to fill the lacuna. The law specified that eligible citizens should possess either the *equus publicus* or the *census equester*.[243] It might initially be thought that the former would be the more probable alternative, especially in light of the mention of the 'withdrawal of the public horse' (*equom adimito*) elsewhere in the law.[244] But this is not the case if we look at the language of the statute and compare it with other pieces of legislation. If the *census equester* was the positive qualification, then the law would also have had to prescribe that a juror must be a full citizen of free birth. This would in fact be the natural way of completing the fragmentary sentence 'who in this state ... '.[245] Crawford has recently observed that there is insufficient room to include both free birth and the *census equester* in the law. He noted that specification of the *equus publicus* alone would fit correctly (since all *equites equo publico* could be assumed to be of free

---

[240] As Hill 1952: 110 notes, the list of magistrates is similar to those from which new senators were recruited during the Second Punic War (Livy 23.23.5–6). Tribunes would become senators by the *lex Atinia* (*c.* 122–102 BC), while quaestors would enter the senate under Sulla in 81 BC (Lintott 1999: 68–9).

[241] Rowland 1965: 365 n. 18 notes the similarity with the *lex Claudia* of 218 BC.

[242] The lacuna occurs at both occasions on which the positive qualification was mentioned (ll. 12: *quei in hac ceivit[ate---]*; l. 16: *quei ha[c ceivitate ---]*). There must have been some positive qualification, or otherwise all non-senatorial citizens would be eligible.

[243] Nicolet 1974: 513–15; Stockton 1979: 142; Lintott 1992: 20; Crawford 1996: 98. The two alternatives were proposed by Mommsen in *CIL* I^1 198 (*census*) and *CIL* I^2 583 (*equus publicus*), respectively (see also Mommsen 1887–8: III, 530 n. 1). Cf. Hill 1952: 110–11, who argues that the law actually imposed the equestrian census for the first time.

[244] *RS* 1, l. 28; Nicolet 1974: 165, 485.

[245] Lintott 1992: 116. Mattingly 1970:168, 1975b: 727 recognised the need to mention free birth, drawing parallels with the *lex de provinciis praetoriis* of 100 BC (see the text in *RS* 12, Delphi Copy, Block C, l. 23).

birth).[246] But given the problems in reconstructing the precise text of the law, the exact lengths of the various lacunae still remain uncertain, and Crawford's observation cannot be decisive.

On the other hand, convincing positive arguments can be mounted for the equestrian census as the primary qualification. As Lintott has pointed out, the *album* of jurors to be drawn up each year numbered 450 men – one quarter of the total of 1,800 *equites equo publico*.[247] From these 1,800 citizens we must subtract the sons of senators, and citizens who held any of the disqualifying magistracies, as well as those under the age of thirty or over sixty.[248] This would surely eliminate a significant number of the *equites equo publico*.[249] An *album* of jurors from the remainder would be drastically reduced – though not impossible.[250] If the qualification was the *census equester*, far greater numbers of citizens would be able to serve. Kay has estimated that there were some 30,000 households in Italy wealthy enough to qualify for the equestrian census at this time. We must discount the significant number of wealthy Italians who were not citizens, and therefore could not be classed as *equites*, as well as those who did not reside in Rome or nearby, whom the law specifically excludes.[251] But this would still result in a much broader pool of potential jurors than if they were defined solely by the *equus publicus*.[252] There is one further piece of evidence that tips the balance in favour of the *census equester*. In the *First Philippic* of 44 BC Cicero refers to three important laws on Roman courts, the *lex Iulia iudicaria* (46 BC), the *lex Pompeia iudicaria* (55 BC) and the *lex Aurelia iudicaria* (70 BC), all of which modified the composition of the juries following Gracchus' law of 123 BC. In these pieces of legislation, he states, the 'census qualification was defined' (*census praefiniebatur*) for the jurors, and 'not only for centurions but also for *equites Romani*' (*non centurioni quidem solum sed equiti etiam Romano*).[253] It is highly probable,

---

[246] Crawford 2001: 432 proposed the restoration *quei h[ac ceivitate equo publico stipendia fecit fecerit d]um* for l. 16.

[247] Lintott 1992: 20–1. The selection process is described by Cic. *Planc.* 41.

[248] Stein 1927: 20–1.

[249] Stone 2005: 78–9 suggested that a body of 600 equestrian *iudices* remained after excluding the ineligible *equites equo publico*, appealing to the authority of Livy, *Per.* 60.

[250] J. S. Richardson 1998: 57 argued that there may not have been too much work involved in drawing up the list of 450 jurors. He suggested that this could have remained consistent from year to year, since the real process of selection came during a trial.

[251] The residence requirement is contained in *RS* 1, ll. 13, 17.

[252] For the calculations, see Kay 2014: 292.

[253] Cic. *Phil.* 1.20, as noted by Mattingly 1975b. However, like Crawford 1996: 99, I am not convinced by Mattingly's argument that cavalry service was a requirement.

therefore, that Gracchus' *lex de repetundis* likewise stipulated a property-based qualification for jurors.[254]

Why did Gaius Gracchus give control of the courts to *equites* without senatorial connections, and how did this fit in with his larger political programme? Appian provides a plausible motivation for the establishment of the court. He wrote that Gaius regarded the *quaestio de repetundis* as corrupt in its existing form, since several senators had recently been acquitted after the senatorial jurors had been bribed.[255] Detailed examination of the *lex de repetundis* reveals that it exhibited significant concern for impartiality.[256] This is shown by the fact that *equites* who had been tribune of the plebs, quaestor or military tribune were also excluded as jurors, even though they were not yet members of the *curia*, because they hoped for a senatorial career. Thus, Pliny the Elder wrote of the Gracchan reforms establishing a specific group of *iudices*, since *equites* with senatorial connections were not actually permitted to sit on the jury.[257] Moreover, Gaius' law made *tribuni militum* and other junior magistrates, who would not have been senators, but *equites*, liable to prosecution.[258] So the division between senators and *equites* was not as entirely clear-cut as the later sources would suggest. But at the same time, however, we should not be so naïve as to suppose that Gaius did not know what he was doing when he gave citizens of equestrian status the authority to sit in judgement on magistrates and members of the senate.[259] Even if he did not set out to create the equestrian order per se,[260] his law established explicit distinctions between Roman aristocrats where they had not existed before. In particular, he invested new political power in those *equites* who had not been magistrates or were not connected to senators, but who were still resident in Rome.

This argument is supported by Gaius' other pieces of legislation, particularly the law concerning the settlement of the province of Asia, which had been constituted after King Attalus III of Pergamum bequeathed his

[254] Furthermore, it is worth noting that Gaius' *lex agraria* specified a jury made up of members of the *prima classis* for tax cases, another census-based qualification. (*RS* 2, ll. 37). See Lintott 1992: 51; Crawford 1996: 168–9.
[255] App. *BC* 1.22; Steel 2013: 24. The men who were acquitted were L. Aurelius Cotta, Livius Salinator and M.' Aquilius. See Gruen 1968: 37–8, 77–8, 297.
[256] Stockton 1979: 141; Sherwin-White 1982. For an overview of the clauses, see Crawford 1996: 51.
[257] Pliny the Elder, *NH* 33.34. This did not supplant the use of the term *equites* in general parlance, however (Ferrary 1980: 316).
[258] Sherwin-White 1982: 19.
[259] See the comments of Meier 1966: 72; Stockton 1979: 152–3; Lintott 1992: 26, 1994: 81.
[260] Note Sherwin-White 1982: 28.

kingdom to Rome.[261] Gaius' *lex Sempronia de provincia Asia* decreed that the tax contracts for the new province would be auctioned off by the censors at Rome, ensuring that the *publicani* would be able to bid for these lucrative opportunities.[262] Even though the *publicani* and *equites* were not synonymous groups, the law on the province of Asia was certainly to the advantage of these wealthy non-senatorial elements in the state.[263] As we have observed earlier in this chapter, the *publicani* and the *equites* usually only came into political conflict with the censors and the senate when they were denied the opportunity to profit from the rewards of empire. The *publicani* and the *equites* were largely reactive groups, who were courted by politicians such as Gracchus who had political vision.

The full impact of Gaius' establishment of the *quaestio de repetundis* empanelled by equestrian jurors was not felt for at least a decade, as Sherwin-White has argued.[264] Indeed, he suggested that *equites* may have initially resented their new political role, since service as a juror in Rome was compulsory, represented a major time commitment, and was subject to significant scrutiny.[265] There is some evidence from Cicero's speeches to support this view, since equestrians evidently resisted the introduction of strictures and penalties designed to regulate their conduct as jurors.[266] This, of course, needs to be set alongside the fact that the equestrians of the late Republic as a whole opposed any diminution of their influence in the criminal courts once it had been given to them. However, this is an example of the primarily reactive political involvement of the *equites*, who only intervened when their interests were affected. By the time of Cicero their right to sit as jurors in the criminal courts was no longer regarded as a novelty, but an accepted privilege of equestrian rank.

Therefore, it was two tribunes – Gaius Gracchus and the anonymous author of the *plebiscitum* – who ended up reshaping the Roman state by instituting new measures designed to benefit their careers and political vision. They never explicitly set out to create an 'equestrian order', though that was the eventual outcome of their laws.[267] At the end of the second century BC we find the first attested use of the term *ordo equester* by the jurist Iunius Congus Gracchanus (so called because he was a friend, and

---

[261] Plut. *T.G.* 14; Livy, *Per.* 58; Badian 1972: 63–5.

[262] Cic. II *Verr.* 2.12. In 66 BC Cicero in *Pro Leg. Man.* 14 declared that the revenues of Asia exceeded all other provinces.

[263] Stockton 1979: 154–5; Brunt 1988: 151; Lintott 1994: 79. For other economic elements of Gaius' legislation that may have benefited the *publicani*, see Rowland 1965.

[264] Sherwin-White 1982: 22–3.   [265] Sherwin-White 1982: 28.

[266] This is discussed in Chapter 2.

[267] Gruen 1968: 90; Badian 1972: 65–6; Brunt 1988: 151–2.

probable supporter, of Gaius Gracchus).[268] It occurs in an excerpt from his work cited verbatim by Pliny the Elder:

> As regards the name for the *ordo equester*, we used to call them *trossuli*, but now we call them *equites*, because they do not understand what the name *trossuli* means, and many are ashamed to be called by this name.[269]

The epithet *trossuli*, which means 'conquerors of Trossulum', refers to an early conflict in which the Italian city of Trossulum was captured by the Roman cavalry.[270] Gracchanus' comment indicates that the *equites* of the late second century BC had no real knowledge of this achievement. Instead, they much preferred to be regarded as a status group, an *ordo*, with a defined function within the state.[271] The next precisely dated appearance of the term *ordo equester* comes in Cicero's *In Verrem* of 70 BC, by which time it is an unexceptional and normal usage.[272] Although prior to this point the *equites* had become increasingly heterogeneous in terms of the pathways they took to gain status and prestige – military service, oratory, law, and the acquisition and display of wealth – they now acquired new political power and influence which could define them as an *ordo* within the *res publica*, sitting alongside, but distinct from, the senate and people.

The question of whether the new *ordo equester* was composed only of *equites equo publico* or all Roman citizens who possessed the *census equester* has generated a significant amount of scholarly controversy. Nicolet, in his fundamental account of the equestrian order, proposed that the only true *equites* were those with the public horse, though his argument has not always been accepted.[273] The matter can be easily settled, however, in favour of the property qualification.[274] Roman citizens who possessed the necessary *census equester* and who served as *equites equo suo* had always been referred to *equites*. As we have seen in this chapter, over the course of the Republican period wealthy Romans with the *census*

---

[268] Pliny the Elder, *NH* 33.36; see also Cic. *Orat.* 1.256; Cic. *De Leg.* 3.49; Rankov 1987.

[269] Pliny the Elder, *NH* 33.36: *quod ad equestrem ordinem attinet, antea trossulos vocabant, nunc equites vocant ideo, quia non intellegunt trossulos nomen quid valeat, multosque pudet eo nomine appellari.*

[270] Pedroni 2010.   [271] Nicolet 1974: 163–5; Ferrary 1980: 316–17.

[272] Cic. I *Verr.* 38; Cic. II *Verr.* 2.175, 3.94, 3.166, 3.223, 3.224, 4.45.

[273] Nicolet 1974: 163–76. See also Stein 1927: 4–6; Demougin 1988: 210–12. Scholars in favour of the *census equester* include M. I. Henderson 1963: 65; Wiseman 1970b; Brunt 1988: 146, 515; Bleicken 1995: 45. The situation in the Augustan and imperial period is much more complicated, and will be discussed in Chapters 4 and 5.

[274] See most recently the forceful statements of Giovannini 2010: 363–4, though I disagree with other aspects of his article, as noted above.

equester withdrew from actual service as mere cavalry troopers and became officers instead, or even chose not to serve in the army at all. But this did not alter their right to be called *equites*, a title that delineated their high status within the *res publica*. This is confirmed by a comment made by Cicero in the speech *Pro Roscio Comoedo* delivered in 76 BC. Referring to the juror C. Cluvius, Cicero proclaimed: 'If you assess him according to his census rating, he is an *eques Romanus*, if you assess him according to his way of life, he is an outstanding man.'[275] The new *ordo equester* therefore encompassed all such citizens who possessed the necessary census property qualification, with the 1,800 *equites equo publico* forming an exclusive elite within the *ordo* at large.

Conclusion: From Warriors to Jurors

The equestrian jurors who sat on Gaius Gracchus' *quaestio de repetundis* had little in common with the mounted warrior aristocrats who roamed across Latium in the eighth to sixth centuries BC. Indeed, the *equites* of the late second century BC would not have recognised the picture of Regal Rome essayed in this chapter – for them it was the world of Romulus and his *Celeres*, Numa and his religious innovations, and Servius Tullius and his centuriate organisation. Such origin myths invested Rome's political and religious institutions of the Republican period with meaning and antiquity. Stories also emerged about the origins of the nascent equestrian order: the *equites* likewise had been created by the kings – and not just any king, but Romulus, the founder of Rome, himself. This meant that the order and its members were not the relatively recent creation of two pieces of legislation, but an ancient and revered component of the Roman state.

The story of the emergence of the equestrian order is much more complicated than the Romans believed. In this chapter we have traced the transformation of the clans of mounted warrior aristocrats into a landed elite which contributed to the Roman *res publica* by serving as the state cavalry. This aristocracy of *equites*, united by their ideology of displaying *virtus* on horseback, changed significantly over the course of the Republican period. *Equites* ceased to be the cavalry of the Roman state after they were supplanted by auxiliary horsemen supplied by the allies, and its members instead served as officers or eschewed army service altogether.

---

[275] Cic. *Rosc. com.* 42: *quem tu si ex censu spectas, eques Romanus est, si ex vita, homo clarissimus est.* See Bleicken 1995: 45; Wiseman 1970b: 74.

The status of *eques* remained much sought after, however, because it provided wealthy Roman citizens with official recognition of their high status within the *res publica*, even if their cavalry service was limited. To this extent, the ceremonial and ideological aspects of equestrian status, such as the *transvectio equitum*, remained crucially important, as they represented the outward manifestation of the *equites'* status and prestige. In sociological terms, an elite that derived its power from military prowess had transformed into one that obtained authority from wealth. For it was wealth that enabled citizens to be classified among the *prima classis* and the *equites* in the first place, and this gave them greater authority in the *comitia centuriata*, a timocratic assembly biased towards the richest elements of the state, as well as the eligibility to stand for senatorial magistracies. This developmental path was typical of the evolution of a pre-modern society that became more politically and socially complex over time.

At the same time, the differences between senatorial and non-senatorial *equites* became more apparent. This was partially because senators acquired status symbols and privileges which other *equites* did not possess, and because of conflicts over control of Rome's new financial resources. Senators had the ability to confirm or block the letting of state contracts to the *publicani*, who were either *equites* themselves or had associates who were. However, in order for the senatorial and non-senatorial *equites* to finally separate into two distinct groups, there needed to be a catalyst. This came in the form of the two laws passed in 129 BC and 123 BC, which compelled all senators to return their public horses and gave *equites* without senatorial relatives a new public role as jurors in the extortion court. These pieces of legislation show that the evolution of the *equites* and the creation of the equestrian order was partially the result of long-term historical changes in the complexity of the Roman state, for which parallels can be found in other pre-modern societies, but also stemmed from the initiative of two remarkable individuals: an anonymous tribune and Gaius Gracchus. It was Gracchus in particular who gave the *equites* a real public role which was unique to them, thus enabling them to emerge as a distinct status group with political clout (though that influence was primarily exercised in a reactive, rather than initiatory, fashion).[276] Service as jurors in the extortion court provided wealthy Roman citizens with further reasons to be invested in the *res publica* which went beyond the prestige of equestrian status itself.

---

[276] Badian 1962: 224.

The removal of senators from equestrian ranks, and the *equites'* own new political role as jurors, led to Romans of the late second century BC conceiving of the equestrians as a new *ordo* which comprised a constituent part of the *res publica*. This helped to provide a sense of unity to what was fundamentally a heterogeneous group of wealthy elites, composed of military officers, orators, poets, businessmen and tax-collectors. The emergence of the new *ordo* did not of course mean that there was a sudden social, economic or 'class' gulf between senators and *equites*, especially since members of the two groups were connected by blood, marriage, friendship and alliances.[277] But they were differentiated by their status, which was no small issue, especially since each *ordo* now possessed power over the other. Senators had authority over letting tax contracts to the *publicani*, whereas equestrians had control over the *quaestio de repetundis*, through which they could convict senators. The political power of the *equites* would be a source of significant tension during the following decades. The new order had arrived.

---

[277] Nicolet 1974: 253–69; Brunt 1988: 148–52; Harris 2011: 18–19.

2 | Cicero's Equestrian Order

Introduction: The Trial of C. Verres

In August 70 BC the thirty-six-year-old senator M. Tullius Cicero began the daunting task of prosecuting C. Verres, the corrupt former governor of Sicily, in the *quaestio de repetundis*. Cicero was a *novus homo*, the first in his family to reach the senate; his ancestors were men of equestrian status from Arpinum, a hill town to the south-east of Rome.[1] If he won the case, Cicero's reputation as an advocate and politician would be enhanced, ensuring future electoral success that would enable him to climb the senatorial *cursus honorum* all the way to the consulship.[2] But the odds were firmly against him. The noted advocate Q. Hortensius was in charge of the defence, and Verres' powerful allies had conspired to limit the time available to Cicero to gather evidence and secure witnesses in Sicily.[3] Moreover, Cicero did not face a jury of *equites* devoid of any senatorial connections, as had been specified under the terms of Gaius Gracchus' *lex de repetundis*. Instead, his jury was composed of senators, as laid down by the legislation of the dictator Sulla, who in 81 BC had ended decades of political wrangling over the law courts by establishing senatorial juries for all *quaestiones perpetuae*.[4] In Cicero's view the new senatorial jurors had proved to be extremely susceptible to bribery and only too willing to acquit their peers of charges of provincial maladministration, something that Gaius Gracchus' equestrian juries had been designed to prevent.[5] The tide would soon turn with the promulgation, later in 70 BC, of the

---

[1] Stockton 1971: 1–3; T. N. Mitchell 1979: 2–9. For the rise of new men in this period, see Wiseman 1971.

[2] For the significance of the case to Cicero's political career, see Vasaly 2009; Tempest 2011: 45–6, 50–3. Cf. T. N. Mitchell 1979: 107–9, who plays down its importance.

[3] Lintott 2008: 84–8; Tempest 2011: 53–5. For Cicero's own take on Hortensius, see *Brut.* 318–20.

[4] Cic. I *Verr.* 37; Vell. Pat. 2.32; Tac. *Ann.* 11.22. The size of the jury was reduced by Sulla's legislation, with the panel at Verres' trial comprising about fifteen men in total. See Lintott 2004: 74, 2008: 87–8.

[5] Vasaly 2009: 107. Cf. Gruen 1974: 30–4.

lex Aurelia iudicaria, which would restore equestrian jurors to the criminal courts.

Cicero was still left in a difficult position, however. He had become a senator himself after his quaestorship in 75 BC, but the *nobiles* in the senate were unlikely to have considered him 'one of us' – he was a new man of equestrian stock, who frequently advocated on behalf of equestrian clients and *publicani*.[6] He chose to adopt a bold and uncompromising rhetorical strategy, exposing the corruption of Sulla's senatorial juries, but urging those jurors who sat in front of him to uphold senatorial dignity on behalf of 'our order'.[7] Rising in court in that summer of 70 BC, Cicero told the assembled senators:

Over the past ten years, since the juries have been handed over to senate, cases have been decided in a disgraceful and heinous manner. Members of the jury, the Roman people will learn from me why, when the equestrian order sat in judgement for nearly fifty straight years, there was never the slightest inkling that an *eques Romanus* serving as a juror had accepted a bribe to influence his decision. They will learn why, when the courts were transferred to the senatorial order, and the power of the Roman people over every man was removed, that Q. Calidus said that an ex-praetor would not be found guilty for less than 300,000 sesterces.[8]

The rhetoric is powerful and persuasive, enabling Cicero to position the trial of Verres as a test case of senatorial integrity. As a new man, he could portray himself as a representative of Rome's traditional morality, undefiled by the recent corruption, and thus urge the senators to return to their former virtue.[9] At the same time as this speech was being delivered, movements were afoot to reform the juries and restore equestrian participation in the courts, and Cicero's language deftly signals his own support for such a measure.[10] The passage is particularly notable for the insight it

---

[6] Cicero states this himself in II *Verr.* 2.181; see also Q. Cic. *Comm. Pet.* 3, 33, 50. See T. N. Mitchell 1979: 100–1.

[7] Cic. I *Verr.* 42. For Cicero's deft rhetorical positioning, see Berry 2003: 224–5; Lintott 2008: 90–1; Vasaly 2009: 105–6, 114, 127–8. His speeches were usually aimed at convincing the specific jury he faced, rather than any other audience (Levene 2004: 122–3).

[8] Cic. I *Verr.* 37–8: ... *quae inter decem annos, postea quam iudicia ad senatum translata sunt, in rebus iudicandis nefarie flagitioseque facta sunt. cognoscet ex me populus Romanus quid sit quam ob rem, cum equester ordo iudicaret, annos prope quinquaginta continuos <in> nullo, iudices, equite Romano iudicante, ne tenuissima quidem suspicio acceptae pecuniae ob rem iudicandam constituta sit: quid sit quod, iudiciis ad senatorium ordinem translatis sublataque populi Romani in unum quemque vestrum potestate, Q. Calidus damnatus dixerit minoris HS triciens praetorium hominem honeste non posse damnari ....*

[9] For the ideology of *novitas*, see Wiseman 1971: 107–16; van der Blom 2010: 50–9, 176.

[10] Cic. *Div. in Caec.* 8; Berry 2003: 225; Vasaly 2009: 128; van der Blom 2010: 176.

provides into the political environment of 70 BC,[11] revealing that we now find ourselves in a world far away from that of Cato the Elder, Scipio Aemilianus, and Gaius Gracchus essayed in the previous chapter. By the time Cicero rose to prosecute Verres, the *ordo equester* was firmly placed as a constituent element in the *res publica* alongside – and in competition with – the *ordo senatorius*.[12]

The power acquired by the new *ordo equester* in the courts proved to be one of the major sources of tension and rivalry between *equites* and senators.[13] This is amply attested by an earlier speech of Cicero delivered in the court dealing with assassinations, the *quaestio de sicariis*, in 80 BC, shortly after Sulla had installed juries composed solely of senators.[14] In this, his first criminal case, Cicero was tasked with defending Sex. Roscius of Ameria on a charge of parricide. In exonerating his client, he had to imply that other parties, including Sulla's Greek freedman Chrysogonus, had conspired to murder the elder Roscius.[15] At that time Cicero was only twenty-six, and still an *eques* himself, defending another *eques* (young Roscius). This meant that he was required to tread very carefully before the senatorial jurors.[16] Yet, in one of the most revealing passages of the speech, he reminded the senatorial nobility that they had to behave in a virtuous fashion if they wished to retain the monopoly over the courts that Sulla had handed to them.[17] For, Cicero cried, 'they should make sure that it is not disgraceful and pitiable that those men who could not endure equestrian brilliance (*equestrem splendorem*) are able to endure the domination of a most wretched slave'.[18] Just as with the *In Verrem*, Cicero's argument was calculated not to attack the senatorial jurors, but to urge them to make the right decision and acquit his client.[19] It is revealing that Cicero spoke of the *equites* not only as a united *ordo*, but also one that had acquired the quality of *splendor* (brilliance), a term that recurs in his

---

[11] Although the *actio prima* and especially the *actio secunda* of the speech were later revised for publication, Cicero wanted to give the impression that they had all been delivered in 70 BC. See Vasaly 2009: 128–33.

[12] The term *equester ordo* is used throughout the *In Verrem* (II *Verr.* 2.175, 3.94, 3.166, 3.223–4, 4.45). For the equestrian order as a part of the Roman state in Cicero's thought, see Bleicken 1995: 58–60.

[13] Brunt 1988: 150–4.   [14] Lintott 2008: 426.

[15] T. N. Mitchell 1979: 90–3; Dyck 2010: 9–10; Tempest 2011: 32–7.   [16] Berry 2003: 224.

[17] Cic. *Rosc. Amer.* 139. See Gruen 1974: 269–70, who argues that the 'freedom of the judiciary' is the theme that permeates the speech.

[18] Cic. *Rosc. Amer.* 140: *videant ne turpe miserumque sit eos qui equestrem splendorem pati non potuerunt servi nequissimi dominationem ferre posse.* The slave is of course Sulla's freedman Chrysogonus.

[19] Lintott 2008: 427. For Sulla's new senators, see further below.

other works with reference to the equestrian order.[20] The equestrian *splendor* was earned through their effective and honourable service in the law courts. Cicero's arguments in both 80 BC and 70 BC show remarkable consistency, despite the transformation of his own personal status from *eques* to senator. He deftly negotiated his own opinions and the expectations of his audience in the courts.

It is through Cicero's speeches, letters, and rhetorical and philosophical works that we gain a vital and priceless contemporary perspective on the politics of the late Roman Republic, and the place of *equites* in the *res publica*. Pliny the Elder gave Cicero a starring role in his potted history of the *ordo equester* from the Gracchi to the mid-first century BC:

Now the Gracchi first of all decided to distinguish the *ordo* with the title of *iudices*, through a disruptive method of courting popularity that insulted the senate. Then, after the significance of this title was thoroughly discredited by various outbreaks of civil discord, it was applied to the *publicani*, and for some time it was these *publicani* who constituted the third part [in the *res publica*]. Marcus Cicero finally established that they would be called the *ordo equester* in the year of his consulship, at the time of the Catilinarian troubles. He proclaimed that he himself had emerged from that very *ordo*, and sought their backing through his own particular methods of campaigning. From that moment, it is clear that the *ordo* became a third constituent part within the *res publica*, and the *ordo equester* was now added to the 'senate and the Roman people'. And it is for this reason that we now write *ordo equester* after the word 'people', since it was the most recent part to be added.[21]

Pliny could not be more precise about the role played by Cicero in establishing the *ordo equester*. But we should be wary. Cicero was closely connected with the *equites* and the *publicani*. He relied on their support to win his cases and to elect him to high office. Without the favour of the *equites*, it is unlikely that Cicero would ever have become consul. They figure prominently in both his personal self-presentation and his political rhetoric.[22] The nature of the surviving evidence means that we view the

---

[20] M. I. Henderson 1963: 70; Berry 2003: 224 n. 10. Either the noun *splendor* or the adjective *splendidus* is used: see *OLD* s.v. *splendidus* 4b. Cf. Nicolet 1974: 213–24, pointing out that *splendidus* was also used to describe some senators.

[21] Pliny the Elder, *NH* 33.34: *iudicum autem appellatione separare eum ordinem primi omnium instituere Gracchi discordi popularitate in contumeliam senatus, mox debellata auctoritas nominis vario seditionum eventu circa publicanos substitit et aliquamdiu tertiae sortis viri publicani fuere. M. Cicero demum stabilivit equestre nomen in consulatu suo Catilinianis rebus, ex eo ordine profectum se celebrans eiusque vires peculiari popularitate quaerens. ab illo tempore plane hoc tertium corpus in re p. factum est, coepitque adici senatui populoque Romano et equester ordo. qua de causa et nunc post populum scribitur, quia novissime coeptus est adici.*

[22] Bleicken 1995: 103–10; Berry 2003.

equites through Cicero's eyes, and we need to be aware of his personal and political agendas. Each of Cicero's works, as we have just seen with the *In Verrem* and *Pro Roscio Amerino*, is the product of a specific place and time, designed to persuade a jury or present a particular point of view, and the *equites* had their own role to play in these arguments.[23]

This chapter will trace the history of the equestrian order from the tribunate of Gaius Gracchus to the mid-first century BC through Cicero's perspective. It will show how the portrayal of *equites* in Cicero's works is crucial to understanding the consolidation of an *ordo equester* distinct from the senate, the problem in defining its role within the *res publica*, and how its members approached their new public roles as jurors. Cicero's speeches portrayed the *equites* as a constituent element of the state along-side the senators and the people, just as Pliny the Elder would later describe the *ordo* at large. Whether they were serving as jurors in the law courts, *publicani* collecting the state's revenues, military officers, or simply acting in their private capacities, *equites* supported the state as good citizens should. Such a perception of the *equites* formed a part of Cicero's vision that the constitution of the *res publica* could only be protected against the actions of ambitious individuals through the *concordia ordinum* ('the harmony of the orders'). This political mantra, which first appears in Cicero's works in the 60s BC, envisaged that all citizens, as part of their constituent *ordines*, would work together to uphold the Roman state, which invested power in the people to elect magistrates, pass legislation, and declare peace and war.[24]

This ideal sat uneasily alongside another view publicly expressed by Cicero, that the *equites* should be somehow exempt from the strictures to which senators were subject as public representatives. We know from Cicero's private letters that he did not genuinely believe that this position was defensible. He advanced these arguments when it was necessary to defend his clients or when it suited his political position. When we consider the Ciceronian corpus as a whole, the *ordo equester* occupies an uncertain place in Cicero's vision of the *res publica* – it was part of the state, its members served the state, yet at the same time they were not always bound by the laws of the state. This chapter will argue that the ambivalent and contradictory picture of equestrians in Cicero's works actually mirrors the political reality of the late Republic, in which the equestrians had only

---

[23] Morstein-Marx 2004: 27–31; Lintott 2008: 3–4, and *passim*.

[24] See N. Wood 1991: 193–9; Lintott 2008: 148. On the *res publica* as a state dependent on unity and consent in Cicero's thought, see Hammer 2014: 46–9. For the part played by the *ordo equester* in this *concordia*, see Nicolet 1974: 637–55, 673–98.

recently come together as an *ordo*, distinct from the senate, and were trying to negotiate their position within the *res publica*. They valued, cherished and guarded their right to sit as jurors in the criminal court; although this may have initially seemed an unwelcome imposition after Gaius Gracchus' law, it soon became an essential aspect of equestrian *dignitas*.[25] But at the same time, the *equites* were wary of any attempt to place further strictures on their service as jurors, nor did they lobby for any new political role. The *equites* as a whole were content to look after their own interests and to win the support of powerful friends, such as Cicero, who could help them accomplish this. This explains why the *equites*, which had evolved from a Weberian status group founded on 'traditional authority' to one centred on 'occupational status' in the transition from the Regal to Republican period, was not entirely transformed into one of Weber's 'political groups' in the late Republic.[26] This is because the political role of the *ordo equester* was specific and circumscribed, reactive rather than proactive.

Equites and the Criminal Courts

The *lex de repetundis* of Gaius Gracchus gave *equites* the ability to exert power and authority over members of the senatorial order outside the confines of the voting assemblies. Senatorial magistrates accused of provincial mismanagement had their cases heard in the *quaestio de repetundis* by a jury which was not composed of their peers, but of *equites* with no senatorial connections. The extortion court was not the only scene of rivalry between *equites* and senators, for there was a range of permanent criminal courts established in the subsequent years, including the courts for electoral corruption, treason and assassinations (*quaestio de ambitu*, *quaestio de maiestate* and *quaestio de sicariis*).[27] It is a matter of debate whether all of these courts had exclusively equestrian juries, or whether they were shared between *equites* and senators.[28] Only one of the relevant laws survives in any detail: the Gracchan law on the *Tabula Bembina*. We therefore need to consider the role and influence of equestrian jurors on a case-by-case basis.

---

[25] Meier 1966: 73.
[26] See the Introduction to the book, which lays out these changes in broad terms.
[27] Brunt 1988: 216–22; Cloud 1992: 510–11 (differing in the chronology of the courts' establishment).
[28] See the divergent views of Brunt 1988: 216–39 (shared courts) and Cloud 1992: 511–12 (exclusively equestrian).

This evidence for the workings of the criminal courts in the years immediately following the death of Gaius Gracchus is very piecemeal, but it does reveal the resentment that the equestrian juries engendered through their convictions of senators.[29] This led the consul of 106 BC, Q. Servilius Caepio, to propose legislation transferring control of the juries to senators.[30] His *lex Servilia* certainly replaced the *equites* with senators on the *quaestio de repetundis*, and the usual description of the statute as a *lex iudicaria* (judiciary law) indicates that it had wider effect, imposing senatorial juries on all criminal courts.[31] One of the law's supporters was the orator L. Licinius Crassus, who had recently served as tribune of the plebs, and may have been eager to win the favour of Caepio.[32] Crassus delivered a famous speech in which he spoke with bitterness about the equestrian jurors and their actions.[33] Addressing the Roman people, Crassus exhorted them to vote to remove equestrian control of the courts:[34]

Rescue us from these misfortunes, rescue us from the jaws of those men, whose cruelty cannot be satisfied except by our blood: ensure that we do not serve anyone, except all of you, whom we can – and must – serve.[35]

Crassus' message was that the senate and its members answered only to the *populus Romanus*, as the sovereign body of the *res publica*, not to the equestrian jurors. His rhetoric was designed to appeal to the Roman people, since they would be naturally suspicious of *equites*, whom nobody elected, possessing this authority.[36] The passing of the *lex Servilia* was long remembered with rancour by the *equites*. In the 80s BC Cicero wrote that one should not praise the law in the presence of *equites*.[37] This is an indication of the fact that once the *ordo* had been granted the privilege of sitting as jurors, they were reluctant to surrender it.

---

[29] See the excellent account of Gruen 1968: 106–56.

[30] Cloud 1992: 511–12. Cf. Gruen 1968: 158–9; Brunt 1988: 204–5, who, based on the evidence of Cassiod. *Chron.* 106 and Obsequens 41 (who themselves drew upon an epitome of Livy), argue that Caepio created mixed senatorial and equestrian panels. However, this limited evidence for mixed panels seems to be undermined by the testimony of Cicero, who refers frequently to equestrian hatred of the law (e.g. Cic. *Inv.* 1.82, *Orat.* 2.199), which implies that the *equites* had been excluded completely.

[31] It is never specified as being a *lex de repetundis*: Gruen 1968: 159; Cloud 1992: 511; J. S. Richardson 1998: 48. Cf. Griffin 1973: 114–15; Brunt 1988: 204–5.

[32] For the speech in the context of Crassus' career, see Fantham 2004: 32–3.   [33] Cic. *Clu.* 140.

[34] Cic. *Brut.* 164 reveals it was addressed to the people.

[35] Cic. *Orat.* 1.225: *eripite nos ex miseriis, eripite ex faucibus eorum, quorum crudelitas nisi nostro sanguine non potest expleri; nolite sinere nos cuiquam servire, nisi vobis universis, quibus et possumus et debemus.*

[36] Morstein-Marx 2004: 235–6.

[37] Cic. *Inv.* 1.92. Similar sentiments can be found in *Orat.* 2.199, in which Cicero, referring to events in the mid-90s BC, writes of equestrian resentment towards Caepio.

Caepio's exclusion of the *equites* from the criminal courts was ultimately short-lived, since it was overturned a few years later, probably in 104 BC, by the tribune C. Servilius Glaucia.[38] This reversal of Caepio's legislation won Glaucia the support and favour of the *equites*.[39] The wrangling over the criminal courts probably led to the demise of Gaius Gracchus' careful procedures for the selection of jurors, which had specifically excluded *equites* with senatorial connections. Lintott has persuasively argued that Glaucia's new law was the first to abandon such provisions, paving the way for all members of the *ordo equester* to serve as *iudices*, regardless of whether they were the sons of senators or had held certain magistracies.[40] Even if we accept Richardson's argument that Gracchus' *repetundae* legislation remained in force,[41] it is likely that after 104/101 BC the majority of prosecutions for provincial maladministration were carried out according to the terms of Glaucia's law.[42] This was a pivotal moment, since it meant that *equites* who were the sons, brothers and fathers of senators could now be empanelled on a jury. Glaucia's tribunician ally, L. Appuleius Saturninus, followed his lead in cultivating the support of the *ordo equester*. During his first tribunate in 103 BC Saturninus established a permanent court to deal with cases of *maiestas populi Romani minuta* ('the reduction of the majesty of the Roman people'), which effectively meant high treason.[43] The new *quaestio de maiestate* was staffed with equestrian jurors, who bitterly remembered the earlier attempt by Servilius Caepio to deprive them of their place in the courts.[44] The *equites* would continue to sit in judgement in the criminal courts until the dictatorship of Sulla.

In speeches delivered throughout his career, Cicero praised the conduct of equestrian jurors during this tumultuous period. He spoke approvingly of their 'strictness' (*severitas*) in convicting senatorial magistrates who had acted unethically in their provinces.[45] He praised the *equites* who sat in judgement on Q. Metellus Numidicus in 111 BC as 'men of the greatest

---

[38] Cic. *Scaur.* quoted in Asc. 21 C, referring to the 'courts in the power of the equestrian order' (*iudicia penes equestrem ordinem*). Asconius calls Glaucia's measure an extortion law, but either he passed additional legislation regarding juries in other courts, or it set a precedent for other courts to use equestrian jurors. For discussion, see Gruen 1968: 166–7; Cloud 1992: 512; Lewis 2006: 222.

[39] Cic. *Brut.* 224. For attitudes to Glaucia, see Cic. *Orat.* 3.164, *Rab. Post.* 14.

[40] Lintott 1992: 21, 27.   [41] J. S. Richardson 1998: 48–51.

[42] Thus in 92 BC M. Aemilius Scaurus was charged with *repetundae* by Q. Servilius Caepio (son of the consul of 106 BC) under the terms of the *lex Servilia* (Cic. *Scaur.* quoted in Asc. 21 C).

[43] Gruen 1968: 167–8; Cloud 1992: 518.   [44] Cic. *Orat.* 2.199.

[45] Cic. *Brutus* 103, I *Verr.* 51, II *Verr.* 3.210, 4.22, 4.133.

authority' (*gravissimis viris*).[46] These remarks formed part of Cicero's strategy to win over the equestrian jurors whom he addressed in the law courts for the bulk of his career.[47] Cicero's *equites* did their duty for the *res publica* by behaving honourably and dispassionately. This did not necessarily mean they always convicted senators, because they did acquit them whenever they were rightfully innocent (in Cicero's view, of course). In 69 BC, the year after his success against Verres, Cicero defended M. Fonteius, his first senatorial client, on a charge of *repetundae*.[48] His speech contained a section in which he praised the conscientious equestrian jurors who acquitted C. Memmius and C. Flavius Fimbria of *repetundae* in the late second century BC.[49] These equestrian jurors possessed 'such great courage and strength' (*tantum animi, tantum roboris*), according to Cicero, because they had not even been swayed by accusations made by the prominent senator M. Aemilius Scaurus against Memmius and Fimbria. This is an important point, because it shows how the criminal courts functioned as a *locus* of senatorial competition, where individual senators could pursue rivalries and petty jealousies by accusing their enemies of corruption or other crimes. The *equites*, far from being the impartial adjudicators envisioned by Gaius Gracchus, were by necessity drawn into this political wrangling.

When the *Pro Fonteio* was delivered, the *equites* had only recently been restored to the jury bench alongside senators and *tribuni aerarii* by the *lex Aurelia* of 70 BC, with which we began this chapter. Cicero therefore had a vested interested in praising their probity in earlier generations when they single-handedly controlled the courts.[50] The portrait of the *equites* as good citizens is developed further in the *Pro Rabirio per duellionis reo*, which Cicero delivered in 63 BC.[51] In this, the year of his consulship, Cicero defended his client, C. Rabirius, on the charge of murdering L. Appuleius Saturninus in 100 BC by throwing the fatal tile that killed the tribune during the attack on the senate house.[52] Cicero painted a picture of how all citizens came together to support the actions taken by the consuls under the *senatus consultum ultimum*, including the members of the *ordo equester*:

---

[46] Cic. I *Verr.* 51, II *Verr.* 3.210, 4.22, 4.133, *Balb.* 11, with Gruen 1968: 132–3. Mattingly 1975a: 261 n. 5 points out that *severus* is different from the more hostile *acerbus*.

[47] Bleicken 1995: 33 notes how Cicero shaped his remarks in accordance with his specific agenda in each speech.

[48] For the context, see Lintott 2008: 101–3; Tempest 2011: 60–2.

[49] Cic. *Font.* 24–6. See Gruen 1968: 174–5.	[50] Berry 2003: 228–9.

[51] This was probably on the Campus Martius (Morstein-Marx 2004: 60 n. 93).

[52] Lintott 2008: 120–5; Tempest 2011: 89. The background to the case is comprehensively discussed by Tyrrell 1978. For the popular rhetoric in the speech, see Morstein-Marx 2004: 214–15, 225–8.

By the immortal gods, what *equites* they were back in our fathers' day, men who played a significant role in supporting the *res publica* and alone maintained the authority of the law courts.[53]

The *Pro Rabirio per perduellionis reo* was delivered in front of the assembly, rather than in a *quaestio*.[54] This did not diminish Cicero's need to win the support of the *equites*, whom he envisaged playing a crucial role in the maintenance of Rome's political system through the *concordia ordinum*, working together with the senate and the people against attempts to subvert the established order by ambitious men.[55] In Cicero's view, therefore, the equestrian jurors of the late second and early first century BC were honest and incorruptible citizens who were acting in the best interests of the Roman *res publica*.

Cicero's praise of the *equites* stands in contrast with other, much later, sources, which portrayed the equestrian jurors as corrupt. This hostility is eloquently demonstrated by the notorious trial of P. Rutilius Rufus for *repetundae* in 92 BC.[56] Rufus had been legate to Q. Mucius Scaevola, proconsul of Asia in 94 BC, and their efforts to put the administration of the province of Asia on a firm footing earned both these men the ire of the *publicani*. Despite his long and distinguished reputation, an equestrian jury convicted Rufus of provincial misgovernment.[57] Velleius Paterculus claimed that the *equites* 'vented their rage on many distinguished and entirely blameless men' (*in multos clarissimos atque innocentissimos viros saevissent*), including Rufus.[58] Asconius, discussing M. Aemilius Scaurus' trial on a charge of *repetundae* in the same year, wrote that 'since P. Rutilius had been condemned there was no one who seemed so innocent that he did not fear it' (*P. Rutilio damnato nemo tam innocens videretur ut non timeret illa*).[59] As for Cicero himself, although he was convinced of Rufus' innocence, he never mentions the actions of the equestrian jurors per se.[60] The case was very much a cause célèbre, serving as a striking demonstration of the influence of the *publicani*

---

[53] Cic. *Rab. perd.* 20: *at quorum equitum, di immortales, patrum nostrorum atque eius aetatis, qui tum magnam partem rei publicae atque omnem dignitatem iudiciorum tenebant.* See also *Rab. perd.* 27, 31, for similar sentiments regarding the *equites*.

[54] Lintott 2008: 120.   [55] See Bleicken 1995: 58–71.

[56] This is traditionally dated to 92 BC, but Kallet-Marx 1990: 129 suggests *c.* 94 BC.

[57] Diod. Sic. 37.5.1–4; Cic. *Brut.* 114–16. For discussion, see Gruen 1968: 204–5 and Badian 1972: 90–2. Kallet-Marx 1990 plays down the emphasis on factional politics found in Gruen and Badian.

[58] Vell. Pat. 2.13. The force of his accusation is underscored by the fact that *clarissimus* was the standard epithet for a senator. For similar sentiments, see Livy, *Epit.* 70; Val. Max. 2.10.5.

[59] Asc. 21C. For the context, see Gruen 1968: 206.   [60] Cic. *Brut.* 115, *Font.* 38.

within the larger *ordo equester*.[61] But there are no firm grounds for
believing that Rufus was as innocent as the ancient sources say, especially
since their version relies primarily on his own memoirs.[62] It is also
important to note that the *publicani* did not work alone: they had powerful senatorial allies, including Gaius Marius, who pursued the case for
their own ends.[63] Consequently, there appears to have been fault on both
sides. On one hand, the equestrian jurors were being pressured by the
publicani to convict Rutilius because of his attempts to curb their authority, as well as by rival factions in the senate. On the other hand, Rutilius
was evidently not the squeaky-clean senator his friends claimed him to
be. The equestrian jurors acquitted as many senators arraigned on
charges of *repetundae* as they convicted.[64] This is not a sign that they
were necessary incorruptible, however, since they could have been bribed
or otherwise induced to clear the names of the accused. This means that
Cicero's positive account of the *equites'* incorruptibility reflected his own
self-interest and that of his clients. The hostile historical tradition against
the *equites* was primarily engendered by the fact that they were regarded
as having improper power over senators, their superiors within the *res
publica*. But at the same time, senators were happy to exploit connections
with the *publicani* and the other *equites* when it suited their interests,
especially if it resulted in the conviction of their enemies or the acquittal
of their friends.

Senatorial resentment at the conviction of Rutilius Rufus inspired the
tribune M. Livius Drusus to attempt another round of jury reform.[65]
In 91 BC Drusus successfully passed a law to add 300 *equites* to the senate,
prescribing that jurors should henceforth be drawn from the 600-strong
curia.[66] This measure was an interesting sleight of hand, effectively restoring the courts to the senate, but at the same time rewarding leading *equites*
with an increase in status. The equestrians-turned-senators would continue to sit on the juries as they had done in the previous decades, but their
new position might prompt a change in outlook – at least that is what

---

[61] Gruen 1968: 205; Kallet-Marx 1990: 138. Cf. Nicolet 1974: 543–9, who denies the connection
between the outcome of the trial and equestrian enmity.
[62] Lintott 1981: 194–5.   [63] Badian 1972: 91–2.
[64] Lintott 1981: 209–12, 1992: 27, who suggests a 50 per cent conviction rate through to 51 BC.
Brunt 1988: 152 has four out of eighteen cases between 123 and 91 BC. The numbers are
indicative only, given the nature of the sources.
[65] Asc. 21C; Gruen 1968: 206–7; Kallet-Marx 1990: 125; Steel 2013: 37.
[66] App. *BC* 1.35; Livy, *Per.* 70–1; Ps.-Aur. Vict. *Vir. Ill.* 66; Gruen 1968: 208–9; Brunt 1988: 206–7.

Drusus' senatorial backers undoubtedly hoped.[67] While the law would have appealed to the select few *equites* promoted to senatorial rank, it would have been rather less well received by the thousands of others who were excluded.[68] Drusus and his ambitious reform programme proved to be short-lived, after his citizenship proposals rapidly earned the ire of his former allies in the senate.[69] Drusus was murdered and his legislation was declared invalid, which meant the senate remained at 300 members, and the *equites* retained their control of the jury panels.[70] The status quo had been restored, but Drusus' actions prompted retributions. In 90 BC the tribune Q. Varius Hybrida passed a new law on high treason (*lex Varia de maiestate*), which was specifically designed to indict the supporters of Drusus.[71] The equestrian jurors who remained would presumably have had a vested interest in convicting the tribune's former associates, and Appian states as much, portraying the *equites* as eager to exact retribution on the senate.[72] There are good reasons, however, for not subscribing to Appian's views wholeheartedly.[73] Our sources frequently deal with conflicts in such broad-brush strokes and sharp dichotomies – *equites* versus senators – that the equestrian jurors appear as 'faceless men', devoid of personality and motivation. Yet in this case we know that some of the senators charged under the *lex Varia de maiestate* defended themselves with speeches written for them by an *eques*, L. Aelius Stilo Praeconinus.[74] Nor was conviction a fait accompli, with senators such as M. Aemilius Scaurus actually being acquitted by the supposedly vengeful equestrian jurors.[75]

In 81 BC the dictator L. Cornelius Sulla attempted to resolve the issue of the criminal courts once and for all, by essentially adopting the same measures proposed by M. Livius Drusus in his tribunate.[76] Sulla increased the size of the senate by adding 300 *equites*, and decreed that all jurors in the *quaestiones perpetuae* should be senators.[77] The measure formed a key part of Sulla's widespread reforms of the permanent courts, the senate and

---

[67] His legislation is generally regarded as 'pro-senatorial': Cic. *Orat.* 1.24, *Brut.* 222; Diod. Sic. 37.10; Vell. Pat. 2.13; Florus 2.5.
[68] Gruen 1968: 208.   [69] Gabba 1992: 111–13.
[70] For the grounds for invalidation, see Asc. 69C, with B. A. Marshall 1985: 244–5.
[71] Asc. 22C; Cic. *Pro Corn.* quoted in Asc. 79C.   [72] App. *BC* 1.37.   [73] Gruen 1968: 216–19.
[74] Cic. *Brut.* 169, 205–7; Gruen 1968: 219.
[75] Cic. *Sest.* 101; Asc. 22C, with B. A. Marshall 1985: 137–8.   [76] Gruen 1968: 256–7.
[77] Senate: Appian, *BC* 1.100; Livy, *Epit.* 89. Courts: Cic. I *Verr.* 37. Vell. Pat. 2.32; Tac. *Ann.* 11.22. It is often assumed that this brought senatorial numbers up to exactly 600, but this figure would have been difficult to maintain, and membership probably numbered about 450–500 initially (Develin 1987; Santangelo 2007: 100).

its magistracies, in order to strengthen the position of the *res publica*.[78] Some of the ancient sources preserve the usual prejudicial rhetoric about the base nature of Sulla's senators, but it is not supported by the more reliable prosopographical evidence.[79] Appian states that Sulla selected approximately 300 of 'the best *equites*' (οἱ ἄριστοι ἱππεῖς), who were chosen by the votes of their respective tribes, for elevation into the *curia*.[80] Since the new jurors were selected from the senate, a much smaller body than the *equites*, senators would have frequently been called up to judge cases. Indeed, Steel has pointed out that the main professional duty of a senator in the post-Sullan age was to staff the juries.[81] This means that there would actually have been significant continuity in the composition of the jury panels, as men who had previously served as *equites* now continued to do so as senators.[82] M. Iuventius Pedo, a juror at the trial of Oppianicus in 74 BC, was one such *eques*-turned-senator who was called up for jury service. Cicero stated that he was 'drawn from those old-school sort of jurors' (*ex vetere illa iudiciorum disciplina*), that is, the *equites* of the pre-Sullan era.[83] Despite Cicero's bombastic rhetoric in the *Pro Roscio Amerino* and the *In Verrem* about the corrupt nature of senatorial jurors and the honesty of their equestrian counterparts, the dividing line between *equites* and the senators on the juries was really very thin, and even non-existent in some cases.[84] In the decade after Sulla's reforms many jurors were the same people, performing the same duty, except they now ranked as senators, not *equites* – it was only their status that had been redefined.

Cicero's rhetoric cannot be dismissed, of course: his arguments were designed to appeal to the perspectives and prejudices of his audiences, which means they provide valuable evidence for the depth of feeling that the issue of criminal juries aroused. The senatorial jurors of 80 BC, listening to the *Pro Roscio Amerino*, would have been stirred up by his reference to 'equestrian brilliance', a reminder of how the equestrian jurors had rankled them in the past. Ten years later the senatorial panel that heard the *actio prima* of the *In Verrem* would have been reminded that they had to behave in a manner befitting the senatorial order, or otherwise the

---

[78] Cloud 1992: 512–30; Seager 1992: 197–207; Keaveney 2005: 140–55; Steel 2013: 126–31.

[79] Sall. *Cat.* 37; Dion. Hal. 5.77. For the Sullan senate, see Hill 1932; Syme 1938a: 22–5; Nicolet 1974: 581–91 (*equites* only); Gabba 1976: 63–7. Cf. Santangelo 2007: 100, who is sceptical about what the prosopographical evidence can tell us.

[80] App. *BC* 1.100. Gabba 1976: 145–7 argues for the authenticity of the tribal selection from men with the *census equester*. Cf. Hill 1932: 172, who suggests that these men were the *equites equo publico*.

[81] Steel 2013: 129.   [82] Hawthorn 1962: 56; Nicolet 1974: 589–91; Gruen 1974: 8, 201–2.

[83] Cic. *Clu.* 107; Nicolet 1974: 587; Wiseman 1971: 236 no. 218.

[84] For example, Q. Titinius, a senator who served on Verres' jury in 70 BC, had an equestrian brother, Cn. Fannius (Cic. II *Verr.* 1.128; Wiseman 1971: 266 no. 433).

courts might be returned to the *equites* who had managed them so well. Even though some of these senators had previously been equestrians, they would have been concerned to maintain the *dignitas* of their new order.[85] The rhetoric of senators versus *equites* had become extremely powerful in the political rhetoric of the post-Gracchan era, overriding the realities of social and familial relationships and appealing to the baser instincts of elite competition.

This brings us back to the summer of 70 BC, where we began this chapter, with Cicero's delivery of *In Verrem*, and the imminent promulgation of the *lex Aurelia iudicaria*. The praetor L. Aurelius Cotta was hardly the type of person one would expect to restore equestrian participation in the courts, if one subscribed to the partisan rhetoric. He was, as Cicero said, 'not sprung from equestrian origin, but came from the noblest stock' (*non ex equestri loco profecto, sed nobilissimo*).[86] The legislation had the support of Cn. Pompeius Magnus, the consul of 70 BC, who had promised to reform the court system if he was elected.[87] Cotta's new law, which applied to both criminal and civil courts, prescribed a jury panel composed of one-third senators, one-third *equites* and one-third *tribuni aerarii* (tribunes of the treasury), drawn from a total *album* of 900 citizens.[88] The *lex Aurelia* defined the *equites* on the jury panel by their census rating, not the possession of the *equus publicus*, just as we have argued that Gaius Gracchus' *lex de repetundis* did.[89] The *tribuni aerarii* are a shadowy group: their title derives from the paymasters of the Roman army, but they had long ceased to perform this function. Most, if not all, possessed the equestrian census, and thus Cicero frequently referred to them as *equites*.[90] Therefore, after 70 BC, two-thirds of the juries were composed of *equites*, giving them the upper hand in the court. This explains why Cicero frequently appealed to the equestrian order in his courtroom speeches, since they had the largest share of the vote.[91] The decades of wrangling over the criminal juries that followed Gaius Gracchus' tribunate ultimately resulted in the confirmation of equestrian participation in the courts. Their status as jurors had given them an official role within the *res*

---

[85] Gruen 1974: 8.   [86] Cic. II *Verr.* 2.174.   [87] Cic. I *Verr.* 1.45.

[88] Asc. 17C, 67C, 78C; Nicolet 1974: 611–13; Brunt 1988: 210. Q. Cicero composed a witty epigram about the law, which seems to have been negative (*Ad Q. Fr.* 1.3). There are suggestions that the law was originally designed to give the courts back to the *equites* wholesale, but this is largely dependent on the rhetoric of Cicero's *In Verrem* (Vasaly 2009: 106–7; cf. the more certain B. A. Marshall 1975: 145–7).

[89] Cic. *Phil.* 1.20; Nicolet 1974: 604–5; Ramsay 2003: 125–6. See Chapter 1 for the terms of Gracchus' law.

[90] See the Addendum to this chapter for detailed discussion on this point.   [91] Berry 2003.

publica, which they jealously guarded. But these equestrian jurors, far from being the impartial observers that Gaius Gracchus intended, were often drawn into senatorial conflicts that clouded their judgements, or delivered verdicts intended to protect the financial interests of *publicani* or other businessmen in Rome's expanding empire.

The Power of the *Publicani*

Cicero's public career would have been impossible without the support of the *ordo equester*. He made his name not as a military man, but as an orator and advocate, the first *novus homo* to reach the consulship by this career path.[92] Cicero's clients, both senators and *equites*, would prove to be successful allies and advocates as he worked his way up the *cursus honorum*. This point was explicitly made by Quintus Tullius Cicero in the guide to electioneering he prepared for his brother's consular campaign in 64 BC.[93] Quintus reminded his brother that his supporters included 'all the *publicani*, almost all the *ordo equester*, many individual towns, and many men of each order whom you have defended'.[94] The *publicani* could exercise their voice through their votes in the *comitia centuriata*, as well as in other less formal ways, such as private alliances and backroom deals. Their political interventions were squarely focused on protecting their economic interests, as we saw in the case of the prosecution of Rutilius Rufus. A new man like Cicero championed the commercial interests of the *publicani* because he needed their votes to secure his election to the senatorial magistracies, especially the consulship. As early as 70 BC, when he was still a young man, not yet praetor, Cicero declared that 'I have occupied a great part of my life in service of the causes of the *publicani*' (*nam quod in publicanorum causis vel plurimum aetatis meae versor*).[95] He continued to cultivate their support and friendship throughout his career, even when he privately disagreed with their ambitions.

It must be pointed out that not all *publicani* were *equites*, nor were all *equites publicani*. But they were understood to be a significant force within the *ordo*, with Cicero famously describing them as 'the flower of the *equites*

---

[92] See the discussion of Steel 2001: 162–73.

[93] The *Commentariolum Petitionis* is now usually regarded as a genuine work (Morstein-Marx 1998: 260–1, with references to earlier studies).

[94] Q. Cic. *Comm. Pet.* 3: *omnis publicanos, totum fere equestrem ordinem, multa propria municipia, multos abs te defensos homines cuiusque ordinis*.

[95] Cic. II *Verr.* 2.181.

Romani' (*flos . . . equitum Romanorum*).[96] The *publicani*, their viewpoints and decisions, often came to be regarded as essentially those of the *ordo equester* itself.[97] For example, there had been tension between *equites* and senators during the early part of the first century BC over the senate's reluctance to annex the kingdom of Cyrene, which had been bequeathed by Apion in 96 BC, and open it up to the *publicani*.[98] The issue of managing Cyrene resulted in 'competition between the different orders' (*diversorum ordinum <certamina>*), according to a fragmentary but suggestive passage from Sallust's *Histories*.[99] The public companies (*societates*) provided venues for *publicani* to meet together as a collective and pass decrees – in short, to act as pressure groups – in a way that was not usually possible for the *ordo equester* in general. These decrees did not institute policies, but were reactive, responding approvingly or disapprovingly to specific events.[100] At a provincial level, the *societates* were the most prominent groupings of *equites*; they would meet and entreat the governor privately, as well as render thanks to him on public occasions.[101] In the speech *De Domo Sua* of 57 BC, Cicero proclaimed that all constituent groups in the *res publica* supported the actions of his consulship, notably the execution of the Catilinarian conspirators, which eventually led to his exile. After describing the backing that he received from the senate in terms of a *senatus consultum*, Cicero turned to the *ordo equester*, which stood 'next to this body in *dignitas*' (*proximus est huic dignitati*). But since the *ordo equester* itself could pass no decrees, Cicero instead referred to the actions of the *publicani*. 'All the companies of all *publicani* produced the most fulsome and eloquent decrees concerning my consulship and my actions at that time,' he declaimed.[102] In order to observe how this relationship developed, we need to turn back to the events of 66 BC, when Cicero delivered his first public political speech.

---

[96] Cic. *Planc*. 23. In Cic. II *Verr*. 2.175, he referred to specific *publicani* as 'those foremost men of the equestrian order' (*istos ipsos principes equestris ordinis*).

[97] Brunt 1988: 165; Rowe 2002: 76–7.   [98] Oost 1963; Harris 1979: 154–5.

[99] Sall. *Hist*. 2.41; McGushin 1992: 207–8. I am grateful to Tom Hillard for this reference.

[100] Note the comments of Meier 1966: 87–88 that the *publicani* only took action when their interests were threatened.

[101] Badian 1972: 72–3. Private audiences: Cic. II *Verr*. 1.137 (these meetings were rather disgraceful in Verres' case, since they were held at the house of his freedwoman, Chelidon). Public occasions: Cic. II *Verr*. 2.172.

[102] Cic. *Domo* 74: *omnes omnium publicorum societates de meo consulatu ac de meis rebus gestis amplissima atque ornatissima decreta fecerunt*. For similar sentiments about the *publicani*, see also Cic. *Sest*. 32, *In Piso*. 41.

The foremost political issue of 66 BC was the Asian command against Mithridates.[103] The senator originally in charge of the war, L. Licinius Lucullus, had reduced the amount of interest owed by the Asian cities to the *publicani*, remitting Sulla's much higher interest rate.[104] The *publicani* worked through their agents in Rome, particularly the plebeian tribunes, to strip Lucullus of his authority, gradually removing provinces from his remit over the course of several years.[105] This was an example of the limited type of political intervention pursued by these businessmen – it was reactive, and motivated by their own interests.[106] The command was then granted to M'. Acilius Glabrio, consul in 67 BC. But in the following year the tribune C. Manilius proposed a law, backed by a coalition of equestrians and senators, to transfer the Asian command to Cn. Pompeius Magnus.[107] Several eminent consulars spoke in favour of this *lex Manilia de imperio Cn. Pompeii*. They were followed by Cicero, who was then only of praetorian rank, but anxious to advance through the *cursus honorum* and obtain the consulship in the first year he was eligible (*suo anno*, literally 'in his own year').[108] In the *Pro lege Manilia* Cicero cast himself in the role of the champion of the *publicani* and the *ordo equester* at large:

Letters come daily from the province of Asia to *equites Romani*, the most respectable men, who have invested significant resources in the collection of your tax revenues. On account of the special relationship I have with their *ordo*, they have reported the situation to me, as it affects the *res publica*, as well as the dangers to their own personal interests.[109]

The context in which Cicero delivered the *Pro lege Manilia* is vital to understanding its significance and impact. It was given not in a closed courtroom in front of the jurors, but from the most prominent public location possible, the *rostra* in the *forum Romanum*.[110] To boast of a 'special relationship' with the *ordo equester* in front of the assembled

---

[103] For the context of the debate and Cicero's role in it, see Steel 2001: 114–56.

[104] Plut. *Luc.* 20.1–4. For the original levels, see Plut. *Luc.* 7.5–6; App. *Bell. Mith.* 63.

[105] Cf. Brunt 1988: 188, 316, who suggests that Lucullus was going to be removed regardless.

[106] Meier 1966: 82–8.   [107] Badian 1972: 98.

[108] Steel 2001: 173–81. Cicero mentions the previous consular speakers in *Leg. Man.* 68. Here I follow Lintott 2008: 429. Cf. Morstein-Marx 2004: 182 n. 95, who suggests that the consulars were in favour of the law, but did not speak.

[109] Cic. *Leg. Man.* 4: *equitibus Romanis, honestissimis viris, adferuntur ex Asia cotidie litterae, quorum magnae res aguntur in vestris vectigalibus exercendis occupatae; qui ad me pro necessitudine quae mihi est cum illo ordine causam rei publicae periculaque rerum suarum detulerunt.*

[110] Cic. *Leg. Man.* 1–3 tells us that this is the first time Cicero had delivered a speech from the *rostra*.

populus Romanus was a calculated political act.[111] It reinforced Cicero's
amicitia with those *equites* whom he genuinely counted as friends and
supporters, while at the same time signalling to the members of the *ordo
equester* who were not yet his firm allies that he was one senator they could
count on.

In a later, particularly emotive, passage Cicero called upon all Roman
citizens to draw their attention to the sufferings of the *equites* in Asia:

For the *publicani*, very distinguished and respectable men, transferred their own
financial investments and resources into that province, and the affairs and fortunes
of these men should be a matter of concern to you. Indeed, since we have always
regarded tax revenues as the sinews of the *res publica*, then it is certainly proper
that we characterise that *ordo* which oversees their collection as the backbone of the
other *ordines*.[112]

The language is flattering and effusive – many provincials would hardly
have called the *publicani* responsible for tax collection 'most distinguished
and respectable men'. But they were not Cicero's intended audience; that
was the assembled citizenry in the forum who would be called to vote on
Manilius' law. Cicero's rhetoric was designed to appeal to the *publicani*
themselves, to show them that he was, and would continue to be,
a guardian of their interests. This would guarantee that they continued to
receive profit from administering the taxes of Rome's expanding empire.
Cicero, on the other hand, was securing his support for his future election
campaign to the consulship.[113] It was a mutually beneficial relationship.
Cicero's intention was to signal this without alienating the other citizens.
Indeed, he argued that the problems of the *publicani* were the concerns of
the entire state.[114] As a piece of political rhetoric, designed to appeal to
equites without isolating other elements in the *res publica*, the *Pro lege
Manilia* was a masterstroke. He had, as Quintus Cicero advised, secured
the 'enthusiasm of the *publicani* and the equestrian order' (*studia publicanorum et equestris ordinis*).[115] But the wider message of the *Pro lege*

[111] The phrase 'special relationship' is used by Berry 2003 to describe Cicero's relationship with
the *equites*, and it is an effective translation of *necessitudo* in this context.
[112] Cic. *Leg. Man.* 17: *nam et publicani, homines honestissimi atque ornatissimi, suas rationes et
copias in illam provinciam contulerunt, quorum ipsorum per se res et fortunae vobis curae esse
debent. etenim, si vectigalia nervos esse rei publicae semper duximus, eum certe ordinem qui
exercet illa firmamentum ceterorum ordinum recte esse dicemus.*
[113] Berry 2003: 225. Note the pointed references to his election as praetor by all the centuries in
Leg. Man. 2.
[114] Cic. *Leg. Man.* 18; Nicolet 1974: 675–6; Steel 2001: 129–30; Lintott 2008: 42. See also Morstein-
Marx 2004: 215, 261 on the *popularis* nature of Cicero's rhetoric in the speech.
[115] Q. Cic. *Comm. Pet.* 50.

Manilia, which appealed to popular sentiment, assured him the allegiance of the people.[116] He was duly elected to one of the consulships of 63 BC *suo anno*, a striking achievement for a *novus homo* with no real military accomplishments.

The *publicani* and their allies frequently sat on criminal juries among the other *equites*, and Cicero often appealed to them specifically in order to win his cases. In 55 BC M. Iuventius Laterensis, a young senator with consular ancestors on both sides of his family tree, stood unsuccessfully for election to the post of curule aedile.[117] Embittered by his defeat, he prosecuted one of his rival candidates, the *novus homo* Cn. Plancius, on the grounds that a new man could have only obtained the magistracy by *ambitus*.[118] In comparison with the distinguished ancestry of his rival Laterensis, Plancius was the son of an *eques Romanus*. His father, also called Cn. Plancius, had been a military tribune in the army of P. Licinius Crassus, served as a juror in the pre-Sullan courts, and was regarded as a leading *publicanus*.[119] In 54 BC Cicero defended young Plancius in the court concerned with electoral corruption. The *Pro Plancio* is remarkable for its expressions of equestrian solidarity. Even though he was by this time a senator of consular standing, Cicero squarely identifies himself with the *ordo equester* and the *publicani*. Countering Laterensis' arguments that a new man could only be elected to a magistracy by underhand means, Cicero proclaims that such a path had always been open to 'men sprung from this equestrian background of ours' (*hominibus ortis hoc nostro equestri loco*).[120] In fact, all of Laterensis' opponents in the election happened to be new men, the sons of *equites Romani*, from the leading families of Italy.[121] Cicero paid particular attention to the fact that Plancius' father was a *publicanus*, something that he imagined an arrogant man of senatorial stock like Laterensis might hold against him. However, as Cicero points out, this was something to be celebrated, not condemned, and had actually aided Plancius' success in the election:

If you like, we can connect this with the issue which you claim counts against my client, namely that his father is a *publicanus*. Who does not know how much support this *ordo* provides to men seeking public office? For the *ordo* of *publicani*

---

[116] Q. Cic. *Comm. Pet.* 51, 53. See Morstein-Marx 1998: 263.   [117] Cic. *Planc.* 18.

[118] See Wiseman 1971: 133, 141–2; Lintott 2008: 219–21.

[119] For the careers of Plancius and his father, see Wiseman 1971: 251; Nicolet 1974: 981–3.

[120] Cic. *Planc.* 17. Similar sentiments are found in Cic. *Mur.* 15, 17. While nobility was obviously an important factor in securing election, it was not the only one (Morstein-Marx 1998: 273–4).

[121] Brunt 1988: 155. The entrance of Italians into the equestrian order is explored in detail in Chapter 3.

comprises the flower of the *equites Romani*, the pride of the state, and the bedrock of the *res publica*. So is there anyone who will deny the exceptional enthusiasm of this *ordo* in assisting Plancius' campaign for public office?[122]

Here, the *publicani* are themselves envisioned as an *ordo* because of the contribution that they make to the state as a collective.[123] It was perfectly acceptable in the Roman conception of their state to have *ordines* within a larger *ordo*.[124] Cicero flattered the *publicani* by claiming that their *ordo* contained the best elements of the larger *ordo equester*. Their influence was crucial to electoral success for all candidates. This is a sign of the largely reactive role of the *publicani* in Roman politics: they did not advocate or advance policies as a group (their decrees being largely decorative displays of ideology), but supported candidates who would work on their behalf to protect their ability to exploit Rome's provinces for financial gain.[125]

We can see this relationship between the interests of *publicani* and Roman administration in action in the criminal courts. In the pre-Sullan courts composed exclusively of equestrian jurors, the *publicani* had wielded significant power. Cicero explicitly made this point in the *In Verrem*: 'Previously, when the *ordo equester* sat in judgement, wicked and greedy magistrates in the provinces submitted to the *publicani*.'[126] This led, so Cicero said, to all *equites* being treated with the utmost respect by governors and other officials, lest an attack on one *eques* be regarded as an attack on the entire *ordo*. This was not empty rhetoric. We have already seen how the *equites* responded when Q. Mucius Scaevola, proconsul of Asia in 94 BC, and his legate P. Rutilius Rufus, had attempted to curtail the influence of the *publicani* in their province. Of course the *publicani* did not work alone – they had powerful senatorial allies – but their hostility towards Scaevola and Rufus was remembered for decades afterwards. In a letter dated December 54 BC, Cicero advised P. Lentulus Spinther, governor of Cilicia, to avoid antagonising the *publicani* in his province for this very reason: 'you are acquainted with the usual behaviour of these men, and you know how serious their hostility was in the case of

---

[122] Cic. *Planc.* 23–24: *adiungamus, si vis, id quod tu huic obesse etiam putas, patrem publicanum; qui ordo quanto adiumento sit in honore quis nescit? flos enim equitum Romanorum, ornamentum civitatis, firmamentum rei publicae publicanorum ordine continetur. quis est igitur qui neget ordinis eius studium fuisse in honore Planci singulare?*

[123] Nicolet 1974: 175; Cohen 1975: 276–9; Harris 2011: 18–19.   [124] Cohen 1975: 280.

[125] See the astute comments of Meier 1966: 82–3.

[126] Cic. II *Verr.* 3.94: *antea cum equester ordo iudicaret, improbi et rapaces magistratus in provinciis inserviebant publicanis.* See also Cic. II *Verr.* 3.168, in which he refers to the possibility of *publicani* serving on juries if they were *equites*.

Q. Scaevola'.[127] In his own speeches to the criminal courts Cicero played up his personal relationship with the *publicani*, since he knew that the equestrian jurors would be responsible for deciding the fate of his clients. In the speech *Pro Murena*, delivered in 63 BC, he praised L. Licinius Murena as a good provincial governor because he enabled 'our men' (*nostri homines*) to recover their debts – the familiar first person plural is generally taken to refer to *equites* with business interests.[128] Later in the speech Cicero almost casually referenced the fact that members of the *societates* of *publicani* were in the court.[129]

The ability of the *publicani* to influence state affairs depended on them establishing networks within the wider *ordo equester* and with senators. They had to have a working relationship with the censors and the senate for the letting of their tax contracts, which Polybius had cited as one of the checks and balances in the Roman constitution.[130] Cicero himself desired this type of balance within the state, since the *concordia ordinum* was his most cherished political dream. He believed that only with senators, *equites* and the people working together could the *res publica* function effectively. In his private letters we can observe the lengths to which Cicero went to pacify the *publicani*, even when he disagreed with their position. The first example comes from 61 BC, when the *publicani* came into conflict with certain senators over the letting of the Asian tax contract. The problem began when one particular *societas*, which had won the right to farm the taxes in Asia, realised that it had significantly overbid for the contract, and wanted it cancelled.[131] According to Polybius, it was within the senate's authority to modify the terms of a contract or to release the bidders from their obligations if necessary.[132] The request made by the Asian *publicani* at this time was not unprecedented, but it proved to be very controversial. As Cicero wrote to his influential equestrian friend T. Pomponius Atticus on 5 December that year:

Now along come the *equites* with another fancy, really almost insupportable – and I have not only borne with it but lent it my eloquence. The farmers who bought the

---

[127] Cic. *Fam.* 1.9.26 [SB 20.26]: *nosti consuetudinem hominum, scis quam graviter inimici ipsi illi Q. Scaevolae fuerint.* The case is also mentioned in Cic. *Planc.* 33.

[128] Cic. *Mur.* 42; Fantham 2013: 144.   [129] Cic. *Mur.* 69.

[130] Polyb. 6.17.1–6; Brunt 1988: 148.

[131] Cic. *Att.* 1.17.9 [SB 17.9]. Dio 37.46.4 refers to the election of censors in this year but does not name them. The identity of the *societas* concerned is likewise unknown: see Baldson 1962: 136–7, refuting the idea of a super-company operating in Asia, Cilicia and Bithynia. Other *societates* were able to bid for provinces opened by Pompeius' conquests (Badian 1972: 99–100).

[132] Polyb. 6.17.5. See Livy 39.44.8 for a particular case.

Asiatic taxes from the censors complained in the senate that they had been led by over-eagerness into making too high an offer and asked for the cancellation of their contract. I was their foremost supporter, or rather foremost but one, for it was Crassus who egged them on to make such an audacious demand. An invidious business! The demand was disgraceful, a confession of recklessness.[133]

Writing privately to his friend Atticus, Cicero was free to vent his frustrations about the greed of the *publicani* in a way that he could never have done in public. For, as he confessed, his official stance was steadfast support for the *publicani* and their requests. The revelation that it was M. Licinius Crassus who urged the Asian *societas* to ask for a cancellation of their contract demonstrates the complex web of relationships that lay behind the dealings in the Roman senate.[134] It reveals that the political power of any individual *societas* depended on having backers who were willing to support them. Cicero championed the interests of this *societas* not only because of his established reputation as an advocate for the *publicani*, but also because he believed that the *concordia* of the state was at risk.

The tax contract was not the only major political issue involving members of the equestrian order in 61 BC. In that year a *senatus consultum* was promulgated that would allow for the prosecution of all jurors, including *equites*, who had previously been exempt. This prompted much opposition from equestrian ranks.[135] Cicero told Atticus that he feared that if the case of the Asian *societas* were to be rejected, the *equites* 'would become completely estranged from the senate' (*plane alienarentur a senatu*). He correspondingly spent two full days in the senate speaking 'about the public standing and harmony of the orders' (*de ordinum dignitate et concordia*).[136] The *concordia ordinum* was something that Cicero regarded as his own personal achievement, and he was prepared to defend it at all costs.[137] Cicero named two opponents to the proposal to alter the tax contract. The first was the consul of 60 BC, Q. Caecilius Metellus Celer, who spoke in opposition to Cicero in early December,

---

[133] Cic. *Att.* 1.17.9 [SB 17.9]: *ecce aliae deliciae equitum vix ferendae! quas ego non solum tuli sed etiam ornavi. Asiam qui de censoribus conduxerunt questi sunt in senatu se cupiditate prolapsos nimium magno conduxisse, ut induceretur locatio postulaverunt. ego princeps in adiutoribus atque adeo secundus; nam ut illi auderent hoc postulare Crassus eos impulit. invidiosa res, turpis postulatio et confessio temeritatis.* I have used the excellent translation of Shackleton Bailey here, with only minor modifications (substituting *equites* for 'knights').

[134] Gruen 1974: 70 notes that this is the only occasion in which Crassus was known to espouse the business interests of *equites*.

[135] Cic. *Att.* 1.17.8 [SB 17.8].   [136] Cic. *Att.* 1.17.9 [SB 17.9].   [137] Cic. *Att.* 1.17.10 [SB 17.10].

61 BC. The second, M. Porcius Cato ('the Younger'), featured prominently in Cicero's letters to Atticus as the primary antagonist.[138]
The controversy dragged on throughout the year, with Cicero lamenting
the separation of 'our *publicani*' (*nostros publicanos*) from the senate
in March, and in June that the *equites* had abandoned the senate
entirely.[139] He reiterated to Atticus that he disagreed with the *publicani*
privately, but publicly he needed to oppose Cato 'for the sake of retaining
the support of the *ordo*' (*retinendi ordinis causa*).[140] This was a view
Cicero maintained to the very end of his life; as he explained in the *De
Officiis*, the union of the equestrian and senatorial orders was necessary
'for the safety of the state' (*ad salutem rei publicae*) to protect it from
ambitious individuals who would seek to invest more power in
themselves.[141]

Cicero's repeated concern for the *res publica* and the *concordia ordinum*
represented a lofty principle, but we should not presume that he was
entirely altruistic. His championing of the *publicani* was, as he wrote to
his brother Quintus when he began his governorship in Asia, necessary for
both their public careers.[142] Cicero obviously wrote this letter with the
knowledge that it might be circulated. It served as a manifesto on
the behaviour of a good governor, who needed to uphold the interests of
the *publicani*.[143] C. Iulius Caesar eventually settled the issue of the Asian
tax contracts, reducing the amount payable by a third in his consulship in
59 BC. This was a move that both Cicero and later historians interpreted as
an attempt to win over the support of the equestrian order.[144] The first man
to cast a vote for Caesar's law was none other than Cn. Plancius the Elder,
the *princeps* of the *publicani*, who had lobbied repeatedly on behalf of the
interests of his order.[145] It is surely no coincidence that the elder Plancius
had served as a *tribunus militum* in Spain under P. Licinius Crassus, the
father of the M. Licinius Crassus who had urged the Asian *societas* to press
their case in the senate.[146] It does not push the boundaries of

---

[138] Metellus and Cato: Cic. *Att.* 1.17.9 [SB 17.9]. Metellus was estranged from Pompeius at this
time (Gruen 1974: 85–6). Cato: *Att.* 1.18.7 [SB 18.7], *Att.* 2.1.8 [SB 21.8], *Off.* 3.88. In general,
Cicero praises Metellus' conduct as consul: *Att.* 1.18.5 [SB 18.5], *Att.* 1.19.4 [SB 19.4], *Att.*
1.20.5 [SB 20.5], *Att.* 2.1.4 [SB 21.4].
[139] Cic. *Att.* 1.19.6 [SB 19.6], *Att.* 2.1.7 [SB 21.7].   [140] Cic. *Att.* 2.1.8 [SB 21.8].
[141] Cic. *Off.* 3.88.
[142] Cic. *Q. Fr.* 1.1, esp. 6–7, 32–4 [SB 1.6–7, 32–4]; Badian 1972: 80–1; Steel 2001: 195–8.
[143] Lintott 2008: 253–4.
[144] Cic. *Att.* 2.16.2 [SB 36.2]; Suet. *Iul.* 20.3; App. *BC* 2.13; Dio 38.7.4. This did not necessarily have
the effect of making the *equites* collectively the wholehearted supporters of Caesar (Brunt
1988: 161).
[145] Cic. *Planc.* 34–5.   [146] L. R. Taylor 1964: 22.

prosopographical plausibility too far to suppose that the so-called first triumvirate of Caesar, Crassus and Pompeius supported the younger Plancius' candidacy for the post of curule aedile in 55 BC.[147] Therefore, the election of Plancius was not only the result of assistance he received from the *publicani*, as Cicero describes in the *Pro Plancio* of 54 BC, but also came about because of wider political support. The *publicani* did not control foreign or domestic policy at Rome, but the members of the *societates* were very much at the heart of the state's administrative apparatus, and they could not afford to be ignored. In the *Pro Plancio*, delivered several years after the affair of the Asia tax contract, Cicero gave no indication of his personal antipathy towards the *societas* that had greedily overbid. Instead he lamented the 'injuries' (*iniuria*) suffered by the *publicani*.[148] The *publicani* and the *ordo equester* were his people.

The Good Governor

In Cicero's letters concerning his provincial governorship in Cilicia in 51–50 BC, he presented himself to his friends as a steadfast supporter of the *publicani*, as well as the protector of the provincials. These relationships played a crucial role in his self-representation as an ideal Roman administrator.[149] The positive reception of Cicero's governorship began before he even reached Cilicia, when he landed in Ephesus in Asia in July 51 BC. There, as he related to Atticus, he was greeted by a crowd of well-wishers, including the *decumani* ('tithe-gatherers'), 'as though I had arrived as their governor' (<*quasi ad se*> *venissem cum imperio*).[150] They were, of course, interested in the terms of the provincial edict under which he intended govern the province. Cicero had previously received a deputation of *publicani* at Samos in advance of his arrival; they specifically requested that he retain a clause from the edict of his predecessor, Appius Claudius Pulcher.[151] When Cicero reached Cilicia he claimed to

---

[147] Gruen 1974: 319.   [148] Cic. *Planc.* 34.
[149] This has often been remarked upon, for example: Nicolet 1974: 678–9; Hutchinson 1998: 89–90; Steel 2001: 197–8; Lintott 2008: 253–55. After prosecuting corrupt provincial governors for many years himself, Cicero had high standards to uphold, a fact he admits to Atticus: 'I am sure you see from this that my professions of these many years past are now put to the test' (*ex quo te intellegere certo scio multorum annorum ostentationes meas nuc in discrimen esse adductas*) (*Att.* 5.13.1) [SB 106.1]. (trans. Shackleton Bailey)
[150] Cic. *Att.* 5.13.1 [SB 106.1]. For the roles of *decumani* within the *societates*, see Badian 1972: 73–4.
[151] Cic. *Fam.* 3.8.4. [SB 70.4].

have found the province in financial disarray on account of Pulcher's mismanagement. Although he personally tried to remain diplomatic in his correspondence with Pulcher, Cicero's letters to Atticus are replete with complaints about Cilician administrative affairs.[152] We know from the correspondence that Atticus was particularly interested in matters that concerned the *publicani*. Cicero was aware of his friend's influence and connections with the tax-farmers, so he was concerned to put him at ease.[153] The *publicani*, as it turned out, were at the centre of the financial corruption, which had been occurring in Cilicia for some time. The terms under which the *publicani* were authorised to collect taxes had imposed excessively high interest rates on the Cilicians, a long-established practice that dated back at least as far as the governorship of P. Servilius Isauricus in 78–74 BC. But the *publicani* had not been receiving their money in a consistent fashion, because of the corruption of local officials and their collusion with the Roman governors, especially Claudius Pulcher, who had been siphoning off money for himself.

Cicero had to take action. His provincial edict reduced the interest rate to 1 per cent each month, ensuring that the rate of payment was manageable for the provincials, and that the *publicani* did receive some money.[154] Cicero's account of these affairs is positive, but not untrustworthy – he did certainly improve conditions in the province out of a desire to be a good governor.[155] But there is also no doubt that he was anxious to be remembered as the protector of the *publicani* and their interests. He went to great lengths to emphasise this in his letters to the influential Atticus, who would communicate it to his own friends and supporters within the *ordo equester*.[156] In February 50 BC Cicero received a letter from Atticus, which contained some complaints about the provincial edict of M. Calpurnius Bibulus, proconsul of Syria. The edict, so Atticus wrote to Cicero, included 'a much too serious precedent against our order' (*nimis gravi praeiudicio in ordinem nostrum*).[157] Cicero responded that his edict included a similar clause, but one that was expressed in a more tactful

---

[152] Lintott 2008: 258–9; Tempest 2011: 154–5.

[153] Cic. *Att.* 6.1.151–6 [SB 115.15–16]. See Hutchinson 1998: 21–2 on Cicero's desire that Atticus 'should understand and think well of his actions'.

[154] For these events, see Cic. *Att.* 6.1.16 [SB 115.16], 6.2.4–5 [SB 116.4–5]; Badian 1972: 113–14; Lintott 2008: 263.

[155] Badian 1972: 155 n. 140; Berry 2003: 227; Tempest 2011: 153.

[156] For Atticus as a distributor of Cicero's works, see Murphy 1998: 495. Judging from the precautions he took to ensure secrecy on occasions, Cicero was aware that friends and colleagues did circulate his letters. He also thought about publication of his letters in the future, though only towards the end of his life (Nicholson 1994: 59–62; Hutchinson 1998: 4).

[157] Cic. *Att.* 6.1.15 [SB 115.15].

manner. His own strategy revealed him to be the master of public relations. As far as the *publicani* were concerned, he assured Atticus, 'I dote upon them, defer to them, butter them up with compliments – and arrange so that they harm nobody'.[158] Cicero communicated the same message to his friend M. Caelius Rufus in Rome, shortly before he left the province, portraying his governorship as a major success:

It's my plan to set out from Cilicia on the Nones of May, since I have now dispensed justice, enriched the city-states, and even ensured that the money from the last cycle has been given to the *publicani*, without a single complaint from the allies. I have ensured that I have received the approval of all men, from the highest to the lowest. When I have reached the legions' summer quarters and addressed the troops, I will leave in accordance with the senatorial decree.[159]

Atticus had a vested interest in ensuring that the *publicani* were protected, and Cicero set his mind at ease. In the final month of his provincial command Cicero boasted to Atticus that, among his many achievements, he had placated the *publicani* while protecting the interests of the cities of Cilicia.[160] Cicero had secured the continuing support of the *publicani* and the provincials, thus fulfilling his promise to be a better governor than the unscrupulous senators he had prosecuted for *repetundae*.[161]

Cicero's positivity in his gubernatorial correspondence was to a large extent political posturing. We have already seen that he had private misgivings over the Asian tax contracts, which he expressed to Atticus, despite his public support for the *publicani*. For instance, Cicero privately blamed the *publicani* for their lack of support during P. Clodius Pulcher's persecution of him for the execution of the Catilinarian conspirators, which eventually led to his exile from Rome in March 58 BC. Writing from Thessalonica to his brother Quintus in August that year, with the wounds still fresh, Cicero lamented the lack of resolve shown by his closest friends.[162] Some of these stung more than others, particularly the

---

[158] Cic. *Att.* 6.1.16 [SB 115.16]: *habeo in deliciis, obsequor, verbis laudo, orno: efficio ne cui molesti sint* (trans. Shackleton Bailey).
[159] Cic. *Fam.* 2.13.4 [SB 94.4]: *mihi erat in animo, quoniam iuris dictionem confe<ce>ram, civitates locupletaram, publicanis etiam superioris lustri reliqua sine sociorum ulla querela conservaram, privatis, summis infimis, fueram iucundus, proficisci in Ciliciam Non. Mai. et, cum primum aestiva attigissem militemque collocassem, decedere ex senatus consulto.*
[160] Cic. *Att.* 6.3.3 [SB 117.3].
[161] Lintott 2008: 255 observes a degree of relief in Cicero's boasting, since he had not given his enemies cause for prosecution.
[162] Cic. *Q. Fr.* 1.4.1 [SB 4.1].

spinelessness of the *publicani*.[163] Cicero remembered this fact several years later, after he had spent his Cilician governorship appeasing and mollifying the *publicani*. Writing to Atticus in April 50 BC, he said that his new arrangements meant that 'I am a prime favourite with the tax farmers. "Grateful men," you might say. I have experienced their gratitude!'[164] The sarcastic tone is clear.[165] But it was rather unfair. *Equites* and *publicani* did lend their support in 58 BC, as Cicero admitted in the *Pro Sestio* (when he was courting the vote of equestrian members of the jury).[166] By December 50 BC Cicero was particularly glum about the state of the *res publica* and the gathering storm between Caesar and Pompeius. He told Atticus that he did not know which of the *ordines* of the state deserved the title of honest men: 'What about the *publicani*, who were never really dependable, and are now Caesar's closest friends, or the money-lenders, or the farmers, who wish for peace most of all?'[167] This is surely the tone of a worried politician, brought on by immediate circumstances. By December 50 BC the dream of the *concordia ordinum* had vanished. Cicero had realised that the *publicani* were more concerned about their own affairs rather than the integrity of the *res publica*.[168] This tension between private interests and public duty within the *ordo equester* was one that Cicero was ultimately unable to resolve, as we shall see.

Otium and *Officium*

In 66 BC, the year of his praetorship, Cicero defended A. Cluentius Habitus, an *eques* from Larinum, on a charge of poisoning, under the terms of Sulla's *lex Cornelia de sicariis et veneficiis* dealing with such cases.[169] In a complicated case of family intrigue, Cluentius' stepbrother, Oppianicus, had charged him with murdering his stepfather, Statius Albius

---

[163] Cic. *Q. Fr.* 1.4.1 [SB 4.4]; Shackleton Bailey 1980: 169. In a letter to Atticus written at about the same time Cicero responded to his friend's serious concern about his state of mind: Cic. *Att.* 3.13.2 [SB 59.2]. He also blamed Atticus for providing him with insufficient advice: Cic. *Att.* 3.15.7–8 [SB 60.7–8]; Shackleton Bailey 1965a: 19–22.

[164] Cic. *Att.* 6.2.5 [SB 116.5]: *itaque publicanis in oculis sumus. 'gratis' inquis 'viris'. sensimus.* I have slightly modified Shackleton Bailey's translation.

[165] See Shackleton Bailey 1968: 259, who interprets this as a reproach against Cicero's 'old allies for their lukewarmness in 58'.

[166] Kaster 2006: 153–4, 175.

[167] Cic. *Att.* 7.7.5. [SB 130.5]: *an publicanos, qui numquam firmi sed nunc Caesari sunt amicissimi, an faeneratores, an agricolas, quibus optatissimum est otium.* As Shackleton Bailey 1968: 305 points out, we do not know what Caesar had done to win over the *publicani*.

[168] Meier 1966: 92; Lintott 2008: 277–8.   [169] For the law, see Ferrary 1991 and *RS* 50.

Oppianicus, and two other men.[170] The case was actually a sequel to a notorious trial of 74 BC, in which Cluentius had accused the elder Oppianicus of attempting to poison him. Oppianicus was eventually found guilty of judicial corruption, since both sides were implicated in an attempt to bribe the members of the jury.[171] Tasked with defending Cluentius on a charge of poisoning in 66 BC, Cicero had to contend with the widespread – and undoubtedly accurate – perception that his client had procured his father-in-law's condemnation less than a decade previously through judicial corruption.[172] Cicero's speech, the *Pro Cluentio*, thus devoted comparatively little attention to the actual crime of which Cluentius had been accused. It instead focused on combating the widespread perception that Cluentius was guilty of judicial murder, that is, of conspiring to fix the outcome of a trial and condemning an innocent man.[173] This is where Cicero was able to play his trump card, since Rome's statute on judicial murder, the *lex Sempronia ne quis iudicio circumveniatur* ('the Sempronian law so that no one should be framed in a law court'), applied only to senators, not to *equites*.[174]

This law had originally been passed by Gaius Gracchus during his first tribunate in 123 BC, but its principles were retained by Sulla in the *lex Cornelia de sicariis et veneficiis*.[175] Although it did not explicitly exclude *equites*, the law stated that its terms only applied to someone who had been tribune of the first four legions, quaestor, tribune of the plebs, as well as anyone who had given his opinion in the senate, and who had been a magistrate. In short, most *equites* were not liable to prosecution.[176] Efforts in 74 BC to extend the ambit of laws on judicial corruption to all *equites* had failed.[177] It was of course ludicrous that *equites*, who made up

---

[170] The complex circumstances of the case are summarised by Hoenigswald 1962: 109–11; Lintott 2008: 36–7.

[171] Cic. I *Verr.* 1.29, 38–9, II *Verr.* 1.157, *Clu.* 77–9, 89–116.

[172] Cluentius' guilt is assumed by modern scholars, e.g. Hoenigswald 1962: 118 n. 23; Lintott 2008: 36.

[173] This was a key part of Cicero's strategy in the case, since it distracted the jury from the actual charge: Hoenigswald 1962: 123; Classen 1978: 609–10; Lintott 2008: 36.

[174] 'Judicial murder' did not apply to the acceptance of a bribe, a crime for which senatorial jurors were charged under the *lex de repetundis* (Cic. *Clu.* 104; the reference is to Sulla's new law on *repetundae*, not that of Gaius Gracchus). Stockton 1979: 124–5 points out that since Cluentius was not a juror in the previous case, the *lex ne quis* must not have been a law against jurors who accepted bribes, but had much wider application.

[175] Cic. *Clu.* 151; Stockton 1979: 122–6. The relevant clause is chapter six of Sulla's law (Ferrary 1991: 426–8).

[176] Cic. *Clu.* 147–8, 156. The exceptions would be those *equites* who had served as tribunes of one of the first four legions.

[177] Cic. *Clu.* 136–7; Gruen 1968: 241.

the majority of the jury panel from 70 BC onwards, and who were intimately involved in a variety of criminal trials, as both plaintiffs and defendants, should be exempt from such charges. This was a product of Gaius Gracchus' original laws, which had envisioned equestrian jurors as impartial arbiters, holding corrupt senators to account. This situation became even more problematic as the *equites* took on roles as jurors across the full range of criminal courts. The case of Cluentius is symptomatic of the tension that existed in the late Republic, as *equites* and senators tried to negotiate the place of the nascent *ordo equester* within the *res publica*. It was true that the vast majority of *equites* had no public role or ambitions, content to ensure that their own interests were protected, as Badian and Meier have argued.[178] At the same time, however, the *equites* who sat on the juries were essentially state officials with undoubted political power.[179] This was a tension that had not previously manifested itself when equestrians had served as military officers, even when they were elected magistrates as tribunes of the first four legions. Army commanders fought for Rome against its enemies, and thus did not play a part in internal political disputes in the same way that jurors did.

In the *Pro Cluentio*, Cicero stated that the exemption of *equites* under the terms of the Gracchan and Sullan legislation was no mere legal loophole, but a recognition of the different roles played by *equites* and senators in Roman society and politics:

Then, what senator ever refused to think that he ought to be subject to the harsher penalties of the laws, since he had achieved his loftier public standing through the favour of the Roman people? How many advantages we forgo, how many troublesome and tiresome problems we suffer! But we are compensated for these things by the perquisites of honour and distinction. Now apply these same strictures of life to the *ordo equester* and the other *ordines*: they would not put up with them. For they think that they should be shielded from the numerous legal penalties and the regulations of the court system, because they have not been able, or have not desired, to ascend to the highest position in our state.[180]

---

[178] Badian 1962: 224; Meier 1966: 72–94.   [179] Nicolet 1974: 704.

[180] Cic. *Clu.* 150: *deinde quis umquam hoc senator recusavit ne, cum altiorem gradum dignitatis beneficio populi Romani esset consecutus, eo se putaret durioribus legum condicionibus uti oportere? quam multa sunt commoda quibus caremus, quam multa molesta et difficilia quae subimus! atque haec omnia tamen honoris et amplitudinis commodo compensantur. converte nunc ad equestrem ordinem atque in ceteros ordines easdem vitae condiciones; non perferent. putant enim minus multos sibi laqueos legum et condicionum ac iudiciorum propositos esse oportere qui summum locum civitatis aut non potuerunt ascendere aut non petiverunt.*

Cicero attempted to define the function of senators and *equites* within the framework of the *res publica* in a way that absolved equestrians of responsibility for their actions under Roman law. Since they did not achieve honours and prestige as senators, they should not face the same legislative penalties. The distinction between the culpability of *equites* and senators stemmed from the fact that the laws were only designed to hold senators and magistrates to account for their actions; it was a tralatician relic, which belied the fact that *equites* had a genuine public role to perform. In pursuing this argument on behalf of his equestrian client, Cicero portrayed himself as an advocate who would uphold the rights, privileges – and exemptions – of the *ordo equester*, a sentiment calculated to appeal to the *equites* on the jury.[181]

There had been previous attempts by senators to close loopholes in the legislation and make equestrian jurors liable to prosecution. Cicero represented these senators as rogue troublemakers who wished to subjugate the *equites*. He contrasted them with the majority of the *curia* who regarded the *ordo equester* as equal partners in the state.[182] One of the magistrates who attempted to rectify the problem was M. Livius Drusus, who passed a law in 91 BC making equestrian jurors liable to the same penalties as senators.[183] Cicero characterised the response of the leading *equites* to Drusus in the following way:

[The *equites* said] that they had noticed the trappings of a senatorial life: it was a brilliant distinction, which came with many status symbols, and a certain public standing. They did not look down upon these things, but were content to remain members of the *ordo equester*, just as their fathers had been. They preferred to follow a life that was peaceful and undisturbed, far from the storms of political turmoil and legal wrangling, as in this very case.[184]

Cicero's hypothetical *equites* thus claimed to value their *quies*, or peace, above the competition for status. They then continued to list the privileges and status symbols available to senators, such as the *toga praetexta* worn by the magistrates, the curule chair, and governorship of provinces.[185]

---

[181] Cic. *Clu.* 157, in which he volunteers to defend any other person (sc. *eques*) who might be unjustly accused. On Cicero's rhetorical strategy here, see Berry 2003: 229–30; Burnand 2004: 286–7.

[182] Cic. *Clu.* 152.

[183] The evidence for this comes from Cic. *Clu.* 151–5 and *Rab. Post.* 15–18. The law was subsequently rescinded, along with Drusus' other legislation.

[184] Cic. *Clu.* 153: *sese vidisse in ea vita qualis splendor inesset, quanta ornamenta, quae dignitas; quae se non contempsisse sed ordine suo patrumque suorum contentos fuisse et vitam illam tranquillam et quietam, remotam a procellis invidiarum et huiusce modi iudiciorum sequi maluisse.*

[185] Cic. *Clu.* 154.

The irony of these sentiments is that by the time Cicero was speaking, the *ordo equester* had come to possess its own status symbols, such as the *trabea*, the gold ring, and the right to sit in the fourteen rows in the theatre, which will be discussed in the next chapter. But this was at odds with Cicero's central conceit in the *Pro Cluenito* that *equites* were fundamentally apolitical creatures, citizens who specifically avoided the contest for power in order to have 'a life that was peaceful and undisturbed'. It was true that *equites* only usually actively intervened in state affairs as a group when their interests were threatened.[186] But at the same time, if they were to sit in judgement on senators and magistrates in the criminal courts, they were taking part in politics as state officials, and had to be prepared to answer for their conduct. Cicero was, in Crawford's memorable phrase, 'shedding crocodile tears' for the *equites*.[187] He used the letter of the law to defeat the spirit of the law, and succeeded in persuading the jurors to acquit Cluentius.[188] Cicero knew exactly what he was doing, and would later boast that 'he had blinded the jurors with a smokescreen' (*se tenebras offudisse iucidibus*).[189]

The strategy was so successful that Cicero used a similar argument in the defence speech *Pro Rabirio Postumo* delivered in late 54 or early 53 BC. The equestrian C. Rabirius Postumus had been charged under the *lex Iulia de repetundis*, in particular the clause 'what has become of the money' (*quo ea pecunia peruenerit*).[190] The charge represented an attempt by the prosecution to recover some of the 10,000 talents that Postumus' associate Aulus Gabinius had been ordered to pay following his own conviction for *repetundae*.[191] In order for Postumus to be prosecuted under the clause, he needed to be named in Gabinius' original trial, which Cicero argued had not occurred.[192] He also proposed that Postumus could not be prosecuted under the *lex Iulia de repetundis* anyway. Only senators and magistrates fell within the scope of the legislation, as had been the case since Gaius Gracchus' original law on provincial maladministration.[193] Cicero urged the equestrian members on the jury bench to stand up for their rights, as they had done when M. Livius

---

[186] Badian 1962: 224; Meier 1966: 85–9.

[187] Crawford 2001: 432. See also Nicolet 1974: 704, 720.

[188] Hoenigswald 1962: 123; Classen 1978: 609–10, 617. For other aspects of Cicero's success, see Hughes 1997: 157–9; Burnard 2004; Goldberg 2007: 58–9.

[189] Quint. *Inst.* 2.17.21. The Latin literally means 'to pour forth shadows'.

[190] For the breadth of Caesar's law, which contained more than one hundred clauses, see Gruen 1968: 240–3.

[191] Siani-Davies 2001: 70, 84–91.

[192] Cic. *Rab. Post.* 10; Siani-Davies 2001: 90, 138–9; Lintott 2008: 246–7.

[193] Cic. *Rab. Post.* 9, 11–12. Cicero explicitly states that 'your *ordo* is not bound by the law' (*at iste ordo lege ea non tenetur*). For discussion, see Gruen 1968: 240–2.

Drusus had attempted to make *equites* liable for judicial murder. Repeating the strategy of the *Pro Cluentio*, he once again introduced hypothetical *equites* who argued that only senators should be subject to the full penalties of the law:[194]

'We have never looked down upon those aspects of your careers,' so the *equites* contended, 'but we have followed this undisturbed and politically neutral life. Since it does not come with public office, it should not come with political pressures.'

  'But you serve as a juror just as I serve as a senator.'

  'That is true, but you sought that position, whereas I am compelled to be a juror. In that case, I should have a choice: either I should be able to decline jury service, or not be held accountable by a law intended for senators.'[195]

The language is nearly identical to the *Pro Cluentio*. In the earlier speech the *equites* claim to pursue 'a life that is peaceful and undisturbed' (*vitam illam tranquillam et quietam*); here it is 'this undisturbed and politically neutral life' (*hanc vitam quietam atque otiosam*). The notion of *quies*, or peace, features in both speeches, but in the *Pro Rabirio Postumo* the adjective *tranquillus* has been replaced by *otiosus*, a change that was not without some meaning. The noun *otium* ('peace' or 'leisure'), from which the adjective *otiosus* derives, has a broad semantic range, made more complicated by the different ways in which Cicero himself used the word. In this example, *otium/otiosus* specifically refers to a life free from public office, which he regarded as the condition of non-senators, including *equites*.[196]

  There was no shame in pursuing *otium*, for such was the natural condition of the *equites* in Cicero's mind. He explicitly made this point in a letter to Atticus from 61 BC: 'a particular ambition led me to seek public office (*ad honorum studium*), whereas an entirely different, but quite understandable, decision led you to follow a respectable private life (*ad honestum otium*)'.[197] Cicero's use of the terms *otiosus* and *otium* in these circumstances needs to be distinguished from references to his own career and

---

[194] Cic. *Rab. Post.* 16–17.

[195] Cic. *Rab. Post.* 17: '*nos ista numquam contempsimus*'—*ita enim disputabant*—'*sed hanc vitam quietam atque otiosam secuti sumus; quae quoniam honore caret, careat etiam molestia.*' '*tam es tu iudex quam ego senator.*' '*ita est, sed tu istud petisti, ego hoc cogor. qua re aut iudici mihi non esse liceat, aut lege senatoria non teneri.*' The manuscript reading *tam es tu iudex quam ego senator* is retained, rather than *tam es tu iudex <eques> quam ego senator*. See Lintott 2008: 247 n. 107.

[196] Nicolet 1974: 700–2; Hanchey 2013: 182–3. For senators, the word could be used in honourable and dishonourable fashions, depending on the intention (Balsdon 1960: 47).

[197] Cic. *Att.* 1.17.5 [SB 17.5]: *quod me ambitio quaedam ad honorum studium, te autem alia minime reprehendenda ratio ad honestum otium duxit.*

necessary retreat into private life, where they mean something quite different.[198] Roman citizens, including *equites*, could serve the *res publica* in an honourable fashion without embarking on the senatorial *cursus honorum*.[199] But this was partly a conceit. Even if *equites* were compelled to serve as jurors, they were still actively playing a role in politics in an official state capacity, and should have been subject to charges of misconduct if they behaved improperly. In the *Pro Rabirio Postumo*, Cicero concluded this argument by exhorting the equestrian jurors to vote in a manner that would not set a precedent for their entire order, and thus make all *equites* liable to prosecution for *repetundae*.[200] He did this in a somewhat conspiratorial manner, reminding them that he himself was once an *eques* and spoke for their *ordo*.[201]

Cicero's arguments in the *Pro Cluentio* and *Pro Rabirio Postumo* served their immediate purpose, since both his clients were acquitted.[202] But they also established a false dichotomy between the political involvement of senators and *equites* that not only belied realities – it was also a state of affairs that Cicero himself knew to be false. In 61 BC a *senatus consultum* was passed which would, if it became a law, allow the prosecution of all jurors, including *equites*, who accepted bribes. Cicero told Atticus that he had defended the *ordo equester*. 'I was stern and eloquent in a cause that was not very respectable,' he confided to his friend.[203] In a second letter, written in mid-60 BC, Cicero revealed that the bill had the support of Cato the Younger (who was simultaneously opposing the remission of the Asian tax contract for the *publicani* at the time, which we noted earlier). Cicero applauded Cato's sentiments, even as he acknowledged that he could not support them publicly:

Cato gives his opinion as if he is in Plato's *Republic*, not Romulus' sewer. What is fairer than a man who sits in judgement being judged himself if he accepts bribes? This is what Cato proposed, and the senate assented, so the *equites* now make war on the senate house (not on me of course, for I didn't agree). What could be more impudent than the *publicani* reneging on their tax contract? Nevertheless, my defeat was necessary in order to retain the support of the *ordo*.[204]

[198] E. A. Marshall 1986: 56–7; Hanchey 2013: 183–91.
[199] Cic. *Sest.* 96–9; Kaster 2006: 322–3.   [200] Cic. *Rab. Post.* 18.
[201] Cic. *Rab. Post.* 15; Berry 2003: 233–4.
[202] For the outcome of Rabirius' trial, see Siani-Davies 2001: 82–4.
[203] Cic. *Att.* 1.17.8 [SB 17.8]: *in causa non verecunda admodum gravis et copiosus fui.* See also Cic. *Att.* 1.18.3 [SB 18.3]. This bill may have been prompted by recent episodes of corruption in the courts (Lintott 2008: 159).
[204] Cic. *Att.* 2.1.8 [SB 21.8]: *dicit enim tamquam in Platonis πολιτείᾳ non tamquam in Romuli faece, sententiam. quid verius quam in iudicium venire qui ob rem iudicandam pecuniam*

Despite Cicero's pessimism, the motion never became law, because it was defeated in the assembly.[205] But the problem of corruption in the courts did not disappear. In 55 BC Cn. Pompeius Magnus passed the *lex Pompeia iudicaria*, which prescribed that jurors would no longer be chosen by the praetor, but would automatically come from the highest census classes of the three *ordines* of senators, *equites* and *tribuni aerarii*.[206] *Equites* were still compelled to serve on a jury if called upon to do so.[207] In the same year there was discussion as to whether the staff of provincial governors, including tribunes, prefects and *scribae* (many of whom would have been *equites*), should be subject to prosecution for *repetundae*. However, the motion was defeated when heard by a full house of the senate.[208] This attempt to make *equites* liable to *repetundae* charges demonstrates that their role in the state was not entirely apolitical, even if the issues on which they were prepared to take an active political stand were limited. They not only served as jurors, sitting in judgement on senatorial governors, but also actively advised and supported governors in the provinces. Equestrians served as tribunes and prefects in the Roman army, fighting for the *res publica*.[209] *Publicani* and other *equites* had alliances and business relationships with senators, and exerted substantial pressure on senators to achieve their goals.[210] The *ordo equester* was intimately connected with the politics and administration of the *res publica* in a way that could not have been entirely anticipated by Gaius Gracchus in 123 BC.

Conclusion: An Elusive Order

Pliny the Elder's statement that Cicero 'established' the name of the *ordo equester* in the year of his consulship cannot be correct: the term was in use well before 63 BC, as we have already seen. But, as so often with Pliny, although his facts might be wrong, he certainly preserved the spirit of Cicero's relationship with the *equites*. There was an important moment

acceperit? censuit hoc Cato et adsensit senatus: equites curiae bellum – non mihi, nam ego dissensi. quid impudentius publicanis renuntiantibus? fuit tam retinendi ordinis causa facienda iactura.
[205] Cic. *Att.* 1.18.3 [SB 18.3]. [206] Cic. *Pis.* 97; Gruen 1974: 231–2.
[207] Cic. *Rab. Post.* 17; Siani-Davies 2001: 161–2.
[208] Cic. *Rab. Post.* 13; Siani-Davies 2001: 150. The *lex Iulia de repetundis* did include members of the governor's staff, but only senators, at least in the Republican period. See Gruen 1974: 240, 242 n. 132; Lintott 2008: 248 n. 108. However, the statute did apply to *equites* serving on the staff of governors in the empire (Brunt 1990a: 62–3, 499–500).
[209] Nicolet 1974: 714–15. Equestrian military officers will be discussed further in Chapter 3.
[210] L. R. Taylor 1968: 472–3.

during Cicero's consulship, on the night of 4 December 63 BC. Then the equestrians currently resident in Rome came together as one, and acquired a leader, if only temporarily, when Atticus took 'the first and last overt political action of his life'.[211] He led the assembled *equites* to the *clivus Capitolinus* to show their support for the senate and to defend the *res publica* against the threat posed by L. Sergius Catilina (better known today as Catiline), who had attempted to seize power for himself.[212] This was a public demonstration of the *concordia ordinum*, to which Cicero would refer in the senate the very next day when he delivered *In Catilinam IV*. He expressed this sentiment in the published version of the speech as follows:

What should I say about the role of the *equites Romani*? These men concede priority in rank and judgement to you, senators, so they can compete with you in displaying their love for the *res publica*. After many years of discord, the events of this very day, and this cause, have joined the men of this *ordo* to you again, since they have been recalled to fellowship and public harmony.[213]

That night, after the execution of the Catilinarian conspirators, a gathering of Roman citizens escorted Cicero home. Atticus' show of support revealed that he and the other *equites* were not entirely apolitical creatures – they only intervened when it suited them. A few years later, in 55 BC, Cicero called Atticus 'a natural politician, but you have no particular bondage' (*natura* πολιτικός, *tamen nullam habes propriam servitutem*) – in contrast to Cicero himself, who had to hold his tongue to please other, more powerful, forces.[214] As Welch has demonstrated, Atticus was the type of 'political operator who worked outside the senate to advise and influence those inside it'.[215] There were many ways of exercising authority and influence in state affairs. Far from being dignified supporters of the status quo as Cicero envisaged, members of the equestrian order intervened in politics as and when it suited them, in a manner that could not be defined constitutionally and which often challenged senatorial authority. The reality, of course, as Cicero admitted to Atticus in late 50 BC, with the shadow of civil war hanging over him, was that the *publicani* and other free citizens were not necessarily concerned about the spectre of kingship 'provided that they are free from political obligation' (*dum modo otiosi*

---

[211] Shackleton Bailey 1965a: 14.   [212] Cic. *Att.* 2.1.7 [SB 21.7], *Sest.* 28, *Leg. Agr.* 2.70–1.

[213] Cic. *Cat.* 4.15: *quid ego hic equites Romanos commemorem? qui vobis ita summam ordinis consilique concedunt ut vobiscum de amore rei publicae certent; quos ex multorum annorum dissensione huius ordinis ad societatem concordiamque revocatos hodiernus dies vobiscum atque haec causa coniungit.*

[214] Cic. *Att.* 4.6.1 [SB 83.1].

[215] K. Welch 1996: 450. See also Nicolet 1984: 125, 'another way of approaching public life'.

essent).[216] Here *otiosus* is still used in the sense of the private life of apolitical *equites*, but it has taken on a slightly bitter tone. If the threat posed by Caesar in 50 BC did not upset their business interests, then there was no need to take a stand.

The crux of the issue is that the *ordo equester* was an elusive order. Its members wanted to be able to have their cake and eat it – they desired privileges and status symbols, power over affairs that affected them, but to remain apolitical when it suited them (such as when threatened with prosecution for judicial murder and *repetundae*).[217] The way in which the *ordo* had evolved since the Gracchan period had resulted in it becoming a political anomaly: originally envisaged as independent arbiters who could hold senatorial magistrates to account in the courts, in reality they turned out to be anything but independent. We have seen how *equites* became embroiled in criminal trials that were vehicles for senatorial rivalries. The *publicani* pressured equestrian juries to indict governors who had wronged them. Cicero was prepared to indulge the *equites'* wishes to remain free from the threat of prosecution, not only because he wanted to win his cases for Cluentius and Postumus, but also because his career depended on their support.[218] This is particularly true of the trial of Cluentius, held in 66 BC, when Cicero was praetor, and desperate to achieve the dream of the consulship *suo anno*.[219] The entirely apolitical *eques*, living a quiet and peaceful life, was something of a mirage within Cicero's own circles and high politics in the city of Rome. Such a reality could only be achieved by an Italian *eques* who was never liable to serve on juries, had no overseas business interests, and rarely travelled to Rome. We should not discount the reality of this silent majority, whose viewpoint no longer survives. But at the same time, the future of the *ordo* as a whole, and its place within the *res publica*, was being contested in Rome.[220]

The influence of Cicero's writings was profound in the fields of Roman political philosophy, oratory and letter writing. He certainly wanted to be remembered, if not as the creator of the *ordo equester*, then as its primary

---

[216] Cic. *Att.* 7.7.5 [SB 130.5].

[217] Note the remarks of Crawford 2001: 432, pointing out the difference between the collective wishes of the *ordo* and the reluctance of individual *equites* to serve if they faced prosecution.

[218] See Lintott 2008: 136 on how Cicero's speech about the equestrian privileges in the theatre (*pro Othone*) fitted into his overall political platform during his consulship.

[219] The *Commentariolum Petitionis* emphasises Cicero's need for equestrian support in these years (Lintott 2008: 132–3).

[220] Note Nicolet's 1974: 720 important comment that even an *eques* with no other political interests was not really a private citizen, because his title gave him a privileged place within the *res publica*. The relationship between Rome and the rest of Italy is discussed in Chapter 3.

benefactor. He defended the integrity of the equestrian jurors in *In Verrem* and other speeches, advocated their exemption from judicial prosecution in the *Pro Cluentio* and *Pro Rabirio Postumo*, and championed the cause of the *publicani* in the *Pro Plancio*. To this we can add the numerous letters to Atticus and friends in which Cicero constantly sought equestrian approval. Yet the problem is, as we have seen, that not even Cicero gives us a consistent picture of the equestrian order. He sometimes expressed different views publicly and privately. The aim of this chapter has not been to convict Cicero of inconsistency in his writings. That would be a rather banal and unfair conclusion to draw about a man whose published work spans a period of almost forty years. Rather, we have argued that his statements about the *ordo equester* reflect the order's own ambivalent position within the *res publica*. We need to remember that it was only in the generation before Cicero that the *ordo* finally acquired an identity separate from the senate. This continued to develop throughout Cicero's own lifetime, as equestrians acquired new privileges and status symbols, as we will see in the next chapter. It is understandable, therefore, that there was debate and dissension in the late Republic about precisely how the *ordo equester* fitted into the state, which Cicero exploited as necessary for his specific political and legal agendas. Cicero's surviving works, extensive though they are, are surely only one part of what was originally a much wider conversation at the time.

Addendum: The *Tribuni Aerarii*

The *lex Aurelia iudicaria* of 70 BC stipulated that one-third of the jury should be composed of *tribuni aerarii*, who had hitherto not played a role in the controversy over the courts. Who exactly were these 'tribunes of the treasury'? In the early and middle Republic they had been responsible for paying Rome's soldiers, before this responsibility was transferred to the quaestors.[221] It has been convincingly argued that these *tribuni aerarii* were wealthy citizens of the *prima classis*, who had to pay the army out of their own funds, then recoup it by collecting the *tributum*.[222] There appear to have been citizens designated *tribuni aerarii* in each voting tribe.[223]

---

[221] Varro, *LL* 5.181; Gell. *NA* 6.10. If the *tribuni aerarii* did not pay the soldiers as requested, the soldiers could mount a legal challenge (Gaius, *Inst.* 4.26–7).

[222] Nicolet 1980: 161–3; Rosenstein 2011: 136–9.

[223] Dion. Hal. 4.15; Nicolet 1974: 608. Evidence from the late Republic comes from Cic. *Planc.* 21, in which Cicero refers to *equites* and *tribuni aerarii* from the tribe Terentia being present in the court to lend their support.

The majority of our evidence for the *tribuni aerarii* in the late Republic can be found in Cicero, but it is somewhat contradictory. When Cicero referred to the social hierarchy of the *res publica*, he explicitly separated the *equites* from the *tribuni aerarii*.[224] The same distinction can be found in some of his private correspondence. When he wrote to his brother Quintus about the trial of Sex. Cloelius, Cicero remarked that the senators voted to acquit Cloelius, the *equites* were split both ways, and the *tribuni aerarii* voted to condemn.[225] In his courtroom speeches, however, Cicero often ignores the *tribuni aerarii* as their own constituent group, referring to the jury as if it were composed only of senators and *equites*.[226] In the *Pro Plancio* of 55 BC, he stated that the jurors included fifty *equites*; since most jury panels were composed of seventy-five members, this figure surely included the *tribuni aerarii* as well as *equites Romani*.[227] Finally, in the *Pro Cluentio*, delivered in 66 BC, Cicero declared that the corruption of the Sullan senatorial juries led to 'the courts being shared with the equestrian order' (*iudicia cum equestri ordine communicata*) under the terms of the *lex Aurelia*.[228] This may initially lead one to conclude, as many scholars have, that the term *tribuni aerarii* referred to all citizens with the *census equester* but not the *equus publicus*.[229]

But there are good grounds for modifying this conclusion. The *tribuni aerarii* appear to be a group analogous to the *scribae*, that is, they existed as an *ordo* because of their official function within the state.[230] Cicero himself implied as much in *In Catilinam IV* when he described the different *ordines* supporting him, which included the *equites, tribuni aerarii,* and the *scribae*.[231] It is likely that the *tribuni aerarii*, as members of the *prima classis*, retained their honorific title long after they ceased to pay the soldiers, in much the same way that *equites* were still known as *equites*

---

[224] Cic. *Planc.* 21, *Cat.* 4.15, *Rab. perd.* 27. In the latter case the reference is to the events of 100 BC, but the mention of the *tribuni aerarii* appears to be standard Ciceronian rhetoric about all the *ordines* coming together, rather than genuine historical evidence for what happened at the time (Hill 1952: 214).

[225] Cic. *Q. Fr.* 2.5.6 [SB 9.4]. In *Q. Fr.* 2.16.3 [SB 20.3], the *tribuni aerarii* voted to acquit a man named Drusus, while the senators and *equites* declared him guilty. For precise breakdowns of jury voting between the three *ordines*, see Nicolet 1974: 595–7.

[226] Cic. *Font.* 36, *Rab. Post.* 13–14, *Flac.* 4, 96.

[227] Cic. *Planc.* 41. For jury size, see Berry 1996: 16; Lintott 2004: 75. The trial of Aemilius Scaurus in 54 BC had a jury composed of twenty-two senators, twenty-three *equites*, and twenty-five *tribuni aerarii* (Asc. 28 C with B. A. Marshall 1985: 157).

[228] Cic. *Cluent.* 130.

[229] See discussion by, *inter alia*, Mommsen 1887–8: III, 192–3, 532–3; Hill 1952: 212–14; M. I. Henderson 1963: 63–4; Wiseman 1970b: 71–2, 79–80; Nicolet 1974: 598–613; Brunt 1988: 210–11; Cloud 1992: 509.

[230] Cohen 1975: 278–9.   [231] Cic. *Cat.* 4.15; Nicolet 1974: 600–4.

long after they had ceased to be the constituent cavalry of the Roman state.[232] We know that each tribe had their own *tribuni aerarii*, and the jurors of the *lex Aurelia* were selected according to their tribes.[233] It may have been the case that only some of the *tribuni aerarii* had sufficient property to qualify for the equestrian census, in much the same way that some *apparitores* were also *equites*. In this case, Cicero would have had good grounds for supposing that at least some *tribuni aerarii* were *equites*.[234] However, an alternative, and more likely, proposition is that all *tribuni aerarii* did possess the equestrian census, but their ancient title made them an exclusive group of citizens within the larger *ordo equester*.[235] An *ordo* within an *ordo* was perfectly acceptable, as we have already discussed with reference to the *ordo* of *publicani* as the flower of the *ordo equester*. This conclusion corresponds with all the Ciceronian evidence. It certainly cannot be concluded that *all* citizens with the equestrian census but not the *equus publicus* were known as *tribuni aerarii*. Not only is there no inkling of this in our sources prior to 70 BC, but these men continued to be described, as they always had been, as *equites*.

---

[232] Hill 1952: 213. Note also the remarks of Crawford 2001: 432, that the *tribuni aerarii* 'must have been definable in terms other than that of a census level for the purpose of Roman legislation'.

[233] L. R. Taylor 1960: 53.

[234] Compare the suggestion of Hill 1952: 214, who proposes that not all *tribuni aerarii* had the *census equester*, only those on the juries.

[235] Thus Bleicken 1995: 38, 'innerhalb der Ritterschaft eine besondere Gruppe'.

3 | Questions of Status

Introduction: A Statue for L. Antonius

On 4 January 43 BC Cicero mounted the Caesarian *rostra* in the Roman forum to address the crowd of citizens summoned there by the tribune P. Apuleius.[1] From that platform he delivered the *Sixth Philippic*, which focused on the embassy that the senate had voted to send to M. Antonius. Cicero argued that the embassy was destined to fail because of the corrupt nature of Antonius and his supporters.[2] Antonius' henchmen included his own brother, L. Antonius, who had supervised the commission for the redistribution of *ager publicus* established in the previous year under the terms of the *lex Antonia agraria*.[3] This law was annulled on the day that Cicero gave his *Sixth Philippic*, so the orator took the opportunity to attack the various constituencies that had expressed their gratitude towards L. Antonius by erecting statues of him in prominent public locations. These included groups of military tribunes and bankers, as well as the members of the thirty-five tribes, who dedicated a gilt statue of L. Antonius in the *forum Romanum*.[4] The members of the *ordo equester* were equally complicit in this sycophantic display, much to Cicero's personal disgust:

Another one was erected by *equites Romani equo publico*: they likewise dedicated it 'to their patron'. Has there ever been anyone whom this order has adopted as its patron? If anyone should have been selected, it ought to have been me. But putting myself aside, did they ever choose a censor or a victorious general as their patron? 'He gave them land,' you say? Those who accepted it are despicable, he who gave it, shameful![5]

---

[1] For the conclusion that Cicero spoke from Caesar's *rostra*, see Manuwald 2007: 792.
[2] The context of the speech is thoroughly discussed by Manuwald 2007: 736–42.
[3] See Manuwald 2007: 574–6 on this law.   [4] Cic. *Phil.* 6.12, 14–15.
[5] Cic. *Phil.* 6.13: *altera ab equitibus Romanis equo publico: qui item ascribunt, 'patrono.' quem umquam iste ordo patronum adoptavit? si quemquam, debuit me. sed me omitto; quem censorem, quem imperatorem? agrum eis divisit. o sordidos qui acceperint, improbum qui dederit!*

Cicero was obviously insulted that he, after all his efforts on behalf of the *ordo equester*, was not chosen as their patron. Instead, the *equites* had been bought by the land distributed through the terms of the *lex Antonia agraria* of June 44 BC.[6] One of the most striking aspects of this speech, at least for our purposes, is that it records the first occasion on which *equites equo publico* came together as a corporate body to elect a patron and dedicate a statue in his honour.

Setting aside Cicero's own righteous indignation for the moment, it is worth considering how this acclamation was accomplished. In the above passage Cicero specifically notes that Antonius was hailed as the patron of the *equites equo publico*, while in the *Seventh Philippic* he calls Antonius the patron of the centuries of *equites Romani*.[7] This suggests that the honour could have been conferred through some sort of vote of the equestrian centuries meeting in the *comitia*.[8] Alternatively, there could have been an acclamation by the *equites* assembled in the fourteen rows at the Theatre of Pompey.[9] The success of such a measure would have depended on leading individuals inside and outside the *ordo equester* who had the clout and influence to organise, or stage-manage, the vote or acclamation. We know that such powerbrokers did exist. In 43 BC Cicero appealed to D. Iunius Brutus for his help in electing L. Lamia to the praetorship, 'since you have in your pocket the centuries of the *equites*, over which you have power' (*quoniam equitum centurias tenes inque iis regnas*).[10] But patronage, or leadership, of the *equites* (as opposed to electoral control) had always been informal, as when Atticus headed the equestrian delegation stationed on the *clivus Capitolinus* in 63 BC. Atticus, despite his prominence, largely eschewed such overt political actions, as we saw in the previous chapter. When, in 44 BC, C. Flavius asked him to lead all the *equites* contributing to a fund for Caesar's assassins, Atticus refused.[11] Cicero's own patronage – despite the immense political capital he expended on behalf of the *ordo*, and derived from them in return – was never acknowledged in such a permanent form as L. Antonius' statue.

What is remarkable about the acclamation of L. Antonius as the *equites*' patron, and the statue erected in his honour, is that it represented the first monumental manifestation of the concept of the equestrian order as a constituent body in the *res publica*, which, as we saw in the previous

---

[6] Manuwald 2007: 796.   [7] Cic. *Phil.* 7.16.

[8] Note that the statue dedicated by the thirty-five tribes was probably voted by the *comitia tributa* (Manuwald 2007: 788–9).

[9] See Rowe 2002: 77–81 on the growing importance of the theatre as an equestrian assembly.

[10] Cic. *Fam.* 11.16.3 [SB 434.3].   [11] Nep. *Att.* 8.3–4. For C. Flavius, see Nicolet 1974: 880–1.

chapter, featured so prominently in Cicero's political rhetoric. This chapter broadly covers the same chronological period as Chapter 2, but from a different angle. It first examines the consolidation of the *ordo equester* as an entity with its own status symbols and privileges, such as the right to wear the gold ring, don the tunic with the narrow stripe, and sit in the first fourteen rows of the theatre. It then proceeds to analyse the role that Italian *equites* played in the *res publica* following the Social War and the enfranchisement of the peninsula. Once again the Ciceronian material looms large in this discussion, as an example of the political discourse of the day. But we will also use inscriptions to analyse the extent to which Italians publicly identified themselves as members of the *ordo equester*. Finally, this chapter will analyse the developments of the triumviral period, which is often portrayed as an age of uncertainty as far as the acquisition and definition of equestrian status was concerned. It will be argued that this level of upheaval has been exaggerated, and that there was actually striking continuity in the definition of equestrian rank and the values of the *ordo* throughout this period, in which Rome transformed into a monarchical *res publica*.

The first century BC was in many ways the most pivotal period of the equestrian order's history, for it witnessed the gradual establishment of the *ordo*'s public status symbols, collective identity, and place within the *res publica* at large. As we discussed in the Introduction, status groups that fail to adopt a coherent ideological justification for their existence are not usually able to survive on a long-term basis. The *ordo equester* – despite being a heterogeneous assortment of businessmen, *publicani*, jurors, military officers, landowners, municipal magistrates, poets and playwrights – was given both cohesion and ideological impetus by adopting the symbols and values of the Republican cavalry, the original *equites*, alongside a range of new perquisites and *insignia*. This did not occur suddenly, but was the result of both gradual changes and specific pieces of legislation which offered the *equites* new privileges. The integration of the newly enfranchised Italian *equites* into the larger *ordo* likewise occurred incrementally over the course of the first century BC, as these men negotiated their new status within the Roman *res publica*, and its relationship to their lives and duties in their own *patriae*. We will see that military service was particularly important in forging connections between Italian communities and the Roman state. Many individual *equites* served as centurions, tribunes and prefects in the Roman army; they filled these state positions in addition to their other business, administrative or artistic interests. For the *equites* of Italian municipalities, officer commands were the most obviously 'Roman' aspect of their public identities, as shown by their honorific and funerary monuments. This demonstrates the continuing importance of the equestrian ideology of *virtus* and martial success in integrating wealthy elites into the *res publica*. The cumulative effect of these processes over the course of the first century BC resulted in the creation of a public equestrian identity which laid the foundations for the long-term continuance, survival and relevance of the *ordo* in the Roman world.

Status Symbols and Collective Identity

As equestrians became an *ordo* distinct from the senate and plebs in the late second century BC, they began to acquire their own symbols and social privileges.[12] Some of these, such as the adoption of the gold ring (*anulus aureus*), the ceremonial *trabea* and the tunic with the narrow stripe (*angustus clavus*), were the result of a slow process of evolution and social acceptance, as the new *ordo* adopted the symbols of the cavalry elite as a way of defining their public status. Other prerogatives, such as the reservation of the first fourteen rows (*XIV ordines*) in the theatre for *equites*, owed their creation to specific pieces of legislation. These privileges allowed members of the *ordo equester* to publicly demonstrate that their status was superior to that of the majority of Roman citizens. They also imposed a sense of collective unity on an *ordo* that was actually quite disparate in nature, since all Romans who were assessed by the censors as possessing the necessary property could claim to be *equites Romani*. The precise number of *equites* in the late Republic is unknown, and scholars have in the past offered a number of estimates, ranging from 5,000 to 10,000.[13] The literary evidence is exiguous and scattered. Plutarch states that nearly all the *equites* changed into mourning dress in a sign of solidarity with Cicero when he was being harassed by Clodius, and that he was often accompanied by 20,000 young men.[14] This seems a very high figure for the *equites* alone, and is probably exaggerated.[15] In the early Augustan period, we know that as many as 5,000 *equites equo publico* were eligible to march in the *transvectio equitum*. This is a more reliable figure, as it comes from the eyewitness report of Dionysius of

---

[12] For the use of status symbols to articulate juridical status at Rome, see Kolb 1977b: 239–41.
[13] See Jongman 1988: 193 (5,000); Scheidel 2006: 50 (10,000). Cf. Goldsmith 1984: 277, who estimates that there were 40,000 members of the *ordo* in the early empire.
[14] Plut. *Cic.* 31.1.
[15] Lintott 2008: 177 suggests that the figure includes both senators and *equites*.

Halicarnassus, but it would not include all the *equites* defined by their census rating.[16] Recent estimates derived from statistical analysis put the number of households with the equestrian census at 15,000 in 50 BC and 20,000–30,000 in the imperial period.[17] Ancient testimony for the deaths of *equites* is consonant with these estimates: 2,600 perished under Sulla; 3,000 at the Battle of Munda in 45 BC; and 2,000 in the proscriptions of the triumvirs.[18] Therefore, we can envisage the *ordo equester* of the Ciceronian period encompassing some 15,000 members. The new status symbols gave these *equites* an identity and collective purpose. They made an *eques Romanus* something more than a citizen who possessed 400,000 sesterces. The *equites* were publicly identified by their dress, personal adornment, and where they sat in the theatre, as a member of a prestigious *ordo* within the *res publica*.

(i) The *Anulus Aureus*

We will begin with the story of the *anulus aureus*. It is conventionally viewed as a symbol of the *ordo equester*, but how and when did it acquire this status? The process was actually very slow and gradual. In the Roman world a ring was regarded as a symbol of *ingenuitas*; the specific metal was a matter of personal choice, though according to Cassius Dio only senators and *equites* were permitted to wear gold.[19] In the late second century BC some senators, but by no means all, had adopted the gold ring. In 111 BC the praetor L. Calpurnius Piso broke his gold ring while serving in Spain and had a new one made for him, while C. Marius began to wear an *anulus aureus* during his third consulship in 103 BC.[20] At the time of the Social War, according to Pliny the Elder, many ex-praetors were still wearing rings made of iron rather than gold.[21] In a famous passage Pliny describes how the *anulus aureus* came to define the *ordo equester* as a distinct corporate body:

Rings distinguished the second *ordo* from the people, as soon as they began to be common items, just as the tunic distinguished the senators from those wearing rings. However, the tunic was a later development, since we find it commonly

---

[16] Dion. Hal. 6.13.4. See further Chapter 5.
[17] Kay 2014: 292–6 (15,000 households in 50 BC); Scheidel and Friesen 2009: 77 (20,000–30,000 *equites* in imperial period).
[18] App. *BC* 1.103 (Sulla); Ps.-Caesar, *Bell. Hisp.* 31 (Munda); App. *BC* 4.5 (triumvirs).
[19] Scholz 2005: 418; Dio 48.45.8.
[20] Calpurnius Piso: Cic. II *Verr.* 4.56. Marius: Pliny the Elder, *NH* 33.21.
[21] Pliny the Elder, *NH* 33.21.

noted that even heralds wore the tunic with the wider purple stripe, as in the case of the father of L. Aelius Stilo, who was dubbed 'Praeconinus' on account of this. But rings clearly inserted this third *ordo* between the people and the senators. The title of *eques*, previously bestowed on military men, is now allocated on the basis of wealth.[22]

Unfortunately, Pliny's idiosyncratic account cannot be read as a straightforward historical narrative, since he used the spread of the gold rings from *nobiles* to senators and then to *equites* to illustrate the diffusion of luxury throughout the Roman world.[23] Moreover, as Wallace-Hadrill notes, Pliny never informs us exactly when the *anulus aureus* became a symbol of the *ordo equester* (an omission which has frustrated Roman historians).[24] His discussion of the purple broad stripe (*latus clavus*) can be situated some time in the late second century BC, since the *eques* L. Aelius Stilo Praeconinus lived around 154–74 BC.[25] What the Plinian version of events does show is that the *anulus aureus* was gradually adopted outside senatorial ranks during the late Republic.

Cicero's *In Verrem* provides valuable contemporary evidence for the significance of the *anulus aureus* in the 70s BC. The orator accused Verres of granting gold rings improperly during his governorship of Sicily by seizing them from the local populace and awarding them to his cronies instead. Cicero says that it had been the custom of Roman *imperatores* to grant gold rings to their *scribae* after great victories as a reward for their services.[26] Verres had sullied that tradition by awarding his *scriba* Maevius a gold ring after he had plundered the wealth of the Sicilian population, rather than following a battle.[27] It is important to note that Cicero does not question the prerogative of *imperatores* to grant the *anulus aureus* to their officials, merely the fact that Verres made a mockery of this action.[28] Cicero does not explicitly say that Maevius became an *eques* as a result of Verres' gesture. Instead, he referred to the *anulus* as the distinction of

---

[22] Pliny the Elder, *NH* 33.29: *anuli distinxere alterum ordinem a plebe, ut semel coeperant esse celebres, sicut tunica ab anulis senatum. quamquam et hoc sero, vulgoque purpura latiore tunicae usos invenimus etiam praecones, sicut patrem L. Aelii Stilonis Praeconini ob id cognominati. sed anuli plane tertium ordinem mediumque plebei et patribus inseruere, ac quod antea militares equi nomen dederant, hoc nunc pecuniae indices tribuunt.*

[23] Wallace-Hadrill 1990a: 90–1, 2008: 349–53.   [24] Wallace-Hadrill 2008: 352.

[25] Nicolet 1974: 765–6.

[26] *Scribae* were one group of many among the *apparitores*, the free public servants of the Roman state. See Purcell 1983.

[27] Cic. II *Verr.* 3.185–7. See also II *Verr.* 1.157, 2.29, 3.175–6.

[28] Nicolet 1974: 935; Bleicken 1995: 51. Improper patronage or enrichment of *scribae* and other *apparitores* was the mark of a corrupt senator (see Purcell 1983: 132 n. 34 for examples).

a 'brave man' (*virum fortem*) and a 'proof of valour' (*testem virtutis*).[29] The equation of the *anulus aureus* with the *ordo equester* may nevertheless have been apparent to Cicero's audience. Elsewhere in the *In Verrem* he refers to unscrupulous *scribae* who bought their way into the upper echelons of Roman society:

Call back those honourable secretaries for me, if you please: don't trot out those men who have scraped together a bit of money from the gifts of their favourites or the donations of actors. When they have purchased a *decuria*, they say that they have moved from the first order of the theatre crowds into the second order of the state.[30]

The implication of Cicero's jibe is that men of humble background could acquire money in disreputable ways, and purchase membership in a *decuria scribarum*. They then boasted that they had entered the *ordo equester*. It was, of course, completely above board for Roman citizens to buy their place in a *decuria*, and there were many *equites* in the colleges.[31] Cicero himself praised his own *scribae* in Sicily as 'truly modest men' (*frugalissimos homines*), and acknowledges the *ordo scribarum* itself as 'upright' (*honestus*).[32] He reserved his odium for the *scribae* who received money in a dishonourable fashion, or who used their influence in an improper way. This can be seen in his characterisation of L. Papirius Potamo, who had been a *scriba* on the staff of Verres' predecessor in Sicily, Q. Caecilius Niger, but had continued in the service of his new governor.[33] Cicero rather sarcastically described Potamo as a 'strict fellow of those old-school equestrian ways' (*hominem severum ex vetere illa equestri disciplina*), implying that he was in fact nothing of the sort, but a new entrant to the equestrian order.[34]

Did the grant of the *anulus aureus* alone make Maevius an *eques*? The answer must be no, since a Roman citizen would still have had to possess the equestrian property qualification.[35] This would not have been hard to come by in Maevius' case, since Verres had siphoned off two-fiftieths (4 per cent) of the funds owed to Sicilian farmers for the *scriba*'s personal use.[36] Maevius' property would have to be assessed by the censors in order to confirm that he met the census requirement, enabling him to be

---

[29] Cic. II *Verr.* 3.187.
[30] Cic. II *Verr.* 3.184: *ad eos me scribas revoca, si placet, noli hos colligere, qui nummulis corrogatis de nepotum donis ac de scaenicorum corollariis, cum decuriam emerunt, ex primo ordine explosorum in secundum ordinem civitatis se venisse dicunt.*
[31] Wiseman 1971: 73; Purcell 1983: 138–9; Badian 1989: 601.   [32] Cic. II. *Verr.* 3.182–3.
[33] Cic. *Caec.* 29, II *Verr.* 3.154.   [34] Cic. II. *Verr.* 3.137; Nicolet 1974: 972–3.
[35] Mommsen 1887–8: III, 518; Stein 1927: 35–45; Badian 1989: 600.   [36] Cic. II *Verr.* 3.181.

officially considered an *eques Romanus*. Cassius Dio understood that 'a man who possesses *imperium*' (ὁ τὸ κράτος ἔχων) could award the gold ring to freedmen as a sign of their *ingenuitas*, which would subsequently allow them enter the *ordo equester*.[37] This is evidently what occurred in the case of the actor Q. Roscius Gallus, who was awarded the *anulus aureus* by Sulla, probably in 81 or 80 BC, though no ancient source specifically says that he was made an equestrian.[38] The grant of the *anulus aureus* in and of itself was an honour from a Roman magistrate, rather than representing automatic elevation into the *ordo equester* (however much it may have been interpreted as such by contemporary Romans).[39]

Two anecdotes from the life of C. Iulius Caesar demonstrate that potential *equites* still had to possess the requisite property qualification. In 49 BC, shortly after crossing the Rubicon, Caesar made a speech to his troops in which he frequently gestured to the ring on his left hand as a way of referring to the affront that had been done to his *dignitas*. Most of the soldiers, however, could not actually hear what he was saying, and thought that he had promised them 'the right of wearing the ring with 400,000 sesterces' (*ius anulorum cum milibus quadrigenis*) which would give them 'the equestrian census qualification' (*equestres census*).[40] A few years later, at Caesar's victory games of 46 BC, the dictator gave the playwright Decimus Laberius 500,000 sesterces and the *anulus aureus* as a way of confirming his equestrian rank.[41] L. Antonius Balbus subsequently imitated this action at Gades in Spain, though he only awarded the actor Herennius Gallus the *anulus aureus*.[42] Whatever the precise legal and juridical technicalities, the gold ring became popularly regarded as the symbol of equestrian status par excellence. The most explicit contemporary reference to this comes in the *Satires* of the poet Q. Horatius Flaccus (better known as Horace), who was himself a member of the *ordo equester*.[43] In *Satire* 2.7, conventionally dated to around 30 BC, the slave Davus refers to Horace changing his appearance for a night on the town:

---

[37] Dio 48.45.8–9. Dio refers the reader to an earlier discussion of the *anulus aureus* in a now lost portion of the *Roman History*.

[38] Macrob. *Sat.* 3.14.13. Cicero's statement in *Pro Roscio Comoedo* 23 that Roscius refused money for his services for ten years has been interpreted to mean that this was forced on him because of his equestrian rank. Cf. Lintott 2008: 61–3.

[39] Reinhold 1971: 279; Nicolet 1974: 95–6, 141; Demougin 1988: 48.

[40] Suet. *Iul.* 33. The expression *ius anulorum* is frequently found in authors of the imperial period (Kolb 1977b: 253 n. 57).

[41] Suet. *Iul.* 39.2; Sen. *Controv.* 7.3.9; Macrob. *Sat.* 2.7.1–3.   [42] Cic. *Fam.* 10.32.2 [SB 415.2].

[43] L. R. Taylor 1925; Nicolet 1974: 914–15; D. Armstrong 1986.

When you cast off these status symbols, the equestrian ring
and your Roman dress, and you turn from a juror into a base
Dama, your sweet-smelling head covered with a cloak,
are you not that person you pretend to be?[44]

The term 'equestrian ring' (*anulus equester*) is found nowhere else in Latin
literature, but its importance as one of the outward representations of
Horace's status is unambiguous.[45] The act of removing the ring and the
toga transformed Horace – or at least his poetic doppelganger – from an
eques to a 'Dama', a common slave name in the Roman world.[46] It shows
that the *anulus aureus* was accepted as one of the distinguishing features of
the equestrian order, even if there was no juridical basis for this
assumption.

The emphasis Cicero placed on the inappropriate way in which Verres
distributed the gold rings to the *scribae* and others in his entourage
suggests a significant degree of anxiety about unworthy men gaining access
to the *ordo equester*, or at least being permitted to wear its status symbols.[47]
As Hopkins has pointed out, an elite group can only be exclusive when
birth is the sole qualification for entry; once other 'criteria of achievement'
are introduced, new men are able to gain membership.[48] This was true of
both the *ordo equester* and the *ordo senatorius* to different degrees. Both
were open to new men, but admission to the senate could at least be tightly
regulated through election to appropriate magistracies. The *ordo equester*
did have a membership qualification, which would have to be assessed by
the censors, but if the census failed to be performed on a regular basis, as
occurred in the first century BC, even qualified *equites* would find it
difficult to have their membership legitimated.[49] Theoretically anyone
could – and did – claim to be an *eques Romanus* by wearing the *anulus
aureus* and other *insignia*, thus giving themselves a higher status than that
to which they were entitled.[50] The high importance that Cicero places on
Verres' abuses of the system is indicative of the growing collective pride of
equestrians as collective group, a real *ordo*. The *anulus aureus* thus functioned as an outward symbol of equestrian unity, but one whose contested
status exposed social tensions.

---

[44] Hor. *Sat.* 2.7.53–6: *tu cum proiectis insignibus, anulo equestri* | *Romanoque habitu, prodis ex
iudice Dama* | *turpis, oderatum caput obscurante lacerna,* | *non es quod simulas?*
[45] L. R. Taylor 1925: 162–3; D. Armstrong 1986: 257–8.
[46] On Horace's poetic persona, see D. Armstrong 1986: 259.
[47] Verres' grants of the rings appear in Cic. II *Verr.* 1.157, 2.29, 3.176, 3.185, 3.187.
[48] Hopkins 1965: 16–17.   [49] This is discussed in greater detail later in this chapter.
[50] Rothfus 2010: 437.

(ii) Equestrian Dress

Members of the *ordo equester* could also be distinguished by their dress, both that worn on ceremonial occasions and in everyday life. The first of these, the *trabea*, a toga with a scarlet band, was a parade uniform worn by *equites equo publico* during the *transvectio equitum*.[51] It was thus originally, like the *anulus aureus*, a symbol of patrician, and later senatorial, identity. However, after the separation of the *ordo equester* from the senate in the late second century BC, the *trabea* became the ceremonial uniform of the *equites*.[52] It was, however, technically confined to those who participated in the yearly parade, that is, the *equites equo publico*. All *equites Romani* were permitted to wear the tunic with the narrow stripe (*angustus clavus*), which distinguished them from senators, who wore a tunic with the broad stripe (*latus clavus*). It is difficult to say precisely when this differentiation came into being: as we saw in Chapter 1, the *latus clavus* had probably become standard senatorial dress by the end of the second century BC. The first evidence for the *angustus clavus* comes in the first century BC.[53] According to Cassius Dio, in 59 BC Cicero laid down his senatorial clothing and instead wore equestrian dress as a sign of humility when he courted supporters while being harassed by Clodius.[54] Later, in 56 BC, the senators collectively set aside their senatorial garb and wore equestrian clothing as a sign of mourning after a year of civil strife.[55] Although Dio does not specifically refer to the *angustus clavus*, it was a commonly accepted mourning ritual for senators to cast aside their *latus clavus*.[56] The *angustus clavus* was certainly known to Varro, who refers to it in his work *De Lingua Latina*, written in the 40s BC, and literary sources show that it was definitely recognised as equestrian dress in the early Augustan period.[57] The archaeological evidence, however, demonstrates that the *angustus clavus* was worn by *equites* much earlier in the first century BC. The famous statue known as *L'Arringatore* (The Orator), now in the Museo Archeologico Nazionale in Florence, dated around 80–60 BC, is of prime importance here. The statue shows Aulus Metellus, a member of the local aristocracy, wearing his tunic with the *angustus clavus* and

---

[51] Dion. Hal. 6.13.4; Val. Max. 2.2.9; Gabelmann 1977: 326–7. By the third century BC the *trabea* was not a tunic, but a longer garment, like a toga (Gabelmann 1977: 346).

[52] Gabelmann 1977: 367–9; Kolb 1977b: 248; Wrede 1988: 384.

[53] Mommsen 1887–8: III, 514; Stein 1927: 48–9.   [54] Dio 38.14.7.   [55] Dio 40.46.1.

[56] Edmondson 2008: 29–31.

[57] Varro, *LL* 9.79; Ovid, *Tristia* 5.10; Vell. Pat. 2.88.2; Suet. *Aug.* 73. See Demougin 1988: 778–9; Rothfus 2010: 437 n. 30. The adjectives *angusticlavius* (Suet. *Otho* 10.1) and its Greek equivalent στενόσημος (Arr. *Epict.* 1.24.12) are very rare.

sporting the *anulus aureus* on his left hand (Figure 3.1).[58] There is little reason to doubt that this was accepted as the dress of *equites Romani* in the age of Cicero, and served as an outward sign of membership of the *ordo*.

(iii) The *XIV Ordines*

These status symbols were accompanied by a new privilege that publicly demarcated *equites* as the second order of the *res publica*. In 67 BC the tribune L. Roscius Otho successfully passed a law (the *lex Roscia theatralis*) reserving the first fourteen rows (*XIV ordines*) in the theatre, immediately behind the orchestra, for members of the *ordo equester*.[59] The earliest reference to the law comes in Cicero's *Pro Murena*, delivered in 63 BC:

Lucius Otho, that steadfast man, my true friend, not only restored public standing to the equestrian order, but also public entertainment. And for that reason his legislation which pertains to the *ludi*, is the most gratifying of all laws, because it restored the enjoyment of pleasure to that most upright order with its brilliance.[60]

This passage does not specifically say that the first fourteen rows were reserved for the *ordo equester*, but that much is apparent from other references to the *lex Roscia*.[61] Cicero's praise for Roscius' initiative in marking out privileged seats for the *equites* would have appealed to the equestrian members of the jury he addressed during his defence of Murena.[62] The *lex Roscia theatralis* was much less well received by the people as a whole, however. In a separate incident, also dated to 63 BC, the theatre audience hissed at and insulted Roscius, who was probably presiding over the *ludi Apollinares* as urban praetor at the time.[63] The people only changed their behaviour after a speech from Cicero, unfortunately now lost, which persuaded them of the error of their ways.[64]

Cicero's language in the *Pro Murena* has prompted debate as to whether Otho's initiative in reserving seats for the *equites* was an original idea. He twice uses the word 'restored' (*restituit* and *est restitutus*), which has led some scholars to suggest that the equestrians had originally been allocated the fourteen rows some time in the second century BC, but that this

---

[58] Demougin 1988: 781–2. For the narrow band on the tunic, see Granger-Taylor 1982: 7.

[59] For discussions, see Stein 1927: 21–30; E. Rawson 1987: 102–5; Demougin 1988: 796–802.

[60] Cic. *Mur.* 40: *L. Otho, vir fortis, meus necessarius, equestri ordini restituit non solum dignitatem sed etiam voluptatem. itaque lex haec quae ad ludos pertinet est omnium gratissima, quod honestissimo ordini cum splendore fructus quoque iucunditatis est restitutus.*

[61] Cic. *Phil.* 2.44; Asc. 79 C; Livy, *Per.* 99.   [62] Fantham 2013: 141.

[63] Plut. *Cic.* 13.2–4 (wrongly placing the *lex Roscia* in 63 BC); Pliny the Elder, *NH* 7.117. For Otho's position as urban praetor, see Ryan 1997.

[64] Cic. *Att.* 2.1.3 [SB 21.3].

Figure 3.1: Statue of *L'Arringatore*, Museo Archeologico Nazionale Florence

privilege had later been rescinded, probably by Sulla.[65] However, Cicero does not say that the seats were restored to the *equites*, but rather 'public

[65] For this argument, see Mommsen 1887–8: III, 519–20; Hill 1952: 160; Nicolet 1974: 99; Badian 1975: 92; Brunt 1988: 159.

standing' (*dignitatem*), 'public entertainment' (*voluptatem*) and the 'enjoyment of pleasure' (*fructus ... iucunditatis*).[66] Most sources emphasise the
revolutionary nature of Roscius' initiative, with the exception of Velleius
Paterculus, who states boldly that 'he restored the seats in the theatre to the
equites' (*equitibus in theatro loca restituit*).[67] This, however, should be
dismissed, since the ancient sources always refer to the *lex Roscia theatralis*,
or its Augustan successor, the *lex Iulia theatralis*, as enshrining the principle of the fourteen rows, rather than an earlier law that Roscius revised.
It may have been, as Wiseman suggested, that the allocation of these seats
to *equites* was originally customary, and it was up to the presiding magistrate to enforce the arrangements prior to Roscius' law.[68] The reaction of
the plebs in 63 BC certainly indicates that the reservation of the best seats
for high-status citizens engendered a certain amount of resentment, as had
been the case when the senators were first allocated seating in 194 BC.
Following Wiseman, the *lex Roscia* could therefore be seen to 'restore'
equestrian *dignitas* which had been affronted in the past.[69]

The *lex Roscia theatralis* must have been an incredibly complicated piece
of legislation.[70] We can do no more than attempt to establish some of its
basic principles using scattered references in the ancient sources, but much
remains uncertain. There has been debate as to whether the primary
qualification for the *XIV ordines* was the *equus publicus* (in which case it
was a very restricted privilege, only for the 1,800 citizens who were enrolled
in the equestrian centuries), or whether eligibility was open to all *equites
Romani*. The literary evidence demonstrates that it was the definition of the
equestrian census that prevailed.[71] When Caesar led Decimus Laberius to
the fourteen rows after granting him the gold ring and 500,000 sesterces in
46 BC, and L. Cornelius Balbus did the same for Herennius Gallus in Gades
only a few years later, there is no indication that these men had been
granted the *equus publicus*.[72] Horace's *First Epistle*, dated to 20/19 BC,

[66] *OLD* s.v. *restituo* 8, with the dative of the person to whom something is restored, in this case *equestri ordini* and *honestissimo ordini*.
[67] Livy, *Per.* 99; Juv. *Sat.* 3.159; Plut. *Cic.* 13.2; Dio 36.42.1; cf. Vell. Pat. 2.32.3. For the argument, see Wiseman 1970b: 80 and 1973: 194–5.
[68] Scamuzzi 1969: 270; Wiseman 1973: 194–6, based on Asc. 78 C, who refers to the 'confirmation' (*confirmavit*) of the privilege.
[69] Wiseman 1973: 195–6.   [70] Crawford 2001: 433.
[71] See Stein 1927: 22–6; Badian 1972: 84; E. Rawson 1987: 102. Wiseman 1970b: 72, 80 originally argued for the *equus publicus* as the major criterion, but subsequently revised his opinion (see Wiseman 1973: 195). Cicero only ever speaks of *equites* being defined by their census (Bleicken 1995: 45). Cf. Linderski 1977: 58; E. Rawson 1987: 102; Demougin 1988: 797–9, who argue that the census was not sufficient in and of itself.
[72] See p. 116 above.

conclusively demonstrates the importance of the census qualification for theatre seating.[73]

> You possess a good head, the right character, eloquence and honour,
> but you're a few thousand sesterces short of 400,000;
> so you'll be one of the masses.[74]

This is the first securely dated piece of evidence for the census qualification being set at 400,000 sesterces. Without this fortune, a Roman citizen would be squatting in the equestrian seats contrary to law.[75] The *lex Roscia* made specific provisions for excluding former *equites* who no longer possessed the equestrian census from the fourteen rows. We know from the accusations made by Cicero about M. Antonius in the *Second Philippic* that there was a special area in the theatre for these bankrupt *equites*:

But it was a mark of your own brand of cockiness that you sat in the fourteen rows, since a designated section had been set aside for bankrupts under the terms of the *lex Roscia*, regardless of whether a man became bankrupt because of his own failings, or mere bad luck.[76]

This is the only reference to the 'designated section' (*certus locus*) for bankrupts in the theatre, but that is not sufficient grounds for disregarding Cicero's testimony.[77] Indeed, it confirms that the census was the primary qualification for sitting in the fourteen rows under the *lex Roscia*, and *equites* who no longer possessed the set amount, even if it had been through no fault of their own, had to sit elsewhere.

It has sometimes been suggested that the *lex Roscia* also reserved the first two rows for military tribunes and ex-tribunes.[78] Horace's *Fourth Epode*, written in the 30s BC, focuses on a freedman who acquired a substantial fortune, rose to the rank of *tribunus militum*, and was eager to show off his new status.[79] Porphyrio's commentary on the poem states that the *lex*

---

[73] See R. Mayer 1994: 10–11 on the date.

[74] Hor. *Epist.* 1.1.57–9: *est animus tibi, sunt mores, est lingua fidesque,* | *sed quadringentis sex septem milia desunt:* | *plebs eris.* For the translation of *sex septem* as 'a few', see R. Mayer 1994: 100.

[75] Horace mentions Roscius explicitly in *Epist.* 1.62. For the same view from the imperial period, see Juv. *Sat.* 3.155, referring to men sitting in the equestrian seats 'whose property is not sufficient under the law' (*cuius res legi non sufficit*).

[76] Cic. *Phil.* 2.44: *illud tamen audaciae tuae quod sedisti in quattuordecim ordinibus, cum esset lege Roscia decoctoribus certus locus constitutus, quamuis quis fortunae uitio, non suo decoxisset.*

[77] Ramsay 2003: 227. Cic. *Att.* 4.7.2 [SB 77.2] contains an enigmatic reference a Greek called Apollonius who has claimed the right of going bankrupt afforded to *equites*. See Shackleton Bailey 1965b: 180.

[78] Stein 1927: 23–4; E. Rawson 1987: 103–4.

[79] For the date and context of the poem, see Mankin 1995: 99–100.

Roscia reserved the first two rows (*duo primi ordines*) for military tribunes.[80] However, the only evidence for the reservation of these first two rows for military tribunes comes from Porphyrio and another scholiast, Psuedo-Acro.[81] Mankin has cogently pointed out that there is no other explicit attestation of this privilege, and it appears to be the interpretation of these later scholiasts based on the poem itself.[82] We have evidence of *equites* who held a post in the vigintivirate sitting alongside tribunes. The poet P. Ovidius Naso (better known as Ovid) was a *decemvir stlitibus iudicandis*. He recalls in his *Fasti* a conversation he had at the *ludi Megalenses* with a *tribunus militum* who was sitting beside him.[83] This shows that the first two rows were not exclusively reserved for tribunes. Even if one argued that the same privilege had been extended to members of the vigintivirate, the whole notion of subdividing the equestrian seating goes against the concept of the *ordo equester* as a united group.[84] We know of no comparable division for the senatorial seats in the theatre or other public entertainment venues either, which suggests that none was enforced.[85]

The *lex Roscia* marked an important stage in defining the collective identity of the new *ordo equester*. The privilege of possessing the *equus publicus* and riding in the *transvectio equitum* was only accorded to a small minority of *equites* enrolled in the equestrian centuries. But now all equestrians were distinguished, and united, by a perquisite which publicly separated them from the populace at large. The *lex Roscia* was undoubtedly a long and complicated law, but we can be certain that the qualification for sitting in the fourteen rows was the *census equester*, probably of 400,000 sesterces, with bankrupt *equites* specifically excluded. Sitting together in the first fourteen rows, wearing their *anulus aureus* and tunic with the *angustus clavus*, the *equites* represented a distinct and privileged social group. The equestrians had no formal meeting place, no official leader, but in the theatre they could be a united *ordo*.

---

[80] Porphyrio on Hor. *Epod.* 4.15.
[81] Though this is accepted by E. Rawson 1987: 103–4; Demougin 1988: 509.
[82] Mankin 1995: 106.   [83] Ovid, *Fasti* 4.383–4.
[84] Thus the bankrupt *equites* were explicitly denied the right to sit in the fourteen rows, rather than being assigned a specific area in the *XIV ordines*. I am grateful to one of the anonymous referees for their comments on this matter.
[85] This changed in the late empire, when specific seating for ex-consuls is attested. See Chapter 8.

Cicero's Italy

The emerging cohesiveness of the *ordo equester*, as represented by its status symbols and social privileges, occurred alongside a significant increase in the number of citizens holding equestrian rank. This was the result of the enfranchisement of Italy following the Social War of 90–88 BC. Equestrian status was fairly limited in Italy prior to this period, since it could only be held by those Italians who had already been granted citizenship. Roman citizenship was generally bestowed as a benefaction to individuals or specific groups, such as citizens or magistrates of a town, or military units.[86] For example, Arpinum, the *patria* of Marius and Cicero, had been awarded citizenship in 303 BC. The ancestors of these two prominent statesmen are classic examples of equestrians among the Italian aristocracy, dubbed the *domi nobiles* ('nobles in their own community'), to distinguish them from the Roman nobility.[87] Individual grants of citizenship are attested only by isolated references in the literary sources. For example, L. Cossinius of Tibur was rewarded with Roman citizenship for a successful prosecution under the terms of the *lex de repetundis* some time before the Social War, and his homonymous son went on to become an *eques Romanus*.[88] These and other scattered examples provide our limited prosopographical evidence for Italian *equites* before the 80s BC: there is no substantial epigraphic basis from which to construct statistical arguments, as there is for the imperial period.[89] It is clear, however, that neither Roman citizenship nor equestrian rank was widespread among the upper echelons of Italian society prior to the Social War.[90]

The vast majority of attested Italian *equites* date from the years after 90 BC, when the *lex Iulia de civitate* and subsequent legislation extended citizenship throughout Italy south of the River Po.[91] Between the censuses of 86/85 and 70/69 BC, the Roman citizen population more than doubled to 910,000.[92] The *domi nobiles* from Italian *municipia* and Roman colonies

---

[86] For citizenship in Roman and Latin colonies, see Brunt 1971: 538–44.

[87] Citizenship: Livy 10.1. Arpinum: Nicolet 1974: 943–5 (Marius), 1052–7 (Tullii Cicerones). The term *domi nobiles* comes from Cic. *Clu.* 23 (see Nicolet 1974: 388).

[88] Cic. *Balb.* 53–4; Nicolet 1974: 855–6.   [89] Nicolet 1974: 406–7.

[90] The idea that Roman citizenship was automatically granted to all Latin magistrates from the 120s BC onwards, or at least before the Social War (Wiseman 1971: 17–18, 89; Sherwin-White 1973: 111–12), has had to be abandoned. See Mouritsen 1998: 99–108, who suggests that the extension of citizenship to these magistrates dates to the late first century BC. Bispham 2007: 128–31 also modifies the traditional view by arguing that Latin magistrates possessed *provocatio*, but not citizenship, in the 120s.

[91] For the laws of enfranchisement, see Sherwin-White 1973: 150–5; Bispham 2007: 161–87.

[92] Wiseman 1970a: 65–6; Brunt 1971: 91–9.

who possessed the necessary property qualification would have been rated by the censors as *equites Romani*. This can be seen in the case of P. Caesius of Ravenna, who was made a citizen by Cn. Pompeius Strabo in 89 BC, and subsequently became an *eques Romanus*.[93] It is not known how many of these citizens were elevated into the more exclusive centuries of *equites equo publico*.[94] The enfranchisement of Italy meant that the wealthiest *domi nobiles* were now eligible to enter the equestrian and senatorial orders and to play their part in the political life of Rome, if they chose to do so.

Where did Italian *equites* come from in the first century BC? It is evident that members of the *ordo equester* were not evenly distributed throughout the peninsula. Even after the Social War, most *equites* still originated in the central regions of Italy, such as Rome and Latium, Campania, Umbria and Picenum.[95] Etruria, on the western side of the peninsula, is strikingly underrepresented in the prosopographical evidence, and there is only a handful of *equites* found north of the River Arno, in towns such as Placentia, Cremona and Verona.[96] There is also a significant dearth of *equites* in the south, particularly in Lucania and Bruttium, but also in Apulia and Calabria. Since the vast majority of *equites* are attested only in literary sources, mainly the works of Cicero, some level of distortion is to be expected.[97] But the general pattern can also be explained by the process of municipalisation in the first century. We know of eight *equites* from Larinum thanks to Cicero's *Pro Cluentio*. It therefore stands out as a prominent outpost of equestrian membership in northern Apulia, where *equites* are otherwise thin on the ground. But this is not entirely distorted by the Ciceronian evidence: Larinum was one of only a handful of *municipia* in this central Adriatic region of Italy, so it is only natural that it had a significant number of *equites*.[98] The regions of Lucania and Bruttium were not heavily municipalised either, and a mere two *equites* can be found in Rhegium from the toe of Italy. In south-western Italy it is only Brundisium and Canusium that turn up two *equites* each.[99] It is not

---

[93] Cic. *Balb.* 50; Gruen 1974: 382.

[94] Wiseman 1971: 7, 123–4, 136. Demougin 1983: 280 emphasises that these municipal equestrians encompassed a broad range of individuals, with varying wealth and property holdings. For the equestrian centuries, see Wiseman 1970a: 70–1.

[95] Nicolet 1974: 1098–9.   [96] See the maps in Nicolet 1974: Appendix III.

[97] Nicolet 1974: 1099. The same pattern is largely reflected for the imperial period (Patterson 2006: 195).

[98] Bispham 2007: 407.

[99] For patterns of municipalisation, see Bispham 2007: 407–8, 462–4. The evidence for numbers of *equites* comes from Nicolet 1974: Appendix III.

surprising, therefore, that *equites* constituted a privileged elite among the wider class of *domi nobiles* in Italy.[100]

The extent to which Italians actually did participate in the Roman assemblies and the political arena in general has been the subject of considerable debate. Some scholars, relying largely on Cicero's testimony – as indeed we all must – have emphasised the importance of the Italian vote in elections.[101] However, more recently, Mouritsen has taken a more sceptical view, arguing that Cicero is a special case, as a new man who concertedly, and perhaps exceptionally, solicited support from all sections of society, including the Italian *domi nobiles*.[102] Mouritsen proposed that Italian notables only tended to participate actively in Roman politics if specifically courted by Roman magistrates, if the issue at stake particularly affected them, or if they lived close enough to make the journey.[103] This is a sensible conclusion, given that the decades after the Social War were a period of adaptation and negotiation: not all newly enfranchised Roman citizens, even those granted high status, would have necessarily identified with, or wanted to play a role in, the Roman *res publica* itself, the way Cicero did.[104] Following Mouritsen's lead, I will argue that Italian *equites* embraced Rome gradually, when it suited their own interests.[105] However, the Ciceronian evidence still has a significant role to play in shaping our understanding of the relationship between Italian *equites* and the state. As explored in the previous chapter, it is necessary to harness Cicero's works for the information they provide about his contribution to the wider political discourse.[106] He envisioned a world in which new Italian *equites* from the municipalities could now take their rightful place within the Roman *res publica*, without forsaking their own *patria*.[107] This vision was somewhat ahead of its time, but it must have appealed to at least

---

[100] The basic qualification of a decurion was 100,000 sesterces, well below that of an *eques Romanus*. See Nicolet 1974: 400–5, who bases his argument on the relatively narrow class of *equites equo publico*. But it is still likely to be true even if (as we have argued), *equites Romani* included all citizens with the requisite property qualification.

[101] For example, L. R. Taylor 1949: 30–1; Wiseman 1971: 123–42.

[102] Mouritsen 1998: 96–9, 2001: 115–25. See also Yakobson 1999: 45, 61.

[103] On this last point, see also Millar 1998: 28–34, 211 and Dench 2005: 131 on the potential ability of Italians to make an impact, if they did want to exercise their vote, though they had to travel to Rome to do so.

[104] Salmon 1972: 75–8; Lomas 2004: 116.

[105] This accords with the politically conservative nature of the *equites* in general (Meier 1966: 68–9).

[106] Dench 2005: 174 makes the important point that Cicero provides us with an idea of what was 'contested and controversial' in his lifetime.

[107] Note famous statement of Cicero that citizens from the Italian municipalities have two *patriae* (*Leg.* 2.5).

some members of Cicero's audience for him to deploy it frequently in his speeches.

Municipal *equites* could choose to travel to Rome to cast their vote in elections or to lend support to their fellow townspeople in the law courts.[108] It was less common to make the journey to vote on laws, which suggests that their interests were focused on promoting local men and protecting municipal interests at Rome rather than shaping the *res publica* itself.[109] Both these motivations are brought to dramatic life in Cicero's *Pro Plancio*, which, as we saw in Chapter 2, was a speech delivered in defence of Cn. Plancius, who was accused of electoral bribery. Cicero successfully argued that it was quite natural for men of equestrian stock like Plancius to be elected to magistracies at Rome. The wide electoral support they received, which included voters from their home communities, made bribery unnecessary, he claimed.[110] In this speech Cicero drew attention to representatives from Plancius' home town of Atina present in the courtroom:

This gathering of men that you now see before you, jurors, dressed in mourning costume and grieving, presents itself as a suppliant to you. There are many *equites Romani* and many *tribunii aerarii* present, for we sent the ordinary people, who were all present at the elections, out of the courtroom. What strength, what *dignitas* did they bring to his campaign?[111]

Cicero proceeded to elaborate on this point in considerable detail. He demonstrated that Plancius not only benefited from the electoral support of the citizens of Atina, but also citizens of nearby communities, including Arpinum, Sora, and Casinum, whose representatives were likewise in the courtroom.[112] This was a striking display of regional municipal solidarity, which, as Bispham points out, cannot be mere rhetoric on Cicero's part: his sentiments would not have been convincing if citizens from these communities had not genuinely turned out to vote for Plancius in the aedilician elections.[113]

---

[108] Millar 1998: 29; Bispham 2007: 425–6; van der Blom 2010: 44–6.   [109] Millar 1998: 30.

[110] Cic. *Planc.* 18–23; Yakobson 1999: 97–8.

[111] Cic. *Planc.* 21: *quam quidem nunc multitudinem videtis, iudices, in squalore et luctu supplicem vobis. hi tot equites Romani, tot tribuni aerarii – nam plebem a iudicio dimisimus, quae cuncta comitiis adfuit – quid roboris, quid dignitatis huius petitioni attulerunt?*

[112] Cic. *Planc.* 21–2. Cf. Mouritsen 2001: 31, who suggests that the actual numbers of voters involved were quite small.

[113] Bispham 2007: 431–4, esp. 433. See also, on similar lines, van der Blom 2010: 45–6. Cf. Mouritsen 1998: 96–7, 2001: 119–20, who reads this as an exceptional case.

The support for Plancius also reveals the importance of *vicinitas* –
connection with one's immediate neighbours – in dictating involvement
in Roman affairs. Men did not travel to Rome simply to support a fellow
Italian; they had to be linked in some deeper way. Cicero's own career
shows that he took specific cases on behalf of Italian clients because they or
their home towns had connections with his own *patria* of Arpinum.[114]
The importance of *vicinitas* in shaping loyalties and coteries can be seen in
the list of advisers on the *consilium* of Cn. Pompeius Strabo at Asculum
during the Social War in 89 BC. The council consisted of five legates,
a quaestor, sixteen military tribunes, thirty-three *equites* who did not hold
a specific post, and four *centuriones primipili* (who were also *equites*).[115]
Of the *equites*, almost half (fourteen out of thirty-three) came from
Picenum, Strabo's own home region.[116] The practice of enlisting armies
from specific regions of Italy was a defining feature of the Social War and
later conflicts in the first century BC.[117] Strabo's *consilium* shows the same
phenomenon of recruitment in action at the officer level as well, since he
turned to Picene equestrians to serve on his staff. *Vicinitas* operated on
both the civilian and military levels in shaping the involvement of Italians
in the affairs of the *res publica*.

How many Italians did actually exercise their prerogative to vote in
elections? Any reader persuaded by the rhetoric of Quintus Cicero's
Commentariolum Petitionis would be left in no doubt that Italian
voters were essential for electoral success.[118] The residents of Italian
municipia are frequently cited by Quintus as necessary supporters of
Cicero's candidacy alongside the *publicani*, *equites* and senators.[119]
Quintus' most striking piece of advice is that his brother should
memorise the map of Italy and its regions, so that he would know
all the *municipia*, colonies, and prefectures intimately, and could
secure representatives there who would canvass on his behalf.[120]
However, as Mouritsen has argued, Cicero appears to have been
something of a trailblazer in this regard, given that his consular
campaign came less than a decade after the census of 70/69 BC,
which enfranchised Italians in great numbers.[121] Cicero went to great
lengths to win the support of Italian communities as a way of harnessing this

[114] Lomas 2004: 111–16.   [115] *CIL* I² 709 = VI 37045 = *ILS* 8888; Criniti 1970: 82.
[116] Syme 1939: 28; Criniti 1970: 88.   [117] Potter 2010: 319–20.
[118] The point has often been noted, e.g. Wiseman 1971: 137; Bispham 2007: 431–2.
[119] Q. Cic. *Comm. Pet.* 3, 24, 50.   [120] Q. Cic. *Comm. Pet.* 30–2.
[121] Mouritsen 1998: 96. See Cic. *Att.* 1.1.2 [SB 10.2] for a plan to campaign in Cisalpine Gaul.

new vote.[122] We do occasionally hear of relationships cultivated by other politicians. For example, L. Murena received support from tribes in Umbria during his consular campaign in 63 BC.[123] The limited evidence for specific cases does not mean that they did not exist, and politicians did undoubtedly use what connections of patronage, *amicitia* and *vicinitas* they possessed.[124] Active campaigning for most Roman senators, however, was probably focused on towns close to Rome itself, since their proximity meant that their residents were more likely to travel to the city to vote.[125]

Equestrian *domi nobiles* sometimes made the journey to Rome as part of embassies despatched by Italian communities in order to express opinions or lend support during trials in the city.[126] The embassy that came from Atina to support Plancius is by no means the only example of such delegations appearing in the courtroom. In 66 BC a group from Larinum travelled to Rome to give testimony on behalf of their fellow citizen, A. Cluentius Habitus, an *eques* who had been charged with poisoning. There was no stopping Cicero's rhetoric on this occasion: apparently every man who could make the journey from Larinum had come to Rome to support Cluentius.[127] This obvious exaggeration aside, representatives from Larinum's neighbours did appear in the courtroom, including *equites* from Teanum and Luceria in Apulia, again displaying the principle of *vicinitas* in action.[128] Cicero pointed out the presence of such delegations in support of his client whenever he could. In the case of M. Caelius Rufus, arraigned on a charge of *vis* (a specific type of 'public' or 'political' violence) in 56 BC, Cicero indicated a delegation from Interamnia Praetuttiorum, including senators and *equites*, present in the courtroom.[129] Cicero emphasised that these embassies were composed of the right sort of Italians: the aristocratic *domi nobiles*, who were fit to play their part in Roman politics.[130] But Cicero's portrayal of the circumstances of these trials sometimes has the effect of obscuring the actual relationship between

---

[122] Cicero often refers to support he receives from Italian communities: Cic. *Fam.* 13.4.1 [SB 318.4] (Volaterrae), *Fam.* 13.7.1 [SB 317.1] (Atella). See Wiseman 1971: 138–9; Bispham 2007: 431–2, for further ties of patronage.

[123] Cic. *Mur.* 42. See also Gruen 1974: 377–8 and Bispham 2007: 434, for the examples of Pompeius and Caesar.

[124] Mouritsen 2001: 108, 123.   [125] Mouritsen 1998: 97, 2001: 120–3.

[126] Millar 1998: 28–9; Crawford 2000: 417; Bispham 2007: 425–6.   [127] Cic. *Clu.* 195.

[128] Cic. *Clu.* 197. Bispham 2007: 410 also notes that these *equites* come from the most muncipalised regions of Italy.

[129] Cic. *Cael.* 3–5. Lomas 2004: 101 argues that this delegation cannot have been very big, while Dyck 2013: 69 cites J. Briscoe's suggestion that it may have been composed of only three men: a senator, an *eques* and one other.

[130] Lomas 2004: 115; Dench 2005: 182–3.

the Italian *domi nobiles* and the *res publica*. The trial of Cluentius, with its familial and municipal rivalries, appears to be a largely parochial conflict, but one which was being played out on the Roman stage.[131] We thus see once again that it was local relationships, interests and conflicts that brought Italians to Rome, rather than an innate desire of citizens from the *municipia* to participate in politics of the *res publica* to the fullest extent. Indeed, as Lomas has pointed out, Cicero's speeches not only reveal the world of the ambitious Plancius, Caelius, and their supporters, but also the *domi nobiles* who showed little interest in running for office at Rome.[132]

Italian *equites* also came to Rome, or became involved in Roman affairs, when necessary to defend their personal business interests. In 63 BC, the year of the Catilinarian conspiracy, one of the main issues of contention was the need for debt relief. Catiline's supporters even included some illustrious debtors from the senatorial and equestrian orders.[133] But for the most part, the moneylenders and *publicani*, equestrian and otherwise, were opposed to any debt relief, and thus readily came Rome in large numbers to lend their support to Cicero.[134] His friend, the equestrian powerbroker Atticus, was probably working hard behind the scenes to prevent the passage of any legislation on debt reform.[135] Apart from Atticus, who famously led the equestrian coterie on the Capitoline, the majority of these *equites* must remain shadowy figures. We can put a face and a name to one additional supporter, L. Aelius Lamia, originally from Formiae.[136] In 58 BC Aulus Gabinius threatened to hold the *equites* to account for their actions during the Catilinarian conspiracy, and banished Lamia to a distance of 200 miles from the city of Rome.[137] It was at this time that Italian towns, colonies and every 'corporation for collecting revenue at Rome' (*Romae societas vectigalium*) passed decrees expressing support for Cicero's actions in 63 BC.[138] The *publicani* would not have been restricted to those who lived and worked in Rome, but probably included men from all over Italy.[139]

---

[131] Dyson 1992: 62, 69–74; Dench 2005: 186–7.   [132] Lomas 2004: 111.

[133] For the crisis from Cicero's point of view, see Cic. *Cat.* 2.4–5, 17–18, *Off.* 2.84, *Fam.* 5.6.2 [SB 4.2]. Despite his rhetoric, the problem was real: Sall. *Cat.* 33; Dio 37.30.2; Gruen 1974: 416–33; Dyck 2008: 4–9.

[134] See, for example, Cic. *Cat.* 1.21, 4.15, *Red. sen.* 12, *Sest.* 28, *Att.* 2.1.7 [SB 21.7]. The equestrian mob could sometimes turn violent, as when they threatened Caesar for advocating leniency for the conspirators (Sall. *Cat.* 49; Suet. *Iul.* 14). For discussion, see Hill 1952: 168.

[135] K. Welch 1996: 462–3.   [136] Nicolet 1974: 762–5.   [137] Cic. *Sest.* 29; Kaster 2006: 184–6.

[138] Cic. *Dom.* 74, *Sest.* 32. For the mob present in Rome, see Millar 1998: 150–1.

[139] Note for example the Italian origins of first-century *publicani* for whom we have such information: Cn. Plancius, from Atina (Cic. *Planc.* 19), C. Rabirius Postumus and his father C. Curtius, both from Campania (Cic. *Rab. Post.* 3).

Cicero was a man devoted both to Italy and to the *res publica* of Rome.[140]
For him, the presence of citizens of equestrian status was a special mark of
honour for an Italian community, a sign that the town had blossomed to
the extent that its inhabitants had reached the upper *ordines* at Rome.
In the *Third Philippic* he was required to defend the standing of Octavian's
family against M. Antonius' jibes. Cicero pointed out that Aricia, the home
town of Octavian's mother, counted senatorial magistrates and 'very many
distinguished *equites Romani*' (*equites Romani lautissimi et plurimi*)
among its citizens.[141] In his defence speeches Cicero used senators and
equites to delineate the relationship between the *res publica* and the Italian
communities, arguing that high status in the local arena should be reflected
in Rome, and vice versa. For example, it was a mark of young Caelius' good
character that he had been enrolled among the *decuriones* of Interamnia,
which Cicero described as 'a *municipium* that is so illustrious and so
respected' (*municipio tam inlustri ac tam gravi*).[142] The fact that both
Cluentius and Caelius had rendered signal service to their respective
municipia stood as testament to their personal standing, which in
Cicero's view should resonate even beyond their communities into *dignitas*
at Rome itself.[143] He expressed the same sentiments privately. Writing to
his brother Quintus concerning the *eques* M. Orfius from Atella, Cicero
described him as 'an outstanding man in his home town, and his influence
even extends beyond its bounds' (*hominem domi splendidum, gratiosum
etiam extra domum*).[144] In Cicero's speeches we can therefore detect him
advocating a 'municipal ideology', as Bispham has aptly characterised it.
The principle of this was that the new Italian *equites* were not subordinate
to their long-enfranchised Roman peers, but equal players in the *res
publica*.[145]

Cicero was of course personally invested in promoting such an ideology.
As he said in the *Pro Caelio*: 'It was from these [municipal] origins that
I emerged to win a reputation among my fellow men' (*ab his fontibus
profluxi ad hominum famam*).[146] In the series of speeches delivered after
58 BC referring to his exile and subsequent recall, Cicero consistently
recalled the role played by the senate, *equites* and 'all Italy' (*cuncta Italia*)
in expressing their shared grief and support for his return to Rome.[147]
In the speech *Post reditum in senatu* Cicero recalled how Cn. Pompeius
Magnus, in his capacity as a local magistrate at Capua, thought that 'it was

[140] Salmon 1972.   [141] Cic. *Phil.* 3.16.   [142] Cic. *Cael.* 5.   [143] Cic. *Clu.* 196, *Cael.* 5.
[144] Cic. *Q. Fr.* 2.13.3 [SB 17.3].
[145] See Bispham 2007: 430–42, esp. 431, for the idea of a 'municipal ideology'.
[146] Cic. *Cael.* 6.   [147] Cic. *Sest.* 25, 87, *Pis.* 11, 14, 27; Nicolet 1974: 397.

necessary to call upon the protection of all Italy to see to my safety' (*Italiae totius praesidium ad meam salutem implorandum*).[148] As Dench has noted, throughout Cicero's speeches Italy largely manifests itself as a 'vast and amorphous moral presence' that lends support to Cicero and condemns his opponents.[149] Cicero came close to admitting the formulaic nature of his rhetoric in a letter to Atticus in 61 BC. He informed his friend of a speech in the senate that included references to the senate, the *concordia ordinum* with the *equites*, and the necessary support of Italy, adding: 'you are already familiar with our thunderous delivery of such matters' (*nosti iam in hac materia sonitus nostros*).[150] Cicero's vision of the *res publica*, founded on the *concordia ordinum*, was not restricted to Rome, but encompassed all of Italy.[151] He was probably somewhat ahead of his time in his political vision, which would later be taken up by Augustus when he emphasised the support he received from 'all Italy' (*tota Italia*).[152] In reality, as we have seen, the integration of Italian *equites* into the *res publica* was a more gradual process, which was only achieved over time alongside the municipalisation of the peninsula. Cicero's distinct contribution was to advocate a coherent vision of how such a process would play out. In the end he proved to be remarkably prescient about the way in which equestrian rank would be valued in the imperial period. An Italian *eques* who never, or rarely, travelled to Rome was still an *eques*; his status and title gave him a connection to the *res publica* that could never be severed. The prominent use of equestrian titles on monuments of the Italian *domi nobiles* of the first century AD and beyond shows the value that they attached to their status.[153] This was equally true of *equites* in the imperial period who hailed from Spain, Asia Minor or North Africa and spent most of their lives in these regions, but who sought, and valued, membership of the equestrian order. Their equestrian rank meant that they were men of *duae patriae* in spirit, if not in law, just as Cicero envisioned.[154]

The integration of Italian *domi nobiles*, including equestrians, into the Roman state in the decades following the Social War was thus a complex phenomenon marked by both adjustment and negotiation. Italian *equites* could travel to Rome to vote for their fellow *municipales* in elections, to

[148] Cic. *Red. sen.* 29. See Nicolet 1980: 295 on these events.
[149] Dench 2013: 128. See also Lomas 2004: 115.   [150] Cic. *Att.* 1.14.4 [SB 14.4].
[151] Wiseman 1971: 7; Nicolet 1974: 415; N. Wood 1991: 198–9.
[152] Wiseman 1971: 10; Bispham 2007: 443–4; Dench 2013: 133–5.
[153] Titles such as *equus publicus* become common in Italy from AD 14/23 onwards (Duncan-Jones 2016: 95).
[154] See Chapter 5 for the articulation of equestrian rank in the imperial period. Only senators actually had two *patriae* in a legal sense since they were supposed to reside in Rome (*Dig.* 50.1.22.6 [Paulus]).

support their family or friends in the law courts, or to protect their own business interests. On one level this reveals a predominant concern for their own affairs, those of their *patria* or their neighbours, rather than an investment in the *res publica* as a whole; evidence for Italian interest in law-making is limited. But the fact that Rome was the venue in which local conflicts and disputes were resolved, and where interests were protected or advocated, shows that their relationship with the *res publica* did matter. In his speeches and other published writings, Cicero tried to articulate the importance to the *res publica* at large of the *domi nobiles* who entered the equestrian and senatorial orders at Rome. His vision was primarily one of integration, expressing the idea that it was possible for citizens from Italian municipalities to have two *patriae*, in their home town and in Rome. This political concept needs to be reconstructed from references in a range of defence speeches, but that does not lessen its importance. There is little doubt that Cicero cultivated his equestrian identity and municipal origin in order to win the support of specific audiences, whether they were jurors, voters or other constituencies, which could influence his political career.[155] Cicero deliberately appealed to those Italian *equites* who, like him, wanted to bridge the distance between their communities and Rome itself, gradually connecting the regions more closely with the centre of politics and government.

The Lives of Others

It is difficult to reconstruct the perspectives of Cicero's equestrian contemporaries in Italy, newly enfranchised and otherwise, since they did not bequeath us the same voluminous corpus of writings. However, an investigation of the use of equestrian ranks and titles in inscriptions can provide an indication of the extent to which Italians publicly identified with the *ordo equester*. Some methodological remarks about this evidence are in order. The number of surviving Republican inscriptions pales in comparison with evidence from the imperial age. There was a significant increase in epigraphic activity in Italy from the late second century BC onwards, though the precise extent varied from region to region.[156] The epigraphic habit manifested itself in the inscribing of decrees, charters and laws on bronze; the erection of funerary monuments with accompanying

---

[155] Note the important comments of Dench 2013: 130–1, that Cicero's '"new man" *persona*' is just one part of his strategy of self-presentation.

[156] Benelli 2001: 8–10; Panciera 2006: 85.

inscriptions; and the creation of inscriptions designed to commemorate the construction of public buildings, such as theatres and temples.[157] When individuals are named, either as dedicators, honorands, or in some other capacity, the texts often include further details about their lives, such as filiation and tribal membership, as well as offices held at the local level and in the Roman army and administration. Municipal magistrates in particular recorded the offices they had held in the form of a *cursus*, or 'career', just as it had been the practice for some Republican senators to do on their sarcophagi. These inscribed careers occur overwhelmingly in a funerary context; their use to honour the living was a feature of the transformation of public epigraphy in the Augustan period.[158] These texts are often called '*cursus* inscriptions', since they record public offices, though the primary object of the inscription was not usually to document the career per se.[159] The level of detail included about official positions or status was a matter of personal choice, and varied depending on the context and purpose of the text.[160] Furthermore, unless they contained specific chronological indications such as the consular year, these inscriptions cannot usually be dated precisely. Many of the texts can only be assigned to general periods, such as 'mid-first century BC' or 'late Republican' on the basis that they reveal evidence of post-Social War municipalisation.[161] However, it is possible to draw some broad conclusions from the inscriptional evidence about the role of equestrian status in the public sphere. I will suggest that equestrian rank only slowly emerged as an element of public self-representation in Italy in the decades after the Social War. This picture of gradual development echoes that which we find in the Ciceronian evidence, as Italian *equites* negotiated their relationship with the Roman *res publica*.

In the late Republic the standard epigraphic term for a member of the equestrian order was *eques*, which was sometimes written out in full, but

---

[157] See Benelli 2001; Pobjoy 2007: 51–62; and Salomies 2015: 158–60 for general overviews of Roman Republican epigraphy and its various forms. Pobjoy 2000 examines types of building inscriptions and the different motivations behind their construction.

[158] Panciera 2006: 91. For the inscribed *cursus* appearing on monuments for the living in the imperial age, see Chapter 6.

[159] Eck 1984: 149–50; Pobjoy 2007: 55–8. On the misnomer of the '*cursus* inscription', see Eck 2009b. For general considerations on this form of text, see Cooley 2012: 145–52. The issue is discussed further in Chapters 6 and 7.

[160] See Bispham 2007: 250 on the Republican evidence. The issue of personal choice more broadly is brought out by Cooley 2012: 52.

[161] On the problems with dating this material, see the sobering remarks of Bispham 2007: 42–4, 247–50.

could also be abbreviated to *eq(ues)*.[162] The earliest securely dated use of this title occurs on a list of Romans citizens initiated into the Samothracian mysteries in 100 BC.[163] A marble stele, discovered at Papa-Vounos in Samothrace, records the names of several officers and advisers who served with the praetor M. Antonius during his campaign against the pirates in 102–100 BC.[164] The men are listed as M. Fannius, *praef(ectus)*, L. Tullius, *praif(ectus)*, P. Petellius, *eq(ues)*, P. Gadienus, *eq(ues)* and C. Menenius. The first two men are evidently prefects of equestrian rank: M. Fannius would later enter the senate, rising to the rank of praetor in 80 BC, while L. Tullius was Cicero's uncle.[165] P. Petellius and P. Gadienus are only styled *eq(ues)*, probably because they did not hold specific military positions.[166] This shows that official posts 'outranked' mere equestrian status in public display. The use of the abbreviation *eq(ues)* to describe a citizen of equestrian status recurs on a second, more fragmentary, list of Roman initiates in Samothrace dating from 67/61 to 45 BC.[167] Apart from these two texts, the term *eq(ues)* does not seem to have been used widely throughout the Mediterranean outside Italy. For example, the businessman L. Agrius Publeianus was honoured with a statue at Ephesus in Asia Minor by 'the Italians who do business at Ephesus' (*Italicei quei | Ephesi negotiantur*).[168] We know from Cicero's *Pro Flacco* that Publeianus was an *eques*, yet this status goes unremarked on the inscribed base on which the statue stood.[169] The use of the term *eq(ues)* in the Samothracian inscriptions represented the beginning of equestrian status being expressed in inscribed and permanent format, but it was by no means a commonplace practice. Indeed, it is striking that on the inscribed bronze tablet recording Cn. Pompeius Strabo's *consilium* at Asculum in 89 BC none of the advisers kown to have been of equestrian rank are actually described as *equites*.[170]

The inscribed use of the title *eques* appears mainly in a handful of funerary texts from Italy dated to the period after the Social War.[171] These vary in the

---

[162] The title *eques* does not refer to a cavalryman unless the inscription also names a specific unit (Nicolet 1974: 243–4).

[163] *SEG* 51, 1092 = Dimitrova 2008 no. 66.   [164] Clinton 2001: 29–30.

[165] Clinton 2001: 32–3. For L. Tullius, see also Cic. *Orat.* 2.2; Nicolet 1974: 1054.

[166] Clinton 2001: 32.

[167] *SEG* 41, 717 D = Dimitrova 2008 no. 49 Side C. The text is very fragmentary, but does record [-] *Vol(tinia) eq(ues)* and C. *Aninius C(ai) f(ilius) eq(ues)*. Cf. Clinton 2001: 32 n. 2, who suggests that the list could date from any time after the mid-second century BC.

[168] *CIL* III 14195.39.   [169] Cic. *Flacc.* 31; Nicolet 1974: 769.

[170] *CIL* I² 709 = VI 37045 = *ILS* 8888.

[171] These have been compiled by Nicolet 1974: 243–5 and Eck 1979b: 108–11. The only text that is not part of a funerary monument is a communal dedication on a fragmentary inscription from Tibur, which refers to something that '*equites* have given...' (*CIL* I² 1489 = XIV 3622: *equites*

amount of detail they provide about the individual equestrian. Some are very taciturn, as in the epitaph of C. Agrius, which simply states: 'Here lie the bones of C. Agrius, son of Caius, *eques*' (*C(ai) Agri C(ai) f(ilii) eq(uitis) | ossa heic sita sunt*).[172] The epitaph of the equestrian M'. Maecius Varus of Visentium, dedicated by his daughter, is more extensive, since it contains a short metrical verse addressed to the passer-by.[173] His personal status, however, is simply given as *eq(ues)*, with no further detail. Some inscriptions allow us to trace links between individual *equites* and the Italian municipal aristocracies, providing comparative evidence for the types of relationships illuminated by Cicero. A funerary monument from Amiternum attests a local magistrate, C. Oviolenus, and his nephew, Quintus:

C. Oviolenus, son of Publius, of the Quirina tribe, *octovir*. Q. Oviolenus, son of Quintus, grandson of Publius, of the Quirina tribe, *eques*.[174]

The family was evidently a prominent one, given that C. Oviolenus held the post of *octovir*, a local magistracy in the Sabine prefecture.[175] The use of the term *eques* to describe his nephew Quintus may suggest a degree of pride in the elevation of a member of the family to equestrian rank in the Roman *res publica*.[176] The funerary monument of the Rosii from Blera in Etruria likewise shows the spread of equestrian status through one particular family. It lists four family members: C. Rosius, *eq(ues)*, his wife Turrania, and their sons, C. Rosius, and C. Rosius Sabinus, *tribunus militum*.[177] It is probable, following the example of the Samothracian inscriptions, that C. Rosius was an equestrian who did not hold any official post, but that his son C. Rosius Sabinus became a military tribune, and therefore did not need also to mention that he was an *eques*.[178]

One final example combines epigraphic and visual evidence. This is the funerary monument of L. Septumius, dated 70–50 BC, which comes from

---

dederunt). Eck 1979b: 111 n. 32 suggested that the Cn. Tituleius of *CIL* IX 3928 should be added to the list of equestrian inscriptions, but Demougin 1992a: 324 has argued that *Eques*, which is written out in full, is actually his cognomen. For the family, see Buonocore 1982: 720–2.

[172] *AE* 1974, 198 = *CIL* VI 40909. There are no firm grounds for identifying this man with C. Agrius, friend of Varro (Nicolet 1974: 768).

[173] *ILLRP* 692a = *AE* 1962, 151; Gasperini 1959: 33–8.

[174] *CIL* I² 1855 = IX 4398 = *ILLRP* 531: *C(aius) Oviolenus P(ublii) [f(ilius)] | Q(uirina tribu) octovir | Q(uintus) Oviolenus | Q(uinti) f(ilius) P(ublii) n(epos) Q(uirina tribu) eque[s]*. For the funerary context, see Segenni 1992: 47.

[175] Sherwin-White 1973: 65–6, 72.   [176] Nicolet 1974: 243, 413.

[177] *AE* 1981, 363; Eck 1979b: 109–11. For Rosius the *tribunus militum*, see *PME* R 10 *bis*.

[178] The family probably came from the municipal aristocracy (Demougin 1983: 288).

Figure 3.2: Funerary relief of L. Septumius, outside Rome

Via Praenestina, to the east of Rome (Figure 3.2).[179] The monument's relief depicts three people: an older man, Septumius' father, on the right; Septumius himself in the centre; and his wife or mother, Hirtuleia, on the left.[180] The inscription reads:

[L. Septumius] quinquennial *magister Capitolinus*. L. Septumius, son of Lucius, of the tribe Arnensis, *eques*. Hirtuleia, daughter of Lucius.[181]

L. Septumius the equestrian was probably a military officer, possibly a tribune, given that he is shown wearing a *paludamentum* (a soldier's cloak) and holding a sword.[182] But rather than noting his military post, as others tribunes chose to do, the inscription gives him only the title *eques*. Septumius' father was a freedman, as indicated by his occupancy of the

---

[179] *PME* S 37; Nicolet 1974: 244–5; Devijver and van Wonterghem 1990: 64–5.
[180] Nicolet 1974: 244. Devijver and van Wonterghem 1990: 65 suggest that Hirtuleia was Septumius' wife, while Keppie 1984: 199 assumes she was his mother.
[181] *CIL* I^2 2992 = VI 40911 = *ILLRP* 697: *[L(ucius) Septumius –] mag(ister) Capitolinus quinq(uennalis), L(ucius) Septumius L(uci) f(ilius) Arn(ensi tribu) eques, Hirtuleia L(uci) f(ilia).*
[182] Devijver and van Wonterghem 1990: 65.

priestly post of *magister Capitolinus*.[183] The acquisition of equestrian rank by his son was therefore a dramatic increase in the family's fortunes, which received permanent commemoration in this funerary monument.

In the broader context of Republican epigraphy, these inscriptions which include the status designation *eq(ues)* are quite exceptional. Apart from this handful of cases, equestrian rank was not indicated on honorific or funerary monuments, or building inscriptions.[184] Instead there was a preference for recording specific municipal magistracies or officer posts in the Roman army.[185] Let us take the case of C. Erucius C. f., *IIIIvir iure dicundo*, who erected eleven altars with his colleague T. Titius Flaccus at Spoletium, where he held his magistracy.[186] Bispham has argued that he is identical with C. Erucius, a man of equestrian rank, who opposed Cicero in the case of Sex. Roscius of Ameria.[187] If Bispham's identification is correct, then Erucius' equestrian status goes unremarked in the inscription attesting his construction of the altars, dated to the 60s BC. It is his local magistracy in Spoletium that is most important in this context, not his equestrian rank. Military men likewise do not often use the title of *eques*. The epitaph of Numerius Granonius, who was buried in Athens after serving under Pompeius Magnus during the civil war with Caesar, records that he was from Luceria in Italy, a *IIIIvir*, and a centurion in two legions.[188] He may have been of equestrian rank, even though it is not recorded, given that the social status of centurions increased significantly in the first century BC to include municipal magistrates and *equites*.[189]

The equestrian status of municipal magistrates can be established with greater confidence when they are attested as officers with the rank of tribune or prefect. For example, C. Atilius Glabrio was commemorated with a funerary monument in Perusia in the Caesarian or triumviral period.[190] The inscription records that Glabrio was a *IIIIvir quinquennalis*, but also includes his two officer commands, as *praefectus fabrum* and *praefectus*

---

[183] Nicolet 1974: 1019; Coarelli 1984: 470; Borg 2012: 42.

[184] Bispham 2007: 473–510 provides a representative sample of such epigraphic texts. For the increase in public building in Italy after the Social War, much of it the responsibility of prominent local families who would go on to enter the senatorial and equestrian orders, see Torelli 1995: 202.

[185] Demougin 1983: 287.   [186] *CIL* XI 4800; Bispham 2007: 323–6.

[187] Bispham 2007: 493, whose autopsy of this monument confirmed its Republican date (*contra* Nicolet 1974: 870).

[188] *CIL* III 6541a = *ILS* 2224 = *ILLRP* 502. For the context of his burial, see Stroszeck 2008: 297–8.

[189] Gruen 1974: 382–3; Potter 2010: 322–5. For the social mobility that could be achieved by centurions, see Harmand 1967: 333–6.

[190] *ILLRP* 638 = *AE* 1979, 245 = *AE* 2011, 365; Nicolet 1974: 789; Bispham 2007: 500–1. For Glabrio, see *PME* A 176; Demougin 1992a no. 69.

cohortis, which provide us with the only indication of his standing as an *eques*.[191] It is apparent, therefore, that Italian municipal magistrates who were also Roman officers did not customarily employ the term *eques* to define themselves publicly on honorific or funerary monuments, or to express their role in the Roman state.[192] This can be explained by the fact that it was their military service that defined the relationship of these men with the *res publica* in commemorative contexts, as Demougin has argued.[193] For example, one might have expected L. Firmius of Sora, who ascended from the rank of *primus pilus* to a military tribunate, to be honoured with an inscription that recorded his status as an *eques*.[194] But a dedication, erected around 30 BC by the colonists of the *legio IIII Sorana*, mentions only his military and municipal positions as a sign of social respectability.[195] The end of the inscription reveals that it was erected 'on account of his honour and valour' (*honoris et virtutis causa*).[196]

The ideal of equestrian *virtus* had a long and proud history. It was expressed in various ceremonies and monuments, such as the *transvectio equitum*, the dedication of a temple of Fortuna Equestris by Q. Fulvius Flaccus, and the construction of equestrian statues of generals in the *forum Romanum*, as we saw in Chapter 1. These same ideals continued throughout the Republican period and into the age of the civil wars.[197] They found public expression in the reliefs and inscriptions commemorating individual equestrian officers erected throughout Italy. This can be seen in the case of the Tillii family tomb located in the Porta Nocera necropolis at Pompeii (Figure 3.3).[198] The tomb contained the remains of [L.? Tillius], a military tribune in Caesar's *legio X Equestris* and a *duovir iure dicundo* at Pompeii, and his brother, C. Tillius, a military tribune in the same legion, and an augur at Verulae.[199] They were interred together with their father, C. Tillius, a municipal magistrate at Arpinum and Pompeii and an augur at Verulae, as well as

---

[191] Bispham 2007: 358–9 discusses his career and the dating of the text.
[192] See Bispham 2007: 359 on magistrates and Roman military service. For other examples from the Caesarian and triumviral periods, see C. Aclutius Gallus, from Venafrum (*PME* A 12; *CIL* X 4876 = *ILS* 2227), C. Baebius, from Forum Livii (*PME* B 4; *CIL* XI 623 = *ILS* 2672 = *AE* 1978, 335), and C. Lactonius, from Sinuessa (*AE* 1986, 154).
[193] Demougin 1983: 287.
[194] *CIL* X 5713 = *ILLRP* 498a; Nicolet 1974: 878; Bispham 2007: 485–6. See also *PME* F 26; Demougin 1992a no. 12.
[195] See the discussions of Demougin 1983: 292 and Bispham 2007: 296–7.
[196] *CIL* X 5713 = *ILS* 2226; Bispham 2007: 296–7.   [197] Syme 1939: 70–1.
[198] Tomb 17 OS; D'Ambrosio and De Caro 1983: 23–4; Devijver and van Wonterghem 1990: 71–2.
[199] *PME* T 17 and 18; Demougin 1992a: nos 1–2.

Figure 3.3: Tomb of the Tillii, Pompeii

their mother, Fadia, and their grandfather, C. Tillius.[200] The statue of one of the Tillii brothers still survives (although it has been erroneously transferred to the neighbouring tomb, where it stands today) (Figure 3.4). He is depicted not as a civilian magistrate, but in the full regalia of an equestrian officer, complete with a cuirass displaying the Gorgon's head.[201] In the funerary inscription, the personal status of the individual family members is represented through municipal magistracies, local priesthoods and officer posts, revealing that service to one's home community and Rome were both important aspects of public representation. Yet the fact that Tillius is represented by a statue of himself in military uniform suggests that he took special pride in the *virtus* he displayed in service to the Roman *res publica*.

---

[200] Hüttemann 2010 no. 76. Fadia was from the municipal aristocracy of Arpinum (Demougin 1992a: 23).

[201] Devijver and van Wonterghem 1990: 69–72.

Figure 3.4: Statue of one of the Tillii brothers, Pompeii

These monuments and inscriptions prompt us to consider the relationship between Rome and the Italian communities. They show that the awards, honours and titles of Rome – an imperial 'centre' in every sense of the word – were not necessarily superior to those available on the 'periphery' in the towns of Italy. As Bispham has argued, municipalisation enabled the Italian communities 'to maintain an individual identity, to be their own *res publicae*.[202] The inscriptions recording municipal magistracies as a mark of personal status indicate the importance of these official positions in their local context.[203] An Italian equestrian could use the title *eques* in an epigraphic text, but it was a personal choice, and, in the late Republic, still a very limited one.[204] Instead of recording equestrian status per se, it was more common to list officer commands in the Roman army. These military posts represented tangible and significant personal achievement, which associated these Italian elites with the proud equestrian tradition of displaying one's *virtus* through military service, thus providing them with a way to integrate themselves into the *res publica*.[205] The presence of both municipal offices and Roman military commands on inscriptions reveals that some *domi nobiles* valued both their positions in their home communities and their army service to the Roman state. Cicero's speeches and the epigraphic evidence are therefore remarkably complementary, revealing in their own ways how Italian *equites* gradually and tentatively negotiated and expressed their relationships with their *duae patriae* in the first century BC. The fact that the title of *eques* was rarely used in inscribed texts in the Republican period shows that equestrian status had not yet achieved suitable cachet as an aspect of public self-commemoration, in comparison with military commands. That would have to wait until the imperial period, when Cicero's vision of Roman equestrian status resonating in the *municipia* would come to fruition.[206]

The Triumviral Period: Turbulence or Status Quo?

The triumviral period is the name given by modern scholars to the years between the assassination of C. Iulius Caesar and the Battle of Actium (44–31 BC). During this period membership of the senate expanded to more than a thousand members, many of whom were regarded as

---

[202] Bispham 2007: 440.

[203] On the persistence of local Italian identities even after the Social War, see Dench 2005: 165–8, 175–8.

[204] Even allowing for the failure of successive censors to complete the *lustrum* between 70/69 and 29/28 BC and thus enrolling all Italian citizens properly, the small number of inscriptions featuring the title *eq(ues)* is still striking. This is especially since we know of military officers who were *equites*, but only referred to their army office in honorific or funerary monuments. For the enrolment of new citizens and *equites*, see further Chapter 5.

[205] For the service of *municipales* as officers, see Harmand 1967: 392–3.   [206] See Chapter 5.

unworthy of senatorial rank.[207] Supporters of the triumvirs, whatever their birth or background, benefited financially from the proscriptions, with many becoming enormously wealthy, and certainly qualifying for the *census equester*.[208] It has frequently been suggested that these wealthy parvenus took advantage of the lack of clarity, or 'fuzziness' (to use Osgood's term), in the definition of equestrian rank to lay claim to the title of *eques Romanus*.[209] This seems to me to be a misreading of the issue. The definition of equestrian status had not changed: *equites Romani* still had to be Roman citizens who possessed the necessary property qualification, while *equites equo publico* had to be members of the eighteen centuries.[210] The importance of the census as the principal method for assessing equestrian status throughout the first century BC is demonstrated by a story in Suetonius' *Life of Augustus*. Augustus allowed *equites* who had become impoverished in the civil wars and no longer possessed the financial qualification to continue to sit in the first fourteen rows of the theatres, as long they or their parents had previously held the requisite equestrian fortune.[211]

The problem was that neither the census nor the *lustrum*, its ceremonial completion, were properly accomplished between 70/69 BC and 29/28 BC.[212] It was only during the census that the property rating of Roman citizens, as well as their moral and physical fitness to receive the public horse and membership of the eighteen centuries, could be formally assessed.[213] There is some evidence for changes in the number of *equites* in this period, but this comes in the form of expulsions rather than enrolments. For example, in 50 BC some *equites* were deprived of their public horse when they were expelled from the *ordo* by the censors (who nevertheless failed to complete the *lustrum*).[214] Caesar appears not to have reviewed the list of *equites equo publico* during his dictatorship.[215] This indicates that by the time of the censorship of Augustus and M. Vipsanius Agrippa in 29/28 BC, the centuries of *equites equo publico* had not

---

[207] Suet. *Aug.* 35.1; Dio 52.42.1; Osgood 2006: 258–60.   [208] Demougin 1988: 34–8.

[209] For example, Linderski 1977: 58 ('baffling lack of clarity in the legal concept and colloquial usage'); Demougin 1988: 34 ('Cette élasticité de l'ordre équestre a joué à plein pendant la période troublée du Triumvirate'); Osgood 2006: 268 ('some fuzziness in its definition').

[210] Cf. Demougin 1983: 286, 1988: 68–9, arguing that the census qualification operated as some type of temporary substitute for equestrian status in the triumviral period.

[211] Suet. *Aug.* 40.1.   [212] Wiseman 1970a; Demougin 1988: 23–4, 156–7.

[213] For the review of the *equites* as an integral part of the census, see Wiseman 1970b: 67–8. The *equites* were not reviewed in 65 BC (Plut. *Crass.* 13), and Cicero attests to the lack of a proper census in the *comitia centuriata* in 55 BC (Cic. *Att.* 4.9.1 [SB 85.1], as interpreted by Wiseman 1970a: 64–5).

[214] Dio 40.63.3.   [215] Wiseman 1970a: 62–3.

increased beyond 1,800 members, and may even have been well below strength.[216] These problems, acute as they were, do not necessarily mean that Romans were uncertain as to the qualifications for equestrian rank, or that there was a 'fuzziness' in its fundamental definition. Rather, the issue was that citizens who possessed the requisite equestrian property qualification could not be officially recognised as *equites* until the next census was taken. The result of this was that new *equites*, whose background was thought unworthy or unbecoming of such high status, and had not been assessed by the censors, were perfect targets for the prejudicial judgements of established equestrians and senators. But this does not suggest that they were not entitled to equestrian rank.

These upwardly mobile parvenus included freedmen who were awarded the *anulus aureus*, which, as we saw in the previous chapter, made them eligible for access to equestrian rank. There were two particularly famous examples from the triumviral period, both of whom were granted the gold ring by Octavian: T. Vinius Philopoemen and Menas (sometimes called Menodorus). Philopoemen became something of a cause célèbre when he famously protected his proscribed patron by hiding him away in an iron chest.[217] Struck by the freedman's loyalty to his master, Octavian made Philopoemen an equestrian. The ancient sources are not entirely clear on how this was accomplished: Suetonius says that Octavian 'honoured him with equestrian status' (*equestri dignitate honoravit*), while Dio uses the more technical expression, 'appointed to the equestrian order' (ἐς τὴν ἱππάδα κατατάξαι).[218] Scholars generally assume that Octavian gave Philopoemen the *anulus aureus*, which was within his powers as a magistrate with *imperium*, as we saw in the case of the gold rings awarded by Verres, Sulla and Caesar.[219] This grant of the gold ring is explicitly attested in the case of the naval commander Menas, who was freed by Octavian after defecting from Sextus Pompeius in 38 BC.[220] The most precise description of Menas' elevation is provided by Cassius Dio, who says that Octavian 'treated him with high honour, bestowed gold rings upon him, and enrolled him in the equestrian order'.[221] Dio then explains,

---

[216] Wiseman 1970a: 70–1, 1970b: 81. In *Comm. Pet.* 33, Quintus Cicero refers to the *equites* in the eighteen centuries as 'few' (*pauci*), a statement that would not be consonant with an increase in their numbers in the late Republic. See Tatum 2002 on the interpretation of this difficult passage.

[217] App. *BC* 4.44.   [218] Suet. *Aug.* 27.2; Dio 47.7.5.

[219] Demougin 1988: 48; Louis 2010: 233–4; Wardle 2014: 208.

[220] Vell. Pat. 2.73.3; Suet. *Aug.* 74; Dio 48.45.7. Note also App. *BC* 5.80, who calls him Menodorus.

[221] Dio 48.45.7: καὶ ἐν τιμῇ μεγάλῃ ἤγαγε δακτυλίοις τε χρυσοῖς ἐκόσμησε καὶ ἐς τὸ τῶν ἱππέων τέλος ἐσέγραψε.

in technical detail that is typical of his style, that the *anulus aureus* granted by a magistrate with *imperium* made freedmen eligible to become *equites*.[222] This was because the ring functioned essentially as a mark of *ingenuitas* which eliminated the stain of their servile upbringing.[223] A freedman honoured in this way would still have to be assessed by the censors as possessing the necessary property before he could technically call himself an *eques Romanus*. Dio's use of the words 'appointed' (κατατάξαι) and 'enrolled' (ἐσέγραψε) suggests that such an enrolment did actually take place in the cases of Philopoemen and Menas.[224] In contrast, the doctor Antonius Musa was honoured with the right to wear gold rings for nursing Augustus back to health, but did not actually become an *eques*.[225]

There was a disjunction between the legality of the award of equestrian rank and the popular perceptions of upwardly mobile freedmen. Legally, the ring conferred free birth on these freedmen, which made them eligible for equestrian status, subject to enrolment by the censors. But at the same time, as we have already seen, the gold ring was popularly regarded as a symbol of equestrian rank – the *anulus equester*, in Horace's words – even though its wearing would not be properly regulated until the reign of Tiberius.[226] This caused a certain amount of resentment and prejudice towards freedmen who possessed the gold ring.

These feelings are perfectly captured in Horace's *Fourth Epode*, probably written around 30 BC, which we have already mentioned briefly above.[227] In this poem Horace launches a stinging satirical attack against an unnamed former slave who acquired a substantial fortune and rose to the rank of *tribunus militum*. Not only does this man parade ostentatiously in an over-length toga, he then has the temerity to take his place front and centre in the theatre: 'He sits in the first rows as if a great *eques*, spurning

[222] Dio 48.45.8–9. [223] Treggiari 1969: 66–7; Nicolet 1974: 141; Mouritsen 2011: 107.
[224] Octavian and the other triumvirs are not generally assumed to have possessed censorial authority (thus Demougin 1988: 25–6), but surviving descriptions of their precise powers are vague (Dio 56.55.3–4; App. *BC* 4.2–3, with the comments of Millar 1973: 51–2). In the Republic there is evidence for consuls being occasionally awarded censorial authority to carry out specific tasks (Ferrary 2009: 105). This may provide some precedent for powers granted to Octavian which have gone unrecorded in our literary sources.
[225] Dio 53.30.3. Musa is generally regarded as being promoted to equestrian rank (e.g. Reinhold 1971: 287; Demougin 1992a: 58; Wardle 2014: 208). If this was the case, it is strange that Dio does not mention the promotion explicitly as he does for Philopoemen and Menas. Ps.-Acro's comment on Hor. *Epist.* 1.15.3 that he received 400,000 HS by a decree of the senate does not carry much weight here.
[226] Hor. *Sat.* 2.7.53. On the Tiberian legislation, see Chapter 5.
[227] For the date and context of the poem, see Mankin 1995: 99–100; L. C. Watson 2003: 145–52.

Otho's law' (*sedilibusque magnus in primis eques | Othone contempto sedet*).[228] This is our only indication that the *lex Roscia* may have specifically forbidden freedmen from occupying the fourteen rows.[229] However, it is best not to treat the poem itself as a source for legal realities, but as a sign of the social anxiety that the nouveau riche engendered.[230] Horace's point is more likely to be that the freedman did not deserve to be an *eques*. Even though the unnamed freedman is certainly a poetic creation, Horace's readers would, as Osgood points out, think of Menas, the freedman admiral-turned-*eques* of Pompeius Magnus and Octavian.[231] The poet's final lament as to why Rome should waste its time fighting against slaves (the forces of Sextus Pompeius or M. Antonius), when a former slave can rise to the post of military tribune, lends the comparison a certain contemporary piquancy.[232] But there is a difference between a freedman, legally granted *ingenuitas* and equestrian rank, sitting in the fourteen rows, and one who had no claim to such status.[233] The ex-slave Sarmentus, who was freed by C. Cilnius Maecenas, is an example of the latter case, since 'he behaved as if he was an *eques Romanus*, and also purchased a scribal *decuria*' (*pro equite Romano ageret, decuriam quoque compararet*).[234] When he tried to sit in the fourteen rows, he was soundly abused.[235] This was a true form of status usurpation, since Sarmentus did not possess equestrian rank, and was not legally entitled to a place in the reserved seats.[236] Such behaviour was most certainly not unique to the triumviral period, given how prominently it features in the poems of both Martial and Juvenal in the late first and early second centuries AD.[237]

The treatment of Sarmentus and Horace's unnamed freedman serve as examples of popular status policing, whereby an individual's rights and privileges were subject to challenge in public. This could happen easily

---

[228] Hor. *Epod.* 4.15–16.   [229] Cf. Bollinger 1969: 5–6; Nicolet 1984: 97.

[230] The extent to which there was a genuine increase in the number of freedmen becoming military tribunes may be doubted. I can find no specific examples of this happening. Freedmen were not usually employed in the Roman army (Mouritsen 2011: 71–2), and are more commonly cited as featuring in the army of Sextus Pompeius (Suolahti 1955: 269).

[231] Osgood 2006: 266. See L. C. Watson 2003: 150 on previous efforts to identify the freedman in question.

[232] Hor. *Epod.* 4.17–20; Mankin 1995: 107 (suggesting that the reference is to the forces of M. Antonius); L. C. Watson 2003: 169–71 (the troops of Sextus Pompeius).

[233] Mankin 1995: 106–7, speculates whether the man's servile origin could just be 'an invention of his enemies'.

[234] *Schol.* on Juv. *Sat.* 5.3–4.

[235] Treggiari 1969: 271–2; Demougin 1992a: 92–3; Osgood 2006: 263–4.

[236] Porphyrio on Hor. *Ser.* 1.5.51 does call him an *eques*. But the purchase of a scribal *decuria* did not automatically make one an *eques Romanus*. Cf. Osgood 2006: 268.

[237] See Chapter 9 for further discussion of these incidents.

given that membership of the *ordo* was, as Reinhold has pointed out, a personal rather than hereditary status – one did not need to be the son of an *eques* to be an *eques*.[238] Anyone who wanted to masquerade as an *eques* could do so simply by sitting in the fourteen rows, provided they had a gold ring and a certain amount of nerve. It would then be up to others to challenge their right to occupy a seat. But at the same time, the odium that might be appropriately levelled against an upstart who illegitimately claimed to be an *eques* could equally be directed at a parvenu who had recently, but legally, acquired the status.[239] Horace himself is an example of this latter category, being the son of an ex-slave, but he was still a legitimate and proper *eques*, *scriba* and *tribunus militum*.[240] He paints a vivid picture of the abuse he received as a freedman's son, which was just as much part of his poetic persona as his elevation to equestrian rank.[241]

Horace was not the only example of this type of social climbing. The most oft-cited comparison is the freedman's son and *tribunus militum* L. Appuleius, whose funerary monument survives today at Mentana in Italy (Figure 3.5).[242] Appuleius is depicted at the centre of a group portrait typical of the period, flanked by his freed parents, L. Appuleius Asclepiades and Appuleia Sophanuba.[243] Appuleius himself appears in heroic nudity, with a *paludamentum* draped over his shoulder, and holding a sword in the parade style.[244] His left hand sports a prominent ring, undoubtedly the *anulus aureus*.[245] The monument is replete with symbols of Appuleius' new status; if the freedman and freedwoman on either side of him are his parents, then this is a striking representation of the family's social mobility.[246] The Appuleius monument is very reminiscent of one we discussed earlier in this chapter: L. Septumius, another freedman's son who bore the title of *eques* in his epitaph. All these men – Horace, Appuleius, Septumius – were legally entitled to their equestrian status, despite any prejudice that might have come

---

[238] Reinhold 1971: 280–1, 284.
[239] Treggiari 1969: 64–5; Osgood 2006: 268–9. As Mouritsen 2011: 261–5 points out, the freedman's son was not a distinct social or legal category.
[240] For his equestrian posts and career, see D. Armstrong 1986.
[241] Hor. *Sat.* 1.6.6, 45–8; D. Armstrong 1986: 259–63. The doubts of Williams 1995 about the truth of Horace's claims seem to me to be too extreme.
[242] *CIL* XIV 3948; Kleiner 1977 no. 55; *PME* A 154.
[243] For comparanda from the same period, see Kleiner 1977: 108. Most scholars generally assume that Appuleius and Appuleia are the tribune's parents (Zanker 1975: 304–5; Kleiner 1977: 33; Demougin 1983: 288; D. Armstrong 1986: 257; Osgood 2006: 270). Cf. Devijver and van Wonterghem 1990: 63, who suggest that they are actually his freedmen.
[244] The heroic nudity in this type of relief is found only in the Augustan period (Kleiner and Kleiner 1975: 260).
[245] Zanker 1975: 305; Devijver and van Wonterghem 1990: 63.
[246] D. Armstrong 1986: 256–7; Osgood 2006: 270–2.

Figure 3.5: Funerary monument of L. Appuleius, Mentana

their way. They were not taking advantage of any uncertainty regarding the definition of an *eques Romanus* in the triumviral period. Freedmen's sons had been able to rise to equestrian and senatorial rank in the past, and though there may have been more opportunities to gain such status, no legal principles were being contravened.[247] This meant that Horace could himself act as a status policeman: his *Fourth Epode* attacking the slave-turned-military tribune serves as a reminder that even parvenus could criticise those lower in the social hierarchy – and perhaps may have been more ready to do so.[248]

---

[247] Treggiari 1969: 64. For opportunities to rise to equestrian status, see the examples in Demougin 1988: 288.

[248] See Mouritsen 2011: 267–8, pointing out that Horace's status was quite different from that of the new *eques* in the poem. Cf. L. C. Watson 2003: 150–2. On new men who were acutely conscious of their origins, note the case of Larcius Macedo (Pliny the Younger, *Ep.* 3.14), who remembered all too well that his own father had been a slave.

In contrast with the traditional picture of confusion within the *ordo equester* during the triumviral period, there is much to be said for emphasising the fundamental similarities between these *equites* and their forebears. This can be seen in the way in which military service was commemorated on the funerary monuments of the upwardly mobile *equites* of freedman origin who became Roman officers, since they are depicted in a very similar fashion to the Italian *domi nobiles* discussed earlier in this chapter. The artistic reliefs on these monuments feature common visual cues, regardless of whether they depict equestrians descended from freedmen or those from long-established families. For example, the depiction of the freedman's son L. Appuleius grasping his sword in the 'parade fashion' is echoed on the funerary monuments of P. Gessius and C. Raecius Perula, both of whom hold their swords in the same manner.[249]

There is continuity from the Republic to empire in the use of military iconography to publicly express one's equestrian status. Italian funerary monuments from the triumviral and early Augustan periods feature the small round equestrian shield (*parma equestris*) and the spears (*hastae*), which were traditionally used by Rome's cavalry. These symbols can be found at Sassina on the tomb of P. Verginius Paetus, a military tribune and local magistrate of the Augustan age,[250] as well as on a funerary monument for an anonymous equestrian officer from Modena (Figure 3.6).[251] The iconographic use of the cavalry weapons to articulate the officers' membership of the *ordo equester* was a particular feature of the late triumviral and Augustan periods.[252]

The performance of military service could be integrated into public honorific monuments, such as the Arch of the Sergii at Pola in Histria. This triumphal arch was surmounted by statues of four members of this prominent municipal family, which included L. Sergius Lepidus, styled *aedilis* and *tribunus militum legionis XXIX*, as well as his father and uncle, both local magistrates.[253] When [L. Corne]lius Menodorus, a native Greek from Asia Minor, was buried in Ephesus, his epitaph did not state that he was an *eques*, but instead proudly noted that he was 'the first military tribune out of those who live in Asia' (*tr(ibunus) mil(itum) primus ex is qui*

---

[249] *ILLRP* 503; *CIL* IX 2532; Devijver and van Wonterghem 1990: 65–6.   [250] *AE* 1966, 120.
[251] Devijver and van Wonterghem 1990: 76–7.
[252] Devijver and van Wonterghem 1990: 74–85, 93–4; see also Devijver 1991b: 253–4.
[253] *CIL* V 50 = *ILS* 2229; Keppie 1983: 203–4.

Figure 3.6: Tomb of an anonymous *eques* showing the *parma* and *hastae*, Modena

in Asia habitant).[254] Taken together, the inscriptions, reliefs and statues of these monuments attest significant collective pride in military service as an equestrian officer.[255] They demonstrate that the sons of freedmen, centurions and municipal magistrates who served in the army were united by their shared equestrian *virtus*, just like their predecessors.[256] The triumviral period was not marked by uncertainty surrounding the definition of equestrian status and what membership of the *ordo* represented – rather, it was a period in which the rapid ascent of new men to equestrian rank engendered resentment and prejudice.

---

[254] *AE* 1993, 1479 = 1997, 1436; Eck 1997: 110–13.

[255] There are also 'civilian'-style tombs and honorific monuments of equestrian officers, which feature limited military iconography, but these tend to date from the late Augustan or Julio-Claudian periods (Devijver and van Wonterghem 1990: 97).

[256] Cf. Osgood 2006: 273: 'The civil wars helped transform the equestrian order from a group of disinterested plutocrats into a corps of officers willing to serve Rome.' This seems to go too far, because there were many wealthy *equites* who did not serve in the Roman army in the last years of the first century BC, and remained content to look after their own interests, as they had done for generations. At the same time, equestrians had long constituted an important part of the officer corps of the Roman army.

Conclusion: A Complementary Perspective

The late Republic was a period in which the position of the equestrian order as a constituent element in the *res publica*, distinct from both the senate and the people, was gradually being shaped and defined. In Chapter 2 we viewed this struggle primarily through the eyes of Cicero and his contribution to contemporary political discourse. His written works are characterised by his vision of the *equites* as good citizens and supporters of the state. Because they did not hold formal magistracies, they were not subject to the same strictures or regulations as senators. As Cicero himself realised, this idealistic formulation was ultimately irreconcilable with the growing political influence exercised by *equites* as voters, jurors, *publicani*, or as a united pressure group, when they were galvanised to act in matters that affected their interests or to protect the prerogatives they had acquired.

This chapter has examined another complicated aspect of the position of the *ordo equester* within the *res publica*, namely the ways in which equestrian status was expressed, collectively and individually, to the wider world. We have seen how in the late Republic the equestrian order came to acquire its own status symbols, such as the tunic with the narrow stripe, the gold ring, and the right to sit in the first fourteen rows of the theatre. These privileges gave the new *ordo equester* and its members their own distinct public image, which distinguished them from the senate and the people. The collective unity of the *ordo* could also be expressed in acts such as the vote of the equestrian centuries to erect a statue of L. Antonius. The fundamental qualifications for equestrian status (the *census equester* and free birth) remained consistent even during the political upheavals of the triumviral period. The uncertainty of this age enabled upwardly mobile freedmen and their sons to enter the equestrian order through benefactions by generals, but they did so legitimately. Nevertheless, their appearances in the fourteen rows of the theatre wearing their gold rings did much to engender resentment among *equites* from established families, who were unhappy that they had to share their rank and its privileges with these new men. This demonstrates the emergence of an equestrian corporate identity in Rome in the late Republic, since a status group needs to recognise and value its own existence before it can police its boundaries.

The new *ordo equester* was very heterogeneous in its membership. When Ovid entered the theatre to watch the *ludi Megalenses* one April, he sat next to a *tribunus militum* who proudly stated that he had earned his seat in the equestrian rows through his military service, rather than any civilian occupations.[257] Army officers who gloried in their *virtus* had to coexist with *equites* like Ovid who saw no military service whatsoever, not to mention the offspring of freedmen like Horace who had only recently been elevated to equestrian rank. Yet the diverse nature of the *ordo* helps us understand its sociological role, particularly why it emerged as a constituent part of the *res publica* in the late Republic, and then remained so integral to the social structure of the state into the imperial period. There were only a limited number of places in the Roman senate available to members of the aristocratic elite, providing them with a title and social distinction. This meant that many wealthy citizens received no such recognition. The *ordo equester* bound all these wealthy non-senatorial Roman citizens together into a collective group and gave them a place in the *res publica*, regardless of differences in their origin or social standing. The title of *eques* had accomplished this in the middle Republic to a certain extent, but the creation of the *ordo* with its own status symbols and privileges consolidated the importance of equestrians and gave them greater public prestige.

By Ovid's day, the composition of the *ordo equester* had changed dramatically, since it was now full of Italian equestrians who came from regions ranging from Umbria to Apulia, as a result of the enfranchisement of Italy after the Social War.[258] The public monuments and inscriptions of these Italian *domi nobiles* include their military positions in the Roman army, as well as municipal magistracies held in their home towns, indicating that service both to the local community and to the Roman *res publica* had important roles to play in their public representation. This is indicative of the process of negotiation between 'centre' and 'periphery' in late Republican Italy which we find in Cicero's speeches. Cicero's own vision was of a united *cuncta Italia* in which Italian *equites*, and other new citizens, could be good citizens of both their *patria* and of Rome.[259] However, the cases discussed in Cicero's speeches show that there was a gradual period of adjustment and negotiation, as Italian *equites* became involved in political affairs in Rome when necessary to protect or champion their own interests, or those of their families or neighbours. The fact that equestrian status was not usually represented on funerary and honorific monuments by the title of *eques*, but through the listing of officer appointments and military iconography, demonstrates the enduring

---

[257] Ovid, *Fasti* 4.383–4.   [258] Crawford 2000: 431–2; Rowe 2002: 71.   [259] Cic. *Leg.* 2.2.5.

importance of *virtus* in defining equestrian public identity, for members of the *ordo* both old and new. After all, even Ovid, who held only civilian posts in the Roman administration, proudly paraded on his public horse in the *transvectio equitum*.[260] But there was one striking feature of Ovid's parade that differed from those undertaken by his predecessors: he rode before an emperor.

---

[260] Ovid, *Tristia* 2.89–90, 2.541–2.

PART II

The Empire

4 | Pathways to the Principate

Introduction: The Return of Monarchy to Rome

In the second century AD Appian of Alexandria, *eques Romanus* and historian of wars foreign and domestic, charted the establishment of one-man rule at Rome in the first century BC. In the preface to his *Roman History*, Appian wrote that the dictator Iulius Caesar 'preserved the appearance of the *res publica*, as well as its name, but he established himself as sole ruler of all men'.[1] In his view this represented the beginning of the Roman imperial monarchy, a form of government that would then be firmly established by Augustus after the defeat of M. Antonius.[2] It was likewise no coincidence that Suetonius chose to start his *On the Lives of the Caesars* with Iulius himself, embracing the delightful ambiguity of whether 'a Caesar' could be considered 'an emperor'.[3] Suetonius' contemporary Cornelius Tacitus acknowledged the power invested in Caesar in the opening passage of his *Annals*, but attributed greater significance to the peace that characterised Augustus' rule. For it was Augustus, 'who, after everything had been exhausted by civil disorder, received the empire with the title of *princeps*'.[4] These different starting points highlight the difficulty that Roman intellectuals of the second century AD faced in pinpointing a single moment of transition from the 'Republic' to the 'Empire'. Perhaps the best ancient understanding of the transformation can be found in Cassius Dio's *Roman History*, written in the third century AD. He wrote that the Republican constitution first gave way to a series of 'great men' or 'dynasts' (δυναστεῖαι), and only then to monarchy under Augustus.[5] This conception reflects the fact that the careers of Sulla, Pompey, Caesar and Antonius placed increasing emphasis on the monarchical element within the *res publica* (to use Polybius' formulation). Octavian, later Augustus,

---

[1] App. Pref. 6: τὸ μὲν σχῆμα τῆς πολιτείας καὶ τὸ ὄνομα ἐφύλαξε, μόναρχον δ'ἑαυτὸν ἐπέστησε πᾶσι.
[2] App. Pref. 14.   [3] This seems to be the point made by J. Henderson 2014: 108–9.
[4] Tac. *Ann.* 1.1: *qui cuncta discordiis civilibus fessa nomine principis sub imperium accepit.*
[5] Dio 52.1.1, with insightful interpretation by Kemezis 2014: 94–8.

can therefore be understood as the last, and most successful, in the line of these dynasts.

Throughout the last generation of the Roman 'Republic' and into the 'Empire', the Roman state remained the *res publica*.[6] Augustus certainly did not claim to 'restore the Republic', according to the typical, but inaccurate, modern formulation.[7] Instead, he stated that he had 'restored laws and rights to the Roman people', ensuring that the *res publica* was truly common property of all citizens.[8] The term *res publica* was also used by Romans to refer to the system of government that existed before Augustus, but this did not become common practice until the early second century AD.[9] Thereafter, *res publica* could refer to both the Roman 'state' – a formulation that existed well into the Byzantine period, as Kaldellis has shown – and the age of the 'Republic'.[10] In this discussion we employ the term *res publica* in the sense of the former meaning, in order to trace the growth of monarchical authority within the state. Augustus' contemporaries certainly knew that they were now living in a different kind of *res publica* from that of their forefathers. The will of one man was paramount, even if his powers were formulated in familiar constitutional terms.[11] Such a model of gradual transition to a monarchical *res publica* is particularly helpful for understanding the role of the *ordo equester* and its members between the 'Republic' and 'Empire'. The Augustan age witnessed the creation of an entire series of new official positions for *equites* in the Roman government and administration, a process which was directly linked to the rise of one-man rule. The Republican 'great men' of the first century BC had themselves employed equestrians as officers, agents and advisers, a situation which laid the groundwork for *equites* achieving a permanent place in the Roman government under Augustus and his successors.[12]

Equites acquired new power and influence in the monarchial *res publica* in two ways.[13] The first was through friendship and intimacy with the *princeps*, acting as his advisers and confidants.[14] Augustus could choose

[6] For the continuance of the *res publica* even under the triumvirs, see Millar 1973: 53–4.
[7] Millar 1973: 63–4; Judge 1974; Rich and Williams 1999: 213.
[8] Rich and Williams 1999: 208–12. This article formally published an Augustan *aureus* of 28 BC with the reverse legend LEGES ET IVRA P(OPVLO) R(OMANO) RESTITVIT.
[9] Judge 1974: 284–5; Wilkinson 2012: 13–16.   [10] Wilkinson 2012: 18–20.
[11] Millar 1973: 65–7.
[12] Throughout this chapter the first Roman emperor is referred to as Octavian in relation to events taking place before 27 BC, and Augustus for events after this year.
[13] Syme 1939: 355 memorably remarked that the *equites* now acquired 'both usefulness and dignity'.
[14] Millar 1977: 110–22; Winterling 1999: 161–94.

whomever he wished to advise him with no need to invest them with any constitutional position. The equestrian members of his coterie included Maecenas and Sallustius Crispus, *equites* who became famous precisely because their power exceeded that of most senators. The second path was through appointment to specific posts in the state administration. In order to put these new official positions for *equites* in context, it is important to understand the dual nature of the *res publica* that emerged under Augustus and his successors. The traditional senatorial magistracies which gave aristocrats access to military and provincial commands were maintained. But at the same time, government essentially became patronal, as all posts, honours and benefactions flowed from the person of the *princeps*.[15] Under the Republic the only official positions in the *res publica* held by *equites* were those of jurors and military officers. Equestrian *publicani* could act as agents of the *res publica*, but they were contracted to undertake specific tasks for a short-term period at the behest of the censors. However, the necessity of maintaining personal control of the empire prompted Augustus to create new official positions in the areas of finance, administration and military command whose occupants were personally answerable to him. Many of these positions he entrusted to equestrians, and still others to freedmen.[16] The new range of civilian offices entrusted to *equites* started to break down the distinction between *equites* and senators as far as government service was concerned, since equestrians could now also serve the *res publica*, even though they were not magistrates or pro-magistrates. In effecting these changes, Augustus was motivated by a need to create an alternative power structure that would reduce his reliance on his senatorial peers, who could pose a threat to his authority. These changes caused understandable anxiety among senators, who resented the ability of equestrians to exercise power outside the traditional framework of the senatorial magistracies. In the brave new world of the monarchical *res publica*, senators had to share and compete for power with equestrians, freedmen, slaves, women and anyone else who earned the emperor's favour.

---

[15] Miller 1977: 7–10, 275–328; Saller 1982: 41–78; Veyne 1990: 255–8, 321–66; Eich 2005: 69–78.
[16] Brunt 1983: 43–4.

The Friends of Caesar

'Does anyone known to the Caesars not think they are a friend?' wrote the exiled Ovid, a man who had certainly lost the friendship of the *princeps*.[17] This line of poetry, more than any other expression from Roman literature, captures the essential quality of court life in the imperial age, the need to be on good terms with the emperor, and the lengths men and women went to in order to achieve this. The competitive world of the Roman imperial court was in many ways a very familiar one, since it had evolved from the coteries of Republican politicians. In the late Republic, Romans of equestrian rank had acted as advisers to prominent senators, either formally as part of a retinue accompanying a governor to his province, or informally as counsellors and confidants over dinner or in the baths. This influence was magnified when senators such Marius, Sulla, Pompeius and Caesar (Cassius Dio's 'dynasts') began to acquire power and authority that went beyond their official magistracies or powers.[18] Their households and personal connections assumed the character of quasi-monarchical 'proto-courts', as Potter has persuasively argued.[19] These Republican grandees were not emperors, but the manner in which they exercised power, through personal charisma, appeals to the gods, financial and political connections, and personal staff, presaged the court of Augustus. His court was essentially a noble Roman household writ large, though one that was heavily influenced by military as well as domestic hierarchies.[20] It was a feature of these 'proto-courts' of the late Republic that they were not restricted to the senatorial establishment, but also encompassed *equites* and freedmen. New men proved to be particularly effective and loyal associates, because they hoped that their patrons would make their careers and fortunes. For example, Cn. Pompeius Magnus' senior officers shared in the wealth of his Asian campaigns.[21] Pompeius bestowed Roman citizenship on his provincial adherents, who were then able to rise to further honours at Rome through membership of the equestrian and senatorial orders.[22] The transition from 'retinue' to a 'court' occurred when these men ceased to be mere advisers and supporters, and began to wield power that was traditionally invested

---

[17] Ovid, *Ep. ex Pont.* 1.7.21: *quis se Caesaribus notus non fingit amicum?*
[18] Crook 1955: 4–7; Nicolet 1974: 718.
[19] Potter 2011: 59–62. The same idea is explored by Sherwin-White 1939: 19–20 and Kienast 2009: 307–8.
[20] Potter 2011. For the military influence on the imperial court, see Winterling 1999: 83–116. On the imperial court under Augustus and his successors, see Crook 1955; Millar 1977: 110–22; Wallace-Hadrill 1996; Paterson 2007; Winterling 1999, 2009: 73–102.
[21] Potter 2011: 67.   [22] Gruen 1974: 63–4.

only in holders of senatorial magistracies. The level of their influence depended not on election by the people, but on proximity to the *princeps*.[23]

The coterie of Caesar shows how such 'proto-courts' consolidated the monarchical element within the *res publica*. L. Cornelius Balbus, an *eques* who benefited from Pompeius Magnus' generosity, went on to become a close partisan of Caesar. During Caesar's dictatorship, Balbus and another equestrian adherent, C. Oppius, served as his representatives at Rome.[24] Balbus was elevated to senatorial rank and became consul in 40 BC; Oppius appears to have declined senatorial honours and remained an equestrian until his death.[25] These men functioned as trustworthy lieutenants for Caesar since they were not members of established senatorial families who could pose a threat to the dictator: they were new men, who depended on him personally for their power as part of a mutually beneficial relationship. The extent of their influence is dramatically brought to life by Cicero's letters. When Caesar was out of Rome, Cicero turned to Balbus and Oppius for help in trying to secure permission for the exiled A. Caecina to remain in Sicily. As Cicero wrote to Caecina in December 46 BC: 'I have noticed that everything Balbus and Oppius do while Caesar is away is usually given his approval.'[26] Balbus is said to have drafted *senatus consulta*, and even added Cicero's name as a supporter without his knowledge, much to his chagrin.[27] Both men played significant roles in shaping Caesar's public image, with Balbus remembered as the man who stopped Caesar from rising to greet the senate, and Oppius as the author of a biography which underlies our later historical accounts of the dictator's life.[28] Caesar's favour reaped rewards for these new men. Balbus' home town of Gades became a *municipium* in 49 BC, the first community outside Italy to be so honoured.[29] Balbus also amassed a vast

---

[23] Wallace-Hadrill 1996: 289.

[24] Syme 1939: 71–3; Alföldi 1976: 31–4; Eich 2005: 91–3. See further K. Welch 1990: 62–9, who argues that they were two of Caesar's prefects of the city.

[25] Cic. *Fam.* 2.16.7 [SB 154.7], dated to 49 BC, states that he had heard of a *toga praetexta* being made for Oppius, which would imply that he was to become a senator. Since nothing else is heard of this, it would imply that he declined such honours (Nicolet 1974: 710). Shackleton Bailey 1977a: 495 argues that Oppius was being elevated to one of the four major priesthoods, but these were only occupied by senators.

[26] Cic. *Fam.* 6.8.1 [SB 235.1]: *omnibus rebus perspexeram quae Balbus et Oppius absente Caesare egissent ea solere illi rata esse.* See Shackleton Bailey 1977b: 403.

[27] Cic. *Fam.* 9.15.4 [SB 196.4]; Shackleton Bailey 1977b: 352.

[28] Balbus and the senate: Plut. *Caes.* 60.7; Suet. *Iul.* 78.1. Oppius' work: Smith and Cornell 2014: 381–2. He also oversaw Caesar's building projects (Cic. *Att.* 4.16.8 [SB 89.8]).

[29] Weinrib 1990: 69.

personal fortune, to the extent that he could leave all Roman citizens a legacy of 100 sesterces each at his death.[30] The influence of Oppius and Balbus continued even after Caesar's assassination, when they transferred their support to his heir, Octavian.[31] Cicero penned a cloying and sycophantic letter to Oppius in mid-44 BC in which he praised his counsel and advice, though this did not represent his true feelings.[32] Continuity from Caesar to Octavian likewise manifested itself in the person of C. Matius, a prominent equestrian friend of Caesar who took charge of the new games of Venus Genetrix (much to the annoyance of Cicero).[33] These 'proto-courts' which formed around leading statesmen allowed equestrians without public office to exercise a political role within the *res publica*.

Cicero's friend T. Pomponius Atticus straddled the transition from Republic to principate in a slightly different way. Atticus eschewed direct political action, and he could not be found drafting laws, overseeing building projects or conducting the business of administration. Instead, he cultivated a network of friends and associates who would protect him and his financial interests. He seems to have accomplished this through his personal charm and charisma, and the relationships he built with Balbus and Oppius secured him safety in the new order.[34] In many ways Atticus was a classic old-school *eques*, becoming involved in political affairs only when his own interests were threatened.[35] Atticus particularly cultivated the friendship of the young Octavian. His biographer, Cornelius Nepos, makes it clear that this was not an attempt to wield power:[36]

Now, although he was satisfied with membership of the equestrian order (for that was his family's background), he came to be a relative by marriage of the emperor, son of the deified one. He achieved such intimacy through that same refined way of life which he had used to charm other leading citizens, who may have been the emperor's equals in their status, but not in their success.[37]

---

[30] Dio 48.32.2.   [31] Alföldi 1976: 43–54; K. Welch 1990: 64.

[32] Cic. *Fam.* 11.29 [SB 335]. Shackleton Bailey 1977b: 486 notes the hypocrisy of Cicero's sentiments, given his private remarks about Oppius to Atticus.

[33] Cic. *Att.* 15.2.3 [SB 379.3]; Tac. *Ann.* 12.60.4. See Cic. *Fam.* 11.28 [SB 349], for Matius' devotion to Caesar.

[34] Shackleton Bailey 1965a: 48–9; K. Welch 1996: 467. For Atticus' charm, see Nep. *Att.* 1.3–4. Note Shackleton Bailey's 1965a: 57 observation that Atticus must have had 'a singularly attractive personality'.

[35] See Chapters 1–3 for the discussion of *equites* predominantly expressing their political will in matters that affected them personally.

[36] Millar 1988: 51–2.

[37] Nep. *Att.* 19.2: *Namque hic contentus ordine equestri, quo erat ortus, in affinitatem pervenit imperatoris, divi filii; cum iam ante familiaritatem eius esset consecutus nulla alia re quam elegantia vitae qua ceteros ceperat principes civitatis dignitate pari, fortuna humiliores.*

The reference to Atticus' equestrian rank is presented as personal modesty, the reticence to seek *potentia* (power) and *honores* (offices). This owes much to the Ciceronian view of equestrian *quies* and *otium*, which was an ideal rather than reality – equestrian rank hardly prevented Oppius and Balbus from grasping at power.[38] The close relationship between Octavian and Atticus manifested itself in daily meetings and correspondence, as well as ties of marriage.[39] Atticus was the sort of man who was useful to Octavian precisely because of his subtle way of doing business and negotiating crises: autocrats did not only need advisers of the Machiavellian sort.[40] Modest rewards came Atticus' way, with Octavian granting him a prefecture in Asia around 38/36 BC. Atticus is known to have accepted such posts only on the condition that he did not have to actually travel anywhere.[41] Nevertheless, the conferral of such honorific offices, no matter how benignly bestowed or accepted, was a crucial component in the emergence of the monarchical *res publica*.[42]

The equestrian confidant par excellence was of course C. Maecenas, a fabulously wealthy patron of the arts, as well as a friend and adviser to the first *princeps*.[43] He famously declined to seek admission to the senatorial order, and his ability to wield power while remaining an *eques* was a continual source of fascination for Roman poets and historians.[44] Tacitus and Dio marvelled at how Octavian frequently placed Maecenas in charge of Rome and Italy during the 30s BC (though his actual authority may have been more circumscribed than they suggest).[45] Horace and Propertius, beneficiaries of Maecenas' patronage, refer his to equestrian status in their poetry as a way of emphasising his modesty and reluctance

[38] For Atticus' reticence to receive honours, see Nep. *Att.* 3.1, 6.1–5, 10.3–6, 12.5; Nicolet 1974: 708–10.

[39] Nep. *Att.* 19.4–20.5. Atticus' daughter, Caecilia Attica, married M. Agrippa, while his granddaughter, Vipsania Agrippina, married the future emperor Tiberius (see Horsfall 1989: 104).

[40] For complementary remarks on Atticus' career and the emergence of monarchy, see Millar 1988: 53–4 and K. Welch 1996: 471.

[41] Prefect in Asia: *SEG* 41, 964, as elucidated by C. P. Jones 1999. On Atticus' prefectures, see Nep. *Att.* 6.4.

[42] Millar 1988: 43.

[43] Bengtson 1988: 14–17. Their relationship seems to have been genuinely warm and friendly, as evidenced by Macrob. *Sat.* 2.4.12, in which the *princeps* teases Maecenas about his writing style.

[44] For Maecenas' decision to remain a senator, see Prop. *Eleg.* 3.9.1–3; Vell. Pat. 2.88.2–3; Dio 55.7.5; Ps.-Acro on Hor. *Carm.* 3.16.20; Porphyrio on Hor. *Sat.* 1.6.68. On the image of Maecenas as an *eques*, see Woodman 1983: 239–44; Cresci 1995; Dakouras 2006; Bodel 2015: 34–6.

[45] Dio 49.16.2, 51.3.5; Tac. *Ann.* 6.11.2; Vell. Pat. 2.88.2. Cf. App. *BC* 5.99, 112, who suggests that he held more limited authority (Dakouras 2006: 226–7).

for power, perhaps as a way of rebutting contemporary criticisms.[46]
As Propertius wrote in *Elegies* 3.9:

> Although you could possess the axes, supreme among Roman offices,
> and lay down the law in the middle of the forum;
> although you could travel through the fighting spears of the Medes,
> and adorn your residence with mounted arms;
> although Caesar gives you the power to accomplish this,
> and riches fall easily into your lap at every moment;
> you refrain from this and keep yourself humbly in the dim shadows . . .[47]

Here Maecenas shuns the traditional symbols of senatorial authority,
such as the *fasces* that represented the magisterial *imperium* of
a consul, and he declines to hold the praetorship and administer the
rule of law.[48] His house is not decorated with the trophies of military
success – although Maecenas did fight during the civil wars, he did
not command armies after that point.[49] Propertius' poem recall
Cicero's argument in the *Pro Cluentio* that the traditional *insignia*
and rewards of the senatorial career were not open to *equites*, who
were thus not subject to the strictures of the *res publica*.[50] One cannot
escape the impression that this image was encouraged by Maecenas
himself, who may have enjoyed the juxtaposition of his ostensible
political reticence against the lives of his illustrious Etruscan
forefathers.[51] At the same time, however, Maecenas' method of obtaining influence in the Augustan regime manifestly circumvented the
accepted notion that authority was invested in senatorial magistrates
elected by the *populus Romanus*.[52] Elections still continued
under Augustus, but the power of Maecenas and others was a potent
reminder of their growing irrelevance.

---

[46] Cresci 1995: 170; Dakouras 2006: 63–7, 94–6.

[47] Prop. *Eleg.* 3.9.23–9: *cum tibi Romano dominas in honore secures | et liceat medio ponere iura foro, | vel tibi Medorum pugnaces ire per hastas | atque ornare tuam fixa per arma domum, | et tibi ad effectum vires det Caesar et omni | tempore tam faciles insinuentur opes, | parcis et in tenues humilem te colligis umbras.*

[48] L. Richardson 1977: 351; Gold 1982: 106–7.

[49] These arms and other military honours would have been affixed at the door to the house (L. Richardson 1977: 351–2).

[50] Cresci 1995: 172–3.

[51] Cairns 2006: 271–4. On Maecenas and Etruria, see Sordi 1995. For Horace's playfulness as regards Maecenius' Etrurian origin in *Carm.* 3.29, see Nisbet and Rudd 2004: 347–8.

[52] Cresci 1995: 173. Bengtson 1988: 17 points out the obvious difference between Agrippa and Maecenas in this regard: the former possessed honour and positions, whereas the latter was happy to be Augustus' friend.

Maecenas was merely the most conspicuous of Augustus' equestrian friends.[53] There were many others, some of whom were interrelated through ties of marriage. C. Proculeius, who was Maecenas' brother-in-law, had been a close associate of the *princeps* since the 30s BC, when he helped secure Cleopatra's capture.[54] His influence remained strong until his death, and Augustus even allegedly considered that he would be a good marriage match for his daughter, Iulia.[55] Proculeius was himself related to C. Sallustius Crispus, who succeeded Maecenas as Augustus' closest equestrian confidant.[56] He was most notorious for his complicity in the death of Augustus' adopted son, Agrippa Postumus, early in Tiberius' reign.[57] But Crispus' influence extended well beyond political machinations. Like Maecenas he was enormously rich, with a vast estate in Rome (the Horti Sallustiani), and a notable patron of the arts. Horace dedicated *Odes* 2.2 to Crispus, portraying him as a paradigm of generosity.[58] This was followed by *Odes* 2.3, addressed to the equestrian Q. Dellius, who seems to have been a particularly unsavoury character, switching sides between Antonius and Octavian several times before settling on the latter.[59] He subsequently obtained the *princeps'* forgiveness and ranked among his foremost friends, according to Seneca.[60] Horace's poems in honour of these equestrian patrons are collected in Book 2 of the *Odes*, kept apart from the senatorial grandees, making them a special class all of their own.[61] Further names suggest themselves, such as C. Matius (mentioned above) and C. Vedius Pollio, both of whom are cited by Tacitus as prominent *equites* in the Augustan regime.[62] Pollio, a freedman's son, was notoriously cruel: he would have thrown one of his slaves to the lampreys for the crime of breaking a cup, if Augustus had not stopped him.[63] But his importance lies in his role as a personal agent of Octavian, administering Asia in his name in around 31/30 BC.[64] These equestrian associates of the first *princeps* did not merely provide advice and cultivate patronal networks as their

[53] Hor. *Carm.* 3.16.20 calls him 'the glory of the *equites*' (*equitum decus*).
[54] Pliny the Elder, *NH* 7.148; Dio 51.11.4, 53.24.2, 54.3.5; Plut. *Ant.* 77–9; Porphyrio on Hor. *Carm.* 2.2.5.
[55] Suet. *Aug.* 63.2; Tac. *Ann.* 4.40.6. There is no evidence that he lost favour with Augustus, as some have supposed (see Rich 1990: 158).
[56] Sen. *Clem.* 1.10.1; Tac. *Ann.* 3.30.2–4. For the relationship between the two men, see Syme 1978b: 295.
[57] Tac. *Ann.* 1.6.3, 3.30. 3.   [58] Nisbet and Hubbard 1978: 33–4.
[59] Sen. *Suas.* 1.7; Vell. Pat. 2.84.2; Nisbet and Hubbard 1978: 51–2.
[60] Sen. *Clem.* 1.10.1; S. M. Braund 2009: 475–6.   [61] Lyne 1995: 84–5.   [62] Tac. *Ann.* 12.60.4.
[63] Dio 54.23.1–6; Pliny the Elder, *NH* 9.77. Their relationship certainly soured, and Augustus demolished his house to make way for the Portico of Livia (Ovid, *Fasti* 6.643–4).
[64] Syme 1961: 28–9. Cf. Atkinson 1962.

forebears had done for Republican politicians: they were also involved in the exercise of government and administration, wielding power tradition- ally invested in the senatorial magistracies.[65]

This does not mean that Augustus lacked senatorial friends; most notably there was his general and right-hand man, the *novus homo* M. Vipsanius Agrippa.[66] Alongside him was another new man, T. Statilius Taurus, one of the *princeps'* generals, who shared the consulship with Augustus as *ordinar- ius* in 26 BC.[67] Augustus carefully cultivated selected supporters from among established families as a way of building wider connections between himself and the aristocracy. One of these was the patrician M. Valerius Messalla Corvinus, who transferred his allegiance from M. Antonius to the young Octavian in the civil wars.[68] Augustus appointed him to the new position of *praefectus urbi* in 26 BC, but he quickly resigned the office.[69] Syme has suggested that this was because Messalla realised that he was being used for his status as a patrician senator, since real power in Rome that year lay with the *novi homines* – Statilius Taurus, consul of 26 BC, as well as Agrippa and Maecenas.[70] Messalla's position echoes the similarly decorative role performed by the senator L. Munatius Plancus – never really a close associate – when he proposed that Octavian should be given the name of Augustus in 27 BC.[71] Messalla himself would later propose that Augustus should be designated as *pater patriae* in 2 BC.[72] Augustus also cultivated the support of the illustrious M. Calpurnius Piso, who was governor of Syria and later served as *praefectus urbi* – the post Messalla had swiftly vacated – for twenty years.[73] Piso obviously realised the potential power inherent in the urban prefecture in the monarchical *res publica*; it would eventually emerge as the most distinguished office in the senatorial *cursus*. Paullus Fabius Maximus, *cos. ord.* 11 BC, who came from a long senatorial and distin- guished family, was another friend of the *princeps*, though he did not serve in many official posts.[74] Nor was he part of a larger aristocratic network or coterie; as Syme put it, he 'remains a curiously isolated figure, his loyalties concentrated on devotion to the ruler'.[75] He was, however, married

---

[65] Brunt 1983: 42; Bodel 2015: 37.   [66] Reinhold 1933; Bengston 1988: 8–14; Tac. *Ann.* 1.3.1.

[67] Vell. Pat. 2.127.1; Syme 1939: 237, 1986: 33–4. For his family, see Benario 1970.

[68] Syme 1939: 237–8, 302; Bengtson 1988: 17–19.   [69] Tac. *Ann.* 6.11.3.

[70] Syme 1986: 211–12.

[71] Vell. Pat. 2.91.1; Suet. *Aug.* 7.2. On the significance of choosing Plancus, see Levick 2010: 72; Wardle 2014: 105.

[72] Suet. *Aug.* 38.1–2. For the similarities in the choice of Plancus and Messalla for these roles, see Syme 1986: 208; Wardle 2014: 393–4.

[73] For Piso's life and career, see Syme 1986: 329–45.   [74] Syme 1939: 376, 1986: 403–20.

[75] Syme 1986: 408. See Ovid, *Ep. Ex. Pont.* 1.2; Tac. *Ann.* 1.5.1 for intimacy with Augustus.

to Augustus' cousin, Marcia.[76] This connection with the *princeps'* family not only offered Fabius Maximus prestige, but also tied his fortunes to those of Augustus. It is important to point out that these senatorial grandees were not guaranteed pre-eminence in the administration (indeed, it could be argued that they were sometimes, as in the case of Messalla Corvinus, used to conceal the real workings of power). Senatorial aristocrats had to compete with new men, both senators and *equites*, for influence with the *princeps*.[77] The prime criterion for access was not status, but intimacy.

Roman writers offered different interpretations of the roles played by Maecenas and Augustus' other equestrian friends. Velleius Paterculus provided a fairly measured portrayal of Maecenas as an example of an *eques* who eschewed ambition, at a time when many men of humble birth were able to rise to senatorial magistracies.[78] Cassius Dio was likewise restrained in his account of Maecenas, because he thought the *eques* did not attempt to exceed his status.[79] Thus, in Dio's mind, he compared favourably with more ambitious *equites*, such as L. Aelius Sejanus, praetorian prefect of Tiberius, and C. Fulvius Plautianus, who held the same position under Septimius Severus.[80] In Dio's *Roman History* it is Maecenas who delivers a speech to Octavian urging him to retain monarchical power in Book 52. Here he emerges as a pragmatic figure, recommending that *equites* should be assigned specific tasks in the imperial administration, but must not rise above their station.[81] Tacitus, in contrast, exhibited anxiety not only about the influence of Maecenas, but all *equites* who obtained some measure of authority in the state.[82] In his account of the year AD 53 Tacitus discussed Claudius' ruling that the decisions of his equestrian procurators should be considered as valid as those of the emperor.[83] This prompted him to embark on an excursus about the growth of equestrian power, which offered a telescoped account of the battle between senators and *equites* over the criminal courts in the late Republic, among other matters. The crucial development, he claimed, came with Oppius and Balbus: 'As a result of Caesar's pre-eminence, they were the first who had

[76] Ovid, *Fasti* 6.804–5; Syme 1978a: 144–5.

[77] Cf. Crook 1955: 33–6, who catalogues the emperor's *amici* but prefers to emphasise their heterogeneous origin.

[78] Vell. Pat. 2.88.2–4; Woodman 1983: 239; Dakouras 2006: 181.   [79] Dio 55.7.4.

[80] Swan 2004: 69–70; Dakouras 2006: 240, 256–61; Kemezis 2014: 134.

[81] Reinhold 1988: 168, 189, 191–2.

[82] On the difference between Tacitus and Dio's perspectives, see Sailor 2008: 138–41; Kemezis 2014: 136–8.

[83] Tac. *Ann.* 12.60.1.

the power to dictate the terms of peace and make judgements on war'
(*primi Caesaris opibus potuere condiciones pacis et arbitria belli tractare*).[84]

This entire excursus initially seems strange coming from the pen of
Tacitus, who wrote his *Annals* at a time in which equestrian administrators
were an accepted part of the Roman system. On one level, it was an
affectation on Tacitus' part to refer to the pre-Augustan 'Republic' as if
its rules and structures still dictated the business of government.[85] This
pretension set up his true purpose, which was to expose the problems of the
monarchy as it developed under Augustus.[86] Sallustius Crispus and
Maecenas are said to possess *potentia*, which means power in the sense
of influence and control (sometimes malevolent), as opposed to *potestas*, or
appropriate constitutional power.[87] In making such a statement, Tacitus
was concerned to highlight the ability of anyone, regardless of whether they
were slaves, freedmen, women or *equites*, to wield power outside the
confines of the traditional senatorial magistrates.[88] In his view, this was
the fundamental problem with the monarchical *res publica*, since the
business of government could now be conducted under the influence of
non-senatorial advisers.[89] It is true that Augustus had created an advisory
committee composed of the senatorial magistrates for each year, as well as
fifteen senators chosen by lot who served for six months.[90] But this was
a clever way of integrating senatorial government into the framework of
the new monarchical *res publica*, and it did not guarantee genuine influence and friendship with the emperor. Tacitus wanted his readers to know
that he was not fooled. His cynicism was a product of the fact that in the
monarchical *res publica* the imperial court sat somewhat uneasily beside
the traditional Republican magistracies.[91] One feature of the Augustan
principate (and indeed that of his successors), as Winterling has pointed
out, is that it did not have a 'court establishment, that is a system of offices
for the nobility to serve the emperor'.[92] This lack of structure – compared
with the French royal court of Versailles – increased suspicion, paranoia
and rivalry among Roman elites, because they were never quite sure of their

[84] Tac. *Ann.* 12.60.4.   [85] Woodman 1983: 244.   [86] Syme 1958: 432.
[87] Tac. *Ann.* 3.30.4; *OLD* s.v. *potentia* 1; Syme 1986: 300.
[88] Sailor 2008: 140–1. On specific cases, see Kehoe 1985; Byrne 1999; Dakouras 2006: 216–17.
[89] Syme 1986: 80. Note especially the secrets to which Sallustius Crispus was privy (Tac. *Ann.*
1.6.3, 3.30.3).
[90] Dio 53.21.4–5; Suet. *Aug.* 35.3. On this committee, see Crook 1955: 8–20, pointing out that the
composition changed significantly under Tiberius, when senatorial membership ceased to
rotate.
[91] Winterling 2009: 31–3.   [92] Winterling 2009: 100.

position in the pecking order.[93] But not everyone possessed Tacitus' cynicism. As Wallace-Hadrill has pointed out, his equestrian coeval C. Suetonius Tranquillus, secretary to the emperors and a true 'courtier', evinces no problem with the business of government being conducted *in camera* rather than in the senate house.[94] For Suetonius, this was the nature of imperial administration.

It is hard to escape the conclusion that the employment of *equites* rather than senators was deliberately encouraged by Caesar in his reliance on Oppius and Balbus, and then Augustus with Maecenas, Sallustius Crispus and his other equestrian friends. These *equites* were valuable to Caesar and Augustus precisely because they depended on the great men themselves for their status and power.[95] It was a mutually dependent relationship – the *princeps* received loyal supporters who would not threaten their position, and the supporters increased their wealth and prestige.[96] Augustus was still a senator whose authority derived from senatorial magistracies and powers (such as the consulship, *imperium* and *tribunicia potestas*), so he could be challenged and threatened by other senators. There were various methods of curbing the ambitions of the old aristocracy, most notably through marriages to Augustus' own family.[97] In contrast, *equites* who wielded power outside the traditional senatorial magistracies, and did not have illustrious ancestry, could not be considered his rivals.[98] Whatever their personal ability as generals might be, they did not have the ancestry of the senator M. Licinius Crassus, who fought and killed the king of the Bastarnae, and had to be neutralised as a threat.[99] The equestrian elites were thus more likely to be invested in supporting and sustaining the monarchical *res publica* that had come into being; they would not question the transformation of the system. The bonds of familiarity between the *princeps* and his equestrian advisers may have been strengthened by the fact that his own family had only recently acquired senatorial status, as Augustus wrote in his autobiography.[100] At the same time, we cannot escape the fact that the *equites* were under a certain compulsion to know their place. As Lyne has pointed out, in order to

[93] Constantine's creation of the orders of *comites* was the first real attempt to create such a structure (Millar 1977: 117–19), though it never approached the institutionalised level of hierarchy such as that found at Versailles.

[94] Wallace-Hadrill 2011: 96.   [95] Nicolet 1984: 106.

[96] On his policy of relying almost exclusively on *equites* in the early years, see Syme 1939: 367–8.

[97] Syme 1939: 373, 378–9.

[98] I must emphasise that this state of affairs applies to the Augustan period: different conditions prevailed by the third century AD, on which see Chapter 11.

[99] On Crassus, see Raaflaub and Samons II 1990: 422–3.   [100] Suet. *Aug.* 2.3.

continue as one of Augustus' equestrian friends one 'would *need* to remain equestrian'.[101] This type of unsteady and fractious political reality – an uneasy tension between the monarchical and aristocratic elements within the *res publica* – was characteristic of the evolution of the Roman system of government. This could be interpreted as Augustus failing to escape the strictures of the Republic as he established one-man rule.[102] But this reading would imply that Augustus was actually trying to abandon Rome's Republican heritage. In fact, the performance of *civilitas* in his relationship with the senators, not to mention his wielding of authority through Republican magistracies and powers, were essential to the strength and plausibility of the new monarchical *res publica*.[103] Augustus' melding of the past and present was designed to keep everyone on their toes.

The Great Prefectures

It was only a short step from Augustus relying on his equestrian friends as advisers to appointing *equites* to occupy official posts as his personal agents outside the traditional senatorial *cursus*, as the examples of Atticus and Vedius Pollio demonstrate. Indeed, the establishment of new administrative positions exclusively reserved for members of the equestrian order proved to be one of Augustus' most significant legacies. These posts offered *equites* an unprecedented range of opportunities to serve the *res publica* and its *princeps*. This was the defining difference between the *ordo equester* in the Republic and the imperial period.[104] It has been suggested that the creation of the administrative roles was largely ad hoc and not the result of systematic planning.[105] That is certainly true in the sense that the system of equestrian posts was not created at one stroke. But other considerations suggest that it is not the full story. The selection of *equites* for government posts reflects the patronal nature of the principate, in which the emperor was the final arbiter of offices and honours. By appointing a wider range of non-senatorial elites to government positions in the *res publica*, Augustus was signalling that he was not beholden to senators. Moreover, it allowed him to appoint other wealthy elites, who would pose less of a threat than senators, to senior positions in the city of Rome and the provinces.[106] This is particularly true of the most prestigious equestrian positions in the administrative hierarchy, which modern scholars call the 'great

---

[101] Lyne 1995: 135.   [102] Winterling 1999: 100–1.
[103] See Wallace-Hadrill 1982 on the performance of *civilitas*.   [104] Nicolet 1984: 104–5.
[105] Brunt 1983; Eck 2009a.   [106] Stein 1927: 442; Bang 2011: 114.

prefectures'.[107] Three of these were based in Rome: the *praefectus praetorio*, who commanded the praetorian guard; the *praefectus annonae*, in charge of Rome's grain supply; and the *praefectus vigilum*, the head of the *vigiles*, or watchmen. The fourth was the provincial governor of Egypt, the *praefectus Aegypti*. The creation of these posts indicates the new form of the monarchical *res publica* and the place of the equestrian order within it.

We will begin with the prefecture of Egypt, which had been established as a Roman province after the defeat of M. Antonius and Cleopatra. The first prefect was C. Cornelius Gallus, an *eques* from Forum Iulii of respectable but not exceptionally prominent family.[108] He developed a significant reputation as a poet, inventing the genre known as the elegy, though only fragments of his work survive today.[109] Gallus served as *praefectus fabrum* under Octavian in Egypt, helping to defeat Antonius' forces and capture Cleopatra in collaboration with another equestrian, C. Proculeius, in 30 BC.[110] Thereafter he remained in Egypt as the first governor of the new province, with the title of *praefectus*. His selection for this pivotal posting can be ascribed to the fact that he was a loyal lieutenant to Octavian, and the man on the scene at the time.[111] Gallus' pride in his achievement is demonstrated by a trilingual inscription, written in Latin, Greek and hieroglyphics, which he erected at the Temple of Isis at Philae in 29 BC. The monument was designed to mark his suppression of a rebellion in the Thebaid and the extension of the borders of Egypt. The Latin text opens with Gallus describing himself in the following manner:

C. Cornelius Gallus, son of Gnaeus, *eques Romanus*, the first prefect of Alexandria and Egypt after the kings had been conquered by Caesar, son of the deified one . . .[112]

---

[107] Sablayrolles 1999 offers the best overview of these prefectures.

[108] Suet. *Aug.* 66.1; Syme 1938b: 41–4.

[109] Hollis 2007: 219–52; R. K. Gibson 2012. Gallus was active in the 40s BC, writing a poem concerned with Caesar's conquests (Anderson, Parsons and Nisbet 1979: 148–55). Gallus' influence on Propertius' elegiac poetry is discussed in great detail by Cairns 2006: 70–249.

[110] Dio 51.9.1; Plut. *Ant.* 79; *AE* 1964, 255 (as *praefectus fabrum*).

[111] Syme 1938b: 39; Brunt 1975: 128; Cairns 2006: 73. The most recent discussions of Jördens 2009: 49–51 and Faoro 2011: 5–25 emphasise Cornelius Gallus' appointment in its immediate context, especially Octavian's use of trusted supporters in ad hoc command posts during the civil wars.

[112] *CIL* III 14147.5 = Hoffmann, Minas-Nerpel and Pfeiffer 2009: 119, ll. 1–2: *C(aius) Cornelius Cn(aei) f(ilius) Gallus, [eq]ues Romanus, pos<t> rege[s] | a Caesare Deivi f(ilio) devictos praefect [us Ale]xandreae et Aegypti primus.* In the Greek text, *eques Romanus* is rendered as [ἱππεὺ]ς Ῥωμαίων and the reference to Alexandria is omitted (Hoffmann, Minas-Nerpel and Pfeiffer 2009: 120, ll. 10–11). The Greek is an interpretation of the Latin original (F. Hoffmann 2010).

Gallus placed himself in succession to the kings of Egypt. Although this may appear self-aggrandising on his part, it actually seems to have been the widespread perception of the prefect's authority.[113] Moreover, the hieroglyphic text, which is much longer than the Latin and Greek inscriptions and is by no means a translation but a separate composition, confirms this impression.[114] The fact that Egypt was given to one of Octavian's personal friends, who conducted campaigns on the *princeps'* behalf, stands in stark contrast to the official rhetoric that it was entrusted to the 'empire of the Roman people' (*imperio populi Romani*).[115]

Proper constitutional procedures were followed, since the province of Egypt and the prefect's *imperium* – his constitutional right of command – were officially authorised by a law.[116] At the same time, there was a certain amount of mystique that surrounded Egypt, which was fomented by the ban on senators and *equites inlustres* (probably those equestrians who held procuratorships or other government posts) travelling there without the *princeps'* express permission.[117] There was a widespread belief among Roman writers, at least in the second and third centuries AD, that such a crucial province, soon to become the breadbasket of Rome, could not be entrusted to a senator, as it would provide a perfect platform for a revolt.[118] This reasoning is usually minimised or dismissed by modern scholars, since realistically, an *eques* at the head of an army was just as dangerous as any senator.[119] But if we consider the immediate context in which Augustus made his decision, it does make sense. The *princeps'* actions show that he wished to maintain as much personal authority over Egypt as possible, and essentially bypassed the senate when he installed

---

[113] Tac. *Hist.* 1.11; Strabo 17.797. Cf. Jördens 2009: 51–2, arguing against the perception that the prefect of Egypt functioned as a type of 'viceroy'.

[114] Minas-Nerpel and Pfeiffer 2010: 269.

[115] *RG* 27.1; *CIL* VI 702; Cooley 2009: 229. Cf. Tac. *Hist.* 1.11, writing somewhat more honestly that it was 'retained by the imperial house' (*domi retinere*).

[116] *Dig.* 1.17.1 (Ulpian); Tac. *Ann.* 12.60.3; A. H. M. Jones 1960: 121–2; Jördens 2009: 48. See Hoffmann, Minas-Nerpel and Pfeiffer 2009: 129–30, who emphasise the technical nature of the language in the inscription.

[117] Tac. *Ann.* 2.59.3. For the *equites inlustres* as procurators, see Mommsen: 1887–8 III.1, 363, and see further Chapter 7. Cf. Dio 51.17.1, who only mentions senators. Despite the ban, Augustus granted both Maecenas and Vedius Pollio estates in Egypt (Capponi 2002). Jördens 2009: 36–41 argues that such a ban probably derived from the immediate political situation at the time, but later became less relevant, while Faoro 2011: 40, who documents cases of senators attested in Egypt, suggests that the *princeps* could grant special dispensation to individual members of the senatorial order.

[118] Dio 51.17.1–2 and Arr. *Anab.* 3.5.7 are most explicit in making this point, but see also Tac. *Ann.* 2.59.1–3, *Hist.* 1.11.1. Cf. Suet. *Iul.* 35.1, who attributes the same motivation to Caesar.

[119] For example, Brunt 1983: 61–2; Bowman 1996a: 680–1; Talbert 1996: 342.

Gallus, a trusted equestrian friend.[120] In the world of the first century BC it was inconceivable that an equestrian could ever emerge as the acknowledged leader of Rome. Status and ancestry mattered, as is shown by M. Antonius' attempts to spread rumours about Octavian's own family.[121]

Gallus soon fell from the *princeps'* favour, after a certain Valerius Largus claimed that he had slandered Augustus, set up images of himself throughout Egypt, and inscribed his own accomplishments on the pyramids.[122] The chronology of his downfall is uncertain, and the official accusations may only have been made after Gallus returned to Rome from Egypt.[123] Augustus formally banned Gallus from his house, and he would have appeared in the *quaestio de maiestate* on a charge of treason, if he had not committed suicide.[124] Augustus then selected another equestrian, C. Aelius Gallus, as prefect of Egypt, and the administration of the province continued in the same vein, regardless of Cornelius Gallus' offences.[125] This was a signal that Cornelius Gallus' appointment was not an aberration, and Egypt would never be entrusted to a senatorial governor. This decision could not have gone unnoticed at time. Indeed, Tacitus included the *praefectus Aegypti* in his excursus on the inappropriate growth of equestrian power in Book 12 of the *Annals*, in which he noted that the prefect's decrees were equal to those of Roman magistrates.[126] The equestrian prefecture of Egypt was therefore conceived as representing a challenge to senatorial authority, since eligibility for appointment was not dependent on having held the magistracy of praetor or consul (as with the proconsuls or *legati Augusti pro praetore*). Instead, it was a symbol of the new monarchical *res publica*.

The three principal equestrian prefectures in the city of Rome were established in the latter half of Augustus' principate. The praetorian prefecture was the first to be created, in 2 BC. In that year Augustus appointed two *equites*, Q. Ostorius Scapula and P. Salvius Aper, as commanders of the nine *cohortes praetoriae*, which numbered approximately 4,500 soldiers in

[120] Eck 2009a: 246. Jördens 2009: 49–50 notes the number of legions stationed in the province, suggesting that there was at least an initial perception that the region needed to be secured.
[121] Suet. *Aug.* 2.3.
[122] Dio 53.23.5–6. Insults towards Augustus seem to be supported by Ovid, *Tristia* 2.446.
[123] Rich 1990: 157–8; Cairns 2006: 73–4.
[124] Suet. *Aug.* 66.2; Dio 53.23.6–7. See also Amm. 17.4.5 for charges of embezzlement, but there is no real evidence that Gallus was staging a revolt (thus Raaflaub and Samons 1990: 423–5).
[125] As Jördens 2009: 53 points out, the equestrian or senatorial status of the governor did not impact how the province was actually administered. However, it did matter politically in Rome.
[126] Tac. *Ann.* 12.60.2.

total.[127] In the Republican army the *cohors praetoria* was an elite unit that protected the general's headquarters (the *praetorium*) and accompanied him on the field.[128] The young Octavian possessed multiple praetorian cohorts, amounting to some 4,000 men, as early as 42 BC.[129] He retained them subsequently as Augustus through his status as proconsul.[130] The praetorians had traditionally been paid at a higher rate than ordinary soldiers, but in 27 BC Augustus decreed that they should receive twice as much as legionaries, in order to ensure their fidelity to him personally.[131] Before 2 BC these praetorian cohorts were commanded by equestrians with the rank of military tribune, who answered to Augustus alone.[132] The creation of two more senior commanders with the title of *praefectus* emphasised their importance, and represented the centralisation of military authority in Augustus' hands – a pivotal element of the transformation of the state into a monarchy.[133] The selection of *equites*, rather than senators, for these prefectures was on one level a logical step given that cohorts were already commanded by equestrian tribunes.[134] But it also sent a very clear message that such important forces could not be entrusted to senators, who were Augustus' peers and rivals. The move signalled that it was the *princeps'* prerogative to institute a new military command structure without reference to the strictures of the senatorial magistracies in the traditional *cursus honorum*.[135] Although Dio provides no reason for the creation of the prefecture in 2 BC, it can plausibly be understood as a response to the political crises of that year, including the downfall and exile of Augustus' daughter, Iulia.[136]

The prosopographical evidence for the lives and careers of the first prefects is scanty, but shows that they possessed connections with Augustus' key equestrian confidants, most notably Sallustius Crispus and Maecenas. Q. Ostorius Scapula, one of the first two prefects, was the

---

[127] Dio 55.10.10. On the numbers of praetorians, Dio 55.24.6 anachronistically gives 10,000 soldiers, but this number would only be achieved under subsequent emperors (Durry 1938: 77–89). Even under Augustus, the numbers fluctuated (Keppie 1996: 107–8).

[128] Durry 1938: 67–74; Keppie 1996: 102–4; Absil 1997: 19–21; Bingham 2013: 9–15.

[129] App. *BC* 5.3; Keppie 1996: 105–6. [130] Keppie 1996: 119–20. [131] Dio 53.11.5.

[132] Brunt 1983: 59; Keppie 1996: 113–14.

[133] Millar 1977: 123. For the rather vague nature of the title of *praefectus*, see Demougin 1988: 722–3.

[134] Bingham 2013: 21. Cf. Durry 1938: 157, who suggests some connection with the equestrian Maecenas and his earlier supervision of Rome in Octavian's absence. There is no evidence, however, that Maecenas was ever prefect (Absil 1997: 197–9).

[135] Note Syme's 1939: 357 remarks about the power of the praetorian prefect exceeding that of a consul.

[136] Syme 1986: 300; Sablayrolles 1999: 360–1; J. S. Richardson 2012: 158–9.

brother of P. Ostorius Scapula, an *eques* who was entrusted with the prefecture of Egypt in AD 3.[137] P. Ostorius Scapula was married to a daughter of C. Sallustius Crispus.[138] L. Seius Strabo, who is attested in office in AD 14, had some senatorial relatives, including consuls, in his family tree.[139] Most importantly, his mother Terentia was the sister-in-law of Maecenas.[140] We should perhaps not push these connections too far: evidence of intermarriage does not prove intimacy, either with the *princeps* or his leading advisers.[141] It is also true that the creation of the praetorian prefecture should not automatically be interpreted as a sinister innovation in the light of the actions of commanders such as Sejanus and Plautianus.[142] For instance, no record exists of either of the first two prefects, Q. Ostorius Scapula and P. Salvius Aper, abusing their power in the manner of these infamous later prefects.

But at the same time, two considerations show that the creation of the praetorian prefecture was emblematic of the change to a monarchical *res publica*. The relationships between the prefects and the emperor's equestrian advisers show some of the networks developing at the imperial court among these equestrian families, whose power and influence was not tied to the traditional framework of the *res publica* in the form of elected magistracies.[143] Moreover, we cannot escape the fact that, while the praetorian guard was paid by the state, its commanders were answerable only to Augustus, and the soldiers were the only men entitled to bear arms in the city of Rome. Their very title of *praefectus praetorio*, literally 'prefect for the *praetorium*', indicated the close connection between the guard commander and the *princeps*' 'headquarters' – that is, his personal household.[144] In the late Republic multiple senatorial generals possessed their own *cohortes praetoriae*, but now only one senator could – Augustus himself.[145]

---

[137] Hanson 1982. Their descendants would enter the senatorial order (Christol and Demougin 1984).

[138] Syme 1968: 79; Hanson 1982: 247.

[139] Vell. Pat. 2.127.3, a description of the family which is undoubtedly intended to be flattering to Sejanus, but is supported by prosopographical studies (Syme 1986: 300–10).

[140] Syme 1958: 384.

[141] Though see Macrob. 2.4.18 for an anecdote featuring Seius Strabo and Augustus which indicates some level of intimacy.

[142] Keppie 1996: 118.

[143] Cf. Tac. *Ann.* 4.3, for unnecessarily pejorative remarks concerning Sejanus' background. We admittedly know virtually nothing about P. Salvius Aper.

[144] Keppie 1996: 122, referring to the emperor's place of residence being described as the *praetorium*.

[145] Note, for example, the multiple cohorts of the members of the second triumvirate (App. *BC* 4.7). No praetorian cohorts existed among the forces commanded by Augustus' governors (Keppie 1996: 121).

The appointment of an equestrian commander, while on one level a relatively straightforward and logical decision based on military hierarchy, also manifestly demonstrated that this position operated outside the traditional constitutional framework of senatorial government.[146] Thus, for Cassius Dio, the guard was prima facie evidence of the monarchical system Augustus had created.[147] Dio was writing in the third century AD when such a system was an accepted and unchangeable reality. It is with the rise of L. Aelius Sejanus as Tiberius' proxy that we can first conjecture contemporary anxiety about these prefects in Velleius Paterculus' spirited defence of the merits of new men from equestrian background.[148] Tiberius' reign saw a significant change in the location of these troops. In Augustus' lifetime the praetorian cohorts had been stationed throughout Italy.[149] But under Sejanus the guard acquired a permanent home in Rome, with all the cohorts being quartered in one camp.[150] Sejanus exerted influence over the *princeps* far above that expected of his status in the social hierarchy. He was the living embodiment of the fear found in Tacitus' remarks about the power of Maecenas and Sallustius Crispus.

Augustus' desire to circumvent senatorial authority and the traditional framework of the *res publica* can be detected in his establishment of the two other equestrian prefectures in Rome.[151] In AD 6 he created the post of *praefectus vigilum* to oversee the seven cohorts of *vigiles*, who were freedmen assigned to fight fires throughout Rome.[152] As with the praetorian prefecture, the institution of the post represented the culmination of a long process.[153] As far back as 22 BC Augustus had established a unit of 600 slaves under the command of the aediles.[154] One such aedile, M. Egnatius Rufus, proved particularly popular when he used his own slaves to extinguish urban fires and began to boast publicly of his achievements.[155] This soon earned him Augustus' displeasure, a development that exposes some of the tensions between the *princeps* and his senatorial peers.[156] In 7 BC the *vicomagistri* assumed responsibility for fire-fighting in their city neighbourhoods.[157] The establishment of the seven cohorts of *vigiles*

---

[146] Absil 1997: 21.   [147] Dio 53.11.5.   [148] Vell. Pat. 2.128.1–4; Woodman 1977: 256–63.

[149] Suet. *Aug.* 49.1; Keppie 1996: 115–16; Wardle 2014: 359.

[150] This was remembered as a major event: see e.g. Suet. *Tib.* 37.1; Tac. *Ann.* 4.2.1; Dio 57.19.6.

[151] Sablayrolles 1999: 356–60; Eck 2009a: 242–5, 247–8.

[152] Dio 55.26.4–5. See also Suet. *Aug.* 30.1; Strabo 5.235.

[153] Sablayrolles 1996: 24–6; Fuhrmann 2011: 116–17.   [154] Dio 52.2.4; *Dig.* 1.15.1 (Paulus).

[155] For the Republican precedents, see Sablayrolles 1996: 6–24.

[156] Dio 54.24.4–6; Furhmann 2011: 119–20. See Rich 1990: 159 on the date (not 26 BC, as Dio implies). Vell. Pat. 2.91.3–92.5 records that Rufus subsequently plotted against the emperor, in 19 BC (Raaflaub and Samons 1990: 427).

[157] Dio 55.8.7.

in AD 6 was initially intended to be a temporary measure in response to an outbreak of fires, but soon became permanent.[158] Unfortunately, the identity of Augustus' first appointee to the post of *praefectus vigilum* must remain a mystery: the first attested prefect is Q. Naevius Macro in the reign of Tiberius.[159] The jurist Iulius Paulus, writing in the third century AD, interpreted the measure, undoubtedly correctly, as one of centralisation: the protection of the city was now the personal concern of the *princeps*, with the *praefectus vigilum* essentially acting as his representative, protecting the inhabitants of Rome, and their property, in his name.[160] There was to be no other Egnatius Rufus from the ranks of the senate.

The delegation of Augustus' personal authority can also be seen in the appointment of the *praefectus annonae*.[161] The responsibility for overseeing the grain supply had traditionally been entrusted to the aediles alongside their other duties. During a grain shortage in 57 BC, which led to riots in Rome, Cn. Pompeius Magnus was entrusted with a five-year extraordinary command to supervise the grain supply (the *cura annonae*).[162] C. Iulius Caesar later made the grain supply and its distribution the sole responsibility of two aediles (known as *aediles cereales*).[163] After another major famine the people pressured Augustus to become dictator and assume responsibility for the *cura annonae* in 22 BC, following the precedent of Pompeius.[164] Although he declined the dictatorship, Augustus readily took on the pressing task of solving the grain problem, and allegedly provided the people with the necessary supplies in a matter of days.[165] He subsequently appointed two senatorial ex-praetors to supervise its distribution.[166] It is probable that Augustus still retained formal oversight of the *annona*, despite the continued existence of the *aediles cereales*, since further famines in AD 6 and 7 prompted him to personally appoint two consular officials to oversee the problem.[167] No ancient source specifically attests the institution of the equestrian *praefectus annonae*, but we know that it must have taken place between AD 7 and 14.[168] The first

---

[158] Dio 55.26.4–5. For the organisation and composition of the units, see Sablayrolles 1996: 27–37.
[159] Sablayrolles 1996: 475–6.
[160] *Dig.* 1.15.3.pref (Paulus). For the prefect's duties, see *Dig.* 1.15.3.1–5 (Paulus), 1.15.4 (Ulpian).
[161] Sablayrolles 1999: 356–61; Eich 2005: 191–3.   [162] Pavis d'Escurac 1976: 3–9.
[163] Dio 43.51.3.   [164] Dio 54.1.3–4; Rich 1990: 172; Pavis d'Escurac 1976: 12–14.
[165] As Augustus himself claimed in *RG* 5.2 (on this, see Cooley 2009: 129).
[166] Dio 54.1.4; Suet. *Aug.* 37.
[167] For the continuing *cura* of Augustus, see Pavis d'Escurac 1976: 17–19. Consular officials: Dio 55.26.1–2, 31.4; Swan 2004: 180, 207; Pavis d'Escurac 1976: 26–8.
[168] Pavis d'Escurac 1976: 29–30; Eck 2009a: 244–5.

known prefect, C. Turranius Gracilis, is attested in office at Augustus'
death in AD 14.[169] He may have been selected based on his experience
as a former prefect of Egypt. The fact that Turranius held the post
until AD 48 (with only a brief interruption under Caligula) suggests
that Augustus' successors were largely content to keep his measures in
place.[170] The equestrian prefect had to work with two senatorial
officials (the *praefecti frumenti dandi*), who were in charge of the
actual distribution of grain within the city of Rome.[171] But the *cura
annonae*, the supervision of the infrastructure and resources necessary
to bring the grain to Italy, was the responsibility of the *princeps* and
his equestrian delegate.

The four equestrian prefects of Egypt, the praetorian guard, the
vigiles and the grain supply were therefore created during the course
of Augustus' lifetime to serve as the *princeps'* personal representatives.
It is important to note that it was not only *equites* who were given
responsibilities in Augustus' administration, as new senatorial posts
were also introduced, such as those in the city of Rome.[172] But these
often originally emerged from efforts to concentrate power in the hands
of his supporters. His right-hand man, the senatorial *novus homo*
Marcus Agrippa, personally managed the water supply of Rome for
more than two decades, with senatorial officials known as *curatores
aquarum* being introduced after his death.[173] The first *curator aquarum*
was a senatorial *nobilis*, Messalla Corvinus. He was already an adherent
of Augustus, a trustworthy patrician who had also been appointed the
first *praefectus urbi* as a safe pair of hands.[174] We must therefore view
these appointments in their contemporary context. Augustus evidently
did not wish to invest too much power in the hands of senators, who
were his peers and potential rivals.[175] The decision to create new
prefectures and select equestrians to hold these posts is a powerful
illustration of the centralisation of power in the *princeps'* hands, outside
the normal bounds of the senatorial magistracies and military commands. It represented the consolidation of the monarchical element
within the *res publica*.

---

[169] Tac. *Ann.* 1.7.2.   [170] Pavis d'Escurac 1976: 317–19; Brunt 1983: 60.   [171] Eich 2005: 191.
[172] Daguet-Gagey 2011.   [173] Eck 2009a: 238–9.   [174] Frontin. *Aq.* 99.4; Syme 1986: 212–13.
[175] This discussion steers a middle course between Pflaum 1950: 4–5, who pits the *equites* and
senators against each other, and the more pragmatic views of Brunt 1983: 59–66, Talbert 1996:
342 and Eck 2009a: 247–9, who play down rivalries and differences. Augustus wanted everyone
kept on their toes.

Managing the Empire

In the Republic, senators had employed freedmen and equestrian *procuratores*, officials who oversaw their property and financial affairs. Augustus possessed a vast array of estates which belonged to him, rather than the *res publica*, and needed to be managed on the same lines. He therefore appointed his own freedmen and equestrian procurators to represent his personal interests and manage his lands throughout the Roman world.[176] Two types of procurators were sent out to the Roman provinces following the 'first settlement' of 27 BC.[177] In the public provinces, such as Achaea, Africa and Asia, which were governed by senatorial proconsuls, the emperor appointed *procuratores patrimonii* who were responsible for managing his estates (his *patrimonium*, or property). Senatorial quaestors continued to be appointed in these provinces, as they had been under the Republic, to oversee the financial affairs of the *res publica*.[178] The remaining, 'imperial', provinces had been allocated to Augustus himself as proconsul in 27 BC, but he ruled these through senatorial *legati Augusti pro praetore* of his own choosing. In these regions, such as Syria and Hispania Citerior, his *procuratores Augusti* possessed authority over both the *princeps'* own affairs and the finances of the *res publica*.[179] Modern scholars usually refer to these officials as 'provincial' or 'financial' procurators to distinguish them from the patrimonial procurators in the public proconsular provinces.[180] The provincial procurators were entrusted with tasks such as the collection of direct taxes, managing the collection of indirect taxes by *publicani*, and paying and supplying the army.[181] The province of Egypt was an exception in terms of its structure, since its administration was adapted from the previous Ptolemaic rulers.[182] Here the deputy of the prefect was another equestrian official known as the *dikaiodotes* or *iuridicus Alexandreae*, who possessed responsibility for judicial affairs, while the head of the *idios logos* was the equivalent of the provincial procurator.[183] All these equestrian officials were paid a regular yearly salary for their service. They were later organised into specific pay

---

[176] This is widely recognised: see, for example, Mommsen 1887–8: III, 557–8; Sherwin-White 1939: 14; Pflaum 1950: 5–9; Nicolet 1974: 425–31; Kienast 2009: 190.

[177] Dio 53.15.3; Brunt 1990c; Burton 1993; Eich 2005: 98–105; Eck 2009a: 232–3.

[178] See A. R. Birley 1981: 12–13 on the appointment of quaestors, and Kantor 2011: 157 on their continuing jurisdiction.

[179] Strabo 17.840. Many of these officials are not firmly attested in the Augustan period, however: see the list in Brunt 1983: 69.

[180] Eich 2005: 104–5.   [181] Brunt 1990b: 165–6; Eck 2009a: 232–3.

[182] Pflaum 1950: 33; Bowman 1996a: 682–6; Eich 2007.   [183] Strabo 17.797.

grades, but this hierarchical system does not seem to have existed under Augustus.[184] Crucially, both the provincial and patrimonial procurators answered directly to Augustus himself, rather than the provincial governor, regardless of whether the governor was a senatorial proconsul or an imperial legate.[185] In this way, much of the Roman empire was managed as a private aristocratic household writ large.

The full title of *procurator Caesaris Augusti* emphasised that these equestrian officials were the personal agents of the *princeps*, not appointees of the *res publica*.[186] Q. Octavius Sagitta, for example, is recorded to have served as 'procurator of Augustus Caesar among the Vindelicans and Raetians and in the Vallis Poenina for four years, in the province of Spain for ten years, and in Syria for two'.[187] But the lines between the property of the *princeps* and that of the *res publica* soon blurred, especially when officials began to overstep their authority.[188] In 4 BC the procurator in Syria, Sabinus, caused significant problems for Augustus' senatorial legate P. Quinctilius Varus when he drove the Jews to revolt and then marched to Jerusalem to seize the property of King Herod, forcing Varus to come and rescue him.[189] In a later case from AD 23, the procurator of the imperial patrimony in the province of Asia, Lucilius Capito, was arraigned before the senate for giving orders to soldiers. The emperor Tiberius noted that this was outside Capito's official remit, which was to manage only 'his slaves and personal assets' (*in servitia et pecunias familiares*).[190] Over the course of the first century AD, however, the authority of patrimonial procurators expanded beyond imperial properties to include duties carried out on behalf of the *res publica*, such as supervising the tax collection.[191] During the principate of Claudius, procurators were officially given additional jurisdictional powers which at least covered imperial properties (and probably extended beyond them) – a measure that was confirmed by

[184] Dio 53.15.4–5; Suet. *Aug.* 36 (with less detail); Pflaum 1950: 30–3. Dio's 'Maecenas' advised Augustus to introduce salaries for senators (52.23.1) and *equites* (52.25.2). For the salary grade system, see Chapter 7.

[185] Eich 2005: 106–24. There was of course no real difference in the way the public and imperial provinces were managed, as shown by Millar 1989.

[186] Sherwin-White 1939: 14–15.

[187] AE 1902, 189 = ILS 9007: *procurat(or) Caesaris | Augusti in Vindalicis et Raetis et in valle Poe | nina per annos IIII et in Hispania provincia | per annos X et in Suria biennium.* The post is to be dated *c.* 15–11 BC, after the initial subjugation of these Alpine regions (Laffi 1977: 376–7).

[188] For discussion, see Millar 1964a: 184; Brunt 1983: 53–4, 1990b: 166–7; Talbert 1996: 340–1. See also Weaver 1972: 267 on freedmen procurators.

[189] Jos. *AJ* 17.250–268, 286–294, *BJ* 2.16–17 (a wonderful example cited by Millar 1965b: 362).

[190] Tac. *Ann.* 4.15.2; Dio 57.23.4–5.

[191] Brunt 1990b: 166–7; Burton 1993: 16–20. Demougin 2007 surveys the procuratorial responsibilities in full.

a *senatus consultum*.[192] The Customs Law of Asia (*lex portorii Asiae*), which dates to AD 62, ordered that disputes between two groups – probably *publicani* and travellers – should be brought before the equestrian procurator of Asia, which was a senatorial proconsular province.[193] It was Claudius' decision to grant such jurisdictional authority to procurators that prompted Tacitus' excursus on the growth of equestrian power as a challenge to the *res publica* and the authority of its magistrates.[194] The return of monarchy to Rome had brought with it a new administrative apparatus to manage the *princeps'* own affairs, but it was inevitable that these officials would eventually become recognised agents of the *res publica* itself.

Equestrians with the title of *praefectus* were also appointed to oversee specific regions of the empire which were usually, though not always, part of a larger area under the authority of a senatorial legate.[195] Some of these had the title of *praefectus civitatium* ('prefect of states') or *praefectus gentium* ('prefect of nations'), which referred to their authority over specific peoples.[196] Strabo recognised this development by writing that it became the accepted practice to appoint equestrian prefects to rule barbarians.[197] Though this is a rather simplistic formulation, it reflects the fact that the regional prefects were often sent to areas recently incorporated into the empire. These were either regions along the frontiers or islands in the Mediterranean, such as the Alpine zones and Raetia, parts of Illyricum, the Balearic islands, and Corsica.[198] In the east of the empire it was the practice to assign former client kingdoms to the control of equestrian prefects, as in the case of Judaea (under Augustus) and Commagene (under Tiberius). The equestrian administrators of both these regions answered to the senatorial governor of Syria.[199] The regional prefects themselves were very often equestrians promoted from military positions.[200] These new positions enabled Augustus to ensure that former

---

[192] Millar 1964a: 187, 1965b: 367; Brunt 1990b: 166–8; Eich 2005: 137–45; Demougin 2007: 275; Kantor 2011. On imperial estates, see Fuhrmann 2011: 196–9.

[193] *ME* ll. 147–9. See the commentary in Cottier et al. 2008: 160–2, developed further with an important new reading in Kantor 2011.

[194] Tac. *Ann.* 12.60.3–4.

[195] Brunt 1983: 55–6; Demougin 1988: 723–4; Eck 2009a: 246–7; Faoro 2011: 81–9, 124–7. For a case study, see the example of Judaea, which is examined by Ghiretti 1985.

[196] Faoro 2011: 124–5.   [197] Strabo 4.6.4.   [198] Faoro 2011: 124–6.

[199] Faoro 2011: 109–14, 116–17. The literary evidence for Judaea long caused problems about the status of the prefect (see A. H. M. Jones 1960: 119, for example), but has now been resolved (Ghiretti 1985; Eck 2008; Faoro 2011: 88–9). The famous Pontius Pilate inscription records his title as *praefectus Iudaeae* (*CIIP* 1277).

[200] Brunt 1983: 55; Demougin 1988: 723; Faoro 2011: 89–106.

independent kingdoms or ethnic groups were under the control of a specific representative of Rome. The selection of equestrians, rather than senators, to fill these roles under Augustus and his successors reflects a certain administrative pragmatism, as Faoro has argued.[201] However, there was no hard and fast rule. For example, M. Iulius Cottius, a former king of the Cottian Alps, became *praefectus civitatium* some time between 13 and 9/8 BC, after the region was subdued by Augustus.[202] Cottius' equestrian status is nowhere made explicit, though it is generally assumed that he had obtained this rank after being granted Roman citizenship and appointed prefect.[203] The Cottian Alps was no ordinary region under the command of an equestrian prefect; it represented a modification of the client-king system through the bestowal of a Roman title on the king, who enthusiastically embraced his new status.[204]

The Augustan principate therefore gave *equites* a range of new opportunities for government employment that had not existed under the Republican system, and which developed further under his successors. It is striking, therefore, that their appointment is all but ignored by the ancient sources. Eck has argued that there was no systematic plan behind the establishment of these posts, which were created on a largely ad hoc basis throughout the Augustan principate.[205] That is certainly true, and we should not attribute to Augustus a grand plan for the creation of an equestrian *cursus honorum*, analogous to the senatorial career path.[206] But at the same time, it is surely significant that he entrusted equestrian officials with a range of judicial, financial and administrative functions, which they had not hitherto possessed. This represented a fundamental shift in the nature of Roman government, as it allowed *equites* to take their place alongside senators as servants of the *res publica*, a state of affairs that would have been inconceivable to Cicero.[207] Suetonius does discuss the rationale behind Augustus' creation of a range of new senatorial positions 'so that more (sc. senators) could share in the administration of the *res publica*' (*quoque plures partem administrandae rei p. caperent*).[208] This was a concerted effort to integrate the senate and its members into the framework of the government, in order to demonstrate that they could still play

---

[201] Faoro 2011: 124.   [202] *RG* 26.3; Roncaglia 2013: 354, 357.

[203] For example, Cooley 2009: 223; Roncaglia 2013: 359; Cornwell 2015: 62. Cottius does not have the title of *eques* or *eques Romanus* on the inscription of the arch of Susa (*CIL* V 7231 = *ILS* 94), but that is to be expected of the epigraphy of the period, and does not mean that he did not possess equestrian status.

[204] Faoro 2011: 89–90. For Cottius' articulation of his *romanitas*, see Cornwell 2015.

[205] Eck 2009a: 229–31.   [206] This is discussed further in Chapter 7.   [207] See Chapter 2.

[208] Suet. *Aug.* 37; Daguet-Gagey 2011.

important roles in the empire, despite the rise of one-man rule.[209] Suetonius may have thought that since the *equites* had never held such official positions, they had no need to be appeased with new posts; hence they were omitted from this discussion.[210] Augustus himself invested significant effort in ensuring that the *ordo equester* had a considerable ideological role to play in his new *res publica*.[211] It would be strange, therefore, if he did not consider their appointment to administrative posts part of this process of integration. Only Cassius Dio's speech of Maecenas presents the creation of the equestrian prefects and procurators as a coherent programme.[212] For, Maecenas argued, their appointments would ensure 'that a large number would benefit and become experienced in government'.[213] This may be the voice of hindsight from the third century AD, but it is more likely that Dio recognised the larger strategy at work. It is clear that Augustus saw untapped potential for members of the equestrian order to serve both him and the *res publica* in a range of financial, administrative and gubernatorial roles.

In the Camp of Augustus

There was a wide range of officer positions available to *equites* in the late Republic, though these were not organised into a coherent system or hierarchy. Members of the equestrian order could stand for election to one of the twenty-four military tribunates selected by the people in the *comitia centuriata*. These positions provided officers for only four legions, with all other tribunates in the gift of senatorial commanders.[214] The post of *tribunus militum* was not an exclusively equestrian one. Senators could also be appointed tribunes, although by the late Republic these commands were not sought after by the most distinguished senatorial families.[215] The total number of *tribuni militum* varied depending on the number of legions in the field. From 25 BC there were twenty-eight standing legions under Augustus' control, three of which perished in the disaster of the

---

[209] Eck 2009a: 230.
[210] This would explain their omission from Suet. *Aug.* 37 for thematic reasons. When the *equites* are dealt with in *Aug.* 38.3–40.1, Suetonius' emphasis is on their collective unity as an *ordo*.
[211] See Chapters 5 and 8.   [212] Dio 52.24.1–25.6.
[213] Dio 52.25.4: ὅπως καὶ ὠφελῶνται ἅμα συχνοὶ καὶ ἔμπειροι τῶν πραγμάτων γίγνωνται.
[214] Suolahti 1955: 35–42; Harmand 1967: 349–58; Demougin 1988: 283–5.
[215] Suolahti 1955: 140–5; Wiseman 1971: 143–7.

Teutoburg Forest in AD 9, bringing the total down to twenty-five.[216] Traditionally, the tribunes took turns to command the legions in pairs, but in the late Republic, especially under Caesar, senatorial *legati* began to assume this responsibility instead.[217] In addition to the tribunes, there were a number of equestrian officers with the title of *praefectus*, who commanded units of non-citizen *auxilia*.[218] These positions included the *praefectus socium*, commander of allied units, as well as the *praefectus equitum* (prefect of the cavalry, in charge of both citizen and non-citizen units), and *praefectus cohortis* (prefect of a cohort, only for non-citizen units).[219] The post of *praefectus equitum* in particular grew in importance during the late Republic, since it constituted an independent command of a unit. It did not eclipse the prestige of the military tribunate, because that was originally a magisterial post elected by the people.[220] To this list we should add the special case of the *praefectus fabrum*, who was a chief staff officer, or aide-de-camp for the commanding officer.[221] The title of *praefectus* could also be bestowed on staff officers with administrative, rather than military, roles.[222] Candidates for these positions were appointed by the overall senatorial commander in charge of the army.

Augustus exercised considerable oversight of the Roman army, reducing the number of legions after the confusion of the triumvirate, imposing fixed tenure of service for soldiers with bonuses on discharge, and creating new taxes and the *aerarium militare* to fund and administer pay and bonuses.[223] He did not, however, institute a sweeping reorganisation of the army officer hierarchy, which continued to evolve during his principate and under his immediate successors. Augustus appointed senatorial legates, rather than tribunes, who were answerable directly to him, to command the legions.[224] Each legion still had six tribunes: one of these would be from a senatorial family, the *tribunus laticlavius*, while the others would be *tribuni angusticlavii*.[225] In theory, these two groups both belonged to the *iuniores* of the *ordo equester*, but the different titles and rank more precisely demarcated their status, in keeping with Augustus'

---

[216] Keppie 1984: 115–25, 177–83. Dio 55.23.2–24.4 provides an overview, to be read with Swan 2004: 158–68. The number of legions continued to fluctuate thereafter: Demougin 1988: 301 provides a useful table of the *tribuni* required in each time period.
[217] Rankov 2007: 38.   [218] Keppie 1984: 98–100; Rankov 2007: 50–2.
[219] Suolahti 1955: 198–205.
[220] Suolahti 1955: 203–4; Harmand 1967: 359–60; Demougin 1988: 283–4, 295–6.
[221] Suolahti 1955: 205–9; Harmand 1967: 362–6; Dobson 1966: 62–4; K. Welch 1995.
[222] Harmand 1967: 360.   [223] Keppie 1984: 146–9; B. Campbell 1984: 157–76.
[224] Devijver 1970: 75; Keppie 1984: 149–50; Saddington 2003: 23.
[225] Suet. *Aug.* 38.2; Dio 53.15.2–3.

other measures to distinguish *equites* and senators.[226] The senatorial *laticlavii* tended to be in their late teens, while the equestrian tribunes ranged in age from eighteen to fifty.[227] Augustus was particularly focused on encouraging senatorial participation in the army, which Suetonius describes as part of his efforts to give senators a prominent role in his new *res publica*.[228] Augustus not only appointed senators' sons to tribunates, but also to cavalry commands, as *praefecti equitum*, allocating two such *laticlavii* per unit.[229] This particular practice seems to have been abandoned after Augustus' reign, after which the cavalry commands were exclusively held by equestrian officers. A further post, that of *praefectus cohortis* commanding an auxiliary infantry or part-mounted unit, was either held by *equites*, if the units were raised within the empire, or by officers from the same tribes as the unit itself, if recruited outside the borders.[230] In the last generation of the Roman Republic, the post of *praefectus fabrum* had been conferred on equestrian members of a general's council to give them a title to match their status, and this pattern continued through the Augustan period.[231] The *equites* eligible for these military posts came from a variety of backgrounds: they could be appointed directly to the post from civilian life, or they could be former chief centurions, known as *primipilares*.[232] Centurions had originally been elected by their fellow soldiers, but the social background of centurions had changed by the first century BC, as we find municipal *domi nobiles* or *equites* attested in the post.[233] There was therefore no overarching systematisation or organisation imposed on the officer commands, apart from a determination to encourage suitably qualified citizens from good backgrounds to seek such posts.

All appointments to equestrian command posts had to be officially approved by Augustus, who sometimes selected the candidates personally.[234] The position therefore functioned as an imperial *beneficium*, an act of special favour.[235] In practice, commissions were granted on the recommendation of the provincial governor, who depended on the advice

[226] Nicolet 1984: 92–3; Demougin 1988: 289; Louis 2010: 314. For membership of the equestrian order in the imperial period, see Chapter 5.
[227] E. Birley 1949: 9–10.
[228] Suet. *Aug.* 37.1–38.2. Though as Louis 2010: 313–14 points out, as far as the military tribunes were concerned, this was not very revolutionary.
[229] Suet. *Aug.* 38.2 anachronistically uses the later title, *praefectus alae* (Wardle 2014: 296).
[230] Demougin 1988: 344–7.   [231] K. Welch 1995: 144–5.
[232] Devijver 1970: 73; Demougin 1988: 290.   [233] Potter 2010: 321–5.
[234] Dio 53.15.2; Millar 1977: 284–5.   [235] *OLD* s.v. *beneficium* 2; Saller 1982: 41–69.

of his peers and friends to nominate suitable candidates.[236] The equestrian officers recognised that they owed their appointment to the *princeps* or one of his representatives. This is demonstrated by the way in which the officer M. Velleius Paterculus describes his own career in his history.[237] Velleius, whose father and grandfather were both equestrian officers, served as *tribunus militum* in Thrace and Macedonia before joining the staff of Gaius Caesar in Syria.[238] He then transferred to Germany in AD 4 to serve as a *praefectus equitum* under Tiberius. Velleius lavished praise on his new commander, declaring that 'for nine straight years as prefect and legate I was a witness to his godlike achievements' (*caelestissimorum eius operum per annos continuos novem praefectus aut legatus spectator*).[239] His appointment immediately followed Tiberius' adoption by Augustus, and so he was understandably keen to point out the connection between his promotion to cavalry commander and the favour of the *princeps'* son.[240]

Velleius' language may initially seem to be nothing more than excessive flattery, but, as Saddington has shown, he was actually quite typical in the way in which he sought to associate himself with the imperial house.[241] The careers of Velleius' equestrian contemporaries are found not in books but on stone, in the form of inscriptions recording their official posts.[242] The first example is inscribed onto a statue base from Saguntum in Hispania Citerior:

To Lucius Fulvius Lesso, son of Lucius, military tribune of the deified Augustus. Quintus Fabius Niger, father of Quintus and Lucius, to their maternal grandfather.[243]

Fabius Niger was a local magistrate and priest, and thus a prominent member of the Saguntine community.[244] By erecting a statue of his father-in-law, Fulvius Lesso, who had served as an officer in the emperor's army, he was drawing a link between the family and the imperial regime, a connection which could only serve to increase their prestige in Saguntum.[245] Our second example is the cenotaph of Cn. Petronius Asellio from

---

[236] E. Birley 1949: 11–13, 16; Saller 1982: 46–7; A. R. Birley 2003: 3–6. Cf. Cotton 1981, who argues that provincial governors had the final say in some circumstances.

[237] Levick 2011 provides an unorthodox account of Velleius' career.

[238] *PME* V 64; Vell. Pat. 2.101.2–3. The date of Velleius' appointment to Syria is probably late AD 1 or 2 (Woodman 1977: 127).

[239] Vell. Pat. 2.104.3.   [240] Woodman 1977: 136–7.   [241] Saddington 2000: 169, 2003.

[242] Devijver 1999: 251–2; Saddington 2000: 168–71.

[243] *PME* F 93; *CIL* II 3852 = II.14.1.336: *L(ucio) Fulvio L(uci) f(ilio) | Lessoni | trib(uno) mil(itum) divi Aug(usti) | Q(uintus) Fabius Niger Q(uinti) et L(uci) | pater avo materno.*

[244] *CIL* II 3863 = II.14.1.360; N. Schäfer 2000: 119.

[245] There are further examples of equestrians described as officers 'of Augustus': M. Iunius Proculus (*CIL* X 6309); Iulius Posiodonius (*IGR* IV 1626, as dated by Demougin 1992a: 151).

Figure 4.1: Cenotaph of Cn. Petronius Asellio, Mainz

Mogontiacum (modern-day Mainz) in Germany (Figure 4.1). This provides a direct parallel for Velleius' career and the favour he earned from Tiberius:

Gnaeus Petronius Asellio, son of Gnaeus, of the voting tribe Pomptina, military tribune, prefect of the cavalry, and *praefectus fabrum* of Tiberius Caesar.[246]

---

[246] *PME* P 21; *CIL* XIII 6816: *Cn(aeus) Petronius | Cn(aei) f(ilius) Pom(ptina tribu) | Asellio | trib(unus) militum | praef(ectus) equit(um) | praef(ectus) fabrum | Ti(beri) Caesaris.*

Asellio served under Tiberius in Germany some time between AD 4 and 12.[247] His pride in his equestrian army service is underlined by the iconography of the stele, which features the equestrian *parma* and *hastae*, the shield and spears, which had become a key part of the military iconography of the *ordo* in the triumviral and Augustan periods.[248] The construction of this cenotaph outside the gates of Mogontiacum was designed to ensure that Asellio would be remembered as an officer favoured by Tiberius, just as Velleius saw to it that his own connection with Tiberius would be immortalised through his history. Velleius' description of his service 'in the camp of Tiberius Caesar' (*castrorum Ti. Caesaris*) is paralleled in other literary and epigraphic texts. Even officers who did not personally answer to the *princeps* or a member of his family used the term 'in the camp of Caesar' (*in castris Caesaris*) as a synonym for military service.[249] The epitaph of M. Aurelius Zosimus, a freedman of the consul M. Cotta Maximus, includes a poem recording the *beneficia* granted by Maximus to Zosimus and his family, including a tribunate for his son Cottanus.[250] According to the epitaph, Maximus 'served bravely in Caesar's camp' (*fortis | castris Caesaris emeruit*). The most striking use of this expression comes in an inscription from Beirut in Syria, which records the career of the *eques* Q. Aemilius Secundus. The inscription actually forms part of the funerary monument for Secundus' son and freedwoman, but these are almost entirely neglected in favour of a detailed account of Secundus' own achievements:

Q. Aemilius Secundus, son of Quintus, of the voting tribe Palatina, in the army of the deified Augustus, under the command of P. Sulpicius Quirinius, legate of Augustus Caesar in Syria, decorated with honours as prefect of the *cohors I Augusta* and prefect of the *cohors II Classica*. After that, on Quirinius' instructions, I conducted the census of the city of Apamea, which registered 117,000 citizens. Then, after I had been sent by Quirinius to attack the Ituraeans on Mount Lebanon, I captured their citadel. Before my military service, I was *praefectus fabrum* registered at the treasury by two consuls,[251] and in the colony I was quaestor, twice aedile, twice magistrate and priest. Here lie my son Q. Aemilius Secundus, son of Quintus, of the voting tribe Palatina, and my freedwoman Aemilia Chia. This tomb will not pass further to the heir.[252]

---

[247] Devijver 1991b: 248–9.   [248] See Chapter 3.

[249] A similar expression is used, for example, by Propertius, *Eleg.* 2.10.4 (*castra ducis*).

[250] *CIL* XIV 2298 = *ILS* 1949.

[251] The *delatio ad aerarium* ('registration at the treasury') confirmed that Secundus was a fully paid-up staff officer (Millar 1964b: 37–8).

[252] *CIL* III 6687 = *ILS* 2683: *Q(uintus) Aemilius Q(uinti) f(ilius) | Pal(atina tribu) Secundus [in] | castris divi Aug(usti) [sub] | P(ublio) Sulpi[c]io Quirinio le[g(ato)] Aug(usti)] | [Ca]esaris Syriae honori | bus decoratus pr[a]efect(us) | cohort(is) Aug(ustae) I pr[a]efect(us) cohort(is) II classicae idem | iussu Quirini censum egi | Apamenae civitatis mil|lium homin(um) civium CXVII | idem missu Quirini adversus | Ituraeos in Libano monte | castellum eorum cepi et ante | militiem (sic) praefect(us) fabrum | delatus a duobus co(n)s(ulibus) ad ae|rarium et in colonia | quaestor*

The manner in which Secundus presents his career in the first person is reminiscent of how an anonymous Roman senator of the second century BC described his achievements in building roads and capturing slaves on the Polla stone.[253] The style lends immediacy and vividness to his years of military service. Secundus' account aptly encapsulates the army command structure of the principate: although under the direct orders of the senatorial *legatus*, P. Sulpicius Quirinus, it was really Augustus' 'camp' in which he served.

These equestrian officer commands acted as a conduit of social mobility. This is shown by two inscriptions. The first is a fragmentary epitaph for an unknown woman from Corfinium, in which she looks back on the achievements of her family with pride:

she reached her final day, married for thirty-nine years to one man in the utmost harmony, and she left behind three surviving children by her husband. The first obtained the greatest municipal offices through the judgement of Augustus Caesar; the second obtained the highest equestrian army posts of the same Augustus Caesar, and is now marked out for the superior order; and a most upright daughter, married to a very virtuous man, and from them two [grandchildren].[254]

The epitaph is composed in such a way that the achievements of the woman's sons are directly connected to the favour of Augustus. Her second child, like Velleius and the other cases discussed above, served in the emperor's army, and after his equestrian military service had even reached senatorial rank. The language of the inscription recalls Valerius Maximus' description of T. Marius of Urbinum, 'who, from the lowest ranks of the army was promoted to the highest equestrian military posts by the favour of the deified Augustus' (*qui ab infimo militiae loco beneficiis divi Augusti imperatoris ad summos castrenses honores*).[255]

The second example is the career of a chief centurion (*primus pilus*) who advanced through a series of command posts, including the new position

---

aedil(is) II duumvir II | pontifexs (sic) | ibi positi sunt Q(uintus) Aemilius Q(uinti) f(ilius) Pal (atina tribu) | Secundus f(ilius) et Aemilia Chia lib(erta) | h(oc) m(onumentum) amplius h(eredem) n(on) s(equetur).

253 *CIL* I² 638. For the unprecedented nature of the Polla stone at its time, see Bernard, Damon and Grey 2014: 971–3.

254 *CIL* IX 3158 = *ILS* 2682: ... *annos XXXVIIII u[n]i | nupta viro summa cum | concordia ad ultumum (sic) | diem pervenit tres ex [e]o | superstites reliquid (sic) liberos | unum maximis municipi(i) honorib(us) | iudiciis Aug(usti) Caesaris usum | alterum castre(n)sibus eiusdem | Caesaris August(i) summis [eq]u[es]|tris ordinis honoribus et iam | superiori destinatum ordini | filiam sanctissimam probissimo | viro coniunctam et ex ea duos | [nepotes]* ...

255 Val. Max. 7.8.6. He is usually identified with Marius Siculus of *CIL* IX 6058 (Nicolet 1974: 946–7; Demougin 1992a: 38–40; Osgood 2006: 272–3). *Summi castrenses honores* was a widely recognised Augustan idiom for the equestrian military commands (Nicolet 1984: 99; Linderski 2002: 578).

of camp prefect, *praefectus castrorum*, created by Augustus. The prefect initially oversaw legions or vexillations stationed together in one camp (hence their title) but later became attached to a specific legion.[256] Our officer came from Arles in Gallia Narbonensis and was commemorated in the following manner:

> By decree of the decurions, on account of his favours towards the community, to [Titus Iulius?], son of Titus, of the voting tribe Teretina, twice *primus pilus*, twice military tribune, twice prefect of the cavalry, prefect of the camp, *praefectus fabrum*, prefect of the fleet, a member of the association of Honour and Valour, twice magistrate, *Augustalis*, priest of Rome and Augustus Caesar.[257]

For Titus and other officers like him who benefited from advancement through a series of officer grades, the enumeration of their career, post by post, in these inscriptions was a way of publicly displaying their pride in their army service. These examples not only show the potential for social mobility through the army and its officer posts in the Augustan period, but also the personal and family pride that resulted in the outward display of these achievements. Augustus had harnessed the traditions of equestrian *virtus* for his own ends, binding Italian and provincial elites to him through the officer corps.[258]

Augustus was particularly keen to ensure that the *domi nobiles* of Italy played their part in the army and the *res publica*. According to Suetonius' *Life of Augustus*:

> And so that no place would lack a substantial number of respectable citizens nor the general population fail to produce offspring, he appointed men who sought an equestrian military post even on the universal recommendation of their towns, and he gave one thousand sesterces per child to those ordinary people who demonstrated to him during his visits to the Italian regions that they had sons and daughters.[259]

---

[256] Saddington 1996: 244–5. For the duties of this office, see R. W. Davies 1989: 37.

[257] PME I 13; *AE* 1954, 104: *d(ecreto) d(ecurionum)* | *[ob] merita in r(em) p(ublicam)* | *[T(ito) Iul]io T(iti) f(ilio) Ter(etina tribu)* | *[prim]o pilo bis* | *[tribu]no militum bis* | *[pr]aefecto [e]quitum bis* | *[pr]aefecto castrorum* | *[p]raefecto [fa]brum* | *praefecto navium* | *ex conlegio Honoris* | *et Virtutis* | *IIvir(o) bis August[ali]* | *flamini Romae et [Aug(usti)]* | *Caesar[is]*. His career is dated early in the reign of Augustus (Demougin 1992a: 80–1).

[258] For equestrian *virtus* under the Republic, see Chapter 3.

[259] Suet. *Aug.* 46: *ac necubi aut honestorum deficeret copia aut multitudinis suboles, equestrem militiam petentis etiam ex commendatione publica cuiusque oppidi ordinabat, at iis, qui e plebe regiones sibi revisenti filios filiasve approbarent, singula nummorum milia pro singulis dividebat.*

Suetonius presents this as part of a series of measures to foster connections between the city of Rome and Italy at large.[260] The crucial point is that Augustus' motive was not to increase the supply of candidates to the officer corps as a way of compensating for a perceived shortfall. Instead, it was to ensure that no community lacked 'a substantial number of respectable citizens' (*honestorum ... copia*): the argument being, therefore, that military tribunes in the community bolstered the ranks of respectable men. This measure, as D'Arms observed, was about status, not the army.[261] We have already observed how military service to Rome formed a new and increasingly important aspect of monumental self-representation in Italy in the latter half of the first century BC.[262] Suetonius largely ignores the bigger picture, namely Augustus' efforts to give equestrians – in this case, those from the towns of Italy – a defined role in his *res publica* (a vision that fulfilled the dreams of Cicero, which we explored in the previous chapter). These measures specifically targeted veterans and their descendants who had settled in the colonies in Italy, and were now firmly established in the municipal aristocracy.[263] Nearly thirty examples of these *equites* are attested in the epigraphic record bearing the title of *tribunus militum a populo* ('military tribune [selected] by the people').[264] Nicolet has conclusively shown that these tribunes are only attested in Italy during the Augustan period, and were elected by their own communities, not by Rome, thus confirming Suetonius' account.[265] They are especially prominent in central Italy, in regions such as Umbria, Latium and Campania, while few examples come from Lucania and Bruttium; this distribution to a large extent replicates the spread of *equites* in Italy during the late Republic.[266] It is an open question as to whether the *tribuni militum a populo* actually served in the army. Nicolet supposed that they did, but D'Arms argued that it was only an honorary post, based on the fact that none of the tribunes recorded the legions or their commanders, which tended to be standard epigraphic practice at the time.[267] They may have constituted a type of decorative 'officer reserve', who could potentially be called up times of warfare, but who were never actually required to serve.

In the age of Augustus equestrian officers did not serve in the 'army of the emperor', for such a formulation would have been anachronistic at that

---

[260] Louis 2010: 262–3; Wardle 2014: 340–6.   [261] D'Arms 1988: 57.   [262] See Chapter 3.

[263] De Blois 1994: 340–5.

[264] Nicolet 1967b collects twenty-six examples, to which should be added P. Verginius Paetus (*AE* 1966, 120) and Aurelius (*AE* 1969/70, 180).

[265] Nicolet 1967b: 52, 55, 75–6, confirming a suggestion of Syme 1939: 364 n. 1. D'Arms 1988: 56 has also noted that these *tribuni* came from towns that produced no senators.

[266] Nicolet 1967b: 55–7.   [267] Nicolet 1967b: 68; D'Arms 1988: 57.

time. Instead, like their Republican forebears who fought under the command of senatorial generals, they were the soldiers of Augustus Caesar, or his adopted son Tiberius, or any of the other princes of the Julio-Claudian family.[268] This continuity in the way in which officers conceived of their military service shows clearly that there was no major break between Republic and principate. The army of one general, Augustus, had become the army of the *res publica*. The language of military service shows that the officers were acutely aware that their fortunes depended on the patronage of Augustus or members of his family. It is unsurprising to see this realisation in the history of Velleius Paterculus, who was intimately associated with prominent members of the new aristocracy.[269] But to detect the same understanding exhibited by the anonymous woman of Corfinium, whose son's advancement 'to the highest offices of the equestrian order' (*summis [eq]u[es]|tris ordinis honoribus*) was indebted to the *princeps*, shows the extent to which the domination of Augustus permeated Roman society. The inscriptions recording the service of the equestrian officers connect their personal achievements with imperial favour. This shows that equestrian military commands, which had always been a key part of the *ordo equester*, had been successfully integrated into the new framework of the new monarchical *res publica*. The equestrian officers served both Rome and the *princeps*.

Jurors and *Publicani* in the New Order

The Augustan principate reconfigured the association between members of the equestrian order and the *res publica*. Power, influence and office were dependent on the person of the *princeps*, who gave *equites* new opportunities to serve in financial and administrative posts to the highest levels. Augustus ensured that equestrians continued to participate in the Roman army by serving in officer commands. But this leaves us with the question of what happened to two familiar equestrian occupations from the age of the Republic: jurors and *publicani*. As we shall see, although both equestrian jurors and *publicani* continued to exist in the imperial period, their political importance declined dramatically in the new *res publica*.[270]

---

[268] See, for example, prefects of Germanicus Caesar (*CIL* XI 969, 5289) and Drusus the Younger (*AE* 1955, 291; *CIL* III 14712).

[269] See the comments of Lobur 2011: 210–15 on Velleius' perspective on the new *res publica*.

[270] Brunt 1983: 43; Demougin 1988: 443.

(i) Jurors

The nature of the criminal courts changed significantly in the early principate. The direct conflict over membership of the jury panels was largely
resolved by the *lex Aurelia* of 70 BC, which divided the juries between
senators, *equites* and *tribuni aerarii*. This did not mean that the *quaestiones*
ceased to be an arena of competition and rivalry, as we saw from Cicero's
speeches and the rhetoric he used to appeal to the equestrian majority on
the jury panels in Chapter 2. C. Iulius Caesar ended the tripartite division
when he removed the *decuria* of *tribuni aerarii* in 46 BC.[271] Only two years
later, however, M. Antonius introduced a new *decuria*, for which the
property qualification was probably membership of the *prima classis*.[272]
Although Antonius' legislation was originally abrogated in 43 BC, it was
subsequently revived under the triumviral administration.[273] These
reforms demonstrate the continuing political relevance of the courts in
the 40s BC. As Ramsay has persuasively argued, Antonius' new *decuria* was
designed to stack the courts with his supporters and ensure judicial immunity for the triumvirs.[274] Once Octavian had defeated Antonius and was
secure in his position, he transferred this third *decuria* to *equites* c. 28 BC.
At some later date, probably as part of a larger judicial reform package
passed in 17 BC, Augustus added a fourth *decuria*, for which the property
qualification was 200,000 sesterces (so these men were called *ducenarii*).[275]
This additional panel primarily dealt with civil, rather than criminal,
cases.[276] The senatorial and equestrian jurors who staffed the courts in
the Augustan period continued to judge crimes such as *maiestas* and
repetundae, and the courts themselves still functioned until the early
third century AD.[277] At the same time, however, these courts were
eclipsed by the senate and the emperor himself as agents of judicial
authority. In the imperial period there was no hard rule as to whether
a case would be heard by the emperor, the senate or a *quaestio*: it often

---

[271] Suet. *Iul.* 41.2; Dio 43.25.1. The overall number of jurors remained consistent, as the numbers
of senators and *equites* were increased to make up for the shortfall (Ramsay 2005: 34).

[272] Cic. *Phil.* 1.2, 5.12b–16; Ramsay 2005: 21–32.   [273] Ramsay 2005: 32–7.

[274] Ramsay 2005: 24, 31–2; Manuwald 2007: 595–6.

[275] Pliny the Elder, *NH* 33.30; Suet. *Aug.* 32.3, as interpreted by Ramsay 2005: 35–7, followed by
Wardle 2014: 265. For the reforms of 17 BC, see Bringmann 1973; Kienast 2009: 186–7; Giltaij
2013.

[276] Wardle 2014: 265.

[277] Bauman 1968. Cf. Garnsey 1967. Senators, at least under Augustus, continued to serve on the
courts (Dio 55.3.2, with Swan 2004: 52), though the extent to which they participated actively
after his reign is debatable (Demougin 1988: 444–9).

depended on the wishes of the prosecutors.[278] Augustus acquired the ability to judge capital crimes early on in his principate, though this was not the result of any particular law.[279] The emperor's justice was often delivered in public places, such as the *forum Romanum* or *forum Augustum*, though as time went on judgments could also take place behind closed doors.[280] The starkest evidence that Rome was now a monarchical *res publica* comes in Ovid's statement that it was not the senate or a jury that condemned him, but the *princeps*.[281]

The influence of equestrian jurors waned with the transfer of courts to the senate in particular. In the early stages of the Augustan principate, the *quaestio de maiestate* continued to sit in judgement on cases of high treason. It tried M. Primus, governor of Macedonia, in late 23 or 22 BC, and would have subsequently heard the case against Cornelius Gallus, if he had not committed suicide.[282] By the reign of Tiberius, however, most of these cases, especially if they concerned senators, were heard by the senate instead, and this continued to be standard practice throughout the principate.[283] A similar point can be made about the charge of *repetundae*. The *senatus consultum Calvisianum* of 4 BC instituted a special senatorial court to deal with provincial misgovernment, which existed alongside the *quaestio de repetundis*, though it does not seem to have operated for an extended period.[284] From AD 22 onwards all cases of *repetundae*, regardless of whether the defendants were senators or *equites*, were heard by the senate or the emperor himself.[285] Augustus introduced a new *quaestio de adulteriis* to deal with cases of adultery, but this tended to only hear cases involving non-elites; senators and *equites* were usually judged by the senate or the emperor.[286] In all three cases, accusations of treason, extortion and adultery formed part of the cut-and-thrust of political life in imperial Rome, as they were used to indict one's enemies, just as under the

---

[278] A. H. M. Jones 1972: 94; Millar 1977: 516–27.

[279] Dio 55.7.2, with Swan 2004: 69. Although Tiberius preferred to have cases heard in the senate or the courts, this was not the case under his successors (Garnsey 1970: 43–64; Bauman 1996: 57–76).

[280] For a resume of locations throughout the principate, see Bablitz 2007: 35–6; de Angelis 2010. For closed hearings under Claudius, see Tac. *Ann.* 11.1–2.1, 13.4.2.

[281] Ovid, *Tristia* 2.131–4.

[282] Primus: Dio 54.3.1–8, with Rich 1990: 174–5 on the date. A. R. Birley 2000a: 741–2 argues that his name was not Marcus Primus, as Dio has it, but Marcius Primus, or perhaps even Marcius Crispus. Maecenas: Dio 52.3.7.

[283] Garnsey 1970: 19, 33–4; A. H. M. Jones 1972: 94; Talbert 1984: 461–2; J. S. Richardson 1997.

[284] Talbert 1984: 464–5; Brunt 1990a: 63–5.

[285] Garnsey 1970: 20; Brunt 1990a: 65–6, 499–500.

[286] For Augustus' law, see Suet. *Aug.* 34.1; Gardner 1986: 127–32; McGinn 2003: 140–215. On the status of the defendants, see Garnsey 1970: 24.

Republic.[287] To take just one example from the notorious Tiberian principate, in AD 26 Claudia Pulchra, cousin of Agrippina and widow of
P. Quinctilius Varus, was accused of adultery and treason by Cn.
Domitius Afer. The trial was, as Tacitus makes clear, part of a calculated
attack on Agrippina.[288] Afer was out to make a name for himself – as
Tacitus says, 'he was better known for his eloquence than his morals'
(*prosperiore eloquentiae quam morum fama fuit*) – and he later prosecuted
Pulchra's son, the younger Quinctilius Varus.[289] The fact that such trials
were now heard in the senate meant that the equestrian jurors played no
role in these machinations, unlike in the Republic, when Cicero would go
to any lengths to win them over to the side of his clients.[290] It is particularly
noteworthy that charges of *repetundae* against senators were now heard by
senators, a move that represented the final reversal of the Gracchan
programme.[291] Somewhat inevitably, the court often ruled in favour of the
senators.[292] Another crime that had played a significant role in Republican
politics was *ambitus* or electoral bribery. This charge continued to be
relevant while elections were held under Augustus, with the *princeps*
passing two new laws on electoral corruption in 18 and 8 BC,
respectively.[293] However, when elections were transferred to the senate,
and securing the emperor's personal approval became the crucial factor for
success, the *ambitus* charge for comitial elections became largely
irrelevant.[294]

These developments, which invested responsibility for criminal judgments in the senate and the emperor, were part of the emergence of the
monarchical *res publica*. These changes were, however, at odds
with Augustus' attempt to ensure that the criminal courts continued to
play an important role in judicial affairs – or at least that they should
be seen to do so. The courts were allocated prominent public space in the
forum Augustum, linking them intimately with the administration of the
new regime.[295] Augustus reviewed the rolls of jurors himself, together with
senatorial assistants, and the *equites* in the three principal *decuriae* bore the
title of *iudices selecti* (but not the *ducenarii*).[296] The equestrian jurors were
also given the privilege of voting in special centuries during the elections, as

[287] Garnsey 1970: 21–2.   [288] Tac. *Ann.* 4.52.1–3.   [289] Tac. *Ann.* 4.52.4, 4.66.1.
[290] Of course, this does not mean that *equites* did not play a role in political intrigue. See, for
example, Tac. *Ann.* 11.4.1–2, on *equites* who had allegedly allowed Mnester and Poppaea to
meet in their house.
[291] Brunt 1990a: 64.   [292] Talbert 1984: 471–3.   [293] Dio 54.16.1, 55.5.3; Suet. *Aug.* 34.1, 40.2.
[294] Wardle 2014: 275, 304.   [295] Suet. *Aug.* 29.1; Bablitz 2007: 28–9; Wardle 2014: 225–6.
[296] Staveley 1953: 208–13; A. H. M. Jones 1955: 16; Bringmann 1973: 242; Duncan-Jones 2006:
206–8, 2016: 116–17. For selection by the emperor and his committee, see Suet. *Aug.* 29.3, *Tib.*

we will see in Chapter 5. Augustus is praised by the ancient sources for allowing the business of the public courts to proceed without apparent interference. For example, when his close friend L. Nonius Asprenas was arraigned on a charge of poisoning 130 people at a banquet, Augustus did not intervene personally, but merely sat in the court, without speaking.[297] Suetonius and Cassius Dio both classified this action as a mark of the emperor's civil behaviour.[298] Tiberius' presence in the courts received a more ambivalent reception. Dio describes him appearing in court as an *assessor*, and Tacitus admits that the emperor's presence had a positive effect on the course of justice.[299] However, Suetonius gives him a more interventionist role, delivering reminders about points of law to the jury while a case was being heard.[300] There were very often legitimate reasons for the emperor or a member of his family to be present, as when the young Marcus Aurelius, heir to Antoninus Pius, acted as an *assessor* as part of the training for his future role as emperor.[301] Of course, even the Augustan incidents, interpreted positively by Suetonius and Cassius Dio, are open to different interpretations: the mere presence of the emperor in the court-room was enough to articulate his will and pervert the course of justice. The most striking demonstration of this is the action of L. Licinius Murena, who was charged with defending Primus on a charge of *maiestas*. When Augustus came into the courtroom, Murena pointedly asked him who had summoned him there.[302] It was this, according to Dio, that led to the conspiracy of Fannius Caepio and Murena against Augustus.[303] The *princeps'* influence was all-pervasive, even when he was not officially acting as a judge.

In addition to, or perhaps as a result of, the centralisation of judicial authority in the hands of the senate and emperor, jury service came to be perceived as a burden by *equites*. This was a marked change from the period from the Gracchi to Cicero, when it was a closely guarded equestrian privilege. The shift actually occurred very quickly in the Augustan period. In response to the unpopularity of jury service, the *princeps* gave each of the *decuriae* a period of exemption (called the *vacatio*) in turn, and

---

41.1, *Claud.* 16.2; Tac. *Ann.* 3.30. Cf. Demougin 1988: 462–78, whose attempt to identify different types of equestrian jurors from different epigraphic titles seems overly optimistic.

[297] Suet. *Aug.* 56.3; Dio 55.4.2–3; Swan 2004: 56–7; Wardle 2014: 384–5.

[298] Rich 1990: 222; Wardle 2014: 384–5.   [299] Dio 57.7.6; Tac. *Ann.* 1.75.1.

[300] Suet. *Tib.* 33; Lindsay 1993: 124.

[301] Fronto, *Ad M. Caes.* 4.13 (vdH² pp. 67–8) = Davenport and Manley 2014: 91–2 (no. 22).

[302] Dio 54.3.3.

[303] Dio 54.3.4–8. On this conspiracy, see Raaflaub and Samons II 1990: 425–6, 432, who consider this the most overt conspiracy against Augustus.

granted them extra holidays.[304] This did not make jury service any more attractive: to take but one example, Pliny the Younger had to remind his friend Romatius Firmus of his duty to actually appear in court.[305] The desire to minimise the time jurors had to devote to their duties prompted Augustus to introduce a fourth *decuria*, and Caligula a fifth. Caligula's panel even included provincials as a way to increase the potential pool of candidates.[306] These provincial equestrians certainly did travel to Italy to sit on the panels. C. Iulius Philippus, who came from Tralles in Asia Minor, is described on an inscription in his home town as an '*eques Romanus* of the select jurors in Rome' (ἱππέα Ῥω|μαῖον, τῶν ἐκλέκτων ἐν Ῥώμῃ δικαστῶν).[307] Indeed, the large number of inscriptions in which *equites* record their membership of the *decuriae* indicates that there was still some inherent value in the status of juror.[308] Selection functioned as a mark of imperial favour, as shown by expressions such as 'adlected into the five jury panels by the deified Hadrian' (*adlectus | in quinq(ue) dec(uriis) a | divo Hadriano*) which appear in these epigraphic texts.[309] But as the opportunities for new honours and dignities, such as procuratorships and prefectures, multiplied in the monarchical *res publica*, service as a juror became a relatively minor distinction. The position required that an *eques* travel to Rome, which could be expensive and burdensome, and serve long hours when empanelled.[310] Nor was there any real opportunity to influence the course of state affairs as under the Republic. It was not necessary for emperors to stack the courts with their supporters as M. Antonius and the triumvirs had done, or to deliver long speeches about the integrity of the *publicani* like Cicero. As politics shifted to the senate and the imperial court, the equestrian jurors lost their political clout.

(ii) *Publicani*

The political power and influence of the *publicani* as a pressure group, courted by leading senators, likewise changed significantly with the emergence of the monarchical *res publica*. The *publicani* did continue to play a crucial role in the financial management of the Roman state, as they were prominently involved in the collection of indirect taxes.[311] These

---

[304] Suet. *Aug.* 32.3; Wardle 2014: 266.   [305] Pliny the Younger, *Ep.* 4.29.
[306] Suet. *Cal.* 16.2, *Claud.* 16.2; Duncan-Jones 2016: 115. For the increase in the number of *equites* in general under Caligula, see Chapter 5.
[307] *OGIS* 499.
[308] Demougin 1988: 477–98. However, given the requirement to appear in Rome, service on the *decuriae* does not seem to have been very popular in areas such as Asia Minor (Kuhn 2010: 25).
[309] *CIL* VIII 22699.   [310] Wardle 2014: 268.
[311] Demougin 1988: 103–12; Brunt 1983: 46–7, 1990c.

included Augustus' 5 per cent tax on the manumission of slaves (*vicesima libertatis*) and on the inheritance of legacies (*vicesima hereditatium*), as well as customs tolls (*portoria*) levelled at key ports and regional borders throughout the empire.[312] The Roman state also let contracts for extractive operations at gold and silver mines and quarries.[313] Imperial officials of both freedmen and equestrian status were appointed to oversee the work of the contractors, but never completely replaced them.[314] The collection of direct tax, known as *tributum*, did change to some degree in the principate. C. Iulius Caesar took the most significant step in 47 BC, when he gave the cities of Asia the responsibility of collecting *tributum* in place of the tax-farmers.[315] There is unfortunately no such unambiguous statement about this development occurring in any other provinces. However, the evidence from the imperial period shows that it did become normal practice for cities to collect direct tax on behalf of the state, though it must be emphasised that *publicani* are still attested in this capacity in some cases.[316] The continuing importance of the *publicani* in all aspects of financial administration is demonstrated by Tacitus' resume of the empire in the reign of Tiberius, in which he remarked that 'the grain-taxes, income from indirect taxes, and the rest of the public revenues are managed by the companies of *equites Romani*'.[317] The manner in which Tacitus equates the *publicani* with *equites* is reminiscent of Cicero, although it cannot be entirely correct: the two groups were never co-extensive, either in the Republic or the principate.[318] It is impossible to quantify the extent to which *publicani* of specifically equestrian rank were involved in tax-farming and other revenue gathering in the empire.[319]

One particularly striking change comes in the nature of our literary evidence. The *publicani* make few appearances in the major historical accounts of the imperial period written by Tacitus, Cassius Dio, Suetonius or indeed other literary sources. This comes as a something of a shock after they feature so prominently in the speeches and letters of

[312] Augustus' taxes: Dio 55.25.5; Brunt 1990c: 402–6. *Portoria*: Cottier et al. 2008.
[313] Hirt 2010: 91–2, 242–4, 274–80; Russell 2013: 45–51.
[314] Brunt 1990c: 385, 399–402, 404–6.   [315] Plut. *Caes.* 48.1; App. *BC* 5.4; Dio 42.6.
[316] Brunt 1990c: 380–1, 388–93 (ascribing changes in all provinces to Caesar); Duncan-Jones 1990: 187–98.
[317] Tac. *Ann.* 4.6.3: *at frumenta et pecuniae vectigales, cetera publicorum fructuum societatibus equitum Romanorum agitanbantur.*
[318] For the situation in the Republic, see Chapters 1 and 2.
[319] Demougin 1988: 109–10 found only one Julio-Claudian *eques* attested as a *publicanus*, Cornelius Senecio (Sen. *Ep.* 101). Duncan-Jones 2016: 118–22 marshals more epigraphic evidence from the later principate.

Cicero, for whom the tax-farmers constituted a major political force worth appeasing at any cost.[320] On one level, this reflects the interests of the major historical and biographical narratives of imperial Rome, which are generally focused on the emperors and the court. For example, Tacitus reports that in AD 58 complaints about the rapacity of the *publicani* prompted Nero to introduce measures to make the companies more accountable.[321] Tacitus' account of this affair seems largely designed to illustrate Nero's fickle and indecisive nature as *princeps*, since the sensible measures were only put into place following the advice of senators: the emperor had allegedly considered scrapping taxes altogether. The same point can be made about the appearance of the *publicani* in Suetonius' *Life of Caligula*, in which they feature in a discussion concerning the emperor's capricious new taxes.[322] In Suetonius' construction of Caligula's character, the creation of new taxes collected by the *publicani* served as evidence of the emperor's acts of plunder.[323] In contrast, abundant information about the *publicani* in the empire can be found in legal texts and, to a lesser extent, in inscriptions, which elucidate the nature of their administrative functions.[324] But the dearth of literary evidence in our major historical and biographical sources is also indicative of the changing role of the *publicani* in the principate: simply put, they no longer had the same clout in the world of high politics. Since elections to senatorial magistracies now depended on imperial favour, there was no longer any need for aspiring senators to court the votes of the *publicani* in the public assemblies, as Cicero had done. Pliny the Younger, our Cicero of the early empire, makes no mention of *publicani* as political agents playing a role in determining the course of his career or those of his peers. Instead, they appear in discussions of his private business affairs.[325] This fits with the prevailing conception of *publicani* and other equestrian businessmen in the popular imagination. They were either recognised as examples of the wealth one could accumulate through successful enterprise, or were viewed as rapacious agents of the state to be appeased and feared by the provincials.[326]

---

[320] Brunt 1990c: 386–7; Andreau 1999b: 282–3.

[321] Tac. *Ann.* 13.50.1–51.2, as interpreted by Brunt 1990c: 360. For the reforms, see Rathbone 2008.

[322] Suet. *Cal.* 40.1. See also Dio 59.28.8–11 for accusations about Caligula's avarice and ways of collecting money.

[323] Wardle 1994: 21, 290–1, with good comments on the moral role of taxes in imperial representation.

[324] See van Nijf 2008, who places a particular emphasis on the material from Asia.

[325] Pliny the Younger, *Ep.* 7.14.

[326] The popular conception of the *publicani* is discussed further in Chapter 5.

The changed political role of *publicani* can be shown by their dependence on the patronage of the emperor. In the Republican period the fortunes of the *publicani* were dependent on maintaining a good working relationship with the censors and the senate, who let their contracts. That relationship also changed in the principate, as the *publicani* relied on friends in high places to grant and renew their contracts, reflecting a shift in power to connections at imperial court. This is effectively illustrated by letters exchanged between the senator and orator M. Cornelius Fronto and his former pupil Marcus Aurelius, the adopted son of the emperor Antoninus Pius, in the 150s AD.[327] Although the correspondence is much later than most of the evidence dealt with in this chapter, it perfectly encapsulates the way in which *publicani* fitted into the monarchical *res publica*. Fronto wrote to Marcus on behalf of Q. Saenius Pompeianus, a *publicanus* who collected taxes in Africa:

I commend him to you, so that when his account (*ratio*) is examined by our lord, your father, you may be induced by my recommendation and your usual practice to treat him with your natural benevolence, which you customarily show to all men.[328]

Since Fronto expressed himself in the elusive language of letters of recommendation, the precise meaning of the term *ratio*, which generally means 'account', has been the subject of some debate. Brunt has suggested that the *ratio* is actually Saenius' contract for tax-collection in Africa, which was dependent upon the favour of Marcus' father, the emperor Antoninus Pius, for its renewal.[329] Alternatively, the letter could be referring to an audit of Pompeianus' account by the imperial administration.[330] Marcus replied to Fronto in the following manner:

Pompeianus has earned my approval as a result of the very same qualities which appealed to you. Therefore I hope that all benefits come to him from the munificence of my father the emperor. For it always brings me joy when things turn out the way that you want them to.[331]

---

[327] For the date, see van den Hout 1999: 209.

[328] Fronto, *Ad M. Caes.* 5.49 (vdH² p. 79): *commendo eum tibi, cum ratio eius a domino nostro patre tuo tractabitur, benignitatem ingenitam tibi, quam omnibus ex more tuo tribuis, ut huic et mea commendatione et tua consuetudine ductus inpertias.*

[329] This is the suggestion of Brunt 1990c: 383 n. 95, who did not think it likely that the emperor would examine the accounts of all *publicani*.

[330] Duncan-Jones 2016: 121.

[331] Marcus, *Ad M. Caes.* 5.50 (vdH² p. 79): *Pompeianus meritis isdem, quibus te sibi conciliavit, me quoque promeruit. quare cupio omnia ei ex indulgentia domini mei patris obsecundare; nam ea, quae tibi ex sententia procedunt, gaudia sunt mea.*

This response is very ambiguous, as Saller has pointed out, since Marcus does not make clear whether he will actually intercede with the emperor, or whether he simply hopes that Pompeianus will be successful.[332] The crucial point is that the *publicani*, just like imperial administrative officials, depended on the emperor's favour for their career. Cicero had written letters of recommendation on behalf of *publicani* and other businessmen to highly placed friends, including senatorial provincial governors.[333] Now, however, the route to such success lay with the emperors themselves. Pompeianus approached Fronto, his contact at the imperial court, but Fronto did not write to the emperor directly – he never had a very close relationship with Antoninus Pius – and instead called upon his former pupil, Marcus Aurelius, asking him to intercede with the emperor.[334] The fact that Pompeianus was commemorated in death with the title *conductor IIII publicorum Africae* (contractor of the four public taxes in Africa) suggests that his contract was renewed, or that he passed his audit successfully, and he maintained his business interests to the last.[335] Pompeianus' career, like much else in the monarchical *res publica*, was dependent upon imperial favour.

Conclusion: Imperial Opportunities

As Tacitus memorably described it, Augustus 'invested in his own person the functions of the senate, the magistrates, and the laws' (*munia senatus magistratuum legum in se trahere*).[336] Although this revolution represented the transformation of the state into a monarchical *res publica*, it also offered members of the equestrian order new ways of serving the state as senior prefects or procurators. These appointments were dependent on the patronage of Augustus himself, who delegated some of his authority to equestrians in the city of Rome (the *praefectus annonae* and *praefectus vigilium*), and in the provinces (the *praefectus Aegypti* and procurators of peoples and regions). Equestrian procurators were employed as Augustus' representatives throughout the provinces to manage his private estates, and in the 'imperial' provinces to control the finances on his behalf. In some of these areas the employment of equestrians rather than senators was clearly a calculated decision, designed to ensure that Augustus' personal position

---

[332] Saller 1982: 174.   [333] On Cicero's letters, see Andreau 1999b: 278–80.
[334] For Marcus Aurelius as the mediator between Fronto and Antoninus Pius, see Davenport and Manley 2014: 78.
[335] *CIL* VI 8588 = *ILS* 1463.   [336] Tac. *Ann.* 1.2.

was not threatened. This can be seen in the case of the appointment of equestrian prefects to command the praetorian guard, the emperor's personal forces, who carried arms in the city of Rome itself. The connection between the *princeps* and the army can be seen in the appointment of equestrian officers, who recognised that their careers were dependent on the favour of the *princeps* and his family. The active encouragement of the best men from Italy to serve in officer posts demonstrates Augustus' commitment to ensuring that the *domi nobiles* of the Italian peninsula continued to be connected to the state, even in its new imperial form. The new range of civilian administrative positions for *equites* was a fundamental change from the Republican age. For the first time, members of the equestrian order could be said to serve the state *domi militiaeque* in a manner comparable to their senatorial peers.[337] This was a privilege, but it also represented the domestication of equestrial elites by the emperor, who ensured that all honours and officers flowed from him.

It is worth asking precisely why *equites* would choose to serve in government positions, given that their political engagement in the Republican period was focused on extending or protecting interests in business, their positions in the law courts, and the careers of friends, family and neighbours. When they did hold official roles, such as jurors on the criminal courts or members of a governor's *consilium*, *equites* had tried to remain as aloof from the strictures of the *res publica* as much as possible.[338] The answer to this problem must be twofold. Firstly, the return of monarchy to Rome altered the structures of power in a profound way, so that politics did not operate in the same manner, especially for previous equestrian 'pressure groups'. The *publicani* could not influence politics through votes on laws or electoral candidates in the *comitia centuriata*, for example. Nor did equestrian jurors have the same influence over senatorial governors or magistrates. Instead, all benefactions ultimately flowed from the emperor. This connects with our second answer, in that individual *equites* still aimed to accumulate wealth for themselves – procuratorships were salaried posts that provided a very substantial income, which came in addition to land or business interests. While the acceptance of a salary from the emperor was a marked change for senators, who were used to

---

[337] This theme will be developed further in Chapters 6 and 7. It is worth emphasising here that I am speaking of the distinct *ordo equester* as it emerged in the late second century BC, not the senatorial *equites* of the middle Republic who of course did serve *domi militiaeque*. This is an indication of the changing nature of group identity throughout the Roman world and how an ethos of service could be attached to different *ordines*, or groups within *ordines*, at different times.

[338] In the case of *equites* on the governor's *consilium*, it is worth recalling the example of C. Rabirius Postumus examined in Chapter 2.

pursuing careers on their own terms, it would not have posed any challenge to the values of *equites*. Indeed, Seneca's brother L. Annaeus Mela preferred to remain an *eques* and make money through procuratorial appointments.[339] Therefore, equestrian procuratorships were not originally established to provide a career or a lifetime of service for *equites*, but instead functioned as short-term honours and rewards, offering money and prestige. An aristocratic elite of service only emerged over the course of the first three centuries AD.[340]

The return of monarchy to Rome also saw significant changes in the influence of jurors and *publicani*. The equestrian jurors had been courted by great men as late as the triumviral period, but their influence waned under Augustus and his successors as the senate and emperor assumed the responsibility of judging political crimes such as *maiestas* and *repetundae*. Membership of a *decuria* was regarded as a status symbol by *equites* (especially those with no greater honours), but the actual service was looked upon as a chore. The *publicani* likewise lost influence as a pressure group, though they remained fundamental to the financial administration of the empire. But as elections for senatorial magistracies ceased to occur, they were no longer courted for their votes in the *comitia centuriata*. The appointments of both jurors and *publicani* now depended upon imperial favour, which they could acquire through their contacts at court.

For the Romans themselves, or at least the members of the senatorial order, the most significant impact of the new monarchy was the growing influence of equestrians who held no official posts. The ancient fascination with the dichotomy between the equestrian status of Maecenas and the real influence he wielded, not to mention Tacitus' excursus about the growth of equestrian power, suggests that these new opportunities for *equites* were not always warmly received by senators. It is true that there was no fundamental difference in social and economic background between the two *ordines*. But the fact that senators, who had exercised their authority through elected magistracies for centuries, now had to compete for influence with *equites*, freedmen, slaves and women was a source of substantial disquiet. To all intents and purposes it was the *princeps* who offered opportunities to succeed in the new *res publica*.

---

[339] Tac. *Ann.* 16.17.3.
[340] For further discussion of the salary payments to *equites*, and the development of a defined equestrian *cursus* over time, see Chapter 7.

5 | An Imperial Order

Introduction: A Poet's Pride

In AD 64 a twenty-something M. Valerius Martialis (better known to us as Martial) arrived in Rome after a long journey from Bilbilis in Hispania Citerior to make his fame and fortune as a poet.[1] He is best remembered today for two works, the *Book of Spectacles*, published in AD 80 to mark the opening of the Colosseum, and his fourteen books of *Epigrams*, the first of which appeared in AD 86.[2] Martial was also a proud member of the *ordo equester*, and he was further rewarded by the emperors with the *ius trium liberorum* and a military tribunate (either the so-called office of *tribunus semestris* or an entirely honorific post).[3] These honours form an integral part of his self-representation, or, more precisely, the development of his poetic *persona* in the *Epigrams*.[4] The first mention of Martial's equestrian status occurs in an epigram from Book Three, in which he satirises the snooty Naevolus, who never deigns to greet him. In response to this snub, Martial refers to his own honours: 'Rome looks upon me as a tribune, | and I sit where Oceanus throws you out' (*vidit me Roma tribunum | et sedeo qua te suscitat Oceanus*).[5] Martial can sit in the rows reserved for *equites*, where the arrogant Naevolus cannot, because he is not a member of the *ordo*. Indeed, the theatre was the prime location in which Martial could show off his equestrian status publicly, and the policing of the fourteen rows is the subject of an entire cycle of poems in his *Epigrams*.[6]

Martial was fiercely proud of his equestrian status, but he was also aware of its precariousness, since it depended on maintaining a fortune of

---

[1] Watson and Watson 2003: 1–2.

[2] Howell 1980: 2, 5–6. Coleman 2006: xlv–lxiv problematises several aspects of the straightforward dating of the *Book of Spectacles* collection to AD 80, but it is clear that most of the poems do refer to the opening of the Colosseum.

[3] Allen et al. 1970: 346–7 suggest that the award of the tribunate and equestrian status pre-date the *ius trium liberorum* under the Flavians. The nature of this tribunate is discussed in Chapter 6.

[4] For equestrian status and the poetic *persona*, see D. Armstrong 2012. [5] Mart. *Ep.* 3.95.9–10.

[6] For the *lex Roscia* cycle of epigrams in Book Five, see Chapter 9.

400,000 sesterces. In one epigram he refers to an unknown and probably hypothetical Roman who possessed all the attributes of an *eques* – 'natural intellect, enthusiasm, character, and birth' (*ingenium studiumque … moresque genusque*) – but unfortunately not the financial qualification, and thus he could not be admitted to the *ordo*.[7] Martial often complained about his financial situation, and the modesty of his clothing and residences.[8] He thus self-consciously positioned himself at the lower end of the equestrian spectrum:

> I am, I confess, a poor man, Callistratus, and always have been;
> but I am also an *eques*, neither ignoble nor held in low regard.[9]

The 'poverty' in which Martial lived was entirely relative – he was enormously wealthy by most standards. But equestrian poets liked to emphasise that they were men of modest means in contrast with the grand members of the senatorial aristocracy.[10] Moreover, the fact that Martial himself is relatively 'poor', but still of high social status by virtue of his equestrian rank, allows him to sneer at those of low birth who try and pass themselves off as *equites*.[11]

Martial's poetry raises a number of issues pertinent to the role and representation of equestrian status in the monarchical *res publica* which we will explore in this chapter. These include the financial and moral qualifications for admission to the *ordo equester*, the part played by the emperor in awarding honours and advancement, the policing of appropriate status boundaries, and the function of equestrian rank in the self-representation of individual *equites*. This develops some of the themes we discussed in Chapter 3 about the articulation and expression of equestrian rank in Rome and Italy during the late Republic. We explored the significance of expressing elevated status through symbols such as the *anulus aureus* and army regalia, and the awarding of privileges, like the fourteen rows, which marked out *equites* as distinct from the populace at large in the Republic. The evolution of the *res publica* into a monarchical state brought with it new challenges to negotiate, in the form of the emperor, his court and the administration. As Martial stated in an epigram, for all his readers to notice: 'Two Caesars have granted me riches and commendation' (*praemia laudato tribuit mihi Caesar uterque*).[12] The presence of the emperor not only

---

[7] Mart. *Ep.* 5.27.1–2.   [8] Kuhn 2015: 21–2.
[9] Mart. *Ep.* 5.13.1–2: *sum, fateor, semperque fui, Callistrate, pauper,* | *sed non obscurus nec male notus eques.*
[10] Allen et al. 1970: 348–9; D. Armstrong 2012: 66–8.   [11] Kuhn 2015: 18.
[12] Mart. *Ep.* 3.95.5. For Martial's obsequiousness to Domitian in particular, see Watson and Watson 2003: 9–12.

transformed the Roman army and administration (as we saw in Chapter 4), but it also altered the way in which membership of the equestrian order was regulated, by investing greater power in the *princeps* himself as the ultimate arbitrator of status. There was also a second significant difference between the age of Cicero and that of Martial: *equites* no longer primarily came from Italy but from across the empire, as in the case of the poet from Bilbilis.[13] The award of equestrian rank to the municipal aristocracies of the Greek east in particular brought greater heterogeneity to the *ordo*.[14] This raises the larger question of how equestrian rank functioned in the world of the *polis*, which had its own traditions and status hierarchies that pre-dated the coming of Rome. We shall explore how membership of the *ordo equester* functioned as a status that bound the provincial elites of the empire into the framework of the monarchical *res publica*, but without diminishing the validity of other cultural and social dignities.

Defining the Imperial Order

This first section will focus on the problematic question of the definition of equestrian status that lay behind apparently straightforward terms such as *eques Romanus*, *eques equo publico* and *ordo equester* in the Roman imperial period. It is vital to unravel the disparate and sometimes contra-dictory evidence for this problem in order to understand how equestrian rank was acquired and articulated under the emperors, and how this changed over the course of the principate. In the Republic, all citizens with the necessary property qualification, as assessed by the censors, were permitted to call themselves *equites Romani*.[15] The *equites equo publico* who voted in the eighteen centuries of the *comitia centuriata* constituted a privileged elite within the larger *ordo equester*. The census and the *equus publicus* were assessed and bestowed by the censors at regular intervals. In the imperial period, the equestrian census qualification – first securely attested as 400,000 HS around 20/19 BC[16] – was regarded as the funda-mental prerequisite for equestrian status, as had been the case under Republic. But there has been considerable scholarly controversy as to whether imperial *equites* also required the *equus publicus* to be considered

---

[13] Duncan-Jones 2016: 89–90, 98–9.
[14] For equestrian status in Asia Minor, see the fundamental study of Kuhn 2010.
[15] See Chapter 1.   [16] See Chapter 3.

official members of the order.[17] Part of the problem is that there was no one single piece of legislation that defined membership of the *ordo equester* either under Augustus or his successors.[18] The principates of Augustus and his adopted son Tiberius witnessed the introduction of new laws and senatorial decrees that sought to define and regulate different aspects of equestrian rank, including membership of the equestrian squadrons and centuries, access to the first fourteen rows in the theatre, and the right to wear the *anulus aureus*. These groups, privileges and status symbols were progressively changed or regulated over a period of approximately fifty years, from around 20 BC to AD 24. The laws and senatorial decrees usually avoided the term *ordo equester*, which figured prominently in ideological pronouncements. Instead, they referred to the various attributes of equestrian status, such as the *equus publicus* or the right to sit in the fourteen rows. This mirrors the situation under the Republic, when Cicero referred to a united *ordo equester*, when in fact this order consisted of two separate groups, the *equites* with the census qualification, and the elite of the *equites equo publico*. Building upon the theses of Mommsen and Wiseman, this chapter will argue that all *equites Romani* became *equites equo publico* by the end of the first century AD, as part of a process of gradual evolution.[19]

We will begin by examining five different aspects of equestrian status under Augustus and Tiberius: (i) the equestrian *turmae*, which marched in the *transvectio* and other ceremonies; (ii) the equestrian *centuriae* in the assembly; (iii) the first fourteen rows in the theatre reserved for the *equites*; (iv) the right to wear the *anulus aureus*; (v) the sons of senators in the *ordo*.

(i) The Equestrian *Turmae*

Dionysius of Halicarnassus preserves the most authoritative account of the Augustan *transvectio equitum* in his *Roman Antiquities*.[20] He noted that the parade's participants were 'those who possessed the *equus publicus*'

---

[17] For the argument that in the empire only the *census equester* was required, as under the Republic, see Brunt 1961: 76–7; M. I. Henderson 1963: 69; Reinhold 1971: 280; Millar 1977: 279–84. Scholars who have proposed that the only imperial *equites* were the *equites equo publico* include Stein 1927:54–7; Nicolet 1974: 177–88; Alföldy 1981: 173 n. 26; Demougin 1988: 189–212; Duncan-Jones 2006: 219–20 and 2016: 94–5; Davenport 2012b: 90–2 (though my earlier views are modified to a certain extent in what follows).

[18] Rowe 2002: 72–3; Duncan-Jones 2016: 89–93.

[19] Mommsen 1887–8: III, 489–91; Wiseman 1970b: 82–3.

[20] The ideological and ceremonial aspects of the ceremony will be examined in greater detail in Chapter 8.

(τῶν ἐχόντων τὸν δημόσιον ἵππον), and that 'sometimes there are five thousand men' (ἄνδρες ἔστιν ὅτε καὶ πεντακισχίλιοι).[21] Dionysius is generally assumed to have witnessed the *transvectio* personally, based on his claim that he learned of the parade and its religious significance from both 'tales and performances' (λεγόμενά τε καὶ πραττόμενα).[22] Since Dionysius arrived in Rome in 30/29 BC, and his first book of the *Roman Antiquities* was published around 8/7 BC, we can presume that he saw the equestrian *transvectio* some time in the intervening period.[23] Between 70/69 and 29/28 BC there was no formal completion of the census, but that does not necessarily mean there was no *recognitio* at all – indeed, the fact that a number of *equites* were deprived of their public horse in 50 BC suggests that there was at least some form of review.[24] Augustus and Agrippa conducted the census in 29/28 BC through a grant of *censoria potestas*.[25] There is no firm evidence that they revised equestrian numbers in their censorship of 29/28 BC, but equally, it is scarcely believable that they did not do so, given that this was the first proper census in more than forty years.[26]

Dionysius of Halicarnassus' statement that as many as 5,000 *equites* could be seen marching in the *transvectio* indicates that Augustus was not content to restrict the numbers of *equites equo publico* to the Republican figure of 1,800.[27] Suetonius states that Augustus had revived the parade 'after a long interval' (*post longam intercapedinem*), but this reference to the *transvectio* is actually part of a much larger passage discussing the formal review of fitness for equestrian rank, the *recognitio equitum*.[28] In the Republic, the *transvectio* parade had always been held every year, but in census years it was combined with the *recognitio*.[29] It seems likely that Augustus incorporated the *recognitio*, which had

---

[21] Dion. Hal. 6.13.4.   [22] Dion. Hal. 6.13.5.

[23] For the date of his arrival in Rome, see Dion. Hal. 1.7.2. The separate publication of the first book is mentioned in 7.70.2. It is generally accepted that Dionysius saw the Augustan parade (e.g. Weinstock 1937a: 19; Swan 2004: 205), though it is uncertain whether he witnessed it in precisely 6 BC, as some have assumed (Demougin 1988: 218; Rebecchi 1999: 196). Cf. Lebek 1991: 68–9, who argues that Dionysius' account is not based on autopsy, but on information from the Republican period.

[24] Dio 40.63.3. For the census in the first century BC, see Chapter 3.

[25] *RG* 8.2; Cooley 2009: 139–41.

[26] Cf. Demougin 1988: 164, who places the first formal review in 18 BC.

[27] This is widely accepted: Brunt 1961: 77; Wiseman 1970b: 76; Demougin 1988: 28; Kienast 2009: 183. Cf. M. I. Henderson 1963: 61, who suggests that the numbers in each century had increased in the late Republic.

[28] Suet. *Aug.* 38.3.

[29] This is a much debated point. For discussion, see J. M. Carter 1982: 150; Nicolet 1984: 96–7; Demougin 1988: 152–5; Lebek 1991: 65–6; Louis 2010: 307–8, 315; Wardle 2014: 297–8.

previously taken place every five years, into the yearly parade, so that the ranks of the *ordo equester* would now be formally reviewed on an annual basis.[30] He was assisted in the process of assessment by a board of ten senators, who reviewed the morals and fitness of the *equites* alongside the *princeps*.[31] How did Augustus accomplish this constitutionally? In 18 BC Augustus conducted the census again, but this time through his consular power, as he tells us himself in his *Res Gestae*.[32] He had been granted *imperium consulare* for life in the previous year.[33] The *princeps* later undertook the census a third time, in AD 14, with Tiberius as his colleague. This was likewise accomplished through his consular power, and a law was passed to enable Tiberius to serve as his colleague.[34] Demougin has plausibly argued that the establishment of the yearly *recognitio equitum* occurred in 18 BC,[35] when Augustus held the census a second time by virtue of his *imperium consulare*. The fact that he had been granted this power for life meant that the ranks of the *equites* could now be reviewed on an annual basis, and the *equus publicus* bestowed or withdrawn without the *princeps* needing to hold the censorship.[36]

Augustus also reorganised the six *turmae* in which the equestrians marched in the *transvectio*. These squadrons came to play a vital role in organising and defining membership of the equestrian order in the imperial period.[37] Each squadron was commanded by an officer of senatorial stock known as a *sevir*, a title not attested in this context before the Augustan period.[38] The number of *turmae* may have been intended to recall the six oldest voting centuries of *equites* in the centuriate assembly, which were known as the *sex suffragia*.[39] The equestrians marched in the *turmae* for other ceremonial occasions, such as state funerals or festivals.[40] The first attested *sevir* of a *turma* is Augustus' adopted son, C. Iulius Caesar (conventionally referred to as Gaius Caesar), who was appointed to the

---

[30] Demougin 1988: 152–5.   [31] Suet. *Aug.* 39.1; Wardle 2014: 291, 299.   [32] *RG* 8.3.
[33] Dio 54.10.5; Cooley 2009: 142. Augustus also declined the office of censor for life, but still assumed many of the powers of the censors (Dio 54.2.1–3).
[34] *RG* 8.4; Suet. *Tib.* 21; Cooley 2009: 143.
[35] Demougin 1988: 150–66, esp. 164, followed by Louis 2010: 315; Wardle 2014: 298.
[36] At some point, probably in AD 14, Augustus established an additional board of three senators with *censoria potestas* to review the ranks of the *equites* (*ILS* 9483). As A. H. M. Jones 1960: 25 points out, Augustus himself did not need *censoria potestas* to review the *equites*; he only gave such powers to senators when he delegated responsibility. However, this innovation did not survive Augustus (Syme 1991c: 152–3).
[37] Dion. Hal. 6.13.4; Tac. *Ann.* 2.83; Pliny the Elder, *NH* 15.19; Weinstock 1937b: 2182–3.
[38] L. R. Taylor 1924: 161–3.   [39] L. R. Taylor 1924: 162–4; Weinstock 1937a: 19.
[40] The *equites* may well have already been divided into *turmae* for the funeral of Drusus the Elder in 9 BC (Dio 55.2.3). For the games, see Rowe 2002: 68.

post in 5 BC. This was the same year he assumed the *toga virilis*, was admitted into the senate, and received the title of *princeps iuventutis*.[41] Inscriptional evidence produces three other *seviri* of senatorial family under Augustus.[42] It was not until the late first century AD, however, that the post commonly came to be recorded as part of the inscribed senatorial *cursus* with the standardised title of *sevir equitum Romanorum*.[43] Although the ceremony of the *transvectio* was probably intended only for the *iuniores* (aged between seventeen and thirty-five) of the equestrian order, it was possible for *seniores* (aged thirty-five and over) to participate if they wished. Actual attendance, however, would be limited to those equestrians who were present in Rome, hence Dionysius' tacit indication that numbers varied from year to year.[44] Inscriptions provide conclusive evidence that all members of the *ordo equester*, regardless of whether they were based in Rome, Italy or the provinces, were allocated to one of the six *turmae*, and that they remembered the squadron to which they were assigned.[45] The *seniores* aged thirty-five and over retained their membership of the order, even if they no longer marched as part of the parade.[46] This meant that each squadron was technically composed of thousands of *equites* and could expand as necessary to account for new members of the *ordo*.[47] This accords with the advice that Cassius Dio's Maecenas gave to Octavian: he told the *princeps* that he should enrol as many *equites* as he liked, without worrying about the numbers.[48]

(ii)   The Equestrian Centuries

The equestrian squadrons, which marched on ceremonial occasions, must be distinguished from the equestrian *centuriae* that voted in the *comitia centuriata*. These institutions represented two fundamentally different ways of configuring the *ordo equester*.[49] The eighteen centuries of *equites equo publico* continued to exist as part of the *comitia centuriata* throughout

---

[41] Zon. 10.35 (ed. Dindorf p. 477); Swan 2004: 90. It is virtually certain that this passage comes from Cassius Dio, and was assigned by Boissevain to Book 55 of the *Roman History* (55.9.9). See also *RG* 14.1–2, which refers to the same honours, though not the post of *sevir*.

[42] C. Pompeius Proculus (*CIL* VI 3530 = *ILS* 1314), P. Numicius Pica Caesianus (*CIL* VI 3835 = *ILS* 911), C. Sulpicius Platorinus (*CIL* VI 40157).

[43] L. R. Taylor 1925: 162. See Demougin 1988: 226–40 for a full list.

[44] Demougin 1988: 180, 223–4. As we will see in Chapter 8, it is clear that some provincials did travel to Rome for the annual parade, though they probably did so only once in their lifetime if they had no other reason to visit the *sacra urbs*.

[45] For examples, see *CIL* X 7285 (*turma* I); *CIL* VIII 11033 (*turma* IIII).

[46] Demougin 1988: 213–17; Swan 2004: 91; Duncan-Jones 2006: 184–5.

[47] Demougin 1988: 225.   [48] Dio 52.19.4   [49] Demougin 1988: 219, 224, 407.

the regimes of Augustus and his successors, though the actual powers of the assembly declined dramatically.[50] Since citizens were permitted to give up their public horse at age thirty-five (though they retained the honour of equestrian membership), the eighteen centuries were primarily composed of *iuniores*.[51] At some point the centuries of *equites* must have expanded to allow more than one hundred members each, on account of the increase in the number of Romans who were granted the *equus publicus* under Augustus.[52] The taking of the *census* and the completion of the *lustrum* in 28 BC were of enormous symbolic value, representing the restoration of order and proper procedures after the period of civil war.[53] It allowed the people of Italy who were not yet properly enfranchised to take their rightful constitutional place in the *comitia centuriata*, as a result of the peace brought by Augustus.[54] More to the point, there were undoubtedly many wealthy citizens in Rome and Italy at large who were eager to receive the official honour of the *equus publicus*.[55] They benefited enormously from the census conducted by Augustus and Agrippa. This represented a fundamental part of Augustus' programme to confirm the place of the *ordo equester* as one of the constituent elements in his new monarchical state and to ensure that the order embraced the *domi nobiles* of Italy.[56]

There were some changes to the way in which the equestrians were organised within the *comitia centuriata* in the early imperial period. Twenty new centuries, composed of both senators and *equites*, were constituted to perform the *destinatio* process in the elections of consuls and praetors.[57] The new centuries had the right to vote first in the elections, and their choices were then announced to the other centuries.[58] Their selections, however, were not binding, and the remaining centuries could still

---

[50] Dio 58.20.4 states that candidates still appeared before the *comitia centuriata* and *comitia tributa* to ratify their election even in his own day. Demougin 1988: 408–9 suggests that the order in which centuries voted remained unchanged from the late Republic.

[51] Suet. *Aug.* 38.3; Brunt 1961: 77; Demougin 1988: 399.   [52] Brunt 1961: 76–7.

[53] *RG* 8.2 specifically notes that it had been forty-two years since the last *lustrum*. See Wiseman 1970a: 71 and Cooley 2009: 141.

[54] *RG* 8.2–4 records the number of Roman citizens increasing in each of Augustus' censuses in 28 BC, 8 BC and AD 14. See the discussion of Cooley 2009: 141–2.

[55] The failure to enrol citizens properly in the classes of the *comitia centuriata* was politically advantageous to those who wished to exclude wealthy Italian *domi nobiles* from power (Wiseman 1970a: 65–7).

[56] Nicolet 1984: 96–8; Demougin 1988: 213–14; Kienast 2009: 185–6.

[57] *RS* 37, *Tabula Hebana* ll. 6–12.

[58] The process is described in explicit detail in *RS* 37, *Tabula Hebana* ll. 16–50. Note especially the remark of Crawford 1996: 539: '*destinatio* is not the result, but the process'.

vote how they wished.[59] The *destinatio* centuries therefore functioned very much like the *centuria praerogativa* in the Republican period, the vote of which was announced in advance of the other centuries.[60] The process of *destinatio* should be distinguished from that of *designatio*, in which the emperor effectively named the candidates he wished to be elected, though the distinction soon disappeared.[61] The *destinatio* method of voting was a new one, invented in AD 5, when the *lex Valeria Cornelia* established ten new centuries in the *comitia centuriata*. These were called the *centuriae Caesarum* in honour of the deceased princes Gaius and Lucius Caesar.[62] The new centuries formed part of a range of measures propagated to commemorate the lives of Augustus' heirs, who had died in AD 2 (Lucius) and 4 (Gaius), respectively.[63] This then set the precedent for the establishment of five new centuries in honour of Germanicus Caesar, who died in AD 19, by the passage of the *lex Valeria Aurelia*.[64] Finally, another five centuries were added in AD 23 to commemorate Tiberius' son, Drusus (the Younger), bringing the total number of *destinatio* centuries to twenty.[65] When the additional voting groups were created for Germanicus and Drusus, the senators and *equites* eligible to be enrolled in the centuries of Gaius and Lucius were now distributed among the larger number of centuries.[66]

The surviving fragments of the *Tabula Hebana* provide precise details of the composition of these new centuries. They were to consist of 'senators and *equites* of all the panels which have been or shall be established for the purpose of the public courts' (*senatores et equites omnium decuriarum quae iudicior(um) publicor(um) caussa constitutae sunt erun[t]*).[67] Therefore, not all members of the *ordo equester* were eligible to be vote in these special centuries, but only those on the lists of the *decuriae*, which was a much more limited group. From around 28 BC there were three judicial *decuriae*, each one thousand strong.[68] As we saw in the previous chapter, the jurors

---

[59] Crawford 1996: 538; Lott 2012: 242–3.

[60] A. H. M. Jones 1955: 14; Brunt 1961: 71; Demougin 1988: 409. For the operation of the *centuria praerogativa*, see L. R. Taylor 1966: 91–9.

[61] Crawford 1996: 538.   [62] *RS* 37, *Tabula Hebana* ll. 5–7.

[63] Hurlet 1997: 139–41; Rowe 2002: 106–19.

[64] *RS* 37, *Tabula Hebana* ll. 7–12. As a result of this, the original ten centuries were renamed the *centuriae Cai et Luci Caesarum* ('centuries of Gaius and Lucius Caesar') to distinguish them from those of Germanicus.

[65] *RS* 38, *Tabula Ilicitana* ll. 4–5. For the identification of this fragment as part of a *rogatio* concerning honours for Germanicus, see Crawford 1996: 512–13 and Lott 2012: 317.

[66] Lott 2012: 242.   [67] *RS* 37, *Tabula Hebana* l. 8 (trans. Crawford, slightly adapted).

[68] See Pliny, *NH* 33.30, with the date proposed by Ramsay 2005: 36, for the change from triumviral arrangements. The *decuriae* continued to include both senators and *equites*, as demonstrated by Bringmann 1973: 238–42. Cf. A. H. M. Jones 1955: 17.

were known as *iudices selecti*, and were appointed by the emperor himself. Augustus later added a fourth *decuria* composed of citizens with a *census* rating of 200,000 HS or more, and Caligula a fifth with the same qualification.[69] Only Roman citizens aged twenty-five years and older were eligible for jury service, which would exclude many, but not all, of the younger *equites*.[70] In the Augustan principate there was also a geographical restriction in that all members of the *decuriae* had to be resident in Italy; it was only later, under Caligula and Claudius, that provincials were admitted.[71] This meant that the equestrians eligible to vote in the *destinatio* centuries under Augustus and Tiberius constituted a subset of the larger *ordo equester*. They were all aged twenty-five and over, lived in Italy, and had been enrolled in the *decuriae*, resulting in a group of no more than three thousand in total. *Equites* did, however, considerably outnumber the senators in the *destinatio* centuries, and the process gave the equestrian *domi nobiles* of Italy a new, if largely symbolic, role in politics of the *res publica*.[72]

The creation of the *destinatio* centuries did not increase the number of total centuries in the *comitia centuriata*, which remained fixed at 193. Rather, as the *Tabula Hebana* reveals, these new centuries were constituted at random by the assignment of senators and *equites* from different tribes, using a complicated balloting process. Therefore, the precise composition of the *destinatio* centuries varied from election to election.[73] This meant that senators and *equites* of the *decuriae* still retained their membership of the centuries to which they were usually assigned. Scholars have often assumed a firm distinction between the eighteen centuries of *equites equo publico*, composed solely of *iuniores*, and the *destinatio* centuries, which admitted more senior *equites*.[74] But why should this be so? If an *eques* was eligible for jury service at twenty-five and was enrolled in a *decuria*, he was not required to relinquish his *equus publicus*. This means that an *eques* between the ages of twenty-five and thirty-five, who was enrolled in the eighteen centuries of *equites equo publico* and was also a member of the

---

[69] Suet. *Aug.* 32.3, *Cal.* 16.2.

[70] Suet. *Aug.* 32.3 states that Augustus reduced the qualifying age from thirty-five to thirty, but this is thought to be an error for thirty to twenty-five, on the basis of the Republican evidence (Brunt 1961: 77–8; Demougin 1988: 458–61; Wardle 2014: 264–6).

[71] Duncan-Jones 2006: 205, 2016: 98. For the evidence, see Pliny, *NH* 33.30; Suet. *Cal.* 16.2, *Claud.* 16.2.

[72] A. H. M. Jones 1955: 17. This did not apply to new citizens, who were forbidden from serving on the juries (Pliny the Elder, *NH* 33.30; Suet. *Tib.* 51.1, with Ramsay 2005: 34–5, suggesting that this measure was instituted in 28 BC).

[73] L. R. Taylor 1966: 89–90; Lott 2012: 247.   [74] Brunt 1961: 78; Demougin 1988: 409, 416–17.

decuriae, could also be called up to vote in the *destinatio* centuries. The surviving evidence does not pose any problem for this theory, so it is best not to draw too firm a line between the *iuniores* and *seniores* in this regard. Rather, the institution of the *destinatio* centuries was a way of involving Italian *equites* more intimately in the political process, integrating them further into the *res publica* in a manner that fulfilled the vision of Cicero.[75] The relevance of these special *centuriae* declined over time together with the significance of the centuriate assembly itself, although it is likely they were never formally abolished.[76]

(iii) The XIV *Ordines*

The *turmae* and the *centuriae* defined equestrian membership in terms of ceremonies and electoral assemblies. But at the same time, the right to sit in reserved seats at the theatre became an increasingly important method of determining who was, and who was not, an equestrian. As discussed in Chapter 3, the *lex Roscia* of 67 BC allowed all *equites Romani* with the census requirement to sit in the first fourteen rows of the theatre (*XIV ordines*); this privilege was not restricted to the narrower group of *equites equo publico*.[77] The first precise reference to 400,000 sesterces as the equestrian property qualification occurs in Horace's *First Epistle*, dated to 20/19 BC.[78] Freedmen who had been granted the *anulus aureus* as a sign of fictive free birth could ascend to equestrian rank and rightly occupy a seat in this area.[79] The provisions of the *lex Roscia* were confirmed as part of the *lex Iulia theatralis*, Augustus' far-reaching legislation on seating and social hierarchy in the theatre, around 20–17 BC.[80] The block of *equites* was further divided into *cunei* of *iuniores*, those between the ages of seventeen and thirty-five, and the *seniores*, aged thirty-five and over.[81] This division cannot be definitely assigned to the *lex Iulia theatralis*, but if it did not form part of this law, it took place at some point during Augustus' reign. The *lex Iulia theatralis* was intended to be applicable throughout Italy and the provinces, though in reality local

---

[75] For Cicero and the *equites* of Italy, see Chapter 3.

[76] Brunt 1961: 71–2. Clarke 1964 shows that they continued interrupted through Augustus and Tiberius' reigns until AD 23. Demougin 1988: 436–7 argues that they were abandoned in the reign of Caligula.

[77] E. Rawson 1987: 102.   [78] Hor. *Epist.* 1.1.57–9.   [79] See further Chapter 3.

[80] Suet. *Aug.* 44.1–3; E. Rawson 1987; Demougin 1988: 802–5; Edmondson 2002: 11–15. In this section we will only examine the theatre for the contribution it makes to the definition of equestrian status, with the social and cultural aspects discussed in Chapter 9.

[81] E. Rawson 1987: 105–6; Edmondson 2002: 14.

considerations meant that the precise number of rows allocated to *equites* varied widely.[82]

The privilege of sitting in the *XIV ordines* was therefore a key method of defining equestrian status, and features as such in two important items of legislation from the reign of Tiberius. The first is the *Tabula Larinas*, a bronze tablet from Larinum in central Italy, which preserves a *senatus consultum* passed in AD 19.[83] The senatorial decree forbade senators, *equites* and their families from performing on stage or fighting in the arena. The manner in which equestrian rank is defined in this document is of crucial importance. Firstly, it commanded that no one should be permitted to perform or be hired out as a gladiator, if their father, paternal or maternal grandfather, brother, or husband (in the case of women) 'had ever had the right of being a spectator in the equestrian seats' (*[ius] fuisset unquam (sic) spectandi in equestribus locis*).[84] A few lines later the *senatus consultum* refers, in a slightly different formulation, to citizens 'who had the right to sit in the equestrian seats' (*quibus sedendi in equestribus locis ius erat*). These individuals willingly incurred public disgrace (*infamia*) if they performed on stage or fought as a gladiator 'in order to make a mockery of the authority of this order' (*eludendae auctoritatis eius ordinis gratia*).[85] The use of the term *ius . . . sedendi* ('right to sit') in the senatorial decree is echoed in other literary sources.[86] But why did the *senatus consultum*, which conceived of equestrians as an *ordo*, define its members solely by the right to sit in the equestrian seats?[87] Other documents of the Augustan and Tiberian periods, such as the *Res Gestae* and the *senatus consultum de Cn. Pisone patre*, likewise use the term *ordo equester*. Why not simply refer to members of the *ordo equester* here too? As Demougin

---

[82] This is discussed in Chapter 9.

[83] *AE* 1978, 145. Levick 1983 presents a text with an English translation. Lebek 1990 offers new readings of the text and a German translation (whence *AE* 1990, 189).

[84] *Tab. Lar.* ll. 7–11 (the quotation is from ll. 8–9). One of the key features of this document is the way in which it refers not only to men, but also to women with equestrian relatives, thus attempting to delineate equestrian families beyond individual *equites* (see Demougin 1988: 564–7). Although this is different from the way in which senatorial rank is specified in the *SC*, it is indebted to Augustan legislation on marriage, which defined senatorial relationships in terms of descent (Levick 1983: 101).

[85] *Tab. Lar.* ll. 11–14 (the quotations are from l. 12). A third and final mention in ll. 13–14 refers either to 'one who withdrew from the equestrian seats of their own accord' (*ei des[civerant sua sponte ex equ]estribus locis*) on the reading of Levick 1983: 98 or 'one who lost the ability to sit in the equestrian seats' (*ei des[ierant posse sedere in eques]tribus locis*), following Lebek 1990: 60.

[86] Demougin 1988: 577–8, citing Tac. *Ann.* 6.3.1; Ps.-Quint. *Decl.* 302.1.

[87] There are three references to the *ordo* in the text (*Tab. Lar.* ll. 5, 12, and 14–15, though the latter is restored).

has rightly pointed out, it was not because the theatre seating was the most appropriate way of defining equestrian membership for the purpose of this specific piece of legislation.[88] The explanation lies in the fact that the *lex Roscia* and *lex Iulia theatralis* were the only laws that had ever attempted to delineate membership of the *ordo equester*, and they undoubtedly specified precisely who was entitled to sit in the fourteen rows.[89] Even though Augustus had increased the numbers of *equites equo publico*, that was still an insufficient way of defining the wider membership of the order, and would not properly account for familial connections stretching back three generations. This explains why the *lex Iulia theatralis* not only played such a crucial part in the *senatus consultum* of AD 19, but also in a second decree passed a few years later, concerning the wearing of the gold ring.[90]

(iv) The *Anulus Aureus*

The gold ring had become popularly accepted as a prominent status symbol of equestrian rank in the first century BC, most notably expressed by Horace's use of the term *anulus equester* in a poem published in about 30 BC.[91] The gold ring was doubly important to freedmen, on whom it could be bestowed by magistrates with *imperium* in order to confer the fictive status of free birth, which would allow them to be formally registered as *equites*.[92] Nevertheless, wearing of the *anulus aureus* became common among men who had no claim to it, because it was a form of status usurpation that could not easily be regulated. Still, the Roman state did eventually try to do so, with the first legislation on the matter passed in the form of a *senatus consultum* in AD 23. Pliny the Elder provides our most extensive account of the issue, which forms part of his idiosyncratic discussion of equestrian rank:

Finally, in the ninth year of Tiberius' rule, the equestrian order became a united body. The authority of rings determined its shape (*forma*), when C. Asinius Pollio and C. Antistius Vetus were consuls, in the 775th year following the foundation of the city. One may express surprise at the rather trivial reason that led to this. It started when C. Sulpicius Galba seized an opportunity to earn the emperor's favour (as young men are wont to do) by imposing penalties on those who managed

---

[88] Demougin 1988: 577.

[89] This is emphasised by the use of the word *ius*, referring to a privilege enshrined in law (*OLD* s.v. *ius* 12; Demougin 1988: 796).

[90] For further discussion of the *Tabula Larinas* in the context of performances by equestrians in the theatre and arena, see Chapter 9.

[91] Hor. *Sat.* 2.7.53.   [92] See Chapter 3 for full discussion.

take-away shops (*popinae*). He complained in the senate that the street hawkers generally showed their rings as a way of evading the penalties due to them. The senate therefore passed a decree on this matter, which specified that no one should have the right to wear the ring unless he, his father, and paternal grandfather were of free birth, possessed the census rating of 400,000 sesterces, and sat in the fourteen rows under the terms of the *lex Iulia theatralis*. Afterwards large numbers of men started to claim this status symbol.[93]

It is evident that the right to wear a gold ring had never been properly regulated prior to this date, even though it was popularly regarded as a symbol of equestrian status.[94] The aim of the *senatus consultum* of AD 23 was to combat status usurpation by men who claimed to be *equites* simply by showing their rings in public. It is important to note that the decree did not seek to define the equestrian order per se, but only the privilege of the wearing the gold ring, which it took for granted as equivalent with membership of the *ordo*.[95] The crucial qualifications, as Pliny the Elder makes clear, were free birth for three generations, the equestrian property qualification, and the right to sit in the first fourteen rows. As we noted above, the *lex Iulia theatralis* was by this time the most definitive piece of legislation on equestrian membership, so it was fitting that the senate referred to it in its decree. This *senatus consultum* did not put an end to status usurpation. There was informal status policing in the form of denouncements by citizens: the equestrian Flavius Proculus infamously reported 400 freedmen to the emperor Claudius as being unqualified to wear the gold ring.[96]

The following year, AD 24, saw the passage of a related law, the *lex Visellia*. This piece of legislation specifically concerned freedmen, rather than the *ordo equester* at large. Our most extensive summary of the law actually appears in a later rescript of the emperors Diocletian and Maximian preserved in the *Codex Justinianus*:

---

[93] Pliny the Elder, *NH* 33.32: *Tiberii demum principatu nono anno in unitatem venit equester ordo, anulorum auctoritati forma constituta est C. Asinio Pollione C. Antistio Vetere cos. anno urbis conditae DCCLXXV, quod miremur, futtili paene de causa, cum C. Sulpicius Galba, iuvenalem famam apud principem popinarum poenis aucupatus, questus esset in senatu, volgo institores eius culpae defendi anulis. hac de causa constitutum, ne cui ius esset nisi qui ingenuus ipse, patre, avo paterno HS CCCC census fuisset et lege Iulia theatrali in quattuordecim ordinibus sedisset. postea gregatim insigne id adpeti coeptum.*

[94] Demougin 1988: 814.

[95] After Arellius Fuscus was deprived of his equestrian status, he only wore silver rings (Pliny the Elder, *NH* 33.152).

[96] Pliny the Elder, *NH* 33.33. Claudius also confiscated the property of freedmen who masqueraded as *equites* (Suet. *Claud.* 25.1).

The *lex Visellia* is applied to men of freed status who dare to assume the offices and *dignitates* of freeborn men or hold the post of decurion, unless they enjoy the right of gold rings which they have obtained from the emperor. For in that case, as long as they shall live they obtain the appearance, but not the status, of being freeborn. They may then perform the public duties of freeborn men without danger.[97]

The law therefore confirmed the practice that the *anulus aureus* conferred a fictive *ingenuitas*, and allowed freedmen to embark on public careers.[98] One of the particularly important aspects of the law was that the *ius aureorum anulorum* – 'the right of the gold rings' – was conferred by the emperor himself, who inherited this privilege from magistrates with *imperium* in the Republican age. Some ancient authors assume that this gift from the emperor effectively made a freedman an *eques*, as in the famous cases of Icelus and Asiaticus, freedmen of Galba and Vitellius, respectively.[99] This assumption undoubtedly derived from the terms of the *senatus consultum* of AD 23, which had restricted the gold ring to *equites*.[100] The senatorial decree of AD 23 and the *lex Visellia* of AD 24 thus approached the wearing of the gold ring from two different perspectives, and there appears to have been no attempt to merge these two pieces of legislation.

(v) The Sons of Senators

The sons of senators were a slightly anomalous group, who were considered to be *equites* until they entered the *curia*, at least in the Julio-Claudian period. Cassius Dio provides crucial evidence for this in his account of the funeral of Drusus the Elder in 9 BC. Dio reported that Drusus' body was carried to the Campus Martius 'by the *equites*, both those who were strictly reckoned among the *ordo*, as well as those who came from senatorial families' (ὑπὸ τῶν ἱππέων, τῶν τε ἐς τὴν ἱππάδα ἀκριβῶς τελούντων καὶ τῶν ἐκ τοῦ βουλευτικοῦ γένους ὄντων).[101] Dio makes the same distinction

---

[97] CJ 9.21.1: *lex Visellia libertinae condicionis homines persequitur, si ea quae ingenuorum sunt circa honores et dignitates ausi fuerint attemptare vel decurionatum adripere, nisi iure aureorum anulorum impetrato a principe sustentantur. tunc enim quoad vivunt imaginem, non statum ingenuitatis obtinent et sine periculo ingenuorum etiam officia peragunt publica.*

[98] *Dig.* 40.10.1.5–6; Mouritsen 2011: 73–4, 106–8.

[99] Icelus is said to have received the ring and assumed an 'equestrian name' (*equestri nomine*), Marcianus, according to Tac. *Hist.* 1.13 (the same story appears in Plut. *Galba* 7; Suet. *Galba* 14.1). In Asiaticus' case, the soldiers are said to have demanded that Vitellius confer equestrian rank on him (*equestri dignitate donaret*), which he did through award of the gold ring (Tac. *Hist.* 2.57; see also Suet. *Vit.* 12). This was probably a symbol of the official award of the *equus publicus*.

[100] Duncan-Jones 2006: 215–16.

[101] Dio 55.2.3; Nicolet 1976: 36–7; Demougin 1988: 262; Swan 2004: 46. Dio also uses the word ἀκριβῶς ('strictly') in his account of the *lex Roscia*, which discriminated *equites* from the plebs.

between the *equites* of senatorial and non-senatorial families in his account of the young men awarded money by Augustus in AD 4.[102] In the Republic, senators' sons were enrolled in the eighteen centuries of *equites*, which meant that they possessed the public horse.[103] This practice presumably continued under Augustus – it is hard to imagine the *princeps* not granting senators' sons such a prestigious honour.[104]

This argument is complicated by a fragmentary portion of the *Tabula Hebana*, which mandates precisely who is supposed to participate in the funeral of Germanicus on the Campus Martius. The text is fragmentary and replete with difficulties:

> also those who shall be of the [equestrian] order, [such of them as] shall have [the ? broad?] stripe, those who shall wish to perform their duty and [shall be able to attend] as far as health and household [religious rites] are concerned, [they] should come into the Campus Martius [without] the stripe, those who shall possess the public horse, they (should come into the Campus Martius) with the *trabea*.[105]

This restoration of the text from *Roman Statutes* divides the *equites* between those with the *latus clavus* (i.e. senators' sons), whose attendance is optional, and those with the *equus publicus*, who must attend, dressed in the *trabea*.[106] Augustus had allowed senators' sons the right to wear the *latus clavus* as soon as they assumed the toga of manhood, as a sign that they were destined for the senate from an early age.[107] While there is nothing unproblematic about separating senators' sons from other *equites*, given the statements of Cassius Dio, this reconstruction of the text does have the effect of implying that senators' sons did not possess the *equus publicus*. The key terms, *[latum cla]uom* ('broad stripe') and *[sine] clauo*

This arrangement of *equites* and senators' sons carrying the bier must be distinguished from the descriptions of the *decursio* around the funeral pyre, which involved both the *equites* and the praetorian cavalry (see Dio 56.42.2, 74.5.5, with the discussions of Demougin 1988: 263–9; Swan 2004: 342; Duncan-Jones 2006: 220).

[102] Dio 55.13.6; Swan 2004: 145–6.   [103] Nicolet 1974: 89–90; Wiseman 1970b: 70.

[104] Nicolet 1976: 36–8; Demougin 1988: 780; E. Rawson 1987: 108; Swan 2004: 46; J. S. Richardson 2012: 151.

[105] *RS* 37, *Tabula Hebana* ll. 55–7 (trans. Crawford): ... *et, qui ordini[s equestris erunt, qui eor(um) ?latum? cla]|uom habebunt, qui eor(um) officio fungi uolent et per ualetudinem perq(ue) domestic[a sacra officio fungi poterunt, ii sine] | clauo, ii qui equom pub(licum) habebunt cum trabeis in campum ueniant;*

[106] Crawford 1996: 541; Lott 2012: 252–3.

[107] Suet. *Aug.* 38.2. Chastagnol 1975 (followed by Nicolet 1984: 92–3; Talbert 1984: 513; Demougin 1988: 166–7) argues that this action meant that young *equites* seeking a senatorial post were no longer allowed to wear the *latus clavus* at all. However, Levick 1991 and Wardle 2014: 295 propose that senators' sons who hoped for office were simply allowed to assume the *latus clavus* earlier than *equites* in the same position.

('without the stripe'), are restorations, and other interpretations are possible.[108] An alternative suggestion, proposed by Demougin, is that the two groups are actually the *seniores* of the *ordo equester* who possess the *angustus clavus*, and the *iuniores* with the *equus publicus*.[109] But the restoration of *Roman Statutes* can be defended. It does not explicitly say that the senators' sons did not possess the *equus publicus*. Instead, it uses the *latus clavus* as the only way of distinguishing between different types of *equites*: senators' sons (who possessed both the *equus publicus* and the *latus clavus*) and other members of the *ordo* (who only had the *equus publicus*).

Therefore, membership of the equestrian order was defined and expressed in various ways in the age of Augustus and Tiberius. *Equites equo publico*, including the sons of senators, were members of the equestrian squadrons and centuries. All *equites* who met the required census qualification, both those with the *equus publicus* and those without it, had the legal right to sit in the first fourteen rows of the theatre, and the privilege of wearing the gold ring. The last two prerogatives, which were the subject of legislation under both Augustus and Tiberius, helped to regulate the outward appearance and status symbols of the *ordo equester*. The most important development of the Augustan principate, which was to have far-reaching consequences, was the increase of the number of *equites equo publico* beyond 1,800 for the first time. This meant that the size of the equestrian *turmae* (for ceremonial purposes, such as the *transvectio* and public funerals), and the *centuriae* (for voting in the assembly) was not restricted and could expand without limit. Dionysius of Halicarnassus' statement that the *transvectio equitum* sometimes included 5,000 *equites* suggests the significant extent of Augustus' generosity in this regard. This resulted in the *equus publicus* being shared more widely among *equites*.

Imperial Benefaction

Augustus incorporated the *recognitio equitum* into the annual *transvectio* ceremony, and he bestowed and withdrew the *equus publicus* without needing to hold the censorship. Three of his successors did assume the office of censor: Claudius, who shared the office with L. Vitellius in AD 47/ 48; Vespasian, who was censor together with his son Titus in AD 73/74; and Domitian, who was sole censor in AD 85 before becoming *censor*

---

[108] See Rowe 2002: 73, whose different translations clearly articulate the problems here.

[109] Demougin 1992b, restoring ll. 55–6 as: *et qui ordini[s equestris erunt, ii qui angustum cla]|uom habebunt.*

perpetuus. From that point onwards the censorship and its powers were formally absorbed into the office of emperor.[110] Claudius and Vespasian both performed a formal review of the equestrian order as part of their censorships, as shown by Suetonius' use of the precise technical terms in his *Lives*.[111] But this does not mean that Augustus' successors needed to hold the censorship in order to supervise the *recognitio* or make grants of the *equus publicus*. For instance, there is no evidence that Caligula ever held the position of censor or conducted a census,[112] but we know that he did supervise the *recognitio* personally, as Suetonius shows:

> He reviewed the *equites Romani* rigorously and carefully, with the appropriate restraint, openly removing the public horse from those men who were judged to have done something scandalous or worthy of disgrace. But in making his official pronouncements, he passed over the names of those men who were thought to have minor faults.[113]

This passage is replete with precise language that leaves one in no doubt that Caligula conducted the *recognitio equitum* as part of the *transvectio* ceremony, following the pattern established by Augustus himself.[114] Cassius Dio describes this action in slightly different terms, which suggest the wider significance of the young emperor's actions:

> Since there were few men in the *ordo equester*, he summoned prominent individuals of good family and abundant wealth from throughout the empire, even from the provinces, and he enrolled them in the *ordo*.[115]

If these provincials possessed the *census equester*, then they were already technically *equites*, following the parameters established under the Republic. Five hundred *equites* are attested at Patavium in Italy and Gades in Spain under Augustus, suggesting that men of equestrian status

---

[110] Millar 1977: 293–5; B. W. Jones 1992: 106–7.

[111] Suet. *Claud.* 16.1 (*recognitione equitum*), *Vesp.* 9.2 (*recenso senatu et equite*).

[112] Barrett 1990: 311 n. 82. Cf. Wiseman 1970b: 70 n. 21, who is open to the possibility that Caligula did so.

[113] Suet. *Cal.* 16.2: *equites R. severe curioseque nec sine moderatione recognovit, palam adempto equo quibus aut probri aliquid aut ignominiae inesset, eorum qui minore culpa tenerentur nominibus modo in recitatione praeteritis.*

[114] Demougin 1988: 178–81; Wardle 1994: 171. The language includes: (i) the verb indicating the formal review ceremony (*recognovit*, see Suet. *Aug.* 37.1, 38.3); (ii) the term for the withdrawal of the public horse (*adempto equo*, see Livy 24.43; Gell. *NA* 7.22); (iii) the legal word for disgrace (*ignominiae*, see Suet. *Aug.* 39.1). The entire passage bears remarkable similarities to the ceremony as described in Suet. *Aug.* 38.3–39.1.

[115] Dio 59.9.5: τοῦ τε τέλους τοῦ τῶν ἱππέων ὀλιγανδροῦντος, τοὺς πρώτους ἐξ ἁπάσης καὶ τῆς ἔξω ἀρχῆς τοῖς τε γένεσι καὶ ταῖς περιουσίαις μεταπεμψάμενος κατελέξατο. For the translation of ἐξ ἁπάσης καὶ τῆς ἔξω ἀρχῆς followed here, see Humphrey 1976: 118–19.

were found in the older provinces.[116] Dio's technical language suggests that Caligula summoned select provincials to Rome, where they were formally granted the *equus publicus* by the emperor as part of the *recognitio*.[117] These actions are often cited as a reaction to the indolence of Tiberius, who is said to have neglected the ranks of the equestrian jury panels in particular.[118] We might doubt the true extent of Tiberius' laxity in this area, for such indolent behaviour is the mark of a 'bad' emperor.[119] Caligula's review of the equestrian order is accordingly classified by Suetonius among his good actions early in his principate.[120]

The fact that Caligula awarded the *equus publicus* without holding the censorship indicates that the paradigm established by Augustus continued under subsequent emperors. This is also supported by Dio's account of the reign of Nero, in which he refers to the 'annual review' of the *equites* (ἐτησίᾳ ... ἐξετάσει) conducted by the emperor, using the correct Greek technical term for the *recognitio*.[121] This meant that Nero likewise granted or withdrew the public horse without holding the office of censor. The censorships of Claudius and Vespasian served specific ideological purposes showing that they were restoring the state following an unpopular predecessor and civil wars.[122] The taking of the census necessarily involved a formal review of the numbers of *equites*. But this did not mean that an emperor could only grant or withdraw the public horse when he formally held the censorship. We should thus envision that there was a gradual increase in the number of *equites* being awarded the *equus publicus* from the reign of Augustus onwards. The reign of Caligula assumed particular importance as a time in which the emperor granted the *equus publicus* to provincials, whom he summoned to Rome to participate in the annual *transvectio*.

The epigraphic evidence for equestrian titulature supports this argument. As we saw in Chapter 3, during the late Republic *eques* was the standard term used in inscriptions to describe a member of the *ordo*. From late in the reign of Augustus the expression *equo publico*, meaning simply 'with the public horse', begins to be employed in epigraphic texts for the

---

[116] Strabo 3.5.3, 5.1.7.
[117] The verb κατελέξατο is the crucial technical term (Humphrey 1976: 119).
[118] Suet. *Tib*. 41; Humphrey 1976: 117–18; Hurley 1991: 80–1; Lindsay 1993: 84–5; Demougin 1988: 175–8.
[119] See Demougin 1988: 542–5 on the lack of firm statistical evidence for this.
[120] See Wardle 1994: 20–1 on the structure of the *Life*.
[121] Dio 63.13.3. Stein 1927: 65 n. 3 pointed out that this must refer to the inspection, not just the parade.
[122] These issues are discussed further in Chapter 8.

first time.[123] It features, for example, in the inscribed account of the career
of M. Minicius of Falerio, one of Augustus' *tribuni militum a populo*.[124]
Soon more complex formulations began to appear in inscriptions, which
noted the specific emperor who had granted the public horse. The first
attested example of this phenomenon comes from Pompeii, where the
epitaph of D. Lucretius Valens records that he 'was honoured with the
equus publicus by Tiberius Claudius Caesar Augustus Germanicus' *(equo
publico honorato ab Ti(berio) Claudio Caesare Au[g(usto)
Ger(manico)])*.[125] The wording of the inscription suggests that Claudius
was still alive when it was erected.[126] A second case comes from Corinth in
Greece, where the base of an honorific statue for C. Iulius Spartiaticus
records that he was 'furnished with the *equus publicus* by the deified
Claudius' *(equo p[ublico] | [ex]ornato a divo Claudio)*.[127] These grants of
the *equus publicus* could have been made during Claudius' censorship; but
if so, the role of his censorial colleague, L. Vitellius, is ignored, and the
honour is portrayed entirely as an imperial benefaction. Finally, the
inscribed statue base of M. Valerius Propinquus Grattius Cerealis, from
Tarraco in Hispania Citerior, reveals that he was 'enrolled among the
equites by the emperor Titus' *(adlecto in | equite* [sic] *a T(ito)
Imp(eratore))*.[128] The presence of Titus alone suggests that Cerialis' adlection occurred during the emperor's reign, not while he was censor with his
father Vespasian in AD 73/74. Senators who received promotions during
that census either recorded the role of both Flavians, or omitted Titus
altogether.[129] Therefore the elevation of Grattius Cerealis to equestrian
rank was evidently performed by Titus alone in AD 79/81.

There are a number of inscriptions from the first century AD which
feature expressions such as *equo publico* or *equo publico ornatus*, without
recording which emperor made the benefaction. It would seem perverse to
insist that all such grants were made during censorships, and very often the
evidence of individual careers rules this out. For example, M. Stlaccius
Coranus served as a *praefectus cohortis* and *tribunus militum* under

---

[123] *CIL* XI 7066 = *ILS* 6598 (for the date, see Duncan-Jones 2006: 219); *CIL* V 7567 = *ILS* 6747
(discriminating between two equestrian brothers, one with the *equus publicus*, one without).
[124] *AE* 1960, 258; *PME* M 57; Nicolet 1967b: 48–9.   [125] *AE* 2004, 405.
[126] A fragmentary inscription from Abellinum may also refer to a grant of the *equus publicus* by
Claudius, but this is uncertain (*AE* 2008, 337).
[127] *Corinth* VIII.2.68. Obviously the inscription was carved after Claudius' death.
[128] *CIL* II 4251 = II.14.2 1171.
[129] *CIL* XI 1834, XIV 2925; *AE* 1925, 126. For the omission of Titus in inscriptions referring to the
censorship, see *CIL* III 335; *AE* 1990, 217.

Claudius, probably in the British invasion of AD 43.[130] The chronology of his career suggests that the award of the *equus publicus* and adlection into the *decuriae* occurred under Tiberius or Caligula.[131] Likewise, M. Iulius Romulus was adlected *inter tribunicios* by Claudius during the censorship of AD 47/48. But Romulus had already received the *equus publicus*, either from Claudius himself at an earlier point in his reign, or from Caligula or Tiberius.[132] In AD 70 the senate rewarded Vespasian's freedman T. Flavius Hormas with equestrian rank.[133] If he was honoured with the *equus publicus*, the grant was surely stage-managed by the Flavian coterie in Rome in Vespasian's name, well before the emperor held the censorship.[134] The evidence of epigraphic and literary sources therefore shows that emperors could and did make grants of the *equus publicus* without specifically holding the censorship. They also had the ability to expel members from the *ordo equester* at will.[135] This led to a change in the perception of the *ordo* over the course of the first century AD, in that it was no longer considered sufficient to simply possess the *census equester* – the *equus publicus* was also required from the emperor. In the second century AD it became much more common for *equites* to record in inscriptions precisely which emperor had granted them the *equus publicus*.[136] By this date equestrian rank was widely accepted as an imperial benefaction which could not be obtained any other way.[137]

Therefore, the distinctions between *equites equo publico* and other *equites Romani* gradually broke down over the course of the first

---

[130] *CIL* VI 3539 = *ILS* 2730.

[131] *PME* S 81. Demougin 1988: 684–5 argues that the post of *praefectus fabrum* and the *equus publicus* were granted when he was a young man.

[132] *AE* 1925, 85; Demougin 1992a no. 448. A comparable case is P. Treptus Atticus, a centurion who received the *equus publicus* before the reign of Claudius, therefore probably under Tiberius or Caligula (*CIL* XI 394; *PME* T 35; Demougin 1992a no. 392).

[133] Tac. *Hist.* 4.39.1.

[134] Technically Domitian was acting as his father's representative, but, as Tacitus makes clear, Mucianus was pulling the strings (Tac. *Hist.* 4.39–40).

[135] This is shown by the case of Arellius Fuscus, during Pliny the Elder's lifetime (*NH* 33.152) and other examples (Suet. *Cal.* 16.2, *Claud.* 24.1).

[136] Mommsen 1887–8: III, 489 n. 4; Demougin 1993: 237. See, for example: *CIL* II 6095 = II.14.2 1138 (Nerva); *CIL* III 607 (Trajan); *CIL* IX 23 = *ILS* 6472 (Hadrian); *CIL* VIII 20144 (Antoninus Pius); *CIL* VI 1586 (Marcus Aurelius and Lucius Verus); *CIL* VI 3550 (Commodus); *ILAfr.* 137 (Severus and Caracalla).

[137] Note in particular the large numbers of second-century emperors who are cited as bestowing the *equus publicus* in inscriptions from North Africa (*AE* 1917/18, 23; *CIL* VIII 11173, 21044, 24017; *ILAfr.* 280, 320, 390). The vast majority of evidence from this region is dated to the second and third centuries AD (Duncan-Jones 1967: 151–2). There is only one papyrological example, dated to the third century AD (*P. Hib.* 2.274, as re-edited by Casanova 2008).

century AD. The process began with Augustus' pivotal decision to increase the numbers of *equites equo publico* for the first time, expanding the size of the equestrian *turmae* and *centuriae*. This went hand in hand with the incorporation of the formal review of the *ordo* (the *recognitio equitum*) into the annual parade (*transvectio equitum*). When a citizen was granted the *equus publicus* he was formally assigned to one of the six squadrons, membership of which he retained for life. Augustus' successors continued this policy of expanding the numbers of *equites equo publico*. The ancient accounts of the reigns of Caligula and Nero show that an emperor did not need to be censor to grant or withdraw the *equus publicus*, a conclusion which is supported by the epigraphic evidence for the careers of individual *equites*. Over time, it became accepted that the census qualification of 400,000 sesterces was insufficient for equestrian rank. Domitian's assumption of the perpetual censorship, and the incorporation of that office's powers into the position of emperor, represented the formal culmination of a century of change. The establishment of the secretariat of the *a censibus*, an imperial department empowered to oversee the census and the qualifications for senatorial and equestrian rank, meant that these powers were now fully amalgamated into the imperial administration.[138]

Some provincials certainly did travel to Rome to participate in the *transvectio* after the reign of Caligula. This cannot have been the case for all *equites*, given the increasing number of equestrians from the provinces and the cost and logistics of undertaking the journey.[139] Sometimes equestrian status could be awarded through an actual meeting with the emperor, as with the case of the sophist Heliodorus, who received the *equus publicus* for both himself and his children after appearing before Caracalla.[140] For most Romans, however, it is likely that they applied for the *equus publicus*, either personally or through a patron, via the office of the *a censibus*, who would assess that they met the property requirement before approving the benefaction.[141] For example, in the third century AD it was the patronage of the chief Vestal Virgin that enabled Aemilius Pardalas to be granted

---

[138] Dio's Maecenas recommends that Augustus should establish the senatorial post of sub-censor to handle such matters, but this did not take place in reality (Dio 52.21.3–5; Reinhold 1988: 191–2).

[139] See further Chapter 8.   [140] Phil. *VS* 626.

[141] Duncan-Jones 1967: 152–4; Demougin 1993: 236–7. Further evidence for imperial regulation of equestrian status is shown by the fact that Caracalla allowed exiled citizens who had been recalled to reclaim their *equus publicus* (*P. Giss.* 40 II = *P. Oxy.* 36.2755 = Oliver 1989 no. 261A). This text has now been shown to be part of the *Constitutio Antoniniana* issued by Caracalla in AD 212 (van Minnen 2016).

membership of the *ordo equester*.[142] As noted at the beginning of the chapter, the argument that there was a change in the criteria of membership of the equestrian order in the first century AD is owed to Mommsen and Wiseman. However, Wiseman places the crucial moment under the Flavians, between Vespasian's censorship and the reign of Domitian, when he assumed the office of censor in perpetuity. In this chapter we have argued that the increase in the number of *equites equo publico* occurred much earlier, under Augustus and the Julio-Claudians. Domitian's reign represented the climax of these changes, rather than a pivotal turning point. This process of evolution shows how membership of the *ordo equester*, like many other aspects of life under the principate, now became a status symbol within the gift of the emperor. This was a fundamental part of the transformation of the Roman state into a monarchical *res publica*.

Provincial Perspectives

Our evidence for the equestrian order is biased towards those *equites Romani* who served as officers in the Roman army or as procurators in the imperial administration, on account of the large numbers of inscriptions that survive recording their official careers.[143] There were probably only 600 *equites* in procuratorial posts at any one time.[144] They therefore represent only a small proportion of the thousands of *equites* who lived in the Roman empire, who numbered around 20,000–30,000 in each generation. The difficulties in relying solely on the evidence of named *equites* for estimating the size of the *ordo* is demonstrated by the fact that only three specific equestrians are attested in Gades.[145] This stands in contrast with Strabo's references to the 500 equestrians resident in both Gades and Patavium, which we noted earlier in this chapter. The extent of the *ordo* can be glimpsed through the groups of *equites* that made corporate dedications, or received handouts, in larger towns such as Saldae in Mauretania Caesariensis, Carmo in Baetica, and Narbo in Gallia Narbonensis.[146] There is also some limited evidence for equestrians being allocated special seats in provincial theatres, similar to the *XIV ordines* in Rome.[147] In Lugdunum

---

[142] *CIL* VI 2131 = *ILS* 4929.

[143] This is strikingly shown by the evidence for the second century AD, for which 80 per cent of known *equites* are officers or procurators (see the table in Demougin 1993: 240).

[144] Bang 2011: 124.   [145] See the figures in Caballos Rufino 1998: 137.

[146] Duncan-Jones 2016: 99; *CIL* VIII 8938 = *ILS* 5078 (Saldae); *CIL* II 1380 (Carmo), XII 4333 = *ILS* 112 (Narbo).

[147] This is discussed in Chapter 9.

there were sufficient numbers of *equites Romani* for them to have their own patron, the merchant M. Inthatius Vitalis.[148] While Chapters 6 and 7 will focus specifically on equestrians as officers and administrators, our aim in this section is to examine how equestrian rank itself functioned as a marker of official status and public identity throughout the Roman world, particularly in the case of those *equites* who never embarked on imperial service. The *ordo equester* embraced a vast range of wealthy non-senatorial aristocrats of Italian and provincial origin, from the praetorian prefect and equestrian procurators, through to town councillors, provincial priests, military officers, *publicani*, businessmen and landowners. Their status as *equites* meant that their wealth and public standing was officially recognised by the *res publica*, providing them with a reason to be invested in the Roman state, its success and longevity. Moreover, as equestrian rank became an imperial benefaction, it made these wealthy elites dependent on the emperor for prestige.

Equestrian rank could be articulated on public statues and funerary monuments through the use of status symbols such as the tunic with the *angustus clavus*, equestrian shoes (*calcei equestres*) and the *anulus aureus*, as well as equestrian titles or positions listed in an accompanying inscription. Personal inscriptions on statue bases, tombs or other monuments incorporated Latin and Greek titles of equestrian rank, which usually following the name of the honorand. In Latin inscriptions the title *eques equo publico* or the briefer *equo publico* are most commonly found in the first and second centuries AD, after which *eques Romanus* becomes the predominant epigraphic status designation.[149] The Greek versions ἱππεὺς Ῥωμαίων and ἱππικός usually appear in inscriptions dating to the second and third centuries AD.[150] These titles were often omitted from the inscribed careers of those who held officer commands or procuratorships. For example, T. Varius Clemens, who rose to become the *ab epistulis* to Marcus Aurelius, was honoured with three statues in his home town of Celeia in Noricum.[151] None of the inscriptions on the statue bases referred to him as an *eques Romanus*, because they did not need to – it was implicit from the listing of prestigious government posts that he possessed this status.

---

[148] *CIL* XIII 1954 = *ILS* 7030. The *ordo equester* at Lugdunum is also referenced in *CIL* XIII 1921 = *ILS* 7024.

[149] Duncan-Jones 2016: 94–5.

[150] Mason 1974: 57; Demougin 1999: 589. The Greek equivalent of *equus publicus*, ἵππος δημόσιος, is attested in epigraphic texts, but it is much rarer (e.g. see *I. Prusias* 54; *I. Eph.* 3048).

[151] *CIL* III 5211 = *ILS* 1362; *CIL* III 5212 = *ILS* 1362a; *CIL* III 5215 = *ILS* 1362b; Eck 2006b: 494–5.

However, for those citizens with no public career to their credit, equestrian rank was a valuable and important honour in and of itself, and the trappings of status formed part of their public self-representation. This can be seen in the statue of the teenage 'Young Togatus' from Aphrodisias in Caria (Figure 5.1). The youth boasts a ring on his left hand, and wears strapless leather shoes, the *calcei equestres*, as a sign of his equestrian status.[152] Although the precise identity of the 'Young Togatus' cannot be confirmed, there are examples of inscriptions of youths from Aphrodisias which give their only status designation as the title of ἱππικός, such as P. Aelius Hilarianus, who was the son of a *primipilaris*.[153] It was not only young men who benefited from the prestige of equestrian rank in Aphrodisias. The doctor M. Aurelius Apollonius was recorded as ἱππικός on his sarcophagus. It was an imperial honour that represented the wealth and social respectability he had acquired, showing that he had been a favoured resident of the city while alive.[154]

Equestrian rank was most visible among the curial classes of the towns of Italy and the provinces. These were the citizens who served as decurions on the town councils and held local magistracies and priesthoods.[155] Equestrian titles often occupied pride of place in inscriptions recording the offices and honours of these municipal aristocrats (or *domi nobiles*) who spent most of their lives in the service of their home towns. The prominent use of the title of *eques equo publico* or *eques Romanus* represented the fulfilment of the vision of Cicero and Augustus that the *equites* of Italy would come to value the status designations of both their home town and of Rome itself.[156] One example of this self-representation can be found inscribed on the base of a statue of P. Nonius Livius Anterotianus (Figure 5.2). This was erected in the 'Plaza of the Corporations' in Ostia:

To Publius Nonius Livius Anterotianus son of Publius, of the Palatina voting tribe, supplied with the *equus publicus* by the Emperor Marcus Aurelius Antoninus Augustus, chosen as a decurion by decree of the decurions, *flamen* of the deified Hadrian, *salius* of *Laurens Lavinas*, aedile, praetor for performing the rites of Volcan. Titus Tinucius Sosiphanes (erected this), for the dearest and most dutiful man. The place was given by a decree of the decurions, and paid for by public money.[157]

---

[152] Smith and Ratté 1997: 21–2; R. R. R. Smith 1998: 69; Smith et al. 2006: 110–11. For equestrian shoes, see Goette 1988: 459–464.

[153] *I. Aph.* 12.17, 12.535.   [154] *I. Aph.* 11.217; Nutton 1997: 192–3.

[155] Duncan-Jones 1967: 151.   [156] See Chapters 3 and 4.

[157] *CIL* XIV 391: *P(ublio) Nonio P(ubli) fil(io)* | *Pal(atina tribu) Livio* | *Anterotiano* | *equo publ(ico)* *exornato ab* | *Imp(eratore) M(arco) Aurelio Antonino Aug(usto)* | *dec(reto) dec(urionum)* *decur(ioni) adlecto* | *flamini divi Hadriani* | *salio Laurent(ium) Lavinatium* | *aedili pr(aetori)* *sacr(is) Volk(ani) faciu(ndis)* | *T(itus) Tinucius* | *Sosiphanes* | *carissimo* | *pientissimo* | *l(ocus)* *d(atus) d(ecreto) d(ecurionum) p(ublice).* There is a companion statue, erected by

Figure 5.1: Statue of the 'Young Togatus', Aphrodisias

Figure 5.2: Inscribed statue base of P. Nonius Livius Anterotianus, Ostia

Anterotianus was an esteemed and prominent citizen in Ostia. He sat on the town council, held local priesthoods, and occupied the priestly office of *salius* of *Laurens Lavinas* at nearby Lavinium.[158] The distinction of the *equus publicus*, granted to him by Marcus Aurelius, comes first in the list of

Anterotianus' grandmother, Livia Marcellina, with near identical wording on the base (*CIL* XIV 390 = *ILS* 6139).

[158] For this priesthood, see Chapter 10.

titles, as it was an imperial honour within the gift of the *princeps*. The fact that there would have been many other *equites Romani* resident in Ostia did not diminish the value of the rank to Anterotianus personally.

In towns where equestrian status was not widespread, such a benefaction would have been an even greater cause for celebration and public commemoration. In Cartima, a town in inland Baetica, the friends and mother of D. Iunius Melinus erected a public statue of him to celebrate the fact that he was 'the first man from the *civitas* of Cartima to be made an *eques Romanus*' (*equiti Romano ex civitate | Cartimitana primo facto*).[159] There were certainly many *equites* resident in Baetica in the Julio-Claudian period, but they were concentrated in the port city Gades and in the provincial capital of Corduba. In Cartima, as the inscription shows, they were a rarity, and Melinus' elevation marked out his superior status among his peers.[160]

Equestrian rank had similar importance among the elites of the Greek provinces, as a mark of imperial status that was recognised and valued by its holders.[161] The ability of provincials in these regions to acquire equestrian status was dependent on patrons or connections with the Roman administration, especially in the early empire.[162] For example, in Achaea the first *equites* were either members of Italian families, or Greeks with Italian connections.[163] These included C. Iulius Spartiaticus of Corinth, who, as we have observed earlier in this chapter, specifically recorded that he received the *equus publicus* from the emperor Claudius.[164] In Asia Minor equestrians are often found in Roman colonies such as Alexandria Troas or Pisidian Antioch during the first century AD, while other Greek cities such as Aphrodisias do not show any *equites* before the second century.[165] The inherent value of equestrian status to Greek-speaking citizens is demonstrated by the case of T. Flavius Gaianus, who was honoured with no fewer than seven public statues by the different tribes of Ancyra in Galatia. The statue bases feature inscriptions outlining his career.[166] The fact that all the inscriptions record Gaianus' official positions and honours in the same order indicates that he personally prepared the main part of the text himself.[167] It reads as follows:

To good fortune! Titus Flavius Gaianus, *eques Romanus*, who twice held the office of first magistrate, and conducted a register of citizens, and three times conducted

---

[159] *CIL* II 1955.   [160] Caballos Rufino 1998: 136–41.   [161] Kuhn 2010: 27, 115, 237–8.
[162] Demougin 1999: 585–6; Kuhn 2010: 35–6.   [163] Spawforth 2002; Zoumbaki 2008: 46–7.
[164] *Corinth* VIII.2.68.   [165] Demougin 1999: 583–4; Kuhn 2010: 132, 217.
[166] *I. Ankara* 96–102.   [167] Mitchell and French 2012: 268.

embassies to the divine Antoninus, and has twice been president of the games of the Galatian *koinon*, and twice of the sacred games called the great isopythian Asclepieia, and was high priest of the Galatian *koinon*, galatarch, sebastophant, founder of the metropolis Ancyra.[168]

Gaianus' title of *eques Romanus* heads the list of his achievements, which consists of a glittering record in the service of Ancyra and Galatia. Even his embassies to Caracalla need not have taken him far from home, since they probably occurred while the emperor was in Bithynia en route to the eastern front in AD 213/14.[169] One wonders whether Gaianus even earned his equestrian status from Caracalla in the course of his ambassadorial duties. We might compare the case of another leading Ancyran *eques*, Tertullus Varus, who received unspecified honours from the emperors in the 250s AD, at the same time that the emperor Valerian was passing through Asia Minor.[170] Equestrian rank was clearly appreciated as a mark of status in the Greek world alongside local honours and dignities, as in the Latin west.

Was equestrian rank, as a status bestowed by the emperor, regarded as intrinsically superior to local positions and honours? The social value of equestrian status is demonstrated by Censorinus in his work *On the Birthday*, in which he referred to the honours achieved by the book's dedicatee, Caerellius:

You have held municipal offices, and you stand tall among the leading men of your city because you have held the distinction of the priesthood, and you have even surpassed provincial rank through the status of the equestrian order.[171]

Censorinus thus outlines a hierarchy of honours that existed within the towns and cities of the Roman world. Municipal magistracies and priest-hoods were significant positions within the civic context, but technically inferior to equestrian rank, which elevated its holder into membership of an empire-wide elite. When Pliny the Younger spoke of granting 300,000 sesterces to his friend, the decurion Romatius Firmus, so that he could

---

[168] *I. Ankara* 99 (trans. Mitchell and French, with minor changes): ἀγαθῆ τύχη. | Τ. Φλ(άουιον) Γαιανὸν ἱππέα Ῥωμαίων | καὶ δὶς τὴν πρώτην ἀρχὴν ἄρξαν|τα καὶ πολειτογραφήσαντα καὶ γ´| πρεσβεύσαντα παρὰ θεὸν Ἀντω|νεῖνον καὶ ἀγωνοθετήσαντα δὶς τοῦ | τε κοινοῦ τῶν Γαλατῶν κὲ [δ]ὶς | τῶν ἱερῶν ἀγώνων τῶν μεγάλων | Ἀσκληπιείων ἰσ[ο]πυθίων κὲ ἀρχι|ερέα τοῦ κοινοῦ τῶν Γαλατῶν, γαλα|τάρχην, σεβαστοφάντην, κὲ κτίστην | τῆς μητροπόλεως Ἀγκύρας. I have omitted the final dedication by the tribe, which is different on each of the inscriptions.
[169] Mitchell and French 2012: 31–3, 268.   [170] *I. Ankara* 119; Mitchell and French 2012: 286–7.
[171] Censorinus, *De Die Natali* 15.4: *tu tamen officiis municipalibus functus, honore sacerdoti in principibus tuae civitatis conspicuus, ordinis etiam equestris dignitate gradum provincialium supergressus.*

become an *eques*, he laid out the reasons 'why I ought to undertake to increase your status' (*cur suscipere augere dignitatem tuam debeam*).[172] In Pliny's mind there was likewise a precise hierarchy of *dignitates*, which proceeded from municipal to imperial honours. The evidence of municipal careers from North Africa demonstrates that local offices usually preceded the award of equestrian rank.[173] The most prominent candidates for elevation to equestrian status were those who could already demonstrate the necessary wealth, distinction and personal qualities to the imperial administration, and service to one's home town was the most effective way to do this.[174] But, at the same time, it is important to emphasise that the promotion to equestrian rank did not exclude Roman citizens from continuing to hold office in their home region. One example of this is L. Maecilius Nepos of Cirta, who occupied all the municipal magistracies, was promoted to equestrian rank, and then became *flamen perpetuus* of the imperial cult.[175] Priests of the imperial cult in the Greek cities of Asia Minor likewise often held the priesthood after becoming *equites* or occupying official government roles.[176] In Ephesus there are even examples of individuals who ascended to important civic positions such as *prytanis* and *grammateus* after receiving equestrian rank.[177] Perhaps the most high-profile example of this type of equestrian is C. Iulius Demosthenes from Oenoanda in Lycia, whose civic offices there followed his military and procuratorial career.[178]

Therefore, despite the comments of Censorinus and Pliny the Younger, it is apparent that equestrian rank did not reduce the prestige inherent in municipal magistracies and civic and provincial priesthoods. The ceremonial duties that Flavius Gaianus undertook as president of the games (*agonothetes*) at Ancyra would have been far more visible, and perhaps more meaningful, to his local audience, than riding in the *transvectio equitum* in far-off Rome, which he would have only done once, if at all.[179] At Oenoanda in Lycia, the *agonothetes* of the festival endowed by C. Iulius Demosthenes was granted the honour of wearing purple and

---

[172] Pliny the Younger, *Ep.* 1.19.   [173] Duncan-Jones 1967: 154–6.

[174] Caballos Rufino 1998: 129–31.   [175] *CIL* VIII 7112 = *ILAlg.* 690.

[176] Frija 2012: 187–8. She distinguishes between Roman colonies in Asia Minor, where the flaminate formed part of the municipal *cursus*, and the Greek cities, where it did not.

[177] Kuhn 2010: 166.

[178] For his career, see Wörrle 1988: 55, 60–2. On Demosthenes and other Greeks who invested in their cities after holding Roman offices, see Salmeri 2000: 58–60.

[179] For provincials taking part in the *transvectio*, see Chapter 8.

a crown decked out with images of Hadrian and Apollo.[180] The festival's procession not only included the *agonothetes* himself, but also civic officials and priests, representing the social and political hierarchy within the town.[181] In these contexts it was the local office that conferred immediate prestige on the individual, and brought them to the attention of members of their community. Equestrian rank complemented these positions, rather than diminishing their importance.

The same point can be made about equestrians who performed acts of euergetism that benefited their local communities. In Ilium, Sex. Iulius Philo was recognised with four statues erected by the city's various tribes:

The Attalis tribe (erected this to) Sextus Iulius Philo, the pride of the city, prefect of the *cohors Flaviana*, the honourable and distinguished gymnasiarch, the first of all time and currently the only man to measure out oil for the city councillors and all the citizens and supply oil for the whole community from tubs.[182]

Although Philo was an equestrian military officer, with his rank and unit duly included in the inscribed text, he was best remembered in Ilium for the scale of his generous benefactions to the community at large.[183] The practice of benefaction was not restricted to the Greek world. For example, M. Licinius Rufus, an equestrian officer from Carthage, was patron of Thugga, where he built the market using his own finances. His combined local and imperial career was inscribed on the market building itself, as well as the base of a statue erected by the council of Thugga on account of this benefaction.[184] In both these cases the honorand's equestrian status was included as part of the list of their achievements. But equestrian rank did not in and of itself provide the basis for their commemoration. It coexisted as an imperial status marker alongside local distinctions.

The interaction between equestrian and municipal status markers in a local context is illustrated by the Augustan epigraphic evidence from Pompeii. No fewer than six *tribuni militum a populo* are attested in Pompeii, constituting the cream of the local elite.[185] Taken as a group,

---

[180] See the discussion of Wörrle 1988: 183–209. Rogers 1991a: 96–7 points out that the use of such imperial imagery altered the nature of the festival.

[181] Zuiderhoek 2009: 97–8.

[182] *IGR* IV 216 = *I.Ilion* 121: ἡ Ἀτταλὶς φυλὴ | Σέξτον Ἰούλιον Φί[λω]|[ν]α, τὸν κόσμον τῆς π[ό]|[λ] εως, ἔπαρχον σπείρης | Φλαβιανῆς, γυμνασιαρ|χήσαντα λαμπρῶς καὶ φι|λοτείμως, καὶ πρῶτον | τῶν ἀπ' αἰῶνος καὶ | μέχρι νῦν μόνον ἐλαι|ομετρήσαντα τούς | τε βουλευτὰς καὶ πο|λείτας πάντας καὶ ἀλ[εί]|ψαντα ἐκ λουτήρων [παν]|δημεί. The other statues are *I.Ilion* 122, 123, 124.

[183] On such distributions of oil, see Zuiderhoek 2009: 109–12.   [184] *AE* 1969/70, 652–3.

[185] For the Augustan post of *tribunus militum a populo*, see Chapter 4.

these tribunes constitute a valuable case study of how equestrian rank figured in public self-representation.[186] One Augustan tribune, M. Lucretius Decidianus Rufus, was honoured with three statues, with his official posts inscribed on the base, in the Pompeian forum. One inscribed base (Figure 5.3) reads:

To Marcus Lucretius Decidianus Rufus, *duumvir* three times, *quinquennalis*,[187] priest, military tribune selected by the people, *praefectus fabrum*, (erected) after his death, (authorised) by a decree of the decurions.[188]

The inscribed text lists Rufus' municipal offices in one group, and his military posts in another, a pattern that can be found on other inscriptions recording the careers of the *tribuni militum a populo*.[189] Unfortunately, since the original statue no longer survives, we cannot be certain whether Rufus was presented in civilian dress or military attire. But the language of the inscription reveals that the local Pompeian offices are not subordinated to his imperial military commands. Indeed, there is a crucial connection between them, since Rufus was recommended by the people of Pompeii to hold the post of *tribunus militum*.

The same point can be made about the representation of the military tribunate on the tomb of A. Veius, a member of a prominent Pompeian family. He was buried in a semicircular *schola* tomb, a form of funerary commemoration unique to Pompeii, in the Porta Ercolano necropolis to the north of the city (Figure 5.4). The inscribed statue base, which is no longer *in situ*, records his career:

To Aulus Veius, son of Marcus, twice *duumvir* with judicial authority, *quinquennalis*, military tribune selected by the people, (authorised) by a decree of the decurions.[190]

The *schola* tombs were reserved for Pompeian citizens who held municipal magistracies, or their family members, and they therefore marked out their holders as members of the local elite. They were designed as semicircular

---

[186] Franklin 2001: 18 styles them the 'core of the Augustan faction in local politics'.

[187] The *duumviri* were the chief magistrates of Pompeii. The *quinquennales* were elected every five years to conduct the census.

[188] *CIL* X 789 = *ILS* 6363c: *M(arco) Lucretio Decidian(o) | Rufo IIvir(o) III quinq(uennali) | pontif(ici) trib(uno) mil(itum) a populo | praef(ecto) fabr(um) ex d(ecreto) d(ecurionum) | post mortem.* The other bases from the forum are *CIL* X 788 = *ILS* 6363b and *AE* 1898, 143 = *ILS* 6363a. His career was also recorded on *CIL* X 851 = *ILS* 6363d, a marble plaque attached to a statue restored by one of his descendants (Nicolet 1967b: 38).

[189] Nicolet 1967b: 39, 63.

[190] *CIL* X 996: *A(ulo) Veio M(arci) f(ilio) IIvir(o) i(ure) d(icundo) | iter(um) quinq(uennali) trib(uno) | milit(um) ab popul(o) ex d(ecreto) d(ecurionum).*

Figure 5.3: Inscribed statue base of M. Lucretius Decidianus Rufus, Pompeii

stone benches, where people could sit and contemplate the statue and read the inscribed achievements of the honorand.[191] Interaction with the local audience was therefore an inherent goal of these monuments.

The *tribuni militum a populo* at Pompeii played a vital role in the life of the city as public benefactors. M. Tullius, who was thrice *duumvir* with

---

[191] Zanker 1998: 122–4; Cormack 2007: 586–8. Not all members of Veius' family chose this form of commemoration, however, as noted by V. L. Campbell 2015: 49–51.

Figure 5.4: *Schola* tomb of A. Veius, Pompeii

judicial authority as well as *tribunus militum a populo*, constructed the Temple of Fortuna Augusta adjacent to the forum out of his own money.[192] Adjoining the temple there is a monumental arch (erroneously dubbed the 'Arch of Caligula'), upon which stood a bronze statue depicting a togate citizen of Pompeii on horseback. It has been plausibly suggested by Welch that this statue represented M. Tullius himself.[193] He wears the *latus clavus*, the *anulus aureus* on his hand, and the *calcei patricii* on his feet.[194] This means that the statue must depict either a Roman senator or a member of Pompeii's decurial class, who were entitled to wear the broad stripe and patrician shoes.[195] If this is a statue of M. Tullius, then he chose to represent himself as a member of the local aristocracy, as well as an *eques Romanus* (through the gold ring), but not as a *tribunus militum angusticlavius*.[196]

The most famous Augustan benefactor from the town is M. Holconius Rufus, who refurbished the large theatre together with M. Holconius Celer (either his brother or son). The renovations were completed in 2 BC, the same year in which Augustus was acclaimed *pater patriae*.[197] Rufus served in numerous magistracies in the Augustan period from around 20 BC onwards, and his career is recorded on a variety of monuments throughout

[192] *CIL* X 820.   [193] K. E. Welch 2007a: 554.

[194] For the differences between the types of aristocratic shoes, see Goette 1988: 450–1.

[195] Spalthoff 2010: 25, 28.

[196] On the status symbols of the decurial class, see Spalthoff 2010: 26–7.

[197] *CIL* X 833–4; D'Arms 1988: 54–6; Zanker 1998: 107–12; Cooley and Cooley 2014: 89–91.

the city, from honorific statue bases to building inscriptions.[198] One inscribed statue base, which now stands on the Via dell'Abbondanza, encapsulates his full career:

To Marcus Holconius Rufus, son of Marcus, military tribune selected by the people, five times *duumvir* with judicial authority, twice *quinquennalis*, priest of Augustus Caesar, patron of the colony.[199]

The statue and its inscribed base formed part of a four-sided arch dedicated to the family of the Holconii, of which only partial remains can be seen today (Figure 5.5).[200] Holconius' statue is remarkable for the fact that it depicts him wearing a breastplate which deliberately imitates the statue of Mars Ultor ('the Avenger') from the *forum Augustum* at Rome (Figure 5.6).[201] His public image was somewhat different from that of M. Tullius, because he emphasised his army commission. The military iconography depicts Holconius as a model for the youth of Pompeii and Italy at large, an emblem of service to their *patria*, the *res publica* and the *princeps*.[202] It was the visual embodiment of Augustus' aims.

The post of *tribunus militum a populo* was evidently important to the public image of these Pompeian magnates, as it was included in the inscribed records of their careers alongside their municipal magistracies, priesthoods, and sometimes other officer commands. As Zanker has argued, the office demonstrated that the honorands' importance was acknowledged both by Augustus, who bestowed all military posts as *beneficia*, and by their local community, which voted for them.[203] These men functioned as inter-mediaries between Pompeii and Rome. For example, men who held the office of *quinquennalis* were required to travel to Rome to officially present the Pompeian census returns.[204] The monuments themselves likewise express the same connection between the imperial 'centre' in Rome and the 'periphery' in Pompeii. In the case of M. Tullius, he was represented on horseback, in the costume and insignia appropriate to his standing as

---

[198] D'Arms 1988: 54–9; Zanker 1998: 109–12.

[199] *CIL* X 830 = *ILS* 6361b: *M(arco) Holconio M(arci) f(ilio) Rufo | trib(uno) mil(itum) a popul(o) | IIvir(o) i(ure) d(icundo) V | quinq(uennali) iter(um) | Augusti Caesaris sacerd(oti) | patrono coloniae.*

[200] D'Arms 1988: 60–2, who suggests that the statue originally stood in the forum, but was later moved to the arch by one of Holconius Rufus' descendants. This is not accepted by all: for example, K. E. Welch 2007a: 577–8 links it with the cult of the Lares at the Crossroads.

[201] Zanker 1981: 349–50, 1998: 112. This interpretation is widely accepted (see, for example, K. E. Welch 2007a: 557; Cooley and Cooley 2014: 185). He also wears patrician shoes, which indicate his membership of the municipal aristocracy of Pompeii, not because he was a senator of patrician rank (Goette 1988: 456–7).

[202] Zanker 1988: 328–9.   [203] Zanker 1998: 112.   [204] Rowe 2002: 106.

Figure 5.5: Inscribed statue base of M. Holconius Rufus, Pompeii

a decurion in Pompeii, rather than a military tribune. The representation of Holconius Rufus, the undisputed *princeps* of Pompeii, went one step further, alluding to imperial iconography in Rome itself. Given that all the *tribuni militum a populo* were contemporaries of each other, it is possible that a certain level of competition and status rivalry can be detected behind the construction of these statues and inscriptions.[205] In any other town, a man like Decidianus Rufus would have been the most prestigious citizen, but in Pompeii he was eclipsed by Holconius Rufus.[206] Augustus' *tribuni militum a populo* perfectly encapsulated the integration of the municipal elite of Italy into the framework of the new *res publica*. They were able to serve the state as equestrian officers, but in a way that was connected to their home communities, the very *populus* that elected them.

The most striking manifestation of the way in which equestrian status could be integrated into the local context can be seen in the foundation of C. Vibius Salutaris at Ephesus.[207] Salutaris was an *eques Romanus* who began his life as a tax-collector, before entering the *militiae equestres* and

---

[205] K. E. Welch 2007a: 554 points out that M. Tullius' equestrian statue would have towered above the other monuments in the forum at Pompeii.

[206] D'Arms 1988: 58–9.

[207] See the comprehensive discussion of Salutaris and his endowment in Kuhn 2010: 172–87.

Figure 5.6: Statue of M. Holconius Rufus, Pompeii

holding procuratorial positions under the emperor Domitian.[208] In AD 103/4 Salutaris made a bequest of 21,500 *denarii*, which would provide sufficient interest for yearly distributions worth 1,935 *denarii* to the people of Ephesus.[209] He also dedicated gold and silver to fund statues of Artemis, as well as images of individuals and personifications of institutions, which

[208] *I. Eph.* 35, 36A–D; Rogers 1991b: 16–17.   [209] *I. Eph.* 27; Rogers 1991b: 26–8, 41–3.

would be carried in a procession from the Temple of Artemis through the streets of Ephesus. This would occur on occasions such as meetings of the assembly, games and festivals – approximately every two weeks throughout the year.[210] The Roman images included the emperor Augustus, the current emperor Trajan and his wife Plotina, as well as personifications of the Roman senate, the Roman people and the equestrian order, each of which were accompanied by representations particular to Ephesus, such as its founder Androclus, the city's tribes, and the *boule, demos* and *ephebeia* (the council, the people, and the youth training organisation).[211] The inclusion of the *ordo equester* in this ceremonial procession gave the order a corporate standing it does not seem to have enjoyed in other Greek cities. Although the *poleis* may have had *equites Romani* as residents, there is no evidence for *equites* existing as coherent organised groups, the way they did in some of the cities of the western provinces such as Narbo. Salutaris' own status and pride in being an equestrian evidently led him to include the *ordo equester* in this procession and to equate it with the *ephebeia*.[212] The result of this was that the status of the *ephebeia* was raised within Ephesian society, elevating it to the level of the *boule* and *demos* in order to mirror the Roman triumvirate of the senate, people and equestrian order.[213] Salutaris' concern for the youth of Ephesus is shown by his endowment of funds especially for the *ephebeia*, and their part in the procession itself.[214] Although ephebes certainly participated in other parades at Ephesus and elsewhere,[215] their role in Salutaris' procession is given greater impetus by their equation with the *equites*.[216] They represented the hope and future of Ephesus in the same way that the *iuventus* of the *ordo equester* did at Rome.[217] It was a perfect illustration of the integration of imperial and civic institutions in the Greek world, demonstrating how equestrian rank could function as a valued indication of social status that complemented traditional offices and honours.[218]

The epigraphic representation of *equites* in the imperial period was therefore much more diverse and varied than in the last generation of the Roman Republic. In the first century BC the conventional term used on inscriptions was *eques*, either written in full, or abbreviated to *eq(ues)*, but, as we saw in Chapter 3, this was very rare indeed, appearing on only a small group of monuments. The appearance of *equo publico* and *ornatus equo*

---

[210] Rogers 1991b: 83.   [211] Rogers 1991b: 84.   [212] *I. Eph.* 27, ll. 170–1.
[213] Kuhn 2010: 179–83.   [214] Rogers 1991b: 58–60; König 2005: 67.   [215] van Nijf 1997: 193.
[216] On associations between the *ephebeia* and the *collegia iuvenum*, see Pleket 1969, 2012.
[217] For the ceremonial roles of the *iuvenes*, see Chapter 8.
[218] See the remarks of Zuiderhoek 2008: 425.

publico (or variations thereof), together with the name of the emperor, in the first century AD, demonstrates that equestrian rank was developing in the popular consciousness as an imperial honour. The use of *eques Romanus* as a personal status designation in Latin epigraphy does not become common until the Severan period.[219] This chronological distribution reflects the fact that by the late second century AD it was acknowledged that admission to the equestrian order was an imperial benefaction, and that all *equites Romani* were *equites equo publico*. The employment of this imperial honour as a form of public self-representation throughout Italy and the provinces shows how the equestrian order bound wealthy non-senatorial elites from across the Mediterranean into the monarchical *res publica*. This did not mean that their local honours – municipal magistracies, priesthoods, presidencies of games and suchlike – lost prestige or significance. Rather, these local positions and membership of the *ordo equester* complemented each other as marks of personal status. This ensured the longevity of equestrian status as a recognised and valuable honour throughout the Roman world.

Pride and Prejudice

The achievement of equestrian rank was very much a matter of personal pride, not only for the *eques* himself, but also for his family. The hard work involved in rising through the social hierarchy is illustrated by a poetic epitaph of L. Aelius Timminus and his wife, who came from Madauros in Africa Proconsularis. The couple's children, who erected the tomb, described Timminus as a man 'enduring of labours, frugal, careful, reasonable, who obtained no small fortune for his household, and thus elevated his family from humble status to equestrian rank'.[220] Trajan rewarded a centurion who fought in his Dacian wars with decorations and also 'transferred him from the army to equestrian status' (*ex militia in equestrem | dignitatem translato*).[221] Some fathers ensured that it was publicly commemorated when their sons obtained equestrian rank. In AD 137 T. Flavius Scopellianus was honoured with a statue in his capacity as patron

---

[219] Duncan-Jones 2016: 95. It is of course attested as early as the Augustan period, as the inscription of Cornelius Gallus from Egypt shows (see Chapter 4).

[220] *CLE* 1868 = *ILAlg.* 2195: *patiens laborum | frugi vigilans sobrius | qui rem paravit haud | mediocrem familiae | domumque tenuem | ad equestrem promovit gradum.*

[221] *CIL* XI 5992. This appears to have been a relatively rare honour, with only two other examples attested (Dobson 1970: 102).

of Privernum in Campania. Taking pride of place in the list of his inscribed honours was the fact that he was 'father of two *equites Romani*' (*duo[r]|um equit(um) Romanor(um) patr[i]*).[222] The practice of recording relatives who obtained equestrian or senatorial rank was especially popular in the Greek world.[223] M. Aurelius Apellas Apellianus of Sebastopolis proclaimed that he was the uncle of *equites*, tribunes and procurators.[224] Sometimes *equites* looked back on what they had achieved not only with a sense of pride, but also a sense of humour. This seems to be the explanation for a graffito etched into the wall of an atrium at Pompeii: 'C. Hadius Ventrio, an *eques Romanus*, was born among the beets and cabbage' (*C. Hadius Ventrio | eques natus Romanus inter | beta(m) et brassica(m)*).[225] Was Ventrio the owner of the house, commemorating his new urban residence and social status with this wry bit of poetry? If the name is intended to be a pun, perhaps 'Mr Belly' was marking other effects of his wealth as well?[226]

Ventrio's witty graffito reminds us that membership of the *ordo equester*, despite the significant amount of the census qualification, was popularly regarded as an elite status that could be sought even by those from the humblest beginnings, a sort of Roman version of the 'American dream'.[227] It was thought to be much more achievable than senatorial status. At the most basic level, this is because there were many more *equites* than senators – at least 20,000–30,000 compared to 600 – and therefore they would have constituted a much more visible presence throughout the towns and cities of the Roman empire. The property qualification for equestrian status was also much lower – 400,000 sesterces compared to 1 million for senators. This was still an enormous amount of money to most Roman citizens, but for those men who were working their way up in the world it was perceived to be an achievable goal.[228] The figure of 400,000 sesterces therefore functioned much like the proverbial 'one million dollars' of the American dream.[229] The way to achieve this wealth in ancient Rome was very often through business enterprise, either by undertaking private contracting or serving the state as *publicani*, who, as we saw in the previous chapter, continued to play a vital role in the imperial period. Poetry offers us the best insights into popular perceptions of the *publicani*. For example, in Juvenal's *Third Satire* the character Umbricius (himself an *eques*), complains about the low-born *publicani* who acquire public contracts for the temples, rivers, harbours and other amenities, including

---

[222] *AE* 1974, 228.   [223] Demougin 1999: 596; Kuhn 2010: 115.   [224] Robert 1954 no. 171.
[225] *CIL* IV 4533 = *ILS* 1319.   [226] On the metre and possible joke here, see Milnor 2014: 120.
[227] For the changing meanings of the 'American dream', see Samuel 2012.
[228] Veyne 1961: 245–6; D. Armstrong 2012: 65–6.   [229] Samuel 2012: 1, 43–4.

public urinals, and then become fabulously wealthy.[230] Wheeling and dealing was a lucrative way to make one's fortune, which could then be transformed into social mobility and high status with the award of equestrian rank.

Tax-collectors and other *publicani* were not highly regarded in Roman imperial society. They notoriously appear as corrupt and grasping figures in the New Testament (where they are grouped together with sinners), and were known for exacting more money than was required of them.[231] Hostile and prejudicial statements abound in the literature of the imperial period, including an infamous list of abusive terms one could hurl at tax-farmers found in Iulius Pollux's *Onomasticon*. These include 'strangler' (ἄγχων), 'plunderer' (ληϊζόμενος) and 'inhuman' (ἀπάνθρωπος).[232] But complaints of Juvenal's Umbricius do not come from prejudice against the *publicani*. In fact, it is quite the opposite, as Armstrong has shown. Umbricius himself lacked the business sense to make it rich like the *publicani*, and thus remained in danger of losing his equestrian rank on account of his personal lack of resources.[233] This reveals the double-sided popular perception of *publicani* and men of commerce in the Roman world: they were subject to criticism and prejudice, but some – the real Umbricii – envied these men because they wanted to be them. *Publicani* and businessmen do not feature prominently in the epigraphic record, or, to put it another way, inscriptions do not usually record their commercial operations conducted privately or on behalf of the Roman state.[234] But the epigraphic texts that do mention business interests suggest that these commercially minded *equites* took special pride in their money-making abilities. For example, the funerary inscription of Aurelius Maximus, who was buried at Tragurium in Dalmatia, styles him 'a most distinguished businessman' (*negotiat[o]ri | cele[be]rrimo*).[235] One *publicanus*, T. Iulius Capito, the farmer of public taxes for the *portorium Illyrici et ripa Thraciae*, was honoured with a public statue, the *ornamenta* of a *IIvir* and *decurio* at Oescus in Moesia Inferior, and received further distinctions from communities in Pannonia Superior, Moesia Superior, and Dacia Superior.[236] This range of honours is testament to the real influence that Capito wielded across these provinces, demonstrating why an 'Umbricius' might want to

---

[230] Juv. *Sat.* 3.29–40.

[231] Matthew 9.10–11, 11.19; Mark 2.15–17; Luke 3.13. For an attempt to reconstruct Jesus' position on the *publicani* from the Bible, see Youtie 1967.

[232] Poll. *Onom.* 9.32 (ed. Bethe p. 155). van Nijf 2008: 281–5 discusses this and other literary opinions.

[233] D. Armstrong 2012: 72–5.   [234] Duncan-Jones 2016: 119.   [235] *CIL* III 14927 = *ILS* 7521.

[236] *CIL* III 753 = *ILS* 1465.

fill his shoes.[237] The inscription also portrays Capito as an agent of the *res publica*, which it shares in common with other epigraphic records of tax-collectors. These inscribed texts show that these men served the *res publica* as agents of the *princeps*, and thus gave their work a public legitimacy and status.[238]

The careers of equestrian *publicani* not only engendered resentment among *equites* like Umbricius who were wary of losing their status. As mentioned above, they could also be aspirational models, giving new men from humble backgrounds something to hope for, in the same way as the American self-made millionaire. Equestrian rank was evidently the aim of the freedman Trimalchio in Petronius' *Satyricon*, who could not dream of becoming a senator, but could certainly become an *eques* like many other freedmen through the acquisition of wealth and the right imperial contacts.[239] This ambition is perfectly articulated by the details in the epitaph Trimalchio composed for his tomb, which parodied the *cursus* inscriptions of *equites*, members of the curial classes and freedmen.[240] His equestrian aspirations also are shown by his assumption of the *agnomen* 'Maecenatianus', a name clearly designed to recall the most famous *eques*, Maecenas.[241] Stories of social climbing by former slaves abound in Roman literature. Juvenal's *First Satire* features a freedman who was born on the Euphrates, but came to own five shops which brought him an equestrian income of 400,000 sesterces – a testament to the power of money to increase social status.[242] Moreover, equestrian rank was eminently achievable for such men, since the requirement of free birth could be overcome by the grant of the *anulus aureus*, which conferred fictive *ingenuitas*.[243]

The advancement of freedmen through business activities was often sneered at, reflecting the traditional conception that birth was better than money, no matter how hard one had worked for it.[244] Greeks were particular targets of such attacks. Juvenal makes a sly remark about *equites* from the province of Asia, whose ankles reveal the brands of fetters, indicating that they were former slaves.[245] Martial likewise referred to a (hypothetical) '*eques* from Cappadocian slave scaffolds' (*Cappadocis*

---

[237] van Nijf 2008: 302 notes that this inscription may conceal an abusive tax-collector who needed to be appeased, or somehow who had 'turned a blind eye' to abuses and thus done men in these communities a favour.

[238] van Nijf 2008: 305.   [239] Veyne 1961: 245–6.

[240] Petr. *Sat.* 71; D'Arms 1981: 108–16; Bodel 1999: 42–3.

[241] D'Arms 1981: 112. For Maecenas' infamous influence and power, see Chapter 4.

[242] Juv. *Sat.* 1.104–6.

[243] Weaver 1972: 282–3; Demougin 1988: 651–2; Mouritsen 2011: 106–8.

[244] Mouritsen 2011: 112–13.   [245] Juv. *Sat.* 7.14–16.

eques catastis).[246] As we observed in Chapter 3, these popular attempts to police equestrian status are a testament to the strong social investment that individual *equites* had in their *ordo*, and their conception of the order as being composed of citizens who were both wealthy and socially respectable. Despite these prejudices, the ascent of freedmen into the municipal elite and the *ordo equester* through the support of patrons seems to have been a largely unexceptional phenomenon.[247] Indeed, it is probable that many *equites* were the descendants of freedmen.[248] Even the great Antonine praetorian prefects, M. Gavius Maximus and T. Furius Victorinus, can be posited to have risen from such humble beginnings.[249] Realisation of this fact is shown by a scene from Tacitus' *Annals*. During a debate set at Nero's court regarding whether the manumission of a slave should be cancelled, it was suggested that 'most of the *equites* and very many senators came from precisely such origin' (*plurimis equitum, plerisque senatoribus non aliunde originem trahi*).[250]

In addition to making money as a businessman, which we have discussed above, service at the imperial court was a key conduit for ex-slaves to advance into the *ordo equester*. For example, Ti. Iulius Aug. lib. was freed by the emperor Tiberius, and became the *a rationibus* early in Vespasian's reign.[251] It was Vespasian who 'led him forth from among the people to the equestrian section' (*in cuneos populo deduxit equestres*) in the theatre, according to Statius' poem for Iulius' son Claudius Etruscus.[252] A fabulously wealthy *eques* himself, Etruscus was the product of Iulius' marriage with a consul's sister.[253] This tradition of rewarding imperial freedmen with equestrian rank continued throughout the centuries: L. Aurelius Nicomedes, the freedman who raised the young Lucius Verus, was elevated to the *ordo equester* by Antoninus Pius.[254] The gratitude of men of this class towards the emperor for their advancement is revealed by a statue from Pola of Septimius Severus, erected by M. Aurelius Menophilus, the son of a freedman:

---

[246] Mart. *Ep.* 10.76.3. Some *equites* with Greek *cognomina* were definitely freedmen (Mouritsen 2011: 125–6).

[247] Garnsey 2010: 38–40; Mouritsen 2011: 261–78.

[248] See the data assembled in Eck 1999a. On the significant freedman population in Rome, see L. R. Taylor 1961, with the caveats of Weaver 1972: 83–90.

[249] Eck 1999a: 21.   [250] Tac. *Ann.* 13.27.   [251] Stat. *Silv.* 3.3.66–87; Weaver 1972: 284–91.

[252] Stat. *Silv.* 3.3.143. This is usually placed in Vespasian's censorship of AD 73/4 (Weaver 1972: 289; Evans 1978: 108).

[253] The baths of Claudius Etruscus were particularly legendary (Stat. *Silv.* 1.5; Mart. *Ep.* 6.42).

[254] *CIL* VI 1598 = *ILS* 1740.

To the Emperor Caesar Lucius Septimius Severus Pius Pertinax Augustus, *pontifex maximus*, holding tribunician power for the sixth time, acclaimed *imperator* for the eleventh time, consul for the second time, *pater patriae*. Marcus Aurelius Menophilus, provided with the *equus publicus* by his decision, *sacerdos Tusculanus*, aedile of Pola, (erected this) with his father Menophilus, freedman of our emperors, and former procurator, to the most indulgent emperor. The place was given by decree of the decurions.[255]

This monument epitomises some of the themes we have examined thus far in this chapter: the pride in acquiring equestrian rank, the ascent of freedmen into the decurial classes and the *ordo equester*, and, most importantly, the role of the emperor as the ultimate source of these benefactions.

The jealous reactions to rich freedmen or *publicani* are more than petty complaints – they reveal just how high the stakes were in the status game. For the benefits of equestrian rank extended far beyond the *eques Romanus* himself: it could increase the status of an entire family. In the Republic and early principate, equestrian rank could be maintained in the male line by retaining the necessary property qualification of 400,000 sesterces.[256] Even when the status became an exclusively imperial benefaction, it would seem perverse to suppose that the son of an *eques* would not himself be formally granted the rank in due course.[257] Holding equestrian rank at the municipal level became a conduit for entrance to the senatorial order in the next generation, a process which Stein has traced in some detail.[258] Given that the members of the senate famously failed to replicate themselves in subsequent generations, the *amplissimus ordo* was in constant need of renewal.[259] The members of the *ordo equester* were the obvious source of new blood, and over time the senate came to encompass the flower of the provincial aristocracy.[260] In the Greek east, *equites* with senatorial sons proudly recorded the social status of their progeny in honorific inscriptions. For example, when Aurelius Septimius Apollonius, high priest of

---

[255] *CIL* V 27: *Imp(eratori) Caes(ari) | L(ucio) Septimio Severo | Pio Pertinaci Aug(usto) | pont(ifici) max(imo) trib(unicia) p(otestate) VI | imp(eratori) XI co(n)s(uli) II p(atri) p(atriae) | M(arcus) Aurel(ius) Menophilus | ornatus iudicio eius | equo publ(ico) sacerdos | Tusculan(us) aedil(is) Polae | cum Menophilo patre | lib(erto) Augg(ustorum) nn(ostrorum) ex procurat(ore) | indulgentissimo | l(ocus) d(atus) d(ecreto) d(ecurionum).*

[256] Demougin 1988: 632–3.   [257] Demougin 1993: 235.   [258] Stein 1927: 213–25.

[259] This is the central conclusion of Hopkins and Burton 1983. See now Duncan-Jones 2016: 61–72 on provincials in senatorial offices.

[260] This was part of the function of the equestrian order as the second *ordo* of the *res publica*. It is a common feature of autocratic regimes that the highest functionaries are replenished from below (Mosca 1939: 402–4).

Asia, was honoured at Olympia, the inscription included the common expression that he was 'father of senators' (πατέρα συν|κλητικῶν).[261]

Equally, some families fell on hard times and lost even their equestrian rank because they failed to maintain the necessary property qualification. This seems to have happened with the father of the poet P. Papinius Statius.[262] Such cases of downward nobility are not unique, and explain the fears of the character Umbricius from Juvenal's *Third Satire*, whom we introduced above. Umbricius felt particularly exposed while sitting in the fourteen rows of the theatre because he no longer had the requisite property qualification due to his lack of business 'know-how'.[263] Juvenal's *Eleventh Satire* features a vignette about an *eques* who was unfortunate enough to actually lose his fortune: 'his ring disappears, and Pollio begs with his unadorned hand' (*exit | anulus, et digito mendicat Pollio nudo*).[264] These lines bring out the very public shame that came with losing equestrian rank, since everyone would be able to see from looking at Pollio's ringless fingers that he was no longer an *eques*. Juvenal brings to life the acute anxiety of *equites* at the bottom end of the spectrum who were constantly clinging to the census, and thus their rank, by their (quite literally) bare hands. One of Pseudo-Quintilian's *Minor Declamations* features a discussion of how young men from wealthy families who fell on hard times resorted to drastic measures to reclaim their fortune – including hiring themselves out as gladiators (as we will discuss in Chapter 9).[265] The loss of equestrian rank by particular families can be determined by reading between the lines of the inscriptional evidence. There are honorific and funerary inscriptions in which the sons and grandsons of *equites Romani* did not describe themselves as *equites*, suggesting that the rank had not been bestowed in subsequent generations, probably because the family had fallen on hard times and lost its fortune.[266] L. Sontius Pineius Iustianus, a member of the municipal elite in Beneventum, described himself as the 'descendant of an *eques Romanus*' (*eq(uitis) R(omani) adne(pos)*), perhaps in the hope of gaining some

---

[261] *SEG* 17, 200. For further examples, see Stein 1927: 295–6, who notes that this formulation was not common in the west.

[262] See *Silvae* 5.3.114–120, discussed by Coleman 1988: xv; B. Gibson 2006: 311–13. The loss of equestrian rank due to lack of funds also appears in Apul. *Apol.* 75.

[263] Juv. *Sat.* 3.152–9, as elucidated by D. Armstrong 2012: 68–70, 74–5.   [264] Juv. *Sat.* 11.42–3.

[265] Ps.-Quint. *Min. Decl.* 260.21–4.

[266] Stein 1927: 76–7. For example, *CIL* VI 3536, 3712, VIII 20706, X 342, XIII 1131. See also the case of L. Staius Rutilius Manilius, who referred to his own father as the son of an *eques Romanus*, suggesting that the rank had definitely not been reconfirmed in later generations (*CIL* IX 1655 = *ILS* 6496).

residual prestige from his ancestor's achievement, since was not himself a member of the *ordo equester*.[267]

Although equestrian rank was fundamentally a personal status bestowed by the emperor, there was a popular conception of equestrian families.[268] Velleius Paterculus, for instance, wrote that Octavian was 'born into an equestrian family' (*equestri genitus familia*) and referred to Maecenas as 'born from stock that was equestrian, but still distinguished' (*equestri sed splendido genere natus*).[269] The belief that both the male and female relatives of *equites* stood above mere Roman citizens was confirmed by legislation in the Julio-Claudian period. The senatorial decree of AD 19 preserved on the *Tabula Larinas* stated that those with equestrian fathers and grandfathers (as well as brothers or husbands, in the case of women), were forbidden to fight as gladiators.[270] In the same year women who were the daughters, granddaughters or wives of *equites* were prohibited from hiring out their bodies as prostitutes.[271] This was a way of protecting the members of the upper *ordines* and their families from social degradation.[272] But it also acknowledged that the dignity inherent in equestrian families continued through both male and female lines, even though women could not themselves be awarded equestrian rank.

This created a problem as to how one should refer to the daughter or wife of an *eques Romanus*.[273] Pliny the Elder, in his potted history of luxury objects, refers somewhat facetiously to the possibility of gold adornments creating 'an equestrian order of women' (*feminarum equestrem ordinem*) in a manner analogous to the *anulus aureus* worn by equestrian men.[274] His frivolous remarks aside, there was certainly no precision in terminology used to refer to female relatives of *equites*. Sometimes women of equestrian lineage specifically referred to themselves in inscriptions as the daughter of an *eques Romanus*, in order to emphasise their descent publicly.[275] From the second century AD a senatorial woman could call herself a *clarissima femina*, the female equivalent of the senatorial honorific *clarissimus vir*. The equestrian women who participated in the Saecular Games under Septimius Severus were simply called 'equestrian matrons'

---

[267] *CIL* IX 1540 = *ILS* 4186. The inscription dates to the third century AD (Torelli 2002: 100).

[268] Stein 1927: 75; Alföldy 1981: 200; Demougin 1988: 587–91. The term is rarer in inscriptions, appearing only in *AE* 1998, 279 and *CIL* VIII 2248, but see also *CIL* IX 3160 = *ILS* 6530 for reference to children with equestrian *dignitas*.

[269] Vell. Pat. 2.59.2, 2.88.2.   [270] *Tab. Lar.* ll. 7–11.

[271] Tac. *Ann.* 2.85; McGinn 2003: 216–19.   [272] This is discussed further in Chapter 9.

[273] See the remarks of Hemelrijk 1999: 10–13. See also Heil 2015: 57, who notes that there is no example of a *femina perfectissima* or *eminentissima*.

[274] Pliny the Elder, *NH* 33.40.   [275] For example, *CIL* III 1217, 14657, X 4790; *AE* 1909, 156.

(*matronae equestres*).[276] New, unofficial titles began to be used to distinguish equestrian women in the late second and third centuries AD, a move which can be interpreted as a popular response to the problem. The first titles to appear were those of *honesta matrona* and *honesta femina*, both indicating a 'respectable woman'. However, these appellations were not restricted to the female relatives of equestrians, but also described women who married members of the curial classes.[277] The title of *honesta femina* could be applied equally to Antonia Diodora, wife of a decurion in Heliopolis in Syria, and Cornelia Valentina Tucciana, who was married to an equestrian military officer, in Thamugadi in Numidia.[278] These titles were the female counterparts of *honestus* or *honestissimus vir* used by men from the municipal aristocracy.[279] Their Greek equivalents were ἀξιολογώτατος and ἀξιολογωτάτη, a title which meant 'most worthy'.[280] For members of the municipal aristocracy, both *equites* and non-*equites*, these honorifics functioned as a way of publicly proclaiming their essential respectability.[281] They delineated their membership of the privileged social strata of *honestiores* with all its attendant privileges, the most notable of which was freedom from baser punishment.[282]

In the third century AD some female equestrian relatives were distinguished with the new social distinction, 'the woman wearing a *stola*', which appears as *femina stolata* in Latin inscriptions, and ματρῶνα στολᾶτα in Greek. This was a title of honour; it did not imply that these women actually wore the *stola*, which by this time was no longer in fashion.[283] These *feminae stolatae* were very often landowners or relatives of equestrian procurators and officers.[284] It might initially be thought that this title was an unofficial one, but such a supposition is disproved by an inscription from Aphrodisias. This refers to a woman whose name is unfortunately lost, but who was the wife of Septimius Chares Aeneias. According to the inscribed text, she was 'honoured on account of the greatness of her family and the unsurpassed distinction of her life by the god Alexander with

---

[276] Raepsaet-Charlier 1999: 215–16.

[277] Pflaum 1970: 182–3; Ladjimi Sebai 1977: 164; Holtheide 1980: 128; Demougin 2015: 72–8.

[278] Diodora: *AE* 1939, 64. Tucciana: *CIL* VIII 17905.

[279] For examples, see *CIL* III 2694, VIII 759–60, 12260.

[280] Pflaum 1970: 184. For examples, see *I. Aph.* 12.522, 12.644.

[281] Cf. Rathbone 1991: 46, who suggests that ἀξιολογώτατος was awarded to *equites* who were not yet procurators.

[282] Garnsey 1970: 221–76; Pflaum 1970: 182.   [283] Holtheide 1980: 128.

[284] Holtheide 1980: 129–30; Rathbone 1991: 48. For the property and landholdings of equestrian women, see Álvarez Melero 2014.

a matron's *stola*.[285] This is unambiguous evidence that this Aphrodisian woman was actually granted an honorific *stola* by Severus Alexander as a mark of her public standing. It appears, therefore, that in an attempt to formally recognise the female members of equestrian families, the imperial government had created a new honour for women, with the grant of the *stola* perhaps intended to be the equivalent of the *equus publicus*. These titles certainly show that the acquisition of equestrian rank held significance for all members of the family, not just the *eques Romanus* himself.

Conclusion: Status and the Individual

One of Martial's *Epigrams* features a scene in the theatre starring a certain Didymus, a social climber who looks down on all the poor men in the audience, and instead 'goes on about theatres and rows and edicts and the *trabea* and the *Ides* and brooches and the census' (*theatra loqueris et gradus et edicta | trabeasque et Idus fibulasque censusque*).[286] This is a wonderful summation of most of the classic markers of equestrian status: the reserved seats in the theatre, marked off from the people at large; the uniform worn at the *transvectio equitum* on the Ides of July; and the property qualification of 400,000 sesterces. These symbols represented the fundamental popular conception of the *eques Romanus*; collectively they represented wealth, prestige, exclusivity and difference from the citizen masses. Perhaps this is why some residences in the insula Arriana Polliana at Pompeii were marketed as 'equestrian apartments' (*cenacula | equestria*) – not because they were restricted to *equites*, but because the very name was synonymous with luxury, in the same way one could advertise an 'executive studio' for lease in high-rise city apartment blocks today.[287] We might imagine the slaves, freedmen and ordinary citizens staring at such a sign and thinking that they could one day call such apartments home. For, as we have explored throughout this chapter, equestrian rank was conceived as a status that could be achieved through hard work, business sense and the right connections at court. Then a man could hope for recognition from the emperor and the official award of the rank as confirmation that he had finally made it.

It was this fact that represented the fundamental transformation of equestrian status in the imperial period. In the Republic any Roman citizen

---

[285] *I. Aph.* 1.187 (trans. C. Roueché): διὰ τὸ με|γαλεῖον τοῦ γένους | καὶ τὴν ἀνυπέρ|βλητον τοῦ βίου | σεμνότητα τει|μηθεῖσαν ὑπὸ θε|οῦ Ἀλεξάνδρου | ματρώνης [[στολῆ]]]. The *stola* itself is not depicted on any of the surviving female statues from Aphrodisias (Smith et al. 2006: 194).

[286] Mart. *Ep.* 5.41.4–5.   [287] *CIL* IV 138 = *ILS* 6035.

assessed by the censors with property of 400,000 sesterces would be entitled to call himself an *eques Romanus*. Admission into the eighteen centuries of *equites equo publico* was more tightly regulated, since only 1,800 places were available. But in the Augustan period these barriers began to break down, as the first *princeps* admitted more citizens to the equestrian centuries. Over the course of the first century AD equestrian rank came to be recognised as a benefaction from the emperor himself, a change consolidated by the permanent investment of the censorship in the imperial office from the reign of Domitian onwards. There was never any single piece of legislation that defined precisely the status of *eques Romanus*, but on the other hand, there did not need to be. There were other laws that regulated the right to sit in the fourteen rows in the theatre, the morality of *equites* and their relatives, and the privilege of wearing the gold ring, so that everyone understood who and what an equestrian was, and, by the end of the first century AD, that it was the emperor who had granted them this status. In the monarchical *res publica* membership of the *ordo equester* was not only a state honour – it was an imperial one.

The age of the emperors witnessed the diffusion of equestrian rank throughout the communities of the Roman empire. The status of *eques Romanus* was awarded to the provincial elites for the same reason that citizenship was extended by emperors – it was a valuable reward that increased their investment in the Roman state, its government, values and beliefs, and thus strengthened the connection between the imperial centre and the periphery. In a sense, the emperors domesticated the wealthy elites of the provinces by encouraging them to look to Rome for rewards and validation. For this reason, it might be thought – and indeed some Romans such as Pliny the Younger and Censorinus did think – that membership of the equestrian order was more prestigious than honours and offices acquired at the local level, such as municipal magistracies, priesthoods or presidencies of games and festivals. However, the honorific and funerary monuments of Roman *equites* from the regions of Italy, North Africa and the Greek east, to name just a few areas, show that equestrian rank was very often publicly portrayed as a status that complemented, rather than superseded or diminished, these local honours. Membership of the equestrian order was something to which a vast range of Roman citizens aspired, but they shared in its rewards and privileges on their own terms. This was perhaps the most important factor in ensuring that equestrian rank was an attractive honour in the monarchical *res publica*.

Introduction: Pliny's Less Successful Friend

In the early years of Trajan's reign Pliny the Younger wrote to the eminent senator L. Neratius Priscus, the consular governor of Germania Inferior, to recommend his equestrian friend, C. Licinius Marinus Voconius Romanus, for a position in the province.[1] Pliny and Romanus were roughly the same age, probably on the cusp of forty when this letter was written. Romanus came from Saguntum in Hispania Citerior, but had been educated at Rome with Pliny, and the two men maintained a close relationship over the years.[2] Pliny basked in imperial favour as he rose through the senatorial *cursus honorum* to the giddy heights of the consulship. Romanus' fortunes were rather less spectacular: he remained an *eques*, and instead of receiving the consular *fasces*, he held the post of *flamen*, or high priest, in his home province.[3] In AD 98 Pliny wrote to Trajan, requesting Romanus' elevation to the senatorial order, but the emperor declined to promote him into the *curia*. Instead, Romanus had to be content with the lesser honour of privileges given to fathers of three children, known as the *ius trium liberorum*.[4]

Pliny then turned to the senator Neratius Priscus, who was related by marriage to both Pliny himself and several of his closest friends, in search of a suitable post for Romanus.[5] Priscus was a senator of consular rank and governor of Germania Superior, which made him well placed to offer patronage. As Pliny himself put it, he could grant a position as a *beneficium*, or 'favour', since he had a large army under his command. Pliny certainly did not hold back when singing Romanus' praises:

---

[1] Pliny the Younger, *Ep.* 2.13 (his full name is found on *CIL* II.14.1 367). For the date of the letter, and the identity of the Priscus to whom it is addressed, see Whitton 2013: 193–5, whose discussion supersedes Sherwin-White 1966: 173–5.

[2] Gibson and Morello 2012: 149–54 note that Romanus was one of Pliny's favourite correspondents.

[3] Syme 1960: 365–6.   [4] Pliny the Younger, *Ep.* 10.4; Syme 1960: 365.

[5] Syme 1985: 339–40, 1991a: 508–9, 1991b; A. R. Birley 2003: 4, 8–9.

His father was a distinguished man of equestrian rank, and his stepfather even more so. More precisely, he was like a second father, earning this title out of his true devotion to Romanus. His mother was from a respectable family. Romanus was very recently the *flamen* of Hispania Citerior, and you know the fine judgement of that province, as well as its great dignity. When we studied together, I showed deep and close affection for him; he has been my comrade both in Rome and in the country; I have shared serious business and pleasurable times with him. For what is more faithful than to have him as a friend, or more pleasant than to have him as a companion? He is wonderfully charming in his conversation, his tone of voice, and his appearance. In addition, he has shown an outstanding character, which is precise, charming, quick-witted, and learned in the law-courts. And as for his letters, well, you would think that the Muses themselves spoke Latin![6]

Pliny conspicuously never names a specific position for which he considered Romanus suitable. It is generally assumed that he is referring to a military tribunate, or possibly a position on the governor's staff.[7] As a member of the *ordo equester*, Romanus was eligible to serve as one of five *tribuni angusticlavii* in a legion. Since Neratius Priscus had three legions under his command, he had fifteen such equestrian tribunates within his gift (provided, of course, that there was a vacancy for Romanus).[8] One of the striking aspects of this letter of recommendation, and others of the same genre, is that it does not focus on specific military or administrative achievements for a particular post, but instead emphasises knowledge of the candidate and their family, as well as their character, education, and personal qualities in general.[9] These were regarded as valuable for whatever position an *eques* held in the Roman imperial government, regardless of whether he was a junior officer, financial procurator, aide-de-camp or superintendent of mines. Over the course of the next two chapters we will explore the many different aspects of equestrian

---

[6] Pliny, *Ep.* 2.13.4–7: *pater ei in equestri gradu clarus, clarior vitricus, immo pater alius (nam huic quoque nomini pietate successit), mater e primis. ipse citerioris Hispaniae (scis quod iudicium provinciae illius, quanta sit gravitas) flamen proxime fuit. hunc ego, cum simul studeremus, arte familiariterque dilexi: ille meus in urbe, ille in secessu contubernalis; cum hoc seria, cum hoc iocos miscui. quid enim illo aut fidelius amico aut sodale iucundius? mira in sermone, mira etiam in ore ipso vultuque suavitas. ad hoc ingenium excelsum subtile dulce facile eruditum in causis agendis; epistulas quidem scribit, ut Musas ipsas Latine loqui credas.*

[7] E. Birley 1949: 12; A. R. Birley 2003: 3, 6–7 (tribunate); Syme 1960: 365 (staff). Pliny was inconsistent in naming the specific post for which he was recommending his friends (Whitton 2013: 193).

[8] Cf. Cotton 1981: 237, who suggests that Priscus would have filled all his tribunates at the start of his governorship.

[9] Fronto, *Ad Amicos* 1.1 (vdH[2] p. 17) = Davenport and Manley 2014: 104–5 (no. 28), gives a brief account of the origin of letters of commendation. See further Cotton 1985 on Cicero; Rees 2007 on developments in the high empire; and A. R. Birley 2003: 4–5, 8 on letters for military commands.

political life in the high empire highlighted in Pliny's recommendation of Voconius Romanus: the qualifications for military and civil office, the use of government posts as social currency, and the development of an equestrian career structure. In the present chapter we will examine the army officer posts open to equestrians, before going on to analyse the administrative, or 'procuratorial', career path in Chapter 7.

It is no surprise that an equestrian of Romanus' background was considered suitable for military service, despite having no apparent prior experience in the army. Martial *virtus* had long been an essential part of equestrian identity, as represented by the *transvectio equitum*, the parade of the *equites* through the streets of Rome dressed in their ceremonial uniform, and the ceremonial *parma* and *hastae*. In Cassius Dio's *Roman History* Maecenas counsels Octavian that senators and *equites* should both be trained in horse riding and military skills from a young age, so that they will be equipped to serve the emperor in the future.[10] Although Augustus did not introduce teachers of military arts as Dio's Maecenas recommended, he did place considerable emphasis on the physical fitness and *virtus* of Rome's aristocratic youth as the reservoir of future talent for the state.[11] If an equestrian such as Romanus had not previously held any army posts, it was simply assumed that he was naturally prepared to be an officer, and possessed the honourable character and aristocratic virtues necessary to succeed. Thus Pliny's remarks in his letter were designed to emphasise Romanus' loyalty: he is called *contubernalis* ('tent-companion' or 'comrade'), *amicus* ('friend'), and *sodalis* ('companion' or 'fellow-member') in quick succession.

Dio's Maecenas likewise portrays the proper training of the aristocratic elite as a way of ensuring their qualifications for all manner of posts, as well as maintaining loyalty to the empire and to the emperor personally.[12] For in the age of the emperors, the idea that senators should be prepared to serve the state *domi militiaeque* could equally be applied to *equites* as well.[13] This was the result of a fundamental change that occurred in the principate of Augustus when *equites*, who had previously served as army tribunes and prefects, were now also eligible, and indeed encouraged, to hold positions throughout the Roman government and administration.[14]

---

[10] Dio 52.26.1–2.   [11] Yavetz 1984: 15–20; Reinhold 1988: 198.

[12] Dio 52.26.2–8, with the important discussion of Saller 1980: 52, 55–6, 1982: 96–7, 102.

[13] B. Campbell 1984: 325–31 (senators); Demougin 1988: 284, 357 (the army and *equites*); Eck 2006b: 488–9 (expected of both senators and *equites*).

[14] We discussed these developments in Chapter 4. Alföldy 1981: 174–82 shows that there was no real distinction between the types of positions held by senators or *equites* in the empire.

Of course, for the vast majority of the tens of thousands of *equites* in the empire, equestrian status was a sufficient distinction in and of itself, as we saw in Chapter 5. But the evolution of the Roman army and administration over the course of the first three centuries AD gave equestrians the opportunity to embark on a *cursus*, or 'career', in the same manner as senators. It is worth remembering that these were not 'careers' in the modern sense, since they did not usually represent a lifetime of employment without a break. Instead, periods in office were interspersed with periods of rest, and a return to one's home in Italy or the provinces. There was likewise no dichotomy between 'amateur' and 'professional' within the Roman aristocracy.[15] Both *equites* and senators were qualified by their background, their personal character and their learning to serve the *res publica*.

The Inscribed *Cursus*

The integration of equestrians into the Roman imperial government is strikingly demonstrated by the fact that they adopted the practice of recording their military and administrative positions as a type of *cursus*, just like senators.[16] This type of evidence will play a significant role in the following two chapters. The '*cursus* format' consisted of lists of offices inscribed on the bases of honorific statues, funerary monuments, building inscriptions and a range of other permanent media. An inscribed base from Ostia, which would have originally supported a statue of the *procurator annonae* Q. Petronius Melior, illustrates how the *cursus* fitted into the overall monumental context (Figure 6.1).[17] The *cursus* format created the impression that the honorand had pursued a successful life in the service of Rome and its emperors.[18] This style of commemoration had been employed by Republican senators in a funerary context; the sarcophagus of L. Cornelius Scipio Barbatus is but one example of this.[19] However, from the age of Augustus the format began to be used to honour senators while

---

[15] Eck 2001: 21; Rankov 2007: 39; A. R. Birley 2000b: 97–8, 116–17 (on senators), 2003: 5 (on *equites*).

[16] On the inscribed *cursus* as a form of self-representation, see Alföldy 1982; Eck 1984, 1995, 2005, 2009b; Maurizi 2013; Bruun 2015; Davenport 2015a.

[17] *CIL* XIV 172 = *ILS* 1429. For other illustrations of the inscribed *cursus* in this book, see Figure 4.1 (equestrian military officer), Figure 5.2 (municipal aristocrat), Figure 5.3 (municipal aristocrat and military officer), Figure 6.3 (municipal aristocrat and military officer), Figure 7.1 (imperial administrator), Figure 10.3 (imperial administrator) and Figure 12.1 (imperial administrator).

[18] Hopkins and Burton 1983: 153; B. Campbell 1984: 327–9, 2007: 186.

[19] *CIL* I² 7 = *ILLRP* 309.

Figure 6.1: Inscribed statue base recording the career of the equestrian military officer and procurator Q. Petronius Melior, Ostia

they were still alive, perhaps inspired by the *elogia* of leading Romans established in the *forum Augustum*. As Eck has pointed out, the senators who initially adopted the *cursus* style of commemoration at this time were overwhelmingly new men, and the format was only later adopted more broadly throughout the senatorial order.[20] The habit of listing one's official posts publicly displayed one's service to the *res publica* and to the *princeps*,

---

[20] Eck 1984: 149–51; Flower 1996: 180–2; Maurizi 2013.

something which *novi homines* were understandably keen to emphasise, as they did not have illustrious ancestors as a source of prestige.[21] This new epigraphic habit was soon taken up by *equites*, reflecting the increased role in the Roman administration that they acquired under Augustus.

Their public careers in the service of the *res publica* had not been commemorated in this way under the Republic because they never had the opportunity to climb a *cursus* like members of the senatorial order (though the listing of posts was sometimes used by municipal magistrates and military officers in the late first century BC).[22] The *cursus* format soon spread widely among all groups who held official posts in the Roman state or local administration, especially if their occupation could be considered in any way 'public', including municipal magistrates, soldiers, slaves and freedmen.[23] The diffusion of the *cursus* format under the empire can be ascribed to a desire to emulate senatorial habits. This was either a way to demonstrate that they worked for the *res publica* or the emperor, or – if they held no official roles – that their occupations could be conceived in similar terms.[24] The enthusiasm for this type of commemoration represented one of the major reasons for the dramatic increase of public epigraphy between Republic and the empire.[25] It emphasised the profound social and cultural impact of the transformation of the Roman *res publica* into its monarchical form, and the primacy of the emperor in the lives of his people.

The inscribed *cursus honorum* was certainly a symbol of pride and distinction. Very often the individual being honoured played a crucial role in shaping the form and content of these inscriptions, as they wished to present their lives and achievements in the best possible light.[26] The genre of the inscribed *cursus* is heavily biased in favour of the successful: officers and administrators who had positions, honours or other marks of imperial favour to boast about.[27] At the same time, however, the *cursus* of the imperial age was an expression of the subservience or 'domestication' of elite Romans, which had quite different connotations from the *elogia* of the Scipios and other great men of the Republic. The Republican testimonials bore witness to their election to magistracies by the people and their military achievements as independent commanders. Under the

---

[21] Compare the study of epitaphs of decurions in Ostia and Pompeii by Mouritsen 2005, who discovered that this form of epigraphic commemoration outside the city was primarily restricted to new men rather than established members of the curial classes.
[22] Eck 2006b, 2009b: 88. For inscriptions of the first century BC, see Chapter 3.
[23] Eck 2009b: 88–90.   [24] Lendon 1997: 100–2, 246–7.   [25] Panciera 2006: 86–95.
[26] Specific examples are discussed by Eck 1995: 218–19, 2009b: 87.
[27] Hopkins and Burton 1983: 156; Saller 2001: 113–15; Thonemann 2011: 204–5.

empire, the *cursus* style of inscription was a testament to a life that was entirely subordinated to the *princeps*. This domestication can also be observed in the placement of statues which had the *cursus* carved on the base. Outside of the city of Rome these statutes were permitted in public places if authorised by the decurions, as they symbolised the connection between local communities, prominent individuals who were employed by the *res publica*, and the emperor. In the city of Rome, however, such commemoration had to occur in private contexts; public statues were only permitted if individuals had rendered exceptional service to the emperor.[28] The adoption of the *cursus* format by *equites* in army and government posts is therefore a testament to their service to the monarchical state in civilian and military roles like their senatorial counterparts. But at the same time, this also meant that they too had been domesticated by the emperor.

Unfortunately, no inscribed *cursus* of Voconius Romanus' official posts survives today. Thanks to the memorable title of an article by Syme, history will forever remember Romanus as one of Pliny's 'less successful friends' – or, less euphemistically, 'a complete failure'.[29] But this title, as wryly amusing as it is, raises important questions about what constituted success or failure for an *eques* in the imperial period. We do not know whether Romanus ever obtained a post from Neratius Priscus, though the evidence tends towards the negative.[30] He might have failed to become a senator or win a tribunate, but the post of *flamen* of Hispania Citerior was certainly a prestigious honour in his home province, confirming his standing in the upper echelons of municipal society.[31] Romanus' own intentions are lost to us today – he may well have preferred a life without high office, and it was only the urging of his friend Pliny that prompted him to seek imperial glories. Indeed, not all senators and *equites* were successful in the competition for office, while some even ostentatiously eschewed this option altogether, preferring to define their lives in other ways.[32] The vast majority of the thousands of *equites* who lived in the imperial period did not hold any military or administrative post, as we noted in Chapter 5 – perhaps as few as 600 *equites* out of 20,000–30,000 in each generation. For these equestrians, service to the *res publica* offered a new source of status and prestige, beyond wealth or municipal or provincial honours. Consequently, *equites* who did occupy such a position came to form an elite within the *ordo* at

---

[28] Alföldy 2001.   [29] Syme 1960: 367.   [30] Syme 1960: 366–7. Cf. Sherwin-White 1966: 180.
[31] For an example of a *flamen* who did enter the *militiae*, see C. Sempronius Fidus (*PME* S 219).
[32] See Talbert 1984: 23–7 on senatorial withdrawal, and Bodel 2015 on equestrians.

large; this elite gradually took on the characteristics of a 'service aristoc-racy', whose members pursued careers in a similar way to senators.[33]

The *Militiae Equestres*

The concept of a specifically equestrian military career path began to emerge in the early imperial period. Velleius Paterculus, whom we met in Chapter 4, uses the term *militia equestris* ('equestrian military service') to refer to his own career, though it probably did not enter common parlance until the middle of the first century AD.[34] This was probably the result of the reforms of the emperor Claudius, who attempted to impose order and structure on the junior officer posts of the Roman army. Although some of Claudius' reforms proved to be short-lived, his actions ensured that there would thereafter be a defined hierarchy to the *militiae equestres* (the plural is used to indicate all the posts).[35] Under Augustus and his immediate successors, both *equites* and senators had been appointed to command the auxiliaries, as prefects of cavalry and infantry units. Former chief centurions (*primipilares*), who were them-selves usually *equites*, were also appointed to these positions.[36] Only the military tribunes of each legion were strictly divided into the senatorial *tribuni laticlavii* and equestrian *angusticlavii*. There was no fixed relation-ship between these posts: although the command of auxiliary cavalry as *praefectus equitum* was generally reserved for more senior men with prior experience, there was no defined progression between the posts of *prae-fectus cohortis* and *tribunus militum*.

Claudius' attempts to bring order to this confusion are classified by the biographer Suetonius among his good administrative acts.[37] He tells us that the emperor imposed a fixed hierarchy, so that the prefect of a cohort became the most junior post, followed by the cavalry command (*praefectus equitum*), and the military tribunate as the most senior position.[38] Suetonius does not record precisely why Claudius did this, though most scholars attribute it, at least in part, to his fondness for tradition. In the Republic the *tribunus militum* had always been the most prestigious officer

[33] The eventual ramifications of this development in the third and fourth centuries AD will be explored in Chapters 11–12.

[34] Vell. Pat. 2.111.3; Demougin 1988: 280–1; Saddington 2003: 20.

[35] E. Birley 1949: 11; Devijver 1970: 73–6 (on which the following paragraph depends).

[36] Dobson 1974: 395–9, 1978: 6–14.   [37] See Hurley 2001: 18 on the structure of the *Life*.

[38] Suet. *Claud.* 25. For examples of officers whose career follow this hierarchy, see *CIL* V 4058, XIV 2960 = *ILS* 2681; *AE* 1966, 124.

command, especially since it was originally an elected magistracy.[39] Military tribunes were in charge of Roman citizens, rather than auxiliaries, which gave them an increased importance.[40] Some scholars have suggested that a military tribunate was a better preparation for a procuratorial career, given the administrative duties it entailed.[41] If this was Claudius' aim, it was not regarded as important, given that the emperor's new hierarchy was soon abandoned. From the reign of Nero onwards a new hierarchy emerged, with *praefectus cohortis* as the most junior position, followed by *tribunus militum* and then *praefectus alae* at the top. Obviously, it was thought that the commander of a cavalry unit needed to have the most military experience. This post's change in title from *praefectus equitum* to *praefectus alae* at this period was one of Claudius' reforms which did endure beyond his reign.[42] The most significant result of these changes was that there was now a coherent grading of officer commands, which were filled exclusively by *equites*, rather than senators.

The final steps in the formulation of the *militiae equestres* took place in the late first and early second centuries AD, when it became a hierarchy of four command grades, with each level consisting of one or two posts.[43] The system that existed from the early second century AD is set out in Table 6.1, following Devijver:[44]

Table 6.1 *The* militiae equestres *in the second century AD*

Grades	Posts available	Officer positions at each grade
militia prima	*c.* 300	(i) *praefectus cohortis quingenariae* ('prefect of a 500-strong infantry cohort')
		(ii) *tribunus cohortis voluntariorum/ingenuorum civium Romanorum* ('tribune of a cohort of volunteer/freeborn Roman citizens')
militia secunda	190	(i) *tribunus angusticlavius legionis* ('legionary tribune with a narrow stripe')
		(ii) *tribunus cohortis milliariae* ('tribune of a 1,000-strong infantry cohort')
militia tertia	90	*praefectus alae quingenariae* ('prefect of a 500-strong cavalry unit')
militia quarta	10	*praefectus alae milliariae* ('prefect of an 1,000-strong cavalry unit')[45]

[39] Syme 1969: 207; Devijver 1970: 78; Hurley 2001: 171. This has some support from Suet. *Claud.* 22.1.
[40] Demougin 1988: 295–6; Levick 1990: 86; C. Thomas 2004: 429.
[41] Devijver 1970: 77; C. Thomas 2004: 429–30.   [42] Devijver 1972: 185 n. 148.
[43] These terms were used by the Romans themselves, e.g. *CIL* VI 2131 = *ILS* 4929; *AE* 2003, 1803 = *CIIP* 1228; *AE* 1933, 208.
[44] Devijver 1989c: 59.
[45] On the *militia quarta*, see E. Birley 1949: 17, 1988: 350–6, who assembled a number of cases in which the *praefectus alae milliariae* was the fourth post. However, see now Duncan-Jones 2016: 12 n. 34, who demonstrates that the command of a thousand-strong *ala* was not always the fourth command. So there was still flexibility in the system.

The epigraphical and papyrological evidence shows that the terms *quattuor militiae* (indicating all four grades) and *tres militiae* (the three main grades) entered common parlance in the mid- to late second century AD; the latter was more common, since the fourth grade was only rarely held.[46] However, it is important to emphasise that even though the *militiae* were organised in a hierarchy, an *eques* did not have to proceed through all the posts in an unbroken sequence.[47] He could, if he wished, seek a commission as a *tribunus legionis* (the *militia secunda*), and then never serve in the army again.[48] Alternatively, he could hold two or more officer posts within the same grade of the *militiae*. Continued employment was contingent on securing a commission through a well-placed recommendation, such as that written by Pliny for Voconius Romanus. It is difficult to determine the precise length of a tour of duty in the *militiae equestres*, given the uncertainly of the evidence.[49] Only the earliest inscribed careers from the Julio-Claudian period tend to mention the years served by equestrian officers. The range which these cover is shown by the cases of T. Aufidius Spinter, who spent five years as a tribune, and Q. Atatinus Modestus, who served for sixteen years as tribune in Spain, then went on to be a cavalry commander and *praefectus fabrum*.[50] The evidence demonstrates that these officer posts were not mere sinecures, and their holders could be expected to be in post from three to four years, on average. It was a serious commitment.

Well over two thousand equestrian officers are known to us today. This is a small fraction of the total number who originally served, but it is sufficient to be able to draw some conclusions about their social and geographical origins. They were not usually the scions of aristocratic households, but were mainly *equites* of municipal background from the curial classes of the towns and cities of the Roman empire.[51] As Eric Birley demonstrated in a classic article, our known officers can be divided into three main groups: (i) young men in their late teens or early twenties, who were comparable in age to the senatorial *tribuni laticlavii*; (ii) *equites* in their

---

[46] Devijver 1989c: 61–9 collects the evidence for these terms in both Latin and Greek.

[47] See especially E. Birley 1949. His arguments have been followed by subsequent scholars: Syme 1969: 208; Devijver 1989c: 57–9; A. R. Birley 2003: 2.

[48] Saller 1982: 87–90 has a useful compilation of the careers of imperial procurators, whose *militiae* ranged from no posts to five.

[49] E. Birley 1949: 9–12; Demougin 1988: 319–24.

[50] Spinter: *CIL* III 399. Modestus: *CIL* IX 3610 = *ILS* 2707.

[51] Ijsewijn 1983/4 documents this in full.

thirties; (iii) *equites* in their forties or beyond. Of these three groups, Birley found that the vast majority came from the second group: after completing their municipal magistracies, they held one or two equestrian officer posts, and then returned to their home communities.[52] The employment of these equestrian *domi nobiles* in the officer ranks represented the fulfilment of Augustus' intention to integrate members of the *ordo equester* into the Roman army and administration alongside senators.[53] As equestrian rank spread throughout the provinces in the imperial period, so the proportion of officers from outside Italy increased accordingly. In the first century AD 65 per cent of attested officers came from Italy, a proportion which reduced to 38 per cent in the second century and 21 per cent in the third.[54] Closer inspection of the data assembled by Devijver enables us to chart the contribution of individual provinces or regions, most notably the dramatic increase of officers from Africa in the second century AD.[55] There are some signs that equestrian officers who came from the eastern provinces preferred to take up posts in those regions.[56] The attractions of equestrian military service – which we will discuss further below – ensured that the system sustained itself with a ready supply of municipal candidates until the late third century AD, when changes in the Roman army and administration brought about the end of the *militiae* as a coherent institution.[57]

There were other options for equestrians to serve in the army beyond the *militiae equestres*. An *eques* could choose to seek a commission as a centurion *ex equite Romano* ('from equestrian rank'), which carried with it a commitment to continuous military service, rather than the more uncertain employment of the *militiae*.[58] Centurions could advance to the rank of *primus pilus* and then, on discharge from the army, earn a 600,000 sesterces bonus, which became standard from the reign of Caligula onwards.[59] It is thus generally assumed that all *primipilares* possessed equestrian status, though it would still have to be formally awarded by the emperor.[60] The pride in achieving these imperial honours is demonstrated by the career of the *primipilaris* L. Gavius Fronto, who

[52] E. Birley 1949: 9–11. His conclusion is widely accepted by scholars who have studied the material in depth, such as Ijsewijn 1983/4: 44; Devijver 1989b: 108–9.

[53] For Augustus' encouragement of *honesti* to serve as officers, see Chapter 4.

[54] Devijver 1989d: 122; Ijsewijn 1983/4: 49.   [55] Devijver 1989d: 112–21.

[56] See Devijver 1989c.   [57] This will be discussed in Chapter 11 and Davenport forthcoming.

[58] On this pathway, see Dobson 1972.   [59] Suet. *Cal.* 44.   [60] Dobson 2000: 142–3.

came from Attaleia in Pamphylia. He was 'honoured with the public horse by the emperor' (ἵππῳ δημοσί|ῳ τετειμημένον ὑπὸ τοῦ Σε|βαστοῦ) and acclaimed as 'the first and only man from his home town' (πρῶτον καὶ μόνον ἐκ | τῆς πατρίδος) to become a *primipilaris* and *praefectus castrorum*.[61] One of the strange features of the Roman army hierarchy was that *primipilares* such as Gavius Fronto did not advance into the *militiae equestres*. Instead, there was a completely separate promotion path for them. This led to the post of legionary *praefectus castrorum*, and then to the 'Rome tribunates' in the *vigiles*, urban cohorts, the praetorian guard, and later, from the time of Trajan, the *equites singulares* (the emperor's horse guard).[62] They could then embark on procuratorial careers in the imperial administration, usually starting at a slightly higher grade than officers in the *militiae*.[63] This distinction between the *primipilaris* career and the *militiae equestres* emerged as the result of Claudius' reforms, and ensured that there was no clear path to officer ranks for ordinary soldiers until the dramatic changes of the mid-third century AD.

Patronage and Promotion

One of the primary attractions of a post in the *militiae equestres* was that an officer commission was officially considered a *beneficium* from the emperor himself (even if he only rubber-stamped a decision made by his administration and provincial governors).[64] It constituted a new form of honour and status distinct from those on offer at the local and provincial level. For example, Ti. Claudius Plotinus boasted that he was 'assigned to the *militiae equestres* by the most sacred emperor Antoninus Caesar' (ἱππικαῖς στρατείαις κε[κοσ]|μημένον ὑπὸ τοῦ θειοτάτο[υ]| Αὐτοκράτορος Καίσαρος Ἀν|τωνείνου).[65] The commission was therefore more than simply a position, but was a tangible sign of imperial favour, which could bring glory to an equestrian family. This was what prompted P. Aelius Blandus, a very proud father from the Italian town of Praeneste, to erect a public statue of his son, P. Aelius Tiro, with the permission of the local council. The inscription on the base read:

---

[61] *SEG* 17, 584; Dobson 1978: 232–3.   [62] Dobson 1974: 399–403, 1978: 68–87.

[63] Dobson and Breeze 1969: 110–11. For *primipilares* as procurators, see Dobson 1978: 92–114.

[64] Millar 1977: 284–6; Lendon 1997: 185. For the continuity of this idea into the late empire, see Eumenius' speech *For the Restoration of the Schools* (*Pan. Lat.* 9(4).5.4).

[65] *I. Perge* 293 = *AE* 2004, 1484. For the expression *ornatus tribus militiis* ('distinguished with the *tres militiae*') used in the Severan period, see Solin 2011: 472–3.

To Publius Aelius Tiro, son of Publius, of the voting tribe Palatina, priest of the Alban citadel, whom Imperator Caesar [[Commodus]] Antoninus Augustus Pius [[Felix]] Germanicus Sarmaticus Britannicus considered worthy of distinguishing with the first grade in the *militia*, as prefect of the 500-strong cavalry unit of Braucones, at the age of fourteen years. His father, Blandus, out of love for his community, reimbursed the town the entire sum and expense (for erecting this). (Authorised) by decree of the decurions.[66]

Although some have regarded young Tiro's appointment as merely honorific, this seems unlikely in view of the precise details of his command which the inscription provided. Nor was such a youthful officer unprecedented, though it was unusual.[67] The favour of Commodus – an emperor known for his fickleness – was thought worthy of commemoration both by the town council of Praeneste, which authorised the monument, and his father Blandus, who took it upon himself to pay for the statue's construction. The record of direct appointment or intervention by specific emperors is sometimes found in other inscribed monuments.[68]

The office of the *ab epistulis* played a crucial role in the administration of these commissions, judging from a celebrated passage in Statius' *Silvae* 5.1.[69] This poem is addressed to T. Flavius Aug. lib. Abascantus, the freedman *ab epistulis* of Domitian, as consolation for the death of his wife. Statius describes some of Abascantus' duties pertaining to military commissions:

Moreover, if our lord were to distribute his swords of loyalty, (it would be his duty) to reveal who should have the power to control a century, an *eques* who is sent among the troops; who should issue orders to a cohort; who should be suitable to receive the greater rank of a distinguished tribune; and who be should more worthy of giving the watchword to the cavalry squadron.[70]

In this passage Statius refers to four military posts open to *equites*: the centurion, commissioned directly from equestrian rank (*ex equite*

---

[66] *CIL* XIV 2947 = *ILS* 2749: *P(ublio) Ael(io) P(ubli) f(ilio) Pal(atina tribu) | Tironi | salio arcis | Albanae quem | Imp(erator) Caes(ar) [[Commo]]|[[dus]] Antoninus | Aug(ustus) Pius [[Felix]] | Germ(anicus) Sarm(aticus) Brit{t}(annicus) | agentem aetatis | annum XIIII | militia prima | praefecturae | equit(um) Brauco|num D exornare | dignatus est | dec(reto) dec(urionum) | Blandus pater | pro amore civi|tatis summam et | sumptum omnem | rei p(ublicae) remisit.*

[67] E. Birley 1949: 9, 1986: 206. Cf. Laes and Strubbe 2014: 168 n. 18, who argue that it was honorific.

[68] *CIL* III 335, XI 6955; *AE* 1992, 577 (Claudius); *CIL* XI 5632 = *ILS* 2735 (Hadrian).

[69] See A. R. Birley 1992: 41–54 for detailed argumentation on this point.

[70] Stat. *Silv.* 5.1. 94–8: *praeterea, fidos dominus si dividat enses, | pandere quis centum valeat frenare, maniplos | inter missus eques, quis praecepisse cohorti, | quem deceat clari praestantior ordo tribuni, | quisnam frenigerae signum dare dignior alae.*

Romano), followed by three commands in the *militiae equestres*, the prefect of a cohort, military tribune, and prefect of a cavalry *ala*.[71] There has been considerable debate regarding the verb 'to reveal' (*pandere*), and precisely to whom the *ab epistulis* was revealing the appointments: to the emperor himself, or the commanding officers in the provinces?[72] Gibson has rightly pointed out that the subjunctives in the passage ('who should. . . ') imply some sort of evaluation or recommendation of candidates on the part of the *ab epistulis*.[73] The holders of this office certainly had enough authority to make appointments on their own initiative, though they sometimes came unstuck later if corruption was discovered. Vespasian, for instance, was said to have obtained command of the *legio II Augusta* thanks to Narcissus, Claudius' *ab epistulis*.[74] Similar intervention can be seen in the case of Caracalla's *ab epistulis* Marcius Claudius Agrippa, who was famously 'kicked upstairs' into the senate for appointing unqualified youths to positions in the *militiae equestres*.[75] These examples show the importance of patronage in securing a command. Even if he did not personally intervene in all cases, the *ab epistulis* was certainly responsible for issuing the commissions to equestrian officers, as these were a key item of imperial correspondence.[76]

Therefore, we propose that the *ab epistulis* played a vital intermediary role in the issuing of equestrian appointments, but one which could vary depending on how and why recommendations were made. Senatorial (and equestrian) governors could choose equestrian officers from their own network of friends or family, or appoint suitable candidates from within the province.[77] They also depended on their peers to recommend suitable candidates, a phenomenon well attested by the letters of recommendation that survive in the collections of Pliny the Younger and Cornelius Fronto. We then have to presume that provincial governors contacted the imperial administration with the names of their candidates, and the *ab epistulis* issued the formal letters of appointment.[78] It is equally possible that *equites* could use their contacts at court to approach the emperor directly: this may

[71] Millar 1977: 286. Cf. B. Gibson 2006: 9, who translates *clari . . . tribuni* as if it refers to the senatorial *tribunus laticlavius*.

[72] *OLD* s.v. *pando, pandere* 6. For the first interpretation of this passage, see E. Birley 1949: 13; Millar 1966: 15, 1977: 286; A. R. Birley 1992: 43–6; B. Gibson 2006: 112–13. For the second, see Cotton 1981: 230–1; Saller 1982: 105–6.

[73] B. Gibson 2006: 112.   [74] Suet. *Vesp.* 4.

[75] Dio 78.13.4, using the appropriate Greek terminology for the *militiae*. See Devijver 1989c: 67–8.

[76] See Millar 1977: 213–28, 313–41 on imperial correspondence, especially with senatorial and equestrian officials.

[77] A. R. Birley 2003: 5. See *AE* 2003, 1803 = *CIIP* 1228 for an example of this.

[78] Austin and Rankov 1995: 138; Devijver 1999: 246–8.

have been how the young Aelius Tiro ended up with his post bestowed by the emperor Commodus.[79] In the third century AD Aemilius Pardalas was able to obtain a commission in the *militia secunda* thanks to the intervention of the chief Vestal Virgin, Campia Severina.[80] The pantomime actor Paris allegedly had the ability to recommend equestrian officers to the emperor Domitian.[81] The precise role of the *ab epistulis* and his evaluation of candidates therefore varied depending on the different ways in which suitable candidates became known to the imperial administration.

The surviving letters of recommendation, like the one written by Pliny the Younger for Voconius Romanus, conform to the expectations of the genre, in that they emphasise the personal character, integrity and loyalty of candidates for equestrian officer posts. Although Pliny never named a specific post for which he considered Romanus suitable, he was more direct in other cases, such as his letter to Q. Pompeius Falco, governor of Judaea in the early second century AD:[82]

You will be less surprised as to why I have petitioned you so relentlessly to award a tribunate to my friend when you know who he is and what sort of man he is. But now that you have promised the post, I am able to reveal his name and describe him to you. He is Cornelius Minicianus – the pride of my home region in both his public distinction and his character. He is a man of excellent family and extremely well-off, but he loves literary study just like men of moderate means. He is also a most proper judge, a very bold advocate, and a truly faithful friend.[83]

The letter reveals that Pliny had been searching for a suitable tribunate for Cornelius Minicianus for some time. Other chronological indications from the letters suggest that Minicianus was probably now in his thirties, making him a typical candidate for the *militiae*.[84] As in the case of Voconius Romanus, no specific military qualities are specified, and instead Minicianus is praised for his fondness for 'literary study' (*studia*). This is echoed by a fragmentary letter of recommendation discovered at Vindolanda, which refers to a candidate's 'love of liberal pursuits'

---

[79] Note also Pliny's letters of recommendation for freedmen and *equites* written directly to Trajan (*Ep.* 10.85, 86A, 86B, 87).

[80] *CIL* VI 2131 = *ILS* 4929.   [81] Juv. *Sat.* 7.88–97.

[82] For Falco, see Sherwin-White 1966: 138–9, 429.

[83] Pliny, *Ep.* 7.22.1–2: *minus miraberis me tam instanter petisse, ut in amicum meum conferres tribunatum, cum scieris, quis ille qualisque. possum autem iam tibi et nomen indicare et describere ipsum, postquam polliceris. est Cornelius Minicianus, ornamentum regionis meae seu dignitate seu moribus. natus splendide abundat facultatibus, amat studia ut solent pauperes. idem rectissimus iudex, fortissimus advocatus, amicus fidelissimus.*

[84] As Sherwin-White 1966: 439 memorably noted, 'he was no chicken when he entered the equestrian service'.

(*liberalium studiorum amore*).[85] These attributes were of course somewhat formulaic, owing much to the education and socialisation of all well-born Roman aristocrats, which emphasised personal character and morals.[86] As Lendon memorably remarked, 'the attributes wanted in a military tribune and in a bridegroom were identical'.[87] But these qualities were not empty and devoid of meaning, as they represented the collective values of the Roman elite.[88]

Pliny's endorsements of Voconius Romanus, Cornelius Minicianus, and his other protégés are hardly out of place when we consider the actual duties of these equestrian officers.[89] The archive of the tribune Postumius Aurelianus from Dura Europos in Syria reveals that he corresponded with officials and civilians in Greek and Latin: a tribune without facility in both these languages would struggle in Syria, or in any other of the eastern provinces.[90] Moreover, the emphasis on judicial and legal capabilities, as noted by Pliny in the case of Minicianus, corresponded with the actual duties of equestrian officers who were required to judge military cases. Some junior officers even exercised jurisdiction in civilian affairs, particularly in the third century AD and later.[91] The decisions of M. Sulpicius Felix, prefect of the *ala II Syrorum civium Romanorum*, earned him the praise of the decurions of Sala in Mauretania Tingitana, who described him as 'an arbitrator who is not too lenient, but fair without exhibiting harshness' (*disceptatorem nec dissolute benignum et iustum sine acerbitate praebendo*).[92]

Pliny's emphasis on education and judicial competence, not to mention loyalty and trustworthiness, is echoed by Aemilius Macer's account of the duties of tribunes in his treatise *De Re Militari* (On Military Affairs), written in the third century AD. The relevant passage is worth quoting in full:

The duty of tribunes, or those men who are in charge of the army, is to confine the soldiers in camp, to lead them out for practice exercises, to take charge of the gate keys, to do the rounds of the watch when required, to oversee the distribution of grain to other soldiers, to test the grain, to prevent embezzlement by the measurers, to punish offences in accordance with the measure of their personal authority, to

---

[85] *Tab. Vind.* III.660, with the comments of Bowman and Thomas 2003, *ad loc.*
[86] Rees 2007: 163–4.   [87] Lendon 1997: 188.
[88] On the socialisation of the elite governing classes in history, see Mosca 1939: 61.
[89] See the thorough study of Devijver 1968, upon which the following paragraphs depend.
[90] *P. Dura.* 66 = Fink 1971 no. 89. See Adams 2003: 599–608 on the languages used by the Roman army in Egypt.
[91] R. W. Davies 1989: 56–7; Pollard 2000: 93–5.   [92] *AE* 1931, 36.

attend the headquarters on a regular basis, to hear complaints of their fellow soldiers, and to examine the invalids.[93]

There is abundant evidence in papyrological and epigraphical sources for these duties being carried out by equestrian officers, so that they can be shown to be fairly consistent throughout the breadth the empire. At Vindolanda in Britain the prefect Flavius Cerialis dealt with petitions for leave, deserters, and requisitions for equipment and clothes.[94] Over in Egypt, Celsianus, prefect of the *cohors III Ituraeorum*, had to manage the enrolment of new recruits in his cohort.[95] The troops likewise had to be well fed and supplied: at Dura Europos, a certain Iustillus, tribune of the *cohors XX Palmyrenorum*, was involved in organising the provision of barley to soldiers, which required him to liaise with an imperial freedman.[96] Supplying the troops assumed prime importance in wartime, and the equestrian officers L. Aburnius Tuscianus and M. Valerius Maximianus played key roles in ensuring provision of the *annona* during Trajan's Parthian War and the Marcomannic Wars of Marcus Aurelius.[97] Numerous further examples could be added.[98] One would expect officers to be literate, loyal and hard-working in order to undertake all these different tasks. In this case, who would decline to appoint Cornelius Minicianus to a tribunate?

As it turned out, Q. Pompeius Falco, *legatus Augusti pro praetore* of the province of Judaea, would. He may well have had no vacant tribunates available, or was perhaps insufficiently impressed by Minicianus' qualities. Falco did offer him a position in his province, but at the lowest level of the *militiae equestres*, as *praefectus* of the *cohors I Damascenorum*.[99] The inscribed account of Minicianus' career reveals that he was later appointed to a tribunate in the *legio III Augusta* in Numidia, followed by a stint in the now largely honorific office of *praefectus fabrum*, the staff officer to a senatorial governor.[100] After what must have amounted to

---

[93] *Dig.* 49.16.12.2: *officium tribunorum est vel eorum, qui exercitui praesunt, milites in castris continere, ad exercitationem producere, claves portarum suscipere, vigilias interdum circumire, frumentationibus commilitonum interesse, frumentum probare, mensorum fraudem coercere, delicta secundum suae auctoritatis modum castigare, principiis frequenter interesse, querellas commilitonum audire, valetudinarios inspicere.*

[94] *Tab. Vind.* II.168–9, 250 (leave), 226 (deserters), 233 (asking for hunting-nets), 255 (being asked for clothes).

[95] *P. Oxy.* 7.1022 = Fink 1971 no. 87.   [96] *P. Dura.* 64 = Fink 1971 no. 91.

[97] Tuscianus: *AE* 1911, 161 = *ILS* 9471. Maximianus: *AE* 1956, 124.

[98] Devijver 1968; R. W. Davies 1989: 33–68.

[99] *CIL* V 5126 = *ILS* 2722; Sherwin-White 1966: 439.

[100] See Dobson 1966: 75–8 on the operations of this post in the high empire.

around a decade – not necessarily continuous – in military posts, he rounded out his days as a priest in Bergomum and Mediolanum. Minicianus was, like Voconius Romanus, a 'less successful friend' in Syme's eyes – but the fact that he almost failed to achieve a command at all highlights the difficulty in gaining a post in the *militiae*, even with a patron as effusive as Pliny.[101] In the reign of Trajan there were thirty legions in existence, so the army required 150 equestrian *tribuni angusticlavii*. This may seem like a large number until one considers that only a certain number of posts were vacant at any one time. Even if we suppose that out of more than 20,000 *equites* resident in the Roman empire in any generation, only a very small minority were of the age and inclination to seek a post in the *militiae equestres*, competition must still have been very fierce.[102] That is why Cornelius Minicianus, despite his qualifications, had to be initially content with the prefecture of a cohort. Disappointment is also apparent in the case of the Gallic noble Ti. Sennius Sollemnis.[103] His patron, Ti. Claudius Paulinus, governor of Britannia Inferior in AD 220, promised Sollemnis a six-months' tribunate as soon as one became available, and in recompense, undertook to send him his salary in advance.[104] However, the tribunate never materialised, and Sollemnis had to be content to serve as his patron's judicial assessor in Britain. Judging from a passage in Artemidorus' *Oneirocritica*, an officer's commission was something that many *equites* could literally only dream of.[105]

The same principles of patronage and promotion can generally be applied to *equites* seeking a direct commission as centurion (*ex equite Romano*). This was an eminently respectable pathway: according to Dio's Maecenas, centurions were worthy of advancement to the senate, while soldiers from lesser ranks were distinctly unwelcome.[106] Military competence was certainly a valid consideration in the appointment process for the centurionate. When Vespasian discovered that a young centurion of good birth turned out to be completely inept at the art of warfare, he had him cashiered honourably.[107] However, patronage and connections were still necessary, as the centurionate was granted by the emperor through the office of *ab epistulis*, as Statius' description of the official's duties makes

---

[101] Note Syme 1960: 364 on Minicianus, whom he characterises as someone who was at least not 'a complete failure'.

[102] See the discussion of the *militiae* and procuratorial posts in Devijver 1999: 244, who comes to the same essential conclusion.

[103] His career is recorded on the famous Marbre de Thorigny (*CIL* XIII 3162); Pflaum 1948; Saller 1982: 132; Benoist 2006.

[104] *CIL* XIII 3162, left face, ll. 13–15.   [105] Artem. *On.* 4.28.   [106] Dio 52.25.7.

[107] Front. *Strat.* 4.6.4.

clear.[108] In addition to recommending suitable individuals for the *militiae*, Pliny obtained a centurionate for Metilius Crispus, an *eques* from his home town of Comum, and even provided him with 40,000 sesterces for his equipment.[109] The centurionate was certainly not a less competitive path than the *militiae*, as we see from the case of the future emperor P. Helvius Pertinax, who originally tried to become a centurion with the support of his father's patron L. Lollianus Avitus. When this failed to eventuate, he had to find a post in the *militiae equestres* instead.[110] Suetonius tells the story of a certain Marcus Probus, who, after many fruitless years of searching, gave up his hope of becoming a centurion and turned to teaching instead.[111]

The difficulty was that an *eques* seeking a direct commission as a centurion had to compete with many other older men, who had worked their way up from the ranks and sought promotion after fifteen to twenty years.[112] However, once an *eques* found a post as centurion, the prospects for continued employment were much more secure than in the *militiae* (providing, of course, that one was not killed in battle, which was something of an occupational hazard).[113] For example, Sex. Pilonius Modestus became a centurion *ex equite Romano* at the age of eighteen, and served as a centurion for nineteen continuous years before dying at thirty-seven.[114] Sometimes equestrian officers even transferred from the *militiae* to a centurionate, as in the case of T. Pontius Sabinus, who, after being decorated as a tribune of the *legio VI Ferrata* in Trajan's Parthian campaign, became centurion of the *legio XIII Gemina*.[115] As we have already noted, one of the strange features of the Roman military hierarchy was that there was no conventional path from the ranks, or even from the centurionate, to the officer posts of the *militiae equestres*, which were only secured by direct appointment from outside the army.[116] This was because the army reforms of the first century AD had reserved them as an imperial benefaction bestowed on *equites*, allowing the emperor to reward and honour the wealthiest elements of the provincial citizenry in the *res publica*.

If an *eques*, having obtained his first post, wished to advance further in the *militiae* he would have to secure support for a second or third

[108] Stat. *Silv.* 5.1. 95–6.
[109] Pliny the Younger, *Ep.* 6.25.3. As it happened, the unfortunate fellow disappeared as he was setting out for his post and was never seen again.
[110] *HA Pert.* 1.5–6; Pflaum 1960: 451–4 (no. 179); Devijver 1988: 208–9.   [111] Suet. *Gram.* 24.
[112] Dobson 1970: 101, 1972: 195.   [113] Dobson 1972: 195, 202–4.
[114] *CIL* II 1480 = *ILS* 2654.   [115] *CIL* X 5829 = *ILS* 2726; Dobson 1972: 196.
[116] Dobson 1972: 195–6. See Chapter 11 for discussion of how this changed in the third century AD.

appointment. This patronage became increasingly important since the number of posts decreased at each level. Only 4 per cent of all officers could hope to make it to the *militia quarta* – a strikingly small number.[117] A recommendation from the provincial governor was crucial, and there is evidence of grateful officers erecting statues of their commanding officers to thank them for their patronal support.[118] These monuments formed part of the ideology of reciprocal benefaction that dictated Roman social relations – the patron secured the military command, and received a statue in return as symbol of his power and beneficent largesse.[119] In the early third century AD the Spanish *eques* M. Vibius Maternus commissioned a statue of his patron, L. Fabius Cilo, the urban prefect of Septimius Severus and Caracalla. The statue stood in Cilo's house on the Aventine hill in Rome, with the following text inscribed on the base:

To Lucius Fabius Septiminus Cilo, son of Marcus, of the Galeria tribe, urban prefect, *clarissimus vir*, twice consul. Marcus Vibius Maternus, a citizen of Iluro, *a militiis*, his candidate (dedicated this).[120]

The inscription shows that Maternus owed his career in the *militiae equestres* to the personal intervention of Cilo.[121] Cilo and Maternus both came from Iluro in the province of Baetica, a connection which helped to secure Maternus' advancement.

These patronal bonds can be traced across the Mediterranean. M. Sempronius Albanus, chief priest and *agonothetes* of Attaleia in Pamphylia, served as prefect of the *ala Augusta Germaniciana*. He cultivated a relationship with the illustrious Sex. Quinctilius Valerius Maximus, whom he styled his friend on the base of a statue which he erected in the senator's honour in Attaleia.[122] The mechanics of these patronal relationships remain obscure, but intelligent conjecture suggests several

---

[117] Devijver 1999: 241.

[118] E. Birley 1949: 13; Devijver 1999: 259–62, with further documentation. See *CIL* III 90 for an example of this.

[119] Saller 1982: 47–8; Duncan-Jones 2006: 198. Occasionally the patronal relationship was noted in an inscription recording the career of the *eques*, as in the case of M. Maenius Agrippa (*CIL* XI 5632 = *ILS* 2735).

[120] *CIL* VI 1410: *L(ucio) Fabio M(arci) fil(io) | Galer(ia tribu) Septimino | Ciloni praef(ecto) urb(i) | c(larissimo) v(iro) co(n)s(uli) II | M(arcus) Vibius Maternus | Ilurensis a militiis | candidatus eius.*

[121] Alföldy 2000: 4694. The word *candidatus* was commonly used by officers, such as centurions, *decuriones* and *beneficiarii*, who obtained promotion to higher rank on account of the provincial governor (Haensch 1998: 286–8). The use of the term here may perhaps indicate that Maternus obtained an equestrian commission from such a post. It was used occasionally to indicate a patronal relationship in civilian contexts, e.g. *AE* 1917/18, 85; *CIL* VIII 25382.

[122] *SEG* 6, 650.

possibilities. Tacitus famously complained about 'the ways of young men who pervert their military service into degeneracy' (*more iuvenum qui militiam in lasciviam vertunt*).[123] This lament was designed to set in relief the upright behaviour of his father-in-law, Cn. Iulius Agricola, who was naturally above such frivolity in his military service. But there may well have been officers who obtained advancement thanks to well-placed drinking buddies and friendships forged over dice games. One never knows what antics lurk behind the inscribed professions of *amicitia* addressed to *commilitones* and *contubernales*. Devijver, in collecting the evidence for such relationships, rather seriously refers to a shared love of literature among these officers.[124] That of course is true, but even the staid Pliny said in his recommendation letter that he had shared 'pleasurable times' (*iocos*) with Voconius Romanus.[125] Vergil's *Aeneid* was not incompatible with, and was possibly improved by, a hearty draught of *mulsum*.

There are other factors in securing promotion that we can document more conclusively, such as military prowess. Although army experience was not usually necessary for the first command, as Pliny's letter for Romanus shows, it assumed greater importance once a man had had the opportunity to prove himself. The honorific and funerary monuments of equestrian officers often document awards for valour or even specific heroic displays of *virtus*. C. Iulius Corinthianus was tribune of the *cohors I Britannicae* and commander of a vexillation of Dacian troops in the Parthian War of Lucius Verus. According to his epitaph, which was erected at Apulum in Dacia, 'the most sacred emperors granted him the mural crown, the untipped spear, and the standard decorated with silver on account of his courage'.[126] At the highest level of military valour, few officers surpassed the achievement of M. Valerius Maximianus, prefect of the *ala I Aravacorum*, who managed to kill the leader of the enemy Naristae in battle.[127] Pliny himself was sure to mention military prowess as a qualification when he wrote on behalf of more experienced equestrian officers. We can see this in the letter he wrote to the emperor Trajan to request a position (probably a tribunate) for the son of a *primipilaris* with whom Pliny had served in Syria:

---

[123] Tac. *Agr.* 5.1. Agricola was of course a *tribunus laticlavius*, but the principle is generally applicable to all tribunes.

[124] Devijver 1999: 263–4.   [125] Pliny the Younger, *Ep.* 2.13.5.

[126] *CIL* III 1193 = *ILS* 2746: *cui |ob virtute sua sacra|tissimi imper(atores) coro|nam muralem hastam | puram et vex[il]lum argent(o)| insignem dederunt.*

[127] *AE* 1956, 124.

Because of these reasons I count the members of his family among my own, most of all his son, Nymphidius Lupus, a young man who is honourable, diligent and entirely worthy of his excellent father. He will be a suitable recipient of your favour, as indeed you can learn from his initial employment, since as *praefectus cohortis* he earned the most fulsome testimonies from the senators Iulius Ferox and Fuscus Salinator. You will ensure my happiness and joy, my lord, by granting a post to his son.[128]

The reports of Ferox and Salinator may well have been sent to Rome, where they were retained by the office of the *ab epistulis* for future consultation.[129] Although the existence of such an imperial records office has been doubted, Pliny's own rather formulaic recommendations of his subordinates to Trajan suggest that the administration did retain such documents, or at least that governors did write 'to whom it may concern'-style letters for them at the completion of their term of office.[130] The overall implication of Pliny's letter is clear – an equestrian officer's further appointments in the *militiae* depended on how he acquitted himself, and the connections he cultivated, in his first post.

The difference between the officer seeking his first commission and more experienced commanders is paralleled in other literary sources, such as two poems of Statius about senatorial military officers. *Silvae* 5.2 concerns the young Crispinus, who is about to take up his first post as *tribunus militium*. The poet describes his character, education and upbringing, which make him suitable for the command, rather than any military ability. In contrast, *Silvae* 3.2 describes the achievements of M. Maecius Celer, who has just been appointed legionary legate: since he has already proven himself in army posts, his martial accomplishments are catalogued by the poet.[131] The same attention to military skill is found in a letter from M. Cornelius Fronto to his friend, the senator Ti. Claudius Iulianus, governor of Germania Inferior in AD 160. Fronto was seeking a post for C. Calvisius Faustinianus, the son of another equestrian associate, C. Calvisius Statianus:

[128] Pliny the Younger, *Ep.* 10.87.3: *quibus ex causis necessitudines eius inter meas numero, filium in primis, Nymphidium Lupum, iuvenem probum industrium et egregio patre dignissimum, suffecturum indulgentiae tuae, sicut primis eius experimentis cognoscere potes, cum praefectus cohortis plenissimum testimonium meruerit Iuli Ferocis et Fusci Salinatoris clarissimorum virorum. meum gaudium, domine, meamque gratulationem filii honore cumulabis.*

[129] E. Birley 1949: 13; A. R. Birley 2003: 5.

[130] See Pliny the Younger, *Ep.* 10.85, 86A. Cf. Saller 1982: 106–7, who is more sceptical.

[131] B. Gibson 2006: 175–8.

You will have to trust me regarding how educated he is – as for his skill in military affairs, everyone under whom he has served confirms it. But he will only consider that he has obtained the rewards of his learning and hard work when he has proved himself to you. Test him in military tasks, test him in judicial hearings, test him in literature – in short, test him in everything large and small that requires good sense and ability: you will discover that he is equal to himself at any time and at any place.[132]

Faustinianus had already served as tribune of the *legio IV Flavia* in Pannonia Inferior, which means that Fronto was most likely petitioning for the higher position of *praefectus alae*.[133] There is little difference in the overall sentiments contained in Fronto's letter compared with those recommending more junior *equites* for tribunates; the most significant addition is the fact that the candidate's military *virtus* has now been confirmed by experience. It is particularly interesting that Faustinianus' father, Statianus, did not write on his son's behalf, but approached Fronto to do so instead. This is despite the fact that Statianus was a high-ranking *eques*, who would himself become *ab epistulis* the following year.[134] It is probable that Statianus did not know Iulianus, whereas he was a genuine friend and regular correspondent of Fronto's, whose letters reveal a real affection for the governor.[135] This demonstrates that patronage was not a mechanical operation, but depended on real connections of both personal and political *amicitia*.[136] Moreover, as these letters and poems show, military experience was not irrelevant, but formed part of a wider set of qualifications for officer posts at the higher level.

The recommendation of suitable candidates for the *militiae equestres* constituted an act of social performance. The consistent and rather formulaic nature of these letters points to the value inherent in the social transaction itself, which conferred honour and distinction on both the recommender and the one being recommended.[137] We can observe this facet of Roman aristocratic society in a letter from Pliny to his friend, and

---

[132] Fronto, *Ad Amicos* 1.5.2 (vdH² p. 175): *quam doctus sit, mihi crede; quam rei militaris peritus, praedicant omnes sub quibus meruit. sed tum demum doctrinae industriaeque suae fructum sese percepisse putabit, ubi se tibi probarit. fac periculum in militiae muneribus, fac periculum in consiliis iudicaris, fac periculum in litteris, omni denique prudentiae et facilitatis usu vel serio vel remisso: semper et ubique eum parem sui invenies.*

[133] Tribunate: *CIL* III 3631–2. *Praefectus alae*: Pflaum 1961: 981 (no. 177 add.); A. R. Birley 2003: 5.

[134] Saller 1982: 139. For his career, see Pflaum 1960: 406–8 (no. 166).

[135] For their relationship, see Fronto, *Ad Amicos* 1.19, 1.20 (vdH² p. 182); Champlin 1980: 34–6.

[136] Saller 1982: 133–9. Cf. Devijver 1999: 263–4, whose view does not really seem to be that different, despite positioning his arguments in opposition to Saller.

[137] Saller 1982: 75–6; Lendon 1997: 185–6.

later biographer of the Caesars, C. Suetonius Tranquillus. He had managed to obtain a tribunate for Suetonius in Britain, but Suetonius wanted it to be transferred to his relative Caesennius Silvanus instead.[138] Pliny's interpretation of this transaction is a masterpiece:

> I even think it is the case that, since it is equally honourable to bestow and to receive favours (*beneficia*), you will simultaneously earn praise on both counts, if you transfer to another something which you earned yourself. Besides, I realise that this will enhance my renown as well, if, as a result of your action, it should not go unnoticed that my friends are not only able to hold the tribunate, but can even grant it as well.[139]

Pliny's rhetoric makes Suetonius' decision to transfer the tribunate to Caesennius Silvanus nothing less than the best possible outcome. Suetonius appears generous and magnanimous towards members of his family, whereas Pliny comes across as influential and connected. Suetonius' father, Suetonius Laetus, had been an equestrian military officer, but there is no sense here that he is disgracing the family heritage.[140] Instead, Pliny praises his friend for showing *pietas*, or duty to his family, which is better than any office.[141] The tribunate thus becomes more than just a military post, but an item of social currency and a mark of personal honour or distinction, like other offices in the Roman world.[142] By publishing his letters, including the many recommendations for his protégés, Pliny demonstrated his influence for all to see, therefore enhancing his personal renown.[143] The honour inherent in military commands is demonstrated by an anecdote told by Macrobius about the emperor Augustus. When a *praefectus equitum* was removed from his post, he asked Augustus if he could retain his salary so that he would not suffer disgrace. The officer then hoped that people would think he had resigned and that Augustus had allowed him to keep the salary.[144] Somewhat surprisingly, the *princeps* agreed. Although the story is probably apocryphal, it nevertheless demonstrates the social processes at work. The military command represented honour, status and imperial favour – to be forcibly stripped of the post was to be deprived of the intangible rewards that came with it.

---

[138] See Sherwin-White 1966: 229–30 for the context.

[139] Pliny the Younger, *Ep.* 3.8.3: *video etiam, cum sit egregium et mereri beneficia et dare, utramque te laudem simul assecuturum, si quod ipse meruisti alii tribuas. praeterea intellego mihi quoque gloriae fore, si ex hoc tuo facto non fuerit ignotum amicos meos non gerere tantum tribunatus posse verum etiam dare.*

[140] Suet. *Otho* 10.1.   [141] Pliny the Younger, *Ep.* 3.8.2.

[142] See Matthews 2010: 105 on this particular case, and more generally, Lendon 1997: 181–5; Griffin 2013: 64.

[143] Rees 2007: 156.   [144] Macrob. *Sat.* 2.4.5.

The value inherent in bestowing or holding an equestrian officer command meant that some men regarded it as attractive to seek a position that only required limited (or no) army service. Pliny wrote to the governor Q. Sosius Senecio to request a position for Varisidius Nepos, the nephew of his friend C. Calvisius Rufus, but specified that he did not desire a long tour of duty:[145]

I ask that you increase this man's personal prestige with the grant of a six months' tribunate, both for his sake, and that of his uncle. You put our friend Calvisius in your debt, as well as Nepos himself, who is no less deserving of being in your debt as you believe that I should be.[146]

The post of *tribunus semestris* was therefore much more than a military command: it was an item of social currency that would bind Pliny, Senecio, Calvisius and Nepos together in a web of mutual obligation. The nature of this position has been the subject of some debate, but it seems best to take its meaning at face value, as a tribunate held only for six months, as opposed to the usual tenure of several years.[147] Its limited tenure is confirmed by a pejorative remark of Juvenal, describing the influence of the pantomime actor Paris with the emperor Domitian: 'It's he who lavishly bestows posts in the army on many, and in six months' time the fingers of poets are ringed with gold.'[148] Juvenal's rather scathing attitude suggests that the post of *tribunus semestris* was not generally well regarded and was seen as a shortcut to prestige.[149] This may have been the type of tribunate awarded to the poet Martial, who proudly described it as a mark of his equestrian status alongside the right to sit in the first fourteen rows of the theatre.[150] Alternatively, Martial could have been awarded an honorary tribunate, which did not require any service at all.[151] It is perhaps no surprise that this honorific office was an invention of Claudius, who may have sympathised with well-born young men who shared his desire for military glory, but conspicuously lacked any aptitude in that arena. According to Suetonius, the emperor 'introduced a type of purely nominal military service, dubbed "supernumerary", which

---

[145] Senecio was probably the governor of Moesia Inferior or Superior (Syme 1964: 755–6).

[146] Pliny the Younger, *Ep.* 4.4.2: *hunc rogo semestri tribunatu splendidiorem et sibi et avunculo suo facias. obligabis Calvisium nostrum, obligabis ipsum, non minus idoneum debitorem, quam nos putas.*

[147] *OLD* s.v. *semestris* 1b (also *semenstris* and *sexmenstris*). For epigraphic attestations, see *CIL* III 130, IX 4885–6, XIII 1850.

[148] Juv. *Sat.* 7.88–9: *ille et militiae multis largitur honorem,| semenstri vatum digitos circumligat auro.*

[149] Dobson 1972: 201 n. 37.   [150] Mart. *Ep.* 3.95.9–10.

[151] Allen et al. 1970: 345–6; Demougin 1988: 197–8.

individuals could hold *in absentia* while receiving the title'.[152] This fiction gave emperors the ability to reward individuals with the honour of a command, without the necessity of having to find a specific vacancy in the *militiae equestres*.

Military Careers and Self-Representation: Regional Dynamics

The vast majority of officers in the *militiae equestres* were, as Birley demonstrated, municipal aristocrats in their thirties, who very often served in only one or two posts before returning to their home communities. Why did they decide to seek military appointments, when they could have lived out their lives in their *patria* undisturbed? In order to reconstruct the different perspectives on equestrian military service, we need to turn to archaeological and epigraphic evidence, notably the honorific and funerary monuments erected to celebrate their lives and achievements. The public monuments for equestrian officers can generally be found outside Rome, in the towns and cities of Italy and the provinces. These were usually the officers' places of origin or communities that had co-opted them as patrons. The only *equites* who tended to be publicly commemorated in the city of Rome itself were the praetorian prefects: no such statues would be authorised in the *sacra urbs* for officers who had not risen beyond the *militiae equestres*.[153] In his home (or adoptive) community an equestrian officer could be honoured with a public statue in a prominent location such as the forum, basilica or theatre. Unfortunately, most of the statues themselves have either been lost or disassociated from their original context, so it is impossible to tell whether *equites* were depicted in civilian dress or wore their military uniform. All that usually survives is the statue base featuring an inscribed record of their offices and achievements at the municipal and imperial level in the *cursus* format. The form and content of these inscriptions can nevertheless provide valuable information about the way in which service in the *militiae equestres* was represented. More iconographical evidence survives from tombs, either in the form of reliefs depicting the dead officer or symbols of military and civilian positions. When combined with the inscribed account of the deceased's life,

---

[152] Suet. *Claud.* 25.1: *stipendiaque instituit et imaginariae militiae genus, quod vocatur supra numerum, quo absentes et titulo tenus fungerentur.* See Hurley 2001: 171–2 for the interpretation of the Latin.
[153] Alföldy 2001: 35–8; Eck 2006b: 492–3.

these monuments help us to interpret the way in which the honorands or their heirs wanted them to be remembered.[154]

Naturally these honorific and funerary monuments are not unvarnished or unguarded representations of *equites*. They are consciously stylised monuments, designed to depict the honorand and his achievements in the best possible light, just as Pliny's *Letters* are designed to present his life, and the lives of his friends, in a specific way. The virtue of these monuments is that they allow us to interpret the lives of a broader range of equestrian military officers than would be possible from the literary sources alone. There was, of course, a wide variety of ways in which equestrian officers could be commemorated, depending on factors such as their cultural and social background and personal choice.[155] But taken collectively, these monuments show that service in the *militiae equestres* – even if it was only a single post – contributed to the idea that an *eques* was a good servant of the *res publica* and the emperor.

Appointment to the *militiae equestres* gave an equestrian the opportunity to share in the status and prestige that came with being an officer. We have already examined how the erection of such monuments in Italy during the Republican and Augustan periods demonstrates the importance of martial *virtus* to the public representation of members of the *ordo equester*.[156] Army service could be emphasised by depicting the equestrian in his military uniform, which usually only survives in funerary contexts, since most public honorific statues have either been lost or are no longer associated with their original bases.[157] Other aspects of military iconography on these monuments include representations of the equestrian *parma* and *hastae* or *dona militaria*, as well as accoutrements such as the short triangular sword called the *parazonium*, and the military standard, the *vexillum*.[158] The *parazonium* was particularly significant as it was one of the attributes of the personification of *virtus*.[159] Such emblems were integrated into the friezes on the outside of mausoleums, as shown by a example of a circular tomb for an

---

[154] See Eck 1995, 2009b on the interplay of inscriptions and monuments. The considerations of Keppie 2003: 41 regarding the funerary commemorations of soldiers apply to equestrian officers as well: sometimes the format of the monument would be prescribed in the will, but at other times it would be left up to the heirs to decide.

[155] Spalthoff 2010: 152–3.   [156] See Chapters 3 and 5.

[157] Devijver 1989a: 425–39; Devijver and Van Wonterghem 1990: 61–74. One rare surviving example of a statue is that of M. Holconius Rufus at Pompeii, which we discussed in Chapter 5.

[158] The different categories are analysed in detailed by Devijver and Van Wonterghem 1990: 94–7 and Spalthoff 2010: 63–109.

[159] Noreña 2011: 82.

anonymous *eques* near Modena.[160] These features also occasionally appear on honorific statue bases, with the *parma* and *hastae* being used as decorative features to indicate equestrian rank.[161] A wonderful example of a commemoration incorporating military decorations is the funerary altar of Q. Sulpicius Celsus, who was prefect of the *cohors VII Lusitanorum* in the Flavian period (Figure 6.2a–b). This monument, discovered along the Via Laurentina to the south of Rome, features striking depictions of his military decorations, including his *torques*, a standard with the *phalera*, and the *corona muralis*.[162] Upon seeing this monument, no one would be left in any doubt that Celsus was an accomplished equestrian military officer.

Service in the *militiae equestres* was very often commemorated as one part of an equestrian's life, which was devoted both to his own community and to the Roman state at large. Our first example of this phenomenon is the funerary monument of Sex. Adgennius Macrinus from Nemausus in Gallia Narbonensis (Figure 6.3).[163] Macrinus was a tribune of the *legio VI Victrix* and *praefectus fabrum*, but the inscription also includes his local service as

Figure 6.2a–b: Funerary altar of Q. Sulpicius Celsus, outside Rome

[160] Devijver and Van Wonterghem 1990: 88. Fragments of a military relief showing a *parazonium*, *phalerae*, *parmae* and *hastae*, dated to the Augustan period, now in the museum at Modena, may be part of the same monument (Spalthoff 2010: 190–1 (no. 77)).

[161] Note, for example, the base of a statue for Q. Arruntius Iustus at Bovianum in Samnium (*CIL* IX 2565 = *ILS* 5017). The list of his imperial posts breaks off in the middle since the base is fragmentary, and therefore we do not know if he actually served in the *militiae*.

[162] *CIL* VI 32934; Spalthoff 2010: 207–8 (no. 110).

[163] *CIL* XII 3175 + 3368; Devijver 1989a: 432–5.

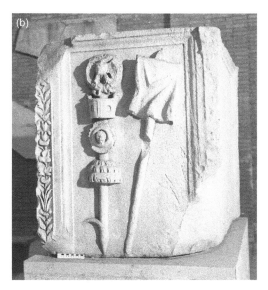

Figure 6.2a–b: (cont)

a magistrate and priest in Nemausus. His wife Licinia Flavilla was equally prominent as a *flaminica Augusta*. The pair was commemorated by their children, who depicted Macrinus as a tribune, wearing a cuirass with the head of Medusa and his *paludamentum*. His civilian post in Nemausus was not neglected in the iconography, however, with the *fasces* of his office shown either side of the central figures. This shows how martial *virtus* contributed to the overall impression that Macrinus served the Roman state as well as the local community.

Nor was it necessary for the military iconography to be as prominent as on the epitaph of Adgennius Macrinus. The circular mausoleum of C. Ennius Marsus from Saepinum is an excellent example of a different style of monument, but with the same overall message.[164] The inscription refers to both Marsus' military achievements for the Roman state and civilian offices held in Saepinum:

To Gaius Ennius Marsus, son of Gaius, of the Voltinia voting tribe, patron of the *municipium*, military tribune, *praefectus fabrum*, duumvir with censorial power,

---

[164] The circular tomb was a fashionable form of burial for municipal elites throughout the Italian peninsula in the early empire. Devijver 1989a: 420 suggests that equestrian officers who travelled outside their home towns were likely to erect such monuments, but his own collection of evidence suggests that they were favoured by Italian municipal elites in general, regardless of whether they had military service. See Devijver and Van Wonterghem 1990: 86 n. 146.

Figure 6.3: Funerary monument of Sex. Adgennius Macrinus, Nemausus

duumvir with judicial power four times, prefect with judicial power twice, quattuorvir, quaestor three times.[165]

The inscribed text seamlessly integrates Marsus' large number of local offices, which undoubtedly occupied most of his adult life, with the one command he held in the *militiae equestres*. The iconography of the tomb does not feature any representation of his army posts, but does include the

---

[165] *AE* 1930, 121: *C(aio) Ennio C(ai) f(ilio) Vol(tinia tribu) Marso | patrono municipi trib(uno) mil(itum) | praef(ecto) fabrum IIvir(o) quinq(uennali) IIvir(o) i(ure) d(icundo) IIII | praef(ecto) i(ure) d(icundo) bis IIIIvir(o) q(uaestori) III.*

sella curulis, the chair of office representing his magistracy in Saepinum.[166] This creates a rounded impression of Marsus – he was not a career officer in any sense of the word, but army service was still a part of his life. These monuments are public representations of the *domi militiaeque* ideology of service.[167]

As we have already seen, it was not an easy task to secure a commission in the *militiae equestres*. For this reason, provincial towns valued and enthusiastically commemorated the achievements of their citizens who held officer commands. For instance, C. Iulius Camillus was honoured with two public statues erected in the forum at Aventicum in Germania Superior, one paid for by the town council, the other by his daughter.[168] The account of his life is identical on both statue bases:

> To Gaius Iulius Camillus, son of Gaius, of the voting tribe Fabia, priest of Augustus, *magister*, military tribune of the *legio IV Macedonica*, awarded the untipped spear and the golden crown by Tiberius Claudius Caesar Augustus Germanicus, when he served in Britannia after he was called up by the emperor. The Colonia Pia Flavia Constans Emerita of the Helvetii (erected this) by a decree of the decurions.[169]

Camillus was from a prominent Helvetian family which obtained Roman citizenship in the late first century BC.[170] His daughter, Iulia Festilla, was the first *flaminica Augusta* of the town of Aventicum.[171] Camillus' sole equestrian military post saw him appointed tribune of the *legio IV Macedonica*, stationed nearby at Mogontiacum. The success of Camillus' exploits in Britain is foregrounded in the inscription, and indeed he must have been something of a novelty in the region: only five equestrian officers from the German provinces are attested in the Julio-Claudian period, and the numbers did not increase in subsequent centuries.[172] For Camillus, his family and the people of Aventicum, his service on campaign with Claudius in Britain was an achievement worth foregrounding, undoubtedly because it was an imperial honour.

---

[166] T. Schäfer 2003: 265–6.   [167] Devijver and Van Wonterghem 1990: 97–8.

[168] *CIL* XIII 5093–4; *PME* I 38.

[169] *CIL* XIII 5093 = *ILS* 2697: *[C(aio)] Iul(io) C(ai) f(ilio) Fab(ia tribu) Camillo | [s]ac(erdoti) Aug(usti) mag(istro) trib(uno) mil(itum) | [l]eg(ionis) IIII Maced(onicae) hast(a) pura | [e]t corona aurea donat[o] | [a] Ti(berio) Claudio Caesare Aug(usto) | Ger(manico) cum ab eo evocatus | [i]n Britannia militasset | [c]ol(onia) pia Flavia constans | Emerita Helvetior(um) | ex d(ecreto) d(ecurionum).*

[170] Syme 1977: 133, 136–7; Lamoine 2003: 201–3.

[171] *CIL* XIII 5064 = *ILS* 7010; Hemelrijk 2005: 157.   [172] Devijver 1989d: 112.

The same pride in the achievements of a local resident can be observed at Caesarea in Mauretania Caesariensis, which boasted the first known equestrian officer from the province, Ti. Claudius Helvius Secundus.[173] Initially appointed as *praefectus fabrum*, Secundus was then selected for the judicial *decuriae* by Nerva, followed by an exceptional five posts in the *militiae equestres*. This represented a substantial period of military service, which probably lasted between fifteen and twenty years in total. Indeed, the inscription on the base of the statue erected in his honour in Caesarea reveals that that Secundus was voted all municipal magistracies *in absentia*.[174] These monuments are merely a small sample, but they illustrate how the inscribed record of an equestrian's career integrated his military and civilian offices into a coherent account of his life, presenting him as a valued citizen of his own community, the Roman state and the emperor. The examples from Germany and North Africa demonstrate that this ethos of serving the Roman *res publica* in a military capacity spread beyond Italy and throughout the western provinces, as membership of the equestrian order encompassed elites from across the empire.

The eastern provinces present a slightly more complicated picture. We need to draw a distinction between officers who were Roman colonists, or descendants of such colonists, and those who were native Greeks.[175] The native Greeks are rarely attested in the *militiae equestres* at first, but gradually became more numerous, especially in the second and third centuries AD.[176] The evidence from the Roman colonies shows that Roman officers were honoured in a comparable fashion to their counterparts in the west, as we would expect. C. Caristanius Fronto Caesianus Iullus was both a military prefect and a magistrate of the colony of Antioch in Pisidia, where he was commemorated with a public statue by decree of the decurions.[177] The language of the inscription listing his official posts is in Latin, and in both form and content it differs little from what is found in Italy in the same period. Turning to Greece itself, Ti. Claudius Dinippus was the first citizen of the Roman colony of Corinth to hold a post in the *militiae*. His precise origins are not on record, but Spawforth has persuasively argued that he was the descendant of Italian businessmen who had been active in the east for several generations.[178] Dinippus was *tribunus*

---

[173] *PME* C 143; Devijver 1991a: 155.

[174] *AE* 1925, 44. See Jarrett 1963: 211–12 and Devijver 1991a on the rarity of North Africans in the *militiae* in the first century AD.

[175] Demougin 1999: 579–85.

[176] Devijver 1986a: 200–2. This analysis does not include Greece and Macedonia, for which see Devijver 1989d: 118.

[177] *AE* 1913, 235 = *ILS* 9502.   [178] Spawforth 1996: 173, 175, 177–8.

militum of the *legio VI Hispana* and thrice *praefectus fabrum* in addition to holding numerous offices in Corinth. There he was *duumvir, duumvir quinquennalis* for taking the census, priest of the cult in honour of Claudius' British victory, curator of the grain supply during a time of famine, and *agonothetes* for the Neronean Caesarean games at Isthmia.[179] This illustrious career in military and civil offices was carved into the base of numerous statues erected by the tribes of Corinth in a range of locations, such as the agora, the Julian Basilica and the South Stoa.[180] It would have been quite impossible escape Dinippus in Neronian Corinth: in a colonial aristocracy largely composed of fellow descendants of merchant families and freedmen, his achievements, both local and imperial, elevated him above other elites.[181] Most of his life was spent in Corinth and environs, but the military posts made him a more fully rounded imperial servant who lived up to the *domi militiaeque* ideal.

The majority of native Greek equestrian officers came from the province of proconsular Asia, where they are attested from the first to the third centuries AD, with numbers increasing in regions such as Lycia and Pamphylia, Syria and Egypt in the second century AD.[182] For these men, a commission in the *militiae* could function as a symbol of imperial favour, a sign that they were well connected with the emperor and his administration. L. Antonius Zeno of Laodicea, the grandson of Polemo I, king of Pontus, served in the *legio XII Fulminata* in Syria in the reign of Augustus.[183] A statue set up in his honour at Apollonia Salbake testifies to his status:

To Lucius Antonius Zeno, son of Marcus Antonius Polemo, great and best, tribune of the *legio XII Fulminata*, honoured by the gods, granted the right to wear royal purple throughout the world by the most noble Augustus, and the high priesthood in Asia by the emperor Caesar Augustus. The monument was established by Attalus and Tata, children of Hermogenes, in accordance with the will of Hermogenes, whose own father was Attalus, on account of his benefactions towards them.[184]

---

[179] *Corinth* VIII.2.89 (statue erected by the decree of the decurions). For his career, see A. B. West 1931: 71–4.

[180] *Corinth* VIII.2.86, 87, 88, 90, VIII.3.158, 159, 160, 161, 162, 163.

[181] For the demographic profile of Corinthian magistrates in the Julio-Claudian period, see Spawforth 1996: 167–75.

[182] Devijver 1986a: 200–12; Bowie 2014: 44–5.

[183] For the Augustan dating, see Thonemann 2004: 144–5, 2011: 209–11. Cf. *PME* A 147, produced before Thonemann's publications, placing him under Claudius or Nero.

[184] *SEG* 37, 855: Λούκιον Ἀντώνιον Μάρκου Ἀντω[νί]|ου Πολέμωνος υἱὸν Ζήνωνα μ[έ]|γαν ἀριστῆ, χιλιαρχήσαντα λεγ[ιῶ]|νος ιβ′ Κεραυνοφόρου, τετειμ[η]|μένον ὑπὸ τοῦ θεῶν ἐνφαν[εσ]|τάτου Σεβαστοῦ βασιλικῇ διὰ τῆς | οἰκουμένης πορφυραφορίᾳ καὶ | ἀρχιερατεύσαντα Αὐτοκράτο|ρος Καίσαρος Σεβαστοῦ ἐν τῇ Ἀσίᾳ· |τὴν ἀνάστασιν ποιησαμέν[ων] | Ἀττάλου καὶ Τατας τῶν Ἑρμ

As Thonemann has pointed out, the right to wear the royal purple was a special distinction unprecedented for any other Roman citizen at the time.[185] We might make a similar point about the military tribunate in its immediate Asian context: as one of the earliest Greeks to hold such a post, Zeno was an exceptional individual.[186] The tribunate was valuable not only as an army command, but also as a mark of imperial favour.

Greek equestrian officers could share the same commitment to serving the state *domi militiaeque* like their counterparts in the west. For example, at Magnesia on the Maeander the tribune Ti. Claudius Democrates erected a statue of the emperor Nero. The inscribed Greek dedication from the base is reproduced below:

Tiberius Claudius Democrates, son of Democrates, of the voting tribe Quirina, priest for life of Germanicus Augustus and tribune of the *legio XII*, and Tiberius Claudius Teimon, son of Tiberii [*sic*], of the voting tribe Quirina, priest of him (sc. Nero) for life, both appointed high priests of Asia, dedicated this.[187]

Democrates had probably been granted Roman citizenship by the emperor Claudius.[188] The majority of his life was spent in his province, serving as *flamen* of Germanicus at Magnesia and as high priest of Asia. Democrates held only one post in the *militiae equestres*, which took him to Syria, before he returned to Magnesia.[189] Nevertheless, the brief military command was all that was required to demonstrate his devotion to the emperors and the imperial regime, alongside his local and provincial service. This reveals that some native Greeks had the same approach to equestrian army commands as the *domi nobiles* in the western provinces.

There are few examples of equestrian monuments with significant military iconography in the Greek east when compared to Italy and the west, and this includes both Roman officers, or descendants of colonists, and native Greeks. One of those in the former category is the funerary monument of L. Pompeius Marcellinus, an equestrian officer from Rome who was buried at Ephesus in the second century AD (Figure 6.4). His tombstone depicts him riding on horseback in his capacity as tribune of the

[o]|γένους τέκνων ἐκ διαθή|κης Ἑρμογένους Ἀττάλου πατρὸς ἰδίου διὰ τὰς ἀπ' αὐ|τοῦ εἰς ἑαυτοὺς εὐεργεσία[ς].

185 Thonemann 2011: 211.
186 The first Greek to hold a military tribunate was Cornelius Menodorus, as discussed in Chapter 3.
187 *I.Magn.* 157b: Τιβέριος Κλαύδιος Δη|μοκράτου υἰὸς Κυρίνᾳ |Δημοκράτης ὁ ἱερεὺς | διὰ βίου τοῦ Σεβαστοῦ | Γερμανικοῦ καὶ χιλίαρ|χος λεγιῶνος ιβ'|καὶ Τιβέριος Κλαύδιος | Τιβερίων υἰὸς Κυρίνᾳ Τεί|μων ὁ ἱερεὺς αὐτοῦ διὰ | βίου οἱ ἀποδεδιγμένοι | τῆς Ἀσίας ἀρχιερεῖς | καθιέρωσαν.
188 Demougin 1992a: 391.
189 The legion, not named in full in the text, is the *legio XII Fulminata*, stationed in Syria.

Figure 6.4: Funerary monument of L. Pompeius Marcellinus, Ephesus

cohors I Ligurica.[190] The style of the monument, which is quite different from others in the region, can be explained by the fact that Marcellinus was Italian, and buried by his mother and sister at the age of only twenty-three. Marcellinus' command of the cohort as an equestrian officer was therefore the defining public office of his short life.

The one example of a native Greek commemorated with ostentatious military iconography is T. Flavius Mikkalus from Perinthus in Thrace.[191] Mikkalus' tomb, erected by his wife Claudia Mak[–], depicts the deceased Mikkalus on horseback, wearing the full uniform of an equestrian cavalry officer (Figure 6.5). The iconography probably shows the moment of his promotion from *tribunus militum* to *praefectus alae*.[192] In the frieze, he rides away from a group of infantry officers on the left, in order to receive the helmet of his new cavalry command from two soldiers on the right. The fragmentary Latin and Greek inscription, carved at the very top of the tomb, reveals that the officer commands were the crowning glory of Mikkalus' life, most of which was spent in Perinthus, where he was president of the games and high priest of the imperial cult, and his wife Claudia was a high priestess. Mikkalus was probably the first member of his family to receive Roman citizenship, which was granted by the Flavian

Figure 6.5: Funerary relief of T. Flavius Mikkalus, Perinthus

---

[190] *CIL* III 7131; Spalthoff 2010: 198 (no. 89); *PME* P 60.

[191] *SEG* 35, 828; Merkelbach 1985; Devijver 1986b; Spalthoff 2010: 114–16.

[192] Devijver 1986b: 254–6, 1989a: 435. Cf. Merkelbach 1985, who suggests that Mikkalus was promoted from the rank of centurion.

emperors.[193] Mikkalus' tomb commemorates both his service to his *patria* and to the Roman state, but in his case the emphasis is firmly on his military service as a shining moment of glory. This style of funerary moment is quite exceptional, however: most Greeks were buried in tombs or sarcophagi which expressed their personal excellence and *arete* through mythological allusions, not Roman military iconography.[194]

When we examine the funerary and honorific monuments for equestrian army officers in the first three centuries AD it is clear that this period witnessed the emergence of a specific sub-group within the *ordo equester* which derived personal status from military service to the Roman state and to the emperor himself. In Chapter 5 we examined how equestrian rank could function as an imperial honour that integrated provincial *domi nobiles* into the framework of the Roman empire at large, without reducing the prestige inherent in their local magistracies, priesthoods and other honours. The same point can be made about officers in the *militiae equestres*, as any other office held in their *patria* after military service still carried great significance. Indeed, the honour of having a former tribune or prefect as a magistrate or *agonothetes* only increased the connections between Rome and the local community. The imperial and local honours complemented each other. The monuments can therefore be viewed as evidence of service *domi militiaeque* both to one's own *patria* and to the Roman *res publica*. Such a claim could not be made by all Roman citizens, or even by all *equites*. These officers should therefore be envisioned as an elite within the *ordo* at large.

Virtus **and** Arete

The examples of Greek equestrians serving in the *militiae* could create the impression that it became an accepted and commonplace choice for *equites* in the eastern half of the empire to take on officer commissions. This seems not to have been the case. Native Greek officers were very much in the minority, both within their own local communities and in the empire at large.[195] L. Mestrius Plutarchus (better known as Plutarch), for example, promoted the idea that Greeks should assist their *polis* by cultivating friends and allies in the imperial administration. But only one of his Greek friends is known to have held a post in the *militiae*: Cn. Cornelius

[193] Devijver 1986b: 254.   [194] Ewald 2004.
[195] Bowie 2014. Cf. Devijver 1986a and Demougin 1999: 585, 587–8, who offer more positive views of Greek involvement in the *militiae*.

Pulcher, tribune of the *legio IV Scythica*.[196] The province of Achaea
furnishes a mere thirteen attested equestrian officers in total, and only
two of these after the mid-second century AD.[197] There is a sole native
Athenian found in the *militiae*, Ti. Claudius Oenophilus, a member of the
Eumolpid family and hierophant at Eleusis, around AD 100. He is recorded
as 'being *praefectus fabrum* of the Roman people, *praefectus* of the *cohors II
Hispanorum*' (ἔπαρχον ἀρχιτεκτόνων δήμου Ῥωμαίων γενόμενον | ἔπαρχον
σπείρης Ἰσπανῶν δευτέρας).[198] The novelty of this equestrian military
service stands out among his other Athenian and Eleusinian positions.
The fact that no other Athenian *eques* repeated his experiment is telling.
If we look at the figures from the province of Asia, which include both
Italian colonists and their descendants as well as native Greeks, there is no
indication that the *militiae equestres* became a more popular option over
time: forty-one officers are attested in the first century AD, and thirty-six
between Trajan and Septimius Severus.[199] To put this in perspective:
current evidence shows Italy furnishing 207 equestrian officers in
the second century AD. The most significant change in the province of
Asia is that fewer Roman colonists appear in the *militiae* after the second
century AD, with most third-century equestrian officers coming from
Greek families.[200] This demands explanation.

Firstly, we need to consider many different local issues, as patterns in
equestrian military service were not consistent. The colony of Alexandria
Troas, for example, only supplied officers after the Flavian period, on
current evidence.[201] Ceramus, in southern Caria, has a single known
officer, the tribune P. Aelius Themistocles, who dates to the mid-second
century AD.[202] Precisely where Themistocles served is unknown, since the
unit is not given in the inscription. Most of his life seems to have been spent
in the province of Asia, where he was an Asiarch, and he is also known to
have minted coins at Miletus and Ceramus.[203] Themistocles evidently saw
some attraction in serving as a Roman officer, but he was very much an
exception among the elites of Ceramus. He may well have acquired
a tribunate through a passing interaction with the governor or another
member of the Roman administration. Sometimes the descendants of
Italians who settled in Asia Minor preferred to hold local positions rather

---

[196] *IG* IV 795, 1600; Swain 1996: 163–4; Bowie 2014: 52, 61.   [197] Devijver 1989d: 118.
[198] *IG* II² 3546 (career), 3548a (full name). For his family, see Woloch 1969: 508.
[199] Devijver 1989d: 118.   [200] Devijver 1986a: 200.
[201] Devijver 1986a: 129. Indeed, there are no equestrians attested at all in the colony in the second
and third century AD (Kuhn 2010: 132).
[202] *I. Keramos* 31; *PME* A 65.
[203] *RPC* IV Online nos. 1072, 1159, 2693, 2697, 2764, 11011 (Miletus), 868–9, 3337 (Ceramus).

than compete for Roman commands in the *militiae equestres*. For example, L. Malius Reginus, a military tribune from Italy, settled at Miletus, where he was a gymnasiarch and stephanephor.[204] His son, L. Malius Saturninus, did not serve in the *militiae*, but followed his father as stephanephor, and his granddaughter Malia Rufina served as a hydrophor of Artemis Pythia at Didyma. The members of the family were prominent local citizens, but there was no return to the *militiae equestres*. We might say that they 'went native'.[205]

In other cities of Asia it was often only one or two families that made the breakthrough that enabled them to hold posts in the *militiae equestres* and beyond. This was the case at Heraclea, where the indigenous Statilii, descended from Trajan's doctor, T. Statilius Crito, can be found in the *militiae equestres* and in procuratorial posts throughout the second century AD.[206] Their only competition from this city at the imperial level came from the family of the Aburnii, who were probably Italian in origin, and may have settled there after Trajan made Heraclea a colony.[207] The first member of the family, L. Alburnius Tuscianus, was an *eques* who wholeheartedly embraced military service as a lifetime commitment. Beginning as a *praefectus fabrum*, he then served in six posts in the *militiae* and was decorated in Trajan's Parthian War.[208] His son and grandson also held equestrian officer commands, but thereafter the family is untraceable.[209] This means that Heraclea's equestrian officers are in fact the product of special circumstances, the result of the connections of T. Statilius Crito, court physician and procurator, and the fact that an elite member of the equestrian military fraternity, L. Alburnius Tuscianus, happened to settle there.[210] Even with such well-connected potential patrons in Heraclea, no other *equites* from the colony were willing or able to serve.[211]

This analysis can be extended to the province of Bithynia and Pontus, where Madsen has suggested that there was particular enthusiasm for 'becoming Roman', based on the record of provincials holding imperial posts.[212] We can certainly detect significant pride among equestrian families who did have imperial connections, and thus formed part of the

---

[204] *I. Didyma* 343; Demougin 1992a: 608.   [205] Demougin 1999: 582–3.

[206] Devijver 1986a: 126; Demougin 1999: 593–4. The history of the Statilii at Heraclea is brilliantly elucidated by Thonemann 2011: 218–27, to whom the following analysis is indebted.

[207] Devijver 1986a: 117, 114; Bowie 2014: 50.   [208] Robert 1954 no. 78 = *ILS* 9471; *PME* A 5.

[209] *PME* A 3–4.   [210] Bowie 2014: 49–50.

[211] Thonemann 2011: 226 points out that there is only one equestrian procurator from Heraclea, P. Aelius Eucritus (Robert 1954 no. 53).

[212] Madsen 2009: 59–81.

elite within the *ordo equester* at large who wished to serve the Roman *res publica*. For example, in the early third century AD M. Iulius Gavinius Secundus was honoured with a statue erected by his nephew at Prusius ad Hypium. The inscription on the base records Secundus' considerable local offices, distinctions and benefactions, including the fact that he was priest of the emperors, twice archon, and *agonothetes* of the games of Zeus Olympius. He also donated money for the restoration of the baths and agora, and 'escorted the great and divine emperors and their sacred campaigns many times' (παραπέμψαντα τοὺς μεγίστους | καὶ θειοτάτους Αὐτοκράτορας | καὶ τὰ ἱερὰ αὐτῶν στρατεύματα | πολλάκις). This desire for a connection to the Roman state can also be detected in Secundus' boast that he was 'the father of one who had twice been a military tribune' (πατέρα δὶς χειλιάρχου).[213] But at the same time, the case of Secundus and his son cannot be typical: there are only twelve equestrian officers in total attested in the province, and Secundus' offspring was one of only four men from Prusias ad Hypium itself who served in the *militiae*.[214] The tribunate was valued by Secundus personally as a mark of his family's distinction, but it does not function as evidence of widespread military service among the equestrians of Bithynia. Instead, it shows the emergence and consolidation of a specific sub-group of Greek *equites* for whom personal and family status could be derived from commands in the Roman army.

Why did more Greeks not choose to serve in the *militiae equestres*? It is true that a certain amount of luck was involved, since candidates needed the right connections in order to secure a commission, as we saw earlier in this chapter. Competition for the officer posts was undoubtedly fierce. But the lack of equestrian military officers can also be attributed to the culture and society of the Greek-speaking provinces. As Bowie has noted, Roman military service plays virtually no role in the Greek literature or culture of the Second Sophistic.[215] The works produced during this period emphasise other forms of achievement, most notably the ability to compose and deliver works of epideictic rhetoric, as a way of displaying *arete*, or personal excellence.[216] From the perspective of the sophists, *arete* was founded on cultural achievement rather than on martial prowess.[217] Literary and intellectual types were not usually found in the *militiae*. The only equestrian officer explicitly attested as a rhetor is an Asiarch, Ti. Claudius

---

[213] *IGR* III 66 = *I. Prusias* 20. This means that his son held two tribunates, not that he had two sons in the *militiae* (Devijver 1986a: 154).

[214] Devijver 1986a: 155–6; Bowie 2014: 51.   [215] Bowie 2014: 58–64.   [216] Bowie 1970.

[217] Asirvatham 2010: 194.

Frontonianus, who came from Ephesus.[218] Sometimes equestrian military service failed to be maintained in a family because subsequent generations chose intellectual and cultural pursuits instead. For example, T. Flavius Varus Calvisius Hermocrates is the only known equestrian officer from Phocaea in Asia. He was twice *praefectus fabrum*, then *praefectus cohortis* and *tribunus legionis*.[219] This was an extensive Roman military career, but his descendants did not seek such a life. One of these was P. Flavius Hermocrates, high priest of Asia, who is called a philosopher in inscriptions.[220] The most famous member of the family, however, was the Severan sophist L. Flavius Hermocrates, who featured in Philostratus' *Lives of the Sophists*.[221] Hermocrates was descended not only from the tribune T. Flavius Hermocrates, but also from L. Antonius Zeno, Augustus' purple-wearing tribune of Laodicea, through M. Antonius Polemo, the great second-century sophist.[222] Hermocrates evidently saw no value in the *militiae* like his ancestors – indeed, he boasted to Septimius Severus that the emperor could not offer him any honours or posts that he and his family did not already have.[223]

The neglect of the *militiae equestres* in imperial Greek literature stands in stark contrast to contemporary works in Latin. To take just one example, the poet Statius composed a lyric ode in honour of P. (?) Vibius Maximus, an *eques* from an Italian family who settled in Dalmatia.[224] The ode celebrated Maximus' service as *praefectus alae*, with Statius envisaging his subject regaling his son with tales of his glorious exploits in the east.[225] It is to be expected that the Greek literature of the Sophistic movement did not contain similar sentiments, since it celebrated the continuing success of Greek *paideia* in the Roman world in a rather self-justifying manner.[226] Perhaps if poems had been written – or had survived – about the military exploits of the equestrian Statilii from Heraclea, then we might have very different evidence with which to contrast the output of Dio Chrysostom, Aelius Aristides and Philostratus. But at the same time, their works are indication of the wider cultural milieu in which potential equestrian officer candidates lived. We should perhaps not be

---

[218] *IG* XII³ 1119; *PME* C 142.   [219] *IGR* IV 1323 = *ILS* 8864; *PME* F 82.

[220] *IGR* IV 1324, 1326; *AE* 1933, 276; C. P. Jones 2003: 127–30.   [221] Phil. *VS* 608–611.

[222] Phil. *VS* 609.   [223] Phil. *VS* 611.

[224] Maximus' birthplace is demonstrated by Stat. *Silv.* 4.7.13–20, and he may be the Vibius Maximus attested as a witness on a military diploma (*CIL* XVI 14 = *ILS* 1991; White 1973: 298). He is not to be identified with the prefect of Egypt of the same name (White 1973; Coleman 1988: 195–6).

[225] Stat. *Silv.* 4.7.45–8; Syme 1957b: 481; Coleman 1988: 195–6, 206–7.

[226] Bowie 1970: 17, 40; Whitmarsh 2005: 13–15.

surprised that only one native Athenian is attested in the *militiae*, since
Athens was the centre of the Greek cultural renaissance under the
empire.[227] It is important to emphasise that these sophists and rhetors
were not opposed to the imperial administration: in fact, they educated the
youth of the Greek world for public service both in their own *polis* and the
Roman state. Many sophists held high posts in the imperial administration
as secretaries and advisers, which they valued as marks of prestige.
However, sophists and intellectuals preferred this type of imperial service
to military commands in the Roman army, as it allowed them to show off
their literary and oratorical talents in a new arena: the emperor's court.[228]

Most Greek elites from the eastern provinces were not sophists who
devoted their lives to writing, performing and teaching rhetoric. So why
are more Greeks not attested seeking commissions in the *militiae equestres*?
The answer must be, as Bowie has argued, that the long and proud tradition
of Greek athletic competitions and festivals already gave young aristocrats
an opportunity to display their *arete*.[229] There were certainly significant
differences in the ways in which the aristocratic youth in the western and
eastern provinces were socialised and trained for their future lives.[230] In the
Greek world *arete* was exhibited on the track and field, rather than through
horseback riding and one-on-one combat, as in Italy and the western
provinces.[231] *Equites* and senators fought in the arena in Rome to display
their *virtus* during the early principate, but they did not usually participate in
athletic festivals.[232] This cultural difference enables us to understand the
novelty of Vibius Salutaris' decision to equate the *ephebeia* of Ephesus with
the *ordo equester*, a connection which was not made formally elsewhere in
the Greek world.[233] Athletic competitions were more popular during the
Roman empire than they had ever been before, at least partly due to patronage by the emperors themselves.[234] Victorious Greek athletes were honoured with statues depicting them in heroic nudity, which was the outward,
monumental embodiment of their inner *arete*.[235] The inscriptions on the

[227] Bowie 1970: 29–30.   [228] This is explored in Chapter 7.
[229] Bowie 2014: 62–4. On athletics and Greek elite identity in the Roman world, see van Nijf 1999,
2001, 2004; König 2005 and Newby 2005.
[230] Greek athletics did grow in popularity in the Roman west (Newby 2005: 41–4), but it did not
supplant horseback riding, hunting and fighting in single combat as methods of displaying
virtus (see Kleijwegt 1991: 109–13, 1994).
[231] Kleijwegt 1991: 115; Kennell 2009: 331–6.
[232] Newby 2005: 273. For senators and *equites* in the arena, see Chapter 9.
[233] See Chapter 5 for discussion of Salutaris' foundation.
[234] König 2005: 28–30, 212–35; Newby 2005: 27–37, 275–6.
[235] van Nijf 2004: 215–21; König 2005: 102–32; Newby 2005: 253–5.

bases of these statues recorded prize-winning victories in great detail.[236] For example, in AD 219 Q. Iulius Dionysius was honoured with a statue in Ancyra, with the inscription on the base listing no fewer than twenty-two games at which he had been victorious, some on multiple occasions, throughout Greece, Asia Minor and Syria.[237]

Young Greek aristocrats were trained in the gymnasium as they had been for generations, as preparation for warfare, although they now did not generally take to the battlefield, but to the sporting field instead.[238] These Greek athletes did sometimes fight for Rome, but tended to do so in local militias, or during serious emergencies, as when the Olympic victor Mnesiboulus took to the field against the invading Costobocs at Elateia in Greece during the reign of Marcus Aurelius.[239] One of the few athletes explicitly attested as being of equestrian status, L. Septimius Flavianus Flavillianus, did not enter the *militiae equestres*, but did assume the civic burden of organising recruits for Severus Alexander's Persian War.[240] This preference for athletics rather than commissions in the *militiae* did not constitute a rejection of Roman authority – far from it. The headquarters of the Universal Guild of Athletes was located in the city of Rome itself.[241] Moreover, the crown festivals authorised by the emperors were strongly associated with the imperial cult, featuring both sacrifices to the Roman rulers and the parading of their images in processions.[242] The Greek elites who lavishly funded these events emerged as local benefactors, as well as intermediaries between the *polis* and the emperor.[243] The difference in the numbers of Greeks and western provincials entering the *militiae* should therefore be understood as the result of cultural preferences, rather than hostility to honours bestowed by the Roman *res publica* and its emperor.

Conclusion: Statues and Letters

In the second century AD the equestrian M. Gavius Bassus was commemorated with a statue in Ephesus by the junior officers under his command. Bassus' official posts are recorded in both Greek and Latin in the *cursus* format on the base of the statue. The inscription includes his service

---

[236] van Nijf 2001: 323–4.
[237] *I. Ankara* 146. Note also the sarcophagus of an athlete from Aphrodisias, the face of which is entirely covered in victory wreaths (Smith et al. 2006: 305, Sarcophagus 3).
[238] König 2005: 47–63; Newby 2005: 168–201.   [239] Paus. 10.34.5; König 2005: 55–6.
[240] *AE* 2011, 1412; Milner 2011.   [241] König 2005: 221–4.
[242] van Nijf 2001: 318–21; König 2005: 71.   [243] van Nijf 2001: 331–3.

in the *militiae equestres*, co-option into the jury panels at Rome, the award
of military decorations in the Dacian war by the emperor Trajan, and his
appointment as *praefectus orae Ponticae maritimae* ('prefect of the Pontic
coast') in the province of Pontus and Bithynia.[244] In a fortunate synchro-
nicity between epigraphy and literature, Bassus emerges once more in the
correspondence of Pliny the Younger, who was governor of Pontus and
Bithynia when he was prefect of the Pontic coast. Pliny had occasion to
write a letter of recommendation for Bassus to the emperor Trajan, in
which he described him as 'irreproachable, upright, and diligent' (*integrum
probum industrium*).[245] It was a rather formulaic missive, without the
warmth found in some of Pliny's recommendations for his friends and
protégés, but it was typical of the 'to whom it may concern' letters governors were expected to pen for their subordinates, in order to ensure their
future employment. In many ways, the inscribed statue base from Ephesus
and Pliny's letter send the same message, that Bassus faithfully did his duty
as a military officer on behalf of both the *res publica* and the emperor. His
army service, like those of countless other equestrian officers, allowed him
to exhibit the *virtus* that was expected of members of the *ordo equester*. But
Bassus' employment as a juror in the courts at Rome, as indicated in the
inscribed *cursus*, meant that he was also employed in a public capacity in
a civilian role. His life was devoted to serving the Roman state *domi
militiaeque*.

Equestrians such as Bassus were expected and encouraged to volunteer
for commands in the *militiae*. In return for three or four years in Pannonia,
Britain or Syria they earned lifetime status and respect as a Roman army
officer. This ethos of service spread throughout Italy and the western
provinces, as it offered opportunities for the *domi nobiles* to display their
virtus. Some native Greeks from Achaea and Asia embraced equestrian
officer commands, which they valued as complements to the positions and
honours in their *polis*, though for the most part easterners preferred to seek
other ways of displaying their personal *arete* or different tokens of imperial
favour. Regardless of one's provincial origin, posts in the *militiae* were not
easy to come by, and depended on necessary vacancies, supportive patrons
and a fair degree of good luck. Eligibility depended not only on possessing
equestrian rank in the first place, but also the education, character and
personal qualities necessary to undertake the administrative, logistical and
diplomatic duties that came with the post. For subsequent appointments,
military aptitude became more important, as by then the *eques* had had the

---

[244] *I. Eph.* 680.   [245] Pliny the Younger, *Ep.* 10.86A.

opportunity to display his talents in that arena. Competition only became fiercer for the more senior posts, as the number of commands diminished at higher ranks of the *militiae*.

The connection between personal qualities and the ethos of serving the *res publica* which features in the letters of recommendation shows that in many ways the lives of *equites* were no different from those of senators who held army commands. Senators occupied more senior command posts such as *tribunus laticlavius, legatus legionis* and provincial governor in control of multiple legions by virtue of their superior status as members of the upper *ordo* of the Roman aristocracy. But the basic principles of selection, recommendation and promotion were the same. Senators had had their individual opportunities for military glory restricted in the transition to the monarchical *res publica*, so that all credit now redounded to the *princeps* himself. They had been domesticated to serve the emperor, their elaborate *cursus* inscriptions denoting both their individual excellence and prestige, as well as their subservience to the *imperator*. Equestrians had always been part of the Roman military machine as junior officers, but with the return of monarchy to Rome their situation changed. A greater range of army positions was made available to *equites*, and they were now organised into hierarchical grades, the *militiae equestres*. This represented the attempts of several emperors, most notably Augustus, Claudius and Nero, to impose order on what had been a haphazard system, and to bind the *domi nobiles* of the provinces to the state in a more active and involved manner than could be achieved by merely holding equestrian rank. These officers therefore constituted an elite sub-group within the *ordo* at large. The result of this was that in the new imperial system senators were domesticated by curtailing their military opportunities, whereas the *equites* were domesticated by offering them new ones.

The elites of Italy and the provinces looked upon the *militiae equestres* as a new form of status and prestige, regardless of whether they held one officer command or four. Their military service was very often commemorated in monumental form when they returned to their *patriae*. Some equestrian officers were honoured with public statues while they were alive, others with impressive tombs or mausoleums in death. The iconographical choices emphasised their personal *virtus* and identification with the equestrian order's military heritage through the use of symbols such as the *parma, hastae* and *vexillum*. These images were very often found side by side with symbols of municipal offices, which were either listed in the inscribed text or displayed iconographically in the form of the *fasces* or the *sella curulis*. Most importantly, the fact that these officers embraced the *cursus*-style inscription used by senators signalled that they shared in the ethos of service *domi militiaeque*. These monuments collectively emphasised their commitment to their *patria*, to the *res publica* and, most importantly, to the emperor himself.

Introduction: The Commission of Marsianus

Q. Domitius Marsianus was one of many *equites* from North Africa who sought positions within the Roman administration in the second century AD.[1] He sat on the equestrian jury panels at Rome, commanded a unit of soldiers as *praefectus*, and managed the collection of the census in Belgica and Germania Inferior – in short, Marsianus embraced the aristocratic ideal of serving the state in both civilian and military capacities.[2] While his official achievements may not have been exceptional in comparison with *equites* who ascended to the prefectures of Egypt or the praetorian guard, Marsianus' employment in imperial service was commemorated in a conspicuous way by his home town of Bulla Regia in Africa Proconsularis. For, when the emperor Marcus Aurelius appointed Marsianus procurator of the imperial *patrimonium* in the province of Narbonensis, the council of Bulla Regia voted to erect an equestrian statue of him. This was no mere token gesture, since the honour of being represented on horseback was both prestigious and expensive.[3] Fortunately for the town's financial health, Marsianus' brother, L. Domitius Fabianus, stepped in to pay for the statue himself.[4] The finished monument does not simply record Marsianus' official posts in the recognisable *cursus* format. Instead, either the council or Domitius Fabianus decided to incorporate an inscribed copy of the letter from Marcus Aurelius awarding Marsianus the procuratorship. The full inscription reads as follows:

---

[1] See Jarrett 1963 for the entrance of equestrians from North Africa into the imperial service.
[2] Pflaum 1971 analyses his career in detail.
[3] For the costs of honorific monuments, see Duncan-Jones 1982: 78–9, 126–7. An equestrian statue of Septimius Severus erected at Uchi Maius cost more than 12,000 sesterces, not including the base (*CIL* VIII 26255 = *ILS* 9401).
[4] The practice of honouring *equites* with equestrian statues only became more common in the provinces from the late first century AD onwards (Eck 2006b: 500).

To Quintus Domitius Marsianus, son of Lucius, of the voting tribe Quirina, procurator of the emperor responsible for imperial property in the province of Narbonensis, procurator of the emperor responsible for the iron mines, procurator of the emperor responsible for the collection of the census in Gaul, specifically the regions of the Tungri and the Frisavones in the province of Belgica, and in the region of the Batavi in Germania Inferior, prefect of soldiers, selected for the jury panels by the Emperors Marcus Aurelius Antoninus Caesar and Lucius Aurelius Verus Caesar.

When the council had decreed that an equestrian statue of him should be erected at public expense, his brother Lucius Domitius Fabianus relieved the community of the burden, and erected it at his own expense.

A copy of the emperor's letter: 'Caesar Antoninus Augustus sends greetings to Domitius Marsianus. Since I have wished to promote you to the distinction of a ducenarian procuratorship for quite some time, I will make use of the opportunity which now presents itself. Therefore, succeed Marius Pudens, with the great expectation of my eternal favour, as long as you retain your sense of integrity, attentiveness, and skills gained by experience. Farewell, my most esteemed Marsianus.'[5]

The juxtaposition of the inscribed *cursus* and the imperial letter, together with the equestrian statue (now sadly lost), portrayed Q. Domitius Marsianus as an important and faithful servant of the *res publica* and the emperor himself. Marsianus was not the only such upwardly mobile resident of Bulla Regia in the Antonine period. C. Memmius Fidus Iulius Albius entered the senate under Marcus Aurelius, rising to become *consul ordinarius* in AD 191. The families of the Agrii, Aradii and Marcii likewise acquired senatorial status in the late second and early third centuries AD.[6] But Marsianus' equestrian service would probably have begun in the 150s, placing him at the vanguard of this movement. Only two other *equites* are attested in the town, both in the early third century AD: the Severan procurator M. Rossius Vitulus, who was not native to Bulla, and a local

---

[5] AE 1962, 183: *Q(uinto) Domitio L(uci) fil(io) Q(uirina tribu) Marsiano | proc(uratori) Aug(usti) patrimoni(i) provin(ciae) | Narbonensis proc(uratori) Aug(usti) ad ferra|rias proc(uratori) Aug(usti) ad census in Gal|lia accipiendos provinc(iae) Belgicae per | regiones Tungrorum et Frisavonum et Ger|maniae inferioris et Batavorum praef(ecto) militum | adlecto in decuri(i)s ab Imperatoribus M(arco) Aurelio | Antonino et L(ucio) Aurelio Vero Caesarib(us), cui cum ordo | equestrem publico sumptu ponendam censuisset, | L(ucius) Domitius Fabianus frater eius remisso rei p(ublicae) sumptu | de suo posuit. exemplum codicillorum. | Caesar Antoninus Aug(ustus) Domitio Marsiano suo salut(em) dicit). | ad ducenariae procurationis splendorem iamdudum te | provehere studens utor opportunitate quae nunc [o]bte|git. succede igitur Mario Pudenti tanta cum spe perpetui | favoris mei, quantam conscientiam retinueris innocen|tiae diligentiae experientiae. vale, mi Marsiane, karissime | mihi.*

[6] Thébert 1973: 287–92; Christol 1978; Corbier 1982: 687–90, 711–15.

magistrate, Q. Lollius Saturninus.[7] In this context we can understand why the council of Bulla Regia awarded Marsianus such a signal honour. The family of the Domitii had themselves not hitherto advanced beyond the ranks of the town council, which explains Fabianus' extraordinary generosity in marking his brother's achievements.[8]

The monument of Domitius Marsianus further elucidates the discussion, begun in the previous chapter, about equestrian careers in the imperial service. The decision to inscribe Marcus Aurelius' letter of appointment provides important insights – and raises significant questions – about the hierarchy of procuratorial posts in the high Roman empire, and the manner in which equestrians came to be appointed to them. For instance, was there a regular and predictable scheme of promotions and promotion criteria for *equites*, as some scholars have argued? The question has significant implications for how we view equestrian careers and the aims and ambitions of those who embarked on them. This chapter will explore how the Roman administrative hierarchy represented an opportunity for *equites* to serve the state *domi militiaeque* in a manner similar to that of senators, and functioned as a conduit for honour, prestige and imperial favour.[9] However, those equestrians who devoted their lives to civilian and military commands through years of service, as represented in the *cursus* inscriptions, were actually in the minority among the *ordo* at large. There were probably only 600 *equites* in procuratorial posts at any one time, out of the 20,000–30,000 members of the *ordo*.[10] There was increasing competition for fewer posts the higher one rose through the procuratorial *cursus*, which meant that many only held one or two administrative positions (though this was still very prestigious). Some *equites* attempted to acquire honorific posts and distinctions, which enhanced their public standing with little work. This suggests that many *equites* were eager for status and honours, but only a few were able – or willing – to devote their lives to the imperial *res publica*. This resulted in the emergence of a sub-group of the *ordo equester* who took on the characteristics of a 'service aristocracy', whose status and prestige derived not merely from membership of the *ordo*, but also, and especially, from their office holding.[11] This was recognised by the

---

[7] Thébert 1973: 286. Vitulus: Pflaum 1960: 593–8 (no. 224). Saturninus: *AE* 2004, 1874.

[8] For the Domitii, see Pflaum 1971: 350; Thébert 1973: 309.

[9] See the comments of Matthews 2000b: 440–1 on Marsianus' inscription as evidence of the 'aristocracy of service' and its ideology.

[10] Bang 2011: 124.

[11] For the historical phenomenon of the service elite, see Mosca 1939: 60. This develops the theme of the previous chapter, which identified *equites* who held multiple officer commands in the *militiae equestres* as an elite among the *ordo*.

historian Tacitus, who described *equites* in imperial service as the 'equestrian nobility' (*equestris nobilitas*).[12]

The Development of the Equestrian Career

One of the most significant innovations of Augustus' principate was his decision to employ *equites Romani* as administrative officials. They were no longer merely the friends, associates or private agents of great men, but representatives of the emperor who could be entrusted with responsibilities comparable to senators. There were some differences between the emerging equestrian career structure and the senatorial *cursus honorum*. The senatorial magistracies were regulated by laws, which determined the precise ages at which the offices of quaestor, aedile, praetor and consul could be held.[13] Senatorial military and administrative posts in the imperial service were all linked to these magistracies: one had to be praetor before becoming a legionary legate, for example.[14] But there were also evident similarities between the senatorial *cursus* and the equestrian career structure, which became more pronounced over the course of the principate. Augustus instituted fixed salaries for senatorial governors – a marked departure from the Republic, which reinforced the subservience and dependence of legates and proconsuls on the *princeps*.[15] He likewise introduced salaries for equestrian officials, thus making the two aristocratic *ordines* equivalent in terms of the basic principle that office-holding was rewarded with a salary. We do not know how much *equites* were paid during Augustus' reign.[16] According to Suetonius, the emperor Claudius granted consular decorations to 'ducenarian procurators' (*procuratoribus ducenariis*), which reveals that at least some equestrian officials were paid 200,000 sesterces per year in the mid-first century AD.[17]

---

[12] Tac. *Agr.* 4.1. The term is used by Tacitus to describe Agricola's grandfathers who both held procuratorships, and thus formed part of this *equestris nobilitas*. The meaning is widely acknowledged (Mommsen 1887–8: III.1, 363; Woodman with Kraus 2014: 96; Duncan-Jones 2016: 91).

[13] Talbert 1984: 16–27.

[14] A. R. Birley 1981: 4–35 remains the best concise overview of the senatorial career in the principate.

[15] Dio 53.15.4–5.

[16] Pflaum 1950: 29–30 argues for the introduction of the salary grades under Augustus. For criticism of this view, preferring to emphasise gradual change, see Millar 1963b; Brunt 1983: 44–5; Talbert 1996: 341; Duncan-Jones 2006: 196–7. For the evolution of the *cursus* in the Julio-Claudian period, see Demougin 1988: 732–9.

[17] Suet. *Claud.* 24.1.

By the second century AD most equestrian procuratorships were cate-
gorised into three grades, according to salary levels: 60,000 sesterces (*sexagenarius*), 100,000 sesterces (*centenarius*), or 200,000 sesterces
(*ducenarius*). In the Antonine period the salaries of some senior court
officials, such as the *a rationibus*, the imperial financial officer, were raised
to 300,000 sesterces per annum (*trecenarius*).[18] Therefore, it is evident that
an equestrian career path did evolve in such a way that there was a clear
hierarchical relationship between the different salary grades that emulated
the senatorial *cursus honorum*, even if it did not precisely replicate it.[19]
The total number of attested equestrian posts increased from fewer than 30
in the reign of Augustus to more than 180 in the mid-third century AD.[20]
They included positions with military responsibilities, such as the prefectures of the fleets, praesidial procuratorships (which entailed command of
auxiliary troops) and the prefectures of the Egypt and the praetorian guard.
These posts could be held along with a wide range of financial and administrative procuratorships, involving duties such as tax collection, management of imperial estates or archives, and supervising water and grain
supplies. The four great prefectures – the praetorian guard, Egypt, the
annona and the *vigiles* – the origins of which we discussed in Chapter 4,
came to sit at the apex of the equestrian career. In the Julio-Claudian period
the prefect of Egypt was the most senior of these posts, and it was only
under the Flavians that it was relegated to second place behind the praetorian prefect.[21] From the end of the first century AD a defined order of
seniority among the great prefectures emerged, with the *praefectus vigilum*
as the most junior post, followed by the *praefectus annonae, praefectus
Aegypti* and *praefectus praetorio*. The combination of positions in the army
and administration enabled equestrians to serve the state *domi militiaeque*,
just like their senatorial counterparts, and thus form a distinct *equestris
nobilitas*.

The expansion of the number of positions available to equestrians, and
the creation of the procuratorial career path, resulted from a series of
decisions made by the imperial administration over the course of the first
two centuries AD. The provincial and patrimonial procurators, who

---

[18] Pflaum 1950: 74, 81, 1974: 43–4, 55–6. Alföldy 1981: 188 argues that that the prefect of Egypt
and the praetorian prefect would have been the equivalent of the *praefectus aerarii Saturni* in
the senatorial *cursus* and thus received a salary 500,000 sesterces.

[19] Millar 1963b: 196; Eck 2000: 259.

[20] Pflaum 1950: 105. The overall increase is still noticeable, even bearing in mind the
methodological point that the first attestation of a post at a particular date does not mean that it
was created then (Brunt 1983: 68–9).

[21] Demougin 1988: 733; Absil 1997: 34–6; Sablayrolles 1999: 368–75.

administered the finances in the provinces, were the bedrock upon which the equestrian *cursus* was built.[22] Roman provincial administration gradually grew more complex by creating new procuratorships to handle duties that had previously been within the purview of these officials, as Eck has demonstrated in his masterful survey of this topic.[23] The collection of the 5 per cent inheritance tax (*vicesima hereditatium*) is an excellent example of these changes. Equestrian procurators in charge of the *vicesima hereditatium* were introduced into Italy by the mid-first century AD.[24] However, the collection of the inheritance tax in the provinces at this time was entrusted to freedmen, as shown by the case of Ti. Claudius Aug. lib. Saturninus, who was *procurator vicesimae hereditatium* in Achaea.[25] Equestrian procurators for the inheritance tax outside Italy are only attested in the second and third centuries AD, when they assumed responsibilities for groups of provinces, such as Baetica and Lusitania, or throughout Asia, Lycia, Pamphylia, Phrygia, Galatia and the Cyclades.[26] These new trans-provincial equestrian procurators were installed above freedmen in the administrative hierarchy.[27] The creation of these officials helped to spread the responsibilities initially invested in the provincial or patrimonial procurator to another post-holder.[28] This process was gradual. For example, it might have been expected that the appointment of equestrian procurators for the *vicesima hereditatium* would have been accompanied by the introduction of comparable officials for the 5 per cent tax on the manumission of slaves (*vicesima libertatis*). But although equestrian procurators for the *vicesima libertatis* are attested in Italy in the first century AD, they are not found in the provinces before the Severan period.[29] This indicates that the Roman state was initially content to entrust the main business of collecting this tax to the *publicani*, but later introduced greater imperial oversight of the process.[30]

Two significant developments in the expansion of the financial administration in the second and third centuries AD created new opportunities for equestrians in government. The first was Hadrian's creation of the post

---

[22] See Chapter 4 for full discussion.

[23] Eck 2000: 238–65. See also Burton 1993: 18–19; Eich 2015: 107–8.

[24] Eck 1979a: 129–32, suggesting AD 58 as a suitable date to coincide with Nero's reforms of the *publicani*.

[25] *CIL* VI 8443 = *ILS* 1546. This is a famous case, noted by Millar 1963b: 196; Brunt 1983: 72; Eck 2000: 242.

[26] Pflaum 1950: 61–2. See the *fasti* in Pflaum 1961: 1048–9, 1054, 1056, 1074, 1077, 1081, 1083, 1086, 1097, with *addenda* in Pflaum 1982: 118, 128, 131.

[27] The process of 'superposition' is discussed by Weaver 1972: 267–81.   [28] Eck 2000: 247–8.

[29] Eck 1979a: 116–18; Brunt 1990c: 404.   [30] Brunt 1990c: 402–6.

of *advocatus fisci*, whose duty it was to represent the interests of the imperial treasury in legal matters.[31] *Advocati fisci* are attested throughout the Roman world by the beginning of the third century AD. They could either assume responsibility for small areas, such as imperial estates, or entire provinces and regions, such as Rome, the Maritime Alps, Spain, Gaul, Gallia Narbonensis, Asia, Phrygia or Egypt.[32] In the early third century a new official is attested at the imperial court itself, the position of *advocatus fisci sacri auditori*, with a high salary of 200,000 sesterces.[33] By the middle of the third century AD A. Vitellius Felix Honoratus could make his career by serving as *advocatus fisci* for several different jurisdictions: the *cursus publicus* in Italy and Noricum, the imperial estates spread through Numidia, and the imperial *patrimonium* in the region of Carthage.[34]

The second major development was the creation of an entirely new office of financial administration in the Antonine period, with the separation of the *patrimonium* (inherited imperial property) and the *ratio privata* (the emperor's private estates).[35] The head of the office at Rome, the *procurator rationis privatae*, was paid 300,000 sesterces a year, reflecting his importance.[36] In the reign of Septimius Severus the department of the *ratio privata* was reorganized as the *res privata*, a new office for imperial estates.[37] New regional procurators of the *res privata* are attested with responsibility for all of Italy, or for specific Italian regions.[38] They also appear in provinces and trans-provincial regions, such as for Gallia Belgica and the two Germanies; Asia, Phrygia, and Caria; Bithynia, Pontus and Paphlagonia; Cilicia; Tripolitania; Mauretania Caesariensis; and Mesopotamia.[39] This new layer of imperial administration was prompted by Severus' confiscation of property from his defeated enemies in the aftermath of the civil wars of the 190s.[40] These examples attest to the expansion and diversification of the financial administration. As new departments (*officia*) and new posts were created, the number of positions

---

[31]   *HA Hadr.* 20.6; Millar 1963a: 31–3, 1977: 287; Brunt 1983: 73–4.

[32]   Pflaum 1961: 1033, 1046–7, 1052, 1056, 1073, 1074, 1087, 1095.

[33]   *AE* 1932, 34; Pflaum 1960: 613–20 (no. 231). An inscription recording the career of M. Cassius Cornasidius Sabinus shows that this was a ducenarian post (*AE* 1960, 257).

[34]   *CIL* VIII 26582 = *ILS* 9018; Pflaum 1960: 936–40 (no. 353).

[35]   Nesselhauf 1964: 75–8; Eck 2000: 246–7. See the helpful collection of evidence in Millar 1977: 625–30.

[36]   *CIL* X 6569 = *ILS* 478.

[37]   Lo Cascio 2000: 139–47; Lo Cascio 2005: 150–2; Lo Cascio 2015: 66–7. Cf. *HA Sev.* 12.4.

[38]   Pflaum 1961: 1036, 1038, 1040; Pflaum 1982: 110.

[39]   Pflaum 1961: 1057, 1073, 1077, 1079, 1095, 1097, 1982: 130.

[40]   Nesselhauf 1964: 85–91; Millar 1977: 171–2; Lo Cascio 2005: 150–2.

requiring equestrians increased, and each of these was ranked in the developing career hierarchy depending on the pay received by the officials.

The management of Rome's water supply provides an excellent illustration of this evolution occurring in non-financial administration. Augustus had initially entrusted the oversight of Rome's water supply to his friend Agrippa on an ad hoc basis, a strategy that was typical of the early principate. After Agrippa's death the position of *curator aquarum* was created, which was held by senators of consular rank.[41] According to Sex. Iulius Frontinus, who was *curator aquarum* under Nerva and the early years of Trajan, Claudius instituted the subordinate post of *procurator aquarum*.[42] Throughout the first century AD these procurators were always freedmen, a situation that continued up to Frontinus' own time. It was once thought, on the basis of the evidence of inscribed water pipes (called *fistulae*), that equestrian procurators replaced the freedmen in the reign of Trajan.[43] However, the officials attested on these pipes are probably not *procuratores aquarum*, but *procuratores patrimonii* or other procurators involved in building works that required a water supply.[44] The first equestrians securely attested with the title of *procurator aquarum* are both of Severan date: Sex. Varius Marcellus and L. Lucilius Pansa Priscilianus.[45] A third equestrian *procurator aquarum*, M. Flavius Marcianus Ilisus, cannot be dated precisely, but may also be Severan.[46] The epitaph of Sex. Varius Marcellus lists the procuratorship as *centenarius*, providing confirmation of its relatively high status in the Severan period. But this grading should not be applied retrospectively.[47] The epigraphic evidence therefore suggests that the equestrian *procurator aquarum* was not instituted by Trajan, but was probably a creation of the Severans.[48] Septimius Severus reorganised the administration of the senatorial curator's office, so that he now became *curator aquarum item et ad fraudes Miniciae* ('the administrator of the water supply and preventer of

---

[41] Bruun 1991: 140–52; Peachin 2004: 102–9.
[42] Frontin. *Aq.* 105.1–2; R. H. Rodgers 2004: 285–7. Only one freedman is specifically attested with the full title of *procurator aquarum* in the first century, Ti. Claudius Aug. lib. Bucolas (*CIL* XI 3612 = *ILS* 1567).
[43] Pflaum 1950: 55; Brunt 1983: 70–1.
[44] Bruun 1991: 263–71, 1999: 32–4, 2005: 14–15, 2006: 102–5.
[45] Marcellus: *CIL* X 6569 = *ILS* 478; Pflaum 1960: 638–42 (no. 237). Priscilianus: *AE* 1947, 89; *I. Eph.* 696A, I and II; Pflaum 1960: 672–77 (no. 249).
[46] *CIL* XIV 4451; Pflaum 1960: 551–2 (no. 206). After serving as *procurator aquarum*, Ilisus was *procurator monetae* of more than one Augustus. This could refer to Marcus Aurelius and Lucius Verus, Marcus Aurelius and Commodus, or Septimius Severus and Caracalla. He could therefore be of Antonine or Severan date (see Bruun 1991: 225–6, favouring the latter option).
[47] Bruun 1991: 236.   [48] Bruun 1991: 267–71; R. Taylor 2010: 208.

fraud of the Minicia').[49] This meant that the senatorial official was now responsible both for the water supply of Rome and for the distribution of grain at the *porticus Miniciae*.[50] The distributions had previously been in the purview of the senatorial *praefectus frumenti dandi*, who was assisted by an equestrian *procurator Augusti ad Miniciam* (first attested in the Trajanic period).[51] Septimius Severus placed the two offices, and their equestrian procurators, under the supervision of one consular *curator* as part of a wide-ranging administrative reform.[52] The evolution of the administration of the water supply in Rome therefore exhibits developments similar to the financial management of the provinces. In both cases we see how new equestrian officials were appointed above existing freedmen, and we can observe a gradual trend towards the centralisation of authority in specific imperial departments.

The *officia palatina*, the administrative and financial positions at the imperial court, eventually ranked as the most prestigious and influential equestrian posts behind the great prefectures. However, they only assumed this place in the second century AD, after the posts had been transferred from freedmen to *equites*. At the beginning of the principate the freedmen and slaves in Augustus' household staff took on responsibilities for administrative tasks.[53] Augustus had offered the equestrian poet Horace a position in charge of his private correspondence, but he declined.[54] The departments of the *a rationibus*, who managed the imperial finances, and the *ab epistulis*, in charge of correspondence, are first attested under Tiberius.[55] These officials, together with the *a studiis*, the head of the imperial archives, and the *a libellis*, the secretary of petitions, bloom into prominence in the reign of Claudius, on account of the strong association between the emperor and his freedmen in the literary sources.[56] We should be wary of placing undue emphasis on this period, since the influence of slaves and freedmen had begun under Claudius' predecessors, and would continue after his death.[57] These freedmen were replaced by *equites* in an inconsistent manner. Indeed, there are cases of equestrians being employed

---

[49] The full title is attested on an inscription recording the offices of its first (presumed) holder, L. Valerius Messalla Helvidius Thrasea Priscus (*AE* 1998, 280).

[50] As persuasively argued by R. Taylor 2010.

[51] R. Taylor 2010: 208; *CIL* XI 5669 = *ILS* 2728; Pflaum 1960: 183–4 (no. 87).

[52] R. Taylor 2010: 211–16.   [53] Millar 1977: 69–74.

[54] Suet. *De Poet. Vit. Hor.* ll. 18–25 (ed. Rostagni); Lindsay 1994: 459.

[55] *CIL* VI 8409c (*a rationibus*), 4249 (*ab epistulis*).

[56] Millar 1966: 14–16; Suet. *Claud.* 28; Tac. *Ann.* 11.29.1–2; Dio 60.30.6b. Polybius may also have been *a libellis* at some stage (see Sen. *Dial.* 11.6.5).

[57] Edmondson 1992: 192.

in palatine offices during the Julio-Claudian period.[58] Both *equites* and freedmen held the post of *a voluptatibus*, the head of imperial entertainment, until the early second century AD.[59] Claudius himself employed equestrian secretaries alongside his more notorious freedmen. These included C. Stertinius Xenophon, who was in charge of Greek *apokrimata* (legal decisions) and Ti. Claudius Balbillus, responsible for embassies and Greek rescripts.[60] Julius Secundus, a noted rhetorician who was either an *eques* or a senator, acted as the secretary *ab epistulis* (ἐπὶ τῶν ἐπιστολῶν) to Otho during his short reign.[61]

The reign of Vitellius is usually cited as a turning point in the service of *equites* within the imperial household. Tacitus states that as soon as Vitellius was proclaimed emperor in Germany, 'he distributed the imperial functions, which were usually performed by freedmen, among *equites Romani*' (*ministeria principatus per libertos agi solita in equites Romanos disponit*).[62] This seems to refer to *equites* who were in Vitellius' entourage in Germany. One such man was Sex. Caesius Propertianus, *tribunus* of the *legio IV Macedonica*, who became 'procurator of the emperor, in charge of the *patrimonium*, inheritances, and petitions' (*proc(uratori) imp(eratoris)* | *a patrim(onio) et heredit(atibus)* | *et a li[b]ell(is)*).[63] But this did not prompt any full-scale change in the imperial household, since Vitellius relied on freedmen in other departments. The same inconsistency can be seen in the position of *a rationibus*. Vespasian elevated his financial secretary, Ti. Iulius Aug. lib., into the equestrian order, but Iulius' successors in this post were freedmen.[64] According to Suetonius, it was Domitian who 'shared some of the greatest offices between freedmen and *equites Romani*' (*quaedam ex maximis officiis inter libertinos equitesque R. communicavit*).[65] This has been interpreted to mean that equestrians and freedmen worked in tandem in the same imperial bureaux, with the

---

[58] Millar 1977: 85–6; Winterling 1999: 111.

[59] Suet. *Tib.* 42.2. On this office and its staff, see Lindsay 1995: 40; Weaver 1972: 253, 1980: 147–8. For the freedmen, see *CIL* XIV 2932 = *ILS* 1569 (Paean Aug. lib); *AE* 1972, 574 = *SEG* 30, 1308 (Ti. Claudius Aug. lib. Classicus).

[60] Xenophon: *SIG*³ 804. Balbillus: *AE* 1924, 78. For their purviews, see Millar 1977: 86, 226, 242–3.

[61] Plut. *Otho* 9.2. His rank is unknown. C. P. Jones 1967: 283–4 suggests that he could have been an *eques* or a senator. For *eques*, see Pflaum 1960: 90; Millar 1977: 88; Lindsay 1994: 457.

[62] Tac. *Hist.* 1.58.1. Cf. Millar 1977: 88–9, who translates *solita* as 'continuously'.

[63] *CIL* XI 5028 = *ILS* 1447; Pflaum 1960: 88–90 (no. 37); Millar 1977: 88–9; Demougin 1992a: 610–11. Freedmen in the post of *a libellis* can be found in the Julio-Claudian period (Weaver 1972: 260–1).

[64] See Weaver 1972: 282–94; Stat. *Silv.* 3.3.143. For his successors, see Weaver 1972: 260.

[65] Suet. *Dom.* 7.2.

freedmen as auxiliary heads.[66] This does not seem to have happened with any apparent systemisation: the freedman T. Flavius Aug. lib. Abascantus was in office as *ab epistulis* for a considerable proportion of Domitian's reign, and was only replaced – or joined by – an *eques*, Cn. Octavius Titinius Capito, shortly before the emperor's death.[67] Jones has plausibly suggested that Domitian became estranged from his freedmen officials over the course of his reign: for example, Entellus, his *a libellis*, was one of those who plotted against him.[68] The senior *officia palatina* were entrusted to equestrians at different times after the reign of Domitian.[69] Although the post of *ab epistulis* seems to have been held by *equites* from Capito onwards, the first equestrian *a cognitionibus* (head of the imperial law court) appears at the beginning of Commodus' reign, although freedmen are attested earlier.[70] The office of the *a memoria*, created some time in the first century AD, was likewise headed by freedmen until the Severan period.[71] In all cases of ministries shared between freedmen and *equites*, the equestrian was manifestly the senior partner, as they formed part of the imperial *consilium*.[72] The senior palatine officials ranked as ducenarian procurators, until they were promoted to trecenarian status, with a salary of 300,000 sesterces per year, in the Severan period.[73]

The Roman administrative system expanded through the creation of deputy or junior procuratorships, establishing a new 'sub-structure' to support the pre-existing officials, and creating new posts for *equites*.[74] The *a rationibus* had acquired a deputy, the *procurator summarum rationum* (procurator of the central finances), by the Antonine period. The creation of the *ratio privata* (later the *res privata*) led to the appointment of the *procurator rationis privatae* to administer this department under the overall authority of the *a rationibus*.[75] This practice of appointing equestrian deputies meant that they replaced the freedmen auxiliary heads of imperial departments.[76] The result of this is that several equestrians are attested in the same bureau, but at a range of different salary

---

[66] Weaver 1972: 259–61, 1994: 357–8; Demougin 1994: 294–7; B. W. Jones 1996: 66.

[67] B. W. Jones 1992: 63, 1996: 66. For Capito, see Pflaum 1960: 143–145 (no. 60).

[68] B. W. Jones 1996: 66–7. Cf. B. W. Jones 1992: 177–9, arguing for a growth in equestrian power under Domitian.

[69] The *HA*'s statement that Hadrian was the first emperor to appoint *equites* as *ab epistulis* and *a libellis* is manifestly wrong (*HA Hadr.* 22.8; Benario 1980: 128).

[70] This is M. Aurelius Papirius Dionysius: Pflaum 1960: 472–6 (no. 181). For freedmen, see Weaver 1972: 261; Millar 1977: 106 n. 37.

[71] Weaver 1972: 264 n. 1; Peachin 1989: 183–4, 187–9. Unfortunately, as Peachin has shown, the exact duties of the *a memoria* during the principate remain uncertain.

[72] Eck 2000: 198–9, 202–3.   [73] Pflaum 1974: 34.   [74] Millar 1963b: 197–8.

[75] Pflaum 1961: 1019–20, 1982: 110.   [76] Weaver 1972: 265–6; Eck 2000: 250.

grades. In the Severan period P. Messius Saturninus served in the office of the *a studiis* at both *sexagenarius* and *centenarius* level.[77] The *a studiis* himself came to carry a new title, that of *magister a studiis* or *magister studiorum*, master of the archives, to distinguish him from his subordinates.[78] The *consiliarii*, judicial advisers on the imperial *consilium*, were also divided into salary grades.[79] M. Aurelius Papirius Dionysius was 'co-opted into the *consilium* at a salary of 60,000 sesterces' (*adsumpto in consilium ad HS LX m(ilia) n(ummum)*) before becoming a *centenarius consiliarius*.[80] The expansion of the department of the *praefectus annonae* can also be traced in some detail.[81] Under the emperor Claudius the office of *procurator annonae* at Ostia was created, replacing the senatorial *quaestor Ostiensis*.[82] A deputy of the *praefectus annonae*, called the *adiutor*, is first attested under the Flavians, and the post may initially have been held by both freedmen and *equites*.[83] By the reign of Marcus Aurelius the position had been upgraded to the grander-sounding *subpraefectus annonae urbis*, and was the exclusive preserve of *equites*.[84] The *praefectus vigilum* had acquired a *subpraefectus* by the early second century, and the praetorian prefect likewise received a new deputy official, the *a commentariis*, both of whom probably ranked as *centenarii*.[85]

The proliferation of the number of equestrian officials at different salary grades can also be found in the provinces.[86] This is most strikingly demonstrated by the *regio Hadrumentina*, an area of North Africa that formed part of the imperial property.[87] The inscribed account of the career of C. Postumius Saturninus Flavianus, *procurator centenarius* of the *regio Hadrumetina*, records that he 'also exercised the post of the *ducenarius* in the same region according to imperial command' (*fun[c]|to etiam partibus duce|nari(i) ex sacro praecepto | in eadem regione*).[88] This indicates that at least two procurators were assigned to this area by the mid-third

---

[77] *AE* 1932, 34; Pflaum 1960: 613–20 (no. 231). The same progression can be found in the mid-third-century career of M. Aurelius Hermogenes: *CIL* XIV 5340; Pflaum 1960: 935–6 (no. 352).

[78] See the *fasti* in Pflaum 1961: 1022–3.

[79] On the *consiliarii* as legal experts, see Eck 2006a: 73–5.   [80] *CIL* X 6662 = *ILS* 1455.

[81] Pflaum 1961: 1030–1; Pavis d'Esurac 1976: 89–97.

[82] Pavis d'Esurac 1976: 105–10; Rickman 1980: 222.

[83] Pavis d'Esurac 1976: 92–3; Rickman 1980: 221.

[84] Pflaum 1961: 1030–1; Pavis d'Esurac 1976: 89–97. For the possibility that the *praefectus annonae* exercised authority over the grain supply in the provinces, see the discussion of Eich 2005: 189–210.

[85] Pflaum 1961: 1030, 1032, 1982: 113–14.   [86] Pflaum 1960: 758–9.

[87] See Eich 2005: 292–3 for the organisation of these domains.

[88] *CIL* VIII 1174 = *ILS* 1440; *CIL* VIII 1175 (with slightly different wording); Pflaum 1960: 757–9 (no. 292 *bis*).

century AD.[89] The provinces themselves also acquired financial procurators at different salary grades. Hispania Citerior had two provincial procurators who ranked as *ducenarii*, one for Asturia and Callaecia, and one
for Tarraconensis. In the Severan period a *procurator centenarius* is
attested, suggesting that another level of administration had been
instituted.[90] The proconsular province of Asia had multiple procurators,
each of whom either supervised different regions or had different responsibilities. When the workers on an imperial estate in Lydia complained
about their treatment at the hands of soldiers, they approached the procurator of the estate, then the *procurator rationis privatae*, and finally the
provincial procurator.[91] From the early second century AD the region of
Phrygia, though still part of the proconsular province of Asia, had its own
procurator who conducted hearings on financial matters, and its own
advocatus fisci.[92] These offices attest to the growing complexity of the
imperial administration in the provinces. The proliferation of posts provided a new range of opportunities for equestrians to serve the *res publica*.

The equestrian procuratorial career came to encompass military as well
as civilian positions, which enabled *equites* to excel *domi militiaeque* in the
same manner as senators. Around 85 per cent of equestrian procurators
had previously served in the *militiae equestres*.[93] After this initial military
experience there were further opportunities for *equites* to occupy more
senior army commands, though the integration of these into the procuratorial hierarchy was a gradual process. Augustus established two fleets
(*classes*) with permanent bases in Italy, one at Misenum on the Tyrrhenian
Sea, and one at Ravenna on the Adriatic, each of which was commanded by
a *praefectus*.[94] Initially, the fleet prefects were promoted straight from
equestrian officer commands in the *militiae*. This changed in the mid-
first century AD, when the emperor Claudius gave these prefects the
official status of procurator.[95] Although the word procurator was later
dropped from the prefects' official titles, this was a seminal move, which
set the stage for the integration of the fleet commands into the developing
equestrian *cursus*.[96] However, at this early stage the prefects were not

---

[89] Christol 2006a: 226–8, 231.
[90] For the ducenarian rank, see Pflaum 1961: 1047–8; *AE* 1998, 282 (Hispania Citerior and
Superior). For the official of centenarian rank, see *CIL* II.14.2 1093.
[91] Keil and von Premerstein 1914: no. 55 = Hauken 1998 no. 3 ll. 19–21. See Hauken 1998: 44–5
for discussion. Cf. Eich 2005: 302–3, suggesting that the lowest-level procurator could be
a freedman.
[92] Kantor 2013: 158–61.   [93] Brunt 1983: 48; Duncan-Jones 2016: 106.
[94] Suet. *Aug.* 49; Tac. *Ann.* 4.5; Starr 1941: 13–26.   [95] Starr 1941: 32; Kienast 1966: 29–32.
[96] Sherwin-White 1939: 21; Pflaum 1950: 47.

drawn exclusively from the equestrian order, with three freedmen commanders of the fleet at Misenum attested (Ti. Iulius Aug. lib. Optatus Pontianus,
Anicetus, and Moschus).[97] In the Flavian period the Misenum and Ravenna
fleets were distinguished with the title of *praetoria classis* (praetorian fleet).[98]
From this point onwards freedmen commanders ceased to be appointed, and
the equestrian prefects obtained the high status of *ducenarii*.[99] The prefecture
of the fleet at Misenum was the more senior post in the hierarchy: prefects
were always promoted from Ravenna to Misenum, and never vice versa.[100]
New provincial fleets were established over the course of the first century AD.
In the eastern provinces the Egyptian *classis*, based at Alexandria, is attested
under Caligula; the Pontic fleet was created by Nero when he integrated the
kingdom of Pontus into the empire in AD 64; and the Syrian fleet was
established by the Flavian period at the latest.[101] In Europe, Claudius was
probably responsible for creating the British and German *classes*, while the
fleets in Pannonia and Moesia are also in evidence during the first
century AD, though the exact date of their introduction is unknown.[102]
The *praefecti* of the British, German, Pontic and Syrian fleets were the most
senior, ranking as *centenarii*, whereas the Moesian, Pannonian and
Alexandrian fleet commanders were *sexagenarii*.[103] There was usually no
attempt to prepare future *praefecti* of the fleets by giving them previous
naval experience; instead, all *equites* were expected to possess the necessary
personal qualities to excel in military roles, as we saw in Chapter 6.[104]

Some equestrian procurators were appointed as provincial governors in
their own right in regions controlled by the *princeps*.[105] Modern scholars
generally refer to them as 'praesidial procurators', from the word *praeses*,
the Latin term for governor.[106] The establishment of provinces under the
control of these equestrian officials was a process that began
under Augustus, but extended far beyond his reign. In AD 6 senatorial
proconsuls of Sardinia were replaced by equestrian governors with military
authority, as a result of a series of attacks by brigands and pirates.[107] This
development represented the transfer of Sardinia into the personal

---

[97] Saddington 2007: 210. Pontianus: *CIL* X 6318 = *ILS* 2185. Anicetus: Tac. *Ann.* 14.3, 7–8, 62;
Dio 61.13.2. Moschus: Tac. *Hist.* 1.87.

[98] Pflaum 1950: 47.   [99] Starr 1941: 33; Kienast 1966: 36.

[100] Pflaum 1950: 248; Eck and Lieb 1993: 85–8.   [101] Saddington 2007: 215.

[102] Saddington 1990: 229–30, 2007: 214.   [103] Pflaum 1950: 47–8.

[104] The anonymous *eques* who commanded the British, German, Moesian and Pannonian fleets,
as well as being sub-prefect at Misenum, is a notable exception (*CIL* VI 1643; Pflaum 1960:
695–6 (no. 259)).

[105] Strabo 17.3.25.   [106] Faoro 2011: 165.

[107] Dio 55.28.1; R. J. A. Wilson 1996: 443. Faoro 2011: 41–9 draws attention to other serious
problems occurring in AD 6, including military revolts on the Danube, which meant that

authority of the *princeps*, with the equestrian *praefectus* acting as his representative.[108] There was flexibility in the system, with Sardinia becoming a senatorial province under Nero, then equestrian again under Vespasian.[109] It is important to note, however, that Sardinia was the only new equestrian province apart from Egypt created during the reigns of Augustus and Tiberius; these two provinces were very much exceptions at this early stage. Over time, however, further independent equestrian governorships were created, particularly in the years AD 37–68.[110] During the principate of Claudius the title of procurator became standard for all equestrian governors of independent provinces, with the exception of the prefect of Egypt.[111] Claudius created several new praesidial procuratorships, such as Thrace, Noricum, Mauretania Caesariensis and Mauretania Tingitana. For example, Thrace was acquired when the death of the client king Rhoemetalces resulted in internal instability which Rome could not allow to continue; Claudius pacified the region through his legate A. Didius Gallus, and it became a procuratorial province. The provincialisation of Thrace formed part of the larger rearrangement of the gubernatorial administration of Greece and the Balkans.[112]

Praesidial procuratorships sometimes evolved from the regional prefectures, as in the case of the Cottian Alps. Cottius I (M. Iulius Cottius), the king turned prefect of the region under Augustus, was succeeded as prefect by his son Donnus II. However, his grandson, Cottius II, was permitted to take the title of *rex* by the emperor Claudius.[113] This emphasises the anomalous place occupied by the Alpine Cottian dynasty, whose members were both governors and client kings.[114] The region became a province in the reign of Nero, following the death of Cottius II.[115] A similar process happened in Judaea, a regional equestrian prefecture from late in Augustus'

---

military security was a priority, and the fact that Sardinia was a grain-producing province needed to supply the city of Rome.

[108] The governor's title initially seems to have been *pro legato* ('in place of a legate') under Augustus (*Eph. Ep.* VIII 782 = *ILS* 105), which indicates it was a provisional appointment (Faoro 2011: 66–9). The title was later standardised as *procurator et praefectus* (A. H. M. Jones 1960: 120; Brunt 1983: 56–7; Faoro 2011: 69–70).

[109] R. J. A. Wilson 1996: 443–5.   [110] Faoro 2011: 84–5, 155–6.

[111] Bowman 1996b: 346; Levick 1990: 54.   [112] Levick 1990: 186; Osgood 2011: 122–4.

[113] Letta 1976 reconstructs the lineage of the Cottian dynasty.

[114] Roncaglia 2013: 357–8; Cornwell 2015: 52–3, 66–7. Note also the case of King Herod of Judaea, who was given the title of procurator of Syria by Augustus in 20 BC, according to Josephus (*BJ* 1.399). Unlike Cottius I, Herod was still king while he held the title of procurator, which appears to be an honorific denoting his status as Augustus' personal representative (see the discussion of Barrett 2009).

[115] Suet. *Nero* 18.2.

principate, which was gradually restored to the client king Herod Agrippa by Caligula and Claudius. However, after Herod's death Judaea became a prefecture again.[116] Finally, the prefecture of Commagene was created by Tiberius, but became a client kingdom again under Caligula, before being firmly integrated into the senatorial province of Syria under Vespasian.[117] As new praesidial procuratorships were created, they fitted into the evolving equestrian *cursus* at one of two grades: some ranked as centenarian positions (the Alpine regions, Judaea and Epirus), while the more senior governorships were ducenarian (Cappadocia, Thrace, Noricum, Raetia, Sardinia and the two Mauretanias).[118] However, it is important to note that this list gives a rather artificial impression, since these provinces were not all simultaneously in the purview of *equites*. Indeed, Cappadocia, Judaea, Thrace, Raetia and Noricum passed into senatorial control over the course of the first and second centuries AD.

The prefect of Egypt and all equestrian praesidial procurators possessed the *ius gladii*, the right to judge Roman citizens and sentence them to death, which they shared with senatorial proconsuls and legates.[119] Praesidial procurators had responsibility for financial administration, as well as other areas of provincial management such as the upkeep of the *cursus publicus*, the construction of new fortifications and repairs to existing ones, infrastructure such as aqueducts, and negotiations with foreign tribes.[120] They were also military commanders, taking charge of the auxiliary forces stationed in their provinces.[121] No equestrians were appointed to govern regions in which legions commanded by senatorial legates were stationed.[122] Legions were quartered in Egypt, but in order to maintain traditional status hierarchies, these were exceptionally commanded by equestrian prefects rather than by senators.[123] The appointment of the equestrian governors in Egypt and Sardinia thus initially represented the delegation of Augustus' personal authority to equestrian officials, but, as with the financial procurators, they soon became to all intents and purposes officials of the Roman state. They operated no differently from senatorial governors.

---

[116] Levick 1990: 196–7; Osgood 2011: 119–22.   [117] Faoro 2011: 142.

[118] Magioncalda 1999: 391; Faoro 2011: 210–12.

[119] *Dig.* 1.18.6.8 (Ulpian); Garnsey 1968: 51–5; Eck 1988: 112–14; Piso 1999: 326; Eich 2005: 153. Cf. Pflaum 1950: 119–20, 1974: 50–1, who suggested that it did not become standard practice until the Severan period. Liebs 1981 argued for gradual extension of these powers during the principate.

[120] Eck 1988. *CIL* III 6123 = *ILS* 231 (*cursus publicus*); *CIL* VIII 20816 = *ILS* 396 (fortifications); *CIL* VIII 2728 = *ILS* 5795 (aqueduct); *AE* 1953, 79 (negotiations).

[121] Eck 1988: 111–12; Bowman 1996b: 351–2; Faoro 2011: 166.   [122] Eck 2000: 272–3.

[123] M. P. Speidel 1982.

The cumulative force of this evidence demonstrates the noticeable similarities in the ways in which equestrians and senators were employed in the monarchical *res publica*. First of all, both *equites* and senators who held state posts received salaries from the reign of Augustus onwards. This did not change the inherent status differential between the two *ordines*, which was rigorously maintained in the form of honours and titles, and senatorial salaries certainly rose to a higher level than those paid to *equites*.[124] But the basic principle of payment for services rendered to the state was a great leveller in and of itself.[125] The second similarity is the career structure itself. The senatorial *cursus honorum* was a carefully regulated hierarchy in which eligibility for imperial positions depended on holding the appropriate magistracies, and their salaries increased as one climbed the *cursus*.[126] Equestrians did not stand for magistracies, but their *cursus* was likewise regulated by salary grades, rising from *sexagenarius* to *trecenarius*. As we have seen, this equestrian administrative hierarchy evolved over time: usually the most senior posts were created first, with the 'sub-structure' of more junior roles instituted over time. The fundamental hierarchy became clear by the second century AD, especially after the transfer of many secretarial offices in the *officia palatina* from freedmen to *equites*. The fact that the equestrian career structure only evolved over time does not mean that it was an unintentional process. This can be observed by the manner in which Claudius made procurator the standard title for equestrian governors, fleet prefects and administrative officials alike; the title showed that, as his personal representatives, they all possessed the same authority. The imperial administration likewise took an active decision to create a hierarchical series of salary grades for equestrian officials. When new posts were created in the second and third centuries AD, such as the *fisci advocatus sacri auditori* or the *subpraefectus annonae urbis*, the different levels of *consiliarii* at court, and the range of additional procuratorships in the provinces, they were assessed and assigned to relevant salary grades.

---

[124] Duncan-Jones 1994: 38. We know that the consular proconsuls of Asia and Africa received 1 million sesterces in the third century AD (Dio 78(77).22.5).

[125] For the need to preserve the essential difference in status between the two *ordines*, see Tac. *Ann.* 2.33.3; Suet. *Vesp.* 9.2.

[126] A. R. Birley 1981: 4–35; Alföldy 1981: 183–7. The evidence for precise salaries is limited, but there is some available information, such as the figure for the pronconsulship of Asia. Dio's Maecenas recommended that the *praefectus urbi* should be paid an unspecified salary (Dio 52.21.7). We also know that Salvius Iulianus received double the usual salary as quaestor (*CIL* VIII 24094 = *ILS* 8973), although we do not have the precise figure.

The process is very much comparable to the developing senatorial *cursus* and the connection of posts in the imperial service to specific magistracies. In the senatorial career it was the praetorship that represented the crucial level, as it gave senators access not only to the posts of legionary legate and provincial governor, but also to a range of other offices, such as curator of roads and prefects of the treasuries. The consulship likewise offered senators the opportunity to hold senior governorships and a range of additional service opportunities, especially curatorships in Rome itself.[127] When new senatorial positions or governorships were created, they were assigned to either the praetorian or consular level. Although they bore the names of the magistracies to which they were attached, this was a holdover from the Republican system, as they were in effect pay grades, with praetorian and consular posts carrying different salaries.[128] Since ducenarian procurators could be adlected to praetorian rank to hold the post of *legatus legionis*, Alföldy suggested that these legionary commanders were paid at least 200,000 sesterces in the Antonine period, and possibly more.[129] Similar analysis of promotions from equestrian to senatorial posts makes it likely that praetorian governors and the treasury prefects were paid 500,000 sesterces per annum.[130] This means that there were salary grades for senators even within the praetorian level itself, attesting to the complexity of the senatorial hierarchy as it developed over the course of the principate.[131] Therefore, there is no escaping these fundamental similarities between the senatorial and equestrian career structures in the monarchical *res publica*, which represented a dramatic change for members of both *ordines* from the workings of government in the last three centuries BC.

The third and final similarity is that both senators and *equites* were eligible to hold a range of civilian and military positions. The majority of

---

[127] Hopkins and Burton 1983: 149, 155–6; Talbert 1984: 20. For details, see A. R. Birley 1981: 15–24 (praetorian career), 26–32 (consular career).

[128] Dio's Maecenas recommended that the new *princeps* introduce salaries for provincial appointments at different levels depending on the importance of the office (Dio 52.23.1). Based on this, Duncan-Jones 2016: 25, 33, suggests that senatorial positions in Rome were not paid. However, I would follow Alföldy 1981: 186–9 in allocating salaries to all senatorial posts. It is true that senators who served on the *consilium* did not receive salaries, while the equestrian *consiliarii* were paid, as Duncan-Jones 2016: 25 points out. But these senatorial advisers did not hold a fixed position, whereas the *consilarii* were paid expert advisers in the imperial administration.

[129] Alföldy 1981: 187.   [130] Alföldy 1981: 188; Duncan-Jones 1994: 38.

[131] The clear hierarchical elements within the praetorian career, with some posts regularly allocated to more senior ex-praetors, have long been noted by scholars (Eck 1974, 2002a: 138–43; A. R. Birley 2005: 6–7).

equestrian procurators had already served in the *militiae equestres*, and there were many additional posts that involved command over army units, such as the fleet prefectures, provincial governorships and the prefecture of the praetorian guard. Indeed, the essential responsibilities of provincial governors differed little regardless of whether the occupant was a senator or an equestrian, as *praesides* from both orders possessed the *ius gladii* and commanded troops in their provinces. This meant that members of both *ordines* could claim to serve the state *domi militiaeque* in a range of administrative and military capacities. This was a remarkable difference from the *res publica* of Cicero, who conceived of the roles of *equites* and senators in the Roman state as being separate and distinct, as we saw in Chapter 2. Of course, not all equestrians chose to embark on extensive careers under the emperors, and those who did constituted an elite group within the *ordo* at large, Tacitus' *equestris nobilitas*. The same point can be made about senators, as it was not compulsory to hold government or army posts, and many did not do so. This meant that the senators who did pursue long careers constituted their own elite: the 'power set', in the words of Hopkins and Burton.[132] They were not necessarily typical of the *ordo* as a whole.[133] Consequently, the administrative and military elite of both the *ordo equester* and the *ordo senatorius* began to take on the characteristics of an aristocracy of service, a change which had become especially apparent by the early third century AD.[134] Although patricians had significant advantages if they wished to occupy high government positions, the system as a whole limited the potential for the formation of a hereditary aristocracy that could pose a challenge to imperial power.[135] Such a development can be understood as the inevitable result of the monarchicalisation of the Roman *res publica*, as the emperors domesticated members of the senatorial order by restructuring their careers and making these elites dependent

---

[132] Hopkins and Burton 1983: 171–5.

[133] *Novi homines* had to take on military and provincial roles as a way of making a name for themselves (Alföldy 1969a: 240). Many patricians only held the Republican magistracies (Alföldy 1977: 37–40), though if they did seek other positions, they were clearly preferred (Duncan-Jones 2016: 8–21). For a number of acute observations about senatorial service, based on statistical analysis, see Duncan-Jones 2016: 19, 25–6, 34–5, 52–7. For senators who deliberately avoided advancement, see Hopkins and Burton 1983: 153–4, 166–9, 174; Talbert 1984: 23–7.

[134] See Hopkins and Burton 1983: 181–2 on the equestrian administrators a 'power set'. The third-century developments are explored in Chapter 11.

[135] For the success of patricians, see Duncan-Jones 2016: 12–18. On the lack of a hereditary aristocracy, see Hopkins and Burton 1983: 174 and *passim*. Challenges to the emperor's position generally came from senators in command of armies, which emphasises the importance of holding office.

on them for both their offices and the salaries that came with them.[136] While senators might thus be said to have had their independence curtailed in the monarchical *res publica*, the new system offered equestrians a vast range of new opportunities. They were certainly domesticated, but in a different manner to senators. If the Roman state had continued to operate along the same lines as under the Republic, there would have been limited opportunities for the *domi nobiles* of the provinces to be integrated into the government of the empire. This would potentially have isolated them from Rome and restricted their potential to progress into the senatorial order. The equestrian imperial service domesticated the provincial elites by offering them the opportunity to be a part of the *res publica* as a group bound together by service to the state and to the emperor himself.

Cultures of Service and Competition

The inscribed *cursus*, listing military and administrative posts and honours, represents the most striking manifestation of the equestrian career under the principate.[137] Through these epigraphic texts we can trace the ascent of individual *equites* as they passed from officer commands in the *militiae*, to procuratorships at a range of salary grades, and in some cases even to the great prefectures. There are very few *cursus* inscriptions for *equites* dated to the first century AD compared to the numbers in the second and third.[138] This section will argue that the gradual adoption of the *cursus*-style commemorative format by *equites* reflects the emergence of the concept of an equestrian administrative career that was analogous to the senatorial *cursus*. For those *equites* who did choose to devote their lives to the Roman state, this became an essential part of their public self-representation. All members of the senatorial order were entitled to the title of *clarissimus vir*. By the mid-second century AD a new range of equestrian statuses and titles (*egregius, perfectissimus,*

---

[136] As artfully described by Syme 1999: 1–6 (a work originally composed in the 1930s). See now Hopkins and Burton 1983: 120–2, 171; Bang 2011: 112–13; Bang and Turner 2015: 17–18.

[137] The point made by Eck 2009b about the term '*cursus* inscription' is well taken, since these careers were carved on a wide range of monuments. But it can be used as term of convenience, provided that one acknowledges the variety of contexts in which these texts are found. This section develops the introduction to the inscribed *cursus* in Chapter 6.

[138] The majority of our evidence for long careers comes from the Flavian period and beyond (Pflaum 1950: 215–16). There are more than 180 *equites* attested holding one official position in the Julio-Claudian period, but only 20 cases with two or more administrative posts on record (Demougin 1988: 714–21, 735–7).

eminentissimus) was introduced to honour *equites* who had held official posts, thus separating them from the *ordo equester* at large into a distinct service aristocracy. At the same time, the substantial corpus of equestrian *cursus* inscriptions should not mislead us into thinking that all members of the *ordo* desired a lifetime of service to the Roman empire. For many *equites* the honour of one or two positions was sufficient as way of demonstrating that they had received imperial favour. The full equestrian career was the ultimate expression of devotion to the imperial *res publica*, but it could only have been achieved by a very small proportion of *equites*. This further separated the service elite from the bulk of the *ordo* at large and emphasised their similarities with the senators who led comparable lives.

Equestrians began to record their official employment in the emperor's service in the Julio-Claudian period. The earliest examples tend to adopt a discursive format, recounting their precise duties in some detail, as opposed to the formulaic listing of official posts that later became standard. This can be seen in the account of the military and civilian occupations of L. Volusenus Clemens, which survives on an inscribed tablet from his home town of Sestinum in Umbria:

> To Lucius Volusenus Clemens, son of Lucius, of the tribe Clustumina, military tribune, prefect of cavalry, prefect of recruits in Gallia Na[rbonen]sis, and he also took [the census] in [Pann]on[ia], having been assigned the task by the deified Augustus. When he was sent by Tiberius Caesar Augustus to deliver justice in Egypt, he died in the province of Aquitania.[139]

Clemens' official career began with military commands, followed by a commission from Augustus to conduct the census in Pannonia. Tiberius then appointed him *iuridicus* of Alexandria in Egypt (*iuridicus Alexandreae*).[140] In the high empire, procurators responsible for taking the provincial census were usually of sexagenarian rank, while the *iuridicus*

---

[139] *CIL* XI 6011 = *ILS* 2691: *L(ucio) Voluseno | L(uci) f(ilio) Clu(stumina tribu) Clementi | trib(uno) mil(itum) praef(ecto) | equit(um) praef(ecto) tir(onum) | Gall(iae) Na[rbonen]]sis it[em in Pan] non[i]a [censum?] | accepit missus a | divo Aug(usto). hic cum | mitteretur a Ti(berio) Caes(are) Aug(usto) | in Aegypt(um) ad iur(is) dict(ionem) | decessit provinc(ia) | Aquitania*. The correct restoration of the second province in line 5 has been the subject of some debate. *CIL* presents *[Aquita]n[icae]*, which has the advantage of explaining why Volusenus was in the province when he died. On the other hand, the stone itself clearly shows the letter O, which is why Firpo 1985, following a suggestion by Mommsen noted in *CIL*, restored *[Pan]non[i]a*. The lacunose lines 5–7, which are not fully inscribed, may have been finished by being painted directly onto the stone (Cenerini 1989: 189–90; Donati 1989: 173). This practice is attested elsewhere in the empire (see M. P. Speidel 1991: 116).

[140] Pflaum 1960: 17–18 (no. 4).

was a much more senior post of ducenarian status.[141] It was also the case
that from the second century AD *equites* tended to hold at least one
centenarian procuratorship before advancing to the more senior
echelons.[142] The course of Clemens' employment confirms that there was
no firm hierarchy at this early stage, and that his career was solely determined by the emperor's decisions.[143] Moreover, rather than giving the
titles of individual posts, the inscription adopts a more discursive approach
to Clemens' career, which is most evident in the description of his commission as *iuridicus*. Although no dedicator is named, the initiative for the
erection of the monument in Clemens' honour probably came from the
community of Sestinum or members of his family, who were prominent
local notables.[144]

Grateful communities who valued their connection with prominent
equestrians often decided to erect a statue of the favoured individual,
inscribing their official government posts and honours on its base.
The level of detail in the inscription could vary, even when the same
individual was honoured within the same public space, as in the case of
the Julio-Claudian *eques* Ti. Claudius Balbillus, from Ephesus. The first
statue base, inscribed in Greek, was discovered in the north-east corner of
the agora there. It reads as follows:

[The *boule* and *demos* h]onoured [Ti. Claudi]us Balbillus, [the excellent] procurator of [the emperor on account of his] continuous reverence [towards the] goddess
and his benefaction [towards the cit]y.[145]

The emphasis is on Balbillus' devotion to Ephesus, since the text only
includes a brief mention of his procuratorship without further elaboration.
A much more detailed account of Balbillus' career was found on a statue
base in the west hall of the agora at Ephesus. The inscription, unfortunately
now very fragmentary, was composed in Latin:

[To Tiberius Claud]ius [Ba]lbillus, son of Tiberius Claudius [Thrasyll]us (?), of the
voting tribe Quirina [...] of the temples of the deified Augustus and ... of the
groves and [all] sacr[ed things wh]ich are in Alexan[dria and in all Aegypt]us and

---

[141] Pflaum 1960: 18.

[142] See the tables of procuratorial career patterns compiled by Saller 1982: 87–91.

[143] Cf. Pflaum 1960: 18, who suggests that Tiberius deviated from the established system in
promoting Clemens in this manner.

[144] For Clemens' two brothers, see *CIL* XI 6016 = *ILS* 5758. For the family and their descendants,
see Cenerini 1989: 189–93.

[145] *I.Eph.* 3041: [ἡ βουλὴ καὶ δῆμος ἐ]τείμησεν | [Τιβ. Κλαύδι]ον Βάλβιλλον | [τὸν κράτιστον]
ἐπίτροπον τοῦ | [Σεβαστοῦ διὰ τὴ]ν ἀδιάλειπτον | [αὐτοῦ εἴς τε τὴν] θεὸν εὐσέβειαν | [καὶ εἰς τήν
πόλι]ν εὐεργεσίαν.

in charge of the mu[s]eu[m] a[nd the Alexandrian] library and high [priest of] Alexandrian [Herm]es for [... years ...] and in charge of [Greek] embassies and res[ponses] of the deified Claudi[us] [Ca]esar Augustus a[nd military tribune of the le]gio XX and prae[fectus] fabrum of the deified Cla[udius and awarded decorations in the triu]m[ph by the deified] Claudius [... the crown and] untipped [spear and flag ...]¹⁴⁶

This second monument, whose dedicator is unfortunately unknown, provides a much more fulsome account of Balbillus' official employment. Even here, however, it is important to note that this is no formulaic *cursus*. All Balbillus' positions are laid out in great detail, and several honours are explicitly positioned as benefactions from the emperor Claudius himself.¹⁴⁷ The difference between the two texts shows that it was not inevitable that these monuments would include a full career. The decision whether to include a *cursus* depended on factors such as the size of the statue base and the space available, as well as the aims of the dedicator. The more detailed a text was, the greater the desire to impress the intended audience with the honorand's achievements in the service of the *res publica*.

The most important feature of the inscribed *cursus* was that it communicated the idea that an equestrian was a loyal servant of the emperor and the Roman state. This essential idea could be deployed for various purposes, such as expressing gratitude to the provincial procurator. We can see this in the case of L. Pupius Praesens, procurator of Galatia, who was honoured with a statue by the city of Iconium during his time in office. The Greek inscription on its base reads:

The people of the Claudiconians honoured L. Pupius Praesens, son of Lucius, of the voting tribe Sabatina, military tribune, prefect of the *ala II Picentiana*, procurator of Caesar with responsibility for the Tiber banks, procurator of Tiberius Claudius Caesar Augustus Germanicus and Nero Claudius Caesar Augustus Germanicus of the province of Galatia, their benefactor and founder.¹⁴⁸

---

¹⁴⁶ I.Eph. 3042: [Ti(berio) Claud]io Ti(beri) Claudi | [Thrasyll]i(?) f(ilio) Quir(ina tribu) | [Ba]lbillo | [...] aedium divi Aug(usti) et | [... e]t lucorum sacro|[rumque omnium qu]ae sunt Alexan| [driae et in tota Aegypt]o et supra mu|[s]eu[m] e[t ab Alexandri]na bybliothece | et archi[erei et ad Herm]en Alexan\dreon pe[r annos ...] et ad legati]ones et res[ponsa Graeca Ca]esaris Aug(usti) | divi Claud[i] e[t trib(uno) milit(um) le]g(ionis) XX et prae[f(ecto)] | fabr(um) divi Cla[udi et d(onis) d(onato) in triu]m[pho a divo] | Claudio [corona ... et hasta] | pura [et vexillo].

¹⁴⁷ See Pflaum 1950: 13–14 on the phenomenon of *equites* mentioning specific emperors in inscriptions during the first half of the first century AD.

¹⁴⁸ IGR III 263 = ILS 8848: [Κ]λαυδ[εικονιέ]||[ω]ν ὁ δῆμος ἐτεί|μησεν| [Λε]ύκιον Πούπιον Λευ||[κ]ίου υἱὸν Σαβατεῖνα | [Π]ραίσεντα, χειλίαρχον,| [ἔ]παρχον ἱππέων ἄλη[ς]||[Π]εικεντεινῆς, ἐπίτρο|[π]

The inscription emphasises imperial connections on a number of levels, from the honorific, emperor-loving name of the 'Claudiconians' themselves, to Praesens' own employment in the administration of at least two emperors.[149] The inscribed *cursus* is augmented by the honorific titles of 'benefactor and founder', which demonstrate that Prasens was not only an important imperial official, but also an integral figure in the public life of Iconium. The ability to connect and communicate both these ideas in one text explains why the inscribed *cursus* became a popular way of commemorating patrons of towns and cities throughout the empire.

This intention can be observed in a very uncomplicated inscription on a statue base from Vasio Vocontiorum in Gallia Narbonensis:

To the patron of the Vasienses Vocontii, Sextus Afranius Burrus, son of Sextus, of the voting tribe Voltinia, military tribune, procurator of the Augusta, procurator of Tiberius Caesar, procurator of the deified Claudius, praetorian prefect, (honoured with) consular decorations.[150]

The *cursus* demonstrates to anyone who could read it the significance of Burrus' patronage of Vasio Vocontiorum. His connections with Livia, and the emperors Tiberius and Claudius, are made abundantly clear, as is his rise through the levels of the administration to the praetorian prefecture. At same time, the rather laconic inscription may seem surprising to modern audiences, who are familiar with Burrus as a major figure in the Julio-Claudian court, as depicted in Tacitus' *Annals*. Although the inscription informs readers that Burrus was praetorian prefect and was awarded consular decorations, there is no real idea of the power he wielded in the Neronian administration. This is an essential part of the genre of the inscribed *cursus*. On the one hand, these texts celebrated and magnified the achievements of individual *equites*, reflecting their success in the competition for status, prestige and imperial favour. However, as the inscriptions became more formulaic and less discursive, they came to emphasise the similarities between all equestrian administrators, from the most important praetorian prefect to a junior procurator, regardless of whether they came from Asia Minor or Gaul. The inscribed *cursus*

ον Καίσαρος προς ὅ|[χ]θαις Τιβέρεως, ἐπίτρο|[π]ον Τιβερίου Κλαυδίου | [Κ]αίσαρος Σεβαστοῦ Γερ|[μ]ανικοῦ καὶ Νέρωνος | [Κ]λαυδίου Καίσαρος Σε[β]α[σ]|[τ]οῦ Γερμανικοῦ [Γ]αλα|[τ]ικῆς ἐ [π]αρχεία[ς, τ]ὸν ἑ|[αυ]τοῦ εὐεργέτην καὶ|[κ]τίστην.

[149] Praesens must have served under Caligula as well, but this is omitted in the text, perhaps deliberately so.

[150] *CIL* XII 5842 = *ILS* 1321: *Vasiens(es) Voc(ontiorum) | patrono | Sex(to) Afranio Sex(ti) f(ilio) | Volt(inia tribu) Burro | trib(uno) mil(itum) proc(uratori) Augus|tae proc(uratori) Ti(beri) Caesar(is) | proc(uratori) divi Claudi | praef(ecto) pra[e]tori(o) orna|me[nt]is consular(ibus).*

demonstrated that these *equites* were devoted to Rome and its emperors, thus symbolising their collective culture of imperial service.

The growing popularity of the *cursus* style of commemoration in the second century AD corresponds with the expansion of the number of posts available to *equites* in the city of Rome, the *officia palatina*, and in the provincial administration. This cannot be a coincidence, but surely reflects the emergence of a defined equestrian career hierarchy, divided into grades, and crowned by the praetorian prefecture. The inscribed career of T. Prifernius Paetus Memmius Apollinaris, from Reate in Italy, is a classic example of an equestrian *cursus* inscription of the early second century AD (Figure 7.1):

To Titus Prifernius Paetus Memmius Apollinaris, son of Publius, of the voting tribe Quirina, *IIIIvir quinquennalis* for delivering justice, master of the youth, prefect of the *cohors III Brevcorum*, tribune of the *legio X Gemina*, prefect of the *ala I Asturum*, awarded military decorations in the Dacian expedition by the Emperor Trajan – the untipped spear, the standard, and the mural crown – procurator of the province of Sicily, procurator of the province of Lusitania, procurator of the 5 per cent inheritance tax, procurator of the province of Thrace, procurator of the province of Noricum. Publius Memmius Apollinaris, son of Publius, of the voting tribe Quirina, (dedicated this) to his most dutiful father.[151]

Prifernus Paetus emerges from this text as the very model of an *eques Romanus* who was a member of the service elite. He was a municipal magistrate in Reate, a decorated officer in the *militiae equestres* and an imperial procurator, rising from centenarian level in Sicily to ducenarian rank from Lusitania onwards, eventually becoming praesidial procurator of both Thrace and Noricum. The inscribed *cursus* is the symbol of his service both to his home community and to the empire at large, *domi militiaeque*. Although the inscription does not state how long Paetus spent in each position, or how much time elapsed between them, we can estimate that his career probably spanned more than two decades.

---

[151] *CIL* IX 4753 = *ILS* 1350; Pflaum 1960: 166–7 (no. 71): *T(ito) Prifernio* | *P(ublii) f(ilio) Qui(rina tribu) Paeto* | *Memmio Apollinari* | *IIIIvir(o) iur(e) dic(undo) quinq(uennali) mag(istro) iu(venum)* | *praef(ecto) coh(ortis) III Breuc(orum) trib(uno) leg(ionis) X* | *Gem(inae) praef(ecto) alae I Asturum donis* | *donato exped(itione) Dac(ica) ab Imp(eratore)* | *Traiano hasta pura vexillo* | *corona murali proc(uratori) provinc(iae)* | *Sicil(iae) proc(uratori) provinc(iae) Lusitan(iae)* | *proc(uratori) XX her(editatium) proc(uratori) prov(inciae) Thrac(iae) proc(uratori) prov(inciae) Noricae* | *P(ublius) Memmius P(ublii) f(ilius) Qui(rina tribu)* | *Apollinaris* | *patri pi(i)ssimo.*

Figure 7.1: Inscribed *cursus* of T. Prifernius Paetus Memmius Apollinaris, Reate

Some equestrians who served for such a length of time were able to rise to the great prefectures, which was a source of great personal pride. Cn. Octavius Titinius Capito commemorated his ascent to *praefectus vigilum* by erecting two statues in the barracks of the *vigiles* in Rome. One was a statue of the emperor Trajan, who had appointed him to this position, while the other was of Volcan, the patron of the *vigiles*. Both statues had an account of Capito's career carved onto the base:

Gnaeus Octavius Titinius Capito, prefect of a cohort, military tribune, decorated with the untipped spear and the rampart crown, procurator *ab epistulis* and *a patrimonio, ab epistulis* for the second time, serving the deified Nerva, awarded *ornamenta praetoria* by that same emperor by a decree of the senate, *ab epistulis* for the third time, serving the Emperor Nerva Caesar Traianus Augustus Germanicus, *praefectus vigilum*, gave this as a gift to Volcan.[152]

The double dedication of the statues together with this inscription left the corps of the *vigiles* in no doubt of their new commander's (self)-importance.[153] The text reveals that the current emperor (Trajan), his deified predecessor and father (Nerva), and the senate had all formally testified to Capito's excellence in serving the *res publica*. Paetus and Capito were both officers in the *militiae equestres* before going on to hold administrative and financial procuratorships, demonstrating their adherence to the *domi militiaeque* ethos.

What was the relationship between service in the *militiae* and the procuratorial career? A substantial majority of procurators – some 85 per cent – had held army posts, as we have already noted. These were not exclusively in the *militiae*: one quarter of procurators were former centurions, who were distinguished from rank-and-file soldiers.[154] The equestrians who progressed from military commands to the procuratorial career represented an elite group within the *ordo*, since most officers did not subsequently obtain procuratorships.[155] Duncan-Jones' analysis of the place of the *militiae equestres* in the careers of procurators has yielded intriguing results.[156] He examined eighty-nine equestrian careers, dating from the reign of Trajan to the mid-third century AD. Equestrians who served in four or more posts in the *militiae equestres* had very successful careers, ending up with an average final procuratorial salary of 230,000 sesterces per year. These *equites* who held four *militiae* were distinguished from their compatriots who served in only three posts. The *equites* with three commands had final average procuratorial salaries of 147,000 sesterces per year, which put them in the same group as men who held one or two *militiae*. This means that the appointment to a fourth *militia* marked out an *eques* as a man to watch, with a promising future in the imperial

---

[152] *CIL* VI 798 = *ILS* 1448: *Cn(aeus) Octavius Titinius Capito | praef(ectus) cohortis trib(unus) milit(um) donat(us) | hasta pura corona vallari proc(urator) ab | epistulis et a patrimonio iterum ab | epistulis divi Nervae eodem auctore | ex s(enatus) c(onsulto) praetoriis ornamentis ab epistul(is) | tertio Imp(eratoris) Nervae Caesar(is) Traiani Aug(usti) Ger(manici) | praef(ectus) vigilum Volcano d(onum) d(edit)*. The other statue base is *CIL* VI 40489.
[153] Eck 2009b: 90–1.   [154] Dio 52.25.7.   [155] Duncan-Jones 2016: 89, 106, 112.
[156] Duncan-Jones 2016: 108–13, the results of which are summarised here.

service. Duncan-Jones discovered that the second most successful group in terms of the average final salary were those *equites* who had no command posts (189,000 sesterces per annum). These constituted twenty-one out of eighty-nine careers, almost a quarter of the sample size. This group included men such as Suetonius, who declined a post in the *militiae equestres*, but found that this was no bar to high office in the administration, for which his literary talents made him eminently suitable.[157] It might also be the case that *equites* of this ilk were able to hold more procuratorships because they had not devoted years of their life to military service, as Duncan-Jones suggested. Between these two extremes, the remaining careers are evenly matched, in the sense that it made little difference to an equestrian's final salary whether he served in one, two or three *militiae*. This analysis demonstrates that there was considerably flexibility in the way in which equestrians could undertake careers in imperial service. Some might hold one *militia* and one procuratorship, others might have no *militiae* but multiple administrative posts – but they all counted as members of the *equestris nobilitas*. There were two especially long-serving groups within this larger service elite identified by Duncan-Jones. The first was composed of those equestrians who occupied four *militiae* and an average of 5.4 procuratorial posts, well above the average of those with one to three *militiae* (which ranged from 3.19–3.45 procuratorships).[158] The second group were the *equites* with no *militiae*, and an average of 5.0 procuratorial positions. We can therefore confidently state that in the second and third centuries AD there was a small group of *equites* – the crème de la crème of the larger *ordo* – who had embraced the possibilities of imperial service.

The *cursus* inscriptions of the second and the third centuries AD, and particularly the use of salary grades in these texts, enable us to trace the emergence of this careerist mentality within the equestrian order. The monument of Domitius Marsianus, with which we began this chapter, is our first epigraphic attestation of the use of the term *ducenarius*. It does not appear in Marsianus' *cursus*, but in the inscribed version of Marcus Aurelius' letter, in which the emperor used the word as if it was a familiar status designation. Within a decade or two, however, *ducenarius* and other salary grades began to be included within the inscribed *cursus* itself,

---

[157] In this context, we should also draw attention to Greek intellectuals who were appointed to senior procuratorships and positions in the *officia palatina* without previous service. These men are discussed later in this chapter.

[158] The *equites* with four *militiae* who later entered the senate also had the most successful senatorial *cursus* (Duncan-Jones 2016: 114).

showing that they had made the transition from administrative terminology to an aspect of public self-representation for *equites*. The career of M. Valerius Maximianus, an equestrian from Poetovio in Pannonia, was inscribed in the 180s AD at Lambaesis in Numidia, where he was serving as governor following his promotion into the senate.[159] The relevant portion of the text notes that he was

... commander of the cavalry of Marcomanni, Naristae, and Quadi tasked with supressing the eastern rebellion, with the honour of centenarian status (*honor(e) centenariae dignitatis*), and then with an increased salary promoted to the procuratorship of Moesia Inferior.[160]

There are two points worth noting here. The first is that the salary grade is referred to as a *dignitas* – that is, an official status conferred by the emperor. The second is that salaries were not inflexible, and could be augmented at the emperor's command, as in the case of Maximianus' appointment to Moesia Inferior.[161] Nor is he the only recorded example of this phenomenon. M. Aurelius Mindius Matidianus Pollio, according to his *cursus* inscribed in Ephesus, was a '*praefectus vehiculorum* honoured by our lord emperor Commodus with the ducenarian salary' (ἐπίτρο|πον ὀχημάτων, τειμηθέντα παρὰ τοῦ κυρίου | αὐτοκράτ[[ορος Κομμόδου σ]] αλαρίῳ δου|κηναρίῳ).[162] Since the *praefectus vehiculorum*, who was in charge of the *cursus publicus* in Italy, was normally a centenarian post, Commodus was showing particular favour to Pollio. The fact that the salary grades were incorporated into inscriptions as far apart as Lambaesis and Ephesus shows that they were intelligible empire-wide as a status designation.

The salary designations could also be used in the inscribed *cursus* to chart an equestrian's rise through the different levels of imperial service.[163] We can observe this phenomenon in the case of M. Iunius Punicus, who paid for statues of Septimius Severus, Iulia Domna, Caracalla and Geta to be erected in the forum at Leptis Magna. Punicus is consistently described on all four statue bases as 'sexagenarian procurator of the province of Thrace, centenarian procurator of the Mercury region in Alexandria' (*proc(urator) sexagena|rius provinciae Thraciae cente|narius Alexan|*

---

[159] Pflaum 1960: 476–94 (no. 181 *bis*).

[160] *AE* 1956, 124: ... *praep(osito) equitib(us) gent(ium) Marcomannor(um) Narist(arum)* | *Quador(um) ad vindictam Orientalis motus pergentium honor(e) centenariae dig|nitatis aucto salario adeptus procurationem Moesiae inferioris* ...

[161] Pflaum 1960: 488.   [162] *I.Eph.* 627, 3056.

[163] See Demougin 2015: 66–7 on salary grades as an honour that distinguished an *eques* from his peers.

driae ad Mercur|ium).[164] These were two relatively unexceptional posts in the administration, but the precise use of the salary titles in all four texts suggests that Punicus wished to emphasise his own ascent through the grades of service, and the high salaries he received. The grades were also precisely delineated on the *cursus* of another Severan *eques,* L. Baebius Aurelius Iuncinus, inscribed on a statue base from Carales in Sardinia:[165]

To Lucius Baebius Aurelius Iuncinus, son of Lucius, of the voting tribe Galeria, procurator of inheritances, procurator of the emperor and prefect of the province of Sardinia, *praefectus vehiculorum* at a salary of 200,000 sesterces, *praefectus vehiculorum* at a salary of 100,000 sesterces, procurator for the grain supply at Ostia at a salary of 60,000 sesterces, procurator of the libraries at a salary of 60,000 sesterces, priest of *Laurens Lavinas.* Quintus Montanius Pollio, *decurio* in the cavalry, his equerry, (erected this) to the *vir egregius,* the most remarkable governor.[166]

The account of Baebius' career was inscribed in Sardinia, undoubtedly on the occasion of his transfer to the post of *procurator hereditatium* in Rome, which is represented as the summation of his ascent through the different levels of the equestrian service. Pflaum suggested that the two pay grades for the post of *praefectus vehiculorum* can be ascribed to the fact that he was in office when Septimius Severus upgraded the salary associated with the post.[167] This may be too schematic a conclusion, since we know that Matidianus Pollio also held the same position at a higher salary of 200,000 sesterces thanks to the favour of Commodus.[168] Moreover, in the reign of Marcus Aurelius, M. Aurelius Papirius Dionysius served as 'ducenarian prefect of the emperor for the *cursus publicus* for provision of supplies on the Flaminian Way' (*ducenario | praef(ecto) vehicul(orum) a copi(i)s Aug(usti) | per viam Flaminiam*).[169] This indicates that emperors had more flexibility than has been supposed in setting salary levels, which could be increased as a mark of imperial favour.[170] These monuments not

[164] *IRT* 392, see also 403, 422, 434. For the duties of the procurator of the Mercury region, involving the grain supply, see Pflaum 1960: 653–4 (no. 244); Rickman 1971: 304–6.

[165] Pflaum 1960: 678–83 (no. 251).

[166] *CIL* X 7580 = *ILS* 1358: *L(ucio) Ba[e]bio L(uci) f(ilio) [G]al(eria tribu) Aurelio | Iuncino proc(uratori) heredit(atium) | proc(uratori) Aug(usti) praef(ecto) prov(inciae) Sard(iniae) | praef(ecto) vehicul(orum) ad HS CC(milia) | praef(ecto) vehicul(orum) ad HS C(milia) | proc(uratori) ad annonam Ostis | ad HS [L]X proc(uratori) b[ib]liothec(arum) | ad HS [L] X(milia) Laurenti[um] | Lavinatium | Q(uintus) Mon[t]an[i]us Po[ll]io | dec(urio) [e]q(uitum) s[t]rator eius | v(iro) e(gregio) praesidi rarissimo.*

[167] Pflaum 1960: 680.   [168] Millar 1963b: 198.

[169] *CIL* X 6662 = *ILS* 1455; *IG* XIV 1072; Pflaum 1960: 472–6 (no. 181).

[170] See the remarks of Eck 2000: 261.

only speak to the consolidation of a hierarchy of equestrian posts, they also show how equestrians embraced the careerist opportunities available to them in the service of the emperor.[171]

The use of salary grades as a public form of self-representation emphasised the large sums of money that equestrian administrators received. Indeed, when converted into gold, procuratorial pay represented the equivalent of between 15 and 75 pounds of gold per annum; a substantial payment from the *res publica* for services rendered, and a significant enticement to hold office.[172] The size of the salaries becomes even clearer when compared with the income of *equites* who possessed the minimum census qualification of 400,000 sesterces (though it should be pointed out that many *equites* were substantially wealthier). The annual income on landed investments in Italy was usually 5–6 per cent per annum.[173] Therefore, an equestrian with the minimum qualification of 400,000 sesterces would expect a return of 20,000–24,000 sesterces per year.[174] This may have been enough for some *equites* to live on comfortably without further income, as White has argued was the case for equestrian litterateurs.[175] However, *equites* would probably have required significantly more than the bare minimum to maintain several houses and estates.[176] Indeed, recent calculations by Scheidel and Friesen put the mean equestrian fortune at >600,000 sesterces, with a mean income of >40,000 sesterces per annum.[177] This is where procuratorships and their high salaries would have proved attractive. The 60,000 sesterces salary paid to a sexagenarian procurator represented either three times the annual income on the equestrian census (assuming a return of 5 per cent), or two-and-a-half times (at 6 per cent), and was also higher than the mean income calculated by Scheidel and Friesen.[178] The order of magnitude increased the higher one rose through the procuratorial cursus to centenarian, ducenarian, or even the rare trecenarian posts. Again, it is worth comparing these salaries with estimated incomes. Duncan-Jones has calculated that 2 million sesterces was the likely wealth of the richest elites in North Africa during the second century AD, though larger fortunes of 3–4 million sesterces are attested.[179] The centenarian salary of 100,000

---

[171] In addition to the examples discussed in detail, the following inscriptions should also be noted: *CIL* X 6569 = *ILS* 478; *CIL* XIV 170; *IG* XIV 1480 = *ILS* 8854; *AE* 1932, 34, 1969/70, 704, 1988, 282, 2010, 1809.

[172] Rathbone 2009: 313.   [173] Duncan-Jones 1982: 33; Frier 1980: 21; Jongman 2007: 600.

[174] For example, 20,000 sesterces a year is the income that Naevolus desires in order to remain an *eques* (Juv. *Sat.* 9.140–1), suggesting that it was the bare minimum return on investment to qualify for the equestrian census.

[175] White 1978: 88–9; Bellandi 2009: 482–3.   [176] Juv. *Sat.* 14.325–6; D. Armstrong 2012: 61.

[177] Scheidel and Friesen 2009: 76–7.   [178] Duncan-Jones 1982: 4.

[179] Duncan-Jones 1963: 164–5, citing the fortunes of Herennius Rufinus (*Apol.* 75, 3 million sesterces), Sicinius Pontianus (*Apol.* 62, 77, 97, 4 million sesterces), and Apuleius himself

sesterces was equivalent to a 5 per cent annual return on a fortune of 2 million sesterces, while the ducenarian salary represented a 10 per cent return.

Procuratorial salaries thus represented a substantial cash payment from the Roman state. This was recognised both by *equites* at the lower end of the scale wishing to make their fortune and by the wealthiest elements eager to enrich themselves further. Administrative posts were widely regarded as way for *equites* to increase their wealth, both through gifts and bribes, and through the salary itself.[180] The most famous example of this is Seneca's brother, L. Annaeus Mela, who preferred to remain an *eques* rather than seek senatorial status, because he wished to hold procurator-ships and obtain the salary that came with them.[181] But he was not alone in this sentiment. Plutarch envisaged prominent men competing with each other to obtain equestrian procuratorships and senatorial governorships, since they were positions that carried large salaries.[182] An *eques* lobbying for an honorary procuratorship without any duties could be suspected of trying to feather his nest by taking the salary without any work. Therefore, when Fronto wrote to the emperor Antoninus Pius to ask for such a sinecure for his friend Appian, he emphasised that Appian merely wanted the status that came with the post, not the payment.[183] The emperor had previously declined such an honour for Appian because he feared that it would lead to many other learned Greeks asking for the same privilege.[184] It would undoubtedly have placed great pressure on the imperial treasury if these sinecures had been granted in an unrestrained fashion. We can therefore state that procuratorial positions were sought after by *equites* because of the salaries they offered, and that the emergence of an eques-trian service elite was driven by a desire for financial reward, among other reasons.[185]

Promotion from the centenarian to the ducenarian salary grade repre-sented a particularly significant step up. An annual payment of 200,000 sesterces was five times the estimated minimum mean equestrian income of 40,000 sesterces, which made such procuratorships very lucrative indeed. They were also something to boast about. In the second century AD equestrians began to highlight that they had reached *ducenar-ius* status by using it as a title. This separated the *ducenarii* from lower-

(*Apol.* 23, 2 million sesterces). The average figure of 2 million comes from his analysis of the outlay of wealthy African elites on public benefactions.
[180] Talbert 1984: 79; Lendon 1997: 176–7.   [181] Tac. *Ann.* 16.17.3. See also Chapter 4.
[182] Plut. *Mor.* 814 D.
[183] Fronto, *Ad Ant. Pium* 10.1–2 (vdH² p. 168) = Davenport and Manley 2014: 122–3 (no. 35).
[184] Fronto, *Ad Ant. Pium* 10.3.   [185] Rathbone 2009: 313.

ranked equestrian administrators and the *ordo equester* at large, indicating their membership of an exclusive elite founded on wealth, office-holding and imperial favour. The title of *ducenarius* is employed in both Greek and Latin inscriptions throughout the provinces, reflecting empire-wide acceptance of the status designation, especially in the third century AD.[186] The equestrian procurator Ti. Claudius Plotinus was styled the 'son of the *procurator ducenarius* Ti. Claudius Heracla' (Τι. Κλ. Ἡρακλᾶ[τος]‖ ἐπιτρόπου δουκηνα[ρίου]‖ υἱὸν) on an inscribed statue base from Perge.[187] The transliteration of the title *ducenarius* into Greek indicates that literate residents of Perge would recognise and understand that Plotinus' father had risen high in the imperial administration.[188] By the third century AD *ducenarius* could be used as shorthand for an entire procuratorial career. For example, L. Titinius Clodianus was honoured at Lambaesis in Numidia in the 240s as 'a man of many ducenarian posts, now *ducenarius* (sc. procurator) of the *ludus magnus*' (*multarum | ducc-(enarium) viro | nunc ducen(arius) | ludi magni*).[189] If an equestrian was referred to as a *vir ducenarius*, then it was recognised that he was, or had been, a high-status servant of the imperial administration.[190] Most procurators never attained such a lofty goal. In the early second century AD M. Aemilius Bassus completed three *militiae*, and served in four sexagenarian positions before being appointed to the procuratorship of Judaea, which carried a salary of 100,000 sesterces.[191] This was the crowning glory of Bassus' official service, since he died soon afterwards.[192] He was not alone in never achieving a commission as a *ducenarius*: the decreasing number of positions available at each grade meant that less than half of those *equites* who held a centenarian post proceeded to a ducenariate procuratorship in the second and third centuries AD.[193] *Vir centenarius* is attested in inscriptions, but is much less common than *ducenarius*, perhaps in view of the reduced prestige it conveyed as a vehicle of self-representation.[194] In the same vein, although *sexagenarius* was

---

[186] Pflaum 1970: 178–90; Christol 2006b: 243–4.   [187] *I. Perge* 293 = *AE* 2004, 1484.

[188] Note, for example, the remarks of Kuhn 2010: 115 on the intelligibility of senatorial and equestrian titles in the Greek world.

[189] *AE* 1917/18, 85; Pflaum 1960: 859–64 (no. 331 *bis*).

[190] Pflaum 1970: 178–9; Chastagnol 1988: 202; Christol 2006b: 249.

[191] Pflaum 1960: 238–40 (no. 103).   [192] *AE* 1915, 58 = *ILS* 9506.

[193] Saller 1982: 116–17. Duncan-Jones 2016: 111 shows that *equites* who served in one *militia* held an average of one ducenarian procuratorship, while those with two and three *militiae* had an average of less than one ducenarian post. This indicates the fierce competition for these offices.

[194] Christol 2006b.

a recognised grade of the imperial administration, no *eques* was explicitly styled a *vir sexagenarius* on a funerary or honorific inscription.

One of the reasons why *equites* were so willing to hold administrative posts from the beginning of the principate is that they would not have felt any compunction in working for the *res publica* in return for financial reward. This is what had motivated *equites* to serve as *publicani* in the Republic.[195] In contrast to this, the payment of salaries to senatorial officials was a marked difference to the conditions under the Republic; it thus represented the curtailment of senators' independence and their subordination to the *princeps*.[196] The economic motive for office-holding does not feature in the discourse of letters of recommendation (unless to deny its existence, as in the case of Fronto), for this would not be in keeping with the aristocratic value system of service to the *res publica* shared by senators and *equites* alike. Instead, administrative posts were referred to as symbols of personal status and prestige, which increased one's honour rather than lining one's pockets.[197] Indeed, Dio's Maecenas advised the *princeps* that the prefect of the city and the sub-censor should be paid officials, not only because they would be deprived of their *otium* to undertake the office, but also because it would offer them status.[198] The connection between payment from the *res publica* and personal status became an established principle under the principate.[199] The higher one rose through the procuratorial *cursus*, the greater the status, and therefore the greater the salary. But the competition was fiercer at the upper echelons, since there were fewer posts available; this concentrated the most lucrative offices in the hands of a small minority. As Duncan-Jones has aptly observed, 'extreme differences of wealth were recognised and even propagated by the state'.[200] The procuratorial salaries therefore served as a way of connecting economic reward with imperial favour, encouraging a steady supply of candidates from the *ordo equester* who would compete for the administrative posts available to them. The result of this was that

---

[195] Dio's Maecenas noted that the salaries for equestrian officials were necessary because they were less wealthy than senators (52.25.3). This is misleading, however, since many *equites* had incomes far exceeding the senatorial threshold. The statement must reflect a need to differentiate senators and equestrians.

[196] The speech of Maecenas explicitly notes that senators' expenditure must be reined in and that a fixed salary is the way to do this (Dio 52.23.1).

[197] Lendon 1997: 176–94.   [198] Dio 52.21.7.

[199] Lendon 1997: 177. See Tac. *Ann.* 4.16.4, on salaries providing an incentive for Romans to hold priesthoods.

[200] Duncan-Jones 1963: 166. See also Jongman 2007: 600; Scheidel 2009c: 351. Dio's Maecenas explicitly notes that the salaries of equestrian officials should be set in relation to their status (Dio 52.25.2).

the *equites* who did hold a series of government positions and were promoted to the highest salaries grades were transformed into an imperial service elite.

The *equestris nobilitas* functioned as a prime source for new senators. We have numerous examples, expertly assembled by Stein, of citizens whose ascent into the *amplissimus ordo* was made possible by the procuratorial careers of their fathers.[201] One specific case study shall serve as an illustration of this phenomenon: the African family of the Marii Perpetui in the second and third centuries AD. They were members of the municipal elite of Thugga in Africa Proconsularis.[202] L. Marius Perpetuus is attested as *scriba quaestorius* to the proconsul of Africa in AD 136/7.[203] His son, also called L. Marius Perpetuus, saw employment as a procurator in a range of financial positions, rising to become procurator of Lugdunensis and Aquitania; he was also co-opted as a *pontifex minor*.[204] His extensive career makes him a textbook member of the *equestris nobilitas*. Both his sons, L. Marius Maximus Perpetuus Aurelianus and L. Marius Perpetuus, entered the senate and held consulships; Aurelianus was especially distinguished, serving as *praefectus urbi* and later holding the consulship for the second time, as *ordinarius*, in AD 223.[205] Their sons in turn became senators and ordinary consuls in AD 232 and 237, respectively.[206] Not all families benefited from such a spectacular ascent through the *ordines*, from a *scriba* to ordinary consul in two generations. But it illustrates the general principle: the procuratorial service provided the launching pad not only for the careers of individuals, but also the ennoblement of families. When the senator Antonius Balbus described his life in a poetic dedication to the god Silvanus, he wrote: 'I was born in this little house, of equestrian family, but I am now proconsul of Africa' (*hac natus casa | equestri genere nunc proco(n)s(ul) Afric(ae))*.[207] There could be no greater statement of the phenomenon of social mobility between the two *ordines*.

The emerging equestrian aristocracy of service was consolidated in the second century AD by the introduction of a new group of *dignitates*.[208] It was in this period that equestrian procurators began to be designated with the status distinction of *egregius* (κράτιστος in Greek) as a way of distinguishing them from ordinary *equites Romani*.[209] The title of

[201] Stein 1927: 236–45, 291–345.   [202] Birley 1999: 205.   [203] *ILAfr.* 592; Syme 1971: 135.

[204] *CIL* XIII 1810 = *ILS* 1389; Pflaum 1960: 411–13 (no. 168). For equestrian priestly offices such as that of *pontifex minor*, see Chapter 10.

[205] See the family tree in Pflaum 1960: 411; Syme 1971: 136–8.   [206] Syme 1971: 143.

[207] *AE* 1998, 279; Várhelyi 2010: 109.   [208] Heil 2015: 56–8.

[209] Seeck 1905: 2006–9; Pflaum 1970: 177–8; Alföldy 1981: 190–1; Löhken 1982: 27. It should be pointed out, however, that κράτιστος could be used in other circumstances as an honorific

egregius could also be combined with the salary grade, with the designation *vir egregius ducenarius* (ὁ κράτιστος δουκηάριος) becoming especially common by the mid-third century AD.[210] In the reign of Marcus Aurelius two new higher statuses which ranked above *egregius* are attested for the first time: *perfectissimus* (διασημότατος) and *eminentissimus* (ἐξοχώτατος).[211] The title of *perfectissimus* was first bestowed on high equestrian officials such as the *praefectus annonae, praefectus vigilum* and *praefectus Aegypti*, while the status of *eminentissimus* was initially reserved for the praetorian prefects alone.[212] Under the Severans the rank of *eminentissimus* was bestowed on the other great prefectures for the first time, though this did not become entrenched practice, since they are also recorded as *perfectissimi* later in the third century.[213] The third century AD also witnessed the extension of the status of *perfectissimus* to a new cadre of officials at the top of the equestrian hierarchy, including the *praefectus classis* at Misenum, and the secretaries in the Palatine bureaux, such as the *a rationibus, ab epistulis, a cognitionibus* and *a studiis*.[214] These new *dignitates* were not merely decorative, but had important implications for one's legal status. For example, Marcus Aurelius ruled that the descendants of *eminentissimi* and *perfectissimi*, down to their great-grandsons, were not subject to plebeian punishments.[215] These changes meant that equestrians who had served at the highest levels of the imperial administration were now precisely and deliberately distinguished from the *ordo equester* at large. The status of *eques Romanus* could be granted by the emperor to all freeborn citizens who possessed the property qualification of 400,000 sesterces, but the higher distinctions were reserved for those who received imperial appointments.[216] The new aristocracy of service was thus marked out by its relationship to the emperor and its legal privileged position within the *res publica*.[217]

Within the equestrian service elite there were many different variations in career pathways. Some *equites* who did not want long years of service

---

designation which did not carry the technical meaning of *vir egregius*. See Demougin 2015: 65–72.

[210] Pflaum 1970: 178–9; Chastagnol 1988: 202; Christol 2006b: 249.

[211] *CJ* 9.41.11. For the Greek equivalents of the Latin titles, see Heil 2015: 57–8.

[212] Ensslin 1937: 664–5; Pflaum 1970: 177–8.   [213] Salway 2006: 123–7.

[214] Ensslin 1937: 665–8; Pflaum 1960: 624.

[215] *CJ* 9.41.11 (Diocletian and Maximian, referring to an earlier ruling by Marcus Aurelius); Garnsey 1970: 142; Alföldy 1981: 199–200.

[216] Christol 2006b: 243–4, 249–50. These statuses could also be granted on an honorific basis, a practice which we will discuss later in the chapter.

[217] Vittinghoff 1980: 43–4.

regarded one or two posts at the lower echelons as sufficient to confer the additional status and prestige they desired. We can observe this in the case of an anonymous equestrian from Lugdunum in Gaul who is attested in a fragmentary inscription dated to the early third century AD. His life was mostly spent in Gaul, holding various offices in the *civitas Senonum*, and then serving as federal priest of the Three Gauls (*sacerdos* of the *ara Caesaris* at the Temple of Roma and Augustus at Lugdunum).[218] However, the inscription records that before he took up this provincial priesthood, 'the deified Aurelius Antoninus gave him the centenarian procuratorship of the province of Hadrumetina' (*cui | divus Aurel(ius) Antoninus | centenariam procuratio(nem) | prov(inciae) Hadrymetinae dedit*).[219] It is notable that our anonymous Gallic *eques* did not have a long career, but was only granted a post of centenarian rank by Caracalla.[220] The procuratorship was an imperial *dignitas* that elevated him above his Gallic peers who did not secure such appointments. Indeed, out of all known federal priests of the Three Gauls, this *eques* was the only one to hold an imperial administrative post.[221]

The variations in equestrian careers can also be observed in the choices made by the men who held the post of *advocatus fisci* in the second and third centuries AD. It could be the first stage of an extensive imperial career, as evidenced by the case of C. Attius Alcimus Felicianus, who was *advocatus fisci* for eleven provinces and later became *praefectus annonae*.[222] Alternatively, many other *equites*, especially in the eastern provinces, held only the position of *advocatus fisci* itself, and progressed no further.[223] These *equites* may have been enticed into service by the fact that they were exempted from undertaking civic *munera* while they were in office as procurators or military commanders.[224] But this privilege only lasted for the length of their commissions, and they were liable for these obligations once again when their positions came to an end.[225]

The equestrian procuratorial system therefore brought with it an entire new series of honours and opportunities for *domi nobiles*, binding the provincial elites of the empire into the framework of the *res publica*.

---

[218] Fishwick 1987: 324–5.　　[219] *CIL* XIII 1684a = *ILS* 1441.

[220] Pflaum 1961: 1094 dates the appointment under Marcus Aurelius, but Fishwick 1987: 324–5 and Christol 2006a: 226 convincingly argue that the 'deified Aurelius Antoninus' is the emperor Caracalla, not Antoninus Pius.

[221] Fishwick 2002: 41.　　[222] *CIL* VIII 822 = *ILS* 1347; Pflaum 1960: 843–9 (no. 327).

[223] Millar 1963b: 196; Brunt 1983: 73–4.

[224] *Dig.* 4.6.32–33 (Modestinus), 4.6.35.2 (Paulus); Millar 1983: 87. The official companions of governors and procurators were also exempt (*Dig.* 50.5.12.1 (Paulus)), but not tax-farmers (*Dig.* 4.6.34 (Javolenus)).

[225] *CJ* 9.48.1 (Carus, Carinus and Numerian). This changed in the late empire, as we will see in Chapter 12.

The financial and honorific rewards enticed both those *equites* who only wanted a single post and those equestrians who sought multiple positions and a lifetime of service. One of the distinguishing features of the Roman imperial state and its administrative hierarchy was the fact that it was flexible enough to accommodate a range of career aspirations.

Advancement, Seniority and Patronage

Members of the *ordo equester* competed with one another to secure official posts and ascend through the procuratorial hierarchy. Even those who eschewed lengthy careers would still have needed sufficient patronage and support to be appointed to one position, given that all procuratorships were officially within the gift of the emperor. Pflaum proposed that appointments were based on the seniority of an individual *eques* – that is, whether it was his turn for promotion or not. There was, he argued, a regular yearly review of appointments and promotions in the equestrian hierarchy, which was not only divided into salary grades, but also into various echelons at centenarian and ducenarian rank.[226] Pflaum's signal achievement in identifying the relative hierarchy of individual posts must be recognised, even if one does not accept his arguments that the salary divisions extended back to the reign of Augustus, or that there were different echelons within the pay grades.[227] Since the publication of his monumental work there has been concerted debate between those scholars who argue that there were specific criteria for the appointment and promotion of equestrians and others who place greater emphasis on the importance of patronage. Eck, for example, has argued that the administrative system was designed to reduce 'arbitrariness' in official appointments, which helped to manage competition among procurators.[228] At the other end of the spectrum, Saller (among others) has emphasised the more unpredictable effects of patronage on equestrian appointments.[229] The problem is an important one, since it goes to the very heart of understanding the workings of the Roman administration, and the place of the *ordo equester* within it.

---

[226] Pflaum 1950: 210–96 lays out the evidence in detail.

[227] Millar 1963b: 195; Saller 1980: 44–5; Eck 2000: 258–9, 2002a: 143–5.

[228] Eck 2000: 260–1, 2002a: 144–6.

[229] Saller 1980, 1982; and see also Millar 1963b; Brunt 1983; Duncan-Jones 2016: 106–8. Several scholars have supported at least parts of Pflaum's analysis, and criticise the undue emphasis on patronage by Saller in particular: Eck 1974; 1982; A. R. Birley 1992; Leunissen 1993; Devijver 1999; Demougin 2001.

The Romans certainly valued rules and regulations in making senatorial appointments.[230] The *lex Villia annalis* of 180 BC firmly established the ages at which senators could stand for public magistracies, the hierarchy of the posts within the *cursus honorum*, and the interval that had to elapse before standing for subsequent magistracies. The exceptions – including, most famously, Cn. Pompeius Magnus – did not undermine these basic principles. The hierarchy of the senatorial *cursus* continued to operate under the Roman empire, though with appropriate modifications, such as the lowering of the age at which senators might stand for magistracies.[231] Various regulations were incorporated into the imperial *cursus*. Augustus, for example, decreed that ex-praetors could only be appointed to provincial governorships five years after they had held the magistracy.[232] This meant that senators did have to reach a certainly level of seniority, at least in terms of age, before they qualified for a provincial command. There was also a degree of expectation among senior senators when it came to balloting for the prestigious proconsulships of Africa and Asia.[233] These rules and expectations did not mean that there was no competition and that senators would simply be appointed automatically. Pliny the Younger, for instance, petitioned Trajan for a praetorship for his friend Attius Sura, after he initially failed to be awarded the magistracy.[234] Although achieving senatorial magistracies below the consulship essentially became a fait accompli by the third century AD, there was still considerable rivalry for other appointments, such as provincial governorships, and distinctions such as priesthoods.[235] Patrons would only put forward sensible candidates within the overall workings of this system: a junior senator would not be recommended for promotion to the consular governorship of Syria Coele, for example.[236] There were, however, various official, imperially sanctioned ways in which senators could achieve rapid promotion, such as qualifying for a year's remission through the *ius trium liberorum* or being designated as the emperor's *candidatus*.[237] There was also the process of adlection (*adlectio*) to a higher rank within the senate. Adlection *inter praetorios*, for example, elevated a senator to the rank of ex-praetor without having to hold the intervening magistracies. Pertinax decreed that those senators who had actually been praetor were more senior than those adlected *inter praetorios*, which understandably annoyed the *adlecti* who had not been previously

---

[230] Eck 2002a: 136–43.   [231] A. R. Birley 1981: 12–16; Talbert 1984: 16–22.

[232] Dio 53.14.2; see also Suet. *Aug.* 36.2. Augustus' measure reinstated one of the provisions of Pompeius' *lex Pompeia de provinciis*, passed in 52 BC (Wardle 2014: 285–6).

[233] Talbert 1984: 349.   [234] Pliny the Younger, *Ep.* 10.12.

[235] On the importance of priesthoods as a sign of prestige and imperial favour, see Duncan-Jones 2016: 7, 11–12.

[236] Leunissen 1993: 107, 117–20.   [237] A. R. Birley 1981: 13–15; Talbert 1984: 16–27.

regarded as junior in rank.[238] There was therefore a set of rules and conventions that regulated the senatorial career in the principate.

Did similar regulations exist for the procuratorial positions held by *equites*? We have no evidence that, for example, the occupant of a sexagenerian post had to wait five years before appointment to the centenarian level, or than an *eques* had to serve in three centenarian posts before advancing to the ducenarian strata. In fact, the prosopographical data suggest that this cannot have been the case.[239] Nor is there any indication in the sources that *equites* felt confident that they would be awarded procuratorships simply because they were the most senior candidates available, either in terms of age or time served. We should not, however, dismiss the seniority principle out of hand, given that it is known to have existed for Roman administrative positions in the fourth and fifth centuries AD.[240] The earliest indication of this comes in a constitution of Constantine, which was issued to Versennius Fortunatus, *consularis aquarum*, in AD 324.[241] The emperor wrote:

The order of advancement must be preserved, so that the highest-ranked official in your department is the one who was appointed earliest by imperial decision.[242]

Constantine's unambiguous declaration of the seniority principle is in keeping with the tone of the legislation that he and Licinius both issued regulating the imperial administration, which comes down to us in edited form through the *Codex Theodosianus*.[243] Indeed, the very hierarchical and regulated nature of the imperial administration in the early fourth century AD, as revealed in the *Codex*, comes as something of a shock after the limited evidence for the third century. The importance of structure, hierarchy and seniority looms large in these imperial constitutions. In AD 341 the emperor Constans made a ruling on the promotion of *exceptores* within the office of the praetorian prefect:[244]

---

[238] *HA Pert.* 6.10–11. In the late empire it was an established principle that men who had held a post ranked higher than those who had achieved it by payment of money, or held it on an honorary basis (Pedersen 1976: 34).

[239] See the tables in Saller 1982: 87–91.

[240] A. H. M. Jones 1964: 563–606; Löhken 1982: 135–47.

[241] The manuscript gives AD 315, but the date must be AD 324, given that Constantine issued it from Thessalonica (Corcoran 2000: 315).

[242] *CTh.* 8.7.1: *promotionis ordo custodiendus est, ut primus in officio sit, qui prior fuerit in consequendo beneficio principali.* Constantine uses the word *promotio* ('advancement' or 'promotion'), which is first attested in the early third century (*CIL* III 14416). See *OLD* s.v. *promotio*.

[243] This will be discussed in Chapter 12.

[244] *CTh.* 8.2.1. This is wrongly attributed to Constantine, but it is part of a larger law given by Constans at Lauriacum in 341 (*CTh.* 12.1.31). See Barnes 1993: 225.

It pleases us that the *exceptores* should advance to the post of *commentarius* and be selected for the administration of these matters in accordance with their status and rank, with all other candidates being rejected. This is so that among the *exceptores*, each man ought to obtain a position in accordance with his rank and merit, as he deserves to have gained this status according to the time he has served.[245]

Constans' declaration was followed by a large number of laws confirming or refining the hierarchy of various government departments and the impact of seniority on promotions.[246] We know too, thanks to the work of John Lydus, that in the Roman empire of the sixth century AD there were established rules about how long a junior bureaucrat had to serve before seeking advancement, and the required intervals between posts.[247]

It is difficult to find evidence for such regulated patterns of advancement for *equites* in the sources for the high empire. However, a letter of Cornelius Fronto to the emperor Marcus Aurelius concerning the promotion of an imperial freedman, Aridelus, provides a crucial piece of the puzzle. Fronto wrote: 'He [sc. Aridelus] now seeks the position of procurator in the proper way, given his status, and since this is an appropriate time' (*petit nunc procurationem ex forma suo loco ac iusto tempore*).[248] There are obvious similarities in language between Fronto's letter and the ruling of Constans, most notably the reference to the status (*locus*) of the man being advanced and the time (*tempus*) already served in the administration. If we take Fronto's letter first, he is arguing that Aridelus is sufficiently senior to be considered for promotion, and not a junior freedman rashly seeking early advancement.[249] Later in the letter Fronto tells Marcus that even if he does not recognise Aridelus' face, he should look out for his name, which suggests that the emperor would actually examine a list of freedmen when it was necessary to fill a vacancy. However, Fronto's letter also suggests that there was no hierarchical list of freedmen ranked from first to last, with the man at the head of the list automatically receiving promotion. The rulings of the emperors Constantine and Constans, issued some two centuries later, do indicate that there was such an order of merit when it came to

---

[245] CTh. 8.1.2: *exceptores placet pro loco et ordine suo ad commentarios accedere et eorum administrationi subrogari ceteris propulsatis, ita ut inter exceptores, prout quisque locum tempore adipisci meruerit, ordine et merito consequatur.*

[246] C. Kelly 2004: 38–43, 211–12.   [247] C. Kelly 2004: 37–8.

[248] Fronto, *Ad M. Caes.* 5.52 (vdH² pp. 79–80) = Davenport and Manley 2014: 107 (no. 29). See the discussion of the passage in Pflaum 1950: 197–9 and Saller 1980: 45–6, who reach different conclusions.

[249] Eck 2002a: 148–9.

promoting staff within the offices of the *consularis aquarum* and the praetorian prefect. This suggests that stricter rules for advancement were put in place, primarily in the lower and middle echelons of government, as the Roman imperial administration became more integrated and complex. But even then, emperors sometimes reserved the right to make their own selections, disregarding the stated criteria.[250]

In the first two centuries AD freedmen occupied many of the clerical and sub-clerical grades in the government, but over the course of the third century AD these positions were transferred to freeborn men. This development created a new integrated career path, from the lowest levels of the clerical staff through to higher positions held by men of equestrian rank.[251] I would argue that it was during this period that seniority became more important as a criterion for promotion of these lower-ranked officials.[252] Words such as *locus* and *tempus*, which Fronto used to refer in an informal way to the freedman Aridelus' standing and suitability for promotion, evolved into technical terms by the fourth century AD and were applied to freeborn officials in the junior ranks of the expanded imperial administration. But did such a seniority principle exist for equestrian procurators during the principate? It is telling that the rigorous procedures for promotion and seniority for junior officials, such as those detailed in the Constantinian constitutions and the work of John Lydus, are not found at all for the most senior grades of the late Roman administration – that is, the fourth- and fifth-century equivalents of the equestrian procurators of the high empire.[253] Appointments were instead based on personal qualities, cultural attainments and honour, just as in the early empire.[254] In the principate, seniority did matter in one sense: an emperor would not usually promote an *eques* from a sexagenarian procuratorship to the prefecture of Egypt, any more than he would appoint an ex-quaestor to govern Syria.[255] But mere time served or the notion that it was one's 'turn' was not enough to qualify an *eques* for the most prestigious offices of state. Instead, this depended on the patronage of courtiers or the friendship of the emperor himself. There were also some positions at court to which *equites* could be appointed directly without any prior service, notably the posts of *ab*

---

[250] C. Kelly 1998: 171–5, 2004: 46–7, 211–12, citing *CTh.* 6.27.3 (AD 380) on the promotion of *agentes in rebus*.

[251] Haensch 2006.

[252] See Pedersen 1976: 30–1 for a good discussion about how the personal qualities expected of officials varied depending on their status.

[253] Pedersen 1976: 33–4, 40.   [254] Lendon 1997: 189–90.

[255] See Brunt 1975 on the selection of prefects of Egypt from among the senior *equites*.

epistulis or *ab epistulis Graecis*, which were often held by Greeks with literary talent but no prior procuratorships to their credit.[256]

In the official discourse of Roman government equestrians were appointed and promoted because they were men of good standing and respectable character who would be faithful servants of the *res publica*.[257] In promoting Domitius Marsianus to his ducenarian procuratorship, Marcus Aurelius hoped that he would retain his 'sense of integrity, attentiveness, and skills gained by experience' (*conscientiam … innocentiae diligentiae experientiae*). When Domitian advanced L. Laberius Maximus from *praefectus Aegypti* to the praetorian prefecture, he referred to Maximus' 'dutifulness' (*pietas*). The emperor noted that when the prefecture became vacant 'I turned my attention immediately to your most devoted loyalty and diligence' (*st[a]tim ad [dev]otissimam f[idem tuam et industri] am respecxi*).[258] The qualities emphasised by these imperial letters are echoed in the correspondence of Pliny the Younger, in which he recommends his friends, associates and junior officials for appointments.[259] As governor of Bithynia, Pliny wrote letters of recommendation for the freedmen and *equites* serving on his staff. He described the freedman procurator Maximus as 'upright and diligent and attentive' (*probum et industrium et diligentem*).[260] Pliny used virtually identical terms to describe the *eques* Gavius Bassus, prefect of the Pontic shore, whom we mentioned in the conclusion to the previous chapter: he was 'irreproachable, upright, diligent' (*integrum probum industrium*).[261] Neither of these letters is very long, and they appear to have been standard references written for administrators when they vacated their posts.[262] The imperial *codicilli* and Pliny's letters of recommendation for his staff are rather formulaic. However, as with the generic nature of the inscribed *cursus*, the formula itself is important. It demonstrates the Roman conception of the personal qualities that made an equestrian a good servant of the *res publica* and marked him out as a member of the *equestris nobilitas*.[263]

---

[256] The different routes to the court office of *ab epistulis* are discussed later in this chapter.

[257] This is something most scholars agree on, regardless of which side of the debate they take (Saller 1982: 103, 111; Eck 2001: 21, 2002a: 138; Demougin 2001: 278).

[258] *P. Berol.* inv. 8334 = ChLA X 417.

[259] The parallels are noted by Eck 2001: 4 (the Marsianus letter); Cugusi 2001: 309–10 (the Maximus letter).

[260] Pliny the Younger, *Ep.* 10.85.　　[261] Pliny the Younger, *Ep.* 10.86A.

[262] Sherwin-White 1966: 681. Pliny was much more fulsome when writing about personal friends. See, for example, his recommendation that Trajan grant Suetonius the *ius trium liberorum* (Pliny the Younger, *Ep.* 10.94).

[263] Eck 2002a: 138; Rees 2007: 159–164.

It is important to emphasise that these characteristics were not unique to equestrian administrators or senatorial governors, but represented the fundamental attributes of a good Roman man. For example, Fronto frequently praised the *probitas* ('uprightness') of his protégés when writing general letters of introduction that were intended to cultivate friendships between aristocrats, rather than recommend friends for promotion.[264] The crucial point here is that an equestrian's conduct in government office was regarded as a reflection of his innate character, just as with any other duty he performed in his life. Describing the accomplishments of the *eques* Terentius Iunior, Pliny wrote that 'he administered the procuratorship in the province of Narbonensis with great integrity' (*etiam procuratione Narbonensis provinciae integerrime functus*).[265] The quality of *integritas* also features in Pliny's account of the equestrian Ti. Claudius Pollio, whom he recommended to his consular colleague, C. Iulius Cornutus Tertullus, as a man worthy of friendship.[266] The two men had known each other since they served together in the army in Syria, when Pliny had been a military tribune and Pollio was a *praefectus* of the *ala Flavia milliaria*.[267] The scrupulous Pliny, who was in charge of auditing the accounts, uncovered widespread corruption among the other commanders, but not Pollio: 'I discovered in his case the utmost integrity, and particular attention to detail' (*ita huius summam integritatem, sollicitam diligentiam inveni*). In his letter to Tertullus, Pliny praised Pollio's continuing probity:

After he was promoted to the most distinguished procuratorships, there was no occasion on which he was corrupted and turned away from his natural sense of propriety. He never put on airs as things went his way. He never sundered his lasting reputation for good conduct during his different postings. He devoted himself to his work with the same resoluteness of spirit with which he now approaches his time out of office.[268]

Pliny did not mention the precise positions Pollio held as procurator, or any specific accomplishments or achievements while he was in post. The focus is instead resolutely on his personal qualities; his sense of

---

[264] Fronto, *Ad Amicos* 1.3 (vdH² pp. 172–3), on Terentius Vanus; *Ad Amicos* 1.4 (vdH² p. 174), on Iulius Aquilinus); *Ad Amicos* 1.8 (vdH² pp. 176–7), on Aemilius Pius. On Fronto's letters of introduction, see Wei 2013: III.18.

[265] Pliny the Younger, *Ep.* 7.25.2.   [266] Pliny the Younger, *Ep.* 7.31.

[267] This was probably early in Domitian's reign (Sherwin-White 1966: 441).

[268] Pliny the Younger, *Ep.* 7.31.3: *postea promotus ad amplissimas procurationes, nulla occasione corruptus ab insito abstinentiae amore deflexit; numquam secundis rebus intumuit; numquam officiorum varietate continuam laudem humanitatis infregit, eademque firmitate animi laboribus suffecit, qua nunc otium patitur.*

abstinentia ('propriety') and his *humanitas* ('good conduct') augmented the *integritas* already mentioned. By recounting Pollio's career in terms of his personal qualities, Pliny made a connection between his friend's character and integrity as a Roman *vir* and his ascent through the procuratorial *cursus*.

This nexus between one's character and the practice of office-holding in the Roman world can be observed in the way in which the inscribed *cursus* developed during the second century AD. In this period the list of municipal and imperial positions and honours began to be augmented by references to the character and virtues of the honorand. Such a practice was not unique to inscriptions for *equites*, but can also be found in texts describing the achievements of senators and municipal elites.[269] This development shows that that the personal qualities found in letters of recommendation and appointment, which were largely private in nature or had limited circulation among elite groups, had made the transition to public commemorative discourse. It is particularly interesting that there is a striking consonance between the virtues highlighted in Pliny's correspondence, such as *integritas* and *abstinentia*, and those that appear in these honorific inscriptions. For example, Irenaeus, an imperial slave working at the port of Ilipa in Baetica, honoured his procurator, L. Cominius Vipsanius Salutaris, with a statue dedicated 'to the best and most upright man' (*optimo viro et integrissimo*).[270] T. Antistius Marcianus impressed the council of the Three Gauls when he was the first *eques* appointed as census collector for the provinces, with the result that they honoured him as 'the most upright and proper procurator' (*inte|gerrim(o) abstinentissimo|que procur(atori)*).[271] Other inscriptions emphasise the virtues of *industria* and *innocentia*, which are found both in imperial *codicilli* and letters of recommendation. In Auzia in Maurentania Caesariensis, the procurator L. Alfenus Senecio was honoured by the town council 'on account of the outstanding diligence of this great man, and for his particular integrity' (*ob egregiam tanti | viri industriam pro|que singulari eius | innocentia*).[272] The council of Bulla Regia took this new habit to its logical conclusion when they inscribed the letter of Marcus Aurelius itself on the monument of Domitius Marsianus; the letter would

---

[269] Alföldy 1982: 47–50; Salomies 1994: 77–82; Neri 1981 (on the late empire). See Forbis 1996: 101–2 for the same pattern in municipal honorific inscriptions in Italy (which of course included senators and *equites*).

[270] *CIL* II 1085 = *ILS* 1406; Pflaum 1960: 629–32 (no. 235).

[271] *CIL* XIII 1680 = *ILS* 1390; Pflaum 1960: 725–6 (no. 272).

[272] *CIL* VIII 9046; Pflaum 1960: 440–4 (no. 176).

then serve as a permanent and incontrovertible testament to his personal qualities. None of the virtues discussed here are especially 'equestrian' in nature, since they are also ascribed to senatorial and municipal elites throughout the empire.[273] This reflects the shared values, culture and outlook of the imperial and provincial aristocracies throughout the Roman world.[274]

These cultural expectations regarding appointments, promotions and office-holding do not mean that experience was not valued, at least in general terms. In the previous chapter we saw how letters of recommendation for candidates seeking a second or third post in the *militiae* did refer to military experience. The same point can be made about administrative positions. In his *Meditations*, Marcus Aurelius described how his father Antoninus Pius depended on the advice of men with specialist knowledge.[275] Marcus himself mentioned *experientia* – skills gained by experience – in his letter appointing Domitius Marsianus to his procuratorship in Narbonensis. Nero is likewise said to have appointed former praetors with *experientia* to take charge of the imperial treasury.[276] But *experientia* does not feature in Pliny or Fronto's letters of recommendation, nor does it appear as a virtue ascribed to governors in honorific inscriptions.[277] The prominent exceptions to this rule were those equestrians who received some sort of professional training, such as lawyers, who were described on inscriptions with the epithet *iurisperitus*, meaning 'skilled in the law'.[278]

In general, senatorial and equestrian administrators were never praised for specialist abilities or achievements. This was because they were supposed to be generalists, Roman citizens who were prepared to serve the *res publica* in whatever capacity they were required. Domitius Marsianus may have possessed general *experientia*, but he had no previous exposure to mining before being appointed procurator of the iron mines, nor did any other imperial officials involved in quarrying or mining operations.[279] This same principle can be found in appointments to other areas of imperial

---

[273] J. Nicols 2014: 272–3.

[274] In the Greek-speaking eastern provinces, honorific inscriptions shifted in a different, but related, manner from the late third century AD onwards. They concentrated on describing virtues and qualities in poetic format, rather than listing official posts. See Slootjes 2006: 129–53.

[275] Marcus, *Med.* 1.16.6.   [276] Tac. *Ann.* 13.29.

[277] Pflaum 1971: 363 cites only a Greek parallel from the late fourth century AD.

[278] For example, *CIL* X 6662 = *ILS* 1455; Eck 2001: 21–3. On this practice in the late empire, see Pedersen 1976: 32.

[279] Hirt 2010: 246–50.

administration. Only one individual, C. Attius Alcimus Felicianus, is known to have been involved in administering the *annona* at a junior grade before becoming *praefectus annonae*.[280] Brunt's detailed examination of prefects of Egypt demonstrated that there was no effort to prepare administrators for this position through prior postings to the province – instead they were selected from among the most senior *equites* thought worthy of the position.[281] Therefore, in the public discourse of Roman imperial government there was a connection between one's personal qualities and appointment and promotion. Wide experience and preparedness, rather than specialism, were central to the *domi militiaequae* ethos of government service shared by equestrians and senators. Even an equestrian who served in only one or two posts, rather than a full career, could be said to espouse this ideal. By interrupting his private life to hold a procuratorship, he was displaying his readiness to serve the *res publica* and showing that he was worthy to be a member of the *equestris nobilitas*.[282]

There was of course a tension between these aristocratic ideals and the realities of imperial government. Cassius Dio's Maecenas advised Octavian to choose his officials in conjunction with his advisers, appointing all candidates on the basis of merit.[283] The ancient sources often evince anxieties about appointments and promotions not going to the most deserving candidates. This illustrates the uncertainties of the imperial administration and its susceptibility to intrigue and manipulation. The emperor – the ultimate source of all official *dignitates* – could not have known all candidates for senatorial and equestrian posts personally, and instead depended on recommendations from friends and associates. This prompted significant anxiety about the influence of inappropriate advisers, such as slaves, freedmen and women, on the appointment process. The *Discourses* of Epictetus include several anecdotes about the need for senators and *equites* to ingratiate themselves with imperial freedmen.[284] The future emperor Vespasian famously owed his command of the *legio II Augusta* to the favour of Claudius' freedman Narcissus.[285] Imperial women were also valuable sources of *beneficia*: the equestrian procurator Gessius Florus is said to have benefited from his wife's intimacy with Nero's consort, Poppaea Sabina.[286] Even the court of Antoninus Pius was not

---

[280] Pavis-D'Esurac 1976: 79.   [281] Brunt 1975.
[282] See Dio 52.21.7 on public office entailing the sacrifice of leisure.   [283] Dio 52.15.1–3, 25.5.
[284] See Millar 1965a: 144–6, who cites several stories from Epictetus (3.7.29–31, 4.1.148, 4.7.19–24).
[285] Suet. *Vesp.* 4.   [286] Jos. *AJ* 20.11.1.

beyond reproach in this regard. The *Historia Augusta* reports a rumour that his praetorian prefect, Sex. Cornelius Repentinus, only gained the post because he had earned the favour of Pius' mistress, the freedwoman Galeria Lysistrate.[287] These stories circulated widely because senators and *equites* resented the influence of marginal figures and the power that they could exercise over their own advancement.

Even when the emperor personally made appointments there was no guarantee that he would choose the most appropriate candidate in the eyes of other members of the aristocratic elite. According to Tacitus, Iulius Paelignus, the procurator of Cappadocia, was 'despised both for his deficient intellect and absurdly comic appearance' (*ignavia animi et deridiculo corporis iuxta despiciendus*).[288] However, Tacitus notes that Paelignus was 'exceedingly intimate' (*perquam familiaris*) with the emperor Claudius, who liked to amuse himself by associating with buffoons. These anecdotes reflect the character and rule of the *princeps*. The appointment of competent and trustworthy officials was regarded a mark of a good emperor, whereas a bad emperor either removed good governors or showed caprice and pique in making appointments.[289] In this context there is a splendid anecdote about the emperor Domitian, who was accompanied to the quaestors' games by a deformed dwarf. As Suetonius tells the story, Domitian was even heard to ask the dwarf if he knew why he had seen fit to appoint M. Mettius Rufus as prefect of Egypt.[290] The emperor's reason remains unknown – he could have regarded Rufus as an exceptional administrator, a mediocrity, or a complete fool whom he wished to remove from court. But that is immaterial to our point: the fact that the story circulated in antiquity shows that Roman senators and equestrians openly discussed the uncertainties of official appointments. They resented decisions made through underhanded means or inappropriate influence, for such actions undermined the fundamental principles of selection on the basis of aristocratic virtues and personal qualities.

The tension between the aristocratic ethos of service, patronage and imperial favour is a feature of monarchical systems of government in which one's status depends, at least partially, on appointments to official positions that lie within the gift of the ruler. There would always be the human equation – the bumbling fool who appealed to the emperor's sense of

---

[287] *HA Ant. Pius* 8.8–9. Her name is attested on *CIL* VI 8972 = *ILS* 1836.

[288] Tac. *Ann.* 12.49.1.   [289] B. Campbell 1984: 337; Lendon 1997: 187–8.

[290] Suet. *Dom.* 4.2. Based on the Latin expression *ordinatione proxima* ('in the next appointment'), Pflaum 1950: 204 suggested that there was a regular round or rounds of appointments each year. There may indeed be some basis for supposing that new prefects of Egypt were appointed at a particular time of year, as shown by Eck 2000: 261.

humour, or the young administrator who had the right connections at court – and there would always be someone ready to criticise the candidate who received the position they coveted. In many ways, the debate about the relative importance of selection criteria and patronage within the equestrian administration is primarily about the aspects of the system one chooses to emphasise.[291] Some scholars prefer to place greater weight on the hierarchy and structure of the equestrian *cursus*, arguing that it could be flexible and adaptable to individual circumstances, while others focus on the anxieties inherent in a patronal society.[292] The most sensible conclusion is that there was probably a multiplicity of reasons for promotion and appointment in the high empire, which could include seniority, merit, recommendations, the family name and good luck.[293] The higher an equestrian rose through the system and the closer he came to the emperor, the more important it was that they had a personal relationship. Factors such as seniority were absent from letters of recommendation written on behalf of equestrians, because it would have been regarded as gauche or inappropriate to recommend an associate on the basis of time served.[294] Instead, a senator or equestrian's character, learning and public standing were much more culturally acceptable reasons for appointment and promotion. The existence of a patronage system did not mean that the candidates who were appointed were undeserving, incompetent or corrupt. Many perfectly competent and talented individuals obtained positions in this way, because their connections were just as important as their abilities. Even the most talented equestrian administrator would have gone unnoticed if he had no friends, relatives or patrons to call upon for help. Moreover, it is probable that senators such Pliny and Fronto would have earned a bad reputation if all their protégés had turned out to be incompetent.[295]

Earlier in this chapter we met Pliny's equestrian friend Claudius Pollio, who held several procuratorships with great probity. Pliny did not specify

---

[291] For example, even Pflaum 1950: 296 recognised the importance of imperial favour in making appointments. Sometimes scholars seem to be talking at cross-purposes (see, for example, Leunissen 1993: 110 n. 42 on Saller's definition of seniority).

[292] In the first category, see Leunissen 1993; Demougin 2001: 32–4, 2007: 273–4; Eck 2001, 2002a; in the second, Saller 1980, 1982.

[293] See the sensible discussion of Eck 2000: 259–60.

[294] Even in the late empire letters of recommendation written by elites were vague, and focused on character and personal qualities (Pedersen 1976: 26–7).

[295] I owe this point to Roger Tomlin.

exactly what those posts were, but fortunately they are set out in Pollio's own record of his career, inscribed on an altar from Rome (Figure 7.2).

To Sol, Luna, Apollo and Diana. Tiberius Claudius Pollio, imperial procurator for the collection of the inheritance tax, procurator of the Alps Graiae, *flamen*

Figure 7.2: Altar dedicated by Tiberius Claudius Pollio, Rome

Carmentalis, praefectus gentium in Africa, *praefectus* of the thousand-strong *ala Flavia* (dedicated this).[296]

This inscribed *cursus* provides a complementary perspective to Pliny's letter about his friend. By recording his career in the imperial army and administration, even on a religious dedication, Pollio was participating in the common cultural practice of defining himself publicly by his official duties.[297] The inscription does not refer to his accomplishments in these positions – but that is not the point of the text. The default interpretation of the *cursus* inscription was that the honorand was a success, a faithful official of the *res publica* and the emperor, who served *domi militiaeque*.[298] Pliny's letter of recommendation for Pollio and his own inscribed altar each reflect the virtues of the imperial service in their own way. Indeed, as we have seen, there are strong connections in language and thought between the letters of patrons such as Pliny and Fronto, the imperial codicils of appointment, and the genre of the *cursus* inscriptions. They are all different manifestations of the ideals and values of the *equestris nobilitas*. The members of this service elite performed their duty for the *res publica* in whatever capacity they were required, carrying out the duties of their offices willingly and honourably in a manner that reflected their personal character and excellence.

Quies **and Sinecures: Alternatives to Careers**

This chapter has thus far traced the emergence of an equestrian career structure and a corresponding aristocracy of service, the *equestris nobilitias*, from the first to the third centuries AD. But equestrian status was not contingent upon office-holding, and the vast majority of *equites* did not have long careers – or indeed hold any office – in the army and administration, as we discussed in Chapter 5. There were fewer than two hundred equestrian positions in the mid-third century AD, compared with the thousands of citizens belonging to the *ordo equester* at large. The *equestris nobilitas* was thus very small group, numbering perhaps only 600 members in a generation.[299] The majority of *equites* were

---

[296] *CIL* VI 3720 = *ILS* 1418: *Soli Lunae | Apollini | Dianae | Ti(berius) Claudius | Pollio | proc(urator) Aug(usti) | XX hereditatium | proc(urator) Alpium | Graiarum | flamen Carmentalis | praef(ectus) gentium in Africa | praef(ectus) alae Flaviae milliari[ae].*

[297] This does not lessen the importance of his religious devotion: see the discussion of this same text from a difference perspective in Chapter 10.

[298] See Chapter 6 for further discussion of this point.

[299] For the total number of equestrian posts, see Pflaum 1974: 43–5.

municipal worthies, the *domi nobiles*, who were either unlikely or unwilling to rise beyond their own community, or they were *publicani*, businessmen, and landowners who eschewed procuratorial positions.[300] For these individuals the status of *eques Romanus* and all its attendant privileges was regarded as a sufficient distinction in and of itself, just as had been the case for thousands of *equites* in the Republican age, who had little interest in politics and government business unless it affected their own interests. The binary opposition between the senatorial politician and the equestrian devoted to his life of *quies* that is familiar to us from the writings of Cicero continued to exert a considerable hold on the Roman imagination until the second century AD.[301] This posed a challenge and counterpoint to the ethos of the developing equestrian service elite, whose lives and careers were no different from those of senators who held military and administrative positions.

The Ciceronian conceit that equestrians led an inherently peaceful life of *quies* can be found in the *Letters* of Pliny the Younger. In his account of the life of the *eques* Minicius Macrinus from Brixia, Pliny stated that Macrinus had declined Vespasian's offer to be elevated into the senate *inter praetorios*: 'He was adamant that he preferred honourable peace to – what should I call it, our ambition or our status?' (*honestam quietem huic nostrae – ambitioni dicam an dignitati? – constantissime praetulit*).[302] *Quies* was thus positioned as an ideal diametrically opposed both to senatorial *dignitas* and to *ambitio*, the desire for such advancement. Pliny was not alone in his conception of distinct and opposite senatorial and equestrian aspirations. In his *Histories*, Tacitus describes the intentions of the equestrian procurator Cornelius Fuscus in similar terms. 'In his early years,' Tacitus wrote, 'he had put aside senatorial ambitions out of a desire for peace' (*prima iuventa quietis cupidine senatorium ordinem exuerat*).[303] *Quies* had become a technical term, which described, in Syme's words, 'a reluctance to bear the dignity, the burdens, and the dangers of the senatorial life'.[304] Yet neither Macrinus nor Fuscus led a life entirely without political involvement. Macrinus, described as 'a prince of the equestrian order' (*equestris ordinis princeps*) – another Ciceronian turn of phrase – probably served in some office or had taken some political action in order to come to

---

[300] *Publicani* of course occupied an ambiguous position here, since they were contractors of the state.

[301] See now Bodel 2015: 37–40, a chapter which nicely parallels the discussion here, citing many of the same examples in pursuit of a complementary argument.

[302] Pliny the Younger, *Ep.* 1.14.5.   [303] Tac. *Hist.* 2.86.

[304] Syme 1937: 7. See also Sherwin-White 1966: 118 and Ash 2007: 339.

Vespasian's attention, just like the other *equites* chosen by that emperor for advancement into the senate.[305] For Cornelius Fuscus, his *quies* was but an interlude early in his life. He soon found plenty of time to be politically active when the events of AD 69 required him to choose sides: as procurator of Illyricum, he entered the civil war on behalf of Vespasian, and eventually became praetorian prefect of Domitian.[306]

The antithesis between senatorial and equestrian careers owes much to the rhetoric of Cicero. In the view of Tacitus and Pliny, equestrians did not face the pressures of the *cursus honorum*, and thus they could simply retire to a life of *quies* at a moment's notice. This was the case with Pliny's friend C. Terentius Iunior, who, after serving in the *militiae equestres* and as procurator of Narbonensis, 'took himself off to his estates, and placed the most peaceful leisure above the offices that awaited him' (*recepit se in agros suos, paratisque honoribus tranquillissimum otium praetulit*).[307] We might compare this statement with Cicero's remarks to Atticus, in which he compared his own pathway of honours with his equestrian friend's *honestum otium*.[308] The manner in which Pliny constructed the identity of the equestrian Maturus Arrianus also has clear echoes of Cicero.[309] Pliny wrote to Arrianus to give an account of the sensational trial of Marius Priscus, proconsul of Africa, who had been arraigned before the senate on a charge of *repetundae*.[310] The opening of the letter is very telling:

It is customary for you to express delight when anything happens in the senate that is worthy of the *ordo*. For although you have withdrawn [sc. from political life] as a result of your desire for peace (*quietis amore*), concern for the dignity of the state sits firm in your heart.[311]

Arrianus' equestrian *quies* is designed to contrast with Pliny's own role in the cut-and-thrust of politics in Rome. For Pliny was not merely observing the trial, but played an active role in it as a member of the prosecution team alongside Cornelius Tacitus (much as Cicero would have done). Arrianus thus appears as the very model of a Ciceronian *eques*, who primarily lives a life of leisure, but still supports and upholds the values of the *res publica*.

---

[305] See Houston 1977: 53–4 on the origins of Vespasian's *adlecti*.

[306] Pflaum 1960: 77–80 (no. 34).   [307] Pliny the Younger, *Ep.* 7.25.2.

[308] Cic. *Att.* 1.17.5 [SB 17.5].

[309] He may be identical with M. Maturus, procurator of the Maritime Alps in AD 69 (whose career is outlined by Pflaum 1960: 95–8 [no. 40 *bis*]).

[310] Pliny the Younger, *Ep.* 2.11. For the context, see Sherwin-White 1966: 56–8, 160; Whitton 2013: 154–8.

[311] Pliny the Younger, *Ep.* 2.11.1: *solet esse gaudio tibi, si quid acti est in senatu dignum ordine illo. quamvis enim quietis amore secesseris, insidet tamen animo tuo maiestatis publicae cura.*

This fits in with the Ciceronian theme of the letter in general, in which Pliny takes on the role of a prosecutor in a case of *repetundae*.[312] That Pliny should turn to Cicero as an epistolary model is understandable, but these passages show the extent to which he adopted his predecessor's rhetoric as a model for a senatorial life in his own day.[313]

Pliny was himself the son of one *eques*, L. Caecilius Secundus, a *praefectus fabrum*, and an adopted son of another, C. Plinius Secundus (better known as the Elder Pliny).[314] But after Pliny the Younger became a senator, and set out to climb the *cursus honorum*, he distanced himself from the equestrian order. Neither his natural nor his adoptive father functioned as an appropriate role model for Pliny's ambitious political life. L. Caecilius Secundus is virtually absent from the *Letters*, and played no role in Pliny's personal self-representation.[315] The Elder Pliny is a more prominent figure in the correspondence, but his nephew did not endorse his life as an example that he should follow. This is because in Pliny's mind the Elder Pliny was an equestrian procurator and thus did not devote himself to the *res publica* in the same way senators were required to do as they ascended the *cursus*.[316] That is not to say that Pliny's uncle was not hard working. When he was in Rome the Elder Pliny would reportedly begin work on his private studies while it was still dark, then pay a visit to the emperor Vespasian before attending to his official responsibilities.[317] His nephew noted that 'after returning home he gave up the remaining time to his studies' (*reversus domum quod reliquum temporis studiis reddebat*). If we follow this literally, it means that Elder Pliny could have only spent a few hours each morning on the duties required by his equestrian post. This was probably the prefecture of the fleet at Misenum: detachments of the fleet were based at Rome and Ostia, and the Elder Pliny probably divided his time between there and Campania.[318] According to his nephew's account, the Elder Pliny followed a similar schedule when he was actually in Misenum, devoting the afternoon to his personal studies

---

[312] Arrianus also received other letters that paint Pliny as a successor of Cicero's writings and career (Whitton 2013: 158).

[313] Gibson and Morello 2012: 74–103.

[314] The career of Pliny's natural father appears on *AE* 1983, 443.

[315] Gibson and Morello 2012: 109.

[316] Suet. *Vir. Ill. Vita Plinii Secundi* records his service in the *militia equestres* then in 'most distinguished procuratorships' (*procurationes . . . splendidissimas*) (ed. Roth, p. 300). Syme 1969 provides a plausible, if still speculative, account of which procuratorships he may have held.

[317] Pliny the Younger, *Ep.* 3.5.9.

[318] Syme 1969: 227. Detachments of the fleet were based at Rome, Ostia/Portus, Puteoli and Centumcellae (Starr 1941: 17–21).

after a period of relaxation, bathing and lunching.[319] This suggests that he spent limited time at fleet headquarters itself, presumably leaving most of the regular business to his staff, and instead focused on his writing whenever possible.[320]

This portrait in the letters revealed to Pliny the Younger's readers why his uncle, although industrious, was not an appropriate role model. As a senator climbing the *cursus honorum*, Pliny the Younger must devote himself to the *res publica* first and foremost, rather than his *studia*.[321] His role models were senators such as Pomponius Bassus and Vestricius Spurinna, who saw their senatorial careers through to their conclusions and climbed to the summit of the *cursus honorum*. Conspicuously, they did not leave their official *cursus* mid-stream (as the *eques* Terentius Iunior was able to do).[322] This was an essential part of Pliny's self-representation as an ideal senator, always working for the good of the state, whose own *otium* would eventually come at the end of his career, as the reward for years of *labor*. It is very telling that the Elder Pliny's own portrayal of his imperial service in the preface to his *Natural History* is somewhat at odds with that of his nephew. The Elder Pliny assured the emperor Titus that he only had time to work on the encyclopaedia at night, since 'we allocate the days for your affairs' (*dies vobis inpendimus*).[323] Like all other equestrian administrators who depended on imperial favour, the Elder Pliny was understandably keen to appear to be a conscientious servant of both the emperor and the *res publica*: there was no question that his imperial service came first before any personal *studia*, a claim diametrically opposed to the portrait in Pliny the Younger's *Letters*. The case of the 'two Plinys' illustrates the tension that emerged during the principate between the enduring Republican conception of *equites* as apolitical individuals and the new equestrian *cursus*, which gave rise to a distinct elite of service with values identical to those of careerist senators.

The dichotomy between senatorial service to the *res publica* and the apparent leisure and flexibility of equestrians is a model that suited Pliny's literary agenda, and the construction of his own identity in the *Letters*. This portrayal would not have accurately characterised Pliny's equestrian contemporaries in the late first and second centuries AD who did embark on

---

[319] Pliny the Younger, *Ep.* 6.16.5.
[320] Even during his procuratorship in Spain, the Elder Pliny took his notebooks with him (Pliny the Younger, *Ep.* 3.5.17).
[321] Bernstein 2008: 205; Gibson and Morello 2012: 115–23.
[322] Pliny the Younger, *Ep.* 3.1 (Vestricius Spurinna), 4.23 (Pomponius Bassus). See Leach 2003: 161–3; Gibson and Morello 2012: 116–23.
[323] Pliny the Elder, *NH pref.* 19.

long careers in the imperial service. But Pliny's description still has some truth in it. Senators did have obligations that equestrians did not, including the requirement to own property in Italy, attend meetings of the senate in Rome, and obtain the emperor's permission before travelling outside Italy. Even if a senator eschewed the attractions and glories of the *cursus honorum* – and there were certainly such men – they still had duties as backbench *pedarii*.[324] It is easy to understand why some elite Romans resisted these restrictions and were content to remain in the *ordo equester*. In eulogising the equestrian Septimius Severus, Statius portrayed him as a man who could have been a senator if he had desired it, but instead preferred to take on occasional legal cases.[325] However, sometimes the emperor's authority left qualified *equites* with no choice but to acquiesce in their promotion to the *curia*. Suetonius noted that if any *equites* refused to become senators, Claudius deprived them of their equestrian rank as well, stripping them of all public honours.[326] One of these must have been the unfortunate Surdinius Gallus, who fled to Carthage to avoid being enrolled in the *curia*, only to be summoned back to Rome by the emperor.[327] Others were more successful in choosing a life of *quies*. For example, L. Iunius Moderatus Columella was a tribune of the *legio VI Ferrata*, before declining further advancement.[328] He settled at Tarentum, perhaps having been sent there to establish a veteran colony composed of soldiers from his former legion.[329] In advocating agriculture as a honourable way to spend his life, Columella criticised those who used money dishonourably to buy 'the glory and power of the *fasces*' (*fascium decus et imperium*).[330] He would have found a boon companion in C. Castricius Calvus Agricola, another military tribune from Forum Livii, who turned to estate management.[331] Agriculture offered a respectable way of life through which to turn a profit and earn monetary rewards.[332] These farmer-*equites* remind us of the real attractions in eschewing advancement to procuratorships or the *curia*, both choices that could entail greater glory, but also greater burdens.

The legacy of the Republican apolitical *eques* meant that equestrian rank could also be used as a cover for political ambitions, at least in the early principate.[333] According to Tacitus, L. Annaeus Mela, the brother of

---

[324] Talbert 1984: 23–6, 249–52.   [325] Stat. *Silv.* 4.5.41–44; Coleman 1988: 168.
[326] Suet. *Claud.* 24.1.   [327] Dio 61.29.1.   [328] *CIL* IX 235 = *ILS* 2923.
[329] Matthews 2010: 89–91.   [330] Col. *RR* I *pref.* 10.
[331] *CIL* XI 600. The fragmentary inscription refers to Agricola only as a tribune, which suggests that he did not seek further employment.
[332] Bodel 2015: 39–40.
[333] This is less true of the Severan period and later, when equestrians did become emperor. See Chapter 11.

Seneca the Younger, had such reasons in mind when he declined senatorial advancement:

He had refrained from seeking senatorial offices on account of the curious ambition that he could rival the power of consuls as an *eques Romanus*. At the same time, he thought the procuratorships for administering the emperor's affairs offered a shorter route for the acquisition of riches.[334]

Mela wanted a life without many restrictions, no *leges annales*, no expenses that came with senatorial office and games, as well as the leisure to pursue his business interests as it suited him, while still receiving a salary as a procurator.[335] His vision therefore combined the equestrian *quies* of the Republic with the new opportunities available under the monarchical *res publica*. Mela's father, the Elder Seneca, envisioned his son's equestrian status as a true renunciation of ambition.[336] But Tacitus' remarks suggest that his aim was actually the opposite, and that like Maecenas and Sallustius Crispus he wished to wield power and influence from outside the *curia*.[337] This experiment in using equestrian rank as a cloak did not save Mela from the *delatores* and the wrath of the emperor Nero, any more than it protected the 300 *equites* allegedly executed by Claudius.[338] Here we see the conflict between the idea of the apolitical *eques* and the reality of the new monarchical state, in which all honours and favours flowed from, or were withdrawn by, the *princeps*.

    The example of Tiberius' praetorian prefect L. Aelius Sejanus reveals similar tensions between equestrian rank and political power in the discourse of the early principate. In Tacitus' *Annals* Tiberius delivers a speech in response to Sejanus' petition to marry Livia, Germanicus' sister, in which the emperor considers whether she will be content to marry an *eques*. Tiberius mentions that Augustus considered marrying his own daughter Iulia to *equites*, who were 'distinguished by their peacefulness of life, and entangled in no political business' (*insigni tranquillitate vitae, nullis rei publicae negotiis permixtos*).[339] Although the emperor says he knows that Sejanus is likewise content 'to remain within the bounds of your rank' (*istum intra locum*), not everyone is convinced and some whisper that the prefect's power has outstripped Augustus' equestrian friends. Tacitus therefore uses Tiberius' speech to dramatise the tension

---

[334] Tac. *Ann.* 16.17.3: *petitione honorum abstinuerat per ambitionem praeposteram ut eques Romanus consularibus potentia aequaretur; simul adquirendae pecuniae brevius iter credebat per procurationes administrandis principis negotiis.*

[335] Duncan-Jones 2006: 193; Matthews 2010: 101.   [336] Sen. *Controv.* 2.pref.3–4.

[337] Thus Ash 2007: 339, 'apparent modesty may mask artfulness'.   [338] Suet. *Claud.* 29.2.

[339] Tac. *Ann.* 4.40.6

between the lesser status of the *equites* and the new power that they could wield under the imperial system. Sejanus, for all his efforts, could not quite cloak his power and ambition with his equestrian status.

Indeed, the plausibility of using equestrian rank as a political cover must have diminished considerably over the course of the principate. In the age of Sejanus and Annaeus Mela the equestrian career structure and the idea of a distinct service elite was in its infancy, but this was certainly not the case in the Flavian and Antonine periods, or beyond. Pliny's characterisation of the senatorial and equestrian orders possessing entirely different aims and goals was at least partially a literary conceit. He was, as we have seen, correct in supposing that *equites* did not have all the same obligations as senators, but he was wrong to deny equestrians any careerist ambitions at all. The same Republican concepts lay behind Tacitus' excursus on the growth of equestrian power in the *Annals*. As we discussed in Chapter 4, this digression was designed to highlight the problems of a monarchical government in which the authority of the senate and its magistrates could be circumvented by courtiers. But the growth of equestrian positions in the imperial administration, as well as their coalescence into a distinct hierarchy and career, lessened the difference between office-holding senators and their equestrian counterparts. Politically ambitious *equites* no longer needed to wield power without office, like Maecenas. Instead, equestrians were appointed to hold senior court posts such as *ab epistulis, a libellis, a rationibus* and *a cognitionibus*, placing them at the very heart of the imperial government.

It is hardly surprising that the idea of the apolitical *eques* is not found prominently in Cassius Dio's *Roman History*, written in the third century AD.[340] In Dio's speech of Maecenas, it is accepted as an uncontroversial fact that equestrians will hold military and administrative offices analogous to senators.[341] Moreover, in Dio's account of contemporary politics under the Severan emperors he does not challenge the idea of *equites* in court posts, as Tacitus did. Instead, his criticism is directed against men of humble background or dubious respectability who gain entrance into the *ordo equester* and thence to high office through imperial favour.[342] Caracalla's *ab epistulis* Marcius Claudius Agrippa was one such undesirable, given that he had begun his life as a slave and hairdresser.[343]

---

[340] His description of Maecenas' power seems to be an exception (Dio 51.3.5).

[341] Dio 52.24.1–25.7.

[342] Similar sentiments can be found in Dio's discussion of such men who entered the senate (see Davenport 2012a: 808–11).

[343] Dio 79(78).13.3–4; Davenport 2012c: 186, 197.

On the other hand, Dio's account of the career of the future emperor M. Opellius Macrinus praises his proper conduct as *praefectus vehiculorum*, procurator and praetorian prefect.[344] By the early third century AD it was unexceptional that *equites* should hold such important administrative posts, which were not perceived as a challenge to senatorial authority.[345]

The idea that equestrians existed outside the framework of government and eschewed official posts for a life of *quies* therefore lost its currency over the course of the principate with the consolidation of the equestrian *cursus* and the emergence of the *equestris nobilitas*. It was replaced by the concept of a sinecure, a position that carried *dignitas* without *labor*. Such honorific positions had their origins in the late Republic, but they became even more significant under the patronal system of the monarchical *res publica*, since they represented personal grants of imperial favour. Even Pliny's equestrian friend Maturus Arrianus, who, it might be remembered, had a love of *quies*, desired such an honorific post. Pliny wrote to the prefect of Egypt, Vibius Maximus, on Arrianus' behalf:[346]

He is free of ambition, and for that reason he has kept himself at equestrian rank, although he could easily climb to the heights of power. However, he must be distinguished and ennobled by me. And so, I judge that there is a real need to increase his public standing, even though he may not consider it, realise it, or perhaps even want it. The post should be one that is distinguished but not burdensome.[347]

The precise office itself is not mentioned, but it may have been the headship of the Library and Museum of Alexandria.[348] In Pliny's argument, the position itself is immaterial (as long as it is not onerous). The crucial point is that it should enhance Arrianus' *dignitas*, and Pliny's in the process. Despite Pliny's characterisation of his friend as free of ambition, there is circumstantial evidence that Arrianus did take up the post when it was offered him.[349]

---

[344] Dio 79(78).11.1–3.

[345] Macrinus' own ascent to the imperial purple was another matter, of course (Davenport 2012c: 196–7).

[346] Pliny the Younger, *Ep.* 3.2.

[347] Pliny the Younger, *Ep.* 3.2.5: *caret ambitu: ideo se in equestri gradu tenuit, cum facile possit ascendere altissimum. mihi tamen ornandus excolendusque est. itaque magni aestimo dignitati eius aliquid astruere inopinantis nescientis, immo etiam fortasse nolentis; astruere autem quod sit splendidum nec molestum.*

[348] Sherwin-White 1966: 210–11.

[349] Sherwin-White 1966: 211, citing Pliny the Younger, *Ep.* 4.8 and 4.12 in which Maturus is not in Italy.

Sometimes an equestrian would seek out a procuratorship with the express intention of declining the honour. Fronto wrote to the emperor Antoninus Pius to thank him for allowing this to happen in the case of his friend Sex. Calpurnius Iulianus:

> In response to my request, you have already increased the public standing (*dignitas*) of one equestrian, my close companion Sextus Calpurnius, by awarding him two procuratorships. I count these two procuratorships as favours that you have actually given four times: twice when you gave him the positions, and twice when you accepted his requests to be excused from holding them.[350]

In the same letter Fronto proceeded to ask Pius for a procuratorship for his friend Appian of Alexandria, assuring the emperor that 'he wishes to acquire this position in order to increase his status in his old age, not out of ambition or from a desire for the procuratorial salary'.[351] Such requests were evidently popular: Pius had previously turned Fronto down on the grounds that it would open the floodgates for a 'torrent of advocates' (*causidicorum scatebra*) asking for such a sinecure. Once again, it was the *dignitas* of the position that was paramount. In the Antonine period even one procuratorship was sufficient to confer the status of *vir egregius*, which would have elevated Appian above his peers in the *ordo equester* into the *equestris nobilitas*. Indeed, Appian proudly remarked in the preface of his *Roman History* that he had pleaded cases before the emperors, and had been rewarded with a procuratorship.[352] These examples from the correspondence of Pliny and Fronto reveal that equestrians who eschewed long administrative careers were not entirely content to renounce the possibility of imperial honours and the prestige that accompanied them. Such was the power of the emperor as the ultimate source of status in the monarchical *res publica*.

Honour among Greeks

The honorary procuratorship awarded to Appian takes us into the world of Greek intellectuals and their attitude to service – or the search for

---

[350] Fronto, *Ad Ant. Pium* 10.1 (vdH² p. 168) = Davenport and Manley 2014: 122–3 (no. 35): *equitis Romani unius contubernalis mei Sexti Calpurnii dignitatem rogatu meo exornasti duabus iam procurationibus datis. ea ego duarum procurationum beneficia quater numero: bis cum dedisti procurationes itemque bis cum excusationes recepisti.*

[351] Fronto, *Ad Ant. Pium* 10.2: *dignitatis enim suae in senectute ornandae causa, non ambitione aut procuratoris stipendii cupiditate optat adpisci hunc honorem.*

[352] App. Pref. 15.

honours – in the Roman government.[353] Two of Plutarch's treatises, *On the Tranquillity of Mind* and *Precepts of Statecraft*, contain important reflections on imperial office-holding. In *On the Tranquillity of Mind* he discussed how some Greeks were never content with their lot, but were always searching for greater rewards. If they were patricians they were upset if they were not yet praetors, and if they were praetors, that they were not yet consul.[354] This remark should not be read as a criticism of Greek involvement in Roman political careers, but a commentary on men who are unable to be content with what life has offered them.[355] Precisely the same sentiment can be found in Seneca's *On Favours*, demonstrating its universality.[356] In *Precepts of Statecraft* Plutarch urged young Greeks to cultivate powerful friends in Rome in order to benefit their own *polis*. He described how Augustus spared the people of Alexandria as a favour to his friend Areius, then comments:

Is there any comparison between such a favour and the procuratorships and governorships of provinces from which many talents may be gained and in pursuit of which most public men grow old haunting the doors of other men's houses and leaving their own affairs uncared for?[357]

Plutarch was not advocating any resistance to Roman rule in making these comments, but the idea that Greeks should work on behalf of their communities.[358] He suggested that if Greeks wanted to benefit their cities, they did not need to hold senatorial and equestrian posts, but should instead seek out powerful Roman friends and allies.[359]

This is something that Plutarch himself did, earning the friendship of prominent Romans, such as the consular Q. Sosius Senecio, and his patron L. Mestrius Florus, in accordance with the advice of *Precepts of Statecraft*.[360] Through Mestrius' patronage Plutarch became a Roman citizen, and he was probably also awarded equestrian status, though this is nowhere recorded definitively.[361] It also seems that Plutarch, like Appian, received an honorary procuratorship. According to the Suda, Trajan granted him 'the status of a consular' (τῆς τῶν ὑπάτων ἀξίας) and authority

[353] See the important discussion in Kuhn 2010: 41–72.   [354] Plut. *Mor.* 470 C.
[355] Swain 1996: 169–70; Kuhn 2010: 63.   [356] Stadter 2014: 46–7; Sen. *Ben.* 2.27.
[357] Plut. *Mor.* 814 D (trans. H. N. Fowler): Ἆρά γ' ἄξιον τῇ χάριτι ταύτῃ παραβαλεῖν τὰς πολυταλάντους ἐπιτροπὰς καὶ διοικήσεις τῶν ἐπαρχιῶν, ἃς διώκοντες οἱ πολλοὶ γηράσκουσι πρὸς ἀλλοτρίαις θύραις, τὰ οἴκοι προλιπόντες.
[358] Swain 1996: 144–86, esp. 170–1; Salmeri 2000: 61.
[359] Stadter 2014: 48. Cf. Nutton 1978: 212–13; Madsen 2006: 65–7.
[360] C. P. Jones 1971: 48–9; Swain 1996: 144–5; Stadter 2014: 8–9.   [361] Stadter 2014: 40.

over Illyricum.[362] Syncellus records that Plutarch became the procurator of Greece (ἐπιτροπεύων Ἑλλάδος) under Hadrian.[363] The historicity of these statements has been the subject of some dispute. It would be strange for Plutarch to be awarded *ornamenta consularia* by Trajan, and a procuratorship by Hadrian, given that the first honour is manifestly the greater, though later Greek writers could easily have confused the two emperors.[364] It is nevertheless probable that Plutarch received some imperial distinction on account of his erudition and learning, possibly obtained through the influence of his prominent Roman friends.[365] This was probably the honorary procuratorship, followed later by the *ornamenta consularia*.[366] Similar contemporary examples can be found, such as Trajan's doctor, T. Statilius Crito, who wrote an account of the emperor's Dacian wars, and was recognised with the sinecure of an honorary procuratorship.[367] Plutarch's imperial *dignitas* did not conflict with the principles of the *Precepts of Statecraft*.[368] It represented Plutarch's acceptance of the Roman imperial system, in which rewards and benefits flowed from the emperor, without forsaking his life and offices in Chaeronea and Delphi.[369]

As with their counterparts from the western provinces, *equites* from Greece and Asia Minor often sought one administrative post as way of both increasing their status and gaining financial reward. This route seems to have been largely preferred to undertaking full careers.[370] The position of *advocatus fisci* was ideal in this regard, as it allowed Greeks to hold a salaried imperial office in the eastern provinces without travelling to Rome or another region in the west. For example, P. Aelius Zeuxidemus Aristus Zeno, high priest of Asia, served as *advocatus fisci* in Phrygia and Asia.[371] Such a post enabled equestrians to continue to engage in traditionally Greek cultural or civic pursuits, perhaps more so than other forms

---

[362] Suda, s.v. Πλούταρχος (ed. Adler π 1793).   [363] Sync. *Ecl. Chron.* (ed. Dindorf p. 659).

[364] Oliver 1970: 70–1 suggests Hadrian granted both honours. This must have been early in his reign, since Plutarch was dead by AD 125 (C. P. Jones 1966: 66).

[365] Stadter 2014: 42.   [366] Bowersock 1969: 57; C. P. Jones 1971: 29–30, 34; Pelling 1988: 2–3.

[367] *I. Eph.* 719. The post is restored in Robert 1954 nos 49, 75. The honorific nature of the office is discussed by Bowersock 1969: 65. For his authorship of the *Getica*, see *FGrH* 200.

[368] Cf. Swain 1996: 171–2, who thinks that the procuratorship is not historical, and it is better 'to allow Plutarch to practise what he preached'.

[369] Cf. Madsen 2006, who draws a distinction between Plutarch's views and those of Greeks in Asia Minor, particularly Bithynia, who did follow official careers.

[370] Kuhn 2010: 27.

[371] *IGR* IV 819; Pflaum 1960: 550–1 (no. 205). His son, P. Aelius Antipater, would go on to further honours at the imperial court, acting as *ab epistulis* to the emperor Septimius Severus and tutor to his sons Caracalla and Geta. See Phil. *VS* 607; Pflaum 1960: 610–13 (no. 230).

of service, such as the *militiae equestres*.[372] This can be seen in the case of the sophist Quirinus of Nicomedia, who was appointed *advocatus fisci* because of his talent for prosecution speeches.[373] Another Greek *eques*, T. Flavius Glaukos of Marathon, described himself as a 'poet and rhetor and philosopher, former *advocatus fisci*' (ποιητὴς καὶ ῥήτωρ καὶ φιλόσοφος | ἀπὸ συνηγοριῶν ταμίου).[374] Glaukos came from a family that had held imperial offices intermittently over several generations. His paternal grandfather, also called T. Flavius Glaukos, was a procurator in the middle of the second century AD, but his family tree shows no other equestrian administrators in the direct line (though there was another branch of the family that entered the senate).[375] The daughter of the procurator Glaukos, [Eury]ale, described her father as a man 'who became the best of the *equites*, and served as procurator of Cyprus in the sea' (ὃς ἄριστος ἐτύχθη | ἱππήων, βυθίην Κύπρον ἐπιτροπέων).[376] This formulation suggests that [Eury]ale, and other Greeks, understood that Glaukos' procuratorship increased his personal status relative to other *equites*, reflecting the same ideas as Tacitus' concept of the *equestris nobilitas*. But imperial accolades were not given excessive pride of place above literary or cultural accomplishments in this family. Glaukos, the poet turned *advocatus fisci*, paid ample tribute to the local priesthoods of his relative Themistokles, and their common ancestry from the poet Sarapion.[377] This represented the integration of traditional Greek honours with new distinctions offered by the empire of Rome.

Emperors bestowed equestrian rank and procuratorships on Greeks whom they valued for their learning and skill.[378] Caracalla lavished several honours on his doctor L. Gellius Maximus, an *eques* from Antioch in Pisidia.[379] The nature of these perquisites is revealed by a number of statues of Maximus which were erected in both his native Antioch and in Sagalassos. On the accompanying inscriptions he is styled 'the *vir egregius* physician and member of the Museum, *ducenarius*' (τὸν κράτιστον | ἀρχίατρον καὶ ἀπὸ | Μουσείου δουκηνά|ριον).[380] Nutton firmly established that the inscriptions refer to the Museum of Alexandria, and that Maximus

---

[372] Though not sophistry, given its extensive demands, as argued by Bowie 1982: 48.
[373] Phil. *VS* 621.   [374] *IG* II² 3704. For his poetry, see Oliver 1949: 248–56.
[375] See Oliver 1949: Fig. 2 (between 248 and 249); Nowakowski 2011: 287.
[376] *IG* II² 3662. Oliver 1949: 253 suggests that the poetic dedication was actually composed by the poet Glaukos.
[377] Geagan 1991: 159–60.   [378] Demougin 1999: 583.
[379] For his Antiochene origin, see Christol and Drew-Bear 2004: 95, 109–10.
[380] Antioch: *SEG* 54, 1368. Sagalassos: *SEG* 50, 1312 = *SEG* 54, 1377. A similar formulation in Latin can be found in *CIL* III 6828 = *AE* 2005, 1479, also from Antioch. Another inscription from the city does not mention the museum post and *ducenarius* title (*SEG* 54, 1369).

was only a member of the institution, rather than its head.[381] Moreover, the title of *ducenarius* must be distinguished from membership of the Museum. Instead, it represents the salary granted by Caracalla to Maximus, as Christol and Drew-Bear have argued.[382] If he ever held a procuratorship, it was likely to have been a purely honorific post, like that granted to Appian of Alexandria.[383] Yet these rewards were sufficient to give Maximus the title of *vir egregius* and *ducenarius*, elevating this Greek doctor above other *equites Romani* without imperial posts and demonstrating to all that the emperor Caracalla had rewarded him financially. The ultimate sinecure was surely that held by Hadrian of Tyre, who occupied the chair of rhetoric at Athens and Rome under Marcus Aurelius and his son Commodus.[384] Hadrian had strong connections with the imperial court, particularly through his friendship with Cn. Claudius Severus, one of the sons-in-law of the emperor Marcus Aurelius.[385] As Hadrian lay on his deathbed, Commodus granted him the post of *ab epistulis* as a final tribute to his literary accomplishments.[386] This is a classic example of how individual positions within the larger equestrian career could function as symbols of imperial favour in and of themselves. The posts were valued by Greek intellectuals as a new form of reward for their talents.

Indeed, in the second and third centuries AD the imperial court became an arena of rivalry for Greek rhetors and sophists, who competed for the positions of *ab epistulis* or *ab epistulis Graecis*.[387] Two types of *equites* held these secretarial offices. The first group was composed of those men who followed a regular equestrian career, such as Valerius Eudaemon, who was procurator of the diocese of Alexandria in Egypt, and of the Greek and Latin libraries, before rising to the rank of *ab epistulis*.[388] For this type of *eques*, the post of *ab epistulis* could lead to the great prefectures, as in the case of Ti. Claudius Vibianus Tertullus (who came from either Pergamum or Selge), who became *a rationibus* and then *praefectus vigilum* under Marcus Aurelius and Commodus.[389] These men were representative of

---

[381] Nutton 1971: 263–9; Christol and Drew-Bear 2004: 111–16.

[382] Christol and Drew-Bear 2004: 110.   [383] Nutton 1971: 270–2.   [384] Phil. *VS* 588–9.

[385] *I. Eph.* 1539; Bowersock 1969: 55.   [386] Phil. *VS* 590.

[387] There were two separate departments, for Greek and Latin letters, at least at the freedman level, from the late first century AD (Weaver 1972: 255, 262–3). The separate equestrian heads, the *ab epistulis Latinis* and *Graecis*, are firmly attested in the late second century AD, but may well pre-date this (Townend 1961b: 379–80; Eck 2000: 249).

[388] *CIL* III 431 = *ILS* 1449; *IGR* III 1077; Pflaum 1960: 264–71 (no. 110). Bowie 2013: 252 calls him a 'career bureaucrat'.

[389] *CIL* III 7136 = *I. Eph.* 651 = *ILS* 1344; Habicht 1969: 28; *I. Selge* 13; *SEG* 53, 1582; Pflaum 1960: 683–4 (no. 252). For the chronology of these offices, see S. Mitchell 2003: 147–8.

the emerging equestrian service elite, with long procuratorial careers and salaries which rose as they ascended the *cursus*. The second group was composed of sophists, rhetors or grammarians who were appointed directly to the position of *ab epistulis Graecis* by the emperor without any previous service.[390] One such man was the sophist Alexander (also known as Peloplaton, the 'Clay-Plato'), whom Marcus Aurelius summoned to his side in Pannonia, where the emperor was based during his wars against the northern tribes.[391] Alexander held no other imperial positions: according to Philostratus, he either died in Gaul while still *ab epistulis Graecis* or in Italy after his retirement from office.[392] The Greek litterateurs selected for this imperial secretarial office benefited from the significant salary it carried. This was 200,000 sesterces under the Antonines, but it became a trecenarian post by the Severan period.[393] While it might be thought that sophists would consider themselves to be above the petty place-seeking at the Roman imperial court – and undoubtedly many did – some were prepared to engage in the competition for the emperor's approval and the large salary that came with an official post.

The sophist T. Claudius Flavianus Dionysius of Miletus was one such competitive Greek intellectual. The emperor Hadrian granted him equestrian rank, the right to eat at the Museum in Alexandria, and two procuratorships (with their salaries, of course), as official recognition for his wisdom.[394] Dionysius' literary and imperial distinctions were recorded on the base of a public statue erected in his honour at Ephesus:

The council and the people. To Titus Claudius Flavianus Dionysius, the rhetor and sophist, twice imperial procurator, Claudius Eutuchus (erected this) to his patron.[395]

Dionysius may well have hoped for elevation to the plum position of *ab epistulis*, but such a reward was not forthcoming from the jealous and paranoid Hadrian. Instead, the emperor decided to actively undermine Dionysius by showering honours on the sophist's rivals.[396] Dionysius is said to have had ongoing rivalry with Caninius Celer, one of the emperor's secretaries, throughout his entire life.[397] He was also particularly spiteful

---

[390] Millar 1977: 82–93, 104–7; Bowie 1982: 39–47.
[391] Phil. *VS* 571 (*ab epistulis*), 576 (student of Dionysius).   [392] Phil. *VS* 576.
[393] Pflaum 1974: 34.   [394] Phil. *VS* 524; Bowie 1982: 48.
[395] *I. Eph.* 3047 = *SEG* 30, 1309: [ἡ βουλὴ καὶ] ὁ δῆμος | [Τ(ίτον) Κλ(αύδιον)] Φ[λαουιαν]ὸν Διονύσιον | [τὸν] ῥήτορα καὶ σοφιστὴν | [δ]ὶς ἐπίτροπον τοῦ Σεβαστοῦ | Κλ(αύδιος) Εὔτυχος τὸν ἑαυτοῦ πάτρωνα.
[396] Dio 69.3.2–4.
[397] Phil. *VS* 524. For the identification of this Celer with Marcus Aurelius' tutor, Caninius Celer, see Bowie 1982: 58.

towards C. Avidius Heliodorus, Hadrian's *ab epistulis*, once remarking: 'Caesar can grant you riches and honour but he cannot make you a rhetor'.[398] This seems to have been a particularly unfair comment, given that Heliodorus' talent later led to his appointment as prefect of Egypt, according to Dio.[399] But it is probable, as Birley suggested, that Dionysius harboured ambitions to be *ab epistulis* himself, and was angry at being denied this prestigious post.[400] The coda to this story is that Dionysius was buried at Ephesus in a sarcophagus that referred to him only as a rhetor, with no imperial honours mentioned.[401] This was markedly different to the inscribed version of his life that accompanied the earlier public statue erected at Ephesus, and leads one to wonder whether the epitaph was an emphatic and deliberate final statement that his talent was the only distinction that mattered.

Some Greek litterateurs certainly felt that their peers who were employed in imperial service were only second-rate writers. Philostratus of Lemnos famously penned the treatise *How to Write Letters* as an indictment of the style of Severus Alexander's *ab epistulis*, the sophist Aspasius of Ravenna.[402] As Bowie has pointed out, the true sophistic life was really not compatible with imperial service, and it is easy to see how many Greek sophists would have believed that a position at the imperial court was subordinate to real accomplishments in the sophistic art.[403] Yet the stories from Cassius Dio and Philostratus reveal that the imperial court continuously attracted Greek sophists, poets and rhetors, because they valued equestrian rank, official posts and salaries as personal rewards and acknowledgement of their *paideia*.[404] For, as Brunt observed, 'their success in the Roman world rested on that which they had already achieved in the Greek'.[405]

These relationships were mutually beneficial to both Greek intellectuals and emperors, as Rome's rulers wanted ensure that they could speak effectively to their Greek subjects through the mouths of the greatest orators of the age. Indeed, Philostratus praised the *ab epistulis Graecis* P. Aelius Antipater for producing compositions that were 'worthy of the imperial image' (ἐπάξια τοῦ βασιλείου προσώπου).[406] The award of equestrian honours and offices to Greek intellectuals thus effectively harnessed

[398] Dio 69.3.5: Καῖσαρ χρήματα μέν σοι καὶ τιμὴν δοῦναι δύναται, ῥήτορα δέ σε ποιῆσαι οὐ δύναται.
[399] Dio 72(71).22.2.   [400] A. R. Birley 1997: 216–17.
[401] *I.Eph.* 426; C. P. Jones 1980: 374. The sarcophagus was found outside the south gate of Ephesus. Cf. Phil. *VS* 526, who says that he was buried in the agora.
[402] Phil. *VS* 628.   [403] Bowie 1982: 48, 50.   [404] Kuhn 2010: 145–6; Kemezis 2014: 215–16.
[405] Brunt 1994: 34.   [406] Phil. *VS* 607; Hogan and Kemezis 2016: 31.

their talents to serve the Roman imperial state, rather than allowing them to become possible mouthpieces of dissent. None of the Greek *equites* discussed thus far offered any genuine resistance to the idea of holding government posts or receiving sinecures from the emperors.[407] Many may have avoided the full careers that required years of service, but, in accepting honorific procuratorships or the post of *ab epistulis Graecis*, they acquiesced in the competition for honours offered by the Roman imperial system.

The writings of Lucian of Samosata provide an indication of the difficulties some Greeks must have felt in deciding whether to accept or decline posts in the Roman administration. Lucian was the author of a treatise entitled *On Salaried Posts in Great Houses*, in which he attacked Greeks who sought the support of Roman grandees. But Lucian later accepted an imperial office in Egypt, probably in the AD 180s, during the last years of his life.[408] He defended this decision in a later work, *The Apology*, in which he argued that his appointment as a salaried official in the imperial administration was very different from the positions held by those who served in private houses like slaves.[409] Lucian had been ensnared by the potential road to honours, proudly remarking that there lay before him the promise of a procuratorship or another imperial position.[410]

One man who would have thought Lucian's arguments rather specious was the former slave and Stoic philosopher Epictetus, who left Rome and taught philosophy at Nicopolis in Epirus.[411] Here was a Greek who represented a genuine oppositional voice. Epictetus characterised all service to Rome and its institutions as a form of slavery, even for those *equites* who obtained the gold ring and held officer commands in the *militiae equestres*.[412] Equestrian procuratorships were grouped together with senatorial provincial governorships, consulships and other imperial honours for which men fight like small children.[413] Epictetus not only took aim at senatorial and equestrian posts in the service of Rome, but also at local Greek civic offices, suggesting that his opposition was actually to all forms of honours, which he regarded as essentially worthless. Instead, he believed

---

[407] Oppositional literature written by Greek and Roman elites usually focused on discussing the best ways to reconcile oneself to the imperial system or living under emperors. For a recent examination of Plutarch and Tacitus in this context, see Kemezis 2016.

[408] Lucian never gives the title of the position. Pflaum 1959 suggested that he was *archistator*, while vander Leest 1985 and C. P. Jones 1986: 20–1 argued that he held the position of *eisagogeus*.

[409] Luc. *Apol.* 11–12.   [410] Luc. *Apol.* 12; C. P. Jones 1986: 21.

[411] Millar 1965a: 141–2; Brunt 2013: 331.   [412] Epict. *Diss.* 4.1.38–40.

[413] Epict. *Diss.* 4.7.21–4. See the discussion of Millar 1965a: 145.

that one should find peace by living life in accordance with Stoic principles.[414] The impact of Epictetus' teaching should not be dismissed, since his audience at Nicopolis included men of senatorial and equestrian rank – including those who held procuratorships and governorships, according to his own account.[415] One of these was an *eques* who had been exiled from Rome and vowed never to seek imperial office again, instead preferring to spend the rest of his days in peace. When this *eques* returned to Rome, however, the emperor offered him a new position, and he eventually became *praefectus annonae*.[416] For Epictetus this was not a sign of success, but a cautionary tale about men who placed too much value in imperial honours. However, most *equites* would have been like Lucian, unable to resist opportunities when they were offered. The power of the emperor was all-encompassing.

Conclusion: The Benefits of Imperial Office

The emperor Augustus employed equestrians as his personal representatives in the Roman administration. They served as financial and patrimonial procurators in the provinces, prefects managing affairs in the city of Rome, prefect of Egypt, and praesidial procurators of other provinces. The appointment of *equites* in these positions was a distinguishing feature of the monarchical *res publica*, as the *princeps* looked outside the senatorial order for new men to assist in managing his empire. These positions formed the core around which a distinct equestrian *cursus* or career structure developed in the centuries after his death. This can be ascribed to several interconnected developments. The first was the replacement or 'superposition' of equestrians over freedmen officials in the provinces, the *officia palatina* and in Rome. The second was the creation of new equestrian procuratorships for specific duties, such as the administration of particular taxes or branches of the financial administration, which relieved the provincial or patrimonial procurators of some of their responsibilities. Both these changes created a range of new administrative positions for equestrians which had not existed under Augustus. The third development was the integration of positions that carried military authority, such as the fleet prefectures and praesidial procuratorships, into the larger procuratorial *cursus*. By the mid-second century AD all these posts were classified

---

[414] A. R. Birley 1997: 60–1; Kuhn 2010: 66; Brunt 2013: 340.   [415] Brunt 2013: 332–3.
[416] Epict. *Diss.* 1.10.2–6. For possibilities as to the identity of this man, see Millar 1965a: 145–6.

at different salary grades, rising from *sexagenarius* to *trecenarius*, thus creating a firm hierarchy through which *equites* could ascend in a manner directly comparable to the senatorial *cursus honorum*. The combination of military and civilian posts in this new career structure meant that members of the equestrian order could also claim to serve the state *domi militiaeque* in the same way as their senatorial counterparts. The equestrians who did hold procuratorships were manifestly favoured by the emperor to the extent that they could be considered a distinct *equestris nobilitas*.

The evolution of the procuratorial *cursus*, and the willingness of *equites* to hold administrative positions, may at first seem at odds with the rather apolitical nature of the members of *ordo equester* in the Republic period. But the procuratorships were first and foremost *dignitates* conferred by the emperor, and they brought with them substantial salaries. These positions therefore conferred both status and financial reward. Moreover, there was significant flexibility, which allowed individual *equites* to decide whether to be satisfied with one procuratorship or whether to compete for the higher, and more lucrative, procuratorships by climbing the equestrian *cursus*. Those *equites* who did secure the patronage and support to achieve this were richly rewarded with advancement to ducenarian and trecenarian posts, and sometimes to the great prefectures. Such a lifestyle was attractive because it could be pursued without the strictures that were placed on senators, such as the obligation to attend meetings in the *curia* or own property in Italy. These incentives meant that procuratorships proved attractive to provincial notables from all over the empire, who saw opportunities to increase their status and their financial position through imperial service. This was beneficial to the Roman state, since it ensured that the provincial *domi nobiles* were invested in the imperial system – not only by accepting equestrian rank itself, but also by holding office. The relationship between *equites* and the monarchical *res publica* was thus mutually advantageous, ensuring a steady supply of *equites* who wished to compete with their peers to acquire procuratorships and the wealth and prestige they carried. It was this competition that sustained the Roman imperial administration over successive generations.

The Ciceronian ideal of equestrian *quies*, as opposed to senatorial office-holding, still lingered in the early empire, as shown by the letters of Pliny the Younger, who used it to define his own self-representation as a dedicated senatorial servant of the *res publica*. But the developing procuratorial career structure meant that the concept of equestrian *quies* had disappeared by the mid-second century AD, to be replaced by the acceptance of *equites* as administrators and officers, as found in the work of Cassius Dio. The nature of this transition is demonstrated by the fact that some *equites* who did not want long careers in government service still sought one or two posts, often as an *advocatus fisci* or a procurator, as a mark of imperial favour. Some even obtained honorific posts that would give them the title and salary of procurator, without actually undertaking the duties. This competition for imperial honours even ensnared Greek rhetors and sophists among the *domi nobiles*, who brought their personal and professional rivalries to the emperor's court. The only serious resistance to this ethos of government service, or the seeking of imperial honours, came from Stoic philosophers such as Epictetus. But this did not represent a significant challenge to the fundamental basis of the principate as a patronal imperial system. After all, if a man was an *eques Romanus*, then he had already accepted a token of the emperor's favour.

The development of the genre of the inscribed equestrian *cursus*, and its use as a medium of public self-representation, is a reflection of the cultural change that saw *equites* integrated into public administration under the monarchical *res publica*. The *cursus* is emblematic of the competition for status, offices and honours bestowed by the emperor. The more of these tokens of favour that an *eques* accumulated, the more extensive and detailed the official, permanent record of his life and career became. Salary grades such as *centenarius* and *ducenarius* were included in the *cursus* as a way of publicly demonstrating an equestrian's ascent through the new hierarchy, as well the significant financial rewards the emperor had bestowed on them in return for their service. By the mid-second century AD equestrian procurators were more strongly delineated as an elite among the *ordo equester* through their new title of *vir egregius*. This status could be earned by serving in only one procuratorship, a prospect that proved attractive to *equites* who did not want a full lifetime of service, or the intense competition it required, but still desired higher status. The most senior equestrian titles of *perfectissimus* and *eminentissimus* were more exclusive, as they could only be earned by holding the highest offices of state and the great prefectures. These lofty posts would usually only be achieved by the crème de la crème of the *ordo* who had spent many years in office, and thus could truly be said to comprise an aristocracy of service.

The formulaic nature of the inscribed *cursus* expressed cohesion, as well as competition, not only among equestrian procurators themselves, but also among senators who embarked on their own *cursus* of imperial office-holding. There was little difference in the types of positions filled by senators and equestrians. Members of both orders commanded military units, delivered justice, and oversaw the infrastructure and administration of the empire. This meant that the specific posts allocated to senators and *equites* were largely regulated by traditional status hierarchies inherited from the Republic and the Augustan era rather than by real distinctions of competence between the two *ordines*. For all practical purposes it did not matter whether an office-holder was an equestrian or a senator, since they were all appointed by imperial favour, not grants of *imperium* by the senate and people. The emergence of a group of careerist equestrians, distinct from the *ordo equester* at large, created the conditions for the transformation of the Roman army and administration in the third century AD.[417]

---

[417] This will be explored in Chapter 11.

PART III

Equestrians on Display

8 | Ceremonies and Consensus

Introduction: The Organisation of Opinion[1]

In 30 BC, the year after the Battle of Actium, the Roman people voted a series of honours for Octavian, including a triumph, arches in Brundisium and Rome, and a yearly supplication to be performed on his birthday.[2] According to Suetonius, the *equites Romani* staged their own two-day birthday celebration each year 'voluntarily and with collective endorsement' (*sponte atque consensu*).[3] Precisely when the equestrian order introduced its festival is unknown, but Suetonius' description perfectly encapsulates the role of the *ordo equester* in the Roman imperial state.[4] The stability and longevity of the new monarchical *res publica* created by Augustus depended on the *princeps* being able to demonstrate that his rule was the result of *consensus* (universal acceptance) by the constituent bodies of the *res publica*: the senate, the equestrian order and the Roman people.[5] The concept of consensus accordingly features prominently in Augustan political discourse, indicating popular approval, continuity and legitimacy, rather than change or revolution.[6] Augustus himself used the Latin terms *consensus* and *universus* in his *Res Gestae* to articulate the wholehearted and spontaneous recognition of his position and powers, emphasising that they were bestowed by the people, not forced upon them.[7] The equestrian order likewise appears in the emperor's *Res Gestae* as a body united in its decision to grant honours to the *princeps* and his family. Augustus wrote that in 5 BC 'the entire body of *equites Romani*' (*equites . . . Romani universi*) acclaimed his adopted son Gaius as *princeps*

---

[1] This is the title of chapter 30 of Syme 1939, which examines the propaganda of the Augustan state. It is deliberately deployed here as part of an analysis which takes a different approach from that of Syme.

[2] Dio 51.19.1–2. For later celebrations, see Dio 54.34.1, 55.6.6, 56.29.1   [3] Suet. *Aug.* 57.1.

[4] Wardle 2014: 387 notes that the second day's festivities is first attested in AD 12.

[5] On the idea of *consensus* representing universal acceptance, see Ando 2000: 30–1, 131.

[6] Lobur 2008: 12–36.   [7] RG 34.1 (*consensus*), 14.2, 35.1 (*universus*); Cooley 2009: 258.

iuventutis.[8] This was followed in 2 BC by the bestowal of the title of *pater patriae* on Augustus by the 'senate and the equestrian order and the entire Roman people' (*sen[atus et e]quester ordo populusq[ue] Romanus universus*).[9] The *equites* were therefore conceived as acting as a united collective, rendering 'corporate recognition' to the emperor and his family, to use Rowe's conceptual terminology.[10]

Displays of consensus are always described as emanating from below, initiated by the senate or individual senators, the people, the *equites*, and sometimes all three groups, rather than from the *princeps* himself. This ideal was vital to underpinning the imperial system that Augustus bequeathed to his successors. In the reign of Caligula the mint at Rome produced a commemorative bronze *dupondius* in honour of Divus Augustus, whose image graced the obverse of the coin. The reverse showed Augustus on a curule chair, with the legend CONSENSV SENAT(VS) ET EQ(VESTRIS) ORDIN(IS) P(OPVLI)Q(VE) R(OMANI) ('by the consensus of the senate and the equestrian order and the Roman people').[11] The reference is probably to Augustus' salutation as *pater patriae* in 2 BC by consensus of all the *ordines*. Caligula himself received this title in September AD 37, six months after his accession.[12] The coin type articulated the fact that the position of the *princeps*, and the monarchical *res publica* in which all Romans now lived, was shaped by universal assent.

Consensus could not be assumed or taken for granted: it had to be articulated and reinforced by performances.[13] This had always been the tradition in the Roman *res publica* – assembly meetings, elections, festivals and triumphs were conducted in public.[14] Therefore, the honours for Augustus and his family members likewise had to be conferred through acclamations, demonstrations and ceremonies – and always voluntarily. The intensity of these performances could be heightened by the *princeps* refusing such distinctions, as in the case of Augustus and the title of *pater patriae*, before finally accepting.[15] Indeed, *recusatio* became an important aspect in defining the monarchical nature of the *res publica* under Augustus and his successors, for such an act was not part of Republican political theatre.[16] The ritual of declining honours or even

---

[8] *RG* 14.2. Coins minted after 2 BC featured both Gaius and Lucius with this title (*RIC* I[2] Augustus 206–12).
[9] *RG* 35.1.   [10] Stein 1927: 57–60; Rowe 2002: 75.   [11] *RIC* 1[2] Caligula no. 56.
[12] For Caligula as *pater patriae*, see Barrett 1990: 70–1; Wardle 1994: 191; Stevenson 2007: 122–3.
[13] Ando 2000: 6–8.   [14] Hillard 2005: 4; Sumi 2005: 1–13.
[15] Suet. *Aug.* 58.1–2; Ando 2000: 146; Lobur 2008: 24–5. Stevenson 2009 discusses the series of factors that led Augustus to accept the title of *pater patriae* in 2 BC.
[16] Wallace-Hadrill 1982: 36–7. For *recusatio* and the title of *pater patriae*, see Stevenson 2007.

the imperial purple itself enabled successive emperors from Tiberius onwards to demonstrate that the Roman people did indeed want a *princeps*. As we will see in this chapter, the performances of Roman political life were important public events in which the *ordo equester* and its members played a vital role.

Collective Action

The *ordo equester* had no assembly. It did not traditionally exist as a formal part of the political and legislative decision-making process of the *res publica*, except as centuries voting in the *comitia centuriata*. This was in contrast with the senate, which met collectively in the *curia* and passed decrees (*senatus consulta*), and the people (including the centuries of *equites*), who gathered in the *comitia* to vote, and who formally endorsed magistrates until the early third century AD.[17] As the equestrian order acquired its own distinct privileges and status symbols in the first century BC, the theatre, in which the *equites* sat in the reserved fourteen rows, became an informal equestrian assembly.[18] It must have been quite a sight to see members of the *ordo* sitting together in the Theatre of Pompey or Marcellus, all clad in their tunic with the *angustus clavus*. It would have been even more impressive when the *equites* made a dramatic gesture, as when they all stood up and removed their cloaks to recognise their occasional patron, the future emperor Claudius, when he entered the theatre.[19] Since the theatre functioned as an ad hoc 'home' of the equestrian order, it was there that they decided to commemorate the deceased Germanicus by renaming the *cuneus* of the equestrian *iuvenes* in his honour.[20] Later, following the death of the younger Drusus in AD 23, the equestrian order is recorded as taking some unspecified action, possibly the performance of acclamations, 'in all the theatres' (*omnibus [t]heatris*).[21] The relationship between the *equites* in the theatre and the *ordo* at large can be seen in an incident from the reign of Nero. Cassius Dio records that the emperor's cheer squad of *Augustiani*, composed of young *equites*, proposed an extravagant 1,000-pound statue of the emperor in honour of Nero's Greek victories, but 'all

---

[17] For attendance at senatorial meetings, see Talbert 1984: 134–52. On the popular assemblies, see Millar 1977: 302–3.

[18] See Chapter 3 for this process.   [19] Suet. *Claud.* 6.1.

[20] Tac. *Ann.* 2.83. For another 'home', the shrine of the Lupercal, see Chapter 10.

[21] *RS* 38, frag. b, col. ii, l. 13; Rowe 2002: 81.

the *ordo equester*' (πᾶν τὸ ἱππικον) had to help pay for it.[22] This was probably the result of a promise made by the *Augustiani* during theatrical acclamations, but this meant that their fellow members of the *ordo* were expected to follow through on the undertaking.

It is therefore plausible that the theatre functioned as the arena in which the *equites* spontaneously vowed birthday celebrations for Augustus and where they bestowed the title of *princeps iuventutis* on his adopted sons Gaius and Lucius (as we will examine in detail later in this chapter). There is certainly strong evidence that it was in the theatre that equestrians offered their support for the conferral of the title of *pater patriae* on Augustus in 2 BC. The role played by the *ordo equester* in this event is emphasised by Augustus himself in the *Res Gestae*, as noted above, but it is not recognised by Suetonius or the *fasti Praenestini*.[23] However, Suetonius does refer to Augustus being hailed as *pater patriae* during 'shows at Rome' (*Romae spectacula*), and Lacey has plausibly suggested that these acclamations would have included the *equites* in the fourteen rows.[24] Ovid, who was himself an *eques Romanus*, highlights the role of the *ordo equester* in this process. As he wrote in his *Fasti*: 'the plebs gave this name to you, the senate gave this name to you, and we the *equites* gave this name to you' (*tibi plebs, tibi curia nomen* | *hoc dedit, hos dedimus nos tibi nomen, eques*).[25] Not all *equites* could genuinely have taken part in the acclamation of Augustus as *pater patriae* or any other displays of consensus mentioned here, for the simple reason that not all of them were present in Rome.[26] But these theatrical acclamations were taken as representative of the *ordo* as a whole, and subsequently enshrined in political rhetoric and documents, as Rowe has convincingly shown.[27] These actions served to demonstrate the *equites*' acceptance of, and participation in, the monarchical *res publica*.[28]

Most, if not all, of these demonstrations of loyalty must have involved some behind-the-scenes negotiations, which would have been orchestrated by leading members of the *ordo*. The mechanics of such manoeuvres are

---

[22] Dio 63(62).18.3.

[23] Suet. *Aug.* 58.1–2; *Inscr. It.* XIII.2, 17. Cf. Dio 55.10.10, who gives a very minimalist account.

[24] Lacey 1996: 195–7.

[25] Ovid, *Fasti* 2.127–8. Stevenson 2009: 103 proposes that Ovid's expression could have been originally composed for an 'equestrian occasion'. Representatives of the *ordo* were probably present in the *curia* when Valerius Messalla saluted Augustus as *pater patriae* on behalf of the people (Louis 2010: 400; Wardle 2014: 393).

[26] Note the important comments of Wardle 2014: 391–2 on the way in which Augustan acclamations were stage-managed.

[27] Rowe 2002: 67–84. See also Bollinger 1969: 52–3; Demougin 1988: 801–2; Slater 1994: 129–31.

[28] Rowe 2002: 82–4.

difficult to trace, given the interests of our literary sources, but the evidence of the late Republican period shows the importance of prominent *equites* as representatives of the *ordo* as a whole. For example, we have already seen that Pomponius Atticus wrote to Cicero on behalf of the *publicani* to complain about the terms of the provincial edict of Cilicia, and that Atticus was later approached to set up a fund for Caesar's murderers.[29] The ability to organise such leadership in the imperial period is shown by the role played by Claudius as a patron of the *equites*. In this capacity he acted as ambassador to the consuls in AD 14 after the death of Augustus and again in AD 31 following the downfall of Sejanus, and to the new emperor Caligula upon his accession to the purple in AD 37.[30] The fact that Suetonius and Cassius Dio refer to Claudius being selected as patron on these specific occasions suggests that the *ordo* may have chosen other representatives at different times.[31] In AD 22, when Livia fell ill, members of the *equester ordo* approached the senate to ask where would be the best place to make a dedication to Fortuna Equestris for the Augusta's well-being. In the senatorial discussion it was discovered that there was a temple of Fortuna Equestris at Antium, so the *equites* accordingly made their dedication there.[32] There were also several religious ceremonies that required the presence of equestrian delegates. For example, select members of each *ordo* brought a gift for Augustus to the Capitoline each year on 1 January, a ceremony which continued until the reign of Claudius.[33] Representatives of the individual *ordines* likewise threw a bronze coin into the *lacus Curtius* in the *forum Romanum* on an annual basis for Augustus' health.[34] The *ordo equester* is also credited with erecting statues to members of the imperial family and high-ranking private citizens, actions which would have to have been co-ordinated by leading *equites*. For example, Tiberius' praetorian prefect Sejanus received statues from the *ordo equester*, the senate and the thirty-five tribes.[35] The epitaph of the senator Q. Veranius records that when he was curator of temples, public works and places under Nero, 'the equestrian order and the Roman people dedicated a statue to him, with the senate's permission' (*[statuam posuit equester] ordo et populus Romanus consentiente senatu*).[36] Such

---

[29] See Chapters 2 and 3.   [30] Suet. *Claud.* 6.1; Dio 59.6.6.
[31] Note the comment of Hurley 2001: 84, '*patronus equitum* was not a standing position'. She makes a plausible argument that Claudius was selected as a spokesperson for matters involving the imperial household.
[32] Tac. *Ann.* 3.71.1.   [33] Suet. *Aug.* 57.1; Rowe 2002: 94; Wardle 2014: 389.
[34] Wardle 2014: 388 suggests that the offering for Augustus' health began during his illness in AD 6.
[35] Dio 58.2.7.   [36] *CIL* VI 41075; Gordon 1952: 257–62.

proposals may have begun life as staged acclamations in the theatre or other venues, before being brought to fruition by specific representatives of the *ordo*.[37]

The power of the theatre as a venue for the expression of equestrian opinion could occasionally backfire on the imperial house. In AD 9 Augustus' step-son Tiberius returned to Rome from Pannonia and was voted a triumph for his achievements. But the image of imperial harmony was soon shattered by a disturbance at the *ludi*, as members of the *ordo equester* chose this moment to call for the overturn of the Augustan legislation on marriage, the *lex Iulia de maritandis ordinibus*.[38] This law of 18 BC was one of the pillars of Augustus' social legislation, prescribing penalties for the unmarried and childless in an attempt to encourage citizens, especially those in the upper *ordines*, to produce heirs.[39] In Suetonius' version of the story Augustus responded to the protests by bringing Germanicus' children to the theatre, cradling them in his lap, and gesturing to the *equites* as if to encourage them to follow the example of the imperial family and father children.[40] Cassius Dio created considerable drama out of the incident in the *Roman History*. In his version Augustus summoned the members of the *ordo equester* into the *forum Romanum* and divided them into two groups, the married and unmarried. Augustus then proceeded to deliver speeches to each group of *equites*; these orations are, of course, not historical, but form part of a dramatic scenario created by Dio to explore the character of the Augustan principate and its moral legislation.[41] However, the initial protest of the equestrians in the theatre was a genuine historical event. Tiberius also felt the wrath of the *equites* in AD 14–15 when he reduced the funds for pantomime performances, and riots coordinated by members of the pantomime-loving equestrian youth broke out in the theatre.[42] These incidents demonstrate how public entertainment venues could allow the *ordo equester* to express a collective will that opposed imperial policy.

These negative incidents should remind us that expression of positive consensus in the form of the voting of honours, titles and statues to the emperor and his family – however stage-managed it might have been – was still the result of willing participation of the *equites*. They were not puppets. In this way, displays of *consensus* – 'universal acceptance' or the 'organisation of opinion' (to return to Syme's phrase) – were not necessarily misleading. Augustus himself enjoyed widespread support throughout all

---

[37] For statues voted in the theatre, see Duncan-Jones 2016: 92–3.
[38] Dio 56.1.1–2; Suet. *Aug.* 34.2.   [39] Treggiari 1991: 60–80.   [40] Suet. *Aug.* 34.2.
[41] Dio 56.1–10; Swan 2004: 226–7.   [42] Slater 1994. See Chapter 9 for full discussion.

levels of society, and there is strong evidence that the Romans wanted him to accept the titles and honours he was granted.[43] The *princeps* had brought peace and stability, which was greeted with genuine relief and acceptance of his rule. Moreover, the ceremonies of consensus were not only vitally important to the imperial house, but also to the *equites* themselves, since they gave form and meaning to the *ordo* and its part in the state. We can detect the pride of individual equestrians in their involvement in imperial ceremonies in the poetry of Ovid and Martial. Ovid's imaginary description of Tiberius' triumph in the *Tristia*, composed when he was in exile at Tomi, features the *equites* celebrating his martial success alongside the other *ordines*: 'the loyal people celebrates, and together with the loyal people, the senate and the equestrian order, of which I was until recently a small part' (*plebs pia cumque pia laetatur plebe senatus,* | *parvaque cuius eram pars ego nuper eques*).[44] Martial describes the celebrations by all the *ordines* in honour of Domitian's return to Rome in AD 93 following his own campaign in Pannonia: 'the people give incense, the thankful equestrian order gives incense, the senate gives incense' (*dat populus, dat gratus eques, dat tura senatus*).[45] Both Ovid and Martial gave prominence to the role of their own order in these events because by doing so they validated their own status. Indeed, shared performances, rituals and costumes have long been significant to the cohesion and identity of status groups, especially to aristocratic elites who need to articulate their exclusivity in order to distinguish themselves from the masses.[46] This was especially important to the *equites*, given that they lacked the formal meeting place that their counterparts in the *ordo senatorius* possessed.

Rituals and ceremonies function as the public expression of the ideological power of status groups in all societies. This is a quality that Mann has termed 'immanence', which represents 'a sense of ultimate significance and meaning in the cosmos'.[47] In the case of the *ordo equester*, its immanence was founded on the idea that it was a body of warriors imbued with martial *virtus*, as the successor of Rome's original cavalry aristocracy.[48] This military heritage was most notably demonstrated through the *transvectio equitum*, the annual parade of the *equites equo publico* through the streets

---

[43] Stevenson 2013: 122. There is also evidence that popular support was building for Augustus to be awarded the title of *pater patriae* before 2 BC (Stevenson 2009: 102, 2013: 135).

[44] Ovid, *Tristia* 4.2.15–16.   [45] Mart. *Ep.* 8.15.3; Sullivan 1991: 135–6.   [46] Weber 1968: 935.

[47] Mann 1986: 519.

[48] This idea remained relevant into the imperial period. In the *Minor Declamations* of Pseudo-Quintilian, which date to the second century AD, the author wrote that the equestrian order 'received its name from outstanding military service' (*ex laude militiae hoc nomen acceperit*) (302.3).

of Rome. In this chapter we will see how this procession not only articulated the ideological power of the *ordo*, but also its role in the monarchical *res publica*, as the ceremony represented the official approval of equestrian rank as bestowed by the emperor. The theatre was a public space which the *equites* had to share with members of the other *ordines*. However, the *transvectio* allowed consensus, and the reciprocal relationship between *ordo* and *princeps*, to be celebrated in a manner that was exclusively equestrian. While the *transvectio* was a Republican ceremony reinvigorated for a new autocratic age, the monarchical state also brought with it new opportunities for public display by the *equites* in the form of public funerals for emperors and their family members. These occasions featured military parades in which members of the *ordo* exhibited their *virtus* and showed their investment in the imperial system. Both the *transvectio* and the funeral ceremonies were distinguished by the prominent involvement of imperial heirs, such as Gaius and Lucius, as *principes iuventutis*. We will explore how, as leaders of the equestrian youth, these princes offered a new and vital connection between the *ordo* and the emperor and his family. The rituals not only acted as displays of *consensus* – they also ensured that *eques Romanus* was no antiquated title devoid of meaning, but a status with real ideological significance.

Morality on Parade

At a first glance, the Augustan poet Ovid might not seem to have much in common with Q. Sittius Faustus, an *eques* who came from the little-known town of Castellum Tidditanorum in Numidia. Ovid was from a very respectable Italian equestrian family, and moved easily in court circles under Augustus before being exiled to Tomi. His poetry, including the *Ars Amatoria* and the *Metamorphoses*, has secured him lasting fame.[49] In contrast, Faustus, who lived in the late second and early third centuries AD, spent most of his life in Numidia, where he was elected to several municipal magistracies. But he did manage to obtain equestrian rank, one of only two such men from Castellum Tidditanorum to enter the upper *ordines* of Roman society (the other was the exceptional Q. Lollius Urbicus, the urban prefect of Antoninus Pius).[50] It may have been Urbicus (or a member of his family) who introduced Faustus to powerbrokers in

---

[49] For Ovid's place in the Augustan principate, see Millar 1993 and White 2001.
[50] Duncan-Jones 1967: 154.

Rome. Faustus' official posts are recorded on the base of a statue of his wife, Apronia Fida, at Castellum Tidditanorum:

To Apronia Fida, daughter of Sextus, wife of Q. Sittius Faustus, son of Quintus, of the voting tribe Quirina, who was approved by the emperors L. Septimius Severus Pius Pertinax Augustus and M. Aurelius Antoninus Augustus, appointed to the five *decuriae* of jurors by the deified M. Antoninus Pius, priest for life, member of the board of three for taking the census, member of the board of three prefects for delivering justice in the colony of Veneria Rusicade, prefect for delivering justice in the colony of Sarnia Milev and prefect for delivering justice of the colony of Minervia Chullu, aedile. His friends erected this by public subscription on account of the good deeds her husband performed for them. The location was authorised by decree of the decurions.[51]

This inscription reveals that Faustus received two key imperial honours. He was first appointed to the jury panels by the emperor Marcus Aurelius, presumably between AD 169 and 176, when he was sole emperor. Then, some time between AD 198 and 209, by which time he would have been in his late sixties, Faustus was 'approved' (*probati*) by Severus and his son Caracalla.[52] This terminology reveals that Faustus had formally been granted the status of an *eques Romanus* through participation in the *transvectio equitum*, which took place every year in Rome on 15 July. The language is identical to that used by Ovid some three centuries before, when he described his own participation in the procession before Augustus. 'But, I remember,' the poet said to the emperor from his place of exile, 'that you used to approve (*probabas*) of my life and character as I passed by on the horse which you had given me'.[53] Ovid and Q. Sittius Faustus were thus connected, across time and space, by their participation in a ceremonial parade in which they were certified as proper representatives of the *ordo equester*.

The *transvectio equitum* was a parade of some antiquity, which was designed to commemorate the role played by the Dioscuri in securing

[51] *CIL* VIII 6711 = *ILAlg.* 2.3610 = *ILS* 6863a: *Aproniae Sex(ti) fil(iae) Fi|dae coniugi | Q(uinti) Sitti (i) Q(uinti) fil(ii) Quir(ina tribu) Faus|ti probati ab | Impp(eratoribus) L(ucio) Septimio Severo | Pio Pertinace Aug(usto) et | M(arco) Aurelio Antonino Aug(usto) | in quinq(ue) decurias allecti a divo | M(arco) Antonino Pio flam(inis) perp(etui) | [III]vir(i) quinq(uennalis) IIIvir(i) praef(ecti) i(ure) d(icundo) | [co]l(oniae) Vener(iae) Rusic(adis) praef(ecti) i(ure) d(icundo) | col(oniae) Sarn(iae) Mil(ev) et praef(ecti) i(ure) d(icundo) | col(oniae) Minerv(iae) Chullu aedil(is) | amici ob merita mariti | [e]ius in se aere conlato | l(ocus) d(atus) d(ecreto) d(ecurionum).*
[52] See Pflaum 1968: 173 for the dates and chronology.
[53] Ovid, *Tristia* 2.89–90: *at, memini, vitamque meam moresque probabas | illo, quem dederas, praetereuntis equo.* See also *Tristia* 2.541–2.

Roman victory at the Battle of Lake Regillus, as we discussed in Chapter 1. Since the Dioscuri were the patron gods of the *equites*, an annual parade of the cavalry was instituted on 15 July, the day of the victory at Lake Regillus and the festival of Castor and Pollux.[54] Dionysius of Halicarnassus provides us with the most complete account of the *transvectio* in the Republican and early Augustan period. The *equites*, dressed in their ceremonial *trabea* and crowned with olive wreaths, assembled outside the walls at the Temple of Mars on the Via Appia, as if they were embarking on a military campaign.[55] They rode on gleaming white horses, recalling the steeds of the Dioscuri themselves.[56] The parade either started at, or passed by, the Temple of Honos and Virtus, which lay near the Porta Capena.[57] The *equites* then rode to the *forum Romanum*, where they processed past the Temple of Castor and Pollux on their way up to the Capitoline hill.[58] The route and dress of the participants recalled that of a Roman triumph, particularly the lesser ceremony of the *ovatio*, in which the recipients wore a *trabea* and olive crown.[59] The parade thus functioned as a display of Roman military might and patriotism and of the commitment of the aristocrats who possessed the *equus publicus* to defending the *res publica*. Every five years, during the taking of the census, the *transvectio* incorporated the formal review of equestrian ranks, called the *recognitio equitum*. This was conducted by the censors, as memorably described by Plutarch in his *Life of Pompey*.[60] In Plutarch's account, the censors L. Gellius and Cn. Lentulus were sitting on a tribunal watching the *equites* parade through the forum when Pompeius turned up to return his *equus publicus* and give an account of his military service. The fact that each *eques* needed to be personally assessed by the censors speaks against the idea that the *recognitio* could take place solely in the course of one day.[61] It is probable that the administrative processes were undertaken prior to the actual *transvectio* parade, which must have functioned as the ceremonial confirmation of the *equus publicus* (Pompeius' dramatic entrance in Plutarch notwithstanding).

Augustus ensured that he personally played a role in reviewing the ranks of *equites*, thus integrating the *ordo equester* into the framework of the new,

---

[54] Dion. Hal. 6.13.4; Weinstock 1937a: 15.

[55] For the uniform, see Dion Hal. 6.13.4; Pliny Elder, *NH* 15.19. The dress was designed to recall that of the Dioscuri themselves (Rebecchi 1999: 192 n. 7). The symbolism of the assembly point is discussed by Spencer 2007: 90.

[56] Weinstock 1937b: 2178–9.

[57] Ps.-Aur. Vict. *Vir. Ill.* 32.3; L. Richardson 1978: 244; McDonnell 2006: 215–16.

[58] Dion. Hal. 6.13.4; Pliny the Elder, *NH* 15.19.

[59] Pliny the Elder, *NH* 15.19; Weinstock 1937a: 15–17, 1937b: 2180.

[60] Plut. *Pomp.* 22.4–6; Rebecchi 1999: 195.   [61] See the comments of Swan 2004: 206 n. 241.

monarchical *res publica*. As we discussed in Chapter 5, under Augustus the formal *recognitio* was incorporated into the process of each year's *transvectio*, so that membership of the equestrian order would henceforth be assessed annually. The most detailed account of his innovations comes from the pen of Suetonius, whose account is worth quoting in full:

He frequently reviewed (*recognovit*) the equestrian squadrons, since he had restored the custom of the parade (*reducto more transvectionis*) after a long interval. But he would not permit anyone riding in the parade to be forced off his horse by an accuser, which used to happen. He also allowed those who were marked out by their old age or frailty to send their horses on ahead in the line, but they had to approach by foot when they were called upon to respond. Later he granted a favour to those men who were more than thirty-five years old and did not wish to retain their public horse the right of returning them.[62]

This assessment incorporated a significant moral dimension, as Augustus scrupulously assessed whether individual citizens were fit to remain in the *ordo*:

Together with ten assessors recruited from the senate, he required each *eques* to give an account of his life. As for those men whom he officially reproached, some suffered punishment, while others were removed with disgrace from the order; a great many received a warning for different reasons. The mildest type of warning occurred when he gave an *eques* a writing tablet in full view of everyone, which he was instructed to read silently right there and then. Some others he reproached because they had borrowed money at rather favourable rates only to invest it for greater returns.[63]

The board of ten assessors was one of Augustus' measures designed to involve members of the senatorial order in the administration of the state. A commission of three men to review the senate itself would be established in AD 4, alongside another board of three for reviewing the *equites* (which did not last beyond his lifetime).[64] But the focus of the ceremony was very

---

[62] Suet. *Aug.* 38.3: *equitum turmas frequenter recognovit, post longam intercapedinem reducto more transvectionis. sed neque detrahi quemquam in travehendo ab accusatore passus est, quod fieri solebat, et senio vel aliqua corporis labe insignibus permisit, praemisso in ordine equo, ad respondendum quotiens citarentur pedibus venire; mox reddendi equi gratiam fecit eis, qui maiores annorum quinque et triginta retinere eum nollent.*

[63] Suet. *Aug.* 39.1: *impetratisque a senatu decem adiutoribus unum quemque equitum rationem vitae reddere coegit atque ex improbatis alios poena, alios ignominia notavit, plures admonitione, sed varia. lenissimum genus admonitionis fuit traditio coram pugillarium, quos taciti et ibidem statim legerent; notavitque aliquos, quod pecunias levioribus usuris mutuati graviore faenore collocassent.*

[64] Suet. *Aug.* 37.1 (no chronological indications); Dio 55.13.2 (senatorial board in AD 4). For discussion, see Demougin 1988: 172–5; Louis 2010: 306–7; Wardle 2014: 299.

much on the *princeps* himself as the final arbiter of morality: it is Augustus who is said to have officially reproached (*notavit*) offending *equites*.

The combined *recognitio* and *transvectio* was designed to publicly censure those *equites* who had not lived up to the moral standards expected of them.[65] Suetonius' description of each individual *eques* being called to give 'an account of his life' (*rationem vitae*) recalls Ovid's remark in the *Tristia* that Augustus approved 'my life and character' (*vitamque meam moresque*).[66] There is also a parallel between the two authors in their use of the Latin verb *noto* to refer to Augustus' censorial actions. Ovid remembered the occasions on which he escaped censure: 'when you were officially reproaching men for their faults, I was an *eques* who passed by time and again without blame' (*cum te delicta notantem | praeterii totiens inreprehensus eques*).[67] Some inscriptions recording the careers of *equites* even referred to this procedure as an 'examination' (*inquisitio*).[68] The *equites* who were confirmed in their status, like Ovid, were granted the official documents of membership, which were represented on funerary reliefs in the form of a *volumen* (a scroll).[69] Equestrians who were found wanting suffered *ignominia*, which entailed official disgrace and relegation from the *ordo*.[70] The inquisitorial nature of Augustus' annual review meant that the *transvectio* was commonly referred to as a *probatio equitum*.[71] This concept was so enduring that the *Codex Calendar of AD 354* listed the festivities of 15 July as *equit(um) Ro(manorum) prob(atio)*.[72] It also explains why Q. Sittius Faustus was said to have been 'approved' by Severus and Caracalla, with the expectation that the readers of the inscription would equate this expression with entrance into the *ordo equester*. Augustus' actions thus ensured that the *transvectio equitum*, and especially the emperor's own role as the arbiter of moral fitness, played an important role in defining the identity of the equestrian order in the imperial period.[73] The *equites* had long since ceased to be the cavalry of the *res publica*, but they continued to symbolise the martial prowess of the aristocratic citizen body.[74] The *transvectio* was designed to inculcate a sense of

---

[65] Once again, it is likely that the actual assessments of the *equites* took place before the ceremony of the *transvectio* itself (Demougin 1988: 155).

[66] Ovid, *Tristia* 2.89–90. See also Suet. *Claud.* 16.2, in which *equites* also give an 'account of their life' (*rationem vitae*) before the emperor.

[67] Ovid, *Tristia* 2.541–2.   [68] *ILAlg.* I.2145; *I. Prusias* 54; Nicolet 1967a.

[69] Rebecchi 1999: 204; Spalthoff 2010: 42.

[70] *OLD* s.v. *ignominia*. Thus Lebek 1991: 50 restores line 12 of the *Tabulas Larinas* as *p[er transvectionem ignominiam] | ut acciperent*.

[71] Demougin 1988: 151–2.   [72] *Inscr. It.* XIII.2, 42. See also Macrob. *Sat.* 2.4.25.

[73] Val. Max. 2.2.9; Nicolet 1984: 96–9; Sumi 2009: 180.

[74] Severy 2003: 82–3; Spencer 2007: 92–4.

belonging and collective pride among equestrians, who would parade together dressed in their *trabea* and wearing their olive crowns.[75]

This was further achieved by Augustus' decision to divide the *equites* into six squadrons under the command of senatorial *seviri*.[76] All equestrians were technically members of one of these *turmae*, and epigraphic evidence shows that they remembered their assigned squadron. Some men, such as C. Iulius Laetitus of Thysdrus, even recorded their advancement to equestrian rank on inscriptions as 'adlection into the squadrons of Roman *equites*' (*allecto in turm[as] | equit(um) Romanor(um)*).[77] On funerary reliefs, the deceased equestrian's membership of a *turma* was symbolised by the ceremonial standard, the *vexillum*.[78] The *transvectio equitum* not only created connections between the *ordo equester* and the emperor, but also between the senatorial aristocracy and members of the wider imperial family, thus ensuring that the *equites* were firmly embedded in Roman society. The *seviri equitum* who commanded the squadrons in the *transvectio* were usually young men of senatorial family, although the post did not occupy a fixed place in the *cursus honorum*.[79] The number of career inscriptions that feature the sevirate, especially from the Flavian period onwards, indicates that it was a significant honour thought worthy of commemoration.[80] These officers were required to mount special games (*ludi Sevirales*) each year in front of the Temple of Mars Ultor in the *forum Augustum*.[81] Such events, staged by the youth of the senatorial order, had special significance, since Roman citizen males now had to visit the Temple of Mars Ultor to register their eligibility for military service.[82] An ideological connection was therefore forged between the equestrian order and young men at other levels of Roman society.

In 5 BC, when Augustus' grandson Gaius Caesar was named *princeps iuventutis* by the equestrian order, he also became a *sevir equitum*.[83] Gaius'

[75] See Pers. *Sat.* 3.27–9: 'Or would it be proper for you to burst open your lungs with puffs of wind because you claim to be one-thousandth-part Tuscan, or because greet your censor while clad in the *trabea*?' (*an deceat pulmonem rumpere ventis | stemmate quod Tusco ramum millesime ducis | censoremve tuum vel quod trabeate salutas?*)

[76] See Chapter 5 for further details of this office.

[77] *CIL* VIII 10501. For other examples, see Demougin 1988: 220. The word *turmae* is sometimes used in literary sources as well to refer to the whole *ordo*, as in Stat. *Silv.* 4.5.47.

[78] Veyne 1960: 106.   [79] Demougin 1988: 241–2; Duncan-Jones 2016: 24–5.

[80] For a prosopography of *seviri*, who are attested until the mid-third century AD, see Demougin 1988: 226–40. On the presence of the post in the inscribed *cursus*, see Duncan-Jones 2016: 84.

[81] Dio 55.10.4; Swan 2004: 98; *HA Marcus* 6.3.

[82] Severy 2003: 176–7. See Lacey 1996: 197–9 on the connection between the army, the Temple of Mars Ultor and the Julian family.

[83] Dio 55.9.9. Lucius Caesar was voted the same honours as Gaius, but it is uncertain whether this included the post as *sevir equitum* (Dio 55.9.10; Swan 2004: 91).

appointment as *sevir* was undoubtedly designed to give him a defined ceremonial role as *princeps iuventutis*, though this precedent was not usually followed by other subsequent holders of the title.[84] The only other member of an imperial dynasty known to have become a *sevir equitum* is Marcus Aurelius, who was appointed to the post in AD 139.[85] It was one of a series of official titles and duties, including the designation of Caesar, that were given to Marcus in that year in order to mark him out as Antoninus Pius' heir.[86] The *transvectio equitum* was also regarded as an appropriate ceremony in which to commemorate the lives of two princes of the imperial house, Germanicus and Drusus, following their deaths in AD 19 and 23, respectively. The equestrian order decreed that that *turmae* should follow behind Germanicus' portrait during the *transvectio*, and voted that a *clupeus argenteus* (silver shield) bearing Drusus' image should be also be paraded following his death.[87] These memorials were not only designed to display the grief of the *ordo equester*, but also to demonstrate their sympathy and solidarity with the imperial family. These changes to the parade of the *transvectio equitum* meant that the ceremony came to be a performative representation of the *ordo*'s acquiescence in imperial rule – a living symbol of consensus.[88] Yet this act of ceremonial consensus not only benefited the emperor and his family, but also the *equites* themselves, as it strengthened their own place within the monarchical state.

The emperor's personal involvement in the annual review of the equestrian order features in the ancient sources as a way of illuminating aspects of their character or style of rule. Suetonius, in his treatment of the initial phase of Caligula's reign, praised the emperor for his scrupulous regard for procedure, after Tiberius' lack of attentiveness to the *ordo equester*.[89] These actions evidently formed part of the main historiographical tradition on Caligula's life and reign. Cassius Dio recorded that Caligula supplemented the declining numbers of *equites* by enrolling men from throughout the empire. This action is explicitly listed among the things the emperor did that were 'good and worthy of commendation' (δὲ καλὰ μέν ἐπαίνου τε ἄξια).[90] Claudius held

---

[84] As Champlin 2011: 98 makes clear, *contra* Poulson 1991: 123, the *princeps iuventutis* was not the leader of the *transvectio equitum* and had no formal role in the parade. The distinction between the *princeps* and *sevir* is discussed by Beringer 1954: 2309–10.

[85] *HA Marcus* 6.3. Cf. Dio 72(71).35.5, with discussion in Beringer 1954: 2304, 2309.

[86] A. R. Birley 1993: 56; Davenport and Manley 2014: 34–5.

[87] Tac. *Ann.* 2.83.4; *CIL* VI 3200 = *RS* 38 col. II ll. 10–11; Lebek 1993: 99, 103.

[88] Rowe 2002: 7–9.

[89] Suet. *Cal.* 16.2. Lindsay 1993: 21, 84–5 discusses this section of the *Life*, which comes before the *divisio*. For Tiberius' failure to enrol men in the equestrian *decuriae*, see Suet. *Tib.* 41.

[90] Dio 59.9.4–5. For the constitutional basis of Caligula's actions, see Demougin 1988: 178–81.

a *recognitio* as part of his censorship of AD 47/48, which Suetonius used as an example of his inconsistency.[91] For, he wrote, some young men of dubious moral character were allowed to remain in the *ordo*. But Claudius removed an *eques* from Greece from the jury panels because he did not know Latin, and others suffered censure because they had left Italy without the emperor's permission.[92] It has been argued that Claudius was following the precedent of his ancestor Appius Claudius, the censor of 213 BC, in showing leniency to *equites* who had strayed from the moral path.[93] Cassius Dio made a brief remark about the *transvectio* under Nero in his discussion of the emperor's inappropriate dress. It was in Nero's reign that the *equites* first used saddle-cloths during the *transvectio*, which is treated as a sign of moral decadence rather than a change in imperial ceremonial.[94] The return to proper order after the reign of Nero and the civil wars of AD 68/69 was, for Suetonius, exemplified by the review of the senate and the *equites* undertaken by Vespasian and Titus in the censorship of AD 73/74.[95] As we have already argued in Chapter 5, the emperor had been able to grant or withdraw the *equus publicus* since the principate of Augustus, regardless of whether he held the censorship of not. The 'set piece' censorships of Claudius and Vespasian were significant for their ideological purposes, exemplifying the maintenance, or restoration, of proper order in each emperor's reign (hence their prominent place in the ancient sources). Although literary descriptions of the ceremony are rare after the Flavian period, it evidently continued until at least the mid-fourth century AD, since it is included in the *Codex Calendar of AD 354*.[96]

Representations of the *transvectio equitum* functioned as a symbol of equestrian status on funerary monuments, a sign of the continuing ideological power of the ceremony. However, the meanings of the scene varied depending on whose life the monuments were intended to commemorate. For the most part, the reliefs can be divided into two groups: (i) adult *equites* who had certainly participated in the *transvectio* in Rome at least once in their life; and (ii) children who were denied this opportunity because of their death at a young age.[97] For the first group, the representation of the *transvectio* was a commemoration of their public life as an *eques*. A most remarkable example of this comes from Comum in north Italy, where large marble fragments survive of a significant funerary monument of an equestrian family

---

[91] The *divisio* is less marked in Suetonius' *Life of Claudius* (Hurley 2001: 18).

[92] Suet. *Claud.* 16.1–2. The last comment about *equites* leaving Italy is strange, but it does seem that Suetonius is referring to equestrians rather than senators. See Ryan 1993: 616 n. 22.

[93] Ryan 1993: 616–17, citing Suet. *Claud.* 24.1 in support of his argument.

[94] Dio 63(62).13.3. This change is confirmed by iconographic evidence (Spalthoff 2010: 40).

[95] Suet. *Vesp.* 9.2. [96] Salzman 1990: 141 suggests an association with the imperial cult.

[97] Rebecchi 1999: 197–8.

(Figure 8.1).[98] Dated to the early first century AD, the upper register depicts two *equites* dressed in their *trabeae* riding in formation, accompanied by attendants. The original monument must have featured a full series of riders, which extended around the circumference of the tomb. The scene is juxtaposed with the representations of sporting and hunting activities, which were common representations of *virtus*, in the lower register.[99] The figures of the *equites* participating in the *transvectio* appear to be generic, indicating that this is an idealised representation of equestrian ceremonial.[100] There are also a number of smaller, more personal, scenes on funerary monuments that highlight different aspects of the ceremony. These generally appear on monuments of young *equites* who did not obtain further positions in the *militiae* or the administration.[101] For example, Sex. Gavius Proculus, who died aged sixteen, is commemorated with the simple inscription 'he passed by on his public horse' (*equo publico | transvectus est*).[102] One of the

Figure 8.1: Relief depicting the *transvectio equitum*, Comum

[98] Veyne 1960: 108–10; Spalthoff 2010: 176–7 (no. 44). Cf. Rebecchi 1999: 198–9, who suggested that the fragments came from a public building, perhaps as a model of inspiration for the youth of Comum. This is unlikely since the fragments came from outside the city limits.

[99] Veyne 1960: 109–10; Spalthoff 2010: 176.   [100] Veyne 1960: 109.

[101] Veyne 1960: 107; Kleijwegt 1991: 215–16. Cf. Crowther 2009: 352, who canvasses the possibility that these young *equites* may have died during an accident in the *transvectio*, though given the idealised nature of children's funerary commemoration, this seems unlikely.

[102] *CIL* XI 3024 = *ILS* 1313.

most evocative narrative scenes comes from the funerary relief of T. Flavius Verus from the the Ostian necropolis (Figure 8.2).[103] Verus is shown riding in the *transvectio*, with the horse being led by one attendant, while another attendant places the olive wreath on his head. Although he is a young man, Verus is styled an *eques Romanus*, suggesting that he had been legitimately granted equestrian rank. The monument was dedicated by Verus' mother, Vibussia Sabina, who is herself depicted to the left of the scene watching her son.

An important representation of the ceremony can also be found on the funerary altar of Ti. Claudius Liberalis, a *praefectus fabrum*, from Tibur. On one side he is shown wearing a *trabea* riding a horse in the *transvectio* (Figure 8.3). On another face he is dressed as a *lupercus* preparing to take part in the Lupercalia (see Figure 10.1).[104] As Veyne has argued, this choice of representation is dictated by the fact that Liberalis died relatively young, before he had a chance to advance through the military or administrative

Figure 8.2: Funerary relief of T. Flavius Verus, Ostia

---

[103] *CIL* XIV 166; Spalthoff 2010: 237 (no. 170); Borg 2013: 27.
[104] *CIL* XIV 3624 = VI 3512; Spalthoff 2010: 237–8 (no. 171). The *luperci* and the Lupercalia are discussed in Chapter 10.

Figure 8.3: Funerary altar of Ti. Claudius Liberalis from Tibur. Face showing the *transvectio equitum*

positions open to equestrians.[105] The funerary monuments often reference the *probatio* aspect of the parade, in which the emperor formally bestowed or confirmed equestrian status. These typically show the *eques* riding on

[105] Veyne 1960: 107.

Figure 8.4: Sarcophagus of Q. Vivius Lucianus, outside Rome

horseback brandishing the *volumen* containing his letter of appointment in his hand.[106] A significant depiction of this appears on the third-century sarcophagus of Q. Vivius Lucianus, found on the Via Appia outside Rome (Figure 8.4).[107] On the left-hand side of the frieze, an equestrian rides on his horse brandishing the crown of olive leaves. On the right-hand side we see the togate *eques* receiving the scroll from an official. This representation appears to depict the two different stages of the *transvectio* ceremony.[108]

The second group of monuments was erected in honour of children who were not specifically described as *equites Romani*, but who were nevertheless shown participating in the *transvectio*.[109] This suggests that they came from an equestrian family, and had expected to be admitted into the *ordo* prior to their untimely deaths. For example, in Rome M. Iunius Rufus was commemorated by his *paedogogus* Soterichus with a marble altar (Figure 8.5). In the lower register Rufus is shown wearing the *trabea* and riding on a horse, which is being led by an attendant.[110] This is juxtaposed with a second image in the upper register of the altar, which depicts the young Rufus being educated by Soterichus. This allowed the freedman the opportunity to integrate himself into the monument, which he dedicated for both of them.[111] The two images are connected, since Rufus' education was designed to prepare him for life as an *eques Romanus* who had the literary talent and cultural background to serve as a tribune, prefect or procurator. Some funerary reliefs are particularly poignant testimonies to the family's misfortunes. The monument of C. Petronius Virianus Postumus, who died aged ten, depicts him riding a horse, wearing the

---

[106] Rebecchi 1999: 204.   [107] *CIL* VI 37103; Spalthoff 2010: 213 (no. 119); Borg 2013: 191–2.
[108] Rebecchi 1999: 201.   [109] Veyne 1960: 107.
[110] *CIL* VI 9752; Spalthoff 2010: 163–4 (no. 15).   [111] Mander 2013: 141–2.

Figure 8.5: Funerary altar of M. Iunius Rufus, Rome

trabea and holding an olive crown, as if he were taking part in the *trans-vectio equitum* (Figure 8.6).[112] Yet the epitaph was not set up by his parents, but by his grandfather, D. Valerius Niceta, suggesting that his parents had already died. It is probable that Niceta was a freedman, commemorating the rise of his family to respectable status, which had now been cruelly cut short.[113] The image of the *transvectio equitum* on these funerary reliefs

---

[112] *CIL* VI 24011; Spalthoff 2010: 208 (no. 111).   [113] Mander 2013: 128.

Figure 8.6: Funerary monument of C. Petronius Virianus Postumus, Rome

enabled the grant of the *equus publicus* to take place in monumental form, even if it did not occur in reality.

Over the course of the first century AD all *equites* became *equites equo publico* and were therefore eligible to march in the *transvectio*.[114] The size and disparate nature of the *ordo*, spread throughout Italy and the provinces

[114] See Chapter 5.

of the empire, meant that not all members of the order did, or could, participate at every ceremony.[115] It is telling that the *transvectio* is predominantly represented on funerary monuments in Italy and the western provinces as an initiation for young *equites*, suggesting that the ceremony had most significance as a rite of passage in these regions closest to Rome.[116] Indeed, reliefs showing the *transvectio* continue to be found in Italy until the late third century AD.[117] A sarcophagus of this date, now in Warsaw, but of unknown provenance, clearly depicts the ceremony, with a central figure on horseback clad in the *trabea* and holding the *corona*, and another man holding the scroll of appointment.[118] The fragmentary sarcophagus of M. Pinnius Faltonius Valens, which shows him accompanied by an attendant, is also dated to the second half of the third century AD.[119] Another fragment, from a sarcophagus in Ravenna, shows an *eques Romanus* on horseback brandishing his *corona*; the monument probably dates from the period around AD 230–250.[120] Such visual representations are rarer in other provinces. There are some examples of *equites* on horseback wearing the *trabea* in western regions, such as Noricum and Germania Superior, but they do not seem to depict the *transvectio* proper.[121] The only attested example of the *transvectio* from the eastern half of the empire is the cenotaph of Gaius Caesar in Limyra in Asia Minor, which is an imperial monument, rather than a relief celebrating the life of an individual *eques*.[122]

In the imperial period it must have been the case that, if a provincial *eques* did take part in the *transvectio*, he did so when he entered the *ordo* for the first time, as in the cases of Q. Sittius Faustus and C. Iulius Laetitus, discussed at the beginning of this section. Inscriptions from Italy, Africa and Asia Minor which refer to the emperor's approval of equestrian rank at the annual parade suggest that the specific *eques* commemorated in these epigraphic texts did indeed travel to Rome for the initiation.[123] This is also demonstrated by the language on the inscribed base of a statue for M. Gavius Gallicus from Attaleia in Pamphylia.[124] The inscription

---

[115] Demougin 1988: 219–25 points out that the imperial *turmae* must have been composed of thousands of men each.

[116] Veyne 1960: 102–3; Rebecchi 1999: 194–5.   [117] Rebecchi 1999: 197.

[118] Spalthoff 2010: 42, 241 (no. 179).   [119] *AE* 1990, 307; Spalthoff 2010: 173 (no. 39).

[120] Spalthoff 2010: 206 (no. 105).

[121] Noricum: Spalthoff 2010: 169–70 (no. 29); Germania Superior: *CIL* XIII 6817; Spalthoff 2010: 189 (no. 73).

[122] This is based on the table included at the back of Spalthoff 2010.

[123] Various different terms are used to indicate this. *Inquisitio*: *ILAlg.* I.2145; *I. Prusias* 54. *Probatio*: *CIL* VIII 6711. *Iudicium*: *CIL* V 27.

[124] *IGRR* 3.778.

records that Gallicus was 'honoured with the public horse in Rome by the emperor, [and] selected as a judge of the jury panels in Rome' (τετει| μημένον ὑπὸ τοῦ Σεβασ|τοῦ ἵππῳ δημοσίῳ ἐν Ῥώ|μῃ, ἐπίλεκτον κριτὴν ἐκ | τῶν ἐν Ῥώμῃ δεκουριῶν).[125] Equestrians resident in Italy were more readily able to visit Rome on a regular basis to participate in the parade, whereas for all other *equites* it was probably only a once in a lifetime event, if it was undertaken at all. But the fact that some equestrians from the provinces did make the journey to Rome indicates that there was inherent value to marching in the parade. The *transvectio* was the ceremonial embodiment of the *virtus* that had defined the equestrian order in the Republican age, and continued to give equestrian status its essential meaning, or ideological immanence (to use Mann's term), in the imperial period. Moreover, the formal *probatio* by the emperor functioned as a demonstration that, in the monarchical Roman state, membership of the *ordo* was conditional on imperial approval.[126] The *ordo* and the emperor were both an integral part of the framework of the *res publica*.

Youth, *Virtus* and the Imperial Succession

> And all the *equites Romani* collectively bestowed upon them shields and spears of silver and proclaimed them each *princeps iuventutis*.[127]

So Augustus wrote of his adopted sons Gaius and Lucius Caesar in chapter fourteen of the *Res Gestae*. The title of *princeps iuventutis*, signifying the leadership of the youth of the *ordo equester*, was a new honour.[128] The phrasing of this statement is of the utmost importance in understanding the interaction between the equestrian order and the imperial house in the early empire. It was not the emperor or the senate, but the *equites Romani universi* – all together and collectively – who decided to honour Augustus' sons in this way, implying that the *ordo* could be considered a corporate body with the ability to make decisions of this

---

[125] Note also the monument for his relative, L. Gavius Fronto, also from Attaleia (*SEG* 17, 584). This inscription contains similar wording, although Rome is not mentioned (ἵππῳ δημοσί|ῳ τετειμημένον ὑπὸ τοῦ Σε|βαστοῦ).

[126] Nicolet 1967a: 415–16; Demougin 1988: 187; Rowe 2002: 74–5.

[127] *RG* 14.2: *equites [a]utem Romani universi principem iuventutis utrumque eorum parm[is] et hastis argenteis donatum appellaverunt.*

[128] The expression had been used in the Republican period, most notably in the plural *principes iuventutis*, but it was never a formal distinction (Beringer 1954: 2297–9).

nature.[129] Furthermore, by granting Gaius and Lucius the title of *princeps iuventutis*, the *equites* for the very first time chose leaders (as opposed to patrons) for themselves, thus reinforcing their status as a unified *ordo* within the Roman social and political hierarchy.

Gaius was named *princeps iuventutis* in 5 BC, about the same time he was made *sevir equitum*, with his younger brother Lucius receiving the title in 2 BC. The naming of Gaius as *princeps iuventutis* in 5 BC probably occurred by acclamations of selected *equites* sitting in the *XIV ordines* in the theatre.[130] There is a fragmentary plaque found near the Theatre of Marcellus in Rome which records such an initiative of the *equites*:

[... to the son of Caesar Augustus], grandson of the [deified J]ulius | [... consul designate], [named prince] of the youth by them [after setting aside] the decorations of [b]oyhood, [the equestrian order] (erected this) [by pe]rmission of the senate.[131]

This inscription, though lacunose, lays out a clear order of events. First Gaius formally set aside his *toga praetexta* and became a man by assuming the *toga virilis*, probably at the festival of the Liberalia on 17 March.[132] This chronology accords with Augustus' own account in the *Res Gestae*, and that of Zonaras (based on Cassius Dio), who says Gaius was enrolled among the *iuvenes*.[133] This was an important occasion, which was marked by a distribution of 60 *denarii* to 320,000 inhabitants of the city of Rome.[134] Gaius' transition to manhood was recognised in different regions of the empire, as shown by an honorific decree of Sardis delivered to Augustus.[135] It was only later in that year that the equestrians acclaimed Gaius *princeps iuventutis*.[136] According to the inscribed plaque from the Theatre of Marcellus, the title was bestowed by the *ordo equester* alone, with permission to erect a statue granted by the senate.[137]

[129] Stein 1927: 58–9; Rowe 2002: 75–6; Horster 2011: 75–7.

[130] Hurlet 1997: 120–1; Rowe 2002: 81–2; Cooley 2009: 165–6.

[131] *CIL* VI 40326: *[--- Caesari Augusti f(ilio) divi I]ulii nepoti | [--- co(n)s(uli) desig(nato) principi] iuventutis a se | [appellato post deposita p]ueritiae insignia | [equester ordo pe]rmissu senatus.* For discussion of this text, see Vassileiou 1984 and Hurlet 1997: 120–1.

[132] Lacey 1996: 195, 197.

[133] *RG* 14.1; Dio 55.9.9 = Zon. 10.35 (ed. Dindorf p. 447). For discussion, see Cooley 2009: 164–5.

[134] *RG* 15.2.   [135] *IGR* IV 1756.

[136] For the chronology of these honours, see Hurlet 1997: 117–25.

[137] Vassileiou 1984: 837–8; Rowe 2002: 81 n. 41. A parallel can be found on the epitaph of the senator Q. Veranius, for whom the 'equestrian order and the Roman people erected a statue with the consent of the senate' (*[statuam posuit equester] ordo et populus Romanus consentiente senatu*) (*CIL* VI 41075).

Zonaras states that it was Augustus who 'proclaimed [Gaius] prince of the youth' (πρόκριτον ἀπέφηνε τῆς νεότητος). We should not be surprised that Dio's Byzantine successor ascribed the agency to the emperor rather than the *ordo equester*. It is hard to imagine that Augustus had no part in the acclamation of Gaius as *princeps iuventutis*. The granting of this new equestrian title and the award of the ceremonial *hastae* and *parma* in the same year in which Gaius assumed the *toga virilis*, became a *sevir*, and first participated in the *transvectio equitum*, cannot be ascribed to coincidence. The series of honours and offices was designed to signal Gaius' introduction to public life as Augustus' son.[138] It was in Augustus' interest to have these marks of favour voluntarily bestowed upon Gaius by the different constituencies in the Roman state, including the *ordo equester*. As so often, it was Tacitus who laid bare the machinery of power, when he wrote that Augustus 'most passionately desired that [Gaius and Lucius] be acclaimed *principes iuventutis* and be designated consuls, although he made a show of refusal'.[139] We should assume, therefore, that the impetus actually came from the emperor and his administration.[140] The members of the *ordo equester* resident in Rome were therefore co-opted into this act of consensus to give legitimacy to Augustus' succession plans. But we should not make them into unwilling participants. The involvement of the *equites* in this performance reinforced the importance of the *ordo* to the *res publica* at large. It was a mutually beneficial partnership.

The title of *princeps iuventutis* was loaded with ideological significance, indicating that Gaius and Lucius would be Augustus' heirs.[141] The title appears prominently in epigraphic documents among the other honours, such as priesthoods and consulships, accorded to the young men.[142] Although there was as yet no formal position of 'emperor' to which they could succeed, it was widely recognised that Augustus was securing the future of the monarchical state.[143] The title of *princeps iuventutis* deliberately echoed Augustus' own assumption of the Republican position of *princeps senatus*, so that both Rome's youth and its elders would be led

---

[138] *RG* 14.1 and *CIL* VI 40360 reveal that Gaius took part in public affairs from this year. For the argument that these actions should be seen as part of a rational programme of designating Augustus' heirs, see Stevenson 2013: 133–4.

[139] Tac. *Ann.* 1.3.2: *principes iuventutis appellari, destinari consules specie recusantis flagrantissime cupiverat.*

[140] Horster 2011: 76.   [141] Cooley 2009: 166.

[142] See, for example, *CIL* II 3267, VI 40325, XIII 2942.

[143] Hurlet 1997: 481–2. Augustus' own sentiments in this matter are expressed in a letter cited by Aulus Gellius: Gell. *NA* 15.7.3.

by members of the Julian family.[144] The idea that Gaius would one day grow
up to replace Augustus as *princeps* is echoed by the poet Ovid, who wrote
that he was 'presently the leader of the youth, but one day of the elders' (*nunc
iuvenum princeps, deinde future senum*).[145] The exemplary role of the
princeps iuventutis extended beyond the imperial *domus* to Roman society
at large: the youth of the *ordo equester*, who paraded through the streets
every 15 July, exhibiting their *virtus* for all to see, were themselves the future
of the *res publica*.[146]

The silver shields and spears (*parmae* and *hastae*), symbols of Rome's
cavalry, bestowed on Gaius and Lucius ensured that the young princes
received permanent memorials of their leadership of the *equites*, and of
their status as paradigms of military *virtus*. The emblems also associated
them with the Dioscuri, the patrons of the *ordo*, though the evidence for
this connection is admittedly limited.[147] The message was given visual
representation on imperial coins minted at Lugdunum between 2 BC
and AD 11 (Figure 8.7).[148] These depict Gaius and Lucius standing side
by side, with their *parmae* and *hastae*, as well as the symbols of their
senatorial priestly offices. On their deaths the shields and spears were
displayed in the *curia* at Rome, a pointed reminder that the *ordo equester*
itself lacked a home.[149] The connection between Gaius and the *ordo
equester* was commemorated on the cenotaph established at his place of
death, Limyra in Asia Minor, which depicts the procession of the *transvectio equitum*.[150] These memorials are important testimony to the public
relationship between Gaius and Lucius and the equestrian order. It must be
remembered, however, that the monuments are only the permanent
reminders of the extensive and varied political actions that followed the
deaths of these princes. As Rowe has shown, communities throughout the
empire actively sought to commemorate the young *principes*, and to communicate their actions to Augustus.[151] For example, when Gaius died the
colony of Pisa in north Italy passed a formal decree to mark his passing and
to establish ceremonies in his honour.[152] An equestrian resident of Pisa,
T. Statulenus Iuncus, was assigned the task of presenting this document

---

[144] Stevenson 2013: 134.   [145] Ovid, *Ars Am.* 1.194.   [146] Rowe 2002: 76.
[147] Champlin 2011: 98; Horster 2011: 84–5. Cf. the more confident Poulson 1991: 123.
[148] *RIC* I² Augustus nos. 205–12.
[149] Dio 55.12.1. Remains of a fragmentary frieze depicting a *parma* suggests that marble versions
might also have been carved into the exterior of Augustus' mausoleum (Spalthoff 2010: 63).
There is no evidence that the shields and spears were carried in the funerary processions for the
young princes (cf. Poulson 1991: 123).
[150] Dio 55.10a.9; Spalthoff 2010: 159–60.   [151] Rowe 2002: 113–14.
[152] *CIL* XI 1421, ll. 42–50 = *ILS* 140.

Figure 8.7: *Aureus* of Augustus (reverse side), showing Gaius and Lucius with their *hastae* and *parmae* (*RIC* 1² Augustus no. 209)

to Augustus in Rome. Iuncus played his part in this performance of support for the imperial regime, because it not only brought prestige to him personally, but also to his entire *ordo*.

The honours for Gaius and Lucius Caesar set the paradigm for the relationship between future princes of the imperial house and the *ordo equester*, although it must be emphasised that there was no fixed way in which this was expressed.[153] As imperial heirs and military commanders, Germanicus and the younger Drusus were both identified with the equestrian order, although neither was formally acclaimed as *princeps iuventutis*.[154] The most explicit evidence for the relationship with the *equites* comes with their deaths: in Germanicus' case, the *cunei* of *iuniores* in the theatre were renamed in his honour, and his image was displayed during the *transvectio equitum*.[155] Drusus received a statue in the Lupercal, and a silver shield bearing his image was likewise carried during the

---

[153] Horster 2011: 89–90 lists the various distinctions and honours that could be conferred on young princes. Poulson 1991 is overly generous in assigning the title to princes who did not actually carry it.

[154] Beringer 1954: 2301–2; Horster 2011: 90–1. The only suggestion comes in Ovid, *Ep. ex Pont.* 2.5.41, in which Germanicus is styled *iuvenum princeps*.

[155] Tac. *Ann.* 2.83. For the theatre, see Chapter 9.

transvectio.[156] Despite not holding the title of *princeps iuventutis*, these young princes were portrayed as models for future generations, especially the youth of the equestrian order. At Germanicus' death the senate published Tiberius' funeral oration for his adopted son because the emperor 'judged that it would be useful for the youth, both our children and the generations to come'.[157]

The next member of the imperial family formally made *princeps iuventutis* was Tiberius' unfortunate grandson, Tiberius Gemellus. After Tiberius' death Caligula adopted Gemellus as his own son, bestowed the *toga virilis* on him, and then acclaimed him *princeps iuventutis.*[158] The connection between the elevation to manhood and the princely title recalled Augustus' promotion of Gaius and Lucius. Caligula cast himself in the role of Augustus in this exchange, which helped to secure his own primacy over Gemellus, who had in fact been named joint heir by Tiberius.[159] Shortly after coming to office Caligula rehabilitated the memory of his dead older brothers, Nero and Drusus, who had been victims of the Tiberian regime. Although they bore the name Caesar and formed part of the imperial family, they had never been acclaimed *principes iuventutis.*[160] In AD 38 Caligula issued bronze coins with an obverse depicting Nero and Drusus riding on horseback, their cloaks flowing behind them (Figure 8.8).[161] The image associated the two sons with the *ordo equester* and their patron deities, the Dioscuri.[162] The coins envision Caligula as the head of the imperial family on the Augustan model, surrounded by his own cadre of princes. The overriding message of dynasty in the years following Augustus' death was that the young men of the imperial family, regardless of whether they actually bore the title of *princeps iuventutis*, served as models of military *virtus* for the youth of the *ordo equester* to emulate.[163] This simultaneously reinforced the place of the *ordo* and the imperial family in the fabric of the Roman state.

The position of the *princeps iuventutis* as the head of the equestrian youth played an important role in the reign of Claudius. In AD 51 the

---

[156] *CIL* VI 3200 = *RS* 38, col. II, 8–12. These honours were explicitly based on those for Germanicus (Tac. *Ann.* 4.9). For the association of the Lupercal with the *ordo equester*, see Chapter 10.

[157] *RS* 37, *Tab. Siar.* frag (b), col. II. l. 17: *esse utile iuventuti liberorum posteriorumque nostrorum iudicaret.*

[158] Suet. *Cal.* 15.2; Dio 59.8.1.

[159] Barrett 1990: 67–8. Note the hostile picture of the adoption in Philo, *Leg.* 26–8.

[160] Beringer 1954: 2302. The *SCPP* l. 147 calls Nero only Caesar and *iuvenis*, and the title does not appear on either of their epitaphs from the Mausoleum of Augustus (*CIL* VI 40373–4).

[161] *RIC* I² Caligula nos. 34, 49.   [162] Poulson 1991: 129.

[163] For the mounted warrior as the symbol of *virtus*, see McDonnell 2006: 150–1.

Figure 8.8: *Dupondius* of Caligula (obverse side), showing his brothers Nero and Drusus (*RIC* I² Caligula no. 49)

emperor's adopted son Nero simultaneously received the *toga virilis*, the title of *princeps iuventutis*, designation to the consulship of AD 55 and proconsular *imperium*; he was also co-opted into all four major priestly colleges.[164] This was a significant demonstration that Nero was Claudius' heir apparent, recalling the introduction of Gaius and Lucius to public life by Augustus.[165] It is interesting that Tacitus presented the award of the title of *princeps iuventutis* as a senatorial initiative: he wrote that Claudius 'freely gave into senatorial flattery' (*adulationibus senatus libens cessit*) on this matter. However, the numismatic evidence has the honour being bestowed by the equestrian order. A *denarius* minted at Rome shows Nero on the obverse bearing the title of CO(N)S(VLI) DESIG(NATO) (Figure 8.9). The reverse depicts the equestrian *parma*, mounted on a *hasta*, with the legend EQVESTER ORDO PRINCIPI IVVENT(VTI) ('the equestrian order to the prince of the youth').[166] Here, for the first

---

[164] Tac. *Ann.* 12.41.1. Suet. *Nero* 7.2 mentions the ceremony of manhood, but not the title of *princeps iuventutis.*

[165] Griffin 1984: 29; Horster 2011: 92–3.

[166] *RIC* I² Claudius nos. 78–9, 108. Other coins dated to AD 51 also feature the *princeps iuventutis* title (*RIC* I² Claudius nos. 75–7, 82, 107). The design was echoed on a cistophoric tetradrachm minted at Pergamum in Asia Minor (*RIC* I² Claudius no. 121).

Figure 8.9a–b: *Aureus* of Claudius, depicting Nero (obverse side) and the award of the title of *princeps iuventutis* (reverse side) (*RIC* I^2 Claudius no. 78)

time since Gaius and Lucius – now half a century in the past – the acclamation of the *princeps iuventutis* was commemorated with the ceremonial weapons of the equestrian order. Tacitus' comments about senatorial sycophancy suggest that the initiative may have originated in the *curia*, after which a proposal was made by leading *equites*, although the exact political machinations are unrecoverable.[167] What we can say is that Nero's debut as prince of the youth was marked by his participation in army exercises in order to display his *virtus*. According to Suetonius, 'he carried forth a shield in his own hand as part of a military exhibition of the praetorians' (*decursione praetorianis scutum sua manu praetulit*).[168] This exercise acted as a ceremonial display of Nero's *virtus* for public consumption, and showed his fitness to succeed Claudius as *princeps*. The involvement of the equestrian order in the designation of Nero as Claudius' heir demonstrates the *ordo*'s continuing importance as an agent of consensus and legitimacy. The members of the *ordo equester* accordingly embraced their role in the imperial system.

The young princes of the Augustan and Julio-Claudian periods featured prominently in another public ceremony, that of the *lusus Troiae* ('game of Troy').[169] This was a mock battle display conducted on horseback, usually in the Circus Maximus, by noble boys and youths, aged between six and fourteen.[170] It was primarily a rite of initiation, the aim of which was to demonstrate that Rome's aristocratic youth were being trained in the ways of their ancestors. They showed that they were fit to fight for the *res publica*, should they be required to do so.[171] The *lusus Troiae* was not a ritual specifically associated with the *ordo equester*, but with the aristocratic youth, which included senators' sons.[172] The *lusus* ritual, composed of intricate military manoeuvres conducted on horseback, came to be closely connected with Augustus' promotion of *virtus* among the upper *ordines*, forming an effective complement to the *transvectio equitum*. The *lusus Troiae* was said to have been of ancient origin, brought to Rome by Aeneas and the Trojans when they fled from Troy. This, at any

---

[167] The *ordo equester* was still involved in voting a range of honours in Rome during the imperial period, as in the case of the statues decreed for Sejanus and Nero (Dio 58.2.7, 63(62).18.3).

[168] Suet. *Nero* 7.2.

[169] For an overview of the ritual and its significance, see Schneider 1927 and Weeber 1974.

[170] Crowther 2009: 351–2 has boys aged six to ten making up the *minores*, and the eleven to fourteen year olds the *maiores*. For the manoeuvres they were required to perform, see Williams 1960: 152; Houston 1981–2: 8.

[171] Schneider 1927: 2065; Houston 1981–2: 9–10; Freyburger-Galland 1997: 628–9; Prescendi 2010: 80–1. The *lusus Troiae* must be distinguished from the 'pyrrhic dance' (πυρρίχη or *pyrrhica*), with which it is sometimes confused. The pyrrhic dances were martial rituals performed by naked men and women dressed as hoplites. They were first introduced to Rome by Caesar (Suet. *Iul.* 39.1), and were later staged by Nero (Suet. *Nero* 12.1) and Hadrian (*HA Hadr.* 19.8). In his description of the funeral of Septimius Severus, Herodian does not seem to be referring to the pyrrhic dance proper, but drawing a comparison between the dance and the rhythmic manoeuvres of the *equites* performing the *decursio* (Herodian 4.2.9).

[172] Weinstock 1971: 88–9. The language used to describe the noble boys is surveyed by Freyburger-Galland 1997: 623–4.

rate, is the aetiology memorably enshrined by Vergil in Book Five of the *Aeneid*, in which the *lusus* features as part of the funeral games for Aeneas' father Anchises.[173] In reality, the ceremony originated in Italy itself (though how this came about is debated), and the association with the foundation of Troy seems to have emerged in the political environment of the first century BC.[174] The first attested staging of the *lusus Troiae* in this period was by Sulla, who sought to capitalise on the association between the myth of Aeneas, son of Venus, and his own divine patronage by the goddess.[175] It was at precisely this time that many Republican families began to claim that they themselves were descended from the original Trojans who came to Italy with Aeneas.[176] These associations gained increasing importance under Caesar, who mounted the *lusus Troiae* during the dedication of the *forum Iulium* and the Temple of Venus Genetrix in 46 BC.[177] It may have been then, as Weinstock suggests, that the role played by Aeneas' son, Iulus (also known as Ascanius), in the transmission of the *lusus* to Rome was invented for the first time.[178]

The performances of the *lusus Troiae* continued throughout the triumviral period, but took on new meaning under Augustus, who staged the ritual very frequently, according to Suetonius.[179] The new *princeps* believed that the *lusus* was an opportunity to display the 'cream of the noble youth' (*clarae stirpis indolem*) to the public at large. But the *lusus Troiae* also enabled Augustus to glorify the past, present and future of the Julian line, since it was now frequently staged at ceremonies of significance for himself and his family, and starred the princes of the imperial house.[180] The *lusus Troiae* featured in the celebrations for the consecration of the Temple of Divus Iulius in 29 BC, and at the Actian games of 28 BC.[181] In one of these games the young Tiberius, Augustus' stepson, took part as the leader of the *maiores*.[182] Gaius Caesar participated in the *lusus* at the dedication of the Theatre of Marcellus in 13 BC, and Agrippa Postumus in 2 BC during

---

[173] Vergil, *Aeneid* 5.545–603.

[174] The association between *Troia* and Troy itself is a false etymology. The word probably derives from the verb *truare*. For discussion of the possible origin myths, see Schneider 1927: 2059–61; Weeber 1974: 171–86.

[175] Plut. *Cat. Min.* 3.1. Sulla and Venus: Weeber 1974: 189–92; Erskine 2001: 244.

[176] Galinsky 1969: 165.   [177] Dio 46.23.6; Erskine 2001: 19–20.

[178] Weinstock 1971: 88. Iulus was one of the three squadron leaders at Anchises' funeral games (Vergil, *Aeneid* 5.546–51, 570–2).

[179] Suet. *Aug.* 43.2; Wardle 2014: 325. The *lusus Troiae* had formed part of Agrippa's *ludi Apollinares* which he mounted as praetor in 40 BC and his games as aedile in 33 BC (Dio 48.20.2, 49.43.2).

[180] For the *lusus* staged at Augustan occasions, see Houston 1981–2: 9.

[181] Dio 51.22.4, 53.1.4.   [182] Suet. *Tib.* 6.4.

the dedication of the Temple of Mars Ultor in the *forum Augustum*.[183] The princes can only have been very young at the time: Tiberius would have been thirteen or fourteen; Gaius, seven; and Postumus, ten. This suggests that these exhibitions were a way of marking their debut in public life.[184] The equestrian exercises were largely symbolic, functioning as displays of military *virtus* rather than actual training for battle.[185] But they were not without their risks: under Augustus, the young Nonius Asprenas suffered from lameness after falling from his horse, and Aeserninus, the grandson of C. Asinius Pollio, broke his leg.[186] This put an end to performances of the *lusus Troiae* after Pollio complained in the senate, some time before AD 4.[187]

The *lusus* fell into abeyance under Tiberius, only to be revived by Caligula, who staged the ceremonial manoeuvres between races at the circus and, more notably, as part of the celebrations for the dedication of the Temple of Divus Augustus and during the funeral of his sister Drusilla.[188] The tradition was continued by Claudius, who had the *lusus Troiae* integrated into the Saecular Games in AD 47.[189] This time the *lusus* featured both the emperor's son, Britannicus, then a mere six years old, and his future adopted son and heir, Nero, aged nine. Nero's performance was particularly successful and was well received by the audience, which acted as a portent for the future (as Tacitus noted wryly).[190] The Saecular Games functioned as a ceremony of renewal for both the *res publica* and the imperial dynasty itself.[191] Although the *lusus Troiae* continued in some form until the third century AD, its association with the princes of the imperial household seems to have dissipated after the Julio-Claudian dynasty.[192]

The title of *princeps iuventutis* continued to be granted to princes of the imperial house under the Flavians and Antonines. The sons of Vespasian – Titus and Domitian – both held the honour, but there is no evidence as to

[183] Gaius: Dio 54.26.1. Postumus: 55.10.6.   [184] Crowther 2009: 351.

[185] Houston 1981–2: 9–10.   [186] Suet. *Aug.* 43.2.

[187] J. M. Carter 1982: 158; Wardle 2014: 326.   [188] Suet. *Cal.* 18.3; Dio 59.7.4, 59.11.2.

[189] Suet. *Claud.* 21.2–3.   [190] Tac. *Ann.* 11.11.2; Suet. *Nero* 7.1.   [191] Malloch 2013: 184.

[192] The *lusus Troiae* featured in the Severan *ludi Saeculares* of AD 204 (*CIL* VI 32326). A reference to the *lusus Troiae* in the Severan period also occurs in Galen (*De Theriaca ad Pisonem* (ed. Kuhn, vol. XIV, p. 212)), who refers to a young noble who fell off his horse while participating in the equestrian dances. See the discussion in L. R. Taylor 1924: 164; Freyburger-Galland 1997: 623; Leigh 2015: 11–18. Ausonius, in his *Riddle of the Number Three* (l. 80), states that there are 'three *turmae* of the *equites*' (*tres equitum turmae*), which may refer to the squadrons in the *lusus Troiae*. This is because Ausonius' figure of three recalls the number of squadrons in the first *lusus Troiae* in which Ascanius participated (*Aeneid* 5.560). Alternatively, Ausonius may be referring to the first three squadrons of cavalry established by Romulus (Livy 1.15.3), on which see Chapter 1. Ausonius' reference does not necessarily mean that the *lusus* continued to be practised during the late fourth century AD.

how it was conferred.[193] Equestrian imagery features particularly prominently on Domitian's coinage as Caesar during Vespasian's reign.[194]
The title of *princeps iuventutis* was often associated with the personification
of Spes on the reverse of imperial coins, articulating the general concept of
expectation and hope that the imperial dynasty would continue in the
future.[195] After Domitian, the next prince to bear the title of *princeps
iuventutis* was Marcus Aurelius. Marcus was associated with the *ordo
equester* as a young man through his appointment as *sevir equitum* and
as *princeps iuventutis*.[196] The Antonine imperial house emphasised their
connections with Rome's legendary past, particularly the arrival of Aeneas
and Ascanius in Italy and the archaic cults of Latium.[197] The image of
Castor, the horseman of the two Dioscuri, appears on the reverse of coins
and medallions for Antonine imperial princes.[198] This began in AD 155
with a medallion of Marcus Aurelius as Caesar on the obverse, and Castor
standing with his horse on the reverse (Figure 8.10).[199] The combination

Figure 8.10: Medallion of Marcus Aurelius as Caesar (reverse side), showing Castor
with his horse

---

[193] Beringer 1954: 2303–4; Horster 2011: 94–5.
[194] McDonnell 2006: 151; *RIC* II[2] Vespasian nos. 539, 672, 679, 959.
[195] Horster 2011: 95; *RIC* II[2] Vespasian nos. 787–8.
[196] *HA Marc.* 6.3; Dio 72(71).35.5. Cf. Horster 2011: 97.
[197] This will be explored in Chapter 10.   [198] Poulson 1991: 134–5; Horster 2011: 88.
[199] Gnecchi 1912: II Marcus no. 39.

returns on coins of Commodus, though they were minted when he was co-Augustus with Marcus, rather than Caesar.[200] In emulation of the Augustan example, Marcus' own son Commodus received the *toga virilis* and the title of *princeps iuventutis* in AD 175, the same year in which he was co-opted into the four senior priestly colleges.[201] The Roman mint even produced coins very similar to Nero's with the shield and legend EQVESTER ORDO PRINCIPI IVVENT(VTI) as a way of marking Commodus' elevation.[202] This emphasis on the equestrian order bestowing the title may well have been the result of the mint reviving an old coin type, rather than any actual historical action undertaken by the *equites*.

The Severan period shows obvious signs of change. The coinage of Septimius Severus's son and Caesar Geta featured images of Castor the horseman, as well as Geta in military uniform and on horseback.[203] There was no reference to the *ordo equester* on these coins. Indeed, it is evident that by the early third century AD the title of *princeps iuventutis* was bestowed by the senate, rather than the equestrian order or its representatives. Cassius Dio provides an account of the senatorial session in AD 217 in which the letters from the new emperor Macrinus were read out in the *curia*. In response to these missives, the senate confirmed Macrinus' position as emperor. His young son Diadumenianus was 'designated' (ἀπεδείχθη) a patrician, *princeps iuventutis* and Caesar.[204] The *ordo equester* played no role in this decision. The coins of Diadumenianus reflected this new reality: the legend PRINC(EPS) IVVENTVTIS accompanied images of Diadumenianus in a cuirass, standing alongside military standards.[205] This suggests that the title had ceased to have a close association with the *equites*.[206] Henceforth almost every imperial heir bore the title *princeps iuventutis* until the middle decades of the fourth century AD.[207] Even some Augusti were erroneously described as *princeps iuventutis* on inscriptions, perhaps due to confusion among provincials as

---

[200] *RIC* III Marcus Aurelius nos. 648, 1579.   [201] *HA Comm.* 10.1–2.1; Dio 72(71).22.2.

[202] *RIC* III Commodus nos. 1534–5.   [203] *RIC* IV Geta nos. 6, 15a–b, 16a–b, 18, 37b.

[204] Dio 79(78).17.1.   [205] *RIC* IV Macrinus nos. 102, 104, 106, 109, 116–17.

[206] Horster 2011: 88–9.

[207] The last *princeps iuventutis* on record is Valentinian II, but he is accorded the title on an inscription from Africa which must date to after AD 375, since he is also called Augustus (*CIL* VIII 14290). Valentinian II had no official titles prior to his acclamation as Augustus in AD 375 (McEvoy 2013: 58), and he is not known to have been made *princeps iuventutis* after this point either. The inscription is therefore likely to preserve incorrect titulature. The demise of the title of *princeps iuventutis* is probably to be associated with the rise of *nobilissimus puer* as a status designation for imperial sons in the late fourth century AD. This title was granted to Jovian's son Varronianus in AD 364, Valentinian I's son Gratian in AD 366, and Valens' son Valentinian Galates in AD 369 (Lenski 2002: 90–2; McEvoy 2013: 49, 52, 58).

to the correct form of imperial titulature.[208] The title *princeps iuventutis* had become a conventional designation for younger members of the imperial family, rather than an emblem of the association between the imperial house and the *ordo equester*. The military iconography on the coins of the *principes iuventutis* reflected the reality of power in the imperial age: the purple was conferred by the army.

The relationship between the *ordo equester* and the title of *princeps iuventutis* therefore changed significantly over the course of the imperial period. In the Augustan age it was a genuine innovation, a new honour given to Augustus' sons Gaius and Lucius by the equestrian order, which in turn provided the *ordo* with a ceremonial leader. The young princes of the imperial house, such as Germanicus and Drusus, were likewise identified as models for the *iuvenes* of the equestrian order, even though there is no record of them being acclaimed with the title of *princeps iuventutis*. Caligula and Claudius cultivated the connection with Augustus' model of imperial succession by bestowing the title on their own heirs. The Flavian and Antonine imperial houses likewise used this association to designate successors to the purple. However, the connection between the *ordo equester* and the *princeps iuventutis* changed over time, as imperial princes were envisaged as more general representatives of military *virtus* rather than true leaders of the equestrian youth. By the early third century AD the title *princeps iuventutis* was evidently within the gift of the senate, and later became a pro-forma honour for every imperial heir, as a way of showing their military qualifications.[209] This change reflected the fact that the late Roman emperor and his heirs most needed the support and approval of the army itself, rather than *ordo equester*, which only represented the military in an ideological sense.[210]

Regimented Grief

There were few more ritualised and choreographed expressions of emotion in the Roman world than the funerals of its emperors.[211] Our best and most reliable accounts of these occasions appear in the histories of Cassius Dio

---

[208] Beringer 1954: 2306–7.

[209] For martial prowess in late Roman imperial ideology, see McEvoy 2013: 29–30.

[210] Note, for example, the agency of the army in the succession of Constantine's sons (Eus. *VC* 4.68.1–2). For other cases, see McEvoy 2013: 39.

[211] See Sumi 2005: 253–61 on the new imperial characteristics of funeral ceremonies as they developed under Augustus.

and Herodian, who have very different motivations for including imperial funerals in their works. Herodian, a Greek official of indeterminate status, described the funeral of Septimius Severus in AD 211 in the manner of an outsider, explaining the 'custom' (ἔθος) of the Romans to his Greek audience.[212] Herodian reveals a superb eye for detail in his explanation of ritual procedure, from the stately processions of the senators and *equites* to the offerings placed on the funeral pyre, giving the account the air of an 'ethnographic excursus'.[213] In contrast, Cassius Dio's description of the funeral of Pertinax in AD 193, while it preserves many of the same details as Herodian's account, is written from the perspective of an insider, since Dio actually took part in the ceremony. His pride in his senatorial status means that he draws specific attention to the communal actions of the order. Dio frequently uses the first person plural 'we' (ἡμεῖς) to refer to senators approaching the effigy of Pertinax, the offerings they carry, the acclamations made during Severus' funeral oration, and their seating around the funeral pyre on the Campus Martius.[214] This aspect of Dio's history is particularly important in the context of imperial funerals because it draws attention to the significance of these ceremonies as expressions of Roman communal identity. The funeral ceremony involved the participation of senators, soldiers, corporations, citizens and *equites* as representatives of the various constituencies that made up the *res publica*, and their involvement validated the state in its monarchical form.[215]

The first state funeral (*funus publicum*) at which the *ordo equester* played a prominent role was that of the dictator Sulla in 78 BC.[216] Sulla's body was accompanied by state priests, followed by the senate and magistrates, the *equites*, and Sulla's legionaries. Each of these groups then raised their voices in lamentation, followed by the Roman people at large.[217] These rituals enshrined the idea that representatives of different corporate groups of the *res publica* should play a role in such commemorations. The ceremony also reveals the significance of the Republican dynasts such as Sulla in laying the groundwork for the monarchy of Augustus and his successors.[218] In the first funeral for a member of Augustus' family, that of Drusus the Elder in 9 BC, the equestrian order carried Drusus' body to the Campus Martius. Dio noted that these *equites* were composed of the sons of senatorial families as well as other

[212] Herodian 4.2.1. On Herodian's position, see the most recent overview of Kemezis 2014: 304–8.
[213] Price 1987: 58.
[214] Dio 75(74).4.4, 4.6, 5.1, 5.4. On Dio's use of the first-person plural in his narrative, see Davenport 2012a: 799–803.
[215] A sentiment expressed by Ps.-Quint. *Decl.* 329.   [216] Hug 1918: 530; Demougin 1988: 261.
[217] App. *BC* 1.106. Cf. Plut. *Sulla* 38, describing the ceremony in less detail.
[218] This idea was explored in Chapter 4.

members of the *ordo*.[219] At the death of Augustus in AD 14, we find the *ordo equester* volunteering to play a prominent role in his funeral procession. The future emperor Claudius was selected as their representative to ask the consuls for permission to carry the *princeps'* body into Rome.[220] The *equites* then met the funeral cortege at Bovillae, and took up the emperor's corpse for the final stage of the journey.[221] The fact that the *equites* specifically asked to take part in the funeral in this manner is an effective illustration of the voluntary consensus of the *ordines* that Augustus sought to foster. It shows that the *ordo equester*, or at least its chief representatives in Rome, were invested in the monarchical *res publica* which the *princeps* had shaped during his life.[222] After the emperor's cremation on the Campus Martius, leading members of the *ordo* sat by Livia's side for five days as she waited for the pyre to cool so that she could collect the remains of her husband.[223] According to Suetonius, barefoot *equites* then took up the ashes for burial in the Mausoleum of Augustus.[224]

Members of the *ordo* continued to have pivotal roles as official escorts or pallbearers in imperial funeral ceremonies, such as when Caligula rehabilitated his deceased mother and brother and had their ashes escorted to the Mausoleum of Augustus by equestrians.[225] However, there appears to have been no official set procedure for their involvement, which varied from ceremony to ceremony. In the funeral of Pertinax the *equites* carried the emperor's bier to the Campus Martius, whereas in the funeral of Septimius Severus members of the *ordo equester* and sons of senators carried the emperor's effigy into the *forum Romanum*.[226] Even though different arrangements were made during each individual funeral, successive generations maintained the belief that the *ordo equester* should play a key role in the ceremony, commensurate with its standing within the *res publica*.

In addition to their role as official escorts, members of the *ordo equester* rode on horseback in the official military parade around the imperial

---

[219] Dio 55.2.3. See also Ps.-Ovid, *Consol. ad Liviam* ll. 202, 207–8.   [220] Suet. *Claud.* 6.1.

[221] Suet. *Aug.* 100.2; Dio 55.31.2. Bovillae was the ancestral home of the Julian family and the location of the shrine of the Gens Iulia (Weinstock 1971: 5–7, 86). In the funeral procession for Germanicus, his body was carried by soldiers. However, *equites* clad in the *trabea* came out to meet the cortège as it processed through Italy (Tac. *Ann.* 3.2).

[222] See the remarks of Price 1987: 83 on the importance of status divisions at funerals in the Augustan period.

[223] Dio 56.42.4.

[224] It had originally been proposed that senatorial priests should fill this role (Suet. *Aug.* 100.2, 4).

[225] Suet. *Cal.* 15.1. Cf. Dio 59.3.5, who says that Caligula deposited their ashes accompanied by lictors.

[226] Pertinax: Dio 75(74).3.2–3.. Septimius Severus: Herodian 4.2.4.

funeral pyre, known as the *decursio*. Like the annual ceremony of the *transvectio*, the *decursio equitum* commemorated the origins of equestrians as the cavalry of the Roman state and their martial *virtus*. Roman soldiers had performed such manoeuvres around the pyres or tombs of deceased generals since the Republic.[227] Circumambulation was a symbol of purification, which explains why circular mausoleums often had winding, maze-like corridors in their interiors.[228] The first attested example of the corporate involvement of the *ordo equester* in the encirclement occurred at the *funus publicum* of Sulla in 78 BC, when the *equites* marched past his pyre with the army.[229] Thereafter, literary references describe *equites* riding in the ceremonial *decursiones* around the funeral pyres of Drusus the Elder, Augustus, Germanicus, Drusilla, Pertinax and Septimius Severus.[230] The ceremony is also enshrined in monumental form on two sides of the base of the Column of Antoninus Pius in Rome (Figure 8.11).[231] It seems probable, therefore, that members of the equestrian order participated in a *decursio* at most, if not all, imperial funerals through to the third century AD.[232]

The regulations for the funeral of Germanicus in AD 19 specified that *equites* with the *equus publicus* should appear in the Campus Martius wearing the *trabea*.[233] The actual procession involved the equestrians on horseback, divided into *turmae* and led by their senatorial *seviri*, just as in the annual *transvectio*; they then performed intricate manoeuvres around the pyre.[234] The praetorian infantry and cavalry accompanied the *equites* in this display.[235] Both Marcus Aurelius and Lucius Verus participated in the *decursio* for their deceased adoptive father Antoninus Pius, leading the *equites* and their *seviri* in formation.[236] In the funeral of Septimius Severus the *decursio* was complemented by the manoeuvres of chariots carrying images of deceased Roman generals and emperors.[237] The *decursio*

---

[227] Toynbee 1971: 55. See Livy 25.17.4.5; Tac. *Ann.* 2.7. For the ancient origin of such manoeuvres, see M. L. West 2007: 502–3.

[228] P. J. E. Davies 2000: 124–6.　[229] App. *BC* 1.106.

[230] Drusus the Elder: Ps.-Ovid, *Consol. ad Liviam* ll. 217–18; Suet. *Claud.* 1.3. Augustus: Dio 56.42.2. Germanicus: *RS* 37, *Tabula Hebana* ll. 55–7. Drusilla: Dio 59.11.2. Pertinax: Dio 75 (74).5.5. Septimius Severus: Herodian 4.2.9.

[231] Vogel 1973: 56–66.　[232] Price 1987: 59–61.

[233] *RS* 37, *Tabula Hebana* l. 57. The *equites* on the Column of Antoninus Pius are shown wearing the *trabea* (Vogel 1973: 59–60).

[234] This is deduced by their depiction on the base of the Column of Antoninus Pius (Vogel 1973: 56–60). Herodian 4.2.9 likens the movements to the pyrrhic dance.

[235] Dio 54.46.2, 59.11.2, 75(74).5.5; Demougin 1988: 263–9; Swan 2004: 342. On the Column of Antoninus Pius, only the praetorian infantry is shown (Vogel 1973: 56–7).

[236] Vogel 1973: 65–6.　[237] Herodian 4.2.10.

Figure 8.11: Base of the Column of Antoninus Pius, Rome, showing the *decursio equitum*

therefore celebrated the past, present and future of the Roman state, giving a leading role to the *ordo equester* and their martial heritage, as well as to the imperial heirs who would succeed to the purple.[238] As with the *transvectio* parade, and the relationship between equestrians and the imperial princes, the funeral ceremonies invested equestrians with ideological immanence, ensuring that membership of the *ordo* remained a status to be esteemed and valued under the empire.

The events of the third century AD seriously disrupted the way in which imperial funerals were conducted. The vast majority of post-Severan emperors were killed in battle, or murdered by their rivals, and therefore did not receive proper funerals at Rome.[239] Of the emperors who reigned between AD 235 and 284, only Gallienus was actually buried at Rome, where he was interred after his murder at Milan in AD 268. His successor, Claudius II Gothicus, ordered Gallienus to be deified, but it is uncertain what sort of ceremony accompanied his burial.[240] The funeral pyre

---

[238] Similar ideas underlie the appointment of equestrians as priests of the state in the imperial period, which will be explored in Chapter 10.

[239] Arce 2000: 120. See the list of imperial deaths and burial places in Johnson 2009: 203–9.

[240] Victor, *Caes.* 33. For Gallienus' mausoleum, see Johnson 2009: 42–7.

continued to appear on *consecratio* coinage for deceased emperors until the
Constantinian period, but this may have simply been a symbol representing the death and apotheosis of the emperor.[241] Indeed, the majority of the
emperors in the third century AD and beyond were buried, rather than
cremated, as part of a wider change in Roman funerary practices.[242]
Without a pyre to process around, there was no role for the *decursio
equitum* in the ceremonies. The porphyry sarcophagus of Constantine's
mother Helena, now in the Vatican, does feature soldiers riding on horseback in a manner reminiscent of the *decursio* on the Column of Antoninus
Pius. It has been suggested that this sarcophagus was originally planned for
a male emperor, either Constantius I, Constantine, or perhaps even
Maxentius.[243] However, the sarcophagus does not depict a ceremonial
procession, since the horsemen are depicted trampling defeated barbarians
as they ride.[244]

It is telling that the equestrian order is nowhere to be found in accounts
of imperial funerals in the fourth century AD. Instead, there is a renewed
emphasis on the role of the army and its officers, as seen in the description
of Constantine's funeral provided by Eusebius of Caesarea. He described
how the emperor's body was carried from the estate outside Nicomedia
where he had died to lie in state at the imperial palace in Constantinople.[245]
There, the most important officials came to pay homage to Constantine:
the army commanders, the *comites* and the 'whole body of magistrates'
(πᾶν τὸ τῶν ἀρχόντων τάγμα). They were followed by the senators, 'all
men according to rank' (οἵ τ' ἐπ' ἀξίας πάντες), and then crowds of the
people.[246] Although these officers and officials undoubtedly included
citizens of equestrian status, who still existed at this time, there is no
mention of the *ordo equester* as a corporate group.[247] Instead, we have
a tripartite division of the Roman state into army, senate and people, with
the military pre-eminent above all.[248] The army assumed a paramount
position, eliminating the need for any involvement of the equestrian order
and its antiquarian displays of *virtus*.[249] The absence of the *ordo equester*
might be also explained by the fact that Constantine's lying in state and

[241] MacCormack 1981: 102; Johnson 2009: 181.   [242] Price 1987: 96–7; Johnson 2009: 15.
[243] Drijvers 1991: 75; Johnson 2009: 118.   [244] Elsner 1998: 21–2.   [245] Eus. *VC* 4.66.1.
[246] Eus. *VC* 4.67.1. An alternative translation for τῶν ἀρχόντων could be 'of the governors'.
[247] For equestrian status in the fourth century AD, see Chapter 12.
[248] Cameron and Hall 1999: 344.
[249] When Constantius II died in AD 361, it was the officer Jovian and the soldiers who escorted the
body to Constantinople (Amm. 21.16.20–1; Greg. Naz. *Or.* 5.17). Arce 2000: 125 says there was
a *decursio equitum* at Constantius II's funeral, but cites no evidence for this, nor have I been
able to find any.

subsequent funeral did not happen in the city of Rome, much to the distress of the city's inhabitants.[250] If Constantine had been buried in Rome like Pertinax and Septimius Severus, there may perhaps have been a greater ceremonial role for the *ordo*'s members.[251] There was no funeral pyre for Constantine in Constantinople, as dictated by the Christian nature of the ceremony, but this also meant that there was no ceremonial *decursio*.[252] The memory of the *decursio equitum* remained, however, so that it was even performed by cavalry at the funeral of Attila the Hun – but these were real warriors.[253]

The symbolic and ceremonial role played by equestrians in public funerals was a result of the emergence and consolidation of the *ordo equester* as a constituent part of the *res publica*. The fact that they are first attested as a defined group at the funeral of Sulla in 78 BC, not long after the Gracchan reforms helped to delineate the shape of the *ordo*, is strongly suggestive of this connection. In the Augustan principate we see more clearly the ways in which the equestrian involvement in these public funerals illustrated their support for the imperial regime. The *decursio* was performed by equestrians, as well as members of the praetorian guard, showing the extent to which the *ordo* was carefully integrated into these state ceremonies. The involvement of *equites* in the funerals helped to promulgate the same message as the *transvectio equitum*, that the *ordo equester* continued to emulate their ancestors with their displays of martial *virtus*. This was as true of the Severan period as it was of the age of Augustus. But the transformations of the third and fourth centuries AD, including the rapid turnover of emperors and the rise of Christian ceremonial, meant that the *ordo* ceased to be a significant participant in these funerals. The *equites* disappeared from such ceremonies, eclipsed by the army, which was the real military force of the Roman empire.

Conclusion: Patterns of Consensus

The Roman emperor Domitian must have been quite an intimidating figure. He supposedly spent his free time stabbing flies with his pen, had

---

[250] Eus. *VC* 4.69.1–2. Equestrian rituals did continue in Rome, such as the *transvectio equitum*, discussed earlier in this chapter.

[251] Price 1987: 100 suggested that any funeral for Constantine in Rome would have been in the traditional 'pagan manner'.

[252] MacCormack 1981: 118–21; Price 1987: 99–101; Cameron and Hall 1999: 346–8.

[253] Jord. *Getica* 49; Arce 2000: 126.

a reputation for bestowing favours on men he intended to execute, and issued letters in which he styled himself 'lord and god' (*dominus et deus*).[254] It is thus understandable that the senatorial order sometimes indulged in excessive displays of sycophancy in order to win Domitian's favour. At one stage the senate voted the emperor a special honour guard which was to accompany him through the streets of Rome when he held the office of consul (which, it seems, was far too often for conservative tastes).[255] The guard would be composed of equestrians, selected by lot, who would wear their military dress uniform, the *trabea*, and brandish their ceremonial *hastae* while processing alongside Domitian.[256] The emperor ended up declining this honour because he was worried that he would one day be killed with a weapon (a remarkably prescient fear, as it turned out). Suetonius used this anecdote to shed light on Domitian's notoriously paranoid personality, but it also demonstrates the important ceremonial role played by the *equites* in displays of imperial power. Although Domitian declined his honour guard, other emperors were more willing to put their lives in the hands of the equestrian order. When Ser. Sulpicius Galba, Nero's governor of Hispania Citerior, claimed the purple, he wanted to demonstrate that he had the support of the different orders. He thus selected leading men among his coterie to serve as a substitute senate, and summoned young men from the *ordo equester* to stand guard around his bedchamber, rather than relying on ordinary soldiers.[257] These two honour guards demonstrate the enduring value of the equestrian youth as representatives of *virtus*, and the ideological importance of their support and protection to the reigning emperor.

The ceremonies of the *ordo equester* functioned as a performative manifestation of its importance to the *res publica*. The *transvectio equitum*, performed on an annual basis on 15 July, reinforced the connection between the equestrians and the emperor, on whose approval their enrolment in the *ordo equester* was contingent. It cast the equestrians as legitimate heirs and successors of the Roman state cavalry, displaying the *virtus* of aristocrats who were prepared to defend the *res publica*. The renewed emphasis on this ceremony in the Augustan principate was connected with the wider corporatisation of the *ordo* and its integration as a constituent part of the *res publica*. Gaius Caesar, Augustus' adopted son and heir, was made a *sevir equitum*, leading his *turma* of equestrians in the parade. The apparently spontaneous, but undoubtedly pre-arranged, conferral of

---

[254] Suet. *Dom.* 3.1, 11.1, 13.2.
[255] For complaints about the number of Domitian's consulships, see Pliny the Younger, *Pan.* 58.4.
[256] Suet. *Dom.* 14.3.   [257] Suet. *Galba* 10.3.

the title of *princeps iuventutis* on Gaius and his brother Lucius cemented this connection between the equestrian order and the princes on a more permanent basis. By making the princes the head of the *ordo*, the equestrians were displaying their approval of, and investment in, the imperial state. Thus it is unsurprising to find equestrians playing crucial roles at imperial funerals in this same period. They actively supported members of the imperial family in their grief, and performed the intricate *decursio* manoeuvres around the pyre alongside military regiments. These performances were designed to function as testimony to the reciprocal nature of the relationship between the *ordo* and the imperial family. They ensured that *equites* were publicly recognised as important agents within the *res publica* on both an individual and collective level, consolidating and extending the recognition that they had received under the Republic. The *ordo equester* benefited from the return of monarchy to Rome.

All these ceremonial elements converged in the Augustan period, at the crucial moment of evolution for the Roman state, and took different paths thereafter. It was part of the political genius of Augustus that he adapted existing institutions, such as the *transvectio equitum*, for his own purposes, and that the changes he made to ceremonial practice resulted in spontaneous displays of consensus which appeared to emanate from the *equites* of their own accord. These may have been stage-managed, but that does not undermine their significance. The *transvectio equitum* was perhaps the most enduring institution, lasting well into the fourth century AD. Its continuing relevance as a rite of passage for members of the *ordo equester* is demonstrated by the inscriptions in which provincial equestrians refer to their participation in this ritual. They knew that they owed their rank and status to the patronage of the emperor. The visual representations of the *transvectio* occur mainly on funerary monuments in Italy, suggesting that equestrians who lived in the peninsula more frequently travelled to Rome to take part in the parade. Provincial *equites* probably participated only once in their life, as a rite of passage, or perhaps not at all.

The association between the *ordo equester* and the *principes iuventutis* declined in the third century AD and beyond, as the award of the title became a conventional part of imperial succession. Instead of a genuine connection between the equestrian order and the princes of the imperial house, we find rather more general images and references to *virtus* thought appropriate for the heir to the throne. These ideas were certainly connected to the values that defined the *ordo equester*, but they were not as explicit as in the Augustan and Julio-Claudian periods. The same transformation can be found in imperial funerals: although the involvement of equestrians as a coherent *ordo* is attested until the Severan period, thereafter the *ordo equester* ceased to play a defining role in these ceremonies. This was the result of changes in the burial places of emperors and the nature of the way in which imperial power was transferred, as well as the Christianity of Constantine and his successors. In the case of both the title of *princeps iuventutis* and imperial funerals, association with the actual army became much more important than the symbolic military presence of the *equites*. Although one must always be wary of the temptation of ascribing all important imperial innovations to the principate of Augustus, in the case of the ceremonies and associated honours that defined the equestrians as an *ordo*, such a conclusion is virtually inescapable. The manner in which the imperial system evolved in subsequent centuries reflects the consolidation and evolution of the monarchical regime he established. The imperial ceremonies and ideology of the later Roman empire were still constructed around the idea that the emperor required the consensus of constituent groups in the *res publica*. But these groups were now the senate, the army and the people – there was no longer a place for the *ordo equester*.[258]

---

[258] Note, for example, Corippus' account of the acclamation of Justin II in AD 565, in which he emphasises the support of the senate, the army and the people, claiming that 'all constituencies' (*omnia … elementa*) approved the emperor (*Cor. Laud. Iust.* I. 360). For the idea of consensus and popular approval in the late Roman and Byzantine state, see Kaldellis 2015.

Introduction: A Problem at Perusia

It is well known that the emperor Augustus had great concern for the maintenance of the proper social order. An anecdote from the biographer Suetonius suggests that he possessed such values from an early age. In 41 BC, when camped outside the walls of Perusia, the Italian town in which his rival M. Antonius sat unhappily besieged, the young Octavian had the occasion to stage games to entertain his troops.[1] This nearly backfired when a common soldier settled down to watch the performance in the first fourteen rows of the theatre, and Octavian asked for him to be removed. A rumour began to circulate that Octavian had not merely ejected the legionary from his prime seating, but had had him tortured and killed. As Suetonius tells the story, the future *princeps* was only saved from the wrath of a furious mob of soldiers when the hapless legionary reappeared, showing no sign of injury. In seeking to eject the soldier from the fourteen rows, Octavian was enforcing the terms of the *lex Roscia theatralis* of 67 BC, which specified that such seats should be reserved exclusively for *equites*. It may be that the soldier did not realise that the legislation applied outside Rome, or that he was trying to see what he could get away with, possibly encouraged by his comrades. As it turned out, the soldier would not be the only spectator at an Italian theatre to arouse the *princeps'* ire. In 26 BC Augustus received word that not a single member of the audience in a crowded theatre at Puteoli had given up their seat for a senator.[2] Augustus was suitably outraged, and a *senatus consultum* was issued decreeing that the front row of seats should be reserved for senators in all theatres throughout the empire. Theatre-going was serious business in ancient Rome, attracting all levels of society from senators and equestrians to common soldiers and beyond. Such was its popularity that

[1] Suet. *Aug.* 14. [2] Suet. *Aug.* 44.1; Dio 53.25.1.

legislative measures had to be put in place to ensure that the rich, powerful and status-conscious received the best seats as befitted their *dignitas*.

This chapter will examine public entertainment venues – theatres, amphitheatres and circuses – as locations in which the status of *equites* could be displayed on an individual and collective level. The reservation of the *XIV ordines*, or the first fourteen rows, for *equites* represented a significant step in consolidating the *ordo equester* as a status group distinct from the senate in the late Republic.[3] The theatre henceforth became a place in which *equites* living in Rome could shout acclamations and thus express their collective political will, in a way that was not possible on purely ceremonial occasions when they appeared together, such as the *transvectio equitum*.[4] This chapter will examine the situation in Rome, as well as Italy and in the provinces, from Gaul to Asia Minor. The regulation of admission to these prestigious seats was the most public representation of the exclusivity of the *ordo equester*. Interlopers or unqualified parvenus were publicly removed from the fourteen rows just like Octavian's hapless soldier. Hierarchy and stratification was an integral part of the regulation of status in the new monarchical *res publica*. These measures helped to give the equestrian order the sense that it was a true group apart from the people, invested with its own ideological significance.

We will also study the ways in which members of the equestrian order transgressed accepted social norms by moving from being spectators to performers. The idea that men (and women) of respectable rank might want to perform as actors and pantomimes, race chariots in the circus or fight in the arena might initially seem somewhat strange. But, as we discussed Chapter 5, the pressures to maintain the necessary equestrian census were extreme, and fighting for pay was one way to save oneself from possible penury. Moreover, the attraction of public performances for the equestrian youth in particular should not be underestimated. Aristocratic young men loved sports and competition, and longed for opportunities to display their *virtus* in a public setting in order to earn fame and renown. The result was that public entertainment venues were characterised by a curious duality, displaying both the proper maintenance of social order and egregious examples of social deviancy and transgression.

---

[3] See Chapter 3.   [4] See Chapter 8.

Seats with a View

The notion of hierarchical allocation of seating at public entertainments reached Rome in 194 BC, when senators had seats set aside from them at the *ludi Romani*.[5] There is some evidence that seating allocations for municipal elites were common in Italy at large by the first century BC.[6] The *equites* had to wait much longer for their assigned seating at Rome, which was allocated by the *lex Roscia theatralis* of 67 BC, as we discussed in Chapter 3. Under the terms of the law proposed by the tribune Roscius Otho, the first fourteen rows of public theatres were to be set aside for the *ordo equester*, based on the census qualification, rather than the *equus publicus*. Augustus subsequently confirmed the allocation of the fourteen rows to the *equites* in his *lex Iulia theatralis*, which established new seating arrangements in the theatre for all social groups, as noted in Chapter 5. Through these two crucial pieces of legislation the 'fourteen rows' (*quattuordecim* or *XIV ordines*) became a defining aspect of equestrian identity in the public sphere. Augustus' seating plan was designed to be a mirror of society at large. The senators, as members of the *amplissimus ordo*, were entitled to sit on seats in the orchestra, while the *ordo equester* occupied the first fourteen rows of the *cavea* (the seating proper) behind them.[7] If we are to take a reference in Juvenal literally, the *equites* not only had some of the best seats in the house, they also sat on cushions, at least by the second century AD.[8] The principle of separate seating for the equestrian order was applied to amphitheatres by Nero's reign at the latest, and was formally extended to circuses by the same emperor in AD 63.[9] Before the latter measure, some *equites* had had to resort to sneaking into the Circus Maximus at night to secure the best possible seats.[10] The arrangements of the *lex Iulia theatralis* were enshrined in stone in the Flavian Amphitheatrum Novum (better known as the Colosseum), where the words 'for the Roman *equites*' (*equiti[bus] Rom[anis]*) were carved into the marble rows.[11]

---

[5] Livy 34.44, 34.54.3–8.   [6] E. Rawson 1987: 107; Jones 2009: 130–1.

[7] Edmondson 2002: 12–13.

[8] Juv. *Sat.* 3.154: *pulvino . . . equestri*. Senators had first sat on cushions in Caligula's reign (Dio 59.7.8).

[9] Tac. *Ann.* 15.32; Pliny the Elder, *NH* 8.21. It does not appear that the full fourteen rows were required in these venues (Edmondson 1996: 89, 2002: 16–18). Cf. Dio 55.22.4, who records a *senatus consultum* of AD 5 allocating *equites* seats in the circus, probably to little effect.

[10] Suet. *Cal.* 26.4: twenty *equites* were killed when Caligula sent henchmen to evict the seat-minders.

[11] *CIL* VI 32098b. See also Stat. *Silv.* 1.6.43–4.

The distinctions between Roman *ordines* prescribed by Augustus' *lex Iulia theatralis* meant that everyone knew their place in his *res publica*. Women and slaves languished at the back; the *pullati* wearing dark clothes were likewise relegated; the citizens, resplendent in their togas, sat in the middle *cavea*; soldiers, married men and the *pueri praetextati* ('boys in the embroidered toga') were allocated to the inner *cavea*, as recognition of their importance to Roman life; and at the front sat the *equites* in their tunics with the *angustus clavus*, and the senators, wearing the *latus clavus*.[12] The equestrians were thus demarcated as an exclusive aristocratic order, as part of a larger social hierarchy that was more stratified and segregated than it had been under the Republic.

Still, it was not necessarily a happy arrangement for all concerned, given the many different ways in which men could gain access to equestrian rank. Watching the *ludi Megalenses* from the first two rows of *equites*, Ovid recalls being addressed by a battle-hardened veteran of Caesar's wars, who said: 'I earned this seat through my military service, but you gained it in peace, because you held a post among the *decemviri*.'[13] Even allowing for a certain measure of poetic licence in the delivery, the sentiment is clear: the *tribunus militum* thought he was more deserving of his place among the *XIV ordines* (and no doubt the title of *eques Romanus* itself) because he had fought for the *res publica* in battle.[14] But all *equites* would have been able to agree on the line separating themselves from other elements of Roman society, especially the soldiers who were directly subordinate to equestrian officers. Tacitus wrote that the emperor Tiberius expelled Iunius Gallio from the senate when he suggested that veterans of the praetorian guard should be allowed to sit in the fourteen rows.[15] The emperor was unwilling for such an honour to be given to the praetorians, even though the maintenance of his authority had long depended on them; such overt recognition would lay bare the true nature of power in his regime, not to mention upset the existing social order. In contrast, Suetonius recorded that Caligula sought to foment discord between the *equites* and the people by actively encouraging the masses to take up places in the fourteen rows.[16] Although Suetonius' anecdote was designed to shed light on the emperor's savagery rather than to serve as meaningful social commentary, it is evident that people did often test traditional status boundaries and sit in equestrian seats.[17]

---

[12] Edmondson 2002: 12–14.

[13] Ovid, *Fasti* 4.383–4: *hanc ego milita sedem, tu pace parasti,* | *inter bis quinos usus honore viros.*

[14] See the perceptive comments of Osgood 2006: 269.   [15] Tac. *Ann.* 6.3.   [16] Suet. *Cal.* 26.4.

[17] Reinhold 1971: 280–3. Quint. *Inst.* 6.3.63 refers to an *eques* who did not want to go home to eat for fear of losing his place.

The emperor Domitian attempted to vigorously enforce the regulations pertaining to theatrical seating in his capacity as *censor perpetuus*.[18] The effects of his measures are display in the '*lex Roscia* cycle' of poems which form part of Book 5 of Martial's *Epigrams*. Many of these feature Romans who try to pass themselves off as *equites* and take a seat in the fourteen rows, until the zealous theatre attendants remove them.[19] The mechanics of Domitian's measure are poorly understood. Martial refers to an imperial edict, which seems to have applied specifically to the seats of the *equites*, rather than any other aspects of theatrical seating arrangements laid down in Augustus' earlier *lex Iulia theatralis*.[20] This explains why no reference is made in the epigrams to the wider provisions of the Augustan law.[21] The poems are solely concerned with Domitian's edict restoring proper dignity to the *ordo equester*. Martial wrote of the *equites* regaining their 'unspoiled rows' (*puros ... ordines*) now that they were 'a more established equestrian [order]' (*certior ... eques*).[22] Martial's concern with the status of the *equites* and approval of Domitian's measures stems from the fact that he had himself been awarded equestrian rank.[23] There can be no doubt that Domitian's edict met with his approval. Members of the *ordo* jealously guarded their privileges, which demonstrated that they were a status group that ranked above the people at large.

Martial gives the impression that it was common for men to take up places illegally in the fourteen rows, as in the case of a Nanneius who did so 'back then when squatting was permitted' (*tunc cum liceret occupare*).[24] Under Domitian's stricter regime Nanneius had to keep getting up and moving from seat to seat, eventually ending up half-standing at the end of a row, trying to pretend that he was an equestrian to his neighbours, but not to the attendants. Other faux *equites* who did try to sit in the fourteen rows often did so in ostentatious coloured cloaks in a naive attempt to fit in as an aristocrat. But their flamboyant dress marked them out immediately as pretenders to the *ordo*.[25] When a certain Phasis ostentatiously proclaimed to the assembled audience that 'the dignity of the *ordo equester* has now been restored' (*nunc est reddita dignitas equestris*), he was swiftly

---

[18] Suet. *Dom.* 8.3; Martial *Ep.* 5.8, 23.   [19] Mart. *Ep.* 5.8, 14, 23, 25, 27, 35, as well as 38 and 41.

[20] Mart. *Ep.* 5.8.1.   [21] For example, Juv. *Sat.* 3.159 (*vano ... Othoni*), 14.324 (*lex Othonis*).

[22] Mart. *Ep.* 5.8.3, 5.23.4.

[23] Sullivan 1991: 4, 35–6, 145. For Martial's equestrian status, see Chapter 5.

[24] Mart. *Ep.* 5.14.2. All the named individuals referred to in these poems are of course entirely fictional characters, but they represent the types of people Martial saw in the theatre.

[25] Mart. *Ep.* 5.8.5 (purple cloak), 5.23.1–5 (green exchanged for purple); see also 2.29. For discussion of purple as a status symbol, see Reinhold 1971: 282–3.

unmasked as an interloper by Leitus, the theatre attendant.[26] One *eques*
had the necessary wealth of 400,000 sesterces to qualify for equestrian rank,
but had not been awarded the status by the emperor; he too was ejected.[27]
A particularly clever epigram deals with two brothers, one of whom
possessed the equestrian census, and the other who did not.[28] The *eques*
is given the *nom de plume* of Castor, while his disenfranchised brother is
Pollux, a nice reference to the fact that it was Castor who was horseman of
the Dioscuri. The comparison has added potency given that the Dioscuri
were the traditional protectors of the *equites*. Imperial favour, of course,
was a great equaliser, admitting many men of previously low status into the
ordo equester. Thus Martial's contemporary, Juvenal, noted wryly that
equites of older families had to share the seats with the upwardly mobile
nouveaux riches – the sons of auctioneers, gladiators and trainers.[29] Once
equestrian status had been legally granted, a new *eques* was legitimately
entitled to enjoy the privileges of membership. The poems also reflect the
uncertainties faced by *equites* who only just scraped by with the minimum
census qualification – if they fell on hard times, then they would be
excluded from the fourteen rows, and everyone would know about it.[30]

How long did these preferential seating arrangements continue to be
mandated in Rome? Several stray references allow us to trace their enforcement throughout the principate. One of the *Minor Declamations* of
Pseudo-Quintilian, dated to the early second century AD, refers to the
qualifications of free birth and the equestrian census as necessary to sit in
the fourteen rows.[31] Philostratus describes senators and *equites* rushing out
of the theatre towards the Athenaeum to hear the sophist Hadrian of Tyre
in the late second century AD.[32] Finally, Herodian notes that senators
and *equites* watched Elagabalus perform sacrifices outside the Temple
of Sol Elagabalus on the Palatine in their theatrical arrangement.[33]
The traditional hierarchies were therefore maintained into the Severan
period. But new social divisions are attested in late third century AD,
when Arnobius described the priests and magistrates taking their assigned
seats in the theatre, but made no reference to *equites*.[34] It is interesting that
in his description Arnobius singled out the 'senators who have held office

---

[26] Mart. *Ep.* 5.8.8.
[27] Mart. *Ep.* 5.35. For equestrian status as an imperial benefaction, see Chapter 5.
[28] Mart. *Ep.* 5.38.   [29] Juv. *Sat.* 3.153–9; Malnati 1987–8: 133–4. Cf. Colton 1966: 157.
[30] See further Chapter 5, where the case of Umbricius from Juvenal's *Third Satire* is discussed.
[31] Ps.-Quint. *Min. Decl.* 302.1.   [32] Phil. *VS* 589.
[33] Herodian 5.5.9. Note also Herodian 1.9.3, a reference to assigned seating in the theatre under
   Commodus.
[34] Arnob. *Adv. Nat.* 4.35.

as consuls' (*consulatibus functi patres*), suggesting that ex-consuls may have had their own designated seats by this time. This was certainly the case in the fifth century AD, when the senatorial order was divided into grades of *viri illustres, spectabiles* and *clarissimi*.[35] Over time, the original allocation of equestrian seating was forgotten: Macrobius thought that the fourteen rows were reserved for senators.[36] With the expansion of senatorial numbers and the absorption of leading equestrian office-holders into their ranks in the fourth century AD, it may have been the case that the more junior senators would have been allocated places in the *cavea* which were previously reserved for the members of the *ordo equester*. This suggests that the seating arrangements changed in the mid-third century AD, when the equestrian order was itself undergoing a transformation into a series of different status grades.[37]

Beyond the *Sacra Urbs*

The ancient literary sources primarily describe the effects of the *lex Roscia theatralis* and the *lex Iulia theatralis* within the city of Rome. These seating arrangements could not be replicated or enforced in precisely the same way throughout Italy and the provinces, given the different social hierarchies involved.[38] The *lex Iulia municipalis* of around 45 BC built on the precedent of the *lex Roscia theatralis* by prescribing the seating arrangements at shows held in Italian *municipia*. It stated that no one should sit in the seats designated for senators or decurions at games or gladiatorial fights.[39] The near contemporaneous *lex Ursonensis* from Urso in Spain (*c.* 44 BC) allocated seats for Roman magistrates, promagistrates, Roman senators and their sons, equestrian *praefecti fabrum* on the governor's staff, local magistrates and decurions.[40] There is no mention of fourteen rows being reserved for *equites* as prescribed by the *lex Roscia*, which may explain the actions of Octavian's errant soldier at Perusia in 41 BC.

---

[35] E. Rawson 1987: 109.   [36] Macrob. *Sat.* 7.3.8.

[37] On the transformation of the equestrian order in the third and fourth centuries AD, see Chapters 11–12.

[38] Demougin 1988: 810–11; Rowe 2007: 79.   [39] *CIL* I² 593 = *RS* 24, l. 138.

[40] *CIL* II² / 5 1022 = *RS* 25, chapters 66, 126–7; Jones 2009: 129–30.

The most commonly cited evidence for the enforcement of the *lex Roscia* in the provinces comes from the Spanish *municipium* of Gades.[41] On 8 June in 43 BC, C. Asinius Pollio wrote to Cicero, regaling him with the activities of the quaestor L. Cornelius Balbus, who staged games in Gades. It is worth quoting the relevant passage in full:

> The following exploits, on the model of C. Caesar as he himself boasts, are in addition to his acts of pilfering and robberies and floggings of provincials. At the games which he gave at Gades he presented a gold ring to an actor, one Herennius Gallus, on the last day of the show, and led him to a seat in the fourteen rows (that being the number he had assigned to the *equites*).[42]

Balbus' primary aim here seems to have been to imitate Caesar's award of 500,000 sesterces and the gold ring to Decimus Laberius, which enabled him to resume his place among the *equites* in the fourteen rows.[43] Would there have been enough *equites* to fill fourteen rows at Gades? Although Strabo remarked that there were 500 *equites* registered in the city in the Augustan period, he also pointed out that most of these did not actually live in Gades.[44] Balbus' actions represented an attempt to reconstruct social hierarchies at Rome in his home town, but the long-term efficacy of his measures seems unlikely as far as the fourteen equestrian rows were concerned. Gades' *equites* simply did not need that much space.

The text of Augustus' *lex Iulia theatralis* is lost to us. Suetonius, however, does specifically note that the law decreed that the first row should be reserved for senators throughout the empire, 'whenever any type of show was publicly staged anywhere' (*quotiens quid spectaculi usquam publice ederetur*).[45] We know that this was enforced in Narbo in Gallia Narbonensis from the inscribed text of a law regarding the provincial *flamen*.[46] A Flavian municipal decree, the *lex Irnitana*, from Irni in Spain, confirmed the seating arrangements in that community for 'categories of men' (*genera hominum*) as specified by the various *senatus consulta* and imperial *edicta*.[47] This presumably included senators, *equites*, decurions and so forth, but the lack of precision leaves the situation

---

[41] Edmondson 2002: 11; Jones 2009: 130.

[42] Cic. *Fam.* 10.32.2 [SB 415.2]: *sed praeter furta et rapinas et virgis caesos socios haec quoque fecit, ut ipse gloriari solet, eadem quae C. Caesar: ludis, quos Gadibus fecit, Herennium Gallum histrionem summo ludorum die anulo aureo donatum in XIIII sessum deduxit (tot enim fecerat ordines equestris loci)* (trans. Shackleton Bailey, slightly adapted).

[43] Suet. *Iul.* 39.2. Reinhold 1971: 279 has pointed out that Balbus did not have the authority to confer the gold ring, since he did not possess *imperium*.

[44] Strabo 3.5.3.   [45] Suet. *Aug.* 44.1. See also Dio 53.25.1; Patterson 2006: 146–7.

[46] *CIL* XIII 6038.   [47] González 1986 = *AE* 1986, 333, section 81.

uncertain. The senatorial decree of AD 19 that regulated the performances of *equites* in the theatre refers to Romans who possessed the 'right of sitting in the equestrian seats' *(sedendi in equestribus locis ius)*.[48] The fact that the *senatus consultum* was inscribed on bronze tablets and publicly displayed in Larinum (in Apulia, close to the Adriatic coast) suggests that both it and the *lex Iulia theatralis* were designed to be applicable throughout Italy.[49]

However, we must bear in mind that the legislation was framed by individuals based in Rome. In reality, the reservation of a whole fourteen rows for *equites* in most other regions would have been completely unnecessary, and the regulations had to be adapted to local circumstances.[50] At Arausio in Gallia Narbonensis there are inscriptions designating 'three rows of *equites*' *(eq(uitum) g(radus) III)* in two central *cunei* of the theatre's *cavea*.[51] These rows must have been restricted to the two marked *cunei* rather than extending the breadth of the theatre (otherwise there would have been far too much space).[52] We know that Italian and provincial communities tended to reserve the orchestra for municipal decurions (many of whom would be of equestrian rank), as noted by Vitruvius in his *On Architecture*.[53] The designation of specifically equestrian spaces does not seem to have been a priority, compared to the needs of the councillors and other groups particular to individual cities.[54] For example, at the odeon at Gerasa in Arabia, one quarter of all seats (275 places) was assigned to members of the city's *boule*.[55] The Theatre of Regilla in Athens had spaces for Athenian citizens and metics, with the citizens then further divided into tribes.[56] At Aphrodisias places were marked out for the ephebes in both the stadium and odeon.[57] Specific seating was assigned to *Augustales* in towns as diverse as Carnuntum, Sarmizgetusa and Veii.[58] Similar circumstances can be found throughout the empire.[59] This suggests that in most towns and cities the decurial class and other local groups were

---

[48] *Tab. Lar.* l. 12.   [49] This decree is discussed in greater detail later in this chapter.
[50] Kolendo 1981: 303; Jones 2009: 127–9.   [51] *CIL* XII 1241 = *ILS* 5655.
[52] Kolendo 1981: 309–10. The only other evidence for equestrian rows is somewhat shaky. Rámon Mélida 1925: 144 no. 711 expands the inscribed letters *E X D* from the *cavea* in the theatre at Augusta Emerita as *E(quites) X D(ecreto) [D(ecurionum)]*, but this seems a very uncertain interpretation.
[53] Vit. *Arch.* 5.6.2; Kolendo 1981: 306; Jones 2009: 129.
[54] See van Nijf 1997: 216–39 for an excellent discussion of seats allocated to associations and other collectives in the Greek east.
[55] Retzleff and Mjely 2004: 37–40.   [56] Small 1987: 86.
[57] Roueché 1993: 94–5, 118, 123, 134–6.   [58] Kolendo 1981: 310; Jones 2009: 131.
[59] Kolendo 1981.

much more important in the immediate context than the *ordo equester*.[60]
Equites resident in these communities fitted much more recognisably into
local categories for the purpose of seating according to rank and office.[61]

The status of individual *equites* could be highlighted by allocating them
specific seats in the theatre. Once again, it was not necessarily their equestrian
rank that earned them this honour. Indeed, out of all seats bearing designations for a particular individual found across the Roman empire, there is only
one inscription which specifically refers to its occupant as an *eques
Romanus*.[62] This comes from Syracuse in Sicily, where a single place on the
podium was reserved for a man of equestrian rank (*[---]ni eq(uitis) R(omani)
lo[cus---]*).[63] At Aphrodisias in Caria there is a seating inscription reserving
a place for Aelius Benuseinos, who bears the designation κράτιστος, the Greek
equivalent of *vir egregius*.[64] He may be identical with M. Aurelius Aelius
Benuseinos, archon of the council at Aphrodisias, in which case he earned the
special seat by virtue of his local office, not equestrian rank per se.[65]

At Pompeii there is striking evidence of the reorganisation of the theatre
under the oversight of the local equestrian dignitary M. Holconius Rufus in
3/2 BC. Rufus modelled the new seating arrangements on Augustus' *lex
Iulia theatralis*.[66] His own place was marked out with his *cursus* inscribed
in the middle of a row of seats in the centre of the theatre (Figure 9.1). This
inscription was carved in such a way that it was designed to frame a *sella
curulis*, which would have been placed in the middle:

For M. Holconius Rufus, son of Marcus, five times magistrate for delivering justice,
and twice magistrate for conducting the census, military tribune elected by the
people, priest of Augustus, patron of the colony, by decree of the decurions.[67]

The only indication of Rufus' equestrian rank is his position as *tribunus
militum a populo*.[68] His commemorative seat was awarded because of his
enormous benefactions to the community of Pompeii, not because he was
an *eques Romanus*. Therefore, although the Augustan theatrical legislation
was intended to set standards throughout the empire, there was less of

---

[60] Dio Chrysostom, *Or.* 34.29–30 accused members of the *boule* of being preoccupied with gaining
honours and status symbols, including seats in the front row of theatres.
[61] The Severan jurist Callistratus referred to *iuvenes* who stirred up the mob in provincial cities
(*Dig.* 48.19.28.3) but the *collegia iuvenum* were not contiguous with the *ordo equester*.
[62] For individual seat assignments, see Kolendo 1981: 312–14.   [63] *CIL* X 7130.1.
[64] *I. Aph.* 8.255.   [65] For the archonship, see *I. Aph.* 5.204.   [66] Jones 2009: 129.
[67] *CIL* X 838: *M(arco) Holconio M(arci) f(ilio) Rufo | IIv(iro) i(ure) d(icundo) quinquiens | iter(um)
quinq(uennali) trib(uno) mil(itum) a p(opulo) | flamini Aug(usti) patr(ono) colo(niae) d(ecreto)
d(ecurionum).*
[68] See Chapter 5.

Figure 9.1: *Cursus* of M. Holconius Rufus inscribed into the theatre seating, Pompeii

a recognisable corporate equestrian presence in the theatre outside Rome. In Italy and the provinces it was usually local hierarchies and groupings that dictated the seating arrangements. This did not lessen the inherent value and significance of equestrian rank outside Rome, but it demonstrates how it was complementary to other markers of status and prestige.[69]

Equites as Performers and Gladiators: Ideology and Regulation

Equestrians did not only enjoy watching shows in the theatre and games in the amphitheatre; a small but not insignificant number of them also liked to participate, especially the younger members of the *ordo*. This enabled them to display their *virtus* or athletic training, and sometimes to receive a financial reward.[70] It additionally had the potential to earn them considerable popularity. For example, Sex. Vetulenus Lavicanus, whose funerary monument at Rome was erected by his fellow youth, was remembered as the 'delight of the people' (*delicium populi*) and is depicted as

---

[69] This argument is set out in full in Chapter 5.

[70] For the latter motive, see Ps.-Quint. *Min. Decl.* 260.21–4; Lebek 1990: 48–9; Wiedemann 1992: 108–9; Bodel 2015: 41–2.

a charioteer.[71] However, receiving payment by hiring oneself out as a performer was a transgressive act that attracted significant social and legal consequences in the imperial period.[72]

C. Iulius Caesar's dictatorship proved to be a watershed moment as far as public performances of *equites* are concerned.[73] At Caesar's victory games 46 BC, the playwright Decimus Laberius, who possessed equestrian rank, acted in one of his own mimes under compulsion from the dictator.[74] By performing on stage, Laberius ran the risk of incurring public disgrace, known as *infamia*, and losing his equestrian status.[75] In response, Caesar granted him 500,000 sesterces and the gold ring, and Laberius moved to take his place in the fourteen rows after his performance.[76] Of course, Laberius did not suddenly cease to be an *eques* the moment he stepped on the stage; that would only happen when the censors removed him formally from the *ordo*.[77] But Caesar's gesture was primarily a symbolic one, a way of demonstrating that through his personal intervention Laberius would not be deprived of equestrian rank.[78] Laberius' actions were not entirely unprecedented, since the actor Q. Roscius had continued to perform on the stage even after being awarded the *anulus aureus* by Sulla.[79] A passage of Cicero's *Pro Roscio Comoedo* has been interpreted to mean that Roscius refused to accept payment thereafter, thus guaranteeing the legality of his actions, but the evidence is inconclusive.[80] Laberius, however, did receive a sum of 500,000 sesterces for his performance, so he could not make the same claim.

The *lex Iulia municipalis* of 45 BC shows that Caesar subsequently took legal steps to clarify the penalties for freeborn men who performed on the stage, banning them from standing for public office.[81] While the *ordo equester* is not directly referenced in the law, the penalties of this legislation would have been applicable to equestrians along with other Roman

---

[71] *AE* 1971, 44. The original publication is Panciera 1970. He was not an *eques*; the purpose of this inscription is to illustrate popular love for performers.

[72] A useful summary of this legislation is provided by Bodel 2015: 31.   [73] Lebek 1990: 44.

[74] For his rank, see Panayotakis 2010: 38–9.

[75] Edwards 1997: 69–71; Ulpian, *Dig.* 3.2.2.5, drawing on earlier opinions from first century AD. The evidence is admittedly later than 46 BC, but Caesar's subsequent grant of the *anulus aureus* suggests something of the legal implications that Laberius faced by performing.

[76] Suet. *Iul.* 39.2; Sen. *Controv.* 7.3.9; Macrob. *Sat.* 2.7.1–3. Panayotakis 2010: 45–56 dates these events to 47 BC, but this does not tally with the evidence of Suetonius, who clearly places it in the context of the games of 46 BC.

[77] Edwards 1997: 72.

[78] Cf. Jory 1988, who proposes that this was a set-up to provide Laberius with the necessary funds to retain equestrian rank.

[79] Macrob. *Sat.* 3.14.13.   [80] Cic. *Rosc. com.* 23; Y. Hunt 2012: 49.   [81] *RS* 24, l. 123.

citizens. Caesar's treatment of Laberius was sufficiently memorable to be imitated by L. Antonius Balbus at Gades, who gave the *anulus aureus* to Herennius Gallus, as we saw earlier. Both gestures were designed to signify the power that Caesar and Balbus possessed over other Romans. This is the only plausible way to explain why the dictator could encourage an *eques* to act on the stage while at the same time legislating against such actions.[82] The vast sums of money paid to actors illustrate the attractions of the theatre to some *equites*, especially those at risk of falling below the census requirement.[83]

Young *equites* also wanted to fight to display their *virtus*. At his games of 46 BC Caesar permitted *equites*, including a praetor's son, to fight in single combat, although he banned senators from taking part because of their higher status.[84] For the earlier funeral games of his daughter Iulia, Caesar had commissioned senators and *equites* to act as gladiatorial trainers, which would imply that they had significant expertise in combat.[85] Such exhibitions continued in the triumviral period, as evidenced by the equestrians who participated in the *venationes* at the *ludi Apollinares* of 41 BC.[86] The equestrian fighters in the Caesarian and triumviral period did not face punishment, since they competed in order to show off their martial abilities, and therefore they were not hired out as gladiators.[87] The legal position regarding being hired as a gladiator was clear. Caesar's *lex Iulia municipalis* specified that anyone 'who has or shall have been hired out for the purpose of fighting as a gladiator' or 'who has or shall have been a trainer of gladiators' was forbidden from holding public office.[88]

The *lux Iulia municipalis* was not the final word on the matter. In 38 BC a young man who had been enrolled in the senate expressed a desire to compete as a gladiator. In response, a *senatus consultum* was passed forbidding senators to engage in such activities.[89] This was probably prompted by a desire to restrict senators from being hired out as professional gladiators.[90] Levick has convincingly argued that this ban was not confined to the arena, but also encompassed senatorial performances in the theatre; crucially, however, it did not seem to apply to the *ordo equester*.[91] It was still permitted for senators to fight to display their *virtus*, providing that they were not hired out. In 29 BC, at the dedication of the Temple of

---

[82] Note the comments of Levick 1983: 110 on the benefits of the privileges given to these men by Sulla, Caesar and Balbus.

[83] Lebek 1990: 47–8; Potter 1999: 269.   [84] Dio 43.23.5; Suet. *Iul.* 39.1.

[85] Suet. *Iul.* 26; Wiedemann 1992: 109.   [86] Dio 48.33.4.   [87] K. E. Welch 2007b: 99.

[88] RS 24, ll. 112–13 (*queive depugnandei | caussa auctoratus est erit fuit fuerit*), 123 (*queive lanistaturam … fecit fecerit*) (trans. C. Nicolet and M. H. Crawford).

[89] Dio 48.43.2.   [90] Lebek 1990: 50.   [91] Levick 1983: 106.

Divus Iulius presided over by Octavian, patrician senators not only competed in chariot races, but one senator, Q. Vitellius, even fought in public.[92]
In the following year Octavian enlisted noble men and boys to participate
in chariot races at the Actian games.[93] Suetonius reports that the chario-
teers, athletes and wild-beast killers who appeared in the arena at this time
were sometimes from 'the noblest youth' (*ex nobilissima iuventute*).[94]
As Lebek has argued, it is highly likely that the nobles competing in 29
and 28 BC were not being paid to perform in these spectacles, but were
simply competing as amateurs in an exhibition of *virtus*.[95] Therefore it is
the case that Octavian initially did not prevent senators from competing in
the arena and circus, because they were not hired for their services.

New measures were soon enforced by Augustus. In 23 BC the aedilician
games staged by Marcellus featured an *eques* as a pantomime dancer; this
was the first time this new form of entertainment was seen at Rome.[96]
Therefore, in 22 BC, despite declining the official post of censor, Augustus
passed sumptuary laws regulating spending on banquets and gladiatorial
exhibitions.[97] Through a *senatus consultum* he forbade senators' descendants and members of the equestrian order from performing as actors and
pantomimes or fighting as gladiators, thus extending the provisions of the
decree of 38 BC to both the upper *ordines* of Roman society. Henceforth,
equites would also risk incurring *infamia*.[98] This is amply demonstrated by
a rhetorical scenario from the *Minor Declamations* of Pseudo-Quintilian,
written in the second century AD. It concerns a Roman man who hired
himself out as a gladiator in order to raise funds for his father's funeral.
After his honourable discharge from the arena, the man eventually earned
enough money to qualify for equestrian status, but he was still prevented
from sitting in the *XIV ordines* in the theatre because of the disgrace he had
suffered.[99]

The law of 22 BC was the opening salvo of Augustus' larger social and
moral programme, which included the *lex Iulia theatralis*, passed between
20 and 17 BC, the *lex Iulia de maritandis ordinibus* of 18 BC, and the *lex
Iulia de adulteriis coercendis*, passed in 17 BC.[100] There is an especially
close connection between the law of 22 BC restricting performances in the
theatre and arena and the later *lex Iulia theatralis*: Roman aristocrats were
supposed to be seated in the proper place as spectators, and were not to

---

[92] Dio 51.22.4. Augustus' personal involvement in the dedication is shown by *RG* 21.2.
[93] Dio 53.1.4.   [94] Suet. *Aug.* 43.2.   [95] Lebek 1990: 50. See also Wardle 2014: 324–5.
[96] Dio 53.31.3. For the date, see Jory 1981; Y. Hunt 2012: 69–71.   [97] Dio 54.2.3–5.
[98] Edwards 1997: 86–9.   [99] Ps.-Quint. *Min. Decl.* 302.pref.
[100] For this legislation, see Treggiari 1996: 886–93.

cross the line that separated them from the performers. This legislation emphasised the place of equestrians as the second highest *ordo* in Augustus' *res publica*, responsible for the maintenance of Roman social norms alongside the *ordo senatorius*. It confirmed their higher social standing, and invested them with a greater sense of significance and meaning as a collective unit. Being an *eques* mattered precisely because the emperor and the *res publica* invested the status with honours and privileges.

At the same time, however, there is a sense that the *ordo equester* was being managed or 'domesticated' by the *princeps*. Welch has plausibly suggested that there may have been additional political reasons behind the *senatus consultum* of 22 BC, as Augustus sought to curtail 'aristocratic self-advertisement in the public sphere'.[101] Valiant and brave fighters were popular in Rome, and the *princeps* could have no rivals in the martial sphere.[102] By limiting the opportunities for aristocrats (both senators and *equites*) to display their valour, Augustus attempted to domesticate the elite to fit into his new *res publica* as a morally upright aristocracy.

There were performances that did contravene this law during the Augustan period, but they were not usually authorised by the *princeps* himself.[103] For example, L. Domitius Ahenobarbus had *equites* participating in mimes in the *ludi* he staged in his praetorship (exact year unknown) and during his consulship of 16 BC; *equites* later performed as pantomimes in 2 BC as well.[104] These equestrians were probably the younger members of the *ordo*, who had the athletic abilities and training in the gymnasia to enable them to perform such dances.[105] On the latter occasion, Dio records that Augustus ignored the affront, since he was more concerned with the escapades of his daughter Iulia, who was flouting his moral legislation in a quite different manner.[106] In AD 8 a senator who had once been wealthy but found himself unexpectedly impoverished fought as a gladiator in Germanicus' games. The senator was undoubtedly competing for financial reward, though we do not know whether he hired himself out, or whether he was fighting as a free man for the prize money.[107] Augustus himself contravened the regulations only once, when the prospect of watching the performing dwarf Lycius proved to be too irresistible to ignore, even

[101] K. E. Welch 2007b: 99.

[102] This is to be connected with Augustus' encroachment on the administration of *munera* in general, on which see Wiedemann 1992: 8.

[103] Wardle 2014: 327.   [104] Suet. *Nero* 4; Dio 55.10.11.

[105] Lebek 1990: 45–8; Slater 1994: 132–8.   [106] Dio 55.10.12.

[107] Dio 55.33.4; Lebek 1990: 52; Swan 2004: 217–18.

though he was 'a young man of respectable origins' (*adulescentulum . . .
honeste natum*); in this case the dwarf received no money.[108]

Matters came to a head in AD 11. Dio reports that in this year *equites*
were actually permitted to fight as gladiators, because they had been
continuously flouting the *senatus consultum* of 22 BC, and did not regard
infamia as a sufficient penalty.[109] Therefore, the senate considered that the
equites might be better deterred by the possibility that they would be killed
in combat, and decided to allow them to fight.[110] As is it turned out, fear for
their lives did not stop *equites* from appearing in the arena, and they even
featured in shows staged by the praetors and watched by Augustus
himself.[111]

The discovery of a fragmentary bronze tablet from Larinum in central
Italy has complicated our understanding of the senatorial decree of AD
11.[112] The *Tabula Larinas*, as it is known today, is inscribed with a *senatus
consultum* dating to AD 19 (we have already discussed this document in
Chapter 5 in relation to the definition of equestrian rank). The *senatus
consultum* refers to an earlier decree of AD 11, which is quite different from
that described by Dio in the *Roman History*. This decree, authorised by M.'
Lepidus and T. Statilius Taurus, the ordinary consuls of AD 11, banned
freeborn women under the age of twenty and freeborn men under the age
of twenty-five from hiring themselves out as gladiators or performing on
the stage.[113] The exceptions to this measure were those individuals
whom Augustus or Tiberius had ruled were exempt. The reasons for
these exemptions are not entirely clear due to the condition of the tablet,
but it may be that the individuals concerned were already *infames*.[114]

The relationship between Dio's measure of AD 11 and the decree of the
same year referred to on the *Tabula Larinas* is somewhat puzzling.
The latter dates to the first half of the year because it was proposed by
the ordinary consuls, and its citation in the *senatus consultum* of AD 19
indicates that it was still in force eight years later. The simplest solution
seems to be to combine our evidence and suggest that in AD 11 *equites*
were indeed permitted to fight as gladiators or perform on the stage as Dio
says, with the exception of those women aged under twenty and men under

---

[108] Suet. *Aug.* 43.3; Wardle 2014: 328.
[109] Dio 56.25.7. Levick 1983: 108–10 argues that Dio uses the Greek ἀτιμία as the equivalent of
infamia.
[110] For this interpretation of the passage, see Lebek 1990: 53, followed by Swan 2004: 282.
[111] Dio 56.25.8.   [112] *AE* 1978, 145 = 1990, 189.
[113] *Tab. Lar.* ll. 17–19, using the text of Lebek 1990: 60–1.
[114] Levick 1983: 104–5; Demougin 1988: 570–2; Lebek 1990: 53–4, 92–6.

twenty-five, respectively.[115] This means that youngest members of the *equester ordo*, who were probably most eager to fight and perform, were still banned from doing so.[116]

Indeed, we do know that the equestrian youth continued to cause problems for the Roman emperors. In AD 15 two *equites* requested permission from the emperor Tiberius to fight in games being staged by his son Drusus. Tiberius, although he evidently granted their request, preferred not to watch himself. When one of the *equites* was killed in the combat, Tiberius stepped in and forbade the other from ever fighting again.[117] Tiberius' reluctance only exacerbated the situation, to the extent that 'the most dissolute youth of both orders' (*ex iuventute utriusque ordinis profligatissimus quisque*) are said to have voluntarily sought to be branded with *infamia* by committing some misdemeanour. Once they were *infames*, they were able to perform on the stage or fight as gladiators, though Tiberius did punish them with exile.[118] These events need to be set in the larger context of Tiberius' reign: he was much less generous than Augustus to senators and *equites* who had fallen on hard times. Lack of money provides a plausible explanation as to why equestrians would seek to serve as professional actors, dancers or gladiators.[119] Such performances could indeed be lucrative. When the young Tiberius had staged games in honour of his grandfather Drusus, he paid retired gladiators 100,000 sesterces each to fight.[120] Prize money varied depending on the generosity of the emperor, but was usually substantial.[121]

As emperor, Tiberius disliked most forms of public entertainment, and his reduction in the amount of public funding made available for pantomimes provoked riots in both AD 14 and 15.[122] These riots were probably fomented by the equestrian youth who sat in the fourteen rows and led many of the theatre claques, as Slater has argued.[123] This is a persuasive

---

[115] Levick 1983: 107.

[116] This is not the only possible interpretation. Baltrusch 1989: 148–9 suggests that there was conflict between the senate and Augustus regarding the issue, resulting in contradictory rulings.

[117] Dio 57.14.3.

[118] Suet. *Tib.* 35.2; Levick 1983: 112–13; Lebek 1990: 55–7; Slater 1994: 140–1. These events are referred to in the *senatus consultum* of AD 19 (*Tab. Lar.* ll. 11–14).

[119] Lebek 1990: 55–7; Wiedemann 1992: 111; Bodel 2015: 41.

[120] Suet. *Tib.* 7.1. For the pay of gladiators, see M. J. Carter 2003: 104–8.

[121] The standard prize was a palm, and later a crown, though this could be supplemented by money. Evidence for monetary reward comes in an anecdote which has Claudius giving out gold pieces (Suet. *Claud.* 21.9) and from Martial's references to offering-plates which had money on them, called *lances* (Mart. *Spec.* 31.5). See further Wiedemann 1992: 122; Potter 1999: 316; Coleman 2006: 146–7, 229–32, 264–5.

[122] Lebek 1990: 54–5; Slater 1994: 123–6.   [123] Slater 1994, esp. 139–44.

thesis: the youth were great lovers of the theatre throughout the Republican period, and especially enjoyed Atellan farces.[124] Nor did one have to be young to show enthusiasm for the theatre and acting. Epictetus' *Discourses* feature a wonderful story about an equestrian procurator of Epirus who had a mob of slaves to cheer on his favourite actor, and ended up engaging in a shouting match with the other spectators.[125] The theatre was a tinderbox for dissent and disturbance.

Given the close associations between aristocrats and pantomimes, Tiberius instituted strong measures in response. Senators were banned from entering the houses of pantomime dancers, and *equites* were not permitted to associate with them in public.[126] We should not necessarily assume that senators and equestrians were visiting the houses of low-born men: indeed, the opposite seems to be the case. The fact that *equites* were themselves performing as pantomimes suggests that Tiberius was trying to isolate them from their peers in the upper *ordines*. In short, the early years of Tiberius' reign saw *equites* actively finding ways to subvert imperial legislation on public performances, and placing collective political pressure on the emperor to reverse his decision. This represents a certain level of resistance from the aristocracy to imperial attempts to curtail their freedoms in the arena of public display. The domestication of the Rome's elites into an aristocracy that supported the monarchical *res publica* was not an entirely smooth process.[127]

The protests of the equestrian youth did not result in changes to the law, as the provisions of the *senatus consultum* of AD 19 make abundantly clear. This measure is not mentioned at all by the literary sources, but is partially preserved on the *Tabula Larinas*. The opening lines refer to men who had been performing on the stage or fighting for payment in the arena, 'contrary to the public standing of their own order' (*contra dignitatem ordinis sui*), as forbidden by previous *senatus consulta* (and by the emperor Tiberius himself).[128] The regulations of AD 19 established that senators and equestrians should not appear as performers, nor hunt wild beasts, hire themselves out as gladiators or undertake similar activities.[129] But rather than simply stating that members of the senatorial or equestrian orders were not to undertake these activities, the *senatus consultum* specified in

---

[124] Livy 7.2.11; Kleijwegt 1994: 88–90. These were also read by the young Marcus Aurelius (Davenport and Manley 2014: 36–7).
[125] Epict. *Diss.* 3.4.   [126] Tac. *Ann.* 1.77.4.
[127] Note also in this regard the protests of the equestrians in the theatre regarding Augustus' marriage legislation, discussed in Chapter 8.
[128] *Tab. Lar.* ll. 5–6.   [129] *Tab. Lar.* ll. 9–11; Levick 1983: 102; Lebek 1990: 75–80.

some detail the relatives of senators and *equites* who were also forbidden. For senators the ban henceforth included their sons, daughters, grandsons, granddaughters, great-grandsons and great-granddaughters. The relationships of the equestrian order are expressed slightly differently, in a retrospective fashion. The senatorial decree covered men and women who had fathers, grandfathers, brothers and husbands who 'had ever held the right of being a spectator in the equestrian seats' (*[ius] fuisset unquam spectandi in equestribus locis*).[130]

The *senatus consultum* of AD 19 played a crucial role in defining the place of the equestrian order in the monarchical *res publica*, by acknowledging that the dignity of equestrian status encompassed both the *equites* themselves and their relatives.[131] The decree possessed a strong moral tone, as with other Augustan and Julio-Claudian legislation, including the measure on adultery passed the same year.[132] It was designed to delineate the appropriate behaviour of the senatorial and equestrian orders – the aristocracy of the monarchical *res publica* – by regulating their forms of public display.

The Augustan and Tiberian legislation established the position of the Roman state on hiring oneself out as a gladiator for the remainder of the principate. Ulpian, writing in the third century AD, stated that free men who subordinated themselves to a gladiatorial trainer (a *lanista*), or received pay for their services, were subject to *infamia*, but not those men who fought solely to display their *virtus*.[133] As Pseudo-Quintilian wrote in the second century AD: 'Therefore, it is not the case that combat is unseemly in and of itself, only combat that is performed for dishonourable reasons' (*non ergo pugna per se turpis est, sed inhonesta pugna*) – that is, as an agent for hire.[134]

Rhetoric and Reality

The measures imposed by the *senatus consultum* of AD 19 did not stop equestrians performing on stage or fighting in the arena. Our major historical accounts of the imperial period, notably those written by Tacitus, Suetonius and Cassius Dio, contain a number of memorable

---

[130] *Tab. Lar.* ll. 7–9.   [131] See Chapter 5.
[132] McGinn 1992 shows that the senatorial decree from Larinum does not refer to the adultery legislation, for which see Suet. *Tib.* 35.2; Tac. *Ann.* 2.85; *Dig.* 48.5.11.2.
[133] Ulpian, *Dig.* 3.1.1.6; Lebek 1990: 49–50; Edmondson 1996: 107–8.
[134] Ps.-Quin. *Min. Decl.* 302.3.

anecdotes about *equites* participating in such events. But were these merely exceptions? How pervasive was the desire to act, dance, sing and fight among members of the *ordo equester*? In attempting to answer these questions, there is a significant methodological problem that we need to confront. The stories preserved by the literary sources are primarily designed to reflect the personalities of the emperors they are discussing.[135] A good emperor – the putative *civilis princeps* – appeared at the theatre and games to receive the acclamations of the people.[136] He enforced legislation regarding who could appear in these events, and imposed penalties on senators and equestrians who disgraced their *ordo*. At the other end of the spectrum, a bad emperor crossed the line between spectator and performer and exhibited himself to the *populus Romanus* as actor, singer, gladiator or charioteer, and encouraged (or forced) senators and *equites* to join him.[137]

Most recorded incidents of this type take place in the city of Rome and its environs. The anecdotes are chronologically restricted as well, since they predominantly come from first century AD. This naturally reflects the coverage provided by the surviving portions Tacitus' *Annals* and *Histories*, and Suetonius' *Lives*. But the pattern can also be detected in Cassius Dio's *Roman History*, which continues up to the late 220s AD. Dio provides a considerable amount of evidence on this matter, which can be explained by his personal distaste for most forms of public entertainment. This led him to record socially aberrant or scandalous behaviour as reflections of the character of particular emperors.[138] Yet the fact that the number of these stories in Dio's narrative declines after the Julio-Claudian and Flavian periods suggests either that such incidents became much less frequent, or that they were of less interest to Xiphilinus, on whose *Epitome* we are largely dependent for reconstructing Dio's *Roman History* after Book 60.[139]

The stories can be roughly divided into two groups, those in which *equites* volunteer to perform or fight, and those in which they are compelled to do so. Regardless of the category, the anecdotes still seem to cluster around 'bad' emperors, such as Caligula, Nero and Domitian. Cassius Dio gives an account of the *eques* Atanius Secundus, who vowed

---

[135] Wiedemann 1992: 130–1; Edmondson 1996: 75–6.
[136] Wallace-Hadrill 1982: 42; Edmondson 1996: 103.   [137] Edmondson 1996: 106.
[138] For Dio's attitude to public entertainment, see Newbold 1975.
[139] For the manner in which Xiphilinus adapts Dio's original narrative, see Mallan 2013. Dio 55.33.4 contains a brief mention of an *eques* fighting as a gladiator. This is preserved by Xiphilinus from Dio's lost account of AD 8.

to fight as a gladiator if the emperor Caligula recovered from a serious illness; he evidently looked forward to some type of financial reward from a grateful emperor.[140] This did not materialise – poor Secundus received only a death sentence for his loyalty – but it does demonstrate the continuing lure of gladiatorial combat for monetary gain. In AD 55 Nero staged games in which thirty members of the *ordo equester* fought in the arena, apparently of their own volition.[141] The stories about imperial compulsion are similarly lurid. Caligula once condemned an equestrian to the arena, where he was killed fighting against wild animals, a death that was manifestly beneath his rank.[142] The emperor was certainly aware of the legal strictures against public performances, and made a show of asking the senate for its permission, even as he forced *equites* and senators to fight in single combat and in battle array.[143] These episodes reflect Caligula's personal interest in all forms of public entertainment, an enthusiasm which he shared with Nero.[144] When Nero staged games to commemorate the erection of his wooden amphitheatre on the Campus Martius in AD 57, Suetonius claims that 400 senators and 600 *equites* were compelled to compete as gladiators and hunt wild beasts.[145] These numbers are so inflated that they are obviously ludicrous, since more than half the *curia* fighting in the arena would have been quite a spectacle.

Although he was not an equestrian, the demise of the consul M.' Acilius Glabrio under Domitian shows the continuing power of these stories as a trope of the bad emperor. Domitian summoned Glabrio to fight against a lion as part of the Iuvenalia which he held at his Alban villa. When Glabrio killed the animal effectively, Domitian is said to have grown jealous, and later executed him on the charge of fighting with wild beasts, among other (probably spurious) transgressions.[146] As Juvenal remarked, 'there was no benefit to the poor fellow when he fought as a naked beast hunter, transfixing Numidian bears at close quarters in the Alban arena'.[147] Glabrio was skilled and accomplished enough with the sword to kill beasts successfully, but he was condemned for fighting because his *virtus* posed

---

[140] Dio 59.8.3; Suet. *Cal.* 14.2, 27.2 (in this version the man is unnamed).

[141] Dio 61.9.1. Champlin 2003: 68–9 emphasises the voluntary nature of many aristocratic performances under Nero.

[142] Dio 59.10.4; Suet. *Cal.* 27.4.   [143] Dio 59.10.1.

[144] On Caligula's own performances, see Dio 59.5.4–5; Suet. *Cal.* 54.1–2.

[145] Suet. *Nero* 12.1. Dio 61.9.5 describes the events, but does not mention the senatorial or equestrian participants.

[146] Dio 67.14.3. For his death, see Suet. *Dom.* 10.2.

[147] Juv. *Sat.* 4.99–101: *profuit ergo nihil misero quod comminus ursos | figebat Numidas Albana nudus harena | venator.*

a challenge to that of the emperor. This returns us to the idea, expressed earlier in this chapter, that the theatrical regulations were as much about regulating aristocratic display and removing rivals to the *princeps* as they were about morality.

Emperors who sought to enforce the proper social order restricted such performances, regardless of whether they were forced or voluntary. Claudius took the unusual step of ordering all *equites* and noble women who had appeared on the stage in Caligula's reign to perform again, so that their disgraceful conduct would be exposed for all to see. After this display they learned their lesson, and such performances were no more.[148] Vitellius issued an edict forbidding *equites* from appearing in public performances in the theatre or the arena, an act which was in reality a confirmation of the principles of the *senatus consultum* of AD 19.[149] But it had the desired effect of distinguishing him from the excesses of Nero's reign: although Vitellius is generally treated in a very hostile fashion by the literary sources, this was one of a handful of acts that showed him conforming to the principles of the *civilis princeps*.[150]

There are cases in which it is difficult to determine whether the equestrian performers were volunteers or conscripts. The *ludi Maximi* of AD 59 featured senators and *equites* acting on stage, dancing as pantomimes, participating in hunts and fighting as gladiators. The games also featured the mind-boggling spectacle of 'a famous Roman *eques* travelling down a tightrope while riding on an elephant'.[151] If this story is to be believed in any form – and even the most credulous minds might take some convincing – the spectacle would have required a considerable investment in training and rehearsal on the part of the *eques*, which suggests that he was a willing participant. Dio discussed the *ludi Maximi* at some length, and claimed that the high-status performers included both volunteers and those who had been forced into the spotlight.[152] Tacitus' account suggests that in reality there may not have been that much of a difference between the two groups:

[Nero] also incited some notable Roman *equites* to offer their services in the arena through significant gifts, but inducements from a man who possesses the power of command is tantamount to compulsion.[153]

---

[148] Dio 60.7.1.   [149] Tac. *Hist.* 2.62.2; Dio 65.6.3.   [150] Davenport 2014b.
[151] Suet. *Nero* 11.2: *notissimus eques Romanus elephanto supersidens per catadromum decucurrit.* The same story features in Dio 61.17.2.
[152] Dio 61.17.3–5.
[153] Tac. *Ann.* 14.14.6: *notos quoque equites Romanos operas arenae promittere subegit donis ingentibus, nisi quod merces ab eo, qui iubere potest, vim necessitatis adfert.*

For Tacitus, the involvement of these *equites* was not the result of threats per se, but financial inducements provided by the emperor. But, as he noted, gifts from the imperial purse did not come without a price. Although Champlin is inclined to dismiss Tacitus' reading of the situation, we should not underestimate the control that the emperor could exert over his subjects, especially those closest to the centre of power.[154] The dependence of *equites* (especially those at risk of falling below the census level) on the emperor's favour and finances was a key aspect of the domestication of the aristocracy in the monarchical *res publica*. On the one hand, senatorial and equestrian elites were supposed to conform to imperial norms by serving as positive moral *exempla* for other *ordines* in the theatre and arena, but on the other hand, the emperor could force them to break those standards. Such was the precarious nature of life in a monarchical state.

We depend solely upon the literary sources for these instances of *equites* transgressing social boundaries, because their gladiatorial or theatrical exploits were not recorded on tombstones or on honorific statue bases.[155] An interesting pattern does emerge of emperors who enforced the legislation concerning high-status performers (Tiberius, Claudius, Vitellius), alternating with those who encouraged such transgressions (Caligula, Nero). This tells us little about how many *equites* were actually participating in these events, and whether it was widespread throughout the empire. There is one significant piece of evidence that does shed some light on this. In his discussion of Vitellius' edict enforcing the ban on equestrian gladiators, Tacitus recorded that young *equites* had been offered financial inducements to fight in Roman *municipia* and colonies.[156] We know from Cassius Dio's discussion of spectacles in the Augustan period that bouts between *equites* drew in the crowds, and Italian communities were always competing with each other for the biggest audiences.[157] Even though such fights are not usually described by our Rome-centric sources, except when they reflect on the regimes of individual emperors, it seems that they probably did take place in other cities in Italy and the western provinces.[158]

---

[154] Cf. Champlin 2003: 70–1.

[155] Compare the funerary monuments for professional gladiators, surveyed by Hope 2000.

[156] Tac. *Hist.* 2.62.2.

[157] Dio 56.25.8; Patterson 2006: 139; Ash 2007: 249. As Sen. *De Prov.* 2.8 pointed out, the greater the respectability of the performer, the greater pleasure the audience derived from it.

[158] Evidence from the Greece east is lacking. Although this might be the result of the perspectives of the literary sources, Greek ephebes were not trained to hunt or fight in the arena like the *iuvenes* of the west (Kleijwegt 1991: 115; see also Kennell 2009: 331–6 on training in the gymnasium). Gladiatorial games did take place in the Greek world, but, as M. J. Carter 2009

One trend that does emerge from our literary accounts is the association between public performances, young emperors and the youth of the *ordo equester* itself. At Nero's Iuvenalia of AD 59 noble men and women performed on the stage and as pantomimes, and even undertook special training for these purposes.[159] It was for this event that Nero formed his corps of *Augustiani*, composed of young *equites* whose task it was to applaud throughout his performances.[160] As Lebek and Slater have demonstrated in their discussion of the Augustan and Tiberian evidence, it was the young *equites* who had the training and agility to dance, sing, act, fight and race in chariots.[161] Dio's Maecenas advised that both senators and *equites* should receive training in horse riding and combat.[162] Imperial encouragement for such activities flourished in the Augustan period, most notably represented by the ceremonial performance of the *lusus Troiae*, which we discussed in the previous chapter.[163]

Some equestrians would have acquired such skills as members of *collegia iuvenum*, which existed throughout Italy and in the western provinces.[164] The members of these *collegia*, who were both of aristocratic and non-aristocratic origin, were trained to simulate the combat of gladiators.[165] The various *collegia iuvenum* in Italy and the provinces staged their own Iuvenalia, which included sword fighting, horse racing and beast hunting.[166] One young man, Sex. Iulius Felicissimus from Aquae Sextiae in Aquitania, was taught to fight in the amphitheatre and to hunt beasts.[167] In Carsulae, C. Cominienus Fortunatianus held the position of *pinn(irapus) iuvenum*, training young men to snatch the feathers from gladiators' helmets.[168] The future emperor Titus had, as a young man, participated in the Iuvenalia held at the Italian town of Reate, fighting in a mock battle with A. Caecina Alienus.[169] Titus was accomplished in horse riding and swordsmanship, and enjoyed the pleasures of the arena as emperor (but in a way that was entirely in keeping with the behaviour of the *civilis princeps*).[170] The arts of the stage also attracted the youth of Italy and the provinces, and

---

has argued, they represented a 'cultural performance' of Roman ideas and values that had been imported into the eastern provinces.

[159] Suet. *Nero* 11.2; Dio 61.19.1–4.
[160] Tac. *Ann.* 14.15. Cf. Dio 61.20.4–5, who says that the *Augustiani* were composed of soldiers.
[161] Lebek 1990; Slater 1994.   [162] Dio 52.26.1; Crowther 2009: 351.
[163] Kleijweget 1991: 113.
[164] For the institution, see Kleijwegt 1994. It is important to note that the *collegia iuvenum* were not exclusively equestrian clubs, though their membership certainly could and did include *equites*.
[165] Wiedemann 1992: 110–11; Edmondson 1996: 108.
[166] Kleijwegt 1991: 109–13, 1994: 85–8; Patterson 2006: 144–5.   [167] *CIL* XII 533.
[168] *CIL* XI 7852 = *ILS* 6635; Kleijwegt 1994: 87.   [169] Dio 65.15.2.   [170] Suet. *Tit.* 3, 8.

pantomime dancers were enormously popular with young men. Two pantomimes of the Antonine and Severan period, M. Aurelius Agilius Septentrio and M. Septimius Aurelius Agrippa, were granted membership of the association of *iuvenes* at Lanuvium and Mediolanum, respectively.[171] The emperor Caracalla was even trained to dance by the pantomime Theocritus, demonstrating how such arts could permeate the uppermost levels of society to the imperial court.[172]

As mentioned at the beginning of this section, the number of anecdotes about emperors staging extravagant theatrical or gladiatorial events featuring equestrians and senators declines after the first century AD. Is this a reflection of our literary sources, or of wider social changes, as Duncan-Jones has suggested?[173] It certainly seems to be the case that imperial compulsion died out by the first half of the second century AD. In the 140s Cornelius Fronto set his pupil, the future emperor Marcus Aurelius, the task of composing a piece on the theme of a consul who publicly fought and killed a lion before the Roman people. The young prince asked Fronto if he was referring to the incident with Acilius Glabrio and Domitian at the Alban hills – if not, he told his tutor, he found such a scenario unbelievable.[174] This indicates that such shocking scenes had not been seen publicly at Rome for some time. The same can be said for the theatre. Trajan and Lucius Verus certainly loved watching pantomimes and enjoyed their company, though this does not seem to have led to any transgressive behaviour on stage itself.[175] Somewhat ironically, it would be Marcus Aurelius' son Commodus who reintroduced the Roman people to the spectacle of elite gladiators, in the form of his own fights in the arena. Both the senators and members of the equestrian order were required to attend his performances.[176] Commodus does not seem to have involved equestrians and senators in his bouts, probably to limit opportunities for aristocratic rivals to display their *virtus*, thus ensuring that he received all the glory himself.

But at the same time, it is clear that enthusiasm for such exploits did not die out among members of the upper *ordines*. The concept of the dissolute aristocrat was still alive in the early second century AD, judging from Juvenal's *Second Satire*, in which the aristocratic Gracchus voluntarily debases himself as a *retiarius* (net-fighter).[177] Such a man was not

---

[171] *CIL* XIV 2113 = *ILS* 5193; *IRT* 606.   [172] Dio 78(77).21.2.   [173] Duncan-Jones 2016: 128.
[174] For the exchange, see Fronto, *Ad M. Caes.* 5.37–38 (vdH² pp. 75–6).
[175] See C. P. Jones 1986: 69–75; Davenport and Manley 2014: 189–90.   [176] Dio 73(72).20.1.
[177] Juv. *Sat.* 2.143–148, see also 8.200–10. The *retiarius* ranked very low on the gladiatorial hierarchy, as S. M. Braund 1996: 159–60 has pointed out.

competing for *virtus*, but for money. Several anecdotes suggest dissolute behaviour in the Severan period as well. Soon after returning to Rome following the defeat of his rival Clodius Albinus, Septimius Severus told the *curia* that he had been shocked to hear of a senator of consular rank engaging in mock fighting with a prostitute who was pretending to be a leopard.[178] Severus brought up this story to censure the senators who had been complaining about being forced to watch the performances of the emperor Commodus in the arena.[179] In Caracalla's reign the equestrian procurator L. Lucilius Priscilianus participated in *venationes* at Tusculum, and allegedly fought against a bear, panther, lion and lioness simultaneously. Caracalla, who shared Priscilianus' fondness for such entertainments, promoted him to the senate.[180] Priscilianus later gained some social respectability as patron of the town of Canusium.[181] It is evident, therefore, that despite a number of senatorial decrees, laws and other measures to restrict performances and exhibitions by equestrians, such practices did continue through to the Severan period. This is because Roman aristocrats, especially the youth, wanted to display the fruits of their rigorous martial training, and this could not entirely be stifled by imperial legislation.

Conclusion: Status Boundaries

Entertainment venues functioned as a way of articulating status boundaries in the Roman world. The assigned seating reserved exclusively for equestrians in the theatre from the late Republic onwards, and in the amphitheatre and circus from the early empire, publicly demarcated the *equites* as the second *ordo* in the Roman social hierarchy, ranking only behind the senatorial order. The enforcement of these privileges by Augustus and Domitian demonstrated imperial concern for the proper maintenance of status, dignity and morality. Equestrians valued their perquisites precisely because they were exclusive, and invested their personal status with meaning and importance. But these venues were also arenas for subverting accepted aristocratic norms. We have explored the ways in which equestrians crossed the line from spectators to performers by acting on stage, or

---

[178] Dio 76(75).8.2. The soldiers whom Severus discharged from the praetorian guard upon coming to power took to service as gladiators or became bandits, according to Dio 75(74).2.5.
[179] Senators and *equites* always attended Commodus' bouts: Dio 73(72).20.1.
[180] Dio 79(78).21.3–5. For Caracalla's love of pantomime dancing, chariot racing, wild-beast hunts and gladiatorial combat, see Dio 78(77).10.1, 17.4, 21.2.
[181] Davenport 2012a: 808–9.

hunting and fighting in the arena. The stories in the literary sources cannot be dismissed. Young men in the Roman world, especially in Rome and Italy itself, were trained from a young age to fight, ride horses, compete in athletic games, recite poetry and sing. This was part of their preparation for life as a Roman man. However, these natural enthusiasms were supposed to manifest themselves in culturally appropriate ways: hunting, serving as military officers, and writing and discussing poetry, music, and literature. Fighting to display one's *virtus* was perfectly acceptable. The problem arose when young men chose to channel these energies into inappropriate performances as actors, pantomimes or gladiators, all professions that incurred legal *infamia*, despite the popularity of both the theatre and amphitheatre in the Roman world. Some equestrians had fallen on hard times and were motivated by the need for money to maintain their estates, while others simply wanted to perform, to revel in the applause and adulation of the crowd.

The allocation of the *XIV ordines* in the theatre to equestrians occurred in 67 BC. This measure represented one of the significant steps in the consolidation of the *ordo* as a constituent body separate from the senate in the Republican period. The meaning and significance of this measure was consolidated and extended under the monarchical *res publica*. Augustus' *lex Iulia theatralis* prescribed seating allocations for all Romans, ensuring that the theatre was a mirror of his idealised social hierarchy. Successive pieces of legislation passed in the period from Caesar to Tiberius enforced the *dignitas* of the senatorial and equestrian *ordines* by forbidding them to perform in the theatre or fight in the arena as gladiators. All these measures were emblematic of the domestication of the aristocracy in the imperial state. Reserved seating was certainly a privilege for *equites*, but it also represented a measure of control – the imperial *lex Iulia theatralis* superseded and replaced Otho's earlier law, subsuming the *equites* into a larger programmatic vision of Roman society. It was in the fourteen rows that the *ordo equester* could shout their acclamations in approval of imperial policies, with these expressions functioning as public displays of consensus.[182] Legislation against public performances by senators and *equites* was designed to keep them firmly in their seats, supporting the emperor and maintaining moral standards, rather than presenting themselves as rivals to the *princeps* in the field of *virtus* or cultivating popular support among the theatre claques.

---

[182] See Chapter 8.

This was an idealised vision of how Roman society was supposed to operate under the emperors, and it did not function so neatly in reality. In Rome, upstarts frequently posed as *equites* in order to try and sit in the fourteen rows, while those who had lost the equestrian census tried to hang on to their privileges. The collective display of equestrian unity in the theatre was not articulated strongly outside Rome, in the towns and cities of Italy and the provinces. Although provincial seating arrangements sought to mirror the legislation of Rome, there was no need to reserve all fourteen front rows for *equites*. In the civic context, equestrians generally benefited from special seating because of the functions and offices they held in these communities, not because of their equestrian rank. Moreover, the legislation against public performances in the theatre and amphitheatre was frequently flouted by *equites* and senators. These activities were fuelled by a succession of young emperors themselves, notably Caligula, Nero, Commodus and Caracalla, who had been trained to act, sing, dance, fight and hunt. Many young *equites* embraced the enthusiasms of their emperors willingly, but other members of the aristocratic *ordines*, both men and women, were forced into fighting and performing. This double standard, in which emperors could flout their own laws and morality, was a manifestation of the power structure of the monarchical *res publica*. The world of public entertainment venues was thus one in which emperors and equestrians played different roles in the ongoing social performance of regulating and subverting social status.

10 | Religion and the *Res Publica*

Introduction: Germanus' Triumph

T. Flavius Germanus was a man of many accomplishments. In the course of his years of service to the *res publica* he supervised the collection of inheritance taxes in Italy, acted as procurator of the gladiatorial school in Rome, and served as major domo of the emperor Commodus' triumph in AD 180. These and a number of other important posts were included in the account of Germanus' career inscribed on the base of a statue, which his three sons and freedman erected in his honour in the central Italian community of Praeneste.[1] But the inscription does not confine itself to the administrative offices held by Germanus: it also tells us that he had 'been distinguished with the most illustrious priesthood of *pontifex minor*' (*exornato | sacerdot(io) splendidissimo pontif(icis) minor(is)*). Germanus was therefore a member of the eminent Roman priestly college, composed of both senatorial *pontifices* and equestrian *pontifices minores*, and headed by the emperor himself as *pontifex maximus*.[2] As one of these equestrian priests, Germanus assisted in the performance of sacrifices on the Capitoline hill, and made official announcements about the calendar.[3] The combination of sacred and secular power in official careers was an accepted part of Roman society.[4] Aristocrats had held both administrative and religious positions since the beginnings of the *res publica*, with magistracies and priesthoods regarded as equally prestigious marks of honour.[5] We can see this manifested in the Praeneste inscription, which draws special attention to Germanus' appointment as *pontifex minor* among his many procuratorial appointments.

The senatorial order dominated the most prestigious priesthoods of the Roman state. The high standing and exclusively senatorial membership of the four *amplissima collegia* was confirmed in 47 BC by C. Iulius Caesar's

---

[1] *CIL* XIV 2922 = *ILS* 1420.　　[2] Rüpke 2008: 7.　　[3] Scheid and Granino Cecere 1999: 88.
[4] Eck 1989: 18–19; Várhelyi 2010: 2–6.
[5] Beard, North and Price 1998: I, 27–30; Rüpke 2007: 215–21.

lex Iulia de sacerdotiis.[6] These colleges were the pontiffs (*pontifices*), augurs (*augures*), the board of fifteen for sacred rites (*quindecimviri sacris faciundis*) and the board of seven for banquets (*septemviri epulonum*).[7] The privilege of belonging to all four *amplissima collegia* was the exclusive domain of the emperor and members of his family, and it was rare for senators to be co-opted into more than one of these colleges, at least before the third century AD.[8] All these public priesthoods (*sacerdotia publica*) had originally been elected offices, but in the monarchical *res publica* such posts lay in the personal gift of the emperor himself, and functioned as a sign of imperial favour.[9] Augustus either revived or increased the status of a range of other priesthoods which were open to senators, including the Arval brothers (*fratres Arvales*), the companions of Titus (*sodales Titii*) and the fetial priests (*fetiales*).[10] The establishment of these colleges allowed more senators to participate in the religious affairs of the state, which helped to ensure they were invested in his *res publica*, restored anew after the violence of the civil wars with the endorsement of the gods.[11] The death and apotheosis of the first *princeps* opened up further opportunities for religious honours, with the establishment of a new senatorial college, the *sodales Augustales*, for the maintenance of Augustus' own cult.[12] Of course, it was paramount that there was some measure of competition for these priesthoods in order to ensure that the status of the priestly colleges was not devalued.[13] It has been estimated that only one quarter to a third of senators could become priests, and such exclusiveness helped to ensure that these positions remained prestigious gifts in the hands of the emperor.[14]

Augustus' religious reforms were not directed exclusively at the senate. One of the characteristics of his principate was his determination to involve all levels of the Roman social hierarchy, from senators to slaves,

[6] Rüpke 2008: 7–8; Várhelyi 2010: 61–2.
[7] Membership of the latter two colleges did not match their names: there seem to have been nineteen *quindecimviri* and ten *septemviri* at any one time (Scheid 2003: 143).
[8] Beard, North and Price 1998: I, 186–8; Várhelyi 2010: 66–7.
[9] Wissowa 1912: 489; Talbert 1984: 345–6; Eck 1989: 25–6.
[10] Suet. *Aug.* 31; Beard, North and Price 1998: 1, 192–6; Scheid 2005: 181–2. Augustus himself was a member of these three priesthoods in addition to the *amplissima collegia* (*RG* 7). On the Arvals, see Scheid 1990a; 1990b.
[11] Scheid 2005: 177. Augustus boasts that 170 of the senators who fought on his side in the civil war went on to become state priests (*RG* 25.3).
[12] Rüpke 2008: 9. Not every deified emperor received his own college, as some had to share priests with other rulers (Várhelyi 2010: 73–5).
[13] Várhelyi 2010: 57–69.
[14] Eck 1989: 29; Beard, North and Price 1998: I, 192. Pliny the Younger, *Ep.* 10.13 is the classic statement of this phenomenon.

in religious affairs.[15] Augustus therefore ensured that a number of state priesthoods were specifically reserved for *equites*.[16] This recognised the important place that the *ordo equester* had assumed within the *res publica* from the late second century BC, when it emerged as a constituent part of the state distinct from the senate and the people.[17] This chapter will examine the appointment, roles and social significance of equestrians serving as priests of the *res publica* in Rome and the surrounding area of Latium.[18] We will begin with the priesthoods specifically located in the city of Rome, most notably the *luperci, pontifices minores* and *flamines*. Then we will turn to the priesthood of *Laurens Lavinas* in Lavinium, and the duties *equites* performed in the maintenance of Roman cult sites in Latium at large. One of the distinctive features of many of the priesthoods allocated to *equites* either by Augustus or one of his successors was that they were religious colleges associated with events such as the coming of Aeneas to Italy, the history of Alba Longa, and the foundation of Rome by Romulus.[19] *Equites* were not co-opted to the new colleges for deified emperors, nor did they have any other priesthoods of a monarchical character created especially for them.[20] The new religious colleges which were instituted under the principate for *equites*, such as the priesthood of *Laurens Lavinas*, had an archaising character which associated the *ordo* with Rome's past.

This impetus towards traditional and even archaic priesthoods was the result of two different, but complementary, motivations. Firstly, the fact that *equites* were given priesthoods in cults associated with the origins of Rome or festivals that had a long-established place in the religious calendar fits in with the late Republican and early imperial preoccupation with writing the equestrian order into Rome's distant past. We have already observed this tendency in our discussion of the association between the *ordo equester* and Romulus' *Celeres*, as well as the web of connections between the *transvectio equitum*, the Dioscuri and celebration of the Battle of Lake Regillus.[21] By envisioning the *ordo equester* as a constituent part of

---

[15] Galinsky 2011: 72–3.

[16] Eck 1989: 22; Scheid and Granino Cecere 1999: 79–80; Rowe 2002: 72; Scheid 2005: 182.

[17] See Chapters 2 and 3.

[18] This chapter does not deal with the range of other priesthoods, such as provincial or civic religious offices, which could be held by men of equestrian rank, alongside Romans of other status. Our focus is on those whose priesthoods whose membership was, at one time or another, restricted to *equites*.

[19] For Augustus' archaic revivals, see Scheid 2005: 177–83.

[20] On new religious opportunities for the Roman people below senatorial and equestrian rank, see Galinsky 2011: 78–80. Mouritsen 2011: 250–61 has an excellent discussion of freedmen *Augustales*, emphasising the flexibility of the institution.

[21] This is discussed in Chapter 1.

the Roman state from the very beginning, Romans ensured that the title of *eques Romanus* was imbued with meaning and significance. The equestrian priesthoods gave the order an essential ideological 'immanence' (to return to Mann's concept of social power) within the framework of the *res publica*, complementing their other performative honours and privileges discussed in the previous two chapters.[22]

This leads into the second reason for reserving membership of traditional or archaising priesthoods for members of the *ordo equester* in the imperial period. The very nature of these religious offices, with their connections to the foundation legends of the Roman state and the city of Rome itself, emphasised tradition and continuity within the *res publica*. It should be pointed out that this was not an attempt to disguise the evolution of the state into its monarchical form under Augustus and his successors. For, as we have seen in Chapter 8, the *equites* were involved in numerous ceremonies and collective performances that validated the emperor and the concept of monarchical succession in the city of Rome. Rather, the priesthoods helped to bind the past (the heritage of Rome and the foundation of the *res publica*), the present (the new monarchical *res publica*) and the future (the continuance of the *res publica*) into one timeless continuum. The priests of the *ordo equester* played an important role in this by ensuring that the Roman state endured with the support of the gods. This connection between past and present was something that was integrated into the practice of Roman religion itself, as Beard has shown in her discussion of the annual festivals which evoked a range of events from different occasions in Rome's past.[23] The equestrian order formed part of this continuum of Roman history, as its members supervised festivals, sacrifices and ceremonies. The equestrian priesthoods, therefore, should not be viewed as collectible honours devoid of any religious significance, whose primary function was to be accumulated like trophies by upwardly mobile *equites*.[24] Religious ceremonies functioned as real and vital expressions of Roman views about the connection between human and divine, since they believed that the support of the gods (the *pax deorum*) was a necessity

---

[22] See the beginning of Chapter 8.

[23] Beard 1987. This article discusses, *inter alia*, how celebrations for Caesar were mapped on to pre-existing festivals, and thus integrated into the religious calendar.

[24] Purcell 1983: 167 noted that some scholars have regarded priesthoods 'as if they were complete ciphers'. For example, Wallace-Hadrill 1983: 5 observed that Suetonius' career included 'some honorific priesthoods'. The significance of Suetonius' post as *flamen Volcanalis* is discussed further below.

for the endurance of the *res publica*.[25] Priesthoods were a way of ensuring that the status of *equites* was articulated not merely in the material terms of procuratorships and salaries, or privileges such as theatre seating or wearing the gold ring, but also through the rituals and performances of religious power, in which they were positioned as intermediaries between gods, men and the emperor.

Initiation and Ideology

When the forty-year-old equestrian M. Ulpius Romanus breathed his last some time in the second century AD, it was up to his dutiful wife to arrange for his burial. His tomb featured an epitaph, which briefly, but poignantly, detailed their life together. She said she had lived together with Romanus for eighteen years, more or less, without any complaint. In addition to their private life, the inscription refers to Romanus' official status, describing him as an '*eques Romanus* who also ran as a *lupercus*' (*eques Romanus qui et | lupercus cucurrit*).[26] Why did Romanus' wife – whose own name remains sadly unknown – choose to record this specific event on his epitaph? What was it about participating in the festival of the Lupercalia that defined M. Ulpius Romanus both as a person and as a member of the *ordo equester*? The Lupercalia, held in the city of Rome each year on 15 February, was one of the most riotous and memorable festivals in the Roman calendar.[27] As befitted the month of February, the Lupercalia was a festival of purification and fertility, as the Romans prepared for the coming of spring.[28] The main attractions of the festival were the priests themselves, the *luperci*. They were young men, naked except for a loincloth, and covered in glistening oil (probably as much to keep out the February chill as for aesthetic reasons), who would run around the Palatine hill to the delight of spectators gathered to witness the event. It was, to use Wiseman's memorable phrase, an occasion of 'sheer sexiness'.[29] But when Ulpius Romanus' wife chose to record his own

---

[25] See Price 1984 on emperor worship, and Beard, North and Price 1998 on Roman religion and society at large. For nuanced studies of the priesthoods themselves, see Beard and North 1990; Várhelyi 2010.

[26] *CIL* VI 2160 = *ILS* 4947.

[27] There are conflicting elements in the ancient descriptions of the ritual (see particularly Dion. Hal. 1.80; Plut. *Rom.* 21.3–8; Ovid, *Fasti* 2.267–452; Val. Max. 2.2.9). Wiseman 1995b: 77–88 and North 2008: 147–8 offer concise overviews of the evidence.

[28] February derived its name from the Sabine *februus*, a ritual of purification (Varro, *LL* 6.13).

[29] Wiseman 1995a: 15.

particular run one cold February day, it is unlikely that she was reminiscing about her husband's glistening appearance. The Lupercalia was a festival that commemorated the very beginnings of the Roman state, and initiation into the ranks of the *luperci* – at least in the imperial period – could mark an important stage in the life of a young *eques Romanus* who lived in the city of Rome and its environs.

The festival began when the college of *luperci* gathered at the site of the Lupercal, located at the base of the south-west flank of the Palatine hill, where the she-wolf was said to have suckled Romulus and Remus.[30] It was there, supervised by Jupiter's own priest, the *flamen Dialis*, that the *luperci* sacrificed goats and a dog to the god of the Lupercal.[31] This was probably the Greek mountain deity Pan, the god of herdsmen. He was identified primarily with the Roman Faunus, but was sometimes syncretised with other deities of fertility, sexual prowess, and warfare.[32] The Romans traditionally ascribed the worship of Pan at this location to the mythical king Evander, who brought the cult with him to Italy from Pallanteum in Arcadia and established a settlement on the Palatine hill.[33] The festival of the Lupercalia was attributed to Romulus, the founder and first king of Rome. Romulus and his brother Remus are said to have run to the site of the Lupercal in a spirit of exuberance after defeating their evil grandfather, Amulius, the king of Alba.[34] The events of the Lupercalia festival therefore included both these elements: the sacrifices to Pan conducted by the priests, followed by the running of the initiates as a way of recreating the original run of Romulus and Remus. The route taken by the *luperci* around the Palatine hill acted as a rite of *lustratio*, following the course of Rome's original settlement as defined by Romulus with his plough.[35] The festival commemorated the very beginnings of Roman power and authority in Latium.[36]

The priests of the *luperci* were organised as a college along traditional lines, under the authority of the *magister*.[37] On the day of the festival the

---

[30] M. Robinson 2011: 725; *LTUR s.v.* 'Lupercal' (F. Coarelli).

[31] The *flamen Dialis* is mentioned only by Ovid, *Fasti* 2.281–2, and his presence is controversial: see M. Robinson 2011: 215–17.

[32] Ovid, *Fasti* 2.267–8; Wiseman 1995a; M. Robinson 2011: 208.

[33] Dion. Hal. 1.80.1; Ovid, *Fasti* 2.271–80.

[34] Plut. *Rom.* 21.3–6; Dion. Hal. 1.32.3–5; Val. Max. 2.2.9.

[35] Varro, *LL* 6.34; Wiseman 1995b: 81–2; Šterbenc Erker 2009: 167–71.

[36] Šterbenc Erker 2009: 154–67.

[37] Wiseman 1995b: 80–1 proposed that only the young initiates actually participated in the run. It is true that Plutarch (*Ant.* 12.2, *Caes.* 61.2) does include the magistrates as well as the youth. However, Plutarch is discussing the Republican Lupercalia, and magistrates do not seem to have run in the imperial period.

initiates were divided into two groups, the *Quintiliani* (representing Romulus) and the *Fabiani* (representing Remus). A third group, the *Iuliani,* named after Iulius Caesar, was added in 45 BC.[38] In the late Republican and imperial period the young *luperci* wore only goatskin loincloths – though this was more modest than in the early days of the ceremony, in which their only protection was a goatskin cape.[39] After the sacrifice of the goats, overseen by the *flamen Dialis* and the *magister lupercorum,* the young men had their foreheads smeared with a mixture of goat's blood and milk.[40] It must have been quite a sight to witness, as the young men were bloodied by their elders. This was ritualistic bonding at its most primal level. The *luperci* proceeded to skin the sacrificial goats and cut the skin into strips, which would serve as whips for the next stage of the festival.[41] Fortified by what was undoubtedly a considerable amount of wine,[42] the young initiates commenced their run, which would have taken them around the foot of the Palatine hill and up the Via Sacra to the *comitium* in the *forum Romanum.*[43] This was not a race per se (there was no winner); rather, the object was for the *luperci* to spend much of the day running around, taunting and teasing the spectators by lashing them with bloodied strips of goatskin. The women in attendance were particular targets of this whipping, which was believed to aid fertility, either by helping women to fall pregnant or promising a favourable birth to those already with child.[44] Pan and Faunus, the gods of the Lupercalia, were both associated with sexual virility and procreation.[45] The use of a goatskin in the festival recalled the fact that it was only after sacrificing a goat to Juno Lucina that Romulus and his men were able to successfully impregnate the Sabine women and give birth to the Roman race.[46] On the face of it, being lashed by a strip of animal hide might seem to be a somewhat violent and aggressive action, but the whole affair seems to have been conducted in a carnival atmosphere. Indeed, many of the young women in attendance extended their arms to be 'caught' by the *luperci.*[47] This festival was

---

[38] Suet. *Iul.* 76.1; Wiseman 1995a: 15, 1995b: 80; Vuković 2016. The different groups are epigraphically attested in the late Republic and Augustan age (*CIL* VI 1933, 33421, XI 3205). The *Iuliani* do not seem to have been a long-lasting innovation (Rüpke 2008: 9; Ferriès 2009: 386–8).

[39] Wiseman 1995a: 12.   [40] Plut. *Rom.* 21.4; North 2008: 148.

[41] Plut. *Rom.* 21.8; Dion. Hal. 1.80.1.   [42] Val. Max. 2.2.9 and, less charitably, Cic. *Phil.* 13.31.

[43] Ovid, *Fasti* 2.31–4, 283–304; Plut. *Rom.* 21.5; Dion. Hal. 1.80.1. For the route, see Wiseman 1995a: 7–8.

[44] Varro, *LL.* 6.34; Plut. *Caes.* 61.2; Wiseman 1995: 14–15; North 2008: 148–151.

[45] See Wiseman 1995a: 8–10; North 2008: 151–2.

[46] Ovid, *Fasti* 2.425–52; M. Robinson 2011: 277–80.

[47] Holleman 1973: 261; North 2008: 152–3.

therefore partially a ritual of purification and partially a fertility rite, which re-enacted the foundation myths of Rome by casting the city's equestrian youth, the future of the *res publica*, as its primary actors.

When and how the equestrian order became associated with such a festival is a complex issue, though the evidence strongly points to the age of Augustus. Valerius Maximus, writing in the reign of Tiberius, described February's Lupercalia as one of two major ritual performances of the *ordo equester* in the Roman calendar, the other being the *transvectio equitum* on 15 July.[48] This must have been a comparatively recent development, because the prosopographical information for the late Republican and triumviral periods reveals a heterogeneous membership of the college of *luperci*. We know of two senatorial *luperci*, L. Herennius Balbus and M. Antonius (the latter famously leading the *Iuliani* in 44 BC), as well as the scions of senatorial families, such as M. Caelius Rufus, Cicero's protégé.[49] The orator's own nephew, Q. Tullius Cicero, was also co-opted into the priesthood in 46 BC, when he would have been twenty years old. Uncle Cicero was not impressed by young Quintus' decision to become a *lupercus*, because two of the family's freedmen were also priests of the college.[50] Epigraphic evidence shows that the admission of freedmen continued until the early Augustan period, but ceased thereafter.[51] It may be that co-opting freedmen was a relatively restricted phenomenon, with senatorial patrons sponsoring their admission as a new type of honour. Freedmen certainly benefited from other opportunities for religious advancement under the Augustan regime.[52] However, from the early first until the late second century AD the membership of the *luperci* was exclusively equestrian, suggesting that Augustus had imposed the new criteria and restricted admission to members of the *ordo equester*.[53]

Yet this does not explain precisely why the Lupercalia and the *luperci*, among all the other festivals and priestly colleges, should be associated with the *ordo equester*. Wiseman has argued that the connection of the Lupercalia and the *equites* can be traced back to 304 BC, the same year in which the censor Q. Fabius Rullianus reformed the *transvectio equitum*.[54] It was then, Wiseman proposed, that the Lupercalia was reorganised and the two groups of runners introduced, so that speed and swiftness played

[48] Val. Max. 2.2.9. For the *transvectio equitum*, see Chapter 8.
[49] North and McLynn 2008: 177. Balbus: Cic. *Cael.* 26. Antonius: Cic. *Phil.* 2.85, 13.31; Dio 44.11.2; Plut. *Caes.* 61.3. Caelius Rufus: Cic. *Cael.* 26.
[50] Cic. *Att.* 12.5.1 [SB 242.1].
[51] Scheid and Granino Cecere 1999: 85, 129–30; Ferriès 2009: 380–1.
[52] Beard, North and Price 1998: I, 357–8.   [53] Ulf 1982: 50–1; Ferriès 2009: 390–1.
[54] Wiseman 1995a: 11–13.

a significant role in the festival. According to Polybius, the Roman cavalry originally fought in a state of near-nakedness, wearing only loincloths, so that they could mount and dismount their horses.[55] Whatever the accuracy of Polybius' statement, the festival of the Lupercalia as reorganised in 304 BC made a definite association between the youth of Rome and the cavalry of the *res publica*, by emphasising the martial elements of the ritual.[56] Wiseman's argument, built upon an erudite philological analysis, is certainly attractive, though it is at odds with the prosopographical evidence that shows non-equestrians being enrolled in the priesthood in the late Republic. It may have been the case that the association of the Lupercalia with the *equites* had diminished over time, before being revived by Augustus.

The *princeps'* precise actions concerning the Lupercalia are shrouded in mystery, however. Suetonius includes it in the lists of religious festivals and ceremonies that had fallen into abeyance before being 'restored' (*restituit*) by Augustus.[57] This may be something of an exaggeration, since the Lupercalia was held in 44 BC, and is not attested as being abolished thereafter (though the senate did withdraw funding from the third group, the *Iuliani*).[58] The only specific detail Suetonius provides about the nature of Augustus' changes is that beardless young men were forbidden to take part. This was undoubtedly a measure of a moral nature, since Suetonius discusses it in the same section as the institution of chaperones for young people attending the Saecular Games; there is no evidence that the ritual itself was any less riotous.[59] In the *Res Gestae*, Augustus boasts that he built the Lupercal itself, though it may be that he actually undertook a substantial rebuilding, since the site was known to exist before his reign.[60] The association of the Lupercal with Romulus meant that Augustus' reconstruction efforts identified him with the founder of Rome. By restricting membership of the *luperci* to *equites*, the emperor wrote the equestrian order into the wider narrative that his *res publica* marked the restoration of religious tradition and public *pietas* after the civil wars.[61]

---

[55] Polyb. 6.25.3–4.   [56] Wiseman 1995a: 13.

[57] Suet. *Aug.* 31.4; North and McLynn 2008: 177–9; Wardle 2011: 284, 2014: 254–5.

[58] This is the most natural understanding of the reference to the *vectigalia Iuliana* ('Julian revenues') in Cic. *Phil.* 13.31. See Ferriès 2009: 386–9.

[59] Suet. *Aug.* 31.4. Cf. North and McLynn 2008: 178–9, who argue that the modest attire of *equites* in imperial reliefs is a 'dress uniform' which differs from the goatskin loincloth worn in the festival itself.

[60] *RG* 19.1; Cooley 2009: 186–7. The importance of the *luperci* to the origins of Rome is underlined by the fact that they featured on the shield of Aeneas (Vergil, *Aeneid* 8.663–6).

[61] For Augustus' aims here, see Scheid 2005: 177.

Since there was a definitive change in the composition of the *luperci* in the Augustan age, with the college becoming exclusively equestrian, the nature of the emperor's revival is best understood as a redefinition of the Lupercalia as an initiation rite specifically for the equestrian youth, as described by Valerius Maximus.[62] It is therefore to be associated with other ceremonies and privileges designed to highlight the importance of the equestrian youth in the Roman state, which we have already explored in Chapters 8 and 9. In Roman thought the notion of restoration 'implied change as well as continuity', and it is clear that Augustus wished to highlight his role in returning the proper religious authority of the past to the Lupercalia.[63] It is plausible to suppose that Augustus also intended to re-emphasise the connections between the swift-footed runners and the *equites* identified by Wiseman.

Two famous reliefs of deceased *equites* from the early empire make the same connection between the Lupercalia and the *transvectio* as Valerius Maximus. The first, a marble funerary altar from Tibur, depicts Ti. Claudius Liberalis on horseback taking part in the annual parade (see Figure 8.3). On another face of the monument Liberalis is shown in the dress of a *lupercus*, holding a whip in his hand (Figure 10.1).[64] The second representation appears on a panel relief from Beneventum (Figure 10.2). The relief shows the deceased *eques* mounted on horseback, taking part in the *transvectio*, on the viewer's right, while on the left he is represented as a *lupercus*.[65] As Veyne has argued, these representations constitute a 'cursus in images', depicting the young *eques Romanus* engaging in two defining public rituals of his initiation into the *ordo*.[66] This *cursus* was very much a creation of Augustus' monarchical *res publica*; indeed, Pliny the Elder, writing in the first century AD, describes images of *luperci* as a recent innovation.[67] Their institution formed part of wider attempts to define and articulate equestrian privileges on funerary and honorific monuments.[68]

The success of the new, or revived, association between the *luperci* and the *ordo equester* is further illustrated by the honours granted to the younger Drusus after his death in AD 23. The equestrian order decreed that a statue of Drusus should be placed in the Lupercal, and a shield bearing his image

[62] Wrede 1983: 186; Scheid and Granino Cecere 1999: 85; Wiseman 1995a: 16; McLynn 2008: 168.

[63] See Galinsky 2011: 76 on the concept of restoration in regards Augustus' religious policies.

[64] *CIL* VI 3512 = XIV 3624, discussed by Veyne 1960: 104–5. Spalthoff 2010: 237–8 dates the monument around AD 50, whereas Wrede 1983: 187 places it in the early second century AD.

[65] Veyne 1960: 105 and Wrede 1983: 187 date the statue to the Antonine period.

[66] Veyne 1960: 105–6.   [67] Pliny the Elder, *NH* 34.18; Wrede 1983: 186, 189–9.

[68] See in particular Chapters 3 and 7.

Figure 10.1: Funerary altar of Ti. Claudius Liberalis from Tibur. Face showing Liberalis as a *lupercus*.

Figure 10.2: Relief from Beneventum showing the *transvectio* and a *lupercus*

should henceforth be carried during the *transvectio equitum* on 15 July.[69] Since there was no longer a temple of Fortuna Equestris in Rome, the Lupercal must have been regarded as the most suitable religious 'home' for the *equites*.[70] The dedication of Drusus' statue at this archaic and venerated cult site, now (re)-appropriated as a place of public initiation for the youth of the *ordo equester*, demonstrates the role played by the equestrian priesthood in connecting the *res publica*'s past (Romulus) with its present and future (the imperial house). The equestrian *luperci* brought validity to the monarchical *res publica* as representatives of the divine, who granted honours to the imperial family with the support of the gods. Moreover, the process of mourning and awarding posthumous honours to the deceased Drusus incorporated multiple equestrian ceremonies and venues, including the theatre, the *transvectio equitum* and the Lupercal. This shows how equestrian status, and its connection with the emperor, was articulated by multiple performances throughout the city of Rome. These helped to give membership of the *ordo* essential meaning and significance in the framework of the monarchical *res publica*, ensuring that the title of *eques Romanus* remained relevant and sought after by elites and non-elites alike.[71]

---

[69] *CIL* VI 31200 = *RS* 38 frag e. + f ll. 8–12; Rowe 2002: 8–9.

[70] Tac. *Ann.* 3.71 states that there was no temple of Fortuna Equestris in Rome in the age of Tiberius, which means the temple built by Q. Fulvius Flaccus (Livy 40.44, 42.10) must have been destroyed by this period.

[71] See Chapter 5 on the view of equestrian rank as inherently achievable.

458   *Religion and the* Res Publica

The Lupercalia was celebrated only in Rome: there were no provincial festivals.[72] This meant that new *luperci* would have to be present in the city in the February in which they were initiated into the priesthood; continuing residence in Rome would have been necessary to participate fully in the life of the college.[73] This may not have been a problem at the beginning of Augustus' reign, when the majority of equestrians were resident in Rome and Italy, but over the course of the first three centuries of empire the *ordo* came to encompass provincial notables from across the Mediterranean. The prosopographical data are too small to draw significant conclusions about the geographical origin of *luperci*. Out of twenty-one priests attested in the imperial period, we know the origins of only elven, including two freedmen attested prior to the Augustan reform. If they are taken out of the equation we are left with three *luperci* from Rome and six from the provinces. In the cases where the origin is not on record, the inscriptions recording the *lupercus'* career come from Rome or Italian communities.[74]

The priests of confirmed provincial origin date to the late second and third centuries AD. Two *luperci* from Nemausus in Gaul, L. Sammius Aemilianus and Q. Solonius Severinus, were also members of the equestrian jury panels, which would have required their presence in Rome.[75] Two further provincial equestrians associated with the Lupercalia, M. Iunius Asclepiades and L. Licinius Secundinus, came from Caesarea in Mauretania.[76] Rather than being styled *luperci*, both men are described as having 'performed the rites of the Lupercalia' (*sacris lupercalibus functus*). This terminology may indicate that they participated in the festival and its rites only on one occasion, before returning to Caesarea, rather than remaining in Rome as members of the college of *luperci*.[77] Our final example is M. Papius Marcianus from Cuicul in Numidia, who was honoured with a public statue in that town by his mother. The inscription on the base recorded that Marcianus 'had been distinguished with the public horse and made a *lupercus* for the

[72] Woolf 2009: 249. Constantine instituted a Lupercalia at his new Rome, Constantinople, but it was a 'pale imitation of the original' (McLynn 2008: 173). The festival was known outside Rome, of course: in the famous mosaic of the months at Thysdrus, February is represented with a depiction of the Lupercalia (Wrede 1983: 185).

[73] Unfortunately, we have no information about the meetings of the *luperci* or the operations of the priestly college.

[74] Scheid and Granino Cecere 1999: 129–34, 185.

[75] Aemilianus: *CIL* XII 3183 = *ILS* 5274; Rüpke 2008: no. 2979. Severinus: *CIL* XII 3184 = *ILS* 6981; Rüpke 2008: no. 3112.

[76] Asclepiades: *CIL* VIII 21063 + *AE* 1924, 41; Rüpke 2008: no. 2106; Secundinus: *CIL* VIII 9405, 9406 = *ILS* 4949; Rüpke 2008: no. 2257.

[77] Rüpke 2008: 771.

performance of public rites' (*equo pu|bl(ico) exornato | et sacrorum | publicorum | causa luperco | facto*).[78] The language strongly suggests that Papius Marcianus was initiated into the ranks of the *luperci* in Rome shortly after receiving the *equus publicus* from the emperor, and presumably remained in the *sacra urbs* to carry out his priestly duties.

The small number of provincial *luperci* indicates that the Lupercalia – far from being a major event in the lives of all *equites* – was primarily a festival of significance for equestrians who were resident in Rome or Italy. Valerius Maximus wrote of the Lupercalia as one of the two defining events for the *ordo equester*, but his perspective was that of a man who lived his life in Rome in the early principate. The same can be said of M. Ulpius Romanus, buried in Rome, who probably spent his entire life in the city: he ran as a *lupercus*, but is not known to have served in any administrative or military posts in the provinces. A number of *apparitores* were co-opted into the college of *luperci*, demonstrating the vital part played by the priesthood in the civic life of Rome for *equites* of all levels.[79] The paucity of provincial *luperci* could, of course, be a reflection of our evidence: it is possible that equestrians who had been co-opted into the priesthood chose not to have the post recorded on honorific or funerary monuments. But this does not seem likely, given the tendency towards inclusiveness, rather than exclusiveness, on such inscriptions. The Lupercalia was a festival that provincial *equites* could participate in if they came to Rome on jury service or other ceremonial duties, as shown by the cases of *equites* from Gaul and Africa discussed above.[80] The connection between the Lupercalia and the *ordo equester* was therefore strongest at a particular historical moment – the Augustan and Julio-Claudian period – when emperors used the priesthood to emphasise the continuity of the *res publica* and its institutions, and when the majority of *equites* lived in Italy, rather than abroad.

The evidence shows that the *luperci* ceased to be an exclusively equestrian priesthood by the Severan period at the latest, when senators are attested as members alongside *equites*.[81] P. Alfius Maximus Numerius Avitus, a patrician who sang in Septimius Severus' Saecular Games as a *clarissimus puer*, is recorded to have been a *lupercus*, as is his contemporary C. Iulius Camilius Asper, the descendant of ordinary consuls.[82]

[78] *AE* 1913, 158; Rüpke 2008: no. 2616.
[79] Purcell 1983: 167–70. For examples, see *CIL* VI 1933 (Rüpke 2008: no. 1289) and *CIL* VI 33421 (Rüpke 2008: no. 3160).
[80] Note the comments of Woolf 2009: 246 that there is no evidence of provincials going on 'pilgrimage' to Rome to participate in religious rituals held only in the *sacra urbs*.
[81] Várhelyi 2010: 62, 222.
[82] Avitus: *CIL* VI 41776; Rüpke 2008: no. 573. Asper: *CIL* VI 41184; Rüpke 2008: no. 2015.

While both Avitus and Asper seem to have been *luperci* in their youth, the same cannot be said for their older contemporary M. Fabius Magnus Valerianus, whose *cursus* records the priesthood between his praetorship and other senatorial offices.[83] The reason for the change in the social composition of the priesthood is not on record; it has been suggested that the college of *luperci* rose in prestige so that it was equivalent in status to the four *amplissima collegia*.[84] Yet it is also likely that the rise in the proportion of provincials in the *ordo equester*, who were not able to travel to Rome, weakened the connection between the priesthood and the *equites* as whole. All senators were supposed to own property in Italy and be resident in Rome for at least part of the year; such restrictions were not imposed on *equites*.[85]

The (admittedly exiguous) evidence suggests that the priesthood was firmly senatorial by the fourth century AD. L. Creperieus Rogatus, a senator of the Tetrarchic period, was styled 'priest of the sun god, *septem-vir*, and distinguished *lupercus*' (*pontifici* | *dei Solis* | *septemviro* | *et insigni* | *luperco*).[86] Rogatus took his role as a *lupercus* very seriously, installing a shrine in his house on the Viminal, which featured a mosaic depicting the she-wolf suckling Romulus and Remus and naked *luperci* brandishing their whips.[87] But there is nothing explicitly equestrian about this icono-graphy, suggesting that by this time the association with the *ordo equester* had been lost. The *luperci* were firmly understood as a senatorial college in literary works dating to the fourth century AD; membership was probably restricted to those members of the senatorial aristocracy resident in Rome or its environs.[88] The sacrificial elements of the cult ceased altogether in the post-Theodosian age, but the Lupercalia itself was still performed, with the run now being undertaken by actors, rather than the scions of senatorial families. By this point the spectacle was more important than the ritual.[89] This transformation of membership of the *luperci* probably reflects changes in the *ordo equester* as whole. The provincialisation of the *ordo* and the

[83] *CIL* XI 2106 = *ILS* 1138; Rüpke 2008: no. 1590.
[84] Rüpke 2008: 9. For a possible parallel, one might note the rise in status of priests of Sol in the third century AD, which was the result of imperial intervention by Aurelian (Hijmans 2010: 385, 404–9).
[85] There appears to have been a transitional period in which *equites* were still accepted as *luperci* before the college became exclusively senatorial. For example, a late third-century AD sarcophagus shows a *lupercus* flanked by the *vexillum*, suggesting equestrian rank (Wiseman 1995a: 16). The evidence, however, is very sparse.
[86] *CIL* VI 1397 = *ILS* 1203; Rüpke 2008: no. 1408.   [87] Wiseman 1995a: 16; Weiland 1992.
[88] Lact. *Div. Inst.* 1.21.45; Prud. *Per.* 2.517–18, discussed by McLynn 2008: 169. The Lupercalia is listed as taking place on February 15 in the *Codex Calendar of AD 354*.
[89] McLynn 2008: 169–70.

growth of an elite equestrian aristocracy of service, which identified with the aims and ambitions of senatorial officials, may have decreased the importance of preserving the initiation rite and priesthood of the *luperci* specifically for *equites*. This resulted in a more heterogeneous membership, which eventually became exclusively senatorial.[90]

A City of Priests

The ritual initiation of new *luperci* at the annual celebration of the Lupercalia gave the youth of the *equites* a religious role in Augustus' *res publica* to accompany their other ceremonial performances. The *princeps'* endeavours did not stop here, however, as he transferred other, more senior, priesthoods in the city of Rome (pontificates and flaminates) to the sole control of members of the equestrian order. The responsibilities of these priests included the supervision of traditional rituals, such as the announcement of the calendar, and major annual festivals, like the Volcanalia and Cerealia. By assigning these long-established priesthoods to *equites*, Augustus gave them important religious roles which befitted the position of the *ordo* as a constituent part of the *res publica*. As discussed in the introduction to this chapter, this action emphasised that his own religious reforms were founded on tradition and restoration, rather than revolution. At the same time, however, the reality of the monarchical *res publica* meant that appointment to priesthoods was not dependent on genuine election, but imperial favour. This is amply demonstrated by the *cursus*-style inscriptions recording equestrian and senatorial careers which incorporate religious offices alongside procuratorships, military commands and other offices bestowed by the *princeps*.[91] The careers of *pontifices* in particular demonstrate that eligibility for appointment to the most senior equestrian religious offices depended on being present in Rome and forging connections with the imperial court.

The most prestigious equestrian priesthood of the *res publica* was the office of *pontifex minor*, which carried with it membership of the pontifical college. The three *pontifices minores* had originally been the pontiffs' assistants, but became priests in their own right by the beginning of

---

[90] For the changes in the *ordo* discussed here, see Chapters 7 and 12.

[91] Members of the senatorial order would usually go to some lengths to highlight their religious offices in *cursus* inscriptions, often placing them immediately after their consulships or in distinct groups in their career hierarchies, as they represented prestigious honours bestowed by the emperor himself. See Várhelyi 2010: 61; Maurizi 2013: 73–89.

the second century BC.[92] In the Republic the post was occupied by plebeian senators, but it was transformed into a specifically equestrian priesthood under Augustus.[93] This formed part of his efforts to ensure that *equites* were integrated into the religious life of the state. The full title of these officials was *pontifex minor publicorum populi Romani sacrorum*, or 'junior pontiff of the public rites of the Roman people', which reflected their duties officiating at sacrificial ceremonies.[94] Membership of the pontifical college created numerous opportunities for *equites* to socialise with senatorial priests, either during the performance of the rituals themselves or while participating in the legendarily decadent feasts of the priesthood.[95]

The office of *pontifex minor* was usually awarded to those who followed administrative careers and formed part of the equestrian service elite, as befitted its seniority within the hierarchy of equestrian priesthoods.[96] Prominent *pontifices minores* include the praetorian prefect and future emperor M. Opellius Macrinus and T. Messius Extricatus, praetorian prefect of Elagabalus, though both men were co-opted into the college fairly early into their careers.[97] The importance of imperial favour is observable in the appointments to the pontificate made by Antoninus Pius. In April AD 142 Pius elevated his *a rationibus* M. Petronius Honoratus into the ranks of the *pontifices minores*.[98] We know the names of Honoratus' two colleagues in the mid-140s AD. They were L. Domitius Rogatus, previously the *ab epistulis* of Hadrian's heir Aelius Caesar and *procurator monetae*, and L. Volusianus Maecianus, who had been *a libellis* to Antoninus Pius when he was still Hadrian's heir apparent, and later worked for him as *a libellis* and *a censibus* during his reign as Augustus.[99] Then, in the 150s AD, a new *pontifex* replaced either Honoratus or Rogatus. This was the freedman L. Aurelius Nicomedes, previously *a cubiculo* of L. Aelius Caesar and *nutritor* of his son Lucius Verus. Pius had elevated Nicomedes to equestrian rank, which enabled him to assume the priesthood.[100] We can therefore

---

[92] Livy 22.57.3; Bleicken 1957: 363–4.

[93] This is based on prosopographical information, since there is no source attesting the change in social composition. See Wissowa 1912: 519 and the *fasti* in Scheid and Granino Cecere 1999: 114–20.

[94] Scheid and Granino Cecere 1999: 88.   [95] Hor. *Carm.* 2.14.28; Mart. *Ep.* 12.48.12.

[96] Scheid and Granino Cecere 1999: 80–1, 186.

[97] Macrinus: Rüpke 2008: no. 2579 (accepting the evidence of *HA Macr.* 7.2). Extricatus: Rüpke 2008: no. 2439; *CIL* VI 41190–1.

[98] Rüpke 2008: no. 2659; *CIL* VI 31834b = *AE* 1987, 138.

[99] Rogatus: Rüpke 2008: no. 1490; *CIL* VI 1607 = *ILS* 1450. Maecianus: Rüpke 2008: no. 3569; *CIL* XIV 5347–8.

[100] Rüpke 2008: no. 850; *CIL* VI 1598 = *ILS* 1740. There is also a later example from the Severan period, of an equestrian who was *a rationibus*, *a libellis*, and *ab epistulis* appointed *pontifex*

observe a strong connection between senior equestrian officials based in the city of Rome, imperial favour, and appointments to the post of *pontifex minor*.[101]

Augustus also transferred the twelve priesthoods classified as *flamines minores* from plebeian senators to members of the *ordo equester*.[102] These priesthoods ranked below the *flamines maiores* of Jupiter, Mars and Quirinus (*flamen Dialis, Martialis* and *Quirinus*), positions which were open only to patrician senators.[103] It is uncertain whether the *flamines minores* were actual members of the pontifical college, but they would have moved in the same social circles.[104] The equestrian flaminates were linked to specific religious festivals. For example, the *flamen Cerialis* presided at the Cerealia, the festival of Ceres, the goddess of grain, which was held on 19 April.[105] As with the sacrificial duties of the *pontifices minores*, the involvement of the *flamines* in these annual events meant that they played a highly visible role in religious ceremonies throughout the city of Rome.[106] The monument for the *praefectus annonae* T. Statilius Optatus, who had been appointed *flamen Cerealis* or *Carmentalis*, features the regalia of his priestly office carved into high relief (Figure 10.3).[107] Although Optatus had served in many senior government posts, his sons Statilius Homullus and Statilius Optatus decided that these priestly implements should accompany the inscribed *cursus*, a choice that should caution us from assuming that it was the administrative offices that mattered most to all equestrians.[108] The *cursus* of Ti. Claudius Pollio, another *flamen Carmentalis*, is not carved into the base of a statue of Pollio himself, but a dedicatory altar to the gods Sol, Luna, Apollo and Diana (Figure 7.2).[109]

---

minor (*AE* 1960, 163; Rüpke 2008: no. 52), which reflects similar connections with the imperial court.

[101] Although the tables in Scheid and Granino Ceccere 1999: 185 show that the geographical origins of the priests were diverse, the *pontifices'* careers had almost without exception brought them to Rome. The last dated example comes from the mid-third century AD (*CIL* VI 1628 = *ILS* 1456).

[102] Rüpke 2008: 44. We only know the names of ten of these *flamines*, however (Vanggaard 1988: 26–9; Pasqualini 2008: 441).

[103] These should be distinguished from the *flamines* of deified emperors, who were usually patrician senators (Várhelyi 2010: 71–4).

[104] Rüpke 2008: 42–5. Cf. Várhelyi 2010: 71.

[105] Scheid and Granino Cecere 1999: 89. Cf. Vanggaard 1988: 112–13, who seems unnecessarily sceptical that the *flamen Cerealis* was involved in this festival.

[106] Pasqualini 2008: 442–7.   [107] Rüpke 2008: no. 3137; *CIL* VI 41272 = *ILS* 9011.

[108] Rüpke 2008: 47 points out that these priestly implements functioned as 'universal symbols', which would be easily understood.

[109] Rüpke 2008: no. 1222; *CIL* VI 31032 = *ILS* 1418. For the importance of recognising the context of the inscribed *cursus*, see Eck 2009b.

Figure 10.3: Monument of T. Statilius Optatus, showing his priestly insignia

Such a dedication shows that priesthoods, and participation in religious life, were valued by members of the equestrian order.[110] The office of *pontifex minor* and the flaminates were especially esteemed because they could only be held in Rome and not in the provinces, even in the colonies.[111] This gave their holders a special cachet among members of

---

[110] The layout of the text on the inscription shows the importance of the dedication itself, with Sol, Luna, Apollo, Diana and Pollio's own name carved in much larger letters than Pollio's career.

[111] See Woolf 2009: 247–8.

the *ordo equester* at large. Sex. Caesius Propertianus was honoured with a statue as patron of the *municipium* of Mevania in Umbria, and the inscription carved on its base lists his priesthood first, immediately after his name, as *flamen Cerialis Romae* – 'at Rome'.[112] The Roman flaminate is thus given pride of place as a special mark of prestige.[113] The same pattern can be found on the honorific statue base of L. Egnatuleius Sabinus, from Thysdrus in Africa Proconsularis, in which his post as *pontifex* (i.e. *flamen*) *Palatualis* in Rome is listed first in the *cursus*, and the municipal office of *flamen Augusti* comes last.[114] This ordering seems to be an important and deliberate choice, since the vast majority of provincial *flamines* did not possess equestrian rank or progress to government careers, which was necessary to be appointed to priesthoods of the *res publica* in the city of Rome.[115] These were regarded a rare honour, as they represented selection by the emperor as a mediator between the earthly and divine. This represents the fulfilment of Augustus' aim that *equites* should be bound more closely into the framework of the *res publica* on a religious, ceremonial and administrative level.

Beneath the *pontifices* and *flamines minores* there was a range of other religious offices for which equestrians were eligible. The *curiones* were priests of the thirty divisions of Roman citizens known as *curiae*; their leader was known as the *curio maximus*.[116] Little is known about the precise details of their responsibilities, though their full title of *curio sacrorum faciendorum* ('curial priest for performing rites') suggests involvement in sacrifices, as with the *pontifices minores*.[117] They presided over the rites of the Fornacalia, staged in honour of the furnace-goddess Fornax.[118] However, although equestrians frequently became *curiones*, it was not an exclusively equestrian priesthood, since several senators are also attested as priests.[119] Indeed, by the third and fourth centuries AD most *curiones* appear to have been senators.[120] Similar points can be made about the college of sixty haruspices (*haruspices de LX*), which included

---

[112] Rüpke 2008: no. 1030; *CIL* XI 5028 = *ILS* 1447.   [113] Pasqualini 2008: 439.

[114] Rüpke 2008: no. 1517; *CIL* VIII 1500 = *ILS* 1409 (for the correction, see Wissowa 1912: 483 n. 1).

[115] See Bassignano 1974 on *flamines* from North Africa, and Wardle 2002: 470–80 on equestrian *flamines* throughout the empire. Cf. *AE* 1953, 73, an inscription recording the career of C. Suetonius Tranquillus, in which the local flaminate is listed first, probably because the posts are in chronological order (for discussion, see Wardle 2002: 469).

[116] Varro, *LL* 5.83; Beard, North and Price 1998: I, 50; Scheid and Granino Cecere 1999: 90–3.

[117] Scheid and Granino Cecere 1999: 90.

[118] Ovid, *Fasti* 2.527–32; Lact. *Div. Inst.* 1.20; M. Robinson 2011: 320–2, 328–9.

[119] Scheid and Granino Cecere 1999: 83–4.

[120] See the lists in Scheid and Granino Cecere 1999: 123–8.

equestrian members, but was not restricted exclusively to members of the *ordo*.[121] The lower-ranked *equites* of apparatorial status were eligible for co-option as *tubicines sacrorum publicorum populi Romani Quiritum* ('trumpeters of the public rites of the Roman citizen populace'). In the Republican period these officials were the trumpet players at religious ceremonies, but they were elevated to the ranks of the priesthood by Augustus.[122] Their promotion can be ascribed to that emperor's desire to involve *apparitores* more closely in the ceremonies of the state.[123] In their priestly capacity the *tubicines* oversaw the rite of the Tubilustrium, which required the purification of their instruments.[124] *Apparitores* also served as *sacerdotes bidentales*, literally 'priests of the two teeth'. This priesthood is not attested before the imperial period; their primary duty was to conduct a ceremony of propitiation after lightning strikes.[125]

The equestrian priesthoods had genuine ritual and religious significance, which gave members of the *ordo* a vital role to play in the maintenance of the *pax deorum* and the endurance of the *res publica*. C. Suetonius Tranquillus, Hadrian's *ab epistulis* and biographer of the Caesars, was also *flamen Volcanalis*, an office he probably held in the reign of Trajan.[126] He would have been required to oversee the festival of the Volcanalia on 23 August, offering sacrificial meats to Volcan and his consort Maia. This probably took place at the site of the Volcanal in the *forum Romanum*, and at the god's temple in the Campus Martius.[127] The *flamen* also oversaw the offerings to Maia on 1 May, as well as the celebrated sacrifice of live fish, which were thrown into the open flames during the *ludi Piscatorii* on 7 June.[128] When we consider the duties undertaken by the *flamen Volcanalis*, Suetonius the biographer becomes less of a solitary bookworm, and instead emerges as a vital participant in the religious life of the *sacra urbs*.[129] In the case of another imperial *eques*, P. Livius Larensis, we are fortunate to have both epigraphic and literary

---

[121] Scheid and Granino Cecere 1999: 86–7.   [122] Scheid and Granino Cecere 1999: 94.

[123] Purcell 1983: 133.   [124] Rüpke 2011: 28.

[125] Scheid and Granino Cecere 1999: 86, 94. A *decuria* of the *sacerdotes bindentales* is associated with the temple of the lightning god Semo Sancus on the Quirinal (*CIL* VI 568 = *ILS* 3473). The name either refers to the teeth of the lightning or to the sacrifice of young sheep (with only two teeth).

[126] *AE* 1953, 73; Rüpke 2008: no. 3168.

[127] Varro, *LL* 6.20; Wissowa 1912: 229–30; Pasqualini 2008: 446.

[128] Macrob. *Sat.* 1.12.18–20; Festus 274 L. Cf. Ovid, *Fasti* 6.239–40; Dumézil 1958.

[129] Cf. Townend 1961a: 102, who suggests that it was a 'quiet and scholarly character' that recommended someone like Suetonius Tranquillus for his priesthood. This overlooks the fact that such a character might not qualify a man to oversee the burning of live fish.

attestation of his religious expertise. If we depended solely on his epitaph for our knowledge of Larensis' life, we would only know that he held the position of *pontifex minor*.[130] But Larensis was also the host of the titular dinner party in Athenaeus' *Deipnosophistae*. Athenaeus' comments show that Larensis' pontificate was no mere sinecure: he was fact deeply interested both in the religious institutions founded by Romulus and Numa and in the political structure of the *res publica*.[131]

We can see genuine religious expertise in the case of P. Flavius Priscus, an equestrian of the mid-third century AD. Priscus was honoured with a statue in the main square of Ostia, the town of which he was patron (Figure 10.4).[132] The inscription includes reference to his administrative and religious offices:

To P. Flavius Priscus, son of Publius, of the tribe Palatina, *vir egregius*, of the equestrian order, promoted to the grade of *centenarius* because of his religious learning, *pontifex* and *dictator Albanus*, first holding this position at the age of 28, magistrate with censorial power, patron of the colony of Ostia, priest of the *genius* of the colony, father of the corporation of bakers and of the corporation of surveyors, patron of the corporation of corn-dealers at Ostia. Dedicated on the Kalends of March in the year in which Aemilianus, for the second time, and Aquilinus were consuls.[133]

Priscus was evidently a prominent figure in Ostia, since he was patron of the colony and of several mercantile corporations, a local magistrate, and *sacerdos* of Ostia's *genius*. His posts as *pontifex* and *dictator Albanus* meant that he was involved in supervising the *feriae Latinae*, and therefore played a role in the wider religious life of Latium.[134] The inscription makes an important reference to his priestly duties, stating that he was 'promoted to the grade of *centenarius* because of his religious learning' (*religiosa disciplina | ad centena provecto*). On first reading, it appears that Priscus was promoted to a centenarian procuratorship in the imperial service. However, the expression *religiosa disciplina* suggests that it was actually

---

[130] Rüpke 2008: no. 2273; *CIL* VI 2126 = *ILS* 2932.
[131] Ath. *Deip.* 2C–2D; Motschmann 2002: 112–14. Cf. D. Braund 2000: 6–8, who suggests that the epitaph does not belong to the Larensis of Athenaeus' work, but to a relative.
[132] Rüpke 2008: no. 1701.
[133] *CIL* XIV 4452 = *ILS* 9507: *P(ublio) Flavio P(ubli) fil(io) Pal(atina tribu) | Prisco e(gregio) v(iro) | equestris ordinis | religiosa disciplina | ad centena provecto | pontifici et dictatori | Albano primo annos | viginti octo agenti | q(uin)q(uennali) c(ensoria) p(otestate) patr(ono) colon(iae) Ost(iensis) | sacerd(oti) Geni(i) colon(iae) | patr(i) corpor(is) pistorum | corp(oris) mensorum | frum(entariorum) Ost(iensis) patron(o) || Dedicata Kale|ndis Marti(i)s | Aemiliano ite|rum et Aquilin|o co(n)s(ulibus)*.
[134] These priesthoods are discussed in detail in the next section of this chapter.

Figure 10.4: Inscribed statue base of P. Flavius Priscus, Ostia

a religious post, possibly that of *haruspex*, which carried a salary of 100,000 sesterces (hence the designation *centenarius*).[135] This argument is supported by the religious career of L. Fonteius Flavianus, who was *haruspex Augustorum C[C?]* (either *centenarius* or *ducenarius*), as well as *pontifex* and *dictator Albanus*.[136] He was a personal *haruspex* of the

[135] Granino Cecere 1996: 299–300; Scheid and Granino Cecere 1999: 87.
[136] Rüpke 2008: no. 1737; *CIL* VI 2161 = *ILS* 4955, discussed by Granino Cecere 1996: 293–5.

emperors, who rewarded him with the salary usually reserved for high procurators.[137] Priscus therefore emerges not as a local politician who accumulated priestly offices merely to adorn his inscribed *cursus*, but as a man of genuine religious expertise, which earned him both imperial favour and financial reward.[138]

Senators and equestrians were prepared to assume such priesthoods from an early age, since religious instruction was an integral part of the socialisation of elite children.[139] Very often this occurred orally and informally, as part of the normal process of child-rearing.[140] However, evidence for more formal education comes from the career of the Elder Papinius, the father of the poet P. Papinius Statius.[141] He is said to have taught young men from all over Italy, whom Statius described as 'noble youth' (*generosaque pubes*) and 'Romulus' stock and leaders of the future' (*Romuleam stirpem proceresque futuros*).[142] The classes included both Greek and Latin literature and religious knowledge, and his students later went on serve as *salii, flamines* and *luperci*.[143] Papinius therefore played an essential part in the socialisation of senatorial and equestrian youth, preparing them for their future roles both as statesmen and as priests.[144] We can see in Statius' account of his father's teachings the inextricable connection between service to the *res publica* and service to the gods in the Roman mindset.[145] This explains the careers and religious interests of *equites* such as Suetonius, P. Livius Larensis and P. Flavius Priscus of Ostia. By enabling members of *ordo equester* to serve as priests of the state, Augustus gave them a real and vital religious role in the *res publica*, emphasising the revival of proper and traditional religious practices under his principate. At the same time, Augustus ensured that *equites* would be dependent on him and his successors for appointment to these priesthoods, effectively domesticating aristocratic religious influence to serve the needs of his regime.

---

[137] For the salary, see Haack 2006: 53.
[138] C. Iulius Domatius Priscus, who was honoured with the *equus publicus* by an unknown emperor, is attested as an assistant to the imperial *haruspices* and *pontifex Albani* (*CIL* VI 2168 = 32402 = *ILS* 4956; Haack 2006: 67–8).
[139] Prescendi 2010.   [140] Bremmer 1995: 37–8.
[141] For his role as a teacher, see McNelis 2002: 73–4.   [142] Stat. *Silv.* 5.3.146, 176.
[143] Stat. *Silv.* 5.3.162–84; B. Gibson 2006: 337–9.   [144] Stat. *Silv.* 5.3.185–190.
[145] Eck 1989: 18–19.

The Sacred Periphery

The involvement of *equites* in the religious life of the *res publica* was not confined to the city of Rome itself, but extended throughout Latium. The region was pregnant with ideological significance, since it was where Aeneas had landed in Italy and established the city of Lavinium, and where his son Ascanius had founded the kingdom of Alba Longa, from which the line of Romulus and Remus emerged. Several new equestrian priesthoods were (re)created at significant cult sites throughout this region during the first century AD. Even though these religious offices were located in communities outside Rome, they still constituted priesthoods of the *res publica*, because it was from this region that the Roman state emerged.[146] The selection of *equites* to serve as priests of cults of Latium during the principate demonstrates that successive Roman emperors wished to continue and strengthen the association between the *ordo equester* and the religious rites of the state. The significance of Rome's legendary past as a way of integrating elites into the framework of the monarchical *res publica* was therefore not restricted to Augustus' reign, but is attested well into the principate, especially in the age of the Antonine emperors.[147]

We turn first to Lavinium, the first city founded by Aeneas when he arrived in Italy, which lay 30 kilometres to the south of Rome[148] He was led to the site of Lavinium by a sow, which proceeded to give birth to thirty piglets. These piglets were then sacrificed by Aeneas to the Penates, the household gods, which he had carried with him to Italy from Troy.[149] Lavinium was an important cult site for the worship of the Penates, who were identified with the Dioscuri, and Vesta, who was described as their companion.[150] After the subjugation of the Latin League in 338 BC Rome renewed its treaty with Lavinium, which had remained loyal throughout the Latin wars. The union was henceforth celebrated on an annual basis during the *feriae Latinae*.[151] This festival was a celebration of some antiquity, having reportedly been established by Tarquinius Superbus as a way of demonstrating the unity of forty-seven tribes in Latium by means of a communal sacrifice to Jupiter Latiaris.[152] Roman magistrates with

---

[146] Wissowa 1912: 520–1. Note for example, Q. Trebellius Rufus, one of the *sacerdotes Caeninenses*, who was styled priest 'of the rites of the Roman people' (ἱερῶν δήμου Ῥωμαίων) (*IG* II² 4193).

[147] For these priesthoods as imperial appointments, see Wissowa 1912: 489.

[148] Livy, 1.1.10–11; Varro, *LL* 5.144. On the site of Lavinium, see Castagnoli 1972.

[149] Dion. Hal. 1.57.1; Vergil, *Aeneid* 8.81–5.

[150] Servius s.v. *Aen.* 2.296; Macrob. *Sat.* 3.4.11; Galinsky 1969: 154–8.

[151] Livy 8.11.15; Cooley 2000: 177.   [152] Simón 2011: 119–21; C. J. Smith 2012: 268–74.

imperium were required to travel to Lavinium each year in order to sacrifice to the Penates and Vesta, with those who failed to fulfil this religious duty suffering ill-fortune.[153]

The community and its cults declined in the second century BC, only to be revived in the first century AD. This probably occurred during the reign of the emperor Claudius, when the equestrian military officer Sp. Turranius Proculus Gellianus led a delegation of Laurentines to renew their treaty with Rome.[154] The priestly college of *Laurens Lavinas* – composed of *praetores, pontifices, flamines, salii* and *sacerdotes* – is thereafter attested until the early fourth century AD. (The bulk of the epigraphic evidence comes from the second and early third centuries AD.)[155] The epigraphic record reveals that all the priests were *equites*, which indicates that there was a conscious decision taken to reserve the college for members of the *ordo equester*. The equestrian priests of *Laurens Lavinas* were geographically and socially diverse.[156] They originated from Gaul, Africa and the Danubian regions, in addition to Rome and Italy, and ranged in rank from *apparitores* to senior equestrian prefects.[157] The one unifying factor that bound them together was that they held administrative posts in Ostia or Rome, often at the imperial court itself, and had won the favour of the emperor.[158] The personal role of the *princeps* is demonstrated by the inscription on the base of a statue for C. Iulius Laetius Fl[–], which was erected in Thysdrus in Africa Proconsularis. This records that he was 'adlected into the squadrons of *equites Romani* by the emperors Caesars Antoninus and Verus Augustus' (*allecto in turm[as]* | *equit(um) Romanor(um) a[b]* | *Imperatoribus Cae|saribus Antonino et* | *Vero Augustis*) and then 'adlected into the body of *Laurentes Lavinates*' (*[alle]cto in numer(o)* | *[Lauren]tium [L]avinatium.*).[159] The equestrian priests did not reside in Lavinium, and may not have spent much time in

---

[153] Galinsky 1969: 146–7. For the continuity of the cult into the imperial period, see C. J. Smith 2012: 274. Cf. Pina Polo 2011: 105–6, who suggests that the consuls themselves did not attend each year, but delegated the duties to others.

[154] *CIL* X 797 = *ILS* 5004. The connection is accepted by a number of scholars: Saulnier 1984: 524–5; Scheid 1993: 120; Scheid and Granino Cecere 1999: 111–12; Cooley 2000: 177–9.

[155] The prosopographical study by Scheid and Granino Cecere 1999: 155–77 lists a total of ninety-four known priests in the college. The last known priests are T. Flavius Vibianus (*IRT* 567–8) and T. Flavinus Frontinus (*IRT* 564).

[156] Saulnier 1984: 530–1; Scheid and Granino Cecere 1999: 101–4.

[157] Scheid and Granino Cecere 1999: 188. For the range in rank, note the cases of L. Fabricius Caesennius Gallus, *scriba* (*CIL* XIV 354), at the lower end of the spectrum and L. Petronius Taurus Volusianus, *praefectus praetorio* (*CIL* XI 1836 = *ILS* 1332), at the upper.

[158] Saulnier 1984: 530–3. One quarter of the priests were provincials from outside Italy, but they had held office in Rome and its environs (Scheid and Granino Cecere 1999: 103).

[159] *CIL* VIII 10501.

the community itself, beyond their official responsibilities.[160] For the most part, their priesthoods are recorded on statue bases or funerary monuments in other communities in Italy or the provinces.[161] It is thus reasonable to imagine the equestrian *Laurentes Lavinates* as a somewhat artificial group, which existed in parallel with the *res publica* of Lavinium itself.[162]

Why did Claudius decide to associate the equestrian order with Lavinium by assigning the priesthood of *Laurens Lavinas* to its members? There was already a strong connection between the senate and the cult site, since consuls and praetors were required to sacrifice there upon taking office; they later renewed the treaty of 338 BC each year ten days after the festival of the *feriae Latinae*.[163] By adding an equestrian priesthood to Lavinium, Claudius ensured that both of Rome's upper *ordines* were represented in religious rituals at the site. Moreover, the Penates, which had been brought by Aeneas from Troy and which were worshipped at Lavinium, were identified with the Dioscuri, the patron deities of Rome's cavalry and later the *ordo equester*.[164] It was fitting, therefore, that *equites* should be established as permanent custodians of the sanctuary. Given Claudius' own antiquarian interests, he may also have recalled that it was not only the residents of Lavinium who had remained loyal to Rome in the fourth century BC, but also the *equites* from Campania. In 338 BC the Romans commemorated the fidelity of Campanian *equites* by establishing a bronze inscription at the Temple of Castor and Pollux in Rome.[165] Hence, there were multiple connections between cavalry service, the Dioscuri and Lavinium, which made it a suitable site for a new equestrian priesthood, connecting members of the imperial *ordo* with significant events in Rome's past.

Emperors were an integral part of the ritual world of Lavinium: they selected the equestrian priests of *Laurens Lavinas*, and were honoured with communal dedications from the college in return.[166] The emperor Antoninus Pius, however, showed special interest in Lavinium and its rites. After his death and deification the community erected a statue of Pius, with the following inscription carved on its base:

To the deified Antoninus Augustus, the Laurentine senate and people (erected this), not only because he safeguarded their privileges, but also because he

[160] Eck 1989: 26 n. 33; Nonnis 1995–6: 255.   [161] Saulnier 1984: 530.
[162] Saulnier 1984: 518; Cooley 2000: 179–80.
[163] Val. Max. 1.6.7; Macrob. *Sat.* 3.4.11; Orlin 2010: 44–5, 50–1; Hartmann 2017.
[164] Galinsky 1969: 154–61.   [165] Livy 8.11.15–16.
[166] Cooley 2000: 180; *CIL* XIV 2069 (for Trajan, Lavinium); *CIL* XIV 2072 (for Iulia Domna, Ostia); *CIL* 2073 (for Caracalla, Ostia).

increased them, under the curatorship of M. Annius Sabinus Libo, *clarissimus vir*, and under the care of Ti. Iulius Nepotianus and P. Aemilius Egnatianus, praetors and magistrates with censorial authority of Laurens Lavinas.[167]

The exact nature of the privileges awarded by Antoninus Pius is uncertain, though there was certainly significant urban expansion in Lavinium during the Antonine period.[168] The privileges may have been bestowed in AD 148, the occasion of the nine-hundredth anniversary of the foundation of the city of Rome.[169] Even if the statue base is not to be connected with that specific anniversary, Antoninus Pius did promote an association between the imperial house and figures from Rome's legendary past as part of his public image.[170] The legend of the sow was commemorated on medallions produced during his reign, featuring alongside a number of other episodes from Rome's early history, including Aeneas carrying Anchises from Troy, and the wolf suckling Romulus and Remus.[171] One particularly significant medallion carries an image of the emperor's heir Marcus Aurelius on the obverse and a scene of sacrifice on the reverse. This depicts Antoninus Pius sacrificing in the guise of Aeneas, and Marcus Aurelius beside him as Ascanius.[172] The imperial family was also iconographically connected to the mythological heritage of the *ordo equester* in their public image. Another medallion of Antoninus Pius featured the Dioscuri, the patrons of the *equites*, and Marcus Aurelius, the Caesar and *princeps iuventutis*, was commemorated with a medallion depicting Castor, as we saw in Chapter 8 (Figure 8.10).[173]

This evidence enables us to build up a web of connections between emperors, gods and the equestrian order, which was articulated in medallions, monuments and rituals. The public image of the imperial family was

---

[167] *CIL* XIV 2070 = *ILS* 6183: *Divo Antonino Aug(usto)* | *senatus populusque Laurens* | *quod privilegia eorum non* | *modo custodierit sed etiam* | *ampliaverit curatore* | *M(arco) Annio Sabino Libone c(larissimo) v(iro)* | *curantibus Ti(berio) Iulio Nepotiano* | *et P(ublio) Aemilio Egnatiano praet(oribus)* | *II q(uin) q(uennalibus) Laurentium* | *Lavinatium.*

[168] Cooley 2000: 180–1.

[169] For the possible connection with the anniversary of Rome's foundation, see Saulnier 1984: 532; Cooley 2000: 187. Pius may have been the recipient of another fragmentary dedication at Lavinium which refers to acts of *indulgentia* bestowed on the community, but other emperors are also a possibility (*CIL* XIV 2071 = *AE* 2000, 268; discussed by Cooley 2000: 181–7, revised in Cooley 2012: 440–8).

[170] Rowan 2014.

[171] Toynbee 1986: 144, 192–3. This series continued themes presented on medallions of Hadrian (Beaujeu 1955: 151–2, 292).

[172] Gnecchi 1912: Pius no. 84. This interpretation is accepted by Beaujeu 1955: 292; Toynbee 1986: 218–19; Cooley 2000: 187.

[173] Gnecchi 1912: Pius no. 95, Marcus no. 39; Beaujeu 1955: 294.

linked to the foundation of Rome itself, and especially to the arrival of
Aeneas in Italy and the foundation of Lavinium. Through their roles as
priests of *Laurens Lavinas*, in which they celebrated Aeneas, the Penates/
Dioscuri and the imperial house, members of the *ordo equester* were
themselves integrated into this rich historical tapestry. The combination
of the past, present and future of Rome resulted in an elaborate 'complex of
times' (to use Beard's evocative phrase), which gave meaning and significance to religious rituals and ideological significance, or 'immanence', to
the *equites* themselves.[174] The fact that the priesthood at Lavinium encompassed *equites* from a variety of regions, from Gaul to the Danube, who
were drawn to Rome through service to the emperor, ensured that the cult
centre remained relevant to the provincialised aristocracy at large.[175] For,
as Scheid has noted, the cult at Lavinium celebrated the very foundations
on which the Roman state was built, a state that by the second century AD
was much more than just Rome and Latium, but an empire that stretched
across the Mediterranean.[176] The interest of Antoninus Pius in Lavinium
shows how post-Augustan emperors constantly renewed the religious
connections with Rome's past in order to ensure that they remained
relevant to its cosmopolitan present.

Only one priest of *Laurens Lavinas*, C. Servilius Diodorus, is attested as
contributing actively to the local community in a personal, rather than
a religious, capacity.[177] Originally from the island of Girba (modern-day
Djerba) off the coast of North Africa, Diodorus had served in the *militiae
equestres* before embarking on a procuratorial career in the Roman administration. In AD 227, while in office as a priest of *Laurens Lavinas*, he
donated the sum of 20,000 sesterces to the *collegium* of *dendrophori* (the
loggers' association) in Lavinium.[178] The 5 percent interest from the
endowment was designed to pay for distributions of money (*sportulae*)
and a public banquet each year.[179] The date for this annual largesse was to
be 12 November, Diodorus' own birthday, ensuring that he would be
linked with the benefaction in perpetuity. In return for his generosity,
the loggers co-opted Diodorus as a patron of their association.[180]

---

[174] Beard 1987.

[175] See Beard 1987: 3 on the shared Graeco-Roman heritage of Roman religious ritual. Hartmann
2017 examines how Roman religion unified members of the imperial aristocracy from both
Italy and the provinces.

[176] Scheid 1993: 112, 118–22.   [177] *AE* 1998, 282. For discussion, see Nonnis 1995–6; Liu 2014.

[178] A. Wilson 2012: 140 argues that the *dendrophoroi* were loggers, rather than an exclusively
religious association, though they were involved in festivals of Magna Mater (Nonnis 1995–
6: 255).

[179] This was a common interest rate in Italy (Nonnis 1995–6: 258).   [180] *AE* 1998, 282, IV.

The letters exchanged between the various parties involved in establishing this foundation were inscribed on a marble statue base alongside a record of Diodorus' official equestrian career.[181] The statue of Diodorus himself, which was dedicated by his wife Egnatia Salviana, stood in front of a large public building with a portico, adjacent to the Via Laurentina.[182] Diodorus' benefaction, and the manner in which it was commemorated in Lavinium, is significant, because he is the first (and currently the only) priest of *Laurens Lavinas* epigraphically attested in the community itself.[183]

The final letter in the epigraphic dossier, from Diodorus himself to the loggers' association, records his hope that his actions will serve as an example for his fellow priests of *Laurens Lavinas*.[184] This may mean that the priests did not usually make a long-term investment in Lavinium. In Diodorus' case, his generosity seems to have been prompted by the actions of his wife, Salviana. As he wrote in a letter to Pontius Fuscus Pontianus, who was probably the senatorial *curator* of Lavinium:

Egnatia Salviana, the mother of my household, on account of her dutifulness towards me has placed a s[tatue] for me in the community of the *Laurentes Lavinates*, where I am a priest. So that her displays of dutifulness might be made greater, I have promised, my lord, that I will give to the association of loggers which is in this same community, 20,000 sesterces.[185]

It was only fitting therefore that the *dendrophoroi* co-opted Egnatia Salviana as a *mater* of their *collegium* in the following year.[186] In this way Servilius Diodorus, an equestrian procurator from Girba, sought to make a permanent mark on the civic life of Lavinium through his benefaction and its subsequent commemoration. However, Diodorus was clearly an exception in this regard, as he was the only priest to make any sort of investment in the community of Lavinium. Indeed, as Liu has suggested, the epigraphic dossier indicates that the *res publica* and the *Laurentes*

---

[181] This is suggested by the reconstruction in *AE* 1998, 282, IIIa: *s[tatuam] mihi in civitate Laurentum Lavinatium*. See further Nonnis 1995–6: 248.

[182] Nonnis 1995–6: 235; Fenelli 1998: 115–16.

[183] Liu 2014: 254 suggests that he may have had commercial interests in the region.

[184] *AE* 1998, 282, V. There was certainly a competitive element in patronage and benefaction where associations were concerned (Liu 2009: 242–3).

[185] *AE* 1998, 282, IIIa: *Egnatia Salviana mater familias mea pro sua pietate rega me s[tatuam] | mihi in civitate Laurentium Lavinatium ubi sacerdotalis su[m po]|suit; eius obsequia amplianda crededi, domine, ut collegi[o den]|drophororum quod est in eadem civitate dem HS XX (milia) n (ummum).*

[186] *AE* 1998, 282, IV. The title of 'mother' (*mater*) was an honour distinct from that of patron or patroness (Hemelrijk 2008: 122–3).

Lavinates did not usually interact in a significant manner.[187] The college of equestrian priests was not integrated into the local community, as it was an imperial rather than municipal religious college. Their focus was elsewhere, on their connections to the emperor and the *res publica* of Rome.

The college of *Laurentes Lavinates* of Lavinium was one of a number of priesthoods in the sacred periphery around Rome reserved for *equites* in the course of the first century AD. These included the *sacerdotes Albani, Cabenses* and *Caeninenses*, which were all public priesthoods of the Roman people based at sites connected with the founding of Rome.[188] They were associated with Alba Longa, the settlement founded by Aeneas' son Ascanius, which later competed with Lavinium for religious primacy.[189] The *sacerdotes Albani* were quartered at Bovillae, a colony of Alba Longa, and the ancestral home of the Julian family. In AD 16 a shrine for the Julian family and a statue of Divus Augustus were erected in the town, and *ludi circenses* were regularly staged there in honour of the Iulii.[190] This revival of interest in Bovillae in the early empire was shaped by the association of Augustus and the Julio-Claudian family with Aeneas and the founding legends of Rome; the connection between Bovillae and the Iulii does not seem to have been particularly strong prior to this point.[191] The first attested *pontifices Albani*, dated to the period of the late Republic, were certainly not equestrians. There is then a gap in our evidence until the second century AD, after which all attested priests are *equites*.[192] It is evident, therefore, that the priesthood was reconfigured in the course of the early principate into an equestrian college. There were three main posts available in the college of the Alban priests: *pontifex, dictator* and *salius* (the last of which were not necessarily of equestrian rank), as well as Vestal Virgins.[193] The selection of priests from the *ordo equester* can be ascribed to an effort to ensure that both of the upper *ordines* were represented at Alba, as was the case at Lavinium. The senatorial priests of the deified Augustus, the *sodales Augustales*, were already involved in cult duties.[194] They were now joined by the equestrian *pontifices*, reflecting the *ordo*'s position within the monarchical *res publica*.

---

[187] Liu 2014: 259–60. Cf. *CIL* XIV 2069, in which the priests' statue of Trajan has been authorised by the decurions.

[188] Wissowa 1912: 520–1; Rüpke 2007: 226.

[189] Galinsky 1969: 141–6; Y. Thomas 1990: 155–62. In the second century AD Juvenal wrote of the 'ruined Alba' (*diruta . . . Alba*) which nevertheless still cared for Vesta and the eternal fire (Juv. *Sat.* 4.60–1).

[190] Tac. *Ann.* 2.41, 15.23.2.   [191] Badian 2009: 14–15.

[192] Scheid and Granino Cecere 1999: 97.

[193] Wissowa 1915: 2–3; Granino Cecere 1996: 284–5, 302–3.   [194] Várhelyi 2010: 74–5.

Two further priestly colleges associated with Alba, the *sacerdotes Cabenses* and the *sacerdotes Caeninenses*, were also transferred to the equestrian order in the first century AD.[195] The *Cabenses* probably derived their name from the settlement of Cabum on the Alban Mount.[196] Together with the *Albani*, the *Cabenses* were involved in the annual celebration of the *feriae Latinae*, which, as we have seen above, commemorated the union of Rome and the Latin League. The emphasis on the union of city-states and the ritual sacrifice before embarking on a war had symbolic resonance for the endurance of Roman hegemony.[197] The *feriae Latinae* continued to be celebrated until the late fourth century AD, which is a sign of the longevity and importance of the festival. The *dictator Albanus* was selected from among the equestrian *pontifices Albani* to oversee the rites of the *feriae Latinae*.[198] The involvement of the *Cabenses* in the festival is apparent in the epigraphic record. An inscription from the late third century AD refers to the religious officials as 'priests of Cabum for the Latin festival on the Alban Mount' (*Caben[ses] | [s]acerdote[s] | [feria]rum Latinarum | mon[tis] Albani*).[199]

The *sacerdotes Caeninenses* derived their name from the town of Caenina, which had ceased to exist by the imperial period.[200] According to tradition, Romulus had defeated Acron, king of the Caenineses, in single combat and dedicated the *spolia opima* (the arms seized in combat) to Jupiter Feretrius.[201] A link can be made between Romulus' actions and Augustus' own dedication of the *spolia opima* at Rome, but this does not necessarily mean that he created the priesthood.[202] The first *sacerdotes* are not attested epigraphically until the late first century AD.[203] Many of them seem to have been young, up-and-coming *equites*, appointed after a municipal career; it therefore constituted an early sign of imperial favour (or represented a useful patron at court).[204] In the case of all three Alban

[195] This is based on epigraphic evidence: see Scheid and Granino Cecere 1999: 98–9, 151–5. The nearby priests of Lanuvium (*sacerdotes Lanuvini*) were also of equestrian rank, though they did not tend to be of high status (Gordon 1937: 46–7). Antoninus Pius also showed an interest in this cult site by restoring temples here (*HA Pius* 8.3; Beaujeu 1955: 293).

[196] Dion Hal. 5.61.3; Pliny the Elder, *NH* 3.64; Granino Cecere 1996: 276.

[197] C. J. Smith 2012: 276–8; Simón 2011: 129–30.   [198] Scheid and Granino Cecere 1999: 106.

[199] *CIL* XIV 2228; Granino Cecere 1996: 276–9. Note also *CIL* VI 2174 = *ILS* 5009.

[200] Pliny the Elder, *NH* 3.68–70.   [201] Plut. *Rom.* 16.1–4; *CIL* X 809 = *ILS* 64.

[202] Cf. Scheid 2005: 180–1, arguing that Augustus was the emperor who changed the priestly college.

[203] See the *fasti* in Scheid and Granino Cecere 1999: 151–5.

[204] Camodeca 1981: 54–5; Scheid and Granino Cecere 1999: 99–100. There are two examples of *equites* appointed to the priesthood prior to their elevation into the senatorial order (*CIL* XI 2699 = *ILS* 5013; *CIL* XI 3103).

religious colleges, we can detect the same motivation behind the creation of an equestrian priesthood: the desire to give the *ordo equester* a role to play in significant ceremonies and rituals of the state that befitted its status as a constituent body of the *res publica*.

This connection was fostered by post-Augustan emperors, such as Claudius and Antoninus Pius, who saw the value in providing equestrians with a part in religious ceremonies that celebrated the foundation of Rome. It invested *equites* from a range of provincial backgrounds in the religion of the monarchical *res publica*. But there is also an element of the imperial domestication of provincial elites at work here (returning to themes which we discussed in earlier chapters).[205] All the Latin priesthoods, as offices of the *res publica*, were formally in the gift of the emperor.[206] This is indicated by the epitaph of the former imperial freedman L. Aurelius Nicomedes, who was granted the *equus publicus* by Antoninus Pius and 'distinguished with the priesthood of Caenina and the post of *pontifex minor* by that same man' (*[sac]erdotio Caeniniensi item pontif(icatu) min(ore) exornatus ab eodem*).[207] The transferral of priesthoods associated with Lavinium and Alba Longa to members of the equestrian order created a range of new honours for which these *equites* could compete in a comparable manner to senators. This broadened the variety of rewards in the emperor's gift beyond equestrian procuratorships, thus enabling him to dispense greater numbers of honours to more members of the *ordo*. The material benefits of these priesthoods could include additional privileges, as shown by the example of Veratius Severianus at Cumae. The town decreed that 'since he was protected by the privilege of the priesthood of Caenina, he could easily be excused offices and civic burdens' (*qui cum privilegio sacer|doti Caeninensis munitus potuisset ab honorib(us) et munerib(us) | facile excusari*).[208] The Latin priesthood, as an *honor* of the *res publica*, was so prestigious that it offered immunity from civic duties in another Italian community. The rewards of empire were many, but they were controlled by one man: the emperor.

---

[205] See Chapters 5–7 in particular.   [206] Wissowa 1915: 4–5.

[207] *CIL* VI 1598 = *ILS* 1740; Camodeca 1981: 54; Fishwick 1998: 87. A fragmentary inscription from Falerii has been restored to read *[sacerdos] Caeniniensis a pon[tificibus creatus]* (*CIL* XI 3103), which suggests that the election was technically in the hands of the pontifical college, although imperial influence would have been decisive.

[208] Rüpke 2008: no. 3459; *CIL* X 3704 = *ILS* 5054. For this interpretation of *munitus*, see Wissowa 1915: 6; Solin 2005: 284–5.

Conclusion: Religion and Prestige

This chapter has sought to explain why new priesthoods were created for, or transferred to, members of the *ordo equester* during the imperial age. These included the *luperci* who ran in the Lupercalia, and the junior *pontifices* and *flamines* of the pontifical college in Rome, all of which were made into equestrian priesthoods by Augustus; the *Laurentes Lavinates* of Lavinium, which were allocated to the *equites* by Claudius; and the Alban priesthoods, which became equestrian at some point in the first century AD. We have argued that these changes can be ascribed to the new monarchical form of the *res publica*, in which it became important to emphasise the continuity of Roman religion, and the connections between the past, present and future of the Roman state. By positioning the members of the *ordo equester* as mediators between human and divine alongside the senators, Augustus and his successors ensured that both aristocratic *ordines* were integrated into the monarchical *res publica*. This had the effect of writing the equestrian order into the events of Rome's foundational legends, associating them with figures such as Aeneas, Romulus and the Dioscuri, their patron deities, making them seem like an inseparable part of the state. This complemented other efforts of the imperial regime to incorporate the *ordo equester* into the framework of the *res publica* through ceremonies, privileges and performances, which we explored in Chapters 8 and 9. These included the creation of the office of *princeps iuventutis*, the honours granted to the imperial princes in parades and at the theatre, and the regulation of moral standards for *equites* to ensure that they were distinguished from the people at large. The creation of equestrian priesthoods not only had the effect of adding further legitimacy to the religious ceremonies of the state that involved the emperor and his family, it also ensured that the equestrian order was not perceived as a new creation of late second and first century BC, but an inherent and timeless component of the *res publica*.

The festival of the Lupercalia offered the most striking demonstration of the role of the *ordo equester* in state religion. The connection between *equites* and the *luperci* was largely a product of Augustus' religious programme, even if he may have revitalised earlier associations dating back to the fourth century BC. The dedication of the statue of Drusus in the Lupercal, a new religious 'home' for the *equites* in Rome, bound the imperial family and the *ordo equester* into the narrative of Rome's history. Valerius Maximus, writing under Tiberius, could classify the Lupercalia and the *transvectio equitum* as the two great annual spectacles in which the *equites* took centre stage. While the *transvectio* parade displayed the equestrian youth in formal array, the Lupercalia was more primeval, a ritual which cast the young men as the successors of Romulus and his band. Their near-naked run was both a ceremony of purification and a fertility rite, as their lashing of female spectators promoted the birth of new generations of Romans. This was Augustus' way of demonstrating the importance of the *ordo equester* in Rome's past, and its future place in the system he had created. The college of *luperci* seemed to have drawn most of its members from Rome and its environs, rather than provincials. Eventually this meant that the Lupercalia ceased to be a ritual exclusive to young equestrians, and senators were admitted to its ranks in the third century AD. The fate of the *luperci* as an equestrian priesthood should be contrasted with the endurance of the *transvectio equitum*, which continued into the mid-fourth century AD.[209] The difference between the survival of the two ceremonies may be ascribed to the fact that the *transvectio* remained important as the paradigmatic ceremony of initiation to the *ordo* at large.

The Augustan religious revival extended well beyond the college of *luperci*, as he reserved the positions of the *pontifices minores* and *flamines minores* for members of the equestrian order. Although we know frustratingly little about the duties and precise practices of these priests, it is clear that they offered equestrians a range of new roles in state rituals. Festivals such as the Cerealia and Volcanalia were presided over by their respective equestrian *flamines*, and the *pontifices minores* assisted the *pontifices* in sacrificial rites as junior members of the pontifical college. Equestrians also received the honour of state priesthoods in Latium, Rome's sacred hinterland, which they held both at Lavinium and the sites associated with Alba Longa and the *feriae Latinae*. These priestly colleges were revived (or introduced) over the course of the first century AD. The institution of the priests of *Laurens Lavinas* should be attributed to Claudius. The members of this college of Lavinium ranged from *apparitores* to senior prefects, and came from as far afield as Africa, Gaul and the Balkans. The one common link was that their careers brought them to Rome and to the attention of the emperor. This largely artificial community of *equites* played a part in continuing the religious traditions allegedly started by Aeneas when he brought the Penates from Troy and founded Lavinium. These ritual associations did not fall dormant, but actually increased in

---

[209] See Chapter 8.

significance, as Rome's empire expanded. The critical mass of *equites* attested as priests at Lavinium in the second century AD, when Antoninus Pius lavished patronage on the community, indicates the relevance of Rome's traditions to a heterogeneous aristocracy drawn from both Italy and the provinces.

The increase in the number of priesthoods available to *equites* in the imperial period meant that emperors were able to offer a greater range of honours to members of the *ordo*, extending their benefactions beyond salaried military posts and procuratorships. The conspicuous series of appointments to the post of *pontifex minor* made by the emperor Antoninus Pius from within his own household in the 140s–150s AD demonstrates the importance of imperial favour in securing these religious positions. They were proudly recorded on *cursus* inscriptions carved on honorific statue bases and funerary monuments, often distinguished among the list of administrative offices. The imperial domestication of the aristocracy would not have been effective if priesthoods were not genuinely attractive to *equites* as religious offices (and not solely tokens of favour). We have observed the enthusiasm and expertise that lay behind the preparation of young Roman aristocrats to serve as religious officials, such as the education provided by Statius' father, and the significance of these priesthoods to individual *equites*, as shown by the priestly emblems on the monument of Statilius Optatus, and the careers of religious experts such as Livius Larensis and Flavius Priscus. Under the monarchical *res publica*, *equites* were able to participate in the maintenance of the *pax deorum* alongside members of other *ordines*, from senators to freedmen. For those *equites* who won the favour of the emperor and secured priestly appointments, it amplified not only their personal *dignitas*, but also earned them the favour of the gods. And that, as the monument of Flavius Germanus tells us, was truly *splendidissimus*.

PART IV

The Late Empire

11 | Governors and Generals

Introduction: A Dedication to Gallienus

In the year AD 267 two Roman officials, T. Clementius Silvius and Valerius Marcellinus, dedicated an altar to the *genius* of the emperor Gallienus at Aquincum, the provincial capital of Pannonia Inferior. The inscription on the monument reads as follows:

> To the *genius* of the Emperor [[Publius Licinius Gallienus]], Unconquered Augustus, Clementius Silvius, *vir egregius*, acting in place of the governor, and Valerius Marcellinus, prefect of the legion, protector of our Augustus, acting in place of the legate, both residents of the province of Raetia, released their vow freely, happily, and deservedly, when Paternus and Archesilaus were consuls.[1]

Although in some respects this text is a typical expression of devotion towards the emperor, the inscription also reveals a dramatic change in the administrative structure of the Roman imperial state. For Pannonia Inferior had traditionally been administered by senatorial legates, and from the reign of Caracalla these governors had been of consular standing.[2] Yet here we have Clementius Silvius, an equestrian *vir egregius*, who is recorded with the title A. V. P., an abbreviation which is to be expanded as *a(gens) v(ice) p(raesidis)*, 'acting in place of the governor'. Valerius Marcellinus, the commander of the *legio II Adiutrix*, is no senatorial general of praetorian status, but a legionary prefect of equestrian rank, described as *a(gens) v(ice) l(egati)*, 'acting in place of the legate'. The appointment of Silvius and Marcellinus to positions hitherto reserved for senators is emblematic of the sweeping changes in the upper echelons of the Roman army and administration in the middle of the third century AD. By the age of the Tetrarchs the majority of provincial governors would be

---

[1] *CIL* III 3424 = *ILS* 545: *Genio | Imp(eratoris) [[P(ubli) Lic(ini) Gallieni]] | Invicti Aug(usti) | Clementius | Silvius v(ir) e(gregius) a(gens) v(ice) p(raesidis) et | Val(erius) Marcellinus | praef(ectus) leg(ionis) prot(ector) | Aug(usti) n(ostri) a(gens) v(ice) l(egati) municipes | ex provincia | Raetia s(olverunt) l(ibentes) l(aeti) m(erito) | Paterno et | Archesilao co(n)s(ulibus).*

[2] A. R. Birley 1981: 26 n. 6.

equites with the rank of *vir perfectissimus*. Senators ceased to command troops in battle, and were replaced by equestrian officers. How did such a transformation come about?

The senator Aurelius Victor, author of the potted history *On the Caesars*, was the only ancient historian who ventured an explanation. Writing in the mid-fourth century AD, he was in no doubt that the end of senatorial military careers should be ascribed to the emperor Gallienus:

> And to add to the problems throughout the Roman world, the senators were insulted by an affront to their own order, because the emperor Gallienus was the first to exclude the senate from military commands and enlistment in the army, because he feared that through his own negligence, the empire would be transferred into the hands of the best of the nobles.[3]

Victor's negative portrait of Gallienus largely adheres to that of the Latin historiographical tradition, in which the emperor is derided as a lazy, profligate and debauched ruler who oversaw the breakup of the Roman empire. If we follow his interpretation, Gallienus excluded senators from their army commands because he feared they would use their positions to unseat him. Victor later revisited the measure, which he dubbed the 'edict of Gallienus' (*edictum Gallieni*), in his account of the short-lived emperor Tacitus, who reigned briefly in AD 275-6.[4] In a pointed diatribe on senatorial excess, he blamed the members of the *amplissimus ordo* for their failure to assert their rights to military command under Tacitus, which 'paved the way for themselves and their descendants to be ruled by the soldiers, and almost by the barbarians'.[5] Of course, it hardly makes sense that senators could pose a vital challenge to Gallienus' authority in the 260s, only to abandon themselves to leisure merely a decade later. This disjointed argument highlights the deficiencies of Victor's work, which combined a brief résumé of each emperor's reign with moralising judgements on social and political changes.[6]

In the face of such a problem the epigraphic evidence offers more positive, but still tentative, guidance regarding the nature of the changes.

---

[3] Victor, *Caes.* 33.33–4: *et patres quidem praeter commune Romani malum orbis stimulabat proprii ordinis contumelia, quia primus ipse metu socordiae suae, ne imperium ad optimos nobilium transferretur, senatum militia vetuit et adire exercitum.*

[4] As Le Bohec 2004: 124 notes, there was no need for Gallienus to issue a formal edict on the matter, since he could decide whom to appoint to military positions. Tacitus himself was probably a former senatorial general (Davenport 2014a), but there is no evidence that he tried to reverse the changes.

[5] Victor, *Caes.* 37.5–7: *munivere militaribus et paene barbaris viam in se ac posteros dominandi.*

[6] Bird 1984: 90–9. On the 'edict of Gallenius', see the recent discussions of Le Bohec 2004; Handy 2006; Cosme 2007.

It shows that no senator is attested in the post of *legatus legionis* after the sole reign of Gallienus (AD 260–8). Yet the epigraphic evidence does not provide the clear-cut confirmation of Victor's statement for which we might have hoped. There are three reasons for this. The first is that senators continue to be attested as governors of consular provinces in which legions were stationed, such as Syria Coele, into the last decades of the third century AD. In some provinces both equestrian *perfectissimi* and senatorial *clarissimi* are found as governors, without any apparent consistency in appointments. Senatorial governors in these regions still had administrative and logistical control over troops, even if they did not lead them into battle. The second reason is that equestrian acting governors with the title of *agens vice praesidis* are attested several decades before the reign of Gallienus. The third and final reason is that there are changes in the army hierarchy earlier in the third century AD which presage some of the later reforms. This has led scholars to argue that equestrians began to replace senators in these posts much earlier in the third century AD, and that Gallienus' decision was merely the climax of a pre-existing trend. This replacement of senatorial legionary legates and governors by appointees of equestrian rank has been conventionally referred to as the 'rise of the *equites*', a model that carries with it a range of assumptions regarding imperial preference for *equites* over senators.[7] Recent scholars have rightly questioned the validity of this rather triumphalist phrase as a way of describing the developments of the period.[8] For, as this chapter will show, the second and third centuries AD witnessed a series of interrelated changes in the hierarchy of the Roman army and administration. These came to a head in the 250s and 260s AD during the reigns of Valerian and Gallienus, when a series of military setbacks and usurpations provided the catalyst for a significant transformation of the army hierarchy.

Pragmatic Administration and Status Hierarchies

The first significant development revealed by the dedication at Aquincum is the title of the governor of Pannonia Inferior, T. Clementius Silvius. He is recorded as V. E. A. V. P., an abbreviation which can be expanded as *v(ir) e(gregius) a(gens) v(ice) p(raesidis)*, '*vir egregius*, acting in place of the *praeses*'. *Praeses* (pl. *praesides*) was a generic term for governor, which was used for senatorial legates and proconsuls as well as equestrian

---

[7] Keyes 1915; Osier 1974. [8] Christol 1999; Heil 2008a.

praesidial procurators.[9] Silvius' official title, incorporated into the dedication to Gallienus, referred to him as a substitute for the *praeses*. The use of an abbreviated formula indicates that the title would be widely known and understood by potential readers.

The roots of this development lie in earlier appointments of acting governors. Such stand-in administrators are attested rarely in the first century AD. They were usually appointed when the governor unexpectedly died in office.[10] When the proconsul of Achaea passed away in AD 6, it was decided (either by the emperor or senate, we are not told) that his quaestor and legate should partition the province between them, with the Isthmus of Corinth forming the dividing line.[11] The precedent was followed when the governor of Crete and Cyrene suddenly expired in AD 15 under Tiberius.[12] This was a pragmatic solution to the problem, since it was clearly preferable to deputise officials already based in the province than to arrange the selection of a replacement proconsul in Rome. Tiberius' decision to select an imperial freedman, Hiberus, to take charge of Egypt following the death of Vitrasius Pollio in AD 32, was more unorthodox.[13] This appointment emphasises that all provincial commands were essentially in the gift of the emperor, who could override the usual divisions of responsibilities between senators, equestrians and freedmen. This was the essence of a monarchical *res publica*: the state could be continually reshaped by the emperor.

The first attested example of an equestrian serving in place of a senatorial governor occurred in Asia during the proconsular year AD 87/88. C. Minicius Italus, the procurator of Asia, replaced the proconsul C. Vettulenus Civica Cerialis, who had been charged with fomenting revolution against the emperor Domitian.[14] The inscribed account of Italus' career from Aquileia states that he was 'procurator of the province of Asia, which he administered on the order of the emperor in place of the proconsul who had died' (*proc(urator) provinciae Asiae quam | mandatu principis vice defuncti proco(n)s(ulis) rexit*).[15] This detailed formulation highlights the exceptional circumstances in which Italus was promoted,

---

[9] *OLD* s.v. *praeses* 2; *Dig.* 1.18.1 (Macer).   [10] Peachin 1996: 154–6.

[11] Dio 55.27.6. On the selection of quaestors and *legati pro praetore*, see Dio 53.14.5–7, with Swan 2004: 186–7 on Dio's terminology.

[12] Dio 57.14.3.

[13] Dio 58.19.6. Hiberus may be identical with Severus, attested as acting governor by Philo, *In Flaccum* 1.2.

[14] Suet. *Dom.* 10.2. B. W. Jones 1992: 182–3 connects his downfall with the appearance of a false Nero in Asia.

[15] *CIL* V 875 = *ILS* 1374; Pflaum 1960: 141–3 (no. 59).

and the fact that his temporary elevation came on the explicit orders of the emperor.[16] There would have been other senatorial officials in Asia who could have replaced Cerialis, since the proconsul was entitled to three senatorial *legati*. They may not have merited consideration by Domitian because they were implicated in Cerialis' treasonous plans. Alternatively, their term of office could have been close to completion, meaning that the equestrian procurator was the most logical choice.[17] The execution of a senatorial legate early in Hadrian's reign led to the appointment of another equestrian, Q. Marcius Turbo, to take temporary command of the provinces of Dacia and Pannonia Inferior.[18] Turbo was kept in office until AD 119/120, during which time he supervised the reorganisation of the Dacian provinces.[19] Although Turbo was an *eques*, he was a trusted associate of Hadrian, and his promotion came at a time when the emperor felt he lacked friends in high places.

The temporary elevations of Minicius Italus and Marcius Turbo, although they set precedents for *equites* to act in place of senatorial governors, did not signal the beginning of a new trend at the time. In the imperial provinces emperors often chose to promote a *legatus legionis* or other senatorial official to act as governor if the incumbent had been removed. This is what happened in Syria c. AD 97/98, when the errant consular legate M. Cornelius Nigrinus Curiatius Maternus was removed from office, and A. Larcius Priscus, commander of the *legio IV Scythica*, served 'in place of the consular legate' (*pro legato consulare*).[20] When Commodus dismissed the consular Ulpius Marcellus from the governorship of Britain in the AD 180s, he appointed the *iuridicus* M. Antius Crescens Calpurnianus as acting governor.[21] Just as senatorial officials proved to be natural acting governors in senatorial provinces, so it was the case that an *eques* usually deputised for the prefect of Egypt. In AD 175 Marcus Aurelius dismissed the prefect, C. Calvisius Statianus, and sent him into exile because he had supported the rebellion of C. Avidius Cassius.[22] In place of Statianus, Marcus appointed C. Caecilius Salvianus, who was already stationed in the Egypt as the senior judicial officer, known as the

---

[16] Syme 1957a: 313 suggests that Italus was also responsible for executing the proconsul.
[17] On the *legati*, see Dio 54.14.7.
[18] *HA Hadr.* 6.7, 7.1, 7.3; Pflaum 1960: 199–216 (no. 94); A. R. Birley 1997: 86–8.
[19] Syme 1962: 87–8; A. R. Birley 1997: 86–91. For the dates of his tenure, see Eck and Pangerl 2011: 241 n. 17.
[20] *AE* 1908, 237; *CIL* VIII 17891= *ILS* 1055. For this particular crisis, see Alföldy and Halfmann 1973.
[21] *CIL* VI 1336 = *ILS* 1151; A. R. Birley 2005: 170–1.   [22] Dio 72(71).28.2–4.

dikaiodotes or *iuridicus Alexandreae*.[23] In a petition from AD 176 Salvianus is formally addressed as '*vir egregius dikaiodotes*, acting in the governor's position' (τῷ κρατίστῳ δικαιοδότῃ, διαδεχομένῳ καὶ τὰ κατὰ τὴν ἡγεμονίαν).[24] Salvianus was the logical replacement for the disgraced Statianus: the *dikaiodotes* was a procurator of ducenarian rank and the second most senior administrative official in Egypt after the prefect himself.[25] These examples of acting appointments all maintained the accepted status hierarchy within senatorial and equestrian provinces.

One important development of the second century AD was the employment of acting governors while the existing governor was still alive. This occurred in times of serious warfare, when the governor was required to be absent from the province temporarily. The first recorded example comes from AD 132, when C. Iulius Severus, legate of the *legio IV Scythica*, was 'managing affairs in Syria when Publicius Marcellus departed from Syria on account of the Jewish disturbance' (διοικήσαντα τὰ ἐν | Συρίᾳ πράγματα, ἡνίκα Που|βλίκιος Μάρκελλος διὰ τὴν κίν(η)|σιν τὴν Ἰουδαικὴν μεταβεβήκει | ἀπὸ Συρίας).[26] This is a clear reference to the circumstances of the Bar Kokhba revolt, which stretched Roman military resources to the limit, and necessitated Marcellus travelling from Syria with the *legio III Gallica* to aid in the war effort.[27] A similar appointment was made in the early AD 170s, during Marcus Aurelius' northern wars, when C. Vettius Sabinianus Iulius Hospes, legionary legate of the *legio XIV Gemina*, was invested 'with jurisdiction over Pannonia Superior' (*cum iurisdicatu Panno|niae superioris*).[28] This temporary promotion was made necessary by the fact that the legate of Pannonia Superior was on campaign with the emperor.[29] The crucial word here is *iurisdicatus*, which suggests that Hospes' primary responsibility was to ensure continuity in legal administration while the governor was absent. This would set an important precedent for the third century AD, to which we will return shortly.

At end of the second and the beginning of third century AD it became much more common to appoint an equestrian procurator to act *vice praesidis*, regardless of whether the province in question was normally

---

[23] Schwartz 1976: 101. For the office of *dikaiodotes/iuridicus Alexandreae*, see Kupiszewski 1954.
[24] *BGU* 1.327 = *M. Chr.* 61.   [25] Stein 1950: 169–71; Kupiszewski 1954: 190–1.
[26] *IGR* III 174 = *I. Ankara* 74. The same wording is found on *IGR* III 175 = *I. Ankara* 75; *AE* 2006, 1476 = *I. Ankara* 76.
[27] A. R. Birley 1997: 268; Eck 1999b: 83.   [28] *AE* 1920, 45 = *ILAfr.* 281.
[29] A. R. Birley 1993: 176.

governed by senators or equestrians. (These examples are collected in Table 11.1). In short, it was the model of Minicius Italus, the procurator-turned-acting-proconsul from the reign of Domitian, that was favoured. This is what happened in Africa in AD 202, after the death of the proconsul, T. Salvius Rufinus Minicius Opimianus.[30] The *Passion of Perpetua and Felicitas* referred to his replacement as 'Hilarianus the procurator, who at that time had received the right of the sword in the place of the proconsul . . . who had died' (*Hilarianus procurator, qui tunc loco proconsulis . . . defuncti ius gladii acceperat*).[31] This official has been identified with P. Aelius Hilarianus, and his office as the *procurator IIII publicorum Africae* ('procurator for administering the four state taxes in Africa').[32] The *Passion* employs Roman juridical language in the correct technical manner. The *ius gladii* refers to the right to sentence Roman citizens to death. This supreme judicial authority was invested in all senatorial and equestrian provincial governors by virtue of their office, as we saw in Chapter 7. The majority of equestrian procurators did not possess this criminal jurisdiction, although they did have judicial author-ity in other areas, such as financial cases.[33] Therefore, in order for Hilarianus to truly act in place of the proconsul, he needed to be officially granted the *ius gladii* by the emperor. The language is paralleled by two inscribed careers, which also date from the Severan period, in which equestrian procurators are recorded as receiving the *ius gladii*. C. Titius Similis is described as 'procurator of the province of Moesia Inferior, holding the *ius gladii* in the same province' (*proc(uratori) prov(inciae) Misiae inferio|ris eiusdem provinciae ius gladii*), while L. Artorius Castus is styled 'procurator *centenarius* of Liburnia with the *ius gladii*' (*proc(urator) cente|nario* [sic] *provinciae Li[burniae iure] gladi(i)*).[34] The technical language suggests that Similis and Castus served as acting governors of Moesia Inferior and Dalmatia, respectively, replacing the senatorial legate in both cases.

---

[30] See Barnes 2010: 305–6; Heffernan 2012: 50–1 for his identity.

[31] *Pass. Perp.* 6.3. The name of the proconsul is omitted here, as it is incorrectly given in the text as Minucius Timinianus, instead of Minicius Opimianus.

[32] Rives 1996: 4; Heffernan 2012: 49–50.

[33] Millar 1965b: 365–6; Eich 2005: 137–45. The *dikaiodotes/iuridicus Alexandreae* was an exception to this, since he always possessed full jurisdiction, which was invested in him by the emperor (Kupiszewski 1954: 191–202).

[34] Similis: *CIL* II 484 = *ILS* 1372; Pflaum 1960: 856–8 (no. 330). Castus: *CIL* III 1919 = *ILS* 2770; Pflaum 1960: 535–7 (no. 196). Sometimes the *ius gladii* was granted to senatorial and equestrian commanders of expeditionary forces, reflecting their higher authority. See *CIL* VIII 20996 = *ILS* 1356 (T. Licinius Hierocles); *CIL* VIII 2582 = *ILS* 1111 (A. Iulius Pompilius Piso).

Table 11.1 *Equestrians acting as governors in senatorial provinces (AD 161–260)*[35]

Date	Name	Acting governor of	Original position	References
198/209	Herennius Gemellinus	Dacia	Procurator	*CIL* III 1625
198/209 or 244/249	Aelius Aglaus	Asia	Procurator	Keil and von Premerstein 1914 no. 55
202	Hilarianus	Africa	Procurator	*Pass. Perp.* 6.3; cf. Tert. *Scap.* 3.1
c.218	C. Furius Sabinius Aquila Timesitheus	Arabia (twice)	Procurator	*CIL* XIII 1807 = *ILS* 1330
c.220	M. Aedinius Iulianus	Lugdunensis	Unknown	*CIL* XIII 3162
221/222	Flavius Sossianus	Numidia	Unknown	*AE* 1995, 1641
Severus Alexander	Badius Comnianus	Lugdunensis	Procurator	*CIL* XIII 3162
225/229	Modius Terventinus	Moesia Inferior	(Procurator?)	Pflaum 1960 no. 317
c.233/235	C. Furius Sabinius Aquila Timesitheus	Germania Inferior	*Procurator patrimonii* of Belgica and the two Germanies	*CIL* XIII 1807 = *ILS* 1330
c.235/236	C. Furius Sabinius Aquila Timesitheus	Pontus and Bithynia	*Procurator patrimonii et rationis privatae* of Bithynia, Pontus, Paphlagonia	*CIL* XIII 1807 = *ILS* 1330[36]

[35] This table depends on earlier lists by Pflaum 1950: 134–5 and Peachin 1996: 229–36, and the *fasti* in Gerhardt and Hartmann 2008. I have excluded several possible cases:

(1) The *procurator ducenarius* who heard the case of Martialis in Hispania Citerior under Decius (Cypr. *Ep.* 67.6.2) could have been conducting a preliminary hearing rather than delivering a sentence (Clarke 1989: 155).

(2) Sex. Acilius Fuscus, procurator of Lugdunensis around AD 258/9. The inscription (*AE* 1934, 161 = *CIL* VI 40704) was originally restored as *proc. Auggg. [n]nn. et [vice praesidis agens]*, but was later read by Alföldy (*CIL* VI *ad loc.*) as *proc. Auggg. [n]nn. et cen[sitore]*.

(3) Appius Alexander (*AE* 2003, 1672 = *SEG* 53, 1329), the procurator of Asia who became *praeses* of Lugdunensis. He was not necessarily acting *vice praesidis* in Lugdunensis: he could have been adlected into the senate.

(4) T. Livius Larensis describes his procuratorship of Moesia in a way that might suggest he was also acting governor, but this is uncertain (Ath. *Deip.* 398E).

[36] This assumes that the correct reading of the stone is *item vice <praes(idis)>*. See Gerhardt and Hartmann 2008: 1167.

Table 11.1 (*cont.*)

Date	Name	Acting governor of	Original position	References
*c.*238/239	C. Furius Sabinius Aquila Timesitheus	Asia	Procurator	*CIL* XIII 1807 = *ILS* 1130
236/238	Q. Axius Aelianus	Dacia (twice)	Procurator of Dacia Apulensis	*CIL* III 1456 = *ILS* 1371
*c.*239/240	P. Aelius Hammonius	Moesia Inferior	Procurator	*IGR* 1.623 = *ILS* 8851
*c.*245/247	Ae[l]ius Fir[mus?]	Macedonia	Procurator of Macedonia	*CIL* VI 41281
*c.*245/247	Ae[l]ius Fir[mus?]	Unknown province	Procurator	*CIL* VI 41281
*c.*244/247	L. Titinius Clodianus	Numidia	Procurator of Numidia	*AE* 1911, 100 = *ILS* 9490; *CIL* VIII 8328–9
245	C. Iulius Priscus	Syria Coele	Prefect of Mesopotamia	*P. Euphr.* 1; cf. Zos. 1.19.2
244/249 (c. 247?)	Marcellus	Syria Coele	Unknown	*P. Euphr.* 2
244/249 (?)	Ulpius [–]	Dacia	Procurator of Dacia Apulensis	*CIL* III 1464 = *ILS* 1370 = *AE* 1980, 758
252/256	Pomponius Laetianus	Syria Coele	Procurator	*P. Euphr.* 3–4; *P. Dura* 97
251/253	Aurelius Marcus	Dacia	Procurator	*AE* 1983, 815, 841
*c.*253/260	Iulius Iulianus	Phrygia and Caria	Procurator	*SEG* 32, 1287
*c.*258/9	Ignotus	Africa	Procurator	*Pass. Mont. et Luc.* 6.1
early IIIc.	L. Artorius Castus	Dalmatia?	Procurator of Liburnia	*CIL* III 1919
early IIIc.	Caecilius Arellianus	Cilicia	*Procurator rationis privatae* in Cilicia	*AE* 1924, 83 = *I. Eph.* 3054
early IIIc.	C. Titius Similis	Moesia Inferior	Procurator of Moesia Inferior	*CIL* II 484 = *ILS* 1372
mid-IIIc.	C. Iulius Senecio	Galatia and Pontus	Procurator of Galatia	*CIL* III 251 = *ILS* 1373 = *I. Ankara* 53; *AE* 1930, 144 = *I. Ankara* 54[37]

[37] He may be identical with the Senecio attested as governor of Bithynia and Pontus in AD 259 (Gerhardt and Hartmann 2008: 1168–9).

Table 11.1 (*cont.*)

Date	Name	Acting governor of	Original position	References
mid-IIIc.	M. Aurelius Tuesianus	Dacia	Procurator of Dacia Apulensis	*AE* 1979, 506
mid-IIIc.	[Ma]gnius Donatus	Baetica	Procurator	*CIL* II.5 1167
mid-IIIc.	M. Aurelius Alexander	Baetica	Procurator	*CIL* II.7 259

In the legal evidence the procurator acting *vice praesidis* first appears in constitutions of the emperor Caracalla. In AD 212 the emperor wrote to a certain Valerius in response to a complaint about the validity of his punishment, stating: 'My procurator, who was not acting in place of the governor, could not enforce the penalty of exile on you' (*procurator meus, qui vice praesidis non fungebatur, exilii poenam tibi non potuit inrogare*).[38] In another rescript dated to AD 215, Caracalla declared that 'my procurator, who is not acting in place of the governor of the province' (*procurator meus, qui vice praesidis provinciae non fungitur*) could not impose a penalty, but was empowered to collect one that had already been laid down.[39] The administrative concept of the acting governor also featured in Ulpian's work *On the Office of Proconsul*, written in AD 213.[40] In the ninth book the jurist discussed the ability of officials to hear cases under the *lex Fabia*: 'In the provinces, this right of jurisdiction belongs to the governors of the provinces, but it does not belong to the emperor's procurator, except if he is discharging the office of the governor in the province.'[41] All these examples are largely negative, referring to what a procurator could not do under normal circumstances. However, by comparing the authority of regular procurators with those empowered to act in the governor's place, these texts reveal that the procurator *vice praesidis* was an established legal and administrative concept by the reign of Caracalla.

---

[38] *CJ* 9.47.2 (AD 212).   [39] *CJ* 3.26.3 (AD 215).
[40] The date is discussed by Honoré 2002: 181–4.
[41] *Coll.* 14.3.2: *in provincia est praesidum provinciarum, nec aliter procuratori Caesaris haec cognitio iniungitur, quam si praesidis partibus in provincia fungatur.* For later rulings of Gordian III on the authority of procurators acting *vice praesidis*, see *CJ* 9.20.4 (AD239), 1.50.1 (AD 240), 3.3.1 (AD 242).

This had probably been the case for at least the previous decade, judging from Hilarianus' appointment as acting governor in Africa AD 202. This is supported by a votive inscription from Dacia, dated to AD 198/209, in which the procurator Herennius Gemellinus is styled '*vir egregius*, procurator of our emperors, acting in place of the governor' (*v(iro) e(gregio) proc(uratore)* | *Augg(ustorum) nn(ostrorum)* | *agente v(ice) p(raesidis)*).[42] The fact that his office could be abbreviated to AGENTE V. P. on the stone indicates that the composer(s) of the text thought that potential readers would be able to readily understand that it should be expanded to read *v(ice) p(raesidis)*, the same term used by Caracalla in his rescripts.[43] One particularly interesting example can be found in a petition from workers on an imperial estate near Philadelphia in Lydia. They complained to two emperors (probably Severus and Caracalla) about the harassment they had received from Roman soldiers.[44] The workers declared that nine of their number had been arrested and sent 'to the procurators of *egregius* status, since the *vir egregius* Aelius Aglaus was discharging the office of the proconsul' (ἐπὶ τοὺς κρατίστους ἐπιτρόπ[ους] | [τοὺς ὑμ] ετέρους διέποντ<ο>ς Αἰλίου Ἀγλαοῦ [τοῦ] | [κρατίσ]του καὶ τὰ τῆς ἀνθυπατείας μέρη).[45] Precise and technical language defines Aglaus' position, using the Greek equivalent of the Latin terminology employed by Ulpian in *On the Office of Proconsul*.[46] The evidence therefore indicates that the appointment of equestrian procurators as acting governors through an official grant of the *ius gladii* had become an accepted administrative practice by the time of the reigns of Septimius Severus and his son Caracalla.

Equestrian procurators are attested acting *vice praesidis* in provinces of both equestrian and senatorial status throughout the following decades of the third century AD.[47] We will deal with each type of province in turn in order to determine why *equites* were chosen, beginning with regions normally governed by equestrian prefects or procurators, as laid out in Table 11.2. In Egypt, as we have already seen, the *dikaiodotes* was the natural choice to deputise for the prefect, since this official already possessed full criminal jurisdiction. But we also find Q. Agrius Rusticianus, the *procurator*

---

[42] *CIL* III 1625 = *IDR* III.2 342; Pflaum 1960: 688 (no. 254). [43] Peachin 1996: 156.

[44] The emperors are either Septimius Severus and Caracalla, or Philip the Arab and his son (Hauken 1998: 42–3, 46).

[45] Keil and von Premerstein 1914: no. 55 = Hauken 1998: no. 3, ll. 6–8.

[46] Mason 1974: 131–2. Ulpian used the plural *partes* to mean function (*OLD* s.v. *pars* 10). Its Greek equivalent was μέρη (*LSJ* s.v. μέρος).

[47] For the standing of provinces at the end of the Severan period, see Glas and Hartmann 2008: 642.

Table 11.2 *Equestrians in acting positions in equestrian provinces (AD 161–260)*

Date	Name	Acting Governor of	Original Position	References
176	C. Caecilius Salvianus	Egypt	*Dikaiodotes (Iuridicus)*	*BGU* 1.327
Severus/ Caracalla	Q. Agrius Rusticianus	Mauretania Caesariensis / Procurator gentium	*Procurator rationis privatae* in Mauretania Caesariensis	*AE* 2003, 1933
After 212	Ignotus	Egypt	*Dikaiodotes (Iuridicus)*	*BGU* 7.1578; Parsons 1967 138 n. 46
215–16	Aurelius Antinous	Egypt	*Dikaiodotes (Iuridicus)*	*P. Oxy.* 33.2671, 47.3347; *W. Chr.* 207, 209
218–19	Callistianus	Egypt	*Dikaiodotes (Iuridicus)*	*P. Oxy.* 43.3117
224/225	Ti. Claudius Herennianus	Egypt	*Dikaiodotes (Iuridicus)*	*P. Harr.* 1.68; *P. Oxy* 34.2705; *P. Oxy.* 42.3076
c. 247–9 or 250–2	Ae[l]ius Fir[mus]	Egypt	*Dikaiodotes (Iuridicus)*	*CIL* VI 41281 = *ILS* 1331
252	Lissenius Proculus	Egypt	*Dikaiodotes (Iuridicus)*	*PSI* 7.870; *P. Oxy.* 42.3050
257–9	L. Mussius Aemilianus	Egypt	Uncertain	*P. Stras.* 5.392–3; *P. Oxy.* 9.1201, 43.3112

rationis privatae of Mauretania Caesariensis, acting in place of the equestrian praesidial procurator in the Severan period. This appointment must have required a grant of the *ius gladii*.[48]

We now turn to the people's provinces, which were governed by senatorial proconsuls of praetorian or consular rank. The proconsuls were accompanied by senatorial *legati pro praetore* and quaestors, who had been the first choice as substitute governors when proconsuls died in the Julio-Claudian period. This practice was not entirely abandoned in the third century AD. Although an equestrian procurator replaced the proconsul of Africa on two occasions (in AD 202 and AD 258/9), there are also

---

[48] *AE* 2003, 1933. Cf. Pflaum 1960: 790–1 (no. 305), an entry written before the discovery of the new inscription.

two senatorial acting governors of the province, Q. Aradius Rufinus Optatus Aelianus and L. Caesonius Lucillus Macer Rufinianus. Aelianus' status prior to his appointment is unknown, but Rufinianus was certainly in Africa already as a legate (see Table 11.3). The thought process that lay behind the decision whether to appoint a legate or a procurator as acting governor is uncertain. It could have depended on factors such as the emperor's relationship with the appointees, or even the time of year at which an acting governor was required. The quaestors and *legati pro praetore* were usually only attached to a specific proconsul, and thus their term expired at the end of the governor's year of office.[49] Procurators were not bound by the timetable of senatorial appointments; hence they could oversee justice and administration until the next proconsul arrived from Rome.[50] In the other proconsulates in which acting governors are known (Asia, Macedonia, Baetica), procurators were preferred to senatorial legates.[51]

We shall now turn to imperial provinces, governed by praetorian and consular *legati Augusti pro praetore*. There were no senatorial officials stationed in the provinces without legions apart from the governors

Table 11.3 *Senators in acting positions in senatorial provinces or offices (AD 161–260)*

Date	Name	Acting as	Original Position	References
Early 170s	C. Vettius Sabinianus Iulius Hospes	Governor of Pannonia Superior	Legionary legate of *legio XIV Gemina*	*AE* 1920, 45 = *ILAfr.* 281
c.185	M. Antius Crescens Calpurnianus	Governor of Britannia	*Iuridicus* of Britannia	*CIL* VI 41177
217/218 or 238	Q. Aradius Rufinus Optatus Aelianus	Proconsul of ʹAfrica	Unknown	*AE* 1971, 490
c.218	Ignotus (= T. Clodius Aurelius Saturninus?)	Legionary Legate · of *legio VII Gemina*[52]	*Iuridicus* of Hispania Citerior	*AE* 1957, 161 = *I. Eph.* 817

---

[49] A. R. Birley 1981: 12–13, 17.   [50] For the proconsular year, see Talbert 1984: 497–8.
[51] See Table 11.1 for the individual cases and references.
[52] The text is restored as *iuridico* | *[prov(inciae) Hisp(aniae) ci]terioris vice <leg(ati)> legionis*. See Alföldy 1969b: 109.

Table 11.3 (*cont.*)

Date	Name	Acting as	Original Position	References
218/225	L. Iulius Apronius Maenius Pius Salamallianus	Governor of Belgica	*Legatus Augusti*	*AE* 1917/18, 51; *CIL* VIII 18270 = *ILS* 1196
230	L. Caesonius Lucillus Macer Rufinianus	Proconsul of Africa	*Legatus pro praetore* of Africa	*CIL* XIV 3902 = *ILS* 1186; *CIL* VIII 26262 = *AE* 2001, 2086 = *AE* 2006, 1688
238/244	[-]us Annianus	Legionary Legate	Military tribune	*CIL* XIII 6763 = *ILS* 1188

themselves, which made an equestrian procurator the most logical choice for an acting *praeses*. In Cilicia it was the *procurator rationis privatae* Caecilius Arellianus who was 'entrusted with the functions of the governor' (τὰ μέρη τῆς | ἡγεμονίας ἐνχειρισθέντα).[53] Badius Comnianus, the procurator who acted *vice praesidis* in Lugdunensis under Severus Alexander, is not given his full title.[54] But he can be plausibly identified as the ducenarian procurator responsible for both Lugdunensis and Aquitania.[55] There is one exception to this pattern: a senator was chosen as governor in Belgica for unknown reasons in the Severan period.[56] In other imperial provinces with no legions, an equestrian procurator was regularly selected as a replacement (Lugdunensis, Dalmatia, Pontus and Bithynia, Phrygia and Caria, Galatia and Pontus).[57] The same point about the lack of senatorial officials can be made about the imperial provinces in which one legion was stationed. In these regions the *legatus legionis* doubled as the provincial governor, leaving the equestrian procurator as the only sensible deputy.[58] When Elagabalus executed Pica Caesianus, legate of the *legio III Cyrenaica* and governor of Arabia in AD 218, it was necessary to turn to C. Furius Sabinius Aquila Timesitheus, the procurator of Arabia, as a temporary replacement.[59] Timesitheus stepped

---

[53] *AE* 1924, 83 = *I. Eph.* 3054.   [54] *CIL* XIII 3162.   [55] Pflaum 1961: 1053.

[56] L. Iulius Apronius Maenius Pius Salamallianus: *AE* 1917/18, 51; *CIL* VIII 18270 = *ILS* 1196. It is generally assumed that *legati Augusti pro praetore* needs to be understood between *vice* and *quinque fascium* (Cotton 2000: 223–5).

[57] See Table 11.1 for the detailed evidence.   [58] Piso 1999: 335.

[59] Dio 80(79).3.4–5. For Timesitheus, see *CIL* XIII 1807 = *ILS* 1330; Pflaum 1960: 811–21 (no. 317).

into the governor's office until a new senator, Flavius Iulianus, was installed as imperial legate.[60]

This brings us to consular imperial provinces, in which there were two or three legions stationed, and thus senatorial *legati* available to act for the governor. Indeed, in the first and second centuries AD it seems to have been accepted practice to employ a legionary legate when the governor died or was on campaign, as we saw above. There was a definite change in the third century AD, when one equestrian is attested acting *vice praesidis* in Germania Inferior; three in Moesia Inferior and Syria Coele, respectively; and five in Dacia.[61] This can only be ascribed to a conscious decision to choose procurators over legionary legates. I would therefore suggest that the emperor and his administration decided that the procurator, since he could be invested with the *ius gladii*, could take care of judicial affairs, in order to leave the legionary legates free for campaigning. An analogy can be found in the appointment of separate senatorial *iuridici* in Britain, which usually occurred during periods of warfare when the governor and his legates were otherwise occupied.[62] It is also important to take an empire-wide view of the problem. The provinces each had varying numbers of senatorial officials: in some regions there was no senator apart from the governor, while others had *legati pro praetore* limited to a year's tenure, and tied to the proconsuls themselves. The one common feature of all provinces, however, regardless of whether they were usually governed by senators or *equites*, or whether they had legions stationed in them or not, was that they had at least one equestrian procurator. The elevation of equestrian officials to acting governors therefore had a certain pragmatic quality about it, as it placed the fundamental operation of government above the allocation of provinces to individuals based on their status. The decision emphasised the role of the *princeps* as the arbiter of appointments within the monarchical *res publica*. But it was also the natural result of the evolution of an equestrian aristocracy of service, the *equestris nobilitas*, over the course of the first two centuries AD, which eroded the distinctions between the roles occupied by *equites* and senators within the *res publica*.[63]

The benefits of this pragmatic approach can be seen in the selection of equestrian administrators who were already stationed in the province to

---

[60] Davenport 2012c: 192.   [61] Table 2.

[62] A. R. Birley 2005: 268. Senatorial *iuridici* were appointed in Hispania Citerior to help the consular legate manage the dispensation of justice in this large province on a regular basis (Alföldy 1969b: 236–46, 2007: 327–32).

[63] See Chapter 7 for full discussion.

replace a dead or disgraced governor.[64] We have observed above how the procurator C. Furius Sabinius Aquila Timesitheus was employed as acting governor of Arabia following Elagabalus' execution of the senatorial legate. Other examples can be surmised from the *damnatio memoriae* signified by the erasure of governor's names in inscriptions.[65] For example, Q. Axius Aelianus, procurator of Dacia Apulensis, served as acting *praeses* of Dacia twice during the reign of Maximinus.[66] One of these temporary promotions was no doubt related to the demise of the consular legate, Iulius Licinianus.[67] Two *legati Augusti* of Moesia Inferior in the period AD 238–44, C. Pe[...] and Tullius Menophilus, also suffered the same fate.[68] Their *damnatio* provides a plausible context for the elevation of the procurator P. Aelius Hammonius as provincial governor.[69] The crowded *fasti* of Moesia Inferior in the years AD 238–44 show that Hammonius' tenure must have been short and caused by political instability.[70]

Such problems also affected the prefecture of Egypt, where there are three examples of the *dikaiodotes* serving as acting governor in a period of only ten years, between AD 215 and 225 (see Table 11.2). These are Aurelius Antinous in AD 215–16, Callistianus in AD 218–19 and Ti. Claudius Herennianus in AD 224/225.[71] Antinous was appointed after Caracalla executed the governor, M. Aurelius Septimius Heraclitus, during his turbulent stay in Alexandria.[72] Callistianus was likewise elevated after Macrinus' prefect, Iulius Basilianus, fled the province when news of the emperor's downfall reached him.[73] Finally, Ti. Claudius Herennianus was promoted to serve as acting prefect after the demise of M. Aurelius Epagathus, who had been responsible for the murder of Severus Alexander's praetorian prefect, Ulpian. Alexander had initially appointed Epagathus *praefectus Aegypti* in order remove him from Rome, but then had him executed.[74] The examples show that political instability affected Egypt just as much as, as if not more than, other provinces, which necessitated temporary appointments from within the existing provincial administration. The appointments of these equestrian procurators as acting

[64] B. Campbell 1984: 404–8.

[65] *Damnatio memoriae* is, of course, not an ancient Roman term (Flower 2006: xix). It is used here merely as a term of convenience.

[66] *CIL* III 1456 = *ILS* 1371; Pflaum 1960: 851–4 (no. 328).   [67] *AE* 1983, 802; Piso 1982: 230–2.

[68] C. Pe[...]: *CIL* III 7606a, 7607; *AE* 1993, 1375. Tullius Menophilus: *IG Bulg* II 641–2.

[69] *IGR* I 623 = *ILS* 8851.

[70] For the governors of these years, see Gerhardt and Hartmann 2008: 1145–7.

[71] The evidence is collected in Table 11.2. The chronology of these prefectures is laid out in Bastianini 1975: 307–9, 1980: 86.

[72] Benoît and Schwartz 1948; Schwartz 1976: 102.   [73] Davenport 2012c: 193.

[74] Dio 80(80).2.4; Modrzejewski and Zawadzki 1967: 600–1; Schwartz 1976: 102–3.

governors cannot be said to be part of deliberate attempt to promote *equites* at the expense of senators, which formed a key part of the old 'rise of the *equites*' paradigm.[75] Instead, it was a practical response to a problem that occurred in both senatorial and equestrian provinces. It was the emperor's prerogative to appoint whomever he wished to act as governor, and it was ultimately a sensible practice to increase the mandate of the procurator.

The downfall of provincial governors cannot account for all the cases of *equites* acting *vice praesidis* (no matter how turbulent the politics of the period). It is probable that procurators were also temporarily promoted to assume the governor's administrative and judicial functions, as Piso has argued.[76] This type of acting governorship is attested in the second century AD during the Bar Kokhba revolt and the Marcomannic Wars, as we have already discussed, but became more common in the third century AD. It seems to be no coincidence that there are equestrian acting governors attested in Germania Inferior, Moesia Inferior, Dacia and Syria Coele. These are all provinces close to major war zones, especially during the 230s–250s, when the number of acting governors increased significantly. In Dacia the procurator of Dacia Apulensis, the senior equestrian official in the province, often assumed some of the consular governor's judicial functions while he was on campaign.[77] This is paralleled by the situation in Syria Coele, where three acting governors are attested in the 240s–250s. The first of these is the *vir perfectissimus* C. Iulius Priscus, brother of the emperor Philip, who held the office of prefect of Mesopotamia, but was also 'exercising consular power' (διέποντι τὴν ὑπατείαν) in Syria Coele in AD 245.[78] A few years later, probably in AD 247, the *vir perfectissimus* Marcellus is attested 'discharging the office of governor' (διέπου[τ]ι τὰ [μέ]ρ[η τῆς] ἡγεμονείας).[79] The two phrases are probably synonyms for each other, and the expression 'exercising consular power' should be disassociated from Priscus' later command over the entire east, when he was *rector Orientis*, around AD 247/249.[80] This is supported by the terminology used to describe the acting governorship of the *eques* Pomponius Laetianus in the 250s. In AD 251 Laetianus appears as *vir egregius* and *procurator* in Syria, and then, some time during AD 252/256, he is also attested 'exercising consular power' (τοῦ τὴν ὑπατίαν διέ[π]οντος). He was never

[75] Cf. Keyes 1915: 4–7; Osier 1974: 75–6.   [76] Piso 1999: 337–45, 2014: 131.

[77] Piso 1999: 337–40.   [78] *P. Euphr.* 1.   [79] *P. Euphr.* 2.

[80] Feissel and Gascou 1995: 82–3; Gerhardt and Hartmann 2008: 1178–9. For example, *IGR* III 1201–2 records Priscus only as prefect of Mesopotamia, which precedes his later appointment as *rector* (*CIL* III 14149.5 = *ILS* 9005). Cf. Vervaet 2007: 134–7, who argues that Priscus was *rector Orientis* when he was 'exercising consular power'.

given a supreme command like Priscus, but appears to have been a regular procurator acting as governor.[81] Laetianus' temporary appointment may be connected with the aftermath of the invasion of Shapur I in AD 252/253, in which 60,000 Roman troops were killed and all the major legionary strong-holds were captured.[82] Since consular legates of Syria Coele continued to be appointed through to the age of the Tetrarchs, the promotion of these eques-trian acting governors was not part of any systematic attempt to replace senators in this position. Instead, it can be attributed to the need to delegate the senatorial governor's judicial responsibilities to the procurator while he was away on campaign.[83]

The promotion of equestrian officials to act *vice praesidis* in the first half of the third century AD has attracted considerable scholarly attention, because it presages the eventual transfer of most provinces to equestrian governors by the age of the Tetrarchs.[84] But it is vitally important to consider the contemporary context of the early third century AD, when such appointments became more frequent, in order to show that this was not an imperial preference for equestrians over senators, as prescribed by the old 'rise of the *equites*' paradigm.[85] For we not only find examples of *equites* acting *vice praesidis* for senatorial and equestrian governors, but also equestrians acting in place of other non-praesidial officials, such as the *dikaiodotes* in Egypt, procurators of specific regions, or officials responsi-ble for collecting taxes (see the list in Table 11.4). Sometimes this may have been the result of serious political upheaval, as in the case of Egypt in AD 217, when the *dioiketes* Heraclides is found as acting *dikaiodotes*, and the *procurator usiacus* Aurelius Terpsilaus appears as acting *dioiketes*. These temporary appointments were evidently connected with the difficult tran-sition between the reigns of Caracalla and Macrinus.[86] Other instances are less readily aligned with political changes; hence they could have resulted from the death of an official, or perhaps a lack of suitable candidates to fill

[81] *P. Dura* 97 (procurator), *P. Euphr.* 3–4 ('exercising consular power'); Feissel and Gascou 1995: 105. For Valerian's Persian campaigns of the 250s, which provide a plausible context for the acting governorship, see Goltz and Hartmann 2008: 234–7, 248–54.

[82] This is discussed later in this chapter in the section entitled 'The Gallienic Transformation'. It is important to point out that Syria had a consular governor in AD 250/1, Atilius Cosminus (*P. Dura* 95, 97). He may have lost his life in Shapur's invasion.

[83] Peachin 1996: 177; Piso 1999: 342–5. For the continuing appointment of senatorial governors, see the *fasti* in Gerhardt and Hartmann 2008: 1178–82.

[84] The bibliography is vast, but see especially Keyes 1915; Osier 1974: 68–93; Petersen 1955; de Blois 1976: 47–54; Pflaum 1976; Heil 2008a: 756–9; Mennen 2011: 137–42.

[85] See B. Campbell 1984: 404–8, 2005a: 117 and Lo Cascio 2005: 159 for arguments against the traditional view that Septimius Severus preferred *equites* to senators.

[86] *P. Oxy.* 43.3092–3, with J. Rea *ad loc.*; Hagedorn 1985: 184–6.

the post immediately. For example, Q. Agrius Rusticianus was stationed in Italy as procurator of the Via Laurentina and Ardeatina when he 'acted in place of the procurator of the five per cent manumission tax' (*vice proc-(uratoris) X[X l]ib[ertatis] functo*).[87] Such a promotion, as with the case of those procurators acting *vice praesidis*, was imperially mandated. This is shown by the example of C. Postumius Saturninus Flavianus, who was '*procurator centenarius* of the Hadrimentine region, also discharging the duty of the *ducenarius* by imperial order in the same region' (*procura|tori centenario regio|nis Hadrimentinae fun[c]|to etiam partibus duce|nari(i) ex sacro praecepto | in eadem regione*).[88] Saturninus' elevation to a senior procuratorship of the *regio Hadrumentina* was not a local decision made by the senatorial governor, but came directly from the emperor himself. The same situation can be posited for all other acting officials, who undoubtedly received imperial letters outlining their appointment to a higher level.[89] These promotions, however temporary they might have been, were recorded in *cursus* inscriptions because they represented a sign of the emperor's favour, which augmented the individual's self-representation as a faithful service of *princeps* and *res publica*.

Table 11.4 *Equestrians acting for other equestrian officials (AD 161–260)*

Date	Name	Acting as	Original Position	References
141	Iulianus	*Dikaiodotes (Iuridicus)*	Dioiketes	*BGU* 4.1019
197	Claudius Diogentus	*Archiereus*	Procurator	*W. Chr.* 81; *P. Oxy.* 8.1113
Severan	C. Postumius Saturninus Flavianus	*Procurator ducenarius regionis Hadrimentinae*	*Procurator centenarius regionis Hadrimentinae*	*CIL* VIII 11174 = *ILS* 1440; *CIL* VIII 11175
Severan	Q. Agrius Rusticianus	*Procurator XX libertatis in Italy*	*Procurator viae Laurentinae et Ardeatinae*	*AE* 2003, 1933
209/211	L. Iulius Victor Modianus	*Procurator tractus Thevestini*	Procurator of Numidia	*CIL* VIII 7053[90]
215	Aurelius Italicus	*Archiereus*	*Procurator usiacus*	*BGU* 2.362

---

[87] *AE* 2003, 1933.

[88] *CIL* VIII 11174 = *ILS* 1440; *CIL* VIII 11175. This parallels the promotion of the *dikaiodotes* Claudius Herennianus to acting governor of Egypt (*P. Oxy.* 42.3076).

[89] All imperial appointees received a codicil from the emperor, as in the case of Q. Domitius Marsianus, discussed at the beginning of Chapter 7.

[90] An example of a senior official substituting for a more junior official (see Pflaum 1960: 733).

Table 11.4 (*cont.*)

Date	Name	Acting as	Original Position	References
217	Heraclides	*Dikaiodotes (Iuridicus)*	*Dioiketes*	*P. Oxy.* 43.3093
217	Aurelius Terpsilaus	*Dioiketes*	*Procurator usiacus*	*P. Oxy.* 43.3092
c. 225	C. Attius Alcimus Felicianus	*Procurator XXXX Galliarum*	*Procurator per Flaminiam, Umbriam, Picenum*	*CIL* VIII 822 = 23963 = *ILS* 1347
c.235/236	C. Furius Sabinius Aquila Timesitheus	*Procurator XXXX portus Bithyniae*	*Procurator patrimonii et rationis privatae* of Bithynia, Pontus, Paphlagonia	*CIL* XIII 1807 = *ILS* 1330
c.238/239	C. Furius Sabinius Aquila Timesitheus	*Procurator XX hereditatium et XXXX portus Asiae*	Procurator of Asia	*CIL* XIII 1807 = *ILS* 1330
241/244	Iulius Magnus	*Subpraefectus vigilum*	*Subpraefectus annonae*	*CIL* XIV 4398 = *ILS* 2159
247/248	Myro	*Archiereus*	Unknown	*W. Chr.* 73
252	Sabinianus	*Archiereus*	Unknown	*P. Oxy.* 50.3567
260/8	Flavius Rufus	*Dioiketes*	*Dikaiodotes (Iuridicus)*	*P. Flor.* 1.89[91]

The practice of appointing acting officials even extended to the highest offices of state. In AD 211/212 Sex. Valerius Marcellus, the *procurator rationis privatae*, deputised for both the praetorian prefects and the urban prefect.[92] Marcellus, a relative of the imperial family, was selected by Caracalla to serve in these posts during the upheavals that followed the death of his father Septimius Severus and the murder of his brother Geta.[93] Subsequent appointments related to the absence of praetorian prefects from the city of Rome, as in the case of Flavius Maternianus, a trusted associate of Caracalla, who remained behind in the city while the emperor and both prefects were in the east.[94] There were no fewer than three acting praetorian prefects in the 240s: Valerius Valens, *praefectus vigilum*; Bassus, whose status is unknown; and C. Attius Alcimus Felicianus, *praefectus annonae*.[95] In the case of Valens, his temporary promotion is certainly

---

[91] This is a rare case in which a senior official acts in place of a more junior official.
[92] *CIL* X 6569 = *ILS* 478; Pflaum 1960: 638–42 (no. 237).
[93] Halfmann 1982: 227–35; Peachin 1996: 157, 236; Davenport 2012a: 806.
[94] Herodian 4.12.4; Dio 79(78).4.2; Peachin 1996: 236 lists him as an *eques*, but his status is not given by the ancient sources.
[95] See Table 11.5 for the full references.

related to the circumstances of Gordian III's Persian War. During this period the praetorian prefects, C. Furius Sabinius Aquila Timesitheus and Iulius Priscus, accompanied the emperor on campaign, but Valens remained in Rome, where he was in charge of the veterans of the *legio II Parthica* who were left behind.[96] Nor were such deputy appointments at the senior echelons of government solely entrusted to *equites*: there are two examples of senators serving in place of the urban prefect in the middle decades of the third century AD (see Table 11.5).

These developments are related to another important change in the Roman imperial government which occurred in the late second and early third centuries AD, namely the appointment of senatorial officials to serve as judicial deputies for the emperor himself. From the beginning of the principate emperors had appointed loyal supporters, whether they were freedmen, *equites* or senators, to manage affairs in their stead, such as Maecenas and Agrippa under Augustus, or Helios under Nero. This was a fundamental aspect of the emperor's ability and authority to delegate

Table 11.5 *Acting urban and praetorian prefects in Rome (AD 161–260)*[97]

Date	Name	Acting as	Original Position	References
211/212	Sex. Valerius Marcellus (*eques*)	Praetorian prefect and Urban prefect (senator)	*Procurator rationis privatae* (in Rome)	*CIL* X 6569 = *ILS* 468
213–217	Flavius Maternianus (status unknown)	Praetorian prefect and Urban prefect?	Unknown	Herodian 4.12.4; Dio 79(78).4.2
241/244	Valerius Valens (*eques*)	Praetorian prefect	*Praefectus vigilum*	*CIL* XIV 4398 = *ILS* 2159; *AE* 1981, 134
244/248	Bassus (*eques*)	Praetorian prefect	Unknown	*CIL* VIII 9611a-b
240s	C. Attius Alcimus Felicianus (*eques*)	Praetorian prefect	*Praefectus annonae*	*CIL* VIII 822 = 23963 = *ILS* 1347; *CIL* VIII 23948
mid-IIIc.	Ignotus (senator)	[P]raef[(ectus) Urbi?][98]	Unknown	*AE* 1961, 37
mid-IIIc.	[–]us Paulinus (senator)	Praetorian prefect and Urban prefect	Unknown	*IG* V.1, 538 = *AE* 1913, 244

[96] *AE* 1981, 134.   [97] This list is based on Peachin 1996: 236–8.
[98] For the restoration of this inscription, see Christol 1986: 306–11.

within the framework of the monarchical system. However, as Peachin has shown, the Severan period witnessed the formalisation of this transfer of powers.[99] Septimius Severus began the practice of appointing senators to judge *vice sacra* (in place of the emperor) when he selected Pollienus Auspex to act as his judicial deputy in Rome in AD 197–202. This was to ensure that the emperor had a representative to deal with his judicial business while he was occupied in the east with the Second Parthian War.[100] This precedent was followed by Severus' successors, with T. Clodius Aurelius Saturninus and L. Caesonius Lucillus Macer Rufinianus filling the same role during the Persian campaigns of Severus Alexander and Gordian III, respectively.[101] The practice of appointing senators as *iudices vice sacra* was a response to the increasing complexity of the Roman administration and the growing amount of judicial business that had to be dealt with by the emperor.[102] On the same analogy, the urban and praetorian prefects both had significant judicial responsibilities, with the *praefectus urbi* possessing jurisdiction in a 100-mile radius around the city of Rome, and the praetorian prefects all of Italy beyond that limit.[103] The authority of the praetorian prefects even expanded to the extent that they acted as a court of final appeal against the decisions of provincial governors.[104] At some point in the third century AD, probably under the Severans, it was decided that there could be no appeal against the praetorian prefect's ruling.[105] Given the extent of the prefects' authority, it was logical that acting praetorian prefects should be appointed in Rome to deal with the judicial business of the office on those occasions when the prefects themselves were occupied with campaigns on the frontiers.[106] The late second and early third centuries AD therefore saw the practice of appointing temporary substitutes in a range of financial, administrative and judicial roles across the empire becoming formalised as a standard practice of the Roman *res publica*. This is demonstrated both by the inscriptional and papyrological evidence and by the writings of Severan jurists such as Ulpian.

When placed in this broader context, the appointment of equestrian procurators to act *vice praesidis* cannot be seen as part of a specific attempt to promote *equites* at the expense of senators, as the old 'rise of the *equites*'

---

[99] Peachin 1996: 154–87.   [100] *IGR* III 618 = *ILS* 8841; Peachin 1996: 93–4.

[101] Peachin 1996: 108–14.   [102] Peachin 1996: 162–3.

[103] Urban prefect: *Dig.* 1.12.1.4 (Ulpian). For the judicial role of the praetorian prefect, see Howe 1942: 32–40; de Blois 2001; Eich 2005: 216–22; Mennen 2011: 169–75.

[104] Eich 2005: 219.   [105] *Dig.* 1.11.1.1 (Charisius); Peachin 1996: 165–6.

[106] The military commands of the praetorian prefects will be explored later in this chapter.

model advocated. Instead, the practice stemmed from the fact that the emperor could appoint the most suitable official as temporary governor, without regard for whether they were a senator or *eques*, in order to ensure the continuity of administration and justice in a specific province. For it remains the case that the majority of equestrian acting governors were not transferred from other provinces, or from civilian life, to deputise for a senatorial legate.[107] Instead, they were already in office in the provinces in which they replaced the governors. Moreover, the epigraphic evidence shows that their appointments were clearly designed to be temporary. For example, the procurator Herennius Gemellinus is attested with the title *vice praesidis* in Dacia at some point between AD 198 and 209, but then in a later inscription, dated AD 209/211, he is referred to only as procurator, signifying that he had returned to his original post.[108] The same point can be made about C. Furius Sabinius Aquila Timesitheus and Q. Axius Aelianus, both of whom served as acting governor of the same province twice, Timesitheus in Arabia, and Aelianus in Dacia.[109] This indicates that they returned to their substantive procuratorial posts in between their acting governorships. Appointments *vice praesidis* did not change the course of equestrian procuratorial careers, which largely continued to adhere to established patterns. For example, L. Titinius Clodianus, temporary *praeses* of Numidia in the 240s, went on to hold procuratorships responsible for collecting taxes and the *ludus magnus* in Rome, before becoming the prefect of Egypt.[110] The exceptional case is that of C. Furius Sabinius Aquila Timesitheus, who served as acting governor of Arabia, Germania Inferior, Pontus and Bithynia, and Asia, as well as deputising as procurator for collecting the customs tax in Bithynia, and as procurator for the inheritance tax and customs tax in Asia. Timesitheus' career cannot be regarded as typical by any means, and must owe something to imperial favour in the 230s, when many of his later posts were held in close succession.[111]

All these temporary appointments demonstrate that the Roman emperor had the authority to select whomever he wished to serve as governor of a province, regardless of existing status hierarchies. This prerogative had been exercised as early as the reign of Tiberius, when he

---

[107] Iulius Priscus, the prefect of Mesopotamia, who exercised consular authority in Syria Coele, was one of the few exceptions to this, probably because he occupied a special position as the emperor's brother.

[108] *CIL* III 7901 = *IDR* III.2 188.

[109] Timesitheus: *CIL* XIII 1807 = *ILS* 1330. Aelianus: *CIL* III 1456 = *ILS* 1371.

[110] Pflaum 1960: 859–64 (no. 331 *bis*).   [111] See the hypotheses of Pflaum 1960: 815–19.

chose the freedman Hiberus to act as governor in Egypt. Over the following centuries the Augustan system of allocating some provinces to senatorial proconsuls, and others to imperial legates or equestrian praesidial procurators, became outmoded. As Eich has argued, this was because the system was at odds with the realities of imperial government, in which all benefactions and appointments flowed from the emperors.[112] In the monarchical *res publica* the distinction between senatorial and equestrian administrators became increasingly irrelevant. *Equites* were appointed to official posts that required the same qualifications and abilities as those given to senators, and which entailed a similar range of duties, as we have seen in several earlier chapters.[113] Provincial procurators had long occupied an ambiguous place within the Roman administration, since they did not answer to the senatorial governor, but to the emperor himself.[114] Since they were already stationed in the provinces, they were the natural choice to act in the governor's stead in special circumstances and emergencies, such as the sudden (natural) death of the incumbent, his fall from favour and execution, or frontier campaigns which necessitated the temporary delegation of judicial authority.

The temporary elevation of these equestrian procurators did not represent the 'rise of the *equites*': they were not selected because of their equestrian status, or because they were inherently more competent or experienced officials than senators. Indeed, the equestrian officials were chosen precisely because, for all intents and purposes, they were just as qualified as senators for governorships – it was only their status that was different.[115] The emergence of the new aristocracy of service (the *equestris nobilitas*) among the *ordo equester* at large meant that there was a group of equestrians willing and able to serve the *res publica* alongside the careerist element in the senatorial order. Therefore, the appointment of *equites* as acting governors was the result of successive emperors prioritising pragmatism over traditionalism, by selecting the most suitable replacements, regardless of their official status. This practice set the stage for the breakdown of traditional status hierarchies among provincial governors in the late third century AD.

---

[112] Eich 2005: 350–4.   [113] See Chapters 4, 6 and 7.

[114] Eich 2005: 98–145. See Chapter 4 for the establishment of the procuratorial system and Chapter 7 for its subsequent development.

[115] Cf. Kulikowski 2014: 138–9, arguing that *equites* were more qualified than senators. As articulated in Chapter 7, I view the equestrian and senatorial aristocracies of service as equivalent groups. I do not regard one as more 'qualified' than the other.

The Ambitions of Soldiers

The second significant development revealed by the dedication at Aquincum is the transfer of legionary commands from senatorial legates to equestrian prefects. Although the circumstances of Gallienus' reign provided the catalyst for this specific change (as we will see later in this chapter), the context in which it occurred needs to be explained with reference to other developments in the Roman army. The first of these concerns the entrance of soldiers and their family members into the ranks of the *ordo equester*, a new phenomenon unattested before the late second century AD.[116] Equestrian rank had never been widespread within the Roman army below the rank of centurion. Even among centurions the status was confined to those commissioned *ex equite Romano*. There are some isolated cases of centurions who were promoted to the *ordo equester* by the emperor, but even then their descendants did not automatically inherit equestrian status.[117] Equestrian rank was usually confined to former chief centurions, the *primipilares*, who had spent a lifetime in the service. A *primipilaris* who remained in the army could then be promoted to the post of *praefectus castrorum*, or to one of the Rome tribunates (in the *vigiles*, urban cohorts, praetorian guard, or *equites singulares*).[118] It is therefore a significant development when we find soldiers' sons elevated to the *ordo equester*, and the soldiers themselves being promoted directly into the *militiae equestres*.

Our first securely dated case of a soldier's son receiving equestrian rank comes in the reign of Commodus:

To the god Hercules. Marcus Aurelius Bassinus, *centurio exercitator* (training officer) of the unit of the *equites singulares*, together with Aurelius Sabinus, *eques Romanus*, his son, willingly discharged his vow.[119]

We know that Bassinus was not a centurion commissioned *ex equite Romano*, since he had risen through the ranks of the *frumentarii*.[120] Therefore, it must be the case that Commodus decided to promote only Bassinus' son, Aurelius Sabinus, into the *ordo equester*. There are twenty-six

---

[116] Stein 1927: 155–60. This section is a revised version of Davenport 2012b.

[117] E. Birley 1953: 104–24; Dobson 1970. For equestrian status as a personal benefaction of the emperor that could not technically be inherited, see Chapter 5.

[118] Dobson 1974: 413–20, 1978: 68–91.

[119] *CIL* VI 273 = M. P. Speidel 1994a: no. 34: [*Deo*] | *Herculi* | *M(arcus) Aur(elius) Bas|sinus* | *7(centurio) ex|ercita(tor) n(umeri)* | *eq(uitum) sing(ularium)* | *cum Aur(elio) Sa|bino eq(uite)* | *R(omano)* | *fil(io) v(otum) l(ibens) s(olvit)*.

[120] M. P. Speidel 1994a: 66.

recorded examples of soldiers' sons with equestrian rank.[121] Although just over half are children of centurions, like Sabinus, others were born to soldiers of lower ranks, such as Iulius Valens (*strator*), Q. Catinius (*signifier*) and C. Artorius Tertullus (*veteranus*).[122] The possibility that they may have usurped this status is ruled out by cases in which the sons are explicitly said to have been 'supplied with the public horse' (*equo publico exornatus*), as in the case of Memmius Victorinus, the son of a veteran.[123] Some of the children honoured were very young indeed. M. Valerius Ulpius, the son of a centurion of the *legio IV Flavia*, had been awarded the *equus publicus* before his death at the age of eight, whereas others were mere babies, aged as young as eight months.[124] Such benefactions to children are not unattested outside the army; for example, C. Velleius Urbanus was granted the *equus publicus* by Antoninus Pius at the age of five.[125] The gesture, which was intended to honour the child's father, was particularly common in the case of imperial freedmen.[126] The same principle seems to have applied to the sons of soldiers. Those who became *equites Romani* were part of a privileged group, whose fathers belonged to units with close proximity to the emperor, such as the praetorian guard, the *equites singulares* or the *legio II Parthica*.[127] Their elevation to equestrian rank represented a way of honouring their fathers' service.

The promotion of military sons into the equestrian order began at about the same time as soldiers started to be appointed directly to officer commands in the *militiae equestres*.[128] There are ten examples of veterans from the legions and the praetorian guard, all of sub-centurion rank, receiving these officer posts. The earliest securely dated case, P. Aelius Valerius, tribune of the *cohors I Campanorum voluntariorum* in AD 212, is described as 'tribune, a former veteran' (*trib(uno) ex vet(erano)*).[129] This implies that there was no intermediate post between his army service and promotion to

---

[121] Stein 1927: 158–60. See the full list in Davenport 2012b: 105.

[122] Valens: *CIL* VI 32878. Catinius: *CIL* VI 3242 = XI 2625. Tertullus: *CIL* VIII 4882.

[123] *CIL* VIII 14344.

[124] Ulpius: *CIL* III 4327. For the youngest, see *CIL* III 14403a (eight months); *AE* 1999, 1335 (one year); *AE* 1976, 494 (two years); *CIL* VI 1596 (four years).

[125] *CIL* X 3924 = *ILS* 6305; Castagnoli 1949/50.

[126] Weaver 1972: 289–90; Demougin 1980: 160; Duncan-Jones 2006: 218, 2016: 125–6.

[127] Duncan-Jones 2006: 216–17, 2016: 124–5. The significance of these units will be discussed later in the chapter.

[128] For a full list, see Devijver 1993: 219–23, updated and revised in Davenport 2012b: 99–100. To this list should be added an example which I previously overlooked: M. Celerinius Augendus (*PME* C 104), an equestrian prefect whose brother was a *miles*, which makes it very likely that he himself came from within the ranks of the army (M. P. Speidel 1991: 117).

[129] *CIL* III 3237.

tribune. Q. Peltrasius Maximus, who served in Britain, referred to himself as 'tribune, a former *cornicularius* of the *viri eminentissimi*, the praetorian prefects' (*trib(unus)* | *ex corniculario* | *praef(ectorum)* *pr[a]etorio* *e|m-(inentissimorum)* *v(irorum)*).[130] These promotions represented a new and unconventional pathway for soldiers, who, after the reign of Claudius, did not advance into the *militiae equestres*, but attained higher rank through the primipilate and the 'Rome tribunates'. The commands of auxiliary units and the legionary tribunates in the *militiae equestres* had largely been the preserve of municipal aristocrats.[131]

In addition to these examples, there are cases of soldiers attested with the title of *militiae petitor* ('petitioner for a post in the *militiae*'). This is a term that indicates that a man had been granted the right to seek a commission in the *militiae equestres*, but had yet to acquire a specific command, presumably because there were currently no vacancies.[132] The earliest example of the term occurs during the reign of Commodus, on the epitaph of M. Ulpius Silvanus:

To the divine shades. To Marcus Ulpius Silvanus, provided with the *equus publicus* by the emperor Commodus Augustus, *militiae petitor*. Atilius Hospitalis made this for his dearest brother.[133]

We know little about Ulpius Silvanus' origin, but he was probably a soldier. The epitaph was dedicated by Atilius Hospitalis to 'his dearest brother' (*dulcissimo fratri*); the strikingly different nomenclature of the two men indicates that they were not brothers by birth, but brothers-in-arms.[134] Although Silvanus had been granted equestrian status before becoming a *militiae petitor*, it is evident that many other men with this designation were not *equites*. Instead, they were veterans from the legions or the praetorian guard, or officers of sub-centurion rank, such as *beneficiarii*.[135] This can be seen in the case of the funerary monument of M. Aurelius Secundinus (Figure 11.1):

To the divine shades. To Marcus Aurelius Secundinus, son of Marcus, veteran of our emperor, from the third praetorian cohort, *militiae petitor*, of Pannonian stock. His heirs, Aelia Valentina, his sister, and Aurelius Secundus, his son, made

---

[130] *RIB* 989 = *ILS* 4721.   [131] See Chapter 6 for full discussion.

[132] Henzen 1868; Stein 1927: 158.

[133] *CIL* VI 3550 = *ILS* 2759: *D(is) M(anibus)* | *M(arco) Ulp(io) Silvano eq(uo)* | *publ(ico) ornato ab* *Imp(eratore)* | *Commodo Aug(usto) pet(i)t(ori)* | *mili(tiae) Atil(ius) Hospitalis* | *fratri dulcissimo* | *fecit.*

[134] On the tendency of soldiers to refer to each other as *fratres*, see Phang 2001: 162.

[135] Stein 1927: 157–8; Davenport 2012b: 100.

Figure 11.1: Funerary monument of M. Aurelius Secundinus from outside Rome

this for a man who well deserved it, who lived 40 years, one month, and four days. M. Aurelius Primus, his freedman, made this while living.[136]

If Secundinus had been an equestrian, the title of *eques Romanus* or *eques equo publico* would surely have been recorded on his epitaph. Instead, his heirs referred to the highest status he possessed, which was that of a *militiae petitor*. Indeed, with one exception, the term *militiae petitor* only appears on epitaphs, presumably because soldiers who were granted this status eventually went on to secure an officer's command, and thus the title became redundant.[137] In the case of the deceased, this honour was recorded on their epitaphs as a way of emphasising their ascent through the army and their potential for officer rank.

The entrance of veterans in the *militiae equestres*, and the ability of other soldiers to apply for these positions as *militiae petitores*, raises serious questions. How could these men have obtained equestrian rank? It is probable that they lacked the financial resources available to achieve the equestrian census.[138] Instead, they were probably granted equestrian status when they were appointed to their commands in the *militiae*. We might compare the case of the *tribunus cohortis* Aemilius Pardalas, who honoured the Vestal Virgin Campia Severina with a statue 'on account of the benefactions of equestrian rank and the second *militia* which have been bestowed on him' (*pro conlatis in se beneficiis | equestr(is) ord(inis) item secundae militiae*). This implies that Pardalas was awarded both distinctions simultaneously.[139] The title of *militiae petitor* was probably granted by the emperor personally to indicate that a soldier had his permission to seek an equestrian officer post. It is surely no coincidence that the majority of *militiae petitores* are epigraphically attested in units such as the praetorian guard which were close to the emperor – as in the case of those soldiers' sons awarded equestrian status. Other *militiae petitores* could have encountered the emperor, or one of his close advisers, at some point in their careers, as has been proposed in the case of C. Tauricius Verus.[140] But such imperial benefactions could also occur through the intercession of powerful patrons, such as prominent senators, equestrians and Vestal

---

[136] *CIL* VI 2488: *D(is) M(anibus) | M(arco) Aur(elio) M(arci) f(ilio) Secundino vet(erano) Aug(usti) | n(ostri) ex coh(orte) III pr(aetoria) mil(itiae) petit(ori) nat(ione) | Pannonio Aelia Valentina | soror et Aur(elius) Secundus filius | heredes bene merenti fecerunt | qui vixit ann(is) XL m(ense) I d(iebus) IIII | M(arcus) Aur(elius) Primus lib(e)rtus viv(u)s fe(cit).*

[137] The term *militiae petitor* only once refers to a living person, Q. Gargilius Martialis (*CIL* VIII 20751), who did not use it subsequently after he had obtained an officer post (*CIL* VIII 9047 = *ILS* 2767).

[138] Davenport 2012b: 101–2.   [139] *CIL* VI 2131 = *ILS* 4929.

[140] For Verus' career, see Haensch 2001.

Virgins. Cassius Timotheus, a former *beneficiarius*, was able to petition for a command in the *militiae* through his connection with Iulius Priscus, prefect of Mesopotamia, and brother of the emperor Philip.[141] It is probable that the equestrian census requirement – still officially in force in the early third century AD – was set aside in the case of these promotions.[142] The same point can be made about the sons of soldiers who became *equites*. Although the children of centurions may have been wealthy enough to meet the 400,000 sesterces qualification based on their father's property, this is unlikely to have been the case with the sons of rank-and-file soldiers. These grants of equestrian rank or equestrian officer commissions to soldiers who did not meet the necessary criteria represent a striking display of imperial prerogative in action. As with the case of acting governors discussed earlier, they show how traditional status hierarchies could be overruled by the emperor. At approximately the same time, we find the title of *vir egregius* being awarded to selected *primipilares* who had not served as procurators.[143] Since this higher equestrian *dignitas* was not awarded to all *primipilares*, it is likely that those who received this title had been granted it as a special honour by the emperor.[144] The titulature of the equestrian aristocracy of service was gradually being extended to the officer commands of the army.

Some scholars have proposed that promotions of soldiers into the *militiae equestres* were made necessary by a shortage of officer candidates from within the equestrians of the municipal aristocracies.[145] The argument primarily arises from Jarrett's interpretation of the epigraphic material from Africa, which shows an increase in the percentage of equestrian officers from the militarised regions, especially in Numidia and Mauretania, in the third century AD.[146] His explanation of this phenomenon is that equestrians from the more urbanised coastal areas were reluctant to serve, and thus recruitment was focused on the former military colonies. Although a shortage of officers is not impossible in and of itself, it seems unlikely to have been a major problem in view of the

---

[141] *IGR* III 1202 = *ILS* 8847.

[142] For a full discussion of the equestrian census in the third century AD, see Chapter 12.

[143] Dobson 1978: 120–1. For example, the *primipilaris* Laberius Gallus, styled *vir egregius* in AD 225 (*CIL* XI 2702 = *ILS* 7217).

[144] This is demonstrated by two funerary inscriptions: (i) the epitaph of Sex. Atilius Rogatianus, *primipilaris*, set up by his heir P. Nonius Felix, a fellow *primipilaris* with the higher status of *vir egregius* (*CIL* VIII 12579); (ii) the tombstone of the *primipilaris* Papirius Sporus, erected by his brother, Papirius Socrates, who possessed the title of *vir egregius* (*CIL* VI 2861).

[145] See, for example, Jarrett 1963: 226; E. Birley 1969: 76–7, 1983: 83; Dobson 1970: 104, 1974: 401; Devijver 1991a: 190, 1992: 221, 1993: 227–30, 1995: 184; Handy 2009: 206–9.

[146] Jarrett 1963: 225–6.

sustained interest shown by municipal elites in serving in the army.[147] Instead, we should consider the reasons why soldiers sought promotion to officer commands in the *militiae equestres*. It is unlikely to have been the pay – which was no better than centurions and *primi pili* – or the security of a continued career, since commissions in the *militiae* were dependent upon vacant posts being available and the support of well-connected patrons, as we saw in Chapter 6. The attractiveness of the *militiae equestres* undoubtedly lay in the status of being an officer, with all its attendant privileges. The traditional route for soldiers from the rank and file to officer commands was by advancement to the post of *primus pilus*, by which time they would have been in their mid-fifties.[148] There were some changes in the hierarchy of new cavalry units in the early third century AD, presaging the career structure of the later Roman army, which did allow soldiers to rise to senior commands.[149] But these appear to be isolated cases, restricted to new units, and they did not alter the established route to officer posts, which was long, convoluted, and unreachable by the majority. Therefore, if a soldier was to be offered a promotion into the *militiae equestres*, allowing him to bypass this long and difficult career path, he would probably have found it difficult to refuse.

The ambitions of soldiers were fostered by the culture of the Roman army, which, while inculcating unity and conformity, remained a highly competitive and hierarchical institution. Differences in military rank were articulated through a complex language of signs and symbols on soldiers' uniforms.[150] When soldiers died and were commemorated by their tent mates and family members, the images on their tombstones carried the distinctions they bore in life. For example, *beneficiarii* were depicted on gravestones with their distinctive lances, while centurions were shown carrying the staff (*vitis*). The monuments were the outward expression of the competition for rank and status that existed within the army itself.[151] The consequence of this hierarchical society was that it encouraged soldiers, many of whom came from quite humble backgrounds, to seek promotion and to aspire to the lifestyle of their senior officers, including those from the senatorial and equestrian orders.[152] This is amply demonstrated by the poems composed by military men, such as those discovered

---

[147] See Davenport 2012b: 118–20; Davenport forthcoming; and Chapter 12.

[148] Breeze 1974: 256–7, 275–8; Dobson 1974: 411.

[149] For the new ranks, see the fundamental works of M. P. Speidel 1977: 703, 1992a, 1994b: 79–81, 2005, 2008: 688. The fourth-century hierarchy appears in Jerome, *Contra Ioh. Hier.* 19, discussed by A. H. M. Jones 1964: 634, 1263–4.

[150] James 2004: 64–5; Coulston 2007: 533–5.   [151] Lendon 1997: 238–47; Coulston 2007: 545.

[152] Lendon 2005: 276–7.

at Bu Njem in Numidia, which were written by centurions without a sophisticated grasp of Latin metre and prosody.[153] The desire for social mobility even extended to soldiers in the auxiliary units, a trend exemplified by the Batavian officers who served at Vindolanda and adopted aspects of the Roman elite lifestyle, throwing sumptuous dinner parties and developing a love of hunting.[154]

The monuments erected in honour of soldiers' sons who achieved equestrian rank illuminate this same phenomenon, but from a slightly different perspective. Many of these *equites* were only children when they died, and their epitaphs encapsulate their parents' grief at their deaths. The epitaph of the three-year-old *eques Romanus* Aurelius Claudianus is particularly poignant (Figure 11.2):

> To the divine shades. To Aurelius Claudianus, *eques Romanus*, who lived three years, ten months, twenty-eight days. Flavius Victor, *protector*, his father, made this for his sweetest son who well deserved it.[155]

On the monument itself Claudianus is shown riding a horse with a wreath in his hand, a scene which was designed to portray the life he would have lived had he survived. This was a particularly common practice on tombs and epitaphs for deceased children.[156] The sarcophagus of the nine-year-old *eques Romanus* Domitius Marinianus, although not a soldier's son, shows the same value system at work (Figure 11.3). Marinianus is depicted in the centre of the sarcophagus in the dress of a military officer, a position that he never achieved.[157] Mouritsen has argued that the epitaphs erected by Roman freedmen for their children not only conveyed their heartfelt grief, but also a profound sense of loss for their family's future and potential rise through the social hierarchy.[158] The inscriptions for these young *equites* reveal that a similar phenomenon occurred in the world of the Roman army: the soldiers were not only mourning their dead sons, but also their ambitions for higher status in future generations.

Service in the *militiae equestres* enabled soldiers to enter the privileged group of individuals who could style themselves *a militiis* or ἀπὸ

---

[153] Adams 1999.   [154] Bowman 2006: 87.

[155] *CIL* VI 1595: *D(is) M(anibus) | Aur(elio) Claudiano | eq(uiti) R(omano) qui vix(it) | annis III m(ensibus) X | die(bus) XXVIII | Fla(vius) Viator | protector | pater | filio dulcissimo | b(ene) m(erenti) fecit.*

[156] B. Rawson 2003: 356–63.

[157] *CIL* VI 41432: 'To Florentio. To Domitius Marinianus, *eques Romanus*, who lived nine years and two months … the sweetest son.' (*Florentio | Domitio Mariniano | eq(uiti) R(omano) qui vixit ann(is) VIIII | mens(ibus) duobus … filio dulcissimo*).

[158] Mouritsen 2005: 61–2.

D   M
AVR·CLAVDIANO
EQ·R· QVI·VIX·
ANNIS·III·M·X
DIES·XXVIII
FLA·VIATOR
PROTECTOR
FRATER
DVLCISSIMO
POSVIT

Figure 11.2: Drawing of the funerary monument for Aurelius Claudianus (now lost), outside Rome

στρατειῶν. These terms are prominent on honorific or funerary inscriptions from the late second century AD onwards.[159] The designations were used even if only one officer post in the *militiae* had been held, in much the same way that anyone who had been employed in one procuratorship ranked as a *vir egregius*. If an officer specifically wished to indicate that

---

[159] Devijver 1989c: 61–72.

Figure 11.3: Sarcophagus of Domitius Marinianus from outside Rome

he had completed three or four *militiae*, more precise terms were employed, such as *a IIII militiis* or *omnibus equestribus militiis perfunctus* ('having held all equestrian officer commands').[160] The use of this terminology indicates a significant degree of pride in military service and membership of the officer corps.[161] More importantly, service in the *militiae equestres* soon merited the award of higher equestrian distinctions, which had previously been granted only to procurators. This is shown by Memmius Valerianus, an officer who served in Numidia in the 240s AD. He proudly styled himself *a IIII militiis v(ir) e(gregius)* on the base of a statue he had erected of his governor.[162] An even earlier example can be found in the case of M. Celerinius Augendus, a Batavian soldier who rose to become prefect of the *ala I Pannoriorum*, stationed at Gemellae in Numidia, in the reign of Severus Alexander.[163] Augendus was one of the soldiers who benefited from imperial advancement to the *militiae* from the ranks. Augendus' brother Celerinius Fidelis died as a mere accountant (*exactus*) on the staff of the procurator of Lugdunensis, while Augudenus rejoiced in the status of *vir egregius* and *a militiis*.[164] It is easy to see why soldiers coveted this route to equestrian status, rather than the long and

---

[160] Variants include *a militiis III* (*CIL* VIII 2399); *a IIII militiis* (*CIL* VIII 2732); ἀπὸ τριῶν χιλιαρχιῶν (*IGR* 4 1204 = *TAM* V.2 913); *omnib(us) equestrib(u)s milit(iis) perfunc(to)* (*CIL* III 1198 = *ILS* 8113); *om[nibu]s militiis equestribus ornato* (*CIL* III 6055).

[161] Devijver 1989c: 71–2.

[162] *CIL* VIII 2732 = *ILS* 1154. For other examples, see T. Cnorius Sabinianus, *praefectus alae* (*CIL* III 4183 = *ILS* 7117; *PME* C 211); M. Lucilius Aufidianus, *a militiis* (*AE* 2007, 1614); T. Varenius Sabinianus (*CIL* III 1198 = *ILS* 8113; Bianchi 1987).

[163] M. P. Speidel 1991: 116–17.   [164] *CIL* XIII 1847 = *ILS* 2389.

convoluted tour via the primipilate. The *militiae equestres* remained an attractive opportunity for officers from municipal aristocracies and the ranks of the army alike through to the middle decades of the third century AD.[165]

This section has advanced the argument that emperors granted soldiers greater access to equestrian rank from the late second century AD as a way of rewarding their army service. This could be achieved either by promoting them into the *militiae equestres* or by conferring the *equus publicus* on their sons. Roman emperors placed great store on their relationship with the troops, which was the ultimate foundation for their authority.[166] The most effective way of ensuring military loyalty was to grant donatives to the soldiers on accession, with further supplements on significant imperial anniversaries.[167] These donatives became more extravagant over the course of the second century AD. The largest single donative on record is the 20,000 sesterces given by Marcus Aurelius and Lucius Verus to the praetorian guard upon their accession in AD 161.[168] During the reign of Commodus specific units also began to be rewarded for their loyalty with the epithet *Commodiana* ('Commodus' own'), and the practice became widespread in the third century AD, with epithets such as *Antoniniana*, *Maximiniana* and *Gordiana* being awarded to legions or auxiliary divisions.[169]

The entrance of soldiers into the *militiae equestres* has traditionally been associated with the army reforms of Septimius Severus.[170] But as we have seen, the practice is actually first attested earlier, in the late second century AD, during the reign of Commodus. It is not necessary, however, to link these changes with any particular emperor. They accumulated over time, as emperors granted equestrian status to the sons of soldiers who had caught their eye, or promoted others into the *militiae equestres* on the recommendation of their trusted associates. The climate of Septimius Severus' reign certainly furthered this process. He was acutely aware that the legions had brought him to power in AD 193, and that their continuing support was integral to the longevity of his regime. He therefore granted soldiers several concessions, including increasing their pay and giving permission for serving *principales* to form *collegia*.[171] These benefits were

---

[165] See Davenport forthcoming for the detailed evidence and discussion.
[166] B. Campbell 1984 is the classic study.   [167] Duncan-Jones 1994: 82–90.
[168] *HA Marcus* 7.9.
[169] B. Campbell 1984: 49–51; M. P. Speidel 1993; Hekster 2002: 164–8. For the third-century epithets, see Fitz 1983.
[170] E. Birley 1969: 63–4; R. E. Smith 1972: 496; Handy 2009: 206.
[171] See Handy 2009 for a recent overview.

the direct result of Severus' generosity towards the soldiers, a connection made by the men themselves in several inscriptions.[172] Severus also granted permission for military men to wear the *anulus aureus*. This did not confer equestrian rank in and of itself, but marked a soldier out as a member of the *honestiores*, with all its attendant legal privileges and exemption from baser punishments.[173] All these various promotions and honours – veterans advanced to the *militiae equestres*, young children from military families awarded equestrian rank, and the award of the gold rings – were the result of emperors responding to the soldiers' desire for greater status and advancement. But the same time, these changes laid the foundation for a wider transformation in the Roman military hierarchy.

The Imperial High Command

The aspirations of soldiers who wished to enter into the *militiae equestres* highlight the often strange and convoluted path to advancement in the Roman army and administration. The usual pattern of promotion from the ranks of the army (via the primipilate and the Rome tribunates) bypassed the equestrian officer commands in the *militiae* and instead led to the procuratorial career. The opportunities for a former soldier to be placed in direct command of troops at a more senior level included the posts of *praefectus classis*, praesidial procurator, or the prefectures of the *vigiles* and praetorian guard. However, there are few indications that the Roman administration actively preferred former soldiers for these posts, and many a *primipilaris* is later found in financial procuratorships.[174] The senior legionary and provincial commands were restricted to senators; experienced *primipilares*, as middle-aged men, were not normally suitable for entrance into the senate.[175] This meant that there was no coherent career path from soldier to general in the principate. The promotion of former soldiers into the *militiae equestres* represented one challenge to this system, but it was not enough in and of itself to prompt the overhaul of the military career structure. This only happened gradually over the course of the late second and third centuries AD.

---

[172] Ginsburg 1940; *CIL* VIII 2554 = *ILS* 2445; *CIL* VIII 2553 = *ILS* 2438; *ILS* 9099; *ILS* 9100.
[173] Garnsey 1970: 245–51; Duncan-Jones 2006: 215–16, 2016: 124–5. For the gold ring in the principate, see Chapter 5.
[174] See Dobson 1974: 421–6, 1978: 92–11, as well as the discussion on this point in Chapter 7.
[175] Dobson 1970: 107–8.

The emperors traditionally invested military authority in their senatorial legates, both the governors of consular and praetorian provinces, as well as any senators appointed to ad hoc supra-provincial commands, as in the case of Cn. Domitius Corbulo or C. Avidius Cassius.[176] Important campaigns requiring significant forces, such as Trajan's Dacian and Parthian Wars, saw the emperor and his senatorial generals assume primary command of the legions.[177] Equestrian officers, usually in the *militiae equestres*, were placed in control of auxiliary troops or smaller detachments.[178] For example, in the Parthian War of Lucius Verus, M. Valerius Lollianus, prefect of the *ala II Flavia Agrippiana*, was appointed *praepositus* of vexillations of auxiliary units in Syria.[179] During this campaign Lollianus answered to the senior senatorial commanders: the governor of Cappadocia, M. Statius Priscus Licinius Italicus, and M. Claudius Fronto, who was *legatus Augusti* in charge of an expeditionary army of legions and auxiliaries.[180] The majority of Marcus Aurelius' senior commanders during his German wars, which occupied most of the 170s, were likewise senatorial generals.[181] The praetorian prefects, who commanded the *cohortes praetoriae* and the imperial horse guard (*equites singulares Augusti*), were the exception to this roster of senatorial commanders.[182] The praetorian prefect was occasionally entrusted with more senior authority, as when Domitian gave Cornelius Fuscus control over the conduct of his First Dacian War after the senatorial governor of Moesia, Oppius Sabinus, was killed in battle.[183] Marcus Aurelius likewise invested his prefect Taruttienus Paternus with command of an expeditionary force at the beginning of his Second German War in AD 177.[184] These short-term appointments did not in and of themselves bring about a change in senatorial military authority.

There was a clear military hierarchy for senators: they could serve as military tribunes, then as legionary legates, then govern a two- or three-legion province. There was no such well-defined path for *equites*, and no opportunity for talented equestrians to lead large expeditionary forces at

[176] Vervaet 2007: 128–9, 132–4.
[177] For the commands in Trajan's wars, see Syme 1958: 239, 242–3, 645–8; Saxer 1967: 25–7; Bennett 2001: 194–5, 200–1.
[178] Saxer 1967: 25–7; R. E. Smith 1979: 264–73; Tully 1998: 230–2.
[179] *CIL* III 600 = *ILS* 2724 = *LIA* 188. For the date, see Haensch and Weiß 2012: 448–50, which supersedes the arguments of D. L. Kennedy 1997 for a Trajanic date.
[180] A. R. Birley 1993: 123, 128–30. Italicus: *CIL* VI 1523 = *ILS* 1092. Fronto: *CIL* VI 41142.
[181] A. R. Birley 1993: 155–7.
[182] Howe 1942: 22; M. P. Speidel 1994b: 99–100; Bingham 2013: 41.
[183] Suet. *Dom.* 6.1; Dio 67.6.5–6; B. W. Jones 1992: 179. Senatorial commanders returned in the Second Dacian War (B. W. Jones 1992: 141).
[184] Dio 72(71).33.3–4[1]; A. R. Birley 1993: 207.

a high rank. This meant that ad hoc solutions had to be devised, as happened in the 160s–170s AD during the reign of Marcus Aurelius. M. Valerius Maximianus, who began his career in the *militiae equestres*, was placed in charge of cavalry units sent to the eastern provinces to assist in suppressing the revolt of Avidius Cassius. Since he had advanced beyond the *militiae*, Maximianus' higher standing was recognised by giving him the status of *centenarius*, the equivalent of a procurator.[185] The same type of promotion was employed for his contemporary, L. Iulius Vehilius Gallus Iulianus, who had also advanced beyond the *militia quarta*.[186] Iulianus was granted the exceptional title of 'procurator Augusti and praepositus of vexillations', as a way of recognising his seniority in several campaigns during this period.[187] These commissions at procuratorial rank represented an attempt to create an equestrian equivalent to the senatorial legionary legate. The only alternative would have been to promote these equestrians into the senate at the rank of ex-praetor. This did eventually occur in the case of M. Valerius Maximianus and two of his Antonine contemporaries, P. Helvius Pertinax and M. Macrinius Avitus Catonius Vindex.[188] But Iulianus remained an *eques*, eventually ascending to the praetorian prefecture under Commodus.[189]

It must be emphasised that these promotions did not represent any attempt to advance hardened soldiers from the ranks to senior commands. Maximianus was from the curial class of Poetovio in Pannonia, while Vindex was the son of the praetorian prefect M. Macrinius Vindex.[190] Pertinax was the son of a freedman, but had obtained equestrian rank and a commission in the *militiae* thanks to prominent senatorial patrons.[191] The origins of Iulianus are unknown, but he certainly began his career in the *militiae*.[192] There was only one seasoned solider on Marcus Aurelius' staff: the praetorian prefect M. Bassaeus Rufus, who was from a poor and humble background, and had risen via the primipilate and a procuratorial

[185] Pflaum 1960: 476–94 (no. 181 *bis*). His title is recorded as *praep(osito) equitib(us)* ... *honor(e) centenariae dig|nitatis* in the inscribed account of his career (*AE* 1956, 124).

[186] Pflaum 1960: 456–64 (no. 180). The award of the *militia quarta* is specified in *SEG* 7, 145 = *AE* 1933, 208.

[187] *CIL* VI 41271.

[188] Pertinax: *HA Pert.* 2.1–5; Pflaum 1960: 451–4 (no. 179). Vindex: *CIL* VI 1449 = *ILS* 1107; Pflaum 1960: 510–13 (no. 188).

[189] *CIL* XIV 4378; Dio 72.14.1.

[190] Maximianus: *AE* 1956, 124; *CIL* VIII 4600. Macrinius Vindex: Pflaum 1960: 388–9 (no. 161).

[191] Dio 74(73).3.1; *HA Pert.* 1.5–6.

[192] He was not Palmyrene as was previously suggested (see Pflaum 1960: 458–9).

career.[193] The wars of Marcus Aurelius therefore introduced some important innovations, which highlighted notable problems with the developing equestrian *cursus*. The second century AD had witnessed the consolidation of the equestrian aristocracy of service, men who were prepared to serve the state *domi militiaeque* in the same manner as senators. Yet there was no clear way for these men to assume high military commands as *equites*, resulting in the creation of ad hoc procuratorial appointments.

The reign of Septimius Severus witnessed important developments for the Roman military establishment, and the place of the equestrian order within it. Severus created three new legions, the *I, II* and *III Parthica*, each of which was placed under the command of an equestrian *praefectus legionis*, not a senatorial legate.[194] The first and third Parthian legions were stationed in the new province of Mesopotamia, which was entrusted to an equestrian prefect on the model of the province of Egypt.[195] The commanders of the legions therefore had to be *equites* in order to avoid having a senator answer to an equestrian governor.[196] This had been the practice of Augustus when he installed the *legio XXII Deiotariana* and the *legio III Cyrenaica* in Egypt under equestrian prefects. The same command structure was maintained in the *legio II Traiana*, which was the sole legion stationed in Egypt in the Severan age.[197] The third new legion founded by Severus, the *legio II Parthica*, was quartered at Albanum just outside Rome, and thus became the first legion to be permanently stationed in Italy. One prefect of the *II Parthica*, T. Licinius Hierocles, is recorded with the exceptional title of *praefectus vice legati* ('the prefect acting in place of the legate'), though this was probably only a formality, since no senatorial legates are on record.[198]

---

[193] *CIL* VI 1599 = *ILS* 1326; Pflaum 1960: 389–93 (no. 162); Dobson 1978: 254–6. On his low birth, see Dio 72(71).5.2–3.

[194] Dio 55.24.4. The province and the legions were established as early as AD 195 (D. L. Kennedy 1987: 59–60; Cowan 2002: 78–81; M. A. Speidel 2007: 408–15).

[195] Dio 75.3.2. The first prefect was Ti. Claudius Subatianus Aquila (*AE* 1979, 625; D. L. Kennedy 1979). The legions were stationed at Nisibis and Singara, respectively (D. L. Kennedy 1987: 60–2).

[196] B. Campbell 1984: 404–5.   [197] Dobson 1982: 322–3; M. P. Speidel 1982.

[198] T. Licinius Hierocles was prefect of the *legio II Parthica* under Severus Alexander (*CIL* VIII 20996 = *ILS* 1356; *AE* 1966, 596). Pflaum 1960: 810 suggested that the term *vice legati* was intended to distinguish Hierocles from the camp prefect. There are three inscriptions from Apamea referring to officials of the *legatus legionis* of the *II Parthica* (*AE* 1971, 469; 1993, 1586–7), which probably also results from the use of standard conventions. Cf. Balty 1988: 102; van Rengen 2000: 410; B. Campbell 2005b: 23–4; Cosme 2007: 103, who all suggest that the legion was at some point commanded by a senator, probably while on campaign.

The career paths for the officers of the Parthian legions followed the pattern of the legions stationed in Egypt. Their tribunates were integrated into the *militiae equestres*, with some tribunes of the Parthian legions going on to procuratorial careers in the usual manner.[199] The traditional route to the prefecture of the *legio II Traiana* in Egypt was via the primipilate and the Rome tribunates.[200] The command of this legion ranked as a ducenarian procuratorship by the Antonine period, and the same status was given to the prefects of the new *legiones Parthicae*.[201] The first prefect of a Parthian legion, C. Iulius Pacatianus, was promoted from the *militiae equestres*, but thereafter the commands appear to have been given to *primipilares*, following the Egyptian precedent.[202] This suggests that Septimius Severus was following traditional status hierarchies when establishing his new Parthian legions. There was certainly no move to replace senatorial legates with equestrian prefects elsewhere in the empire. This had been attempted by Sex. Tigidius Perennis, Commodus' praetorian prefect, after the British legions acclaimed the senatorial legionary legate Priscus as emperor.[203] When Perennis tried to place equestrians in command of the legions, this punitive measure provoked a military revolt that eventually led to his downfall.[204] Severus was not about to repeat this mistake, and therefore his new legions fitted with existing equestrian paradigms and career paths.

The foundation of the Parthian legions did, however, lead to changes in the expeditionary forces, particularly their overall command structure. The *legio II Parthica* was designed to accompany the emperor on campaign, a role it performed during Septimius Severus' two Parthian wars and

[199] See the cases of Q. Petronius Quintianus (*PME* P 2; *AE* 1958, 239–40); Ulpius Victor (*CIL* III 1464 = *ILS* 1370 = *AE* 1980, 758; Pflaum 1960: 691–4 (no. 257)); T. Caesius Anthianus (*AE* 1908, 206 = *ILS* 9014; Pflaum 1960: 827–8 (no. 321)).

[200] Pflaum 1960: 229; Dobson 1978: 71–4, 1982: 322–4.

[201] For the *II Traiana*, see L. Cominius Maximus, who is styled *praef(ecto) leg(ionis) II Troianae* [sic] *fortis CC* (*CIL* XIV 3626 = *ILS* 2742; Pflaum 1960: 513–14 (no. 189)). For the *legio II Parthica*, see Iulius Iulianus (*CIL* III 99).

[202] Pacatianus: *CIL* XII 1856 = *ILS* 1353; Pflaum 1960: 605–10 (no. 229); Cowan 2002: 80–2. For later careers, the best attested example is T. Licinius Hierocles (Pflaum 1960: 808–10 (no. 316)). Other cases, such as Aelius Triccianus, are discussed below.

[203] *HA Comm.* 6.2; Dio 73(72).9.2²–10.1. This Priscus may be identical with the polyonomous senator commemorated on the fragmentary inscription from Rome (*CIL* VI 41127), as suggested by Alföldy *ad loc.*

[204] For this reconstruction of events, see A. R. Birley 2005: 168–9, 260–1. Cf. Herodian 1.9.1–10, who states that Perennis' demise was precipitated by the revolt of his sons against Commodus in Pannonia. Kolb 1977a: 467–8 speculatively suggests that one of Perennis' sons was actually an equestrian commander appointed in Britain.

his British expedition.[205] The question of whether the legion came under the direct command of the *praefectus praetorio* is a vexed one. In Cassius Dio's *Roman History* the character Maecenas advises Octavian that the praetorian prefect should control all the forces stationed in Italy, a statement that could be taken refer to the situation in Dio's own lifetime.[206] As an official imperial *comes* during Severus' Parthian campaigns, the prefect Fulvius Plautianus certainly joined the emperor in the east, but he is not mentioned in any specifically military capacity, in contrast with the abundant evidence for Severus' senatorial generals leading troops in battle.[207] It seems likely, therefore, that the authority of the praetorian prefect over the *legio II Parthica* evolved gradually.[208] During Caracalla's campaign against the Parthians his expeditionary force was composed of the *legio II Parthica*, the *cohortes praetoriae*, and the *equites singulares Augusti*, as well as vexillations of legions based on the German, Danubian and Syrian frontiers, totalling some 80–90,000 soldiers.[209] This is what scholars call a 'field army', a modern term of convenience used to describe a large force composed of vexillations from a range of legions and auxiliary forces, which accompanied emperors or their leading generals on campaigns.[210] Apart from the *legio II Parthica*, the only other legion that may have participated in Caracalla's campaign as a complete unit was the *legio II Adiutrix* of Pannonia.[211] This meant that the *legio II Parthica* was effectively the central core of the force and – although no ancient source explicitly attests this – the logical commander of the field army would be the praetorian prefect. Both of Caracalla's prefects, M. Opellius Macrinus and M. Oclatinius Adventus, are known to have accompanied him to the east.[212] This necessitated the appointment of a substitute prefect in Rome to handle the judicial responsibilities of the position (a problem we examined earlier in the chapter).

The *legio II Parthica* later formed the core of the forces marshalled by Severus Alexander and Gordian III for their eastern campaigns against the revived Persian empire.[213] Indeed, it is during Gordian III's reign that the connection between the legion and the praetorian prefect is shown clearly for the first time. Both the emperor's praetorian prefects, C. Furius

---

[205] E. Birley 1969: 78; A. R. Birley 1999: 175, 2007: 367; Cowan 2002: 83–4, 89–92, 136–7; M. P. Speidel 2008: 676.

[206] Dio 52.24.3.

[207] Cowan 2002: 83–4. For Plautianus on campaign, see *CIL* VI 225; *CIL* VI 1074 = *ILS* 456. For Severus' generals, see Mennen 2011: 194–215.

[208] Howe 1942: 21–31; Eich 2005: 214–16; Mennen 2011: 166–9.   [209] Cowan 2002: 136–55.

[210] See Strobel 2009: 917 for an overview of the field armies of the third century.

[211] Cowan 2002: 143–5.   [212] Dio 79(78).14.1–4; Herodian 4.14.1–2.

[213] The legion was stationed at Apamea in Syria (Balty 1998: 97–100; Ricci 2000: 399).

Sabinius Aquila Timesitheus and C. Iulius Priscus, formed part of the retinue that left Rome for the Persian front in AD 242.[214] In the same year, Valerius Valens, *praefectus vigilum*, is attested in Rome 'acting in place of the praetorian prefect' (*vice praef(ecti) praet(orio) agentis*). In this capacity he oversaw the discharge of the veteran soldiers of the *legio II Parthica*. These men had originally enlisted in AD 216, and had been left behind in Rome rather than journeying to the east.[215] The prefects on campaign with their emperor became enormously powerful individuals: C. Iulius Philippus, who succeeded Timesitheus, was able to arrange the downfall of Gordian III in the east, and returned to Rome as emperor.[216] Successianus, an equestrian commander on the Black Sea in the 250s, was summoned by Valerian to serve as his praetorian prefect in the east, where he commanded the field army against the Persians.[217] The composition of Valerian's army is strikingly demonstrated by the account of the Roman forces in the account of the Persian king Shapur, known as the *Res Gestae divi Saporis*. This includes the detail that the praetorian prefect was captured by the Persians in AD 260 alongside the emperor and members of the senate.[218] The employment of the *legio II Parthica* as a permanent core of the emperor's own field army enhanced and consolidated the position of the praetorian prefect as a senior military commander in addition to the senatorial generals.

The rise of the field armies attached to the emperor and the praetorian prefect sometimes offered new opportunities to soldiers of other ranks. In the previous section we observed the marked correspondence between soldiers who served in the praetorian guard, the *equites singulares*, and the *legio II Parthica*, and those who obtained advancement into the *militiae equestres* or the promotion of their sons to equestrian rank. Proximity to the emperor and his senior staff on campaign evidently had its advantages. The same phenomenon can be observed in the careers of prefects of the *legio II Parthica*, which, since it accompanied Caracalla to the east, was intimately bound up with the political machinations of the years AD 217–18. In this period the empire passed from Caracalla to his prefect Macrinus and then to the boy emperor Elagabalus, with the crucial battles

---

[214] Howe 1942: 78–80; Huttner 2008: 185–7. The *HA Gord.* 27.2 attributes the success of the campaign to Timesitheus before his untimely death, and his co-ordinating role is alluded to by Zos. 1.18.

[215] *AE* 1981, 134; see also *CIL* XIV 4398 = *ILS* 2159; Holder 1994. Tomlin 2008: 152–3 makes the point that the field army troops were chosen from the younger members of the legions.

[216] Zos. 1.18–19; *HA Gord.* 28–30; Victor, *Caes.* 27.8.   [217] Zos. 1.32.1–2.

[218] For the composition of the forces, see Loriot 2006. The argument that Successianus was the captured prefect has been made by Howe 1942: 80–1; Gerhardt and Hartmann 2008: 1172–3.

all happening in Syria. The commanders of the *legio II Parthica* included Aelius Triccianus, who had begun his career as a rank-and-file soldier in Pannonia and *ostiarius* ('door-keeper') to the governor.[219] Other *ostiarii* are attested as being promoted to centurion, so it is likely that Triccianus himself became a centurion and *primus pilus*, a career path attested for comparable equestrian legionary prefects.[220] This was a spectacular career, but not unprecedented or improper. The same can be said for P. Valerius Comazon, who served as a soldier in Thrace early in his career, before rising to become *praefectus* of the *legio II Parthica*.[221] Again, there is nothing truly exceptional in and of itself about soldiers who ascended to the Rome tribunates or camp prefecture via the primipilate.[222] But the command of the *legio II Parthica* offered connections to the imperial court, and the favour of Macrinus and Elagabalus, respectively, enabled Aelius Triccianus and Valerius Comazon to enter the ranks of the senate. Their promotion earned the ire of the senatorial historian Cassius Dio, who disliked the progression of soldiers into the *amplissimus ordo*.[223] Dio did not resent the advancement of equestrians per se, but the elevation of soldiers who were able to enter the equestrian order and then into the *curia*. Triccianus and Comazon were quite different from M. Valerius Maximianus, who originated from the curial classes of Pannonia. Such opportunities would only become more common as emperors spent more time on campaign with their field armies.

In addition to the creation of the Parthian legions and the growing importance of the field army, the first half of the third century AD witnessed *equites* appointed to ad hoc procuratorial military commands. We have already noted this phenomenon in the wars of Marcus Aurelius, when M. Valerius Maximianus and L. Iulius Vehilius Gallus Iulianus commanded army detachments with the rank of a procurator, as a way of compensating for the lack of any defined military pathway for equestrians after the *militiae*. In the reign of Severus Alexander, P. Sallustius Sempronius Victor was granted the *ius gladii* with a special commission to clear the sea of pirates, a command that was probably associated with his existing procuratorship in Bithynia and Pontus.[224] This creation of new

---

[219] Dio 79(78).13.3–4, 80(79).4.3; *HA Cara.* 6.7.

[220] Fitz 1978; Dobson 1978: 291–2. There are two comparable cases of *ostiarii* who became centurions (*AE* 1910, 77 = *ILS* 9074; *AE* 1949, 108).

[221] Dio 80(79).3.5–4.2; Pflaum 1960: 752–6 (no. 290). This was suggested by Pflaum 1960: 754–5, and followed by Syme 1971: 141; Dobson 1978: 293; Salway 2006: 124–5.

[222] See the career paths of *primipilares* discussed by Dobson 1978: 16–51.

[223] Davenport 2012c: 186–7, 197.

[224] *IGR* IV 1057; Pflaum 1960: 840–2 (no. 325); Herz 1995: 196–8.

military commands within the procuratorial hierarchy can also be seen vividly in the case of Ae[l]ius Fir[mus].[225] Following a series of financial procurator-ships in Pontus and Bithynia and Hispania Citerior (high-ranking posts in and of themselves), Fir[mus] was placed in charge of vexillations of the praetorian fleet, detachments of a *legio I* (possibly *Parthica* or *Adiutrix*), and another group of vexillations, in the Parthian War of Gordian III.[226] In this capacity he ranked as an army commander and procurator at the ducenarian level, without actually holding a standing military post (such as fleet prefect, praesidial procurator or praetorian prefect). The adaptability of the equestrian careers to meet the new demands is demonstrated by the case of a certain Ulpius [–].[227] After series of administrative procuratorial positions, Ulpius was *praepositus* of the *legio VII Gemina*. Since this legion was normally stationed in northern Spain, Ulpius probably commanded vexillations of the legion in a war conducted in the reign of Philip.[228] He then returned to the usual procuratorial *cursus*, serving as *sub- praefectus annonae* in Rome.

Some equestrians were given special appointments as *dux* with respon-sibility for a specific province or series of provinces.[229] This can be observed in Egypt, where generals with the title of *dux* or στρατηλάτης appear in the 230s–240s. The archaic Greek word στρατηλάτης is rarely used in the imperial period before the third century AD; the only exception is inscribed account of the career of the Trajanic senator and general C. Iulius Quadratus Bassus at Ephesus.[230] But it makes a reappearance in the third century AD to describe senior equestrian military commanders.[231] The first Egyptian example is M. Aurelius Zeno Ianuarius, who replaced the prefect in some, or probably all, of his functions in AD 231. His military responsibilities should be connected with the beginning of Severus Alexander's Persian War.[232] The second *dux*/στρατηλάτης is attested ten years later, in AD 241/2, which is precisely when war broke out between Romans and Persians again under Gordian III. This time, the *dux* was Cn.

---

[225] *CIL* VI 41281.   [226] Nasti 1997: 284–6.

[227] *CIL* III 1464 = *ILS* 1370 = *AE* 1980, 758. Pflaum 1960: 691–4 (no. 257) is now superseded by the discussion of Piso 1980.

[228] Piso 1980: 282.

[229] The title of *dux* does not always indicate such a post, however. For example, Iulius Iulianus, prefect of the *legio I Parthica*, was described colloquially as 'the most devoted general' (*duci devotis|simo*) (*CIL* III 99 = *ILS* 2771). The *dux ripae* ('general of the banks') attested at Dura Europos was probably a more minor official than originally supposed, and was not a regional *dux* like those found in the fourth century AD. See Edwell 2008: 128–43.

[230] Habicht 1969: no. 21.

[231] Mason 1974: 13, 87. In the fourth century AD it is used as the Greek equivalent of *magister militum* (*LSJ* s.v. στρατηλάτης).

[232] *P. Lond.* 3.946; *P. Oxy.* 42.3077; *SB* 22.15468; *ChLA* 5.281; Parsons 1970: 393–5.

Domitius Philippus, the *praefectus vigilum*, who appears to have been sent directly to Egypt while retaining his post as commander of the *vigiles*.[233] In both cases the new military command was an ad hoc addition to their usual equestrian *cursus*.[234] The final example occurs in the 250s, when M. Cornelius Octavianus, *vir perfectissimus*, is attested as 'general across Africa, Numidia and Mauretania' (*duci per Africam | Numidiam Maureta|niamque*), with a commission to campaign against the Bavares.[235] This substantial command was in succession to his appointment as governor of Mauretania Caesariensis.[236] Octavianus then departed to become prefect of the fleet at Misenum, working his way to a senior post in the equestrian procuratorial *cursus*.

All these cases show the essential adaptability of the imperial system, which allowed third-century emperors to appoint equestrians to senior military commands when it suited them. This may have been because an equestrian was the person the emperor trusted most in the circumstances; for example, Cn. Domitius Philippus, as *praefectus vigilum*, was one of the most senior officials in the empire. This represents the same pragmatic approach we saw in the appointment of equestrians as acting governors. On a practical level, it did not matter whether an army commander was an *eques Romanus* or a senator, because the military tasks that he was capable of performing, and was entrusted with by the emperor, were essentially the same. The new ad hoc army commands gave members of the *equestris nobilitas* further opportunities to serve the state *domi militiaeque* alongside the senatorial service elite.

At the same time, it is necessary to point out that these changes did not lead to senators being ousted from military commands prior to the reign of Gallienus. Rich epigraphic evidence, combined with the testimony of Dio and Herodian, preserves a long list of Septimius Severus' senatorial generals. P. Cornelius Anullinus, L. Fabius Cilo, L. Marius Maximus, Ti. Claudius Candidus and L. Virius Lupus commanded Severus' troops as *duces* or *praepositi* in one, or both, of his civil wars against Pescennius Niger and Clodius Albinus.[237] Candidus also participated in the emperor's

---

[233] *P. Oxy.* 19.2231; *P. Berl. Leihg.* 1.9; *CIL* VI 1092. See especially Rea 1970, with Parsons 1970: 395–6; Gilliam 1961: 390–2. For Philippus' career, see Sablayrolles 1996: 509–11.

[234] Parsons: 1970: 396.

[235] *CIL* VIII 12296 = *ILS* 2774; Pflaum 1960: 905–23 (no. 347 *bis*); Gerhardt and Hartmann 2008: 1139. For discussion of Octavianus' career, see now Christol 1997: 236–7, 2003: 155–7.

[236] *AE* 1954, 136. The order of commands is strongly suggested by a fragmentary text which contains the phrase *et in | [p]riori praesidatu | [e]t post(ea) in ducatu* (*AE* 1907, 4 = *ILS* 9006).

[237] Anullinus: Dio 75(74).7.1, 75(75).3.2. Cilo: *AE* 1926, 79; *CIL* VI 1408 = *ILS* 1141. Maximus: *CIL* VI 1450 = *ILS* 2935. Candidus: *CIL* II 4114 = *ILS* 1140. Lupus: Dio 76(75).6.2. We should add to the list a certain [–]anus (*AE* 2003, 1189 = 2011, 764), whose recently discovered career matches that of no other known Severan general.

Parthian campaigns, alongside Ti. Claudius Claudianus, T. Sextius Lateranus, Claudius Gallus, Iulius Laetus and a certain Probus.[238] These senators were rewarded with a range of honours, from consulships and governorships to wealth and property (the sole exception was Laetus, who was executed for being too popular with the troops).[239] In the face of such overwhelming testimony, it proves difficult to marshal support for the still-popular scholarly argument that Severus prioritised equestrian officers over senators.[240] Equestrian commanders continued to participate in campaigns as subordinates to the senatorial generals, as we see in the case of L. Valerius Valerianus, who commanded the cavalry at the Battle of Issus under the authority of the consular legate, P. Cornelius Anullinus.[241]

The same pattern can be found in Severus Alexander's Persian War of AD 231-3.[242] Herodian's *History*, our major historical account of this conflict, is notoriously deficient in prosopographical detail.[243] Yet senators are attested in inscriptions, as in the case of the senior consular *comes*, T. Clodius Aurelius Saturninus, who accompanied Alexander to the east.[244] The senator L. Rutilius Pudens Crispinus, praetorian governor of Syria Phoenice and legate of the *legio III Gallica*, also served as a commander of vexillations during this conflict.[245] But we only know about Crispinus' command from an inscription from Palmyra, which recounts the assistance rendered by the local dignitary Iulius Aurelius Zenobius to Alexander, Crispinus and the Roman forces.[246] The inscribed account of Crispinus' career from Rome merely states that he was *legatus Augusti pro praetore* of Syria Phoenice.[247] It is probable that senatorial governors, such as D. Simonius Proculus Iulianus, consular legate of Syria Coele, continued to play important roles in eastern conflicts

---

[238] Claudianus: *CIL* VIII 7978 = *ILS* 1147. Lateranus: Dio 75(75).2.3. Gallus: *AE* 1957, 123. Laetus: Dio 75(75).2.3, 3.2, 76(75).6.8, 9.1, 10.3; Herodian 3.7.3 Probus: Dio 75(75).3.2.

[239] Mennen 2011: 204-8.

[240] See, for example, de Blois 1976: 67-8; Christol 1986: 38; Lo Cascio 2005: 160; Strobel 2007: 272; Rankov 2007: 73. The more measured view of B. Campbell 1984: 408-9, 2005b: 9-10, is to be preferred.

[241] *AE* 1985, 829; Dio 75(74).7.1; Pflaum 1982: 75-8 (no. 297A). For Valerianus' role in completing the Mesopotamian expedition, see M. P. Speidel 1985: 323.

[242] Cf. Heil 2008a: 747, who states that no senators participated.

[243] Herodian 6.5.1-7. For the likely composition of Alexander's army, see Edwell 2008: 161-2.

[244] *AE* 1972, 792 = *I. Eph.* 657.   [245] *IGR* III 1033 = *OGIS* 640.

[246] *IGR* III 1033 = *OGIS* 640.

[247] *CIL* VI 41229. A fragmentary inscription from Tarraco now reveals that his *praenomen* was Lucius (*CIL* II.14.2 992a).

under Gordian III.[248] Indeed, the evidence for equestrian procurators acting *vice praesidis* in Syria Coele, discussed above, suggests that the procurator assumed judicial responsibilities while the consular governor was preoccupied with warfare. This indicates that senatorial governors continued to play a major part in military campaigns, even if it was not specifically noted in inscriptions recording their *cursus*.

This argument is supported by the literary sources that show senators assuming military commands through to the middle decades of the third century AD. We can observe this in particular in the Danubian and Balkan region, which was a near-continuous conflict zone.[249] Tullius Menophilus fought against the Goths as *legatus Augusti pro praetore* of Moesia Inferior in the reign of Gordian III.[250] During the incursion of the Goths under Cniva in AD 250/1, the Moesian governor C. Vibius Trebonianus Gallus successfully defended the town of Nova.[251] In AD 253 M. Aemilius Aemilianus, governor of one of the Moesian provinces, pursued the fight against the Goths, before being acclaimed emperor.[252] Senators also continued to receive special commands, as in the case of C. Messius Quintus Decius Valerinus and P. Licinius Valerianus, both future emperors, who were placed in charge of expeditionary forces by the emperors Philip and Aemilius Aemilianus, respectively.[253] In Numidia, the governor C. Macrinius Decianus conducted a major campaign against several barbarian tribes in the middle of the 250s.[254] In fact, if we examine the backgrounds of the generals who claimed the purple up to and including the reign of Gallienus, the majority of them were actually senators, a fact obscured by the common use of the term 'soldier emperor' for rulers of this period.[255] Decius, one of the few known senators from Pannonia, successfully allied himself with an Etruscan senatorial family when he married the eminently suitable Herennia Cupressenia Etruscilla.[256] His successor, Trebonianus Gallus, was of remarkably similar background to Etruscilla,

---

[248] *CIL* VI 41232 = *ILS* 1189.   [249] Heil 2008b: 723–4.

[250] Petrus Patricius, frag 8. = *FHG* IV 186; *IG Bulg.* II 641–2; Dietz 1980: 233–45.

[251] Jord. *Getica* 102; Zos. 1.23.2. His senatorial status is confirmed by two inscriptions referring to his earlier governorship of Thrace (*AE* 2006, 1249–50).

[252] Victor, *Caes.* 31.1; Zos. 1.28.1–2; Huttner 2008: 215–16. Aemilianus' exact province is unknown: it was probably Moesia Superior since coins were minted in his name at Viminacium (Peachin 1990: 293).

[253] Decius: Victor, *Caes.* 29.1; Zos. 1.21.1–3. Valerian: Victor, *Caes.* 32.2; Eutrop. 9.7. There is also the case of an anonymous senator who had a command *[per No]|ricum et R(a)etia[m]* (*AE* 1993, 672) during the mid-third century AD.

[254] *CIL* VIII 2615 = *ILS* 1194; Christol 2003: 143–8.

[255] Alföldi 1939: 196; Syme 1983: 346, 356; Heil 2006: 421–2, 2008a: 753.

[256] Syme 1971: 197, 1983a: 341.

coming from Perusia in central Italy.[257] The emperor Valerian likewise had close links with the Italian senatorial aristocracy, marrying into the family of the Egnatii.[258] Some of the more ephemeral emperors deserve notice too, such as Ti. Claudius Marinus Pacatianus, the descendant of a Severan senatorial governor, who rebelled in the reign of Philip.[259] P. Cassius Regalianus, who was probably consular legate of Pannonia Superior when he began an insurrection against Gallienus in 260, was himself descended from a Severan suffect consul.[260] These men were not soldiers promoted from the ranks, but senatorial generals who used their positions to make a play for the imperial purple.

The Roman military hierarchy in the first half of the third century AD was therefore characterised by a mixture of continuity and change. The creation of the *legio II Parthica*, and the necessity for the emperor and his praetorian prefects to campaign on a regular basis, meant that emperor was in close contact with members of the expeditionary forces. Officers in the field army could receive imperial favour and embark on spectacular careers, like Aelius Triccianus or Valerius Comazon, or even Iulius Philippus, the praetorian prefect who snatched the purple from Gordian III while in the east. It is no coincidence that many of the soldiers' sons attested with equestrian rank belonged to the praetorian guard, the *equites singulares* and the *legio II Parthica*. At the same time, the imperial state tried to create senior army roles for promising *equites* in a manner analogous to senatorial legates by instituting ad hoc procuratorial commands (as seen in the case of Valerius Maximianus and Vehilius Gallus Iulianus). This gave members of the *equestris nobilitas*, the equestrian aristocracy of service, access to army officer commands beyond the *militiae equestres*. It should be noted that for the most part these men were not lowborn ingénues from the ranks, but members of the municipal aristocracy who served the *res publica* in a comparable manner to senators, as their predecessors had before them. It is also imperative to point out the endurance of tradition within the high command. Senatorial legates and generals still commanded armies in the emperor's foreign wars on the

---

[257] Syme 1983: 342. His wife was Afinia Gemina Baebiana (*CIL* XI 1927 = *ILS* 527), herself probably of consular stock.

[258] His wife, Egnatia Mariniana, was the daughter and sister of consular senators (Christol 1986: 192).

[259] Zos. 1.20.2; Zon. 12.19. He was descended from Claudius Sollemnius Pacatianus (governor of Arabia under Severus Alexander) and may well be identical with his son, the *clarissimus puer* C[-] Marinus (*CIL* III 94).

[260] Victor, *Caes.* 33.2; Eutrop. 9.81. Regalianus' command is placed in Pannonia Superior by Gerhardt and Hartmann 2008: 1163. For his family, see Eck 2002b. Syme 1971: 198 noted that his wife Sulpicia Dryantilla was from a Lycian family of some standing.

Rhine, Danube and Euphrates frontiers. Their military authority continued to make them viable and desirable candidates for the purple in the first
half of the third century AD. There was as yet no attempt to undermine the
positions of senatorial tribunes or legionary legates. It was the dramatic
developments in the 250s–260s that provided the catalyst to set the empire
on a radically different path.

The Gallienic Transformation

The first important development occurred in the joint reign of Valerian and
his son Gallienus (AD 253–60), with the creation of a new military institution,
the protectorate. *Protectores* were originally guards, drawn from the corps of
the *equites singulares*, who served on the staff of provincial governors and the
praetorian prefect.[261] In the late 250s, however, tribunes of the praetorian
guard are attested as *protectores Augusti*, an honorific title denoting their close
association with the emperor.[262] The most famous example is L. Petronius
Taurus Volusianus, who was 'tribune of the first praetorian cohort and
protector of our emperors' (*trib(uno) | coh(ortis) primae praet(oriae) protect-
(ori) | Augg(ustorum) nn(ostrorum)*).[263] The title of *protector* was also granted
to centurions and chief centurions, but only if they served in legions or
detachments of legions that formed part of the field armies, as Christol has
shown.[264] For example, the career of an anonymous soldier records that he
was promoted from centurion in the *legio III Augusta* to the *legio IV Flavia*.[265]
Since he served in vexillations of the *IV Flavia*, which formed part of a field
army, he received the new title of *centurio protector*. The officer in question
was then promoted to the higher rank of *primipilaris protector*. There are
several comparable examples of other centurions who were distinguished with
the title *protector* when promoted into vexillations in field armies.[266]

---

[261] M. P. Speidel 1978: 130–3, 1986: 451–2.

[262] See Mommsen 1884: 126–8, though he places their creation earlier, under Philip or Decius.

[263] *CIL* XI 1836 = *ILS* 1332. The post is to be dated to the late 250s, since he was *praefectus vigilum*
around AD 259 (Sablayrolles 1996: 515). Other examples of praetorian tribunes as *protectores*
from this period include an unknown tribune dated around AD 256/260 (*CIL* III 3126; Dobson
1978: 310–11); and Aurelius Sabinianus, who must be placed in the early 260s at the latest (*CIL*
III 3126).

[264] Christol 1977: 402–8. See Strobel 2009: 917–18 on the different field armies under Valerian
and Gallienus.

[265] *AE* 1954, 135; Christol 1977: 405–6. For vexillations of the *legio IV Flavia* in the field army, see
Alföldi 1929: 254; Nicasie 1998: 36; Strobel 2009: 917 n. 19.

[266] For example, Traianus Mucianus (*IGBulg* III.2, 1570) and Aurelius Processanus (*CIL* XI 837 =
ILS 2778).

The award of the new distinction of *protector* was especially significant because of the way the Roman military machine was changing in the mid-third century AD. It had usually been the practice for detachments to return to their home legions after serving as part of larger armies in major campaigns. But now these legionary vexillations ceased to return to their bases, and instead stayed with the field armies.[267] This meant that the expeditionary forces, and their officers, built up their own characters that were distinct from their original units. By granting centurions and praetorian tribunes the honorific title of *protector*, Valerian and Gallienus effectively cast themselves in the role of patrons to these officers.[268] It was more prestigious to serve in the field army than in other units. In many ways the institution of the protectorate was the culmination of earlier developments in train since the late second century AD, notably the advancement of soldiers and their sons who had served in the *legio II Parthica*, the praetorian guard or the *equites singulares* to equestrian rank or officer posts in the *militiae equestres*. Now, they could receive new distinctions while remaining part of the imperial field armies, and consolidating their connections with the praetorian prefect and the emperor.

The second development concerns the senatorial military officers of the legion, the *tribunus laticlavius* and *legatus legionis*. Senatorial *tribuni laticlavii* disappear entirely from the inscriptional record in this period: the last known officers in this post can be placed in the 250s and early 260s.[269] Senatorial legionary commanders are last definitively attested in AD 262/3 in the provinces controlled by Gallienus, and AD 262/6 in the Gallic empire of Postumus. The last known senatorial tribunes and legates are listed in Tables 11.6 and 11.7.[270]

Table 11.6 *The last attested senatorial legionary tribunes*

Date	Name	Legion	Reference
249	T. [–] Tiberianicus	*X Gemina*	*CIL* III 4558
early 250s	M. Flavius ... Honoratus	Unknown	*CIL* VI 1478
early 250s	Ignotus	[*Adiu?/Vic?*]*trix*	*AE* 1957, 325
late 250s	Axilius [H]onoratus	III ...	*CIL* V 8921
c.260	P. Balsamius Sabinianus	Unknown	*CIL* III 8571

[267] M. P. Speidel 2008: 674–84; Tomlin 2008: 151–2.
[268] Ensslin 1939: 378; de Blois 1976: 46–7; Christol 1977: 407.
[269] Christol 1986: 40–3; Le Bohec 2004: 124–5.
[270] These tables are based on the work of Christol 1982 and 1986: 35–44, with necessary updates.

Table 11.7 *The last attested senatorial legionary legates*

Date	Name	References
Legio II Augusta (Britannia Superior)		
early 250s	T. Flavius Postumius Varus	*RIB* 316
253–8	Vitulasius Laetinianus	*RIB* 334
Legio VI Victrix (Britannia Inferior) [Gallic empire][271]		
262/266	Octavius Sabinus	*RIB* 605 = *ILS* 2548
Legio III Cyrenaica (Arabia)		
253/256	M. Aelius Aurelius Theo	*CIL* III 89 = *ILS* 1193; *CIL* III 90
253/260	Germanus	*AE* 1996, 1602a
250s	Virius Lupus	*CIL* VI 41235 = *ILS* 1210
256/257	?—philus	*AE* 2000, 1536
259/260	[-]ius Gallonianus	*AE* 1953, 231; *IGR* 3.1326
?260/2	Coc(ceius) Rufinus	*AE* 1905, 213; *IGR* 3.1288
262/263	Iunius Olympus	*IGR* 3, 1286 = *SEG* 50, 1519
Legio III Augusta (Numidia)		
253/254	C. Macrinius Decianus	*CIL* VIII 2615 = *ILS* 1194
254/256	C. Pomponius Magnus	*CIL* VIII 2748; *AE* 1917/18, 76
256–8	L. Magius Valerianus	*AE* 1950, 63
258–9	M. Veturius Veturianus	*CIL* VIII 2634 = *ILS* 2296
After 260	C. Iulius Sallustius Fortunatianus	*AE* 1971, 508–10
Unknown legions		
early 250s	Ignotus	*AE* 1966, 376

Vitulasius Laetinianus, legate of the *legio II Augusta* in Britannia Superior between AD 253 and 256, is the last attested senator in command of a legion in a two- or three-legion province. In the one-legion provinces of Arabia and Numidia the legates of the *legio III Cyrenaica* and *legio III Augusta* also served as the provincial governor. In Arabia there is a clear and decisive change after AD 262/3, as Iunius Olympus' successors were all equestrian governors.[272] The case of Numidia is more speculative. C. Iulius Sallustius Saturninus Fortunatianus is definitively attested under Gallienus as both governor of the province and legate of the *legio III Augusta*.[273]

---

[271] A. R. Birley 2005: 337, 365 proposed that Postumus may not have implemented the Gallienic reforms, which is very likely. This is discussed further below.

[272] See Gerhardt and Hartmann 2008: 1100–1.

[273] *CIL* VIII 2797 = *ILS* 2413. This inscription is fragmentary, but Fortunatianus' identity is secured by the fact that the *beneficiarius* who erected the statue also dedicated one to the legate's wife (*AE* 1917/18, 52). See A. R. Birley 1991: 601–2, who placed his governorship early in the 260s, though the exact dates are unknown (Le Bohec 2004: 125).

The traditional command structure of the *III Augusta* seems to have been maintained at this time, since Fortunatianus was the superior of Aurelius Syrus, *vir egregius* and *praefectus (castrorum) legionis*.[274] There is unfortunately no end date for Fortunatianus' tenure on record, and the next governor, the equestrian Tenagino Probus, is not attested until AD 267.[275] We cannot therefore assign any decision made by Gallienus to stop appointing senatorial legionary legates to a particular year, and indeed it was probably a gradual process.[276]

Over the course of the 260s senatorial legionary legates were replaced by officers of equestrian rank. These new officers bore the title of *praefectus legionis*, like the commander of the *legio II Traiana* in Egypt and the *legiones Parthicae*. The new prefects are collected in Table 11.8.

M. Aurelius Veteranus is styled *praefectus legionis*, which means that we cannot entirely exclude the possibility that he served under a senatorial legate, like Aurelius Syrus. However, the officers with stars next to their names are recorded with the title of *praefectus legionis a(gens) v(ice) l(egati)*, indicating that they had replaced the senatorial general. These new equestrian prefects had the rank of *vir egregius*, as had been the case with the previous *praefecti castrorum* in the third century AD.

No senator is ever again attested as a legionary legate after the reign of Gallienus. But there is a question as to whether this transfer of authority from senatorial legates to equestrian prefects had started before the 260s. Piso has recently published two statue bases from Potaissa in Dacia, which

Table 11.8 *Legionary prefects (AD 260–285)*

Date	Name	Legion	References
260/268	M. Aurelius Veteranus	*XIII Gemina*	*CIL* III 1560 = *ILS* 3845
261/267	P. Aelius Aelianus*	*II Adiutrix*	*CIL* III 3529; *AE* 1965, 9
267	Clementius Valerius Marcellinus*	*II Adiutrix*	*CIL* III 3425 = *ILS* 545
268	Aurelius Frontinus	*II Adiutrix*	*CIL* III 3525 = *ILS* 2457
268	Aurelius Montanus*	*X Gemina*	*AE* 2011, 1007[277]
269	Aurelius Superinus*	*I Adiutrix*	*CIL* III 4289 = *ILS* 3656
270/275	M. Aurelius Fortunatus	*III Augusta*	*CIL* VIII 2665 = *ILS* 584
283/5	Aelius Paternianus*	*II Adiutrix*	*CIL* III 3469

---

[274] *AE* 1971, 508; Piso 2014: 142 n. 106.   [275] Gerhardt and Hartmann 2008: 1156.

[276] See Le Bohec 2004: 124 on previous attempts to date the change to AD 262.

[277] This inscription was originally published as *CIL* III 14359.27 = *ILS* 9268, but the readings and dating underwent substantial revision in Alföldy 2011.

date to the reign of Aemilius Aemilianus (AD 253). These attest a certain M. Publicianus Rhesus as *praef(ectus) alae Bat(avorum) (milliariae) agens vice praef(ecti) leg(ionis)* ('prefect of the thousand-strong cavalry wing of Batavi, acting in place of the prefect of the legion'). The legion in question was the *V Macedonica*, which was stationed at Potaissa.[278] Was the prefect whom Rhesus replaced merely the *praefectus castrorum* who answered to a senatorial legate, or was he the legionary commander? Piso argued that it is unlikely that he was the *praefectus castrorum*, since it is difficult to accept that the equestrian prefect of a nearby auxiliary unit (the the *ala I Batavorum milliaria* was stationed at Salinae to the south of Potaissa) would be seconded to this post. This raises the prospect that a certain Donatus, attested as *praefectus legionis* of the *V Macedonica* in AD 255, was also an independent legionary commander, rather than being the *praefectus castrorum*.[279] Piso's argument is certainly possible, but without further information we cannot be confident that Rhesus did not deputise for a *praefectus castrorum*. The jury must remain out for now. What we can say for certain is that the epigraphic evidence shows that senatorial tribunes and legates ceased to be appointed after the reign of Gallienus, even if the process may have begun earlier in the 250s.

It remains the case that senators continued to command expeditionary forces through to the 250s. Indeed, it was from such a post that the emperor Valerian was himself able to claim the purple. From the sole reign of Gallienus onwards, however, such forces were only placed under the control of equestrians, most of whom had risen from the ranks of the army, rather than through a procuratorial career.[280] For example, the officer responsible for overseeing the fortification of Verona in AD 265 was Aurelius Marcellinus, a *vir perfectissimus*, who bore the hitherto unattested title 'general of generals' (*duc(e) duc(um)*).[281] The new hierarchy is best demonstrated by the officers involved in combating the invasions in Asia Minor and the Balkans.[282] The overall command of the campaign against the Goths in AD 268 was in the hands of Aurelius Marcianus.[283] An inscribed statue base from Philippopolis in Thrace gives his full title as 'the *vir perfectissimus* Marcianus, *protector* of our unconquered lord Gallienus Augustus, praetorian tribune, *dux* and

---

[278] Piso 2014: 125–8.   [279] *CIL* III 875 = *ILS* 4345; Piso 2014: 129.
[280] Heil 2008a: 753–4; Mennen 2011: 244–5.
[281] *CIL* V 3329 = *ILS* 544. This reading, as opposed to *duc(e) duc(enario)*, is supported by an inscription from Numidia attesting Marcellinus with the same title, *duci ducum*, without requiring expansion (*AE* 2006, 1803). See Buonopane 2008: 129–33.
[282] Goltz and Hartmann 2008: 283–7.
[283] Zos. 1.40.1; *HA Gall.* 13.10; Goltz and Hartmann 2008: 286–7.

general' (τὸν διασημότατον | Μαρκιανόν, προτήκτο|ρα τοῦ ἀνεικήτου δεσπό|του ἡμῶν Γαλλιηνοῦ Σεβ(αστοῦ)| τριβοῦνον πραιτωριανῶν | καὶ δοῦκα καὶ στρατηλάτην).²⁸⁴ The reappearance of the Greek term στρατηλάτης, denoting a senior general, previously applied to Zeno Ianuarius and Domitius Philippus in Egypt, emphasises the importance of his command. Marcianus was supported in this conflict by vexillations of the *legio II Parthica* and *legio III Augusta*, stationed in Macedonia under the command of the *dux* Aurelius Augustianus and the *praepositus* Clyentus Synforianus.²⁸⁵ Similar field army brigades are attested on the Danubian front under Gallienus. Vexillations of German and British legions, as well as their auxiliary forces, were stationed Sirmium in Pannonia under the command of the *praepositus* Vitalianus.²⁸⁶ L. Flavius Aper, *vir egregius*, commanded detachments of the *legio V Macedonica* and *legio XIII Gemina*, based at nearby Poetovio.²⁸⁷

Many of the new legionary prefects and field army commanders carried the title of *protector*.²⁸⁸ This indicates that they had been promoted through the field army positions of praetorian tribune, centurion or chief centurion. This was the case with the first praetorian prefect appointed by Gallienus after the death of his father Valerian, L. Petronius Taurus Volusianus, who was a praetorian tribune and *protector* before becoming *praefectus vigilum*.²⁸⁹ Aurelius Marcianus, the commander against the Goths in AD 268, was a *vir perfectissimus* and praetorian tribune, demonstrating that Gallienus was selecting generals directly from the field army. In previous generations Marcianus, as a 'Rome tribune', would have been eligible for a procuratorial career, which would have involved financial and administrative posts. Under Gallienus he was deployed directly into a military command. Other *protectores* promoted to senior military posts include the *praepositus* Vitalianus, and two of the *praefecti legionis*, Clementius Valerius Marcellinus and P. Aelius Aelianus. Aelianus, prefect of the *legio II Adiutrix*, was the son of P. Aelius Martialis, who had served as keeper of the armaments (*custos armorum*) in the same legion.²⁹⁰ One

---

²⁸⁴ *AE* 1965, 114 = *IGBulg.* V 5409. He is probably identical with the Aurelius Marcianus honoured on Rhodes with the same title (*SEG* 47, 1256).

²⁸⁵ *AE* 1934, 193 = *IG* X 2.2, 364.

²⁸⁶ *CIL* III 3228 = *ILS* 546; M. P. Speidel 2008: 675. There is further evidence for vexillations of British legions serving in Europe (*RIB* II.3, 2427.26*; *CIL* XIII 6780).

²⁸⁷ *AE* 1936, 53–4, 57.

²⁸⁸ Christol 1977; Goltz and Hartmann 2008: 279; Mennen 2011: 227–31.

²⁸⁹ Gerhardt and Hartmann 2008: 1073.

²⁹⁰ *CIL* III 3529: 'To the divine shades of the memory of P. Aelius Martialis, onetime veteran and former keeper of the armaments of the *legio II Adiutrix*, his father, and Flavia Agathe, his

officer who worked his way up through the different grades of *protector* in the reign of Gallienus was Traianus Mucianus, who began his army career as a humble *miles* in an auxiliary cohort. His transfer to the *legio II Parthica* brought him into the field army, and he would end up playing a pivotal commanding role in Aurelian's campaigns against Zenobia in the 270s.[291] The advancement was made possible by the patronage of Gallienus' praetorian prefect, the *vir eminentissimus* Aurelius Heraclianus, whom Traianus honoured with a statue in his home town of Augusta Traiana, praising him as his benefactor.[292] It must be pointed out that not all of Gallienus' appointees were so humble. The praetorian prefect Volusianus was actually from a traditional municipal Italian background, having been granted the *equus publicus* and serving in the *decuriae* before being commissioned as a centurion *ex equite Romano*. Now *equites* from the municipal aristocracies like Volusianus fought alongside men who rose from the ranks, such as Aelius Aelianus and Traianus Mucianus. This new career path, which led from soldier to general, was only possible because of the changes which took place in the late second to third centuries AD.[293]

Gallienus' second significant innovation was his use of cavalry units, which were especially mobile forces suited for moving quickly between different fronts. It has been suggested that Gallienus established a new cavalry strike force, composed of the *equites singulares Augusti* and a range of other mounted auxiliary units.[294] The ancient sources refer to a supreme cavalry commander under Gallienus, a post first held by Aureolus and then by the future emperor Claudius II.[295] Aureolus certainly played a major role in campaigns on several fronts, not only in the Danubian wars against the Goths, but also against Postumus in Gaul.[296] It is highly likely that Aureolus and Claudius were both tribunes of the *equites singulares Augusti*.[297] From the reign of Septimius Severus onwards there were two such officers at any one time, overseeing the *castra nova* and *castra priora* ('new camp' and 'old camp') of the *equites singulares*.[298]

---

mother…' (D(is) M(anibus) | memoriae P(ublii) Ael(i) Martialis q(uon)d(am) | vet(erani) ex c(ustode) a(rmorum) leg(ionis) II Adi(utricis) patris et | Flaviae Agathes matris …).

[291] *IGBulg*. III.2 1570.

[292] *IG Bulg*. III.2 1568, 1569. For the careers of these men, see Christol 1976, 1977.

[293] Handy 2006: 75–9.   [294] Ritterling 1903; D. Hoffmann 1969/70: I, 247–8.

[295] Ritterling 1903: 346; Zos. 1.40.1; Zon. 12.24 (ed. Dindorf p. 143); *HA Aurel*. 18.1. For acceptance of this theory, see M. P. Speidel 1994b: 72; Nicasie 1998: 37.

[296] Goltz and Hartmann 2008: 288. Danube: *HA Gall*. 3.3. Postumus: Zos. 1.40.1; Victor, *Caes*. 33.17; *HA Gall*. 4.6, 7.1.

[297] M. P. Speidel 1987: 376–7. For Claudius, see Zon. 12.25 (ed. Dindorf pp. 148–9), 12.26 (ed. Dindorf p. 150); D. Hoffmann 1969/70: I, 247.

[298] M. P. Speidel 1994b: 59–60, 95.

The tribunes, who ranked as *viri egregii*, were usually former *primipilares.*[299] The importance of cavalry units in Gallienus' field army increased the standing of their commanders.[300] Aurelius Valentinus, one of the tribunes of the horse guard, is attested with the senior equestrian rank of *vir perfectissimus.*[301] The command hierarchy of the auxiliary cavalry units also changed as new junior officer posts, which were within reach of the ordinary cavalrymen, were introduced. The positions of *centenarius* and *ducenarius*, which ranked above centurions, are first attested in cavalry *alae* in the reign of Gallienus.[302] One of these officers was Aurelius Processanus, who was promoted from his post as centurion in the sixth praetorian cohort to become a *protector ducenarius* in the cavalry.[303]

An inscribed dedication to the emperor Claudius II Gothicus at Grenoble illuminates the new military hierarchy that crystallised in the reign of Gallienus (Claudius' immediate predecessor). It was erected in AD 269 by the army preparing to invade the Gallic empire:

> To the Emperor Caesar Marcus Aurelius Claudius, Dutiful, Fortunate Unconquered Augustus, greatest conqueror of Germany, *pontifex maximus*, holding tribunician power for the second time, consul, father of the fatherland, proconsul, the vexillations and cavalry units and *praepositi* and *ducenarii protectores* encamped in the province of Narbonensis, under the command of Iulius Placidianus, *vir perfectissimus, praefectus vigilum*, devoted to his spirit and majesty.[304]

The supreme commander of the field army unit was Iulius Placidianus, a *praefectus vigilum* deployed outside Rome, much like Domitius Philippus had been in Egypt in the reign of Gordian III. The next year Placidianus would be elevated to the praetorian prefecture while still in Gaul.[305] His subordinates were equestrian *praepositi*, who were in charge of the infantry vexillations, and the *ducenarii protectores* commanding the cavalry

---

[299] Dobson 1974: 417–20.   [300] Cosme 2007: 107–9.

[301] *IG* X.2.1, 151; M. P. Speidel 1994a: 102–3.

[302] M. P. Speidel 2005: 206–7, 2008: 681. These should be distinguished from the identical procuratorial titles.

[303] *CIL* XI 837 = *ILS* 2778.

[304] *CIL* XII 2228 = *ILS* 569: *Imp(eratori) Caesar[i] | M(arco) Aur(elio) Claudio | Pio Felici Invicto | Aug(usto) Germanico | max(imo) p(ontifici) m(aximo) trib(uniciae) potes|tatis II co(n)s(uli) patri pa|triae proc(onsuli) vexil|lationes adque | equites itemque | praepositi et duce|nar(ii) protect(ores) ten|dentes in Narb(onensi) | prov(incia) sub cura Iul(ii) | Placidiani v(iri) p(erfectissimi) prae|fect(i) vigil(um) devoti | numini maiesta|tiq(ue) eius.*

[305] *CIL* XII 1551.

divisions. This field army now had its own distinct identity as a complete unit under the command of officers of equestrian rank.

One question remains. Why did senators cease to be appointed as legionary legates and commanders of expeditionary forces? It was probably the result of several factors. Firstly, the vicissitudes of near-constant warfare on both the northern and eastern frontiers in the 240s–250s had divided standing legions into vexillations, which were sent far from their home base, and to which they often did not return, instead being quartered at new locations.[306] The *legio III Italica* in Raetia is a good example of this. It was traditionally commanded by a senatorial legate of praetorian rank, who also served as governor of the province. In the middle of the third century AD vexillations from this legion served under P. Licinius Valerianus, when he was still a senator and had been entrusted with a special command by the emperor Aemilius Aemilianus.[307] During Valerian's own reign detachments from the *legio III Italica* formed part of the imperial field army that fought unsuccessfully against the Persians under Shapur at the Battle of Edessa in AD 260.[308] It is highly likely that the senatorial legionary legate accompanied the vexillations of the legion on this disastrous expedition. For we know that in AD 260 Raetia had an acting equestrian governor, M. Simplicinius Genialis, *vir perfectissimus*. Genialis defeated the invading Semnones and Iuthungi while in charge of an army composed of troops from Raetia, Germany and the local populace, an act subsequently commemorated on a famous victory altar.[309] The *legio III Italica* is not mentioned at all in this inscription, and the fact that Genialis' army included what amounted to a local militia suggests that a significant proportion of the legion had been sent as vexillations under the command of the senatorial legate to participate in Valerian's field army. The *Res Gestae divi Saporis* recorded that senators were captured along with the emperor Valerian after the Roman defeat at Edessa.[310] This leads to the conclusion that a large number of leading senatorial officers were lost in this disaster.[311]

The Battle of Edessa was the latest in a series of defeats which had caused dramatic losses in Roman manpower in the middle decades of the third century.[312] The slaughter of Trajan Decius, Herennius Etruscus and their troops at the Battle of Abrittus in AD 251 must have deprived the army of

---

[306] Strobel 2009: 916–19.   [307] Victor, *Caes.* 32.1; Eutrop. 9.7.   [308] Loriot 2006: 329.
[309] *AE* 1993, 1231; Piso 2014: 141.   [310] *Res Gestae divi Saporis* line 22 (ed. Huyse).
[311] Cosme 2007: 106–7. Duncan-Jones 2016: 79 also makes a connection between the impact of Valerian's defeat and the change in the military hierarchy.
[312] Potter 2004: 251.

both men and commanders.[313] Furthermore, in AD 252 or 253 the Persian
king Shapur invaded Roman territory in the east, massacring a Roman
army of 60,000 at Barbalissus, and capturing Antioch on the Orontes.[314]
As Potter has pointed out, the list of cities Shapur claims to have taken
include the major legionary strongholds.[315] Some time between AD 252
and 256 an equestrian acting governor, Pomponius Laetianus, is attested in
Syria Coele, perhaps because the senatorial incumbent had been killed or
because he needed to delegate his judicial authority to the procurator.[316]
The crisis of AD 260 was thus the culmination of a decade of military
setbacks resulting in the attrition of Roman forces and officers. It is
plausible to propose, therefore, that Gallienus sought to fill the legionary
commands left vacant after senatorial legates had been captured or killed at
the Battle of Edessa by promoting soldiers from within the army hierarchy.
The most logical choice would be officers at the rank of *praefectus castrorum* who were now deputised to act in place of legate, hence the title
praefectus agens vice legati which we find in the epigraphic sources.[317] Such
an action would have been in keeping with the Roman government's
pattern of replacing deceased officials with acting substitutes, as we
explored earlier in the chapter.

There is an additional reason for a shortage of senators to command the
legions during Gallienus' sole reign: he did not control substantial portions
of the empire. In the summer of AD 260 M. Cassianius Latinius Postumus,
the governor of Germania Inferior, revolted.[318] Gallienus' son and Caesar,
P. Cornelius Licinius Saloninus Valerianus (known as Saloninus for short),
was murdered at Colonia Agrippina during this usurpation, together with

---

[313] For this defeat, see Zos. 1.23; Potter 2004: 242; Drinkwater 2005: 39.
[314] *Res Gestae divi Saporis* lines 9–13 (ed. Huyse); Zos. 1.27. For the date of AD 252, see Potter 2004: 249; for AD 253, see Barnes 2009.
[315] Potter 2004: 249.   [316] *P. Euphr.* 3–4.
[317] See Heil 2008a: 755 n. 6, for a possible connection between the post *praefectus castrorum* and the later *praefectus legionis*. Of course, those *praefecti castrorum* who accompanied the legionary vexillations to Persia would not have been viable candidates, as they too would have been killed or captured. We are referring here to *praefecti castrorum* who commanded units or vexillations that did not form part of the expeditionary force.
[318] The exact sphere of Postumus' command is uncertain, but the consensus is now that he was governor of Germania Inferior (Eck 1985: 222–3; Drinkwater 1987: 25–6, 2005: 45; Potter 2004: 257; Gerhardt and Hartmann 2008: 1125–6). The case for this province is a strong one. If Postumus had been governor of Belgica, Lugdunensis, Aquitania or Gallia Narbonensis he would have had no legions under his command with which to mount an insurrection. Postumus was almost certainly of senatorial status, as he claimed his second consulship in 261 (Peachin 1990: 100), which means that he had already been consul before his usurpation (Drinkwater 1987: 67, 168 n. 121).

the praetorian prefect Silvanus.[319] This was a major blow to the emperor, who had lost his eldest son and Caesar, P. Licinius Cornelius Valerianus, in AD 258, and his father and co-Augustus Valerian earlier in AD 260.[320] Now Gallienus was the sole remaining member of the imperial college.[321] When Postumus revolted Gallienus himself was occupied elsewhere, dealing with the invasion of Italy by the Alamanni and Iuthungi.[322] Over the course of the next year Postumus' territory expanded to include a significant portion of the western empire, including Gaul, Spain, and even Britain.[323] The insurrection of Postumus not only deprived Gallienus of control of these provinces, but also separated him from the senatorial and equestrian elites who remained in the territories under Postumus' control.[324] The admittedly exiguous epigraphic evidence from Postumus' provinces shows one senator, Octavius Sabinus, still in command of troops (the *legio VI Victrix*) in his realm, suggesting that he did not replace senatorial legionary legates as Gallienus did.[325] It is also highly likely that Ulpius Cornelius Laelianus, who rebelled against Postumus himself in AD 268, was either the senatorial governor of Germania Superior or the legate of the *legio XXII Primigenia* stationed in Mogontiacum.[326] The 'Gallic' empire therefore did still employ some senators as legionary commanders, perhaps in conjunction with equestrian officials.[327]

The revolt of Postumus was not the only usurpation to trouble Gallienus in AD 260; indeed, the capture of his father Valerian initiated an unprecedented series of revolts across the empire, many of which were staged by senatorial governors. These included Ingenuus, governor of one of the Danubian provinces, and P. Cassius Regalianus, who was in charge of Pannonia Superior.[328] Although these were dealt with relatively swiftly,

---

[319] Zos. 1.38.2; Zon. 12.24 (ed. Dindorf p. 144); *Epit.* 32.3. For Silvanus, see also Zos. 1.37.2; Howe 1942: 81; Drinkwater 1987: 88–9.

[320] Valerianus Caesar had died in AD 258 on the Danube frontier (Victor, *Caes.* 33.3; *Epit.* 33.1; Drinkwater 2005: 43).

[321] Marinianus, the consul of AD 268, may have been a third son or nephew of Gallienus (Grandvallet 2006).

[322] Zos. 1. 37.1–38.1; Victor, *Caes.* 33.3; Drinkwater 2005: 43–4, 2007: 56–7.

[323] Lafaurie 1975: 869–72; Drinkwater 1987: 27; A. R. Birley 2005: 364.

[324] Kulikowski 2014: 142. Senators were officially supposed to reside in Rome, but could obtain imperial permission to live elsewhere (*Dig.* 50.1.22.6 (Paulus); Salzman 2002: 31). This means that a number of senators would have been caught on either side of the empires of Postumus and Gallienus during the 260s.

[325] A. R. Birley 2005: 337, 365.   [326] Luther 2008: 333.

[327] The senators may well have been members of the senate of the 'Gallic' empire, rather than that of Rome. For the Gallic origin of Laelianus and other emperors of this region, see Drinkwater 1987: 34–9.

[328] Goltz and Hartmann 2008: 262–6. The revolt of Ingenuus may have been long in gestation, if we can trust an anecdote that Gallienus' wife Salonina suspected the governor's ambitions (*Anon. Cont. Dio.* frag. 5 = *FHG* IV p. 194).

there were further insurrections in the east. Valerian's surviving praetorian prefect Ballista and the *a rationibus* T. Fulvius Macrianus elevated the latter's two sons, T. Fulvius Iunius Macrianus and T. Fulvius Iunius Quietus, to the imperial purple.[329] Coins minted in Antioch, Nicaea and Byzantium show that they were recognised throughout Syria and Asia Minor until their defeat in AD 261.[330] The proclamation of the Macriani led to confusion and upheaval throughout the eastern provinces. The proconsul of Achaea, a senator known only as Valens, was acclaimed emperor, either in opposition to the rule of the Macriani or to Gallienus himself.[331] His revolt collapsed, possibly suppressed by another aristocratic general loyal to the Macriani.[332]

The loss of senatorial life at the Battle of Edessa and the secession of Postumus' 'Gallic' empire are part of the story, but this series of revolts lends some credence to Aurelius Victor's suggestion that the exclusion of senators from the direct command of troops was prompted by Gallienus' fear of usurpation.[333] Indeed, in the light of the insurrections of Postumus, Ingenuus and Regalianus, not to mention the deaths of his father and son, it is not surprising that Gallienus felt that he could not trust his senatorial peers. It is important to point out, however, that he excluded not only senators as legionary legates and field army commanders, but also the equestrian procuratorial elite, who, as we have seen, constituted an aristocracy of service. These were the sort of *equites* who had held ad hoc military commands with the rank of procurator since the reign of Marcus Aurelius. They were probably also regarded as potential challengers for the purple by Gallienus, given the revolts orchestrated by prominent *equites* such as Ballista and Macrianus. Instead, Gallienus specifically turned to the field army for his new officers – that is, men promoted from the ranks, rather than the procuratorial *cursus*. The fact that senatorial generals were replaced by praetorian tribunes, *praepositi* and *praefecti* from among the corps of *protectores* fostered by Valerian and Gallienus cannot be a random coincidence. It is highly unlikely, of course, that Gallienus actually

---

[329] Goltz and Hartmann 2008: 259–62.   [330] Peachin 1990: 38, 366.

[331] Valens appears in the *HA Gall.* 2.2–3 and *Trig. Tyr.* 19.1–3, but his historicity is borne out by mentions in other sources (*Epit.* 32.4; Amm. 21.16.10).

[332] The *HA* records that Macrianus sent a consular named Piso to execute Valens, which prompted Valens to usurp the throne (*HA Trig. Tyr.* 19.1–3). Piso only appears in the *HA Gall.* 2.2 and *Trig. Tyr.* 19.2–3, 21.1–7, and thus it is uncertain whether he even existed. However, Amm. 21.16.10 says that Valens was called Thessalonicus, while the *HA* (*Gall.* 2.4; *Trig. Tyr.* 21.1) gives Piso a very similar name (Thessalicus). There may have only been one usurper in Achaea, which the *HA* turned into two characters in order to add another rebel to his account of the *Tyranni Triginta*.

[333] De Blois 1976: 82; Le Bohec 2004: 129–30.

promulgated an edict regarding the appointment of senators, as Victor contends. Edicts were only addressed to the population of the empire – emperors did not issue them to themselves.[334] Instead, he simply stopped selecting senators for military commands as tribunes and legates in the regions of the empire he controlled. Once the precedent was set, it was never reversed.

The restructuring of military commands precipitated the demise of the *militiae equestres* as a coherent series of officer posts.[335] The last securely dated attestation of the terms *a militiis* and ἀπὸ στρατειῶν occurs in the 280s.[336] Promotion to officer commands now came via the protectorate, which was transformed from an honorific title to an actual position in the course of the 270s. The *protectores* constituted an elite corps of junior officers, primed for promotion to higher posts, as *tribunus*, *praepositus*, *praefectus alae*, and *praefectus legionis*.[337] The *protectores* therefore filled the role previously occupied by *primipilares*, since the office of *primus pilus*, the senior centurion of the legion, changed to a military supply post after the reign of Gallienus.[338] These officers did not have to be of equestrian status before obtaining their commands: instead, they received the title of *vir egregius* upon their appointment. Equestrian rank had therefore become a reward for service as a military officer, rather than a precondition for it, and was not dependent on the *census equester*. This change would have appealed to the soldiery, given their desire for access to officer commands and equestrian rank which we have already traced in the late second and early third centuries AD.

Where did this leave the members of the municipal aristocracies who had previously monopolised the posts in the *militiae*? Judging from the evidence of the late Roman law codes, the curial classes still tried to obtain direct commissions as *protectores* in the fourth century AD, since this would provide them with immunity from municipal liturgies. Army families also gained preferential treatment in the new system. When the sons of military officers and civilian officials chose to enter the army in the fourth century AD they were appointed as *protectores*, rather than having to rise through the ranks.[339] There was one significant difference, however: unlike the *militiae equestres*, service as a *protector* carried a commitment to many years in the Roman army.[340] Therefore, members of the curial cases

[334] Le Bohec 2004: 124.   [335] This argument is laid out in full in Davenport forthcoming.
[336] *AE* 1973, 550; *AE* 1987, 1084; *AE* 1989, 869.   [337] M. P. Speidel 2008: 687–8.
[338] Dobson 1978: 139–45; M. P. Speidel 2008: 688.
[339] A. H. M. Jones 1964: 641–2; Matthews 1989: 77–80, 270, 519 n. 33.
[340] Trombley 1999: 18–21.

who became *protectores* followed a similar career path to those who were commissioned as centurions *ex equite Romano* in the high empire.

Gallienus' reforms had important ramifications for the appointment of provincial governors as well. Since the legions had been transferred from senatorial *legati* to equestrian *praefecti*, senators no longer continued to administer the one-legion provinces in which the legionary commander doubled as the governor (Arabia, Britannia Inferior, Noricum, Numidia, Raetia and Syria Phoenice).[341] This probably began as an interim measure: we have already discussed the case of M. Simplicinius Genialis, appointed *agens vice praesidis* in Raetia when the senatorial legate was probably in the east with Valerian. In the province of Arabia there is a clear break between the senator Iunius Olympus, who held office AD 262/3, and the *vir egregius* Statilius Ammianus, who is recorded as acting governor (διέποντος τὴν ἡγεμονίαν) in AD 263/4.[342] Later in the 260s an anonymous *vir perfectissimus*, who was perhaps even Ammianus' immediate successor, was 'entrusted with the governorship' (ἐγκεχ(ειρισμένου) τὴν ἡγεμον(ίαν)).[343] A similar situation occurs in the praetorian provinces without legions, such as Macedonia and Thrace. In Macedonia the *vir egregius* M. Aurelius Apollinarius is attested under Gallienus as 'imperial procurator, managing the office of the proconsul' (ἐπί|τροπον τοῦ Σεβ(αστοῦ), πράσσοντα | τὰ μ[έ]ρη τῆς ἀν[θ]υπατείας).[344] This title shows that he was already in office as financial procurator when he was promoted to deputise for the proconsul, using the same procedure that had become common over previous decades. In AD 267/8 this same Apollinarius appears as provincial governor of Thrace, but as a *vir perfectissimus* 'governing the province' (ἡγούμενον [τῆς] | ἐπαρχείας).[345] Apollinarius had made a transition from being a procurator, exercising temporary gubernatorial authority in one province, to being a governor in his own right in another region. This transition may well have been assisted by the fact that he was the brother of Aurelius Heraclianus, the praetorian prefect of the emperor Gallienus.[346] The epigraphic evidence suggests that this transformation was not uniform throughout the empire, as provinces acquired equestrian *praesides* at different times throughout the 260s and 270s.

The situation in the consular provinces is equally complicated. We are best informed about the hierarchy in Pannonia Inferior, thanks to a number of inscriptions which survive from that province. A series of

[341] Glas and Hartmann 2008: 662; Heil 2008a: 750.   [342] *IGR* III 1287.   [343] *SEG* 16, 810.

[344] *IG* X 2.1, 140; Pflaum 1982: 97–8 (no. 357A).

[345] *IGBulg.* III.2 1569; Christol 1976: 870–4.

[346] This relationship is explicitly stated in the text of *IGBulg.* III.2 1569.

equestrian prefects is attested in command of the *legio II Adiutrix* in the 260s, demonstrating the transfer of legionary commands: P. Aelius Aelianus (AD 261/7), Clementius Valerius Marcellinus (AD 267) and Aurelius Frontinus (AD 268). Marcellinus and Frontinus both served under the governor Clementius Silvius, who was a *vir egregius*. In the first inscription, from AD 267, Silvius has the title *a(gens) v(ice) p(raesidis)*, but in AD 268 he is attested as *praeses*.[347] Since he also has the title of *a(gens) v(ice) p(raesidis)* on a third, undated, inscription, we should not read too much into the distinction.[348] The same issue occurs with L. Flavius Aper, a *vir perfectissimus* attested as governor of Pannonia Inferior under Aurelian, who is attested as *a(gens) v(ice) p(raesidis)* and *praeses* on different inscriptions.[349] In the light of the fact that neither Silvius nor Aper is given the title of procurator, it is probable that they were appointed directly to the province of Pannonia Inferior as governor. Officially, as equestrians, their title was *a(gens) v(ice) p(raesidis)* standing in for the senatorial governor, but for all intents and purposes they were effectively the *praeses*. The use of the title *a(gens) v(ice) p(raesidis)* was not merely an outdated relic of traditionalism: it signalled that senators could still be appointed to govern the province. Indeed, under Probus the senator M. Aurelius Valentinianus appears as governor of Pannonia Inferior with the traditional title of *legatus Augusti pro praetore*.[350] In nearby Moesia Inferior an acting governor, Titius Saturninus, is attested in AD 268/70, but then two senatorial *legati Augusti pro praetore*, Sallius Aristaenetus and M. Aurelius Sebastianus, appear in office under Aurelian.[351] The same pattern recurs in Syria Palaestina: Aurelius Maron was procurator and acting governor in the 260s or later, but two senatorial *praesides* are attested under Probus.[352]

Although Gallienus ceased appointing senators to legionary commands, there was no systematic plan to deprive them of provincial governorships.[353] Indeed, on current evidence, senators governed the key consular province of Syria Coele through to the Tetrarchic period.[354] All

---

[347] *CIL* III 3425 = *ILS* 545; *CIL* III 3525 = *ILS* 2457 = *AE* 1993, 1310.   [348] *CIL* III 10424.
[349] *AE* 2003, 1417b; *CIL* III 15156.   [350] *CIL* III 3418 = *ILS* 3654.
[351] Saturninus: *AE* 1993, 1377. Aristaenetus: *AE* 1994, 1532. Sebastianus: *SEG* 44, 635 = *SEG* 50, 688; *IGR* I 591 = *SEG* 50, 679.
[352] Maron: *AE* 1978, 824. The senatorial governors were Acilius Cleobulus (*AE* 1993, 1620) and Clodius Passenianus (*AE* 1993, 1623).
[353] Glas and Hartmann 2008: 663–4.
[354] See the *fasti* in Gerhardt and Hartmann 2008: 1180–2. For the Tetrarchic period, note the case of L. Aelius Helvius Dionysius (*CIL* VI 1673 = *ILS* 1211).

provincial governors, regardless of whether they were senators or *equites*, still must have had oversight of troops stationed in these provinces, as Le Bohec has pointed out.[355] This was certainly the case in the early fourth century AD, where we can observe a number of governors involved in military construction and logistics throughout the empire.[356] It must be the case, therefore, that emperors of the late third century AD appointed both senators and equestrians to administer provinces without paying attention to whether the position of governor was reserved for senators of praetorian or consular status, as it had been in the past.

In some cases this led to the final breakdown of the traditional division between senatorial proconsulates and the imperial provinces. Both Baetica and Macedonia ceased to be governed by proconsuls, and instead received senatorial and equestrian *praesides*.[357] With the transfer of at least some of the proconsulates to imperial appointees, the post of provincial quaestor disappeared, being last attested in AD 260.[358] Proconsuls still continued to be appointed in Achaea, as well as in the consular provinces of Asia and Africa, which remained prestigious appointments for senators.[359] These developments acknowledged the practical reality that it did not matter whether a *praeses* was of equestrian or senatorial status, because members of both *ordines* were equally well equipped to undertake the duties required. This was the result of the emergence and consolidation of the equestrian service elite whose offices and responsibilities were very similar to senators. It was only under the Tetrarchs that the vast majority of provincial governorships were standardised with equestrian *viri perfectissimi* as governors, as we shall see in the next chapter.

Gallienus was murdered in AD 268 by a cabal of his senior officers, not by senators. In the end the *protectores* turned on their emperor, and elected the cavalry commander M. Aurelius Claudius (better known as Claudius II Gothicus) as his successor from among their own number. The promotion of the officers to senior military commands meant that these men were now in a position to become emperors themselves. The senate's reaction to

[355] Le Bohec 2004: 125–8.
[356] A. H. M. Jones 1964: 43–4; Bowman 1978: 33; Davenport 2010: 353–6.
[357] Baetica: Alföldy 1995. Macedonia: Gerhardt and Hartmann 2008: 1136–8.
[358] Christol 1986: 84.
[359] Achaea: Davenport 2013: 225–6. Asia and Africa: Gerhardt and Hartmann 2008: 1090–5, 1102–8. The only exception occurred in AD 276, when the procurator of Asia deputised for the proconsul (*AE* 1924, 70). But this was clearly a temporary appointment, along the lines of earlier examples, such as Minicius Italus under Domitian.

this news was evidently a joyous one, as they ordered Gallienus' supporters to be thrown off the Gemonian steps and organised the murder of his family members in Rome.[360] This provides some sense of the senate's reaction to Gallienus' decision to stop appointing them to military posts, an act which represented an 'affront to their own order', as Aurelius Victor put it. The emperor was remembered with open hostility in Latin historiography of the fourth century AD, most notably in the accounts of Victor, Eutropius and the *Historia Augusta*.[361] The *Historia Augusta* even devoted a whole book to chronicling the thirty tyrants – many of them completely fictional – who challenged Gallienus' decadent regime.[362] Senators never regained their access to legionary commands, though the *curia* and its members did not automatically become politically impotent in the decade after Gallienus' death. They continued to pose a challenge to emperors, such as Aurelian, who rose from the new military elite, although their revolts were ultimately unsuccessful.[363] We have argued here that Gallienus' original intention was to replace senatorial legionary legates who perished in the east with equestrian prefects promoted from within the field army. In a time of crisis, including senatorial revolts across the empire and the loss of the Gallic provinces under Postumus, he turned to a group of officers he could trust. But these actions proved to be a catalyst that brought a number of long-simmering challenges to the traditional hierarchies of the Roman army and administration to a head, giving soldiers readier access to officer commands and equestrian rank, and equestrian procurators access to provinces which were previously the domain of senators.

Conclusion: The Remaking of the Roman State

This chapter has proposed that the third-century transformation of the Roman state was the result of a series of interrelated factors. The first was the demise of established status hierarchies, which had traditionally divided provinces into senatorial imperial provinces, senatorial

---

[360] Victor, *Caes.* 33.21; Zon. 12.26.

[361] Victor, *Caes.* 33.3, 15, 29, 33–4; Eutrop. 9.7–8; *HA Gall.* 1.1, 3.6–9, 4.3, 9.3–8, 16.1–18.6. The Greek historical tradition, as represented by Zos. 1.38–41 and Zon. 12.25, does not rely on these *topoi* of a dissolute emperor.

[362] See the *HA Trig. Tyr.*, where rebellion and revolt is frequently attributed to Gallienus' love of pleasure (e.g. 5.1, 8.9, 9.1, 11.1, 12.8).

[363] Davenport 2014a.

proconsulates and equestrian praesidial procuratorships. This division was essentially artificial, the result of Augustus building his monarchical *res publica* on the foundations of the framework of Republican government. Over the course of the principate a new group of careerist equestrian administrators emerged (the *equestris nobilitas*), which shared the senatorial ethos of serving the state *domi militiaeque*. The responsibilities and competencies of this group were no different from those of senators.[364] The appointment of equestrian procurators as acting governors to assume the governors' judicial responsibilities, or to deputise for them in times of death or crisis, represented the logical extension of this development. These procurators were not promoted as part of an imperial policy to replace senators with equestrians. Instead, the emperors practised a policy of administrative substitution, in which deputies for a wide range of imperial officials – from the emperor himself to prefects, governors and procurators – were selected from among the most suitable candidates, rather than on the basis of their senatorial or equestrian status. Although this challenged existing hierarchies, the essential inertia of the Roman administrative system did not lead to any long-term changes at this stage.

The second development related to the Roman army. The circuitous route to officer commands through the primipilate had stymied soldiers who were ambitious for greater opportunities. From the late second century AD these soldiers petitioned for officer commands in the *militiae equestres*, which were granted to them by emperors who wanted to consolidate their relationship with the army. Many of these soldiers served in the praetorian guard, the *equites singulares*, or the newly founded *legio II Parthica*, which made up the core of the imperial field army that accompanied the emperors on campaign. The favour shown towards these soldiers can also be seen in imperial grants of equestrian rank to their sons. It is very unlikely that these troops, most of whom were below the rank of centurion, possessed the necessary property qualification for equestrian status, either for themselves or their sons. Instead, they were granted equestrian rank as an imperial benefaction. The favour shown to field army troops was formalised in the 250s, when Valerian and Gallienus gave praetorian tribunes and centurions in the field army the honorific title of *protector Augusti*. These developments, although significant, did not in and of themselves challenge the military authority of senators, who continued to serve as tribunes, legionary legates and generals of expeditionary forces through to the mid-third century. Even the appointment of

---

[364] See Chapters 6–7.

equestrians to command posts as part of the procuratorial *cursus* did not constitute an attempt to deprive senators of their authority. Instead, it represented a pragmatic approach to administration, recognising that senators and equestrians were equally suitable for such commands, despite their difference in status.

It took a major crisis to finally overturn the established order. In AD 260 the emperor Valerian was captured by the Persians, along with his praetorian prefects and senatorial generals. In the same year his son Gallienus, now sole Augustus, faced a series of revolts from provincial governors across the empire. In order to replace deceased senatorial legionary legates, and to compensate for the loss of the manpower of the Gallic provinces that had defected to Postumus, Gallienus turned to his *protectores*, the field army officer corps which he and his father had promoted and fostered. What started as an emergency response soon became accepted practice, as he ceased to appoint senators as legionary legates or as the commanders of expeditionary forces. Nor did he turn to members of the equestrian procuratorial elite to hold these positions. Instead, these commands were filled by soldiers who had risen from the ranks, and now earned the equestrian status of *vir egregius* by virtue of their new commands. The result of this decision was that senators were no longer appointed to govern one-legion provinces in which the legate also served as the governor. The practice spread to other provinces as well, though without any apparent consistency: sometimes the governor was an equestrian *vir egregius* or *perfectissimus*, at other times a senatorial *vir clarissimus*. Although initially equestrians were made 'acting governors', as they had been in temporary appointments since the Severan period, they soon became acknowledged as *praesides* in their own right.

This analysis has by necessity concentrated on the most revolutionary impacts of Gallienus' reforms, such as the ascent of military officers from the army to equestrian status, and the breakdown of the traditional army and provincial hierarchies. But it leaves us with one significant question. What happened to the members of the *ordo equester* who, in previous generations, advanced through the procuratorial *cursus*? These were the *equites Romani* who served in the *militiae equestres*, then held financial and administrative posts, perhaps even ascending to the great prefectures. They had been the officials who had deputised for governors *vice praesidis*, ensuring the continuity of government and justice in the provinces. In short, what was the fate of the equestrian service elite, the *equestris nobilitas*? As we shall see in the next chapter, these administrators remained the bedrock of the late Roman imperial state. But by the late fourth century AD, when they managed the imperial finances, issued letters and edicts in the emperor's name, and governed the provinces, they did not do so as equestrians, but as senators.

12 | The Last *Equites Romani*

Introduction: The Edict of Licinius

On 21 July in AD 317 the emperor Licinius issued an edict to the people of the province of Bithynia.[1] The edict, which can be partially reconstructed from the *Codex Theodosianus* and *Codex Justinianus*, specified precisely who was, and who was not, permitted to acquire the *dignitates* of *egregius, centenarius, ducenarius* and *perfectissimus*. These were all grades of equestrian status – only the most prestigious rank of *eminentissimus* was absent – though the *ordo* itself was not mentioned on this occasion. Instead, Licinius referred to these *dignitates* as if they could be acquired or bestowed without reference to membership of the equestrian order. Since the edict was addressed specifically to the Bithynians, it is plausible that Licinius issued the pronouncement in response to a provincial embassy.[2] The contents of the decree suggest that the Bithynians were concerned about government officials and members of the curial class unjustly acquiring these *dignitates* and then claiming immunity from their compulsory civic obligations, known as *munera*.

Three excerpts from Licinius' edict in the *Codex Theodosianus* deal with the ability of specific groups to access these equestrian ranks: *primipilares* (who administered the *annona militaris*), *Caesariani* (officials of the *res privata*), and *monetarii* (imperial minters).[3] The primipilate was by now a military supply post, and a hereditary one at that, so that it officially constituted a public *munus*.[4] Licinius therefore authorised that *primipilares* could be granted the status of *egregius, centenarius, ducenarius* and *perfectissimus* 'after the completion of service' (*post emeritam militiam*).

---

[1] For the attribution of this edict to Licinius, rather than Constantine, see Corcoran 2000: 193, 283–4.

[2] Millar 1983: 93.

[3] *CTh.* 8.4.3 (*primipilares*), *CTh.* 10.7.1. (*Caesariani*), *CTh.* 10.20.1 = *CJ* 11.8.1 (*monetarii*).

[4] For the transformation of the primipilate, see *CJ* 12.62.1 (AD 253/60); *Frag. Vat.* 278 (AD 286); and Dobson 1978: 139–45.

The *Caesariani* had a notorious reputation as corrupt and menacing representatives of the imperial administration, and it would have been a poor political move for the emperor to honour them with the status of *egregius* or above while in service.[5] However, Licinius did allow *Caesariani* to acquire equestrian dignity on discharge if their account books were correctly balanced (i.e. they were shown not to be corrupt).[6] On the other hand, the imperial mint officials were expressly forbidden from the equestrian dignities because 'they must always remain in their natural status' (*in sua semper durare condicione oportet*).[7] The *monetarii* and their offspring were bound to imperial service, which meant that they could only escape if they acquired equestrian status through underhand means.[8]

The final surviving part of Licinius' edict ruled that the equestrian *dignitates* could be granted to imperial officials and decurions who had performed the required *munera* in their cities. It is worth quoting in full because the legislative rhetoric provides important insights into the way in which the *dignitates* were regarded by the imperial government in the early fourth century AD:

Those men who have served in the palace, those men to whom provinces have been assigned, those men who through service in the most distinguished offices have gained the status of *perfectissimus* or *egregius*, and likewise those men who, having been appointed *decuriones* or *principales*, have fulfilled all the *munera* of their place of residence, ought to enjoy the *dignitas* they have been awarded. But if a *decurio* has earned the *dignitas* of *perfectissimus* or *ducenarius* or *centenarius* or *egregius* by means of a purchased recommendation, because he desires to avoid his curial obligations, after giving up his letter of appointment, he must be returned to his actual status, so that he may obtain any privilege according to the local law, after he has endured an examination of all his local offices and civic *munera*. As for a man who has been summoned to serve his local *curia* on account of his place of birth, residence, or property ownership, the *dignitas* of *perfectissimus* gained by

---

[5] For the *Caesariani*, see Corcoran 2000: 183–4, 347–52, 2007: 235–6, 2012: 267–9; Haensch 2006; Dillon 2012: 91–2, 207–8.

[6] They were now freeborn *officiales*, not freedmen (Haensch 2006: 162; Corcoran 2012: 268).

[7] *CTh.* 10.20.1. The version in the *Codex Justinianus* (11.8.1) omits the equestrian dignities and instead says that *monetarii* 'must not be freed from this kind of condition by the privilege of any type of status' (*oportet nec dignitatis cuiuscumque privilegio ab huiusmodi condicione liberari*).

[8] See A. H. M. Jones 1964: 435–6 (who notes that many *monetarii* became quite wealthy), and Bond 2016: 241–3. Constantius II later confirmed that *monetarii* and other low-grade functionaries 'should not attempt to enjoy any *dignitas*' (*aliqua frui dignitate pertemptet*) (*CJ* 12.1.6 (AD 357/60)). Women who married *monetarii* faced the downgrading of their legal status under the terms of the *senatus consultum Claudianum*, which forbade marriage between free women and slaves (*CTh.* 10.20.10 = *CJ* 11.8.7, AD 379). Cf. Constantine's legislation on unions between women and slaves, discussed by Evans-Grubbs 1995: 263–77.

patronage does not protect him, and after it has been given up, he ought to be handed over to the *curia*.[9]

Licinius' rhetoric is elevated, fulsome and opaque. The overall effect is to emphasise the emperor as the source of all benefactions and *dignitates* for those who serve in his administration.[10] This, as we have seen in previous chapters, was a fundamental aspect of the emperor's domestication and control over elites in the monarchical *res publica*. Imperial officials were all entitled, by imperial permission, 'to enjoy the *dignitas* they have been awarded' (*frui ... dignitate indulta*), with the same privilege extended to *curiales* on the proviso that they had completed their *munera*. Licinius then went on to reveal the rather startling fact that some citizens had acquired the equestrian dignities, not through the emperor's personal benefaction, but 'by means of a purchased recommendation' (*suffragio comparato*).[11] This indicates that by the early fourth century AD members of the curial classes were able to purchase formal imperial letters (*codicilli*) granting them equestrian *dignitates*, presumably from imperial officials, and were using them to evade their curial obligations. It may well have been this particular outrage that prompted the embassy from the provincial council of Bithynia, which was concerned about decurions claiming exemption from their *munera* by virtue of acquired *dignitates*.

This was not a problem unique to Bithynia, or to Licinius' eastern half of the empire, which he was administering in an uneasy detente with his western counterpart, Constantine.[12] For Constantine had been forced to rule on similar issues regarding members of the curial classes in response to questions from his own governors and officials. In January of AD 317, the year of Licinius' edict, Constantine had responded to Octavianus, *comes* of the diocese of Hispania, regarding the privileges of decurions.[13]

---

[9] *CTh.* 12.1.5: *eos qui in palatio militarunt et eos quibus provinciae commissae sunt quique merito amplissimarum administrationum honorem perfectissimatus vel egregiatus adepti sunt, nec non et illos, qui decuriones vel principales constituti cuncta suae patriae munera impleverunt, frui oportet dignitate indulta. si vero decurio suffragio comparato perfectissimatus vel ducenae vel centenae vel egregiatus meruerit dignitatem declinare suam curiam cupiens, codicillis amissis suae condicioni reddatur, ut omnium honorum et munerum civilium discussione perfunctus iuxta legem municipalem aliquam praerogativam obtineat. eum quoque, qui originis gratia vel incolatus vel ex possidendi condicione vocatur ad curiam, perfectissimatus suffragio impetrati dignitas non defendit, qua remota tradi eum curiae oportebit.*

[10] Dillon 2015: 52–3.

[11] See C. Kelly 2004: 293–4 for the translation of *suffragio comparato* as 'a purchased recommendation'.

[12] Constantine and Licinius had only recently concluded peace after a brief civil war, 'the war of Cibalae', when this edict was issued (Barnes 2011: 103–4).

[13] *CTh.* 12.1.4.

He ruled that men 'who have chosen to claim the decorations of an unmerited office' (*qui honoris indebiti arripere insignia uoluerunt*) should be forced to stand in the local *curia*, allowing decurions the privilege of sitting. It used to be thought that Constantine's legislation on this matter prompted Licinius' own ruling in July, but they actually deal with related, but not identical, issues.[14] A more appropriate parallel to Licinius' edict on the equestrian *dignitates* is a constitution from Constantine addressed to a certain Paternus Valerianus, which cannot be dated more closely than AD 312/337.[15] The emperor wrote:

Men who have obtained letters of appointment should enjoy the status of *perfectissimus* if they are not of servile origin, or indebted to the imperial treasury or their *curia*, or if they have not been bakers, or engaged in any business, or have bought this status by a purchased recommendation, or have administered anyone's affairs.[16]

The implications of Constantine's ruling are clear. It is accepted that the emperor can grant the status of *perfectissimus* via imperial codicil. But these letters were also being acquired illegitimately through a 'purchased recommendation' (*venali suffragio*). In both Licinius' edict of AD 317 and this letter of Constantine, *suffragium* is qualified by adjectives to show that the emperors are not referring to mere patronage, but *dignitates* that have been bought. By AD 338, however, the word *suffragium* without further qualification could refer to 'a purchased recommendation', depending on the context.[17] This suggests that the idea of buying honours, favours and offices had become ingrained in the Roman administration.[18]

The stern rulings of Licinius, Constantine and numerous other late Roman emperors on this subject were not designed to put an end to the practice of patronage, but rather to ensure that the emperors themselves were regarded as the sole source of benefaction.[19] An emperor could grant the status of *egregius* or *perfectissimus* as a standard reward for a period of service to the state or directly to an individual as a benefaction. This marked a change from the high empire, when an *eques* had to serve as

---

[14] Corcoran 2000: 283; Barnes 2011: 104.

[15] *CTh* 6.38.1 (fragmentary) = *CJ* 12.32.1 (complete). Seeck 1919: 165 dated this letter to 19 January, AD 317, based on the earlier letter to Octavianus on that date, but that is uncertain.

[16] *codicillis perfectissimatus fruantur, qui impetraverint, si abhorreant a condicione servili vel fisco aut curiae obnoxii non sint vel si pistores non fuerint vel non in aliquo negotio constiterint nec sibi honorem venali suffragio emerint nec rem alicuius administraverint.*

[17] C. Kelly 2004: 293–4.   [18] A. H. M. Jones 1964: 391–6; C. Kelly 1998, 172–3, 2004: 211–16.

[19] C. Kelly 1998: 152.

a procurator to earn such a title.[20] The receipt of a codicil signed by the emperor embodied his personal role in conferring high rank or office.[21]

Licinius and Constantine shared a common belief in the sort of men who were not suitable beneficiaries of equestrian *dignitates*. The concept that holders of all *dignitates* in the Roman world should be free from moral or criminal defects still existed, as Constantine made clear in a ruling to Volusianus, urban prefect of Rome, in AD 314.[22] But the legislation on equestrian status in the early fourth century AD suggests that emperors had much broader aims: they wished to ensure that even respectable, free-born men could not gain a higher status if it did not suit the imperial administration. Slaves, mint-workers and even decurions were not to rise beyond their *condicio* ('natural status') through the acquisition of equestrian *dignitates*, and even bakers were forbidden access to the perfectissimate.[23] Not all these groups were created equal – the *condicio* of a slave was quite different from that of a decurion, for instance. But they all needed to remain in their natural status for the good of the Roman empire. The Roman administration required mint-workers to ensure the steady production of coinage, bakers to provide for the imperial bread supply in Rome and Constantinople, and *curiales* to take on costly liturgies at the local and provincial level on behalf of the state.[24] The various equestrian *dignitates* provided exemption from their burdens, and so the government sought to limit their acquisition by men from these groups. *Curiales* were the most privileged of these, but even they could only acquire high equestrian status after completing their civic obligations. It is understandable why they would be driven to pay for codicils of the *egregiatus* or *perfectissimatus* in order to gain immunity from these burdens. The imperial government was thus somewhat self-defeating: emperors ruled that *dignitates* could only be granted by them personally or earned through official imperial service; but at the same time, state bureaucrats were busily engaged in selling off these *dignitates*.[25]

The issues raised in Licinius' edict and the contemporaneous rulings of Constantine show the wider social impact of the division of the *ordo*

---

[20] See Chapter 7.   [21] C. Kelly 1998: 151–2, 2004: 193–4.

[22] *CJ* 12.1.2. For the other parts of this ruling, concerning Roman citizens who status had been reduced by Maxentius, see *CTh*. 5.8.1, 13.5.1 (Corcoran 2000: 304).

[23] On *condicio*, see Garnsey 1970: 225–7.

[24] For the supply of bread to Rome and Constantinople from the third century AD, see Erdkamp 2005: 252–4.

[25] On imperial rhetoric directed against the emperor's own officials, see Dillon 2012: 159–91. The overlapping and often competing aims of the imperial administration are examined by C. Kelly 1998: 171–80.

equester into several status grades. When titles such as *egregius* and *perfectissimus* were introduced in the second century AD, they served as a way of distinguishing equestrian procurators and high-level administrators from among the *equites Romani* at large. However, as we saw in Chapter 7, it soon became possible to be counted as *egregius* by holding only one procuratorship, even if it was purely honorary. This revealed a desire to acquire status and privilege without undertaking necessary imperial service, which, when left unchecked, resulted in the situation we find in the early fourth century AD, of such honours being bought and sold. In this chapter we will explore the changing significance of the equestrian status grades and the privileges they afforded, a process which occurred in parallel with the transformation of the Roman army and administration in the third century AD, which we discussed in the last chapter. We will then move on to examine the ramifications of the third-century upheavals in government in terms of appointments to procuratorships and provincial governorships. This brought an end to the combined civilian–military equestrian *cursus* and resulted in the consolidation of a separate military career path. Finally, we will consider the continuance of the *ordo equester* as a constituent part of the *res publica* into the late fourth to mid-fifth centuries AD. The demise of the *ordo equester* has exercised a considerable hold on the scholarly imagination, but it did continue to exist until at least the mid-fifth century AD. It is therefore equally worth asking why the *ordo* survived for so long.

The End of the Census Qualification

There were three essential qualities shared by members of the *ordo equester* in the high Roman empire. They possessed free birth (*ingenuitas*), the census qualification of 400,000 sesterces, and had been formally granted equestrian status by the emperor.[26] Although precise references to the census figure appear predominantly in literary sources of the first and early second centuries AD, there is no indication that the monetary qualification was adjusted on account of inflation or other problems in the following century.[27] The Severan historian Cassius Dio, who tended to note differences between his own age and preceding periods of Roman

---

[26] See Chapter 5.

[27] Demougin 1988: 78–9. Ps.-Quint. *Min. Decl.* 302 pref., written in the early second century AD, refers to laws establishing the equestrian census which were still in operation, but does not specify the amount. A letter of Fronto, dated to AD 139, refers to Marcus Aurelius possessing

history, made no comment on the equestrian census per se in the surviving books of his work, though he did discuss the senatorial property qualification.[28] The equestrian census continued to be enforced in the early third century AD, since membership of the *ordo* was overseen by an official known as the *a censibus equitum Romanorum* ('secretary for the census assessment of *equites Romani*').[29]

Although no ancient source refers to the abolition or abandonment of the property qualification, the evidence suggests that at some point it did cease to be one of the prime criteria for equestrian status. The commentators on Horace and Juvenal from the fifth century AD refer to the census qualification as if it was a relic of a past time.[30] Pseudo-Acro, commenting on Horace's mention of the census in *Ars Poetica* 382–3, noted: 'For it was not previously permitted to become an *eques Romanus* unless one possessed a certain amount of money, that is 400,000 sesterces'.[31] The *Scholia Vetera* on Juvenal glossed Juvenal *Satires* 1.106 with the comment: '400,000 was previously the census of *equites Romani*'.[32] The late antique scholiasts are well known for changing the present tense verbs of earlier commentators to imperfects in order to more accurately reflect the differences between the past and present circumstances.[33] Romans of the fifth century AD needed to be reminded that there was once a census qualification for *equites*, who sat in reserved seats in the first fourteen rows of the theatre.[34]

It is a long way from Dio's *Roman History* of the Severan period to the scholiasts of the fifth century AD. In Chapter 11 we examined how veterans from the legions and the praetorian guard had secured officer commissions

---

[28] significantly more than the equestrian census qualification, but does not give a precise figure (Fronto, *Ad M. Caes.* 4.3.6 [vdH² pp. 56–9] = Davenport and Manley 2014: 22–6 no. 1).

[28] This was originally set at 400,000 sesterces by Augustus before being raised to 1 million sesterces (Dio 54.17.3, 54.26.3–5).

[29] The office was held by M. Aquilius Felix (Pflaum 1960: 598–601 (no. 225)). The emperor Elagabalus scandalously appointed an actor to this post (Herodian 5.7.7). The third-century scholiast Porphyrio explains the census qualification in his comment on Hor. *Epist.* 1.1.62 (*quibus census et SS CCCC*), but this does not indicate whether or not it was still in force when he was writing.

[30] A reference to the census from the fourth century AD occurs in Symmachus' description of the famous scene of Pompey leading his horse into the forum (*Or.* 3.8, delivered in AD 369 or 370). However, Symmachus passes no comment on whether the census qualification still applied in his day.

[31] Ps.-Acro on Hor. *Ars P.* 382–3: *non enim licebat antea equitum Romanum fieri nisi habuisset certam summam pecuniae, hoc est quadringentorum sestertiorum.*

[32] *Schol.* on Juv. *Sat.* 1.106: *quadringenta qui erat census antea equitum Romanorum.* For the date of this scholiast, see Cameron 2010.

[33] Cameron 2011: 576–8.

[34] Cf. Macrob. *Sat.* 7.3.8, who states that the *XIV ordines* were reserved for senators. See Chapter 9.

in the *militiae equestres* directly, without possessing the requisite equestrian census qualification. In the reign of Gallienus these officers were awarded the higher equestrian status of *egregius* or *perfectissimus* when they replaced senators as commanding officers of the legions. But this did not stop the emperor from making grants of equestrian status in the normal way to citizens of free birth who possessed the *census equester*. Municipal aristocrats with the title of *eques Romanus* are attested in inscriptions from Africa, Italy and the eastern provinces through to the Tetrarchic period.[35] As late as AD 284 the Pannonian M. Aurelius Clemens could refer to having received the *equus publicus*.[36] Aurelius Sempronius Serenus Dulcitius, a local notable from Leptis Magna, is styled an '*eques* of the Ausonians' ([ἱπ]πεὺς Αὐσονίων) in an inscribed honorific epigram of the early fourth century AD.[37] It is thus unsurprising that Diocletian's *Edict of Maximum Prices*, dated to AD 301, contains entries for *calicae equestres* ('equestrian shoes') alongside prices for senatorial and patrician shoes.[38] This does not of course prove that the property qualification was still enforced at the level of 400,000 sesterces, which would have been worth considerably less by the time of Diocletian than in the Severan period.[39] But there is other evidence concerning the salaries of equestrian officials which strongly suggests that the census was not altered until the early fourth century AD.

Equestrian administrators in the imperial government were graded according to salary.[40] Cassius Dio noted that in the early third century AD the titles of these grades, such as *centenarius* and *ducenarius*, matched the actual payments received by the officials.[41] Somewhat surprisingly, we know that this continued to be the case in AD 297/8, when the Gallic orator Eumenius delivered his speech *For the Restoration of the Schools*.[42] In this public oration Eumenius revealed that he had received the salary of 300,000 sesterces as *magister memoriae* of the emperor Constantius I, and would henceforth be paid double that amount to

---

[35] Chastagnol 1988: 201; Lepelley 1999: 632. For example, Aelius Exuperatus (*AE* 2003, 1421, AD 286), Cocceius Donatus (*CIL* VIII 2480, 2481, AD 286/293), M. Rutilius Felix Felicianus (*AE* 1920, 15, AD 295), Flavius Diophanes (*SEG* 51, 916 = *AE* 2001, 1743, early fourth century AD). The evidence is especially abundant in North Africa: see the tables in Duncan-Jones 1967 and Lefebure 1999.

[36] *AE* 2003, 1420.

[37] *SEG* 53, 1166. On another statue base he receives the more standard designation of *eq(ues) R(omanus)* (*IRT* 559).

[38] *Edictum de pret. max.* IX.7–9.   [39] Cf. the comments of Stein 1927:30; Demougin 1988: 79.

[40] See Chapter 7 for full discussion.

[41] Dio 53.15.4–5, see also the recommendations in the speech of Maecenas (52.25.2–3).

[42] For the date, see Nixon and Rodgers 1994: 148.

serve as head of the school of rhetoric, the Maenianae, at Autun.[43]
Eumenius' remarks indicate that the salaries of equestrian officials had
not been altered over the course of the third century AD.[44] This continuity
is also suggested by the career of one of Eumenius' direct contemporaries,
C. Caelius Saturninus. At the beginning of his imperial service, probably in
the court of Maximian or Constantius I, Saturnius served as *sexagenarius
studiorum adiutor, sexagenarius a consiliis,* and *ducenarius a consiliis*.[45] It is
generally assumed that the titles of *sexagenarius* and *ducenarius* refer to the
actual salary Saturninus received, as in the case of Eumenius.[46]
The promotion to different pay levels as *a consiliis* is paralleled by the
career of the Antonine administrator M. Aurelius Papirius Dionysius.[47]
Salary grade promotions are also explicitly attested for the post of *a studiis*
in the mid-third century AD, when M. Aurelius Hermogenes was 'elevated
from the post of *procurator a studiis* of our emperor at 60,000 sesterces to
100,000 sesterces'.[48] Third-century equestrian officials therefore continued
to receive the salaries that matched their titles.[49] If the pay of Tetrarchic
administrators such as Eumenius and Caelius Saturninus was the same as
their Severan predecessors, and continued to be calculated in sesterces,
then there is little reason to suppose that the equestrian census qualification had been altered either.[50] This conclusion is plausible when considered in the context of recent scholarship on the Roman economy in the
third century AD, which has shown that despite the consistent debasement
of the silver coinage, significant inflation did not take place until after the
reign of Aurelian.[51]

---

[43] *Pan. Lat.* 9(4).11.2.   [44] Segrè 1943: 103–6; A. H. M. Jones 1953: 306, 1964: 51.

[45] *CIL* VI 1704 = *ILS* 1214; *PLRE* I Saturninus 9.

[46] Segrè 1943: 108. See also Chastagnol's comments included in Pflaum's paper on inflation and
equestrian titles (Pflaum 1978: 314).

[47] Note also the mid-third century case of Caecilius Hermianus, 'ducenarius on the emperor's
consilium' ([δ]ουκινά[ριο]ν ἐπὶ συμβουλίου τοῦ Σεβ(αστοῦ)), a position he filled while the
emperor Valerian was campaigning in in the east (*I. Ankara* 116; Mitchell and French
2012: 283).

[48] *CIL* XIV 5340: *proc(uratori) a studi(i)s Aug(usti) n(ostri) ad HS LX (milia) n(ummum)
provect(o)* | *HS C (milia) n(ummum)*; Pflaum 1960 935–6 (no. 352).

[49] This does not mean that salaries were always consistently paid at the level they were supposed to
be, if the complaint of grammarian Lollianus under Valerian and Gallienus is anything to go by.
His annual salary was 2,000 sesterces, but this was paid in poor-quality wine and grain (Parsons
1976).

[50] It is interesting to note that equestrian procuratorial salaries did not increase in the third
century AD, while those of soldiers did so substantially. This meant that the army occupied
a much larger proportion of the imperial budget in the third century AD (Duncan-Jones 1994:
45). However, despite these increases, the basic salary of soldiers remained insufficient and had
to be supplemented by donatives (Rathbone 2009: 312).

[51] Rathbone 1996.

The situation was to change rapidly in the age of the Tetrarchs, making Eumenius of Autun one of the last equestrian officials to receive a salary that matched his grade in the administration. Imperial officials of the fourth century AD tended to be paid in kind, rather than in cash.[52] Eumenius' pay of 600,000 sesterces as professor of rhetoric at Autun is the last attested salary for a state professor recorded as a cash value, rather than in cash and in kind.[53] The career inscription of C. Caelius Saturninus, which recorded his early appointments so precisely at the different grades, makes no further mention of salaries after his promotion from *ducenarius a consiliis*. Saturninus' posts were held in the late third century AD, at the same time as those of Eumenius, so we can say that this title matched his actual salary, as with Eumenius. The change therefore occurred after this point, in the early fourth century AD. The last securely dated appearance of the grade of *sexagenarius* occurs in a letter from Constantine to Aelianus, proconsul of Africa, dated to late AD 313 or 314, in which he refers to imperial tax officials at this level.[54] Of course, this ruling does not confirm that *sexagenarii* were actually paid the equivalent of 60,000 sesterces for their services, but only that the title was still in use.

The best evidence for the change comes from Licinius' edict of AD 317, which referred to *ducenarius* and *centenarius* as grades of equestrian status between *egregius* and *perfectissimus*.[55] Moreover, as Licinius made clear, the emperor could grant *codicilli* awarding these statuses after the completion of administrative service. This firmly indicates that the *ducena* or *centena dignitas* bore no relationship to salaries by this time. Nor did Licinius mention any property qualification necessary to achieve these *dignitates* or those of *egregius* or *perfectissimus*. In a piece of imperial legislation that delineated the award of rank so precisely, one would have expected the census qualification to be explicitly stated if it was relevant. Finally, we know from a law of Gratian, Valentinian II and Theodosius I dated to AD 380 that the emperor Constantine conferred the *equestris ordinis dignitas* to the *navicularii* ('shipmasters') *en masse*.[56] The original law of Constantine does not survive, nor is the precise date known, though it may have been issued in AD 329, since that is when the emperor granted

---

[52] A. H. M. Jones 1964: 396–8. For pay in cash and in kind to soldiers under Diocletian, see Duncan-Jones 1990: 105–15.

[53] Kaster 1988: 116. For Eumenius' salary as professor, see *Pan. Lat.* 9(4).11.2, 14.5; B. S. Rodgers 1989: 256–8.

[54] *C.Th.* 11.1.2, 11.7.1 = *CJ* 10.9.1 (AD 313 or 314). For the different dates, see Barnes 1982: 170; Corcoran 2000: 304.

[55] Lepelley 1999: 632; Christol 2006: 248.   [56] *CTh.* 13.5.16.pr. (AD 380).

other privileges to *navicularii*, including immunity from civic *munera*.[57] The block grant of equestrian rank to a particular group strongly suggests that the census qualification had finally been abandoned.[58] Given the evidence presented here, the change most likely occurred between Eumenius' speech in AD 297/8 and Licinius' edict of AD 317. During these twenty years the economic reforms of Diocletian and Constantine dramatically overhauled the Roman currency system, which rendered the fiscal system of the principate effectively meaningless.[59]

The Structure and Privileges of Equestrian Status

The demise of the census qualification in the early fourth century AD did not, however, mark the end of equestrian status and its significance. This was because the *ordo equester* was now divided into a series of grades, with the higher equestrian *dignitates* of *egregius* and *perfectissimus* granting privileges that were worth competing for. In Chapter 7 we saw how these statuses could only be earned in the high empire through service in the imperial army and administration. Officials of *egregius* rank often used the additional titles of *centenarius* or *ducenarius* in inscriptions to show that they had been advanced to higher procuratorships by the emperor. The various *dignitates* were significant in defining a hierarchy of status groups within the equestrian order. Marcus Aurelius decreed that the sons, grandsons and great-grandsons of *eminentissimi* and *perfectissimi* should not be subject to plebeian punishments.[60] In Marcus' reign these titles were restricted to the praetorian prefects, the other 'great prefects' and some court officials. The social legislation of the Julio-Claudian period specified the greater dignity inherent in the male and female relatives of *equites*, even if they were not of equestrian rank themselves, which distinguished them from ordinary Roman citizens. Therefore, they were forbidden from engaging in base professions.[61] The ruling of Marcus approached the nature of status from a different angle by granting a privilege which

[57] *CTh.* 13.5.5 (AD 329). In a letter to Verinus, prefect of Rome, in AD 324, Constantine refers to *equites Romani* and *navicularii* as separate categories (*CTh.* 2.17.1.2), indicating that the grant of equestrian rank was after this date.

[58] Davenport 2012b: 107–8.

[59] Corbier 2005: 335–8; Abdy 2012: 584–92. A new salary system for provincial governors was introduced in the late empire (Rathbone 2009: 312–13).

[60] *CJ* 9.41.11 (Diocletian and Maximian, referring to an earlier ruling of Marcus Aurelius); Garnsey 1970: 141–2; Alföldy 1981: 199–200.

[61] See the discussion in Chapter 5.

confirmed the members of these procuratorial families as *honestiores* to several generations.

In the Severan period the jurist Ulpian wrote that the same principle – immunity from plebeian punishments – also applied to decurions and their sons.[62] Since it would be strange for the higher-ranking *viri egregii* and *equites Romani* to be excluded from a privilege that was granted to the curial class, they probably shared the exemption from such base treatment, with their descendants also receiving immunity, at least to the first generation.[63] In the third century AD *viri egregii* emerged in popular consciousness as a distinct higher group within the *ordo*. A rescript from Valerian to the senate in AD 258 regarding the appropriate penalties to be inflicted on high-ranking Christians cited *viri egregii* and *equites Romani* separately.[64] This is demonstrated in a letter from Cyprian to his fellow bishop Successus:

> And these matters are in truth as follows, that it is said that Valerian has replied to the senate that bishops, presbyters, and deacons should be punished with death immediately, but that senators, *viri egregii*, and *equites Romani* must have their *dignitas* removed, and then their property confiscated.[65]

There is no mention of *eminentissimi* and *perfectissimi*, but Cyprian is reporting the substance of the rescript, not providing a verbatim quotation. The bishop may have specifically mentioned *viri egregii* because there were many men of this rank living in Africa, since it could be acquired by serving in only one official post (as discussed in Chapter 7).[66] The notion that *egregii* were now numerous enough to be considered an exclusive group above ordinary *equites* is suggested by an inscription from Zucchabar in Mauretania Caesariensis. This describes a certain Manlia Secundilla as the 'sister of brothers and uncles who are *egregii viri* and *equites Romani*' (*sorori fra|trum et av(u)nculor(um) e(gregiorum) v(irorum) et | eq(uitum) Romanor(um)*).[67] This demonstrates that although the equestrian order was still a constituent *ordo* within the *res publica*, the higher equestrian status grades offered significant prestige and privileges beyond the title of *eques Romanus*.[68]

---

[62] Ulpian is cited in the same ruling of Diocletian and Maximian (*CJ* 9.41.11)

[63] Garnsey 1970: 241–2.   [64] Seeck 1905: 2006.

[65] Cypr. *Ep.* 80: *quae autem sunt in vero ita se habent, rescripsisse Valerianum ad senatum ut episcopi et presbyteri et diacones in continenti animadvertantur, senatores vero et egregii viri et equites Romani dignitate amissa etiam bonis spolientur.*

[66] In Pontius' *Vita Cypriani* (14.3), written shortly after the bishop's death, he describes how Cyprian was encouraged to go into exile by 'very many men of *egregius* and *clarissimus* rank and blood' (*plures egregii et clarissimi ordinis et sanguinis*).

[67] *CIL* VIII 9616.

[68] Inscriptions from Rome and Ostia still refer to the *ordo equester* in the mid-third century AD (*CIL* VI 2131 = *ILS* 4929, AD 240; *CIL* XIV, 4452 = *ILS* 9507, AD 249; *CIL* XIV 42 = *ILS* 526, AD 251/3).

By the end of the third century AD the rank of *egregius* was held by Roman citizens who had never served in the imperial army and administration. Instead, it could be awarded on the basis of municipal offices, notably the post of *curator rei publicae*.[69] This position had changed from an external official selected by the emperor to oversee the city's finances into a local administrator appointed from among the curial classes.[70] The *vir egregius* Aelius Rufus, who was *flamen perpetuus* and *curator rei publicae* of Lambaesis in the reign of Aurelian or Probus, is an early example of this phenomenon.[71] Many other examples can be found from Italy and North Africa in the Tetrarchic period.[72] These *curatores* probably received the *egregiatus dignitas* in order to denote their higher status within their local communities.[73] Holders of the priestly post of *flamen perpetuus* also ranked as *egregii*.[74] The careful status gradations this could produce in the civic context are demonstrated by an inscribed dedication to Jupiter Optimus Maximus made by two *quinquennales* of Aquincum in AD 284. M. Aurelius Polideuces and M. Aurelius C(l)emen(s) were both magistrates, but since Polideuces was also a *flamen*, he ranked as *vir egregius*, while Clemens was only styled *equo publico*.[75]

In the early fourth century AD it became typical for all *decuriones* who completed their municipal obligations to receive the title of *vir egregius*, as Licinius confirmed in his edict to the Bithynians in AD 317. L. Aurelius Dorotheus, *vir egregius* and *patronus* of his home community of Puteoli in Italy, was honoured by the local *ordo* after 'he had undertaken all offices, burdens and liturgies honestly' (*omnibus honoribus | oneribus muneribusq-(ue) | honeste perfuncto*).[76] The *viri egregii* essentially constituted a new high-ranking elite within the municipalities, among which equestrian rank was now widespread.[77] In Lambaesis in Numidia several municipal notables, including three at the rank of *egregius*, contributed to the construction

---

[69] Millar 1983: 87–94; Chastagnol 1988: 201–2.

[70] Lucas 1940: 63–4; Burton 1979: 473–4, 477–9. The culmination of this process is demonstrated by a ruling of Constantine from AD 331 in which he decreed that a decurion could not become a *curator* until he had completed all his civic obligations (*CTh.* 12.1.20).

[71] *CIL* VIII 2661 = *ILS* 5788.

[72] Selected examples: Iulianus, *curator* of Casena after AD 275 (*CIL* XI 556); Rupilius Pisonianus, *curator* of Mactar and Mididi in AD 290/3 (*CIL* VIII 11774); C. Umbrius Tertullus, *curator* of Thuburiscu Numidarum in AD 286/305 (*AE* 1904, 5; 1940, 18).

[73] Although local officials, they were still associated with the state (A. H. M. Jones 1964: 726; Corcoran 2006: 48).

[74] The evidence is especially abundant in North Africa (*CIL* VIII 1646, 5142, 25834; *AE* 1966, 512).

[75] *AE* 2003, 1420.

[76] *AE* 1983, 196. For other examples of this phenomenon, see *CIL* III 5111 (Noricum); *CIL* V 4333 (Brixia, Italy).

[77] Lepelley 1986: 237.

of a portico in AD 283/4.[78] No less than six equestrian *viri egregii* are attested at Lavinium in Campania erecting a statue of their patron, the senator Virius Lupus, in the late third century AD.[79] In his polemic *On the Deaths of the Persecutors* Lactantius wrote of the emperor Galerius torturing both decurions and 'leading men of the cities' (*primores ... civitatum*) who held the status of *egregius* or *perfectissimus*.[80] A bronze patronage tablet from Rome dated to AD 322 brilliantly illustrates this final stage in the spread of the *egregiatus dignitas* within the municipal aristocracies. In that year the senator Q. Aradius Valerius Proculus became patron of Zama Regia in North Africa. According to the tablet, he was visited by a delegation of its *decemprimi* ('the leading ten men') headed by the *curator rei publicae*, C. Mucius Brutianus Faustinus Antonianus.[81] Antonianus and his nine colleagues had all held the major priesthoods in Zama Regia, and they all ranked as *viri egregii*. An equestrian status that was once a reward for service in the Roman imperial army and administration was by this point widespread throughout the provincial aristocracy of the empire.

The spread of the status of *egregius* could not have occurred without the assent of the emperors, given that it was a benefaction that remained in their hands. In extending this rank, it is likely that they were responding to pressure from below.[82] Leading municipal citizens who had held the positions of *flamen* or *curator rei publicae* wanted to distinguish themselves from their fellow decurions who were also *equites Romani*. They could, of course, seek appointments in the imperial administration. For example, M. Aurelius Achilleus alias Ammon became *procurator usiacus* after completing his liturgies in Oxyrhynchus.[83] But these posts depended on graft and patronage, and were by no means guaranteed. It was preferable to obtain the *dignitas* without such service, much like Appian of Alexandria and others who applied for honorific procuratorships in the second century AD.[84] We do in fact possess evidence of a successful petition by a municipal notable asking to be granted the κρατιστία (the

---

[78] *AE* 1989, 869.   [79] *CIL* XIV 2078 = *ILS* 1209.

[80] Lact. *DMP* 21.3; Barnes 1973: 137; Millar 1983: 93. Lact. *Div. Inst.* 5.14.18 also refers to the three key statuses of *egregius, perfectissimus* and *clarissimus*, but he does so metaphorically to make a religious point.

[81] *CIL* VI 1686 = *ILS* 6111c.

[82] Compare our discussion of the ambitions of soldiers in Chapter 11. See also Kautsky 1997: 213–17 and Dillon 2015: 56 on the aristocratic 'need for differentiation', i.e. the need for elites to define their place in relation to each other, and to have higher honours to which they could aspire.

[83] Bagnall 1991: 289–93; *P. Oxy.* 12.1514 (AD 274 or 280).   [84] This is discussed in Chapter 7.

Greek translation of *egregiatus*). A papyrus from AD 299 preserves a transcript of a case held before the *katholikos* of Egypt, in which a certain Aurelius Plutarchus claimed that his status as an *egregius* granted him an exemption from undertaking the obligations to which he had been nominated:[85]

In an attempt to find relief from municipal liturgies, Plutarchus, *vir egregius*, who presents himself here before Your Virtue, some time previously petitioned the Sacred Fortune of our lords the *Augusti* and *Caesares* for the *dignitas* of the *egregiatus*. Their Sacred Fortune assented to this and bestowed the status on him, and he now possesses it.[86]

The argument on which Plutarchus based his application to Diocletian and his colleagues for the *egregiatus* is not known. From the other sections of the petition it seems that he had played some role in the discharge of soldiers on the order of the prefect of Egypt. However, this service was not in and of itself sufficient to be awarded the status of *vir egregius*.[87] If one was not a procurator or army officer, the status had to be obtained by imperial benefaction, and the emperors evidently assented to Plutarchus' request. There are also examples of *curatores rei publicae* and *flamines* attested as *perfectissimi* in Italy, Sicily and North Africa as early as the 290s, with no service in the army and administration recorded.[88] This shows that the emperors were not only in the habit of granting the rank of *egregius* to municipal elites, but also the status of *perfectissimus*. If the case of Aurelius Plutarchus is any indication, there were many who wanted these honours in order to avoid their curial burdens.

This must have been a relatively recent change, since imperial officials, whether soldiers or administrators, had only ever possessed immunity from civic *munera* so long as they were engaged in state service. They were still liable to these obligations when they returned home.[89] In AD 282

---

[85] *P. Oxy.* 9.1204. The papyrus uses the Greek terms κράτιστος and κρατιστία, which I have translated using their Latin equivalents. For discussion of this important text, see A. H. M. Jones 1964: 70; Carrié 1979: 221–3; Millar 1977: 289, 1983: 91–2.

[86] *P. Oxy.* 9.1204, ll. 13–16: ἀπαλλαγὴν εὕρασθαι πειρώμενος ὁ παρεστὼς τῇ σῇ ἀρετῇ Πλούταρχος ὁ κράτιστος τῶν πολειτικῶν λειτουργιῶν δεδέηται τῆς θείας τύχης ἔτι ἄνωθεν τῶν δεσποτῶν ἡμῶν τῶν Σεβαστῶν καὶ τῶν Καισάρων μεταδοῦναι αὐτῷ τοῦ τῆς κρατιστίας ἀξιώματος, καὶ ἐπένευσεν ἡ θεία τύχη αὐτῶν καὶ μετέδωκεν, καὶ νῦν ἐστιν ἐν αὐτῷ.

[87] Millar 1983: 92.

[88] C. Valerius Pompeianus, *curator* of Lilybaeum (*Eph. Ep.* 696, dated to AD 293/304, following Barnes 1982: 165), Lucius Vo[-]amus, *flamen perpetuus* in Sabratha (Tantillo and Bigi 2010: no. 93, dated AD 303/315), L. Domitius Iustus Aemilianus, *curator* of Leptis Magna (Tantillo and Bigi 2010: no. 45, dated AD 280/320), Iulius Larentius, *curator* of Praeneste (*CIL* XIV 2919 = *ILS* 1219, dated to AD 333). For further examples, see Ensslin 1937: 672; Millar 1983: 93.

[89] See the fundamental discussion of Millar 1983: 87–94, to which this section is indebted.

the emperors Carus, Carinus and Numerian had ruled that even procurators (who would be *viri egregii* at the minimum) had to undertake their
civic *munera*.[90] Less than two decades later – unfortunately the precise date
is uncertain – Diocletian gave a landmark ruling that represented a change
in imperial policy.[91] In response to an embassy from the chief magistrates
of Antioch, he decreed: 'We have granted to men possessing certain
dignitates an immunity from civic and personal *munera*, specifically to
former *protectores* and *praepositi.*'[92] The fact that Diocletian only mentions
military officers probably relates to the specific case he was called to rule
upon; it would have been very strange if equestrian procurators were not
also immune from such obligations.

Indeed, the principle that imperial service could grant all Roman citizens
permanent relief from their curial obligations was extended throughout the
lower hierarchies of the administration.[93] In an edict of AD 314, addressed
to palatine officials (*palatini*) who had recently been discharged from his
service, Constantine outlined their privileges:[94]

As regards the *palatini*, who honestly perform their duties in our personal household, as well as those who are employed in our administrative offices of the
magister memoriae, magister epistularum, and *magister libellorum*, we order that
they should be kept far away from malicious prosecutions, nor should they be
nominated to perform *munera*. We order that this act of generosity shall apply to
their sons and grandsons related by blood. These men, along with their moveable
property and urban slaves, will enjoy immunity from all base and personal *munera*,
and no one should impose such injustices upon them. If anyone disregards these
orders, he shall pay the penalty, regardless of his *dignitas*.[95]

Constantine therefore confirmed the close connection between imperial
service, the reward of equestrian rank, and exemption from civic *munera*
for life, both for the officials themselves and their descendants for two

---

[90] *CJ* 10.48.1.

[91] *CJ* 10.48.2. Corcoran 2000: 254–5 dates the text prior to AD 293 on the basis that only
the Augusti Diocletian and Maximian are mentioned, in which case it would have to date to the
late 280s, when Diocletian was in Syria (Barnes 1982: 51). However, Potter 2004: 395 prefers AD
299 or 300, when a number of Diocletianic constitutions place him in Antioch.

[92] *CJ* 10.48.2: *certis dignitatibus data a nobis indulgentia est munerum civilium et personalium, id
est his, qui aut ex protectoribus sunt aut ex praepositis.*

[93] Millar 1983: 84.   [94] *CTh.* 6.35.1 = *CJ* 12.28.1. See also *CTh.* 6.35.4 (AD 328).

[95] *a palatinis tam his, qui obsequiis nostris inculpata officia praebuerunt, quam illis, qui in scriniis
nostris, id est memoriae epistularum libellorumque, versati sunt, procul universas calumnias sive
nominationes iubemus esse summotas, idque beneficium ad filios eorum atque nepotes ipso
ordine sanguinis pervenire atque inmunes eos a cunctis muneribus sordidis et personalibus
permanere cum universis mobilibus et mancipiis urbanis, neque iniurias eis ab aliquibus inferri,
ita ut, qui haec contempserit, indiscreta dignitate poenas debitas exigatur.*

generations.[96] This meant that the status of *egregius* and *perfectissimus* now only conferred such privileges if they had been earned through imperial employment, rather than through other means (such as purchase or direct grant). Some time between AD 318 and 326 Constantine wrote to a senior administrator called Severus, explicitly targeting members of the curial classes who had not seen imperial service.[97] He wrote: 'Regardless of whether they are *perfectissimi* or have been established among the rank and file of the *egregii*, they should be named as decurions.'[98] Then, in AD 327, Constantine wrote to Annius Tiberianus, *comes* of the diocese of Africa, asking him to communicate the decision to all governors that veterans' sons should act as decurions, as should *perfectissimi*.[99]

In AD 299 Aurelius Plutarchus had claimed that the status of *egregius* conferred immunity from civic *munera*, but by the 320s even the *dignitas* of *perfectissimus* was insufficient to obtain this privilege, unless one had earned it through holding an army or government post.[100] The change represented a desire on the part of the imperial administration to restrict privileges to those who had engaged in service to the Roman state. The fourth-century Romans who were described on their epitaphs and honorific inscriptions as *ex praesidibus, ex comitibus, ex procuratoribus* and *ex rationalibus* ('former governors, former companions, former pro-curators, former financial officers') emphasised their imperial employment. This meant that in the status hierarchy they ranked above equestrians who merely had the title of *eques Romanus, egregius* or *perfectissimus*, but had never held imperial offices.[101] The same trend can be detected among military men as well. At some point in the mid-fourth century AD *protectores* gained the rank of *perfectissimus*.[102] The fact that the *protectores* are so rarely attested with the title of *perfectissimus* in inscriptions suggests that it was the least valuable of their status designations.[103] However, the designation of *protector, ex protectoribus* or *ex protectore* occurs much more frequently in epitaphs.[104] This indicates that when soldiers were commemorated epigraphically, their military rank and army service were regarded as the most important distinctions. This was a striking change from the mid-third century AD, when the *praefecti*

---

[96] Millar 1977: 108–9, 1983: 94–5.   [97] *CTh.* 6.22.1.

[98] *CTh.* 6.22.1: *sive perfectissimi sunt sive inter egregiorum ordinem locumque constiterint, decuriones nominentur.*

[99] *CTh.* 12.1.15; Barnes 1982: 146.   [100] Ensslin 1937: 674–5.

[101] See Millar 1983: 94–5 for the privileges given to these officials.   [102] G. Kelly 2008: 131–2.

[103] For a solitary epigraphic example from the mid/late fourth century AD, see *CIL* III 4185.

[104] Some examples include *AE* 1939, 45; *AE* 1981, 731; *CIL* III 371, 7440, 8741; *CIL* V 6226; *CIL* VI 32945; *CIL* XI 835.

and *protectores* who rose from the ranks proudly proclaimed their status as *egregius* and *perfectissimus*.

Let us pause here to sum up these complicated developments, which occurred in four stages. In the first stage, over the course of the second century AD, the imperial administration granted the *dignitates* of *egregius* and *perfectissimus* only to equestrians who held high office in the army and administration. In the second stage, during the late third century AD, they bestowed the same honours on Roman citizens of the municipal aristocracy who had not occupied any imperial posts. Complication occurred at the third stage, during the Tetrarchy, when emperors granted immunity from curial duties to *egregii* and *perfectissimi* who had seen imperial service, as well as to senior military officers. This meant that Roman citizens who had not held official positions, such as Aurelius Plutarchus, began to claim that their rank of *egregius* and *perfectissimus* also exempted them from their *munera*. This led to the fourth stage, in the reign of the emperor Constantine, who decreed that only those who had earned the *egregiatus* and *perfectissimatus* through imperial employment received such immunity. The result was that the Roman state once again confirmed service in the army and administration as the basis for the most significant honours and rewards within the emperor's gift, effectively closing the loophole that had emerged in the Tetrarchic period.

Where did this leave the municipal *equites* who had not held imperial office but had acquired the status of *perfectissimus*? The rank remained significant in the sense that it delineated the highest ranks of the municipal aristocracy, whose members had discharged their curial obligations in keeping with the wishes of the imperial administration. Constantine's social legislation of the 320s and 330s separated the *perfectissimi* from citizens of lesser equestrian status, and instead grouped them together with senatorial *clarissimi*, creating what Harper has termed a 'community of honour'.[105] Constantine's legislation on marriage and inheritance modified two Augustan laws, the *lex Iulia de adulteriis coercendis* and the *lex Iulia et Papia*.[106] One particular piece of legislation forbade high-status men to claim as legitimate, or bequeath property to, the children born from intercourse with low-status women, such as slaves, actresses, tavern keepers, degraded women and the daughters of pimps and gladiators. The original law does not survive, but may have been passed in AD 326.[107] Its main terms are described in a constitution from the year

---

[105] Harper 2011: 424.   [106] Evans Grubbs 1995: 350–2; Harper 2011: 444–54.

[107] Evans Grubbs 1995: 286; Harper 2011: 449–50. For other social legislation from AD 326, see *CTh.* 9.7.1 = *CJ* 9.9.28; *CTh.* 9.24.1 = *CJ* 7.13.3; *CTh.* 9.7.2 = *CJ* 9.9.29; *CJ* 5.26.1.

AD 336, which Constantine addressed to Gregorius, praetorian prefect of Africa.[108] The citizens to which the law referred were 'senators or *perfectissimi*, or those who in the cities are decorated with the distinctions of the post of *duumvir* or *quinquennalis* or *flamen* or *sacerdos* of the province'.[109] The legislation thus grouped together senators, *perfectissimi* and selected curial officials and priests throughout the Roman empire into one collective elite.[110] This represented a significant change from the Augustan marriage legislation, which had concentrated on the exclusivity of the senatorial order, and had actually permitted marriages between equestrians and freedwomen.[111] The fact that Constantine only included *perfectissimi* in this ruling indicates that lower-ranked equestrians (namely *ducenarii, centenarii, egregii* and mere *equites Romani*) were not generally regarded as part of this new higher social group, unless they had held the municipal posts of *duumvir, quinquennalis, sacerdos* or *flamen*.[112] Equestrian rank was now common among the curial elites, so that its highest privileges could only be accorded to those who had completed their civic duties.

With the spread of the higher equestrian *dignitates* throughout the curial classes in the late third and early fourth century AD, the proud title of *eques Romanus* effectively disappeared from the epigraphic record after the age of the Tetrarchs.[113] This can be explained by the fact that lowest level of equestrian status lacked the necessary social prestige to be considered worthy of being recorded in inscriptions, compared with the higher *dignitates* of *egregius* and *perfectissimus*. There were still *equites Romani*, of course: the disappearance of the title in epigraphic sources does not mean that the status itself was abolished. Constantine's block grant of equestrian rank to the *navicularii* in AD 329, discussed above, is but one piece of

---

[108] *CTh.* 4.6.3 = *CJ* 5.27.1, read at Carthage on 31 July, AD 336. This and the previous constitution (*CTh.* 4.6.2) had been prompted by the specific case of the 'son of Licinianus' who improperly acquired an imperial codicil granting him senatorial rank. This was not the son of the emperor Licinius (Evans Grubbs 1995: 285–6; McGinn 1999: 62–3; Corcoran 2000: 291).

[109] *senatores seu perfectissimos, vel quos in civitatibus duumviralitas vel quinquennalitas vel flamonii vel sacerdotii provinciae ornamenta condecorant.*

[110] The absence of the rank of *egregius* in the law of AD 336 does not mean that it had been abolished. Constantine does not mention *centenarii* and *ducenarii* in the ruling either, and we know that these ranks continued to exist into the 380s (*CTh.* 6.30.7 = *CJ* 12.23.7 (AD 384)). See Davenport 2015b on the title of *egregius*.

[111] Evans Grubbs 1995: 289–90; McGinn 1999:60.

[112] Matthews 2000b: 434–5 notes the absence of *curiales* who are not magistrates, as well as other free Roman citizens from this law, which is indicative of Constantine's attempt to delineate an imperial elite.

[113] Chastagnol 1988: 201–2, 205; Lepelley 1986: 240, 1999: 632.

evidence demonstrating its continuing existence.[114] Moreover, equestrian status remained still valuable in and of itself, both for the *navicularii* and for other Roman citizens, since it confirmed them as *honestiores* and gave them immunity from baser punishments.[115] Therefore, we cannot talk in terms of 'status inflation' whereby the rank of *eques Romanus* became 'devalued', as Dillon has cogently argued.[116] Instead, it is apparent that the title *eques Romanus* no longer had the same cachet as an element of public self-representation among the municipal aristocrats of the cities, which explains its disappearance as an honorific in inscriptions.

The same fate soon befell the status of *egregius*, which largely disappeared from the epigraphic record after the middle of the 320s.[117] The *curator rei publicae* Claudius Aurelius Generosus from Leptis Magna, who is on record as a *vir egregius* in AD 324/6, is often presumed to be the last attested holder of the title who can be precisely dated.[118] Chastagnol even proposed that Constantine abolished the rank of *egregius* in AD 326, a conclusion which has been questioned by more recent scholars.[119] Indeed, some isolated later examples of the title *egregius* can still be found in epigraphic texts from North Africa. The *sacerdos* Valerius is given the title of *v(ir) e(gregius)* on a dedicatory inscription on the base of a statue for the deified Gratian (the father of Valentinian I and Valens). This was erected in Constantina in Numida in AD 364/7.[120] Chastagnol assumed that the status designation was simply an error, but there are no convincing reasons to regard it as such.[121] There is also a fragmentary text from Mididi in Byzacena, which records the restoration of a monument 'through the agency of the [*vir*] *egregius curator* Volusius Calpurnianus' (*per instantiam [v(iri)] e(gregii) Vol(usii) Calpurniani curat(oris)*).[122] The inscription would seem to date to the early fifth century AD on the basis of the imperial titulature, and thus the editors of *L'année épigraphique*

---

[114] *CTh.* 13.5.16.pr. (AD 380) cites the now-lost constitution of Constantine.

[115] Lepelley 1986: 238, 1999: 640; Dillon 2015: 49.   [116] Dillon 2015: 43–5.

[117] The last citation of *egregius* in the law codes occurs in *CTh.* 6.22.1. The date of this constitution is debated: Barnes 1982: 130, 144 (emended to AD 318); Seeck 1919: 172–3 (emended to AD 324); Mommsen 1905: 268 (emended to AD 325/6). The last attestation of the Greek equivalent κράτιστος occurs in *P. Stras.* 6.560, which should be dated to AD 326 (Davenport 2015b. Cf. Coles 1985; Sirks 1995).

[118] Tantillo and Bigi 2010: no. 71.

[119] Chastagnol 1966: 549–50, 1970: 309, 1988: 205–6. See now Lepelley 1986: 238; Lizzi Testa 2009: 114; Davenport 2015b.

[120] *CIL* VIII 7014.

[121] Chastagnol 1966. See now *LSA* 2320 (U. Gehn), which also expands the abbreviation VE as *v(ir) e(gregius)*.

[122] *AE* 2000, 1661.

dismissed the restoration *[v(iri)] e(gregii)* as impossible, citing Chastagnol's arguments that the rank was abolished in AD 326. But the restoration should be allowed to stand.[123] The status of *vir egregius* was therefore not discontinued by Constantine in AD 326, but instead declined as a title used in public self-representation.

This process would have been accelerated by the increase in the number of *perfectissimi* in the municipal aristocracies. Constantine made liberal grants of the rank of *perfectissimatus* in the period after his defeat of Licinius in AD 324.[124] This was an attempt by Constantine to reward the cream of the curial classes and create a new elite loyal to him, especially in the eastern provinces that he acquired from Licinius.[125] As Dillon has pointed out, the extension of the *perfectissimatus* did not cost the emperor Constantine and his *fiscus* anything more than awarding the *egregiatus*, since the honours were no longer attached to salary grades and therefore did not involve financial outlay.[126] Moreover, Constantine's social legislation demonstrated that it was now only these *perfectissimi* who could be associated with the senatorial *clarissimi* in his 'community of honour' (to use Harper's term again).[127] This is perfectly encapsulated by a statue of L. Aradius Valerius Proculus, patron of Puteoli, which was erected in AD 340 by 'the *viri perfectissimi* and the *principales* and the most splendid council and people of Puteoli'.[128] The inscription clearly distinguishes the *perfectissimi* and the leading magistrates, but not the *egregii*. This meant that *vir egregius* was no longer as valuable as an aspect of one's public identity as it had been in the past. As with the title of *eques Romanus*, that of *vir egregius* largely disappeared from inscriptions.

---

[123] Note also two further cases: (ii) A statue of Iulius Sulpicius Successus, *vir egregius* and procurator of the port of Puteoli, which probably dates to the mid-fourth century AD (D'Arms 1972; *AE* 1972, 79); (ii) Tannonius Boionius Chrysantius, who is styled *puer egregius* on a statue base from Puteoli (*CIL* X 1815). He was the son of a prominent patron of the town in the late fourth century AD. However, this may well be an informal use of the adjective *egregius*. See Camodeca 1980–1: 121.

[124] Eus. *VC* 4.1.2. The passage in question is unfortunately mistranslated by Cameron and Hall 1999: 154, as they render the Greek term διασημότατοι into Latin as *clarissimi* (the rank of senators), rather than the correct equestrian title of *perfectissimi*.

[125] Heather 1994: 12–16; C. Kelly 2006: 195–7.   [126] Dillon 2015: 48–9.

[127] For the impact of this, see the *album* of Thamugadi in Numidia, dated to the 360s; this lists ten patrons as *viri clarissimi* and two *viri perfectissimi*, but no lower equestrian dignities (*CIL* VIII 2403).

[128] *CIL* VI 1691: *viri perfectissimi et prin|cipales, et splendidissimus or|do et populus Puteolanorum.*

Where did these changes leave the *ordo equester* as a constituent part of the Roman state? Firstly, it is important to point out that there was still formally an *ordo equester* and *equites Romani*. The endurance of equestrian rank in the fourth century AD can be ascribed to the fact that it was a comprehensible distinction which articulated status and privilege. Hence, Constantine's bestowal of equestrian status to the *navicularii* in around AD 329 was a way of recognising their important role in ensuring that the grain supply reached the *sacra urbs*. The annual parade of *equites* through the city of Rome continued every 15 July at least until the mid-fourth century AD, as shown by the *Codex Calendar of AD 354*; this remained an important ceremony in the ritual calendar for local *equites*.[129] But it is also true to say that many other aspects of community cohesion that had defined the *equites* as an *ordo* had been lost by the age of Constantine, such as the participation in imperial funerals, the fourteen rows in the theatre, and the exclusively equestrian priesthoods.[130] Without such rituals and performances, one of the crucial aspects of equestrian unity was lost, namely the sense of 'immanence', the idea than an *eques Romanus* was part of a collective elite with a firm place in the *res publica*.[131] Indeed, it is questionable whether members of the military corps who had worked their way up through the ranks of the army to achieve officer commands and the status of *egregius* and *perfectissimus* identified themselves with the larger *ordo equester*. Despite their own army background, it is doubtful that they would have travelled to Rome to participate in the *transvectio equitum*.[132] The status of *eques Romanus* no longer ranked immediately below a senator, as there now were *egregii, centenarii, ducenarii*, and especially *perfectissimi*, between them and the *clarissimi*. The *ordo equester* was now a firmly divided series of status grades, each of which carried its own inherent value and prestige. But these equestrian ranks remained an integral part of the Roman state and the social hierarchy of honour and privilege regulated by the emperors and their administration.[133]

---

[129] Stein 1927: 457. Zos. 2.29.5 does not seem to be a reference to the *transvectio equitum*, but to the triumph.

[130] See Chapters 8, 9 and 10.

[131] For the concept of immanence, see Mann 1986: 519, and Chapter 8.

[132] For example, some of the Danubian military officers who became emperors, like Galerius, had never even seen the city of Rome (Lact. *DMP* 27.2).

[133] Note in this regard the comment of Matthews 2000b: 436 that the extension of equestrian rank, and especially the perfectissimate, with all its attendant privileges, represented the administration's 'greater intervention in the lives of its subjects'.

The Government Made New

In parallel with these changes in the *ordo equester* at large, the equestrian *cursus* underwent its own transformation in the period from Gallienus to Constantine. The nature of the changes is complicated and difficult to reconstruct, especially because of the declining number of *cursus* inscriptions for *equites* in the late third century AD.[134] In this section we will first consider the structure of the equestrian procuratorial career, including the fiscal and administrative posts and provincial governorships. This will largely focus on developments in equestrian office-holding up to the 310s (though there is the use of evidence from the later fourth century AD to illustrate earlier changes). We will then proceed to examine the transferral of governorships and senior positions from equestrian to senatorial rank in the reign of Constantine, and the ramifications that this had for the relationship between the upper *ordines* and the imperial government.

Traditional procuratorial careers within the provincial administration and the imperial court, which would not have been out of place in the high empire, are still observable in the 260s and 270s. For example, C. Claudius Firmus served in procuratorial posts in Rome, Gaul, Spain and Galatia, before becoming prefect of Egypt in AD 264/5, and *corrector* of the same province in AD 274.[135] At Rome itself, Iulius Achilleus advanced from the court post of the deputy *a memoria* to the ducenarian procuratorship of the *ludus magnus* (the imperial gladiatorial establishment), either under Gallienus or one of his immediate successors.[136] However, we do know that the structure of the traditional equestrian career path changed in two significant ways. Firstly, equestrians ceased to serve in the *militiae equestres* before advancing to a procuratorial career. This development was the result of the demise of the *militiae* as a coherent institution and the creation of the new separate officer career path via the protectorate, as we saw in the previous chapter.[137] Secondly, the entire structure of the financial administration of the provinces was progressively revised. Financial officials

---

[134] This was partially the result of a decline in the epigraphic habit, and a move towards other forms of self-representation, on which see Borg and Witschel 2001.

[135] *SEG* 27, 846; S. Mitchell 1977: 67–70.

[136] *CIL* VI 41286; Peachin 1989: 175. His sarcophagus was built into the Aurelianic wall, so he must have died before this (Pflaum 1950: 317–18).

[137] The last examples of procurators who were previously in the *militiae* come from mid-third century AD: M. Aurelius Hermogenes (*CIL* XIV 5340; Pflaum 1960: 935–6 (no. 352)); Statilius Ammianus (Pflaum 1982: 98–9 (no. 358)); and two anonymous *equites* recorded at Rome (*CIL* VI 41295; Pflaum 1982: 70–2 (no. 278 A); *CIL* VI 1641; Pflaum 1960: 941–7 (no. 355)). On the end of the *militiae equestres*, see Davenport forthcoming.

known as *rationales*, who were representatives of the *summa res* (the central finance department), superseded provincial procurators. This was not an entirely unanticipated development, as it was presaged in various ways in Egypt earlier in the third century AD.[138] The process was evidently a gradual one, as provincial procurators responsible for financial management are still attested in Asia and Palaestina into the Tetrarchic period.[139] The *res privata* (the emperor's private finances) came to be managed by *magistri rei privatae* in the provinces, though procurators continued to be appointed in some regions.[140] The provincial financial officers answered to two court officials based at Rome, either the senior *magister rei privatae* (previously the *procurator rationis privatae*), or the *rationalis summae rei* (previously known as the *a rationibus*).[141] The central reorganisation must have started at Rome by the 270s at the latest, since *rationales rei privatae* and *summae rei* with the rank of *vir perfectissimus* are attested in the city from the reign of Aurelian onwards.[142] This demonstrates that significant changes to the Roman imperial administration pre-date the reign of Diocletian.

The marble base of a statue of C. Caelius Saturninus preserves one of the few examples of inscribed equestrian careers from the Tetrarchic and Constantinian periods. The statue, dated to around AD 324, was erected in Saturninus' residence in Rome after he had been advanced into the senate (Figure 12.1).[143]

In honour of Dogmatius. To C. Caelius Saturninus, *vir clarissimus*, adlected among the ex-consuls on the petition of the senate, *comes* of our lord Constantine Victor Augustus, *vicarius* of the urban prefecture, judge of the imperial court, twice *vicarius* of the praetorian prefects in the city of Rome, and through the Moesian provinces, inquisitor throughout Italy, *praefectus annonae* of Rome, *rationalis* of the *res privata*, *vicarius* of the *rationalis summae rei*, *rationalis vicarius* through the Gallic provinces, *magister* of the census, *vicarius* to the imperial *a consiliis*, *magister studiorum*, *magister libellorum*, *a consiliis* with a salary of 200,000 HS, *a consiliis* with a salary of 60,000 HS, assistant to the *magister studiorum* with a salary of 60,000 HS, *advocatus fisci* throughout Italy. C. Flavius Caelius Urbanus, *vir clarissimus*, of consular rank (erected this) for his father.[144]

[138] Delmaire 1989: 178–85; Eich 2005: 164–75.

[139] Asia: *AE* 1924, 70 (dated to AD 276); *AE* 1966, 433 (dated to AD 293/305). Palaestina: *AE* 1966, 494 (dated AD 284/6); Pflaum 1950: 320–1; M. P. Speidel 1981.

[140] A. H. M. Jones 1964: 47–8, 413–14, 428; Delmaire 1989: 172–8, 207–17.

[141] A. H. M. Jones 1964: 50.   [142] Delmaire 1989: 26–8.

[143] See *LSA* 1266 (C. Machado) for discussion of the inscribed base and *LSA* 903 (J. Lenaghan) for the statue.

[144] *CIL* VI 1704 = *ILS* 1214: *Dogmatii | honori | C(aio) Caelio Saturnino v(iro) c(larissimo) | allecto petitu senatus inter | consulares comiti d(omini) n(ostri) Constantini | Victoris Aug(usti) vicario praefecturae | urbis iudici sacrarum cog(nitionum) vicario | praeff(ectorum) praetorio bis in urbe*

Figure 12.1: Statue of C. Caelius Saturninus on top of an inscribed base recording his career, Rome

The inscription captures the complexity of the Roman administration in the late third and early fourth centuries AD, as well as the career paths of equestrian officials, in a way that few other contemporary documents can manage.[145] Although the statue was dedicated in the 320s, Saturninus' extensive career in the government had begun in the Tetrarchic period, probably under Diocletian's co-emperor Maximian. He first held the post of treasury advocate in Italy, and was then assistant in the archives office, before serving on the imperial *consilium* at two salary grades, a path that recalls earlier examples from the Antonine and Severan periods (as we observed earlier in this chapter in our discussion of the equestrian *census*). Saturninus then became head of the department of imperial petitions as *magister libellorum* (previously the *a libellis*) and the archives as *magister studiorum* (previously the *a studiis*).

Saturninus' career trajectory can help us to shed light on the backgrounds of other high equestrian court functionaries of the same period whose earlier careers are not attested. These included Cominius Priscianus, *magister studiorum* in the late third century AD; Gregorius, who was *magister libellorum* under both Carinus and Diocletian; and Aurelius Arcadius Charisius, *magister libellorum* to Maximian and Diocletian.[146] Gregorius and Charisius both advanced from *magister libellorum* to become *magister epistularum Latinarum* (the position previously known as *ab epistulis Latinis* in the high empire).[147] The first stages of their *cursus* were probably quite similar to those of Saturninus, holding positions as *a consiliis* at different levels and serving in the lower rungs of the imperial bureaux before rising to hold the magisterial posts. The praetorian prefecture, the summit of the equestrian career, could be held either by this type of administrator or by army officers. This is illustrated by one pair of Tetrarchic *praefecti*: Diocletian's prefect Aurelius Hermogenianus was a former *magister libellorum*, while Maximian's prefect was Iulius Asclepiodotus, a military man who commanded troops in the invasion of Britain.[148]

Roma | et per Mysias examinatori per Ita|iiam [sic] praefecto annon(a)e urbis ratio|nali privat(a)e vicario summae rei | rationum rationali vicario per | Gallias magistro censu(u)m vicario | a consiliis sacris magistro stu|diorum magistro libellorum duce|nario a consiliis sexag(enario) a consiliis | sacris sexag(enario) studiorum adiutori | fisci advocato per Italiam | C(aius) Fl(avius) Caelius Urbanus v(ir) c(larissimus) | consularis patri.

[145] For the chronology of Saturninus' career, see Liebs 2010: 86–8, 92–4.

[146] Priscianus: *CIL* X 1487. Gregorius and Charisius: Corcoran 2000: 90–1; Liebs 2010: 82–4.

[147] Corcoran 2000: 90–1; Liebs 2010: 82–4.

[148] *AE* 1987, 456; Corcoran 2000: 87–90; Liebs 2010: 85–6. There were only two praetorian prefects in office at this time (Porena 2003: 131–52).

One of the distinguishing features of Saturninus' career is that he had several financial positions. He was employed in Gaul as *rationalis vicarius* before returning to Rome as *vicarius*, or deputy, to the *rationalis summae rei*, the head of the imperial fiscus.[149] Saturninus then became chief of the *res privata* and was appointed to one of the great prefectures, serving as *praefectus annonae*, probably in the early fourth century AD. Although the titles of the positions are different, the career trajectory is not in and of itself dissimilar to that of equestrian officials in the high empire who advanced from *a rationibus* to *praefectus annonae*.[150] While Saturninus himself largely remained in the imperial bureaux in Gaul and Italy, some of his contemporaries had careers that took them from financial posts to provincial governorships instead. For example, T. Atilius was promoted from the post of *rationalis* in the city of Rome to *praeses* of Mauretania Sitifensis,[151] while C. Valerius Antoninus, *rationalis* of Numidia and Mauretania in AD 303/5, was subsequently appointed governor of Numidia Cirtensis in AD 306.[152] Multiple governorships are attested in the case of Vinicius Caecilianus, who started his career as a *rationalis* in Rome and Africa, before becoming *praeses* of Lusitania and *corrector* of Apulia and Calabria in the early fourth century AD.[153] As a coda to this discussion, it is particularly interesting that Saturninus was commemorated with a second-century togate statue which had equestrian, rather than senatorial, shoes. This probably reflects the fact that the statue was chosen before his promotion into the senate.[154] The combination of the *cursus* inscription listing his administrative offices and the statue displaying his equestrian shoes shows the continuity of the service elite, the *equestris nobilitas*, into the early fourth century AD.

The integration of most provincial governorships into the equestrian career path was a significant development of the Tetrarchic period. In the reigns of Gallienus and his immediate successors there was no consistency in the appointment of equestrian or senatorial governors in the praetorian and consular provinces, as we discussed in Chapter 11. Diocletian divided the existing provinces into smaller units, thereby effectively doubling the number of provinces from fifty-four to more than one hundred, based on

---

[149] The large number of inscriptions recording the presence of *rationales* in the city of Rome itself indicates that the most senior officials in the western administration continued to be based there in the age of the Tetrarchs and Constantine (e.g. *CIL* VI 1133, 1701, 31380).

[150] For this career path, see Sablayrolles 1999: 363.   [151] *CIL* VIII 8484 = 20349.

[152] *Rationalis: CIL* VIII 7067 = *ILS* 674. Numidia: *AE* 1895, 80; *CIL* VIII 4766; *CIL* VIII 5526 = 18860 = *ILS* 651.

[153] *CIL* XI 831 = *ILS* 1218. For the dating of his career, see Porena 2006.

[154] Lenaghan 2016: 270–1, 276.

the evidence of the Verona List.[155] This was a major undertaking which loomed large in the memory of those whose experienced it: Lactantius memorably described the proliferation of officials which resulted after Diocletian 'sliced and diced the provinces' (*provinciae in frusta concisae*).[156] The provincial divisions were initiated around AD 293 at the same time as the reform of the imperial mints and the appointment of the Caesars Constantius and Galerius. The reforms probably also included the creation of dioceses, regional groups of provinces, headed by *vicarii* of *perfectissimus* rank.[157] The divisions of the provinces themselves were not accomplished overnight, and probably continued for several years.[158] Most of the provinces were now administered by equestrian *praesides* with the rank of *perfectissimus*, with the exception of the proconsulates of Asia and Africa and some Italian regions.[159] This instituted a sense of order following the inconsistences of the post-Gallienic period. It also meant that the old hierarchy of the equestrian, senatorial praetorian and senatorial consular provinces effectively disappeared. For example, the *praefectus Aegypti* had long ranked among the great equestrian prefectures, second only to the praetorian prefect. In the Tetrarchic period we find a governor promoted from Egypt to the province of Numidia, which had been under the command of a praetorian senator during the principate.[160]

Why did Diocletian place most provinces in the hands of *equites*? Was it because he was the 'hammer of the aristocracy' and was opposed to senators, as Arnheim thought?[161] This was not the case, as scholars now know, given the evidence for continuing employment of senators in high office. Although he preferred fellow soldiers from the army as imperial colleagues, Diocletian actively tried to work with senators.[162] These included L. Aelius Helvius Dionysius, whom he appointed governor of Syria and *iudex sacrarum cognitionum totius Orientis* ('judge of imperial

---

[155] Barnes 1982: 224–6; Bowman 2005: 76. It should be pointed out that provincial divisions had occurred earlier in the third century AD, but these were not on the scale of the Diocletianic reorganisation. See Wilkes 2005 for an account of the new divisions.

[156] Lact. *DMP* 7.4. The pithy translation is that of Corcoran 2006: 46.

[157] The institution of the *vicarii* and the diocesan system has traditionally been ascribed to Diocletian (e.g. Barnes 1982: 140–7, 224–5). Zuckerman 2002 mounted a convincing case that the new dioceses were created by Constantine and Licinius in AD 314 (a conclusion accepted by Barnes 2011: 92; Davenport 2013: 231). This has been complicated by a new fragment from Diocletian's currency edict of AD 301, which clearly includes the term *[d]ioecesi* (Chaniotis and Fujii 2015).

[158] Bowman 2005: 76; Davenport 2013: 227–8.

[159] It should be noted that even then some other regions had senatorial governors, such as Aelius Flavianus, *vir clarissimus* and *praeses* of Palaestina in AD 303 (*AE* 2008, 1569). He could have been adlected into the senate during his governorship. See Davenport 2010: 352.

[160] *PLRE* I Diogenes 7.   [161] The regrettable phrase is that of Arnheim 1972: 39.

[162] Lepelley 1999: 633. Cf. Arnheim 1972: 5, 48–9; Chastagnol 1992: 233–4.

hearings throughout the entire East') in the 290s, while he was himself occupied with his Persian campaigns.[163] Diocletian's aim was not to exclude senators, but to introduce a level of standardisation in provincial appointments to correct the uncertainty that followed Gallienus. Theoretically, he could have reversed the appointment of *equites* and tried to restore the old hierarchy of provinces, but this would have been difficult given the changes in the legionary command structure. Moreover, since Diocletian's administration had twice the number of provinces, he therefore required twice the number of governors – over a hundred at any one time. The senatorial order only had 600 members, which was plainly insufficient to fill the number of praesidial posts, whereas the *ordo equester* had no such limit and numbered tens of thousands. This explains the decision to standardise most provinces at the rank of *perfectissimus*.[164]

It remains true, however, that the doubling of the number of provinces still represented a significant increase in the number of senior posts that needed to be filled by high-ranking *equites*. Where did these *praesides* come from? Our ability to answer this question is compromised to a certain extent by a lack of prosopographical evidence. For example, we know the name of at least one governor for only seventy-one provinces (and often it is just one solitary *praes*, who usually remains little more than a name).[165] Nevertheless, it is possible to identify two major groups of *equites* who became *praesides*. The first was composed of former soldiers who had acquired equestrian rank through elevation to office posts, including members of Gallienus' corps of *protectores*. For example, P. Aelius Aelianus and Clementius Valerius Marcellinus, both prefects of the *legio II Adiutrix* in the 260s, were later promoted to administer Mauretania Caesariensis and Tingitana, respectively.[166] Other men in this category included M. Aurelius Decimus, former *princeps peregrinorum*, and Flavius Flavianus, a former *cornicularius*, who served as *praesides* of Numidia in the 280s.[167] Even when we cannot identify precise career paths, nomenclature is often an effective guide to origin, as in the case of Aurelius Dizzo, *praeses* of Moesia Inferior in the late third century AD; Dizzo is a name common to Thrace, and suggests a military

---

[163] *CIL* VI 1673 = *ILS* 1211; Barnes 1982: 63; Peachin 1996: 167–82.

[164] One must also point out that such a system could not have been reversed after Diocletian's retirement, because of the fracturing of the empire. The reign of Maxentius (AD 306–12) isolated Rome and its senate from most other provinces. See Salway 2015: 203.

[165] This is based on Barnes 1981, as well as my own prosopographical data collected for my D.Phil. (Davenport 2009).

[166] Gerhardt and Hartmann 2008: 1140, 1142.   [167] *PLRE* I Decimus 1; *PLRE* I Flavianus 9.

background.[168] The rise of men from the Danubian provinces to governor-ships through the army is exemplified by the career of the future emperor Constantius I, who became *praeses* of Dalmatia after his service as a *protector* and *tribunus*.[169] Valerius Firmilianus, governor of Palaestina under Galerius and Maximinus Daza, had previously served in the army.[170] However, the route from officer commands to provincial governorships changed in the early fourth century, when regional military commanders with the title of *dux* or *comes rei militaris* were appointed for the first time.[171] The first attested example is Aurelius Maximinus, the *dux* of Egypt, the Thebaid and Libya in AD 308/310.[172] Henceforth, army officers were usually promoted to these regional offices, rather than the post of provincial *praeses*. This change represented the consolidation of a separate military hierarchy after the upheavals of the mid-third century AD.

The second, larger, group of governors was composed of *equites* from the curial classes, who followed administrative careers with virtually no army service.[173] We have already highlighted several cases of *rationales* who were advanced to the position of provincial *praeses*. Many of the equestrian *praesides* of the late third and early fourth centuries AD, parti-cularly in the eastern provinces, bore the *nomen* Aurelius. This indicates that their families received Roman citizenship in AD 212 through the *Constitutio Antoniniana*.[174] These *equites* were not parvenus of humble birth, given that wealthy families from the east would only have qualified for equestrian status after enfranchisement by Caracalla.[175] We know of several examples among prominent landowners in Egypt, including the *eques* Aurelius Appianus; his daughter married Antonius Philoxenos, a former procurator and *vir egregius*.[176] We can posit a similar background

---

[168] *AE* 1980, 793b; Chastagnol 1988: 204.   [169] *PLRE* I Constantius 12; Anon. Val. *Origo* 2.

[170] *PLRE* I Firmilianus 2; Eus. *Mart. Pal.* (L) 8.1; *AE* 1993, 1618. Further examples can be found: (i) Aurelius Maximianus (*PLRE* I Maximianus 4), prefect of the *legio IV Flavia Felix* (*CIL* III 1646 = *ILS* 2292) before being appointed governor of Numidia (*CIL* VIII 2572 = *ILS* 5786; *CIL* VIII 2660 = *ILS* 5787). It should be noted, however, that no one inscription securely identifies the prefect and the praeses; (ii) Aurelius Reginus (*PLRE* I Reginus), prefect of the *legio III Augusta* (*CIL* VIII 2761), is probably to be identified with the homonymous *praeses* of the Thebaid in 301 (*AE* 1934, 9); (iii) Valerius Concordius (*PLRE* I Concordius 4), recorded as governor of Numidia in 295 (*AE* 1920, 15; *CJ* 9.9.27), could be the *dux* in an inscription from Trier dated to 293–305 (*CIL* XIII 3672).

[171] A. H. M. Jones 1964: 43–4, 125–6, 609–10.   [172] *AE* 1934, 7–8; *AE* 2004, 1636, 1641.

[173] A. H. M. Jones 1964: 44–5.

[174] For the argument that the eastern Aurelii predominantly received their citizenship from Caracalla, rather than previous Antonine emperors, see Blanco-Pérez 2016.

[175] Garnsey 2004: 134. This argument draws on Davenport forthcoming.

[176] Aurelius Appianus, the owner of a substantial estate in Arsinoe, had obtained equestrian status by AD 231/232. See Rathbone 1991: 46, 51–2. For other Aurelii of equestrian status in third-century Egypt, see Rowlandson 1996: 109–10.

for governors such as Aurelius Aurelianus, *praeses* of Galatia in the late third century AD, whose son Aurelius Philadelphus was honoured by the *colonia* of Iconium.[177] Many of the Aurelii who served as provincial *praesides* in the late third century AD may have been new men, but that does not mean they were from undistinguished backgrounds. Indeed, it is highly unlikely that the Roman state uncovered some untapped source of administrative manpower in the late third century AD. Instead, it continued to recruit *equites* from the municipal aristocracies to serve the *res publica*, just as they had in preceding centuries.[178]

This evidence indicates that it continued to be possible for *equites* to pursue long careers in the imperial service, holding administrative, legal and financial posts. These could lead either to high office at court (as in the case of Caelius Saturninus) or to provincial governorships. The imperial bureaucracy demanded literate and educated officials to fill these roles, and they continued to be found in the ranks of the municipal aristocracies from Italy and the provinces.[179] C. Vesedius Rufinus of Beneventum, son of the city's leading citizen, Vesedius Iustus, was one such man, who was 'elevated to the post of *advocatus fisci* of the imperial treasury by imperial decision' (*advocato fisci | summ(a)e rei iudicio | sacro promoto*).[180] These curial elites often came to the attention of the central administration on the basis of their legal or oratorical abilities.[181] They included men such as Eumenius, the professor of rhetoric from Autun in Gaul (whom we have already met in our discussion of salary grades). Eumenius served as *magister memoriae* at the western imperial court in the 290s, and was praised by Constantius I for his 'eloquence and seriousness of character' (*eloquentiam et gravitatem morum*).[182] Another Gallic notable, Aemilius Magnus Arborius, was an advocate before being summoned to act as tutor one of the sons of Constantine.[183]

The best evidence for the scions of the provincial aristocracy moving into the imperial administration comes from the pen of the anonymous orator who delivered a panegyric of Constantine in AD 310. He concluded the speech by commending his children to the emperor – one of his offspring was already serving as *advocatus fisci*.[184] The orator also referred to the achievements of his pupils, who had advanced to posts in the palatine *officia* and to provincial governorships. In a manner reminiscent

---

[177] *RECAM* IV 2.   [178] A. H. M. Jones 1964: 48–9.   [179] A. H. M. Jones 1964: 741.
[180] *CIL* IX 1682 = *ILS* 6502. For his father, see *CIL* IX 1683 = *ILS* 6501.   [181] Kaster 1988: 104.
[182] *Pan. Lat.* 9(4).6.2, 11.2. 14.3 (for quotation); B. S. Rodgers 1989: 250–2; Nixon and Rodgers 1994: 128; Corcoran 2000: 91, 132–3, 268–9.
[183] Hopkins 1961: 240–3; Kaster 1988: 100–6.   [184] *Pan. Lat.* 6(7).23.1.

of Pliny the Younger's letters of recommendation he declaimed: 'I rejoice in the successes of these men, and I regard their distinction as if it were my own' (*quorum successibus laetor omniumque honorem pro meo duco*).[185] The post of governor was particularly attractive to well-educated elites such as lawyers, so much so that this career path was parodied in the late Roman joke-book, the *Philogelos*.[186] It seems to be no coincidence that several of these equestrians, from the anonymous orator's son to Caelius Saturninus, began their careers as *advocati fisci*. Constantine, in a letter to his praetorian prefect Pacatianus in AD 334, emphasised the need for *advocati* to be selected and promoted on their basis of their integrity, literary talent and trustworthiness.[187] The qualities were no different from those prized among such equestrian administrators in the high empire, revealing an essential continuity in the ethos of the Roman imperial government.[188]

One new aspect of the administrative system was that it became possible for men to rise to high office and equestrian status from positions within the imperial service. In the principate even the lowest rank on the procuratorial ladder, the grade of *sexagenarius*, was restricted to pre-existing members of the equestrian order. The subaltern officials of the palatine bureaux were all imperial freedmen, while the offices of the provincial governors were staffed by soldiers on secondment. However, the third century AD witnessed a reduction in the roles of freedmen, who were largely replaced by freeborn men.[189] These included the *Caesariani*, the officials of the *res privata*, whom we met at the beginning of this chapter: they could gain equestrian rank if they completed their service honourably. In the later Roman empire all provincial governors, to say nothing of the diocesan *vicarii* and the praetorian prefects, required their own staff.[190] These positions were filled by free Roman citizens known as *cohortales*, rather than soldiers, as had previously been the case.[191] The evolution of this new hierarchy resulted in the introduction of a complex system of rules and regulations regarding appointments and promotions, especially in the lower levels.[192] The *cohortales* were notionally prevented from rising up the bureaucratic ladder and attaining higher positions. Indeed, the emperor Constantine ruled that sons were expected to succeed their fathers in the same post.[193] But this appears to have been a theoretical distinction, since

---

[185] *Pan. Lat.* 6(7).23.2.   [186] *Philogelos* 202. See also *AE* 1904, 108 = *ILS* 8376; Amm. 29.3.6.

[187] *CTh.* 10.15.2; Pedersen 1976: 30–2.

[188] See Chapters 6 and 7 for letters of recommendation in the high empire.

[189] A. H. M. Jones 1964: 564–6, 594–5; Lepelley 1999: 630; Haensch 2006.

[190] As memorably described by Lact. *DMP* 7.4.   [191] Heather 1994: 21.

[192] See the discussion about seniority and advancement in Chapter 7.

[193] *CTh.* 7.22.3 (AD 331).

we know of some exceptional cases of social mobility. The lowly Flavius Ablabius rose from the staff of the governor of Crete to become praetorian prefect and ordinary consul in AD 331, while Datianus, the son of a bath-attendant, advanced from service as a *notarius* to the consulship in AD 358.[194] These careers are detailed in a speech of Libanius, and although genuine, they are used to disparage the new senators who inhabited the *curia* of Constantinople, and should be regarded as exceptional cases.[195] Many *cohortales* actually came from middling curial families, which possessed sufficient wealth and property to allow for further education and training, enabling their offspring to become successful court officials.[196] As they worked their way up through the administration these men gained access to equestrian status (if they did not already possess it), and the higher *dignitates* of *egregius* and *perfectissimus*. This pathway offered new opportunities for Roman citizens of modest means (but still well-off in comparison to most people) to advance in government service.[197]

Equestrian governors were prime candidates for entrance into the senatorial order itself, which always needed to be replenished by new men, as Hopkins and Burton have demonstrated.[198] There were definite connections between the two orders. For example, the daughter of M. Ulpius Iulianus, *praeses* of Macedonia in the late third century AD, was a *clarissima femina*, a status she probably acquired through marriage.[199] Many senators share the same names as *equites*, suggesting that they may have been new men. There is Aurelius Aurelianus, *praeses* of Galatia, mentioned above, and a senatorial Aurelius Aurelianus, governor of Arabia and consul designate.[200] We have two senatorial governors, father and son, with the name M. Aurelius Valentinianus, who administered Pannonia Inferior and Hispania Citerior, respectively, under the emperors Gallienus and Carus.[201] They shared their names with a homonymous equestrian *praeses* of Pontus in the Tetrarchic period.[202] The administrative elites and the curial classes continued to enter the Roman senate via the

---

[194] *PLRE* I Ablabius 4; *PLRE* I Datianus 1. Although Ablabius reached the apogee of his career under Constantine, his post in the governor's office would have been in the Tetrarchic period, given that he was *vicarius* of Asiana in AD 324/6 (*CIL* III 352 = 7000).

[195] Lib. *Or.* 42.23–4; Heather 2008: 112–13; Skinner 2013: 22–28.

[196] A. H. M. Jones 1964: 595; Matthews 1975: 41–3; Heather 1994: 21.

[197] This returns us to the point of Mosca 1939: 404, discussed in the Introduction, that in autocratic regimes there is always a reservoir of lower elites who are ready and able to ascend to higher office and dignities. The curial classes were the reservoir of the Roman administration throughout the imperial period. See Heather 1998.

[198] Hopkins and Burton 1983.   [199] *AE* 2002, 1283.   [200] *AE* 1965, 23.

[201] Pannonia Inferior: *AE* 2008, 1142. Hispania Citerior: *CIL* II 4102, 4103.

[202] *CIL* III 14184.31 = *AE* 1986, 663a.

crucial channel of equestrian rank. Apart from some spectacular examples of praetorian prefects promoted to the ranks of the *clarissimi* (who would always remain the exception rather than the rule), this was not the path followed by the new military elites.[203] Municipal aristocrats who gained equestrian rank, equestrian administrators who became senators – the story seems very familiar from the high empire.[204] But in the world of the Tetrarchic regime there was now a crucial difference: the equestrians who, in previous generations, would have been adlected into the *curia* in order to take up provincial commands could now be appointed to govern provinces directly, without the need to make them senators. After several centuries this represented the final acknowledgement that there was no difference in the abilities and competencies of equestrians and senators, and that they could hold the same positions with identical responsibilities.[205]

The status hierarchy of administrative offices and provincial governorships established by Diocletian was not long lasting, as the system began to change again under Constantine. The senior prefectural positions – *praefectus vigilum*, *praefectus annonae* and *praefectus praetorio* – were all upgraded to the status of *clarissimi*; this meant that the title of *eminentissimus* disappeared from use, as it was no longer awarded to any officials after about AD 325.[206] The deputies of the praetorian prefects, known as *vicarii*, who administered the provincial dioceses, were likewise upgraded from *perfectissimi* to senatorial status.[207] Finally, Constantine raised governors to the rank of *clarissimus* in a number of provinces. Achaea became a proconsulship again around AD 317, taking its place alongside Asia and Africa as a senior senatorial governorship.[208] Syria Coele, Phoenice, Bithynia, Europa and Thracia, Byzacena, Numidia and most Italian regions were likewise henceforth governed by *clarissimi*.[209] Many of these provinces were areas in which the wealthiest senatorial aristocrats had significant landholdings.[210] This was a gradual process which took place from AD 312 to AD 324, as Constantine acquired control over the city of Rome, Italy and Africa from Maxentius, and then later the eastern provinces that had previously been under the authority of Licinius.[211] In these new senatorial provinces the title of the governor was changed from *praeses*

[203] See the next section.   [204] See Chapter 7.

[205] This theme has been traced through Chapters 4, 6–7 and 11.

[206] Salway 2006: 132–3, 2015: 203, 213; Lizzi Testa 2009: 115.   [207] A. H. M. Jones 1964: 106–7.

[208] Davenport 2013: 233–4.

[209] See the provincial *fasti* in Barnes 1982, with Arnheim 1972: 52.   [210] Wickham 2005: 163.

[211] Dillon 2015: 46–7. See Davenport 2013: 231–2 on the process in the east.

to *consularis*, though one did not actually need to have been a consul to be selected.[212]

These senatorial governorships were particularly important, because Constantine allowed equestrians to be granted the status of *clarissimus* on appointment to the position.[213] The senatorial rank of *clarissimus* thus became a reward for government service, rather than a precondition for it.[214] The *equites* who were elevated to senators on their appointment received new privileges. Equestrian status could not technically be inherited, nor could the higher ranks of *egregius* or *perfectissimus*, for they were all personal honours, attached to the individual.[215] However, the senatorial *dignitas* of *clarissimus* could be passed down through successive generations, so that the sons of these governors became *clarissimi* themselves.[216] This meant that there was an increase in the number of *clarissimi* both in the present (since the rank was awarded on appointment to office) and in the future (since the sons of the new *clarissimi* inherited the rank). The number of new senators created by Constantine in this way is impossible to quantify. Chastagnol proposed a rapid proliferation of *clarissimi*, at least in the western provinces, between AD 312 and 326, but other scholars have been more cautious about the extent and pace of the increase.[217] The size of the senatorial order, including the senates at both Rome and Constantinople, did not reach the oft-quoted number of 2,000 members until much later in the fourth century AD.[218] It is important to note that Constantine did not elevate all provinces to senatorial status, as many of the smaller regions remained under the control of equestrian *praesides*. But he had initiated a change that would eventually see all provincial governors possess the rank of *clarissimus* by the early fifth century AD.[219]

---

[212] Arnehim 1972: 56. See Bagnall et al. 1987: 2 n. 14 on the lack of consular qualification. The first Constantinian senatorial governor of Syria Phoenice (by now referred to simply as Phoenice), Iulius Iulianus, drew attention to his new appointment by noting that he was the *primus consularis* (*AE* 2005, 1566).

[213] A. H. M. Jones 1964: 106–7, 526–7; Lizzi Testa 2009: 114–16.

[214] A. H. M. Jones 1964: 525–30. See Chapter 11 for soldiers gaining higher equestrian dignities.

[215] Even the legislation of Marcus Aurelius granting privileges to the progeny of *perfectissimi*, discussed earlier in this chapter, did not alter this, since the descendants did not actually acquire the status of *perfectissimi* themselves.

[216] A. H. M. Jones 1964: 107; Dillon 2015: 45–6, 50.

[217] Chastagnol 1992: 236–41. Cf. now the revisionist and more balanced account of Lizzi Testa 2009: 113–15. Much of Chastagnol's early evidence is derived from the rhetoric of imperial panegyric (*Pan. Lat.* 12(9).20.1, delivered in AD 313, and *Pan. Lat.* 4(10).35.2, from AD 321).

[218] A. H. M. Jones 1964: 527; Heather 1994: 13; Salzman 2002: 31; Lizzi Testa 2009: 114–16.

[219] This is discussed later in this chapter.

The result of Constantine's reforms was that the positions in the provinces and the court administration could be held by former equestrians who gained senatorial status through their imperial service, as well as by senatorial aristocrats from established families.[220] Men of similar background to Caelius Saturninus and the other equestrian administrators discussed above are attested in the new consular governorships. For example, one of Constantine's appointees as *consularis Syriae*, Flavius Dionysius, was a former advocate.[221] Another senatorial governor, C. Iulius Rufinianus Ablabius Tatianus, who was *consularis* of Aemila and Liguria and *corrector* of Tuscia and Umbria, had been adlected into the senate after service as a *patronus fisci*.[222] These men rubbed shoulders with grandees such as L. Aradius Valerius Proculus, who came from a family that had been of consular rank since the Severan period. Proculus served as *praeses* of Byzacena, *consularis* of Europa and Thrace, and *consularis* of Sicily.[223]

The form of the new career can be seen in the inscribed *cursus* of another senatorial aristocrat, M. Maecius Placidus, which was carved on a statue base in Puteoli:

To Marcus Maecius Memmius Furius Baburius Caecilianus Placidus, *vir clarissimus, pontifex maior*, public augur of the Roman people and its citizens, *quindecemvir sacris faciundis, corrector* of Venetia and Histria, *praefectus annonae* of the sacred city with the *ius gladii, comes* of the first rank, *comes Orientis* of Egypt and of Mesopotamia, judge of the imperial court, judge for the second time by imperial delegation, praetorian prefect, and judge of the imperial court for the third time, *consul ordinarius*. The Palatine region erected this for its most distinguished patron.[224]

Placidus' *cursus* took him from a provincial governorship to the prefecture of the grain supply, and he then ascended through further posts as *comes Orientis* (the equivalent of *vicarius* in the east) and praetorian prefect before receiving the honour of the ordinary consulship. This *cursus* represented a combination of positions that had previously been of equestrian

---

[220] Dillon 2015: 46–7.   [221] *PLRE* I Dionysius 11; Lib. *Or.* 1.36.

[222] *PLRE* I Tatianus 4; *CIL* X 1125 = *ILS* 2942. For the *patronus fisci*, see Delmaire 1989: 83 n. 100.

[223] *PLRE* I Proculus 11; *CIL* VI 1690 = *ILS* 1240.

[224] *PLRE* I Placidus 2; *CIL* X 1700 = *ILS* 1231: *M(arco) Maecio Memmio Furio Baburio | Caeciliano Placido c(larissimo) v(iro) | pontifici maiori auguri pu|blico p(opuli) R(omani) Quiritium quindecem|viro sacris faciundis correc|tori Venetiarum et Histriae | praefecto annonae urbis | sacrae cum iure gladii comiti | ordinis primi comiti orienti | Aegypti et Mesopotamiae iudi|ci sacrarum cognitionum | [tertio] iudici iterum ex de|legationibus sacris prae|fecto praetorio et iudici | sacrarum cognitionum | tertio consuli ordinario | patrono pr(a)estantissimo | regio Palatina | posuit.*

status in the high empire and those that had always been senatorial – they were now all merged into one senatorial career.[225] Indeed, after the Constantinian period the inscribed *cursus honorum* was no longer used as a form of public self-representation by lower-ranked equestrian officials, and instead became the embodiment of the senatorial career.[226] This was in many ways a fitting conclusion to the emergence of an equestrian service elite which shared the same values and commitment to serving the *res publica* as members of the senatorial order.[227]

The reasons behind Constantine's administrative decisions are nowhere on record, but it is possible to advance some plausible hypotheses. First of all, the elevation of the senior prefectures (such as the *praefectus annonae* and *praefectus praetorio*), as well as other high-ranking officials, like the diocesan *vicarii*, to senatorial rank eliminated a certain level of status friction within the Roman administrative hierarchy. Henceforth, senatorial *clarissimi* would not be required to answer to men of equestrian rank. The selection of *equites* for the great prefectures was a decision made by Augustus at the birth of the principate, when he was trying to install men who would not pose a challenge to his regime in key positions.[228] Such a distinction no longer mattered in the fourth century AD when emperors primarily emerged from the Roman army. Secondly, the Diocletianic reforms – as logical as it had been at the time to standardise most governorships at the rank of *perfectissimus* – had flattened out the hierarchy of administration. This meant that there was really no difference in status between the vast majority of provinces – one could govern Libya Superior, Epirus Vetus, Narbonensis Prima or Valeria all at the same rank. In essence, the fact that there was no *cursus*, no higher offices to strive for, was a problem for the Roman aristocrats – for, like all elites, they thrived on status distinctions which set them apart from their peers.[229] As we observed in Chapter 7, the genre of the inscribed *cursus* adopted by senators and *equites* in the imperial period represented both their collective unity as members of the aristocratic *ordines* of the *res publica* and their desire to climb the greasy pole to acquire new honours, rewards and privileges. By elevating some prestigious provinces to senatorial rank, and making new governors eligible for the status of *clarissimus* on

---

[225] It is interesting to note that the evidence of consular appointments and precedence shows that the emperor valued service at the imperial court above noble birth (Salway 2015: 219–20).

[226] Davenport 2015a: 281–3.   [227] See Chapter 7 for the origins of these developments.

[228] See Chapter 4.

[229] For aristocratic competition in empires in general, see Kautsky 1997: 212–17; Scheidel 2013: 19–20. For relevance to Constantine's government, see Dillon 2015: 56.

appointment, Constantine returned a level of competition to provincial administration.

Thirdly, by selecting senators (both those from established families and new men from equestrian ranks) for these new governorships, Constantine won himself allies and supporters in the highest levels of administration.[230] It has long been acknowledged that one of the primary aims of Constantine's regime was to unify the aristocratic elements throughout the empire into a governing elite loyal to him.[231] This was a necessary and important task because Constantine only progressively acquired suzerainty over the entire Roman empire between AD 306 and 324. After his defeat of Licinius, Constantine was the first emperor in two generations to rule the entire empire as sole Augustus. Several of his initiatives, such as the grant of the *perfectissimatus* to municipal aristocrats (recorded by Eusebius) and the creation of three new grades of imperial *comites*, serve as evidence for Constantine's desire to create strong links between himself and the elites of the provinces.[232] The strategy was essentially one of imperial domestication, as practised by Augustus and his successors. The Roman aristocracy relied and depended on the emperors for honours and privileges – essentially, all forms of validation stemmed from the imperial centre.[233]

The benefits of imperial service exercised such a powerful attraction that they enticed members of the curial elites who did not want a full career in the administration. As we discussed in Chapters 6 and 7, during the high empire it was very common for equestrians from the municipal aristocracies to seek one or two commands in the *militiae equestres*, or perhaps a single procuratorship, before returning to their home communities. Their military and administrative posts gave them increased prestige, and even the title of *vir egregius*, if they had been a procurator. In the fourth century AD imperial service also conferred an additional privilege, the much-coveted immunity from curial *munera*. Tenure as a governor was therefore particularly attractive in a way that it had not been during the high empire. Former governors were able to retire to their home towns with the status of *ex praesidibus*, which exempted them from their curial obligations. Many provincial governors only held office for one to two

---

[230] Dillon 2015: 52.   [231] Heather 1994: 14–16.

[232] On the *comites*, see A. H. M. Jones 1964: 104–5, 333–4. For Constantine's 'regime building', see Heather 1994; Dillon 2015: 50–1.

[233] For the state as an organising force in societies, see Mann 1986: 267–70; Poulantzas 1978: 127. For the turn of curial elites towards the imperial government, see Skinner 2013: 49–50; Sirks 2015: 301.

years, less than the average tenure of senatorial legates in the principate, which tended to be about three years.[234]

The rapid turnover of governors was an acknowledged reality in the mid-fourth century AD, as revealed by Libanius' famous remark that officials were always looking behind them to see if their successor had arrived.[235] Indeed, the late Roman state actively prevented men from holding several governorships. When the unfortunate lawyer Africanus petitioned Valentinian I for a second term as a *praeses*, the emperor had him executed.[236] This might initially be thought to be an atypical example, but it was actually forbidden to hold the post of *praeses* twice by the fifth century AD.[237] As I have suggested elsewhere, there are striking parallels between the ambitions of municipal aristocrats who held one or two officer posts in the *militiae equestres* in the high empire and their equivalents in the fourth century AD who served as governors.[238] While some men such as C. Caelius Saturninus had long careers in the palatine and provincial administration, others eschewed this pathway for a single governorship in a province closer to home. For example, a Greek from Caria might choose to act as governor of his home province for a year or two, with his brief tenure in the imperial administration being commemorated with a statue and inscription praising his virtues.[239] This offered a lasting memorial that he was a faithful servant of the Roman state. The changes in the structure of government, the titles of positions and the status of officials did not alter the ambitions of men.

Senators and Soldiers

Military officers did not quite fit into this new senatorial aristocracy. Gallienus' generals who worked their way up from the ranks of the legions in the third century AD were from a different background to senatorial aristocrats, municipal worthies and the equestrian procuratorial elite. The members of the new officer corps banded together, unified by their shared army service, and this enabled them to rise to the purple themselves. The emperor Diocletian, a former commander of the *protectores*, specifically selected his imperial colleagues, Maximian, Constantius and Galerius, from among the ranks of the tribunes and *protectores*.[240] Galerius later

---

[234] A. H. M. Jones 1964: 381.
[235] Lib. *Or.* 2.42; Liebeschuetz 1972: 111–12; Roueché 1998: 34–5; Slootjes 2006: 25–7.
[236] Amm. 29.3.6. [237] *CTh.* 9.26.4 (Honorius). [238] Davenport forthcoming.
[239] Horster 1998; Slootjes 2006: 25–6. [240] Barnes 1982: 32–8 reviews their careers.

advocated the appointment of Severus and Licinius to fill vacant positions in the imperial college because they had been faithful military officers, indicating that he wanted colleagues who shared his inclinations and values.[241] The emperor Maximian was a soldier from Sirmium in Pannonia, but unlike Marcus Aurelius' Pannonian general M. Valerius Maximianus, his parents were not members of the curial class, but common labourers.[242] Maximianus' Antonine contemporary Pertinax had to acquire an influential senatorial patron and secure adlection into the *amplissimus ordo* before he was able to govern the most important frontier provinces. In the changed world of the post-Gallienic era, this career could be accomplished within the army itself – and some former soldiers were not ashamed to acknowledge it. M. Aurelius Decimus, governor of Numidia in AD 284, recorded his status as a former *princeps peregrinorum* on more than ten inscriptions.[243] One of Decimus' successors, Flavius Flavianus, erected several dedicatory inscriptions in which he stated that he was a former *cornicularius* of the praetorian prefects.[244] The fact that many of these inscriptions were erected by Decimus and Flavianus themselves (their names appear in the nominative case) means that they must have personally authorised the inclusion of their former posts. Their ascent from the army was evidently central to their public self-representation.

One prominent place where the new military elites were not represented is the epigraphic and statue record of the city of Rome. There are no public or private statues or inscriptions honouring their achievements in the late third or early fourth centuries AD.[245] On one level this reflects the fact that their careers were focused around the army in the provinces or in the mobile imperial *comitatus*, with the result that they did not move to Rome. But the lack of public statues to honour the *equites* who defended the borders of the empire stands in stark comparison with the commemoration of Marcus Aurelius' senatorial generals for their service during the Marcomannic Wars.[246] This indicates that these equestrian officers did not yet possess sufficient social prestige to be recognised with honours in the *sacra urbs*.

---

[241] Severus: Lact. *DMP* 18.12; Anon. Val. *Origo* 9. Licinius: Lact. *DMP* 20.2.   [242] *Epit.* 40.10.

[243] *PLRE* I Decimus 1. For his title of *p(raeses) p(rovinciae) Numidiae ex principe peregrinorum*, see *CIL* VIII 2529 = *ILS* 2291, VIII 2530, 2663, 2670, 4578, 7002, 18288; *AE* 1919, 26, 28; 1973, 630; 1993, 1769a–b.

[244] *PLRE* I Flavianus 9; *CIL* VIII 4325; *AE* 1916, 18, 21.

[245] Davenport 2015a: 278–81. The exceptions are praetorian prefects who became *clarissimi*, who are noted below.

[246] For these statues, see Chenault 2012: 118–22.

This fact speaks to a certain level of tension between the new military elite and the senatorial and equestrian administrators. The Tetrarchic emperors and other officers such as Decimus and Flavianus did consciously choose to emphasise their army backgrounds, because it was a qualification that senators no longer possessed.[247] This is amply shown by panegyrics delivered in honour of Maximian in the late third century AD, which trumpet the emperor's *virtus* and military excellence as the prime qualifications for the purple, while praising his civilian achievements as well. Only the emperor could now rule *domi militiaeque* in the world envisioned by these orators; the senators and the senate were reduced to a venerable ceremonial role.[248] After the reign of Gallienus senators were, as a general rule, no longer appointed to command troops in battle, although they could be employed as imperial *comites*.[249] There is only one, quite exceptional, example of a senator leading troops in the early fourth century AD: C. Ceionius Rufius Volusianus, *praefectus praetorio* of the usurper Maxentius, who was despatched to Africa in order to subdue the rebellion of L. Domitius Alexander.[250] Military command was therefore a vital ability which the equestrian officer corps possessed and most senators did not.

At the same time, however, there were evident connections between the two groups. Army officers, including Gallienus' *dux* Iulius Marcellinus and M. Aurelius Fortunatus, prefect of the *legio III Augusta* under Aurelian, married women from senatorial families.[251] These wives were not downgraded to equestrian rank, but retained their high standing as *clarissimae feminae*.[252] At the very highest level praetorian prefects continued to be awarded the ordinary consulship in the late third century AD, officially entering the senatorial order.[253] This group included Ti. Claudius Aurelius Aristobulus, *cos. suff.* AD 285, Afranius Hannibalianus, *cos. ord.* AD 292, and Iulius Asclepiodotus, *cos. ord.* AD 292.[254] Aristobulus even became proconsul of Africa and urban prefect, ascending to the heights of the senatorial *cursus*.[255] Former military officers evidently had

---

[247] On the last generation of senatorial generals, see Davenport 2014a: 182–4.

[248] Davenport 2016. See also Symm. *Or.* 1, delivered in honour of Valentinian I, in which the catalogue of the emperor's military achievements is followed by a section on his civilian government (*Or.* 1.23). The message was that Valentinian I excelled both *domi* and *militiae*.

[249] For examples, see Pomponius Bassus (*CIL* VI 3836 = 31747 = *IGR* I 137) under Gallienus and Caesonius Bassus (*AE* 1964, 223 = *AE* 1980, 215) during the eastern expedition of Carus and Numerian.

[250] Zos. 2.14.2 (noting that he was accompanied by a general, Zenas); Victor, *Caes.* 40.18.

[251] *AE* 2006, 1803; *CIL* III 2665 = *ILS* 584.   [252] Evans Grubbs 1993: 133–4.

[253] Salway 2006: 129–30.   [254] For Aristobulus' consulship as suffect, see Barnes 1996: 537.

[255] *PLRE* I Aristobulus.

a desire to share in the honours and offices of the senatorial life, as a way of gaining recognition for their seniority and importance as generals.

Indeed, the upper echelons of the officer corps were proud of their military service, and the bonds forged through the army, but this did not mean that they always rejected the existing senatorial *mentalité*. As Wallace-Hadrill has shown, cultural identity can be best understood as a type of 'code-switching', whereby individuals emphasise the aspects of their identity most appropriate to individual situations.[256] The military elite, while certainly espousing the values and ideals of Roman soldiers, did sometimes seek integration with, or validation from, the senatorial order, and its members could emphasise a cultured, aristocratic identity when necessary. In Chapter 11 we discussed how there was already a culture of aspiration within the Roman army of the principate, as soldiers sought to share the lifestyles of their officers. We can see this same characteristic in fourth-century monuments, such as the epitaph erected by Valeria for her deceased husband, the tribune Dassianus.[257] The inscription not only emphasises his rise through the ranks, but also his personal bravery in two lines which are reminiscent of the *Aeneid*.[258] Another poetic epitaph, erected for Flavius Aemilianus, a fourth-century officer from the diocese of Dacia, shows similar cultural aspirations. The inscription is, in the words of Drew-Bear, 'characterised by a curious combination of a low level of literary culture on the one hand and repeated, strenuous attempts at elegance in expression on the other'.[259] The level of education and cultural attainment increased depending on the background and opportunities available to officers. The fourth-century evidence shows that *protectores* were often literate and cultured, of which Ammianus Marcellinus is merely the most notable example.[260] At the highest levels of society we find Constantine, himself a former army officer, fostered in the bosom of the Tetrarchs, being consistently depicted in the sources, both pagan and Christian, as an intelligent and literate man.[261] Educated at

---

[256] Wallace-Hadrill 2008: 63–4.

[257] Drew-Bear, Malay and Zuckerman 2004 = *AE* 2004, 1396a.

[258] Lines 8–9 of the text refer to Vergil, *Aeneid* 5.67 (Drew-Bear, Malay and Zuckerman 2004: 412).

[259] *AE* 1977, 806; Drew-Bear 1977: 259.

[260] Trombley 1999. For Ammianus' origin and background, see Matthews 1989: 77–80; G. Kelly 2008: 119–32.

[261] Eus. *VC* 3.13.1–2; Eutrop. 10.7.2; *Epit.* 41.14. Only one writer notes deficiencies: Anon. Val. *Origo* 2.

Diocletian's court in Nicomedia, Constantine spoke both Latin and Greek well, though like all Roman emperors he used Latin when engaged in official business.[262]

The fact that senior military officers, such as the new regional *duces* appointed from the early fourth century AD onwards, ranked as *perfectissimi* meant that they were automatically included in Constantine's 'community of honour' (to return to Harper's useful phrase) on the basis of their status. But they were markedly excluded from the *clarissimi*. The praetorian prefects, who had been made senators under Constantine's reforms, did not lose all military responsibilities, as some prefects are attested campaigning with the emperor until the middle decades of the fourth century AD.[263] By the 340s at the latest the position of a new senior general, the *magister militum*, had been created. There were usually two of these at any one time, a *magister peditum* for the infantry and a *magister equitum* for the cavalry.[264] These new posts formed a natural apex at the top of the empire's military command structure, which previously had lacked such generals; instead, as we have seen throughout this book, leadership was delegated to senatorial governors or praetorian prefects commanding the field army. The *magistri militum* held the status of *clarissimi* and were first appointed to ordinary consulships under Constantine's sons. The first examples are Flavius Bonosus, *cos. ord.* AD 344, and Flavius Eusebius, *cos. ord.* AD 347.[265] These generals were likewise part of the 'community of honour'.

There was, however, some feeling that military men, especially lower down the hierarchy, were not suitable for senatorial office. For example, Ammianus praised Constantius II for not elevating *duces* into the senatorial order: 'In his reign, no *dux* was exalted with the clarissimate. For they were – as we ourselves remember – *perfectissimi*.'[266] This was a somewhat surprising sentiment given that Ammianus was himself a *protector*. But he firmly believed in the separation of civilian and military authority, noting that it was equally appropriate that 'no one, except those hardened by the dust of warfare, was placed in charge of soldiers'.[267] Ammianus' remarks

---

[262] See the remarks of Barnes 1981: 73–4; Corcoran 2000: 259–60, 263–4.

[263] Barnes 1992: 241, 251.

[264] Barnes 2011: 153–6. Cf. Zos. 2.33.2, who states that Constantine instituted the post of *magister militum*. The evidence for the office's creation is inconclusive, hence we have adopted the position that it came into being by the 340s at the latest.

[265] *PLRE* I Bonosus 4; *PLRE* I Eusebius 49.

[266] Amm. 21.16.2: *nec sub eo dux quisqum cum clarissimatu provectus est. erant enim (ut nos quoque meminimus), perfectissimi.* The evidence for *duces* as *perfectissimi* is collected by Ensslin 1937: 671–2.

[267] Amm. 21.16.3: *non nisi pulvere bellico indurati, praeficiebantur armatis.*

are important, because they reveal that the separation of civilian and military career paths in the late third century AD had had a real and significant impact on the Roman world. For Ammianus it was simply inconceivable that army officers should be senators or obtain civilian commands – they most certainly did not serve *domi miltiaeque*.

Such a viewpoint would have suited aristocratic senators. Despite the efforts of Maximian's panegyrists to argue that the true combination of military and civilian virtues lay only in the person of the emperor, and Ammianus' belief that only battle-hardened men should command troops, senators from noble and established senatorial families still claimed the *domi militiaeque* ethos for themselves. In their *cursus* inscriptions, senators referred to their service as *comites* on imperial campaigns as if it carried real military authority.[268] When Q. Aurelius Symmachus acted as the senate's ambassador to Valentinian I and spent several years at court in Trier in AD 368–70, he earned the distinction of *comes ordinis tertii*. This provided him with an honour that offered a tangible connection to the emperor himself.[269] Symmachus subsequently used his visit to the imperial court, with all its military connotations, to bolster his image with other aristocrats. Despite his negligible involvement in Valentinian I's campaigns, he was anxious to emphasise his presence on the frontier in his letters to Ausonius.[270] In his first panegyric to Valentinian I, delivered in AD 368, Symmachus made extraordinary claims about the relationship between civilian and military elites under the emperor's government:

The camp and the *curia* are now on equal footing, since you can see the praetorian cohorts obeying nobles and lictors parading with the symbols of civilian office before well-deserving *duces*. We often exchange our togas for military cloaks, and frequently deck out armed soldiers in the *trabea*.[271]

Symmachus' vision of the Roman state, which had been set to rights under the good government of Valentinian I, was clearly anachronistic. Part of this passage recalled a section from Pliny's *Panegyricus* in which he portrayed

---

[268] Davenport 2015a: 284–5.
[269] For the date and circumstances of this visit, see Sogno 2006: 2–3, 8–9. For the office of *comes*, see *CIL* VI 1699 = *ILS* 2946; *AE* 1966, 518. Symmachus was following in the footsteps of his father, who served as ambassador many times (*CIL* VI 1698 = *ILS* 1257). On the use of the title *comes* as a way of emphasising one's connection with the emperor, see Horster 1998: 51; Humphries 2003: 33–5.
[270] Matthews 1989: 284–5, citing Symm. *Ep.* 1.14, 1.32.
[271] Symm. *Or.* 1.23: *castrorum curiaeque parem nunc esse fortunam, cum uideas praetorianas cohortes parere nobilibus et ante emeritos duces urbana insignia gestare lictores. togas paludamentis saepe mutamus, armatis trabeas frequenter induimus . . .* The text unfortunately breaks off at this crucial point.

Trajan behaving in the manner of Republican generals who 'exchanged their magisterial togas for military cloaks' (*paludamento mutare praetextam*).[272] Rather than describing the emperor moving from civilian to military life in this fashion, Symmachus transferred the reference to himself and other nobles – that is, the senatorial *comites* who travelled from Rome to the frontiers.[273] Symmachus was fond of using military metaphors in letters he sent to generals, as if to claim some sort of familiarity with their world.[274] The rhetorical strategy of Symmachus' speeches and letters was assisted by the fact that all administrative service in the late empire was known as *militia*, and the uniforms of these officials were military in nature.[275] Nevertheless, he pushed his vision into the realm of fantasy when he imagined aristocratic senators actually undertaking military duties. There was an ideological tension between the army commanders and the senators over who could claim to be the true heirs of the great generals of the *res publica*.

The world of Ammianus and Symmachus changed in AD 372, when the emperors Valentinian I and Valens integrated the military and civilian branches of the Roman imperial state into one cohesive hierarchy. They regulated the status and order of precedence of all officials within the imperial army and the administration, from the highest ranks of the *praefectus urbi*, *praefecti praetorio* and *magistri militum* down through provincial governors and other senatorial office-holders.[276] It was at this time that *duces* were promoted from *perfectissimi* to *clarissimi*, formally making them part of the wider senatorial order.[277] Ammianus lamented the declining standards that this represented:

And since this work gives us the opportunity of speaking what we feel, let us speak plainly: this emperor was the first of all to increase the arrogance of military men, causing damage to our commonwealth, by elevating their status and rewards to greater heights.[278]

In reality, however, these promotions were necessary to give the *duces* a status that befitted their seniority within the Roman imperial state, given

---

[272] Pliny the Younger, *Pan.* 56.4. G. Kelly 2013: 273 n. 41 suggests that Symmachus and Pliny drew independently on Sall. *Hist.* 1.87.

[273] B. S. Rodgers 2015: 17 n. 95.   [274] Tomlin 1976: 191–2.

[275] On *militia* and the uniforms of officials, see A. H. M. Jones 1964: 564–6; C. Kelly 1998: 168; Halsall 2007: 110.

[276] *CTh.* 6.7.1, 6.9.1, 6.11.1, 6.14.1, 6.22.4; A. H. M. Jones 1964: 142–4; Schmidt-Hofner 2008: 103–16.

[277] A. H. M. Jones 1964: 144, 527.

[278] Amm. 27.9.4: *et quoniam adest liber locus dicendi quae sentimus, aperte loquemur: hunc imperatorem omnium primum in maius militares fastus ad damna rerum auxisse communium, dignitates opesque eorum sublimius erigentem.*

the vast expansion of the ranks of the *perfectissimi* over the course of the fourth century AD. The legislation of Valentinian I and Valens meant that all branches of the imperial government, both military and civilian, were henceforth unified by one system of precedent and hierarchy, which culminated in the award of senatorial status.[279] The social impact of this change is demonstrated by the commissioning of full-length portrait statues of officials in the new-style toga and *chlamys* of the imperial administration (rather than reusing togate bodies from the second-century AD).[280] This acted as a form of recognition that civilian and military officials were bound together in the service of the emperor.

At the very end of the fourth century AD Flavius Stilicho, the *magister equitum et peditum*, was honoured with several public statues in the *forum Romanum*. The inscriptions on the bases recorded his commitment to military and administrative service from the beginning of his life in the traditional *cursus* format.[281] The same style of commemoration would be adopted on the inscribed statue bases of Flavius Aetius and Flavius Constantius in the fifth century AD.[282] These inscriptions celebrated their consulships and status as patricians alongside the army command posts, such as *magister utriusque militiae*. Generals like Stilicho and Aetius were also effectively the chief ministers of state affairs for their respective emperors, Honorius and Valentinian III.[283] This development had been a long time in the making – one and a half centuries since senators had ceased commanding troops in battle and the promotion of Gallienus' *protectores* to officer rank in the mid-third century AD. The status and prestige of senior generals had finally caught up with members of the senatorial aristocracy, because they had themselves become senators.[284] This united aristocracy of *clarissimi*, *spectabiles* and *illustres* could not entirely mask tensions that continued to exist between senators from aristocratic families and generals of senatorial rank.[285] No title would ever convince established nobles that new men really shared their values. But in a way, the tension between the senatorial aristocracy and the men from the army did forge a sense of unity. Each side wanted something else the other possessed: the military men wished to be acknowledged with honours and prestige and given respect for their efforts in defending the

---

[279] Heather 1998: 188.   [280] R. R. R. Smith 2016: 19.

[281] *CIL* VI 1730 = *ILS* 1277; *CIL* VI 1731 = *ILS* 1278; *CIL* VI 41381. For the exceptional position of Stilicho and his relationship with the imperial family, see McEvoy 2013: 153–86.

[282] Aetius: *CIL* VI 41389. Constantius: *CIL* VI 1719, 1720; Chenault 2012: 125–9.

[283] McEvoy 2013: 153–86, 251–72.   [284] Davenport 2015a: 285.

[285] Salzman 2006: 352–60; Lee 2007: 153–63.

frontiers, whereas senatorial aristocrats still made a claim on their martial heritage. This tension prevented a firm line of demarcation from emerging between a civilian aristocracy with no interest in the army and a true warrior aristocracy whose members held no civilian government office.[286] By the time of Stilicho, both aristocrats and generals could, in some sense or another, say that they served the empire *domi militiaeque*.

The Survival of Equestrian Rank

In the fourth century AD the ultimate goal of an imperial administrative career became admission into the senatorial order by acquiring the status of *clarissimus*. After AD 358 imperial laws issued to prevent members of the curial classes from becoming *perfectissimi* disappeared, because this rank had become insufficient to escape one's municipal obligations. The *curiales* now required, and sought, the higher status of *clarissimus* instead.[287] This became the entry-level senatorial grade, beyond which one could aim for the higher dignities of *spectabilis* and *illustris*.[288] But senatorial status remained the apex of an administrative career, which would require many years of service for officials attempting to rise from low-level bureaucratic posts. The many different equestrian grades within the imperial service are demonstrated by an imperial law of AD 384. In that year the emperors Gratian, Valentinian II and Theodosius I wrote to Trifolius, the *comes sacrarum largitionum*, establishing the *dignitates* to which the various officials in his department were entitled.[289] The status of *perfectissimus* was divided into the first, second and third class (*ordo primus, secundus* and *tertius*). Below the *perfectissimi* came the *ducenarii* and *centenarii*, followed by the *epistulares*, who were also of equestrian status (they may have been ranked as *egregii*).[290] Then came the lower-level grades (called *formae*), whose members constituted three-quarters of all administrators in the office of the *comes sacrarum largitionum*.[291] The top-ranked

---

[286] The army officers of the later Roman empire were therefore not the equivalent of the warrior aristocracy of the Huns (on which see Maenchen-Helfen 1973: 190–9).

[287] A. H. M. Jones 1964: 528; Lepelley 1999: 642–3; Dillon 2015: 53–4, 64–5.

[288] A. H. M. Jones 1964: 143–4, 528; Heather 1998: 190. Valentinian I and Valens' successors continued to legislate on these matters as a way of regulating the ever-expanding ranks of the senatorial order. See *CTh.* 6.7.2 (AD 380), 6.6.1 (AD 382) and 6.5.2 (AD 384).

[289] *CTh.* 6.30.7 (fragmentary) = *CJ* 12.23.7 (given at Heraclea on 10 June, AD 384).

[290] A. H. M. Jones 1964: 584. The confirmation of the continuing existence of the ranks of *ducenarius* and *centenarius* is welcome, given the decline in the epigraphic habit, which reduces the extent of our evidence. One isolated example is a [Ma]rcianus *ducenarius* attested at Madauros in Africa Proconsularis in the reign of Julian (*ILAlg.* 2100).

[291] A. H. M. Jones 1964: 583–4; C. Kelly 2004: 42.

perfectissimi of the *ordo primus* were a rare breed indeed, since only the heads of the department of the silver coinage and clothing requisitions merited this status.[292] The value of the *perfectissimatus* was therefore a matter of perspective. Although it was no longer sought by decurions anxious to escape their curial obligations, for bureaucrats working their way through the ranks of the administration it remained a valuable title, only acquired after promotion through many subordinate grades. It is often easy to forget about these officials, because the decline in the epigraphic habit makes it difficult to reconstruct their presence in the wider social landscape.

The upgrading of provinces to senatorial rank begun by Constantine continued throughout the fourth century AD, so that by the end of the century only a few regions remained under control of *praesides* who ranked as *perfectissimi*.[293] These included the three Mauretanias (Caesariensis, Sitifensis, and Tingitana), as well as Tripolitania and Libya Superior in North Africa, and Samnium, Apulia and Calabria, and Sardinia in Italy.[294] In areas with a steady epigraphic habit these governors continued to record their status as *vir perfectissimus* on inscribed statue bases, a sign that the title still carried some prestige.[295] A significant body of our evidence comes from Leptis Magna in Tripolitania, which had a very strong statue and epigraphic practice. Governors with the designation *vir perfectissimus* are attested there until AD 378.[296]

The title of *perfectissimus* also appears in late fourth-century inscriptions in the city of Rome. For example, Flavius Maximus, the prefect of the *vigiles*, used the title on the bases of statues he erected of the emperors Valentinian I and Gratian.[297] In AD 379 a certain Flavius Claudius Rufus, *vir perfectissimus*, dedicated a statue of his patroness Tyrrania Anicia Iuliana, wife of the prominent senator and consular Q. Clodius Hermogenianus Olybrius.[298] Since Rufus listed no official government positions, it may be presumed that he held a private grant of the *perfectissimatus*. The same point can be made about Flavius Pompeianus, who is styled 'vir perfectissimus and *ex comitibus*' (τοῦ διασημοτάτου καὶ | ἀπὸ κομίτων) on the base of the statue he erected of Flavius Rufus, proconsul of

---

[292] *CJ* 12.23.7.12–13.   [293] Heather 1998: 190. See the tables in A. H. M. Jones 1964: 1451–61.
[294] *PLRE* I Fasti, 1083–1110.   [295] See also Bodnaruk 2016: 157–8.
[296] Tantillo and Bigi 2010: nos. 35–43. Note especially no. 42, dated precisely to AD 378.
[297] *CIL* VI 1180 = *LSA* 1291 (C. Machado); *CIL* VI 1181 = *LSA* 1292 (C. Machado). The fact that he had this title at all is strange, since the prefects of the watch became *clarissimi* under Constantine. Therefore, it may be the case that these statues were erected directly before his promotion (Ensslin 1937: 669).
[298] *CIL* VI 1741 = *LSA* 1270 (C. Machado).

Achaea in the late fourth century AD.[299] He was a member of the curial elite, for whom his equestrian title remained a part of his public image, especially when combined with the honorific *ex comitibus*.[300]

The last precisely dated official represented epigraphically with the title of *vir perfectissimus* is Flavius Sexio, *corrector* of Apulia and Calabria in AD 379/395. He was responsible for erecting an equestrian statue of the deified Theodosius the Elder, father of the emperor Theodosius I.[301] The rank of *perfectissimus* therefore continued to have some significance as an element of public self-representation in regions with a strong epigraphic tradition up to the late fourth century AD.[302] This is a sign that it continued to be valued as an item of status currency. If the epigraphic habit had been as prevalent in other regions of the empire, we might have many more *perfectissimi* on record. In the early fifth century AD all remaining equestrian governors became *clarissimi*.[303] After this point the status of *perfectissimus* continued to be granted to members of the imperial administration. But the government bureaucrats were no longer commemorated with *cursus* inscriptions listing their careers, as this had become the preserve of the united senatorial aristocracy of service.

The longevity of equestrian status itself is a vexed question. There is only one entry under the heading *De Equestri Dignitate* (On Equestrian Status) in both the *Codex Theodosianus* and *Codex Justinianus*.[304] The sole law found under this title was issued by Valentinian I and Valens in October AD 364 to Claudius Mamertinus, *praefectus praetorio* of Italy, Africa and Illyricum:

Equites Romani, whom we wish to hold the *dignitas* of the second grade of all people in the city, should be chosen from those who are natural-born Romans and citizens, as well as from foreign-born men who are not required to serve in guilds. And since it is not fitting that these men should be without perquisites of this sort, they should not be troubled by the fear of corporal punishments and prosecutions,

---

[299] *IG* II/III² 13274 = *LSA* 103 (U. Gehn, who discusses the date).

[300] For evidence of honorary *comites* among municipal elites, see *CTh.* 12.1.41 (AD 339).

[301] *CIL* IX 333 = *LSA* 1695 (C. Machado). See also *CIL* VIII 8480 = *ILS* 5596, which is dated to AD 388/392. The title of *vir perfectissimus* for Fl. Maecius Constans, the governor of Mauretania Sitifensis, is only restored, but it is likely that the original text included it.

[302] Bodnaruk 2016.

[303] A. H. M. Jones 1964: 142–3, 528, 1221. In *Not. Dig. Occ.* xlv the *praeses* of Dalmatia is still given the title of *perfectissimus*, which A. H. M. Jones 1964: 1221 suggests is an error, reflecting that this governorship only became clarissimate in the early fifth century AD.

[304] *CTh.* 6.37 = *CJ* 12.31.

and they will be classified as immune from those exactions which apply to the senatorial order.[305]

The imperial ruling confirms that equestrian status was still a privilege that existed in the 360s. It distinguished its holders from ordinary plebeians, who were subjected to baser tortures. The wording of Valentinian I and Valens' constitution, referring as it does to those 'in the city' (*in urbe*), may initially suggest that the juridical status of *eques Romanus* was now essentially confined to the city of Rome, where it was carried by respectable citizens.[306] However, we need to be careful about drawing sweeping assumptions from this one statement: Valentinian I and Valens could have been replying to a specific inquiry from Mamertinus regarding the privileges of *equites* in Rome itself. It does not necessarily follow that *equites Romani* only existed in this one city. In AD 380 the emperors Gratian, Valentinian II and Theodosius wrote to the guild of *navicularii*, stating: 'We confirm the *dignitas* of the *ordo equester* which was extended to you by the deified Constantine and Julian, eternal emperors.'[307] This is the last precisely dated law which explicitly mentions the equestrian order in the *Codex Theodosianus*. The fact that there was an entry headed *De Equestri Dignitate* in the *Codex* indicates that equestrian status was still relevant at the time of its promulgation in AD 438. The emperors Theodosius II and Valentinian III had specifically laid down principles of relevance to all legislation in the *Codex*.[308] Why include a section on equestrian status if there were no *equites Romani* to whom the law could be

---

305 *CTh.* 6.37.1: *equites Romani, quos secundi gradus in urbe omnium optinere volumus dignitatem, ex indigenis Romanis et civibus eligantur, vel his peregrinis, quos corporatis non oportet adnecti. et quia vacuos huiusmodi viros esse privilegiis non oportet, corporalium eos iniuriarum et prosecutionum formido non vexet, ab indictionibus quoque, quae senatorium ordinem manent, habebuntur immunes.* The version in *CJ* 12.13.1 is slightly different (see below).

306 For the argument that *equites* were now confined to Rome, see Stein 1927: 458; Lepelley 1986: 237–9; Chastagnol 1988: 205; Marcone 1998: 339, 359. In this context, *CTh.* 2.17.1, addressed to the *praefectus urbi* of Rome, Verinus, in AD 323–5, is cited as evidence for the urban character of the equestrian order since *equites* are requested to appear before the *praefectus vigilum* to prove their status. However, the law is specifically applicable to Rome, as it instructs other residents to appear before officials stationed in the *sacra urbs*: senators before the urban prefect, *perfectissimi* before the *vicarius*, and shipmasters before the *praefectus annonae*. This does not mean that members of all these groups were restricted to Rome.

307 *CTh.* 13.5.16.pr.: *delatam vobis a divo Constantino et Iuliano principibus aeternis equestris ordinis dignitatem nos firmamus.*

308 *CTh.* 1.1.5 (AD 429), 1.1.6 (AD 435). On the principles of relevance, see Matthews 2000a: 57–71.

applied?[309] We can therefore conclude that equestrians and equestrian status continued to exist until at least the mid-fifth century AD.

The sixth-century *Codex Justinianus* also retains the sections *De Equestri Dignitate* and *De Perfectissimatus Dignitate* as Titles Thirty-One and Thirty-Two of Book Twelve, respectively.[310] The first section on equestrian status contains a heavily truncated and revised version of the ruling which Valentinian I and Valens sent to Mamertinus in AD 364: 'We order *equites Romani* to hold the second grade below the *dignitas* of *clarissimus*' (*equites Romanos secundum gradum post clarissimatus dignitatem obtinere iubemus*).[311] Jones has suggested that the presence of this section in Justinian's law code may have been the result of administrative inertia.[312] In support of this argument, one could cite another ruling in the *Codex Justinianus* on the social status of minters, which does edit out specific equestrian ranks (*perfectissimus*, *ducenarius*, *centenarius* and *egregius*) from the equivalent entry in the *Codex Theodosianus*.[313] This suggests that the compilers did exercise some editorial control in excising *dignitates* that were no longer pertinent in the sixth century AD. On the other hand, the fact that the title *De Equestri Dignitate* was retained in the *Codex Justinianus* may indicate that it met the criteria for conclusion.[314] Moreover, the editors went to the trouble of revising and abridging the sole entry under this title, rather than removing it altogether.[315] This indicates that the compilers thought that equestrian status remained relevant, even if it only formed part of an antiquarian conception of the shape of the Roman *res publica*. More surprisingly, equestrian rank features in the Byzantine law code known as the *Basilika*, a Greek version of the entire Justinianic legal corpus, which was compiled in the ninth century AD.[316] Book Six, Title Thirty-Four of the *Basilika* is headed: 'On the equestrian dignity and the dignity of former prefect' (περὶ ἱππέως ἀξιώματος καὶ ἀπὸ ἐπάρχων ἀξιώματος).[317] The first entry is a Greek version of the *Codex Justinianus*' entry of the law of Valentinian I and Valens, listed above: 'The *equites Romani* are to be placed after the *clarissimi* in rank' (οἱ ἱππεῖς

---

[309] See Sirks 2015: 292: 'the arrangement of the law reflects a view on the arrangement of society'.
[310] *CJ* 12.31, 12.32.   [311] *CJ* 12.31.1.
[312] A. H. M. Jones 1964: 1221. See also Stein 1927: 458, suggesting that it is a tralatician reference reflecting sixth-century understanding of the equestrian order.
[313] *CTh.* 10.20.1 and *CJ* 11.8.1.
[314] For the editorial process and the principles of relevance of the *Codex Justinianus*, see *Const. Haec* 2; *Const. Summa* 1, 3; Corcoran 2016: xcix, cx–cxiii.
[315] This was permitted by Justinian in *Const. Summa* 3.   [316] Corcoran 2016: cxix.
[317] I owe this reference to Stein 1927: 458 n. 2.

Ῥωμαίων μετὰ τοὺς λαμπροτάτους τῇ τάξει ταττέσθωσαν).[318] This certainly appears to be a case of mere institutional memory, because the *Basilika* did not systematically revise the *Codex Justinianus*, but rather incorporated earlier Greek versions of the code.[319]

Why, then, did equestrian rank continue into the fifth and perhaps even to the sixth century AD? The Romans did not tend to abolish the officials and institutions that made up their *res publica* – they were either allowed to continue, as in the case of the senate and the consulship, or they evolved or were reinvented in new forms, as we see with the status of patrician and the office of praetorian prefect. Established names and titles invested offices and individuals with meaning and purpose. So it was with the *equites Romani* of the fifth century AD. They were certainly not nobles, but their equestrian status marked them out as a group that retained privileges and dignities, even if they were quite different from their forebears who bore the same title. *Equites* who wished to acquire higher status and advancement into the senatorial order as *clarissimi* would need to enter the imperial service. In many ways this development was the natural product of the process, begun by Augustus and accelerated by his successors, particularly Constantine, of integrating elites into the framework of the monarchical *res publica* by making honours primarily dependent on service to the emperor.

Conclusion: The More Things Change . . .

In AD 326 the imperial mints of Thessalonica and Nicomedia celebrated the twentieth year of Constantine's reign by issuing a series of multiple *solidi* medallions These paid tribute to the constituent elements of the Roman state: the people, the senate and the equestrian order, with each of these groups being honoured with its own medallion.[320] The medallion minted for the *ordo equester* featured a reverse image of a man on horseback, accompanied by the legend EQVIS ROMANVS (the one-and-a-half *solidus* medallion issued at Nicomedia graces the cover of this book).[321] This was a fitting way of recognising the long and proud history of the equestrian order and its place within the *res publica*. It symbolised the idea

---

[318] *Basil.* 6.34.1. The next entry, 6.34.2, is similar to *CTh.* 12.32.1, but renders the Latin *perfectissimi* with the Greek ἀπὸ ἐπάρχων.

[319] Stolte 2014: 66–7; Corcoran 2016: cxix–cxx.

[320] Alföldi 1947: 13–14; Toynbee 1986: 116–17.

[321] *RIC* VII Thessalonica 145, Nicomedia 99–100.

that Constantine's regime was supported by the consensus of the people, senate and *equites*, just like the principate of Augustus.[322] But this would be the last time that the *ordo equester* would feature in such an ideological display of consensus. The medallion was struck at a time when upwardly mobile Roman citizens were no longer content with the title of *eques Romanus*, and instead strove for higher *dignitates*. They wanted to be known as an *egregius, centenarius, ducenarius, perfectissimus*, or even as a senatorial *clarissimus*. The equestrian order was still technically an *ordo*, but it had now been firmly divided into a series of status grades, each of which carried greater prestige and privileges than equestrian rank itself. Imperial legislation of the fourth century AD, such as that issued by Licinius and Constantine, continually emphasised that these higher statuses were only bestowed at the behest of the emperor. This was the culmination of the process of domesticating the aristocracy that had started with Augustus.

Despite these changes, we can observe striking continuities between the Roman empire of the fourth century AD and the principate. There were still equestrians who desired long careers in the service of the state; these men could hold a wide variety of administrative posts in the course of their *militia*, which now climaxed in admission to the senate. This was the end result of the emergence of the equestrian service elite of the high empire, whose members were employed in a variety of capacities similar to senators. All that had distinguished them was their status. In the fourth century AD they were unified, both nobles and new men, into one senatorial aristocracy of service. Military officers were initially excluded from this model, which was a product of the third-century transformations which had seen the army career path separated from the mainstream administration. However, by the late fourth century AD they had been brought back into the fold again, with *duces* and *magistri militum* achieving senatorial status and consulships. This meant that the Roman empire did not witness the evolution of a distinct military caste, but an aristocracy which – despite the different origins of its members – was united by the ethos of serving the state *domi militiaeque.*

The other important element of continuity can be seen in the choices made by those elites who did not want long careers in the imperial administration, but still desired its privileges. In the same way that Appian of Alexandria had his friend Fronto petition for

---

[322] For consensus and empire, see Chapter 8.

a procuratorship, or an *eques* from Mutina might hold only one military tribunate before returning to his home town, Rome of the fourth century AD provided opportunities for limited (or honorary) imperial service that conferred status and privileges. In Late Antiquity many municipal aristocrats chose to hold governorships in their home provinces, or nearby regions, for a year or two. This service earned them exemption from their curial obligations, as well as a statue and inscription praising their virtues, a fine reward for a year's *labor*.

Although the *ordo equester* and the *dignitas equestris* continued to exist until at least the mid-fifth century AD, equestrian status lost its aristocratic significance. In his speech of thanks to Gratian for his consulship in AD 379, the emperor's former tutor Ausonius boasted that he had no need to campaign or flatter the people to earn the honour of the consulship, as his Republican predecessors would have had to do. He proclaimed:

> The Roman people, the *Campus Martius*, the equestrian order, the *rostra*, the voting pens, the senate, and the *curia* – it is Gratian himself who is all these things for me.[323]

The influence and prestige of the *ordo equester* – and its role as a constituent body in the *res publica* – was thus expressly positioned by Ausonius as a relic of a bygone age.[324] The *ordo equester* ceased to be celebrated as a constituent part of the *res publica*. When Sidonius Apollinaris delivered a panegyric for the emperor Majorian in AD 458 he proclaimed that 'every order gave kingship to you in turn – the plebs, the senate, and the soldiery' (*ordine vobis | ordo omnis regnum dederat, plebs, curia, miles*).[325] The *equites Romani* who lived in the late Roman empire still earned the title through imperial benefaction.[326] They still had privileges that surpassed ordinary men, but this was far below what members of their *ordo* had possessed in the days of Cicero, Augustus, or Marcus Aurelius. Now one had to enter imperial service and become a senator, a *vir clarissimus*, to earn the rewards that had once been granted to equestrians. The domestication of status in the monarchical *res publica* had made elites dependent on the emperor for privileges, honours and status, all of which he could refashion at his will.

---

[323] Aus. *Grat.* 3: *Romanus populus, Martius campus, equester ordo, rostra, ovilia, senatus, curia, unus mihi omnia Gratianus.*

[324] Lepelley 1999: 643.   [325] Sid. Apoll. *Carm.* 5.386–7.

[326] See the ruling of Valentinian and Valens included in the *Codex Theodosianus* (6.37.1), which emphasised that *equites* 'are chosen' (*eligantur*).

In April of AD 244 L. Arellius Petronius Karus was honoured with a public statue at the central Italian town of Praeneste. The inscription on the base reads as follows:

To Lucius Arellius Petronius Karus, son of Lucius, of the voting tribe Fabia, illustrious *eques Romanus*, *flamen* of the deified Augustus, *duumvir*, aedile and quaestor of the colony, the worshippers of the cult of Jupiter Arcanus in the market region (erected this) for their most deserving patron. The place was allocated by a decree of the decurions. Dedicated five days before the Ides of April, in the year of the consulship of Arrianus and Papus, under the supervision of Tiberius Claudius Victor, *sevir Augustalis*.[1]

Four letters which followed Karus' name summed up his standing in the Roman *res publica* – SP EQ R. The abbreviations should be expanded as *sp(lendido) eq(uiti) R(omano)*, 'the illustrious *eques Romanus*'. Karus shared this distinction with tens of thousands of other Roman citizens, many of whom were themselves honoured with inscriptions proclaiming their status as *eques Romanus*, *eques equo publico*, ἱππεὺς Ῥωμαίων or ἱππικός. They also received statues, which would have depicted them in military dress or wearing the status symbols of the order, such as the *calcei equestres* or the *anulus aureus*. By the third century AD Rome's *ordo equester* had existed as a constituent part of the *res publica* for more than four hundred years, and there had been *equites* for many centuries before that. Although Karus and most of his peers did not ride in the cavalry, the status and title of *eques Romanus* still mattered to them, as it did its associations with *virtus*, honour, distinction and imperial favour. The endurance of *equites* and the *ordo equester* for more than a millennium clearly demonstrates their fundamental importance to the social and political fabric of the Roman state.

---

[1] *AE* 1998, 286: *L(ucio) Arellio L(uci) f(ilio) Fab(ia tribu) | Petronio Karo | sp(lendido) eq(uiti) R(omano) fl(amini) divi Aug(usti) | IIvir(o) aed(ili) q(uaestori) col(oniae) | cultores Iovis | Arkani | regionis macelli | patrono | dignissimo | l(ocus) d(atus) d(ecreto) d(ecurionum) | Dedicata V Idus April(es) | Arriano et Papo co(n)s(ulibus) | cur(ante) Ti(berio) Cl(audio) Victore | IIIIIIvir(o) Aug(ustali).*

Roles and Functions

We began this book with three aims. The first was to examine the range of capacities in which *equites* served the *res publica*, and how these roles changed and developed over time. During the Archaic period in the eighth to sixth centuries BC, Rome was ruled by kings and dominated by a mounted warrior aristocracy, much like many other pre-modern societies. The evolution of the Roman polity from a monarchy to a *res publica* changed the nature of the warrior elites, so that by the fifth century BC they had become a landed aristocracy, which constituted the cavalry of the nascent Roman *res publica*. This process meant that the mounted warriors transformed from a collective which derived power from their 'traditional authority' – their ability to ride on horseback, subjugate rival clans and display martial valour – to an 'occupational status group', defined by its official function in the state (to use Weber's terms outlined in the Introduction). In the Roman *res publica* the citizen body was the army, in which its wealthiest citizens served as the cavalry (the *equites*). These aristocrats still derived authority and prestige from military achievement, in particular from their *virtus*, as the warrior elites had before them. The difference was that in the Republican state they were now also defined by their wealth and moral standing, which was regulated by the Roman censors. The citizens registered by the censors in the eighteen centuries of *equites* in the *comitia centuriata* received the honour of the *equus publicus*, which came in the form of public funds to buy and maintain one's horse for combat. These *equites equo publico* marched in regimented formation through the streets of Rome on 15 July each year, displaying their *virtus* and aristocratic cohesion for all to see. Such a ceremony gave the *equites* their 'immanence', a sense of purpose articulated through shared values and the ideology of service to the *res publica*. Even as the roles filled by *equites* in the Roman state expanded over subsequent centuries, the significance of their original status as cavalrymen and protectors of the *res publica* continued to invest the title *eques Romanus* with antiquity, authority and purpose.

With the expansion of the Roman state during the middle Republic, the numbers of citizens who met the property requirement necessary to be classified as *equites* increased, and the aims and ambitions of members diversified. Military service remained a necessary and important obligation as a Roman citizen, though with the increasing reliance on auxiliary cavalry, *equites* came to serve as officers, rather than ordinary cavalrymen.

Non-senatorial *equites* invested in lucrative forms of private enterprise beyond their land-holding interests. In the pursuit of this aim many *equites* sought temporary employment as contractors for the Roman state. These *publicani*, as they were known, kept the army fed, collected taxes and duties, and oversaw public works. Their service to the Roman state was not driven by altruism, but by a desire for profit. They were not an expressly political group – they had no policies or vision for social change – but they did interfere in the political arena when their own interests were threatened.

At the end of the second century BC senators were excluded from the equestrian centuries, a change which resulted in the formation of a distinct *ordo equester*. It was at this time that the *equites* unexpectedly acquired a new form of political influence. They were employed as jurors in the criminal courts, since the tribune Gaius Gracchus believed that *equites* without senatorial connections could act as a check on the corruption and graft of senators. The *equites* did not collectively lobby for such an influential role, but once they had acquired this prerogative they resented any attempts to deprive them of it. As jurors, the *equites* were servants of the *res publica*, but they were reluctant to accept the restrictions and obligations that came with such duties, most notably accepting accountability for their actions before the law. They were aided in this agenda by senatorial politicians such as Cicero, who needed the support of equestrians to progress his own political career. This cynical attitude stood in contrast with the ideals articulated by the monuments of equestrian officers of the late Republican, triumviral and early Augustan periods, which proudly depicted *equites* as valiant defenders of the *res publica*. The difference between the two perspectives can be explained by the fact that military service and *virtus* had always been a defining factor of equestrian collective identity. But the employment of *equites* as jurors – and their potential to influence political affairs, which were often being played out in the criminal courts – represented a recent development. *Equites* were keen to use this new role to their advantage, and thus pressed to avoid penalties and prosecution. The new *ordo equester* never quite made the transition to a Weberian 'political status group', even in this period of the late Republic, because they did not have a monopoly on political powers, nor did they seek to extend their authority to acquire it.

The return of monarchy to Rome under Augustus brought new opportunities for members of the *ordo equester*. In the monarchical *res publica* equestrians not only served as officers, jurors and *publicani* – they could henceforth also be employed as financial and administrative officials in

Rome and the provinces. Over the course of the principate these positions were shaped into an equestrian career structure which was in many ways analogous to the senatorial *cursus honorum*. Equestrians could serve in both civilian and military capacities (*domi militiaeque*) and work their way up through the various salary grades before reaching the great prefectures. This resulted in the emergence of an equestrian service aristocracy, the *equestris nobilitas*, which constituted an elite among the *ordo* at large. Augustus' motivations for employing *equites* as his personal officials are clear. The *princeps* wanted to ensure that all elites – senators, *equites* and others – were primarily dependent on him for sources of prestige. This process of 'domestication' was a common one among pre-industrial monarchical societies. Augustus was also driven by a desire to employ equestrians in senior posts, because they were not able to pose a challenge to his regime in the same way that his senatorial peers could. At the beginning of the monarchical state it was inconceivable that an *eques* could occupy the *statio* of *princeps*.

What about the motivations of the *equites* themselves? Why did they take on official positions in the new monarchical *res publica*, when political engagement in the Republican period was primarily focused on their own interests? Part of the answer lies in the way in which the government of the state evolved slowly over several centuries. When Augustus employed *equites* as his personal agents, he was following the tradition that had begun under 'proto-emperors' such as Pompeius and Caesar in the last generation of the Roman Republic. Moreover, Augustus paid *equites* substantial salaries as an inducement to serve at his pleasure. *Equites* of this period did not sign up to an 'administrative career', but to act as Augustus' representatives, and to receive the honours and rewards he offered. If they had refused such distinctions from Augustus, there would have been nowhere else to turn for validation of personal status in the monarchical state. Soon, however, the distinction between officials and agents of the *princeps* and those of the *res publica* was elided. A real administrative system emerged, and developed under Augustus' successors. The expansion of the number of military and administrative posts available to *equites*, together with the growth of a distinct equestrian career structure, particularly in the second and third centuries AD, reflected the development and consolidation of Rome as an ostentatiously monarchical state.

The new *res publica* was still able to accommodate the different ambitions of members of the *ordo*. For members of the *equestris nobilitas*, their commitment to serving the state *domi militiaeque* was expressed through the genre of the inscribed *cursus*. By the second century AD they were granted new titles which set them apart from the *ordo equester* at large. The artificiality of the division of responsibilities between senatorial and equestrian officials, which was based on the traditional status hierarchies of the Republic and their adaptation by Augustus, became marked over time. The equestrian service elite embraced the opportunities of the monarchical state, but the system was flexible enough to enable *equites* who did not want to devote their lives to government service to take part. They could hold one or two commands in the *militiae equestres* or a single procuratorship. For all equestrians, regardless of whether they embarked on full careers or not, military service and office-holding was regarded as a reflection of their personal character and qualities. These honours and rewards only flowed to good, honest and upright individuals, an ideal which is present in letters from aristocratic patrons and emperors alike. This ideology of service represented a reformulation of equestrian identity for a monarchical world. The reality, of course, was much messier. Some *equites* were not motivated by lofty ideals of service: procuratorships came with lucrative salaries and offered a road to wealth without the strictures of senatorial life. Graft and corruption were the inevitable by-products of empire. From the imperial centre flowed military commands, procuratorships and priesthoods, not to mention the dignity of equestrian rank itself. Since the emperor could not know all citizens personally, he depended on the advice of his friends and courtiers, some less suitable – or more susceptible to bribes – than others. *Equites* joined in the intrigues of petty place-seeking at the imperial court alongside senators, freedmen, slaves and women.

Between the late second and the early fourth centuries AD, changes to the hierarchy of the Roman army and administration dramatically altered the framework of the Roman state. This was the result of a series of interconnected factors. Firstly, equestrian rank had been much coveted among the sub-officer ranks of the army, for whom there was no coherent path to further officer commands. Emperors began to grant equestrian status to these soldiers and their children to consolidate their own links with the army (which had assumed a prime position as a power-broker in the imperial age). Secondly, the consolidation of the equestrian aristocracy of service meant that there was little difference between the official responsibilities of the *equestris nobilitas* and the senators. The result of this was that *equites* were employed as acting officials in positions that had previously been allocated exclusively to senators. Both these developments provide crucial context for understanding the changes that occurred in the second half of the third century AD. When Gallienus decided to cease appointing senators to command the armies in battle (for a variety of logistical and political reasons) he turned to equestrians promoted from within the ranks of the army. At the same time, equestrian procurators started to serve as regular governors of provinces in place of senators. This acknowledged that the primary difference between senators and equestrians was one of status, not competence or experience.

In the fourth century AD Constantine and his successors combined the equestrian and senatorial career paths into one coherent aristocracy of service. Personnel and positions that were formerly of equestrian status now became senatorial. They remained the same type of people, holding the same types of government positions – except they now did so as *clarissimi*.[2] In the late Roman imperial administration status became a reward for service, rather than a precondition for it. But the positions that carried equestrian rank became progressively less prestigious: they were now clerks and supervisors in the imperial bureaux rather than senior financial and administrative officials. The number and nature of official posts open to *equites* thus changed alongside the transformation of the Roman state itself, from monarchy to Republic, then into a monarchical *res publica*. This was partially the result of the growing complexity of the state, a process Rome shared in common with many other pre-industrial societies.[3] But there were also peculiarly Roman circumstances which explain the public roles of *equites*: the laws of Gaius Gracchus; the political manipulations of Cicero; and the decisions of Augustus, Gallienus and Constantine. Nor should we forget the aims and ambitions of *equites* themselves, who embraced opportunities and honours, both intrinsic and material, offered to them by these points of crisis, transition and transformation.

Articulating Status

The second aim of this book has been to examine how equestrian status functioned on an individual and collective level, in Rome, Italy and the provinces. We have examined precisely who constituted an *eques Romanus* and how this status came to be awarded, both in the Republic and imperial periods. In the *res publica* all Roman citizens with the necessary property qualification – 400,000 sesterces from the late Republic – could consider

---

[2] See Heather 2008: 116 for similar remarks about the curial classes of the late Roman empire.
[3] This is developed below in the last section of the Conclusion.

themselves *equites*. The 1,800 *equites equo publico* enrolled by the censors in the equestrian centuries constituted an elite among the *ordo*. This changed under the empire, as Augustus increased the numbers of *equites equo publico* for the first time, a practice continued by his successors. By the end of the first century AD at the latest, all *equites* – now probably some 20,000–30,000 of them – were *equites equo publico*. Equestrian rank thus became an imperial benefaction, functioning as the primary way for emperors to reward the wealthy elites of the provinces, integrating them into the socio-political framework of the Roman state. The emperor's favour was not only lavished on citizens who were resident in Rome and Italy, but also on inhabitants throughout the empire, so that *equites* could be found throughout the provinces, from Gades to Gerasa. Equestrian rank was regarded as complementary to municipal and provincial offices and dignities, rather than being viewed as inherently superior. This meant that it could be widely adopted throughout the empire. Service in the *militiae equestres* may never have been very popular with native Greeks from Asia Minor, for instance, but they still valued equestrian status itself. Others held government positions, such as that of *advocatus fisci*, which did not require extensive travel or commitment of time. There seems to have been little real resistance to the honours and privileges that flowed from Rome, apart from those whose philosophical inclinations made them inherently recalcitrant. Even *equites* who performed on stage or who fought as gladiators did not challenge the essential process of benefaction itself; they merely wished to circumvent it to indulge their predilections.

Military valour, or *virtus*, has emerged as an important, even paradigmatic, aspect of the articulation of equestrian personal and public identity. Even as the aristocratic *equites* ceased to constitute the actual cavalry of the state, equestrians still served as officers into the late Republican period, often combining military commands with their business interests, legal advocacy or literary pursuits. In the age of the emperors, equestrian officer posts were reorganised into a coherent series of grades. Although service was not compulsory, many provincials did seek commissions in the *militiae equestres*. Even though they may have held only one or two army posts, preparedness to take on military commands was recognised as an important quality possessed by members of the equestrian order. This was demonstrated both by the honorific and funerary monuments of *equites* and by the letters of recommendation penned by the senators Pliny the Younger and Cornelius Fronto.

When the *ordo equester* emerged as a 'third part' of the *res publica* distinct from the senate, it appropriated the ceremonies and status symbols of the Roman cavalry. These included the annual procession of the *trans-vectio equitum*, which weaved its way through the centre of Rome every July. This was a vital social performance that publicly articulated the collective *virtus* of the equestrians and their importance to the *res publica*. The members of the *ordo* also adopted the ceremonial dress known as the *trabea*, and the cavalry shield and spears (the *parma* and *hastae*), which often featured on monuments of individual *equites*. In the imperial period the youth of the equestrian order represented the reserve of manpower upon which the state could draw in times of war. All members of the *ordo* were officially registered in a squadron (*turma*); these *turmae*, led by senatorial *seviri*, took part in events such as the *transvectio* and imperial funerals. There were even leaders of the youth, the *principes iuventutis*, who were drawn from the imperial family. The first occupants of this position were Augustus' sons and heirs, Gaius and Lucius, who were granted the *parma* and *hastae* – the order's very own military symbols – in recognition of their position. It was only fitting that during the crisis of the third century AD the origins of the equestrian order were commemorated with the creation of the *ala Celerum* ('the unit of the swift ones'), recalling one of the stories told about Rome's early cavalry.[4]

Membership of the *ordo equester* brought with it a range of perquisites and status symbols. These included the right to sit in the first fourteen rows of the theatre, and to wear a gold ring (*anulus aureus*) and the tunic with the narrow stripe (*angustus clavus*). Such privileges were jealously guarded by the *equites* themselves, who resented any attempt by interlopers to squat in their seats, and reported upstarts who ostentatiously wore rings to which they were not entitled. The Roman state because increasingly interested in regulating these and other forms of status in the imperial period. Emperors such as Augustus, Tiberius and Domitian legislated to protect the privileges and *dignitas* of the senatorial and equestrian orders. After all, if the perquisites of the *equites* were not regulated, then the prestige of equestrian rank itself would be diluted. This meant that members of the upper *ordines* were expected to adhere to certain aristocratic social and moral standards as befitted their place within the *res publica*. The proud military tradition of the *equites* as cavalry gave them a sense of purpose and meaning well into the imperial period, while the additional privileges and perquisites brought dignity and prestige. These combined to make equestrian status inherently desirable and sought after by elites across the empire.

---

[4] M. P. Speidel 1992.

We have thus far emphasised the aspects of commonality that united members of the *ordo equester*, but there was also significant variation, in both geographic and temporal senses. All equestrians had the privilege of sitting in the first fourteen rows of the theatre, a distinction that was designed to be applicable in Italy and the provinces as much as in Rome. But this perquisite never quite worked in the same way outside the *sacra urbs*, as municipal offices and organisations proved to be more important ways of articulating status hierarchies in the local context. Equestrians could come to Rome to serve on the juries, to march in the *transvectio*, run naked in the Lupercalia, or hold a priesthood in Latium. There were provincials who made this effort, either because they valued the prestige these positions gave them, or because they had already made the decision to embark on a military and administrative career which would take them across the empire, even to Rome itself. But many could not, and did not, share in these ceremonies and rituals, because of the geographically diverse nature of the *ordo*. This explains why, for example, monuments celebrating the *transvectio equitum* were more commonly erected for *equites* resident in Italy itself, even though each member of the *ordo* was registered in a *turma*.

The significance of equestrian privileges, rituals and honours changed over time. The *transvectio equitum* was the most enduring of these, extending from the fifth (or possibly fourth) century BC until at least the mid-fourth century AD. Its continued existence testifies to the role of the ceremony in the initiation of new members of the *ordo* and the importance of martial *virtus* to the equestrian order's sense of purpose. The practice of allocating the first fourteen rows to the *equites* in theatres at Rome was also long-lasting, being initiated by *lex Roscia* in 67 BC, confirmed under Augustus and Domitian, then continuing until the late third century AD. Other attributes of the *ordo* are best associated with the period of the early empire, being introduced under Augustus or one of his successors, before eventually falling by the wayside at various points between the late second and fourth centuries AD. The acclamation of imperial heirs as *princeps iuventutis* and leaders of the *equites* had its heyday from the Augustan to Antonine periods. By the third century AD there was a strong association between imperial princes and martial *virtus*, but the precise connection with the *ordo equester* had been lost, as support for the army itself was much more important than a status group which only represented military power in a symbolic and ideological fashion. Likewise, the involvement of *equites* in imperial funerals is attested from Augustus until the Severan period, after which they ceased to be a part of such ceremonies, because of factors such as the changing place of imperial burials and the rise of Christianity. Members of the *ordo equester* had previously marched with the army and its officers in these events, but now, in the late empire, ceded precedence to the army alone. This acknowledged the fact that the real military was more important in the transfer of imperial power – and as a constitutent element of the monarchical *res publica* – than the equestrians. Finally, Augustus and his Julio-Claudian successors either revived or created new priesthoods of the *res publica* in Rome and in Latium which were reserved exclusively for members of the *ordo*. These priesthoods gave *equites* a religious role in the state which they had lacked under the Republic, and enjoyed particular prominence in the cosmopolitan world of the Antonine age. After this point priesthoods such as the *luperci* lost their specifically equestrian associations, and diversified to include senators in their number.

We cannot avoid the fact the principate of Augustus was central to so many of these developments. It was under his auspices that innovations were introduced or pre-existing elements of the *ordo equester* were given new significance. This was because the Augustan age witnessed nothing less than the remaking of the Roman *res publica*, as it was transformed into a monarchical state. Augustus needed to demonstrate the essential continuity of the Roman state and its institutions, and to show that his rule was supported by the voluntary consensus of all the elements of the *res publica*: the senate, the *equites* and the people. This explains his personal role in the *transvectio*, reviewing the ranks of the *equites*, and the creation of the post of *princeps iuventutis* for Gaius and Lucius, as well as the creation of a new range of opportunities for *equites* to serve as procurators and prefects. Yet we should not entirely view this process from a 'top-down' perspective: members of the *ordo equester* enthusiastically embraced the opportunities offered by the new monarchical *res publica*, both on an individual and collective level, as it brought them honours, rewards and privileges.

There was still an *ordo equester* in the fourth century AD, and Roman citizens continued to be made *equites Romani* into the fifth, and possibly even the sixth, century AD. But by the late empire the census qualification had been abandoned, and equestrian rank was itself fragmented into a series of status grades, each of which carried new exemptions, privileges and honours. This was the result of a desire for differentiation, common among all aristocrats in pre-industrial societies, which had come to the fore in the second and third centuries AD. From the high empire onwards senior members of the *ordo* serving in high government posts had had their superior status acknowledged with more exalted titles, such as *eminentissimus, perfectissimus* and *egregius*, or designations that ostentatiously showed how much they were paid, such as *centenarius* and *ducenarius*. This drive for differentiation was rewarded by the emperors, who depended on the service elite to staff the senior procuratorships of the empire. But they did not forget provincial elites who merely desired equestrian status, rather than imperial employment. Soon these municipal aristocrats too shared in higher designations, such as *egregius*. The effects of this imperial largesse can be seen in patterns of epigraphic representation, as the titles of *eques Romanus* and *vir egregius* ceased to carry the cachet they had once possessed, and disappeared from inscriptions in the Tetrarchic and Constantinian periods, respectively (with a few exceptions). With the upgrading of formerly equestrian posts such as provincial governorships and prefectures to senatorial rank, government officials and army officers alike craved the higher senatorial *dignitates*. From the time of Constantine onwards, the status of *eques Romanus* was valuable in and of itself as a privilege that conferred immunity from baser punishments, but it was a far cry from the aristocratic prestige it had possessed the past. These changes affected the way in which the consensus of the *res publica* was expressed in displays of imperial legitimacy. In late Roman imperial ideology the emperor depended on the support of the senate, the army and the people – not the *ordo equester*.

The Endurance of the *Ordo Equester*

The third aim of the book has been to examine the sociological function of the equestrian order in the Roman world. Why did Rome have *equites Romani* for more than a thousand years? The first answer to this must be that equestrian status in both the Republican and imperial periods provided a wide range of wealthy non-senatorial elites with official recognition from the *res publica*. Membership of the senate was limited, as the *curia* usually accommodated only 300–600 senators (though numbers did fluctuate). But there could be thousands of *equites*, who were awarded equestrian status if they met the appropriate moral and financial qualifications.[5] This became especially important in the imperial period, as it enabled the emperors to dispense honours to provincial elites both in the form of equestrian status itself and offices such as procuratorships, prefectures and priesthoods. The fact that the emperor was the ultimate source of benefactions assisted in the process of domesticating aristocrats in Italy

---

[5] The numbers of *equites equo publico* were of course limited to 1,800 until the Augustan age.

and the provinces. This was one of the great advantages of equestrian rank: it offered Roman citizens status, prestige and privileges, not to mention opportunities for religious, military or administrative honours, without forsaking or compromising other aspects of their lives. Of course, acting, prostitution and paid gladiatorial combat were usually out of the question, given the aristocratic status of *equites*, but there were many other more respectable occupations that were compatible: composing poetry, declaiming oratory, farming land, making money, practising law, sponsoring athletics festivals, or even, like Uncle Pliny, writing a *Natural History* in thirty-seven books. The sands shifted, however, as Rome moved into the world of Late Antiquity. When, in the fourth century AD, the numbers of senators expanded dramatically beyond the earlier limit of 600, the status of *clarissimus* eclipsed that of *eques Romanus* as a unifying distinction for the elites of the empire.

Secondly, the *ordo equester* provided the Roman state with structure and cohesion. The gradual separation between the senatorial and non-senatorial *equites* over the course of the middle Republic indicated that the *res publica* needed greater status differentiation among its elites. The *plebiscitum* of 129 BC and Gaius Gracchus' legislation of 123 BC provided the catalyst for the emergence of a distinct *ordo equester* as a social stratum between the senate and ordinary citizens. The political discourse of the late Republic, as revealed through the writings of Cicero, shows that this process did not occur without negotiation of the place of the new *ordo* within the *res publica*. But the acquisition of status symbols and perquisites, such as the right to sit in the first fourteen rows of the theatre, and the collective actions exhibited by *equites* in voting statues for patrons or creating leaders such as the *princeps iuventutis*, gave the *ordo equester* a real corporate identity (at least in the city of Rome) during the late Republic and early empire. It meant that equestrian rank became an aspirational status for Romans of middling wealth who could never dream of entering the senate, but whose business interests might one day make them enough money to possess property worth 400,000 sesterces. The place of the *ordo equester* in the *res publica* was consolidated by Augustus and his successors, as it brought much-needed definition to the state in its monarchical form. *Equites* could be seen as a cohesive group voting honours to the imperial family and participating in ritual events that supported the monarchical regime.

Thirdly, the success of the *ordo equester* in achieving these aims can be ascribed to the honours, ceremonies, *insignia* and official posts that gave the order and its members a sense of purpose. Regimes and status groups alike throughout history have needed an ideological basis to justify their existence. In short, *equites* had to believe there was relevance and meaning – or 'immanence' – in their status for it to be regarded as something worth striving for and valuing. In the case of the *ordo equester*, immanence was created through the ideology of martial *virtus*, displayed in ceremonies, dress and monuments. Related to this was the sense that the *equites* supported the *res publica*, and later its emperor. In the Republic this could be articulated through serving in the cavalry, by making important gestures at key moments of political crisis (such as the equestrian crowd led by Atticus on the Capitoline during the Catilinarian conspiracy), by voting to pass just legislation or electing the right sort of people to magistracies. In the imperial period *equites* could perform religious rituals, march in funeral ceremonies, and serve *domi militiaeque* to show their position as a bulwark of the *res publica*. This last point is particularly important. One of the great differences between the place of *equites* in the Republic and the empire came in the form of the numerous financial, administrative and military capacities in which they could be employed. These new opportunities initially arose because Augustus wanted to place non-senators in senior positions; but over time, as we have seen, there emerged a distinct equestrian aristocracy of service. This elite sub-group of the *ordo* developed its own ideology based on the idea that *equites* were Renaissance men, who could serve the state in both civilian and military roles, *domi militiaeque*, just like senators. This promoted aristocratic cohesion and prevented the formation of a separate militaristic caste in the late Roman empire.

The longevity of the *ordo equester* over many centuries can be ascribed to a series of fictions. When the *ordo* emerged as a separate constituent part of the *res publica* in the late Republic, traditions were invented about the origins of the order which were designed to connect the present-day *publicani*, businessmen, jurors and officers with the cavalry of Romulus and the other kings of Rome. The (re-)invention of tradition played a prominent role in the empire, as the *princeps* inserted himself into the *recognitio* and *transvectio* ceremonies as the ultimate arbiter of equestrian status (a duty previously invested in the censors). Equestrians were allocated newly created or revived priesthoods associated with the founding of Rome and Alba Longa, as a way of connecting the *ordo* with the origins of the state and making it part of the larger continuum of Roman history. In this way, new 'imperial' actions of the *ordo*, such as the acclamation of Augustus as *pater patriae* or his heirs as *princeps iuventutis*, did not seem inherently revolutionary, but an intrinsic part of the gradual evolution of the Roman state. Augustus and his successors had to ensure that equestrian status remained a relevant and sought-after honour in order to guarantee that provincial elites believed that it was a token of social prestige worth competing for.

The late empire brought challenges to the prestige and function of the *ordo equester* in Roman society, even though it formally remained a constituent part of the *res publica* (as shown by the medallion of Constantine on the cover of this book). The emergence of a defined equestrian aristocracy of service (with its own status grades of *egregius, perfectissimus* and *eminentissimus*) during the second to third centuries AD posed a challenge to the unity of the *ordo*. The lines between the equestrian service elite and their senatorial equivalent became progressively less distinct. The tension was resolved in the fourth century AD during the reign of Constantine, who effectively combined the separate equestrian and senatorial career structures into one government hierarchy. Now a Roman could begin his career in the lowest clerical grades of the imperial administration, acquiring equestrian and then senatorial rank as he worked his way up through the hierarchy. The reforms of Valentinian I and Valens integrated the military establishment into this new imperial system, which enabled all imperial servants to become senators.

These changes did not fundamentally alter the many pre-existing facets and habits of Roman elites. The *curiales* of the provinces still constituted the prime source of new imperial officials and for the senatorial order. Nor was it compulsory to have long careers – Romans could still serve in one or two posts to gain new dignities before retiring to their home towns, as their forebears had done by holding one post in the *militiae equestres* or a single procuratorship in the high empire. But at the same time, individual *equites* must have come to identify less as members of the *ordo equester*, a change which was paralleled by the decline in equestrian privileges, status symbols and ceremonies. This development reflected the diminishing position of the *ordo* in the status pyramid. By the late fourth century AD equestrian rank sat beneath the senatorial *illustres* and *spectabiles* (titles that could only be earned through service), and the hereditary rank of senatorial *clarissimi*, who numbered in their thousands. It was the *clarissimi* who now provided the reservoir of talent for the higher imperial offices, a role which had previously been filled by members of the *ordo equester* itself. Below the *clarissimi* came the *perfectissimi* and various equestrian sub-grades, such as *centenarii* and *ducenarii*, before one finally arrived at the status of *eques Romanus*. The title still carried privileges which elevated *equites* as *honestiores* above ordinary Roman citizens, but it had ceased to be a high aristocratic status, and that is what mattered. The emperors of the late Roman world did not refer to the *consensus* of the senatorial order, the *equites* and the plebs, as Augustus had done.

The status of *eques Romanus* survived into the fifth century AD because Rome did not abandon titles, but rather refashioned to them to serve new purposes. *Eques Romanus* had value as a recognisable legal distinction of the Roman state, and so it was retained. The late Roman *equites* were members of groups such as the shipmasters, who ensured that the grain supply continued to reach Rome and Constantinople throughout the year, or citizens in the lower grades of the imperial administration. By the fifth century AD the attributes of the *ordo equester* were antiquarian relics. The *equites* of this period may have read the works of Horace and Juvenal, in which they would have learnt that citizens of equestrian standing used to possess 400,000 sesterces worth of property and had the privilege of sitting in the first fourteen rows of the theatre. They may have walked down the Via Ostiensis, admiring the tombs of their predecessors sporting gold rings, priestly decorations or military uniforms. And maybe, just maybe, one or two of them even owned a horse.

Glossary

This glossary elucidates key Latin and Greek terms used in the text of the book.

IIIvir: triumvir, member of a board of three.

IIIvir capitalis (sing.); *IIIviri capitales* (pl.):   member of the board of three for capital punishments.

IIIIvir iure dicundo: member of the board of four for the administration of justice.

IIIIvir quinquennalis: member of the board of four and quinquennial magistrate for conducting the census.

XIV ordines: the first fourteen rows in the theatre, reserved exclusively for *equites* under the provisions of the *lex Roscia* of 67 BC.

a censibus equitum Romanorum: imperial secretary for assessing the census of Roman *equites*.

a cognitionibus: imperial secretary for the emperor's law court.

a commentariis: administrative secretary of the praetorian prefect.

a libellis: imperial secretary for petitions.

a memoria: imperial secretary, the precise duties of which are uncertain during the principate.

a militiis: a term used from the late second century AD onwards to indicate that an equestrian had held a post in the *militiae equestres*.

a rationibus: imperial financial secretary.

a studiis: head of the imperial archives.

a voluptatibus: head of imperial entertainment.

ab epistulis: imperial secretary of correspondence.

ab epistulis Graecis: imperial secretary of Greek correspondence.

actio prima and *actio secunda:*   first and second parts of a criminal trial, as established by the *lex Servilia* of 111 BC.

advocatus fisci (sing.); *advocati fisci* (pl.):   advocate representing the imperial treasury in court cases.

aerarium militare: Roman military treasury, established by Augustus in AD 6.

aes equestre: funds from the Roman treasury allocated for the purchase of the *equus publicus*.

aes hordiarium: funds from the Roman treasury allocated for the upkeep of the public horse.

ager publicus: public land of the Roman state.

agnomen: additional Roman name referring to military conquests, personal qualities and character, or physical characteristics.

agonothetes: president of the games in the Greek world.

album: board or official list.

ambitus: the charge of electoral bribery.

amicitia: friendship, both personal and political.

amplissima collegia: the four most distinguished priestly colleges, comprising the pontiffs, the augurs, the board of fifteen for sacred rites, and the board of seven for banquets.

amplissimus ordo: the most distinguished order, a term used to describe the senatorial order.

angustus clavus: the narrow stripe on the tunic worn by *equites*.

annona: the grain supply.

annona militaris: supply of provisions for the Roman army.

anulus aureus: gold ring, which became a distinguishing feature of the *equites* in the first century BC.

anulus equester: the equestrian ring, another way of referring to the gold ring.

apokrimata: a Greek term referring to imperial replies to petitions.

apparitores: public servants of the Roman state.

arete: a Greek term for excellence, courage, valour.

assessor: judicial adviser.

auxilia: the auxiliary troops of the Roman army.

beneficiarius (sing.); *beneficiarii* (pl.):   staff officers in the Roman army.

beneficium (sing.); *beneficia* (pl.):   benefaction, favour.

Caesariani: low-ranking officials employed in the *res privata* in the later Roman empire.

calcei equestres: equestrian shoes.

calcei patricii: patrician shoes.

candidatus: designated as the emperor's candidate.

cavea: area of the theatre with seats for spectators.

censor perpetuus: censor for life, a title held by the emperor Domitian; after this, censorial powers became inherent in the imperial office.

censoria potestas: censorial power.

census: assessment of Roman citizens and their property.

census equester: minimum qualification for equestrian rank, set at 400,000 sesterces from the first century BC until the early fourth century AD.

centenarius: (i) imperial official paid 100,000 sesterces per year; (ii) a rank in the later Roman army.

centuria (sing.), *centuriae* (pl.):   century, or division of the Roman people in the centuriata assembly (*comitia centuriata*), which had 193 such centuries.

centuria praerogativa: one of the centuries selected by lot to vote first.

clarissima femina: most distinguished women, a title given to female relatives of senators.

clarissimus vir: most distinguished man, a title given to senators.

classis (sing.), *classes* (pl.): (i) class, or division, of the Roman people based on property, of which there were six in the *comitia centuriata*; (ii) a fleet.

clivus Capitolinus: road from the *forum Romanum* up to the Capitoline hill.

codicilli: imperial letters of appointment.

cohors praetoria (sing.), *cohortes praetoriae* (pl.): praetorian cohort and cohorts, originally attached to all commanders in the Republic, but only to the emperor in the principate.

collegia iuvenum: official associations of elite youth, found in the western cities of the Roman empire.

comes: official imperial companion, later divided by the emperor Constantine into three grades (*primus, secundus, tertius*).

comes sacrarum largitionum: head of the Roman treasury in the later Roman empire.

comitia centuriata: 'centuriate assembly' of all Roman citizens, believed by the Romans to have been created by the king Servius Tullius (r. 578–534 BC).

commentarius: administrative official in the late Roman government.

concordia ordinum: 'the harmony of the orders', a political vision advocated by Cicero.

conductor IIII publicorum Africae: contractor of the four public taxes in Africa.

consul ordinarius: the consul who gives his name to the year. There were two such *consules ordinarii.*

corona muralis: 'mural crown', a Roman military decoration given to the first man to scale the wall of an enemy city.

cuneus (sing.), *cunei* (pl.): 'wedge', a section of the theatre.

cura annonae: supervision of the Roman grain supply.

curator aquarum (sing.), *curatores aquarum* (pl.): supervisor of the water supply.

curia: (i) the senate house at Rome; (ii) the council of colonies and municipalities.

curialis (sing.), *curiales* (pl.): member of a municipal council.

cursus honorum: 'course of offices', a way of describing the senatorial career.

cursus publicus: imperial postal and transport service.

decemvir stlitibus iudicandis: one of the board of ten men for judging lawsuits.

decumani: collectors of tithes in Sicily.

decuria (sing.), *decuriae* (pl.): a panel of jurors (*iudices*).

decuria scribarum: organisation of clerks, administrative officials of the Roman state.

decurio (sing.), *decuriones* (pl.): a member of the council in a Roman colony or municipality.

delator (sing.), *delatores* (pl.): political informer.

designatio: the process by which the emperor named the senatorial candidates he wished to be elected to office.

destinatio: a special recommendation process in the elections of consuls and praetors in the imperial period.

dignitas: (i) public standing and personal honour; (ii) an official dignity of the Roman state.

domi militiaeque: an expression meaning 'both at home and on campaign', the ideal that a Roman senator would excel in civilian and military affairs.

domi nobiles: 'nobles in their own community', an expression used by Cicero (*Clu.* 23) to describe the municipal aristocracies.

dona militaria: military decorations awarded by the Roman emperor.

ducenarius (sing.), *ducenarii* (pl.): (i) an imperial official with an annual salary of 200,000 sesterces; (ii) a rank in the later Roman army.

duumvir iure dicundo: member of the board of two for delivering justice, who were the chief magistrates of Roman colonies (including Pompeii).

epistulares: secretaries in the late Roman administration.

eques (sing.), *equites* (pl.): (i) a member of the equestrian centuries; (ii) a member of the equestrian order; (iii) a cavalryman.

eques Romanus (sing.); *equites Romani* (pl.): a member of the Roman equestrian order.

eques equo publico (sing.), *equites equo publico* (pl.): equestrians with the public horse, members of the equestrian centuries.

equites equo suo: equestrians serving on their own horses; they possessed the equestrian census, but not the public horse.

equus publicus: the 'public horse', granted by the Roman state in the form of money to buy and maintain a horse.

exceptor (sing), *exceptores* (pl.): stenographer in the late Roman administration.

fasti Praenestini: the calendar of the Italian city of Praeneste.

femina stolata: 'woman wearing a *stola*', an honorific title given to elite women in the third century.

feriae Latinae: Latin festival in honour of Jupiter Latiaris, reportedly established by Tarquinius Superbus.

flamen: (i) a type of priest in the Roman pontifical college charged with the worship of one god only; (ii) priests of the cult of the emperor outside Rome.

flamen perpetuus: 'priest for life', a priest of the imperial cult in the provinces.

flaminica: the wife of a *flamen*.

funus publicum: a Roman funeral held at public expense.

hasta (sing.), *hastae* (pl.): spear, specifically the spear carried by the *equites*, usually along with their *parma*, a round shield.

honesta femina: 'respectable woman', an honorific term used to refer to female relatives of *equites* and *curiales* in the second and third centuries AD.

honestiores: a legal category introduced in the second century AD denoting Roman citizens who were free from baser punishments such as torture and condemnation to the mines.

honestus vir: 'respectable man', an honorific title used by Roman citizens of the curial classes in the second and third centuries AD.

imperator (sing.), *imperatores* (pl.):   originally an acclamation meaning 'victorious general' in the Republican period. It was later adopted as a name by Augustus and came to mean 'emperor'.

imperium: power of Roman magistrates in peace and war, including power over Roman citizens.

infamia: public disgrace; if an equestrian incurred *infamia*, he would be removed from the order.

ingenuitas: free birth, a condition for entrance into the equestrian order.

insignia: status symbols appropriate to a specific office or status.

iudex (sing.), *iudices* (pl.):   (i) judge; (ii) juror.

iudices selecti: the title given to jurors in the imperial *decuriae* as they were selected by the emperor.

iudicium publicum: trial by the Roman state on a charge related to the *res publica*.

iuniores: members of the equestrian order aged between seventeen and thirty-five.

iurisperitus: a term meaning 'skilled in the law'.

ius aureorum anulorum: 'the right of the gold rings', that is, the prerogative of a magistrate with *imperium*, and later the Roman emperor, to grant a gold ring as a sign of free birth (*ingenuitas*).

ius gladii: 'right of the sword', the power to judge Roman citizens and sentence them to death.

ius trium liberorum: the privilege of those with three children, which conferred various political advantages on its holders, including the right to stand for office earlier.

iuvenes: (i) the Roman citizen youth who had been granted the toga of manhood (*toga virilis*), aged fourteen to thirty-five; (ii) also used to specifically refer to *equites* aged between fourteen and thirty-five.

latus clavus: broad strip on the tunic worn by members of the senatorial order.

legatus (sing.), *legati* (pl.):   legate, a representative of a magistrate in the late Republic, and of the emperor in the imperial period.

legatus Augusti pro praetore (sing), *legati Augusti pro praetore* (pl.):   legate of Augustus (sc. the emperor) with praetorian power.

legatus legionis: legionary legate, the senatorial commander of a legion.

lex (sing.), *leges* (pl.):   law, usually followed by the family name of the magistrate who proposed it (e.g. *lex Claudia* of 218 BC).

libertas: freedom, one of the fundamental rights of citizens in the *res publica*.

lupercus (sing.), *luperci* (pl.):   priests of the Lupercal; they were of equestrian rank from the time of Augustus to the Severan period.

lustratio: a ritual of purification performed by means of a circular procession.

lustrum: an act of *lustratio* performed on the Campus Martius by one of the censors to signify that the taking of the *census* had been officially completed.

magister a studiis/magister studiorum: the new title of the *a studiis* from the third
    century AD.

magister equitum et peditum: 'master of the cavalry and infantry', the title of
    a senior Roman general who commanded both branches of the army service
    (sometimes also called *magister utriusque militiae*).

magister militum: 'master of the soldiery', the title of senior Roman generals from
    the mid-fourth century AD.

militiae equestres: the equestrian military career established under the principate
    (see also *tres militiae* and *quattuor militiae*).

militiae petitor (sing), *militiae petitores* (pl.):   petitioner for a post in the *militiae*,
    a term which appears in inscriptions from the late second century AD
    onwards.

monetarius (sing), *monetarii* (pl.):   imperial minters, who were forbidden from
    acquiring equestrian rank by an edict of Licinius in AD 317.

municipium (sing.), *municipia* (pl.):   self-governing urban community of Roman
    citizens.

munus (sing.), *munera* (pl.):   obligatory duty (in terms of both service and pay-
    ment) performed for one's community.

navicularii: shipmasters; they were granted equestrian rank by Constantine.

nobilis (sing.), *nobiles* (pl.):   'noble'; in the Republican period this generally meant
    a senator from a family which had already held a curule magistracy.

notarius: administrative official of the later Roman empire, sometimes sent on
    special missions.

novus homo (sing.), *novi homines* (pl.):   'new man', a political term used to refer to
    the first man in a family to enter the senate, or the first to hold a consulship.

officia: departments of the Roman administration.

officia palatina: departments of the Roman administration associated with the
    person of the emperor, such as imperial letters, petitions and archives.

ordo (sing.), *ordines* (pl.):   a status group within the Roman *res publica*.

ordo equester: the equestrian order.

ordo senatorius: the senatorial order.

ornamenta: decorations or marks of honour, usually of a particular office.

paideia: Greek education, and the cultural attainment that stemmed from it.

palatini: a term used to refer to officials of the imperial court in the later Roman
    empire.

paludamentum: a soldier's cloak.

parazonium: a short triangular sword, an attribute of Virtus.

parma (sing.), *parmae* (pl.):   the small round shield used by the Roman cavalry,
    later a symbol of the equestrian order.

pater patriae: 'father of the fatherland', a title granted to Augustus in 2 BC.

patria (sing.), *patriae* (pl.):   'fatherland', the origin or birthplace of a Roman
    citizen.

patrimonium: the property of the Roman emperor, administered by patrimonial
procurators in the public provinces and by the financial procurators in the
emperor's provinces. This *patrimonium* was inherited by all emperors upon
their accession.

phalerae: ceremonial bosses that decorated the horses of *equites*.

plebiscitum: a decree of the plebeians (non-patrician citizen body), passed by the
concilium plebis. After the passing of the *lex Hortensia* in 287 BC, all such
decrees had the force of law.

populus Romanus: the Roman people.

portoria: customs tolls levied by the Roman state.

praefectus (sing.) *praefecti* (pl.):   prefect, a generic title which could be applied to
administrative and military officials.

praefectus Aegypti: equestrian prefect of Egypt.

praefectus alae: prefect of a cavalry unit.

praefectus annonae: equestrian prefect for the grain supply.

praefectus castrorum: prefect of the camp.

praefectus civitatium: prefect of communities or states.

praefectus cohortis: prefect of a cohort.

praefectus equitum: prefect of the cavalry.

praefectus fabrum: 'prefect of engineers', later an aide-de-camp or staff officer.

praefectus gentium: prefect of nations or peoples.

praefectus legionis: prefect of the legion, an equestrian officer who replaced the
legionary legate as the commanding officer in the third century AD.

praefectus praetorio: equestrian prefect, commander of the praetorian cohorts in
the principate. The post gradually acquired powers of legal jurisdiction and
transformed into an administrative office in the fourth century AD.

praefectus socium: prefect of allies.

praefectus urbi: senatorial prefect of the city of Rome.

praefectus vigilum: equestrian prefect of the watch and fire-fighting brigade
(*vigiles*).

praeses (sing.), *praesides* (pl.):   a generic term for governor.

praetorium: the general's headquarters.

prima classis: the first infantry class in the *comitia centuriata*.

primipilaris (sing.), *primipilares* (pl.):   former chief centurion; from the mid-third
century AD onwards the office was in charge of administering the *annona
militaris*.

primus pilus (sing.), *primi pili* (pl.):   chief centurion of a legion.

princeps iuventutis (sing.), *principes iuventutis* (pl.):   'prince of the youth', a title
given to Augustus' adopted sons Gaius and Lucius Caesar and subsequently
bestowed on other imperial heirs.

pro legato: acting in place of an emperor's legate.

procurator (sing.), *procuratores* (pl.):   in the Republic, an official in charge of
  property and finances. Subsequently used from the reign of Augustus onwards
  to refer to imperial officials of freedmen and equestrian rank.

procurator Augusti (sing.), *procuratores Augusti* (pl.):   procurator of Augustus (sc.
  the emperor), who managed all financial affairs in the imperial provinces,
  both those of the emperor and the *res publica*.

procurator patrimonii (sing.); *procuratores patrimonii* (pl.):   patrimonial procurator, who managed the emperor's personal property and estates in the
  provinces.

provocatio: the right of a Roman citizen to appeal against the actions of
  a magistrate.

publicanus (sing.); *publicani* (pl.):   contractors employed to carry out services
  connected with the public property of the Roman state.

quaestio de ambitu: criminal court for electoral bribery.

quaestio de maiestate: criminal court for treason.

quaestio de repetundis: criminal court for provincial misgovernment.

quaestio de sicariis: criminal court for assassinations.

quaestio perpetua (sing.), *quaestiones perpetuae* (pl.):   permanent criminal court.

quattuor militiae: four posts in the *militiae equestres*, a shorthand for the
  equestrian military career. The fourth echelon was introduced in the late first
  century AD.

quinquennalis (sing.), *quinquennales* (pl.):   municipal magistrates elected every
  five years to conduct the *census.*

ratio privata: the imperial department for the emperor's private estates (as
  opposed to the *patrimonium*, the inherited imperial property). The *ratio
  privata* was reorganised as the *res privata* in the reign of Septimius Severus.

recognitio equitum: formal review of the moral and physical fitness of equestrians, assessing whether they were qualified to retain the public horse. Also
  referred to as the *probatio equitum.*

repetundae: 'things that must be recovered', a term for the charge of provincial
  maladministration or extortion.

res privata: the name given to the imperial department for the emperor's private
  estates from the reign of Septimius Severus onwards.

res publica: 'public property' or 'commonwealth', that is, the Roman state.

rex (sing.), *reges* (pl.):   king; on the traditional chronology, Rome was ruled by
  kings from 753 to 509 BC.

rostra: speaker's platform in the *forum Romanum.*

sacerdotia publica: the public priesthoods of the Roman state.

scriba (sing.), *scribae* (pl.):   clerk, the highest ranked office among the Roman
  state officials called *apparitores.*

sella curulis: the curule chair, used by curule magistrates at Rome, as well as
  municipal magistrates outside Rome.

senatus consultum (sing.), *senatus consulta* (pl.):   decree of the senate.

senatus consultum ultimum: 'final decree of the senate', empowering the consuls to see that the state comes to no harm.

seniores: members of the equestrian order aged thirty-five and over.

sevir equitum Romanorum: commander of a squadron (*turma*) of *equites*.

sex suffragia: six centuries of *equites* which played a privileged role in voting in the *comitia centuriata*.

sexagenarius: equestrian official paid a yearly salary of 60,000 sesterces.

societas (sing.), *societates* (pl.): corporation of *publicani*.

summa res: central finance department of the late Roman state.

tertium corpus: 'third part', Pliny the Elder's term to describe the place of the equestrian order in the *res publica*. The first and second parts of the state were the senate and the people.

toga virilis: toga of manhood, traditionally bestowed on Roman boys at the age of fourteen.

torques: neck rings, military decorations bestowed for valour.

trabea: a short red or purple toga, part of the parade uniform of the *equites*.

transvectio equitum: the annual parade of *equites equo publico* held every year in Rome on 15 July.

trecenarius: equestrian official paid a salary of 300,000 per year.

tres militiae: the 'three military posts', an expression referring to the equestrian army career.

tribuni aerarii: 'tribunes of the treasury', originally the paymasters of the legions. For their status in the late Republic, see the Addendum to Chapter 2.

tribunus angusticlavius (sing.), *tribuni angusticlavii* (pl.): equestrian military tribune with a narrow stripe; there were five such tribunes per legion under the empire.

tribunus laticlavius (sing.), *tribuni laticlavii* (pl.): senatorial military tribune with the broad stripe; there was one per legion under the empire.

tribunus militum (sing.), *tribuni militum* (pl.): military tribune.

tributum: direct tax levied by the Roman state.

turma (sing.), *turmae* (pl.): squadron of *equites* which marched in the *transvectio equitum*.

vectigalia: rents and indirect taxes levied by the Roman state.

vexillum: military standard; each of the equestrian *turmae* had its own *vexillum*.

vice sacra: to act in place of the emperor, usually as a judge.

vicomagistri: magistrates of a neighbourhood (*vicus*) in Rome.

vigiles: watchmen, the imperial fire brigade in Rome founded by Augustus.

virtus: military valour, manliness, courage, personal excellence: the sum total of what it mean to be a Roman man (*vir*).

vis: a specific charge of political violence in the late Republic.

Bibliography

Abdy, R. (2012), 'Tetrarchy and the house of Constantine', in W. E. Metcalf (ed.), *The Oxford Handbook of Greek and Roman Coinage*, Oxford: 584–600.

Absil, M. (1997), *Les préfets du prétoire d'Auguste à Commode*, Paris.

Adams, J. N. (1999), 'The poets of Bu Njem: language, culture and the centurionate', *JRS* 89: 109–34.

(2003), *Bilingualism and the Latin Language*, Cambridge.

Alföldi, A. (1929), 'The numbering of the victories of the emperor Gallienus and of the loyalty of his legions', *NC* 5th series 9: 218–79.

(1939), 'The crisis of the empire (AD 249–270)', in *CAH* XII[1]: 165–231.

(1947), 'On the foundation of Constantinople: a few notes', *JRS* 37: 10–16.

(1952), *Der frührömische Reiteradel und seine Ehrenabzeichen*, Baden-Baden.

(1968), '(*Centuria*) *procum patricium*', *Historia* 17: 444–60.

(1976), *Oktavians Aufsteig zur Macht*, Bonn.

Alföldy, G. (1969a), 'Die Generalität des römischen Heeres', *Bonner Jahrbücher* 169: 233–46.

(1969b), *Fasti Hispanienses: Senatorische Reichsbeamte und Offiziere in den spanischen Provinzen des römischen Reiches von Augustus bis Diokletian*, Wiesbaden.

(1977), *Konsulat und Senatorenstand unter den Antoninen: Prosopographische Untersuchungen zur senatorischen Führungsschicht*, Bonn.

(1981), 'Die Stellung der Ritter in der Führungsschicht des Imperium Romanum', *Chiron* 11: 169–215.

(1982), 'Individualität und Kollektivnorm in der Epigraphik des römischen Senatorenstandes', in S. Panciera (ed.), *Epigrafia e ordine senatorio* I, Rome: 37–53.

(1984), *The Social History of Rome*, trans. D. Braund and F. Pollock, London.

(1995), 'Der Status der Provinz Baetica um die mitte des 3. Jahrhunderts', in R. Frei-Stolba and M. A. Speidel (eds.), *Römische Inschriften – Neufunde, Neulesungen und Neuinterpretationen: Festschrift für Hans Lieb*, Basel: 29–42.

(2001), '*Pietas immobilis erga principem* and ihr Lohn: Öffentliche Ehrenmonumente von Senatoren in Rom während der Frühen und Hohen Kaiserzeit', in G. Alföldy and S. Panciera (eds.), *Inschriftliche Denkmäler als Medien der Selbstdarstellung in der römischen Welt*, Stuttgart: 11–46.

(2007), '*Fasti* und Verwaltung der hispanischen Provinzen: Zum heutigen Stand der Forschung', in R. Haensch and J. Heinrichs (eds.), *Herrschen und*

Verwalten: Der Alltag der römischen Administration in der Hohen Kaiserzeit, Cologne: 325–56.

(2011), 'Eine umstrittene Altarinschrift aus Vindobona', *Tyche* 26: 1–22.

Alföldy, G. (ed.) (2000), *Corpus Inscriptionum Latinarum: Volumen Sextum – Inscriptiones Urbis Romae Latinae, Pars Octava, Fasciculus Tertius*, Berlin.

Alföldy, G. and Halfmann, H. (1973), 'M. Cornelius Nigrinus Curiatius Maternus, General Domitians und Rivale Trajans', *Chiron* 3: 331–73.

Allen, W. et al. (1970), 'Martial: knight, publisher, and poet', *CJ* 65: 345–57.

Álvarez Melero, A. (2014), 'Du foyer au forum: la place des matrones équestres dans les activités économiques', in G. de Kleijn and S. Benoist (eds.), *Integration in Rome and in the Roman World*, Leiden: 161–86.

Anderson, R. D., Parsons, P. J. and Nisbet, R. G. M. (1979), 'Elegiacs by Gallus from Qaṣr Ibrîm', *JRS* 69: 125–55.

Ando, C. (2000), *Imperial Ideology and Provincial Loyalty in the Roman Empire*, Berkeley.

Andreau, J. (1999a), *Banking and Business in the Roman World*, trans. J. Lloyd, Cambridge.

(1999b), 'Intérêts non agricoles des chevaliers romains (IIe siècle av. J.-C.–IIIe siècle ap. J.-C.)', in S. Demougin, H. Devijver and M.-T. Raepsaet-Charlier (eds.), *L'ordre équestre: histoire d'une aristocratie (IIe siècle av. J.-C.–IIIe siècle ap. J.-C.)*, Rome: 271–90.

Arce, J. (2000), 'Imperial funerals in the later Roman empire: change and continuity', in F. Theuws and J. L. Nelson (eds.), *Rituals of Power from Late Antiquity to the Early Middle Ages*, Leiden: 115–29.

Armstrong, D. (1986), 'Horatius *eques* et *scriba*: Satires 1.6 and 2.7', *TAPA* 116: 255–88.

(2012), '*Juvenalis eques*: a dissident voice from the lower tier of the Roman elite', in S. Braund and J. Osgood (eds.), *A Companion to Persius and Juvenal*, Oxford and Malden, MA: 59–78.

Armstrong, J. (2016), *War and Society in Early Rome: From Warlords to Generals*, Cambridge.

Arnason, J. P. and Raaflaub, K. A. (eds.) (2010), *The Roman Empire in Context: Historical and Comparative Perspectives*, Oxford and Malden, MA.

Arnheim, M. T. W. (1972), *The Senatorial Aristocracy in the Later Roman Empire*, Oxford.

Ash, R. (ed.) (2007), *Tacitus: Histories Book II*, Cambridge.

Asirvatham, S. R. (2010), 'His son's father? Philip II in the Second Sophistic', in E. Carney and D. Ogden (eds.), *Philip II and Alexander the Great: Father and Son, Lives and Afterlives*, Oxford: 193–204.

Astin, A. E. (1967), *Scipio Aemilianus*, Oxford.

(1978), *Cato the Censor*, Oxford.

(1988), 'Regimen Morum', *JRS* 78: 14–34.

Atkinson, K. M. T. (1962), 'The *constitutio* of Vedius Pollio at Ephesus and its analogies', *RIDA* 9: 261–89.

Austin, N. J. E. and Rankov, N. B. (1995), *Exploratio: Military and Political Intelligence in the Roman World from the Second Punic War to the Battle of Adrianople*, London.

Bablitz, L. (2007), *Actors and Audience in the Roman Courtroom*, London.

Bachrach, B. S. (1999), 'Early medieval Europe', in K. Raaflaub and N. Rosenstein (eds.), *War and Society in the Ancient and Medieval Worlds: Asia, the Mediterranean, Europe, and Mesoamerica*, Cambridge, MA: 271–307.

Badian, E. (1962), 'From the Gracchi to Sulla (1940–59)', *Historia* 11: 197–245.

(1972), *Publicans and Sinners: Private Enterprise in the Service of the Roman Republic*, Oxford.

(1989), 'The *scribae* of the Roman Republic', *Klio* 71: 582–603.

(2009), 'From the *Iulii* to Caesar', in M. Griffin (ed.), *A Companion to Julius Caesar*, Oxford and Malden, MA: 11–22.

Badian, E. and Birley, A. R. (eds.) (1979–91), *Ronald Syme: Roman Papers*, 7 vols, Oxford.

Bagnall, R. (1991), 'Notes on Roman and Byzantine documents', *CdÉ* 66: 282–96.

Bagnall, R. et al. (1987), *Consuls of the Later Roman Empire*, Atlanta, GA.

Balot, R. K. (2006), *Greek Political Thought*, Oxford and Malden, MA.

Balsdon, J. V. P. D. (1960), '*Auctoritas, dignitas, otium*', *CQ* 10: 43–50.

(1962), 'Roman history, 65–50 BC: five problems', *JRS* 52: 134–41.

Baltrusch, E. (1989), *Regimen Morum: Die Reglementierung des Privatlebens der Senatoren und Ritter in der römischen Republik und frühen Kaiserzeit*, Munich.

Balty, J. C. (1988), 'Apamea in Syria in the second and third centuries AD', *JRS* 78: 97–104.

Bang, P. F. (2011), 'Court and state in the Roman empire: domestication and tradition in comparative perspective', in J. Duindam, T. Artan and M. Kunt (eds.), *Royal Courts in Dynastic States and Empires*, Leiden: 103–28.

(2013), 'The Roman empire II: the monarchy', in P. F. Bang and W. Scheidel (eds.), *The Oxford Handbook of the State in the Ancient Near East and Mediterranean*, Oxford and New York: 412–72.

Bang, P.F. and Turner, K. (2015), 'Kingship and elite formation', in W. Scheidel (ed.), *State Power in Ancient China and Rome*, Oxford: 11–38.

Bang, P. F. and Scheidel, W. (eds.) (2013), *The Oxford Handbook of the State in the Ancient Near East and Mediterranean*, Oxford and New York.

Barber, R. (1995), *The Knight and Chivalry*, revised edition, Woodbridge.

Barker, G. and Rasmussen, T. (1998), *The Etruscans*, Oxford and Malden, MA.

Barnes, T. D. (1973), 'More missing names (AD 260–395)', *Phoenix* 27: 135–55.

(1981), *Constantine and Eusebius*, Cambridge, MA.

(1982), *The New Empire of Diocletian and Constantine*, Cambridge, MA.

(1992), 'Praetorian prefects, 337–361', *ZPE* 94: 249–60.

(1993), *Athanasius and Constantius*, Cambridge, MA.

(1996), 'Emperors, panegyrics, prefects, provinces and palaces (284–317)', *JRA* 9: 532–52.

(2009), 'The Persian sack of Antioch in 253', *ZPE* 169: 294–6.

(2010), *Early Christian Hagiography and Roman History*, Tübingen.

(2011), *Constantine: Dynasty, Religion and Power in the Later Roman Empire*, Oxford and Malden, MA.

Barnish, S. J. B. (1988), 'Transformation and survival in the western senatorial aristocracy, *c.*AD 400–700', *PBSR* 56: 120–55.

Barrett, A. A. (1990), *Caligula: The Corruption of Power*, London.

(2009), 'Herod, Augustus, and the special relationship: the significance of the procuratorship', in D. M. Jacobson and N. Kokkinos (eds.), *Herod and Augustus: Papers held at the IJS Conference, 21st–23rd June 2005*, Leiden: 281–302.

Bassignano, S. (1974), *Il flaminato nelle province romane dell'Africa*, Rome.

Bastianini, G. (1975), 'Lista dei Prefetti d'Egitto dal 30ᵃ al 299ᴾ', *ZPE* 17: 263–328.

(1980), 'Lista dei Prefetti d'Egitto dal 30ᵃ al 299ᴾ: aggiunte e correzioni', *ZPE* 38: 75–89.

Bauman, R. A. (1968), 'Some remarks on the structure and survival of the *quaestio de adulteriis*', *Antichthon* 2: 68–93.

(1996), *Crime and Punishment in Ancient Rome*, London.

Beard, M. (1987), 'A complex of times: no more sheep on Romulus' birthday', *PCPhS* 33: 1–15.

Beard, M. and North, J. (eds.) (1990), *Pagan Priests: Religion and Power in the Ancient World*, Ithaca, NY.

Beard, M., North, J. and Price, S. (1998), *Religions of Rome*, 2 vols., Cambridge.

Beaujeu, J. (1955), *La religion romaine à l'apogée de l'empire*, vol. I: *La politique religieuse des Antonins (96–192)*, Paris.

Bellandi, F. (2009), '*Naevolus cliens*', in M. Plaza (ed.), *Oxford Readings in Classical Studies: Persius and Juvenal*, Oxford: 469–505.

Benario, H. W. (1970), 'The family of Statilius Taurus', *Classical World* 64: 74–6.

(1980), *A Commentary on the Vita Hadriani in the Historia Augusta*, Atlanta.

Bendix, R. (1978), *Kings or People: Power and the Mandate to Rule*, Berkeley.

Benelli, E. (2001), 'The Romanization of Italy through the epigraphic record', in S. Keay and N. Terrenato (eds.), *Italy and the West: Comparative Issues in Romanization*, Oxford: 7–16.

Beness, J. L. (2005), 'Scipio Aemilianus and the crisis of 129 BC', *Historia* 54: 37–48.

Bengtson, H. (1988), 'Die Freunde des Augustus', in F. Seibert (ed.), *Gesellschaftsgeschichte: Festschrift für Karl Bosl zum 80 Geburtstag*, Munich: 9–21.

Bennett, J. (2001), *Trajan: Optimus Princeps*, 2nd edition, London.

Benoist, S. (2006), 'Le marbre de Thorigny, une oeuvre au clair', in S. Demougin, X. Loriot, P. Cosme and S. Lefebvre (eds.), *H.-G. Pflaum, un historien du XXe siècle*, Geneva: 285–303.

Benoît, P. and Schwartz, J. (1948), 'Caracalla et les troubles d'Alexandrie en 215 apres J.-C.', *Études de Papyrologie* 7: 17–33.

Beringer, W. (1954), '*Princeps iuventutis*', *RE* 22, 2: 2296–2311.

Bernard, S. G., Damon, C. and Grey, C. (2014), 'Rhetorics of land and power in the Polla inscription (*CIL* I² 638)', *Mnemosyne* 67: 953–85.

Bernstein, N. W. (2008), 'Each man's father served as his teacher: constructing relatedness in Pliny's *Letters*', *Classical Antiquity* 27: 203–30.

Berry, D. H. (1996), *Cicero: Pro P. Sulla Oratio*, Cambridge.

(2003), '*Equester ordo tuus est*: did Cicero win his cases because of his support for the *equites*?', *CQ* 53: 222–34.

Bianchi, L. (1987), 'Il sarcofago dei Vareni', in *Studi per Laura Breglia, Parte III: Archeologia e Storia*, Rome: 159–63.

Bingham, S. (2013), *The Praetorian Guard: A History of Rome's Elite Special Forces*, Waco.

Bird, H. W. (1984), *Sextus Aurelius Victor: A Historiographical Study*, Liverpool.

Birley, A. R. (1981), *The Fasti of Roman Britain*, Oxford.

(1991), 'A persecuting *praeses* of Numidia under Valerian', *JThS* 42: 598–610.

(1992), *Locus virtutibus patefactus? Zum Beförderungssystem in der Hohen Kaiserzeit*, Opladen.

(1993), *Marcus Aurelius: A Biography*, London.

(1997), *Hadrian: The Restless Emperor*, London.

(1999), *Septimius Severus: The African Emperor*, London.

(2000a), 'Q. Lucretius Vespillo (*cos. ord.* 19)', *Chiron* 30: 711–48.

(2000b), 'Senators as generals', in G. Alföldy, B. Dobson and W. Eck (eds.), *Kaiser, Heer, und Gesellschaft in der römischen Kaiserzeit: Gedenkschrift für Eric Birley*, Stuttgart: 97–120.

(2003), 'The commissioning of equestrian officers', in J. J. Wilkes (ed.), *Documenting the Roman Army: Essays in Honour of Margaret Roxan*, London: 1–18.

(2005), *The Roman Government of Britain*, Oxford.

(2007), 'The frontier zone in Britain: Hadrian to Caracalla', in L. de Blois and E. Lo Cascio (eds.), *The Impact of the Roman Army (200 BC–AD 476)*, Leiden and New York: 355–70.

Birley, E. (1949), 'The equestrian officers of the Roman army', *Durham University Journal* 41: 8–19.

(1953), *Roman Britain and the Roman Army*, Kendal.

(1969), 'Septimius Severus and the Roman army', *Epigraphische Studien* 8: 63–82.

(1983), 'A Roman altar from Old Kilpatrick and interim commanders of auxiliary units', *Latomus* 42: 73–83.

(1986), 'Some military inscriptions from Chester (Deva)', *ZPE* 64: 201–8.

(1988), 'Alae and cohortes milliariae', in *The Roman Army: Papers 1929–1986*, Amsterdam: 349–64. (Originally published in *Corolla Memoriae Erich Swoboda Dedicata*, 1966: 54–67.)

Bispham, E. (2007), *From Asculum to Actium: The Municipalization of Italy from the Social War to Augustus*, Oxford.

Blanco-Pérez, A. (2016), 'Nomenclature and dating in Roman Asia Minor: *(M.) Aurelius/a* and the 3rd century AD', *ZPE* 199: 271–93.

Blanshard, A. J. L. (2010), 'War in the law-court: some Athenian discussions', in D. Pritchard (ed.), *War, Democracy and Culture in Classical Athens*, Cambridge: 203–24.

Bleicken, J. (1957), 'Oberpontifex und Pontifikalkollegium: eine Studie zur römischen Sakralverfassung', *Hermes* 85: 346–66.

(1995), *Cicero und die Ritter*, Göttingen.

Bodel, J. (1999), 'The *Cena Trimalchionis*', in H. Hofmann (ed.), *Latin Fiction: The Novel in Context*, London, 38–51.

(2015), 'Status dissonance and status dissidents in the equestrian order', in A. B. Kuhn (ed.), *Social Status and Prestige in the Graeco-Roman World*, Munich: 29–44.

Bodnaruk, M. (2016), 'Administering the empire: the unmaking of an equestrian elite in the 4th century AD', in R. Varga and V. Rusu-Bolindet (eds.), *Official Power and Local Elites in the Roman Provinces*, London: 145–67.

Bollinger, T. (1969), *Theatralis Licentia: Die Publikumsdemonstrationen an den öffentlichen Spielen im Rom der früheren Kaiserzeit und ihre Bedeutung im politischen Leben*, Winterthur.

Bond, S. (2016), 'Currency and control: mint workers in the later Roman empire', in K. Verboven and C. Laes (eds.), *Work, Labour, and Professions in the Roman World*, Leiden: 227–45.

Borg, B. E. (2012), 'The face of the social climber: Roman freedmen and elite ideology', in S. Bell and T. Ramsby (eds.), *Free at Last! The Impact of Freed Slaves on the Roman Empire*, London: 25–49.

(2013), *Crisis and Ambition: Tombs and Burial Customs in Third-Century CE Rome*, Oxford.

Borg, B. E. and Witschel, C. (2001), 'Veränderungen im Repräsentationsverhalten der römischen Eliten während des 3. Jhs. n. Chr.', in G. Alföldy and S. Panciera (eds.), *Inschriftliche Denkmäler als Medien der Selbstdarstellung in der römischen Welt*, Stuttgart: 47–120.

Bottomore, T. (1993), *Élites and Society*, 2nd edition, London.

Bowersock, G. W. (1969), *Greek Sophists in the Roman Empire*, Oxford.

Bowie, E. (1970), 'Greeks and their past in the Second Sophistic', *P&P* 46: 3–41.

(1982), 'The importance of sophists', *YCS* 27: 29–59.

(2013), 'Libraries for the Caesars', in J. König, K. Oikonomopoulou and G. Woolf (eds.), *Ancient Libraries*, Cambridge: 237–60.

(2014), 'Becoming wolf, staying sheep', in J. M. Madsen and R. Rees (eds.), *Roman Rule in Greek and Latin Writing: Double Vision*, Leiden: 39–78.

Bowman, A. K. (1978), 'The military occupation of Upper Egypt in the reign of Diocletian', *BASP* 15: 25–38.

(1996a), 'Egypt', in *CAH* X^2: 676–702.

(1996b), 'Provincial administration and taxation', in *CAH* X^2: 344–70.

(2005), 'Diocletian and the first Tetrarchy, AD 284–305', in *CAH* XII^2: 67–89.

(2006), 'Outposts of empire: Vindolanda, Egypt, and the empire of Rome', *JRA* 19: 75–93.

Bowman, A. K. and Thomas, J. D. (eds.) (2003), *The Vindolanda Writing Tablets*, Tabulae Vindolandenses 3, London.

Braund, D. (2000), 'Learning, luxury and empire: Athenaeus' Roman patron', in D. Braund and J. Wilkins (eds.), *Athenaeus and His World: Reading Greek Culture in the Roman Empire*, Exeter: 3–22.

Braund, S. M. (1996), *Juvenal Satires Book 1*, Cambridge.

(2009), *Seneca: De Clementia*, Oxford.

Breeze, D. J. (1974), 'The organisation of the career structure of the *immunes* and *principales* of the Roman army', *Bonner Jahrbücher* 174: 245–92.

Bremmer, J. N. (1995), 'The family and other centres of religious learning in antiquity', in J. W. Drijvers and A. A. MacDonald (eds.), *Centres of Learning: Learning and Location in Pre-Modern Europe and the Near East*, Leiden: 29–38.

Briant, P. (1999), 'The Achaemenid empire', in K. Raaflaub and N. Rosenstein (eds.), *War and Society in the Ancient and Medieval Worlds: Asia, the Mediterranean, Europe, and Mesoamerica*, Cambridge, MA: 105–28.

Bringmann, K. (1973), 'Zur Gerichtsreform des Kaisers Augustus', *Chiron* 3: 235–44.

Briscoe, J. (2008), *A Commentary on Livy Books 38–40*, Oxford.

(2012), *A Commentary on Livy Books 41–45*, Oxford.

Brock, R. and Hodkinson, S. (2001), 'Introduction: alternatives to the democratic polis', in R. Brock and S. Hodkinson (eds.), *Alternatives to Athens: Varieties of Political Organization and Community in Ancient Greece*, Oxford: 1–32.

Brown, P. (1992), *Power and Persuasion in Late Antiquity*, Madison.

(2000), 'The study of elites in late antiquity', *Arethusa* 33: 321–46.

Brown, T. S. (1984), *Gentlemen and Officers: Imperial Administration and Aristocratic Power in Byzantine Italy, AD 554–800*, London.

Brunt, P. A. (1961), 'The *lex Valeria Cornelia*', *JRS* 51: 71–83.

(1971), *Italian Manpower, 225 BC–AD 14*, Oxford.

(1975), 'The administrators of Roman Egypt', *JRS* 65: 124–47.

(1983), '*Princeps* and *equites*', *JRS* 73: 42–75.

(1988), *The Fall of the Roman Republic and Related Essays*, Oxford.

(1990a), 'Charges of provincial maladministration under the early principate', in P. A. Brunt, *Roman Imperial Themes*, Oxford: 53–95, 487–506. (Revised version with *addenda* of the original in *Historia* 10 (1961), 189–227.)

(1990b), 'Procuratorial jurisdiction', in P. A. Brunt, *Roman Imperial Themes*, Oxford: 163–87. (Revised version of the original in *Latomus* 25 (1966): 461–87.)

(1990c), 'Publicans in the principate', in P. A. Brunt, *Roman Imperial Themes*, Oxford: 354–432.

(1994), 'The bubble of the Second Sophistic', *BICS* 39: 25–52.

(2013), *Studies in Stoicism*, ed. M. Griffin and A. Samuels with M. Crawford, Oxford.

Bruun, C. (1991), *The Water Supply of Ancient Rome: A Study of Roman Imperial Administration*, Helsinki.

(1999), 'Imperial *procuratores* and *dispensatores*: new discoveries', *Chiron* 29: 29–42.

(2005), 'Puzzles about procurators in Rome', *Arctos* 39: 9–24.

(2006), 'Der Kaiser und die stadtrömischen *curae*: Geschichte und Bedeutung', in A. Kolb (ed.), *Herrschaftsstrukturen und Herrschaftspraxis: Konzepte, Prinzipien und Strategien der Administration im römischen Kaiserreich*, Berlin: 89–114.

(2015), 'Roman government and administration', in C. Bruun and J. Edmondson (eds.), *The Oxford Handbook of Roman Epigraphy*, Oxford: 274–98.

Bumke, J. (1977), *The Concept of Knighthood in the Middle Ages*, trans. W. T. H. Jackson and E. Jackson, New York.

Buonocore, M. (1982), 'Monumenti funerari romani con decorazione ad Alba Fucens', *MEFRA* 94: 715–41.

Buonopane, A. (2008), 'Un *dux ducum* e un *vir egregius* nell'iscrizione di porta Borsari a Verona (*CIL*, V, 3329)', in P. Basso et al. (eds.), *Est enim ille flos Italiae: Vita economica e soiale nella Cisalpina Romana*, Rome: 125–36.

Burnand, C. (2004), 'The advocate as a professional: the role of the *patronus* in Cicero's *Pro Cluentio*', in J. Powell and J. Paterson (eds.), *Cicero the Advocate*, Oxford: 277–90.

Burnett, A. (2012), 'Early Roman coinage and its Italian context', in W. E. Metcalf (ed.), *The Oxford Handbook of Greek and Roman Coinage*, Oxford: 297–314.

Burton, G. P. (1979), 'The *curator rei publicae*: towards a reappraisal', *Chiron* 9: 465–87.

(1993), 'Provincial procurators and the public provinces', *Chiron* 23: 13–28.

Byrne, S. (1999), 'Pointed allusions: Maecenas and Sallustius in the *Annals* of Tacitus', *RhM* 142: 339–45.

Caballos Rufino, A. (1988), 'Cities as the basis for supraprovincial promotion: the *equites* of Baetica', in S. J. Keay (ed.), *The Archaeology of Early Roman Baetica*,

Journal of Roman Archaeology Supplementary Series 29, Portsmouth, RI: 123–46.

Cairns, F. (2006), *Sextus Propertius: The Augustan Elegist*, Cambridge.

Cameron, A. (2010), 'The date of the *Scholia vetustiora* on Juvenal', *CQ* 60: 569–76.

  (2011), *The Last Pagans of Rome*, Oxford.

Cameron, A. M. and Hall, S. G. (eds.) (1999), *Eusebius: Life of Constantine*, Oxford.

Camodeca, G. (1980–1), 'Ricerche su Puteoli tardoromana (fine III–IV secolo)', *Puteoli* 4–5: 59–128.

  (1981), 'La carriera del prefetto del pretorio Sex. Cornelius Repentinus in una nuova iscrizione puteolana', *ZPE* 43: 43–56.

Campbell, B. (1984), *The Emperor and the Roman Army*, Oxford.

  (2005a), 'The Army', in *CAH* XII²: 110–30.

  (2005b), 'The Severan Dynasty', in *CAH* XII²: 1–27.

  (2007), 'Anthony Birley', *CR* 57: 184–6.

Campbell, V. L. (2015), *The Tombs of Pompeii: Organization, Space, and Society*, London.

Capponi, L. (2002), 'Maecenas and Pollio', *ZPE* 140: 181–4.

Carrié, J.-M. (1979), 'Bryonianus Lollianus de Sidé ou les avatars de l'ordre équestre', *ZPE* 35: 213–24.

Carter, J. M. (1982), *Suetonius: Divus Augustus*, Bristol.

Carter, M. J. (2003), 'Gladiatorial ranking and the *SC de Pretiis Gladiatorum Minuendis* (*CIL* II 6278 = *ILS* 5163)', *Phoenix* 57: 83–114.

  (2009), 'Gladiators and *monomachoi*: Greek attitudes to a Roman cultural performance', *International Journal of the History of Sport* 26: 298–322.

Casanova, G. (2008), '"A caval donato … .": *P. Hib.* II 274 riesaminato', *Aegyptus* 88: 127–36.

Castagnoli, F. (1949/50), 'Sul limite di età degli *equites*', *Bullettino della Comissione Archeologica Comunale di Roma* 73: 89–90.

  (1972), *Lavinium I: Topografia generale, fonti e storia delle ricerche*, Rome.

Cenerini, F. (1989), 'Notabili e famiglie curiali sestinati', in *Sestinum: Comunità antiche dell'Appennino tra Etruria e Adriatico*, Rimini: 189–98.

Champlin, E. (2003), *Nero*, Cambridge, MA.

  (2011), 'Tiberius and the heavenly twins', *JRS* 101: 73–99.

Chaniotis, A. and Fujii, T. (2015), 'A new fragment of Diocletian's currency regulation from Aphrodisias', *JRS* 105: 227–33.

Chastagnol, A. (1966), 'Un gouverneur constantinien de Tripolitaine: Laenatius Romulus, *praeses* en 324–326', *Latomus* 25: 539–52.

  (1970), 'L'évolution de l'ordre sénatorial aux IIIe et IVe siècles de notre ère', *RH* 244: 305–14.

  (1975), '*Latus clavus* et *adlectio*: l'accès des hommes nouveaux au sénat romain sous le Haut-Empire', *RHD* 53: 375–94.

  (1988), 'La fin de l'ordre équestre: reflexions sur la prosopographie des derniers chevaliers romains', *MEFRM* 100: 199–206.

(1992), *Le sénat romain à l'époque imperial*, Paris.

Chenault, R. (2012), 'Statues of senators in the Forum of Trajan and the Roman Forum in Late Antiquity', *JRS* 102: 103–32.

Chenu, M.-D. (1968), *Nature, Man, and Society in the Twelfth Century: Essays on New Theological Perspectives in the Latin West*, ed. and trans. J. Taylor and L. K. Little, Chicago.

Cheynet, J.-C. (2006), 'The Byzantine aristocracy (8th–13th centuries)', in J.-C. Cheynet, *The Byzantine Aristocracy and its Military Function*, Aldershot: 1–43.

Christol, M. (1976), 'Une carrière équestre sous le règne de l'empereur Gallien', *Latomus* 35: 866–74.

(1977), 'La carrière de Traianus Mucianus et l'origine des *protectores*', *Chiron* 7: 393–408.

(1978), 'A propos des Aradii: le stemma d'une famille sénatoriale au IIIe siècle ap. J-C.', *ZPE* 28: 145–50.

(1982), 'Les réformes de Gallien et la carrière sénatoriale', in S. Panciera (ed.), *Epigrafia e ordine senatorio* I, Rome: 143–66.

(1986), *Essai sur l'évolution des carrières sénatoriales dans la seconde moitié du IIIe siècle ap. J.C.*, Paris.

(1997), 'M. Simplicinius Genialis: ses fonctions (*vir perfectissimus, agens vice praesidis*)', *CCG* 8: 231–41.

(1999), 'L'ascension de l'ordre équestre: un thème historiographique et sa rèalité', in S. Demougin, H. Devijver and M. T. Raepsaet-Charlier (eds.), *L'ordre équestre: histoire d'une aristocratie (IIe siècle av. J.-C.–IIIe siècle ap. J.-C.)*, Rome: 613–28.

(2003), 'Les gouverneurs de Numidie sous Valérien et Gallien et l'histoire militaire de la province entre 253 et 260', *L'Antiquité classique* 72: 141–59.

(2006a), 'L'administration et la gestion des ressources de la province d'Afrique à la transition du Haut-Empire et du Bas-Empire', *CCG* 17: 219–46.

(2006b), '*Vir centenarius*', *ZPE* 158: 243–50.

Christol, M. and Demougin, S. (1984), 'Notes de prosopographie équestre II: Gens Ostoria', *ZPE* 57: 171–8.

Christol, M. and Drew-Bear, T. (2004), 'Caracalla et son médecin L. Gellius Maximus à Antioche de Piside', in S. Colvin (ed.), *The Greco-Roman East: Politics, Culture, Society*, Yale Classical Studies 31, Cambridge: 85–118.

Clarke, G. W. (1964), 'The *destinatio* centuries in AD 14', *Historia* 13: 383–4.

Clarke, G. W. (ed.) (1989), *The Letters of St. Cyprian of Carthage*, IV, New York.

Classen, C. J. (1978), 'Cicero, the laws, and the law-courts', *Latomus* 37: 597–619.

Clinton, K. (2001), 'Initiates in the Samothracian Mysteries, September 4, 100 BC', *Chiron* 31: 27–35.

Cloud, D. (1992), 'The constitution and public criminal law', in *CAH* IX^2: 491–530.

Coarelli, F. (1984), 'Iside Capitolina, Clodio e i mercanti di schiavi', in N. Bonoacasa and A. di Vita (eds.), *Alessandria e il Mondo ellenistico-romano: Studi in onore di Achille Adriani*, Rome: 461–75.

Cohen, B. (1975), 'La notion d'ordo dans la Rome antique', *Bulletin de l'Association Guillaume Budé*, 259–82.

Coleman, K. M. (1988), *Statius: Silvae IV*, Oxford.

(2006), *Martial: Liber Spectaculorum*, Oxford.

Coles, R. (1985), 'Caecilius [Cons]ultius, *Praefectus Aegypti*', *BASP* 22: 25–7.

Colton, R. E. (1966), 'Juvenal and Martial on the Equestrian Order', *CJ* 61: 157–9.

Cooley, A. E. (2000), 'Politics and religion in the *ager Laurens*', in A. E. Cooley (ed.), *The Epigraphic Landscape of Roman Italy*, London: 173–91.

(2012), *The Cambridge Manual of Latin Epigraphy*, Cambridge.

Cooley, A. E. (ed. and trans.) (2009), *Res Gestae Divi Augusti: Text, Translation, and Commentary*, Cambridge.

Cooley, A. E. and Cooley, M. G. L. (2014), *Pompeii and Herculaneum: A Sourcebook*, 2nd edition, London.

Corbier, M. (1982), 'Les familles clarissimes d'Afrique proconsulaire (Ier–IIIe siècle)', in S. Panciera (ed.), *Epigrafia e ordine senatorio* II, Rome: 685–754.

(2005), 'Coinage and taxation: the state's point of view', in *CAH* XII^2: 327–92.

Corcoran, S. (2000), *The Empire of the Tetrarchs: Imperial Pronouncements and Government, AD 284–324*, revised edition, Oxford.

(2006), 'Before Constantine', in N. Lenski (ed.), *The Cambridge Companion to the Age of Constantine*, Cambridge: 35–58.

(2007) 'Galerius's jigsaw puzzle: the *Caesariani* dossier', *AntTard* 15: 221–50.

(2012) 'Emperors and *Caesariani* inside and outside the *Code*', in S. Crogiez-Pétrequin and P. Jaillette (eds.), *Société, économie, administration dans le Code Théodosien*, Villeneuve d'Ascq: 265–84.

(2016), 'The Codex of Justinian: the life of a text through 1,500 years', in B. W. Frier (ed.), *The Codex of Justinian: A New Annonated Translation, with Parallel Latin and Greek Text*, Cambridge: xcvii–clxiv.

Cormack, S. (2007), 'The tombs of Pompeii', in J. J. Dobbins and P. W. Foss (eds.), *The World of Pompeii*, London: 585–606.

Cornell, T. J. (1995), *The Beginnings of Rome: Italy and Rome from the Bronze Age to the Punic Wars (c.1000–264 BC)*, London.

Cornwell, H. (2015), 'The king who would be prefect: authority and identity in the Cottian Alps', *JRS* 105: 41–72.

Cosme, P. (2007), 'À propos de l'édit de Gallien', in O. Hekster, G. de Kleijn and D. Slootjes (eds.), *Crises and the Roman Empire: Proceedings of the Seventh Workshop of the International Network Impact of Empire, Nijmegen, June 20–24, 2006*, Leiden and Boston: 97–110.

Cottier, M. et al. (eds.) (2008), *The Customs of Law of Asia*, Oxford.

Cotton, H. M. (1981), 'Military tribunates and the exercise of patronage', *Chiron* 11: 229–38.

(1985), '*Mirificum genus commendationis*: Cicero and the Latin letter of recommendation', *AJPh* 106: 328–34.

(2000), 'Cassius Dio, Mommsen, and the *quinquefascales*', *Chiron* 30: 217–34.

Coulston, J. (2007), 'Art, culture and service: the depiction of soldiers on funerary monuments of the 3rd century AD', in L. de Blois and E. Lo Cascio (eds.), *The Impact of the Roman Army (200 BC–AD 476): Economic, Social, Political, Religious and Cultural Aspects*, Leiden: 529–65.

Cowan, R. H. (2002), 'Aspects of the Severan Field Army: The Praetorian Guard, Legio II Parthica, and Legionary Vexillations, AD 193–238', Ph.D. thesis, University of Glasgow.

Crawford, M. (1985), *Coinage and Money under the Roman Republic: Italy and the Mediterranean Economy*, London.

(1992), *The Roman Republic*, 2nd edition, London.

(2000), 'Italy and Rome from Sulla to Augustus', in *CAH* X²: 414–33.

(2001), 'Review of J. Bleicken, *Cicero und die Ritter*', *CR* 51: 431–3.

Crawford, M. (ed.) (1996), *Roman Statutes*, London.

Cresci, G. (1995), 'Maecenas, *equitum decus*', *RSA* 25: 169–76.

Criniti, N. (1970), *L'epigrafe di Asculum di Gn. Pompeo Strabone*, Milan.

Crone, P. (1980), *Slaves on Horses: The Evolution of the Islamic Polity*, Cambridge.

(2003), *Pre-Industrial Societies: Anatomy of the Pre-Modern World*, 2nd edition, Oxford.

Crook, J. (1955), *Consilium Principis*, Cambridge.

Crowther, N. B. (2009), 'Observations on boys, girls, youths and age categories in Roman sports and spectacles', *International Journal of the History of Sport* 26: 343–64.

Cugusi, P. (2001), 'Note esegetiche, linguistiche e testuali su papiri latini', *Aegyptus* 81: 307–21.

D'Agostino, B. (1990), 'Military organization and social structure in archaic Etruria', in O. Murray and S. Price (eds.), *The Greek City from Homer to Alexander*, Oxford: 59–82.

D'Ambrosio, E. and De Caro, S. (1983), *Un impegno per Pompei: fotopiano e documentazione della necropoli di Porta Nocera*, Milan.

D'Arms, J. (1972), 'A new inscribed base from fourth-century Puteoli', *PP* 27: 255–70.

(1981), *Commerce and Social Standing in Ancient Rome*, Cambridge, MA.

(1988), 'Pompeii and Rome in the Augustan age and beyond: the eminence of the *gens Holconia*', in R. I. Curtis (ed.), *Studia Pompeiana et Classica in Honour of Wilhelmina F. Jashemski*, New Rochelle: 51–74.

Daguet-Gagey, A. (2011), 'Auguste et la naissance des services publics à Rome', in S. Benoist et al. (eds.), *Figures d'empire, fragments de mémoire: pouvoirs et identités dans le monde romain impérial IIe s. av. n. è–VI s. de n. è.*, Lille: 341–60.

Dakouras, P. (2006), 'Maecenas Eques: A Study in the Creation and Development of an Image', Ph.D. thesis, New York University.

Davenport, C. (2009), 'The Senatorial and Equestrian Orders in the Roman Army and Administration, AD 235–337', D.Phil. thesis, Oxford University.

  (2010), 'The building inscription from the fort at Udruh and Aelius Flavianus, Tetrarchic *praeses* of Palaestina', *JRA* 23: 349–57.

  (2012a), 'Cassius Dio and Caracalla', *CQ* 62: 796–815.

  (2012b), 'Soldiers and equestrian rank in the third century AD', *PBSR* 80: 89–123.

  (2012c), 'The provincial appointments of the emperor Macrinus', *Antichthon* 46: 184–203.

  (2013), 'The governors of Achaia under Diocletian and Constantine', *ZPE* 184: 225–34.

  (2014a), 'M. Claudius Tacitus: senator or soldier?', *Latomus* 73: 174–87.

  (2014b), 'The conduct of Vitellius in Cassius Dio's *Roman History*', *Historia* 63: 96–116.

  (2015a), 'Inscribing senatorial status and identity, AD 200–350', in A. B. Kuhn (ed.), *Social Status and Prestige in the Graeco-Roman World*, Stuttgart: 269–89.

  (2015b), 'The prefecture of Caecilius [Cons]ultius', *BASP* 52: 275–81.

  (2016), 'Fashioning a soldier emperor: Maximian, Pannonia, and the panegyrics of 289 and 291', *Phoenix* 70: 381–400.

  (forthcoming), 'The end of the *militiae equestres*', in D. Rathbone and A. Wilson (eds.), *Documents and the Mechanics of Roman Rule*, Cambridge.

Davenport, C. and Manley, J. (eds.) (2014), *Fronto: Selected Letters*, London.

Davies, P. J. E. (2000), *Death and the Emperor: Roman Imperial Funerary Monuments from Augustus to Marcus Aurelius*, Austin.

Davies, R. W. (1989), *Service in the Roman Army*, Edinburgh.

de Angelis, F. (2010), 'The emperor's justice and its spaces in Rome and Italy', in F. de Angelis (ed.), *Spaces of Justice in the Roman World*, Leiden: 127–59.

de Blois, L. (1976), *The Policy of the Emperor Gallienus*, Leiden.

  (1994), 'Sueton, *Aug.* 46 und die Manipulation des mittleren Militärkaders als politisches Instrument', *Historia* 43: 324–45.

  (2001), 'Roman jurists and the crisis of the third century AD in the Roman empire', in L. de Blois (ed.), *Administration, Prosopography and Appointment Policies in the Roman Empire*, Amsterdam: 136–53.

De Ste. Croix, G. E. M. (1981), *The Class Struggle in the Archaic Age to the Arab Conquests*, London.

Delmaire, R. (1989), *Largesses sacrées et res privata: l'aerarium impérial et son administration du IVe au VIe siècle*, Rome.

Demandt, A. (1980), 'Der spätrömische Militäradel', *Chiron* 10: 609–36.

Demougin, S. (1980), '*Eques*: un surnom bien romain', *Annali del Seminario di Studi del Mondo Classico, Archeologia e Storia Antica* 2: 158–69.

(1983), 'Notables municipaux et ordre équestre à l'époque des dernières guerres civiles', in *Les 'bourgeoisies' municipales italiennes aux IIe et Ier siècles av. J.C.*, Paris: 279–98.

(1988), *L'ordre équestre sous les Julio-Claudiens*, Rome.

(1992a), *Prosopographie des chevaliers romains julio-claudiens (43 av. J.-C.-70 ap. J.-C.)*, Rome.

(1992b), 'Un proposition de restitution des lignes 54 à 57 de la *Tabula Hebana*', *Athenaeum* 80: 65–77.

(1993), 'Appartenir à l'ordre équestre au IIème siècle', in W. Eck (ed.), *Prosopographie und Sozialgeschichte: Studien zur Methodik und Erkenntnismoglichkeit der kaiserzeitlichen Prosopographie*, Cologne: 233–50.

(1994), 'L'ordre équestre sous Domitien', *Pallas* 40: 289–99.

(1999), 'L'ordre équestre en Asie mineure: histoire d'une romanisation', in S. Demougin, H. Devijver and M.-T. Raepsaet-Charlier (eds.), *L'ordre équestre: histoire d'une aristocratie (IIe siècle av. J.-C.-IIIe siècle ap. J.-C.*, Rome: 579–612.

(2001), 'Considérations sur l'avancement dans les carriéres procuratoriennes équestres', in L. de Blois (ed.), *Administration, Prosopography and Appointment Policies in the Roman Empire*, Amsterdam: 24–34.

(2007), 'L'administration procuratorienne au quotidien: affaires de chancellerie', in R. Haensch and J. Heinrichs (eds.), *Herrschen und Verwalten: Der Alltag der römischen Administration in der Hohen Kaiserzeit*, Cologne: 271–88.

(2015), 'Titres officiels, titres officieux', in A. B. Kuhn (ed.), *Social Status and Prestige in the Graeco-Roman World*, Munich: 63–85.

Dench, E. (2005), *Romulus' Asylum: Roman Identities from the Age of Alexander to the Age of Hadrian*, Oxford.

(2013), 'Cicero and Roman Identity', in C. Steel (ed.), *The Cambridge Companion to Cicero*, Cambridge: 122–38.

Develin, R. (1987), 'Sulla and the senate', *AHB* 1: 130–4.

Devijver, H. (1968), 'Die Aufgabe eines Offiziers im römischen Heer: Kommentar zu Aemilius Macer, Dig. XLIX, xvi, 12, 2', in J. Cerfaux (ed.), *Antidorum W. Peremans sexagenario ab alumnis oblatum*, Studia Hellenistica 16, Leuven: 23–37.

(1970), 'Suétone, Claude, 25, et les milices équestres', *Ancient Society* 1: 69–81.

(1972), 'The career of M. Porcius Narbonensis (*CIL* II 4239): new evidence for the reorganization of the *militiae equestres* by the emperor Claudius?', *Ancient Society* 3: 165–91.

(1976–2001), *Prosopographia militiarum equestrium quae fuerunt ab Augusto ad Gallienum*, 6 vols., Leuven.

(1986a), 'Equestrian officers from the East', in P. Freeman and D. Kennedy (eds.), *The Defence of the Roman and Byzantine East*, Oxford: 109–225.

(1986b), 'T. Flavius Mikkalus, Ritteroffizier aus Perinthos', *ZPE* 64: 253–6.

(1988), 'Les *militiae equestres* de P. Helvius Pertinax', *ZPE* 75: 207–14.

(1989a), 'Equestrian officers and their monuments', in H. Devijver, *The Equestrian Officers of the Roman Imperial Army*, Amsterdam: 416–49.

(1989b), 'Equestrian officers in the East', in D. H. French and C. S. Lightfoot (eds.), *The Eastern Frontier of the Roman Empire*, Oxford: 77–111.

(1989c), 'Some observations on Greek terminology for the *militiae equestres* in the literary, epigraphical and papyrological sources', in H. Devijver, *The Equestrian Officers of the Roman Imperial Army*, Amsterdam: 56–72. (Originally published in *Zetesis. Album amicorum E. de Strycker*, Antwerp–Utrecht (1973): 549–65.)

(1989d), 'The geographical origins of equestrian officers', *Bulletin of the Institute of Archaeology* 26: 107–26.

(1991a), 'Equestrian officers from North Africa', *L'Africa Romana* 8: 127–201.

(1991b), 'The monument of the equestrian officer Cn. Petronius Asellio (*CIL* XIII 6816 – Mogontiacum)', *Ancient Society* 22: 245–54.

(1992), '*Successoribus acceptis militare desinunt* (*Digesta*, XXVIIII, 1, 21)', in H. Devijver, *The Equestrian Officers of the Roman Imperial Army: Volume II*, Stuttgart: 212–21.

(1993), 'Veränderungen in der Zusammensetzung der ritterlichen Offiziere von Septimius Severus bis Gallienus', in W. Eck (ed.), *Prosopographie und Sozialgeschichte*, Cologne: 205–31.

(1995), 'Les milices équestres et la hiérarchie militaire', in Y. Le Bohec (ed.), *La hiérarchie (Rangordnung) de l'armée romaine sous le haut-empire*, Paris: 175–91.

(1999), 'Les relations sociales des chevaliers romains', in S. Demougin, H. Devijver and M.-T. Raepsaet-Charlier (eds.), *L'ordre équestre: histoire d'une aristocratie (IIe siècle av. J.-C.–IIIe siècle ap. J.-C.)*, Rome: 237–69.

Devijver, H. and van Wonterghem, F. (1990), 'The funerary monuments of equestrian officers of the late Republic and early empire in Italy (50 BC–100 AD)', *Ancient Society* 21: 59–98.

Dietz, K. (1980), *Senatus contra principem*, Munich.

Dillon, J. N. (2012), *The Justice of Constantine: Law, Communication, and Control*, Ann Arbor.

(2015), 'The inflation of rank and privilege: regulating precedence in the fourth century AD', in J. Wienand (ed.), *Contested Monarchy: Integrating the Roman Empire in the Fourth Century AD*, New York: 42–66.

Dimitrova, N. M. (2008), *Theoroi and Initiates in Samothrace: The Epigraphical Evidence*, Hesperia Supplements 37, Princeton.

Dobson, B. (1966), 'The *praefectus fabrum* in the early principate', in M. G. Jarrett and B. Dobson (eds.), *Britain and Rome: Essays Presented to Eric Birley on his Sixtieth Birthday*, Kendal: 61–84.

(1970), 'The centurionate and social mobility during the principate', in C. Nicolet (ed.), *Recherches sur les structures sociales dans l'Antiquité classique*, Paris: 99–115.

(1972), 'Legionary centurion or equestrian officer? A comparison of pay and prospects', *Ancient Society* 3: 193–207.

(1974), 'The significance of the centurion and *primipilaris* in the Roman army and administration', in *ANRW* II.I: 392–434.

(1978), *Die Primipilares: Entwicklung und Bedeutung, Laufbahnen und Persönlichkeiten eines römischen Offiziersranges*, Bonn.

(1982), '*Praefectus castrorum Aegypti*: a reconsideration', *CdÉ* 57: 322–7.

(2000), 'The *primipilares* in army and society', in G. Alföldy, B. Dobson and W. Eck (eds.), *Kaiser, Heer, und Gesellschaft in der Römischen Kaiserzeit: Gedenkschrift für Eric Birley*, Stuttgart: 139–52.

Dobson, B. and Breeze, D. J. (1969), 'The Rome cohorts and the legionary centuriate', *Epigraphische Studien* 8: 100–24.

Donati, A. (1989), 'La produzione epigrafica sestinate', in *Sestinum: Comunità antiche dell'Appennino tra Etruria e Adriatico*, Rimini: 167–74.

Drew-Bear, T. (1977), 'A fourth-century Latin soldier's epitaph from Nakolea', *HSPh* 81: 257–74.

Drew-Bear, T., Malay, H. and Zuckerman, C. (2004), 'L'épitaph de Valeria, veuve du tribun Dassianus', in Y. Le Bohec and C. Wolff (eds.), *L'armée romaine de Dioclétien à Valentinien Ier: Acts du Congrès de Lyon, 12–14 Septembre 2002*, Lyons: 409–18.

Drews, R. (2004), *Early Riders: The Beginnings of Mounted Warfare in Asia and Europe*, London.

Drijvers, J. W. (1991), *Helena Augusta: The Mother of Constantine the Great and the Legend of her Finding of the True Cross*, Leiden.

Drinkwater, J. F. (1987), *The Gallic Empire: Separatism and Continuity in the North-Western Provinces of the Roman Empire, AD 260–274*, Stuttgart.

(2005), 'Maximinus to Diocletian and the "Crisis"', in *CAH* XII²: 28–66.

(2007), *The Alamanni and Rome 213–496: Caracalla to Clovis*, Oxford.

Drogula, F. K. (2015), *Commanders and Command in the Roman Republic and Early Empire*, Chapel Hill.

Duby, G. (1976), 'Die Ursprünge des Rittertums', in A. Borst (ed.), *Das Rittertum im Mittelalter*, Darmstadt: 349–69.

(1980), *The Three Orders: Feudal Society Imagined*, trans. A. Goldhammer, Chicago.

Dumézil, G. (1958), 'Les pisciculi des Volcanalia', *REL* 36: 121–30.

Duncan-Jones, R. P. (1963), 'Wealth and munificence in Roman Africa', *PBSR* 31: 159–77.

(1967), 'Equestrian rank in the cities of the African provinces under the principate: an epigraphic survey', *PBSR* 35: 147–86.

(1982), *The Economy of the Roman Empire: Quantitative Studies*, 2nd edition, Cambridge.

(1990), *Structure and Scale in the Roman Economy*, Cambridge.

(1994), *Money and Government in the Roman Empire*, Cambridge.

(2006), 'Who were the *equites*?', in C. Deroux (ed.), *Studies in Latin Literature and Roman History XIII*, Brussels: 183–223.

(2016), *Power and Privilege in Roman Society*, Cambridge.

Durry, M. (1938), *Les cohortes prétoriennes*, Paris.

Dyck, A. R. (ed.) (2008), *Cicero: Catilinarians*, Cambridge.

(2010), *Cicero: Pro Sexto Roscio*, Cambridge.

(2013), *Cicero: Pro Marco Caelio*, Cambridge.

Dyson, S. L. (1992), *Community and Society in Roman Italy*, Baltimore and London.

Eck, W. (1974), 'Beförderungskriterien innerhalb der senatorischen Laufbahn, dargestellt an der Zeit von 69 bis 138 n. Chr.', in *ANRW* II.1: 158–228.

(1979a), *Die staatliche Organisation Italiens in der hohen Kaiserzeit*, Munich.

(1979b), 'Iscrizioni nuove dall'Etruria meridionale', *Epigraphica* 41: 89–118.

(1982), 'Einfluß korrupter Praktiken auf das senatorisch-ritterliche Beförderungswesen in der Hohen Kaiserzeit?' in W. Schuller (ed.), *Korruption im Alterum*, Munich: 135–51.

(1984), 'Senatorial self-representation: developments in the Augustan period', in F. Millar and E. Segal (eds.), *Caesar Augustus: Seven Aspects*, Oxford: 129–67.

(1985), *Die Statthalter der germanischen Provinzen vom 1.–3. Jahrhundert*, Cologne.

(1988), 'Die Leitung und Verwaltung einer prokuratorischen Provinz', in M. Vacchina (ed.), *La valle d'Aosta et l'arco alpino nella politica del mondo antico*, St Vincent: 102–17.

(1989), 'Religion und Religiosität in der soziopolitischen Führungsschicht der Hohen Kaiserzeit', in W. Eck (ed.), *Religion und Gesellschaft in der römischen Kaiserzeit: Kolloquium zu Ehren von Friedrich Vittinghoff*, Cologne and Vienna: 15–51.

(1995), '"Tituli honorarii", curriculum vitae und Selbstdarstellung in der Hohen Kaiserzeit', in H. Solin (ed.), *Acta colloquii epigraphici Latini Helsingiae 3.–6. sept. 1991 habiti*, Helsinki: 211–37.

(1997), 'Zu kleinasiatischen Inschriften (Ephesos; Museum Bursa)', *ZPE* 117: 107–16.

(1999a), '*Ordo equitum romanorum, ordo libertorum*: Freigelassene und ihre Nachkommen im römischen Ritterstand', in S. Demougin, H. Devijver and M.-T. Raepsaet-Charlier (eds.), *L'ordre équestre: histoire d'une aristocratie (IIe siècle av. J.-C.–IIIe siècle ap. J.-C.)*, Rome: 5–29.

(1999b), 'The Bar Kokhba revolt: the Roman point of view', *JRS* 89: 76–89.

(2000), 'Government and civil administration', in *CAH* XI^2: 195–292.

(2001), 'Spezialisierung in der staatlichen Administration des Römischen Reiches in der Hohen Kaiserzeit', in L. de Blois (ed.), *Administration, Prosopography and Appointment Policies in the Roman Empire*, Amsterdam: 1–23.

(2002a), 'Imperial administration and epigraphy: in defence of prosopography', in A. K. Bowman et al. (eds.), *Representations of Empire: Rome and the Mediterranean World*, Proceedings of the British Academy 114, Oxford: 131–52.

(2002b), 'Prosopographische Bemerkungen zum Militärdiplom vom 20. 12. 202 n. Chr.: Der Flottenpräfekt Aemilius Sullectinus und das Gentilnomen des Usurpators Regalianus', *ZPE* 139: 208–10.

(2005), 'Auf der Suche nach Personen und Persönlichkeiten: *Cursus honorum* und Biographie', in K. Vössing (ed.), *Biographie und Prosopographie: Internationales Kolloquium zum 65. Geburtstag von Anthony R. Birley*, Stuttgart: 53–72.

(2006a), 'Der Kaiser und seine Ratgeber: Überlegungen zum inneren Zusammenhang von *amici, comites* und *consiliarii* am römischen Kaiserhof', in A. Kolb (ed.), *Herrschaftsstrukturen und Herrschaftspraxis: Konzepte, Prinzipien und Strategien der Administration im römischen Kaiserreich*, Berlin: 67–77.

(2006b), 'Sozio-politische Macht und öffentliche Repräsentation: der *equester ordo*', in S. Demougin, X. Loriot, P. Cosme and S. Lefebvre (eds.), *H.-G. Pflaum, un historien du XXe siècle*, Geneva: 485–502.

(2008), 'Die Benennung von römischen Amtsträgern und politisch–militärisch–administrativen Funktionen bei Flavius Iosephus: Probleme der korrekten Identifizierung', *ZPE* 166: 218–26.

(2009a), 'The administrative reforms of Augustus: pragmatism or systematic planning?' in J. Edmondson (ed.), *Augustus*, Edinburgh: 229–49.

(2009b), 'There are no *cursus honorum* inscriptions: the function of the *cursus honorum* in epigraphic communication', *SCI* 28: 79–92.

Eck, W. and Lieb, H. (1993), 'Ein Diplom für die classis Ravennas vom 22. November 206', *ZPE* 96: 75–88.

Eck, W. and Pangerl, A. (2011), 'Drei Konstitutionen im Jahr 123 für Truppen von Dacia Porolissensis unter dem Präsidialprokurator Livius Gratus', *ZPE* 176: 234–42.

Edmondson, J. (1992), *Dio: The Julio-Claudians. Selections from Books 58–63 of the Roman History of Cassius Dio*, London.

(1996), 'Dynamic arenas: gladiatorial presentations in the city of Rome and the construction of Roman society during the early empire', in W. J. Slater (ed.), *Roman Theatre and Society: E. Togo Salmon Papers 1*, Ann Arbor: 69–112.

(2002), 'Public spectacles and Roman social relations', in T. Nogales Basarrate and A. Castellanos (eds.), *Ludi Romani: Espectáculos en Hispania Romana*, Madrid: 9–29.

(2008), 'Public dress and social control in late Republican and early imperial Rome', in J. Edmondson and A. Keith (eds.), *Roman Dress and the Fabrics of Roman Culture*, Toronto: 21–46.

Edwards, C. (1997), 'Unspeakable professions: public performance and prostitution in ancient Rome', in J. Hallett and M. Skinner (eds.), *Ancient Sexualities*, Princeton: 66–95.

Edwell, P. M. (2008), *Between Rome and Persia: The Middle Euphrates, Mesopotamia and Palmyra under Roman Control*, London.

Eich, P. (2005), *Zur Metamorphose des politischen Systems in der römischen Kaiserzeit: Die Entstehung einer 'personalen Bürokratie' im langen dritten Jahrhundert*, Berlin.

(2007), 'Die Administratoren des römischen Äegyptens', in R. Haensch and J. Heinrichs (eds.), *Herrschen und Verwalten: Der Alltag der römischen Administration in der Hohen Kaiserzeit*, Cologne: 378–99.

(2015), 'The common denominator: late Roman imperial bureaucracy from a comparative perspective', in W. Scheidel (ed.), *State Power in Ancient Rome and China*, Oxford: 90–149.

Eisenstadt, S. N. (1993), *The Political Systems of Empires*, revised edition, New Brunswick and London.

Elias, N. (1982), *The Civilizing Process*, vol. II: *State Formation and Civilization*, Oxford.

(1983), *The Court Society*, trans. E. Jephcott, Oxford.

Elsner, J. (1998), *Imperial Rome and Christian Triumph*, Oxford.

Ensslin, W. (1937), 'Perfectissimus', in *RE* XIX.1: 664–83.

(1939), 'The end of the principate", in *CAH* XII[1]: 352–82.

Erdkamp, P. (1995), 'The corn supply of the Roman armies during the third and second centuries BC', *Historia* 44: 168–91.

(2005), *The Grain Market in the Roman Empire: A Social, Political and Economic Study*, Cambridge.

Erskine, A. (2001), *Troy between Greece and Rome: Local Tradition and Imperial Power*, Oxford.

Evans, J. K. (1978), 'The role of *suffragium* in imperial political decision-making: a Flavian example', *Historia* 27: 102–28.

Evans Grubbs, J. (1993), '"Marriage more shameful than adultery": slave–mistress relationships, "mixed marriages" and late Roman law', *Phoenix* 47: 125–54.

(1995), *Law and Family in Late Antiquity: The Emperor Constantine's Marriage Legislation*, Oxford.

Everdell, W. R. (2000), *The End of Kings: A History of Republics and Republicans*, revised edition, Chicago.

Ewald, B. (2004), 'Men, muscle, and myth: Attic sarcophagi in the cultural context of the Second Sophistic', in B. E. Borg (ed.), *Paideia: The World of the Second Sophistic*, Berlin: 229–75.

Fantham, E. (2004), *The Roman World of Cicero's De Oratore*, Oxford.

(2013), *Cicero's Pro L. Murena Oratio*, Oxford.

Faoro, D. (2011), *Praefectus, procurator, praeses: Genesi delle cariche presidiali equestri nell'Alto Impero Romani*, Florence and Milan.

Farris, W. W. (1999), 'Japan to 1300', in K. Raaflaub and N. Rosenstein (eds.), *War and Society in the Ancient and Medieval Worlds: Asia, the Mediterranean, Europe, and Mesoamerica*, Cambridge, MA: 47–70.

Feissel, D. and Gascou, J. (1995), 'Documents d'archives romains inédits du moyen Euphrate', *Journal des Savants*: 65–119.

Fenelli, M. (1998), 'Lavinium', in L. Drago Troccoli (ed.), *Scavi e ricerche archeologiche dell'Università di Roma 'La Sapienza'*, Rome: 109–19.

Ferguson, R. B. (1999), 'A paradigm for the study of war and society', in K. Raaflaub and N. Rosenstein (eds.), *War and Society in the Ancient and Medieval Worlds: Asia, the Mediterranean, Europe, and Mesoamerica*, Cambridge, MA: 389–437.

Ferrary, J.-L. (1980), 'Pline, *N. H.* XXXIII, 34, et les chevaliers Romains sous la République', *REL* 58: 313–37.

(1991), '*Lex Cornelia de sicariis et veneficiis*', *Athenaeum* 79: 417–34.

(2009), 'The powers of Augustus', in J. Edmondson (ed.), *Augustus*, Edinburgh: 90–136.

Ferriès, M. (2009), 'Luperci et Lupercalia de César à Auguste', *Latomus* 68: 373–92.

Fink, R. O. (1971), *Roman Military Records on Papyrus*, Ann Arbor.

Finley, M. I. (1999), *The Ancient Economy*, updated edition with a new foreword by I. Morris, Berkeley.

Firpo, G. (1985), '*CIL* XI 6011 e la grande rivolta dalmatico-pannonica del 6–9 d. C.', *Epigraphica* 47: 21–33.

Fishwick, D. (1987), *The Imperial Cult in the Latin West: Studies in the Ruler Cult of the Western Provinces of the Roman Empire. Volume I.2*, Leiden and New York.

(1998), 'Our first high priest: a Gallic knight at Athens', *Epigraphica* 60: 83–112.

(2002), *The Imperial Cult in the Latin West: Studies in the Ruler Cult of the Western Provinces of the Roman Empire. Volume III: Provincial Cult. Part 2: The Provincial Priesthood*, Leiden and Boston.

Fitz, J. (1978), 'Die Laufbahn des Aelius Triccianus', *ActaArchHung* 26: 21–7.

(1983), *Honorific Titles of Army Units in the Third Century*, Budapest.

Flower, H. I. (1996), *Ancestor Masks and Aristocratic Power in Roman Culture*, Oxford.

(2006), *The Art of Forgetting: Disgrace and Oblivion in Roman Political Culture*, Chapel Hill.

(2010), *Roman Republics*, Princeton.

Forbis, E. (1996), *Municipal Virtues in the Roman Empire: The Evidence of Italian Honorary Inscriptions*, Stuttgart.

Forsythe, G. (2005), *A Critical History of Early Rome: From Prehistory to the First Punic War*, Berkeley.

Fouracre, P. (2000), 'The origins of the nobility in Francia', in A. J. Duggan (ed.), *Nobles and Nobility in Medieval Europe: Concepts, Origins, Transformations*, Woodbridge: 17–24.

Franklin, J. L. (2001), *Pompeis difficile est: Studies in the Political Life of Imperial Pompeii*, Ann Arbor.

Frederiksen, M. W. (1968), 'Campanian cavalry: a question of origins', *Dialoghi di archeologia* 2: 3–31.

Freyburger-Galland, M.-L. (1997), 'Dion Cassius et le carrousel troyen', *Latomus* 53: 619–29.

Friday, K. F. (2003), *Samurai, Warfare and the State in Early Medieval Japan*, London.

Frier, B. W. (1980), *Landlords and Tenants in Imperial Rome*, Princeton.

Frija, G. (2012), *Les prêtres des empereurs: Le culte imperial civique dans la province romaine d'Asie*, Rennes.

Fuhrmann, C. (2011), *Policing the Roman Empire: Soldiers, Administration, and Public Order*, Oxford.

Gabba, E. (1976), *Republican Rome, the Army and the Allies*, trans. P. J. Cuff, Berkeley.

  (1992), 'Rome and Italy: the Social War', in *CAH* IX^2, 104–28.

Gabelmann, H. (1977), 'Die ritterliche trabea', *JDAI* 92: 322–74.

Galinsky, G. K. (1969), *Aeneas, Sicily, and Rome*, Princeton.

  (2011), 'Continuity and change: religion in the Augustan semi-century', in J. Rüpke (ed.), *A Companion to Roman Religion*, Oxford and Malden, MA: 71–95.

Gardner, J. F. (1986), *Women in Roman Law and Society*, London.

Garnsey, P. (1967), 'Adultery trials and the survival of the *quaestiones* in the Severan age', *JRS* 57: 56–60.

  (1968), 'The criminal jurisdiction of governors', *JRS* 58: 51–9.

  (1970), *Social Status and Legal Privilege in the Roman Empire*, Oxford.

  (2004), 'Roman citizenship and Roman law in the late Empire', in S. Swain and M. Edwards (eds.), *Approaching Late Antiquity: The Transformation from Early to Late Empire*, Oxford: 133–55.

  (2010), 'Roman patronage', in S. McGill, C. Sogno and E. Watts (eds.), *From the Tetrarchs to the Theodosians: Later Roman History and Culture, 284–450 CE*, Cambridge: 33–54.

Gasperini, L. (1959), 'Nuove iscrizioni Etrusche e Latine di Visentium', *Epigraphica* 21: 31–50.

Geagan, D. J. (1991), 'The Sarapion monument and the quest for status in Roman Athens', *ZPE* 85: 145–65.

Gerhardt, T. and Hartmann, U. (2008), '*Fasti*', in K.-P. Johne, U. Hartmann and T. Gerhardt (eds.), *Die Zeit der Soldatenkaiser: Krise und Transformation des römischen Reiches im 3. Jahrhundert n. Chr. (235–284)*, 2 vols., Berlin: 1055–1198.

Ghiretti, M. (1985), 'Lo status della Giudea dall'età Augustea all'età Claudia', *Latomus* 44: 751–66.

Gibson, B. (2006), *Statius: Silvae 5*, Oxford.

Gibson, R. K. (2012), 'Gallus: The first Roman love elegist', in B. K. Gold (ed.), *A Companion to Roman Love Elegy*, Oxford and Malden, MA: 172–86.

Gibson, R. and Morello, R. (2012), *Reading the Letters of Pliny the Younger: An Introduction*, Cambridge.

Gilliam, J. F. (1961), 'Egyptian "duces" under Gordian', *CdÉ* 36: 386–92.

Giltaij, J. (2013), 'The problem of the content of the *lex Iulia iudiciorum publicorum*', *Tijdschrift voor Rechtsgeschiedenis* 81: 507–25.

Ginsburg, M. (1940), 'Roman military clubs and their social functions', *TAPA* 71: 149–56.

Giovannini, A. (2010), 'Cheval public et ordre équestre à la fin de la République', *Athenaeum* 98: 354–64.

Glas, T. and Hartmann, U. (2008), 'Die Provinzverwaltung', in K.-P. Johne, U. Hartmann and T. Gerhardt (eds.), *Die Zeit der Soldatenkaiser: Krise und Transformation des römischen Reiches im 3. Jahrhundert n. Chr. (235–284)*, 2 vols., Berlin: 641–72.

Gnecchi, F. (1912), *I Medaglioni Romani*, 3 vols., Milan.

Gold, B. K. (1982), 'Propertius 3.9: Maecenas as *Eques, Dux, Fautor*', in B. K. Gold (ed.), *Literary and Artistic Patronage in Ancient Rome*, Austin: 103–17.

Goldberg, S. M. (2007), 'Performing theory: variations on a theme by Quintilian', in T. Beghin and S. Goldberg (eds.), *Haydn and the Performance of Rhetoric*, Chicago: 39–60.

Goldsmith, R. W. (1984), 'An estimate of the size and structure of the national product of the early Roman empire', *Review of Income and Wealth* 30: 263–88.

Goltz, A. and Hartmann, U. (2008), 'Valerianus und Gallienus', in K.-P. Johne, U. Hartmann and T. Gerhardt (eds.), *Die Zeit der Soldatenkaiser: Krise und Transformation des römischen Reiches im 3. Jahrhundert n. Chr. (235–284)*, 2 vols., Berlin: 223–96.

González, J. (1986), 'The *Lex Irnitana*: a new copy of the Flavian municipal law', *JRS* 76: 147–243.

Gordon, A. E. (1938), *The Cults of Lanuvium*, Berkeley.

   (1952), *Quintus Veranius, Consul AD 49: A Study Based upon his Recently Identified Sepulchral Inscription*, Berkeley.

Goette, H. R. (1988), 'Mulleus – Embas – Calceus: Ikonografische Studien zu römischen Schuhwerk', *JDAI* 103: 401–64.

Graff, D. A. (2002), *Medieval Chinese Warfare, 300–900*, London.

Grandvallet, C. (2006), 'Marinianus, successeur désigné de Gallien?', *AC* 75: 133–41.

Granger-Taylor, H. (1982), 'Weaving clothes to shape in the ancient world: the tunic and toga of the Arringatore', *Textile History* 13: 3–25.

Granino Cecere, M. G. (1996), '*Sacerdotes Cabenses* e *sacerdotes Albani*: la documentazione epigrafica', in A. Pasqualini (ed.), *Alba Longa: mito, storia, archeologia: atti dell'incontro di studio Roma–Albano Laziale, 27–29 gennaio 1994*, Rome: 275–316.

Grieve, L. J. (1987), '*Proci patricii*: a question of voting order in the centuriate assembly', *Historia* 36: 302–17.

Griffin, M. T. (1973), 'The *leges iudiciariae* of the pre-Sullan era', *CQ* 23: 108–21.

(1984), *Nero: The End of a Dynasty*, London.

(2013), *Seneca on Society: A Guide to De Beneficiis*, Oxford.

Gruen, E. (1968), *Roman Politics and the Criminal Courts*, Cambridge, MA.

(1974), *The Last Generation of the Roman Republic*, Berkeley.

(1984), *The Hellenistic World and the Coming of Rome*, Berkeley.

Haack, M.-L. (2006), *Prosopographie des haruspices romains*, Pisa and Rome.

Habicht, C. (1969), *Altertümer von Pergamon VIII.3: Die Inschriften des Asklepieions*, Berlin.

Haensch, R. (1998), 'Statthalterinschriften', *ZPE* 122: 286–92.

(2001), '*Veteranus ex beneficiario consularis, equestris militiae petitor*: mögliche Gründe für einen außergewöhnlichen Aufstieg', *Kölner Jahrbuch* 34: 135–9.

(2006), 'Von den *Augusti liberti* zu den *Caesariani*', in A. Kolb (ed.), *Herrschaftsstrukturen und Herrschaftspraxis: Konzepte, Prinzipien und Strategien der Administration im römischen Kaiserreich*, Berlin: 153–64.

Haensch, R. and Weiß, P. (2012), 'Ein schwieriger Weg: Die Straßenbauinschrift des M. Valerius Lollianus aus Byllis', *MDAI (RA)* 118: 435–54.

Hagedorn, D. (1985), 'Zum Amt des διοικητής im römischen Aegypten', *YClS* 28: 167–210.

Haldon, J. F. (1990), *Byzantium in the Seventh Century: The Transformation of a Culture*, Cambridge.

(2004), 'The fate of the Late Roman senatorial elite: extinction or transformation', in J. F. Haldon and L. I. Conrad (eds.), *Elites Old and New in the Byzantine and Early Islamic Near East*, Princeton: 179–234.

(2009), 'Social élites, wealth and power', in J. F. Haldon (ed.), *A Social History of Byzantium*, Oxford and Malden, MA: 168–211.

Halsall, G. (2007), *Barbarian Migrations and the Roman West, 376–568*, Cambridge.

(2010), *Cemeteries and Society in Merovingian Gaul: Selected Studies in History and Archaeology, 1992–2009*, Leiden.

Halfmann, H. (1982), 'Zwei syrische Verwandte des severischen Kaiserhauses', *Chiron* 12: 217–35.

Hammer, D. (2014), *Roman Political Thought: From Cicero to Augustine*, Cambridge.

Hanchey, D. (2013), '*Otium* as civic and personal stability in Cicero's *Dialogues*', *CW* 106: 171–97.

Handy, M. (2006), 'Bemerkungen zum *edictum Gallieni*', in M. Frass et al. (eds.), *Akten des 10 Österreichen Althistorkertages*, Vienna: 73–81.

(2009), *Die Severer und das Heer*, Berlin.

Hanson, A. E. (1982), 'Publius Ostorius Scapula: Augustan prefect of Egypt', *ZPE* 47: 243–53.

Harmand, J. (1967), *L'armée et le soldat a Rome de 107 à 50 avant notre ère*, Paris.

Harper, K. (2011), *Slavery in the Late Roman World, AD 275–425*, Cambridge.

Harris, W. V. (1979), *War and Imperialism in Republican Rome, 327–70 BC*, Oxford.

(2011), *Rome's Imperial Economy: Twelve Essays*, Oxford.

Hartmann, A. (2017), 'Between Greece and Rome: forging a primordial identity for the imperial aristocracy', in W. Vanacker and A. Zuiderhoek (eds.), *Imperial Identities in the Roman World*, London: 16–35.

Hassig, R. (1999), 'The Aztec world', in K. Raaflaub and N. Rosenstein (eds.), *War and Society in the Ancient and Medieval Worlds: Asia, the Mediterranean, Europe, and Mesoamerica*, Cambridge, MA: 361–87.

Hauken, T. (1998), *Petition and Response: An Epigraphic Study of Petitions to Roman Emperors 181–249*, Bergen.

Hawley, R. (2007), 'Lords of the rings: ring-wearing, status, and identity in the age of Pliny the Elder', in E. Bispham and G. Rowe (eds.), *Vita Vigilia Est: Essays in Honour of Barbara Levick*, London: 103–12.

Hawthorn, J. R. (1962), 'The senate after Sulla', *G&R* 9: 53–60.

Heather, P. (1994), 'New men for mew Constantines? Creating an imperial elite in the eastern Mediterranean', in P. Magdalino (ed.), *New Constantines: The Rhythm of Imperial Renewal in Byzantium, 4th–13th Centuries*, Aldershot: 11–33.

(1998), 'Senators and senates', in *CAH* XIII: 184–210.

(2005), *The Fall of the Roman Empire: A New History*, London.

(2008), 'Running the empire: bureaucrats, curials and senators', in D. M. Gwynn (ed.), *A. H. M. Jones and the Later Roman Empire*, Leiden and Boston: 97–119.

Heffernan, T. J. (2012), *The Passion of Perpetua and Felicity*, New York.

Heil, M. (2006), '"Soldatenkaiser" als Epochenbegriff', in K. P. Johne, T. Gerhardt and U. Hartmann (eds.), *Deleto paene imperio Romano: Transformationsprozesse des Römischen Reiches im 3. Jahrhundert und ihre Rezeption in der Neuzeit*, Stuttgart: 411–28.

(2008a), 'Der Ritterstand', in K.-P. Johne, U. Hartmann and T. Gerhardt (eds.), *Die Zeit der Soldatenkaiser: Krise und Transformation des römischen Reiches im 3. Jahrhundert n. Chr. (235–284)*, 2 vols., Berlin: 737–61.

(2008b), 'Der Senat', in K.-P. Johne, U. Hartmann and T. Gerhardt (eds.), *Die Zeit der Soldatenkaiser: Krise und Transformation des römischen Reiches im 3. Jahrhundert n. Chr. (235–284)*, 2 vols., Berlin: 715–36.

(2015), 'Die Genese der Rangtitel in den ersten drei Jahrhunderten', in A. B. Kuhn (ed.), *Social Status and Prestige in the Graeco-Roman World*, Munich: 45–62.

Hekster, O. (2002), *Commodus: An Emperor at the Crossroads*, Amsterdam.

Hemelrijk, E. (1999), *Matrona Docta: Educated Women in the Roman Élite from Cornelia to Julia Domna*, London.

(2005), 'Priestesses of the imperial cult in the Latin west: titles and function', *L'Antiquité classique* 74: 137–70.

(2008), 'Patronesses and "mothers" of Roman *Collegia*', *Classical Antiquity* 27: 115–62.

Henderson, J. (2014), 'Was Julius a Caesar?', in T. Power and R. K. Gibson (eds.), *Suetonius the Biographer: Studies in Roman Lives*, Oxford: 81–110.

Henderson, M. I. (1963), 'The establishment of the *equester ordo*', *JRS* 53: 61–72.

Henzen, G. (1868), 'Monumenti: iscrizione militare', *Bullettino dell'Instituto di Corrispondenza Archeologica*: 71–3.

Herz, P. (1995), 'Kampf den Piraten? Zur Deutung zweier kaiserzeitlicher Inschriften', *ZPE* 107: 195–200.

Hijmans, S. (2010), 'Temples and priests of Sol in the city of Rome', *Mouseion* 10: 381–427.

Hill, H. (1930), 'Livy's account of the *equites*', *CPh* 25: 244–9.

(1932), 'Sulla's new senators in 81 BC', *CQ* 26: 170–7.

(1938), '*Equites* and *celeres*', *CPh* 33: 283–90.

(1939), '*Census equester*', *AJPh* 60: 357–62.

(1943), '*Aes equestre, aes hordearium*, and *triplex stipendium*', *CPh* 38: 132–4.

(1952), *The Roman Middle Class in the Republican Period*, Sheffield.

Hillard, T. W. (2005), '*Res publica* in theory and practice', in K. Welch and T. W. Hillard (eds.), *Roman Crossings: Theory and Practice in the Roman Republic*, Swansea: 1–48.

Hirt, A. M. (2010), *Imperial Mines and Quarries in the Roman World: Organizational Aspects 27 BC–AD 235*, Oxford.

Hoenigswald, G. S. (1962), 'The murder charges in Cicero's *Pro Cluentio*', *TAPA* 93: 109–23.

Hoffmann, D. (1969/70), *Das spätrömische Bewegungsheer und die Notitia Dignitatum*, 2 vols., Düsseldorf.

Hoffmann, F. (2010), 'Lost in translation? Beobachtungen zum Verhältnis des lateinischen und griechischen Textes der Gallusstele', in K. Lembke, M. Minas-Nerpel and S. Pfeiffer (eds.), *Tradition and Transformation: Egypt under Roman Rule*, Leiden: 149–58.

Hoffmann, F., Minas-Nerpel, M. and Pfeiffer, S. (2009), *Die dreisprachige Stele des C. Cornelius Gallus*, Berlin.

Hogan, P. P. and Kemezis, A. M. (2016), 'Introduction: the empire's second language?', *Classical World* 110: 31–42.

Holcombe, C. (1994), *In the Shadow of the Han: Literati Thought and Society at the Beginning of the Southern Dynasties*, Honolulu.

Holder, P. A. (1994), '*Legio II Parthica* in the reigns of Gordian III and Philip', *LCM* 19: 145–6.

Holleman, A. W. J. (1973), 'Ovid and the Lupercalia', *Historia* 22: 260–8.

Hollis, A. (2007), *Fragments of Roman Poetry*, Oxford.

Holtheide, B. (1980), '*Matrona stolata – femina stolata*', *ZPE* 38: 127–34.

Honoré, T. (2002), *Ulpian: Pioneer of Human Rights*, 2nd edition, Oxford.

Hope, V. (2000), 'Fighting for identity: the funerary commemoration of Italian gladiators', in A. Cooley (ed.), *The Epigraphic Landscape of Roman Italy*, London: 93–113.

Hopkins, K. (1961), 'Social mobility in the later Roman empire: the evidence of Ausonius', *CQ* 11: 239–49.

(1965), 'Elite mobility in the Roman empire', *P&P* 32: 12–26.

Hopkins, K. and Burton, G. (1983), 'Ambition and withdrawal: the senatorial aristocracy under the emperors', in K. Hopkins, *Death and Renewal*, Cambridge: 120–200.

Horsfall, N. (1989), *Cornelius Nepos: A Selection, Including the Lives of Cato and Atticus*, Oxford.

Horster, M. (1998), 'Ehrungen spätantiker Statthalter', *AntTard* 6: 37–59.

(2011), '*Princeps iuventutis*: concept, realisation, representation', in S. Benoist et al. (eds.), *Figures d'empire, fragments de mémoire: Pouvoirs et identités dans le monde romain impérial IIe s. av. n. è–VI s. de n. è.*, Lille: 73–103.

Houston, G. W. (1977), 'Vespasian's adlection of men *in senatum*', *AJPh* 98: 35–63.

(1981–2), 'The *lusus Troiae* and Augustan patriotism', *The Augustan Age* 1: 8–12.

Howe, L. L. (1942), *The Pretorian Prefect from Commodus to Diocletian (AD 180–305)*, Chicago.

Howell, P. (1980), *A Commentary on Book One of the Epigrams of Martial*, London.

Hug, A. (1918), '*Funus publicum*', in *RE* Suppl. III: 530–2.

Hughes, J. J. (1997) '*Inter tribunal et scaenam*: comedy and rhetoric in Rome', in W. J. Dominik (ed.), *Roman Eloquence: Rhetoric in Society and Literature*, London: 150–62.

Hula, E. (1900), 'Clavus 2', in *RE* IV.1: 4–9.

Humm, M. (2015), 'From 390 BC to Sentium: political and ideological aspects', in B. Mineo (ed.), *A Companion to Livy*, Oxford and Malden, MA: 342–65.

Humphrey, J. W. (1976), 'An Historical Commentary on Cassius Dio's Roman History Book 59 (Gaius Caligula)', Ph.D. thesis, University of British Columbia.

Humphries, M. (2003), 'Roman senators and absent emperors in Late Antiquity', *Acta ad Archaeologiam et Artium Historiam Pertinentia* 17: 27–46.

Hunt, P. (2007), 'Military forces', in P. Sabin, H. van Wees and M. Whitby (eds.), *The Cambridge History of Greek and Roman Warfare*, vol. I: *Greece, the Hellenistic World and the Rise of Rome*, Cambridge: 108–46.

Hunt, Y. (2012), 'Imperial Policies towards Pantomime and Public Entertainment'. Ph.D. thesis, University of Queensland.

Hurlet, F. (1997), *Les collègues du prince sous Auguste et Tibère*, Rome.

Hurley, D. W. (1991), 'A Historical and Historiographical Commentary on Suetonius' Life of C. Caligula', Ph.D. thesis, Columbia University.

Hurley, D. W. (ed.) (2001), *Suetonius: Divus Claudius*, Cambridge.

Hutchinson, G. O. (1998), *Cicero's Correspondence: A Literary Study*, Oxford.

Hüttemann, A. (2010), *Pompejanische Inschriften*, Stuttgart.

Huttner, U. (2008), 'Von Maximinus Thrax bis Aemilianus', in K. P. Johne, T. Gerhardt and U. Hartmann (eds.), *Deleto paene imperio Romano: Transformationsprozesse des Römischen Reiches im 3. Jahrhundert und ihre Rezeption in der Neuzeit*, Stuttgart: 161–221.

Hyland, A. (1990), *Equus: The Horse in the Roman World*, New Haven.

Ijsewijn, E. (1983/4), 'Gli *ordines decurionum* come base di reclutamento delle *militiae equestres* sotto il Principato', *BIHBR* 53–4:41–63.

Jackson, W. H. (1990), 'Knighthood and the Hohenstaufen imperial court under Frederick Barbarossa (1152–1190)', in C. Harper-Bill and R. Harvey (eds.), *The Ideals and Practice of Medieval Knighthood III*, Woodbridge: 101–20.

James, S. (2004), *The Excavations at Dura-Europos conducted by Yale University and the French Academy of Inscriptions and Letters 1928 to 1937, Volume 7: Arms and Armour*, London.

Jarrett, M. G. (1963), 'The African contribution to the imperial equestrian service', *Historia* 12: 209–26.

Johnson, M. J. (2009), *The Roman Imperial Mausoleum in Late Antiquity*, Cambridge.

Jones, A. H. M. (1953) 'Inflation under the Roman empire', *Economic History Review* n.s. 5: 293–318.

  (1955), 'The elections under Augustus', *JRS* 45: 9–21.

  (1960), *Studies in Roman Government and Law*, Oxford.

  (1964), *The Later Roman Empire, AD 284–602*, Oxford.

  (1972), *The Criminal Courts of the Roman Republic and Principate*, Oxford.

Jones, B. W. (1992), *The Emperor Domitian*, London.

Jones, B. W. (ed.) (1996), *Suetonius: Domitian*, London.

Jones, C. P. (1966), 'Towards a chronology of Plutarch's works', *JRS* 56: 61–74.

  (1967), 'Julius Naso and Julius Secundus', *HSCPh* 72: 279–88.

  (1971), *Plutarch and Rome*, Oxford.

  (1980), 'Prosopographical notes on the Second Sophistic', *GRBS* 21: 373–80.

  (1986), *Culture and Society in Lucian*, Cambridge, MA.

  (1999), 'Atticus in Ephesus', *ZPE* 124: 89–93.

  (2003), 'Epigraphica IV–V', *ZPE* 142: 127–33.

Jones, T. (2009), 'Pre-Augustan seating in Italy and the West', in T. Wilmott (ed.), *Roman Amphitheatres and Spectacula: A 21st-Century Perspective*, Oxford: 127–39.

Jongman, W. M. (1988), *The Economy and Society of Pompeii*, Amsterdam.

  (2007), 'The early Roman empire: consumption', in W. Scheidel, I. Morris and R. Saller (eds.), *The Cambridge Economic History of the Greco-Roman World*, Cambridge: 592–618.

Jördens, A. (2009), *Statthalterliche Verwaltung in der römischen Kaiserzeit: Studien zum Praefectus Aegypti*, Stuttgart.

Jory, E. J. (1981), 'The literary evidence for the beginnings of imperial pantomime', *BICS* 28: 147–61.

(1988), 'Publilius Syrus and the element of competition in the theatre of the Republic', in N. Horsfall (ed.), *Vir bonus discendi peritus: Studies in Celebration of Otto Skutsch's Eightieth Birthday*, London: 73–81.

Judge, E. A. (1974), '"Res publica restituta": a modern illusion?', in J. A. S. Evans (ed.), *Polis and Imperium: Studies in Honour of Edward Togo Salmon*, Toronto: 279–311.

Kaeuper, R. W. (2009), *Holy Warriors: The Religious Ideology of Chivalry*, Philadelphia.

Kaldellis, A. (2015), *The Byzantine Republic: People and Power in New Rome*, Cambridge, MA.

Kallet-Marx, R. (1990), 'The trial of Rutilius Rufus', *Phoenix* 44: 122–39.

Kamen, D. (2013), *Status in Classical Athens*, Princeton.

Kantor, G. (2011), 'Procuratorial jurisdiction in the *lex portorii Asiae*', *ZPE* 179: 155–8.

(2013), 'Law in Roman Phrygia: rules and jurisdictions', in P. Thonemann (ed.), *Roman Phrygia: Culture and Society*, Cambridge: 143–67.

Kay, P. (2014), *Rome's Economic Revolution*, Oxford.

Kaster, R. A. (1988), *Guardians of Language: The Grammarian and Society in Late Antiquity*, Berkeley.

Kaster, R. A. (ed.) (2006), *Cicero: Speech on Behalf of Publius Sestius*, Oxford.

Kautsky, J. H. (1997), *The Politics of Aristocratic Empires*, revised edition, New Brunswick.

Kazhdan, A. P. and Wharton Epstein, A. (1985), *Change in Byzantine Culture in the Eleventh and Twelfth Centuries*, Berkeley.

Keaveney, A. (2005), *Sulla: The Last Republican*, 2nd edition, London.

Kehoe, D. (1985), 'Tacitus and Sallustius Crispus', *CJ* 80: 247–54.

Keil, J. and von Premerstein, A. (eds.) (1914), *Bericht über eine dritte Reise in Lydien und den angrenzenden Gebieten Ioniens*, Vienna.

Kelder, J. M. (2012), 'Horseback riding and cavalry in Mycenaean Greece', *Ancient West and East* 11: 1–18.

Kelly, C. (1998), 'Emperors, government and bureaucracy', *CAH* XIII: 138–83.

(2004), *Ruling the Later Roman Empire*, Cambridge, MA.

(2006), 'Bureaucracy and government', in N. Lenski (ed.), *The Cambridge Companion to the Age of Constantine*, Cambridge: 183–204.

Kelly, G. (2008), *Ammianus Marcellinus: The Allusive Historian*, Cambridge.

(2013), 'Pliny and Symmachus', *Arethusa* 46: 261–87.

Kemezis, A. M. (2014), *Greek Narratives of the Roman Empire under the Severans: Cassius Dio, Philostratus, and Herodian*, Cambridge.

(2016), '*Inglorius labor*? The rhetoric of glory and utility in Plutarch's *Precepts* and Tacitus' *Agricola*', *Classical World* 110: 87–177.

Kennedy, D. L. (1979), 'Ti. Claudius Subatianus Aquila, "First Prefect of Mesopotamia"', *ZPE* 36: 255–62.

(1987), 'The garrisoning of Mesopotamia in the late Antonine and early Severan period', *Antichthon* 21: 57–66.

(1997), 'The special command of M. Valerius Lollianus', in E. Dabrowa (ed.), *Donum Amicitiae: Studies in Ancient History*, Krakow: 79–81.

Kennedy, G. (1972), *The Art of Rhetoric in the Roman World*, Princeton.

Kennell, N. M. (2009), 'The Greek ephebate in the Roman period', *International Journal of the History of Sport* 26: 323–42.

Keppie, L. (1983), *Colonisation and Veteran Settlement in Italy, 47–14 BC*, London.

(1984), *The Making of the Roman Army: From Republic to Empire*, London.

(1996), 'The praetorian guard before Sejanus', *Athenaeum* 84: 101–24.

(2003), 'Having been a soldier: the commemoration of military service on funerary monuments of the early Roman empire', in J. J. Wilkes (ed.), *Documenting the Roman Army: Essays in Honour of Margaret Roxan*, London: 31–53.

Keyes, C. W. (1915), 'The Rise of the Equites in the Third Century of the Roman Empire', Ph.D. thesis, Princeton University.

Kienast, D. (1966), *Untersuchungen zu den Kriegsflotten der römischen Kaiserzeit*, Bonn.

(2009), *Augustus: Prinzeps und Monarch*, 4th edition, Darmstadt.

Kleijwegt, M. (1991), *Ancient Youth: The Ambiguity of Youth and the Absence of Adolescence in Greco-Roman Society*, Amsterdam.

(1994), '*Iuvenes* and Roman imperial society', *Acta Classica* 37: 79–102.

Kleiner, D. E. E. (1977), *Roman Group Portraiture: The Funerary Reliefs of the Late Republic and Early Empire*, New York and London.

Kleiner, D. E. E. and Kleiner, F. S. (1975), 'A heroic funerary relief on the Via Appia', *AA* 90: 250–64.

Kolb, F. (1977a), 'Der Aufstand der Provinz Africa Proconsularis im Jahr 238 n. Chr: Die wirtschaftlichen und sozialen Hintergründe', *Historia* 26: 440–78.

(1977b), 'Zur Statussymbolik im antiken Rom', *Chiron* 7: 239–59.

Kolendo, J. (1981), 'La répartition des places aux spectacles et la stratification sociale dans l'Empire Romain: à propos des inscriptions sur les gradins des amphithéâtres et théâtres', *Ktema* 6: 301–15.

König, J. (2005), *Athletics and Literature in the Roman Empire*, Cambridge.

Kuhn, A. B. (2010), 'Senatorial and Equestrian Rank in the Cities of Roman Asia Minor, *c.*30 BC–AD 212', D.Phil. thesis, University of Oxford.

(2015), 'The dynamics of social status and prestige in Pliny, Juvenal and Martial', in A. B. Kuhn (ed.), *Social Status and Prestige in the Graeco-Roman World*, Stuttgart: 9–28.

Kulikowski, M. (2014), 'Regional dynasties and imperial court', in J. Wienand (ed.), *Contested Monarchy: Integrating the Roman Empire in the Fourth Century AD*, New York: 135–48.

Kupiszewski, H. (1954), 'The *Iuridicus Alexandreae*', *JJP* 7–8:187–204.

Lacey, W. K. (1996), *Augustus and the Principate: The Evolution of the System*, Leeds.

Ladjimi Sebai, L. (1977), '*Egregiae memoriae filia*? À propos d'une inscription inedited d'Haidra (Tunisie)', *Antiquités africaines* 11: 161–5.

Laes, C. and Strubbe, J. (2014), *Youth in the Roman Empire: The Young and the Restless Years?*, Cambridge.

Lafaurie, J. (1975), 'L'empire gaulois: apport de la numismatique', in *ANRW* II.2: 853–1012.

Laffi, U. (1977), 'La procuratela quadriennale di Q. Octavius Saggita in Vindalicis et Raetis et in valle Poenina', *Athenaeum* 55: 369–79.

Lamoine, L. (2003), 'Préteur, vergobret, *princeps* en Gaule Narbonnaise et dans les trois Gaules: pourquoi faut-il reprendre le dossier?', in M. Cébeillac-Gervasoni and L. Lamoine (eds.), *Les élites et leurs facettes: les élites locales dans le monde hellénistique et romain*, Rome: 187–204.

Le Bohec, Y. (2004), 'Gallien et l'encadrement senatorial de l'armée romaine', *REMA* 1: 123–32.

Leach, E. W. (2003), '*Otium* as *luxuria*: economy of status in the Younger Pliny', *Arethusa* 36: 147–65.

Lebek, W. (1990), 'Standeswürde und Berufsverbot unter Tiberius: das SC der Tabula Larinas', *ZPE* 81: 37–96.

(1991), 'Das SC der Tabula Larinas: Rittermusterung und andere Probleme', *ZPE* 85: 41–70.

(1993), 'Roms Ritter und Roms Pleps in den Senatsbeschlüssen für Germanicus Caesar und Drusus Caesar', *ZPE* 95: 81–120.

Lee, A. D. (2007), *War in Late Antiquity: A Social History*, Oxford and Malden, MA.

Lefebure, S. (1999), 'Donner, recevoir: les chevaliers dans les hommages publics d'Afrique', in S. Demougin, H. Devijver and M.-T. Raepsaet-Charlier (eds.), *L'ordre équestre: histoire d'une aristocratie (IIe siècle av. J.-C.–IIIe siècle ap. J.-C)*, Rome: 513–78.

Leigh, R. (2015), *On Theriac to Piso, Attributed to Galen*, Leiden.

Lenaghan, J. (2016), 'Re-use in fourth-century portrait statues', in R. R. R. Smith and B. Ward-Perkins (eds.), *The Last Statues of Antiquity*, Oxford: 267–79.

Lendon, J. E. (1997), *Empire of Honour: The Art of Government in the Roman World*, Oxford.

(2005), *Soldiers and Ghosts: A History of Battle in Classical Antiquity*, New Haven.

Lenski, N. (2002), *Failure of Empire: Valens and the Roman State in the Fourth Century AD*, Berkeley.

Lepelley, C. (1986), 'Fine dell'ordine equestre: le tappe dell'unificazione della classe dirigente romana nel IV secolo', in A. Giardina (ed.), *Società romana et impero tardoantico* I, Rome: 228–44.

(1999), 'Du triomphe à la disparition: le destin de l'ordre équestre de Dioclétien à Théodose', in S. Demougin, H. Devijver and M.-T. Raepsaet-Charlier (eds.), *L'ordre équestre: histoire d'une aristocratie (IIe siècle av. J.-C.–IIIe siècle ap. J.-C.)*, Rome: 629–46.

Letta, C. (1976), 'La dinastia dei Cozii e la romanizazzione delle Alpi occidentali', *Athenaeum* 54: 37–76.

Leunissen, P. M. M. (1993), 'Conventions of patronage in senatorial careers under the Principate', *Chiron* 23: 101–20.

Levene, D. S. (2004), 'Reading Cicero's narratives', in J. Powell and J. Paterson (eds.), *Cicero the Advocate*, Oxford: 117–46.

Levick, B. (1983), 'The *senatus consultum* from Larinum', *JRS* 73: 93–115.

(1990), *Claudius*, London.

(1991), 'A note on the *latus clavus*', *Athenaeum* 79: 239–44.

(2010), *Augustus: Image and Substance*, London.

(2011), 'Velleius Paterculus as senator: a dream with footnotes', in E. Cowan (ed.), *Velleius Paterculus: Making History*, Swansea: 1–16.

(2013), 'C. Plinius Secundus', in T. J. Cornell et al. (eds.), *The Fragments of the Roman Historians*, Oxford: 525–34.

Lewis, R. G. (2006), *Asconius: Commentaries on Speeches of Cicero*, Oxford.

Leyser, K. (1994), 'Early medieval canon law and the beginnings of knighthood', in T. Reuter (ed.), *Communications and Power in Medieval Europe: The Carolingian and Ottonian Centuries*, London: 51–71.

Liebeschuetz, J. H. W. G. (1972), *Antioch: City and Imperial Administration in the Later Roman Empire*, Oxford.

Liebs, D. (1981), 'Das *ius gladii* der römischen Provinzgouverneure in der Kaiserzeit', *ZPE* 43: 217–23.

(2010), *Hofjuristen der römischen Kaiser bis Justinian*, Munich.

Linderski, J. (1977), 'Review of C. Nicolet, *L'ordre équestre a l'époque républicaine (312–43 av. J.-C.). Vol. 2: Prosopographie des chevaliers romains*', *CPh* 72: 55–60.

(2002), 'Romans in the province of Pesaro and Urbino', *JRA* 15: 577–80.

Lindsay, H. (1994), 'Suetonius as *ab epistulis* to Hadrian and the early history of the imperial correspondence', *Historia* 43: 454–68.

Lindsay, H. (ed.) (1993), *Suetonius: Caligula*, London.

(1995), *Suetonius: Tiberius*, London.

Lintott, A. (1981), 'The *leges de repetundis* and associate measures under the Republic', *ZSS* 98: 162–212.

(1992), *Judicial Reform and Land Reform in the Roman Republic*, Cambridge.

(1994), 'Political history, 146–95 BC', *CAH* IX^2: 40–103.

(1999), *The Constitution of the Roman Republic*, Oxford.

(2001), 'Aristotle and the mixed constitution', in R. Brock and S. Hodkinson (eds.), *Alternatives to Athens: Varieties of Political Organization and Community in Ancient Greece*, Oxford: 152–66.

(2004), 'Legal procedure in Cicero's time', in J. Powell and J. Paterson (eds.), *Cicero the Advocate*, Oxford: 61–78.

(2008), *Cicero as Evidence: A Historian's Companion*, Oxford.

Liu, J. (2009), *Collegia Centonariorum: The Guilds of Textile Dealers in the Roman West*, Leiden.

(2014), 'AE 1998, 282: A case study of public benefaction and local politics', in N. Dimitrova and J. Bodel (eds.), *Ancient Documents and their Contexts*, Leiden: 248–62.

Lizzi Testa, R. (2009), 'Alle origini della tradizione pagana su Costantino e il senato romano', in P. Rousseau and M. Papoutsakis (eds.), *Transformations of Late Antiquity: Essays for Peter Brown*, Farnham: 85–128.

Lo Cascio, E. (2000), *Il Princeps e il suo Impero: Studia di storia amministrativa e finanziaria romana*, Bari.

(2005), 'The emperor and his administration', in *CAH* XII²: 131–83.

(2015), 'The imperial property and its development', in P. Erdkamp, K. Verboven and A. Zuiderhoek (eds.), *Ownership and Exploitation of Land and Natural Resources in the Roman World*, Oxford: 62–70.

Lobur, J. A (2008), *Consensus, Concordia, and the Formation of Roman Imperial Ideology*, London.

(2011), 'Resuscitating a text: Velleius' history as cultural evidence', in E. Cowan (ed.), *Velleius Paterculus: Making History*, Swansea: 203–18.

Löhken, H. (1982), *Ordines Dignitatum: Untersuchungen zur formalen Konstituierung der spätaniken Führungsschicht*, Cologne and Vienna.

Lomas, K. (2004), 'A Volscian mafia? Cicero and his Italian clients in the forensic speeches', in J. Powell and J. Paterson (eds.), *Cicero the Advocate*, Oxford: 96–116.

Loriot, X. (2006), 'Les contingents de l'armée de Valérien', in M.-H. Quet (ed.), *La 'crise' de l'Empire romain de Marc Aurèle à Constantin*, Paris: 329–44.

Lott, J. B. (2012), *Death and Dynasty in Early Imperial Rome: Key Sources, with Text, Translation, and Commentary*, Cambridge.

Louis, N. (2010), *Commentaire historique et traduction du Diuus Augustus de Suétone*, Brussels.

Low, P. (2002), 'Cavalry identity and democratic ideology in early fourth-century Athens', *PCPhS* 48: 102–22.

Lucas, C. (1940), 'Notes on the *curatores rei publicae* of Roman Africa', *JRS* 30: 56–74.

Luscombe, D. E. and Evans, G. R. (1988), 'The twelfth-century renaissance', in J. H. Burns (ed.), *The Cambridge History of Medieval Political Thought, c.305–1450*, Cambridge: 306–38.

Luther, A. (2008), 'Das gallische Sonderreich', in K.-P. Johne, U. Hartmann and T. Gerhardt (eds.), *Die Zeit der Soldatenkaiser: Krise und Transformation des Römischen Reiches im 3. Jahrhundert n. Chr. (235–284)*, 2 vols., Berlin: 325–42.

Lyne, R. O. A. M. (1995), *Horace: Behind the Public Poetry*, New Haven.

MacCormack, S. G. (1981), *Art and Ceremony in Late Antiquity*, Berkeley.

Madsen, J. M. (2006), 'Intellectual resistance to Roman hegemony and its representativity', in T. Bekker-Nielsen (ed.), *Rome and the Black Sea Region: Domination, Romanisation, Resistance*, Aarhus: 63–84.

(2009), *Eager to be Roman: Greek Response to Roman Rule in Pontus and Bithynia*, London.

Maenchen-Helfen, O. J. (1973), *The World of the Huns: Studies in their History and Culture*, ed. Max Knight, Berkeley.

Magioncalda, A. (1999), 'I governatori delle province procuratorie: carriere', in S. Demougin, H. Devijver and M.-T. Raepsaet-Charlier (eds.), *L'ordre équestre: histoire d'une aristocratie (IIe siècle av. J.-C.–IIIe siècle ap. J.-C.)*, Rome: 391–462.

Mallan, C. T. (2013), 'The style, method, and programme of Xiphilinus' *Epitome* of Cassius Dio's *Roman History*', *GRBS* 53: 610–44.

Malloch, S. J. V. (ed.) (2013), *The Annals of Tacitus: Book 11*, Cambridge.

Malnati, T. P. (1987–8), 'Juvenal and Martial on social mobility', *CJ* 83: 133–41.

Mander, J. (2013), *Portraits of Children on Roman Funerary Monuments*, Cambridge.

Mankin, D. (ed.) (1995), *Horace: Epodes*, Cambridge.

Mann, M. (1986), *The Sources of Social Power*, vol. I: *A History of Power from the Beginning to AD 1760*, Cambridge.

Manuwald, G. (ed.) (2007), *Cicero, Philippics 3–9: Introduction, Translation and Commentary*, Berlin.

Marcone, A. (1998), 'Late Roman social relations', in *CAH* XIII: 338–70.

Marshall, B. A. (1975), 'Q. Cicero, Hortensius and the *lex Aurelia*', *RhM* 118: 136–52.

(1985), *A Historical Commentary on Asconius*, Columbia, MO.

Marshall, E. A. (1986), 'A Biography of Titus Pomponius Atticus', Ph.D. thesis, Harvard University.

Mason, H. (1974), *Greek Terms for Roman Institutions: A Lexicon and Analysis*, Toronto.

Massa-Pairault, F.-H. (1995), '"Eques Romanus – eques Latinus" (Ve–IVe siècle)', *MEFRA* 107: 33–70.

Mathisen, R. W. (1993), *Roman Aristocrats in Barbarian Gaul: Strategies for Survival in an Age of Transition*, Austin.

Matthews, J. F. (1975), *Western Aristocracies and Imperial Court*, Oxford.

(1989), *The Roman Empire of Ammianus*, London.

(2000a), *Laying Down the Law: A Study of the Theodosian Code*, New Haven.

(2000b), 'The Roman empire and the proliferation of elites', *Arethusa* 33: 429–46.

(2010), *Roman Perspectives: Studies in the Social, Political and Cultural History of the First to Fifth Centuries*, Swansea.

Mattingly, H. B. (1970), 'The extortion law of the *Tabula Bembina*', *JRS* 60: 154–68.

(1975a), 'The extortion law of Servilius Glaucia', *CQ* 25: 255–63.

(1975b), 'The jury-panel of the *lex repetundarum*', *Latomus* 34: 726–28.

Maurizi, L. (2013), *Il cursus honorum senatorio da Augusto a Traiano: sviluppi formali e stilistic nell'epigrafia latina e greca*, Helsinki.

Maxfield, V. (1981), *The Military Decorations of the Roman Army*, Berkeley.

Mayer, E. (2012), *The Ancient Middle Classes: Urban Life and Aesthetics in the Roman Empire, 100 BCE–250 CE*, Cambridge, MA.

Mayer, R. (ed.) (1994), *Horace: Epistles Book 1*, Cambridge.

McCall, J. B. (2002), *The Cavalry of the Roman Republic: Cavalry Combat and Elite Reputations in the Middle and Late Republic*, London.

McCormick, M. (1986), *Eternal Victory: Triumphal Rulership in Late Antiquity, Byzantium and the Early Medieval West*, Cambridge.

McDonnell, M. (2006), *Roman Manliness: Virtus in the Roman Republic*, Cambridge.

(2011), '*Virtus* as a specialization in the middle Republic', in W. Blösel and K.-J. Hölkeskamp (eds.), *Von der militia equestris zur militia urbana: Prominenzrollen und Karrierefelder im antiken Rome*, Stuttgart: 29–42.

McEvoy, M. A. (2013), *Child Emperor Rule in the Late Roman West, AD 367–455*, Oxford.

(2016), 'Becoming Roman? The not-so-curious case of Aspar and the Ardaburii', *Journal of Late Antiquity* 9: 482–511.

McGinn, T. A. J. (1992), 'The *SC* from Larinum and the repression of adultery at Rome', *ZPE* 93: 273–95.

(1999), 'The social policy of emperor Constantine in *Codex Theodosianus* 4,6,3', *Tijdschrift voor Rechtsgeschiedenis* 67: 57–73.

(2003), *Prostitution, Sexuality, and the Law in Ancient Rome*, Oxford.

McGushin, P. (ed.) (1992), *Sallust: The Histories. Volume I*, Oxford.

McLynn, N. (2008), 'Crying wolf: the pope and the Lupercalia', *JRS* 98: 161–75.

McNelis, C. (2002), 'Greek grammarians and Roman society during the early empire: Statius' father and his contemporaries', *Classical Antiquity* 21: 67–94.

Meier, C. (1966), *Res Publica Amissa: Eine Studie zu Verfassung und Geschichte der späten römischen Republik*, Wiesbaden.

Mennen, I. (2011), *Power and Status in the Roman Empire, AD 193–284*, Leiden.

Merkelbach, R. (1985), 'Grabmal eines *tribunus militum* aus Perinthos', *ZPE* 59: 40.

Millar, F. G. B. (1963a), 'The *fiscus* in the first two centuries', *JRS* 53: 29–42.

(1963b), 'Review of H.-G. Pflaum, *Les carrières procuratoriennes équestres sous le haut-empire romain*', *JRS* 53: 194–200.

(1964a), 'Some evidence on the meaning of Tacitus, *Annals* XII.60', *Historia* 13: 180–7.

(1964b), 'The *aerarium* and its officials under the empire', *JRS* 54: 33–40.

(1965a), 'Epictetus and the imperial court', *JRS* 55: 141–8.

(1965b), 'The development of jurisdiction by imperial procurators: further evidence', *Historia* 14: 362–7.

(1966), 'Emperors at work', *JRS* 57: 9–19.

(1973), 'Triumvirate and principate', *JRS* 63: 50–67.

(1977), *The Emperor in the Roman World*, London.

(1983) 'Empire and city, Augustus to Julian: obligations, excuses and status', *JRS* 73: 76–96.

(1984), 'The political character of the classical Roman Republic, 200–151 BC', *JRS* 74: 1–19.

(1986), 'Politics, persuasion and the people before the Social War (150–90 BC)', *JRS* 76: 1–11.

(1988), 'Cornelius Nepos, "Atticus" and the Roman Revolution', *G&R* 35: 40–55.

(1989), 'Senatorial provinces: an institutionalized ghost', *Ancient World* 20: 93–7.

(1993), 'Ovid and the Domus Augusta: Rome seen from Tomoi', *JRS* 83: 1–17.

(1998), *The Crowd in Rome in the Late Republic*, Ann Arbor.

(2002), *The Roman Republic in Political Thought*, Hanover and London.

Milner, N. P. (2011), 'Athletics, army recruitment and heroisation: L. Sep. Fl. Flavillianus of Oinoanda', *AS* 61: 151–67.

Milnor, K. (2014), *Graffiti and the Literary Landscape in Roman Pompeii*, Oxford.

Minas-Nerpel, M. and Pfeiffer, S. (2010), 'Establishing Roman rule in Egypt: the trilingual stela of C. Cornelius Gallus from Philae', in K. Lembke, M. Minas-Nerpel and S. Pfeiffer (eds.), *Tradition and Transformation: Egypt under Roman Rule*, Leiden: 265–98.

Mitchell, S. (1977), 'R.E.C.A.M. notes and studies no. 1: inscriptions of Anycra', *AS* 27: 63–103.

(2003), 'Inscriptions from Melli (Kocaaliler) in Pisidia', *AS* 53: 139–59.

Mitchell, S. and French, D. (2012), *The Greek and Latin Inscriptions of Ankara (Ancyra)*, vol. I: *From Augustus to the End of the Third Century AD*, Munich.

Mitchell, T. N. (1979), *Cicero: The Ascending Years*, New Haven and London.

Mittag, A. and Mutschler, F.-H. (2008), 'Epilogue', in F.-H. Mutschler and A. Mittag (eds.), *Conceiving the Empire: Rome and China Compared*, Oxford: 421–47.

Modrzejewski, J. and Zawadzki, T. (1967), 'La date de la mort d'Ulpien et la préfecture du prétoire au début du règne d'Alexandre Sévère', *RD* 40: 565–611.

Momigliano, A. (1966), '*Procum patricium*', *JRS* 56: 16–24.

Mommsen, T. (1884), '*Protectores Augusti*', *Ephemeris Epigraphica* 5: 121–41.

(1887–8), *Römisches Staatsrecht*, 3 vols., Leipzig.

(1905), *Theodosiani libri XVI cum constitutionibus Sirmondianis et leges novellae ad Theodosianum pertinentes*, Berlin.

Morris, C. (1978), '*Equestris ordo*: chivalry as a vocation in the twelfth century', *Studies in Church History* 15: 87–96.

Morstein-Marx, R. (1998), 'Publicity, popularity and patronage in the *Commentariolum Petitionis*', *Classical Antiquity* 17: 259–88.

(2004), *Mass Oratory and Political Power in the Late Roman Republic*, Cambridge.

Mosca, G. (1939), *The Ruling Class*, ed. A. Livingston, trans. H. D. Kahn, New York.

Motschmann, C. (2002), *Die Religionspolitik Marc Aurels*, Stuttgart.

Mouritsen, H. (1998), *Italian Unification: A Study in Ancient and Modern Historiography*, Bulletin of the Institute of Classical Studies Supplement 70, London.

(2001), *Plebs and Politics in the Late Roman Republic*, Cambridge.

(2005), 'Freedmen and decurions: epitaphs and social history in imperial Italy', *JRS* 95: 38–63.

(2011), *The Freedman in the Roman World*, Cambridge.

Murphy, T. (1998), 'Cicero's first readers: epistolary evidence for the dissemination of his works', *CQ* 48: 492–505.

Mutschler, F.-H. and Mittag, A. (eds.) (2008), *Conceiving the Empire: Rome and China Compared*, Oxford.

Näf, B. (1995), *Senatorisches Standesbewusstsein in spätrömischer Zeit*, Freiburg.

Nasti, F. (1997), 'Il prefetto del pretorio di *CIL* VI 1638 (= D. 1331) e la sua carriera', *ZPE* 117: 281–90.

Neri, V. (1981), 'L'elogio della cultura e l'elogio delle virtù politiche nell'epigrafia latina del IV secolo d. C.', *Epigraphica* 43: 175–201.

Nesselhauf, H. (1964), '*Patrimonium* and *res privata* des römischen Kaisers', *BHAC* 1963, Bonn: 73–94.

Newbold, R. F. (1975), 'Cassius Dio and the games', *L'Antiquité Classique* 44: 589–604.

Newby, Z. (2005), *Greek Athletics in the Roman World: Victory and Virtue*, Oxford.

Nicasie, M. (1998), *Twilight of Empire: The Roman Army from the Reign of Diocletian until the Battle of Adrianople*, Amsterdam.

Nicholson, J. (1994), 'The delivery and confidentiality of Cicero's letters', *Classical Journal* 90: 33–63.

Nicolet, C. (1962), '*Les equites campani* et leurs répresentations figurées', *MEFRA* 74: 463–517.

(1967a), '*Eques Romanus ex inquisitione*: à propos d'une inscription de Prousias de l'Hypios', *BCH* 91: 411–22.

(1967b), '*Tribuni militum a populo*', *MEFRA* 79: 29–76.

(1974), *L'ordre équestre a l'époque républicaine (312–43 av. J.-C.)*, 2 vols., Paris. (Vol. I originally published in 1966.)

(1976), 'Le cens senatorial sous la Republique et sous Auguste', *JRS* 66: 20–38.

(1980), *The World of the Citizen in Republican Rome*, trans. P. S. Falla, Berkeley.

(1984), 'Augustus, government, and the propertied classes', in F. Millar and E. Segal (eds.), *Caesar Augustus: Seven Aspects*, Oxford: 89–128.

Nicols, J. (2014), *Civic Patronage in the Roman Empire*, Leiden.

Nicols, M. (2010), 'Contemporary perspectives on luxury building in second-century BC Rome', *PBSR* 78: 39–61.

Nisbet, R. G. M. and Hubbard, M. (1978), *A Commentary on Horace: Odes Book II*, Oxford.

Nisbet, R. G. M. and Rudd, N. (2004), *A Commentary on Horace: Odes Book III*, Oxford.

Nixon, C. E. V. and Rodgers, B. S. (1994), *In Praise of Later Roman Emperors: The Panegyrici Latini*, Berkeley.

Nonnis, D. (1995–6), 'Un patrono dei dendrofori di Lavinium: onori e munificenza in un dossier epigrafico di età severiana', *RPAA* 68: 235–62.

Noreña, C. (2011), *Imperial Ideals in the Roman West: Representation, Circulation, Power*, Cambridge.

North, J. A. (1990), 'Democratic politics in Republican Rome', *P&P* 126: 3–21.
  (2008), 'Caesar at the Lupercalia', *JRS* 98: 144–60.

North, J. A. and McLynn, N. (2008), 'Postscript to the Lupercalia: from Caesar to Andromachus', *JRS* 98: 176–81.

Nowakowski, P. (2011), 'The family of Titus Flavius Glaukos, procurator of βυθίη Κύπρος', *Cahier du Centre d'Études Chypriotes* 41: 283–8.

Nutton, V. (1971), 'L. Gellius Maximus, physician and procurator', *CQ* 21: 262–72.
  (1977), 'Archiatri and the medical profession in antiquity', *PBSR* 45: 191–226.
  (1978), 'The beneficial ideology', in P. D. A. Garnsey and C. R. Whittaker (eds.), *Imperialism in the Ancient World*, Cambridge: 209–21.

Oakley, S. P. (1985), 'Single combat in the Roman Republic', *CQ* 35: 392–410.
  (1998), *A Commentary on Livy Books VI–X. Volume II: Books VII–VIII*, Oxford.
  (2005a), *A Commentary on Livy Books VI–X. Volume III: Book IX*, Oxford.
  (2005b), *A Commentary on Livy Books VI–X. Volume IV: Book X*, Oxford.

Ogilvie, R. M. (1970), *A Commentary on Livy Books 1–5*, Oxford.

Oliver, J. H. (1949), 'Two Athenian poets', in *Commemorative Studies in Honour of Theodore Leslie Shear*, Hesperia Supplements 8: 243–58.
  (1970), *Marcus Aurelius: Aspects of Civic and Cultural Policy in the East*, Princeton.
  (1989), *Greek Constitutions of Early Roman Emperors from Inscriptions and Papyri*, Philadelphia.

Oost, S. I. (1963), 'Cyrene, 96–74 BC', *CP* 58: 11–25.

Orlin, E. (2010), *Foreign Cults in Rome: Creating a Roman Empire*, Oxford.

Osgood, J. (2006), *Caesar's Legacy: Civil War and the Emergence of the Roman Empire*, Cambridge.
  (2011), *Claudius Caesar: Image and Power in the Early Roman Empire*, Cambridge.

Osier, J. F. (1974), 'The Rise of the Ordo Equester in the Third Century of the Roman Empire', Ph.D. thesis, University of Michigan.

Panayotakis, C. (ed.) (2010), *Decimus Laberius: The Fragments*, Cambridge.

Panciera, S. (1970), 'Tra epigrafia e topografia (I)', *Archeologia Classica* 22: 131–63.

(2006), 'L'epigrafia Latina nel passaggio dalla repubblica all'impero', in *Epigrafi, epigrafia, epigrafisti*, Rome: 83–101.

Parsons, P. J. (1967), 'Philippus Arabs and Egypt', *JRS* 57: 134–61.

(1970), 'M. Aurelius Zeno Januarius', in D. H. Samuel (ed.), *Proceedings of the Twelfth International Congress of Papyrology, Ann Arbor, 1968*, Toronto: 329–97.

(1976), 'Petitions and a letter: the grammarian's complaint', in *Collectanea Papyrologica: Texts Published in Honor of H. C. Youtie*, Bonn: 409–46.

Pasqualini, A. (2008), 'Mappa liturgica dei flamini minori di Roma', in M. L. Caldelli, G. L. Gregori and S. Orlandi (eds.), *Epigrafia 2006: Atti della XIV recontre sur l'epigraphie in onore di Silvio Panciera con altri contributi di colleghi, allievi e collaboratori*, Rome: 437–52.

Paterson, J. (2007), 'Friends in high places: the creation of the court of the Roman emperor', in A. J. S. Spawforth (ed.), *The Court and Court Society in Ancient Monarchies*, Cambridge: 121–56.

Patterson, J. R. (2006), *Landscapes and Cities: Rural Settlement and Civic Transformation in Early Imperial Italy*, Oxford.

Pavis d'Escurac, H. (1976), *La préfecture de l'annone: service administratif impérial d'Auguste à Constantine*, Rome.

Peachin, M. (1989), 'The office of the memory', in E. Chyrsos (ed.), *Studien zur Geschichte der römischen Spätantike: Festgabe für Professor Johannes Straub*, Athens: 168–208.

(1990), *Roman Imperial Titulature and Chronology, AD 235–284*, Amsterdam.

(1996), *Iudex vice Caesaris: Deputy Emperors and the Administration of Justice during the Principate*, Stuttgart.

(2004), *Frontinus and the curae of the curator aquarum*, Stuttgart.

Pedersen, F. S. (1976), *Late Roman Public Professionalism*, Odense.

Pedroni, L. (2010), 'Il nome die cavalieri Romani in età medio-Repubblicana', *REA* 112: 353–61.

Pelling, C. (1988), *Plutarch: Life of Antony*, Cambridge.

Petersen, H. (1955), 'Senatorial and equestrian governors in the third century AD', *JRS* 45: 47–57.

Pflaum, H.-G. (1948), *Le marbre de Thorigny*, Paris.

(1950), *Les procurateurs équestres sous le Haut-Empire romain*, Paris.

(1959), 'Lucien de Samosate, *Archistator Praefecti Aegypti*, d'après une inscription de Césarée de Maurétanie', *MEFRA* 71: 281–6.

(1960), *Les carrières procuratoriennes équestres sous le Haut-Empire romain*, vols. I–II, Paris.

(1961), *Les carrières procuratoriennes équestres sous le Haut-Empire romain*, vol. III, Paris.

(1968), 'Les juges des cinq décuries originaires d'Afrique romaine', *Antiquités africaines* 2: 153–95.

(1970), 'Titulature et rang social sous le Haut-Empire', in C. Nicolet (ed.), *Recherches sur les structures sociales dans l'antiquité classique*, Paris: 159–85.

(1971), 'Une lettre de promotion de l'empereur Marc Aurele pour un procur-ateur ducenaire de Gaule Narbonnaise', *BJ* 171: 349–66.

(1974), *Abrégé des procurateurs équestres*, Paris.

(1976), 'Zur Reform des Kaisers Gallienus', *Historia* 25: 109–17.

(1978), 'Les salaires des magistrats et fonctionnaires du Haut-Empire', in *Les 'dévaluations' à Rome: époque républicaine et impériales. Volume 1.* Paris: 311–15.

(1982), *Les carrières procuratoriennes équestres sous le Haut-Empire romain: Supplèment*, Paris.

Phang, S. E. (2001), *The Marriage of Roman Soldiers (13 BC–AD 235): Law and Family in the Imperial Army*, Leiden.

Pina Polo, F. (2011), 'Consuls as *curatores pacis deorum*', in H. Beck et al. (eds.), *Consuls and Res Publica: Holding High Office in the Roman Republic*, Cambridge: 97–115.

Piso, I. (1980), 'Beiträge zu den Fasten Dakiens im 3. Jahrhundert', *ZPE* 40: 273–82.

(1982), 'Maximinus Thrax und die Provinz Dazien', *ZPE* 49: 225–38.

(1999), 'Les chevaliers romains dans l'armée impériale et les implications de l'*imperium*', in S. Demougin, H. Devijver and M.-T. Raepsaet-Charlier (eds.), *L'ordre équestre: histoire d'une aristocratie (IIe siècle av. J.-C.–IIIe siècle ap. J.-C.)*, Rome: 321–50.

(2014), 'Zur Reform des Gallienus anläßlich zweier neur Inschriften aus den Lagerthermen von Potaissa', *Tyche* 29: 125–46.

Pleket, H. W. (1969), '*Collegium iuvenum Nemesiorum*: a note on ancient youth-organisations', *Mnemosyne* 22: 281–98.

(2012), 'Ephebes and horses', *Mnemosyne* 65: 324–8.

Pobjoy, M. (2000), 'Building inscriptions in Republican Italy: euergetism, respon-sibility, and civic virtue', in A. E. Cooley (ed.), *The Epigraphic Landscape of Roman Italy*, London: 77–92.

(2007), 'Epigraphy and numismatics', in N. Rosenstein and R. Morstein-Marx (eds.), *A Companion to the Roman Republic*, Oxford and Malden, MA: 51–80.

Pollard, N. (2000), *Soldiers, Cities, and Civilians in Roman Syria*, Ann Arbor.

Porena, P. (2003), *Le origini della prefettura del pretorio tardoantica*, Rome.

(2006), 'L'Italia prima di Ponte Milvio e la carrier di Caecilianus', *Epigraphica* 68: 117–54.

Potter, D. S. (1999), 'Entertainers in the Roman empire', in D. S. Potter and D. J. Mattingly (eds.), *Life, Death, and Entertainment in the Roman Empire*, Ann Arbor: 256–325.

(2004), *The Roman Empire at Bay, AD 180–395*, London.

(2010), 'Caesar and the Helvetians', in G. Fagan and M. Trundle (eds.), *New Perspectives on Ancient Warfare*, Leiden: 305–29.

(2011), 'Holding court in Republican Rome (105–44)', *AJPh* 132: 59–80.

Poulantzas, N. (1978), *State, Power, Socialism*, trans. P. Camiller, London.

Poulson, B. (1991), 'The Dioscuri and ruler ideology', *Symbolae Osolenses* 66: 119–46.

Powis, J. K. (1984), *Aristocracy*, Oxford.

Prag, J. R. W. (2007), '*Auxilia* and *gymnasia*: a Sicilian model of Roman imperialism', *JRS* 97: 68–100.

    (2010), 'Troops and commanders: *auxilia externa* under the Roman Republic', in D. Bonanno, R. Marino and D. Motta (eds.), *Truppe e Comandanti nel mondo antico*, Palermo: 101–13.

    (2011), 'Provincial governors and auxiliary soldiers', in N. Barrandon and F. Kirbihler (eds.), *Les gouverners et les provinciaux sous la République romaine*, Rennes: 15–28.

Prescendi, F. (2010), 'Children and the transmission of religious knowledge', in V. Dasen and T. Späth (eds.), *Children, Memory, and Family Identity in Roman Culture*, Oxford: 73–93.

Price, S. R. F. (1984), *Rituals and Power: The Roman Imperial Cult in Asia Minor*, Cambridge.

    (1987), 'From noble funerals to divine cult: the consecration of Roman emperors', in D. Cannadine and S. R. F. Price (eds.), *Rituals of Royalty: Power and Ceremonial in Traditional Societies*, Cambridge: 56–105.

Purcell, N. (1983), 'The *apparitores*: a study in social mobility', *PBSR* 51: 125–73.

Raaflaub, K. (1999), 'Archaic and Classical Greece', in K. Raaflaub and N. Rosenstein (eds.), *War and Society in the Ancient and Medieval Worlds: Asia, The Mediterranean, Europe, and Mesoamerica*, Cambridge, MA: 129–61.

Raaflaub, K. and Rosenstein, N. (eds.) (1999), *War and Society in the Ancient and Medieval Worlds: Asia, The Mediterranean, Europe, and Mesoamerica*. Cambridge, MA.

Raaflaub, K. A. and Samons II, L. J. (1990), 'Opposition to Augustus', in K. A. Raaflaub and M. Toher (eds.), *Between Republic and Empire: Interpretations of Augustus and his Principate*, Berkeley: 417–54.

Raber, K. and Tucker, T. J. (eds.) (2005), *The Culture of the Horse: Status, Discipline, and Identity in the Early Modern World*, New York.

Raepsaet-Charlier, M.-T. (1999), '*Matrones equestres*: la parenté feminine de l'ordre équestre', in S. Demougin, H. Devijver and M.-T. Raepsaet-Charlier (eds.), *L'ordre équestre: histoire d'une aristocratie (IIe siècle av. J.-C.–IIIe siècle ap. J.-C.)*, Rome: 215–36.

Ramón Mélida, J. R. (1925), *Catálogo Monumental de España: Provincia de Badajoz*, vol. I, Madrid.

Ramsay, J. T. (2005), 'Mark Antony's judiciary reform and its revival under the triumvirs', *JRS* 95: 20–7.

Ramsay, J. T. (ed.) (2003), *Cicero: Philippics I–II*, Cambridge.

Rankov, B. (1987), 'M. Iunius Congus the Gracchan', in M. Whitby, P. Hardie and M. Whitby (eds.), *Homo Viator: Classical Essays for John Bramble*, Bristol: 89–94.

(2007), 'Military forces', in P. Sabin, H. van Wees and M. Whitby (eds.), *The Cambridge History of Greek and Roman Warfare*, vol. II: *Rome from the Late Republic to the Late Empire*, Cambridge: 30–75.

Rathbone, D. (1991), *Economic Rationalisation and Rural Society in Third Century AD Egypt*, Cambridge.

(1993), 'The *census* qualifications of the *assidui* and the *prima classis*', in H. Sancisi-Weerdenburg, R. J. Van der Spek, H. C. Teitler and H. T. Wallinga (eds.), *De Agricultura: In Memoriam Pieter Willem de Neeve (1945–1990)*, Amsterdam: 121–52.

(1996), 'Monetisation, not price-inflation, in third-century AD Egypt', in C. E. King and D. G. Wigg (eds.), *Coin Finds and Coin Use in the Roman World*, Berlin: 329–33.

(2008), 'Nero's reforms of *vectigalia* and the inscription of the *lex portorii Asiae*', in M. Cottier et al. (eds.), *The Customs Law of Asia*, Oxford: 251–78.

(2009), 'Earnings and costs: living standards and the Roman economy', in A. Bowman and A. Wilson (eds.), *Quantifying the Roman Economy: Methods and Problems*, Oxford: 299–326.

Rawlings, L. (1998), '*Condottieri* and clansmen: early Italian raiding, warfare and the state', in K. Hopwood (ed.), *Organised Crime in Antiquity*, London: 97–128.

Rawson, B. (2003), *Children and Childhood in Roman Italy*, Oxford.

Rawson, E. (1971), 'The literary sources for the pre-Marian army', *PBSR* 39: 13–31.

(1987), '*Discrimina ordinum*: the *lex Julia theatralis*', *PBSR* 55: 83–114.

Rea, J. (1970), 'Cn. Domitius Philippus, *praefectus vigilum, dux*', in D. H. Samuel (ed.), *Proceedings of the Twelfth International Congress of Papyrology, Ann Arbor, 1968*, Toronto: 427–9.

Rebecchi, F. (1999), 'Per l'iconograpfia della *transvectio equitum*: altre considerazioni e nuovi documenti', in S. Demougin, H. Devijver and M.-T. Raepsaet-Charlier (eds.), *L'ordre équestre: histoire d'une aristocratie (IIe siècle av. J.-C.–IIIe siècle ap. J.-C.)*, Rome: 191–214.

Rees, R. (2007), 'Letters of commendation and the rhetoric of praise', in R. Morello and A. D. Morrison (eds.), *Ancient Letters: Classical and Late Antique Epistolography*, Oxford: 149–68.

Reinhold, M. (1933), *Marcus Agrippa: A Biography*, Geneva, NY.

(1971), 'Usurpation of status and status symbols', *Historia* 20: 275–302.

(1988), *From Republic to Principate: An Historical Commentary on Cassius Dio's Roman History Books 49–53 (36–29 BC)*, Atlanta.

Retzleff, A. and Mjely, A. M. (2004), 'Seat inscriptions in the Odeum at Gerasa (Jerash)', *BASOR* 336: 37–48.

Ricci, C. (2000), 'Legio II Parthica: una messa a punto', in Y. Le Bohec and C. Wolff (eds.), *Les légions de Rome sous le Haut-Empire*, 2 vols., Lyons: 397–406.

Rich, J. W. (1990), *Cassius Dio: The Augustan Settlement (Roman History 53–55.9)*, Warminster.

Rich, J. W. and Williams, J. H. C. (1999), '*Leges et iura p. R. restituit*: a new aureus of Octavian and the settlement of 28–27 BC', *NC* 159: 169–213.

Richard, J. C. (1995), 'Patricians and plebeians: the origins of a social dichotomy', in K. Raaflaub (ed.), *Social Struggles in Archaic Rome: New Perspectives on the Conflict of the Orders*, Oxford and Malden, MA: 107–27.

Richardson, J. S. (1976), 'The Spanish mines and the development of provincial taxation in the second century BC', *JRS* 66: 139–52.

(1987), 'The purpose of the *lex Calpurnia de repetundis*', *JRS* 77: 1–12.

(1997), 'The senate, the courts, and the *SC de Cn. Pisone patre*', *CQ* 47: 510–18.

(1998), 'Old statutes never die: a brief history of abrogation', in M. Austin, J. Harries and C. Smith (eds.), *Modus Operandi: Essays in Honour of Geoffrey Rickman*, London: 47–61.

(2012), *Augustan Rome, 44 BC to AD 14: The Restoration of the Republic and the Establishment of the Empire*, Edinburgh.

Richardson, L., Jr. (1978), '*Honos et Virtus* and the *Sacra Via*', *AJA* 82: 240–6.

Richardson, L., Jr. (ed.) (1977), *Propertius: Elegies I–IV*, Norman.

Rickman, G. E. (1971), *Roman Granaries and Store Buildings*, Cambridge.

(1980), *The Corn Supply of Ancient Rome*, Oxford.

Ritterling, E. (1903), 'Zum römischen Heerwesen des ausgehenden dritten Jahrhunderts', in *Festschrift zu Otto Hirschfelds*, Berlin: 345–9.

Rives, J. B. (1996), 'The piety of a persecutor', *JECS* 4: 1–25.

Robert, L. (1954), *La Carie II: Le plateau de Tabai et ses environs*, Paris.

Robinson, M. (2011), *Ovid: Fasti, Book 2*, Oxford.

Robinson, O. F. (2007), *Penal Practice and Penal Policy in Ancient Rome*, London.

Rodgers, B. S. (1989), 'Eumenius of Augustodunum', *AncSoc* 20: 249–66.

(2015), *Symmachus. Oration 1. To Valentinian. 25 February 368 or 369*. www.uvm.edu/~bsaylor/rome/Symmachus1.pdf.

Rodgers, R. H. (2004), *Frontinus: De Aquaeductu Urbis Romae*, Cambridge.

Rogers, G. M. (1991a), 'Demosthenes of Oenoanda and models of euergetism', *JRS* 81: 91–100.

(1991b), *The Sacred Identity of Ephesos: Foundation Myths of a Roman City*, London and New York.

Roncaglia, C. (2013), 'Client prefects? Rome and the Cottians in the western Alps', *Phoenix* 67: 353–72.

Rosenstein, N. (2007), 'Military command, political power, and the Republican elite', in P. Erdkamp (ed.), *A Companion to the Roman Army*, Oxford and Malden, MA: 132–47.

(2008), 'Aristocrats and agriculture in the middle and late Republic', *JRS* 98: 1–26.

(2009), 'War, state formation, and the evolution of military institutions in ancient China and Rome', in W. Scheidel (ed.), *Rome and China: Comparative Perspectives on Ancient World Empires*, Oxford: 24–51.

(2011), 'War, wealth and consuls', in H. Beck (ed.), *Consuls and Res Publica*, Cambridge: 133–57.

Rostagni, A. (1944), *Suetonio: De Poetis e Biografi Minori*, Turin.

Rothfus, M. A. (2010), 'The *gens togata*: changing styles and changing identities', *AJPh* 131: 425–52.

Roueché, C. (1993), *Performers and Partisans at Aphrodisias in the Roman and Late Roman Periods*, London.

(1998), 'The functions of the governor in late antiquity: some observations', *AntTard* 6: 31–6.

Rowan, C. (2014), 'Showing Rome in the round: reinterpreting the "Commemorative Medallions" of Antoninus Pius', *Antichthon* 48: 109–25.

Rowe, G. (2002), *Princes and Political Cultures: The New Tiberian Senatorial Decrees*, Ann Arbor.

Rowland, R. J. (1965), 'C. Gracchus and the *equites*', *TAPA* 96: 361–73.

Rowlandson, J. (1996), *Landowners and Tenants in Roman Egypt: The Social Relations of Agriculture in the Oxyrhynchite Nome*, Oxford.

Rüpke, J. (2007), *Religion of the Romans*, trans. R. Gordon, London.

(2008), *Fasti Sacerdotum: A Prosopography of Pagan, Jewish, and Christian Religious Officials in the City of Rome, 300 BC to AD 499*, Oxford.

(2011), *The Roman Calendar from Numa to Constantine: Time, History and the Fasti*, Oxford and Malden, MA.

Russell, B. (2013), *The Economics of the Roman Stone Trade*, Oxford.

Ryan, F. X. (1997), 'The praetorship of L. Roscius Otho', *Hermes* 125: 236–40.

(1993), 'Some observations on the censorship of Claudius and Vitellius, AD 47–48', *AJPh* 114: 611–18.

Sabin, P. and De Souza, P. (2007), 'Battle', in P. Sabin, H. van Wees and M. Whitby (eds.), *The Cambridge History of Greek and Roman Warfare*, vol. I: *Greece, the Hellenistic World and the Rise of Rome*, Cambridge: 399–460.

Sablayrolles, R. (1996), *Libertinus Miles: les cohortes de vigils*, Rome.

(1999), '*Fastigium equestre*: les grades préfectures équestres', in S. Demougin, H. Devijver and M.-T. Raepsaet-Charlier (eds.), *L'ordre équestre: histoire d'une aristocratie (IIe siècle av. J.-C.–IIIe siècle ap. J.-C.)*, Rome: 351–89.

Saddington, D. B. (1990), 'The origin and nature of the German and British fleets', *Britannia* 21: 223–32.

(1996), 'Early imperial *praefecti castrorum*', *Historia* 45: 244–52.

(2000), '"Honouring" Tiberius on inscriptions, and in Valerius Maximus: a note', *Acta Classica* 43: 166–72.

(2003), 'An Augustan officer on the Roman army: *militaria* in Velleius Paterculus and some inscriptions', in J. J. Wilkes (ed.), *Documenting the Roman Army: Essays in Honour of Margaret Roxan*, London: 19–29.

(2007), '*Classes*: the evolution of the Roman imperial fleets', in P. Erdkamp (ed.), *A Companion to the Roman Army*, Oxford and Malden, MA: 201–17.

Sailor, D. (2008), *Writing and Empire in Tacitus*, Cambridge.

Saller, R. P. (1980), 'Promotion and patronage in equestrian careers', *JRS* 70: 44–63.

(1982), *Personal Patronage under the Early Empire*, Cambridge.

(2001), 'The family and society', in J. Bodel (ed.), *Epigraphic Evidence: Ancient History from Inscriptions*, London: 95–117.

Salmeri, G. (2000), 'Dio, Rome and the civic life of Asia Minor', in S. Swain (ed.), *Dio Chrysostom: Politics, Letters, and Philosophy*, Oxford: 53–92.

Salmon, E. T. (1972), 'Cicero, *Romanus an Italicus anceps*', in J. R. C. Martyn (ed.), *Cicero and Vergil: Studies in Honor of Howard Hunt*, Amsterdam: 75–86.

Salomies, O. (1994), 'Observations on the development of the style of Latin honorific inscriptions during the empire', *Arctos* 28: 63–106.

(2015), 'The Roman Republic', in C. Bruun and J. Edmondson (eds.), *The Oxford Handbook of Roman Epigraphy*, Oxford: 153–77.

Salway, R. W. B. (2006), 'Equestrian prefects and the award of senatorial honours from the Severans to Constantine', in A. Kolb (ed.), *Herrschaftsstrukturen und Herrschaftspraxis: Konzepte, Prinzipien und Strategien der Administration im römischen Kaiserreich*, Berlin: 115–35.

(2015), 'Redefining the Roman imperial elite in the fourth century AD', in P. Briks (ed.), *Elites in the Ancient World*, Szczecin: 199–220.

Salzman, M. R. (1990), *On Roman Time: The Codex-Calendar of 354 and the Rhythms of Urban Life in Late Antiquity*, Berkeley.

(2002), *The Making of a Christian Aristocracy: Social and Religious Change in the Western Roman Empire*, Cambridge, MA.

(2006), 'Symmachus and the "barbarian" generals', *Historia* 55: 352–67.

Samuel, L. R. (2012), *The American Dream: A Cultural History*, Syracuse.

Santangelo, F. (2007), *Sulla, the Elites and the Empire: A Study of Roman Policies in Italy and the Greek East*, Leiden.

Saulnier, G. (1984), '*Laurens Lauinas*: quelques remarques à propos d'un sacerdoce équestre à Rome', *Latomus* 43: 517–33.

Saxer, R. (1967), *Untersuchungen zu den Vexillationen des römischen Kaiserheeres von Augustus bis Diokletian*, Cologne.

Scamuzzi, U. (1969), 'Studio sulla *lex Roscia theatralis*', *Rivista di Studi Classici* 17: 133–65, 259–319.

Schäfer, N. (2000), *Die Einbeziehung der Provinzialen in den Reichsdienst in augusteischer Zeit*, Stuttgart.

Schäfer, T. (2003), 'Die Rezeption römischer Herrschaftsinsignien in Italien und im Imperium Romanum im 1. und 2. Jh. n. Chr.', in G. Weber and M. Zimmerman (eds.), *Propaganda-Selbstdarstellung-Repräsentation im römischen Kaiserreich des I. Jhs. n. Chr*, Stuttgart: 243–73.

Scheid, J. (1990a), *Le collège des frères arvales: Études prosopographique du recrutement (69–304)*, Rome.

(1990b), *Romulus et ses Frères: Le College des Frères arvales. Modèle du culte public dans la Rome des empereurs*, Rome.

(1993), 'Cultes, mythes et politique au début de l'Empire', in F. Graz (ed.), *Mythos in mythenloser Gesellschaft: Das Paradigma Roms*, Stuttgart 109–27.

(2003), *An Introduction to Roman Religion*, trans. J. Lloyd, Bloomington and Indianapolis.

(2005), 'Augustus and Roman religion: continuity, conservatism, and innovation', in K. Galinsky (ed.), *The Cambridge Companion to the Age of Augustus*, Cambridge: 175–93.

Scheid, J. and Granino Cecere, M. G. (1999), 'Les sacerdoces publics équestres', in S. Demougin, H. Devijver and M.-T. Raepsaet-Charlier (eds.), *L'ordre équestre: histoire d'une aristocratie (IIe siècle av. J.-C.–IIIe siècle ap. J.-C.)*, Rome: 79–189.

Scheidel, W. (2006), 'Stratification, deprivation and quality of life', in M. Atkins and R. Osborne (eds.), *Poverty in the Roman World*, Cambridge: 40–59.

(2009a), 'Introduction', in W. Scheidel (ed.), *Rome and China: Comparative Perspectives on Ancient World Empires*, Oxford: 1–10.

(2009b), 'From the "Great Convergence" to the "First Great Divergence": Roman and Qin-Han state formation and its aftermath', in W. Scheidel (ed.), *Rome and China: Comparative Perspectives on Ancient World Empires*, Oxford: 11–23.

(2009c), 'New ways of studying Roman incomes', in A. Bowman and A. Wilson (eds.), *Quantifying the Roman Economy: Methods and Problems*, Oxford: 346–52.

(2009d) *Rome and China: Comparative Perspectives on Ancient World Empires*, Oxford.

(2013), 'Studying the state', in P. F. Bang and W. Scheidel (eds.), *The Oxford Handbook of the State in the Ancient Near East and Mediterranean*, Oxford: 5–57.

Scheidel, W. (ed.) (2015), *State Power in Ancient China and Rome*, Oxford.

Scheidel, W. and Friesen, S. J. (2009), 'The size of the economy and the distribution of income in the Roman empire', *JRS* 99: 61–91.

Schmidt-Hofner, S. (2008), *Reagieren und Gestalten: der Regierungsstil des spätrömischen Kaisers am Beispiel der Gesetzgebung Valentinians I*, Munich.

Schneider, K. (1927), 'Lusus Troiae', in *RE* XIII: 2059–67.

Scholz, P. (2005), 'Zur öffentlichen Repräsentation römischer Senatoren und Magistrate: einige Überlegungen zur (verlorenen) materiellen Kultur der republikanischen Senatsaristokratie', in T. L. Kienlin (ed.), *Die Dinge als Zeichen: Kulturelles Wissen und materielle Kultur*, Bonn: 409–31.

Schwartz, J. (1976), 'Préfecture d'Egypt et intérim', *ZPE* 20: 101–7.

Seager, R. (1992), 'Sulla', in *CAH* IX^2, 165–207.

Seeck, O. (1905), 'Egregiatus', in *RE* V.2: 2006–10.

(1919), *Regesten der Kaiser und Päpste für die Jahre 311 bis 476 n. Chr.*, Stuttgart.

Segenni, S. (1992), 'Amiternum – Ager Amiterninus', *Supplementa Italica* 9: 11–209.

Segrè, A. (1943), 'A note on the classes of Roman officials in the age of Diocletian', *TAPA* 74: 102–8.

Sekunda, N. V. (2013), 'War and society in Greece', in B. Campbell and L. A. Tritle (eds.), *The Oxford Handbook of Warfare in the Classical World*, Oxford: 199–215.

Severy, B. (2003), *Augustus and the Family at the Birth of the Roman Empire*, London.

Shackleton Bailey, D. R. (ed.) (1965a), *Cicero's Letters to Atticus*, vol. I: *68–59 BC*, Cambridge.

(1965b), *Cicero's Letters to Atticus*, vol. II: *58–54 BC*, Cambridge.

(1968), *Cicero's Letters to Atticus*, vol. III: *51–50 BC*, Cambridge.

(1977a), *Cicero: Epistulae ad Familiares*, vol. I: *62–47 BC*, Cambridge.

(1977b), *Cicero: Epistulae ad Familiares*, vol. II: *47–43 BC*, Cambridge.

(1980), *Cicero: Epistulae ad Quintum Fratrem et M. Brutum*, Cambridge.

Shatzman, I. (1975), *Senatorial Wealth and Roman Politics*, Brussels.

Sherwin-White, A. N. (1939), 'Procurator Augusti', *PBSR* 15: 11–26.

(1966), *The Letters of Pliny: A Historical and Social Commentary*, Oxford.

(1973), *The Roman Citizenship*, 2nd edition, Oxford.

(1982), 'The *lex repetundarum* and the political ideals of Gaius Gracchus', *JRS* 72: 18–31.

Siani-Davies, M. (ed.) (2001), *Marcus Tullius Cicero: Pro Rabirio Postumo*, Oxford.

Simón, F. M. (2011), 'The *feriae Latinae* as religious legitimation of the consuls' *imperium*', in H. Beck et al. (eds.), *Consuls and Res Publica: Holding High Office in the Roman Republic*, Cambridge: 116–32.

Sirks, A. J. B. (1995), 'Aurelius Neilammon alias Hiërax and Caecilius [Cons]ultius, prefect of Egypt, in a case of extortion (*P. Strasb.* VI 560)', *Tyche* 10: 179–84.

(2015), 'Status and rank in the Theodosian Code', in A. B. Kuhn (ed.), *Social Status and Prestige in the Graeco-Roman World*, Munich: 291–302.

Skinner, A. (2013), 'Political mobility in the later Roman empire', *P&P* 218: 17–53.

Slater, W. J. (1994), 'Pantomime riots', *Classical Antiquity* 13: 120–44.

Slootjes, D. (2006), *The Governor and his Subjects in the Later Roman Empire*, Leiden.

Small, D. B. (1987), 'Social correlations to the Greek cavea in the Roman period', in S. Macready and F. H. Thompson (eds.), *Roman Architecture in the Greek World*, London: 85–93.

Smith, C. J. (2012), 'The *feriae Latinae*', in J. Rasmus Brandt and J. W. Iddeng (eds.), *Greek and Roman Festivals: Content, Meaning, and Practice*, Oxford: 267–88.

Smith, C. J. and Cornell, T. J. (2014), 'C. Oppius', in T. J. Cornell (ed.), *The Fragments of the Roman Historians*, Oxford: 380–3.

Smith, R. E. (1972), 'The army reforms of Septimius Severus', *Historia* 21: 481–500.

(1979), '*Dux, praepositus*', *ZPE* 36: 263–78.

Smith, R. R. R. (1998), 'Cultural choice and political identity in honorific portrait statues in the Greek east in the second century AD', *JRS* 88: 56–93.

(2016), 'Statue practice in the late Roman empire: numbers, costumes, and style', in R. R. R. Smith and B. Ward-Perkins (eds.), *The Last Statues of Antiquity*, Oxford: 1–27.

Smith, R. R. R. et al. (2006), *Roman Portrait Statuary from Aphrodisias (Aphrodisias II)*, Mainz.

Smith, R. R. R. and Ratté, C. (1997), 'Archaeological research at Aphrodisias in Caria', *AJA* 101: 1–22.

Sogno, C. (2006), *Q. Aurelius Symmachus: A Political Biography*, Ann Arbor.

Solin, H. (2005), '*Munitus*', in S. Kiss et al. (eds.), *Latin et langues Romanes*, Tübingen: 283–6.

(2011), 'Una nuova iscrizione con carriera equestra da Limatola', in S. Cagnazzi et al. (eds.), *Scritti di stori per Mario Pani*, Bari: 469–75.

Sordi, M. (1995), 'La centralità dell'Etruria nella politica di Mecenate', *RSA* 25: 149–56.

Spalthoff, B. H. (2010), *Repräsentationsformen des römischen Ritterstandes*, Rahden.

Spawforth, A. J. S. (1996), 'Roman Corinth: the formation of a colonial elite', in A. D. Rizakis (ed.), *Roman Onomastics in the Greek East: Social and Political Aspects*, Athens: 167–82.

(2002), 'Italian elements among the Roman knights and senators from Old Greece', in C. Müller and C. Hasenohr (eds.), *Les Italiens dans de monde grec: IIe siècle av. J.-C.–Ier siècle ap. J.-C. (circulation, activités, integration)*, Paris: 101–7.

Speidel, M. A. (2007), 'Ein Bollwerk für Syrien: Septimius Severus und die Provinzordnung Nordmesopotamiens im dritten Jahrhundert', *Chiron* 37: 405–33.

Speidel, M. P. (1977), 'The Roman army in Arabia', in *ANRW* II.8: 687–730.

(1978), *Guards of the Roman Armies: An Essay on the Singulares of the Provinces*, Bonn.

(1981), 'The last of the procurators', *ZPE* 43: 363–4.

(1982), 'Augustus' deployment of the legions in Egypt', *CdÉ* 57: 120–4.

(1985), 'Valerius Valerianus in charge of Septimius Severus' Mesopotamian campaign', *CPh* 80: 321–6.

(1986), 'The early *protectores* and their *beneficiarius* lance', *AKB* 16: 451–4.

(1987), 'The later Roman field army and the guard of the high empire', *Latomus* 46: 375–9.

(1991), 'The shrine of the *dii campestres* at Gemellae', *AntAfr* 27: 111–18.

(1992), '*Ala Celerum Philippiana*', *Tyche* 7: 217–20.

(1993), 'Commodus the god-emperor and the army', *JRS* 83: 109–14.

(1994a), *Die Denkmäler der Kaiserreiter Equites Singulares Augusti*, Cologne.

(1994b), *Riding for Caesar: The Roman Emperors' Horseguard*, London.

(2005), 'The origin of the late Roman army ranks', *Tyche* 20: 205–7.

(2008), 'Das Heer', in K.-P. Johne, U. Hartmann and T. Gerhardt (eds.), *Die Zeit der Soldatenkaiser: Krise und Transformation des Römischen Reiches im 3. Jahrhundert n. Chr. (235–284)*, 2 vols., Berlin: 673–90.

Spence, I. G. (1993), *The Cavalry of Classical Greece: A Social and Military History with Particular Reference to Athens*, Oxford.

(2010), 'Cavalry, democracy and military thinking in classical Athens', in D. Pritchard (ed.), *War, Democracy and Culture in Classical Athens*, Cambridge: 111–38.

Spencer, D. (2007), 'Rome at a gallop: Livy, on not gazing, jumping, or toppling into the void', in D. H. J. Larmour and D. Spencer (eds.), *The Sites of Rome: Time, Space, Memory*, Oxford: 61–101.

Stadter, P. (2014), *Plutarch and his Roman Readers*, Oxford.

Starr, C. G. (1941), *The Roman Imperial Navy, 31 BC–AD 324*, New York.

Staveley, E. S. (1953), '*Iudex selectus*', *RhM* 96: 201–13.

Stein, A. (1927), *Der römische Ritterstand: Ein Beitrag zur Sozial- und Personengeschichte des römischen Reiches*, Munich.

(1950), *Die Präfekten von Ägypten in der römischen Kaiserzeit*, Bern.

Steel, C. W. (2001), *Cicero, Rhetoric, and Empire*, Oxford.

(2013), *The End of the Roman Republic, 146 to 44 BC: Conquest and Crisis*, Edinburgh.

Šterbenc Erker, D. (2009), 'Das Lupercalia-Fest im augusteischen Rom: Performativität, Raum und Zeit', *Archiv für Religionsgeschichte* 11: 145–78.

Stevenson, T. R. (2007), 'Roman coins and refusals of the title *pater patriae*', *NC* 167: 119–41.

(2009), 'Acceptance of the title *pater patriae* in 2 BC', *Antichthon* 43: 97–108.

(2013), 'The succession planning of Augustus', *Antichthon* 47: 118–39.

Stockton, D. (1971), *Cicero: A Political Biography*, Oxford.

(1979), *The Gracchi*, Oxford.

Stolte, B. H. (2014), 'Codification in Byzantium: from Justinian to Leo IV', in J. Hudson and A. Rodríguez (eds.), *Diverging Paths? The Shapes of Power and Institutions in Medieval Christendom and Islam*, Leiden: 55–74.

Stone, A. M. (2005), '*Optimates*: an archaeology', in K. Welch and T. W. Hillard (eds.), *Roman Crossings: Theory and Practice in the Roman Republic*, Swansea: 59–94.

Strobel, K. (2007), 'Strategy and army structure between Septimius Severus and Constantine the Great', in P. Erdkamp (ed.), *A Companion to the Roman Army*, Malden, MA: 267–85.

(2009), 'From the imperial field army of the principate to the late Roman field army', in A. Morillo, N. Hanel and E. Martín (eds.), *Limes XX: Estudios sobre la frontera romana*, Madrid: 913–27.

Stroszeck, J. (2008), 'Römische Gräber und Grabbauten vor dem Dipylon', in S. Vlizos (ed.), *Η Αθήνα κάτα τη ρωμαϊκή εποχή: Πρόσφατες ανακαλύψεις, νέες έρευνες. Akten des Symposions im Benakimuseum Oktober 2006, Μουσείο Μπενάκι Suppl. 6*, Athens: 291–309.

Sullivan, J. P. (1991), *Martial, the Unexpected Classic: A Literary and Historical Study*, Cambridge.

Sumi, G. S. (2005), *Ceremony and Power: Performing Politics in Rome between Republic and Empire*, Ann Arbor.

(2009), 'Monuments and memory: the *aedes Castoris* in the formation of Augustan ideology', *CQ* 59: 167–86.

Suolahti, J. (1955), *The Junior Officers of the Roman Army in the Republican Period: A Study on Social Structure*, Helsinki.

Swain, B. (2016), 'Goths and Gothic identity in the Ostrogothic kingdom', in J. J. Arnold, M. S. Bjornlie and K. Sessa (eds.), *A Companion to Ostrogothic Italy*. Leiden: 203–33.

Swain, S. (1996), *Hellenism and Empire: Language, Classicism, and Power in the Greek World, AD 50–250*, Oxford.

Swan, P. M. (2004), *The Augustan Succession: An Historical Commentary on Cassius Dio's Roman History Books 55–56 (9 BC–AD 14)*, Oxford.

Syme, R. (1937), 'The colony of Cornelius Fuscus: an episode in the *bellum Neronis*', *AJPh* 58: 7–18.

(1938a), 'Caesar, the senate and Italy', *PBSR* 14: 1–31.

(1938b), 'The origin of Cornelius Gallus', *CQ* 32: 39–44. (*Roman Papers* I: 47–54.)

(1939), *The Roman Revolution*, Oxford.

(1957a), 'Antonine Relatives: Ceionii and Vettuleni', *Athenaeum* 35: 306–15. (*Roman Papers* I: 325–32.)

(1957b), 'C. Vibius Maximus, prefect of Egypt', *Historia* 6: 480–7. (*Roman Papers* I: 353–60.)

(1958), *Tacitus*, 2 vols., Oxford.

(1960), 'Pliny's less successful friends', *Historia* 9: 362–79. (*Roman Papers* II: 477–95.)

(1961), 'Who was Vedius Pollio?', *JRS* 51: 23–30. (*Roman Papers* II: 518–29.)

(1962), 'The wrong Marcius Turbo', *JRS* 52: 87–96. (*Roman Papers* II: 541–56.)

(1964), 'Pliny and the Dacian wars', *Latomus* 23: 750–9. (*Roman Papers* VI: 142–9.)

(1968), 'The Ummidii', *Historia* 17: 72–105. (*Roman Papers* II: 659–93.)

(1969), 'Pliny the procurator', *HSCPh* 73: 201–36. (*Roman Papers* II: 742–73.)

(1971), *Emperors and Biography*, Oxford.

(1977), 'Helvetian aristocrats', *Museum Helveticum* 24: 129–40. (*Roman Papers* III: 986–97.)

(1978a), *History in Ovid*, Oxford.

(1978b), 'Sallust's wife', *CQ* 28: 292–5. (*Roman Papers* III: 1085–9.)

(1983), 'Emperors from Etruria', *BHAC* 1979/1981, Bonn: 333–60.

(1985), 'Correspondents of Pliny', *Historia* 34: 324–59. (*Roman Papers* V: 440–77.)

(1986), *The Augustan Aristocracy*, Oxford.

(1991a), 'Consular friends of the elder Pliny', in A. R. Birley (ed.), *Roman Papers* VII, Oxford: 496–511.

(1991b), 'Domitius Apollinaris', in A. R. Birley (ed.), *Roman Papers* VII, Oxford: 588–602.

(1991c), 'M. Favonius, Proconsul of Asia', in A. R. Birley (ed.), *Roman Papers* VI, Oxford: 150–3.

(1999), *The Provincial at Rome and Rome and the Balkans 80 BC–AD 14*, edited by A. R. Birley, Exeter.

Talbert, R. J. A. (1984), *The Senate of Imperial Rome*, Princeton.

(1996), 'The senate and senatorial and equestrian posts', in *CAH* X²: 324–43.

Tanner, J. J. (2000), 'Portraits, power, and patronage in the late Roman Republic', *JRS* 90: 18–50.

Tantillo, I. and Bigi, F. (2010), *Leptis Magna: una città e le sue iscrizioni in epoca tardoromana*, Cassino.

Tatum, W. J. (2002), 'Q. Cicero, *Commentariolum Petitionis* 33', *CQ* 52: 394–8.

Taylor, L. R. (1924), '*Seviri equitum Romanorum* and municipal *seviri*: a study in pre-military training among the Romans', *JRS* 14: 158–71.

(1925), 'Horace's equestrian career', *AJPh* 46: 161–70.

(1949), *Party Politics in the Age of Caesar*, Berkeley.

(1960), *The Voting Districts of the Roman Republic*, Rome.

(1961), 'Freedmen and freeborn in the epitaphs of imperial Rome', *AJPh* 82: 113–32.

(1964), 'Magistrates of 55 BC in Cicero's *Pro Plancio* and Catullus 52', *Athenaeum* 42: 12–28.

(1966), *Roman Voting Assemblies from the Hannibalic War to the Dictatorship of Caesar*, Ann Arbor.

(1968), 'Republican and Augustan writers enrolled in the equestrian centuries', *TAPA* 99: 469–486.

Taylor, R. (2010), 'Bread and water: Septimius Severus and the rise of the *curator aquarum et Miniciae*', *MAAR* 55: 199–220.

Tempest, K. (2011), *Cicero: Politics and Persuasion in Ancient Rome*, London.

Thébert, Y. (1973), 'La romanisation d'une cité indigène d'Afrique: Bulla Regia', *MEFRA* 85: 247–312.

Thomas, C. (2004), 'Claudius and the Roman army reforms', *Historia* 53: 424–52.

Thomas, Y. (1990), 'L'institution de l'origine: *sacra principiorum populi romani*', in M. Detienne (ed.), *Tracés de fondation*, Leuven: 143–70.

Thonemann, P. (2004), 'Polemo, son of Polemo (Dio, 59.12.2)', *EA* 37: 144–50.

(2011), *The Maeander Valley: A Historical Geography from Antiquity to Byzantium*, Cambridge.

Tomlin, R. S. O. (1976), 'Notitia dignitatum omnium, tam civilium quam militar-ium', in R. Goodburn and P. Bartholomew (eds.), *Aspects of the Notitia Dignitatum: Papers presented to the Conference in Oxford, December 13 to 15, 1974*, Oxford: 189–209.

(2008), 'A. H. M. Jones and the army of the fourth century', in D. M. Gwynn (ed.), *A. H. M. Jones and the Later Roman Empire*, Leiden: 143–65.

Torelli, M. (1995), *Studies in the Romanization of Italy*, trans. H. Fracchia and M. Gualtieri, Edmonton.

(2002), *Benevento Romana*, Rome.

Townend, G. B. (1961a), 'The Hippo inscription and the career of Suetonius', *Historia* 10: 99–109.

(1961b), 'The post of ab epistulis in the second century', *Historia* 10: 375–81.

Toynbee, J. M. C. (1971), *Death and Burial in the Roman World*, London.

(1986), *Roman Medallions*, New York.

Treggiari, S. (1969), *Roman Freedmen during the Late Republic*, Oxford.

(1991), *Roman Marriage: Iusti Coniuges from the time of Cicero to the time of Ulpian*, Oxford.

(1996), 'Social status and social legislation', in *CAH X²*: 873–904.

Trombley, F. (1999), 'Ammianus and fourth-century warfare: a protector's approach to historical narrative', in J. W. Drijvers and D. Hunt (eds.), *The Late Roman World and its Historian: Interpreting Ammianus Marcellinus*, London: 17–28.

Tully, G. D. (1998), 'The στρατάρχης of legio VI *Ferrata* and the employment of camp prefects as vexillation commanders', *ZPE* 120: 226–32.

Tyrrell, W. B. (1978), *A Legal and Historical Commentary to Cicero's Oratio pro C. Rabirio perduellionis reo*, Amsterdam.

Ulf, C. (1982), *Das römische Lupercalienfest: Ein Modellfall für Methodenprobleme in der Altertumswissenschaft*, Darmstadt.

vander Leest, J. (1985), 'Lucian in Egypt', *GRBS* 26: 75–82.

van den Hout, M. P. J. (1999), *A Commentary on the Letters of M. Cornelius Fronto*, Leiden.

van der Blom, H. (2010), *Cicero's Role Models: The Political Strategy of a Newcomer*, Oxford.

van Minnen, P. (2016), 'Three edicts of Caracalla? A new reading of P. Giss. 40', *Chiron* 46: 205–21.

van Nijf, O. (1997), *The Civic World of Professional Associations in the Roman East*, Amsterdam.

(1999), 'Athletics, festivals and Greek identity in the Roman east', *PCPhS* 45: 176–200.

(2001), 'Local heroes: athletics, festivals and elite self-fashioning in the Roman east', in S. Goldhill (ed.), *Being Greek under Rome: Cultural Identity, the Second Sophistic and the Development of Empire*, Cambridge: 306–34.

(2004), 'Athletics and *paideia*: festivals and physical education in the world of the Second Sophistic', in B. E. Borg (ed.), *Paideia: The World of the Second Sophistic*, Berlin and New York: 203–27.

(2008), 'The social world of Roman tax-farmers and their personnel', in M. Cottier et al. (eds.), *The Customs Law of Asia*, Oxford: 279–311.

van Rengen, W. (2000), 'La IIe légion parthique à Apamée', in Y. Le Bohec and C. Wolff (eds.), *Les légions de Rome sous le Haut-Empire*, Lyon: 407–10.

Vanggaard, J. H. (1988), *The Flamen: A Study in the History and Sociology of Roman Religion*, Copenhagen.

Várhelyi, Z. (2010), *The Religion of Senators in the Roman Empire: Power and the Beyond*, Cambridge.

Vasaly, A. (2009), 'Cicero, domestic politics, and the first action of the Verrines', *Classical Antiquity* 28: 101–37.

Vassileiou, A. (1984), 'Caius ou Lucius Caesar proclamé *princeps iuuentutis* par l'ordre équestre', in H. Walter (ed.), *Hommages à Lucien Lerat 2*, Paris: 827–40.

Vervaet, F. (2007), 'The reappearance of the supra-provincial commands in the late second and early third centuries CE: constitutional and historical considerations', in O. Hekster, G. de Kleijn and D. Slootjes (eds.), *Crises and the Roman Empire*, Leiden: 125–39.

Veyne, P. (1960), 'Iconographie de la "transvectio equitum" et des lupercales', *REA* 62: 100–12.

(1961), 'Vie de Trimalcion', *Annales: Économies, Sociétés, Civilisations* 16: 213–47.

(1990) *Bread and Circuses: Historical Sociology and Political Pluralism*, trans. B. Pearce, London.

Vittinghoff, F. (1980), 'Soziale Struktur und Politisches System der hohen römischen Kaiserzeit', *Historische Zeitschrift* 230: 31–55.

Vogel, L. (1973), *The Column of Antoninus Pius*, Cambridge, MA.

Vuković, K. (2016), 'Roman myth and ritual: groups of Luperci and epigraphic evidence', *Epigraphica* 78: 43–52.

Walbank, F. W. (1956), *A Historical Commentary on Polybius I*, Oxford.

Wallace-Hadrill, A. (1982), 'Civilis princeps: between citizen and king', *JRS* 72: 32–48.

(1983), *Suetonius*, London.

(1990a), 'Pliny the Elder and man's unnatural history', *G&R* 37: 80–96.

(1990b), 'Roman arches and Greek honours: the language of power at Rome', *PCPhS* 36: 143–81.

(1996), 'The imperial court', in *CAH* X²: 283–308.

(2008), *Rome's Cultural Revolution*, Cambridge.

(2011), 'The Roman imperial court: seen and unseen in the performance of power', in J. Duindam, T. Artan and M. Kunt (eds.), *Royal Courts in Dynastic States and Empires*, Leiden: 91–102.

Wardle, D. (2002), 'Suetonius as *ab epistulis*: an African connection', *Historia* 51: 462–80.

(2011), 'Augustus and the priesthoods of Rome: the evidence of Suetonius', in J. H. Richardson and F. Santangelo (eds.), *Priests and State in the Roman World*, Stuttgart: 271–89.

Wardle, D. (ed.) (1994), *Suetonius' Life of Caligula*, Brussels.

(2014), *Suetonius: Life of Augustus*, Oxford.

Watson, A. (2005), 'Bacchanalian rewards: Publius Aebutius and Hispala Faecenia', *Fundamina* 11: 411–14.

Watson, L. C. (2003), *A Commentary on Horace's Epodes*, Oxford.

Watson, L. C. and Watson, P. (eds.) (2003), *Martial: Select Epigrams*, Cambridge.

Weaver, P. R. C. (1972), *Familia Caesaris: A Social Study of the Emperor's Freedman and Slaves*, Cambridge.

(1980), 'Two freedman careers', *Antichthon* 14: 143–56.

(1994), 'Confusing names: Abascantus and Statius, *Silvae* 5.1', *ECM* 38: 333–64.

Weber, M. (1968), *Economy and Society: An Outline of Interpretive Sociology*, ed. G. Roth and C. Wittich, Berkeley.

Webster, D. (1999), 'Ancient Maya warfare', in K. Raaflaub and N. Rosenstein (eds.), *War and Society in the Ancient and Medieval Worlds: Asia, the Mediterranean, Europe, and Mesoamerica*, Cambridge, MA: 333–60.

Weber, K.-H. (1974), 'Troiae lusus: Alter und Entstehung eines Reiterspiels', *Ancient Society* 5: 171–96.

Wei, R. (2013), 'Fronto and the rhetoric of friendship', *Cahiers des études anciennes* 50. URL: http://etudesanciennes.revues.org/558.

Weiland, A. (1992), 'Bemerkungen zur Datierung der ehemaligen Luperkal-Kapelle im Vicus Patricius zu Rome', in *Memoriam Sanctorum Venerantes: Miscellanea in onore di Monsignor Victor Saxer*, Vatican City: 773–93.

Weinrib, E. J. (1990), *The Spaniards in Rome: From Marius to Domitian*, London.

Weinstock, S. (1937a), 'Römische reiterparade', *Studi e materiali di storia delle religioni* 13: 10–24.

(1937b), 'Transvectio equitum', in *RE* VIA: 2178–87.

(1971), *Divus Iulius*, Oxford.

Weisweiler, J. (2015), 'Domesticating the senatorial elite: universal monarchy and transregional aristocracy in the fourth century AD', in J. Wienand (ed.), *Contested Monarchy: Integrating the Roman Empire in the Fourth Century AD*, Oxford and New York: 17–41.

Welch, K. (1990), 'The *praefectura urbis* of 45 BC and the ambitions of L. Cornelius Balbus', *Antichthon* 24: 53–69.

(1995), 'The office of *praefectus fabrum* in the late Republic', *Chiron* 25: 131–45.

(1996), 'T. Pomponius Atticus: a banker in politics?', *Historia* 45: 450–71.

Welch, K. E. (2007a), 'Pompeian men and women in portrait sculpture', in J. J.
    Dobbins and P. W. Foss (eds.), *The World of Pompeii*, London: 550–84.
  (2007b), *The Roman Amphitheatre: From its Origins to the Colosseum*.
    Cambridge.
West, A. B. (ed.) (1931), *Corinth: Results of Excavations Conducted by the American
    School of Classical Studies at Athens. Volume VIII. Part II: Latin Inscriptions
    1896–1926*, Cambridge, MA.
West, M. L. (2007), *Indo-European Poetry and Myth*, Oxford.
White, P. (1973), 'Vibius Maximus, the friend of Statius', *Historia* 22: 295–301.
  (1978), '*Amicitia* and the profession of poetry in early imperial Rome', *JRS* 68:
    74–92.
  (2001), 'Ovid and the Augustan milieu', in B. W. Boyd (ed.), *Brill's Companion to
    Ovid*, Leiden: 1–25.
Whitmarsh, T. (2005), *The Second Sophistic*, Greece and Rome New Surveys in the
    Classics 35, Oxford.
Whitton, C. (ed.) (2013), *Pliny the Younger: Epistles Book II*, Cambridge.
Wickham, C. (1984), 'The other transition: from the ancient world to feudalism',
    P&P 103: 3–36.
  (2005), *Framing the Early Middle Ages*, Oxford.
Wiedemann, T. (1992), *Emperors and Gladiators*, London.
Wilkes, J. (2005), 'Changes in Roman provincial organization, AD 193–337', in
    CAH XII²: 705–23.
Wilkinson, S. (2012), *Republicanism during the Early Roman Empire*, London.
Williams, G. W. (1995), '*Libertino patre natus*: true or false?', in S. J. Harrison (ed.),
    Homage to Horace, Oxford: 296–313.
Williams, R. D. (ed.) (1960), P. *Vergili Maronis Aeneidos Liber Quintus*, Oxford.
Wilson, A. (2012), 'Raw materials and energy', in W. Scheidel (ed.), *The Cambridge
    Companion to the Roman Economy*, Cambridge: 133–55.
Wilson, R. J. A. (1996), 'Sicily, Sardinia and Corsica', in *CAH X²*: 434–48.
Winterling, A. (1999), *Aula Caesaris: Studien zur Institutionalisierung des
    römischen Kaiserhofes in der Zeit von Augustus bis Commodus (31 v. Chr–
    192 n. Chr.)*, Oldenbourg.
  (2009), *Politics and Society in Imperial Rome*, Oxford and Malden, MA.
Wiseman, T. P. (1970a), 'The census in the first century BC', *JRS* 59: 59–75.
  (1970b), 'The definition of *eques Romanus* in the late Republic and early empire',
    Historia 19: 67–83.
  (1971), *New Men in the Roman Senate 139 BC–AD 14*, Oxford.
  (1973), 'Review of E. Badian, *Publicans and Sinners: Private Enterprise in the
    Service of the Roman Republic*', *Phoenix* 27: 189–98.
  (1995a), 'The god of the Lupercal', *JRS* 85: 1–22.
  (1995b), *Remus: A Roman Myth*, Cambridge.
Wissowa, G. (1912), *Religion und Kultus der Römer*, 2nd edition, Munich.

(1915), 'Die römischen Staatspriestertümer altlatinischer Gemeindekult', Hermes 50: 1–33.

Woloch, M. (1969), 'Four leading families in Roman Athens (AD 96–161)', Historia 18: 503–10.

Wood, I. (1994), The Merovingian Kingdoms 450–751, London and New York.

Wood, N. (1991), Cicero's Social and Political Thought, Berkeley.

Woodman, A. J. (ed.) (1977), Velleius Paterculus: The Tiberian Narrative (2.94–131), Cambridge.

(1983), Velleius Paterculus: The Caesarian and Augustan Narrative (2.41–93), Cambridge.

Woodman, A. J., with Kraus, C. S. (eds.) (2014), Tacitus: Agricola, Cambridge.

Woolf, G. (2009), 'Found in translation: the religion of the Roman diaspora', in O. Hekster, S. Schmidt-Hofner and C. Witschel (eds.), Ritual Dynamics and Religious Change in the Roman Empire, Leiden: 239–52.

Wörrle, M. (1988), Stadt und Fest im kaiserzeitlichen Kleinasien, Munich.

Woytek, B. E. (2012), 'The denarius coinage of the Roman Republic', in W. E. Metcalf (ed.), The Oxford Handbook of Greek and Roman Coinage, Oxford: 315–34.

Wrede, H. (1983), 'Statuae Lupercorum habitu', MDAI (RA) 90: 185–200.

(1988), 'Zur trabea', JDAI 103: 381–400.

Yakobson, A. (1999), Elections and Electioneering in Rome: A Study in the Political System of the Late Republic, Stuttgart.

Yates, R. D. S. (1999), 'Early China', in K. Raaflaub and N. Rosenstein (eds.), War and Society in the Ancient and Medieval Worlds: Asia, the Mediterranean, Europe and Mesoamerica, Cambridge, MA: 7–45.

Yavetz, Z. (1962), 'The policy of C. Flaminius and the plebiscitum Claudianum', Athenaeum 40: 325–44.

(1984), 'The Res Gestae and Augustus' public image', in F. Millar and E. Segal (eds.), Caesar Augustus: Seven Aspects, Oxford: 1–36.

Youtie, H. C. (1967), 'Publicans and sinners', ZPE I: 1–20.

Zanker, P. (1975), 'Grabreliefs römischer Freigelassener', JDAI 90: 267–315.

(1981), 'Das Bildnis des M. Holconius Rufus', AA 1981: 349–61.

(1988), The Power of Images in the Age of Augustus, trans. A. Shapiro, Ann Arbor.

(1998), Pompeii: Public and Private Life, Cambridge, MA.

Zetzel, J. E. G. (ed.) (1995), Cicero: De Re Publica. Selections, Cambridge.

(1999), Cicero: On the Commonwealth and On the Laws, Cambridge.

Zmora, H. (2001), Monarchy, Aristocracy, and the State in Europe, 1300–1800, London.

Zoumbaki, S. (2008), 'The composition of the Peloponnesian elites in the Roman period and the evolution of their resistance and approach to the Roman rulers', Tekmeria 9: 25–51.

Zuckerman, C. (2002), 'Sur la Liste de Vérone et la province de Grande Arménie, la division de l'Empire de la date de la création des diocèses', *Travaux et Mémoires* 14: 617–37.

Zuiderhoek, A. (2008), 'On the political sociology of the imperial Greek city', *GRBS* 48: 417–45.

    (2009), *The Politics of Munificence in the Roman Empire: Citizens, Elites and Benefactors in Asia Minor*, Cambridge.

Index

For EU product safety concerns, contact us at Calle de José Abascal, 56–1°,
28003 Madrid, Spain or eugpsr@cambridge.org.

www.ingramcontent.com/pod-product-compliance
Ingram Content Group UK Ltd.
Pitfield, Milton Keynes, MK11 3LW, UK
UKHW030857150625
459647UK00021B/2769